THE Java™ Class Libraries

Second Edition, Volume 1

Supplement for the
Java™ 2 Platform
Standard Edition, v1.2

The Java™ Series

Lisa Friendly, Series Editor
Tim Lindholm, Technical Editor
Ken Arnold, Technical Editor of The Jini™ Technology Series
Jim Inscore, Technical Editor of The Java™ Series, Enterprise Edition

---

Ken Arnold, James Gosling, David Holmes
The Java™ Programming Language, Third Edition

Joshua Bloch
Effective Java™ Programming Language Guide

Greg Bollella, James Gosling, Ben Brosgol, Peter Dibble, Steve Furr, David Hardin, Mark Turnbull
The Real-Time Specification for Java™

Mary Campione, Kathy Walrath, Alison Huml
The Java™ Tutorial, Third Edition: A Short Course on the Basics

Mary Campione, Kathy Walrath, Alison Huml, Tutorial Team
The Java™ Tutorial Continued: The Rest of the JDK™

Patrick Chan
The Java™ Developers Almanac 2000

Patrick Chan, Rosanna Lee
The Java™ Class Libraries, Second Edition, Volume 2: java.applet, java.awt, java.beans

Patrick Chan, Rosanna Lee
The Java™ Class Libraries Poster, Sixth Edition, Part 1

Patrick Chan, Rosanna Lee
The Java™ Class Libraries Poster, Sixth Edition, Part 2

Patrick Chan, Rosanna Lee, Doug Kramer
The Java™ Class Libraries, Second Edition, Volume 1: java.io, java.lang, java.math, java.net, java.text, java.util

Patrick Chan, Rosanna Lee, Doug Kramer
The Java™ Class Libraries, Second Edition, Volume 1: Supplement for the Java™ 2 Platform, Standard Edition, v1.2

Kirk Chen, Li Gong
Programming Open Service Gateways with Java™ Embedded Server

Zhiqun Chen
Java Card™ Technology for Smart Cards: Architecture and Programmer's Guide

Li Gong
Inside Java™ 2 Platform Security: Architecture, API Design, and Implementation

James Gosling, Bill Joy, Guy Steele, Gilad Bracha
The Java™ Language Specification, Second Edition

Jonni Kanerva
The Java™ FAQ

Doug Lea
Concurrent Programming in Java™, Second Edition: Design Principles and Patterns

Rosanna Lee, Scott Seligman
JNDI API Tutorial and Reference: Building Directory-Enabled Java™ Applications

Sheng Liang
The Java™ Native Interface: Programmer's Guide and Specification

Tim Lindholm and Frank Yellin
The Java™ Virtual Machine Specification, Second Edition

Vlada Matena and Beth Stearns
Applying Enterprise JavaBeans™: Component-Based Development for the J2EE™ Platform

Roger Riggs, Antero Taivalsaari, Mark VandenBrink
Programming Wireless Devices with the Java™ 2 Platform, Micro Edition

Henry Sowizral, Kevin Rushforth, and Michael Deering
The Java 3D™ API Specification, Second Edition

Kathy Walrath, Mary Campione
The JFC Swing Tutorial: A Guide to Constructing GUIs

Seth White, Maydene Fisher, Rick Cattell, Graham Hamilton, and Mark Hapner
JDBC™ API Tutorial and Reference, Second Edition: Universal Data Access for the Java™ 2 Platform

Steve Wilson, Jeff Kesselman
Java™ Platform Performance: Strategies and Tactics

The Jini™ Technology Series

Eric Freeman, Susanne Hupfer, Ken Arnold
JavaSpaces™ Principles, Patterns, and Practice

Jim Waldo/Jini™ Technology Team
The Jini™ Specifications, Second Edition, edited by Ken Arnold

The Java™ Series, Enterprise Edition

Rick Cattell, Jim Inscore, Enterprise Partners
J2EE™ Technology in Practice: Building Business Applications with the Java™ 2 Platform, Enterprise Edition

Patrick Chan, Rosanna Lee
The Java™ Class Libraries Poster, Enterprise Edition, version 1.2

Nicholas Kassem, Enterprise Team
Designing Enterprise Applications with the Java™ 2 Platform, Enterprise Edition

Bill Shannon, Mark Hapner, Vlada Matena, James Davidson, Eduardo Pelegri-Llopart, Larry Cable, Enterprise Team
Java™ 2 Platform, Enterprise Edition: Platform and Component Specifications

http://www.javaseries.com

THE Java™ Class Libraries

Second Edition, Volume 1

Supplement for the Java™ 2 Platform Standard Edition, v1.2

Patrick Chan
Rosanna Lee
and
Douglas Kramer

ADDISON–WESLEY

Boston • San Francisco • New York • Toronto • Montreal
London • Munich • Paris • Madrid
Capetown • Sydney • Tokyo • Singapore • Mexico City

The publisher offers discounts on this book when ordered in quantity for special sales. For more information, please contact:

Pearson Education Corporate Sales Division
One Lake Street
Upper Saddle River, NJ 07458
(800) 382-3419
corpsales@pearsontechgroup.com

Visit AW on the Web: www.awl.com/cseng/

Library of Congress Cataloging-in-Publication Data
Chan, Patrick, 1961-
The Java class libraries / Patrick Chan, Rosanna Lee, and Douglas Kramer -- 2nd ed.
p. cm. -- (The Java series)
Includes index.
ISBN 0-201-48552-4
1. Java (Computer program language) I. Lee, Rosanna, 1960-, Kramer, Douglas, 1950- II. Title. III. Series.
QA76.73.J38C47 1999
005.13'3--dc21 97-33423
CIP

ISBN 0201485524
Text printed on recycled paper
4 5 6 7 8 9 10—CRS—04 03 02 01
4th printing, June 2001

In Loving Memory

Fai Chan

—P.C. & R.L.

To my sibs

Dan, Judy,
Greg,
Chip, David

—D.K.

Contents

Addendum

List of Figures

Package Overviews

Alphabetical Reference of Classes

List of Tables

Package Overviews

Alphabetical Reference of Classes

Preface

How to Use This Book

This book is a companion to *The Java Class Libraries, Second Edition, Volume 1*. It contains descriptions of the new packages and classes in the Java™ 2 Platform, Standard Edition, Version 1.2. It also provides details of how the classes and methods have changed from the Java™ Developement Kit (JDK™) Version 1.1 to Version 1.2. It is important to understand that some of the material in this book is not complete and refers to material in *The Java Class Libraries, Second Edition, Volume 1*.

Like *The Java Class Libraries, Second Edition, Volume 1*, this book is intended as a reference rather than a tutorial. Its format is similar to a dictionary's in that it is designed to optimize the time it takes for you to look up information about a class or class member. For a tutorial-style presentation of the class libraries, see *The Java™ Tutorial* by Mary Campione and Kathy Walrath. *The Java™ Class Libraries* does not explain any part of the Java language. There are several books you can use to learn the language. These include *The Java™ Programming Language*, by Ken Arnold and James Gosling, and *The Java™ Language Specification*, by James Gosling, Bill Joy, and Guy Steele.

Following is an overview of this book.

Package Overviews

This part briefly describes each package and all of the classes in it. Also included are diagrams that show the inheritance hierarchy of the classes that appear in a package.

Each overview contains not only a general description about the package, but also descriptions of the changes in the package for Version 1.2. Each class that has been introduced in Version 1.2 is labeled with a **1.2** tag. Each class that has been changed for Version 1.2 is labeled with a **Δ** tag.

Alphabetical Reference of Classes

This part covers the alphabetical listing of the classes from the following ten packages:

```
java.io                 java.net
java.lang               java.text
java.lang.ref           java.util
java.lang.reflect       java.util.jar
java.math               java.util.zip
```

Only those classes that have been changed or added in Version 1.2 are included. Moreover, within the changed classes, only those members that have been changed or added are included. See the Table of Contents for a list of the classes and members in this book. For information about the classes that are changed, see *The Java Class Libraries, Second Edition, Volume 1*.

Like *The Java Class Libraries, Second Edition, Volume 1*, the classes are ordered alphabetically without regard to package name or version.

Each class is described in its own chapter. Each chapter contains a picture of the class hierarchy, a class description, a "Changes for Version 1.2" section for classes that have changed, a class example, a member summary, and descriptions for each member that is changed or new in Version 1.2. Chapters for classes that have changed (as opposed to those that were introduced in Version 1.2) have the label **CHANGES FOR VERSION 1.2** in their footer.

Class Hierarchy Diagram

Each chapter starts with a class diagram. The class diagram shows all of the ancestors of the class, its siblings, its immediate descendents, and any interfaces that the class implements. In these diagrams, if a package name precedes a class or interface name, the class or interface is not in the same package as the current class.

In the diagrams, the different kinds of Java entities are distinguished visually as follows:

- The interface: A rounded rectangle
- The class: A rectangle
- The abstract class: A rectangle with an empty dot
- The final class: A rectangle with a black dot
- Classes with subclasses: A rectangle with a small black triangle in the lower-right corner

Most of these elements are shown in Figure i. The class or interface being described in the current chapter is shaded grey. A solid line represents `extends`, while a dotted line represents `implements`.

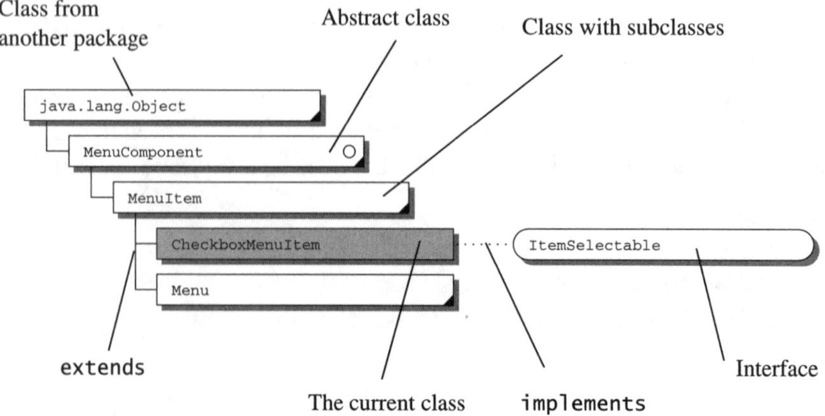

FIGURE i: Class Hierarchy Diagram.

Class Description

In the class description, we describe all of the properties of the class. For example, the properties of the `Graphics` class include the current color, font, paint mode, origin, and clipping area. Describing in one place all of a class's available properties and how the properties behave makes learning all of the capabilities of a class much easier than if the property descriptions were scattered throughout the member descriptions.

Any terminology used in the member descriptions is introduced and described in the class descriptions. If you find that the member description lacks detail, go to the class description for more information.

If the class is newly introduced in Version 1.2, its class description is complete. If the class is one that is changed in Version 1.2, the class description is only a summary of the class; the complete class description is in *The Java Class Libraries, Second Edition, Volume 1.*

Changes for Version 1.2

If the class is one that is changed in Version 1.2, the chapter contains a "Changes for Version 1.2" section that describes the changes, including the new methods that have been added and how existing methods have changed.

Class Example

Most of the chapters for new classes have a class example that illustrates how to use the class. Some of the chapters for the changed classes have a class example. For some of the changed classes, the changes are so minor that the class example in *The Java Class Libraries, Second Edition, Volume 1* is still relevant.

Member Summary

The member summary is intended to help the reader quickly grasp the key points of the class. It groups the members of the class into categories that are specific to that class. For example, in the `List` class the Selection Methods category lists all methods having to do with selections. It is meant to be a quick summary of the class's members, so it does not contain any syntax information other than the name of the member.

The member summary for both changed and new classes is complete. In a changed class, changed members are labeled with a Δ tag, while new members are labeled with a 1.2 tag. Only those members with one of these two tags are documented in the chapter. The documentation for unlabeled members in is *The Java Class Libraries, Second Edition, Volume 1.*

For example, following is the member summary for `ZipInputStream`.

MEMBER SUMMARY		
	Constructor	
	ZipInputStream()	Constructs a ZipInputStream instance.
	Entry Methods	
	closeEntry()	Closes the current ZipEntry.
1.2	createZipEntry()	Creates an instance of ZipEntry.
	getNextEntry()	Reads the next ZIP entry from this ZipInputStream.
	Stream Methods	
Δ	available()	Determines whether this ZipInputStream has been closed.
	close()	Closes this ZipInputStream.
	read()	Reads decompressed data from this ZipInputStream.
	skip()	Discards decompressed data from this ZipInputStream.

In Version 1.2, ZipInputStream has one new member, createZipEntry(), and one changed member, available(). The chapter for ZipInputStream contains member descriptions for createZipEntry() and available(). All other members of ZipInputStream are described in *The Java Class Libraries, Second Edition, Volume 1.*

Member Descriptions

The member descriptions appear in alphabetical order within a class chapter regardless of what kind of method or field they are. This is done to make locating a member proceed as fast as possible.

Overloaded methods are placed together in one member description because they share very similar functionality. The different overloaded forms are typically provided as a convenience for the programmer when specifying parameters. For instance, some overloads eliminate parameters by providing common defaults. To describe overloads with missing parameters, we use a phrase of the form "if the parameter p is not specified, it defaults to the value 3.14." Other overloads take different representations of a value. For example, one overload could take a particular parameter as an integer, while another could take the same parameter as a string containing an integer.

In a changed class, each member heading is labeled with either a Δ or a 1.2 tag. Δ indicates a member whose behavior has changed in Version 1.2. The changes might include an addition of an overloaded form, deprecation, or any other change in the semantics of the member. 1.2 indicates that the member was introduced in Version 1.2. Following are examples of each tag.

Δ compareTo()

1.2 unscaledValue()

Each member description contains some or all of the following fields.

PURPOSE	A brief description of the purpose of this member
SYNTAX	The syntactic declaration of this member
DESCRIPTION	A full description of this member
PARAMETERS	The parameters accepted by this member, if any, listed in alphabetical order
RETURNS	The value and its range returned by this member, if any
EXCEPTIONS	The exceptions and errors thrown by this member, if any, listed in alphabetical order
SEE ALSO	Other related classes or members, if any, listed in alphabetical order
OVERRIDES	The method that this member overrides, if any
EXAMPLE	A code example that illustrates how this member is used. This is sometimes a reference to an example that illustrates the use of this method in another member example or class example.

If an overloaded form has been added to an existing member, the overloaded form has a *SINCE 1.2* tag. For example, in Version 1.1 the `String` class has a form of `compareTo()` that accepts a `String` parameter. In Version 1.2, the `String` class has two overloaded forms of `compareTo()`, one that accepts an `Object` and one that accepts a `String`. `String.compareTo()`'s syntax field looks as follows.

SYNTAX
```
public int compareTo(String str)
```
SINCE 1.2
```
public int compareTo(Object str)
```

A changed member, in addition to having its member heading labeled with a Δ tag, always includes the following field.

1.2 CHANGES Description of the old behavior or what has changed in Version 1.2

Deprecation

A method or class is *deprecated* if its use is no longer recommended. A deprecated method appears in the Member Summary under the Deprecated Methods section. In the chapter body, the deprecated method is annotated by a "deprecated" tag in its method heading. For example, `Component.size()` is a deprecated method. It has the following method heading.

size() ***DEPRECATED***

If not all of the overloaded forms of the method are deprecated, a *DEPRECATED* tag appears beside the syntax of each deprecated form. For example, the second of the two forms of `BorderLayout.addLayoutComponent()` is deprecated. This is indicated by the *DEPRECATED* tag, as follows.

SYNTAX `public void addLayoutComponent(Component comp, Object location)`
DEPRECATED `public void addLayoutComponent(String location, Component comp)`

The method description contains a deprecation section with instructions on how to replace the usage of the deprecated method, like this.

DEPRECATION A description of how to replace the usage of this deprecated method

Where to Download the Examples

All of the code examples in this book have been compiled and run on the FCS version of the Java™ 2 SDK, Standard Edition, Version 1.2 (formerly "JDK™ 1.2") either on Solaris or Windows NT or both. Most of the complete examples are available on-line. You can access them and other information about this book by at `http://java.sun.com/books/Series`.

Typographical Conventions Used in This Book

`Lucida Sans Typewriter` is used for examples, syntax declarations, class names, method names, values, and field names. *Italic* is used when defining a new term and for emphasis.

Acknowledgments

We want to thank the many people who made this book possible.

Mike Hendrickson, the Executive Editor for this book, helped coordinate the many tasks and people needed to complete it.

The accuracy and quality of this book were improved immensely as the result of the feedback provided by the following individuals: Cynthia Bloch, Joshua Bloch, Gilad Bracha, Steve Byrne, David Connelly, Joseph Fialli, Li Gong, Peter Jones, Sheng Liang, Alan Liu, Jeff Nisewanger, Mark Reinhold, and Roland Schemers.

Sarah Weaver, Rosemary Simpson, Lisa Friendly, Katherine Kwack, Jason Jones, and Laura Michaels all played a part in the production of this book and were wonderful to work with.

Patrick Chan
Rosanna Lee
Palo Alto, California
March, 1999

I have many people to thank for supporting me in contributing the `java.text` package to this book.

First, I want to thank my coauthors, Patrick and Rosanna, for whom I have a great deal of respect. They have set the standards very high for this book, meaning the effort but also the rewards are high.

Lisa Friendly, my manager at Sun's Java Software, has fully supported my desire to contribute to this extracurricular project. While it has sapped my free time, I think its payback has been worthwhile for Sun.

The Internationalization team helped improve the quality of this book by reviewing content and providing contacts. For this edition, I want especially to thank Laura Werner, Alan Liu, Rich Gillam, and Kathleen Wilson of IBM and Norbert Lindenberg and Naoto Satoh of Java Software.

Some French translations were provided by Isabelle and Lionel Gilet, my good friends.

Thanks also to Mike Hendrickson at Addison-Wesley and the Addison-Wesley production team.

My precious dog, Lady, has been by my side throughout the time spent working on this book, keeping me company. Lastly, I thank the other book authors in my family: my father and mother, Chuck and Jan, who have always given me their undying love.

Douglas Kramer
Palo Alto, California
March, 1999

java.io

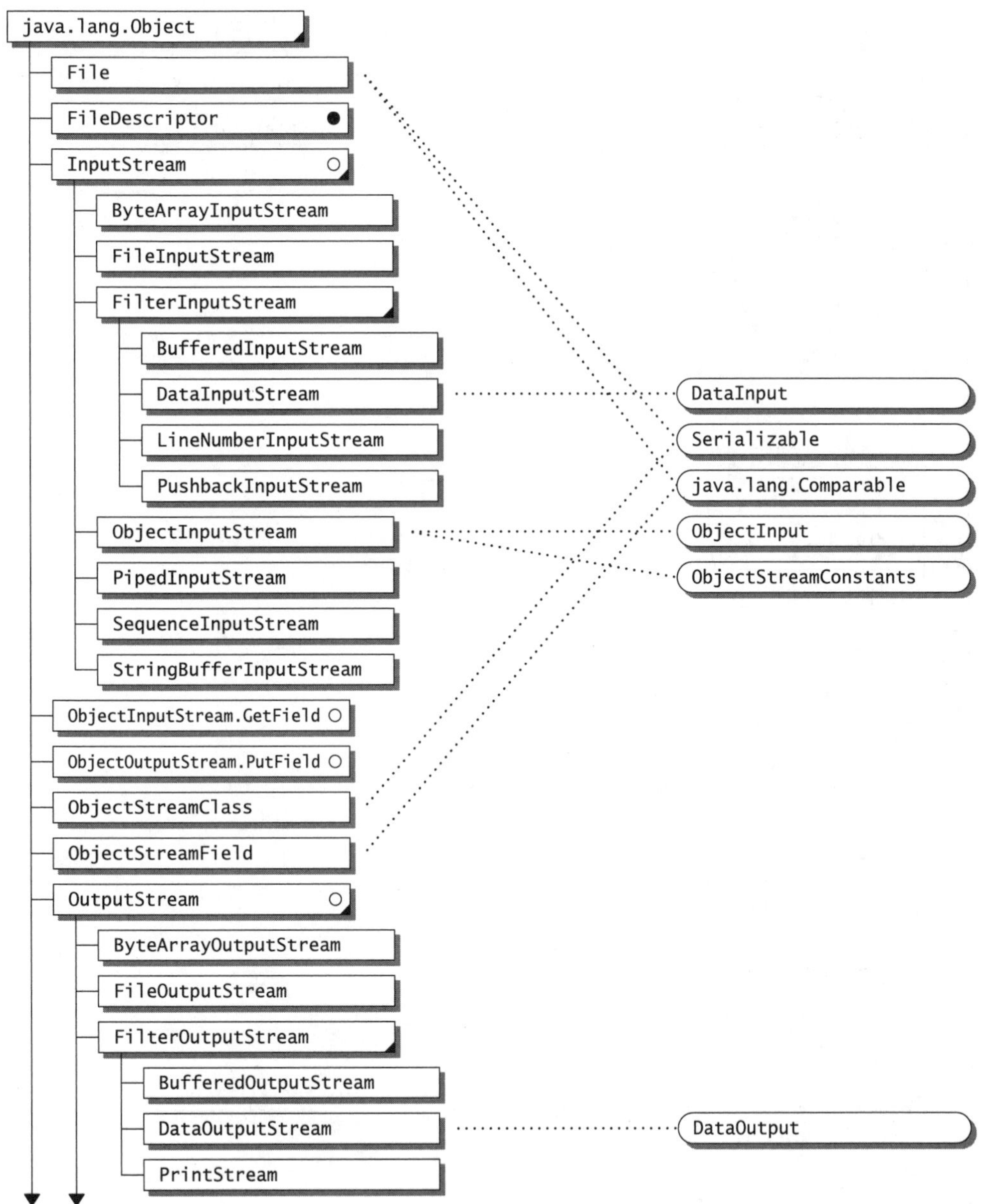

java.lang.Object
File
FileDescriptor
InputStream
ByteArrayInputStream
FileInputStream
FilterInputStream
BufferedInputStream
DataInputStream
LineNumberInputStream
PushbackInputStream
ObjectInputStream
PipedInputStream
SequenceInputStream
StringBufferInputStream
ObjectInputStream.GetField
ObjectOutputStream.PutField
ObjectStreamClass
ObjectStreamField
OutputStream
ByteArrayOutputStream
FileOutputStream
FilterOutputStream
BufferedOutputStream
DataOutputStream
PrintStream
DataInput
Serializable
java.lang.Comparable
ObjectInput
ObjectStreamConstants
DataOutput

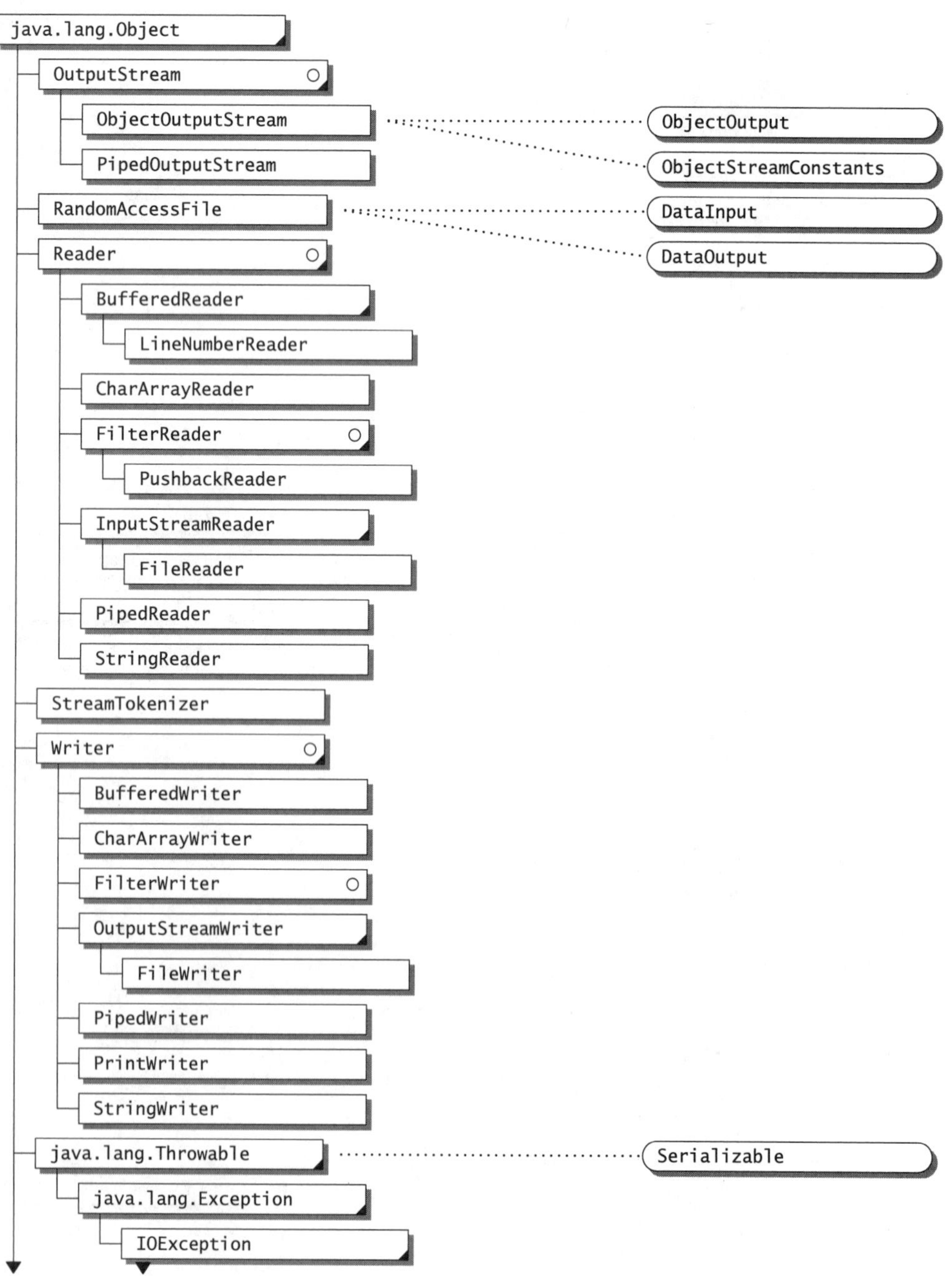
java.lang.Object
OutputStream
ObjectOutputStream
PipedOutputStream
RandomAccessFile
Reader
BufferedReader
LineNumberReader
CharArrayReader
FilterReader
PushbackReader
InputStreamReader
FileReader
PipedReader
StringReader
StreamTokenizer
Writer
BufferedWriter
CharArrayWriter
FilterWriter
OutputStreamWriter
FileWriter
PipedWriter
PrintWriter
StringWriter
java.lang.Throwable
java.lang.Exception
IOException
ObjectOutput
ObjectStreamConstants
DataInput
DataOutput
Serializable

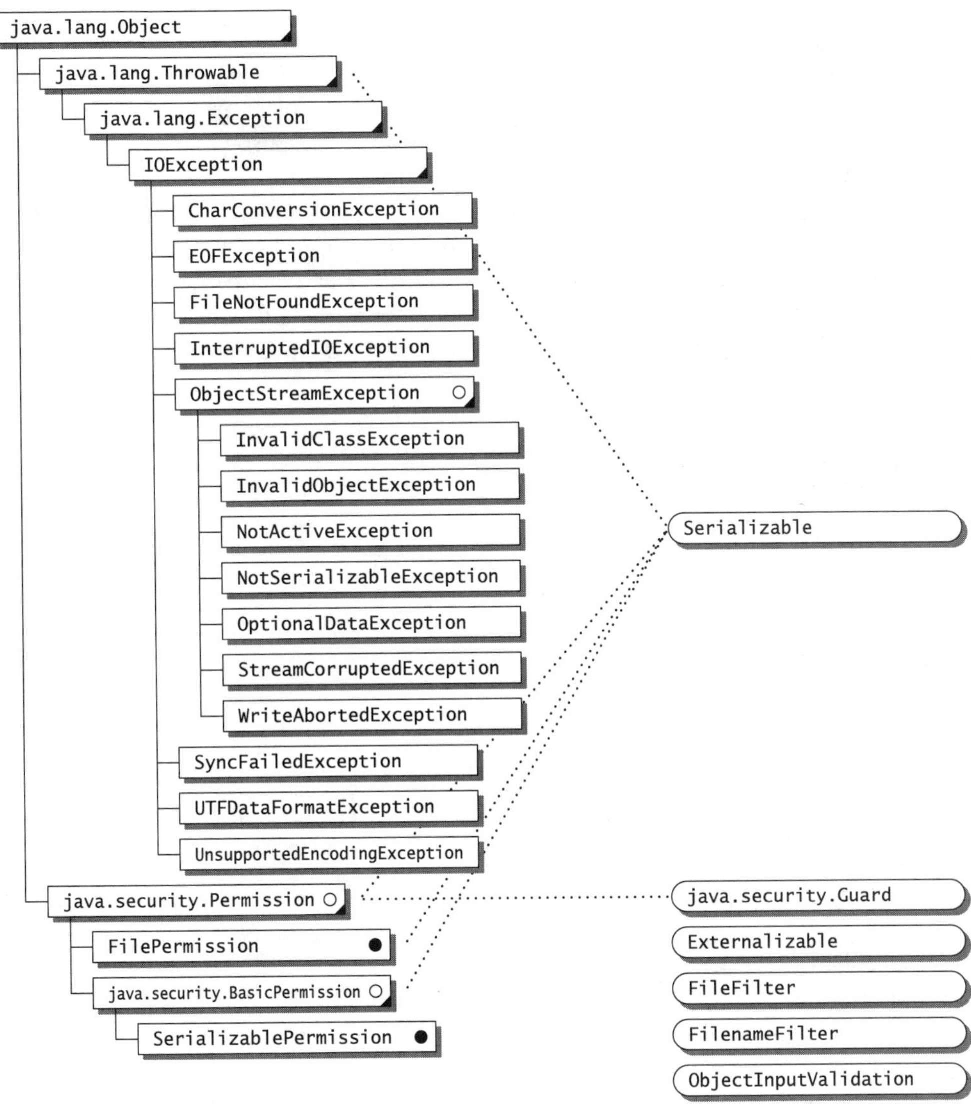

Description

The `java.io` package contains three main groups of classes and interfaces:

- Classes for building data streams
- Classes and interfaces for serialization
- Classes and interfaces for dealing with the file system

Data Streams

A *data stream* is either an *input* stream for reading values from a data source, such as an HTTP server or a Java string, or an *output* stream for writing values to a data repository, such as a file or an array of bytes. The data can be bytes or characters. The `java.io` package contains separate classes for dealing with byte streams and character streams. It also has classes for converting between byte streams and character streams.

A data container such as a file typically provides a method that returns an input stream for reading its contents or an output stream for storing values to it. These streams can be composed to form a chain of streams through which data flows and can be transformed by each stream. For example, after an input stream is obtained for a file, a data input stream could be added that transforms a stream of bytes into higher-level Java types, such as strings and integers, as shown in Figure 1.

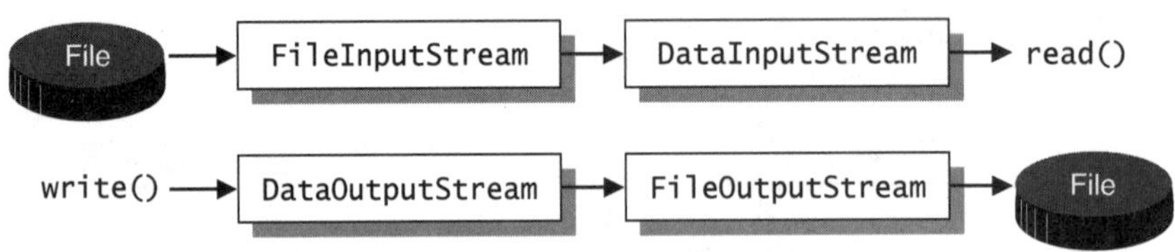

FIGURE 1: Composing IO Streams.

Serialization

Serialization of an object means to convert its state into a byte stream in such a way that the byte stream can be restored into a copy of the object. Not all objects can be serialized. An object that can be serialized is *serializable*. A Java object is serializable if its class or any of its superclasses implement the `Serializable` interface or its subinterface `Externalizable`.

Deserialization is the process of converting the serialized form of an object into a copy of the object.

Data values that are of Java primitive types, arrays, strings, and objects can all be serialized. Figure 2 shows how object serialization and deserialization works. Primitive types can be serialized/deserialized by using methods in the `DataInputStream`/`DataOutputStream` classes.

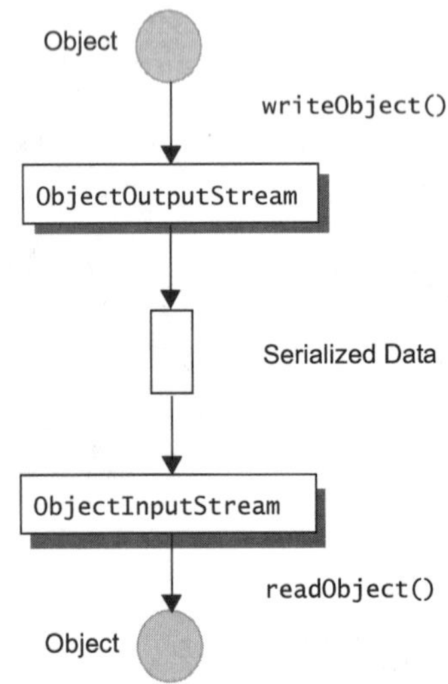

FIGURE 2: Object Serialization and Deserialization.

Files

The `java.io` package also contains classes for operating on files, such as creating and removing files, in a platform-independent way. Data in files can be treated as bytes or characters.

Changes for Version 1.2

Data Streams

The changes in the data stream classes consist primarily of the addition of overriding methods such as `close()`, `read()`, `ready()`, and `write()` so as to better match the semantics of the class.

The `PrintStream` constructors are no longer deprecated.

`PrintWriter`'s internal implementation has been modified to allow for easier subclassing.

Serialization

`ObjectInputStream` and `ObjectOutputStream` allow for more flexible subclassing. They also provide for a more uniform way of getting and setting serializable fields by using the new abstract classes `ObjectInputStream.GetField` and `ObjectOutputStream.PutField`. Object Serialization uses the Version 1.2 security model and the new `SerializablePermission` class to control customize serialization.

Files

The `File` class has been expanded to support the creation of temporary and lock files. There are new methods also for deleting files and changing a file's modification time and read-only status.

The `File`, `FileOutputStream`, and `RandomAccessFile` constructors have been modified to consistently throw a `FileNotFoundException` instead of an `IOException` if the supplied string name identifies a nonexistent file.

The `RandomAccessFile` has a new method for setting the length of a file, thus allowing a file to be easily truncated or expanded.

All file access has been changed to use the Version 1.2 security model, via the new `File-Permission` class.

Class and Interface Summary

Superclasses

The following abstract classes define a minimum set of operations that a stream must implement. `InputStream` and `OutputStream` are for byte streams, while `Reader` and `Writer` are for character streams.

`InputStream`	The superclass of all byte input streams. Provides basic input methods for reading data from a byte stream.
`OutputStream`	The superclass of all byte output streams. Provides basic output methods for writing data to a byte stream.
`Reader`	The superclass of all character input streams. Provides basic input methods for reading characters from a character stream.
`Writer`	The superclass of all character output streams. Provides basic output methods for writing characters to a character stream.

Byte Stream-to-Character Stream Converters

The following classes allow a program to convert a byte stream to a character stream.

`InputStreamReader`	Reads bytes from a byte stream, and converts them to characters.
`OutputStreamWriter`	Converts characters to a byte encoding, and writes them to a byte stream.

Filter Streams

A *filter stream* performs some "processing," or "filtering" as data is passed through it. A filter output stream performs processing on the data *before* it is written to its eventual destination, while a filter input stream performs processing on the data *after* it is read from its original source. `FilterInputStream` and `FilterOutputStream` are for byte streams, while `FilterReader` and `FilterWriter` are for character streams.

`FilterInputStream`	The superclass of all byte input filter streams.
`FilterOutputStream`	The superclass of all byte output filter streams.
`FilterReader`	The superclass of all character input filter streams.
`FilterWriter`	The superclass of all character output filter streams.

Buffered Streams

A *buffered stream* is a filter stream that *buffers* the data that flows through it in order to improve the performance of small read and write operations. `BufferedInputStream` and `BufferedOutputStream` are for byte streams, while `BufferedReader` and `BufferedWriter` are for character streams.

	Class	Description
Δ	`BufferedInputStream`	A filter input stream that maintains a buffer of bytes read from the original input stream.
	`BufferedOutputStream`	A filter output stream that maintains a buffer of bytes to be written to its destination output stream.
	`BufferedReader`	A filter input stream that maintains a buffer of characters read from the original character input stream.
	`BufferedWriter`	A filter output stream that maintains a buffer of characters to be written to its destination character output stream.

Files

The following classes provide file-related operations available in Java. `FileInputStream` and `FileOutputStream` are for reading/writing bytes to files, while `FileReader` and `FileWriter` are for reading/writing characters to files. The `RandomAccessFile` class allows random access to the contents of a file.

	Class	Description
Δ	`File`	A file that has methods for operating on a file.
	`FileDescriptor`	A handle to an open file.
1.2	`FileFilter`	An interface for filtering files by their `File` objects.
	`FileInputStream`	A filter input stream for reading bytes from a file.
Δ	`FileOutputStream`	A filter output stream for writing bytes to a file.
	`FilenameFilter`	An interface for filtering files by their filenames.
1.2	`FilePermission`	Permission to access a file or directory.
	`FileReader`	A filter input stream for reading characters from a file.
	`FileWriter`	A filter output stream for writing characters to a file.
Δ	`RandomAccessFile`	A class for accessing the contents of a file nonsequentially.

Serialization

The following classes are used to serialize (and deserialize) Java primitive data, arrays, strings, and objects in a compact binary form. They are typically used to save and retrieve values and objects in a file or exchange them via a network connection. The `DataInput/DataOutput`-related methods are for serializing/deserializing Java primitive types. The `ObjectInput/ObjectOutput`-related methods are for serializing/deserializing Java objects.

	Class	Description
	`DataInput`	An interface for deserializing Java primitive data.
	`DataInputStream`	A filter input stream for deserializing Java primitive data.
	`DataOutput`	An interface for serializing Java primitive data.
	`DataOutputStream`	A filter output stream for serializing Java primitive data.
	`Externalizable`	An interface to indicate that instances of a class can be serialized into a class-specific "external" format.
	`ObjectInput`	An interface for deserializing Java primitive data and objects.
Δ	`ObjectInputStream`	An input stream for deserializing Java primitive data and objects.
1.2	`ObjectInputStream.GetField`	Serializable fields read from an `ObjectInputStream`.
	`ObjectInputValidation`	An interface for validating a deserialized object.
	`ObjectOutput`	An interface for serializing Java primitive data and objects.
Δ	`ObjectOutputStream`	An output stream for serializing Java primitive data and objects.
1.2	`ObjectOutputStream.PutField`	Serializable fields to be written to an `ObjectOutputStream`.
Δ	`ObjectStreamClass`	A class descriptor.
1.2	`ObjectStreamConstants`	Constants used by Object Serialization.
1.2	`ObjectStreamField`	A serializable field.
	`Serializable`	An interface to indicate that instances of a class can be serialized.
1.2	`SerializablePermission`	Permission to perform certain serialization operations.

In-Memory Streams

The following classes use in-memory data structures as IO streams.

	Class	Description
Δ	`ByteArrayInputStream`	An input stream that reads data from a `byte` array.
Δ	`ByteArrayOutputStream`	An output stream that writes its data to a `byte` array.
Δ	`CharArrayReader`	An input stream that reads data from a `char` array.
	`CharArrayWriter`	An output stream that writes its data to a `char` array.
Δ	`StringReader`	An input stream that reads data from a `StringBuffer`.
Δ	`StringWriter`	An output stream that writes its data to a `StringBuffer`.

Pipes

The following two pairs of classes can be used to create a stream of data between two threads. Such a stream of data is called a *pipe*. One thread can write into one end of the pipe, while the other thread can read from the other end of the pipe. `PipedInputStream` and `PipedOutputStream` are for byte streams, while `PipedReader` and `PipedWriter` are for character streams.

	`PipedInputStream`	An input stream for reading bytes from a pipe.
	`PipedOutputStream`	An output stream for writing bytes to a pipe.
Δ	`PipedReader`	An input stream for reading input from a pipe.
Δ	`PipedWriter`	An output stream for writing output to a pipe.

Streams for Parsing

The following classes are useful when building parsers.

Δ	`PushbackInputStream`	A filter input stream that allows bytes to be unread from the stream.
Δ	`PushbackReader`	A filter input stream that allows characters to be unread from the stream.
	`StreamTokenizer`	A filter input stream for parsing the stream into a sequence of tokens.

Input Stream Sequence

The following class is used to combine a sequence of input streams into a single input stream. When one input stream is exhausted, the class seamlessly starts reading from the next input stream.

`SequenceInputStream`	Creates a single input stream from two or more input streams.

Miscellaneous Filter Streams

The following classes implement various useful streams.

	`LineNumberReader`	A buffered character input stream for counting the number of lines.
Δ	`PrintStream`	A filter output stream for converting Java primitive types and objects to a printable form.
Δ	`PrintWriter`	A character output stream for converting Java primitive types and objects to a printable form.

Serialization-Related Exceptions

Following are the serialization-related exceptions declared in this package. They are not subclasses of `RuntimeException`, so they must be either caught or declared in the `throws` clause.

Exception	Description
`InvalidClassException`	Thrown if a problem occurs that is related to the class of object being serialized/deserialized.
`InvalidObjectException`	Thrown if validation of the deserialized object fails.
`NotActiveException`	Thrown if certain methods in `ObjectInputStream`/`ObjectOutputStream` are invoked when an object is not being serialized/deserialized.
`NotSerializableException`	Thrown if an attempt is made to serialize an object that does not implement the `Serializable` or `Externalizable` interface.
`ObjectStreamException`	The superclass of serialization-related exceptions.
`OptionalDataException`	Thrown if unexpected data is encountered in the serialization stream.
`StreamCorruptedException`	Thrown if data in the serialization stream does not match its associated control data.
`WriteAbortedException`	Thrown when the stream indicates that it contains incomplete serialization data because the writer aborted the serialization process.

All Other IO Exceptions

Following are the nonserialization-related exceptions declared in this package. They are not subclasses of `RuntimeException`, so they must be either caught or declared in the `throws` clause.

Exception	Description
`CharConversionException`	Thrown if the byte-to-character or character-to-byte conversion fails.
`EOFException`	Thrown if end-of-file has been reached when reading from a data input stream.
`FileNotFoundException`	Thrown if attempting to access a nonexistent file.
`IOException`	The superclass of input/output-related exceptions.
`InterruptedIOException`	Thrown if a stream operation has been interrupted.
`SyncFailedException`	Thrown if the attempt to flush internal system buffers to the corresponding physical device has failed.
`UnsupportedEncodingException`	Thrown if the specified character-to-byte or byte-to-character encoding is not supported.
`UTFDataFormatException`	Thrown if a Unicode string in a malformed Unicode Transfer Format has been encountered.

Deprecated Classes

The following classes have been deprecated.

`LineNumberInputStream`	Replaced by `LineNumberReader`.
`StringBufferInputStream`	Replaced by `StringReader`.

java.lang

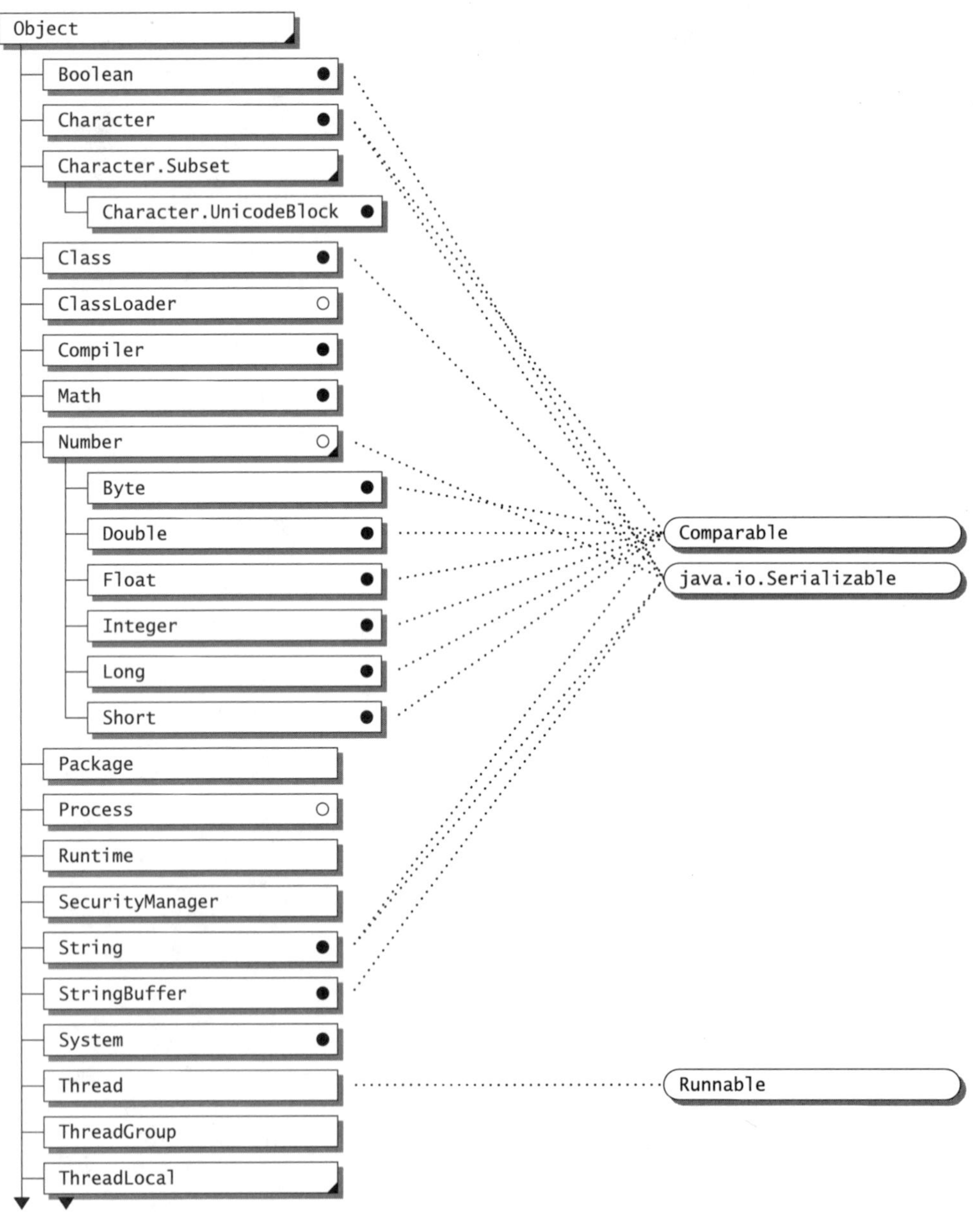

Object
Boolean
Character
Character.Subset
Character.UnicodeBlock
Class
ClassLoader
Compiler
Math
Number
Byte
Double
Float
Integer
Long
Short
Package
Process
Runtime
SecurityManager
String
StringBuffer
System
Thread
ThreadGroup
ThreadLocal
Comparable
java.io.Serializable
Runnable

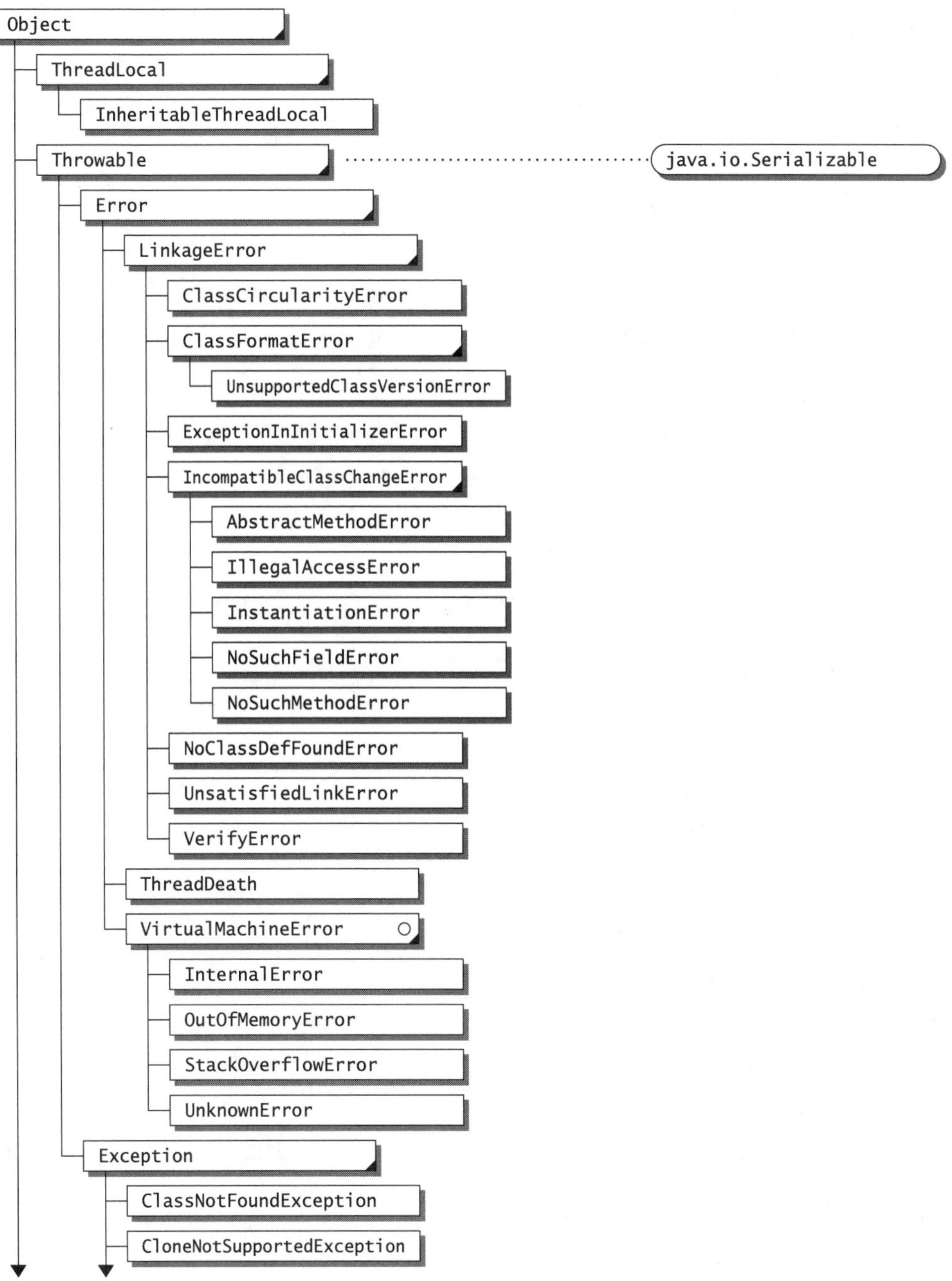
Object
ThreadLocal
InheritableThreadLocal
Throwable
java.io.Serializable
Error
LinkageError
ClassCircularityError
ClassFormatError
UnsupportedClassVersionError
ExceptionInInitializerError
IncompatibleClassChangeError
AbstractMethodError
IllegalAccessError
InstantiationError
NoSuchFieldError
NoSuchMethodError
NoClassDefFoundError
UnsatisfiedLinkError
VerifyError
ThreadDeath
VirtualMachineError
InternalError
OutOfMemoryError
StackOverflowError
UnknownError
Exception
ClassNotFoundException
CloneNotSupportedException

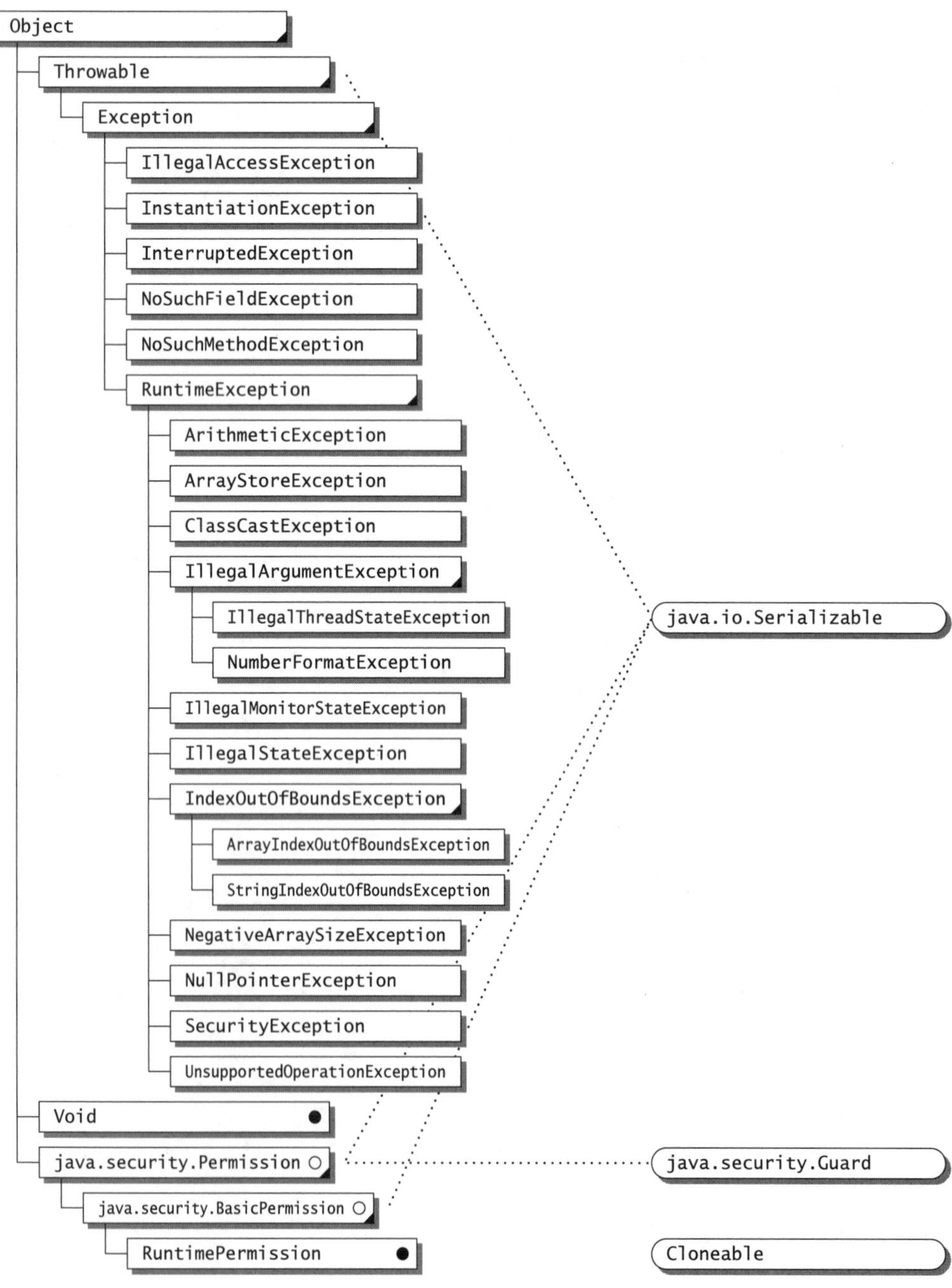

Object
Throwable
Exception
IllegalAccessException
InstantiationException
InterruptedException
NoSuchFieldException
NoSuchMethodException
RuntimeException
ArithmeticException
ArrayStoreException
ClassCastException
IllegalArgumentException
IllegalThreadStateException
NumberFormatException
IllegalMonitorStateException
IllegalStateException
IndexOutOfBoundsException
ArrayIndexOutOfBoundsException
StringIndexOutOfBoundsException
NegativeArraySizeException
NullPointerException
SecurityException
UnsupportedOperationException
Void
java.security.Permission
java.security.BasicPermission
RuntimePermission
java.io.Serializable
java.security.Guard
Cloneable

Description

The java.lang package contains classes that are integral to the Java language. These include Object, Throwable, String, and Thread. If any class in this package is missing, the runtime will not start. The classes in this package are automatically imported into every Java program, so there is no need to explicitly import them.

All errors and exceptions that can be thrown by the Java virtual machine appear in this package. Also included are classes for accessing system resources, primitive type object wrappers, a math class, and a security class.

Changes for Version 1.2

Wrapper Classes

The wrapper classes, Byte, Character, Double, Float, Integer, Long, and Short, implement the new Comparable interface. This allows arrays containing instances of these classes to be easily sorted, for example by using the collection classes (see java.util.Collection). A few parsing methods have been added to some of these classes so that they all have the set of parsing routines.

New classes Character.Subset and Character.UnicodeBlock have been added to make categorizing Unicode characters easier.

Classes and Class Loading

Version 1.2 includes a new class loader architecture that implements a delegation algorithm in which a class loader always consults its parent class loader before attempting to load the class itself. The parent in turn consults its parent, and so on. So the current class loader gets involved only when *all* of the ancestor class loaders cannot find the class. This same delegation algorithm is employed for loading resources.

Related to this new architecture is the refinement of the Version 1.1 concept of *system class loader,* which is responsible for loading system classes and system resources, into a *bootstrap class loader* and a *system class loader.* The system class loader's parent is the bootstrap class loader.

The concept of a package has been formalized in the new class Package. Class and ClassLoader provide methods for getting packages of a class and a class loader, respectively. They use the Version 1.2 security model to control access to a class loader.

Threads

Methods in the Thread and ThreadGroup classes that relate to thread suspension and stoppage were deprecated because they could too easily be misused to create misbehaving programs.

New methods have been added to the Thread class for getting a thread's *context* class loader—this is useful when writing library code.

InheritableThreadLocal and ThreadLocal have been added to allow multithreaded programs to more easily use thread-local data structures.

System

The Version 1.2 security model provides a fine-grained permission model. `SecurityManager` has been rewritten to use this new model. See `SecurityManager` for details. The new class `RuntimePermission` is used to represent runtime-related permissions.

`runFinalizationOnExit()` was deprecated in `Runtime` and `System` because it might have resulted in unsafe programs.

Methods have been added to `Math` for converting angles specified in degrees to and from radians.

String Processing

`String` implements the new `Comparable` interface. It also has new methods for doing case-insensitive comparisons and sorts.

Several new methods have been added to `StringBuffer` to allow the deletion and replacement of portions of the buffer.

Errors and Exceptions

`UnsupportedClassVersionError` and `UnsupportedOperationException` have been added.

`ClassNotFoundException` and `ExceptionInInitializationError` override `printStackTrace()` to print the stack trace of the root exception.

Class and Interface Summary

Root Classes

The `Object` class is the superclass of all classes, so the methods defined in this class are inherited by all other classes. A `Class` object encapsulates information about a Java class that has been loaded into the system; there is one `Class` object for each loaded class. The `Throwable` class is the root of all Java errors and exceptions. A class that represents an error or an exception must inherit from `Throwable`.

Δ	`Class`	Used to obtain information about a Java class.
	`Object`	The superclass of all Java objects.
	`Throwable`	The superclass of all Java errors and exceptions.

Basic Interfaces

The `Cloneable` interface is used by classes that want to support the `clone()` method. Unless a class implements this interface, an attempt to clone an object will result in a `CloneNotSupportedException` being thrown. The `Comparable` interface is used for classes whose items can be ordered.

	Cloneable	An interface that a class must implement in order to support the `clone()` method.
1.2	Comparable	An interface that a class implements so that instances of it can be sorted.

Strings
The following classes provide Java's string manipulation capabilities. A `String` object is immutable. This means that any operation on it always results in a new `String` object, with the original object left intact. A `StringBuffer` object maintains an expandable sequence of characters and should be used in applications when you expect to modify a string a lot. In most applications, `String` objects are typically used and result in fewer programming errors. Consider using a `StringBuffer` object only if efficiency becomes an issue.

Δ	String	An immutable sequence of characters with lots of string-related operations.
Δ	StringBuffer	A mutable, expandable sequence of characters with lots of string-related operations.

Math

Δ	Math	A collection of mathematical operations for doing trigonometry, for rounding, and for finding logs and square roots.

System
The following classes are used to access system-related services such as the current time, processes, garbage collector, and memory management.

Δ	ClassLoader	Used to load Java classes and define loading policies.
1.2	Package	Represents a package.
	Process	Used to obtain information about and communicate with processes spawned to execute system programs.
Δ	Runtime	Used to perform environment-related and system-related operations, such as loading libraries, executing system programs, and performing garbage collection.
Δ	System	Used to examine and manipulate system-related information such as the current time and system properties in a platform-independent manner. Contains fields for standard input, output, and error.

java.lang

Threads

Threads allow a program to have multiple threads of execution occurring concurrently. The following classes provide the support for defining, creating, and manipulating Java threads. There also are classes for representing thread-local variables.

1.2	`InheritableThreadLocal`	A thread-local variable that is inherited from a parent thread by child threads.
	`Runnable`	An interface that a class can implement to be runnable by a thread.
Δ	`Thread`	Used to define, create, and manipulate a thread.
Δ	`ThreadGroup`	Used to create and manipulate a set of threads.
1.2	`ThreadLocal`	A thread-local variable.

Primitive Type Wrappers

The following classes are used to work around the fact that primitive types such as `int` and `float` are not Java objects and that Java does not support templates. For example, classes that implement a data structure such as a tree or a hash table are typically implemented to handle objects so as to achieve maximal reusability. This means that a primitive type like `int` cannot be used with the class. When an `Integer` object is wrapped around an `int` value, the `int` value can then be used by the class. Of course, this introduces some overhead, so if efficiency is absolutely critical, you need to implement a version of the data structure specifically for the desired primitive type.

	`Boolean`	An object wrapper for a `boolean` value.
Δ	`Byte`	An object wrapper for a `byte` value.
Δ	`Character`	An object wrapper for a `char` value.
Δ	`Double`	An object wrapper for a `double` value.
Δ	`Float`	An object wrapper for a `float` value.
Δ	`Integer`	An object wrapper for an `int` value.
Δ	`Long`	An object wrapper for a `long` value.
	`Number`	The abstract superclass for the number objects (`Byte`, `Double`, `Float`, `Integer`, `Long`, `Short`, `BigDecimal`, and `BigInteger`).
Δ	`Short`	An object wrapper for a `short` value.
	`Void`	Holds a reference to a `Class` object for `void`. Cannot be instantiated.

Character Ranges

These classes are for getting ranges of Unicode character ranges.

1.2	`Character.Subset`	Holds constants for subsets of the Unicode character set.
1.2	`Character.UnicodeBlock`	Defines ranges of characters defined by Unicode 2.0.

Security

The `SecurityManager` class is used to define the security policies of a Java application. It controls what a Java application or applet can and cannot do. It is typically used by an application that executes Java applets, such as a Web browser. It can be set once and cannot be removed. If an applet or application fails a security check, a `SecurityException` is thrown.

1.2	`RuntimePermission`	Represents permission to perform a runtime operation.
	`SecurityException`	A runtime exception that is thrown when the program is denied access to perform an operation due to security reasons.
Δ	`SecurityManager`	Used to define the security policy for a Java program.

Compiler

The `Compiler` class is used to control a compiler that compiles Java byte codes directly into machine code for a particular platform. Such a compiler is not included in the Java development kit from Sun Microsystems and must be obtained from a third-party source.

`Compiler`	Used to compile Java byte codes into machine code.

Errors

A Java *error* is a type of exception thrown by the Java virtual machine to indicate that an unrecoverable erroneous condition has occurred. For example, an error would be thrown if there was an attempt to load a corrupted class.

`AbstractMethodError`	Thrown if an attempt is made to invoke an abstract method.
`ClassCircularityError`	Thrown if an attempt is made to load classes that have cyclic class inheritance.
`ClassFormatError`	Thrown if an attempt is made to load a class that is not in an acceptable format.
`Error`	The superclass of all error classes.

Continued

Δ	`ExceptionInInitializerError`	Thrown if an exception is encountered in a static initializer.
	`IllegalAccessError`	Thrown if an attempt is made to access a member of a class to that cannot be accessed due to the Java programming language protection modes (such as `protected` and `private`).
	`IncompatibleClassChangeError`	The superclass of errors that are thrown if an attempt is made to access a member of a class in a way that violates Java language semantics.
	`InstantiationError`	Thrown if an attempt is made to instantiate an abstract class or an interface.
	`InternalError`	Thrown if the Java virtual machine encounters an unrecoverable error that involves the virtual machine's internal logic.
	`LinkageError`	The superclass of errors that result when an attempt is made to load a class that has changed in an incompatible manner and consequently cannot be loaded.
	`NoClassDefFoundError`	Thrown if the system's default class loader cannot find the class to load.
	`NoSuchFieldError`	Thrown if an attempt is made to access a nonexistent field of a class.
	`NoSuchMethodError`	Thrown if an attempt is made to access a nonexistent method of a class.
	`OutOfMemoryError`	Thrown if the Java runtime runs out of memory and consequently cannot continue execution.
	`StackOverflowError`	Thrown if the Java execution stack limit has been exceeded during the execution of a thread.
	`ThreadDeath`	Thrown by the runtime to indicate that the current thread is about to be terminated.
	`UnknownError`	Thrown if a condition that cannot be described by any other error has occurred.
	`UnsatisfiedLinkError`	Thrown if a library cannot be loaded and linked successfully.
1.2	`UnsupportedClassVersionError`	Thrown if the Java virtual machine encounters a class file with a major or minor version number that it does not support.
	`VerifyError`	Thrown if a class cannot be loaded because it violates the Java byte code specification.
	`VirtualMachineError`	The superclass of errors that are thrown if the Java virtual machine encounters an unrecoverable error, such as lack of memory or lack of stack size.

Runtime Exceptions

The following exceptions inherit from `RuntimeException`, so it is not necessary to catch them or declare them in a `throws` clause. However, exceptions of this type are considered programming bugs and should be corrected.

Exception	Description
`ArithmeticException`	Thrown if an attempt is made to perform an illegal arithmetic operation (such as division by zero).
`ArrayIndexOutOfBoundsException`	Thrown if an attempt is made to access an array element with an index that is outside of the array bounds.
`ArrayStoreException`	Thrown if an attempt is made to store an object of the wrong type in an array.
`ClassCastException`	Thrown if an attempt is made to cast an object to an incompatible class.
`IllegalArgumentException`	Thrown if an illegal argument has been passed to a method.
`IllegalMonitorStateException`	Thrown if a thread calls an object's synchronized method but does not own the object's lock.
`IllegalStateException`	Thrown if a method is invoked on an object while it is in an unsuitable state.
`IllegalThreadStateException`	Thrown if an attempt is made to perform an operation on a thread while the thread is in a state unsuitable for that operation.
`IndexOutOfBoundsException`	The superclass of exceptions that are thrown when an attempt is made to access an element with an index that is out of bounds.
`NegativeArraySizeException`	Thrown if an attempt is made to create an array that has a negative size.
`NullPointerException`	Thrown if an attempt is made to dereference a `null` reference.
`NumberFormatException`	Thrown if a string is not in a format that can be parsed into a number of the desired type.
`RuntimeException`	The superclass of all runtime exceptions that indicate a programming error.
`StringIndexOutOfBoundsException`	Thrown if attempting to access an element of a string using an index that is outside of the bounds of the string.
1.2 `UnsupportedOperationException`	Thrown if a method is invoked that is not supported.

Exceptions

The following exceptions directly inherit from `Exception`, so they must be either caught or declared in the `throws` clause. Exceptions of this type typically indicate some error condition that can sometimes arise in an operation. For example, when a class is going to be loaded the operation normally returns a reference to the class. However, if the class cannot be found, a `ClassNotFoundException` is raised. A program should catch this error, notify the user of the error, and then continue running.

Δ	`ClassNotFoundException`	Thrown if a class loader cannot find the class to load on explicit instructions from the program (rather than implicitly by the runtime, which loads classes as they are referenced).
	`CloneNotSupportedException`	Thrown if an attempt is made to clone an object that belongs to a class that does not implement the `Cloneable` interface.
	`Exception`	The superclass used for representing exceptional conditions that must be caught.
	`IllegalAccessException`	Thrown if not permitted to access a member of a class.
	`InstantiationException`	Thrown if an attempt is made to instantiate an abstract class or an interface.
	`InterruptedException`	Thrown when a thread receives an interrupt invoked by another thread.
	`NoSuchMethodException`	Thrown if an attempt is made to access a nonexistent method of an object.
	`NoSuchFieldException`	Thrown if an attempt is made to access a nonexistent field of an object.

java.lang.ref

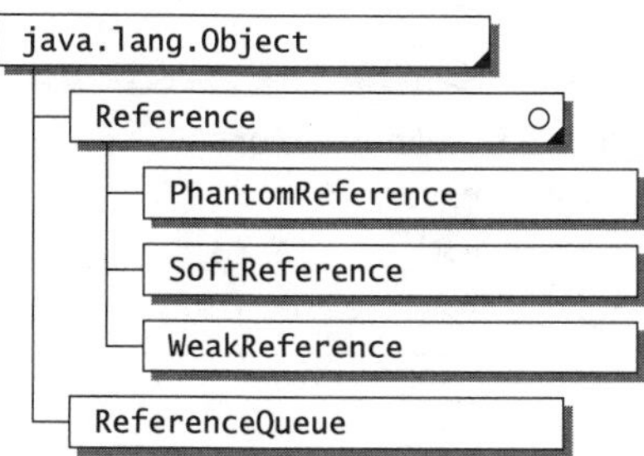

Description

The `java.lang.ref` package provides classes for manipulating *reference objects*. A reference object is used to determine when an object is garbage collected. This capability is typically used to free resources associated with the object when the object is no longer being used.

Reference objects are used in the following way. If you want to know when some object `obj` is garbage collected, you create a reference object to refer to `obj` (the *referent*). When `obj` is no longer used, the garbage collector collects it and enqueues all reference objects to it to a *reference queue*. You can then determine that `obj` has been garbage collected by polling the reference queue until the reference object appears. See Figure 3.

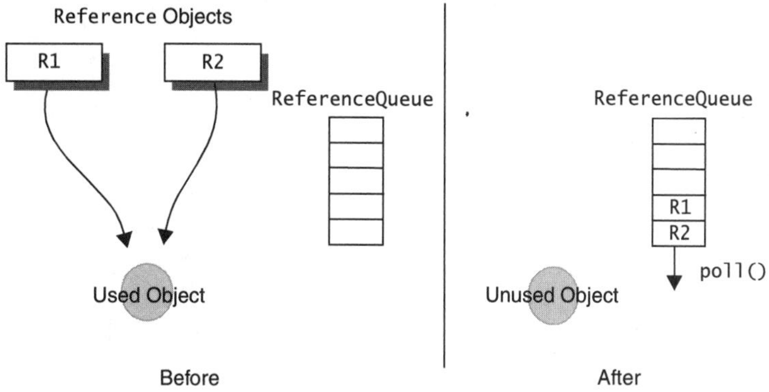

FIGURE 3: The Enqueuing of Reference Objects to an Unused Object.

Class and Interface Summary

References

The following classes represent the different types of references.

`PhantomReference`	Used to schedule post-mortem cleanup actions.
`Reference`	The abstract base class of references.
`SoftReference`	Represents a soft reference object.
`WeakReference`	Used to implement simple caches.

Reference Queue

`ReferenceQueue` holds registered reference objects appended to by the garbage collector after the appropriate reachability changes are detected.

`ReferenceQueue`	Holds registered reference objects.

java.lang.reflect

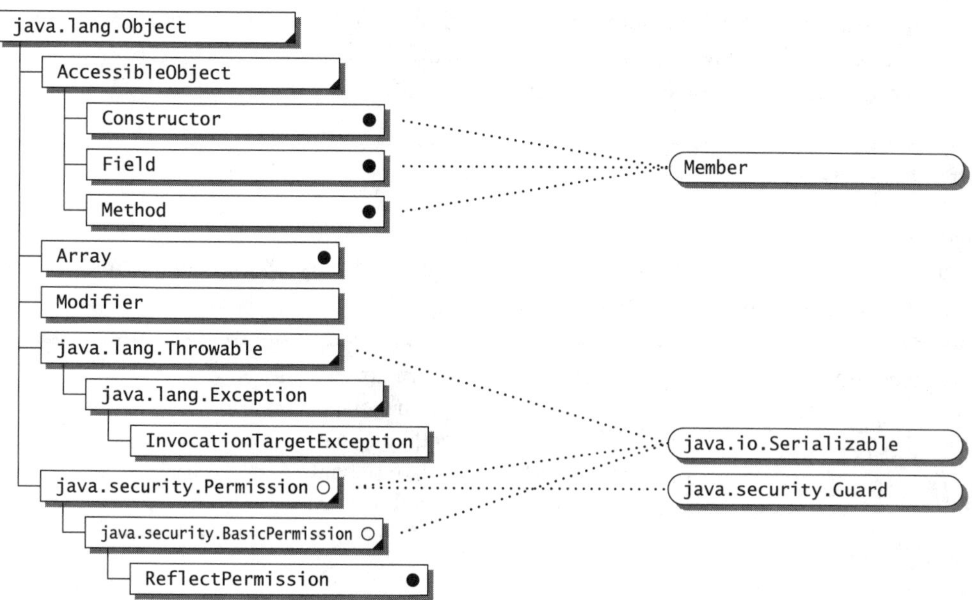

Description

The `java.lang.reflect` package provides classes and interfaces for obtaining *reflective information* about Java classes and objects. Reflective information includes information about the members that a class has, the signatures of a class's constructors and methods, and the types of its fields. With it, you also can create new objects, access and change an object's fields, and invoke an object's methods.

This package is typically used by programs such as debuggers, interpreters, object inspectors, and class browsers and by Java runtime services such as Object Serialization and JavaBeans.

Security

An application can get reflective information about a class or object only if it has been granted permission to do so by the security manager. If it does not have permission, a `SecurityException` is thrown. See `SecurityManager.checkMemberAccess()` and `ReflectPermission`.

In addition, gaining access to reflective information does not automatically grant the holder of that information special privileges as far as the Java language is concerned. Specifically, the holder can access nonpublic members if, and only if, it was able to do so without using reflection.

Changes for Version 1.2

Constructor, Field, Member, and Method have a new base class, AccessibleObject, that provides the ability to suppress the default Java programming language access control checks for the purposes of reflection. This ability is controlled by using ReflectPermission.

The Java programming language has a new modifier, strictfp. The Modifier class has a new constant and method for supporting this new modifier.

Class and Interface Summary

Members

Instances of Constructor, Field, and Method are created only by the Java virtual machine. They are returned by methods in java.lang.Class.

Constructor	Represents a constructor in a class.
Field	Represents a field in a class.
Member	The interface containing methods common to Constructor, Field, and Method.
Method	Represents a method in a class.

Utility Classes

AccessibleObject provides the ability to suppress the default Java programming language access control checks for the purposes of reflection. Array and Modifier are useful for dealing with Java arrays and modifiers.

1.2	AccessibleObject	Base class for Constructor, Field, Member, and Method.
	Array	Used to create, access, and modify arrays. Cannot be instantiated.
Δ	Modifier	Used to decode the modifiers associated with a class and members of a class. Cannot be instantiated.
1.2	ReflectPermission	Represents a permission for reflective operations.

Exception

There is one exception declared in this package. It extends directly from Exception, so it must be either caught or declared in the throws clause.

Δ	InvocationTargetException	Thrown if the invoked method or constructor throws an exception.

java.math

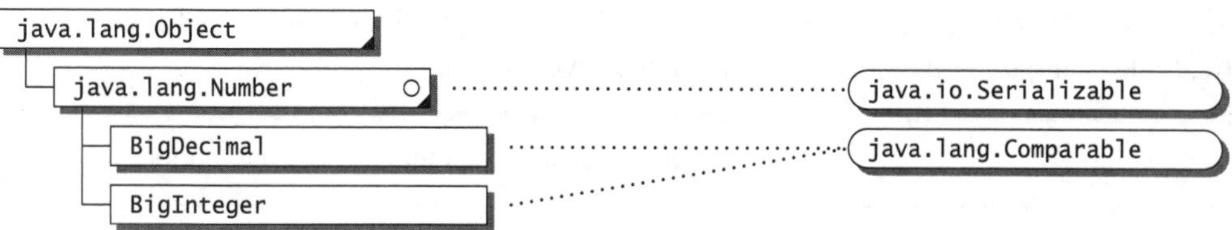

Description

The `java.math` package contains classes for performing arithmetic and bit manipulation on arbitrary-precision decimal and integer numbers. `BigInteger` and `BigDecimal` are analogous to Java's primitive types—`double` and `long`, respectively—except that they have arbitrary precision. Hence, operations on them do not overflow or lose precision.

Changes for Version 1.2

`BigInteger` and `BigDecimal` now implement the new `Comparable` interface. This allows arrays containing instances of these classes to be easily sorted, for instance with the collection classes (see `java.util.Collection`).

A new method, `BigDecimal.unscaledValue()`, has been added to retrieve the big decimal value that does not have a decimal point.

For convenience, two new `BigInteger` constants have been added: `ZERO` and `ONE`.

Class Summary

BigInteger

A `BigInteger` is represented in two's-complement notation. The class provides corresponding methods for all Java operations on `int` and `long`. The semantics of these operations are analogous to those of corresponding Java operations on `int` and `long`, except that operations on `BigInteger` do not overflow.

`BigInteger` also provides methods for modular arithmetic, GCD calculation, primality testing, prime generation, single-bit manipulation, and many methods corresponding to those in `java.lang.Math`.

Δ	`BigInteger`	Represents an arbitrary-precision integer.

BigDecimal

A `BigDecimal` represents an arbitrary-precision decimal number consisting of an arbitrary-precision integer value and a nonnegative integer *scale*. The scale represents the number of decimal digits to the right of the decimal point. This class provides operations for basic arithmetic, scale manipulation, comparison, format conversion, and hashing.

Δ	`BigDecimal`	Represents an arbitrary-precision decimal number.

java.net

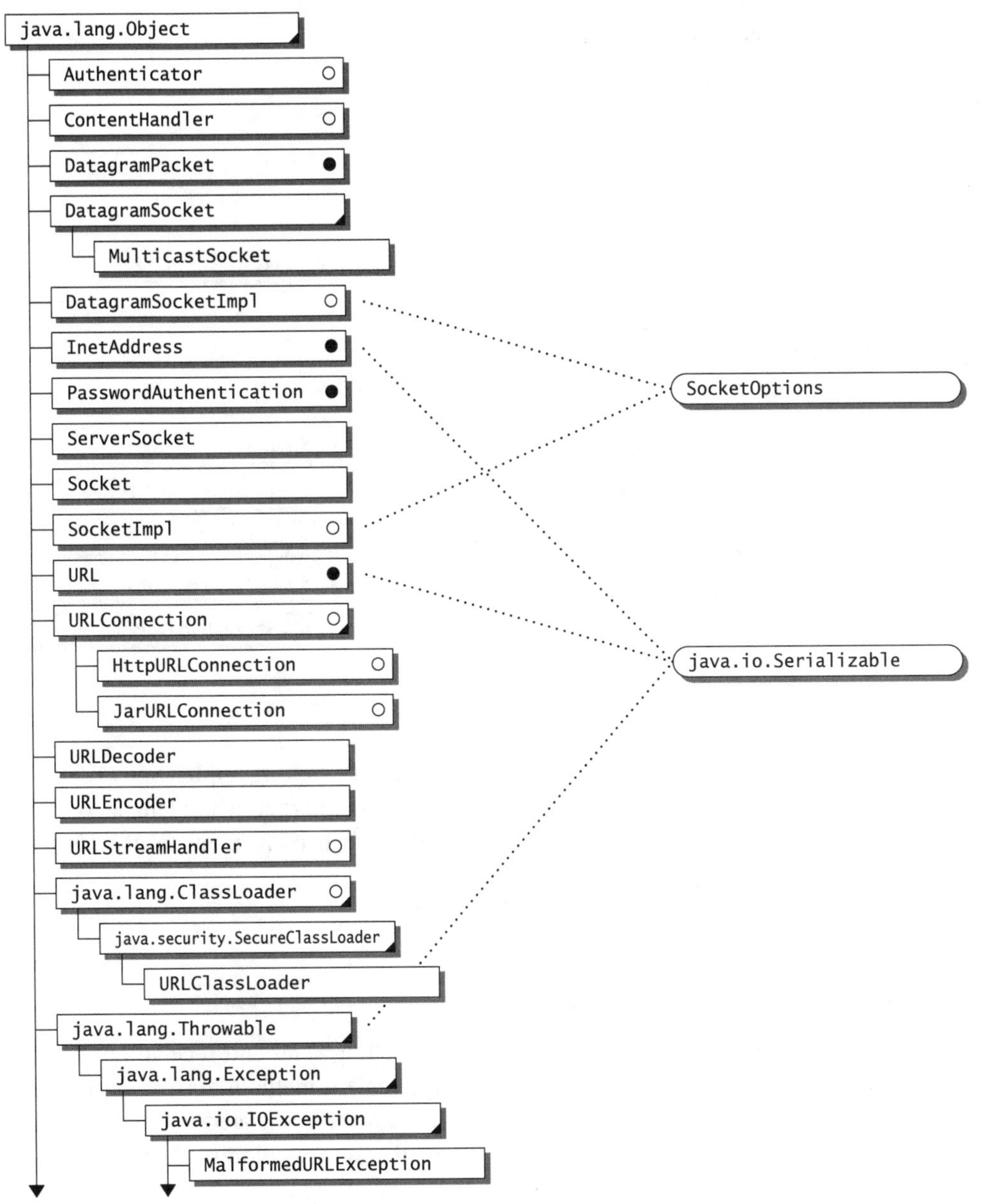

java.lang.Object
Authenticator
ContentHandler
DatagramPacket
DatagramSocket
MulticastSocket
DatagramSocketImpl
InetAddress
PasswordAuthentication
ServerSocket
Socket
SocketImpl
URL
URLConnection
HttpURLConnection
JarURLConnection
URLDecoder
URLEncoder
URLStreamHandler
java.lang.ClassLoader
java.security.SecureClassLoader
URLClassLoader
java.lang.Throwable
java.lang.Exception
java.io.IOException
MalformedURLException
SocketOptions
java.io.Serializable

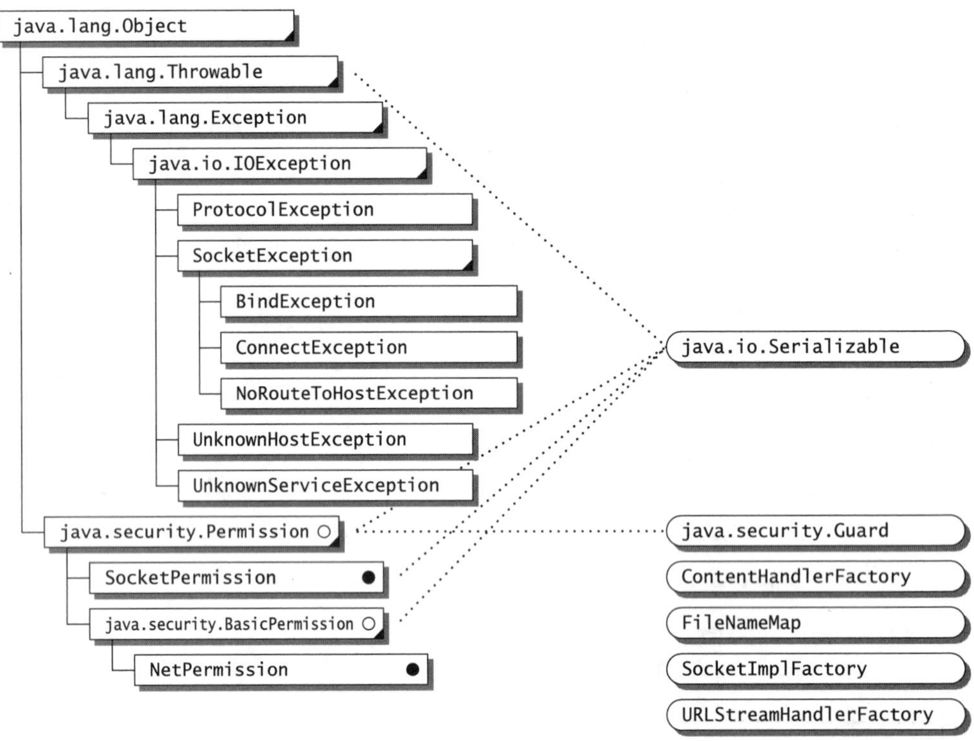

Description

The `java.net` package contains classes for implementing networking applications. Using the socket classes, you can communicate with any server on the Internet or implement your own Internet server.[1] A number of classes are provided to make it convenient to use *Universal Resource Locators* (URLs) to retrieve data on the Internet.

Changes for Version 1.2

Sockets

`Socket` and `DatagramSocket` now support getting and setting send and receive buffer sizes. `DatagramSocket` and `MulticastSocket` have more convenient methods for setting the time-to-live values. `DatagramSocket` allows a remote address to be associated with the socket so that it can send and receive datagram packets only from that remote address. Access to sockets

1. Restrictions may be placed by the security manager regarding with which servers you can communicate. For example, some Web browsers allow applets to communicate only with the server from which the applet was loaded.

is now controlled using the Version 1.2 security model via the `SocketPermission` class. The `SocketOptions` interface has been added for socket implementation developers to use for setting and getting socket options.

URL

The `URL` class has new constructors that allow you to supply a `URLStreamHandler` instead of using the system-supplied default handler. A `URLDecoder` class has been added for decoding URLs embedded within MIME-formatted documents (to complement the existing `URLEncoder`).

You can now load classes over the network easily using the new `URLClassLoader` class.

`URLConnection` and `HttpURLConnection` have a new method, `getPermission()`, to determine the permissions required to use that connection. `HttpURLConnection` also has a new method, `getErrorStream()`, for getting the optional HTML document that might accompany HTTP error headers. `JarURLConnection` has been added to allow you to get the contents of a JAR using a `URLConnection`.

Authentication

The `Authenticator` and `PasswordAuthentication` classes have been added for network connections to obtain authentication information from users.

Security

The `java.net` package and its supporting implementation classes use the Version 1.2 security model via the `SocketPermission` and `NetPermission` classes to control access to the network.

Class and Interface Summary

Host Name Resolution

The `InetAddress` class is used to resolve a host name to an Internet address.

`InetAddress`	Represents an Internet address with methods for resolving a host name to an Internet address.

Sockets

The following classes provide the necessary functionality for communicating with servers on the Internet. These classes can also be used to implement an Internet server. See Figure 4.

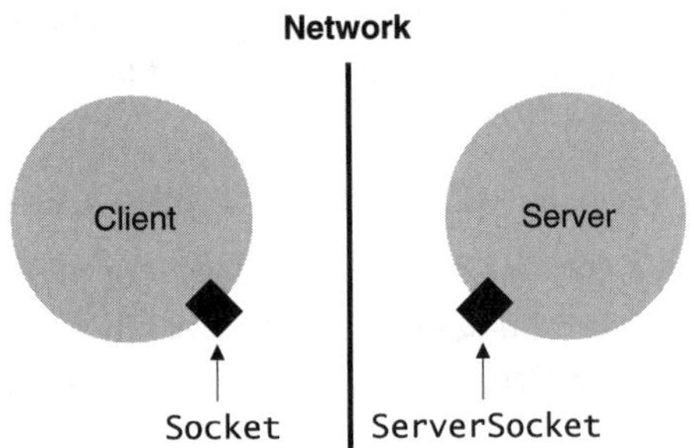

FIGURE 4: Socket and ServerSocket.

	Class	Description
Δ	`DatagramPacket`	A datagram used in a connectionless protocol such as UDP.
Δ	`DatagramSocket`	Used to send and receive datagrams.
Δ	`DatagramSocketImpl`	The abstract superclass for a datagram socket implementation. Not directly used.
Δ	`MulticastSocket`	Used to send and receive multicast datagrams.
	`ServerSocket`	Used by a server in a connection-oriented protocol such as TCP.
Δ	`Socket`	Used by a client or server in connectionless or connection-oriented protocols.
1.2	`SocketOptions`	An interface for getting and setting socket options.
	`SocketImpl`	The abstract superclass for a stream socket implementation. Not directly used.
	`SocketImplFactory`	A factory that creates `SocketImpl` objects. Not directly used.

URL

The following classes make it convenient to use URLs to retrieve data on the Internet. The data can be retrieved as a complete object or as a stream. Figure 5 shows the use of the `URL` and `URLConnection` classes in accessing Web services.

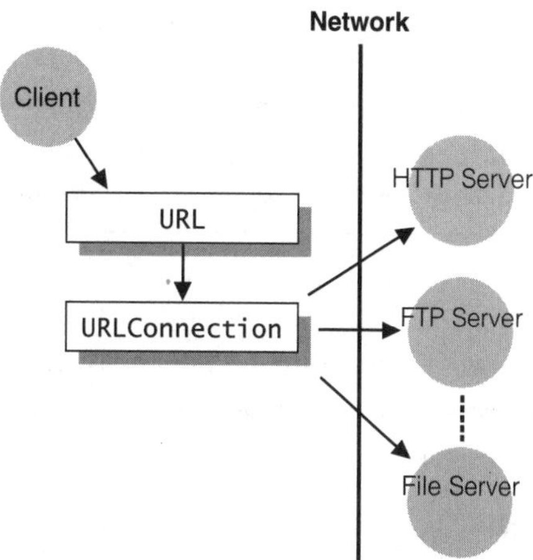

FIGURE 5: Use of `URL` and `URLConnection` to Access Web Services.

	Class	Description
	`ContentHandler`	The abstract superclass of content handlers for producing an object based on a MIME type. Not directly used.
	`ContentHandlerFactory`	A factory that returns a new `ContentHandler` object based on a MIME type. Not directly used.
	`FileNameMap`	An interface for mapping a filename to a MIME type.
1.2	`JarURLConnection`	Used to read the contents of a JAR file as a URL connection.
Δ	`HttpURLConnection`	Used to create an HTTP connection.
Δ	`URL`	Represents a URL with methods for parsing the URL and creating a connection to the URL's host.
1.2	`URLClassLoader`	Used to load classes over the network.
Δ	`URLConnection`	Used to create a connection to a URL's host and retrieve the data.
1.2	`URLDecoder`	Used to convert strings in `www-form-urlencoded` format.
	`URLEncoder`	Used to encode a string in `x-www-form-urlencoded` format.
	`URLStreamHandler`	The abstract superclass for URL protocol handlers (for example, "http," "ftp," and "telnet"). Not directly used.
	`URLStreamHandlerFactory`	A factory that creates instances of `URLStreamHandler` for different URL protocols. Not directly used.

Network Authentication

The following classes are used by browsers to obtain authentication information from a user.

	Class	Description
1.2	`Authenticator`	Used to authenticate a user for a network connection.
1.2	`PasswordAuthentication`	Represents a user name/password pair.

Permissions

The following classes are used to check network-related permissions.

	Class	Description
1.2	`NetPermission`	Represents permissions for network authentication and using stream handlers.
1.2	`SocketPermission`	Represents permissions for making and accepting socket connections.

Exceptions

Following are the exceptions declared in this package. They are not subclasses of `RuntimeException`, so they must be either caught or declared in the `throws` clause.

Exception	Description
`BindException`	Thrown when an attempt is made to bind a socket to a local address and port, but they cannot be assigned to the requesting program.
`ConnectException`	Thrown when an attempt is made to connect a socket to a remote address and port.
`MalformedURLException`	Thrown if arguments to the `URL` constructor are invalid.
`NoRouteToHostException`	Thrown if the machine cannot be reached because there is no route to it.
`ProtocolException`	Thrown if an attempt is made to connect to a socket of the wrong type.
`SocketException`	Thrown if an attempt is made to create a socket to an unsupported service or to install a socket implementation factory when one has already been installed.
`UnknownHostException`	Thrown if a host name to an Internet address cannot be resolved.
`UnknownServiceException`	Thrown if an attempt is made to use a service that is not supported by a URL connection.

java.text

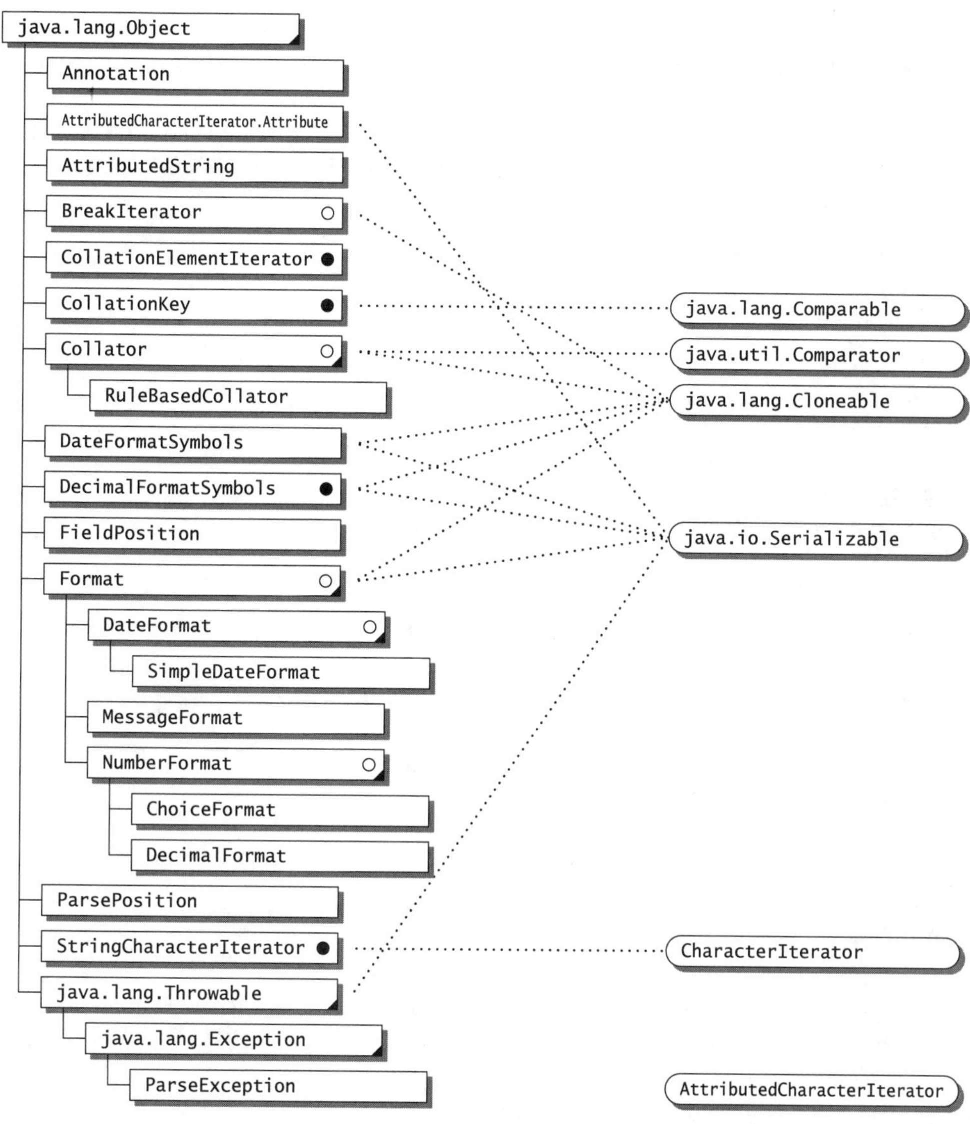

java.text

Description

The `java.text` package contains classes and interfaces for handling text, dates, numbers, and messages in a manner independent of natural languages. This means that your main application or applet can be written either to be language-independent and to call upon separate, dynamically linked localized resources. This allows the flexibility of adding localizations for new languages at any time.

These classes can format dates, numbers, and messages; parse; search and sort strings; and iterate over characters, words, sentences, and line breaks. This package contains four main groups of classes and interfaces:

- Classes for formatting and parsing
- Classes for string collation
- Classes for string iteration
- Classes for associating attributes with text

Classes for Formatting and Parsing

As shown in Figure 6, *formatting* is basically the conversion of number and date objects to strings, while *parsing* is the reverse operation of converting strings to number and date objects.

Dates and numbers are represented internally in a locale-independent way. For example, dates are kept as milliseconds since epoch (January 1, 1970, 00:00:00 GMT). When these objects are printed or displayed, they must be converted to localized strings. The locale-specific parts of a date string, such as the time zone string, are separately imported from a locale-specific resource bundle.

The `format()` method converts the `Date` object from –604656780000 milliseconds to the form "Tuesday, November 3, 1997 9:47am CST" for the U. S. English locale. Figure 6 shows how the `format()` method of subclasses of `Format` enable instances of `Number`, `Date`, `String`, and other objects to be formatted to locale-specific strings.

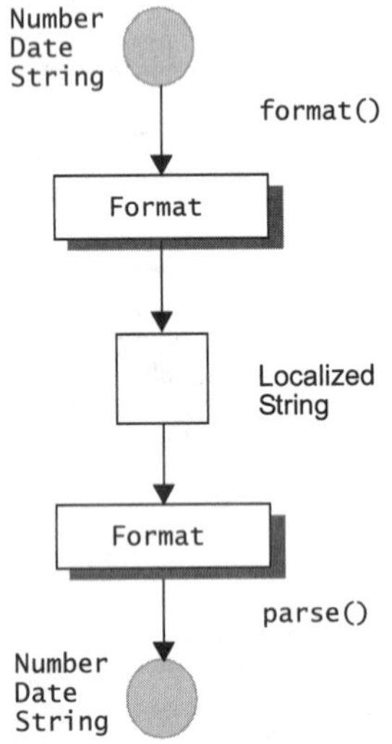

FIGURE 6: Object Formatting and String Parsing.

Conversely, the `parseObject()` method (and `parse()` method in subclasses) performs the reverse operation of parsing localized strings and converting them to `Number`, `Date`, and `String` objects. Figure 6 shows how the `parse()` method is complementary to `format()`. Any `String` formatted by `format()` is guaranteed to be parseable by `parseObject()`.

The `java.text` package provides six subclasses of `Format` for formatting dates, numbers, and messages: `DateFormat`, `SimpleDateFormat`, `NumberFormat`, `DecimalFormat`, `ChoiceFormat`, and `MessageFormat`.

String Collation

The term *collate* means to determine the proper sort sequence for two or more strings. It can also tell if two strings are equal for searching. The `Collator` class and its subclass `RuleBasedCollator` perform locale-sensitive string comparison. You use these classes to build searching and alphabetical sorting routines for natural language text. They can distinguish characters based on base character, accent marks, and uppercase/lowercase properties.

`Collator` is an abstract base class. Subclasses implement specific collation strategies. One subclass, `RuleBasedCollator`, is currently provided and is applicable to a wide set of languages. Other subclasses may be created to handle more specialized needs. `CollationElementIterator` provides an iterator for stepping through each character of a locale-specific string according to the rules of a specific `Collator` object. `CollationKey` enables the fast sorting of strings by representing a string as a sort key under the rules of a specific `Collator` object.

String Iteration

While the Java types `char` and `Character` represent Unicode characters, sometimes Unicode characters combine to form a more complex character, called a *user character*, which has its own semantic value. The `BreakIterator` class makes it possible to iterate over these user characters. A break iterator can find the location of a character, word, or sentence boundary or potential line-break boundary. This makes it possible for a program to properly select characters for text operations such as highlighting a character, cutting a word, moving to the next sentence, or word-wrapping at a line ending. These operations are performed in a locale-sensitive manner, meaning that they honor the boundaries of text for a particular locale.

Figure 7 shows how the French word "théâtre" with seven user characters could be constructed of nine Unicode characters. A user character can be made of one stroke or multiple, disconnected strokes. In Latin languages (with the alphabet A–Z), a character is part of a larger word, but in ideographic languages (for example, Chinese, Japanese, and Korean), a character can carry a complete idea or may be part of a larger word. Examples of user characters include "ä" (accent mark) and characters in some Middle East and Asian languages.

User Characters	|t|h|é|â|t|r|e|
Unicode Characters	|t|h|e|'|a|^|t|r|e|

FIGURE 7: User Characters.

Text Attributes

Text can have *attributes*, such as language, pronunciation, font, size, and style. Each attribute has a key and an associated value. Each character in the text can have a set of key/value pairs, where no two keys are the same. Key/value pairs can be added to one or more ranges of characters. For example, a string with the `LANGUAGE` attribute might have the `JAPANESE` locale as its value. One portion of the string might have a `READING` attribute that defines how it is pronounced—its value is a pronunciation string. This string would be wrapped in an *annotation* to indicate that it cannot be merged with adjacent attributes. Multiple attributes and annotations can be applied to different overlapping subranges of a string. The string attribute classes allow for the definition of attribute constants and annotation values, for the storage of attributed strings, and for the iteration over characters and their attribute key/value pairs.

Locale-Sensitive Classes

Many of the classes in `java.text` are locale-sensitive, meaning you have to create a different instance for each locale. Table 1 lists both locale-sensitive and locale-independent classes.

Locale-Sensitive Classes	Locale-Independent Classes
`NumberFormat`	`Format`
`DecimalFormat`	`ChoiceFormat`
`DecimalFormatSymbols`	`FieldPosition`
`MessageFormat`	`ParsePosition`
`DateFormat`	`ParseException`
`SimpleDateFormat`	`StringCharacterIterator`
`DateFormatSymbols`	`CharacterIterator`
`Collator`	`AttributedString`
`RuleBasedCollator`	`AttributedCharacterIterator`
`CollationElementIterator`	`AttributedCharacterIterator.Attribute`
`CollationKey`	`Annotation`
`BreakIterator`	

TABLE 1 Locale-Sensitive and Locale-Independent Classes.

Changes for Version 1.2

Format Classes

`SimpleDateFormat` has new setter and getter methods for indicating where to interpret the start of 2-digit years in the format string.

`DecimalFormat` has four new methods for setting the maximum and minimum number of fraction and integer digits. More Unicode digits (such as superscripts) can be recognized and parsed as decimal digits. The `"E"` exponent character has been added as a pattern symbol. Also, a new separator has been introduced: *monetary decimal separator.* The monetary decimal separator is used when the currency sign (`\u00a4`) is in the pattern; otherwise, the normal decimal separator is used.

`DecimalFormatSymbols` has new setter and getter methods for currency symbols and monetary decimal separators.

`FieldPosition` has new setter methods for the begin and end indexes, used when creating subclasses of `Format`.

`ParsePosition` has new setter and getter methods for the error index, used for pinpointing parse errors.

Collation Classes

CollationElementIterator has new methods for accessing the offset, setting text, getting the maximum expansion, and for moving the iterator backwards.

CollationKey has been modified to implement interface Comparable.

Collator has been modified to implement interface Comparator. It no longer implements Serializable. In Version 1.1, serialization of Collator was not implemented and always threw an exception.

RuleBasedCollator has a new overloaded form of getCollationElementIterator() that takes a CharacterIterator object as parameter.

Iterator Classes

BreakIterator no longer implements Serializable. In Version 1.1, serialization of BreakIterator was not implemented and always threw an exception. Two convenience methods have been added: isBoundary() and preceding().

In CharacterIterator and StringCharacterIterator, the semantics for current(), first(), last(), next(), previous(), and setIndex() have changed such that they can accept the position returned by getEndIndex().

Text Attribute Classes

The text attributes classes: AttributedCharacterIterator, AttributedCharacterIterator.Attribute, AttributedString, and Annotation have been added to the java.text package.

Class and Interface Summary

General Format

The Format class defines the operations for formatting a Date or Number object (or number primitive) to a localized string and parsing a localized string to a Number, Date, String, or other object. The format() methods accept a FieldPosition object as a parameter. Some syntax forms of the parse() method accept a ParsePosition object.

	Format	The abstract superclass of all format classes. Provides the basic methods for formatting and parsing numbers, dates, strings, and other objects.
Δ	FieldPosition	A concrete class for holding the field constant and the begin and end indices for number and date fields.
Δ	ParsePosition	A concrete class for holding the current position in a string during parsing.

Number Format

The following classes define the operations for formatting a `Number` object or number primitive to a localized string and parsing a localized string to a `Number` object. `NumberFormat` is the abstract superclass; `DecimalFormat` and `ChoiceFormat` are its subclasses. `DecimalFormat` uses `DecimalFormatSymbols`.

	Class	Description
	`NumberFormat`	The abstract superclass that provides the basic fields and methods for formatting `Number` objects and number primitives to localized strings and parsing localized strings to `Number` objects.
Δ	`DecimalFormat`	A concrete class for formatting `Number` objects and number primitives to localized strings and parsing localized strings to `Number` objects.
Δ	`DecimalFormatSymbols`	A concrete class for accessing localized number strings, such as the grouping separators, decimal separator, and percent sign. Used by `DecimalFormat`.
	`ChoiceFormat`	A concrete class for mapping strings to ranges of numbers and for handling plurals and names series in user messages.

Date and Time Formats

The following classes define the operations for formatting a `Date` object to a localized string and parsing a localized string to a `Date` object. `DateFormat` is the abstract superclass, and `SimpleDateFormat` is its subclass.

	Class	Description
	`DateFormat`	The abstract superclass that provides the basic fields and methods for formatting `Date` objects to localized strings and parsing date and time strings to `Date` objects.
Δ	`SimpleDateFormat`	A concrete class for formatting `Date` objects to localized strings and parsing date and time strings to `Date` objects.
	`DateFormatSymbols`	A concrete class for accessing localized date-time formatting strings, such as names of the months, days of the week, and the time zone. Used by `DateFormat`.

Message Format

The Message class is used to produce language-specific user messages. It is a subclass of Format.

MessageFormat	A concrete class for producing a language-specific user message that contains numbers, currency, percentages, dates, times, and string variables.

Exception

The ParseException exception is the only exception declared in this package. It is not a subclass of RuntimeException, so it must be either caught or declared in the throws clause.

ParseException	Thrown when an unexpected error has been encountered while parsing a string.

String Collation

The following classes define the operations for performing locale-sensitive string comparisons for searching and alphabetical sorting for natural language text. Collator is the abstract superclass, and RuleBasedCollator is its subclass. RuleBasedCollator uses both CollationElementIterator and CollationKey.

Δ	Collator	The abstract superclass for performing locale-sensitive string comparisons for searching and alphabetical sorting for natural language text.
Δ	RuleBasedCollator	A concrete class for performing locale-sensitive string comparisons for searching and alphabetical sorting for natural language text.
Δ	CollationElementIterator	A concrete iterator class used to step through each character of a locale-specific string according to the rules of a specific Collator object.
Δ	CollationKey	A concrete class that represents a sort key for a string under the rules of a specific Collator object. Used for fast sorting of strings.

String Iteration

The following classes define the operations for finding and getting the position of logical breaks in a string of text based on user characters.

	Class	Description
Δ	`BreakIterator`	An abstract class that defines the operations for finding and getting the position of logical breaks in a string of text: characters, words, sentences, and potential line breaks.
Δ	`StringCharacterIterator`	A concrete class for forward and backward iteration over a string of Unicode characters. Implements `CharacterIterator`.
Δ	`CharacterIterator`	An interface for forward and backward iteration over a string of Unicode characters.

Text Attribute Classes

The text attribute classes provide the ability to associate attributes with a piece of text. An attribute is a characteristic such as language, pronunciation, font, size, or color. These classes allow for the definition of attribute key/value pairs and annotation values, for the storage of attributed strings, and for iteration over attribute key/value pairs.

	Class	Description
1.2	`AttributedCharacterIterator`	An interface for iterating through text and its attribute information, for getting attribute keys and values and for determining how far attributes run.
1.2	`AttributedCharacterIterator.Attribute`	A static inner class that defines attribute key constants and useful methods for serializing, comparing, sorting, and debugging those keys.
1.2	`Annotation`	A concrete class used as a wrapper for a text attribute value when this value applies only to its current range of text, such as pronunciation.
1.2	`AttributedString`	A concrete class for holding text and attribute information.

java.util

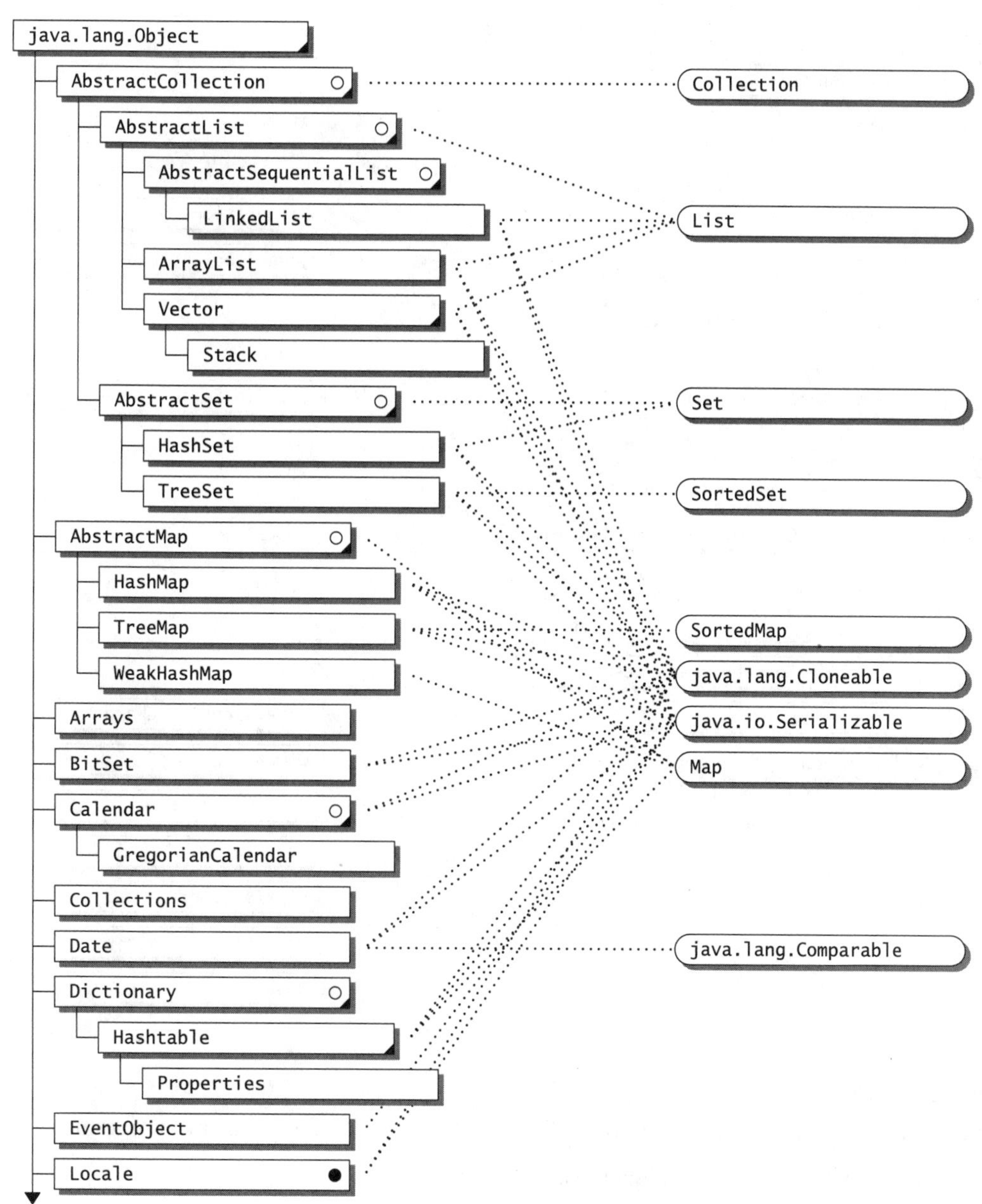

java.util

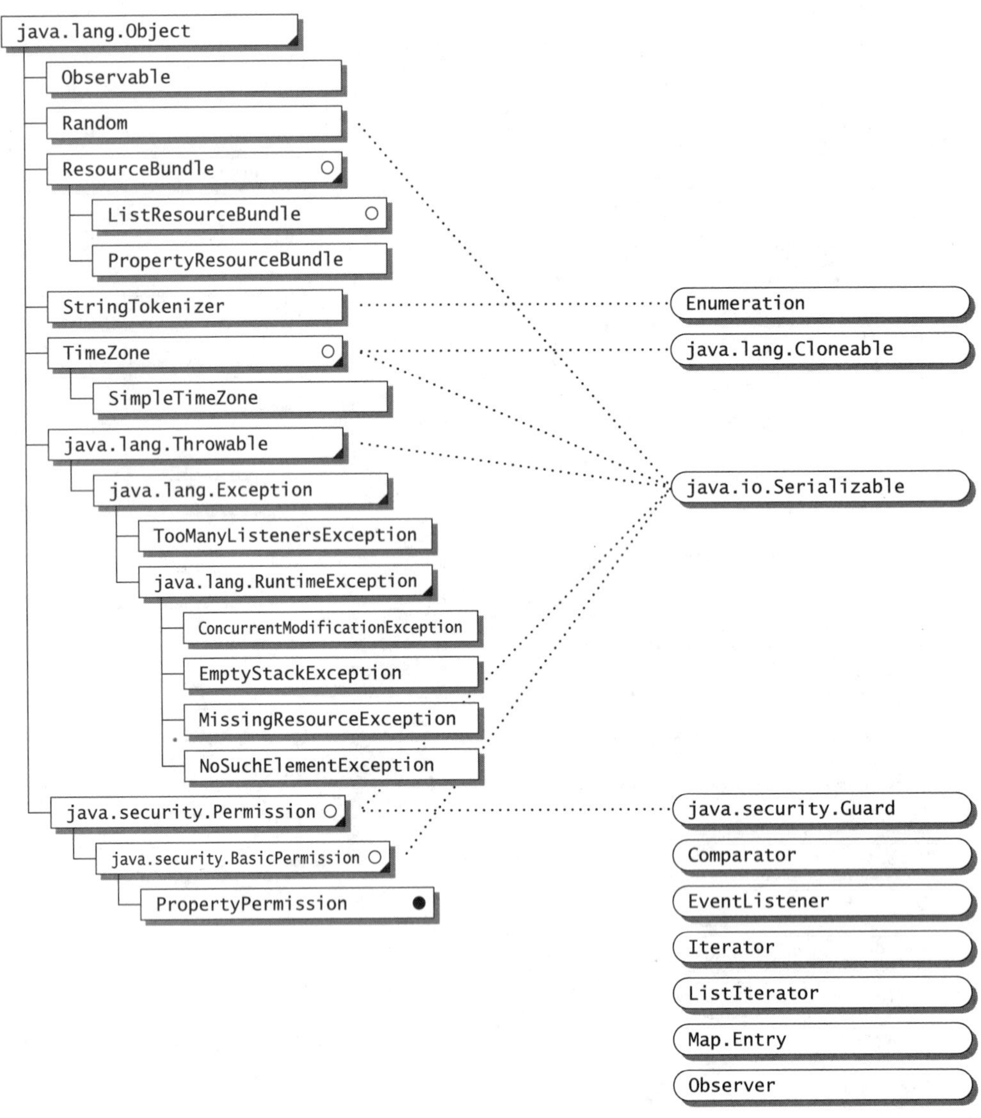

Description

The `java.util` package contains utility classes that are useful in typical Java programs:

- Collection classes that implement useful data structures
- Date- and time-related classes
- Internationalization and localization classes
- Root interfaces for events
- Miscellaneous classes, including a string tokenizer and a random-number generator

Changes for Version 1.2

The Collections Framework

A *collection* is a container of objects. There are several kinds of containers available for different situations. If the available set of containers does not meet your needs, you can define your own kind of container.

There are several interfaces and classes that are related to collections. These collectively make up what is called *The Collections Framework*. This framework is based on *interfaces* that characterize common types of collections, such as sets and maps. It provides *implementations* of these interfaces, including hash tables, linked lists, and balanced trees, and *abstract classes* designed to help you implement your own collection. It also provides various utilities that help with the use of collections, for example, utilities for sorting or reversing lists.

`Hashtable` and `Vector` have been retrofitted to use The Collections Framework. `Hashtable` now implements the `Map` interface, while `Vector` implements the `List` interface.

Other Data Structures

Two new methods have been added to `BitSet`: `andNot()`, which adds to the set of available `boolean` operations, and `length()`, which returns the logical length of a bit set.

Date and Time

A method was added to `Calendar` to retrieve the actual maximum value, when given the current date. For example, the maximum day is 30 if the current month is April. The `Date` class now implements `Comparable` so that `Date` instances can be sorted using the collection classes. Many more time zone ids have been added to the `TimeZone` class. The `SimpleTimeZone` has been enhanced to handle several more types of rules for when daylight savings time starts and ends.

Properties and Random

`Properties` has two new methods: `setProperty()` for setting the value of a property and `store()` for writing properties to an output stream.

`nextBoolean()` and an overloaded form of `nextInt()` have been added to `Random`.

Class and Interface Summary

Root Event Interfaces

The `EventObject` class is the superclass of all events (such as `AWTEvent`). `EventListener` is the interface from which all event listener interfaces extend.

`EventListener`	An interface to indicate that a class is an event listener.
`EventObject`	Represents an event fired by objects.

The Collections Framework and Other Data Structures

1.2	`AbstractCollection`	A skeletal implementation of the `Collection` interface.
1.2	`AbstractList`	A skeletal implementation of the `List` interface.
1.2	`AbstractMap`	A skeletal implementation of the `Map` interface.
1.2	`AbstractSequentialList`	A skeletal implementation of the `List` interface optimized for sequential access.
1.2	`AbstractSet`	A skeletal implementation of the `Set` interface.
1.2	`ArrayList`	A resizable-array implementation of the `List` interface.
1.2	`Arrays`	Contains static methods for sorting and searching arrays.
Δ	`BitSet`	A space-efficient bit vector that automatically expands.
1.2	`Collection`	The root interface in the collections class hierarchy.
1.2	`Collections`	Contains static methods that operate on or return `Collection`.
1.2	`Comparator`	An interface for performing total ordering of objects in a collection.
	`Dictionary`	The abstract superclass for data structures that maintain a set of key/value pairs.
	`Enumeration`	An interface consisting of methods for enumerating a list of objects.
1.2	`HashMap`	A hash table-based implementation of the `Map` interface.
1.2	`HashSet`	A hash table-based implementation of the `Set` interface.
Δ	`Hashtable`	A hash table for efficiently associating an object with another object.
1.2	`Iterator`	An iterator over a `Collection`.
1.2	`LinkedList`	A linked-list implementation of the `List` implementation.
1.2	`List`	An ordered `Collection`.
1.2	`ListIterator`	An iterator over a `List`.
1.2	`Map`	A collection that maps a key to a value.
1.2	`Map.Entry`	A key-value pair.
1.2	`Set`	A `Collection` with no duplicates.
1.2	`SortedMap`	An ordered `Map`.
1.2	`SortedSet`	An ordered `Collection` with no duplicates.
	`Stack`	A last-in/first-out stack of objects.
1.2	`TreeMap`	A red-black, tree-based implementation of the `Map` interface.
1.2	`TreeSet`	An implementation of `Set`, backended by a `TreeMap`.
Δ	`Vector`	An array of objects that automatically expands.
1.2	`WeakHashMap`	A hash table-based `Map` with entries that will be automatically removed when their key is no longer in use.

Date and Time

The following classes are used to represent date- and time-related information.

	Class	Description
Δ	`Calendar`	The abstract superclass for extracting calendar-related attributes from a `Date` value.
Δ	`Date`	Represents a date and time with the resolution of milliseconds.
Δ	`GregorianCalendar`	Represents a Gregorian calendar.
Δ	`SimpleTimeZone`	Represents a time zone for use with a Gregorian calendar.
Δ	`TimeZone`	The abstract superclass for representing a time zone.

Internalization and Localization

A *resource bundle* is a set of resources such as strings and images. It is the primary means for localizing Java applications. A *locale* is Java's standard means of identifying a language for the purposes of internationalization.

Class	Description
`ListResourceBundle`	An abstract class representing a resource bundle whose values are known at the time the bundle is instantiated. Not used directly.
`Locale`	Used to identify a language and dialect for the purposes of internalization and localization.
`PropertyResourceBundle`	Represents a resource bundle whose values are stored in a properties file.
`ResourceBundle`	An abstract class representing a set of resources used for localizing an application.

Observer

An *observable object* is an object that holds some data that is constantly modified. An observer is an object that when registered with an observable object gets notifications whenever the data held by the observable object changes.

Class	Description
`Observable`	The superclass of observable objects.
`Observer`	The interface that an observer must implement.

Random Numbers

The `Random` class is used to generate pseudorandom numbers of the Java primitive number types.

	Class	Description
Δ	`Random`	Used to generate pseudorandom numbers.

Properties

A *property* is a key/value pair; both the key and value are strings. The `Properties` class is used to implement system properties (`java.lang.System.getProperties()`), as well as `PropertyResourceBundle`. It contains methods for saving and retrieving all of the data to/from a properties file.

Δ	`Properties`	A set of properties that has methods for saving and retrieving those properties.
1.2	`PropertyPermission`	Represents permissions to read and update system properties.

Parser

The `Parser` class is used to separate a string into smaller strings based on a set of characters that define the separators. The separators are typically whitespace characters, such as the space and the tab.

`StringTokenizer`	Used to parse a string to a sequence of tokens.

Exceptions

Following are the exceptions declared in this package. They are subclasses of `RuntimeException` and so should not be caught or declared in the throws clause.

	`EmptyStackException`	Thrown if an attempt is made to access an element on an empty stack.
1.2	`ConcurrentModificationException`	Thrown if concurrent modification to a data structure has been detected.
	`MissingResourceException`	Thrown if a resource bundle or a resource could not be found.
	`NoSuchElementException`	Thrown if an attempt is made to access an element in an enumeration after the enumeration is exhausted.
	`TooManyListenersException`	Thrown if an attempt is made to add a listener to an object that does not support multiple listeners.

java.util.jar

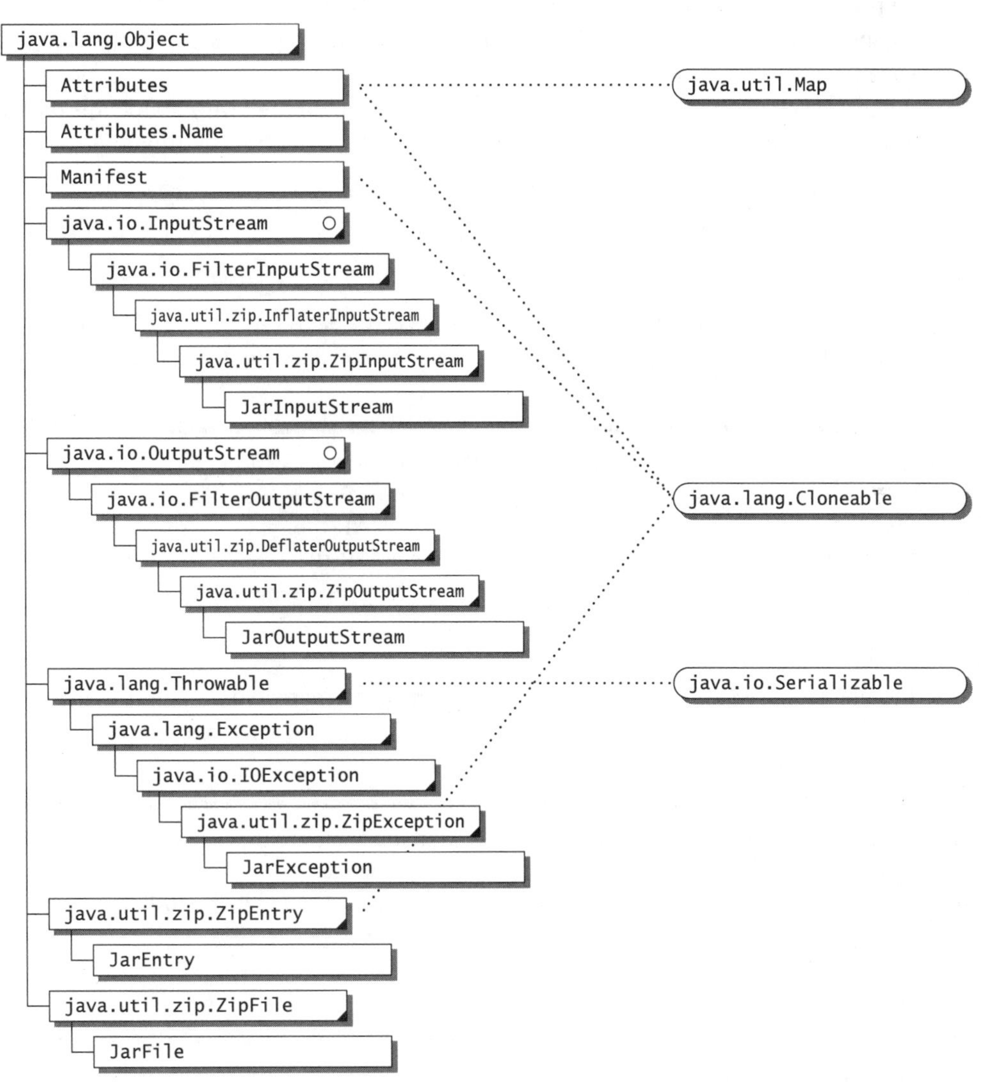

Description

The `jar.util.jar` package contains classes for manipulating a *Java Archive* (JAR). A JAR specifies a platform-independent file format for archives. The Java archive tool, `jar`, available on Solaris and Windows platforms, allows you to create a JAR archive using multiple class and resource (such as image and sound) files.

See `http://java.sun.com/products/jdk/1.1/docs/guide/jar/` for details on JAR and the `jar` command.

Class and Interface Summary

JAR File

A JAR file consists of a *manifest* and one or more pieces of data. Each piece of data is represented by a *JAR entry.* `JarFile` and `JarInputStream` are used to read JAR files, while `JarOutputStream` is used to create JAR files.

`JarEntry`	Represents a JAR entry in a JAR file.
`JarFile`	Used to read JAR entries from a JAR file.
`JarInputStream`	A stream for reading a JAR file.
`JarOutputStream`	A stream for writing a JAR file.

Manifest

A JAR file contains a *manifest*, which is a set of attributes (name/value pairs) that provide additional information about the JAR file and about entries in the JAR file. For example, if a class is signed, its digest is kept in the manifest. .

`Attributes`	Maps manifest attribute names to their string values.
`Attributes.Name`	Represents an attribute name.
`Manifest`	Contains manifest entry names and their attributes.

Exceptions

There is one exception declared in this package. It extends from `ZipException` and must be either caught or declared in the `throws` clause.

`JarException`	Thrown if the JAR data is invalid or corrupted.

java.util.zip

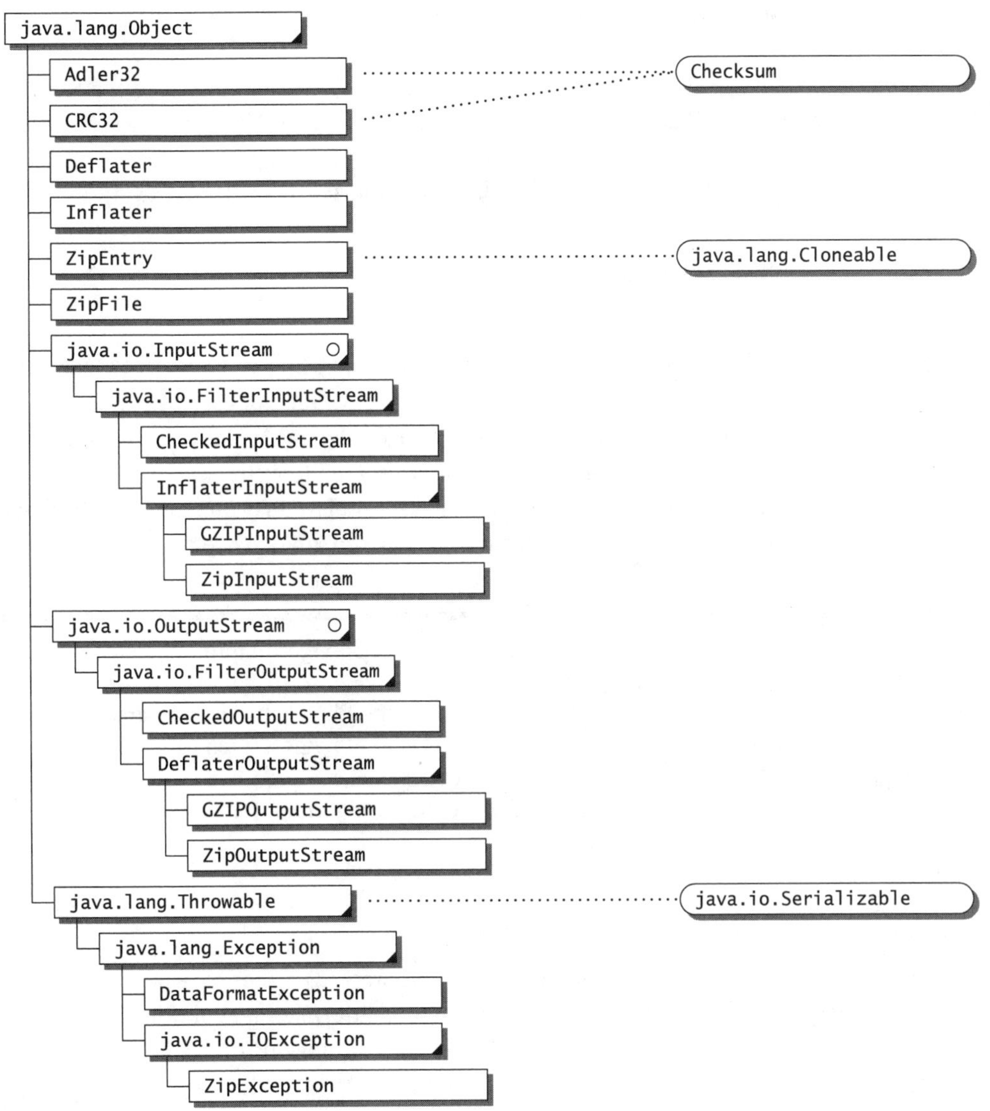

Description

The `java.util.zip` package contains classes for computing checksums of data and for compressing and decompressing data.

Changes for Version 1.2

`ZipInputStream` and `InflaterInputStream` override `available()` and `close()` to track better when the stream has been closed and when end-of-stream has been reached so that the rest of the methods in these classes can throw an `IOException` if the stream has ended or been closed.

`ZipEntry` can be more easily copied because its `clone()` method has been made public and it has a new constructor that accepts another `ZipEntry` as input. You can also set the compressed size of a `ZipEntry` using the new `setCompressedSize()` method.

`ZipFile` has a new method for getting the number of entries in a ZIP file.

Class and Interface Summary

Checksum

This package provides implementations for two checksum algorithms: ADLER-32 and CRC-32. The ADLER-32 algorithm is faster than the CRC-32 algorithm, but CRC-32 produces better-quality checksums. `CheckedInputStream` and `CheckedOutputStream` use one of these algorithms to compute a checksum for data read from or written to a stream.

To implement your own checksum algorithm, declare a class that implements `Checksum`. This allows your checksum algorithm to be used with `CheckedInputStream` and `CheckedOutputStream`.

`Adler32`	Implements the ADLER-32 algorithm for computing checksums.
`CheckedInputStream`	Computes the checksum of bytes read from a stream.
`CheckedOutputStream`	Computes the checksum of bytes written to a stream.
`Checksum`	The interface for checksums.
`CRC32`	Implements the CRC-32 algorithm for computing checksums.

ZIP Files

A ZIP file consists of one or more compressed (or uncompressed) pieces of data. Each piece of data is represented by a *ZIP entry*. The ZIP entry contains information about the data, such as its uncompressed size, its checksum value, and its location in the ZIP file. `ZipFile` is used to read ZIP files, while `ZipOutputStream` is used to create ZIP files.

Δ	`ZipEntry`	Represents a ZIP entry in a ZIP file.
Δ	`ZipFile`	Used to read the contents of a ZIP file.

Compression

This package contains the following classes for *deflating* (compressing) data. A *deflater* is used to compress data. It is typically used with the `DeflaterOutputStream` class to compress a stream of data.

`GZIPOutputStream` and `ZipOutputStream` are subclasses of `DeflaterOutputStream` that produce compressed output in a specific format. A GZIP file differs from a ZIP file in that it contains only one piece of data, while a ZIP file may contain multiple pieces of data. Each piece of data in a ZIP file can be either compressed or uncompressed. See the `GZIPOutputStream` and `ZipEntry` for more information about these formats.

`Deflater`	Compresses a data stream of arbitrary length using the DEFLATE compression algorithm and data format.
`DeflaterOutputStream`	An output stream for compressing data using `Deflater`.
`GZIPOutputStream`	An output stream for creating a compressed file in GZIP format.
`ZipOutputStream`	An output stream for creating a ZIP file.

Decompression

This package contains the following classes for *inflating* (decompressing) data. An *inflater* is used to decompress data. It is typically used with the `InflaterOutputStream` class to decompress a stream of compressed data.

`GZIPInputStream` and `ZipInputStream` are subclasses of `InflaterOutputStream` that read and decompress compressed data in a specific format. A GZIP file differs from a ZIP file in that it contains only one piece of data, while a ZIP file may contain multiple pieces of data. Each piece of data in a ZIP file can be either compressed or uncompressed. See the `GZIPOutputStream` and `ZipEntry` for more information about these formats.

	`Inflater`	Decompresses a data stream that was compressed using the DEFLATE compression algorithm and data format.
Δ	`InflaterInputStream`	An input stream for decompressing data using the `Inflater` class.
	`GZIPInputStream`	An input stream for reading and decompressing a compressed file in GZIP format.
Δ	`ZipInputStream`	An input stream for reading a ZIP file.

Exceptions

Two exceptions are declared in this package. They extend directly from `Exception`, so they must be either caught or declared in the `throws` clause.

`DataFormatException`	Thrown if the compressed data is invalid or corrupted.
`ZipException`	Thrown if the data is not in ZIP format or if an error occurs while a new ZIP file is being created.

AbstractCollection

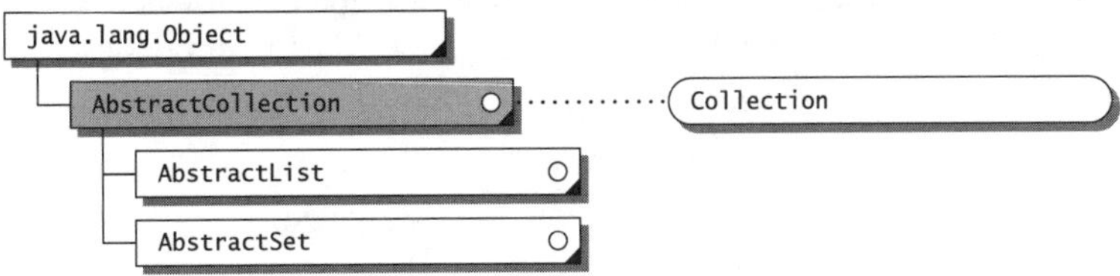

Syntax

```
public abstract class AbstractCollection implements Collection
```

Description

The `AbstractCollection` abstract class is a partial implementation of the `Collection` interface. Its purpose is to minimize the effort in building your own collection classes by providing default implementations for most of the methods required by the `Collection` interface.

This class does not implement any kind of storage. It is more like a veneer over some data storage that you provide. You "layer" this class over your data storage by overriding some of the methods in this class. For example, this class declares a `size()` method that returns the number of elements in the collection. You must implement this abstract method in order to return the number of elements in your data storage.

The methods in this class fall into three groups: required, optional, and convenience.

Required Methods

A subclass of `AbstractCollection`, to be instantiable, must implement the following two abstract methods:

`iterator()`	Creates an iterator for the collection.
`size()`	Returns the number of elements in the collection.

Implementing these two methods results in a usable but nonmodifiable collection.

Optional Methods

To allow elements to be added to the collection, you must override the `add()` method. To allow elements to be removed from the collection, you must implement the `remove()` method in the iterators returned by `iterator()`.

Convenience Methods

All other methods are convenience methods. All are written in a way that uses only `iterator()` and `size()`. If you are concerned about performance, you can override any of the convenience methods for a more efficient implementation.

A

Fail-Fast Iterators

Most collections do not allow modifications while an iterator on the collection is in use. These collections might implement a *fail-fast iterator.* A fail-fast iterator watches for modifications on the collection and throws an exception if it detects one. This feature is used to detect programming errors. See `Iterator` for more details.

MEMBER SUMMARY	
Modification Methods	
`add()`	Adds an element to this collection.
`addAll()`	Adds all elements in a collection to this collection.
`clear()`	Removes all of the elements in this collection.
`remove()`	Removes an element from this collection.
`removeAll()`	Removes all of the elements from this collection that are in another collection.
`retainAll()`	Removes all of the elements in this collection that are not in another collection.
Query Methods	
`contains()`	Determines if this collection contains a particular element.
`containsAll()`	Determines if this collection contains all of the elements in another collection.
`isEmpty()`	Determines if this collection has no elements.
`size()`	Returns the number of elements in this collection.
Iterator Method	
`iterator()`	Creates an iterator for the elements in this collection.
Conversion Method	
`toArray()`	Returns all of the elements in this collection in an array.
Object Method	
`toString()`	Generates a string representation of this collection.

See Also

`Collection`.

Example

This example demonstrates the use of this class by implementing a simple, limited-sized collection. The collection behaves like a set, except that it will hold duplicate elements. The collection cannot grow beyond a size that is specified in the collection's constructor. The collection internally uses an `Object` array to store the elements.

```
import java.util.*;

class Main {
    public static void main(String[] args) {
        Collection col = new FixedCol(3);

        System.out.println(col.add("dog"));      // true
        System.out.println(col.add("dog"));      // true
        System.out.println(col.add("cat"));      // true
        System.out.println(col);                 // [dog, dog, cat]

        // The collection is full
        // System.out.println(col.add("pig"));   // IllegalStateException

        System.out.println(col.remove("pig"));   // false
        System.out.println(col.remove("dog"));   // true
        System.out.println(col.remove("dog"));   // true
        System.out.println(col);                 // [cat]
    }
}

class FixedCol extends AbstractCollection {
    private Object[] array;
    int size = 0;

    FixedCol(int capacity) {
        array = new Object[capacity];
    }

    FixedCol() {
        this(10);  // Default capacity is 10
    }

    FixedCol(Collection c) {
        int cSize = c.size();
        array = new Object[(cSize*110)/100];  // Allow 10% for growth
        c.toArray(array);
        size = cSize;
    }

    public boolean add(Object e) {
        if (size == array.length)
            throw new IllegalStateException();
        array[size++] = e;
        return true;
    }

    public Iterator iterator() {
        // This is not a fail-fast iterator
        return new Iterator() {
            private int cursor = 0;
            private boolean removeProhibited = true;
            public boolean hasNext() {
                return cursor < size;
            }
            public Object next() {
                if (cursor==size)
                    throw new NoSuchElementException();
                removeProhibited = false;
                return array[cursor++];
```

```
                }
                public void remove() {
                    if (removeProhibited)
                        throw new IllegalStateException();
                    array[--cursor] = array[--size];
                    array[size] = null;   // Eliminate "false reference"
                    removeProhibited = true;
                }
            };
        }

        public int size() {
            return size;
        }
    }
```

add()

PURPOSE Adds an element to this collection.

SYNTAX `public boolean add(Object e)`

DESCRIPTION This method adds the element `e` to this collection. Some collections, such as sets (see `Set`), do not store duplicate elements; in this case, this call is ignored. The `equals()` method of `e` is used to determine whether two elements are the same.

Some collections do not accept `null`. If `null` is added to such a collection, an `NullPointerException` should be thrown.

Some collections might accept only elements of a certain type. If an incompatible element is added to such a collection, a `ClassCastException` should be thrown.

The default implementation throws `UnsupportedOperationException`. If a subclass supports this operation, it must override this method.

PARAMETERS

`e` The possibly `null` element to be added to this collection.

RETURNS `true` if this collection was modified.

EXCEPTIONS

`ClassCastException`
If the class of `e` is not compatible with this collection.

`IllegalArgumentException`
If some aspect of `e` prevents it from being added to this collection.

`NullPointerException`
If `e` is `null` and this collection does not accept `null` elements.

`UnsupportedOperationException`
If this method is not supported by this collection.

SEE ALSO `addAll()`.

EXAMPLE See `Set.add()`.

addAll()

PURPOSE Adds all of the elements in a collection to this collection.

SYNTAX `public boolean addAll(Collection c)`

DESCRIPTION This method adds all of the elements in the collection `c` to this collection. It is equivalent to calling `add()` for each of the elements in `c`.

The collection `c` should not be modified while this method is being called; otherwise, the results are undefined.

The default implementation throws `UnsupportedOperationException`. If a subclass supports this operation, it must override this method.

PARAMETERS

`c` A non-`null` collection of elements to be added to this collection.

RETURNS `true` if this collection was modified.

EXCEPTIONS

`ClassCastException`
If the class of an element in `c` is not compatible with this collection.

`ConcurrentModificationException`
If `c`'s iterators are fail-fast and `c` is being modified during this method call.

`IllegalArgumentException`
If some aspect of an element in `c` prevents it from being added to this collection.

`NullPointerException`
If some element in `c` is `null` and this collection does not accept `null` elements.

`UnsupportedOperationException`
If this method is not supported by this collection.

SEE ALSO `add()`.

EXAMPLE See `Set.addAll()`.

clear()

PURPOSE Removes all of the elements in this collection.

SYNTAX `public void clear()`

DESCRIPTION This method removes all of the elements in this collection. After it is called, the collection will be empty.

The default implementation throws `UnsupportedOperationException`. If a subclass supports this operation, it must override this method.

EXCEPTIONS

`UnsupportedOperationException`
If this method is not supported by this collection.

EXAMPLE See `Set.clear()`.

contains()

PURPOSE Determines if this collection contains a particular element.

SYNTAX `public boolean contains(Object e)`

DESCRIPTION This method determines if this collection contains the element `e`. It returns `true` if some element in this collection is equal to `e`. Two elements are equal if both are `null` or if the `equals()` method determines that they are equal.

PARAMETERS

`e` A possibly `null` element.

RETURNS `true` if some element in this collection is equal to `e`.

EXCEPTIONS

`ClassCastException`
If the class of `e` is not compatible with this collection.

`NullPointerException`
If `e` is `null` and this collection does not accept `null` elements.

SEE ALSO `containsAll()`, `equals()`.

EXAMPLE See `Set.contains()`.

containsAll()

PURPOSE Determines if this collection contains all of the elements that are in another collection.

SYNTAX `public boolean containsAll(Collection c)`

DESCRIPTION This method determines if this collection contains all of the elements that are in `c`. If all of the elements in `c` appear in this collection, this method returns `true`. Two elements are equal if both are `null` or if the `equals()` method determines that they are equal.

PARAMETERS

`c` A non-`null` collection.

A

RETURNS `true` if all of the elements in `c` appear in this collection.

EXCEPTIONS

`NullPointerException`

If some element in `c` is `null` and this collection does not accept `null` elements.

SEE ALSO `contains()`, `equals()`.

EXAMPLE See `Set.containsAll()`.

isEmpty()

PURPOSE Determines if this collection has no elements.

SYNTAX `public boolean isEmpty()`

RETURNS `true` if this collection contains no elements.

SEE ALSO `size()`.

EXAMPLE See `Set.isEmpty()`.

iterator()

PURPOSE Creates an iterator for all of the elements in this collection.

SYNTAX `public Iterator iterator()`

DESCRIPTION This method creates and returns an iterator (see `Iterator` for more details) for all of the elements in this collection. The order in which the elements are presented by the iterator depends on the class that created the iterator. Some classes might guarantee an ordering, while others might not.

In most cases, the collection should not be modified while the returned iterator is in use. Otherwise, a `ConcurrentModificationException` is thrown. However, there might be some collections that allow this; check its documentation.

RETURNS A non-`null` iterator.

SEE ALSO `ConcurrentModificationException`, `Iterator`.

EXAMPLE See `Set.iterator()`.

remove()

PURPOSE Removes an element from this collection.

SYNTAX `public boolean remove(Object e)`

DESCRIPTION If this collection contains one or more elements that are equal (according to the `equals()` method) to `e`, this method removes one of those elements and returns `true`. Otherwise, this method does not modify this collection and returns `false`.

The default implementation throws `UnsupportedOperationException`. If a subclass supports this operation, it must override this method.

PARAMETERS

`e` The possibly `null` element to be removed from this collection.

RETURNS `true` if this collection was modified.

EXCEPTIONS

`UnsupportedOperationException`
If this method is not supported by this collection.

SEE ALSO `removeAll()`, `retainAll()`.

EXAMPLE See `Set.remove()`.

removeAll()

PURPOSE Removes all of the elements from this collection that are in another collection.

SYNTAX `public boolean removeAll(Collection c)`

DESCRIPTION This method removes all of the elements in this collection that are in `c`. The `equals()` method is used to determine whether two elements are equal. After this call returns, this collection will contain no elements in common with `c`. This operation can be thought of as a subtraction operation, in which `c` is subtracted from this list.

The default implementation throws `UnsupportedOperationException`. If a subclass supports this operation, it must override this method.

PARAMETERS

`c` A non-`null` collection of elements to be removed from this collection.

RETURNS `true` if this collection was modified.

EXCEPTIONS

`ConcurrentModificationException`
If `c`'s iterators are fail-fast and `c` is being modified during this method call.

`UnsupportedOperationException`
If this method is not supported by this collection.

SEE ALSO `remove()`, `retainAll()`.

EXAMPLE See `Set.removeAll()`.

retainAll()

PURPOSE Removes all of the elements in this collection that are not in another collection.

SYNTAX `public boolean retainAll(Collection c)`

DESCRIPTION This method removes all of the elements in this collection that are not in `c`. The `equals()` method is used to determine whether two elements are equal. This operation can be thought of as an intersection operation.

The default implementation throws `UnsupportedOperationException`. If a subclass supports this operation, it must override this method.

PARAMETERS

`c` A non-`null` collection of elements to retain.

RETURNS `true` if this collection was modified.

EXCEPTIONS

`ConcurrentModificationException`
If `c`'s iterators are fail-fast and `c` is being modified during this method call.

`UnsupportedOperationException`
If this method is not supported by this collection.

SEE ALSO `remove()`, `removeAll()`.

EXAMPLE See `Set.retainAll()`.

size()

PURPOSE Returns the number of elements in this collection.

SYNTAX `public int size()`

RETURNS The non-negative number of elements in this collection.

SEE ALSO `isEmpty()`.

EXAMPLE `Set.size()`.

toArray()

PURPOSE Returns all of the elements in this collection that are in an array.

SYNTAX
```
public Object[] toArray()
public Object[] toArray(Object arr[])
```

DESCRIPTION This method fills `arr` with all of the elements in this collection and returns `arr`. If `arr` is not large enough, a new array is created, filled, and then returned. The new array is just large enough to hold all of the elements in this collection, and its type is identical to the type of `arr`.

If `arr` is larger than the total of all of the elements in this collection, `arr[size()]` is set to `null`. This `null` value can be used to determine the number of returned elements. However, it is not helpful if the collection may contain `null` elements.

The order of the elements in the returned array matches the order (if any) of the elements returned by an iterator on this collection.

If `arr` is not specified, it defaults to `new Object[0]`.

PARAMETERS

`arr` The non-`null` array into which the elements of this collection will be copied.

RETURNS The array `arr` or a new array whose length equals `size()`.

EXCEPTIONS

`ArrayStoreException`

If some element in this collection cannot be assigned to an element in `arr`. This exception is never thrown if arr is an `Object` array.

EXAMPLE See `Set.toArray()`.

toString()

PURPOSE Generates a string representation of this collection.

SYNTAX `public String toString()`

DESCRIPTION This method returns a string showing all of the elements in this collection.

RETURNS A non-`null` string representation of this collection.

OVERRIDES `java.lang.Object.toString()`.

EXAMPLE See the class example.

AbstractList

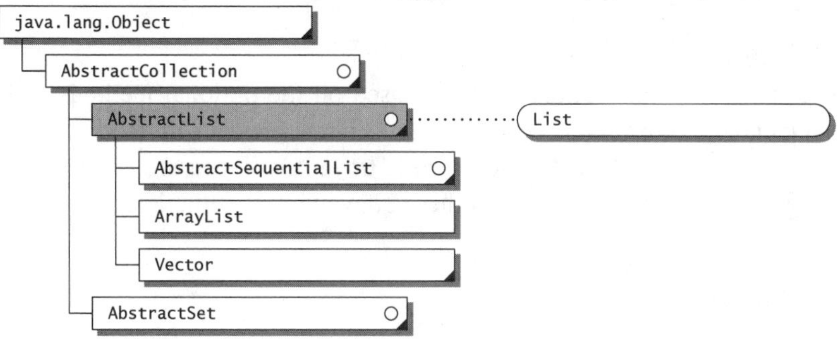

Syntax

```
public abstract class AbstractList extends AbstractCollection implements List
```

Description

The `AbstractList` abstract class is a partial implementation of the `List` interface. Its purpose is to minimize the effort in building your own list classes by providing default implementations for most of the methods required by the `List` interface.

This class does not implement any kind of storage. It is more like a veneer over some data storage that you provide. You "layer" this class over your data storage by implementing or overriding some of the methods in this class. For example, this class declares a `size()` method that returns the number of elements in the list. You must implement this abstract method in order to return the number of elements in your data storage.

The methods in this class fall into three groups: required, optional, and convenience.

Required Methods

A subclass of `AbstractList`, to be instantiable, must implement the following two abstract methods:

`get(int)`	Returns an element at an index.
`size()`	Returns the number of elements in the list.

Optional Methods

These are methods that have implementations that simply throw an `UnsupportedOperationException`. Which methods you override depend on the capabilities of your list. For example, if your list is read-only, you don't have to override any optional methods. If your list is modifiable, you need to override `set(int,Object)`. If your list can grow, you need to override `add(int, Object)`. And so on. Here is the list of optional methods and capabilities they can enable if you override them.

`add(int index, Object e)`	Enables a list that can grow.
`remove(int index)`	Enables a list that can shrink.
`set(int index, Object e)`	Enables a list that can be modified.

Convenience Methods

These methods have implementations that are based on the optional methods and so do not need to be overridden. For example, `add(Object)` is a convenience method whose implementation is based on the optional method `add(int, Object)`. If you are concerned about efficiency, you might want to override some of these convenience methods, listed as follows.

`add(Object)`
`addAll(int, Collection)`
`addAll(Collection)`—*inherited*
`clear()`
`contains(Object)`—*inherited*
`containsAll(Collection)`—*inherited*
`indexOf(Object)`
`iterator()`
`isEmpty()`—*inherited*
`lastIndexOf(Object)`
`listIterator()`
`listIterator(int)`
`remove(Object)`—*inherited*
`removeAll(Collection)`—*inherited*
`void removeRange(int, int)`—*protected*
`retainAll(Collection)`—*inherited*
`subList(int, int)`
`Object[] toArray()`—*inherited*
`Object[] toArray(Object[])`—*inherited*

Usage

This class is meant to be subclassed. You should implement a constructor with no parameters to make it convenient for your class to be instantiated. You should also provide a constructor that accepts a `Collection` object. This latter constructor constructs a new list initialized with the elements from the supplied collection, thereby making it easy to copy any collection. You might want to provide other constructors as well. You must also, at a minimum, implement the two abstract methods—`get(int, Object)` and `size()`—in order for the subclass to be instantiable. Implementing only these two methods results in a read-only list. If you want the list to have more capabilities, you will have to override some of the optional methods. See the previous subsection, "Optional Methods," for more details.

Fail-Fast Iterators

Most lists do not allow modifications while an iterator on the list is in use. These lists should implement a *fail-fast iterator.* A fail-fast iterator watches for modifications on the list and throws an exception if it detects a modification. This feature is used mainly to avoid programming errors. See `Iterator` for more details.

The `modCount` field in this class is used to implement fail-fast iterators. This integer should be incremented every time the list is modified. The default implementation of the iterator in this class automatically uses this field to detect whether the list has been modified.

AbstractList versus AbstractSequentialList

The `List` interface has two partial implementations. Which one you use depends on how elements are accessed in your data storage. If your data storage makes it easy to access elements by an integer index, then you should use `AbstractList`. If your data storage is more like a linked list, in which you have to traverse the structure in order to get at an element, then you should use `AbstractSequentialList`.

Both `AbstractList` and `AbstractSequentialList` have exactly the same methods. They differ mainly in which are required, optional, and convenient. In `AbstractList`, `get(int)` is required, while `iterator()` is not. In `AbstractSequentialList`, `iterator()` is required, while `get()` is not. See `AbstractSequentialList` for more details.

MEMBER SUMMARY	
Element Retrieval Methods	
`get()`	Retrieves the element at a particular index in this list.
`indexOf()`	Determines the index of the first occurrence of an element in this list.
`lastIndexOf()`	Determines the index of the last occurrence of an element in this list.
Modification Methods and Field	
`add()`	Inserts or appends an element to this list.
`addAll()`	Inserts or appends all elements of a collection to this list.
`clear()`	Removes all of the elements in this list.
`modCount`	Contains the number of times this list has been modified.
`remove()`	Removes an element from this list.
`removeRange()`	Removes a range of elements from this list.
`set()`	Replaces an element with another element.
Iterator Methods	
`iterator()`	Creates an iterator for all of the elements in this list.
`listIterator()`	Creates a list iterator for the elements in this list.
Sublist Method	
`subList()`	Creates a sublist of a range of elements in this list.
Object Methods	
`hashCode()`	Computes the hash code for this list.
`equals()`	Determines if this list is equal to another object.

See Also

`AbstractSequentialList`, `Iterator`, `ListIterator`.

Example

This example demonstrates the use of this class by implementing a simple, limited-sized list. The list cannot grow beyond a size that is specified in the list's constructor. The list internally uses an `Object` array to store the elements.

```
import java.util.*;

class Main {
    public static void main(String[] args) {
        List list = new FixedList(2);
        list.add("dog");
        list.add("cat");
        //list.add("pig");              // IllegalStateException
        list.remove("dog");
        list.add("pig");
        System.out.println( list );     // [cat, pig]

        Iterator it = list.iterator();
        list.remove("cat");
        //it.next();                    // ConcurrentModificationException
    }
}

class FixedList extends AbstractList {
    int size;
    Object[] array;

    FixedList(int capacity) {
        array = new Object[capacity];
    }

    FixedList() {
        this(10);  // Default capacity is 10
    }

    FixedList(Collection c) {
        int cSize = c.size();
        array = new Object[(cSize*110)/100];  // Allow 10% for growth
        c.toArray(array);
        size = cSize;
    }

    public void add(int index, Object e) {
        if (index < 0 || index > size) {
            throw new IndexOutOfBoundsException();
        }
        if (size==array.length) {
            throw new IllegalStateException();
        }
        System.arraycopy(array, index, array, index+1, size-index);
        array[index] = e;
        size++;
        modCount++;
    }
```

```
    public Object get(int index) {
        checkIndex(index);
        return array[index];
    }

    public Object remove(int index) {
        checkIndex(index);
        Object e = array[index];
        System.arraycopy(array, index+1, array, index, size-index-1);
        size--;
        array[size] = null;  // Eliminate "false reference"
        modCount++;
        return e;
    }

    // This method is not strictly necessary, but it speeds up the
    // clear method on this list and its sublists.
    protected void removeRange(int fromIndex, int toIndex) {
        // Needn't check indices, as this is only used internally
        int numMoved = size - toIndex;
        System.arraycopy(array, toIndex, array, fromIndex, numMoved);

        //  Eliminate "false references" to help garbage collector
        int newSize = size - (toIndex-fromIndex);
        while (size != newSize)
            array[--size] = null;
    }

    public Object set(int index, Object e) {
        checkIndex(index);
        Object o = array[index];
        array[index] = e;
        return o;
    }

    public int size() {
        return size;
    }

    // Utility method.
    private void checkIndex(int index) {
        if (index < 0 || index >= size) {
            throw new IndexOutOfBoundsException();
        }
    }
}
```

add()

PURPOSE Inserts or appends an element to this list.

SYNTAX

```
public boolean add(Object e)
public void add(int ix, Object e)
```

DESCRIPTION This method inserts or appends `e` at index `ix`. If `ix` is not specified, the method defaults to `size()`.

A

If `e` is `null` and this list does not accept `null` elements, a `NullPointerException` is thrown.

`add(int, Object)` is an optional method that must be overridden for a growable list. `add(Object)` is a convenience method whose implementation uses `add(int, Object)`. If the iterators on this list are fail-fast, an override to `add(int, Object)` needs to increment `modCount` (see `modCount`).

PARAMETERS

`e` The possibly `null` element to insert or append to this list.

`ix` The index at which `e` is to be inserted or appended. `0` ≤ `ix` ≤ `size()`.

RETURNS The overloaded method that returns a `boolean` always returns `true`.

EXCEPTIONS

`ClassCastException`
If `e`'s type is not compatible with this list.

`IllegalArgumentException`
If some aspect of `e` prevents it from being added to this list.

`IndexOutOfBoundsException`
If `ix` < `0` or `ix` > `size()`.

`NullPointerException`
If `e` is `null` and this list does not accept `null` elements.

`UnsupportedOperationException`
If this method is not overridden and is used.

EXAMPLE For a usage example, see `List.add()`. For an override example, see the class example.

addAll()

PURPOSE Inserts or appends all elements of a collection to this list.

SYNTAX

```
public boolean addAll(Collection c)
public boolean addAll(int ix, Collection c)
```

DESCRIPTION This method inserts or appends all elements from `c` to this list at index `ix`. The elements are inserted or appended in the same order as they would appear from an iterator on `c`. If `ix` is not specified, the method defaults to `size()`.

If some element in `c` is `null` and this list does not accept `null` elements, a `NullPointerException` is thrown.

This method is a convenience method whose implementation uses `add(int, Object)`.

PARAMETERS

`c` The non-`null` collection of elements to be inserted or appended to this list.

`ix` The index where `e` is to be inserted or appended. `0` ≤ `ix` ≤ `size()`.

RETURNS `true` if this list was modified.

EXCEPTIONS

`ClassCastException`
If the class of an element in `c` is not compatible with this list.

`ConcurrentModificationException`
If `c`'s iterators are fail-fast and `c` is being modified during this method call.

`IndexOutOfBoundsException`
If `ix` < `0` or `ix` > `size()`.

`NullPointerException`
If some element in `c` is `null` and this list does not accept `null` elements.

`UnsupportedOperationException`
If `add(int, Object)` is not overridden and this method is used.

SEE ALSO `add()`.

EXAMPLE See `List.addAll()`.

clear()

PURPOSE Removes all of the elements in this list.

SYNTAX `public void clear()`

DESCRIPTION This method removes all of the elements in this list. After it is called, the list will be empty. This implementation calls the `removeRange()` method.

The default implementation throws `UnsupportedOperationException`. If a subclass supports this operation, it must override this method.

EXCEPTIONS

`UnsupportedOperationException`
If this method is not supported by this list.

EXAMPLE See `Set.clear()`.

equals()

PURPOSE Determines if this list is equal to another object.

SYNTAX `public boolean equals(Object c)`

DESCRIPTION This method determines if this list is equal to the object `c`. It returns `true` if, and only if, `c` is a `List` instance and the elements in `c` and this list match in number and in order. For all non-`null` elements, the `equals()` method of an element in this list is applied to the corresponding element in `c`.

This method is a convenience method whose implementation uses `listIterator()`.

PARAMETERS

c — The possibly `null` object to be compared with this list.

RETURNS — `true` if `c` is equal to this list.

OVERRIDES — `java.lang.Object.equals()`.

SEE ALSO — `hashCode()`.

EXAMPLE — See `List.equals()`.

get()

PURPOSE — Retrieves the element at a particular index in this list.

SYNTAX

```
public abstract Object get(int ix)
```

DESCRIPTION — This method returns the element located at index `ix`. It is required and must be implemented in order for a subclass to be instantiable.

PARAMETERS

`ix` — The index of the element to return. $0 \le$ `ix` $<$ `size()`.

RETURNS — The possibly `null` element at index `ix`. `null` if element is `null`.

EXCEPTIONS

`IndexOutOfBoundsException`
If `ix` < `0` or `ix` ≥ `size()`.

EXAMPLE — For a usage example, see `List.get()`. For an override example, see the class example.

hashCode()

PURPOSE — Computes the hash code for this list.

SYNTAX

```
public int hashCode()
```

DESCRIPTION — This method computes the hash code for this list. The hash code is an integer value that is based on the hash codes of all of the list's elements. Two equal lists will have the same hash code. Unequal lists might also have the same hash code, although the hash code algorithm minimizes this possibility. The hash code is typically used as the key in a hash table.

This implementation of this method implements the algorithm described in `List.hashCode()`.

RETURNS This list's hash code.

OVERRIDES `java.lang.Object.hashCode()`.

SEE ALSO `equals()`, `List.hashCode()`.

EXAMPLE See `java.lang.Object.hashCode()`.

indexOf()

PURPOSE Determines the index of the first occurrence of an element in this list.

SYNTAX `public int indexOf(Object e)`

DESCRIPTION This method searches this list, from the beginning, for any element that equals `e` (using `equals()`). If one is found, its index is returned; otherwise, `-1` is returned.

This a convenience method whose implementation uses `listIterator()`.

PARAMETERS

`e` The possibly `null` element for which to search.

RETURNS The index of the first occurrence of `e` in this list or `-1` if `e` is not in this list.

SEE ALSO `java.lang.Object.equals()`.

EXAMPLE See `List.indexOf()`.

iterator()

PURPOSE Creates an iterator for all of the elements in this list.

SYNTAX `public Iterator iterator()`

DESCRIPTION This method creates and returns an iterator (see `Iterator` for more details) for all of the elements in this list. The order in which the elements are presented by the iterator matches the order of the elements in this list.

Note: The `remove()` method of the returned iterator will throw an `UnsupportedOperationException` unless this list's `remove()` method is overridden.

This is a convenience method whose implementation uses `get(int)`, `remove(int)`, and `size()`.

RETURNS A non-`null` iterator.

SEE ALSO `Iterator`, `listIterator()`, `modCount`.

EXAMPLE See `List.iterator()`.

A

lastIndexOf()

PURPOSE Determines the index of the last occurrence of an element in this list.

SYNTAX `public int lastIndexOf(Object e)`

DESCRIPTION This method searches this list backward, starting from the end, for any element that equals `e` (using `equals()`). If one is found, its index is returned; otherwise, `-1` is returned.

This a convenience method whose implementation uses `listIterator()`.

PARAMETERS

`e` The possibly `null` element for which to search.

RETURNS The index of the last occurrence of `e` in this list or `-1` if `e` is not in this list.

SEE ALSO `java.lang.Object.equals()`.

EXAMPLE See `List.lastIndexOf()`.

listIterator()

PURPOSE Creates a list iterator for the elements in this list.

SYNTAX
```
public ListIterator listIterator()
public ListIterator listIterator(int ix)
```

DESCRIPTION This method creates and returns a list iterator (see `ListIterator` for more details) for all elements in this list starting at index `ix`. The order in which the elements are presented by the list iterator matches the order of the elements in this list. If `ix` is not specified, it defaults to `0`.

If `ix` > `0`, the elements preceding `ix` are not "hidden" from the list iterator. In other words, you can use the list iterator to move backward beyond the element at `ix`. However, you cannot move beyond the first element of this list.

Note: The `add()`, `remove()`, and `set()` methods of the returned iterator will throw an `UnsupportedOperationException` unless this list's `add()`, `remove()`, and `set()` methods are overridden.

This is a convenience method whose implementation uses `add(int)`, `get(int)`, `remove(int)`, `set(int)`, and `size()`.

PARAMETERS

`ix` The index of the first element to be returned by the list iterator. `0` ≤ `ix` ≤ `size()`.

RETURNS A non-`null` list iterator for this list.

EXCEPTIONS

`IndexOutOfBoundsException`

If `ix` < `0` or `ix` > `size()`.

SEE ALSO `iterator()`, `ListIterator`, `modCount`.

EXAMPLE See `List.listIterator()`.

modCount

PURPOSE Contains the number of times this list has been modified.

SYNTAX `protected transient int modCount`

DESCRIPTION This is a field that tracks the number of times this list has been modified. When an iterator is created on this list, it remembers the current value of `modCount`. If the iterator discovers an unexpected change in the value, it throws a `ConcurrentModificationException`.

This field should be incremented whenever a modification is made to the list. For example, if any of the three optional methods—`add(int, Object)`, `set(int, Object)`, and `remove(int)`—are overridden, they should increment `modCount` when they result in a modification to the list. Also, if any of the convenience methods that modify the list are overridden, they also need to increment `modCount`. `modCount` should never be decremented or cleared.

Note: A modification method might decide to increment `modCount` even though no modification was made. Thus a `ConcurrentModificationException` thrown by an iterator might mean only that an *attempt* to modify the list was made. Also, you cannot call a modification method that you know will not result in a modification (such as to remove a nonexistent element) and assume that an iterator won't throw `ConcurrentModificationException`.

The use of this field is optional. If the iterators on your subclass don't need to be fail-fast, you don't need to increment this field. However, if you do use this field, all modification methods must increment this field. That is, you can't have `set()` increment the field and `remove()` not increment the field.

Note: The default implementations of the iterators in this class require that each call to one of the modification methods not increment `modCount` by more than one.

EXAMPLE See the class example.

A

remove()

PURPOSE Removes an element from this list.

SYNTAX `public Object remove(int ix)`

DESCRIPTION This method removes and returns the element at index `ix` from this list.

It is an optional method and must be overridden for lists that can shrink. If the iterators on this list are fail-fast, an override to this method needs to increment `modCount` (see `modCount`).

PARAMETERS

`ix` The index of the element to remove. `0` ≤ `ix` < `size()`.

RETURNS The possibly `null` element that was removed.

EXCEPTIONS

`IndexOutOfBoundsException`
If `ix` < `0` or `ix` ≥ `size()`.

`UnsupportedOperationException`
If this method is not overridden and is used.

SEE ALSO `removeAll()`, `retainAll()`.

EXAMPLE For a usage example, see `List.remove()`. For an override example, see the class example.

removeRange()

PURPOSE Removes a range of elements from this list.

SYNTAX `protected void removeRange(int fromIx, int toIx)`

DESCRIPTION This method removes all of the elements between `fromIx` (inclusive) and `toIx` (exclusive) from this list.

This protected method is a convenience method. Overriding this method can *significantly* improve the performance of the `clear` operation on this list and its sublist views. If this operation is not overridden and the `listIterator().remove()` operation runs in linear time, the `clear` operation will run in quadratic time.

PARAMETERS

`fromIx` The index of the first element to be removed. `0` ≤ `fromIx` ≤ `size()`.

`toIx` The element at `toIx-1`, the last element to be removed. `fromIx` ≤ `toIx` ≤ `size()`.

EXCEPTIONS

`UnsupportedOperationException`
If neither this method nor the `remove(int)` method is overridden.

EXAMPLE See the class example.

set()

PURPOSE Replaces an element with another element.

SYNTAX `public Object set(int ix, Object e)`

DESCRIPTION This method replaces the element at `ix` with `e` and returns the element previously at `ix`.

This method is an optional method and must be overridden for lists that can be modified. If the iterators on this list are fail-fast, an override to this method needs to increment `modCount` (see `modCount`).

PARAMETERS

`e` The possibly `null` element to be stored at `ix`.

`ix` The index of the element to replace. `0` ≤ `ix` < `size()`.

RETURNS The possibly `null` element that was replaced.

EXCEPTIONS

`ClassCastException`
If the class of `e` is not compatible with this list.

`IllegalArgumentException`
If some aspect of `e` prevents it from being added to this list.

`IndexOutOfBoundsException`
If `ix` < `0` or `ix` ≥ `size()`.

`UnsupportedOperationException`
If this method is not overridden and is used.

EXAMPLE For a usage example, see `List.set()`. For an override example, see the class example.

subList()

PURPOSE Creates a sublist of a range of elements in this list.

SYNTAX `public List subList(int fromIx, int toIx)`

DESCRIPTION This method creates and returns a sublist containing all of the elements between `fromIx` (inclusive) and `toIx` (exclusive). The element at `toIx` is not included. The order of these elements in the sublist exactly matches the order of the elements as they appear in this list. The size of the new sublist is `toIx` minus `fromIx`. The index of the first element in the sublist is `0`. The sublist cannot access any element in this list that is outside the range of `fromIx` to `toIx`.

A sublist does not have its own storage. Rather, it shares the storage with this list. If you modify the sublist, the modifications also appear in this list. If this list is modified directly or through another sublist, the sublist is no longer valid and should be discarded.

Some implementations of `subList()` will watch for modifications of the underlying list. If a method of the sublist detects a modification, it will throw a `ConcurrentModificationException`.

PARAMETERS

`fromIx` The index of the first element to be included in the sublist. `0` ≤ `fromIx` ≤ `size()`.

`toIx` The element at `toIx-1`, the last element to be included in the sublist. `fromIx` ≤ `toIx` ≤ `size()`.

RETURNS A non-`null` list containing the elements from this list in the range of `fromIx` to `toIx-1`.

EXCEPTIONS

`IndexOutOfBoundsException`
If `fromIx` < `0`, or `toIx` < `fromIx`, or `toIx` > `size()`.

EXAMPLE See `List.subList()`.

AbstractMap

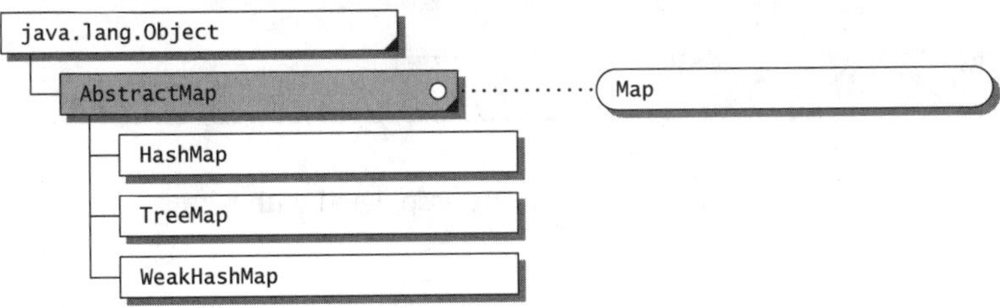

Syntax

```
public abstract class AbstractMap implements Map
```

Description

The `AbstractMap` abstract class is a partial implementation of the `Map` interface. Its purpose is to minimize the effort in building your own map classes by providing default implementations for most of the methods required by the `Map` interface.

This class does not implement any kind of storage. It is more like a veneer over some data storage that you provide. You "layer" this class over your data storage by implementing or overriding some of the methods in this class.

To use this abstract class, you need to implement one method: `entrySet()`. All other methods are based on `entrySet()`.

Usage

This class is meant to be subclassed. You should implement a constructor with no parameters to make it convenient for your class to be instantiated. You should also provide a constructor that accepts a `Map` object. This constructor constructs a new map initialized with the elements from the supplied map. It makes copying any map easy. You might want to provide other constructors as well. You must also, at a minimum, implement the abstract method `entrySet()` in order for the subclass to be instantiable. Implementing this method results in a read-only map.

To be able to add entries to your map, you must override `put()`. If you want to be able to remove entries from your map, you must implement the `remove()` method on the iterators from sets returned by `entrySet()`.

All other methods are convenience methods. All of these are written in a way that uses only `entrySet()`. If you are concerned about performance, you can override any of the convenience methods for a more efficient implementation.

Fail-Fast Iterators

Some maps do not allow modifications while an iterator on the map is in use. These maps should implement a *fail-fast iterator* (see `Iterator`). A fail-fast iterator watches for modifications on the map and throws an exception if it detects one. This feature is used mainly to avoid programming errors. See `Iterator` for more details.

MEMBER SUMMARY	
Retrieval Method	
`get()`	Retrieves the value associated with a key.
Query Methods	
`containsKey()`	Determines if this map contains a particular key.
`containsValue()`	Determines if this map contains a particular value.
`isEmpty()`	Determines if this map has no entries.
`size()`	Returns the number of entries in this map.
Modification Methods	
`clear()`	Removes all of the entries in this map.
`put()`	Adds a key/value pair to this map.
`putAll()`	Adds key/value pairs from another map to this map.
`remove()`	Removes an entry from this map.
Set Methods	
`entrySet()`	Returns a set view of all of the key/value pairs in this map.
`keySet()`	Returns a set view of all of the keys in this map.
`values()`	Returns a collection view of all of the values in this map.
Object Methods	
`equals()`	Determines if this map is equal to another object.
`hashCode()`	Computes the hash code for this map.
`toString()`	Generates a string representation of this map.

See Also

`Iterator`, `Map`.

Example

This example demonstrates the use of this class by implementing a simple, limited-sized map. The map cannot grow beyond a size that is specified in the map's constructor. The list internally uses `Object` arrays to store the keys and values. This map does not provide a constructor that has no parameters, since it requires that a capacity be specified.

```
import java.util.*;

class Main {
    public static void main(String[] args) {
        Map map = new FixedMap(2);
        map.put("dog", "spot");
        map.put("cat", "luck");
```

```
        // map.put("pig", "babe");

        System.out.println(map.get("dog"));
        System.out.println(map.put("dog", "ruff"));
        System.out.println(map.remove("cat"));
        System.out.println(map);

        System.out.println(map.put("cat", "luck"));
        System.out.println(map.keySet());
        System.out.println(map.values());

        System.out.println(map.keySet().remove("dog"));
        System.out.println(map);
        System.out.println(map.values().remove("luck"));
        System.out.println(map);
    }
}

class FixedMap extends AbstractMap {
    private Entry[] entry;
    int size = 0;

    FixedMap(int capacity) {
        entry = new Entry[capacity];
        for (int i=0; i<capacity; i++)
            entry[i] = new Entry();
    }

    FixedMap() {
        this(10);  // Default capacity is 10
    }

    FixedMap(Map m) {
        entry = new Entry[(m.size()*110)/100];  // Allow >= 10% for growth
        putAll(m);
    }

    public Object put(Object key, Object value) {
        for (int i=0; i<size; i++) {
            if (eq(entry[i].key, key)) {
                Object oldVal = entry[i].value;
                entry[i].value = value;
                return oldVal;
            }
        }
        if (size == entry.length)
            throw new IllegalStateException();
        entry[size].key = key;
        entry[size++].value = value;
        return null;
    }

    public Set entrySet() {
        return new AbstractSet() {
            public int size() {
                return size;
            }
            public Iterator iterator() {
                return new Iterator() {
                    private int cursor = 0;
```

```
                        private boolean removeProhibited = true;
                        public boolean hasNext() {
                            return cursor < size;
                        }
                        public Object next() {
                            if (cursor==size)
                                throw new NoSuchElementException();
                            removeProhibited = false;
                            return entry[cursor++];
                        }
                        public void remove() {
                            if (removeProhibited)
                                throw new IllegalStateException();
                            entry[--cursor].key = entry[--size].key;
                            entry[cursor].value = entry[size].value;
                            entry[size].key = entry[size].value = null;
                            removeProhibited = true;
                        }
                    };
                }
            };
        }

        private static class Entry implements Map.Entry {
            Object key, value;
            public Object getKey() {
                return key;
            }
            public Object getValue() {
                return value;
            }
            public Object setValue(Object v) {
                Object oldVal = value;
                value = v;
                return oldVal;
            }
            public boolean equals(Object o) {
                if (!(o instanceof Map.Entry))
                    return false;
                Map.Entry e = (Map.Entry) o;
                return eq(e.getKey(), key) && eq(e.getValue(), value);
            }
            public int hashCode() {
                return hash(key) ^ hash(value);
            }
            public String toString() {
                return key + "=" + value;
            }
        }

        private static boolean eq(Object o1, Object o2) {
            return (o1==null ? o2==null : o1.equals(o2));
        }
        private static int hash(Object o) {
            return (o==null ? 0 : o.hashCode());
        }
    }
```

clear()

PURPOSE Removes all of the entries in this map.

SYNTAX `public void clear()`

DESCRIPTION This method removes all of the entries in this map. After it is called, this map will be empty.

The default implementation throws `UnsupportedOperationException`. If a subclass supports this operation, it must override this method.

EXCEPTIONS

`UnsupportedOperationException`
If this method is not supported by this map.

EXAMPLE See `Map.clear()`.

containsKey()

PURPOSE Determines if this map contains a particular key.

SYNTAX `public boolean containsKey(Object k)`

DESCRIPTION This method determines if this map contains the key `k`. It returns `true` if some key in this map is equal to `k`. For all non-`null` keys, the `equals()` method is used to determine if two keys are equal.

PARAMETERS

`k` A possibly `null` key.

RETURNS `true` if some key in this map is equal to `k`.

EXCEPTIONS

`ClassCastException`
If the class of `k` is not compatible with this map.

`NullPointerException`
If `k` is `null` and this map does not accept `null` keys.

SEE ALSO `equals()`.

EXAMPLE See `Map.containsKey()`.

containsValue()

PURPOSE Determines if this map contains a particular value.

SYNTAX `public boolean containsValue(Object v)`

DESCRIPTION This method determines if this map contains a particular value. It returns `true` if some value in this map is equal to `v`. For all non-`null` values, the `equals()` method is used to determine if two values are equal.

PARAMETERS

`v` A possibly `null` value.

RETURNS `true` if some value in this map is equal to `v`.

EXCEPTIONS

`ClassCastException`
If the class of `v` is not compatible with the class of this map.

`NullPointerException`
If `v` is `null` and this map does not accept `null` values.

SEE ALSO `equals()`.

EXAMPLE See `Map.containsKey()`.

entrySet()

PURPOSE Returns a set view of all of the key/value pairs in this map.

SYNTAX `public abstract Set entrySet()`

DESCRIPTION This method returns a set containing all of the key/value pairs in this map. The key/value pairs are represented by `Map.Entry` objects. See `Map.Entry` for information about retrieving a key or value from an entry.

The returned set and this map share the same storage. This means that changes to the map are immediately reflected in the set and changes to the set are immediately reflected in the map.

This is the only method in this class that must be implemented in order for a subclass to be instantiable.

RETURNS A non-`null` set containing all entries in this map.

SEE ALSO `Collection`, `keySet()`, `Map.Entry`, `values()`.

EXAMPLE For a usage example, see `Map.entrySet()`. For an override example, see the class example.

A

equals()

PURPOSE Determines if this map is equal to another object.

SYNTAX `public boolean equals(Object c)`

DESCRIPTION This method determines if this map is equal to the object `c`. It returns `true` if, and only if, `c` is a `Map` object and both this map and `c` have exactly the same entries (see `Map.Entry`). `Map.Entry.equals()` is used to determine if two entries match. Basically, two entries match if the keys and values of one are equal to those of the other.

PARAMETERS

`c` The possibly `null` object to be compared with this map.

RETURNS `true` if `c` is equal to this map.

OVERRIDES `java.lang.Object.equals()`.

SEE ALSO `hashCode()`.

EXAMPLE See `Map.equals()`.

get()

PURPOSE Retrieves the value associated with a key.

SYNTAX `public Object get(Object k)`

DESCRIPTION This method searches this map for an entry with the key `k` and returns the associated value. `null` is returned if `k` is not in this map. A return value of `null` is ambiguous if the map accepts `null` values. You can use `containsKey()` to unambiguously determine if `k` is in this map.

PARAMETERS

`k` A possibly `null` key.

RETURNS The possibly `null` value associated with `k` or `null` if `k` is not in this map.

EXCEPTIONS

`ClassCastException`
If the class of `k` is not compatible with this map.

`NullPointerException`
If `k` is `null` and this map does not accept `null` keys.

SEE ALSO `containsKey()`.

EXAMPLE See `Map.get()`.

hashCode()

PURPOSE Computes the hash code for this map.

SYNTAX `public int hashCode()`

DESCRIPTION This method computes the hash code for this map. The hash code is the sum of the hash codes of all of the entries in the map. The hash code for an entry is the exclusive-OR of the key and the value. The hash code for a `null` key or value is `0` (see `Map.Entry.hashCode()` for more information).

Two equal maps will have the same hash code. Unequal maps might also have the same hash code, although the hash code algorithm minimizes this possibility. The hash code is typically used as the key in a hash table.

RETURNS This map's hash code.

OVERRIDES `java.lang.Object.hashCode()`.

SEE ALSO `equals()`, `MapEntry.hashCode()`.

EXAMPLE See `java.lang.Object.hashCode()`.

isEmpty()

PURPOSE Determines if this map has no entries.

SYNTAX `public boolean isEmpty()`

RETURNS `true` if this map contains no entries.

SEE ALSO `size()`.

EXAMPLE See `Map.clear()`.

keySet()

PURPOSE Returns a set view of all of the keys in this map.

SYNTAX `public Set keySet()`

DESCRIPTION This method returns a set containing all of the keys in this map.

The set and this map share the same storage. This means that changes to the map are immediately reflected in the set and changes in the set are immediately reflected in the map.

RETURNS A non-`null` set containing all of the keys in this map.

SEE ALSO `Collection`, `entrySet()`, `values()`.

EXAMPLE See `Map.keySet()`.

A

put()

PURPOSE Adds a key/value pair to this map.

SYNTAX `public Object put(Object k, Object v)`

DESCRIPTION This method adds a new entry with the key `k` and value `v` into this map. If an entry with the key `k` already exists in this map, it is replaced with the new entry. In this case, the previous value is returned.

The default implementation throws `UnsupportedOperationException`. If a subclass supports this operation, it must override this method.

PARAMETERS

`k` A possibly `null` key.

`v` A possibly `null` value.

RETURNS If `k` already exists in this map, then the possibly `null` old value is returned; otherwise, `null` is returned.

EXCEPTIONS

`IllegalArgumentException`

If some aspect of `k` prevents it from being added to this map.

`ClassCastException`

If the class of `k` is not compatible with this map.

`NullPointerException`

If `k` or `v` is `null` and this map does not accept `null` keys or values.

`UnsupportedOperationException`

If this method is not supported by this map.

EXAMPLE See `Map.put()`.

putAll()

PURPOSE Adds key/value pairs from another map to this map.

SYNTAX `public void putAll(Map m)`

DESCRIPTION This method adds key/value pairs from the map `m` to this map. Every entry from `m` is added to this map. If the key for some entry from `m` already exists in this map, the entry in this map is replaced by the one from `m`.

The default implementation throws `UnsupportedOperationException`. If a subclass supports this operation, it must override this method.

PARAMETERS

`m` A non-`null` map.

EXCEPTIONS

`ConcurrentModificationException`
If `m`'s iterators are fail-fast and `m` is being modified during this method call.

`ClassCastException`
If the class of some entry in `m` is not compatible with this map.

`IllegalArgumentException`
If some aspect of some entry in `m` prevents it from being added to this map.

`NullPointerException`
If the key or value of some entry in `m` is `null` and this map does not accept `null` keys or values.

`UnsupportedOperationException`
If this method is not supported by this map.

SEE ALSO `put()`.

EXAMPLE See `Map.putAll()`.

remove()

PURPOSE Removes an entry from this map.

SYNTAX `public Object remove(Object k)`

DESCRIPTION This method searches for the first occurrence of an entry with key `k` in this map and removes the entry from this map. It uses `equals()` to determine equality.

The default implementation throws `UnsupportedOperationException`. If a subclass supports this operation, it must override this method.

PARAMETERS

`k` The possibly `null` key of the entry to remove.

RETURNS The possibly `null` value associated with `k` or `null` if `k` does not match any keys in this map.

EXCEPTIONS

`UnsupportedOperationException`
If this method is not supported by this map.

EXAMPLE See `Map.remove()`.

size()

PURPOSE Returns the number of entries in this map.

SYNTAX `public int size()`

RETURNS The non-negative number of entries in this map.

SEE ALSO `isEmpty()`.

EXAMPLE See `clear()`.

toString()

PURPOSE Generates a string representation of this map.

SYNTAX `public String toString()`

RETURNS A non-`null` string containing all of the keys and values in this map.

OVERRIDES `java.lang.Object.toString()`.

EXAMPLE

```
HashMap map = new HashMap();
map.put("dog", "spot");
map.put("cat", "luck");

System.out.println( map.toString() );   // {cat="luck, dog=spot}
```

values()

PURPOSE Returns a collection view of all of the values in this map.

SYNTAX `public Collection values()`

DESCRIPTION This method returns a collection containing all of the values in this map. Unlike `keySet()`, the returned collection is not a set because there could be duplicates of values (sets don't allow duplicate elements).

The returned collection and this map share the same storage. This means that changes to the map are immediately reflected in the collection and changes in the collection are immediately reflected in the map.

RETURNS A non-`null` collection containing all of the values in this map.

SEE ALSO `Collection`, `entrySet()`, `keySet()`.

EXAMPLE See `Map.values()`.

java.util

AbstractSequentialList

A

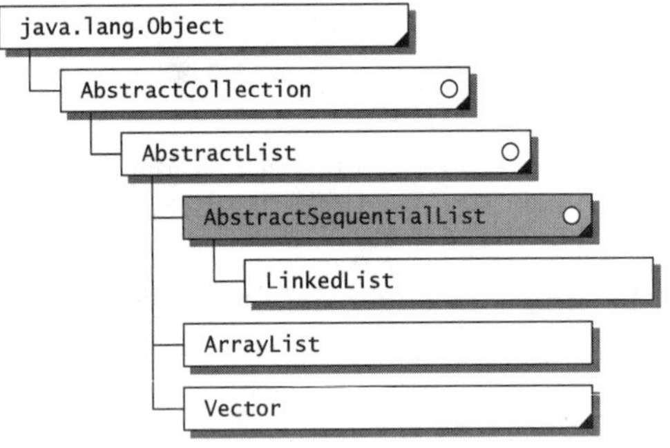

Syntax

```
public abstract class AbstractSequentialList extends AbstractList
```

Description

The `AbstractSequentialList` abstract class is a partial implementation of the `List` interface. Its purpose is to minimize the effort in building your own list classes by providing default implementations for most of the methods required by the `List` interface. This class differs from the more commonly used `AbstractList` in that it is designed for list data structures that are *sequential* in nature.

This class does not implement any kind of storage. It is more like a veneer over some data storage that you provide. You "layer" this class over your data storage by implementing some of the abstract methods in this class. For example, this class declares a `size()` method, which returns the element at `index`. You must implement this abstract method to return the number of elements in your data storage.

The methods in this class fall into two groups: required and convenience. There are two required methods:

`listIterator(int)`	Creates a list iterator.
`size()`	Returns the number of elements in the list.

These abstract methods must be implemented before you can instantiate a subclass of `AbstractSequentialList`.

All other methods are convenience methods. All are written in a way that uses only `listIterator()` and `size()`. If you are concerned about performance, you can override any of the convenience methods for more efficient implementations. Note that if iterators on the subclass are fail-fast, the override needs to increment `AbstractList.modCount`. See `AbstractList.modCount` for more details.

The List Iterator

The implementation of the list iterator determines what operations are allowed on the list. In particular, to implement the minimum read-only list, you need to implement the methods `hasNext()`, `next()`, `hasPrevious()`, `previous()`, `nextIndex()`, and `previousIndex()`.

- To implement a list whose elements can be modified, you need to implement `set()`.
- To implement a list that can grow, you need to implement `add()`.
- To implement a list that can shrink, you need to implement `remove()`.

If a capability is not implemented, simply have the method throw an `UnsupportedOperationException`.

Usage

The `AbstractSequentialList` class is meant to be subclassed. You should implement a constructor with no parameters so as to make it convenient to instantiate. You should also provide a constructor that accepts a `Collection` object. This latter constructor constructs a new list initialized with the elements from the supplied collection, thereby making it easy to copy any collection. You might want to provide other constructors as well.

Also, for the subclass to be instantiable, you must, at a minimum, implement the two abstract methods, `listInterator()` and `size()`. Implementing only these two methods results in a read-only list. If you want the list to have more capabilities, you must override some of the optional methods in the superclass `AbstractList`. For more details, see the subsection "Optional Methods" for the class `AbstractList`.

Fail-Fast Iterators

Some lists do not allow modifications while an iterator on the list is in use. These lists should implement a *fail-fast iterator*. A fail-fast iterator watches for modifications on the list and throws an exception if it detects one. The feature is used mainly to avoid programming errors. See `Iterator` for more details.

The `modCount` field in the parent of this class is used to implement fail-fast iterators. This integer should be incremented every time the list is modified. See `AbstractList.modCount` for more details.

AbstractList versus AbstractSequentialList

There are two skeletal implementations of the `List` interface available. Which one you use depends on how elements are accessed in your data storage. If your data storage makes it easy to access elements by an integer index, then you should use `AbstractList`. If your data storage is more like a linked list, in which you have to traverse the structure in order to get at an element, then you should use `AbstractSequentialList`.

Both classes have exactly the same methods. They differ mainly in which methods are required and which are convenient. In `AbstractList`, `get(int)` is required while `iterator()` is not. In `AbstractSequentialList`, `iterator()` is required while `get(int)` is not. See `AbstractList` for more details.

MEMBER SUMMARY	
Element Retrieval Method	
`get()`	Retrieves the element at a particular index in this list.
Modification Methods	
`add()`	Inserts an element into this list.
`addAll()`	Inserts all of the elements of a collection into this list.
`remove()`	Removes an element at an index from this list.
`set()`	Replaces an element with another element.
Iterator Methods	
`iterator()`	Creates an iterator for the elements in this list.
`listIterator()`	Creates a list iterator for the elements in this list.

See Also

`AbstractList`, `Iterator`, `ListIterator`, `LinkedList`.

Example

This example demonstrates the use of the `AbstractSequentialList` class by implementing a simple linked list. This list is very similar to `LinkedList`, but it is a bit simpler.

The methods `getModCount()` and `incModCount()` are needed because the inner class cannot access inherited protected field such as `modCount`. *Note*: In the future, this restriction might be relaxed to allow inner classes to access inherited protected fields, since the inner class is currently allowed to access protected fields that are declared in the enclosing class.

```
import java.util.*;

class Main {
    public static void main(String[] args) {
        List list = new SimpleLinkedList();

        // Test the list.
        list.add("dog");
        list.add("cat");
        list.remove("dog");
        list.add("pig");
        System.out.println( list );    // [cat, pig]
        list.set(list.size()-1, "dog");
        System.out.println( list );    // [cat, dog]

        // Traverse the list backwards
        for (ListIterator it=list.listIterator(list.size());
            it.hasPrevious(); ) {
            System.out.println( it.previous() );
        }    // dog cat

        // Modify the list while an iterator is active.
        Iterator it = list.iterator();
        list.remove("cat");
```

```
        it.next();                   // ConcurrentModificationException
    }
}

class SimpleLinkedList extends AbstractSequentialList {
    private Node header = new Node(null, null, null);
    private int size = 0;

    public SimpleLinkedList() {
        header.next = header.previous = header;
    }

    public SimpleLinkedList(List l) {
        super();
        addAll(l);
    }

    public ListIterator listIterator(int index) {
        return new OurListIterator(index);
    }

    public int size() {
        return size;
    }

    private static class Node {
        Node(Node next, Node previous, Object element) {
            this.next = next;
            this.previous = previous;
            this.element = element;
        }
        Node next;
        Node previous;
        Object element;
    }

    private class OurListIterator implements ListIterator {
        private Node next;
        private int nextIndex;
        private Node lastReturned = null;
        private int expectedModCount = getModCount();

        OurListIterator(int index) {
            if (index < 0 || index > size) {
                throw new IndexOutOfBoundsException("Index: " + index);
            }

            // Iterate from front or back, whichever is closer
            if (index < size/2) {
                next = header.next;
                for (nextIndex=0; nextIndex<index; nextIndex++) {
                    next = next.next;
                }
            } else {
                next = header;
                for (nextIndex=size; nextIndex>index; nextIndex--) {
                    next = next.previous;
                }
            }
        }
```

```
public void add(Object o) {
    checkForComodification();
    Node newNode = new Node(next, next.previous, o);
    next.previous = newNode;
    newNode.previous.next = newNode;
    size++;
    nextIndex++;
    lastReturned = null;
    incModCount();
    expectedModCount++;
}

public boolean hasNext() {
    return nextIndex < size;
}

public boolean hasPrevious() {
    return nextIndex > 0;
}

public Object next() {
    checkForComodification();
    if (!hasNext()) {
        throw new NoSuchElementException();
    }
    lastReturned = next;
    next = next.next;
    nextIndex++;
    return lastReturned.element;
}

public int nextIndex() {
    checkForComodification();
    return nextIndex;
}

public Object previous() {
    checkForComodification();
    if (!hasPrevious()) {
        throw new NoSuchElementException();
    }
    next = lastReturned = next.previous;
    nextIndex--;
    return lastReturned.element;
}

public int previousIndex() {
    checkForComodification();
    return nextIndex-1;
}

public void remove() {
    if (lastReturned==null) {
        throw new IllegalStateException();
    }
    checkForComodification();
    if (next==lastReturned) {
        next = lastReturned.next;
    } else {
        nextIndex--;
```

```
            }
            lastReturned.previous.next = lastReturned.next;
            lastReturned.next.previous = lastReturned.previous;
            lastReturned = null;
            size--;
            incModCount();
            expectedModCount++;
        }

        public void set(Object o) {
            if (lastReturned==null) {
                throw new IllegalStateException();
            }
            checkForComodification();
            lastReturned.element = o;
        }

        private void checkForComodification() {
            if (getModCount() != expectedModCount) {
                throw new ConcurrentModificationException();
            }
        }
    }

    // "Bridge methods" required to give inner class access to protected field
    private int getModCount() {
        return modCount;
    }
    private void incModCount() {
        modCount++;
    }
}
```

add()

PURPOSE Inserts an element into this list.

SYNTAX `public void add(int ix, Object e)`

DESCRIPTION This method inserts the element `e` at index `ix`.

This is a convenience method whose implementation creates a list iterator starting at `ix` and then uses the list iterator's `add()` method to append `e` to the list.

PARAMETERS

`e` The possibly `null` element to add to this list.

`ix` The index at which `e` is to be inserted. `0` ≤ `ix` ≤ `size()`.

RETURNS The overloaded method that returns a `boolean` always returns `true`.

EXCEPTIONS

`IllegalArgumentException`

If some aspect of `e` prevents it from being added to this list.

`IndexOutOfBoundsException`
If `ix` < `0` or `ix` > `size()`.

`NullPointerException`
If `e` is `null` and this list does not accept `null` elements.

`UnsupportedOperationException`
If this list does not support this method.

EXAMPLE See `List.add()`.

addAll()

PURPOSE Inserts all of the elements of a collection into this list.

SYNTAX

```
public boolean addAll(Collection c)
public boolean addAll(int ix, Collection c)
```

DESCRIPTION This method inserts all of the elements from `c` into this list at index `ix`. The elements are inserted in the same order as they would appear from an iterator on `c`. If `ix` is not specified, it defaults to `size()`.

This is a convenience method whose implementation uses the `add()` method of a list iterator on this list.

PARAMETERS

`c` The non-`null` collection of elements to be inserted into this list.

`ix` The index at which `e` is to be inserted. `0` ≤ `ix` ≤ `size()`.

RETURNS `true` if this list was modified.

EXCEPTIONS

`ClassCastException`
If the class of an element in `c` is not compatible with this list.

`ConcurrentModificationException`
If `c`'s iterators are fail-fast and `c` is being modified during this method call.

`IllegalArgumentException`
If some aspect of an element in `c` prevents it from being added to this list.

`IndexOutOfBoundsException`
If `ix` < `0` or `ix` > `size()`.

`NullPointerException`
If some element of `c` is `null` and this list does not accept `null` elements.

`UnsupportedOperationException`
If this list does not support this method.

SEE ALSO `add()`.

EXAMPLE See `List.addAll()`.

get()

PURPOSE Retrieves the element at a particular index in this list.

SYNTAX `public Object get(int ix)`

DESCRIPTION This method returns the element located at index `ix`.

This is a convenience method whose implementation creates a list iterator starting at `ix` on this list and then uses the list iterator's `next()` method to retrieve the element.

PARAMETERS

`ix` The index of the element to return. `0` ≤ `ix` < `size()`.

EXCEPTIONS

`IndexOutOfBoundsException`

If `ix` < `0` or `ix` ≥ `size()`.

EXAMPLE See `List.get()`.

iterator()

PURPOSE Creates an iterator for the elements in this list.

SYNTAX `public Iterator iterator()`

DESCRIPTION This method creates and returns an iterator (see `Iterator` for more details) for all of the elements in this list. The order in which the elements are presented by the iterator matches the order of the elements in this list.

This is a convenience method whose implementation simply returns a list iterator on this list.

RETURNS A non-`null` iterator.

SEE ALSO `Iterator`, `listIterator()`, `modCount`.

EXAMPLE See `List.iterator()`.

listIterator()

PURPOSE Creates a list iterator for the elements in this list.

SYNTAX `public abstract ListIterator listIterator(int ix)`

DESCRIPTION This method creates and returns a list iterator (see `ListIterator` for more details) for all of the elements in this list. The cursor of the list iterator is initialized to `ix`. This means that the first element returned by the list iterator is the element at `ix`. The elements preceding `ix` are also available to the list iterator. If `ix` is not specified, it defaults to `0`.

The order of the elements returned by the list iterator is exactly the same order in which the elements appear in the list.

This is a required method that must be implemented in order for a subclass to be instantiable.

PARAMETERS

`ix` The initial value of the list iterator's cursor. `0` ≤ `ix` ≤ `size()`.

EXCEPTIONS

`IndexOutOfBoundsException`
If `ix` < `0` or `ix` > `size()`.

SEE ALSO `iterator()`.

EXAMPLE For a usage example, see `List.listIterator()`. For an override example, see the class example.

remove()

PURPOSE Removes an element at an index from this list.

SYNTAX `public Object remove(int ix)`

DESCRIPTION This method removes and returns the element at index `ix` from this list.

This is a convenience method whose implementation creates a list iterator starting at `ix` on this list and then uses the list iterator's `remove()` method to remove the element at `ix`.

PARAMETERS

`ix` The index of the element to remove. `0` ≤ `ix` < `size()`.

RETURNS The possibly `null` element that was removed.

EXCEPTIONS

`IndexOutOfBoundsException`
If `ix` < `0` or `ix` ≥ `size()`.

`UnsupportedOperationException`
If this list does not support this method.

SEE ALSO `removeAll()`, `retainAll()`.

EXAMPLE See `List.remove()`.

set()

PURPOSE Replaces an element with another element.

SYNTAX `public Object set(int ix, Object e)`

DESCRIPTION This method replaces the element at `ix` with `e` and returns the element previously at `ix`.

This is a convenience method that creates a list iterator on this list starting at `ix` and then uses the list iterator's `set()` method to replace the element at `ix`.

PARAMETERS

`e` The possibly `null` element to be stored at `ix`.

`ix` The index of the element to replace. `0` ≤ `ix` < `size()`.

RETURNS The possibly `null` element that was replaced.

EXCEPTIONS

`ClassCastException`
If the class of `e` is not compatible with this list.

`IllegalArgumentException`
If some aspect of `e` prevents it from being added to this list.

`IndexOutOfBoundsException`
If `ix` < `0` or `ix` ≥ `size()`.

`NullPointerException`
If `e` is `null` and this list does not accept `null` elements.

`UnsupportedOperationException`
If this list does not support this method.

EXAMPLE See `List.set()`.

java.util
AbstractSet

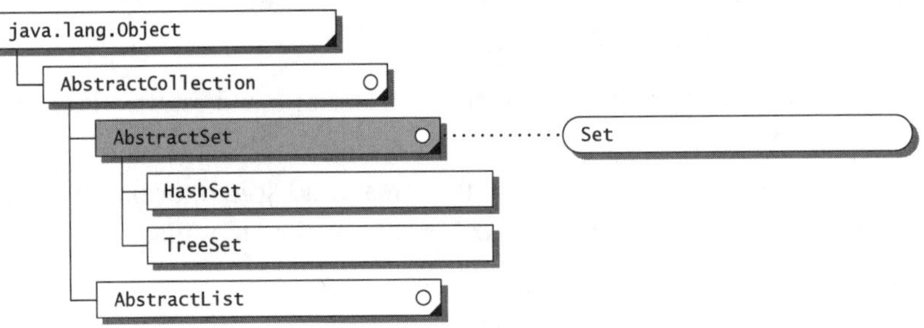

Syntax

`public abstract class AbstractSet extends AbstractCollection implements Set`

Description

The `AbstractSet` abstract class is a partial implementation of the `Set` interface. Its purpose is to minimize the effort in building your own set classes by providing default implementations for most of the methods required by the `Set` interface.

This class does not implement any kind of storage. It is more like a veneer over some data storage that you provide. You "layer" this class over your data storage by overriding some of the methods in this class. For example, this class declares a `size()` method that returns the number of elements in the set. You must implement this abstract method to return the number of elements in your data storage.

Usage

This class is meant to be subclassed. You should implement a constructor with no parameters to make it convenient for your class to be instantiated. You should also provide a constructor that accepts a `Collection` object. This constructor constructs a new set initialized with the elements from the supplied collection. It makes copying any collection easy.

A subclass, to be instantiable, must implement the following two abstract methods:

`iterator()`	Creates an iterator for the set.
`size()`	Returns the number of elements in the set.

Implementing only these two methods results in a read-only set.

To allow elements to be added to the set, you must override the `add()` method.

To allow elements to be removed from the set, you must implement the `remove()` method in the iterators returned by `iterator()`.

All other methods are convenience methods. All are written in a way that uses only `iterator()` and `size()`. If you are concerned about performance, you can override any of the convenience methods for a more efficient implementation.

Fail-Fast Iterators

Some sets do not allow modifications while an iterator on the set is in use. These sets should implement a *fail-fast iterator.* A fail-fast iterator watches for modifications on the set and throws an exception if it detects one. This feature is used mainly to avoid programming errors. See `Iterator` for more details.

MEMBER SUMMARY	
Object Methods	
`equals()`	Determines if this set is equal to another object.
`hashCode()`	Computes the hash code for this set.

See Also

`HashSet, Set, TreeSet.`

Example

This example demonstrates the use of this class by implementing a simple, limited-sized set. The set cannot grow beyond a size that is specified in the set's constructor. The set internally uses an `Object` array to store the elements. It does not provide a constructor that has no parameters, since it requires that a capacity be specified.

```
import java.util.*;

class Main {
    public static void main(String[] args) {
        Set set = new FixedSet(2);

        System.out.println(set.add("dog"));     // true
        System.out.println(set.add("cat"));     // true
        System.out.println(set);                // [dog, cat]

        // The set is full
        // System.out.println(set.add("pig")); // IllegalStateException

        // Add an identical element
        System.out.println(set.add("dog"));     // false
        System.out.println(set);                // [dog, cat]

        // Remove some elements.
        System.out.println(set.remove("pig")); // false
        System.out.println(set.remove("cat")); // true
        System.out.println(set);                // [dog]
    }
}

class FixedSet extends AbstractSet {
    private Object[] array;
    int size = 0;

    FixedSet(int capacity) {
```

```
        array = new Object[capacity];
    }

    FixedSet() {
        this(10);  // Default capacity is 10
    }

    FixedSet(Collection c) {
        array = new Object[(c.size()*110)/100];  // Allow >= 10% for growth
        addAll(c);
    }

    public boolean add(Object e) {
        if (contains(e))
            return false;
        if (size == array.length)
            throw new IllegalStateException();
        array[size++] = e;
        return true;
    }

    public Iterator iterator() {
        // This is not a fail-fast iterator
        return new Iterator() {
            private int cursor = 0;
            private boolean removeProhibited = true;
            public boolean hasNext() {
                return cursor < size;
            }
            public Object next() {
                if (cursor==size)
                    throw new NoSuchElementException();
                removeProhibited = false;
                return array[cursor++];
            }
            public void remove() {
                if (removeProhibited)
                    throw new IllegalStateException();
                array[--cursor] = array[--size];
                array[size] = null;   // Eliminate "false reference"
                removeProhibited = true;
            }
        };
    }

    public int size() {
        return size;
    }
}
```

A

equals()

PURPOSE Determines if this set is equal to another object.

SYNTAX `public boolean equals(Object c)`

DESCRIPTION This method determines if this set is equal to the object `c`. It returns `true` if, and only if, `c` is a `Set` object and both this set and `c` have exactly the same elements. For all non-`null` elements, the `equals()` methods of the elements are used to determine if two elements match.

PARAMETERS

`c` The possibly `null` object to be compared with this set.

RETURNS `true` if `c` is equal to this set.

OVERRIDES `java.lang.Object.equals()`.

SEE ALSO `hashCode()`.

EXAMPLE See `Set.equals()`.

hashCode()

PURPOSE Computes the hash code for this set.

SYNTAX `public int hashCode()`

DESCRIPTION This method computes the hash code for this set. The hash code is the sum of the hash codes of all of the elements in the set. The hash code of a `null` element has the value `0`. Two equal sets will have the same hash code. Unequal sets might also have the same hash code, although the hash code algorithm minimizes this possibility. The hash code is typically used as the key in a hash table.

RETURNS This set's hash code.

OVERRIDES `java.lang.Object.hashCode()`.

SEE ALSO `equals()`.

EXCEPTIONS

`ConcurrentModificationException`

If this set's iterators are fail-fast and are being modified during this method call.

EXAMPLE See `java.lang.Object.hashCode()`.

java.lang.reflect

AccessibleObject

A

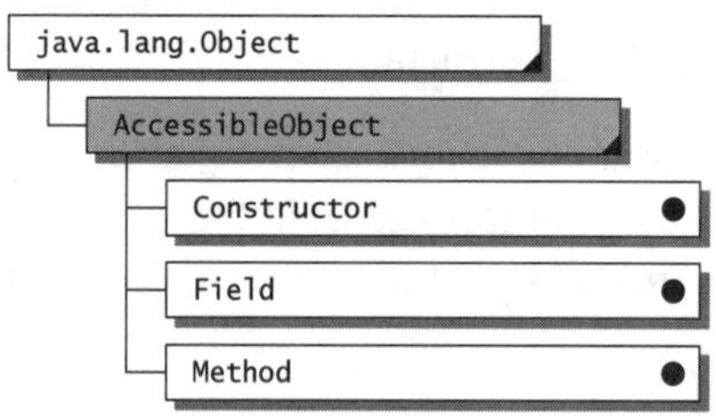

Syntax

```
public class AccessibleObject
```

Description

The `AccessibleObject` class is the superclass of all reflection objects—`Constructor`, `Field`, and `Method`. It contains a method to allow a reflection object to suppress the Java language access checks that are in effect when you use the reflection object. For example, if you have a `Field` object for a private field, accessing the field through the `Field` object would normally cause an `illegalAccessException` because the Java language access checks forbid access to another object's private fields. However, if your code has been granted appropriate permission, you can use the methods in this class to suppress those checks and use the `Field` object to access the private fields.

This capability is typically needed by applications such as a debugger.

Accessibility

All reflection objects have an *accessible* property that indicates whether the Java access checks should be suppressed for that reflection object. If the reflection object already has access to the constructor, field, or method (as in the case of a public field), the value of this property has no effect on the reflection object. However, if the reflection object does not have access to the constructor, field, or method according to the Java language access rules, then setting the accessible property to `true` will allow it access. See *The Java Language Specification, First Edition*, Section 6.6.1, for the Java language's accessibility rules.

The default value of the accessible property of a reflection object is always `false`. It can be changed to `true` using the `setAccessible()` method if permitted to do so by the security manager.

Note that the name of this property can be confusing. Setting the accessible property to `false` has no effect on public members—they are always accessible. This property affects only members that are inaccessible due to the Java language access checks.

Security Considerations

There are two permissions related to reflection objects: `RuntimePermission("accessDeclaredMembers")` and `ReflectPermission("surpressAccessChecks")`. The `RuntimePermission` determines whether you can obtain the reflection object, for example by using `Class.getField()`. Once you get obtain the reflection object, the `ReflectPermission` determines whether you can use it to access the object that it reflects, for example to examine the value stored in the field. It is the `ReflectPermission` that is used by `setAccessible()`. See `ReflectPermission` for more information about this permission.

Usage

There is no reason to subclass and create instances of this class. This class is always used in the context of a reflection object created by calling the appropriate reflection methods in `Class`. For example,

```
Field f = c.getClass().getDeclaredField(fieldname);
f.setAccessible(true);
```

Since `Constructor`, `Field`, and `Method` are the only subclasses of `AccessibleObject`, these methods are useful only on instances of these subclasses.

MEMBER SUMMARY	
Constructor	
`AccessibleObject()`	Constructs a new `AccessibleObject` instance.
Accessible Methods	
`isAccessible()`	Determines if this reflection object is accessible.
`setAccessible()`	Attempts to make this reflection object accessible.

See Also

`Constructor`, `Field`, `Member`, `Method`, `ReflectPermission`, `java.lang.Class`, `java.lang.RuntimePermission`.

Example

This example declares a class `C` with a private and public `int` field. It demonstrates how to set the accessible property of a `Field` object. It also demonstrates that even though the accessible property of a `Field` object is `false`, you might still be able to access the field value if it has been declared public.

```
import java.lang.reflect.*;

class Main {
    public static void main(String[] args) {
        C c = new C();
```

```
        try {
            Field f = c.getClass().getDeclaredField("i");

            System.out.println( f.isAccessible() ); // false

            // The private field is not accessible so exception occurs.
            //System.out.println( f.getInt(c) );    // IllegalAccessException

            // Make Field object accessible.
            f.setAccessible(true);
            System.out.println( f.isAccessible() ); // true
            System.out.println( f.getInt(c) );      // 10

            // Examine a public field.
            f = c.getClass().getDeclaredField("j");
            System.out.println( f.isAccessible() ); // false
            System.out.println( f.getInt(c) );      // 20
        } catch (NoSuchFieldException e) {
            e.printStackTrace();
        } catch (IllegalAccessException e) {
            e.printStackTrace();
        }
    }
}

class C {
    private int i = 10;
    public int j = 20;
}
```

AccessibleObject()

PURPOSE Constructs a new `AccessibleObject` instance.

SYNTAX `protected AccessibleObject()`

DESCRIPTION This constructor should never be used. It is used only by the Java Virtual Machine when creating reflection objects.

All newly created accessible objects are initially inaccessible. That is, `isAccessible()` returns `false`.

isAccessible()

PURPOSE Determines if this reflection object is accessible.

SYNTAX `public boolean isAccessible()`

RETURNS `true` if this reflection object is accessible; `false` otherwise.

EXAMPLE See the class example.

setAccessible()

PURPOSE Attempts to make this reflection object accessible.

SYNTAX

```
public void setAccessible(boolean newVal) throws
   SecurityException
public static void setAccessible(AccessibleObject[] arr, boolean
   newVal) throws SecurityException
```

DESCRIPTION This method tries to make this reflection object accessible by setting its accessible property to `newVal`. If `arr` is specified, this method tries to set the accessible property of all reflection objects in `arr` to `newVal`. This method will throw `SecurityException` if the caller does not have permission to change the accessible property value on the target object(s). If the caller fails to change the accessible property on any one element of `arr`, the entire operation fails with a `SecurityException`.

If `newVal` is `true`, the Java language access checks should be suppressed for this reflection object or the objects in `arr`. If `newVal` is `false`, the checks should be enforced on this reflection object or the objects in `arr`.

PARAMETERS

`arr` A non-`null` array of `AccessibleObject` objects.

`newVal` The new value for the accessible property.

EXCEPTIONS

`SecurityException`

If the caller does not have permission to make the reflection object(s) accessible.

SEE ALSO `ReflectPermission`.

EXAMPLE See the class example.

java.text
Annotation

A

```
java.lang.Object
  └─ Annotation
```

Syntax

`public class Annotation extends Object`

Description

An `Annotation` object is a special type of attribute value. (For the definition of the term *attribute*, see the `AttributedCharacterIterator` class description.) An annotation is used as a wrapper for a text attribute value to give it "annotation" characteristics, thereby making it behave as a "lump" attribute. The wrapper prevents the attribute values from being considered part of a larger attribute run or from being broken up into smaller runs. Following are the annotation characteristics.

- The text range that the attribute key/value pair is applied to is critical to the semantics of the range. This means that the attribute cannot be applied to subranges of its text range. In addition, if two adjacent text ranges have the same value for this attribute key, the attribute still cannot be applied to the combined range as a whole.
- The attribute key or its value usually no longer apply if the underlying text is changed.

There are at least three places where this has an effect.

- Methods `getRunStart()` and `getRunLimit()` in `AttributedCharacterIterator` consider adjacent annotations as separate attribute runs.
- When an iterator is created that does not fully span an instance of annotation, that annotation value is returned as `null` by `getAttribute()`.
- When an `AttributedString()` constructor creates a new attributed text object from an existing one, any attributes whose values are wrapped by an `Annotation` object are discarded if the specified subrange does not fully enclose the annotation's range.

Not all attributes make sense wrapped in an annotation. An example in which annotation is useful is "reading" information (known in Japanese as "yomi"), which is the manner in which text is pronounced. In the following example, the French verb "aimez," for "like," is pronounced "eme" (using French phonetics). This pronunciation applies only to the entire word, so "eme" will be returned by `getValue()` only if the iterator spans the entire "aimez" word. Also notice that "aimez" appears as adjacent annotations—it would not make sense to merge them. (These sentences translate to English as "You like it? Do you like the automobile?")

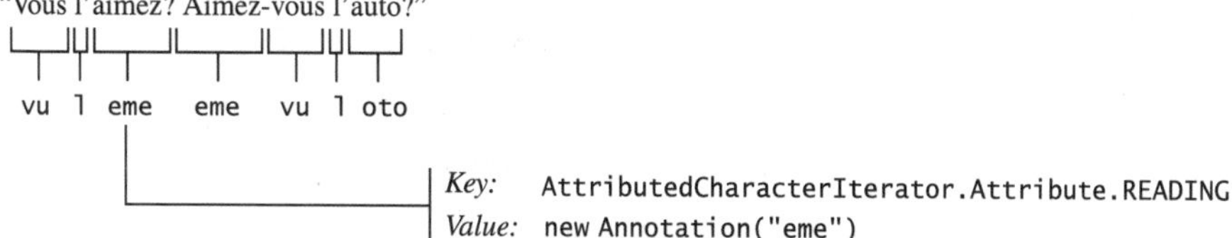

Another example of annotation is grammatical information attached to a sentence. For the first sentence in the example, you can say that "vous" is the subject and "l'aimez" is the predicate, but you cannot say the same about parts of the predicate: "l," "aimez," or "aim." When the text is changed, the grammatical information typically becomes invalid.

Wrapping the attribute value into an `Annotation` object guarantees that adjacent text runs are not considered a single attribute run by the iterator, even if the attribute values are equal (such as "eme" in the example). Doing this also indicates to text storage objects that the attribute key/value pair should be discarded if the underlying text is modified.

Two predefined attributes in the `AttributedCharacterIterator.Attribute` class currently allow their values to be `Annotation` objects: `INPUT_METHOD_SEGMENT` and `READING`.

Usage

To "promote" an attribute value to an annotation value, you create an annotation object, supplying it with the attribute value. You then add the annotation to the attributed text as the attribute value. This is demonstrated as follows.

1. Given a string, you create an instance of `AttributedString` or your own attributed text object:

```
AttributedString attrStr = new AttributedString(
    "A grown man has seen a million things schemed.");
```

2. To create a *predefined* annotation, call the `Annotation()` constructor and pass in an attribute value. The following adds pronunciation text for the word "million" with the key `READING` to the subrange 23 to 30.

```
attrStr.addAttribute(AttributedCharacterIterator.Attribute.READING,
    new Annotation("mil-yen"), 23, 30);
```

   Repeat for each subrange that needs an annotation.

3. To create a *custom* annotation key, subclass `Attribute` and define your own static field. The following example creates a static field called `GRAMMAR` that can identify the subject and predicate of a sentence, as shown in the following diagram:

```
public class MyAttr extends AttributedCharacterIterator.Attribute {
    public static final MyAttr GRAMMAR = new Attribute("grammar");
}
attrStr.addAttribute(MyAttr.GRAMMAR, new Annotation("subject"), 0, 12);
attrStr.addAttribute(MyAttr.GRAMMAR, new Annotation("predicate"), 12, 46);
```

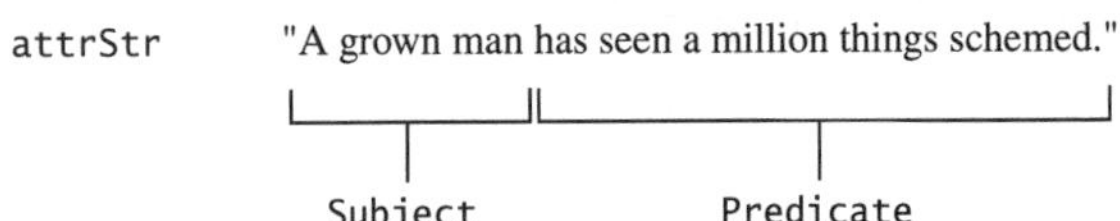

4. Use the `getIterator()` method in `AttributedString` to get an iterator for retrieving these annotations by key over the entire range or a selected subrange.

```
AttributedCharacterIterator iter = attrStr.getIterator();
```

You can then use any of the methods in `AttributedCharacterIterator` or those it inherits from `CharacterIterator` to move to any character or annotation and to get the start and end character positions of runs of one or more annotations.

MEMBER SUMMARY	
Constructor	
`Annotation()`	Constructs an `Annotation` instance that has an attribute value.
Attribute Method	
`getValue()`	Retrieves the value of this `Annotation` instance.
Debugging Method	
`toString()`	Generates the string representation of this `Annotation` instance.

See Also

`AttributedCharacterIterator`, `AttributedCharacterIterator.Attribute`.

Example

This example creates an attributed string with the `READING` attribute key with pronunciation strings added to each of its words. Each pronunciation string is encapsulated in an `Annotation` instance to indicate that it applies only to the whole word. An iterator is then created that spans the first two words but only half of the last word (to illustrate how it handles partial words). The attribute runs are then printed out. Notice that the pronunciation strings (values of annotation) are printed for the first two words, but not for the partial word "aim" (which is part of the French word "aimez").

```
import java.text.AttributedString;
import java.text.AttributedCharacterIterator;
import java.text.Annotation;
import java.util.Locale;
```

```
class Main {
    // Assign READING constant to a variable (to save typing).
    static AttributedCharacterIterator.Attribute attrREAD =
        AttributedCharacterIterator.Attribute.READING;

    public static void main(String[] args) {
        // Create an attributed string.
        AttributedString attrStr = new AttributedString("Vous l'aimez.");

        // Add reading attribute key/value pairs for each subrange.
        attrStr.addAttribute(attrREAD, new Annotation("vu"), 0, 4);   // Vous
        attrStr.addAttribute(attrREAD, new Annotation("l"), 5, 7);    // l'
        attrStr.addAttribute(attrREAD, new Annotation("eme"), 7, 12); // aimez

        AttributedCharacterIterator.Attribute[] matchAttr =
            new AttributedCharacterIterator.Attribute[] {
                attrREAD
            };

        // Create an iterator for the attributed string.
        AttributedCharacterIterator iter =
           attrStr.getIterator(matchAttr, 0, 10);

        // Print each run of the READING attribute.
        while (iter.current() != AttributedCharacterIterator.DONE) {
            printToRunLimit(iter);
        }
    }

    // Print the run start, run limit, string and attribute.
    public static void printToRunLimit(AttributedCharacterIterator aci) {
        // Get the run limit of the READING attribute.
        int runStart = aci.getRunStart(attrREAD);
        printInColumn("" + runStart, 5);
        int runLimit = aci.getRunLimit(attrREAD);
        printInColumn("" + runLimit, 5);
        Object attr = aci.getAttribute(attrREAD);

        // Print characters to the run limit
        System.out.print("\"");
        while (aci.getIndex() < runLimit) {
            System.out.print(aci.current());
            aci.next();
        }
        System.out.print("\"    ");
        printInColumn("", 10 - (runLimit - runStart));
        if (attr != null) {
            if (attr.getClass() == Annotation.class) {
                System.out.println(((Annotation)attr).getValue());
            }
        } else {
            System.out.println(attr);
        }
    }

    // Print string, then pad spaces to a particular vertical column
    static void printInColumn(String str, int col) {
        System.out.print(str);
        for (int p = str.length(); p < col; ++p) {
            System.out.print(" ");
```

```
            }
        }
    }
```

Output

```
> java Main
0    4    "Vous"          vu
4    5    " "             null
5    7    "l'"            l
7    10   "aim"           null
```

Annotation()

PURPOSE Constructs an `Annotation` instance that has an attribute value.

SYNTAX `public Annotation(Object val)`

DESCRIPTION This method constructs an `Annotation` instance containing `val`. You can then use this `Annotation` instance in place of the attribute value in an attribute key/value pair. An `Annotation` instance encapsulates the attribute value.

The value may be `null`. The attribute `INPUT_METHOD_SEGMENT` (in `AttributedCharacterIterator.Attribute`) takes an annotation whose value is `null`.

PARAMETERS

`val` A possibly `null` value of this annotation.

EXAMPLE See the class example.

getValue()

PURPOSE Retrieves the value of this `Annotation` instance.

SYNTAX `public Object getValue()`

DESCRIPTION An `Annotation` object contains a single value that it receives when it is created by the `Annotation()` constructor. This method returns that value.

RETURNS The value of this `Annotation` instance, which can be `null` if the instance was created with a value of `null`.

EXAMPLE See the class example.

toString()

PURPOSE Generates the string representation of this `Annotation` instance.

SYNTAX `public String toString()`

DESCRIPTION This method generates the string representation of this `Annotation` instance. The string representation includes the class name and the annotation's value.

RETURNS The non-`null` string representation of this `Annotation` instance.

OVERRIDES `Object.toString`.

EXAMPLE This example creates an `Annotation` instance for a locale value and prints its string representation.

```
import java.text.Annotation;
import java.util.Locale;

class Main {
    public static void main(String[] args) {

        // Create an annotation.
        Annotation annot = new Annotation(java.util.Locale.FRENCH);

        System.out.println(annot.toString());
    }
}
```

OUTPUT

```
> java Main
java.text.Annotation[value=fr]
```

java.util
ArrayList

java.lang.Object
AbstractCollection
AbstractList
ArrayList
AbstractSequentialList
Vector
List
java.lang.Cloneable
java.io.Serializable

Syntax

```
public class ArrayList extends AbstractList implements List, Cloneable,
   java.io.Serializable
```

Description

An `ArrayList` object is a collection for storing objects in a particular order. Each element in the list has an index that is used to access the element. This list will store any arbitrary number of elements, and it supports all of the modification operations, so you can add, remove, and replace elements in the list.

`ArrayList` internally uses an array to store the elements. This means that accessing an element using an index involves a quick array access, while adding and removing an element from the list involves shifting elements around in the array. However, adding and removing elements at the end of the list is efficient.

This class is one of three implementations of the `List` interface. The others are `Vector` and `LinkedList`, which internally uses a doubly linked list to store its elements. This means that adding and removing elements involves updating two links, while accessing an element with an index involves traversing the linked list.

Usage

You can create either an empty `ArrayList` or one that is initialized from a collection, as follows.

```
ArrayList list;
list = new ArrayList();
list = new ArrayList(collection);
```

Once the list is created, you can use various modification methods such as `add()` to add elements to the list or `remove()` to remove elements from the list.

Capacity

`ArrayList` internally uses an array to store its elements. The size of the array is usually larger than the number of elements in the `ArrayList` so as to minimize the number of the reallocations of the array. The size of the array is called this list's *capacity*. The capacity does not limit the number of elements that the list can hold because the capacity is increased as necessary.

If you are concerned about performance, you can control the capacity to optimize performance. For example, if you are about to insert 100 elements, you should make the capacity at least `100` plus the current size. This ensures that no reallocations of the internal array occurs during the additions. See `ensureCapacity()` for more details.

You can increase or decrease the capacity, but you cannot determine the current capacity.

Iterators

This list implements fail-fast iterators. It should not be modified while the returned iterator is in use or the iterator will throw a `ConcurrentModificationException`. See `Iterator` for more details.

Serialization

When the list is serialized, all of the elements are serialized. An attempt to serialize a list that contains an element that is not serializable results in a `NotSerializableException`. The capacity of the list is restored when it is deserialized.

Synchronization

This list allows more than one thread to read from it. However, if a thread wants to modify the list, there should not be any thread reading from it at the same time. If reads and modifications need to be able to occur concurrently, you can create a synchronized version of the list by calling `Collections.synchronizedList()` on the list. This creates a version of the list in which all of the methods are synchronized. Note that although each method is synchronized, you might still need to synchronize a sequence of method calls. See the `Collections` class description for more details.

MEMBER SUMMARY	
Constructor	
`ArrayList()`	Constructs a new `ArrayList` instance.
Element Retrieval Method	
`get()`	Retrieves the element at a particular index in this list.
Capacity Methods	
`ensureCapacity()`	Increases the capacity of this list.
`trimToSize()`	Trims the capacity of this list to be the list's current size.
	Continued

MEMBER SUMMARY	
Modification Methods	
`add()`	Inserts an element into this list.
`addAll()`	Inserts the elements of a collection into this list.
`clear()`	Removes all of the elements in this list.
`remove()`	Removes an element from this list.
`set()`	Replaces an element with another element.
Query Methods	
`contains()`	Determines if this list contains a particular element.
`isEmpty()`	Determines if this list has no elements.
`indexOf()`	Determines the index of the first occurrence of an element in this list.
`size()`	Returns the number of elements in this list.
`lastIndexOf()`	Determines the index of the last occurrence of an element in this list.
Conversion Method	
`toArray()`	Returns an array containing all of the elements in this collection.
Object Method	
`clone()`	Creates a copy of this list.

See Also

`Collections`, `Iterator`, `LinkedList`, `ListIterator`.

add()

PURPOSE Inserts an element into this list.

SYNTAX
```
public boolean add(Object e)
public void add(int ix, Object e)
```

DESCRIPTION This method inserts the element `e` at index `ix`. If `ix` is not specified, it defaults to `size()`.

PARAMETERS

`e` The possibly `null` element to add to this list.

`ix` The index at which `e` is to be inserted. `0` ≤ `ix` ≤ `size()`.

RETURNS The overloaded method that returns a `boolean` always returns `true`.

EXCEPTIONS

`IndexOutOfBoundsException`
If `ix` < `0` or `ix` > `size()`.

SEE ALSO addAll(), remove(), set().

EXAMPLE See List.add().

addAll()

PURPOSE Inserts the elements of a collection into this list.

SYNTAX
```
public boolean addAll(Collection c)
public boolean addAll(int ix, Collection c)
```

DESCRIPTION This method inserts all of the elements from c into this list at index ix. The elements are inserted in the same order as they would appear from an iterator on c. If ix is not specified, it defaults to size().

PARAMETERS

c The non-null collection of elements to be inserted into this list.

ix The index at which the elements in c are to be inserted. 0 ≤ ix ≤ size().

RETURNS true if this list was modified.

EXCEPTIONS

ConcurrentModificationException

If c's iterators are fail-fast and c is being modified during this method call.

IndexOutOfBoundsException

If ix < 0 or ix > size().

EXAMPLE See List.addAll().

ArrayList()

PURPOSE Constructs a new ArrayList instance.

SYNTAX
```
public ArrayList()
public ArrayList(int initialCapacity)
public ArrayList(Collection c)
```

DESCRIPTION This constructor constructs a new ArrayList instance. The new instance will have a capacity of initialCapacity and will contain the elements in c. The order of the elements in the new list is the same as the order of elements presented by an iterator on c. The references to the elements from c are copied into the new list so that subsequent modifications to c will not affect this list.

If c is not specified, the new list is empty. Otherwise, the capacity of the list is 110 percent of the size of c. If initialCapacity is not specified, it defaults to 10.

PARAMETERS

`c` The non-`null` collection of elements to be added to this list.

`initialCapacity`
The initial capacity of the `ArrayList`. `initialCapacity` ≥ `0`.

EXAMPLE

```
ArrayList list = new ArrayList();
list.add("dog");

// Create a second list based on the first.
ArrayList list2 = new ArrayList(list);
System.out.println( list2 );        // [dog]

// Now add an element to the first list.
list.add("cat");
System.out.println( list );         // [dog, cat]

// The change to the first list does not affect the second.
System.out.println( list2 );        // [dog]
```

clear()

PURPOSE Removes all of the elements in this list.

SYNTAX `void clear()`

DESCRIPTION This method removes all of the elements in this list. After this method is called, the list will be empty.

EXAMPLE See `List.clear()`.

clone()

PURPOSE Creates a copy of this list.

SYNTAX `public Object clone()`

DESCRIPTION This method makes a shallow copy of this list. Only the list itself is cloned, not the elements. Both this list and the new list share references to the same elements. The capacity of the new list matches the size of the list.

RETURNS A new non-`null` list that contains the same elements.

OVERRIDES `java.lang.Object.clone()`.

EXAMPLE

```
StringBuffer buf = new StringBuffer("dog");
ArrayList list = new ArrayList(
    Arrays.asList(new Object[]{buf, null, "cat"}));
System.out.println( list );        // [dog, null, cat]
```

```
ArrayList list2 = (ArrayList)list.clone();
System.out.println( list2 );       // [dog, null, cat]

// This shows that the cloned list shares the same elements
// as the original list.
buf.append("fish");
System.out.println( list2 );       // [dogfish, null, cat]
```


contains()

PURPOSE Determines if this list contains a particular element.

SYNTAX `public boolean contains(Object e)`

DESCRIPTION This method determines if this list contains the element `e`. It returns `true` if some element in this collection is equal to `e`. For all non-`null` elements, the `equals()` method is used to determine if two elements are equal.

PARAMETERS

`e` A possibly `null` element.

RETURNS `true` if some element in this list is equal to `e`.

SEE ALSO `List.containsAll()`, `List.equals()`.

EXAMPLE See `List.contains()`.

ensureCapacity()

PURPOSE Increases the capacity of this list.

SYNTAX `public void ensureCapacity(int minCap)`

DESCRIPTION If the current capacity of this list is less than `minCap`, this method increases its capacity to `minCap`.

It is not strictly necessary to call this method, since the capacity of the list is automatically increased when necessary. However, increasing the capacity incurs some cost (allocation of new storage and copying from old storage), which you might want to avoid in certain cases. In particular, if you are about to add some number of elements to the list, you can increase its capacity so that it is large enough to hold all of the new elements. This guarantees that none of the added elements will cause the capacity to be increased.

PARAMETERS

`minCap` The desired minimum capacity of the list.

EXAMPLE

```
// This method adds a range of integers to the list.
public void addInts(ArrayList list, int start, int end) {
```

```
        list.ensureCapacity(list.size() + end-start+1);
        for (int i=start; i<=end; i++) {
            list.add(new Integer(i));
        }
    }
```


get()

PURPOSE Retrieves the element at a particular index in this list.

SYNTAX `public Object get(int ix)`

DESCRIPTION This method returns the element located at index `ix` in this list.

PARAMETERS

`ix` The index of the element to return. `0` ≤ `ix` < `size()`.

RETURNS The possibly `null` element at index `ix`. `null` if element is `null`.

EXCEPTIONS

`IndexOutOfBoundsException`

If `ix` < `0` or `ix` ≥ `size()`.

EXAMPLE See `List.get()`.

indexOf()

PURPOSE Determines the index of the first occurrence of an element in this list.

SYNTAX `public int indexOf(Object e)`

DESCRIPTION This method searches this list, from the beginning, for any element that equals `e` (determined by using `equals()`). If an element is found, its index is returned; otherwise, `-1` is returned.

PARAMETERS

`e` The possibly `null` element for which to search.

RETURNS The index of the first occurrence of `e` in this list or `-1` if `e` is not in this list.

SEE ALSO `java.lang.Object.equals()`.

EXAMPLE See `List.indexOf()`.

isEmpty()

PURPOSE Determines if this list has no elements.

SYNTAX `public boolean isEmpty()`

RETURNS `true` if this list contains no elements.

SEE ALSO `size()`.

EXAMPLE See `clear()`.

lastIndexOf()

PURPOSE Determines the index of the last occurrence of an element in this list.

SYNTAX `public int lastIndexOf(Object e)`

DESCRIPTION This method searches this list backward, starting from the end, for any element that equals `e` (determined by using `equals()`). If one is found, its index is returned; otherwise, `-1` is returned.

PARAMETERS

`e` The possibly `null` element for which to search.

RETURNS The index of the last occurrence of `e` in this list or `-1` if `e` is not in this list.

SEE ALSO `java.lang.Object.equals()`.

EXAMPLE See `List.lastIndexOf()`.

remove()

PURPOSE Removes an element from this list.

SYNTAX `public Object remove(int ix)`

DESCRIPTION This method removes the element at index `ix` from this list.

PARAMETERS

`ix` The index of the element to remove. `0` ≤ `ix` < `size()`.

RETURNS The possibly `null` element that was removed.

EXCEPTIONS

`IndexOutOfBoundsException`
If `ix` < `0` or `ix` ≥ `size()`.

SEE ALSO `removeAll()`, `retainAll()`.

EXAMPLE `List.remove()`.

set()

PURPOSE Replaces an element with another element.

SYNTAX `public Object set(int ix, Object e)`

DESCRIPTION This method replaces the element at `ix` with the element `e` and returns the element previously at `ix`.

PARAMETERS

`e` The possibly `null` element to be stored at `ix`.

`ix` The index of the element to replace. `0` ≤ `ix` < `size()`.

RETURNS The possibly `null` element that was replaced.

EXCEPTIONS

`IndexOutOfBoundsException`
If `ix` < `0` or `ix` ≥ `size()`.

EXAMPLE See `List.set()`.

size()

PURPOSE Returns the number of elements in this list.

SYNTAX

```
public int size()
```

RETURNS The non-negative number of elements in this list.

SEE ALSO `isEmpty()`.

EXAMPLE See `List.size()`.

toArray()

PURPOSE Returns an array containing all of the elements in this collection.

SYNTAX

```
Object[] toArray()
Object[] toArray(Object arr[])
```

DESCRIPTION This method fills `arr` with all of the elements in this list and returns arr. If `arr` is not large enough, a new array is created, filled, and then returned. The new array is just large enough to hold all of the elements in this list, and its type is identical to the type of `arr`.

If `arr` is larger than all of the elements in this list, `arr[size()]` is set to `null`. This `null` value can be used to determine the number of returned elements but only if the list is known not to contain any `null` elements.

The order of the elements in the returned array matches the order of the elements in the list.

If `arr` is not specified, it defaults to `new Object[0]`.

PARAMETERS

`arr` The non-`null` array into which the elements of this list will be copied.

RETURNS The array `arr` or a new array whose length equals `size()`.

EXCEPTIONS

`ArrayStoreException`

If some element in this list cannot be assigned to an element in `arr`.

EXAMPLE See `List.toArray();`

trimToSize()

PURPOSE Trims the capacity of this list to be the list's current size.

SYNTAX `public void trimToSize()`

DESCRIPTION If the array capacity does not already match the size of the list, this method reduces the space used by the array so that it exactly matches the size of the list. This method might be useful if you don't anticipate adding any more elements to the list. As with all performance optimizations, it should be used with caution. It copies the array and then discards it. Thus while you reduce the amount of space your array needs, your code takes longer to run.

This method is not a part of the `List` interface. Using it makes your program less maintainable because changing from one implementation of the `List` interface to another becomes more difficult.

EXAMPLE This example reads lines from standard input and stores them in an `ArrayList`. The list is created with a fairly large capacity so as to minimize the number of times the capacity needs to be increased. After all of the lines are read, the list's capacity is trimmed in order to minimize the space used by the list.

```
import java.util.*;
import java.io.*;

class Main {
    public static void main(String[] args) {
        BufferedReader in = new BufferedReader(
            new InputStreamReader(System.in));
        ArrayList list = new ArrayList(1000);
        String line;

        try {
            while ((line = in.readLine()) != null) {
                list.add(line);
                System.out.println(line);
            }
            in.close();
        } catch (Exception e) {
            e.printStackTrace();
        }
        list.trimToSize();
    }
}
```

java.util
Arrays

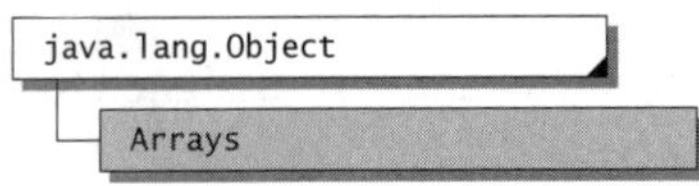

A

Syntax

`public class Arrays`

Description

The `Arrays` class contains various utility methods for dealing with arrays, such as searching and sorting.

Usage

Some of the methods in this class assume that your array is full. If your array is not full, you will need to create another array of exactly the right size and then copy the contents of your array into the more compact array. Here's a simple utility method for doing this.

```
public static Object[] compact(Object[] arr, int len) {
    if (arr.length == len) {
       return arr;
    }
    Object[] newarr = (Object[])Array.newInstance(
       arr.getClass().getComponentType(), len);
    System.arraycopy(arr, 0, newarr, 0, len);
    return newarr;
}
```

MEMBER SUMMARY	
Search Method	
`binarySearch()`	Searches a sorted array for a value.
Fill Method	
`fill()`	Sets array elements with a particular value.
Sort Method	
`sort()`	Sorts an array of values.
Conversion Method	
`asList()`	Creates a list from an array.
Object Method	
`equals()`	Determines if two arrays are equal.

asList()

PURPOSE Creates a list from an array.

SYNTAX `public static List asList(Object[] arr)`

DESCRIPTION This method creates a list using `arr` as storage. Any modifications to the elements of `arr` will appear in the list, and any modifications to the list will appear in `arr`.

The list is fixed-sized. This means that you cannot add elements to or remove elements from the list.

PARAMETERS

`arr` A non-`null` array.

RETURNS A non-`null` list containing the elements in `arr`.

EXAMPLE

```
String[] arr = {"dog", "cat"};
List l = Arrays.asList(arr);

//System.out.println( l.add("pig") );     // UnsupportedOperationException
//System.out.println( l.remove("cat") );  // UnsupportedOperationException

// Change the list and check the contents of the array.
System.out.println( l.set(1, "pig") );    // cat
System.out.println( Arrays.asList(arr) ); // [dog, pig]


// Change the array and check the contents of the list.
arr[0] = "gnu";
System.out.println( l );                  // [gnu, pig]
```

binarySearch()

PURPOSE Searches a sorted array for a value.

SYNTAX

```
public static int binarySearch(byte[] arr, byte e)
public static int binarySearch(char[] arr, char e)
public static int binarySearch(short[] arr, short e)
public static int binarySearch(int[] arr, int e)
public static int binarySearch(long[] arr, long e)
public static int binarySearch(float[] arr, float e)
public static int binarySearch(double[] arr, double e)
public static int binarySearch(Object[] arr, Object e)
public static int binarySearch(Object[] arr, Object e, Comparator
   comp)
```

DESCRIPTION This method searches the array `arr` for the element `e`. The array `arr` must be sorted; otherwise, the results are undefined. If `e` appears more than once in `arr`, there is no guarantee as to which instance will be found. The array `arr` is assumed to be full; that is, you can't specify how many elements in `arr` are actually being used.

A

This method uses a binary searching algorithm to find `e`. This means that it requires no more than log_2(`arr.length`) accesses to find `e`.

If `arr` has the type `Object[]`, the comparator `comp` is used to sort the elements. However, if `comp` is not specified or is `null`, the elements in `arr` must implement `Comparable`. In this case, the element's `compareTo()` method is used to compare elements.

If `e` is found, this method returns its index. If `e` is not found, this method returns a negative value. If you negate the negative result and then subtract `1`, the result specifies an *insertion index* in `arr`. The insertion index is the index at which `e` should be inserted into `arr` to maintain a sorted list.

PARAMETERS

`arr` A non-`null` array to be searched.

`comp` A non-`null` comparator.

`e` A possibly `null` element for which to search.

RETURNS The index of `e` in `arr` if `e` appears in `arr`. Otherwise, a negative value representing the insertion index is returned. See the description for more information. The returned value is always `-arr.length-1` ≤ `result` < `arr.length`.

EXCEPTIONS

`ClassCastException`

If `arr` has the type `Object[]` and some element in `arr` cannot be compared to some other element in `arr`.

SEE ALSO `java.lang.Comparable`, `sort()`.

EXAMPLE

```
String[] arr = {"cat", "dog", "gnu", "pig"};
System.out.println( Arrays.binarySearch(arr, "dog") ); // 1
System.out.println( Arrays.binarySearch(arr, "ape") ); // -1
System.out.println( Arrays.binarySearch(arr, "yak") ); // -5

int[] ints = {3, 5, 7};
System.out.println( Arrays.binarySearch(ints, 5) );    // 1
System.out.println( Arrays.binarySearch(ints, 0) );    // -1
System.out.println( Arrays.binarySearch(ints, 9) );    // -4
```

A

equals()

PURPOSE Determines if two arrays are equal.

SYNTAX
```
public static boolean equals(boolean[] a1, boolean[] a2)
public static boolean equals(byte[] a1, byte[] a2)
public static boolean equals(char[] a1, char[] a2)
public static boolean equals(short[] a1, short a2[])
public static boolean equals(int[] a1, int a2[])
public static boolean equals(long[] a1, long a2[])
public static boolean equals(float[] a1, float[] a2)
public static boolean equals(double[] a1, double[] a2)
public static boolean equals(Object[] a1, Object[] a2)
```

DESCRIPTION In general, this method returns `true` if `a1` and `a2` have the same length and `a1[i].equals(a2[i])` for `0` ≤ *i* < `a1.length`. Two elements are the same if they are both `null`. Also, two arrays are the same if they are both `null`.

PARAMETERS

`a1` A possibly `null` array.

`a2` A possibly `null` array.

RETURNS `true` if `a1` and `a2` are equal.

OVERRIDES `java.lang.Object.equals()`.

EXAMPLE
```
String[] a1 = {"cat", "dog", "gnu", "pig"};
String[] a2 = {null, "dog", "gnu", "pig"};
System.out.println( Arrays.equals(a1, a2) );     // false;

a2[0] = "cat";
System.out.println( Arrays.equals(a1, a2) );     // true;

a1 = null;
a2 = null;
System.out.println( Arrays.equals(a1, a2) );     // true;
```

fill()

PURPOSE Sets array elements to a particular value.

SYNTAX
```
public static void fill(boolean[] arr, boolean val)
public static void fill(boolean[] arr, int fromIx, int toIx,
   boolean val)
public static void fill(byte[] arr, byte val)
public static void fill(byte[] arr, int fromIx, int toIx, byte
   val)
public static void fill(char[] arr, char val)
```

```
public static void fill(char[] arr, int fromIx, int toIx, char
   val)
public static void fill(short[] arr, short val)
public static void fill(short[] arr, int fromIx, int toIx, short
   val)
public static void fill(int[] arr, int val)
public static void fill(int[] arr, int fromIx, int toIx, int val)
public static void fill(long[] arr, long val)
public static void fill(long[] arr, int fromIx, int toIx, long
   val)
public static void fill(float[] arr, float val)
public static void fill(float[] arr, int fromIx, int toIx, float
   val)
public static void fill(double[] arr, double val)
public static void fill(double[] arr, int fromIx, int toIx,
   double val)
public static void fill(Object[] arr, Object val)
public static void fill(Object[] arr, int fromIx, int toIx,
   Object val)
```

DESCRIPTION

This method sets all elements in `arr[fromIx]` to `arr[toIx-1]` to `val`. If `fromIx` is not specified, it defaults to `0`. If `toIx` is not specified, it defaults to `arr.length`.

If `fromIx` ≥ `toIx`, no elements are set.

PARAMETERS

`arr`	A non-`null` array.
`fromIx`	The beginning index, inclusive, of the element to be set. `0` ≤ `fromIx` ≤ `arr.length`.
`toIx`	The ending index, exclusive, of the last element to be set. `fromIx` ≤ `toIx` ≤ `arr.length`.
`val`	A possibly `null` value to be stored in all elements of the array.

EXCEPTIONS

`ArrayIndexOutOfBoundsException`
If `fromIx` < `0`, or `fromIx` > `arr.length`, or `toIx` < `0` or `toIx` > `arr.length`.

`IllegalArgumentException`
If `fromIx` > `toIx`.

EXAMPLE

```
String[] arr = new String[3];

Arrays.fill(arr, 1, 2, "cat");             // [null, cat, null]
System.out.println( Arrays.asList(arr) );

Arrays.fill(arr, "dog");
System.out.println( Arrays.asList(arr) ); // [dog, dog, dog]
```

```
Arrays.fill(arr, 3, 3, "pig");
System.out.println( Arrays.asList(arr) ); // [dog, dog, dog]

Arrays.fill(arr, 3, 0, "pig");      // IllegalArgumentException
System.out.println( Arrays.asList(arr) );
//Arrays.fill(arr, 0, 4, "dog");    // ArrayIndexOutOfBoundsException
```


sort()

PURPOSE Sorts an array of values.

SYNTAX

```
public static void sort(byte[] arr)
public static void sort(byte[] arr, int fromIx, int toIx)
public static void sort(char[] arr)
public static void sort(char[] arr, int fromIx, int toIx)
public static void sort(short[] arr)
public static void sort(short[] arr, int fromIx, int toIx)
public static void sort(int[] arr)
public static void sort(int[] arr, int fromIx, int toIx)
public static void sort(long[] arr)
public static void sort(long[] arr, int fromIx, int toIx)
public static void sort(float[] arr)
public static void sort(float[] arr, int fromIx, int toIx)
public static void sort(double[] arr)
public static void sort(double[] arr, int fromIx, int toIx)
public static void sort(Object[] arr)
public static void sort(Object[] arr, int fromIx, int toIx)
public static void sort(Object[] arr, Comparator comp)
public static void sort(Object[] arr, int fromIx, int toIx,
   Comparator comp)
```

DESCRIPTION If the component type for `arr` is a primitive type, this method sorts the array `arr` in ascending numerical order using the quick-sort algorithm. (This algorithm is adapted from Jon L. Bentley and M. Douglas McIlroy's *Engineering a Sort Function*, "Software-Practice and Experience," Vol. 23 (11) (November 1993), 1249–1265.

If `arr` has the type `Object[]`, this method sorts the array `arr` using the comparator `comp` and the merge-sort algorithm. The sort is *stable*, meaning that the order of equal elements in `arr` will be the same after the sort.

If `arr` has the type `Object[]` and you do not provide a comparator, the elements in `arr` must implement `Comparable`. In this case, the element's `compareTo()` method is used to compare elements.

This method sorts all of the elements in `arr[fromIx]` to `arr[toIx-1]`. If `fromIx` is not specified, it defaults to `0`. If `toIx` is not specified, it defaults to `arr.length`.

PARAMETERS

`arr` The non-`null` array to sort.

`comp` A non-`null` comparator.

`fromIx` The beginning index, inclusive, of the element to be sorted. `0` ≤ `fromIx` ≤ `arr.length`.

`toIx` The ending index, exclusive, of the last element to be sorted. `fromIx` ≤ `toIx` ≤ `arr.length`.

EXCEPTIONS

`ArrayIndexOutOfBoundsException`
If `fromIx` < `0`, or `fromIx` > `arr.length`, or `toIx` < `0` or `toIx` > `arr.length`.

`ClassCastException`
If some element in `arr` is not comparable to all other elements in `arr`.

`IllegalArgumentException`
If `fromIx` > `toIx`.

SEE ALSO `binarySearch()`, `java.lang.Comparable`.

EXAMPLE

```
String[] strs = {"dog", "pig", "cat"};
Arrays.sort(strs);
System.out.println( Arrays.asList(strs) );    // [cat, dog, pig]

int[] ints = {9, 5, 1, 7};
Arrays.sort(ints);
for (int i=0; i<ints.length; i++) {
    System.out.print( ints[i]+" " );          // 1 5 7 9
}
```

AttributedCharacterIterator

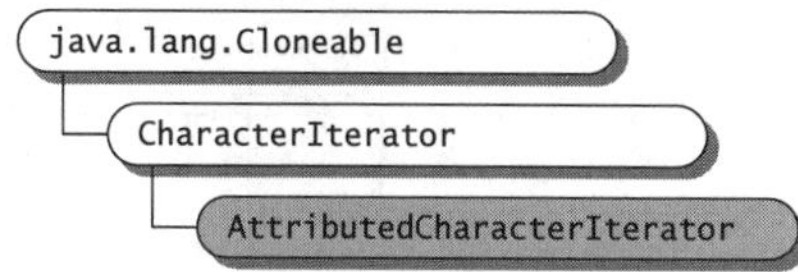

Syntax

```
public interface AttributedCharacterIterator extends CharacterIterator
```

Description

`AttributedCharacterIterator` is an interface that declares methods for iteration through *attributed text*, which is made up of Unicode characters and some associated attribute information. The purpose of this iterator is to allow you to retrieve not only the characters but also all attribute keys and values, as well as the character indexes at which the attribute runs start and stop. The returned character indexes are limited to the range of the iterator. The returned attribute information is limited to runs that contain the current character.

This iterator is created by calling `getIterator()` on the text storage object. The `java.text` package includes one implementation of attributed text: `AttributedString`. This text storage object is based on `String`. Alternatively, the text storage container can be a custom storage type based on another type of container of characters. The following sections describe the terms *attribute*, *attribute key*, *attribute value*, and *attribute run*.

Attributes

An *attribute* is a characteristic that can be added to text to enrich or identify it. Attributes include language, pronunciation, font, size, style, justification, color, run direction, superscript, width, and so on. Each attribute can be added to the entire range or to a subrange of text. An attribute is composed of a key/value pair, where the key must be of the type `AttributedCharacterIterator.Attribute` and the value is any arbitrary object and `null`. A particular key might require values of a particular type.

A given character position can have associated with it one or more unique keys, each with no value or one possibly `null` value. Adding another value for a key at a character position will overwrite the previous value.

In Figure 8, the key `LANGUAGE` has the value `Locale.ENGLISH` for the first part of the text, and `Locale.FRENCH` for the second part. The key `SIZE` has the value `12` (meaning 12-point type) for the entire length of the text.

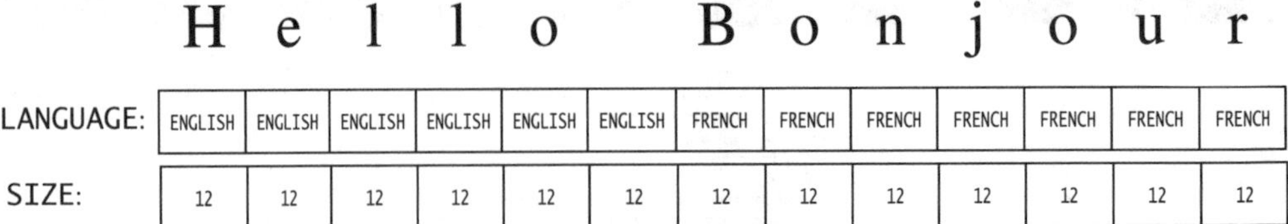

FIGURE 8: Each Character Allowed at Most One Value per Attribute.

Note: The term *attribute* is not used consistently throughout the `java.text` package; this inconsistency at times can be confusing. It refers to three different things, depending on context: attribute key, attribute value, or attribute key/value pair. For example, the class `AttributedCharacterIterator.Attribute` defines attribute keys, the method `getAttribute()` (in `AttributedCharacterIterator`) returns an attribute value, and the method `getAttributes()` returns attribute key/value pairs. To combat this confusion, this book always uses the full terms *attribute key* and *attribute value* when referring to, respectively, a key and a value and uses either *attribute key/value pair* or (infrequently) *attribute* to mean a key/value pair.

Attribute Keys

Attribute keys are used in `AttributedCharacterIterator` (and `AttributedString`) instances to identify useful meta information that you can add to ranges of text. Examples are `LANGUAGE`, `FONT`, `SIZE`, and `WEIGHT`. Attribute keys must be unique and must be of type `AttributedCharacterIterator.Attribute`. Each attribute key can be associated with a value by way of a map of key/value pairs.

Attribute keys are defined by the inner class `AttributedCharacterIterator.Attribute` or one of its subclasses. This class also defines useful methods for serializing, comparing, sorting, and debugging those keys. The particular attribute keys defined in this class are the static field constants `LANGUAGE`, `READING`, and `INPUT_METHOD_SEGMENT`. Other attribute keys, such as `FONT`, `SIZE`, and `WEIGHT`, are defined in subclasses such as `java.awt.font.TextAttribute`.

You can use the predefined keys, or you can create your own attribute keys by subclassing the `AttributedCharacterIterator.Attribute` class. For efficiency, attribute keys must be guaranteed to be unique. That is, an attribute key must be represented by one and only one object. This allows you to compare attribute keys by using the == operator rather than `equals()`.

Attribute Values

An attribute value may be either undefined, `null`, or a value of an allowable type (as specified in its field description in this book). For example, the `LANGUAGE` key requires a `Locale` value. Attribute values are immutable or must not be mutated by clients or storage. They are always passed by reference and not cloned. The reason for this is for performance and to prevent other objects from changing the attribute values "behind the back" of the iterator.

Adding and Getting Key/Value Pairs

You can add attribute key/value pairs by using methods in the storage class, such as `addAttribute()` in `AttributedString`. You can get attribute key/value pairs by using methods in `AttributedCharacterIterator`, such as `getAttribute()`. The method `addAttribute()` does not check the value's type; as long it is passed is an object (and not a primitive), it accepts the value.

Multiple attribute key/value pairs can be collected into maps. This enables setting and getting multiple attributes at once, such as by using `addAttributes()`.

Because an attribute value can be an annotation, when getting attributes from an iterator, you should consider testing whether the value might be an annotation.

Attribute Runs

It is convenient to define *attribute run* for an instance of `AttributedCharacterIterator`. An attribute run is a maximum text range for which the attribute key and value are unchanged. To be more precise, a run is defined where:

- The attribute value is undefined or `null` over the entire range, or
- The attribute value is defined and has the same non-`null` value for the entire range

The `getRunStart()` and `getRunLimit()` methods return indexes for runs of text; these runs are limited to the range of the iterator.

For all of the `get` methods in this class, the returned attribute information is limited to runs that contain the current character.

Annotations

An `Annotation` object is a special type of attribute value that acts like a "lump" attribute. The wrapper prevents the attribute values from being considered part of a larger attribute run or from being broken up into smaller runs. Following are the characteristics of an annotation.

- The text range that the attribute key/value pair is applied to is critical to the semantics of the range. This means that the attribute cannot be applied to subranges of the text range to which it applies, and, if two adjacent text ranges have the same value for this attribute key, the attribute still cannot be applied to the combined range as a whole.
- The attribute key or its value usually no longer apply if the underlying text is changed.

For more about annotations, see the `Annotation` class.

Usage

Given attributed text, you call `getIterator()` to create an iterator for it:

```
AttributedCharacterIterator iter = attrStr.getIterator();
```

You can then use any of the methods in `AttributedCharacterIterator` or those it inherits from `CharacterIterator` to move to any character or attribute, and to get the start and end character positions of runs of one or more attributes.

MEMBER SUMMARY	
Attribute Key/Value Methods	
`getAllAttributeKeys()`	Retrieves the set of all attribute keys defined over this iterator's text range.
`getAttribute()`	Retrieves the attribute value for a particular key at the current character.
`getAttributes()`	Retrieves a map of the key/value pairs at the current character.
Attribute Run Methods	
`getRunStart()`	Retrieves the index of the first character of the attribute run containing the current character.
`getRunLimit()`	Retrieves the index of the character following the attribute run containing the current character.

See Also

`AttributedCharacterIterator.Attribute`, `AttributedString`, `Annotation`.

Example

This example creates an attributed string initially with no attributes and then adds two attributes to it. It adds the French language attribute to the entire string and then adds the reading attribute to describe how to pronounce each word. For example, the French word "vous" is pronounced "vu" (using French phonetics). The pronunciation string is a `READING` attribute value that is encapsulated in an annotation. Each annotation object ensures that a pronunciation applies only to its original word and not to a substring or superstring of the word (see the `Annotation` class). The reading attribute runs are then printed out.

```
import java.text.AttributedString;
import java.text.AttributedCharacterIterator;
import java.text.Annotation;
import java.util.Locale;

class Main {
    public static void main(String[] args) {
        // Create an attributed string.
        AttributedString attrStr = new AttributedString("Vous l'aimez.");

        // Add a French language attribute key/value pair to entire string.
        attrStr.addAttribute(
            AttributedCharacterIterator.Attribute.LANGUAGE,
            Locale.FRENCH);

        // Assign READING constant to a variable.
        AttributedCharacterIterator.Attribute attrREAD =
            AttributedCharacterIterator.Attribute.READING;

        // Add reading attribute key/value pairs for each subrange.
        attrStr.addAttribute(attrREAD, new Annotation("vu"), 0, 4);  // Vous
        attrStr.addAttribute(attrREAD, new Annotation("l"), 5, 7);   // l'
```

```
        attrStr.addAttribute(attrREAD, new Annotation("eme"), 7, 12); // aimez

        // Get the string's iterator and print the string.
        AttributedCharacterIterator iter = attrStr.getIterator();
        printText(iter);

        // Print each run of the READING attribute.
        iter.first();
        while (iter.current() != AttributedCharacterIterator.DONE) {
            printToRunLimit(iter);
        }
    }

    public static void printText(AttributedCharacterIterator aci){
        // print the entire text using the character iterator
        do {
            System.out.print(aci.current());
            aci.next();
        } while (aci.current() != AttributedCharacterIterator.DONE) ;
        System.out.println("");
    }

    // Print the run start, run limit, string and attribute value.
    public static void printToRunLimit(AttributedCharacterIterator aci) {
        // Get the run limit of the READING attribute.
        int runStart = aci.getRunStart(
            AttributedCharacterIterator.Attribute.READING);
        printInColumn("" + runStart, 5);
        int runLimit = aci.getRunLimit(
            AttributedCharacterIterator.Attribute.READING);
        printInColumn("" + runLimit, 5);
        Object attr = aci.getAttribute(
            AttributedCharacterIterator.Attribute.READING);

        // Print to the run limit
        System.out.print("\"");
        while (aci.getIndex() < runLimit) {
            System.out.print(aci.current());
            aci.next();
        }
        System.out.print("\"   ");
        printInColumn("", 10 - (runLimit - runStart));
        System.out.println(attr);
    }

    // Print string, then pad spaces to a particular vertical column
    static void printInColumn(String str, int col) {
        System.out.print(str);
        for (int p = str.length(); p < col; ++p) {
            System.out.print(" ");
        }
    }
}
```

Output

```
> java Main
Vous l'aimez.
0    4    "Vous"          java.text.Annotation[value=vu]
4    5    " "             null
```

```
5   7   "l'"        java.text.Annotation[value=l]
7   12  "aimez"     java.text.Annotation[value=eme]
12  13  "."         null
```

A

getAllAttributeKeys()

PURPOSE Retrieves the set of all attribute keys defined over this iterator's text range.

SYNTAX `public abstract Set getAllAttributeKeys()`

RETURNS The non-`null` set of all attribute keys defined over this iterator's text range. The set is empty if no attributes are defined. (By definition, a set contains no duplicates.)

EXAMPLE This example creates an `AttributedString` instance of one word and then adds the `LANGUAGE` and `READING` attributes to it. It then prints all keys using `getAllAttributeKeys()`, then prints all attribute key/value pairs using `getAttributes()`.

```
import java.text.AttributedString;
import java.text.AttributedCharacterIterator;
import java.text.Annotation;
import java.util.Locale;

class Main {
    public static void main(String[] args) {

        // Create an attributed string.
        AttributedString attrStr = new AttributedString("Vous");

        // Add a French language attribute key/value pair to entire string.
        attrStr.addAttribute(
            AttributedCharacterIterator.Attribute.LANGUAGE,
            Locale.FRENCH);

        // Assign READING constant to a variable.
        AttributedCharacterIterator.Attribute attrREAD =
            AttributedCharacterIterator.Attribute.READING;

        // Add reading attribute key/value pairs for each subrange.
        attrStr.addAttribute(attrREAD, new Annotation("vu"), 0, 4);  // Vous

        // Get the string's iterator and print the string.
        AttributedCharacterIterator iter = attrStr.getIterator();
        iter.getAttributes();

        // Print each of the keys.
        iter.first();
        System.out.println("Keys: ");
        printAttrKeys(iter);
        System.out.println("");

        // Print each of the key/value pairs.
        iter.first();
        System.out.println("Key/Value Pairs: ");
```

```
        printAttrKeyValuePairs(iter);
    }

    // Print each of the keys.
    public static void printAttrKeys(AttributedCharacterIterator aci) {
        Object[] attrArray = aci.getAllAttributeKeys().toArray();
        for(int i=0; i<attrArray.length; i++) {
            System.out.println(attrArray[i]);
        }
    }

    // Print each of the key/value pairs.
    public static void printAttrKeyValuePairs(
                                    AttributedCharacterIterator aci) {
        Object[] attrKeyArray = aci.getAttributes().keySet().toArray();
        Object[] attrValueArray = aci.getAttributes().values().toArray();
        for(int i=0; i<attrKeyArray.length; i++) {
            System.out.println(attrKeyArray[i]);
            System.out.println(attrValueArray[i]);
            System.out.println("");
        }
    }
}
```

OUTPUT

```
> java Main
Keys:
java.text.AttributedCharacterIterator$Attribute(language)
java.text.AttributedCharacterIterator$Attribute(reading)

Key/Value Pairs:
java.text.AttributedCharacterIterator$Attribute(language)
fr

java.text.AttributedCharacterIterator$Attribute(reading)
java.text.Annotation[value=vu]
```

getAttribute()

PURPOSE Retrieves the attribute value for a particular key at the current character.

SYNTAX

```
public abstract Object getAttribute(
    AttributedCharacterIterator.Attribute attribute)
```

PARAMETERS

`attribute` The non-`null` key of the attribute whose value is requested.

RETURNS The value of the specified attribute for the current character of this iterator. Returns `null` if either the attribute key or attribute value is not defined for this character, or if the attribute value is `null`.

EXAMPLE See the class example.

A

getAttributes()

PURPOSE Retrieves a map of the key/value pairs at the current character.

SYNTAX
```
public abstract Map getAttributes()
```

RETURNS A map of attribute key/value pairs defined at the current character. (By definition, a map cannot contain duplicate keys.)

EXAMPLE See `getAllAttributeKeys()`.

getRunLimit()

PURPOSE Retrieves the index of the character following the attribute run containing the current character.

SYNTAX
```
public abstract int getRunLimit()
public abstract int getRunLimit(
   AttributedCharacterIterator.Attribute attribute)
public abstract int getRunLimit(Set attributes)
```

DESCRIPTION This method looks at the attribute run containing the current character and returns as an `int` the index (zero-based character position) of the first character following that run. All forms are based on runs containing the current character.

The first form returns the index of the first character following the run for all attribute keys. This run is the maximum range of text for which all attributes are unchanged.

The second form returns the index of the first character following the run for the given attribute key.

The third form returns the index of the first character following the run for the given set of attribute keys. This run is the maximum range of text for which all those attributes are unchanged.

PARAMETERS

`attribute` The attribute key, an instance of `AttributedCharacterIterator.Attribute`, whose run limit is requested.

`attributes` The set of attribute keys whose run limit is requested. These keys are instances of `AttributedCharacterIterator.Attribute`.

RETURNS The index of the first character following the run for the specified attributes containing the current character.

EXAMPLE See the class example.

A

getRunStart()

PURPOSE Retrieves the index of the first character of the attribute run containing the current character.

SYNTAX
```
public abstract int getRunStart()
public abstract int getRunStart(
    AttributedCharacterIterator.Attribute attribute)
public abstract int getRunStart(Set attributes)
```

DESCRIPTION This method looks at the attribute run containing the current character and returns as an `int` the index (zero-based character position) of the first character of that run. All forms are based on runs containing the current character.

The first form returns the first character of the run of all attributes.

The second form returns the index of the first character of the run for the given attribute key.

The third form returns the index of the first character of the run for the given set of attribute keys. This run is the maximum range of text for which that set of attributes is unchanged.

PARAMETERS

`attribute` The attribute key, an instance of `AttributedCharacterIterator.Attribute`, whose run limit is requested.

`attributes` The set of attribute keys whose run limit is requested. These keys are instances of `AttributedCharacterIterator.Attribute`.

RETURNS The index of the first character of the run for the specified attributes containing the current character.

EXAMPLE See the class example.

java.text
AttributedCharacterIterator.Attribute

A

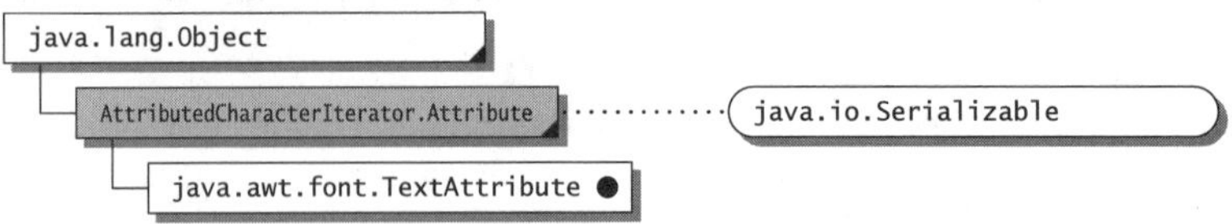

Syntax

```
public static class AttributedCharacterIterator.Attribute extends Object
    implements Serializable
```

Description

An *attribute* is a characteristic that can be added to text to enrich or identify it. Attributes include language, pronunciation, font, size, style, justification, color, run direction, superscript, width, and so on. The `AttributedCharacterIterator.Attribute` class represents the key from each attribute key/value pair. For a description of the terms *attribute*, *attribute key*, *attribute value*, and *attribute run*, see `AttributedCharacterIterator`.

Each attribute has a key and a value. In the following diagram, the key `LANGUAGE` takes the value `Locale.ENGLISH` for the first part of the string and the value `Locale.FRENCH` for the second.

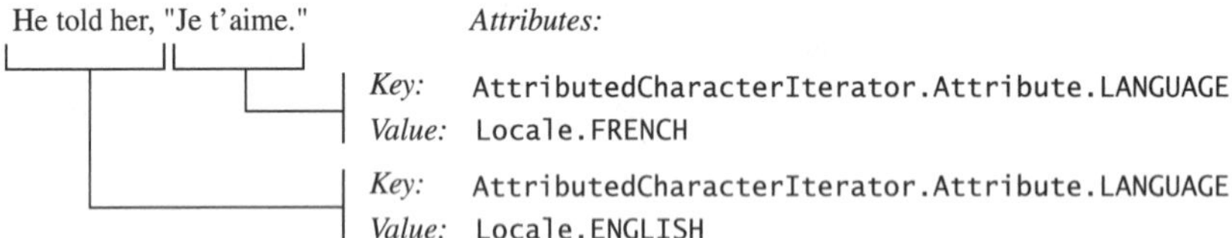

Note: The term *attribute* is not used consistently throughout the `java.text` API; this at times can be confusing. It refers to three different things, depending on context: attribute key, attribute value, or attribute key/value pair. For example, the class `AttributedCharacterIterator.Attribute` defines attribute keys, the method `getAttribute()` (in `AttributedCharacterIterator`) returns an attribute value, and the method `getAttributes()` returns attribute key/value pairs. To combat this confusion, this book always uses the full terms *attribute key* and *attribute value* when referring to, respectively, keys and values and uses either *attribute key/value pair* or (infrequently) *attribute* to mean a key/value pair.

Attribute Keys

The class `AttributedCharacterIterator.Attribute` defines attribute keys and useful methods for serializing, comparing, sorting, and debugging those keys. The attribute keys defined in this class are the static field constants `LANGUAGE`, `READING`, and `INPUT_METHOD_SEGMENT`. More attribute keys are defined in subclasses, such as `java.awt.font.TextAttribute`. These keys are used in `AttributedCharacterIterator` and `AttributedString` instances to add useful meta information to ranges of text.

You can use the predefined keys, or you can create your own attribute keys by subclassing this `AttributedCharacterIterator.Attribute` class. For efficiency, attribute keys must be guaranteed to be unique. That is, an attribute key must be represented by one and only one object. This allows you to compare attribute keys by using the `==` operator rather than `equals()`.

Attribute keys can be serialized and deserialized. When deserializing, `readResolve()` ensures that there is only one instance of each static constant. When creating attribute keys, make sure to define attribute key names that are unique to all instances of your class so that `readResolve()` can differentiate the instances.

Attribute Names

An attribute key's *name* is a predefined string that identifies the key. For example, the name of the `INPUT_METHOD_SEGMENT` key is "input method segment." The `readResolve()` method uses this name to distinguish the different instances when these instances are deserialized.

Usage: Using An Attribute

A typical use of `AttributedCharacterIterator.Attribute` is as follows.

1. Given a string, you create an instance of `AttributedString`:

   ```
   AttributedString attrStr = new AttributedString(
       "A grown man has seen a million things schemed.");
   ```

2. Add to that instance *predefined* attribute keys with appropriate values, where an attribute key is a static field of the `AttributedCharacterIterator.Attribute` class or its subclass `TextAttribute`. Each key requires a specific kind of value. For example, a `LANGUAGE` key requires a `Locale` value and a `READING` key requires an `Annotation` instance that holds a pronunciation string. Assign these attribute key/value pairs to substrings or to the entire string, as appropriate. Here, English applies to the entire string, while the pronunciation "mil-yen" applies only to the word *million*.

   ```
   attrStr.addAttribute(AttributedCharacterIterator.Attribute.LOCALE,
       Locale.ENGLISH);
   ```

   ```
   attrStr.addAttribute(AttributedCharacterIterator.Attribute.READING,
       new Annotation("mil-yen"), 23, 30);
   ```

   Repeat adding the `READING` key with different values for each subrange that gets an attribute.

3. Use the `getIterator()` method in `AttributedString` to get an iterator for retrieving these attributes by key over the entire range or a selected subrange:

   ```
   AttributedCharacterIterator iter = attrStr.getIterator();
   ```

   You can then use any of the methods in `AttributedCharacterIterator` or those it inherits from `CharacterIterator` to move to any character or attribute, and to get the start and end character positions of runs of one or more attributes.

Usage: Creating an Attribute

Here is the procedure for creating your own attribute. Another example is shown in the description of the constructor `AttributedCharacterIterator.Attribute()`.

1. Create a *custom* attribute by subclassing `Attribute` and defining your own static field. You must implement `readResolve()`. In addition, this example implements an `instanceMap`, which holds (a) the unique names used by `readResolve()`, (b) a constructor `MyAttr()`, and (c) the attribute itself, `DIALOG`, which is an instance of this class. This attribute is called `DIALOG` and identifies which person (in this case, "David") is to speak the text in a screenplay.

```
public class MyAttr extends AttributedCharacterIterator.Attribute {
    // Table of all instances in this class, used by readResolve.
    private static final Map instanceMap = new HashMap(2);

    // Constructor to create an instance of MyAttr with given name.
    protected MyAttr(String name) {
        super(name);
        if (this.getClass() == MyAttr.class) {
            instanceMap.put(name, this);
        }
    }

    // Resolves instances being deserialized to predefined constants.
    protected Object readResolve() throws InvalidObjectException {
        if (this.getClass() != MyAttr.class) {
            throw new InvalidObjectException(
                "subclass didn't correctly implement readResolve");
        }

        MyAttr instance =
                    (MyAttr) instanceMap.get(getName());
        if (instance != null) {
            return instance;
        } else {
            throw new InvalidObjectException("unknown attribute name");
        };
    }

    // New attribute named DIALOG.
    public static final MyAttr DIALOG = new Attribute("dialect");
}
```

2. Use the custom attribute by calling `addAttribute()`, as in the previous section:

```
attrStr.addAttribute(MyAttr.DIALOG, "David");
```

MEMBER SUMMARY	
Constructor	
`AttributedCharacterIterator.Attribute()`	Constructs an attribute key that has the given name.
Attribute Constants	
`INPUT_METHOD_SEGMENT`	An attribute key that indicates that a range of text is considered an unbroken unit by an input method.
`LANGUAGE`	An attribute key for a `Locale` value for a range of text.
`READING`	An attribute key for the pronunciation of a range of text.
Serialization Methods	
`getName()`	Retrieves the name of this attribute key.
`readResolve()`	Resolves a deserialized attribute to a predefined constant.
Object Methods	
`equals()`	Compares this attribute object with another object for equality.
`hashCode()`	Computes the hash code of this attribute object.
`toString()`	Generates the string representation of this attribute key.

See Also

`AttributedCharacterIterator`, `AttributedString`, `Annotation`, `java.awt.font.TextAttribute`.

Example

See the class example in `AttributedCharacterIterator`.

AttributedCharacterIterator.Attribute()

PURPOSE Constructs an attribute key that has the given name.

SYNTAX `protected AttributedCharacterIterator.Attribute(String name)`

DESCRIPTION This method constructs an attribute key, an instance of `AttributedCharacterIterator.Attribute`, that has the name `name`. It is protected and so can be called only by a subclass. You create a new instance of an attribute key by subclassing `AttributedCharacterIterator.Attribute`.

PARAMETERS

`name` The non-`null` string used to identify this attribute key. When subclassing and creating your own attribute constants, you should choose a name unique to instances of the class so as to avoid name collisions by `readResolve()`.

A

EXAMPLE This example defines an attribute key `MyTextAttribute` that is a subclass of `AttributedCharacterIterator.Attribute`. It then creates the static fields, `GLOSSARY_DEFINITION` and `SYLLABLES`. While the constructor of this class does not call this constructor by name, it does call it using `super(name)`. This example source file should be named `MyTextAttribute.java`.

```
import java.text.AttributedCharacterIterator.Attribute;
import java.util.Map;
import java.util.HashMap;
import java.io.InvalidObjectException;

public final class MyTextAttribute extends Attribute {
    // Table of all attribute constants in this class, used by readResolve
    private static final Map instanceMap = new HashMap(2);

    // Constructs an instance of MyTextAttribute with the given name.
    protected MyTextAttribute(String name) {
        super(name);
        if (this.getClass() == MyTextAttribute.class) {
            instanceMap.put(name, this);
        }
    }

    // Resolves instances being deserialized to the predefined constants.
    protected Object readResolve() throws InvalidObjectException {
        if (this.getClass() != MyTextAttribute.class) {
            throw new InvalidObjectException(
                "subclass didn't correctly implement readResolve");
        }

        MyTextAttribute instance =
                        (MyTextAttribute) instanceMap.get(getName());
        if (instance != null) {
            return instance;
        } else {
            throw new InvalidObjectException("unknown attribute name");
        };
    }

    // Attribute key for glossary definition
    public static final MyTextAttribute GLOSSARY_DEFINITION =
        new MyTextAttribute("glossary definition");

    // Attribute key for syllable breaks
    public static final MyTextAttribute SYLLABLES =
        new MyTextAttribute("syllables");
}
```

equals()

PURPOSE Compares this attribute key with another object for equality.

SYNTAX `public final boolean equals(Object obj)`

DESCRIPTION This method compares this attribute key instance with the object `obj` for equality. If, and only if, this attribute key and `obj` refer to the same object does this method return `true`. This method is final and therefore guarantees this equality for all subclasses. If this attribute key and `obj` refer to different objects, this method returns `false`.

It is preferable to use the == operator rather than this `equals()` method. The == operator is more efficient because there can be only one unique object to represent an attribute key.

PARAMETERS

`obj` The possibly `null` object to compare.

RETURNS Returns `true` only if `obj` and this `Attribute` refer to the same object; `false` otherwise.

OVERRIDES `java.lang.Object.equals()`.

EXAMPLE This example tests two attribute keys for equality and then computes the hash code of the first one.

```
import java.text.AttributedCharacterIterator;

class Main {
    public static void main(String[] args) {
        // Create attribute.
        AttributedCharacterIterator.Attribute attr1 =
                AttributedCharacterIterator.Attribute.LANGUAGE;
        System.out.println("First attribute key:");
        System.out.print("    ");
        System.out.println(attr1.toString());
        // java.text.AttributedCharacterIterator$Attribute(language)

        AttributedCharacterIterator.Attribute attr2 =
                AttributedCharacterIterator.Attribute.READING;
        System.out.println("Second attribute key:");
        System.out.print("    ");
        System.out.println(attr2.toString());
        // java.text.AttributedCharacterIterator$Attribute(reading)

        // Print equality comparison.
        System.out.println(attr1.equals(attr2));   // false
    }
}
```

OUTPUT

```
> java Main
First attribute key:
    java.text.AttributedCharacterIterator$Attribute(language)
Second attribute key:
    java.text.AttributedCharacterIterator$Attribute(reading)
```

getName()

PURPOSE Retrieves the name of this attribute key.

SYNTAX `protected String getName()`

DESCRIPTION This method retrieves the name, a `String`, of this attribute key. The name is defined as the string passed in when the attribute key was created. For example, predefined attribute keys have predefined names, as in, the name of the `LANGUAGE` key is "language." This method is used primarily by `readResolve()` to look up the corresponding predefined instance of an attribute key when it is deserializing an instance. This method is also used by `toString()`.

RETURNS The name of this attribute.

EXAMPLE See `AttributeCharacterIterator.Attribute()`.

hashCode()

PURPOSE Computes the hash code of this attribute key.

SYNTAX `public final int hashCode()`

DESCRIPTION Returns a hash code value, an `int`, for this attribute key. This version of `hashCode()` is identical to the one in `Object`, except that it is final.

RETURNS This attribute key's hash code value., an `int`.

OVERRIDES `java.lang.Object.hashCode()`.

EXAMPLE See `java.lang.Object.hashCode()`.

INPUT_METHOD_SEGMENT

PURPOSE An attribute key that indicates that a range of text is considered an unbroken unit by an input method.

SYNTAX
```
public static final AttributedCharacterIterator.Attribute
   INPUT_METHOD_SEGMENT
```

DESCRIPTION This constant is an attribute key for input method segments, indicating that the range of text is considered to be an unbroken unit. Input methods often break up text into segments, which usually correspond to words. Each segment is a subrange of characters that are presented to the user to be composed together. This key and its value can be paired in an `AttributedString` instance. The value is an instance of `Annotation` holding a `null` reference. A different instance of `Annotation` must be created for each subrange of text.

SEE ALSO `Annotation`.

EXAMPLE This example defines input method segments at word boundaries for the following Japanese text.

祖父がクリスマスに芝居を見に行き、とても感激したと言ってました。

```
import java.text.AttributedString;
import java.text.AttributedCharacterIterator;
import java.text.Annotation;
import java.util.Locale;

class Main {
    public static void main(String[] args) {

        // Create an attributed string.
        AttributedString attrStr = new
AttributedString("\u7956\u7236\u304c\u30af\u30ea\u30b9\u30de\u30b9\u306b\u829d
\u5c45\u3092\u898b\u306b\u884c\u304d\u3001\u3068\u3066\u3082\u611f\u6fc0\u3057
\u305f\u3068\u3044\u3063\u3066\u307e\u3057\u305f\u3002");

        // Add a Japanese language attribute key/value pair to entire string.
        attrStr.addAttribute(
            AttributedCharacterIterator.Attribute.LANGUAGE,
            Locale.JAPANESE);

        // Set up variables.
        AttributedCharacterIterator.Attribute attrIMS =
            AttributedCharacterIterator.Attribute.INPUT_METHOD_SEGMENT;

        // Add INPUT_METHOD_SEGMENT attribute key/value pairs
        // for each word.
        attrStr.addAttribute(attrIMS, new Annotation(null),  0,  2 );
        attrStr.addAttribute(attrIMS, new Annotation(null),  2,  3 );
        attrStr.addAttribute(attrIMS, new Annotation(null),  3,  8 );
        attrStr.addAttribute(attrIMS, new Annotation(null),  8,  9 );
        attrStr.addAttribute(attrIMS, new Annotation(null),  9, 11 );
        attrStr.addAttribute(attrIMS, new Annotation(null), 11, 12 );
        attrStr.addAttribute(attrIMS, new Annotation(null), 12, 13 );
        attrStr.addAttribute(attrIMS, new Annotation(null), 13, 14 );
        attrStr.addAttribute(attrIMS, new Annotation(null), 14, 15 );
        attrStr.addAttribute(attrIMS, new Annotation(null), 15, 16 );
        attrStr.addAttribute(attrIMS, new Annotation(null), 16, 17 );
        attrStr.addAttribute(attrIMS, new Annotation(null), 17, 20 );
        attrStr.addAttribute(attrIMS, new Annotation(null), 20, 22 );
        attrStr.addAttribute(attrIMS, new Annotation(null), 22, 24 );
        attrStr.addAttribute(attrIMS, new Annotation(null), 24, 25 );
        attrStr.addAttribute(attrIMS, new Annotation(null), 25, 31 );
        attrStr.addAttribute(attrIMS, new Annotation(null), 31, 32 );
    }
}
```

LANGUAGE

PURPOSE An attribute key for a `Locale` value of a range of text.

SYNTAX
```
public static final AttributedCharacterIterator.Attribute
   LANGUAGE
```

DESCRIPTION This constant is an attribute key for the language of a range of text. A value is an instance of `Locale`. This key and its value can be paired in an `AttributedString` instance.

SEE ALSO `java.util.Locale`.

EXAMPLE See the class example.

READING

PURPOSE An attribute key for the pronunciation of a range of text.

SYNTAX
```
public static final AttributedCharacterIterator.Attribute
   READING
```

DESCRIPTION This constant is an attribute key for the pronunciation of some text. In languages for which the written form and the pronunciation of a word are only loosely related (such as Japanese), it is often necessary to store the reading (pronunciation) along with the written form. A value is an `Annotation` instance that holds the pronunciation string. This key and its value can be paired in an `AttributedString` instance.

SEE ALSO `Annotation`, `AttributedString`.

EXAMPLE See the class example.

readResolve()

PURPOSE Resolves a deserialized attribute to a predefined constant.

SYNTAX
```
protected Object readResolve() throws InvalidObjectException
```

DESCRIPTION This method ensures that upon deserialization, there is only one instance of each static constant. This allows for efficiencies in comparison and other operations. Subclasses *must* override this method.

When this class is loaded, *predefined* instances of its static constants are created. When an object containing an attribute key is deserialized, a new instance of that static constant is created. This method is automatically called at that point to resolve references in the deserialized object to the predefined constant instead of to this new instance. (The new instance is then allowed to be garbage collected.) The mechanism is to look up the name of the deserialized attribute using `getName()` and then get and return the predefined instance by that name.

EXCEPTIONS

`InvalidObjectException`
If a subclass did not correctly implement `readResolve()`, or if the deserialized attribute name is unknown.

RETURNS The value of the attribute key; `null` if the attribute key's name is unknown.

EXAMPLE See `AttributeCharacterIterator.Attribute()`.

toString()

PURPOSE Generates the string representation of this attribute key.

SYNTAX `public String toString()`

DESCRIPTION This method returns `String`, the string representation of an attribute key, which includes the concatenation of the class name, the character "(", the attribute key's name, and the character ")".

RETURNS The string representation of this attribute key.

OVERRIDES `java.lang.Object.toString()`.

EXAMPLE See `equals()`.

java.text
AttributedString

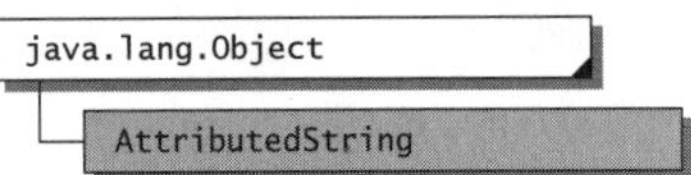

Syntax

```
public class AttributedString extends Object
```

Description

An AttributedString holds text and related attribute information. It is an example of a text storage object that is based on a string, for which an AttributedCharacterIterator object can be created. You may use it as the actual data storage in some cases in which a text reader wants to access attributed text through the AttributedCharacterIterator interface.

An *attribute* is a characteristic that can be added to text to enrich or identify it. Attributes include language, pronunciation, font, size, style, justification, color, run direction, superscript, width, and so on. Each attribute can be added to the entire range or to a subrange of text. For a further description of the terms *attribute*, *attribute key*, *attribute value*, and *attribute run*, see AttributedCharacterIterator.

Adding Attributes

AttributedString lets you add attribute key/value pairs either one at a time, by using addAttribute(), or as maps of pairs, by using addAttributes(). Both of these methods allow you to add attribute key/value pairs either to the entire range or to a subrange of text.

The method addAttribute() does not check the value's type; as long as it is passed an object (and not a primitive), it accepts the value. Attribute values are immutable; that is, they must not be mutated by clients or storage. They are always passed by reference, not cloned. The reason for this is for performance and to prevent other objects from changing the attribute values "behind the back" of the iterator.

An attribute key can have an associated value of an allowable type (as specified in its field description in this book). For example, the LANGUAGE key requires a Locale value. This allowable type can include an Annotation object. See the Annotation class for more details.

Clearing Attributes

To clear an attribute value, you add the attribute key with a value of null.

Retrieving Attributes

For a given AttributedString instance, you can create one or more instances of AttributedCharacterIterator by using the method getIterator(). Such an iterator has a getAttribute() method that lets you retrieve attribute keys and their values. There is no such method in AttributedString.

Usage

Given a string, you create an instance of `AttributedString` using its constructor. You can then associate attribute key/value pairs one at a time to the entire string or to a particular substring by using `addAttribute()`. Or you can add maps of attribute key/value pairs by using `addAttributes()`. With `getIterator()`, you can create an iterator that enables you to retrieve the characters, attribute key/value pairs, and runs of attribute key/value pairs.

MEMBER SUMMARY	
Constructor	
`AttributedString()`	Constructs an `AttributedString` instance that has specified text and attribute key/value pairs.
Attribute Methods	
`addAttribute()`	Adds an attribute key/value pair to this `AttributedString`.
`addAttributes()`	Adds a map of attribute key/value pairs to a subrange of this `AttributedString`.
Iterator Creation Method	
`getIterator()`	Creates an `AttributedCharacterIterator` instance that provides access to the specified contents of this `AttributedString`.

See Also

`AttributedCharacterIterator`, `AttributedCharacterIterator.Attribute`, `Annotation`.

Example

This example demonstrates how to create an `AttributedString` instance from a subrange of a larger `AttributedString` instance. The larger attributed string is created with the `POSTURE` and `LANGUAGE` attributes. The `POSTURE_OBLIQUE` value is the italic style of the font. We want the new, shorter instance to contain only `POSTURE` attributes, so the matching attributes array `matchingAttrs[]` is created with only that attribute. This example uses the form of `AttributedString` constructor that copies into the new, shorter `AttributedString` only those attribute key/value pairs whose attribute keys are in `matchingAttrs[]`.

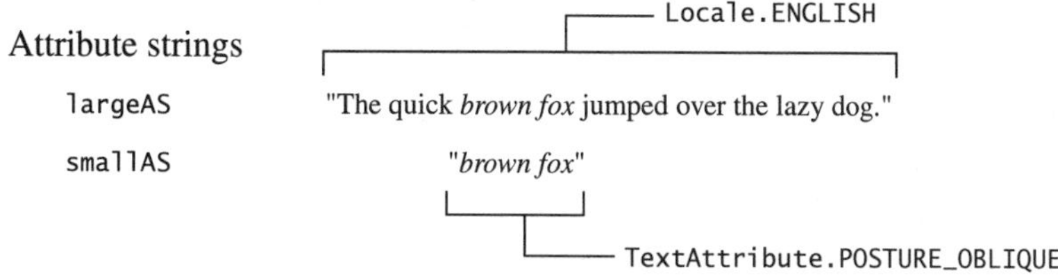

```
import java.text.AttributedString;
import java.text.AttributedCharacterIterator;
import java.awt.im.InputMethodHighlight;
import java.awt.font.TextAttribute;
import java.util.HashMap;
import java.util.Locale;

class Main {
    public static void main(String[] args) {
        // Create a large attributed string. (OK, it's not very large)
        AttributedString largeAS = new AttributedString(
                  "The quick brown fox jumped over the lazy dog.");

        // Add LANGUAGE attribute key/value pair to entire attribute string.
        largeAS.addAttribute(AttributedCharacterIterator.Attribute.LANGUAGE,
            Locale.ENGLISH);

        // Add POSTURE attribute key/value pair to part of attribute string.
        largeAS.addAttribute(TextAttribute.POSTURE,
                             TextAttribute.POSTURE_OBLIQUE, 10, 19);

        // Get the iterator for the large string and print the string.
        AttributedCharacterIterator largeACI = largeAS.getIterator();
        System.out.println("Large string:");
        printText(largeACI);

        // Print the attribute key/value pairs for the large string.
        System.out.println("\nAttribute key/values in large string:");
        printAttrs(largeACI, 15);
        System.out.println();

        // Create an array of attribute keys for matching.
        TextAttribute[] matchingAttrs = new TextAttribute[]{
            TextAttribute.POSTURE};

        // Create an attributed substring from the larger string.
        AttributedString smallAS =
            new AttributedString(largeACI, 10, 19, matchingAttrs);

        // Get iterator for the small string and print the string.
        AttributedCharacterIterator smallACI = smallAS.getIterator();
        System.out.println("Small string:");
        printText(smallACI);

        // Print the attribute key/value pairs for the small string.
        System.out.println("\nAttribute key/values in small string:");
        printAttrs(smallACI, 5);
    }

    public static void printText(AttributedCharacterIterator aci) {
        // Print the entire text using the character iterator
        while (aci.current() != AttributedCharacterIterator.DONE) {
            System.out.print(aci.current());
            aci.next();
        }
        System.out.println("");
    }

    // Print all keys and the value at a particular character position.
    public static void printAttrs(AttributedCharacterIterator aci, int pos) {
```

```
        aci.setIndex(pos);
        Object[] attrArray = aci.getAllAttributeKeys().toArray();
        for(int i=0; i<attrArray.length; i++) {
            System.out.print(attrArray[i] + "     ");
            System.out.println(aci.getAttribute(
                (AttributedCharacterIterator.Attribute)attrArray[i]));
        }
    }
}
```


Output

```
> java Main
Large string:
The quick brown fox jumped over the lazy dog.

Attribute key/values in large string:
java.text.AttributedCharacterIterator$Attribute(language)     en
java.awt.font.TextAttribute(posture)     0.2

Small string:
brown fox

Attribute key/values in small string:
java.awt.font.TextAttribute(posture)     0.2
```

addAttribute()

PURPOSE Adds an attribute key/value pair to this `AttributedString`.

SYNTAX

```
public void addAttribute(
   AttributedCharacterIterator.Attribute key, Object value)
public void addAttribute(
   AttributedCharacterIterator.Attribute key, Object value,
   int beginIndex, int endIndex)
```

DESCRIPTION This method adds the attribute key/value pair to the subrange of this `AttributedString` from `beginIndex` (inclusive) to `endIndex` (exclusive). If the `AttributedString` already has values in this range, this method overwrites those values. If `beginIndex` and `endIndex` are not specified, the attribute is added to the entire attributed string.

PARAMETERS

`beginIndex` The non-negative index of the first character of the range at which the attribute is to be added.

`endIndex` The index of the character following the last character of the range at which the attribute is to be added. The value `endIndex` must be greater than `beginIndex` and no greater than the length of the string.

`key` The non-`null` attribute key to be added.

`value` The possibly `null` value of the attribute to be added.

EXCEPTIONS

`IllegalArgumentException`

If `beginIndex` and `endIndex` are not specified and if the string held in this `AttributedString` has length of zero. (Attributes cannot be added to a zero-length range.)

If `beginIndex` and `endIndex` are specified and if `beginIndex` is less than zero, or `endIndex` is greater than the length of the string, or `beginIndex` and `endIndex` together do not define a nonempty subrange of the string.

EXAMPLE This example first creates an `AttributedString` instance with no attributes. Then it adds a language attribute key (`LANGUAGE`) and value (`Locale.FRENCH`) to the `AttributedString` instance.

```
import java.text.AttributedString;
import java.text.AttributedCharacterIterator;
import java.util.Locale;

class Main {
    public static void main(String[] args) {

        // Create an attributed string with no attributes.
        String str = "Je t'aime parce que tu est coquette.";
        AttributedString attrString = new AttributedString(str);

        // Add the attributes to the attributed string.
        attrString.addAttribute(
            AttributedCharacterIterator.Attribute.LANGUAGE,
            Locale.FRENCH, 0, str.length());
    }
}
```

addAttributes()

PURPOSE Adds a map of attribute key/value pairs to a subrange of this `AttributedString`.

SYNTAX
```
public void addAttributes(Map attributes, int beginIndex,
   int endIndex)
```

DESCRIPTION Use this method if you have more than one attribute key/value pair that you want to add to a particular range of this `AttributedString`. This method adds the map of attribute key/value pairs to the subrange of the string from `beginIndex` (inclusive) to `endIndex` (exclusive). If this `AttributedString` already has values in this range, this method overwrites those values. (Note that a map cannot have duplicate keys.)

PARAMETERS

`attributes` The non-`null` map of attribute key/value pairs to be added to this `AttributedString`.

`beginIndex` The non-negative index of the first character of the range at which the attributes are to be added.

`endIndex` The index of the character following the last character of the range at which the attributes are to be added. The value `endIndex` must be greater than `beginIndex` and no greater than the length of the string.

EXCEPTIONS

`IllegalArgumentException`

If `beginIndex` is less than zero, or if `endIndex` is greater than the length of this string, or if `beginIndex` and `endIndex` together do not define a nonempty subrange of the string and the attributes parameter is not an empty `Map`.

EXAMPLE This example first creates an `AttributedString` with no attributes. Then it creates a map, puts two attributes into the map, and adds the map to the `AttributedString` instance.

```
import java.text.AttributedString;
import java.text.AttributedCharacterIterator;
import java.awt.font.TextAttribute;
import java.util.HashMap;
import java.util.Locale;

class Main {
    public static void main(String[] args) {
        // Create an attributed string with no attributes.
        String str = "Je t'aime parce que tu est coquette.";
        AttributedString attrString = new AttributedString(str);

        // Create a map to hold attribute key/value pairs.
        HashMap attrMap = new HashMap();

        // Put a LANGUAGE key/value pair into the map.
        attrMap.put(AttributedCharacterIterator.Attribute.LANGUAGE,
            Locale.FRENCH);

        // Put a SIZE key/value pair into the map.
        attrMap.put(TextAttribute.SIZE, new Float(12f));

        // Add the attributes to the attributed string.
        attrString.addAttributes(attrMap, 0, str.length());
    }
}
```

AttributedString()

PURPOSE Constructs an `AttributedString` instance that has specified text and attribute key/value pairs.

SYNTAX

```
public AttributedString(String text)
public AttributedString(String text, Map attributes)
public AttributedString(AttributedCharacterIterator text)
```

```
public AttributedString(AttributedCharacterIterator text,
   int beginIndex, int endIndex)
public AttributedString(AttributedCharacterIterator text,
   int beginIndex, int endIndex,
   AttributedCharacterIterator.Attribute[] matchingKeys)
```


DESCRIPTION This constructor creates an instance of `AttributedString` from `text`. Some forms of the constructor create it with attributes, and others without. If `beginIndex` and `endIndex` are specified, this `AttributedString` is constructed from the specified subrange of the given text; otherwise, it is constructed from the entire range of `text`. If `matchingKeys` is not specified, it defaults to `null`.

The first form constructs an `AttributedString` instance with the given text, applying no attributes to the text.

The second form constructs an `AttributedString` instance with the given text and adds to the entire text the set of attribute key/value pairs specified by the `Map` instance.

The third form constructs an `AttributedString` instance with the attributed text represented by the given `AttributedCharacterIterator`.

The fourth form constructs an `AttributedString` instance with the subrange of text and attributes from `beginIndex` (inclusive) to `endIndex` (exclusive) of the given attributed text. All attribute key/value pairs within that subrange are kept. However, if the given subrange is empty of text, all attribute key/value pairs will be discarded. Note that any attribute whose value is wrapped by an `Annotation` object is discarded if the given subrange does not fully enclose the annotation's range.

The fifth form, like the fourth form, constructs an `AttributedString` instance with the subrange of characters from `beginIndex` (inclusive) to `endIndex` (exclusive). However, it adds to this `AttributedString` only those attribute key/value pairs present in the original `AttributedCharacterIterator` whose keys match any of the attribute keys in `matchingKeys`. This enables you to create a new `AttributedString` with only the attributes that are of interest. The same conditions apply. That is, if the given subrange is empty of text, all attribute key/value pairs will be discarded. Any attribute whose value is wrapped by an `Annotation` object is discarded if the given subrange does not fully enclose the annotation's range.

PARAMETERS

`attributes` The non-`null` map of attribute key/value pairs that apply to the entire string.

`beginIndex` The non-negative index of the first character of the range.

`endIndex` The index of the character following the last character of the range. The value `endIndex` must be greater than `beginIndex` and no greater than the length of the string.

`matchingKeys`
: The attribute keys to match with the original `AttributedCharacterIterator` instance. If `null`, all available attributes will be copied to the new `AttributedString`.

`text`
: The text for this `AttributedString`.

EXCEPTIONS

`IllegalArgumentException`
: In the second form, if the text has length of zero and the attributes parameter is not an empty `Map` (attributes cannot be added to a zero-length range). In the fourth and fifth forms, if the subrange given by `beginIndex` and `endIndex` is out of the text range.

SEE ALSO `Annotation`.

EXAMPLE This is an example of the second form of the constructor. It creates an instance of a `HashMap` and puts into that map a key/value pair of the `LANGUAGE` attribute key for the `FRENCH` locale. It then creates an `AttributedString` instance from a French string, with this attribute map applied to the entire string.

```
import java.text.AttributedString;
import java.text.AttributedCharacterIterator;
import java.util.HashMap;
import java.util.Locale;

class Main {
    public static void main(String[] args) {

        // Create a map to hold the attribute key/value pair.
        HashMap attrMap = new HashMap();

        // Put a key/value pair into the map.
        attrMap.put(AttributedCharacterIterator.Attribute.LANGUAGE,
            Locale.FRENCH);

        // Create an attributed string.
        AttributedString attrString = new AttributedString(
                  "Je t'aime parce que tu est coquette.",
                  attrMap );
    }
}
```

getIterator()

PURPOSE Creates an `AttributedCharacterIterator` instance that provides access to the specified contents of this `AttributedString`.

SYNTAX

```
public AttributedCharacterIterator getIterator()
public AttributedCharacterIterator getIterator(
   AttributedCharacterIterator.Attribute[] matchingKeys)
```

```
public AttributedCharacterIterator getIterator(
   AttributedCharacterIterator.Attribute[] matchingKeys,
   int beginIndex, int endIndex)
```


DESCRIPTION This method creates an `AttributedCharacterIterator` instance that lets you retrieve characters of this `AttributedString` and the attribute key/value pairs associated with those characters. If `beginIndex` and `endIndex` are specified, the iterator spans the subrange of this string from `beginIndex` (inclusive) to `endIndex` (exclusive). Otherwise, the iterator spans the entire contents of this `AttributedString`.

If `matchingKeys` is specified, this method creates an iterator with access to the subrange of this `AttributedString` instance whose attribute keys match any of the specified attribute keys in `matchingKeys`. The resulting iterator thus restricts access to only that subrange whose attributes are of interest. Information about attributes *not* listed in `matchingKeys` need not be made accessible through the iterator.

Any attribute whose value is wrapped by an `Annotation` object is not accessible by the iterator unless the given subrange fully encloses the annotation's range.

PARAMETERS

`beginIndex` The non-negative index of the first accessible character of the created iterator.

`endIndex` The index of the character following the last character of the created iterator. The value `endIndex` must be greater than `beginIndex` and not greater than the length of the string.

`matchingKeys`

A list of attribute keys that the caller is interested in accessing. If `null`, all available attributes should be made accessible.

RETURNS A new `AttributedCharacterIterator` instance.

EXCEPTIONS

`IllegalArgumentException`

If `beginIndex` is less than `zero`, or `endIndex` is greater than the length of the string, or `beginIndex` is greater than `endIndex`.

EXAMPLE See the class example.

Attributes

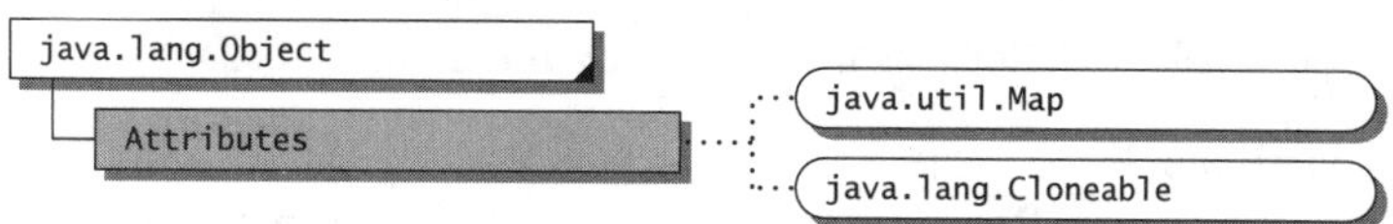

Syntax

```
public class Attributes implements Map, Cloneable
```

Description

The `Attributes` class represents a map (see `Map`) for holding attributes. An *attribute* is a name/value pair in which the name and value are both strings. The attribute name is case-insensitive and must follow certain syntax rules. The value is any non-`null` arbitrary string.

An *attributes map* stores the attribute name encapsulated in an `Attributes.Name` object. The purpose of the `Attributes.Name` class is to check the attribute name's syntax and to implement case-insensitive versions of the `equals()` and `hashCode()` methods. See `Attributes.Name` for details about the special attribute naming syntax. Almost all of the methods in this class deal with the attribute name as an `Attributes.Name` object rather than a string.

Attributes in Manifests

This class is used by the `Manifest` class to hold attributes. In particular, `Attributes` objects are used to hold the main attributes of a manifest and to hold the attributes for each manifest entry. See `Manifest` for more information about manifests.

Usage

This class implements the `Map` interface and therefore behaves much like a map. A common mistake when using the methods in this class is to pass in a string for an attribute name instead of an `Attributes.Name` object. Similarly, you might forget that a returned attribute name is an `Attributes.Name` object rather than a string. The current implementations of the methods do not always check the type of its parameters. Therefore accidentally passing in objects of the wrong type will not necessarily result in exceptions. Be careful.

MEMBER SUMMARY	
Constructor	
`Attributes()`	Constructs a new `Attributes` instance.
Value Retrieval Methods	
`get()`	Retrieves the value associated with an attribute name.
`getValue()`	Retrieves the value associated with an attribute name.
Query Methods	
`containsKey()`	Determines if this attributes map contains a particular attribute name.
`containsValue()`	Determines if this attributes map contains a particular attribute value.
`isEmpty()`	Determines if this attributes map has no attributes.
`size()`	Returns the number of attributes in this attributes map.
Modification Methods	
`clear()`	Removes all entries in this attributes map.
`put()`	Adds an attribute to this attributes map.
`putAll()`	Adds the attributes from another attributes map to this attributes map.
`putValue()`	Adds an attribute to this attributes map.
`remove()`	Removes an attribute from this attributes map.
Collection View Methods	
`entrySet()`	Returns a `Set` containing all name/value pairs in this map.
`keySet()`	Returns a `Set` containing all attribute names in this map.
`values()`	Returns a `Collection` containing all values in this map.
Protected Field	
`map`	Field holding the `Map` object used to store the attributes.
Object Methods	
`clone()`	Creates a copy of this attributes map.
`equals()`	Determines if this attributes map is equal to another object.
`hashCode()`	Computes the hash code for this attributes map.

See Also

`Attributes.Name`.

Example

This example is a simple demonstration of the use of an attributes map. It demonstrates that the attribute name is case-insensitive. For an example of the use of an attributes map while creating a Java Archive (JAR) file, see the `JarOutputStream` class example.

```
import java.io.*;
import java.util.*;
import java.util.jar.*;
class Main {
    public static void main(String[] args) {
        Attributes a = new Attributes();
        a.put(new Attributes.Name("dog"), "spot");
        print(a);                             // {dog=spot}
        a.put(new Attributes.Name("DOG"), "spot");
        print(a);                             // {dog=spot}; ignore case of name
        a.put(new Attributes.Name("DOG"), "ruff");
        print(a);                             // {dog=ruff}

        a.putValue("dog", "spot");
        print(a);                             // {dog=spot}
        a.putValue("DOG", "ruff");
        print(a);                             // {dog=ruff}
    }
    static void print(Attributes a) {
        System.out.print("{");
        boolean first = true;
        for (Iterator it=a.keySet().iterator(); it.hasNext(); ) {
            if (first) {
                first = false;
            } else {
                System.out.print(", ");
            }
            Object key = it.next();
            System.out.print(key+"="+a.get(key));
        }
        System.out.println("}");
    }
}
```

Attributes()

PURPOSE Constructs a new `Attributes` instance.

SYNTAX
```
public Attributes()
public Attributes(int initCap)
public Attributes(Attributes attr)
```

DESCRIPTION This constructor creates a new attributes map initialized with the attributes from `attr`. If `attr` is not specified, the new attributes map is empty.

`initCap` is the initial capacity of the attributes map. See `HashMap` for information about the capacity. If `initCap` is `0`, an initial capacity of `1` is used. If `initCap` is not specified, it defaults to `101`.

PARAMETERS

`attr`	A non-`null` attributes map.
`initCap`	The non-negative initial capacity of the attributes map.

EXCEPTIONS

`IllegalArgumentException`
If `initCap` < `0`.

EXAMPLE See the class example.

SEE ALSO `java.util.HashMap`.

clear()

PURPOSE Removes all entries in this attributes map.

SYNTAX `public void clear()`

DESCRIPTION This method removes all entries in this attributes map. After this method is called, this attributes map will be empty.

EXAMPLE See `java.util.Map.clear()`.

clone()

PURPOSE Creates a copy of this attributes map.

SYNTAX `public Object clone()`

DESCRIPTION This method creates a copy of this attributes map. Modifications to the returned copy will not affect this attributes map.

This method is implemented by calling the following constructor:

```
return new Attributes(this);
```

RETURNS A non-`null` copy of this attributes map.

OVERRIDES `java.lang.Object.clone()`.

EXAMPLE

```
Attributes a1 = new Attributes();
a1.putValue("dog", "spot");
a1.putValue("cat", "luck");

// Create a clone and modify it.
Attributes a2 = (Attributes)a1.clone();
print(a2);                              // {cat=luck, dog=spot}
a2.remove(new Attributes.Name("dog"));
print(a2);                              // {cat=luck}

// The modification does not affect the original.
print(a1);                              // {cat=luck, dog=spot}

// Note: see the class example for the implementation of print().
```

containsKey()

PURPOSE
Determines if this attributes map contains a particular attribute name.

SYNTAX
`public boolean containsKey(Object nameObj)`

DESCRIPTION
This method determines if this attributes map contains the attribute name `nameObj`. It returns `true` if `nameObj` is equal to (according to `equals()`) an attribute name in this attributes map.

PARAMETERS

`nameObj` A possibly `null` `Attributes.Name` object. If `null`, this method returns `false`.

RETURNS
`true` if `nameObj` is present in this map.

EXAMPLE

```
Attributes a1 = new Attributes();
a1.putValue("dog", "spot");
a1.putValue("cat", "luck");

System.out.println( a1.containsKey(null) );      // false
System.out.println( a1.containsKey("dog") );     // false; wrong type

System.out.println( a1.containsKey(new Attributes.Name("dog")) );
                                                 // true
System.out.println( a1.containsKey(new Attributes.Name("Dog")) );
                                                 // true
```

containsValue()

PURPOSE
Determines if this attributes map contains a particular attribute value.

SYNTAX
`public boolean containsValue(Object value)`

DESCRIPTION
This method determines if this attributes map contains the attribute value `value`. It returns `true` if an attribute value in this attributes map is equal to `value`.

PARAMETERS

`value` A possibly `null` `String` object. If `null`, this method returns `false`.

RETURNS
`true` if `value` is equal to an attribute value in this attributes map.

EXAMPLE

```
Attributes a1 = new Attributes();
a1.putValue("dog", "spot");
a1.putValue("cat", "luck");

System.out.println( a1.containsValue(null) );     // false
System.out.println( a1.containsValue("dog") );    // false

System.out.println( a1.containsValue("spot") );   // true
System.out.println( a1.containsValue("luck") );   // true
```

entrySet()

PURPOSE Returns a Set containing all name/value pairs in this map.

SYNTAX `public Set entrySet()`

DESCRIPTION This method returns a Set containing all of the name/value pairs in this map. The name/value pairs are represented by Map.Entry objects. See Map.Entry for information on retrieving a name or value from a Map.Entry object.

The returned Set and this map both share the same storage. This means that changes to the map are immediately reflected in the Set and changes to the Set are immediately reflected in the map.

The returned Set does not support add() or addAll().

RETURNS A non-null Set containing a Map.Entry object for each attribute in this attributes map.

SEE ALSO java.util.Map, java.util.Map.Entry, keySet(), values().

EXAMPLE

```
Attributes attr = new Attributes();
attr.putValue("dog", "spot");
attr.putValue("cat", "luck");

// Get entries
Set set = attr.entrySet();

// Remove attribute with the name "dog".
Attributes.Name dog = new Attributes.Name("Dog");
for (Iterator it=set.iterator(); it.hasNext(); ) {
    Map.Entry e = (Map.Entry)it.next();

    if (e.getKey().equals(dog)) {
        it.remove();
        break;
    }
}
print( attr );                              // {cat=luck}

// Add to the attributes map and check the set
attr.put("yak", "yolk");
System.out.println( set );                  // {cat=luck, yak=yolk}

// You can't add to the set
set.add("bess");                            // UnsupportedOperationException

// Note: see the class example for the implementation of print().
```

equals()

PURPOSE Determines if this attributes map is equal to another object.

SYNTAX `public boolean equals(Object o)`

DESCRIPTION This method determines if this attributes map is equal to `o`. It returns `true` if, and only if, `o` is an `Attributes` object and both this attributes map and `o` have exactly the same attributes. Two attributes maps match if their names (case-insensitive) and values (case-sensitive) are equal to each other.

PARAMETERS

`o` The possibly `null` object to be compared with this attributes map.

RETURNS `true` if `o` is equal to this attributes map.

OVERRIDES `java.lang.Object.equals()`.

EXAMPLE

```
Attributes a1 = new Attributes();
a1.putValue("dog", "spot");
a1.putValue("cat", "luck");

Attributes a2 = new Attributes();
a2.putValue("DOG", "spot");

System.out.println(a1.equals(null));     // false
System.out.println(a1.equals(a2));       // false

a2.putValue("Cat", "Luck");
System.out.println(a1.equals(a2));       // false

a2.putValue("Cat", "luck");
System.out.println(a1.equals(a2));       // true
```

get()

PURPOSE Retrieves the value associated with an attribute name.

SYNTAX `public Object get(Object nameObj)`

DESCRIPTION This method searches this attributes map for an attribute with the name `nameObj` and returns the associated value. `null` is returned if `nameObj` is not in this attributes map.

PARAMETERS

`nameObj` A possibly `null` `Attributes.Name` object.

RETURNS The value associated with `nameObj` or `null` if `nameObj` is not found.

EXAMPLE

```
Attributes a = new Attributes();
a.putValue("dog", "spot");
```

```
System.out.println( a.get(null) );                          // null
System.out.println( a.get("dog") );                         // null
System.out.println( a.get(new Attributes.Name("DOG")) );    // spot

System.out.println( a.getValue("DOG") );                    // spot
System.out.println( a.getValue(new Attributes.Name("DOG")) ); // spot

// The following won't compile since it's ambiguous which
// getValue() should be called.
//System.out.println( a.getValue(null) );                   // null
```

A

getValue()

PURPOSE Retrieves the value associated with an attribute name.

SYNTAX
```
public String getValue(String aname)
public String getValue(Attributes.Name nameObj)
```

DESCRIPTION This method searches this attributes map for an attribute with the case-insensitive name `aname` or `nameObj` and returns the associated value. `null` is returned if `aname` or `nameObj` is not in this attributes map.

`aname` must be a valid attributes name. See `Attributes.Name` for more details.

If `aname` is specified, the implementation of this method is

```
return (String)get(new Attributes.Name(aname));
```

If `nameObj` is specified, the implementation of this method is

```
return (String)get(nameObj);
```

PARAMETERS

`aname` The non-`null` attribute name.

`nameObj` A non-`null` `Attributes.Name` object.

RETURNS The value associated with `aname` or `nameObj`; `null` is returned if `aname` or `nameObj` is not found.

EXCEPTIONS

`IllegalArgumentException`
If `aname` is invalid.

EXAMPLE See `get()`.

hashCode()

PURPOSE Computes the hash code for this attributes map.

SYNTAX `public int hashCode()`

DESCRIPTION This method computes the hash code for this attributes map.The hash code of an attributes map is the sum of the hash codes of all attributes in the map. The hash code for an attribute is the exclusive-OR of the attribute name and the value.

Two equal attributes maps will have the same hash code. Note that unequal maps might also have the same hash code, although the hash code algorithm reduces this possibility. The hash code is typically used as the key in a hash table.

RETURNS This attributes map's hash code.

OVERRIDES `java.lang.Object.hashCode()`.

SEE ALSO `equals()`, `java.lang.Object.equals()`.

EXAMPLE See `java.lang.Object.hashCode()`.

isEmpty()

PURPOSE Determines if this attributes map has no attributes.

SYNTAX `public boolean isEmpty()`

RETURNS `true` if this attributes map contains no attributes.

EXAMPLE See `java.util.Map.clear()`.

keySet()

PURPOSE Returns a `Set` containing all attribute names in this attributes map.

SYNTAX `public Set keySet()`

DESCRIPTION This method returns a `Set` containing all of the attribute names in this attributes map. The elements in the `Set` are `Attributes.Name` objects. The `Set` and this attributes map both share the same storage. This means that changes to the attributes map are immediately reflected in the `Set` and changes in the `Set` are immediately reflected in the attributes map.

The returned `Set` does not support `add()` or `addAll()`.

RETURNS A non-`null` `Set` containing all of the attribute names in this attributes map.

SEE ALSO `Collection`, `entrySet()`, `values()`.

EXAMPLE

```
Attributes attr = new Attributes();
attr.putValue("dog", "spot");
attr.putValue("cat", "luck");
```

```
// Get all keys
Set set = attr.keySet();

// Remove attribute with the name "dog".
Attributes.Name dog = new Attributes.Name("Dog");
set.remove(dog);

print( attr );                              // {cat=luck}

// Add to the attributes map and check the set
attr.put("yak", "yolk");
System.out.println( set );                  // {cat, yak}

// You can't add to the set
set.add("bess");                            // UnsupportedOperationException

// Note: see the class example for the implementation of print().
```

map

PURPOSE Field holding the `Map` object used to store the attributes.

SYNTAX `protected Map map`

put()

PURPOSE Adds an attribute to this attributes map.

SYNTAX `public Object put(Object nameObj, Object val)`

DESCRIPTION This method adds a new attribute with the name `nameObj` and value `val` to this attributes map. If an attribute with the name `nameObj` already exists in this attributes map, its value is replaced with `val`; in this case, the previous value is returned.

PARAMETERS

`nameObj` A non-`null` `Attributes.Name` object.

`val` A non-`null` string.

RETURNS If `nameObj` already exists in this attributes map, the non-`null` old value is returned; otherwise, `null` is returned.

EXCEPTIONS

`ClassCastException`

If `nameObj` is not a `Attributes.Name` or `val` is not a string (not yet implemented).

EXAMPLE See the class example.

A

putAll()

PURPOSE Adds the attributes from another attributes map to this attributes map.

SYNTAX `public void putAll(Map attr)`

DESCRIPTION This method adds the attributes from `attr` to this attributes map. If the name for some attribute from `attr` already exists in this attributes map, the attribute in this map is replaced by the one from `attr`.

PARAMETERS

`attr` A non-`null` attributes map.

SEE ALSO `put()`.

EXAMPLE

```
Attributes a1 = new Attributes();
a1.putValue("dog", "spot");
a1.putValue("cat", "luck");

Attributes a2 = new Attributes();
a2.putValue("DOG", "ruff");
a2.putValue("pig", "babe");

a1.putAll(a2);
print(a1);              // {cat=luck, dog=ruff, pig=babe}

// Note: see the class example for the implementation of print().
```

putValue()

PURPOSE Adds an attribute to this attributes map.

SYNTAX `public String putValue(String aname, String val)`

DESCRIPTION This method adds a new attribute with the case-insensitive name `aname` and value `val` into this attributes map. If an attribute with the name `aname` already exists in this attributes map, its value is replaced with `val`; in this case, the previous value is returned.

`aname` must be a valid attributes name. See `Attributes.Name` for more details.

The implementation of this method is

```
return (String)put(new Attributes.Name(aname), val);
```

PARAMETERS

`aname` The non-`null` attribute name.

`val` The non-`null` attribute value.

RETURNS If `aname` already exists in this attributes map, the non-`null` old value is returned; otherwise, `null` is returned.

EXCEPTIONS

`IllegalArgumentException`
If `aname` is invalid.

EXAMPLE See `put()`.

A

remove()

PURPOSE Removes an attribute from this attributes map.

SYNTAX `public Object remove(Object nameObj)`

DESCRIPTION This method searches this attributes map for an attribute whose name matches `nameObj` (according to `equals()`) and, if found, removes the attribute and returns its value. If `nameObj` is not found, `null` is returned.

PARAMETERS

`nameObj` A possibly `null` `Attributes.Name` object. If `null`, this method does nothing and returns `null`.

RETURNS If `nameObj` exists in this attributes map, its non-`null` value is returned; otherwise, `null` is returned.

EXAMPLE

```
Attributes a = new Attributes();
a.putValue("dog", "spot");
a.putValue("cat", "luck");

System.out.println( a.remove(null) );                            // null
System.out.println( a.remove("dog") ); // null; not an Attributes.Name

System.out.println( a.remove(new Attributes.Name("DOG")) ); // spot
print(a);                                                        // {cat=luck}

// Note: see the class example for the implementation of print().
```

size()

PURPOSE Returns the number of attributes in this attributes map.

SYNTAX `public int size()`

RETURNS The non-negative number of attributes in this attributes map.

SEE ALSO `isEmpty()`.

EXAMPLE See `java.util.Map.clear()`.

values()

PURPOSE Returns a `Collection` containing all values in this map.

SYNTAX `public Collection values()`

DESCRIPTION This method creates a `Collection` from all of the values in this map. All elements in the returned `Collection` are `Strings`. Unlike `keySet()`, the returned `Collection` is not a `Set` because there could be duplicate values (`Sets` don't allow duplicate elements).

The returned `Collection` and this map both share the same storage. This means that changes to the map are immediately reflected in the `Collection` and changes in the `Collection` are immediately reflected in the map. Removing a duplicate value from the returned `Collection` results in the removal of only one of the attributes with that value.

The returned `Collection` does not support `add()` or `addAll()`.

RETURNS A non-`null` `Collection` containing all of the attribute values in this attributes map.

SEE ALSO `Collection`, `entrySet()`, `keySet()`.

EXAMPLE

```
Attributes attr = new Attributes();
attr.putValue("dog", "spot");
attr.putValue("cat", "luck");
attr.putValue("pig", "spot");

Collection c = attr.values();

// Remove an attribute with the value "spot".
c.remove("spot");
print( attr );                              // {cat=luck, pig=spot}

// Remove all attributes with the value "spot".
for (Iterator it=c.iterator(); it.hasNext(); ) {
    String v = (String)it.next();

    if (v.equals("spot")) {
        it.remove();
    }
}
print( attr );                              // {cat=luck}

// Add to the attributes map and check the collection
attr.put("yak", "yolk");
System.out.println( c );                    // [luck, yolk]

// You can't add to the collection
c.add("bess");                              // UnsupportedOperationException

// Note: see the class example for the implementation of print().
```

java.util.jar
Attributes.Name

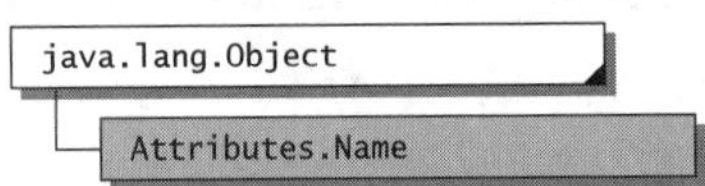

Syntax

```
public static class Attributes.Name
```

Description

A Java Archive (JAR) file contains a manifest file (see `Manifest`), which in turn contains a number of *attributes*. An attribute is a name/value pair in which the name and value are both strings. Although the value can be any non-`null` string, the attribute name is case-insensitive and must follow certain syntax rules. In particular, an attribute name is a nonempty string of any length but must consist only of any combination of the following characters:

digits: `0` to `9`
letters: `a` to `z` and `A` to `Z`
underscore: `_`
minus: `-`

Examples of valid attribute names are "Version_1" and "0–1". Examples of invalid attribute names are "a.b" or "#1".

The syntax rules for an attribute name is described in detail in

`http://java.sun.com/products/jdk/1.2/docs/guide/jar/manifest.html`

Usage

The `Attributes.Name` class represents an attribute name. It is meant to be used in conjunction with the `Attributes` class. An `Attributes` object is essentially a map (see `java.util.Map`) whose keys are `Attributes.Name` objects. To update or retrieve values from an `Attributes` object, you can specify an attribute name by using an `Attributes.Name` object.

MEMBER SUMMARY	
Constructor	
`Attributes.Name()`	Constructs a new `Attributes.Name` instance.
Object Methods	
`equals()`	Determines if this `Attributes.Name` object is equal to another object.
`hashCode()`	Computes the hash code for this `Attributes.Name` object.
`toString()`	Returns the attribute name.

A

MEMBER SUMMARY	
Predefined Attribute Names	
`CLASS_PATH`	Name of attribute for specifying additional JAR files.
`CONTENT_TYPE`	Name of attribute for specifying the type of a JAR entry.
`MAIN_CLASS`	Name of attribute for specifying the entry point of an application.
`IMPLEMENTATION_TITLE`	Name of attribute containing the implementation title of a package.
`IMPLEMENTATION_VERSION`	Name of attribute containing the implementation version of a package.
`IMPLEMENTATION_VENDOR`	Name of attribute containing the implementation vendor of a package.
`MANIFEST_VERSION`	Name of attribute for specifying the version of the manifest file.
`SEALED`	Name of attribute for sealing a package.
`SIGNATURE_VERSION`	Name of attribute containing the signature version of the JAR file.
`SPECIFICATION_TITLE`	Name of attribute containing the specification title of a package.
`SPECIFICATION_VERSION`	Name of attribute containing the specification version of a package.
`SPECIFICATION_VENDOR`	Name of attribute containing the specification vendor of a package.

See Also

`Attributes`, `Manifest`.

Example

See the `Attributes` class for examples that use this class.

Attributes.Name()

PURPOSE Constructs a new `Attributes.Name` instance.

SYNTAX `public Name(String aname)`

DESCRIPTION This constructor creates a new `Attributes.Name` object containing `aname`. The nonempty string `aname` can be any length but must consist only of any combination of the following characters:

```
digits: 0 to 9
letters: a to z and A to Z
underscore: _
minus: -
```

PARAMETERS

`aname` A non-`null` string.

EXCEPTIONS

`IllegalArgumentException`
If `aname` is invalid.

EXAMPLE

```
Attributes.Name an;

// Some valid attribute names.
an = new Attributes.Name("Version");
an = new Attributes.Name("_-0123456789");

// Some invalid attribute names.
//an = new Attributes.Name("a.b");     // IllegalArgumentException
//an = new Attributes.Name("a b");     // IllegalArgumentException
```

CLASS_PATH

PURPOSE Name of attribute for specifying additional JAR files.

SYNTAX `public static final Name CLASS_PATH`

DESCRIPTION This constant contains the name of the attribute for specifying additional JAR files. If the contents of a JAR file depend on other JAR files, you can name these additional JAR files using the `CLASS_PATH` attribute. When the class loader searches for a class or resource, it will also search these JAR files.

The value of the `CLASS_PATH` attribute is a set of URLs separated by spaces. Each URL must refer to a JAR file. The URL can be absolute or relative. If relative, it is relative to the JAR file that contains the `CLASS_PATH` attribute. The `CLASS_PATH` attribute must be specified in the main attributes set (see `Manifest`) of a manifest file.

The value of this constant is `"Class-Path"`.

EXAMPLE See `Package.isSealed()`.

CONTENT_TYPE

PURPOSE Name of attribute for specifying the type of a JAR entry.

SYNTAX `public static final Name CONTENT_TYPE`

DESCRIPTION This constant contains the name of the attribute for specifying the type of a JAR entry. The value of the `CONTENT_TYPE` attribute is a MIME type (*RFC 2046*). An example of a MIME type is "image/gif" or "audio/basic." This information can be used by a viewer to determine how to display the JAR entry. See `MimeType` for more information about MIME types.

The `CONTENT_TYPE` attribute can be specified as a main attribute. This means its value will apply to all entries in the JAR file. It can then be overridden for individual entries.

The value of this constant is `"Content-Type"`.

equals()

PURPOSE Determines if this `Attributes.Name` object is equal to another object.

SYNTAX `public boolean equals(Object obj)`

DESCRIPTION This method determines if this `Attributes.Name` object is equal to `obj`. It returns `true` only if `obj` is a non-`null` instance of `Attributes.Name` and `toString().equalsIgnoreCase(obj.toString())` returns `true`.

PARAMETERS

`obj` A possibly `null` object.

RETURNS `true` if `obj` is not `null` and is equal to this `Attributes.Name` object.

OVERRIDES `java.lang.Object.equals()`.

SEE ALSO `hashCode()`.

EXAMPLE

```
Attributes.Name an1 = new Attributes.Name("version");
Attributes.Name an2 = new Attributes.Name("VERSION");

// Show that attribute names are not case-sensitive.
System.out.println(an1.equals(an2));     // true
System.out.println(an1.hashCode());      // 351608024
System.out.println(an2.hashCode());      // 351608024

System.out.println(an1.toString());      // version
System.out.println(an2.toString());      // VERSION
```

hashCode()

PURPOSE Computes the hash code for this `Attributes.Name` object.

SYNTAX `public int hashCode()`

DESCRIPTION This method computes the hash code for this `Attributes.Name` object. Two equal `Attributes.Name` objects (see `equals()`) will have the same hash code. Note that unequal `Attributes.Name` objects might also have the same hash code, although the hash code algorithm reduces this possibility. The hash code is typically used as the key in a hash table.

RETURNS This `Attributes.Name` object's hash code.

OVERRIDES `java.lang.Object.hashCode()`.

SEE ALSO `equals()`, `java.lang.Object.equals()`.

EXAMPLE See `equals()`.

IMPLEMENTATION_TITLE

PURPOSE Name of attribute containing the implementation title of a package.

SYNTAX `public static final Name IMPLEMENTATION_TITLE`

DESCRIPTION This constant contains the name of the attribute containing the implementation title of a package. See `Package.getImplementationTitle()` for information about the value of the `IMPLEMENTATION_TITLE` attribute.

To apply the `IMPLEMENTATION_TITLE` attribute to a package `p.q`, for example, you need to add it to a manifest entry named "p/q/":

```
Name: p/q/
Implementation-Title: Demo API Implementation for Solaris
```

In this example, the value of the `IMPLEMENTATION_TITLE` attribute is "Demo API Implementation for Solaris".

The `IMPLEMENTATION_TITLE` attribute can be specified as a main attribute. This means its value will apply to all packages in the JAR file. It can then be overridden for individual packages.

The value of this constant is `"Implementation-Title"`.

SEE ALSO `java.lang.Package.getImplementationTitle()`.

EXAMPLE See the `java.lang.Package` class example.

IMPLEMENTATION_VERSION

PURPOSE Name of attribute containing the implementation version of a package.

SYNTAX `public static final Name IMPLEMENTATION_VERSION`

DESCRIPTION This constant contains the name of the attribute containing the implementation version of a package. See `Package.getImplementationVersion()` for information about the value of the `IMPLEMENTATION_VERSION` attribute.

To apply the `IMPLEMENTATION_VERSION` attribute to a package `p.q`, for example, you need to add it to a manifest entry named "p/q/":

```
Name: p/q/
Implementation-Version: 1.2.3
```

In this example, the value of the IMPLEMENTATION_VERSION attribute is "1.2.3".

The IMPLEMENTATION_VERSION attribute can be specified as a main attribute. This means its value will apply to all packages in the JAR file. It can then be overridden for individual packages.

The value of this constant is "Implementation-Version".

SEE ALSO java.lang.Package.getImplementationVersion().

EXAMPLE See the java.lang.Package class example.

IMPLEMENTATION_VENDOR

PURPOSE Name of attribute containing the implementation vendor of a package.

SYNTAX `public static final Name IMPLEMENTATION_VENDOR`

DESCRIPTION This constant contains the name of the attribute containing the implementation vendor of a package. See Package.getImplementationVendor() for information about the value of the IMPLEMENTATION_VENDOR attribute.

To apply this attribute to a package p.q, for example, you need to add it to a manifest entry named "p/q/":

```
Name: p/q/
Implementation-Vendor: Chan, Lee, Kramer
```

In this example, the value of the IMPLEMENTATION_VENDOR attribute is "Chan, Lee, Kramer".

The IMPLEMENTATION_VENDOR attribute can be specified as a main attribute. This means its value will apply to all packages in the JAR file. It can then be overridden for individual packages.

The value of this constant is "Implementation-Vendor".

SEE ALSO java.lang.Package.getImplementationVendor().

EXAMPLE See the java.lang.Package class example.

MAIN_CLASS

PURPOSE Name of the attribute for specifying the entry point of an application.

SYNTAX `public static final Name MAIN_CLASS`

DESCRIPTION This constant contains the name of the attribute for specifying the entry point of an application. The value of the MAIN_CLASS attribute is the fully qualified

A

name of a class (such as "java.lang.String"). The `MAIN_CLASS` attribute must appear in the main attributes set (see `Manifest`) of a manifest file. The named class must be `public` and appear in the JAR file and should have a method with the signature

```
public static void main(String[] args)
```

The value of this constant is `"Main-Class"`.

EXAMPLE This example demonstrates the use of this attribute. It defines a manifest file that specifies the main class to be `p.Main`. The example then creates a JAR file using the manifest file. Finally, the JAR file is invoked using the `java -jar` command.

p/Main.java

```
package p;
class Main {
    public static void main(String[] args) {
        System.out.println("Hello World");
    }
}
```

manifest.mf

```
Manifest-Version: 1.0
Main-Class: p.Main
```

OUTPUT

```
> jar cfm main.jar manifest.mf p/Main.class
> java -jar main.jar
Hello World
```

MANIFEST_VERSION

PURPOSE Name of attribute for specifying the version of the manifest file.

SYNTAX `public static final Name MANIFEST_VERSION`

DESCRIPTION This constant contains the name of the attribute for specifying the version of the manifest file. The `MANIFEST_VERSION` attribute is a required main attribute for all manifest files. (See `Manifest`.) At the moment, the latest version is 1.0.

The value of this constant is `"Manifest-Version"`.

EXAMPLE See `MAIN_CLASS`.

SEALED

PURPOSE Name of attribute for sealing a package.

SYNTAX `public static final Name SEALED`

DESCRIPTION This constant contains the name of the attribute for sealing a package. (See `Package` for more information about sealed packages.)

The value of the `SEALED` attribute can be either `"true"` or `"false"`. To seal, for example, a package `p.q`, you need to add the `SEALED` attribute to a manifest entry named "p/q/":


```
Name: p/q/
Sealed: true
```

The `SEALED` attribute can be specified as a main attribute. This means its value will apply to all packages in the JAR file. It can then be overridden for individual packages.

The value of this constant is `"Sealed"`.

SEE ALSO `java.lang.Package.isSealed()`.

EXAMPLE See `Package.isSealed()`.

SIGNATURE_VERSION

PURPOSE Name of attribute containing the signature version of the JAR file.

SYNTAX `public static final Name SIGNATURE_VERSION`

DESCRIPTION This constant contains the name of the attribute containing the signature version of the JAR file. The `SIGNATURE_VERSION` attribute is a required main attribute in a *signature manifest file*. The signature manifest file is typically generated automatically by tools that sign JAR files. For more details about this attribute, see

`http://java.sun.com/products/jdk/1.2/docs/guide/jar/manifest.html`

The value of this constant is `"Signature-Version"`.

SPECIFICATION_TITLE

PURPOSE Name of attribute containing the specification title of a package.

SYNTAX `public static final Name SPECIFICATION_TITLE`

DESCRIPTION This constant contains the name of the attribute containing the specification title of a package. See `Package.getSpecificationTitle()` for information about the value of the `SPECIFICATION_TITLE` attribute.

To apply the `SPECIFICATION_TITLE` attribute to a package `p.q`, for example, you need to add it to a manifest entry named "p/q/":

```
Name: p/q/
Specification-Title: Demo API Specification
```

In this example, the value of the SPECIFICATION_TITLE is "Demo API Specification".

The SPECIFICATION_TITLE attribute can be specified as a main attribute. This means its value will apply to all packages in the JAR file. It can then be overridden for individual packages.

The value of this constant is "Specification-Title".

SEE ALSO java.lang.Package.getSpecificationTitle().

EXAMPLE See the java.lang.Package class example.

SPECIFICATION_VERSION

PURPOSE Name of attribute containing the specification version of a package.

SYNTAX `public static final Name SPECIFICATION_VERSION`

DESCRIPTION This constant contains the name of the attribute containing the specification version of a package. See Package.getSpecificationVersion() for information about the value of the SPECIFICATION_VERSION attribute.

To apply the SPECIFICATION_VERSION attribute, for example to a package p.q, you need to add it to a manifest entry named "p/q/":

```
Name: p/q/
Specification-Version: 1.2.3
```

In this example, the value of the SPECIFICATION_VERSION is "1.2.3".

The SPECIFICATION_VERSION attribute can be specified as a main attribute. This means its value will apply to all packages in the JAR file. It can then be overridden for individual packages.

The value of this constant is "Specification-Version".

SEE ALSO java.lang.Package.getSpecificationVersion().

EXAMPLE See the java.lang.Package class example.

SPECIFICATION_VENDOR

PURPOSE Name of attribute containing the specification vendor of a package.

SYNTAX `public static final Name SPECIFICATION_VENDOR`

DESCRIPTION This constant contains the name of the attribute containing the specification vendor of a package. See Package.getSpecificationVendor() for information about the value of the SPECIFICATION_VENDOR attribute.

To apply the `SPECIFICATION_VENDOR` attribute to a package `p.q`, for example, you need to add it to a manifest entry named "p/q/":

```
Name: p/q/
Specification-Vendor: Chan, Lee, Kramer
```

In this example, the value of the `SPECIFICATION_VEENDOR` is "Chan, Lee, Kramer".

The `SPECIFICATION_VENDOR` attribute can be specified as a main attribute. This means its value will apply to all packages in the JAR file. It can then be overridden for individual packages.

The value of this constant is `"Specification-Vendor"`.

SEE ALSO `java.lang.Package.getSpecificationVendor()`.

EXAMPLE See the `java.lang.Package` class example.

toString()

PURPOSE Returns the attribute name.

SYNTAX `public String toString()`

DESCRIPTION This method returns this `Attributes.Name` object's string representation. The returned string is identical to the one supplied to the constructor.

RETURNS A non-`null` attribute name.

OVERRIDES `java.lang.Object.toString()`.

EXAMPLE See `equals()`.

java.net

Authenticator

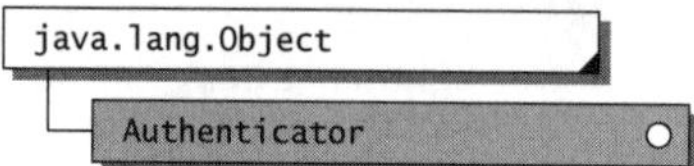

A

Syntax

```
public abstract class Authenticator
```

Description

The `Authenticator` class is used to authenticate users to network connections. It is used by networking applications, such as Web browsers, that deal with authenticating users to network services. Except for applications that write protocol handlers, most applications do not use this class directly.

Usage

The application must define a subclass of `Authenticator`, override `getPasswordAuthentication()` appropriately, and install it as follows:

```
Authenticator.setDefault(new SomeAuthenticator());
```

When the user of the application subsequently attempts to access a (security-) protected site or service, for example by specifying a URL, the networking connection (see `URLStreamHandler` and `URLConnection`) receives a request from the site for the user to authenticate itself to the site. This request is called a *challenge*. The networking connection extracts information from the challenge and invokes `Authentication.requestPasswordAuthentication()`, which will call the overridden `getPasswordAuthentication()` method.

```
PasswordAuthentication pa =
    Authenticator.requestPasswordAuthentication(
        server, 80, "http/1.1", "payingCustomers", "basic");
```

For example, the authenticator installed by the Web browser might obtain this password information by prompting the user of the browser by popping up a dialog window for the user to enter the password.

Information for Authentication

Different network protocols (and corresponding services) have different authentication schemes and hence might require different authentication information. Even though this class could be used for other protocols, it was designed primarily with the HTTP protocol in mind.

In the HTTP protocol, authentication is based on a challenge/response protocol. First, the entity requests a service by sending a request to the server. The server, noting that the request is for a protected resource, responds with a *challenge*, asking the client to identify itself. The client must use the information in the challenge to compose an appropriate response to the server. If the server is satisfy with the response, the authentication completes successfully and the client is granted access to the protected resource.

In HTTP, the challenge consists of an authentication *scheme*, a *realm*, and possibly additional authentication parameters depending on the scheme. The authentication scheme is a case-insensitive string that identifies the scheme (for example, "basic"). The realm is a case-sensitive string that identifies the *protection space* on the server. For example, a server might have set up several protection spaces, each with a different authentication scheme depending on how strongly the information contained therein needs to be protected. Clients wanting to gain access to a particular protection domain must be registered in that domain and must supply the necessary credentials. The names of realms are determined by the server.

See *RFC 2068* for information about the HTTP 1.1 protocol and its authentication mechanisms.

Using this information from the challenge, as well as the network address of the server requesting the authentication, the `Authenticator` subclass must return a user/password pair that can be used by the underlying protocol to generate a satisfying authentication response to the server.

MEMBER SUMMARY	
Installation Method (static)	
`setDefault()`	Installs the authenticator for this application.
Authentication Methods	
`requestPasswordAuthentication()`	Retrieves user/password information from the installed authenticator.
`getPasswordAuthentication()`	Called by `requestPasswordAuthentication()` to obtain the user/password pair.
Access Methods	
`getRequestingPort()`	Returns the remote port number of the network connection requiring authentication.
`getRequestingPrompt()`	Returns a prompt string from the server's authentication request.
`getRequestingProtocol()`	Returns the string identifying the protocol to use for the network connection.
`getRequestingScheme()`	Returns the string identifying the authentication mechanism to use.
`getRequestingSite()`	Returns the network address of the server requesting the authentication.

See Also

`NetPermission`, `PasswordAuthentication`, `URL`, `URLStreamHandler`.

Example

This example defines a subclass of `Authenticator`, called `SomeAuthenticator`, and installs it. The `Main` program has a "Login" button. Each time the Login button is pushed, `Authenticator.requestPasswordAuthentication()` is invoked to get user/password information.

Main.java

```
import java.net.*;
import java.awt.*;
import java.awt.event.*;

public class Main extends Frame implements ActionListener {
    Main() {
        super("Authenticator Example");

        Button b = new Button("Login");
        b.addActionListener(this);
        add(b, BorderLayout.NORTH);

        pack();
        show();
    }

    public void actionPerformed(ActionEvent evt) {
        // Try to get authentication information
        try {
            PasswordAuthentication pw =
                Authenticator.requestPasswordAuthentication(
                InetAddress.getLocalHost(),
                555,    // port
                "foo",  // protocol
                null,   // prompt
                "cleartext");

            if (pw != null) {
                System.out.println("username: " + pw.getUserName());
               System.out.println("password: " + new String(pw.getPassword()));
            } else {
                System.out.println("No password entered");
            }
        } catch (UnknownHostException e) {
            e.printStackTrace();
        }
    }

    public static void main(String[] args) {
        // Install authenticator
        Authenticator.setDefault(new SomeAuthenticator(new Main()));
    }
}
```

SomeAuthenticator.java

```
import java.net.*;
import java.awt.*;
import java.awt.event.*;

public class SomeAuthenticator extends Authenticator {
    private Frame parent;
```

```
private PasswordAuthentication pw;
private boolean done = false;

public SomeAuthenticator(Frame parent) {
    this.parent = parent;
}

// Override default to ask user for password
protected PasswordAuthentication getPasswordAuthentication() {
    pw = null;
    done = false;

    new LoginDialog(parent,
        getRequestingSite(),
        getRequestingPort(),
        getRequestingProtocol(),
        getRequestingScheme(),
        getRequestingPrompt());

    // Wait until user enters something
    while (!done) {
        try {
            System.out.println("sleeping");
            Thread.sleep(5000);
        } catch (InterruptedException e) {
        } // ignore interrupts
    }
    return pw;
}

// Popup Dialog window for user to enter password
class LoginDialog extends Dialog implements ActionListener {
    private TextField passwd = new TextField("", 5);
    private TextField username = new TextField("", 5);
    private Button ok = new Button("OK");
    private Button dismiss = new Button("DISMISS");

    LoginDialog(Frame f,
        InetAddress src, int port, String protocol,
        String scheme, String prompt) {
        super(f, "Login", true);

        setLayout(new GridLayout(0, 2));

        passwd.setEchoChar('*');

        add(new Label("User Name:"));
        add(username);

        add(new Label("Password:"));
        add(passwd);

        if (src != null) {
            add(new Label("Server:"));
            add(new Label(src.getHostName()));

            add(new Label("Port:"));
            add(new Label(port + ""));
        }
        if (protocol != null) {
```

```
                add(new Label("Protocol:"));
                add(new Label(protocol));
            }
            if (scheme != null) {
                add(new Label("Authentication:"));
                add(new Label(scheme));
            }
            if (prompt != null) {
                add(new Label("Prompt:"));
                add(new Label(prompt));
            }

            ok.addActionListener(this);
            dismiss.addActionListener(this);

            add(ok);
            add(dismiss);

            addWindowListener(new WindowEventHandler());

            pack();
            show();
        }

        public void actionPerformed(ActionEvent evt) {
            if (evt.getSource() == ok) {
                String pwstr = passwd.getText();
                char[] pwbuf = new char[pwstr.length()];
                pwstr.getChars(0, pwbuf.length, pwbuf, 0);

                pw = new PasswordAuthentication(username.getText(), pwbuf);
            }
            done = true;
            dispose();
        }

        class WindowEventHandler extends WindowAdapter {
            public void windowClosing(WindowEvent evt) {
                dispose();
            }
        }
    }
}
```

getPasswordAuthentication()

PURPOSE Called by `requestPasswordAuthentication()` to obtain the user/password pair.

SYNTAX `protected PasswordAuthentication getPasswordAuthentication()`

DESCRIPTION This method should be overridden by the `Authenticator` subclass. It should use information recorded by this `Authenticator` to query the user (perhaps by using a dialog window) for password information.

The default implementation returns `null`.

RETURNS — A possibly `null` instance of `PasswordAuthentication` containing the user/password information.

SEE ALSO — `requestPasswordAuthentication()`.

EXAMPLE — See the class example.

getRequestingPort()

PURPOSE — Returns the remote port number of the network connection requiring authentication.

SYNTAX
```
protected final int getRequestingPort()
```

DESCRIPTION — This method returns the remote port number of the network connection requiring authentication. The port number is one of the parameters supplied to `requestPasswordAuthentication()`.

RETURNS — The remote port number of the network connection.

SEE ALSO — `getRequestingProtocol()`, `getRequestingSite()`, `requestPasswordAuthentication()`.

EXAMPLE — See the class example.

getRequestingPrompt()

PURPOSE — Returns a prompt string from the server's authentication request.

SYNTAX
```
protected final String getRequestingPrompt()
```

DESCRIPTION — This method returns a prompt string from the server's authentication request. This string is one of the parameters supplied to `requestPasswordAuthentication()`. For the HTTP protocol, the prompt corresponds to the *realm*. See the class description for a brief description of realms. See *RFC 2068* for information about the HTTP protocol, realms, and authentication mechanisms.

RETURNS — A possibly `null` string containing authentication request information.

SEE ALSO — `getRequestingScheme()`, `requestPasswordAuthentication()`.

EXAMPLE — See the class example.

getRequestingProtocol()

PURPOSE — Returns the string identifying the protocol to use for the network connection.

SYNTAX
```
protected final String getRequestingProtocol()
```

DESCRIPTION This method returns the string identifying the protocol to use for the network connection. The format of the string is an identifier that specifies the protocol to use (see `URL.getProtocol()`) followed by an optional version string. The version string starts with a forward slash character (/) and is followed by the version number of the protocol. Examples of requesting protocol are `"http"` or `"http/1.1"`. This is one of the parameters supplied to `requestPassword-Authentication()`.

RETURNS A non-`null` string identifying the protocol.

SEE ALSO `URL.getProtocol(), requestPasswordAuthentication().`

EXAMPLE See the class example.

getRequestingScheme()

PURPOSE Returns the string identifying the authentication mechanism to use.

SYNTAX `protected final String getRequestingScheme()`

DESCRIPTION This method returns the string identifying the authentication mechanism to use. This string is one of the parameters supplied to `requestPasswordAuthen-tication()`. It identifies the authentication scheme that the server has requested. See the class description for a brief description of authentication mechanisms. See *RFC 2068* for information about the HTTP protocol and authentication mechanisms.

RETURNS A non-`null` string identifying the authentication mechanism.

SEE ALSO `getRequestingPrompt(), requestPasswordAuthentication().`

EXAMPLE See the class example.

getRequestingSite()

PURPOSE Returns the network address of the server requesting the authentication.

SYNTAX `protected final InetAddress getRequestingSite()`

DESCRIPTION This method returns the network address of the server requesting the authentication. This address is one of the parameters supplied to `requestPassword-Authentication()`. A value of `null` means that the address is not available.

RETURNS The possibly `null InetAddress` of the server requesting the authentication.

SEE ALSO `getRequestingPort(), getRequestingProtocol(), requestPasswordAuthentication().`

EXAMPLE See the class example.

requestPasswordAuthentication()

PURPOSE Retrieves user/password information from the installed authenticator.

SYNTAX
```
public static PasswordAuthentication
   requestPasswordAuthentication( InetAddress addr, int port,
   String protocol, String prompt, String scheme)
```

DESCRIPTION This method uses the authenticator that has been installed to obtain user/password information. The caller typically collects information to use as parameters by using data it reads from the network connection. See the class description for details. This method is typically called by protocol handlers. Except for applications that write protocol handlers, most applications do not call this method directly.

If no authenticator has been installed, this method returns `null`.

PARAMETERS

`addr` The possibly `null` `InetAddress` of the machine requesting authorization.
`port` The remote port number of the network connection.
`protocol` A non-`null` string identifying the protocol.
`prompt` A possibly `null` string containing authentication request information.
`scheme` A non-`null` string identifying the authentication mechanism.

RETURNS A possibly `null` `PasswordAuthentication` instance; `null` means the authentication information is not available.

SEE ALSO `getPasswordAuthentication(), NetPermission, setDefault().`

EXCEPTIONS

`SecurityException`
If the caller has not been granted permission to call this method.

EXAMPLE See the class example.

setDefault()

PURPOSE Installs the authenticator for this application.

SYNTAX
```
public synchronized static void setDefault(Authenticator auth)
```

DESCRIPTION This method installs the authenticator for this application, setting it to `auth`. It can be executed only if permitted by the security manager. If permitted, it can be executed only once for a non-`null` `auth` during the lifetime of the application. If `auth` is `null` or if a non-`null` authenticator has been previously installed, this method does nothing.

After `auth` has been installed, subsequent invocations of `requestPassword-Authentication()` will use `auth.getPasswordAuthentication()` to obtain authentication information.

PARAMETERS

`auth` A possibly `null` authenticator.

SEE ALSO `NetPermission`, `requestPasswordAuthentication()`.

EXCEPTIONS

`AccessControlException`
If the caller has not been granted permission to call this method.

EXAMPLE See the class example.

BigDecimal

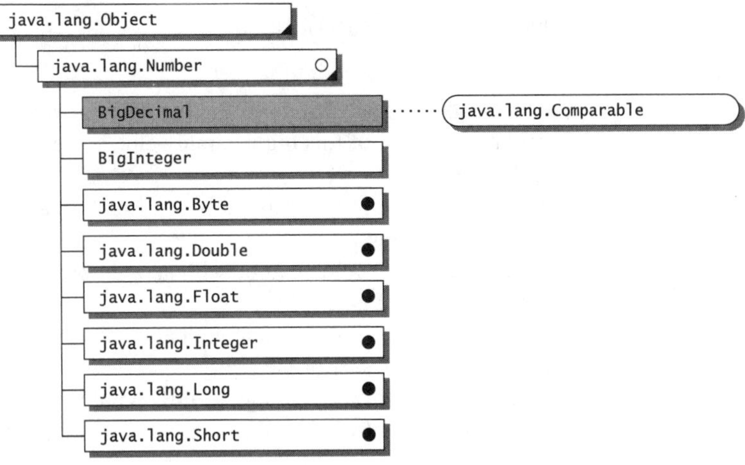

Syntax

```
public class BigDecimal extends Number implements Comparable
```

Description

A `BigDecimal` object represents an arbitrary-precision decimal number. The *scale* of a big decimal value is the number of digits to the right of the decimal point. For example, in the value `123.4560`, the scale is 4. Zeros at the end of the fractional part of a big decimal value are significant and are never automatically truncated to reduce the scale. For example, some operators do not consider `1.0` to be equal to `1.00`.

A `BigDecimal` object is immutable. That is, it contains a value that cannot be changed. Most big decimal operations yield a new `BigDecimal` object that holds the result of the operation. Big decimal values never overflow.

See *The Java Class Libraries, Second Edition, Volume 1* for more information about this class.

Changes for Version 1.2

This class now implements `Comparable`. This makes it possible for `BigDecimal` objects to be sorted with the collection classes (see `Collection`).

A new method, `unscaledValue()`, retrieves the big decimal value without a decimal point.

B

MEMBER SUMMARY

Constructor	
`BigDecimal()`	Constructs a `BigDecimal` instance.
Math Methods	
`abs()`	Calculates the absolute value of this big decimal value.
`add()`	Calculates the sum of this big decimal value and another big decimal value.
`divide()`	Calculates the result of dividing this big decimal value by another big decimal value.
`max()`	Compares this big decimal value with another big decimal value and returns the greater of the two.
`min()`	Compares this big decimal value with another big decimal value and returns the lesser of the two.
`movePointLeft()`	Returns the result of moving the decimal point to the left.
`movePointRight()`	Returns the result of moving the decimal point to the right.
`multiply()`	Calculates the product of this big decimal value and another big decimal value.
`negate()`	Calculates the product of this big decimal value and `-1`.
`signum()`	Determines the sign of this big decimal value.
`subtract()`	Calculates the difference of this big decimal value and another big decimal value.
Comparison Methods	
`equals()`	Determines if this big decimal value is equal to another object.
Δ `compareTo()`	Compares this big decimal value with another big decimal value.
Conversion Methods	
`doubleValue()`	Converts this big decimal value to a `double` value.
`floatValue()`	Converts this big decimal value to a `float` value.
`intValue()`	Converts this big decimal value to an `int` value.
`longValue()`	Converts this big decimal value to a `long` value.
`toBigInteger()`	Converts this big decimal value to a big integer value.
`valueOf()`	Returns a `BigDecimal` instance for a primitive integer value.
Scaling Methods	
`scale()`	Retrieves the scale of this big decimal value.
`setScale()`	Returns the result of changing the scale of this big decimal value.
1.2 `unscaledValue()`	Retrieves the value of this big decimal value without a decimal point.
Rounding Mode Constants	
`ROUND_CEILING`	Rounding mode that specifies rounding toward positive infinity.
`ROUND_DOWN`	Rounding mode that specifies rounding toward zero.
`ROUND_FLOOR`	Rounding mode that specifies rounding toward negative infinity.

B

MEMBER SUMMARY	
`ROUND_HALF_DOWN`	Rounding mode that specifies rounding toward the nearest neighbor; if equidistant, rounding is toward zero.
`ROUND_HALF_EVEN`	Rounding mode that specifies rounding toward the nearest neighbor; if equidistant, rounding is toward the even new tail digit.
`ROUND_HALF_UP`	Rounding mode that specifies rounding toward the nearest neighbor; if equidistant, rounding is away from zero.
`ROUND_UNNECESSARY`	Rounding mode that specifies that loss of precision must not occur.
`ROUND_UP`	Rounding mode that specifies rounding away from zero.
Object Methods	
`hashCode()`	Computes the hash code of this big decimal value.
`toString()`	Generates a string representing this big decimal value.

See Also

`java.lang.Comparable`, `java.util.Collection`.
`BigDecimal` in *The Java Class Libraries, Second Edition, Volume 1*.

Δ compareTo()

PURPOSE — Compares this big decimal value with another big decimal value.

SYNTAX
```
public int compareTo(BigDecimal val)
public int compareTo(Object val)
```
SINCE 1.2 (second form)

DESCRIPTION — This method compares this big decimal value with another big decimal value, `val`. If this big decimal value is less than `val`, `-1` is returned. If it is equal to `val`, `0` is returned. If it is greater than `val`, `1` is returned.

The equals test used in this method differs from `equals()`. In particular, with `equals()`, not only must the values be numerically equal but so must their scales. For example, `equals()` would not consider `1.0` and `1.00` equal. `compareTo()` compares only the numerical values and hence would consider `1.0` and `1.00` to be equal.

1.2 CHANGES — The method that takes an `Object` is new in Version 1.2.

PARAMETERS
`val` — A non-`null` `BigDecimal` object.

RETURNS — `-1`, `0`, or `1`, depending on how this big decimal value compares with `val`.

SEE ALSO — `equals()`.

EXAMPLE

```
// Some sample output.
BigDecimal a = new BigDecimal("1.23");
BigDecimal b = new BigDecimal("1.234");
System.out.println(a.compareTo(b));                 // -1
System.out.println(b.compareTo(a));                 // 1

a = new BigDecimal("1.23");
b = new BigDecimal("1.2300");
System.out.println(a.compareTo(b));                 // 0
System.out.println(a.equals(b));                    // false

//System.out.println( a.compareTo("A String") );   // ClassCastException
//System.out.println( a.compareTo(null) );         // NullPointerException

// Sorting a list of big decimal numbers.
List list = new ArrayList();
for (int i=0; i<5; i++) {
    list.add(new BigDecimal(Math.random()));
}
Collections.sort(list);
for (int i=0; i<5; i++) {
    System.out.println( list.get(i) );
}
```

1.2 unscaledValue()

PURPOSE Retrieves the value of this big decimal value without a decimal point.

SYNTAX `public BigInteger unscaledValue()`

DESCRIPTION This method retrieves the unscaled value of this big decimal. The unscaled value of a big decimal value is the value of the big decimal value without a decimal point. For example, if a big decimal value is `1.23`, the unscaled value would be `123`.

RETURNS The unscaled value of this big decimal value.

SEE ALSO `BigDecimal(BigInteger, int)`.

EXAMPLE

```
BigDecimal n = new BigDecimal("1.23");
System.out.println( n.unscaledValue() );    // 123

n = new BigDecimal("-1.234");
System.out.println( n.unscaledValue() );    // -1234

n = new BigDecimal("00.000");
System.out.println( n.unscaledValue() );    // 0
```

BigInteger

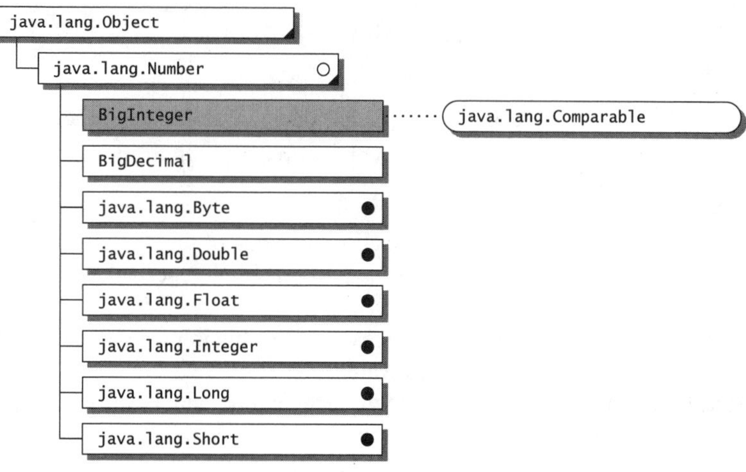

Syntax

```
public class BigInteger extends Number implements Comparable
```

Description

A `BigInteger` object represents an arbitrary-precision integer. A big integer value provides a means to do calculation on a value that is too big to be represented by a 64-bit `long` value. The operations in this class provide the same kind of operations (and more) that are available for `long` values. They are semantically identical to the Java integer operations, except that big integer values never overflow. See *The Java Language Specification, First Edition*, for details about Java integer operations.

A `BigInteger` object is immutable. That is, it contains a value that cannot be changed. Most big integer operations yield a new `BigInteger` object that holds the result of the operation.

See *The Java Class Libraries, Second Edition, Volume 1* for more information about this class.

Changes for Version 1.2

This class now implements `Comparable`. This makes it possible for `BigInteger` objects to be sorted with the collection classes (see `Collection`).

For convenience, two new big integer constants have been added: `ZERO` and `ONE`.

B

MEMBER SUMMARY	
Constructor	
`BigInteger()`	Constructs a `BigInteger` instance.
Constants	
1.2 `ONE`	A big integer value constant containing the value `1`.
1.2 `ZERO`	A big integer value constant containing the value `0`.
Math Methods	
`abs()`	Calculates the absolute value of this big integer value.
`add()`	Calculates the sum of this big integer value and another big integer value.
`divide()`	Calculates the result of this big integer value divided by another big integer value.
`divideAndRemainder()`	Calculates the quotient and remainder of two big integers.
`gcd()`	Calculates the greatest common denominator of this big integer value and another big integer value.
`isProbablePrime()`	Guesses whether this big integer value is prime.
`max()`	Compares this big integer value with another big integer value and returns the greater of the two.
`min()`	Compares this big integer value with another big integer value and returns the lesser of the two.
`mod()`	Calculates the residue of this big integer modulo another big integer.
`modInverse()`	Calculates the modular multiplicative inverse of this big integer value.
`modPow()`	Calculates the residue of this big integer value raised to a power and modulo another big integer value.
`multiply()`	Calculates the product of this big integer value and another big integer value.
`negate()`	Calculates the product of `-1` and this big integer value.
`pow()`	Calculates the result of raising this big integer value to a power.
`remainder()`	Calculates the remainder of dividing this big integer value by another big integer value.
`signum()`	Determines the sign of this big integer value.
`subtract()`	Calculates the difference between this big integer value and another big integer value.
Comparison Methods	
Δ `compareTo()`	Compares this big integer value with another big integer value.
`equals()`	Determines if this big integer value is equal to an object.

B

MEMBER SUMMARY	
Bit Methods	
`and()`	AND's this big integer value with another big integer value.
`andNot()`	AND's this big integer value with the inverse of another big integer value.
`bitCount()`	Counts the number of zeroes or ones in the two's complement representation of this big integer value.
`bitLength()`	Determines the number of bits in the minimal representation of this big integer value, exclusive of sign bits.
`clearBit()`	Returns the result of clearing a bit in the two's complement representation of this big integer value.
`flipBit()`	Returns the result of reversing a bit in this big integer value.
`getLowestSetBit()`	Finds the rightmost one bit in the two's complement representation of this big integer value.
`not()`	Complements all of the bits in this big integer value.
`or()`	OR's the bits in this big integer value with another.
`setBit()`	Returns the result of setting a bit in the two's complement representation of this big integer value.
`shiftLeft()`	Shifts to the left the bits in the two's complement representation of this big integer value.
`shiftRight()`	Shifts to the right the bits in the two's complement representation of this big integer value.
`testBit()`	Determines if some bit is set in the two's complement representation of this big integer value.
`xor()`	XOR's this big integer value with another big integer value.
Conversion Methods	
`doubleValue()`	Converts this big integer value to a `double` value.
`floatValue()`	Converts this big integer value to a `float` value.
`intValue()`	Converts this big integer value to an `int` value.
`longValue()`	Converts this big integer value to a `long` value.
`toByteArray()`	Creates an array containing the bits of this big integer value.
`valueOf()`	Returns a `BigInteger` instance for a primitive integer value.
Object Methods	
`hashCode()`	Computes the hash code of this big integer value.
`toString()`	Generates a string representing this big integer value.

See Also

`java.lang.Comparable`, `java.util.Collection`.
`BigInteger` in *The Java Class Libraries, Second Edition, Volume 1*.

B

Δ compareTo()

PURPOSE Compares this big integer value with another big integer value.

SYNTAX `public int compareTo(BigInteger val)`
SINCE 1.2 `public int compareTo(Object val)`

DESCRIPTION This method compares this big integer value with another big integer value, `val`. If this big integer value is less than `val`, `-1` is returned. If it is equal to `val`, `0` is returned. If it is greater than `val`, `1` is returned.

1.2 CHANGES The method that takes an `Object` is new in Version 1.2.

PARAMETERS

`val` A non-`null` `BigInteger` object.

RETURNS `-1`, `0`, or `1`, depending on how this big integer value compares with `val`.

SEE ALSO `equals()`.

EXAMPLE This example starts with some sample output. It then reads a list of big integers from standard input, sorts the big integers, and prints them to standard output.

```
// Some sample output.
BigInteger bi = BigInteger.valueOf(100);
System.out.println( bi.compareTo(BigInteger.ZERO) );// 1
System.out.println( BigInteger.ZERO.compareTo(bi) );// -1
//System.out.println( bi.compareTo("A String") );   // ClassCastException
//System.out.println( bi.compareTo(null) );         // NullPointerException

// Read numbers from standard in.
BufferedReader is =
    new BufferedReader(new InputStreamReader(System.in));
String line;
List list = new ArrayList();

// Add the big integers to the list.
try {
    while ((line = is.readLine()) != null) {
        list.add(new BigInteger(line));
    }
} catch (Exception e) {
    e.printStackTrace();
}

// Sort the list.
Collections.sort(list);

// Print sorted list.
for (int i=0; i<list.size(); i++) {
    System.out.println(list.get(i));
}
```

INPUT

```
2903429847238942
92384729847294729874
03294823984938439483
```

```
203489204823904823908420842094820948293
83478278437843784
2387284732
29348723904820984032948
28347238472947294729748923749238
```

OUTPUT

```
2387284732
2903429847238942
83478278437843784
3294823984938439483
92384729847294729874
29348723904820984032948
28347238472947294729748923749238
203489204823904823908420842094820948293
```

1.2 ONE

PURPOSE A big integer value constant containing the value 1.

SYNTAX `public static final BigInteger ONE`

DESCRIPTION This object is a convenient constant containing the value 1.

EXAMPLE

```
BigInteger bi = BigInteger.valueOf(100);
bi = bi.add(BigInteger.ONE);
System.out.println( bi );                                    // 101

System.out.println( bi.compareTo(BigInteger.ZERO) );         // 1
System.out.println( BigInteger.ZERO.compareTo(BigInteger.ONE) ); // -1
```

1.2 ZERO

PURPOSE A big integer value constant containing the value 0.

SYNTAX `public static final BigInteger ZERO`

DESCRIPTION This object is a convenient constant containing the value 0. It is typically used when big integer values need to be compared with 0.

EXAMPLE See ONE.

java.util
BitSet

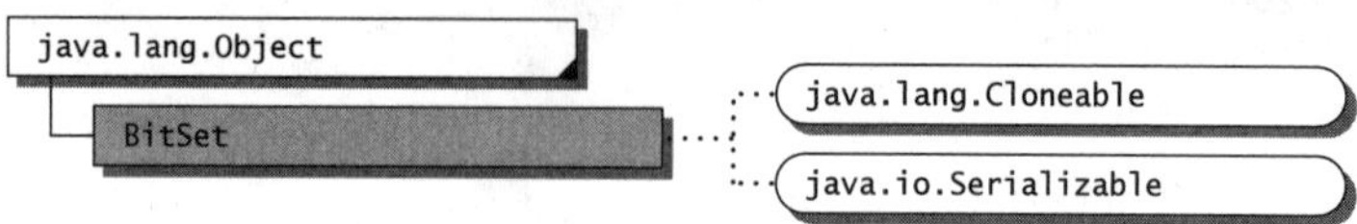

B

Syntax

```
public final class BitSet implements Cloneable, Serializable
```

Description

The `BitSet` class is used to represent a bit set.[1] Each element in the bit set is a bit that is either set (`1`) or cleared (`0`). You create a bit set with an initial size. The bit set will grow automatically as bits beyond its initial size are set/cleared. You can access and update the bits in the set individually via their indices, and you can perform bitwise logical operations on the entire set.

See *The Java Class Libraries, Second Edition, Volume 1* for more information about this class.

Changes for Version 1.2

The new `andNot()` method adds to the set of available `boolean` operations. Another new method, `length()`, returns the logical length of a bit set.

In Version 1.1, this class was thread-safe, thereby allowing multiple threads to safely query and modify a `BitSet` object concurrently. If thread safety is needed, all threads sharing a `BitSet` object now must enclose each method call to the object in a `synchronized` statement. However, all `boolean` operations that operate on two bit sets still properly handle the case in which both bit sets are the same object.

MEMBER SUMMARY	
Constructor	
`BitSet()`	Constructs a `BitSet` instance with all bits initialized to `0`.
Object Override Methods	
`clone()`	Makes a copy of this `BitSet`.
`equals()`	Determines if this `BitSet` is equal to another object.
`hashCode()`	Computes the hash code of this `BitSet`.
`toString()`	Generates the string representation of this `BitSet`.

1. `BitSet` is a misnomer because "sets" are unordered. `BitVector` would be a more correct class name.

MEMBER SUMMARY	
Bit Manipulation Methods	
`and()`	Applies the logical AND of this `BitSet` with another `BitSet`.
1.2 `andNot()`	Calculates the logical NOT of another `BitSet` and logically ANDs it with this `BitSet`.
`clear()`	Clears a bit in this `BitSet`.
`get()`	Retrieves a bit from this `BitSet`.
`or()`	Applies logical OR of this `BitSet` with another `BitSet`.
`set()`	Sets a bit in this `BitSet`.
`xor()`	Applies logical XOR of this `BitSet` with another `BitSet`.
Size Methods	
1.2 `length()`	Determines the logical size of this `BitSet`.
`size()`	Determines the number of bits internally used by this `BitSet`.

See Also

`BitSet` in *The Java Class Libraries, Second Edition, Volume 1.*

1.2 andNot()

PURPOSE Calculates the logical NOT of another `BitSet` and logically ANDs it with this `BitSet`.

SYNTAX `public void andNot(BitSet bs)`

DESCRIPTION This method applies logical AND of this `BitSet` with the logical NOT of the `BitSet` `bs`. For all indices of this `BitSet`, the *i*th bit in this `BitSet` is cleared if the *i*th bit in `bs` is set. Otherwise, the *i*th bit will be cleared. If `bs` has fewer bits than this `BitSet`, the rest of the bits in this `BitSet` are not changed. If `bs` has more bits than this `BitSet` does, the extra bits are ignored.

PARAMETERS

`bs` The non-`null` `BitSet` with which to logically AND.

SEE ALSO `and()`, `or()`, `xor()`.

EXAMPLE

```
import java.util.*;

class Main {
    public static void main(String[] args) {
        BitSet bs1 = new BitSet();
        bs1.set(0);
        bs1.set(2);
        print(bs1);            // 101
```

```
            BitSet bs2 = new BitSet();
            bs2.set(0);

            bs1.andNot(bs2);        // 100
            print(bs1);
        }

        public static void print(BitSet bs) {
            for (int i=bs.length()-1; i >= 0; i--) {
                System.out.print(bs.get(i) ? "1" : "0");
            }
            System.out.println();
        }
    }
```

B

1.2 length()

PURPOSE Determines the logical size of this `BitSet`.

SYNTAX `public int length()`

RETURNS This method returns the index of the highest set bit plus 1.

SEE ALSO `size()`.

EXAMPLE

```
BitSet bs = new BitSet();
System.out.println( bs.length()+" "+bs.size() );    // 0 64

bs.set(0);
System.out.println( bs.length()+" "+bs.size() );    // 1 64

bs.set(64);
System.out.println( bs.length()+" "+bs.size() );    // 65 128

bs.set(1000);
bs.clear(1000);
System.out.println( bs.length()+" "+bs.size() );    // 65 1024
```

java.text
BreakIterator

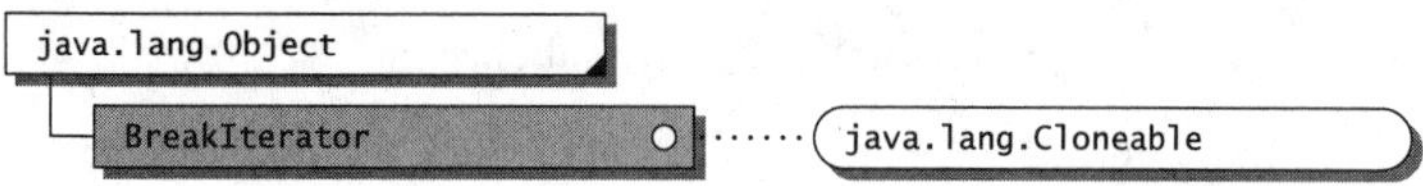

B

Syntax

```
public abstract class BreakIterator extends Object implements Cloneable
```

Description

`BreakIterator` is an abstract class that indirectly implements methods for finding and getting the position of four different kinds of logical breaks, or boundaries, in a string of text, based on user characters (rather than Unicode characters).

See *The Java Class Libraries, Second Edition, Volume 1* for more information about this class.

Changes for Version 1.2

`BreakIterator` is no longer declared `Serializable`—serialization never was implemented and always threw an exception. Two new convenience methods have been added: `isBoundary()` and `preceding()`. Example 2 in *The Java Class Libraries, Second Edition, Volume 1* had the wrong screen shot. Figure 9 shows the correct one.

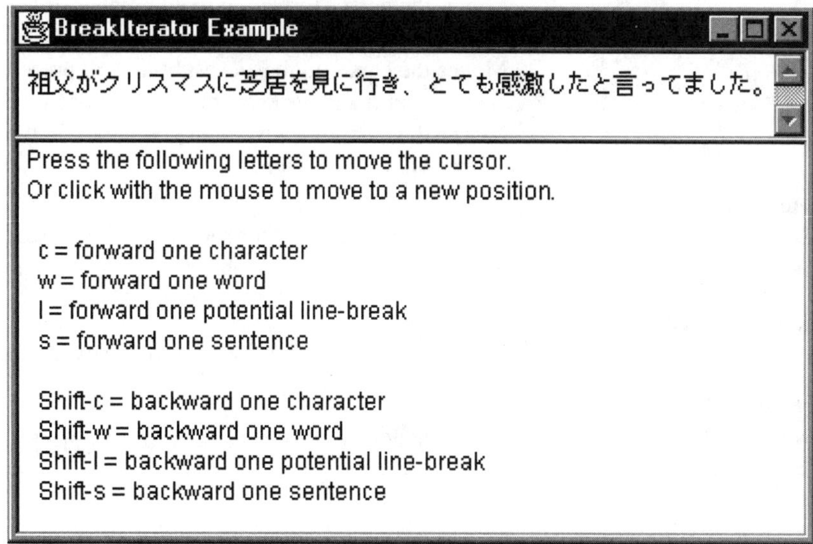

FIGURE 9: `BreakIterator` for Japanese Text.

B

MEMBER SUMMARY	
Constructor	
`BreakIterator()`	Constructor used by subclasses.
Break Iterator Creation Methods	
`getCharacterInstance()`	Creates a new break iterator that locates character boundaries.
`getLineInstance()`	Creates a new break iterator that locates line-break boundaries.
`getSentenceInstance()`	Creates a new break iterator that locates sentence boundaries.
`getWordInstance()`	Creates a new break iterator that locates word-break boundaries.
Locale Method	
`getAvailableLocales()`	Gets the locales for which break iterators are installed.
Movement Methods	
`current()`	Retrieves the current position of the cursor.
`first()`	Moves the cursor to the first boundary in the text and retrieves the position.
`following()`	Moves the cursor to the first boundary following a boundary position and retrieves the position.
1.2 `isboundary()`	Determines if a character position is a boundary.
`last()`	Moves the cursor to the last boundary in the text and retrieves the position.
`next()`	Moves the cursor forward a fixed number of boundaries in the text and retrieves the position.
1.2 `preceding()`	Moves the cursor to the closest boundary preceding a character position and retrieves the position of that boundary.
`previous()`	Moves the cursor backward one boundary in the text and retrieves that position.
Text Methods	
`getText()`	Gets the character iterator for the text being scanned.
`setText()`	Sets a new string to be scanned for text boundaries.
Termination Constant	
`DONE`	Returned when this iterator tries to go beyond the end of text.
Object Method	
`clone()`	Creates a copy of this `BreakIterator` object.

See Also

`CharacterIterator`, `StringCharacterIterator`.
`BreakIterator` in *The Java Class Libraries, Second Edition, Volume 1.*

1.2 isBoundary()

PURPOSE

Determines if a character position is a boundary.

SYNTAX

```
public boolean isBoundary(int pos)
```

DESCRIPTION

This method checks whether the position `pos` is at a boundary. If it is, the method moves the cursor there and returns `true`. Otherwise, it moves the cursor to the first boundary following `pos` and returns `false`. Note that the start and end of the iteration range are boundary positions by definition. Therefore, if you check the first position of the iteration range, `isBoundary()` will return `true` and move the cursor there.

When subclassing `BreakIterator`, you will almost always want to override `isBoundary()` for greater efficiency rather than use the default implementation.

When implementing a search engine, you can use `isBoundary()` to create a "whole words only" option using a word break iterator `wb`. When you find an occurrence of the search string, you can check the leading boundary with `wb.isBoundary()`. If `wb.isBoundary()` returns `true`, then call `wb.next()` to go to the subsequent boundary, checking to see if it is the same position as the trailing edge of the search string. If `matchStart` is the position at which the matching text starts and `matchEnd` is the position at which the matching text ends, the following code checks for whole words.

```
if (isBoundary(matchStart)) {
    while (getIndex() < matchEnd)
        next();
    return getIndex() == matchEnd;
}
return false;
```

When you are searching for a single word, `wb.next()` will be faster than `wb.isBoundary()` to find the trailing edge. This is due to the implementation of `isBoundary()`, which backs up one position before it starts moving forward. You would first have to move the iterator forward one character and then call `wb.isBoundary()` to find the next boundary.

PARAMETERS

`pos` The character position to check. `first()` ≤ `pos` ≤ `last() - 1`.

RETURNS

`true` if `pos` is at a boundary; `false` otherwise.

EXAMPLE

This example checks to see if the word-break cursor is at a word boundary initially (which it is). It then moves the character-break cursor forward two characters and checks if the character-break cursor is now at a word boundary (it is not).

```
import java.text.BreakIterator;

class Main {
    public static void main(String args[]) {
        String str = "Thanks! Hi-ho \n bye.";

        // Create word break iterator.
        BreakIterator wb = BreakIterator.getWordInstance();
        wb.setText(str);

        // Is the iterator's cursor at a boundary?
        System.out.println(wb.isBoundary(0));           // true
        System.out.println(str.charAt(0));              // 'T'

        System.out.println(wb.isBoundary(5));           // false
        System.out.println(str.charAt(5));              // 's'

        System.out.println(wb.isBoundary(6));           // true
        System.out.println(str.charAt(6));              // '!'

        System.out.println(wb.isBoundary(7));           // true
        System.out.println(str.charAt(7));              // ' '

        System.out.println(wb.isBoundary(10));          // true
        System.out.println(str.charAt(10));             // '-'
    }
}
```

1.2 preceding()

PURPOSE Moves the cursor to the closest boundary preceding a character position and retrieves the position of that boundary.

SYNTAX `public int preceding(int pos)`

DESCRIPTION This method moves this break iterator's cursor to the closest boundary preceding the character position `pos` and retrieves the position of that boundary. If the cursor is at the start of the iteration range, then calling this method returns `BreakIterator.DONE` and does not move the cursor.

As with other movement methods, what `preceding()` considers a boundary depends on what kind of iterator this is. The `preceding()` method can move by characters, words, sentences, or potential line breaks.

When subclassing `BreakIterator`, you will almost always want to override `preceding()` for greater efficiency rather than use the default implementation.

PARAMETERS

`pos` The character position from which to begin scanning backward. `first()` ≤ `pos` ≤ `last() - 1`.

RETURNS The character position of the closest boundary preceding `pos`, or `BreakIterator.DONE`.

EXAMPLE

This example creates a line-break iterator and then moves the cursor to the closest potential line-break boundary preceding various character positions. The character at position 6 is the "n" in the word "thank". The boundary at position 3 is the character "t".

```
import java.text.BreakIterator;

class Main {
    public static void main(String args[]) {
        String str = "We thank you.";

        // Create line-break iterator.
        BreakIterator lb = BreakIterator.getLineInstance();
        lb.setText(str);

        // Move to boundary preceding various character positions.
        System.out.println( lb.preceding(0) );      // -1
        System.out.println( lb.preceding(6) );      //  3
        System.out.println( lb.preceding(12) );     //  9
    }
}
```

java.io

BufferedInputStream

B

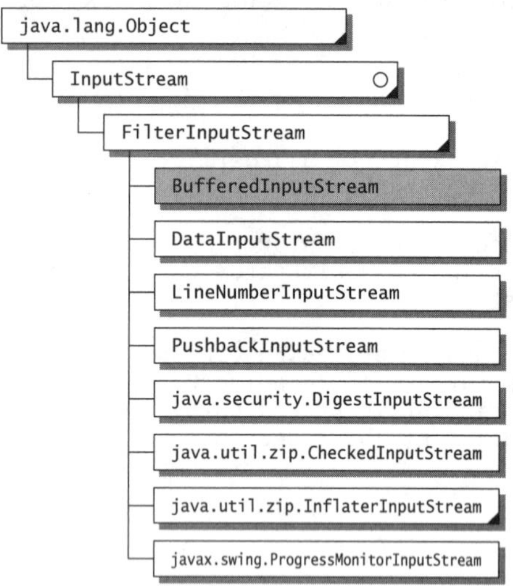

Syntax

```
public class BufferedInputStream extends FilterInputStream
```

Description

The `BufferedInputStream` class implements a *buffered input stream.* A buffered input stream is a filter input stream. You can compose it with an existing input stream to allow buffering of input when reading from that stream. The buffered input stream maintains a buffer of bytes read from the original input stream. Requests to read from the buffered input stream retrieve bytes from this buffer, rather than performing read operations on the original input stream. When all bytes from the buffer have been read, the buffer is refilled with input from the original input stream.

See *The Java Class Libraries, Second Edition, Volume 1* for more information about this class.

Changes for Version 1.2

The `close()` method has been overridden to release resources used by the `BufferedInputStream`.

B

MEMBER SUMMARY	
Constructor	
`BufferedInputStream()`	Constructs a `BufferedInputStream` instance for an input stream.
Input Methods	
`read()`	Reads bytes from this `BufferedInputStream`.
`skip()`	Skips the specified number of bytes in this `BufferedInputStream`.
Mark/Reset Methods	
`mark()`	Marks the current position in this `BufferedInputStream`.
`markSupported()`	Determines whether this `BufferedInputStream` supports rereading of its data.
`reset()`	Repositions this `BufferedInputStream` to the last marked position.
Stream Methods	
`available()`	Determines the number of bytes that can be read without being blocked.
Δ `close()`	Closes this `BufferedInputStream`.
Protected Fields	
`buf`	The buffer that stores the input stream data.
`count`	The number of bytes in the buffer.
`marklimit`	The maximum read-ahead allowed before the mark is invalidated.
`markpos`	The position in the buffer of the current mark.
`pos`	The current read position in the buffer.

See Also

`BufferedInputStream` in *The Java Class Libraries, Second Edition, Volume 1.*

Δ close()

PURPOSE Closes this `BufferedInputStream`.

SYNTAX `public synchronized void close() throws IOException`

DESCRIPTION This method closes the underlying input stream and releases the resources used by this `BufferedInputStream`.

1.2 CHANGES In Version 1.1, this method was inherited from `FilterInputStream`, which called `close()` on the underlying input stream.

EXCEPTIONS

`IOException`

If an IO error occurred while closing this stream.

OVERRIDES `FilterInputStream.`

EXAMPLE See the `InputStream` class example in *The Java Class Libraries, Second Edition, Volume 1.*

Byte

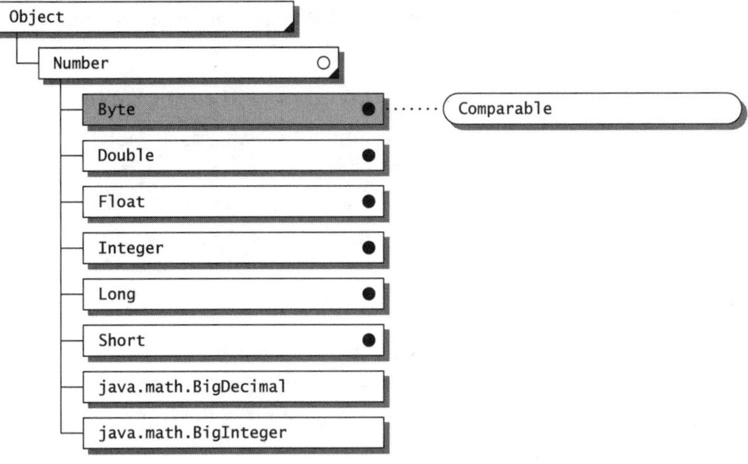

Syntax

```
public final class Byte extends Number implements Comparable
```

Description

The `Byte` class provides an object wrapper for a `byte` data value. A *`byte` data value* in Java is a 8-bit signed integer. This object wrapper allows bytes to be passed to methods in Java class libraries that accept Java objects as parameters. This class also provides methods that convert values to and from `byte` values.

See *The Java Class Libraries, Second Edition, Volume 1* for more information about this class.

Changes for Version 1.2

The `Byte` class implements the `Comparable` interface and has two overloaded forms of the `compareTo()` method used for comparing and ordering `Byte` objects. This allows arrays of `Byte` objects to be sorted, as shown in this example.

```
Byte[] ba = new Byte[]{new Byte((byte)10),
                       new Byte((byte)-4), new Byte((byte)48)};
Arrays.sort(ba);
for (int i = 0; i < ba.length; i++) {
    System.out.println(ba[i]);
}
// -4, 10, 48
```

B

MEMBER SUMMARY	
Constructor	
`Byte()`	Constructs a `Byte` instance using a `byte` value or a string.
Number Methods	
`byteValue()`	Retrieves the value of this `Byte` as a `byte`.
`doubleValue()`	Retrieves the value of this `Byte` as a `double`.
`floatValue()`	Retrieves the value of this `Byte` as a `float`.
`intValue()`	Retrieves the value of this `Byte` as an `int`.
`longValue()`	Retrieves the value of this `Byte` as a `long`.
`shortValue()`	Retrieves the value of this `Byte` as a `short`.
`byte`-Related Constants	
`MAX_VALUE`	The minimum value a `byte` can have.
`MIN_VALUE`	The maximum value a `byte` can have.
`TYPE`	The `Class` object representing the primitive type `byte`.
Comparison Methods	
1.2 `compareTo()`	Compares the signed numeric value of this `Byte` with that of another `Byte`.
`equals()`	Determines if this `Byte` is equal to another object.
String Conversion Methods	
`decode()`	Parses the string representation of an 8-bit signed integer into a `Byte`.
`parseByte()`	Parses the string representation of an integer into a `byte`.
`valueOf()`	Creates a `Byte` instance using its string representation.
`toString()`	Generates the string representation of a `byte` or a `Byte`.
Object Method	
`hashCode()`	Computes the hash code of this `Byte`.

See Also

`Comparable`, `java.util.Arrays`.
`Byte` in *The Java Class Libraries, Second Edition, Volume 1.*

1.2 compareTo()

PURPOSE Compares the signed numeric value of this `Byte` with that of another `Byte`.

SYNTAX
```
public int compareTo(Byte anotherByte)
public int compareTo(Object anotherByte)
```

DESCRIPTION This method compares this `Byte`'s (signed) numeric value with that of `anotherByte`. It returns an integer indicating whether the two numeric values are equal and, if they are not, the ordering of the two values. It returns `0` if the two numeric values are the same. It returns a negative number if the numeric value of this `Byte` is less than the numeric value of `anotherByte`. It returns a positive number if the numeric value of this `Byte` is greater than the numeric value of `anotherByte`.

If `anotherByte` is not an instance of `Byte`, a `ClassCastException` is thrown.

PARAMETERS

`anotherByte` The non-`null` `Byte` to be compared.

RETURNS `0` if the numeric values of this `Byte` and `anotherByte` are the same; a negative number if this `Byte`'s value is less than that of `anotherByte`; a positive number if this `Byte`'s value is greater than that of `anotherByte`.

EXCEPTIONS

`ClassCastException`

If `anotherByte` is not an instance of `Byte`.

SEE ALSO `Comparable`.

EXAMPLE

```
Byte b = new Byte((byte)100);
System.out.println(b.compareTo(new Byte((byte)-1)));    // positive
System.out.println(b.compareTo(new Byte((byte)100)));   // 0
System.out.println(b.compareTo(new Byte((byte)-100)));  // positive
System.out.println(b.compareTo(new Byte((byte)101)));   // negative
System.out.println(b.compareTo("abc")); // ClassCastException
```

java.io

ByteArrayInputStream

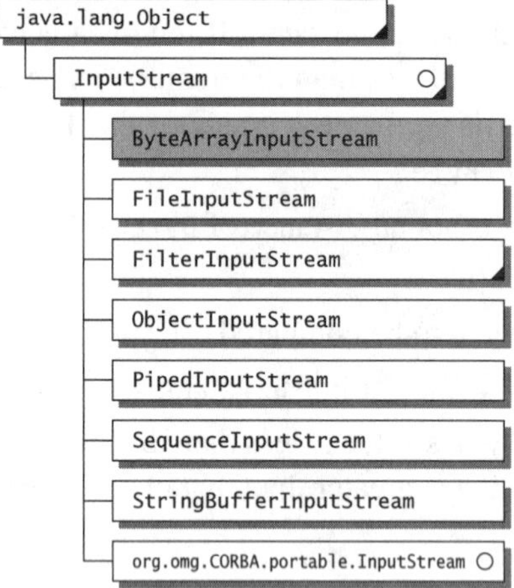

Syntax

```
public class ByteArrayInputStream extends InputStream
```

Description

The `ByteArrayInputStream` class implements a byte array input stream. You can use this stream to turn a `byte` array into an input stream on which you can perform read operations. Requests to read from the stream retrieve bytes from the original `byte` array.

See *The Java Class Libraries, Second Edition, Volume 1* for more information about this class.

Changes for Version 1.2

The `close()` method has been overridden to mark that the `ByteArrayInputStream` has been closed.

The `reset()` method now treats the byte array offset correctly.

MEMBER SUMMARY	
Constructor	
`ByteArrayInputStream()`	Constructs a `ByteArrayInputStream` instance using a `byte` array.
Input Methods	
`read()`	Reads bytes from this `ByteArrayInputStream`.

MEMBER SUMMARY	
`skip()`	Skips the specified number of bytes in this `ByteArrayInputStream`.
Mark/Reset Methods	
`mark()`	Marks the current position in this `ByteArrayInputStream`.
`markSupported()`	Determines whether this `ByteArrayInputStream` supports rereading of its data.
Δ `reset()`	Resets the buffer to the previously marked position of the `byte` array.
Stream Methods	
`available()`	Determines the number of unread bytes in this `ByteArrayInputStream`.
Δ `close()`	Closes this `ByteArrayInputStream`.
Protected Fields	
`buf`	The `byte` array containing the bytes to be read.
`count`	The ending index of the `byte` array to be read.
`mark`	The position of the mark.
`pos`	The current read position in the `byte` array.

See Also

`ByteArrayInputStream` in *The Java Class Libraries, Second Edition, Volume 1.*

Δ close()

PURPOSE Closes this `ByteArrayInputStream`.

SYNTAX `public synchronized void close() throws IOException`

DESCRIPTION This method closes this `ByteArrayInputStream`. It sets an internal flag to indicate that the stream has been closed but otherwise does nothing.

1.2 CHANGES In Version 1.1, this method was inherited from `InputStream`, which does nothing.

EXCEPTIONS

`IOException`

If an IO error occurred while closing this stream.

OVERRIDES `InputStream.close()`.

EXAMPLE See the `InputStream` class example in *The Java Class Libraries, Second Edition, Volume 1.*

Δ reset()

PURPOSE Resets the buffer to the previously marked position of the `byte` array.

SYNTAX `public synchronized void reset()`

DESCRIPTION This method resets the current read position of this stream to the previously marked position. If no mark has been set, it is set to the offset specified in the constructor (or to zero if no offset was specified). The ending index of the `byte` array to read (that calculated originally using `offset` and `count` arguments to the constructor) remains unchanged.

1.2 CHANGES In Version 1.1, the offset specified in the constructor was not used by `reset()`. If no mark has been set, `reset()` always resets to the beginning of the `byte` array (zero). For example, regardless of whether `offset` was `10` or zero, `reset()` always sets the current read position to zero.

OVERRIDES `InputStream.reset()`.

SEE ALSO `count`, `pos`, `mark`, `mark()`, `read()`, `skip()`.

EXAMPLE See the class example in *The Java Class Libraries, Second Edition, Volume 1*.

ByteArrayOutputStream

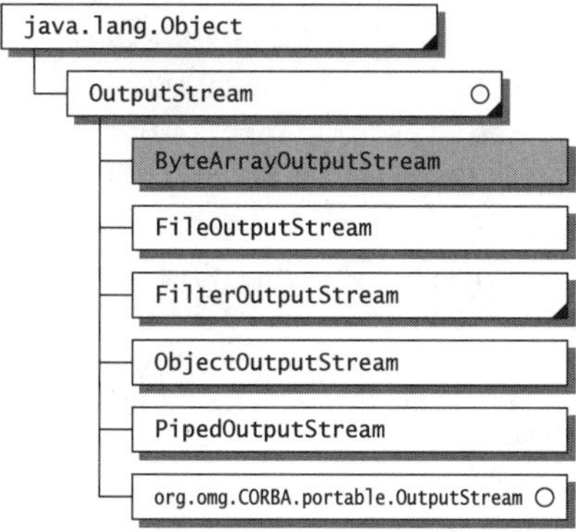

Syntax

```
public class ByteArrayOutputStream extends OutputStream
```

Description

The `ByteArrayOutputStream` class implements a `byte` array output stream. You can use a `byte` array output stream to treat a `byte` array as an output stream on which you can perform write operations. Requests to write bytes to the stream store the bytes into an automatically expandable `byte` array whose contents can later be retrieved as a `byte` array or as a string. This is helpful when you want to capture output from methods that operate on output streams in the form of a `byte` array.

See *The Java Class Libraries, Second Edition, Volume 1* for more information about this class.

Changes for Version 1.2

The `close()` method has been overridden to mark that the `ByteArrayOutputStream` has been closed.

MEMBER SUMMARY	
Constructor	
`ByteArrayOutputStream()`	Constructs a `ByteArrayOutputStream` instance.
Output Method	
`write()`	Writes bytes to this `ByteArrayOutputStream`.
	Continued

B

MEMBER SUMMARY	
Stream Methods	
Δ `close()`	Closes this `ByteArrayOutputStream`.
`reset()`	Resets this `ByteArrayOutputStream` so that it can be reused.
`size()`	Retrieves the number of bytes in this `ByteArrayOutputStream`.
Output Method	
`write()`	Writes bytes to this `ByteArrayOutputStream`.
Externalizing Methods	
`toByteArray()`	Retrieves the contents of this `ByteArrayOutputStream` as a `byte` array.
`toString()`	Retrieves the contents of this `ByteArrayOutputStream` as a string.
`writeTo()`	Writes the contents of this `ByteArrayOutputStream` to another `ByteArrayOutputStream`.
Protected Fields	
`buf`	The buffer in which data of this `ByteArrayOutputStream` is stored.
`count`	The number of bytes in this `ByteArrayOutputStream`.

See Also

`ByteArrayOutputStream` in *The Java Class Libraries, Second Edition, Volume 1.*

Δ close()

PURPOSE Closes this `ByteArrayOutputStream`.

SYNTAX `public synchronized void close() throws IOException`

DESCRIPTION This method closes this `ByteArrayOutputStream`. It sets an internal flag to indicate that the stream has been closed but otherwise does nothing.

1.2 CHANGES In Version 1.1, this method was inherited from `OutputStream`, which does nothing.

EXCEPTIONS

`IOException`

If an IO error occurred while closing this stream.

OVERRIDES `OutputStream.close()`.

EXAMPLE See the `OutputStream` class example in *The Java Class Libraries, Second Edition, Volume 1.*

Calendar

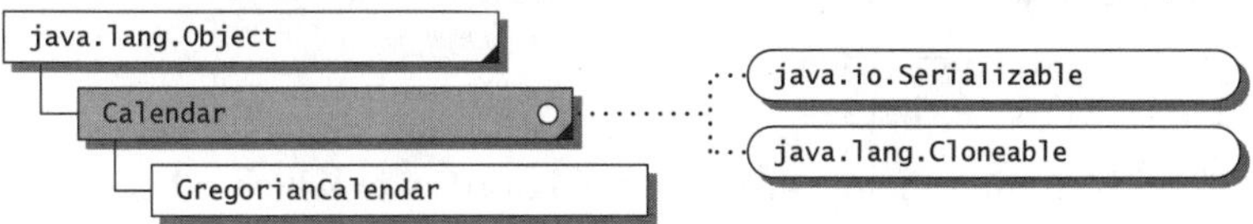

Syntax

```
public abstract class Calendar implements Serializable, Cloneable
```

Description

The `Calendar` class is designed to support different kinds of calendar systems. It provides functionality that is common to most calendar systems and makes that functionality available to subclasses. The subclasses of this class are used to calculate calendar-related information of a particular calendar system. For example, you could use `GregorianCalendar`, a subclass of this class, to determine the day of the week of December 25, 2000 in the Gregorian calendar system.

See *The Java Class Libraries, Second Edition, Volume 1* for more information about this class.

Changes for Version 1.2

Two methods are new to this class: `getActualMaximum()` and `getActualMinimum()`. Also new is an overloaded form of `roll()` and overrides for `equals()`, `hashCode()`, and `toString()`. See the method descriptions for information about these.

A new way is included for how a `Calendar` object handles the case in which not all of its fields have been set. In Version 1.1, there was a particular order in which fields were examined when you tried to get enough information to construct a date (see `Calendar.set()` in *The Java Class Libraries, Second Edition, Volume 1*). Previously, this method caused much confusion in that if you modified a field that was lower down on the list, you might not see any change, for example if you changed the `DAY_OF_YEAR` field and tried to recalculate the date. To see a change, you had to remember to first clear the month field before recalculating the date.

In Version 1.2, a time-stamp has been added to the fields. Now, when you change a field and construct a date from the new information, the `Calendar` object uses the most recently changed field. Here is an example of the effects of the change.

```
Calendar cal = new GregorianCalendar();
System.out.println( cal.getTime().toString() );

cal.set(Calendar.DAY_OF_YEAR, 180);
System.out.println( cal.getTime().toString() );
```

In Version 1.1, this program produced

```
Sun Jan 17 15:11:08 PST 1999
Sun Jan 17 15:11:08 PST 1999
```

In Version 1.2, it produces

```
Sun Jan 17 15:11:08 PST 1999
Tue Jun 29 15:11:08 PST 1999
```

For a couple of fields, setting them causes an ambiguity as to which other field to use in the date calculation. For example, if you set the `DAY_OF_WEEK` field, either the `WEEK_OF_MONTH` or `DAY_OF_WEEK_IN_MONTH` field could be used in the calculation. In such a case, the algorithm resorts to the order described in `Calendar.set()` in *The Java Class Libraries, Second Edition, Volume 1*. Therefore, if you set the `DAY_OF_WEEK` field, the algorithm uses `WEEK_OF_MONTH` to calculate the new date.

MEMBER SUMMARY	
Constructor	
`Calendar()`	Used by a subclass to construct a `Calendar` instance.
Creation Method	
`getInstance()`	Creates a `Calendar` instance.
Month Constants	
`APRIL`	Specifies April.
`AUGUST`	Specifies August.
`DECEMBER`	Specifies December.
`FEBRUARY`	Specifies February.
`JANUARY`	Specifies January.
`JULY`	Specifies July.
`JUNE`	Specifies June.
`MARCH`	Specifies March.
`MAY`	Specifies May.
`NOVEMBER`	Specifies November.
`OCTOBER`	Specifies October.
`SEPTEMBER`	Specifies September.
`UNDECIMBER`	Artificial name specifying the thirteenth month for lunar calendars.
Day-of-Week Constants	
`FRIDAY`	Specifies Friday.
`MONDAY`	Specifies Monday.
`SATURDAY`	Specifies Saturday.
`SUNDAY`	Specifies Sunday.
`THURSDAY`	Specifies Thursday.
`TUESDAY`	Specifies Tuesday.
`WEDNESDAY`	Specifies Wednesday.

C

MEMBER SUMMARY

Calendar Field Constants	
AM_PM	Specifies the A.M./P.M. field.
DATE	Specifies the date calendar field.
DAY_OF_MONTH	Specifies the day-of-month calendar field.
DAY_OF_WEEK	Specifies the day-of-week calendar field.
DAY_OF_WEEK_IN_MONTH	Specifies the day-of-week-in-month calendar field.
DAY_OF_YEAR	Specifies the day-of-year calendar field.
DST_OFFSET	Specifies the daylight-savings-time calendar field.
ERA	Specifies the era calendar field.
FIELD_COUNT	Specifies the number of calendar fields.
HOUR	Specifies the hour (12-hour clock) calendar field.
HOUR_OF_DAY	Specifies the hour-of-day (24-hour clock) calendar field.
MILLISECOND	Specifies the millisecond calendar field.
MINUTE	Specifies the minute calendar field.
MONTH	Specifies the month calendar field.
SECOND	Specifies the second calendar field.
WEEK_OF_MONTH	Specifies the week-of-month calendar field.
WEEK_OF_YEAR	Specifies the week-of-year calendar field.
YEAR	Specifies the year calendar field.
ZONE_OFFSET	Specifies the zone-offset calendar field.
Time Constants	
AM	Represents A.M. in a 12-hour clock.
PM	Represents P.M. in a 12-hour clock.
Comparison Methods	
Δ after()	Determines if the time of this Calendar is later than that of another object.
Δ before()	Determines if the time of this Calendar is before that of another object.
Calendar Field Methods	
add()	Increments/decrements a calendar field.
clear()	Clears the values of time fields.
get()	Retrieves the value of a calendar field.
getTime()	Computes this Calendar's Date value.
isSet()	Determines if a calendar field has been set.
Δ roll()	Rolls a calendar field.
set()	Sets the values for the year, month, date, hour, minute, and second fields.
setTime()	Sets this Calendar's current date and time.

Continued

C

MEMBER SUMMARY

Calendar Property Methods	
`getFirstDayOfWeek()`	Retrieves this `Calendar`'s first day-of-week.
`getMinimalDaysInFirstWeek()`	Retrieves the minimal number of days required in the first week of the year.
`isLenient()`	Determines if this `Calendar` is lenient.
`setFirstDayOfWeek()`	Sets this `Calendar`'s first day-of-week.
`setLenient()`	Sets the leniency property of this `Calendar`.
`setMinimalDaysInFirstWeek()`	Sets the minimal number of days required in the first week of the year.
Range Methods	
1.2 `getActualMaximum()`	Calculatets the maximum value of a field using the current date.
1.2 `getActualMinimum()`	Calculates the minimum value of a field using the current date.
`getGreatestMinimum()`	Retrieves the greatest minimum value for a calendar field.
`getLeastMaximum()`	Retrieves the least maximum value for a calendar field.
`getMaximum()`	Retrieves the maximum value for a calendar field.
`getMinimum()`	Retrieves the minimum value for a calendar field.
Locale Method	
`getAvailableLocales()`	Retrieves the set of locales in which the current date can be printed.
Time Zone Methods	
`getTimeZone()`	Retrieves this `Calendar`'s time zone.
`setTimeZone()`	Sets the time zone.
Protected Methods	
`complete()`	Computes either the `Date` value or the calendar fields.
`computeFields()`	Computes the values for the calendar fields from this `Calendar`'s `Date` value.
`computeTime()`	Converts the calendar fields into a `Date` value.
`getTimeInMillis()`	Computes this `Calendar`'s `Date` value and returns it as a `long`.
`internalGet()`	Retrieves the current value of a calendar field.
`setTimeInMillis()`	Sets this `Calendar`'s current `Date` value.
Protected Fields	
`areFieldsSet`	Indicates whether any fields have been cleared.
`fields`	Holds the calendar field values.
`isSet`	Holds the set state of each calendar field.
`isTimeSet`	Indicates if the time field is valid.
`time`	Holds this `Calendar`'s current date and time.

MEMBER SUMMARY	
Object Methods	
`clone()`	Creates a clone of this `Calendar`.
Δ `equals()`	Determines if this `Calendar` is equal to another object.
Δ `hashCode()`	Computes the hash code of this Calendar.
Δ `toString()`	Generates the string representation of this `Calendar`.

C

See Also

`GregorianCalendar`.
`Calendar` in *The Java Class Libraries, Second Edition, Volume 1.*

Δ after()

PURPOSE Determines if the time of this `Calendar` is later than that of another object.

SYNTAX `public boolean after(Object cal)`

DESCRIPTION This method determines if the time of this `Calendar` is later than the time of `cal`. It returns `true` if `cal` is an instance of this `Calendar` and `getTimeInMillis() > cal.getTimeInMillis()`. Note that the comparison is independent of the time zone.

As needed, this method recomputes the time fields of this `Calendar` and `cal` using their calendar fields before doing the comparison.

1.2 CHANGES This method was abstract in Version 1.1.

PARAMETERS

`cal` A possibly `null` object.

RETURNS `true` if this `Calendar`'s time is later than `cal`'s time.

EXCEPTIONS

`IllegalArgumentException`

If there is insufficient information to recompute the calendar fields of this `Calendar` and `cal`.

SEE ALSO `before()`.

EXAMPLE

```
Calendar cal1 = Calendar.getInstance();
Calendar cal2 = Calendar.getInstance(TimeZone.getTimeZone("GMT"));

// Make sure both calendars have identical times.
Date date = new Date();
cal1.setTime(date);
cal2.setTime(date);
```

```
// Demonstrates that calendar times are independent to the time zone.
System.out.println(cal1.after(cal2));         // false
System.out.println(cal2.after(cal1));         // false

cal2.set(1000, Calendar.JANUARY, 1);
System.out.println(cal1.after(cal2));         // true

cal2.set(3000, Calendar.JANUARY, 1);
System.out.println(cal1.after(cal2));         // false
```


Δ before()

PURPOSE Determines if the time of this `Calendar` is before that of another object.

SYNTAX `public boolean before(Object cal)`

DESCRIPTION This method determines if the time of this `Calendar` is before the time of `cal`. It returns `true` if `cal` is an instance of this `Calendar` and `getTimeInMillis() < cal.getTimeInMillis()`. Note that the comparison is independent of the time zone.

As needed, this method recomputes the time fields of this `Calendar` and `cal` using their calendar fields before doing the comparison.

1.2 CHANGES This method was abstract in Version 1.1.

PARAMETERS

`cal` A possibly `null` object.

RETURNS `true` if this `Calendar`'s time is earlier than `cal`'s time.

EXCEPTIONS

`IllegalArgumentException`
If there is insufficient information to recompute the calendar fields of this `Calendar` and `cal`.

SEE ALSO `after()`.

EXAMPLE

```
Calendar cal1 = Calendar.getInstance();
Calendar cal2 = Calendar.getInstance(TimeZone.getTimeZone("GMT"));

// Make sure both calendars have identical times.
Date date = new Date();
cal1.setTime(date);
cal2.setTime(date);

// Demonstrates that calendar times are independent to the time zone.
System.out.println(cal1.before(cal2));        // false
System.out.println(cal2.before(cal1));        // false

cal2.set(1000, Calendar.JANUARY, 1);
System.out.println(cal1.before(cal2));        // false
```

```
cal2.set(3000, Calendar.JANUARY, 1);
System.out.println(cal1.before(cal2));        // true
```

Δ equals()

PURPOSE Determines if this `Calendar` is equal to another object.

SYNTAX `boolean equals(Object obj)`

DESCRIPTION This method determines if this `Calendar` is equal to the object `obj`. It returns `true` if `obj` is a `Calendar` whose class is an instance of this class and its properties are identical. The properties that are compared are first day-of-week, minimum days-in-first-week, time zone, leniency, and actual date.

1.2 CHANGES This method was abstract in Version 1.1.

PARAMETERS

`obj` A possibly `null` object.

RETURNS `true` if `obj` is a `Calendar` and has properties that are identical to this `Calendar`; `false` otherwise.

OVERRIDES `java.lang.Object.equals()`.

EXAMPLE

```
Calendar cal1 = Calendar.getInstance();
Calendar cal2 = (GregorianCalendar)cal1.clone();

System.out.println(cal1.equals(null));                  // false
System.out.println(cal1.equals(cal2));                  // true

// Create one with a different time zone.
cal2 = Calendar.getInstance(TimeZone.getTimeZone("GMT"));
cal2.setTime(cal1.getTime());
System.out.println(cal1.equals(cal2));                  // false
```

1.2 getActualMaximum()

PURPOSE Calculates the maximum value of a field using the current date.

SYNTAX `public int getActualMaximum(int fld)`

DESCRIPTION This method calculates the maximum value of the field `fld` using the values of the current date. It differs from `getMaximum()`, which returns the maximum value of `fld` regardless of the current date. For example, if the current month is February, this method will return `28` and if the current month is January, this method will return `31`.

This method determines the return value by incrementally rolling the field (see `roll()`). Subclasses should implement a more efficient algorithm.

PARAMETERS

`fld` One of the valid calendar field constants.

RETURNS The maximum value of the field `fld` using the current date.

SEE ALSO `getActualMinimum()`, `getLeastMaximum()`, `getGreatestMinimum()`, `getMaximum()`, `getMinimum()`.

EXAMPLE

```
Calendar cal = Calendar.getInstance();
System.out.println( cal.getTime().toString() );
    // Sun Jan 10 23:05:23 PST 1999

System.out.println( cal.getActualMinimum(Calendar.DAY_OF_MONTH) );    // 1
System.out.println( cal.getActualMaximum(Calendar.DAY_OF_MONTH) );    // 31

cal.set(Calendar.MONTH, Calendar.FEBRUARY);
System.out.println( cal.getActualMinimum(Calendar.DAY_OF_MONTH) );    // 1
System.out.println( cal.getActualMaximum(Calendar.DAY_OF_MONTH) );    // 28
```

1.2 getActualMinimum()

PURPOSE Calculates the minimum value of a calendar field using the current date.

SYNTAX `public int getActualMinimum(int fld)`

DESCRIPTION This method calculates the minimum value of the field `fld` using the values of the current date. It differs from `getMinimum()`, which returns the minimum value of `fld` regardless of the current date. For the Gregorian calendar, this method always returns the same value as `getMinimum()` and `getGreatestMinimum()`.

This method determines the return value by incrementally rolling the field (see `roll()`). Subclasses should implement a more efficient algorithm.

PARAMETERS

`fld` One of the valid calendar field constants.

RETURNS The minimum value of the field `fld` using the current date.

SEE ALSO `getActualMaximum()`, `getLeastMaximum()`, `getGreatestMinimum()`, `getMaximum()`, `getMinimum()`.

EXAMPLE See `getActualMaximum()`.

Δ hashCode()

PURPOSE Computes the hash code of this `Calendar`.

SYNTAX `public int hashCode()`

DESCRIPTION This method computes the hash code of this `Calendar`. A calendar's hash code is calculated using its first day-of-week, minimum days-in-first-week, time zone, and leniency properties. Two equal `Calendars` will have the same hash code. However, unequal `Calendars` might also have the same hash code. The hash code is typically used as the key in a hash table.

Note: The hash code calculation does not include the date. This allows you to change the date of a `Calendar` while it is in a hash table. The downside to this "feature" is that the resulting hash code value is not very good, since most `Calendars` will be placed in the same hash table bucket.

1.2 CHANGES In Version 1.1, this method was inherited from `java.lang.Object`.

RETURNS This object's hash code.

OVERRIDES `java.lang.Object.hashCode()`.

SEE ALSO `equals()`, `getFirstDayOfWeek()`, `getMinimalDaysInFirstWeek()`, `Hashtable`.

EXAMPLE

```
GregorianCalendar cal = new GregorianCalendar();
System.out.println( cal.hashCode() );    // 584930835

// Hashcode is independent to date.
cal.set(1980, Calendar.JANUARY, 1);
System.out.println( cal.hashCode() );    // 584930835
```

Δ roll()

PURPOSE Rolls a calendar field.

SYNTAX `abstract public void roll(int fld, boolean up)`

SINCE 1.2 `public void roll(int fld, int amt)`

DESCRIPTION This method increments or decrements the calendar field `fld`. If `up` is `true`, the field is incremented by `1`. If `up` is `false`, the field is decremented by `1`. If `amt` is positive, the field is incremented by `amt`. If `amt` is negative, the field is decremented by `-amt`.

If `up` is `true` and `get(fld) == getMaximum(fld)`, the calendar field is set to `getMinimum(fld)`. If `up` is `false` and `get(fld) == getMinimum(fld)`, the calendar field is set to `getMaximum(fld)`. This process is called *rolling*.

Rolling the calendar field can also affect other calendar fields. For example, if the current date is January 31 and the `WEEK_OF_MONTH` field is `5`, rolling up the `DATE` field causes the `WEEK_OF_MONTH` field to be `1`.

The leniency of a `Calendar` has no effect on this method. `fld` cannot be either `DST_OFFSET` or `ZONE_OFFSET`.

1.2 CHANGES The overload with the `amt` parameter is new in Version 1.2.

PARAMETERS

`amt` A positive or negative increment to apply to the field `fld`.

`fld` One of the valid calendar field constants.

`up` If `true`, rolls the calendar field up by `1`; if `false`, rolls the calendar field down by `1`.

C

EXCEPTIONS

`IllegalArgumentException`

If `fld` is either `DST_OFFSET` or `ZONE_OFFSET`.

SEE ALSO `add()`.

EXAMPLE

```
Calendar cal = Calendar.getInstance();
DateFormat df = DateFormat.getInstance();

cal.set(1997, Calendar.JANUARY, 31);

System.out.println(df.format(cal.getTime()));      // 1/31/97 9:54 AM
cal.roll(Calendar.MONTH, false);
System.out.println(df.format(cal.getTime()));      // 12/31/97 9:54 AM
cal.roll(Calendar.DATE, true);
System.out.println(df.format(cal.getTime()));      // 12/1/97 9:54 AM

cal.set(1997, Calendar.JANUARY, 31);

System.out.println(df.format(cal.getTime()));      // 1/31/97 9:54 AM
cal.roll(Calendar.MONTH, -2);
System.out.println(df.format(cal.getTime()));      // 11/30/97 9:54 AM
cal.roll(Calendar.DATE, 2);
System.out.println(df.format(cal.getTime()));      // 11/2/97 9:54 AM

//cal.roll(Calendar.DST_OFFSET, true);             // IllegalArgumentEx
//cal.roll(Calendar.ZONE_OFFSET, true);            // IllegalArgumentEx
```

Δ toString()

PURPOSE Generates the string representation of this `Calendar`.

SYNTAX `public String toString()`

DESCRIPTION This method constructs a string representing all of the state of this `Calendar`. This includes the date, in the form of a `Date` value (see `Date`); the time zone; the leniency setting; first day-of-week; minimum days-in-first-week; and the values of all of the fields. This method is typically used for debugging purposes.

1.2 CHANGES In Version 1.1, this method was inherited from `java.lang.Object`.

RETURNS The non-`null` string representation of this `Calendar`.

OVERRIDES `java.lang.Object.toString().`

EXAMPLE

```
Calendar cal = Calendar.getInstance();
System.out.println( cal.toString() );
```

OUTPUT

```
java.util.GregorianCalendar[time=916620401553,areFieldsSet=true,areAllFieldsSe
t=true,lenient=true,zone=java.util.SimpleTimeZone[id=America/Los_Angeles,off-
set=-
28800000,dstSavings=3600000,useDaylight=true,startYear=0,startMode=3,startMont
h=3,startDay=1,startDayOfWeek=1,startTime=7200000,endMode=2,endMonth=9,end-
Day=-
1,endDayOfWeek=1,endTime=7200000],firstDayOfWeek=1,minimalDaysInFirstWeek=1,ER
A=1,YEAR=1999,MONTH=0,WEEK_OF_YEAR=4,WEEK_OF_MONTH=4,DAY_OF_MONTH=17,DAY_OF_YE
AR=17,DAY_OF_WEEK=1,DAY_OF_WEEK_IN_MONTH=3,AM_PM=1,HOUR=4,HOUR_OF_DAY=16,MINUT
E=46,SECOND=41,MILLISECOND=553,ZONE_OFFSET=-28800000,DST_OFFSET=0]
```

java.lang

Character

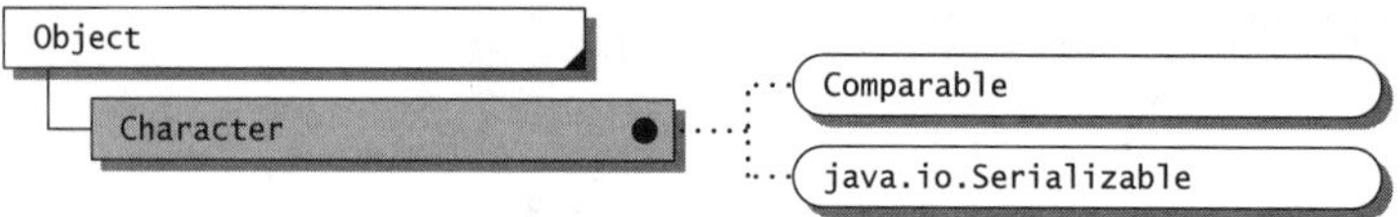

C

Syntax

`public final class Character extends Object implements Serializable, Comparable`

Description

The `Character` class provides an object wrapper for a `char` data value. A *`char` data value* in Java represents a Unicode character. Information about *The Unicode Standard, Version 2.0* is available at `http://www.unicode.org`. Detailed descriptions about characters are available from *The Java Language Specification, First Edition*, Section 20.5.

The `Character` class allows characters to be passed to methods in Java class libraries that accept Java objects as parameters. In addition, it provides methods that operate on characters, such as determining whether a character is uppercase or lowercase and converting a character to its numeric value.

See *The Java Class Libraries, Second Edition, Volume 1* for more information about this class.

Changes for Version 1.2

The `Character` class implements the `Comparable` interface and has two overloaded forms of the `compareTo()` method used for comparing and ordering `Character` objects. This allows arrays of `Character` objects to be sorted, as shown in this example.

```
Character[] ca = new Character[]{new Character('C'),
                 new Character('t'), new Character('a')};
Arrays.sort(ca);
for (int i = 0; i < ca.length; i++) {
    System.out.println(ca[i]);
}
// 'C', 'a', 't'
```

C

MEMBER SUMMARY	
Constructor	
`Character()`	Constructs a `Character` instance using a `char` value.
Digit Character Constants and Methods	
`digit()`	Retrieves the numeric value of a digit character in the specified radix.
`forDigit()`	Retrieves the `char` value (digit character) of a number in the specified radix.
`getNumericValue()`	Retrieves the Unicode numeric value of a character.
`isDigit()`	Determines if a character is a digit character.
`MAX_RADIX`	The maximum radix available for converting a digit character to or from a number.
`MIN_RADIX`	The minimum radix available for converting a digit character to or from a number.
Character Value Constants and Method	
`charValue()`	Retrieves the value of this `Character` as a `char`.
`MAX_VALUE`	The maximum value that a `char` can have.
`MIN_VALUE`	The minimum value that a `char` can have.
Comparison Methods	
1.2 `compareTo()`	Compares the `char` value of this `Character` with that of another `Character`.
`equals()`	Determines if this `Character` is equal to another `Character`.
`isDefined()`	Determines if a character is defined in Unicode.
`isJavaIdentifierStart()`	Determines if a character is a valid first character in a Java identifier.
`isJavaIdentifierPart()`	Determines if a character is a valid nonfirst character in a Java identifier.
`isIdentifierIgnorable()`	Determines if a character is ignorable in a Java or Unicode identifier.
`isISOControl()`	Determines if a character is an ISO control character.
`isLetter()`	Determines if a character is a letter.
`isLetterOrDigit()`	Determines if a character is a letter or a digit.
`isUnicodeIdentifierStart()`	Determines if a character is a valid first character in a Unicode identifier.
`isUnicodeIdentifierPart()`	Determines if a character is a valid nonfirst character in a Unicode identifier.
Space Methods	
`isSpaceChar()`	Determines if a character is a Unicode space character.
`isWhitespace`	Determines if a character is an ISO-LATIN-1 space character.

Continued

C

MEMBER SUMMARY	
Case Methods	
`isLowerCase()`	Determines if a character is lowercase.
`isTitleCase()`	Determines if a character is a titlecase character.
`isUpperCase()`	Determines if a character is uppercase.
`toLowerCase()`	Retrieves the lowercase form of a character.
`toTitleCase()`	Retrieves the titlecase form of a character.
`toUpperCase()`	Retrieves the uppercase form of a character.
Unicode Category Method	
`getType()`[a]	Retrieves the Unicode category of a character.
Object Methods and Constant	
`hashCode()`	Computes the hash code of this instance.
`toString()`	Generates the string representation of this `Character`.
`TYPE`	Represents the `Class` object for the primitive type `char`.
Deprecated Methods	
`isJavaLetter()`	Replaced by `isJavaIdentifierStart()`.
`isJavaLetterOrDigit()`	Replaced by `isJavaIdentifierPart()`.
`isSpace()`	Replaced by `isWhitespace()`.

a. The constants defined in the `Character` class returned by `getType()` are not listed in this Member Summary. They can be found in Table 7 in *The Java Class Libraries, Second Edition, Volume 1*.

See Also

`Character.Subset`, `Character.UnicodeBlock`, `Comparable`, `java.util.Arrays`.
`Character` in *The Java Class Libraries, Second Edition, Volume 1*.

1.2 compareTo()

PURPOSE Compares the `char` value of this `Character` with that of another `Character`.

SYNTAX
```
public int compareTo(Character achar)
public int compareTo(Object achar)
```

DESCRIPTION This method compares this `Character`'s Unicode value with that of `achar`. It returns an `int` indicating whether the two values are equal and, if they are not, the Unicode ordering of the two values. It returns `0` if the two values are the same. It returns a negative number if the Unicode value of this `Character` is less than the Unicode value of `achar`. It returns a positive number if the Unicode value of this `Character` is greater than the Unicode value of `achar`.

If `achar` is not an instance of `Character`, a `ClassCastException` is thrown.

PARAMETERS

achar — The non-null Character with which to compare.

RETURNS — 0 if the Unicode values of this Character and achar are the same; a negative number if this Character's value is less than that of achar; a positive number if this Character's Unicode value is greater than that of achar.

EXCEPTIONS

ClassCastException

If achar is not an instance of Character.

SEE ALSO — Comparable.

EXAMPLE

```
Character ch = new Character('B');

System.out.println(ch.compareTo(new Character('b')));      // negative
System.out.println(ch.compareTo(new Character('\u3521'))); // negative
System.out.println(ch.compareTo(new Character('B')));      // 0
System.out.println(ch.compareTo(new Character('A')));      // positive
System.out.println(ch.compareTo(new Byte((byte)64))); // ClassCastException
```

java.lang
Character.Subset

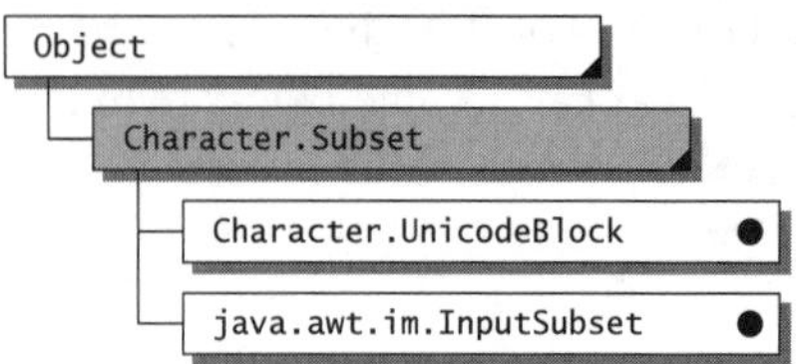

C

Syntax

`public static class Character.Subset`

Description

The `Character.Subset` class is used to represent a subset of a character set. For example, it is used by `Character.UnicodeBlock` to represent various subsets of the Unicode character set.

This class contains no new methods. It is simply a wrapper around a name (a `String`). It overrides the `Object.equals()` and `Object.hashCode()` to declare them `final` so that they cannot be overridden by subclasses.

Usage

This class is meant to be subclassed. You cannot create a `Character.Subset` directly. See the class example.

MEMBER SUMMARY	
Constructor	
`Character.Subset()`	Constructs a new `Character.Subset` instance.
Object Methods	
`equals()`	Determines whether an object is equal to this `Character.Subset`.
`hashCode()`	Computes the hash code for this object.
`toString()`	Returns the string representation of this `Character.Subset`.

See Also

`Character.UnicodeBlock.`

Example

This example creates a subclass of `Character.Subset` called `MaryJohnSubsets`. It contains a single method `of()` that returns the constant `MARY` if a character is one of the letters M, A, R, or Y and returns the constant `JOHN` if a character is one of the letters J, O, H, or N.

```
public class Main {
    static public class MaryJohnSubsets extends Character.Subset {
        private MaryJohnSubsets(String name) {
            super(name);
        }
        public static final MaryJohnSubsets MARY = new MaryJohnSubsets("MARY");
        public static final MaryJohnSubsets JOHN = new MaryJohnSubsets("JOHN");

        public static MaryJohnSubsets of(char c) {
            switch (c) {
            case 'M':
            case 'A':
            case 'R':
            case 'Y':
                return MARY;

            case 'J':
            case 'O':
            case 'H':
            case 'N':
                return JOHN;
            }
            return null;
        }
    }

    public static void main(String[] args) {
        System.out.println(MaryJohnSubsets.of('R'));    // MARY
        System.out.println(MaryJohnSubsets.of('O'));    // JOHN
    }
}
```

Character.Subset()

PURPOSE: Constructs a new `Character.Subset` instance.

SYNTAX: `protected Subset(String name)`

DESCRIPTION: This constructor constructs a new instance of `Character.Subset` with the name `name`.

PARAMETERS

`name`: A non-`null` string that is the name of the subset.

equals()

PURPOSE Determines whether an object is equal to this `Character.Subset`.

SYNTAX `public final boolean equals(Object obj)`

DESCRIPTION This method determines whether an object, `obj`, is equal to this `Character.Subset`. `obj` is equal to this `Character.Subset` if it has the same reference as this `Character.Subset` (that is, they are the same object). It is declared `final` so that subclasses cannot override it.

PARAMETERS

`obj` The possibly `null` object to compare.

RETURNS `true` if `obj` is this `Character.Subset`; `false` otherwise.

OVERRIDES `Object.equals()`.

SEE ALSO `hashCode()`.

EXAMPLE See the `Character.UnicodeBlock` class example.

hashCode()

PURPOSE Computes the hash code for this object.

SYNTAX `public final int hashCode()`

DESCRIPTION This method computes the hash code for this object. It simply returns `super.hashCode()` (that is, `Object.hashCode()`). It is declared `final` so that it cannot be overridden by subclasses.

RETURNS An `int` representing the hash code of this object.

OVERRIDES `Object.hashCode()`.

SEE ALSO `equals()`.

EXAMPLE See `Object.equals()`.

toString()

PURPOSE Returns the string representation of this `Character.Subset`.

SYNTAX `public final String toString()`

RETURNS A non-`null` string that is the name of this `Character.Subset`.

EXAMPLE See the class example.

Character.UnicodeBlock

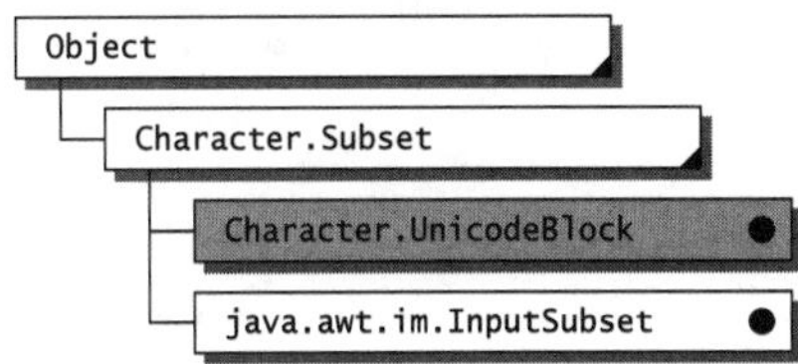

Syntax

```
public static final class Character.UnicodeBlock extends Character.Subset
```

Description

The `Character.UnicodeBlock` class defines constants representing character blocks defined by the Unicode 2.0 specification. It defines a single static method `of()` for determining to which block a character belongs. Table 2 contains a list of the names of the blocks defined by this class and the (inclusive) Unicode range they represent.

Unicode Block Name	Begin char	End char
BASIC_LATIN	\u0000	\u07F
LATIN_1_SUPPLEMENT	\u0080	\u0FF
LATIN_EXTENDED_A	\u0100	\u017F
LATIN_EXTENDED_B	\u0180	\u024F
IPA_EXTENSIONS	\u0250	\u02AF
SPACING_MODIFIER_LETTERS	\u02B0	\u02FF
COMBINING_DIACRITICAL_MARKS	\u0300	\u036F
GREEK	\u0370	\u03FF
CYRILLIC	\u0400	\u04FF
Not used	\u0500	\u052F
ARMENIAN	\u0530	\u058F
HEBREW	\u0590	\u05FF
ARABIC	\u0600	\u06FF
Not used	\u0700	\u08FF
DEVANAGARI	\u0900	\u097F
BENGALI	\u0980	\u09FF
GURMUKHI	\u0A00	\u0A7F
GUJARATI	\u0A80	\u0AFF

TABLE 2: `Character.UnicodeBlock` Constants.

Unicode Block Name	Begin char	End char
ORIYA	\u0B00	\u0B7F
TAMIL	\u0B80	\u0BFF
TELUGU	\u0C00	\u0C7F
KANNADA	\u0C80	\u0CFF
MALAYALAM	\u0D00	\u0D7F
Not used	\u0D80	\u0DFF
THAI	\u0E00	\u0E7F
LAO	\u0E80	\u0EFF
TIBETAN	\u0F00	\u0FBF
Not used	\u0FC0	\u109F
GEORGIAN	\u10A0	\u10FF
HANGUL_JAMO	\u1100	\u11FF
Not used	\u1200	\u1DFF
LATIN_EXTENDED_ADDITIONAL	\u1E00	\u1EFF
GREEK_EXTENDED	\u1F00	\u1FFF
GENERAL_PUNCTUATION	\u2000	\u206F
SUPERSCRIPTS_AND_SUBSCRIPTS	\u2070	\u209F
CURRENCY_SYMBOLS	\u20A0	\u20CF
COMBINING_MARKS_FOR_SYMBOLS	\u20D0	\u20FF
LETTERLIKE_SYMBOLS	\u2100	\u214F
NUMBER_FORMS	\u2150	\u218F
ARROWS	\u2190	\u21FF
MATHEMATICAL_OPERATORS	\u2200	\u22FF
MISCELLANEOUS_TECHNICAL	\u2300	\u23FF
CONTROL_PICTURES	\u2400	\u243F
OPTICAL_CHARACTER_RECOGNITION	\u2440	\u245F
ENCLOSED_ALPHANUMERICS	\u2460	\u24FF
BOX_DRAWING	\u2500	\u257F
BLOCK_ELEMENTS	\u2580	\u259F
GEOMETRIC_SHAPES	\u25A0	\u25FF
MISCELLANEOUS_SYMBOLS	\u2600	\u26FF
DINGBATS	\u2700	\u27BF
Not used	\u27C0	\u2FFF
CJK_SYMBOLS_AND_PUNCTUATION	\u3000	\u303F
HIRAGANA	\u3040	\u309F
KATAKANA	\u30A0	\u30FF
BOPOMOFO	\u3100	\u312F

TABLE 2: `Character.UnicodeBlock` Constants.

Unicode Block Name	Begin char	End char
HANGUL_COMPATIBILITY_JAMO	\u3130	\u318F
KANBUN	\u3190	\u31FF
ENCLOSED_CJK_LETTERS_AND_MONTHS	\u3200	\u32FF
CJK_COMPATIBILITY	\u3300	\u33FF
Not used	\u3400	\u4DFF
CJK_UNIFIED_IDEOGRAPHS	\u4E00	\u9FFF
Not used	\uA000	\uABFF
HANGUL_SYLLABLES	\uAC00	\uD7A3
Not used	\uD7A4	\uD7FF
SURROGATES_AREA	\uD800	\uDFFF
PRIVATE_USE_AREA	\uE000	\uF8FF
CJK_COMPATIBILITY_IDEOGRAPHS	\uF900	\uFAFF
ALPHABETIC_PRESENTATION_FORMS	\uFB00	\uFB4F
ARABIC_PRESENTATION_FORMS_A	\uFB50	\uFDFF
Not used	\uFE00	\uFE1F
COMBINING_HALF_MARKS	\uFE20	\uFE2F
CJK_COMPATIBILITY_FORMS	\uFE30	\uFE4F
SMALL_FORM_VARIANTS	\uFE50	\uFE6F
ARABIC_PRESENTATION_FORMS_B	\uFE70	\uFEFE
SPECIALS	\uFEFF	\uFEFF
HALFWIDTH_AND_FULLWIDTH_FORMS	\uFF00	\uFFEF
SPECIALS	\uFFF0	\uFFFF

TABLE 2: `Character.UnicodeBlock` Constants.

Usage

You use the static method `of()` to find out to which block a character belongs, as follows.

```
System.out.println(Character.UnicodeBlock.of('u597d'));
                                        // CJK_UNIFIED_IDEOGRAPHS
```

You can also check whether two characters are in the same Unicode block, as follows.

```
Character.UnicodeBlock.of('u597d').equals(
    Character.UnicodeBlock.of('u5929'));
```

MEMBER SUMMARY	
Subset Determination Method	
`of()`	Finds the Unicode block of a character.

See Also

`Character.Subset.`

of()

PURPOSE Finds the Unicode block of a character.

SYNTAX `public static UnicodeBlock of(char c)`

DESCRIPTION This method finds the Unicode block range that `char c` is in and returns the corresponding `Character.UnicodeBlock` constant for that block. If `c` does not belong to any Unicode block, it returns `null`.

PARAMETERS

`c` The character to check.

RETURNS The `Character.UnicodeBlock` instance representing the Unicode block to which `c` belongs or `null` if `c` is not a member of any Unicode block.

EXAMPLE See the usage section in the class description.

CharacterIterator

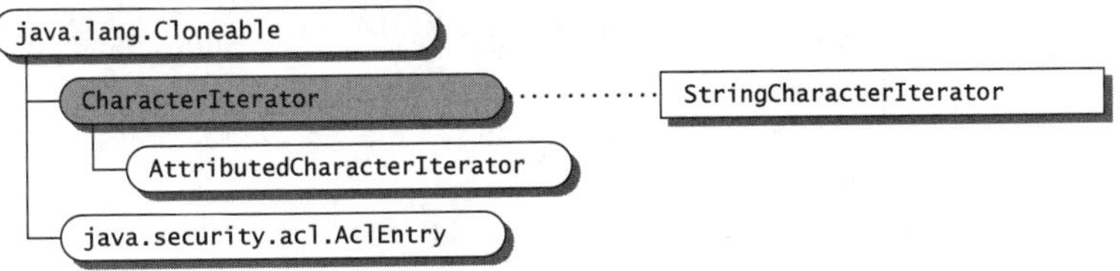

Syntax

```
public interface CharacterIterator extends Cloneable
```

Description

`CharacterIterator` is an interface that defines a protocol for iterating forward and backward over Unicode characters. A class should implement this interface if it wants to move about within a range of text and return individual Unicode characters or their index values.

See *The Java Class Libraries, Second Edition, Volume 1* for more information about this class.

Changes for Version 1.2

In Version 1.2, the semantics for `current()`, `first()`, `last()`, `next()`, `previous()`, and `setIndex()` are changed in order to fix one bug in Version 1.1. Now they accept the position returned by `getEndIndex()`. All of the changes in this class and `StringCharacterIterator` derive from this change.

For example, in the following diagram, the method `getEndIndex()` returns 8, whereas `last()` returns the last character, "!", which is at position 7. In Version 1.1, the iterator was allowed only to point to actual character positions. Thus there was nowhere for it to point if the iteration range was empty or if you tried to move the iterator to position 8; you would just get an exception. This meant that client code would have to special-case these conditions so that they never tried to create an iterator over an empty string or tried to move to the end of the substring. In Version 1.2, this is fixed by making the end index a legal position for the iterator and having `current()` return `DONE` when sitting there. Because these changes affect semantics, these bugs will never be fixed in the Version 1.1 series.

```
|T|h|e| |e|n|d|!|
0 1 2 3 4 5 6 7 8
|               |
          getEndIndex()
```

MEMBER SUMMARY	
Movement Methods	
Δ `first()`	Moves the index to the beginning of the text subrange, and retrieves the character at that index.
Δ `last()`	Moves the index to and retrieves the last character within the text subrange.
Δ `next()`	Increments the index by 1, and retrieves the character at the new index.
Δ `previous()`	Decrements the index by 1, and retrieves the character at the new index.
Δ `setIndex()`	Moves the index to a position, and retrieves the character at the new index.
Character and Index Getter Methods	
Δ `current()`	Retrieves the character at the current index.
`getIndex()`	Retrieves the current index.
`getBeginIndex()`	Retrieves the index at the beginning of the text subrange.
`getEndIndex()`	Retrieves the index at the end of the text subrange.
Constant	
`DONE`	Returned when this iterator tries to go beyond either end of text.
Object Method	
`clone()`	Creates a copy of this `CharacterIterator`.

See Also

`StringCharacterIterator`, `AttributedCharacterIterator`.
`CharacterIterator` in *The Java Class Libraries, Second Edition, Volume 1.*

Δ current()

PURPOSE Retrieves the character at the current index.

SYNTAX `public abstract char current()`

DESCRIPTION This method gets the character at the current index, or `StringCharacterIterator.DONE` if the text subrange is empty (that is, if `getBeginIndex()` and `getEndIndex()` return the same value). This is the same index returned by `getIndex()`. This method does not move the current index.

1.2 CHANGES In Version 1.1, if the text subrange was empty this method threw a `StringIndexOutOfBoundsException`. In Version 1.2, it returns `CharacterIterator.DONE` if the text subrange is empty.

RETURNS The character at the current index, or `StringCharacterIterator.DONE` if the text range is empty.

SEE ALSO `getIndex()`.

EXAMPLE See `StringCharacterIterator.next()`.

Δ first()

PURPOSE Moves the index to the beginning of the text subrange, and retrieves the character at the new index.

SYNTAX `public abstract char first()`

DESCRIPTION This method moves the index to the beginning of the text subrange and returns the character at the first position. This new index is the same as that returned by `getBeginIndex()`. If the text subrange is empty, this method does not move the iterator but just returns `CharacterIterator.DONE`. (The subrange is empty if `getBeginIndex()` and `getEndIndex()` return the same value.)

1.2 CHANGES In Version 1.1, if the text subrange was empty this method threw a `StringIndexOutOfBoundsException`. In Version 1.2, it returns `CharacterIterator.DONE` if the text subrange is empty.

RETURNS The first character in the text subrange, or `CharacterIterator.DONE` if the text subrange is empty.

SEE ALSO `getBeginIndex()`.

EXAMPLE See `StringCharacterIterator.next()`.

Δ last()

PURPOSE Moves the index to and retrieves the last character within the text subrange.

SYNTAX `public abstract char last()`

DESCRIPTION This method moves the index to the last character in the text subrange and retrieves that character. The resulting index is the same as that returned by `getEndIndex() - 1`, or `getEndIndex()` if the text subrange is empty. This is special-cased for the empty subrange so that `last()` does not move the current index *ahead of* the subrange. If the text subrange is empty, this method does not move the index but just returns `CharacterIterator.DONE`. (The subrange is empty if `getBeginIndex()` and `getEndIndex()` return the same value.)

1.2 CHANGES In Version 1.1, if the text subrange was empty this method set the index to `getEndIndex() - 1` and threw a `StringIndexOutOfBoundsException`. In Version 1.2, it returns `CharacterIterator.DONE` if the text subrange is empty.

RETURNS The last character in the text subrange, or `CharacterIterator.DONE` if the text subrange is empty.

SEE ALSO `getEndIndex()`.

EXAMPLE See `StringCharacterIterator.next()`.

Δ next()

PURPOSE Increments the index by 1, and retrieves the character at the new index.

C

SYNTAX `public abstract char next()`

DESCRIPTION This method increments the current index by 1 and returns the character at the new index. The current index is always pinned to the range from `getBeginIndex()` to `getEndIndex()`, inclusive. If the iterator attempts to increment past the end of the text subrange, the current index remains at that position and a value of `CharacterIterator.DONE` is returned. If the text subrange is empty, calling `next()` does not move the iterator but just returns `CharacterIterator.DONE`. (The subrange is empty if `getBeginIndex()` and `getEndIndex()` return the same value.)

1.2 CHANGES In Version 1.1, if the text subrange was empty this method threw a `StringIndexOutOfBoundsException`. In Version 1.2, it returns `StringCharacterIterator.DONE` if the text subrange is empty.

RETURNS The character at the new index, or `CharacterIterator.DONE`.

SEE ALSO `CharacterIterator.DONE`.

EXAMPLE See `StringCharacterIterator.next()`.

Δ previous()

PURPOSE Decrements the index by 1, and retrieves the character at the new index.

SYNTAX `public abstract char previous()`

DESCRIPTION This method decrements the current index by 1 and returns the character at the new index. The current index is always pinned to the range from `getBeginIndex()` to `getEndIndex()`, inclusive. If the iterator attempts to decrement past the beginning of its range, `getBeginIndex()`, the current index remains at that position and `CharacterIterator.DONE` is returned. If the text subrange is empty, calling `previous()` does not move the iterator but just returns `CharacterIterator.DONE`. (The subrange is empty if `getBeginIndex()` and `getEndIndex()` return the same value.)

1.2 CHANGES In Version 1.1, if the text subrange was empty this method threw a `StringIndexOutOfBoundsException`. In Version 1.2, it returns `StringCharacterIterator.DONE` if the text subrange is empty.

RETURNS The character at the new index, or `CharacterIterator.DONE`.

SEE ALSO `CharacterIterator.DONE`.

EXAMPLE See `StringCharacterIterator.next()`.

Δ setIndex()

C

PURPOSE Moves the index to a position, and retrieves the character at the new index.

SYNTAX `public abstract char setIndex(int idx)`

DESCRIPTION This method sets the current index to `idx` and returns the character at that new index. Currently, if a value outside of the subrange is passed in, this method throws an exception.

1.2 CHANGES In Version 1.1, the call `iterator.setIndex(iterator.getEndIndex())` threw an exception, which is considered a bug. If the text subrange was empty, `setIndex(iterator.getBeginIndex())` also threw an exception. In Version 1.2, both of these return `CharacterIterator.DONE`.

PARAMETERS

`idx` The position within the text. Valid values are in the range `getBeginIndex()` ≤ `idx` ≤ `getEndIndex()`.

RETURNS The character at the specified position, or `CharacterIterator.DONE` if the specified position is equal to `getEndIndex()`.

EXCEPTIONS

`IllegalArgumentException`
If `idx` is outside of its valid range.

EXAMPLE See `StringCharacterIterator.next()`.

java.io
CharArrayReader

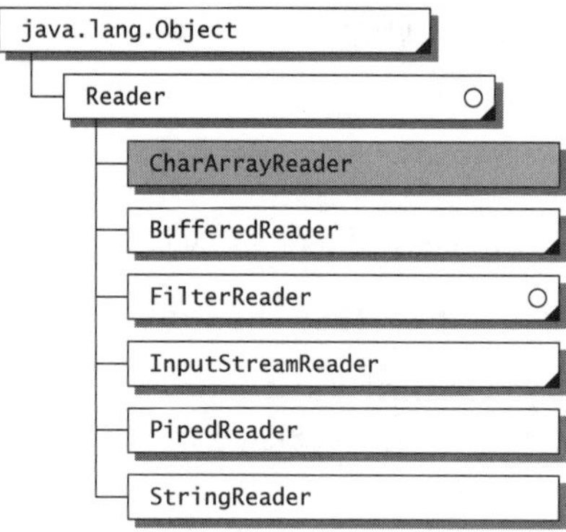

C

Syntax

```
public class ByteArrayInputStream extends InputStream
```

Description

The `CharArrayReader` class implements a `char` array input stream, or *`char` array reader.* You can use a `char` array reader to turn a `char` array into an input stream on which you can perform character-read operations. Requests to read from the `char` array reader retrieve characters from the original `char` array.

See *The Java Class Libraries, Second Edition, Volume 1* for more information about this class.

Changes for Version 1.2

The `reset()` method now treats the `char` array offset correctly.

MEMBER SUMMARY	
Constructor	
`CharArrayReader()`	Constructs a `CharArrayReader` instance using a `char` array.
Mark/Reset Methods	
`mark()`	Marks the current position in this `CharArrayReader`.
`markSupported()`	Determines whether this `CharArrayReader` supports rereading of its data.
Δ `reset()`	Resets the current read position of this `CharArrayReader` to the previously marked position.

MEMBER SUMMARY	
Input Methods	
`read()`	Reads one or more characters from this `CharArrayReader`.
`skip()`	Skips a specified number of characters in this `CharArrayReader`.
Stream Methods	
`close()`	Closes this `CharArrayReader`.
`ready()`	Determines whether this `CharArrayReader` is ready to be read without being blocked.
Protected Fields	
`buf`	The `char` array containing the characters to be read.
`count`	The ending index of the `char` array to be read.
`markedPos`	The position of the mark.
`pos`	The current read position in the `char` array.

C

See Also

`CharArrayReader` in *The Java Class Libraries, Second Edition, Volume 1.*

Δ reset()

PURPOSE Resets resets the current read position of this `CharArrayReader` to the previously marked position.

SYNTAX `public  void reset() throws IOException`

DESCRIPTION This method resets the current read position of this `CharArrayReader` to the previously marked position. If no mark was set, the current read position is set to the offset specified in the constructor (or to zero if no offset was specified). The ending index of this reader (the index calculated originally using the `offset` and `count` arguments to the constructor) remains unchanged.

1.2 CHANGES In Version 1.1, the offset specified in the constructor was not used by `reset()`. In Version 1.2, if no mark has been set, `reset()` always resets to the beginning of the `char` array (zero). For example, regardless of whether `offset` is `10` or zero, `reset()` always sets the current read position to zero.

OVERRIDES `Reader.reset()`.

SEE ALSO `count, pos, markedPos, mark(), read(), skip()`.

EXAMPLE See the class example in *The Java Class Libraries, Second Edition, Volume 1.*

java.text
ChoiceFormat

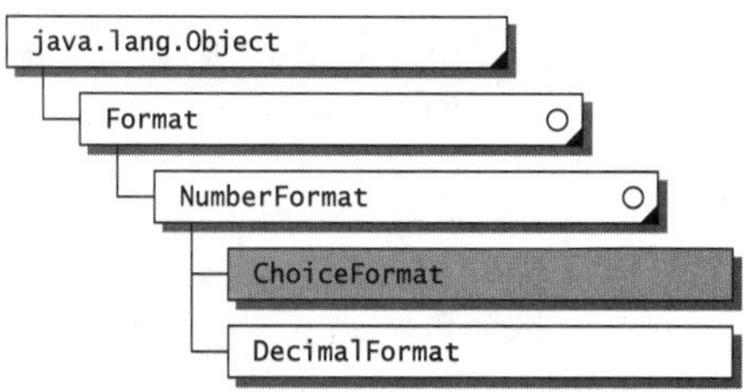

C

Syntax

```
public class ChoiceFormat extends NumberFormat
```

Description

A `ChoiceFormat` is like a switch statement for choosing strings, whereby a numeric value determines which string is chosen. A simple use of a `ChoiceFormat` is to choose the singular or plural form of a noun based on its quantity. First, you define contiguous and non-overlapping ranges along a number line, assign strings to those ranges, and turn those ranges into a pattern. Then, the `format()` method generates an output string from a number based on the range in which the number falls.

See *The Java Class Libraries, Second Edition, Volume 1* for more information about this class.

Changes for Version 1.2

The values you specify in a pattern for +Infinity and –Infinity are `\u221E` and `-\u221E`, respectively, which represent the Unicode characters displayed as ∞ and –∞. These values were valid in Version 1.1 but were undocumented. This added information modifies step 2c and adds step 2d in the following procedure. Plus, this modifies the one-line example patterns at the end of the procedure. Other than that, this procedure is identical to what it was in *The Java Class Libraries, Second Edition, Volume 1.*

Usage: Constructing a Pattern

Constructing a pattern requires three steps. Starting with the number line, you first break it up into ranges and define the strings you want for each range. Next, you encode each range using pattern symbols. Finally, you produce the pattern string.

1. **Determine the ranges.**
   Write down the ranges you want to use, using <= (less than or equal to) and < (less than), with the string results for each range. Make sure that the following holds.
   - There are *no* gaps or overlaps. That is, every number from –Infinity to +Infinity

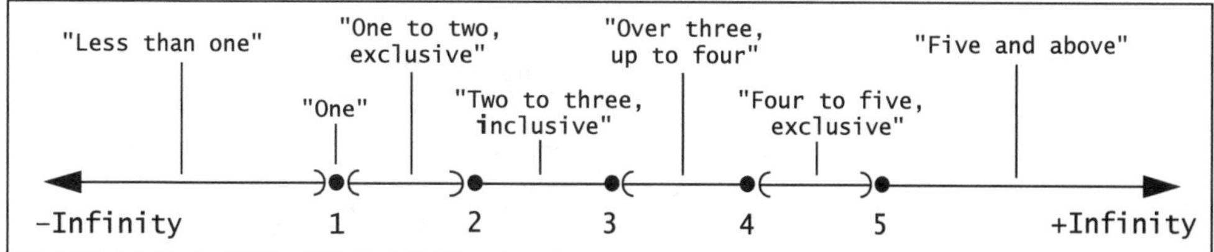

FIGURE 10: Example of Breaking Up a Number Line into Ranges.

belongs to *exactly* one range.

- The ranges are in ascending order.

Example: This example shows every combination of ranges using ≤ and <. See Figure 10 and Table 3. Note that if you want exactly one number, you use two ≤ signs, as shown in the second and last rows in Table 3.

Lower Limit	Lower Relation	String Result	Upper Relation	Upper Limit
`-Infinity`	≤	`"Less than one"`	<	`1.0`
`1.0`	≤	`"One"`	≤	`1.0`
`1.0`	<	`"One to two, exclusive"`	<	`2.0`
`2.0`	≤	`"Two to three, inclusive"`	≤	`3.0`
`3.0`	<	`"Over three, up to four"`	≤	`4.0`
`4.0`	<	`"Four to five, exclusive"`	<	`5.0`
`5.0`	≤	`"Five and above"`	≤	`+Infinity`

TABLE 3: Example of Ranges in a `ChoiceFormat` Pattern.

2. Encode each range using pattern symbols.

a. Drop the uppermost relation and upper limit.

b. For ≤, substitute either # or `\u2264` (the Unicode symbol for ≤).

c. In place of +Infinity, use `\u221E` (the Unicode symbol for ∞).

d. In place of –Infinity, use `-\u221E` (the Unicode symbol for –∞). You can optionally substitute any valid number in the first range. The number you choose will be the number returned by the `parse()` method for a string whose value matches this range.

Table 4 shows the results of these steps in reduced form, using –1.0 as the lower limit rather than –∞ (for the reason stated in step d).

Lower Limit	Lower Relation	String Result
-1.0	#	"Less than one"
1.0	#	"One"
1.0	<	"One to two, exclusive"
2.0	#	"Two to three, inclusive"
3.0	<	"Over three, up to four"
4.0	<	"Four to five, exclusive"
5.0	#	"Five and above"

TABLE 4: Reduction of Table 3 Using Pattern Symbols.

3. Compose the pattern string by appending each range, with strings separated from each other by a vertical bar "|".

Example:

```
pattern = "-1.0#Less than one"
        + "|1.0#One"
        + "|1.0<One to two, exclusive"
        + "|2.0#Two to three, inclusive"
        + "|3.0<Over three, up to four"
        + "|4.0<Four to five, exclusive"
        + "|5.0#Five and above";
```

For clarity, this example is shown broken up on separate lines.

If you want to do the reverse and figure out *exactly* what a complicated pattern means, just reverse this process to find the original ranges.

Note: You can always figure out what the missing upper elements in the range are as follows.

- The upper bound is always the same as the next lower bound.
- The upper relation is always the opposite of the next lower relation (for example, < and # or # and <).

Other examples of patterns follow. In each case, the text in the string (negative, zero, positive, and so on) indicates the range that the string covers.

```
"-\221E#Negative|0.0#Zero|0.0<Positive"
"-\221E#Non-Positive|0.0<Positive"
"-\221E#Negative|0.0#Non-Negative"
```

See Also

`ChoiceFormat` in *The Java Class Libraries, Second Edition, Volume 1.*

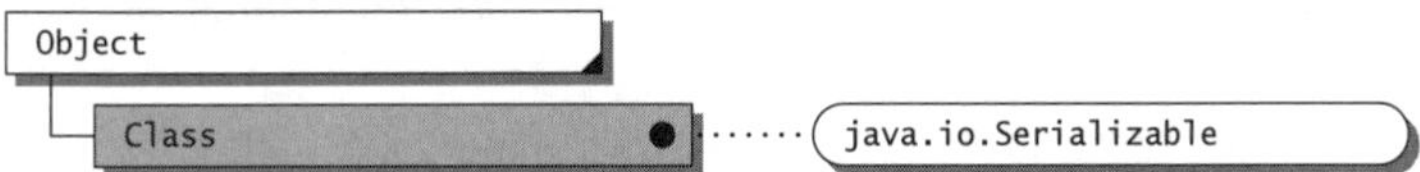

Syntax

```
public final class Class implements Serializable
```

Description

The `Class` class provides methods that return information about a class, as well as a method to generate new instances of the class. Every object in Java is an instance of a class. For each class, Java maintains an immutable `Class` object that contains information about the class. We say that the `Class` object *represents* or *reflects* the class. The `Class` object contains information that includes the class's string name, the superclass it extends, the interfaces it implements, and the class loader used to load this class.

The `Class` object is also used to give information about interfaces, although an interface does differ from a class. When talking about a `Class` object, we will often loosely speak of the "class" it reflects, with the understanding that the `Class` object may in fact reflect an interface, not a class.

See *The Java Class Libraries, Second Edition, Volume 1* for more information about this class.

Resource Names

A *resource* is a piece of data such as an image or audio file or an HTML file that is used by the program. Resources are typically packaged with a JAR file or stored with the class files that use them. The `Class` class contains the methods `getResource()` and `getResourceAsStream()` for retrieving a resource using a *resource name*. If a resource name does not have a leading forward slash character ("/"), the name used to locate the resource has the class's package name as the prefix, with all of the dot characters (".") replaced by forward slashes characters. For example, invoking `getResource("index.html")` on the class `p.C` requests the resource `"p/index.html"`. If a resource name has a leading forward slash character, the resource being requested is the resource with the name without the leading slash. For example, invoking `getResource("/index.html")` on the class `p.C` requests the resource `"index.html"`.

This algorithm of mapping a resource name to a resource is used by the `getResource()` and `getResourceAsStream()` methods, which are described in *The Java Class Libraries, Second Edition, Volume 1*. Note that it is not used by the resource-related method in `ClassLoader`.

C

Changes for Version 1.2

A new overloaded form of `forName()` allows you to specify the class loader to use when retrieving the `Class` object of a class. This is useful for library code that wants to load classes on behalf of another entity.

A new class, `Package`, represents a package. You can now ask a class for its package using the `getPackage()` method.

In the Version 1.2 security model, each class has associated with it a *protection domain* that specifies the *code source*—where the class was loaded from and who signed it—and the permissions granted to that code source. You can ask for a class's protection domain using the `getProtectionDomain()` method. See `SecurityManager` for an overview of the new security model.

In Version 1.1, `getClasses()`, `getDeclaredClasses()` and `getDeclaringClass()` were not implemented. In Version 1.2, they are implemented. See Addendum for their method descriptions.

MEMBER SUMMARY	
Class Retrieval Methods	
Δ `forName()`	Retrieves the `Class` object specified by the class's type descriptor.
Δ `getClasses()`	Retrieves an array of `Class` objects for all public class and interface members.[a]
Δ `getDeclaredClasses()`	Retrieves an array of `Class` objects for all class and interface members.[a]
`getSuperclass()`	Retrieves the superclass that this `Class` extends.
Instance Creation Method	
`newInstance()`	Constructs an instance of the class represented by this `Class` object.
Resource Methods	
`getResource()`	Finds a resource associated with the class represented by this `Class` object.
`getResourceAsStream()`	Finds and creates an input stream on a resource associated with the class represented by this `Class` object.
Object Type Query Methods	
`isArray()`	Determines if this `Class` object represents an array type.
`isAssignableFrom()`	Determines if the class represented by this `Class` object is a superclass of a class.
`isInstance()`	Determines if an object is an instance of the class represented by this `Class` object.
`isInterface()`	Determines if this `Class` object represents an interface.
`isPrimitive()`	Determines if this `Class` object represents a primitive Java type.

MEMBER SUMMARY	
Name and Package Methods	
getName()	Retrieves the type descriptor for this Class object.
1.2 getPackage()	Retrieves the Package object for this Class object.
Reflection Methods	
getComponentType()	Retrieves the component type of an array.
getConstructor()	Retrieves a Constructor object for a public constructor.
getConstructors()	Retrieves the Constructor objects for all public constructors.
getDeclaredConstructor()	Retrieves a Constructor object for a constructor.
getDeclaredConstructors()	Retrieves the Constructor objects for all constructors.
getDeclaredField()	Retrieves a Field object for a declared field.
getDeclaredFields()	Retrieves the Field objects for all declared fields.
getDeclaredMethod()	Retrieves a Method object for a declared method.
getDeclaredMethods()	Retrieves the Method objects for all declared methods.
Δ getDeclaringClass()	Retrieves the declaring class of this Class object.[a]
getField()	Retrieves a Field object for an accessible public field.
getFields()	Retrieves the Field objects for all accessible public fields.
getInterfaces()	Retrieves the interfaces being implemented by this Class.
getMethod()	Retrieves a Method object for an accessible public method.
getMethods()	Retrieves the Method objects for all accessible public methods.
getModifiers()	Retrieves the Java language modifiers for the class represented by this Class object.
Security Methods	
1.2 getProtectionDomain()	Retrieves the ProtectionDomain for this Class object.
getSigners()	Retrieves the signers of this Class.
Class Loader Method	
getClassLoader()	Retrieves the class loader for this Class.
Object Method	
toString()	Generates the string representation of this Class object.

a. See Addendum for method description.

See Also

ClassLoader.loadClass(), Package, SecurityManager.
Class in *The Java Class Libraries, Second Edition, Volume 1.*

C

C

Δ forName()

PURPOSE Retrieves the `Class` object specified by the class's type descriptor.

SYNTAX
```
public static Class forName(String className) throws
    ClassNotFoundException
```
SINCE 1.2
```
public static Class forName(String className, boolean init,
    ClassLoader loader) throws ClassNotFoundException
```

DESCRIPTION This method retrieves the `Class` object specified by the type descriptor in `className`. The syntax of `className` is that of the string returned by `getName()`. See the class description in *The Java Class Libraries, Second Edition, Volume 1* for details on the type descriptors of `Class` objects.

This method cannot be used to retrieve the `Class` objects for primitive types. See the class description in *The Java Class Libraries, Second Edition, Volume 1* for ways to do this.

The first form of this method retrieves the `Class` object for `className`. If the class has not been loaded yet, this form causes the class to be loaded using the class loader of the calling method and initialized.

The second form of this method retrieves the `Class` object for `className`. If the class has not been loaded yet, this form causes it to be loaded using `loader`. `init` should be set to `false` to load a class without initialization. The initialization causes performance problems for some applications, such as class introspection tools, that simply want to load a class and use reflection without creating an instance or otherwise accessing the class. The `init` parameter is for use by the Java virtual machine to optimize its class loading. It does not in any way affect how the loaded class can be used in the future. For example, if `init` was set to `false` when the class was loaded, then the first time the program requests that an instance of the class be created the Java virtual machine will automatically link and initialize it. If `loader` is `null`, the class loader of the calling method is used.

Because the second form of this method accepts an explicit `loader` parameter, you can use it instead of `loader`'s public `loadClass()` method. This overload of `forName()` is often a better choice because `loadClass()` does not handle array class names.

1.2 CHANGES The second form of this method is new in Version 1.2. In Version 1.1, `forName()` threw an `IllegalArgumentException` if `className`'s syntax was invalid. In Version 1.2, a `ClassNotFoundException` is thrown if `className`'s syntax is invalid.

In Version 1.2, the first form of `forName()` always performs class initialization before returning the class when the class is first loaded. In Version 1.1, whether initialization is performed was unspecified.

C

PARAMETERS

`className`	The non-`null` type descriptor of a `Class` object (for example, `"java.lang.String"`).
`init`	If `true`, link and initialize the class so that it is ready for creating new instances; if `false`, do not initialize.
`loader`	The possibly `null` class loader to use. If `null`, use the caller's class loader.

RETURNS The non-`null` `Class` object represented by `className`.

EXCEPTIONS

`ClassNotFoundException`
If the class cannot be found by the class loader.

`ExceptionInInitializerError`
If the static initialization of the class fails.

`LinkageError`
If the class cannot be linked due to an error.

`SecurityException`
If the caller does not have `RuntimePermission("getClassLoader")`.

SEE ALSO `ClassLoader.loadClass()`, `getName()`, `RuntimePermission("getClassLoader")`, `Thread.getContextClassLoader()`.

EXAMPLE See *The Java Class Libraries, Second Edition, Volume 1* for examples that use the first form of this method. See `getProtectionDomain()` and `Thread.getContextClassLoader()` for an example that uses the second form of this method.

1.2 getPackage()

PURPOSE Retrieves the `Package` object for this `Class` object.

SYNTAX `public Package getPackage()`

DESCRIPTION Each class loader maintains a list of packages of classes that it has loaded. This method uses this `Class`'s class loader (`getClassLoader()`) to get the class's `Package` object.

RETURNS The possibly `null` `Package` object of this `Class` object. If `null`, no package information was recorded by the class loader that loaded this class.

SEE ALSO `ClassLoader.getPackage()`, `ClassLoader.getPackages()`, `getClassLoader()`, `Package`.

EXAMPLE See `Main.java` in the `ClassLoader` class example.

C

1.2 getProtectionDomain()

PURPOSE Retrieves the `ProtectionDomain` of this class.

SYNTAX `public ProtectionDomain getProtectionDomain()`

DESCRIPTION This method retrieves the protection domain of this class. When a class is loaded, its class loader records the class's *protection domain*. The protection domain specifies the class's *code source* (the location from which it was loaded and the certificates used to sign its code) and the permissions granted to the code source by the Java runtime's security policy. This method returns the protection domain that was recorded for this class. If none was recorded, this method returns a protection domain consisting of a `null` code source (which means that the code is unsigned and its source is unknown) and all permissions.

The caller must have `RuntimePermission("getProtectionDomain")` to use this method; otherwise, a `SecurityException` is thrown.

RETURNS A non-`null` `ProtectionDomain` for this class.

EXCEPTIONS

`SecurityException`

If a security manager exists and it does not allow the caller to get the `ProtectionDomain`.

SEE ALSO `java.security.ProtectionDomain`, `RuntimePermission("getProtectionDomain")`.

EXAMPLE

```
try {
    Class c = Class.forName("ShowFiles", true,
        ClassLoader.getSystemClassLoader());

    ProtectionDomain pd = c.getProtectionDomain();
    System.out.println("code source: " + pd.getCodeSource());
    System.out.println("permissions: " + pd.getPermissions());
} catch (ClassNotFoundException e) {
    System.out.println(e);
}
```

OUTPUT

```
# java -Djava.security.policy=.policy -cp showfiles.jar\:. Main > o.txt
code source: (file:/tmp/lang/Class/getProtectionDomain/showfiles.jar [
[
  Version: V1
  Subject: CN=Duke, OU=JavaSoft, O=Sun, L=Cupertino, ST=CA, C=US
  Signature Algorithm: SHA1withDSA, OID = 1.2.840.10040.4.3

  Key:  Sun DSA Public Key
    Parameters:DSA
        p:     fd7f5381 1d751229 52df4a9c 2eece4e7 f611b752 3cef4400 c31e3f80
b6512669
```

```
    455d4022 51fb593d 8d58fabf c5f5ba30 f6cb9b55 6cd7813b 801d346f f26660b7
    6b9950a5 a49f9fe8 047b1022 c24fbba9 d7feb7c6 1bf83b57 e7c6a8a6 150f04fb
    83f6d3c5 1ec30235 54135a16 9132f675 f3ae2b61 d72aeff2 2203199d d14801c7
        q:     9760508f 15230bcc b292b982 a2eb840b f0581cf5
        g:     f7e1a085 d69b3dde cbbcab5c 36b857b9 7994afbb fa3aea82 f9574c0b
3d078267
    5159578e bad4594f e6710710 8180b449 167123e8 4c281613 b7cf0932 8cc8a6e1
    3c167a8b 547c8d28 e0a3ae1e 2bb3a675 916ea37f 0bfa2135 62f1fb62 7a01243b
    cca4f1be a8519089 a883dfe1 5ae59f06 928b665e 807b5525 64014c3b fecf492a

  y:
    e5ca7e17 db82e902 c62235fe 8c053101 6e59a7d8 997b06db 7feafed2 b39c96b9
    1e26019c 8c67597a a101e063 bd3a5435 3bdec61a eab09bef a2d6d46d ace66710
    967357a9 6fbfc158 5a214078 cb69cb39 83bb69c2 189651bd 48b343d3 e6d3cb22
    7497bc31 4f2cb08d 840ac659 01c05794 64947c5b 1df8a931 f28283e6 00850e6e

  Validity: [From: Fri Sep 04 12:10:13 GMT-07:00 1998,
               To: Tue Jan 20 11:10:13 GMT-08:00 2026]
  Issuer: CN=Duke, OU=JavaSoft, O=Sun, L=Cupertino, ST=CA, C=US
  SerialNumber: [    35f03b15 ]

]
  Algorithm: [SHA1withDSA]
  Signature:
0000: 30 2C 02 14 6F D1 AD 78   B3 80 C6 7E 65 BB 94 52  0,..o..x....e..R
0010: 9F F7 CC 37 B2 49 E3 89   02 14 35 53 73 FF 75 41  ...7.I....5Ss.uA
0020: D5 65 DA AF 63 74 41 A5   FF CB 73 4B ED 41        .e..ctA...sK.A

])
permissions: java.security.Permissions@60a7101c (
 (java.net.SocketPermission localhost:1024- listen,resolve)
 (java.util.PropertyPermission java.specification.name read)
 (java.util.PropertyPermission java.version read)
 (java.util.PropertyPermission java.specification.version read)
 (java.util.PropertyPermission java.vm.vendor read)
 (java.util.PropertyPermission java.vm.specification.version read)
 (java.util.PropertyPermission os.arch read)
 (java.util.PropertyPermission java.vendor.url read)
 (java.util.PropertyPermission line.separator read)
 (java.util.PropertyPermission os.name read)
 (java.util.PropertyPermission java.vendor read)
 (java.util.PropertyPermission java.vm.specification.vendor read)
 (java.util.PropertyPermission java.specification.vendor read)
 (java.util.PropertyPermission java.vm.name read)
 (java.util.PropertyPermission java.vm.specification.name read)
 (java.util.PropertyPermission java.class.version read)
 (java.util.PropertyPermission os.version read)
 (java.util.PropertyPermission java.vm.version read)
 (java.util.PropertyPermission path.separator read)
 (java.util.PropertyPermission file.separator read)
 (java.lang.RuntimePermission stopThread )
 (java.lang.RuntimePermission exitVM )
 (java.io.FilePermission /tmp/lang/Class/getProtectionDomain/showfiles.jar
read)
 (java.io.FilePermission /tmp/lang/Class/getProtectionDomain/- read)
)
```

ClassLoader

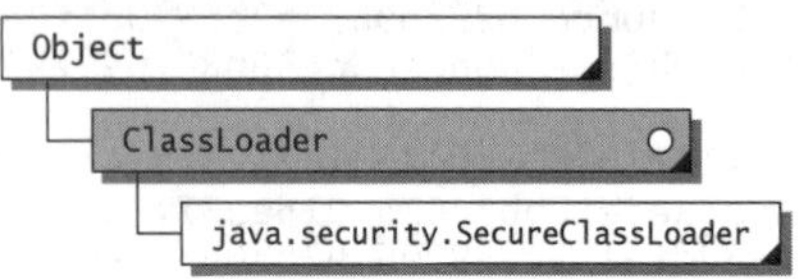

Syntax

```
public abstract class ClassLoader
```

Description

The `ClassLoader` class is used to define policies for loading Java classes into the runtime environment. Such policies include the format in which the classes are stored (for example, bytecode, ZIP, or compressed), the source for the classes (for example, a file system or a network), how to locate the classes within the source (for example, the directories to search, the JAR files to use, the machines to contact), and security conditions to apply when loading the classes.

See *The Java Class Libraries, Second Edition, Volume 1* for more information about this class.

Changes for Version 1.2

Subclass Implementations

In Version 1.1, to create a new class loader you had to subclass `ClassLoader`, provide the implementation for the abstract method `loadClass(String name, boolean resolve)`, and override `getResource()` and `getResourceAsStream()` as appropriate.

In Version 1.2, `loadClass(String name, boolean resolve)` is no longer abstract. Instead, it implements a delegation algorithm in which it always consults its parent class loader before attempting to load the class itself. The parent in turn consults its parent and so on. So it is only when *all* of the ancestor class loaders cannot find the class that the current class loader gets involved. The subclass provides an implementation for `findClass(String name)` to load classes for the class loader. It also should provide implementations for `findResource()`, `findResources()`, and `findLibrary()`, if appropriate. This same delegation algorithm is employed for loading resources. A class loader that needs to deal with protection domains and permissions should subclass from `SecureClassLoader` instead of `ClassLoader`.

Default System Class Loader

In Version 1.1, *system* classes and resources referred to all of those classes and resources accessible from the classpath specified for the application, including the classes and resources that comprise the Java runtime. The *system class loader* was responsible for loading system classes and system resources. If you asked for the class loader of a class using `Class.getClassLoader()`, an answer of `null` meant that the class was loaded by the system class loader.

In Version 1.2, this same notion of "system" still applies, but there is now a finer-grain distinction among system classes and resources. Specifically, classes and resources that comprise the Java runtime are referred to as *bootstrap* classes/resources and are loaded by the *bootstrap class loader*. If you ask for the class loader of a class using `Class.getClassLoader()`, an answer of `null` means that the class was loaded by the bootstrap class loader. Application classes and resources found in the classpath of the application are called *application* classes/resources and are loaded by the *application class loader*, also called the *system class loader*. If you ask for the class loader of an application class using `Class.getClassLoader()`, the system class loader is returned. The parent of the system class loader is the bootstrap class loader. Therefore the bootstrap class loader is always asked to load the class before the system class loader is asked to load the class.

Specifying the Classpath

Some commands in the Java 2 SDK, Version 1.2 (formerly JDK 1.2) allow you to set the classpath via the `-cp` and `-classpath` options. These have been changed as follows.

- `-cp` and `-classpath` set the application classpath (not the bootstrap classes). In Version 1.1, this used to set the classpath for *both* application classes and bootstrap classes. In Version 1.2, `-Xbootclasspath` sets the bootstrap class loader's classpath.
- The system property `java.boot.class.path` contains the classpath used by the bootstrap class loader, while the system property `java.class.path` is the application classpath.

Final Methods

The `getSystemResource()` and `getSystemResourceAsStream()` methods are no longer final.

	MEMBER SUMMARY	
	Constructor	
Δ	`ClassLoader()`	Constructs a `ClassLoader` instance.
	Methods for Getting Class Loaders	
1.2	`getParent()`	Retrieves the parent class loader of this `ClassLoader`.
1.2	`getSystemClassLoader()`	Retrieves the system class loader.
	Methods Provided by Subclass	
1.2	`findClass()`	Loads a class using this `ClassLoader`.
1.2	`findLibrary()`	Returns the absolute pathname of a native library.
1.2	`findResource()`	Retrieves a resource using this `ClassLoader`.
1.2	`findResources()`	Retrieves all resources with a given name accessible by this `ClassLoader`.

Continued

MEMBER SUMMARY		
	Methods for Loading Classes/Resources	
Δ	`getResource()`	Retrieves a resource using this `ClassLoader` or its ancestors.
Δ	`getResourceAsStream()`	Retrieves a resource as a stream using this `ClassLoader` or its ancestors.
1.2	`getResources()`	Retrieves all resources with a given name accessible by this `ClassLoader` or its ancestors.
	`getSystemResource()`	Retrieves a resource using the system class loader or its ancestors.
	`getSystemResourceAsStream()`	Retrieves a resource as a stream using the system class loader or its ancestors.
1.2	`getSystemResources()`	Retrieves all resources with a given name accessible by the system class loader or its ancestors.
Δ	`loadClass()`	Loads a class using the policy defined by this `ClassLoader` and its ancestors.
	Methods for Implementing `findClass()`	
Δ	`defineClass()`	Generates a `Class` object using an array of bytecodes.
1.2	`definePackage()`	Generates a `Package` object using information about the package.
1.2	`getPackage()`	Retrieves a package defined by this `ClassLoader` or its ancestors.
	`setSigners()`	Records the signers for a class.
	Miscellaneous Methods	
	`resolveClass()`	Links a class so that it can be executed.
	`findLoadedClass()`	Finds a class previously loaded by this `ClassLoader`.
Δ	`findSystemClass()`	Loads a class using the system class loader.
1.2	`getPackages()`	Retrieves all packages defined by this `ClassLoader` and its ancestors.

See Also

`Class`, `Package`, `RuntimePermission("createClassLoader")`, `RuntimePermission("getClassLoader")`, `RuntimePermission("setContextClassLoader")`, `System.loadLibrary()`, `System.mapLibraryName()`, `Thread.getContextClassLoader()`, `Thread.setContextClassLoader()`.

`ClassLoader` in *The Java Class Libraries, Second Edition, Volume 1.*

C

Example

This example implements a class loader that loads bytecodes from files in a directory. Note that no subdirectories are allowed within the directory. If a class is from a package, the package name is stripped from the class's name before the name is used to construct the name of the class file from which the bytecodes will be read.

FlatClassLoader.java

```
import java.io.*;
import java.net.*;
import java.util.Enumeration;
import java.util.NoSuchElementException;

// Class loader for loading bytes codes from a file.
public class FlatClassLoader extends ClassLoader {
    String path;

    public FlatClassLoader(String path) {
        this.path = path;
    }

    // Loads the bytes from file
    byte[] getBytecodes(String classname) throws ClassNotFoundException {
        // To get file name, remove the package name, if any.
        String filename;
        if (classname.indexOf(".") >= 0) {
            filename = classname.substring(classname.lastIndexOf(".")+1);
        } else {
            filename = classname;
        }
        // Make sure the filename ends with .class
        filename += ".class";

        File fullname = new File(path, filename);
        System.out.println("class file name: " + fullname);
        try {
            // Read in the byte codes.
            InputStream is = new FileInputStream(fullname);
            int bufsize = (int)fullname.length();
            byte buf[] = new byte[bufsize];
            is.read(buf, 0, bufsize);
            is.close();

            return buf;
        } catch (Exception e) {
            throw new ClassNotFoundException(classname);
        }
    }

    protected synchronized Class findClass(String className)
        throws ClassNotFoundException {
            byte[] buf = getBytecodes(className);

            // Check if package needs to be defined
            if (className.indexOf('.') != -1) {
               String pkg = className.substring(0, className.lastIndexOf('.'));
                if (getPackage(pkg) == null) {
                  definePackage(pkg, null, null, null, null, null, null, null);
                }
```

```
            }

            return defineClass(className, buf, 0, buf.length);
        }

    // Returns a URL containing the location of the named resource.
    protected URL findResource(String name) {
        try {
            File file = new File(path, name);
            String absPath =
                file.getAbsolutePath().replace(file.separatorChar, '/');

            // If leading character is not '/', add for URL.
            if (absPath.charAt(0) != '/') {
                absPath = '/' + absPath;
            }

            System.out.println("resource name: " + absPath);
            return new URL("file:" + absPath);
        } catch (MalformedURLException e) {
            e.printStackTrace();
        }
        return null;
    }

    // Returns an enumeration containing URLs of the named resource.
    protected Enumeration findResources(String name) throws IOException {
        // We only look in one place;
        return new SingleEnum(findResource(name));
    }

    private static class SingleEnum implements Enumeration {
        Object element;
        SingleEnum(Object element) {
            this.element = element;
        }
        public boolean hasMoreElements() {
            return element == null;
        }

        public Object nextElement() {
            if (element == null) {
                throw new NoSuchElementException();
            } else {
                Object answer = element;
                element = null;
                return answer;
            }
        }
    }
}
```

Main.java

```
import java.net.*;
import java.io.*;

class Main {
    public static void main(String[] args) {
        if (args.length != 3) {
```

```
            System.err.println(
                "usage: java Main <dir> <classname> <resource>");
            System.exit(-1);
        }

        try {
            ClassLoader cl = new FlatClassLoader(args[0]);

            // See who cl's parent is
            System.out.println("Parent: " + cl.getParent());

            // Load a class
            Class c = cl.loadClass(args[1]);

            System.out.println("Class: " + c);
            System.out.println("Package: " + c.getPackage());
            System.out.println("Resource: " + cl.getResource(args[2]));
            System.out.println("Resource Stream: " +
                cl.getResourceAsStream(args[2]));

        } catch (ClassNotFoundException e) {
            e.printStackTrace();
        }
    }
}
```

Output

```
# java Main /tmp/testdir p.C manifest.mf
Parent: sun.misc.Launcher$AppClassLoader@ce49dba9
class file name: /tmp/testdir/C.class
Class: class p.C
Package: package p
resource name: /tmp/testdir/manifest.mf
Resource: file:/tmp/testdir/manifest.mf
resource name: /tmp/testdir/manifest.mf
Resource Stream: java.io.BufferedInputStream@2781dba8
```

Δ ClassLoader()

PURPOSE Constructs a `ClassLoader` instance.

SYNTAX
`protected ClassLoader()`
SINCE 1.2 `protected ClassLoader(ClassLoader parent)`

DESCRIPTION The first form of this constructor creates a `ClassLoader` instance whose parent is the system class loader (`getSystemClassLoader()`). The second form creates a `ClassLoader` instance whose parent is `parent`. This new `ClassLoader` instance always consults its parent to see if the parent can load a class/resource before attempting the task itself. A `parent` that is `null` means the parent is the bootstrap class loader.

The constructor(s) of a subclass of `ClassLoader` will invoke one of these two constructors. When a security manager has been installed, a class loader can be created only if the caller has been granted `RuntimePermission("create-`

ClassLoader") by the Java runtime's security policy. Otherwise, a SecurityException is thrown.

1.2 CHANGES The second form of this construct is new in Version 1.2. In Version 1.1, there was no notion of "parent" class loader. This concept is new in Version 1.2.

PARAMETERS

parent A possibly null class loader to use as this class loader's parent. If null, use the bootstrap class loader as the parent.

C

EXCEPTIONS

SecurityException
If the Java runtime's security policy does not allow the caller to create a class loader.

SEE ALSO getSystemClassLoader(), RuntimePermission("createClassLoader"), SecurityManager.checkCreateClassLoader().

EXAMPLE See the FlatClassLoader in the class example.

Δ defineClass()

PURPOSE Generates a Class object using an array of bytecodes.

SYNTAX
```
protected final Class defineClass(String className, byte[]
   bytecode, int offset, int length) throws ClassFormatError
```
SINCE 1.2
```
protected final Class defineClass(String className, byte[]
   bytecode, int offset, int length, ProtectionDomain pDomain)
   throws ClassFormatError
```
DEPRECATED
```
protected final Class defineClass(byte[] bytecode, int offset, int
   length) throws ClassFormatError
```

DESCRIPTION The Java compiler compiles Java programs into a machine-independent representation called *bytecodes* to be used by the Java interpreter and runtime system. defineClass() converts bytecodes into a Class object and places that object into a cache so that the class can be retrieved using findLoadedClass().

When a new ClassLoader is defined, the implementation of findClass() should use definePackage() to add the class's package to the list of known packages and then use defineClass() to turn the bytecodes that it loads into a Class object.

The protection domain of a class consists of its code source—the location from which it was loaded and the certificates used to sign it—and the permissions granted to that code source. If no protection domain is specified for a class, the default protection domain is used. The default protection domain is for unsigned code whose origin is unknown.

1.2 CHANGES The form of `defineClass()` that accepts a `ProtectionDomain` parameter has is new in Version 1.2.

DEPRECATION The form of this method that does not accept a class name has been deprecated. Use the first form instead, which allows the Java runtime system to verify that the bytecodes being defined indeed represent the class identified by `className`. If the class name is not known, supply `null` as the name. For example, instead of using

```
Class c = defineClass(buf, 0, buf.length);
```

use

```
Class c = defineClass(className, buf, 0, buf.length);
```

or

```
Class c = defineClass(null, buf, 0, buf.length);
```

PARAMETERS

`bytecode` A non-`null` array of bytes containing the bytecodes for the class.

`className` The possibly `null` name of the class being defined. This is the fully qualified class name (for example, "`java.lang.String`").

`offset` The start position in `bytecode` of the class's bytecodes. `0` ≤ `offset` < `bytecodes.length`.

`length` The number of bytes occupied by the class's bytecodes. `0` ≤ `length` ≤ `bytecodes.length-offset`.

`pDomain` A possibly `null` protection domain of the class. If `null`, use the default protection domain.

RETURNS A non-`null` `Class` object generated by using given bytecodes.

EXCEPTIONS

`ClassFormatError`
If the bytes in `bytecode` are not in the correct format.

SEE ALSO `definePackage()`, `java.security.CodeSource`, `java.security.ProtectionDomain`.

EXAMPLE See `FlatClassLoader` in the class example.

1.2 definePackage()

PURPOSE Generates a `Package` object using information about the package.

SYNTAX

```
protected Package definePackage(String pkgName, String
    specTitle, String specVers, String specVendor, String
    implTitle, String implVers, String implVendor, URL sealBase)
    throws IllegalArgumentException
```

DESCRIPTION This method generates a `Package` object using information about the package and adds it to the list of packages known by this `ClassLoader`. It should be called before classes in the package named pkgName are defined (by defineClass()). A package must be defined only once (by this class loader and its ancestors); otherwise, an IllegalArgumentException is thrown. You can use getPackage() to find out whether a package has been defined.

PARAMETERS

implTitle	A possibly null string specifying the package's implementation title. If null, the package does not have an implementation title.
implVendor	A possibly null string specifying the package's implementation vendor. If null, the package does not have an implementation vendor.
implVers	A possibly null string specifying the package's implementation version. If null, the package does not have an implementation version.
pkgName	A non-null string containing the package's name.
sealBase	A possibly null URL specifying the codebase with which the package has been sealed. If null, the package is not sealed.
specTitle	A possibly null string specifying the package's specification title. If null, the package does not have a specification title.
specVendor	A possibly null string specifying the package's specification vendor. If null, the package does not have a specification vendor.
specVers	A possibly null string specifying the package's specification version. If null, the package does not have a specification version.

RETURNS A non-null Package for pkgName.

EXCEPTIONS

IllegalArgumentException

If a package by the same name has already been defined by this class loader or one of its ancestors.

SEE ALSO defineClass(), getPackage(), Package.

EXAMPLE See the FlatClassLoader in the class example.

1.2 findClass()

PURPOSE Loads a class using this ClassLoader.

SYNTAX

```
protected Class findClass(String className) throws
    ClassNotFoundException
```

DESCRIPTION This method is used by loadClass() to find and load the class file for the class named className using the policy local to this ClassLoader. loadClass() invokes this method if it cannot load the class from this class loader's ancestors.

This method's default implementation throws a `ClassNotFoundException`. It should be overridden to first get the bytecodes (using this class loader's own policy) and then call `defineClass()` to turn the bytecodes into a `Class` object. This method should also invoke `definePackage()` when it encounters a package that it has never loaded before. It should check whether the package has been previously defined by this class loader or its ancestors by using `getPackage()`.

PARAMETERS

`className` A non-`null` string containing the fully qualified name of the class (for example, "`java.lang.String`").

RETURNS The non-`null` `Class` object representing the class that has been loaded.

EXCEPTIONS

`ClassNotFoundException`

If the class could not be found.

SEE ALSO `findResource()`, `findResources()`, `loadClass()`.

EXAMPLE See `FlatClassLoader` in the class example.

1.2 findLibrary()

PURPOSE Returns the absolute pathname of a native library.

SYNTAX `protected String findLibrary(String libname)`

DESCRIPTION When the classes loaded using this class loader invoke `System.loadLibrary()` or `Runtime.loadLibrary()` to load the native library with the name `libname`, the Java virtual machine uses this method to obtain `libname`'s absolute pathname. If a nonabsolute pathname is returned, an `UnsatisfiedLinkError` is thrown. If this method returns `null`, the Java virtual machine will search for the library in the search path specified by the system properties `sun.boot.library.path` and `java.library.path`. Each of these properties contains a list of directories to search; each item on the list is separated using `File.pathSeparator`. The Java virtual machine first maps `libname` to a platform-specific string representing a native library by using `System.mapLibraryName()` and then tries to load a library with that name from the directories specified in the two system properties.

The default implementation of this method returns `null`.

PARAMETERS

`libname` A non-`null` string containing the native library's name.

RETURNS The possibly `null` absolute path of the native library.

SEE ALSO `Runtime.loadLibrary()`, `System.loadLibrary()`, `System.mapLibraryName()`.

1.2 findResource()

PURPOSE Retrieves a resource using this `ClassLoader`.

SYNTAX `protected URL findResource(String name)`

C

DESCRIPTION This method is used by `getResource()` to find and retrieve the first resource with the name `resName` using the same (local) policy that this `ClassLoader` uses for loading classes. `getResource()` invokes this method if it cannot find the resource from this `ClassLoader`'s ancestors.

This method's default implementation returns `null`. It should be overridden to implement the policy that this `ClassLoader` uses for finding resources.

PARAMETERS

`resName` A non-null forward slash character ("/")-separated pathname that identifies the resource (for example, `"app/index.html"`).

RETURNS A possibly `null URL` of the resource. It is `null` if no such resource is found or the caller does not have permission to access the resource.

SEE ALSO `findResources()`, `getResource()`, `getResourceAsStream()`.

EXAMPLE See `FlatClassLoader` in the class example.

1.2 findResources()

PURPOSE Retrieves all resources with a given name accessible by this `ClassLoader`.

SYNTAX

```
protected Enumeration findResources(String resName) throws
    IOException
```

DESCRIPTION This method is used by `getResources()` to find and retrieve all resources with the name `resName` using the same (local) policy that this `ClassLoader` uses for loading classes. `getResources()` invokes this method and merges its results with those obtained by consulting this `ClassLoader`'s ancestors to get all resources with the name `resName` from the ancestors.

This method's default implementation returns an empty enumeration. It should be overridden to implement the policy that this `ClassLoader` uses for finding resources.

PARAMETERS

`resName` A non-`null` forward slash character ("/")-separated pathname that identifies the resource (for example, `"app/index.html"`).

RETURNS A non-`null` enumeration of `URL` instances.

EXCEPTIONS

`IOException`

If an `IO` error occurred while getting the resources.

SEE ALSO `findResource()`, `getResources()`.

EXAMPLE See `FlatClassLoader` in the class example.

Δ findSystemClass()

PURPOSE Loads a class using the system class loader.

SYNTAX

```
protected final Class findSystemClass(String className) throws
   ClassNotFoundException
```

DESCRIPTION This method loads a class using the system class loader. The system class loader loads a class by first using the bootstrap class loader. If the class is not found, it then looks for the class in the application's classpath.

Since `loadClass()` automatically uses the parent class loader, which will percolate the call up the ancestor chain until the system class loader is used, there is seldom a need to use this method explicitly.

1.2 CHANGES In Version 1.1, the `Class` object returned by this method always returned `null` when `getClassLoader()` was invoked on it. In Version 1.2, the `Class` object returned by this method can have a `null` class loader, meaning it was loaded by the bootstrap class loader, or a non-`null` class loader, which is the system class loader that loaded the application. See the class description for details.

PARAMETERS

`className` A non-`null` string containing the fully qualified name of the class to load (for example, "`java.lang.String`").

RETURNS A new `Class` object with the name `className`.

EXCEPTIONS

`ClassNotFoundException`

If the class with the name `className` could not be found by the system class loader or its ancestor.

SEE ALSO `getParent()`.

1.2 getPackage()

PURPOSE Retrieves a package defined by this `ClassLoader` or its ancestors.

SYNTAX

```
protected Package getPackage(String pkgName)
```

DESCRIPTION This method returns a Package instance for the package named pkgName that has been defined by this class loader or any of its ancestors.

When a class loader loads a class from a package that the class loader (or its ancestors) has not seen before, the class loader *defines* the package. It does this by recording the package's name, the specification and implementation information, and the code source from which it came if the package was sealed. This allows the class loader to determine whether subsequent classes from the same package violate the sealing rule. (See Package for details.)

PARAMETERS

pkgName A non-null string representing the package's name (for example, "java.lang").

RETURNS A possibly null Package instance. It is null if the package has not been defined by this class loader or its ancestors.

SEE ALSO definePackage(), getPackages(), Class.getPackage(), Package.

EXAMPLE See FlatClassLoader in the class example.

1.2 getPackages()

PURPOSE Retrieves all packages defined by this ClassLoader and its ancestors.

SYNTAX `protected Package[] getPackages()`

DESCRIPTION This method returns an array of the packages of classes that have been loaded using this ClassLoader and its ancestors.

When a class loader loads a class from a package that the class loader (or its ancestors) has not seen before, the class loader *defines* the package. It does this by recording the package's name, the specification and implementation information, and the code source from which it came if the package was sealed. This allows the class loader to determine whether subsequent classes from the same package violate the sealing rule. (See Package for details.)

RETURNS A non-null Package array.

SEE ALSO definePackage(), getPackage(), Class.getPackage(), Package.

1.2 getParent()

PURPOSE Retrieves the parent class loader of this ClassLoader.

SYNTAX `public final ClassLoader getParent()`

DESCRIPTION This method retrieves the parent class loader of this ClassLoader. When a class loader is created, it is created with a *parent* class loader. When this

ClassLoader is asked to load a resource or class, it always consults the parent class loader before it attempts to load the resource or class itself. If the parent is null, the parent is the bootstrap class loader.

When a security manager has been installed, if the caller was not loaded using this class loader or an ancestor of this class loader, the caller must have been granted RuntimePermission("getClassLoader"). Otherwise, a SecurityException is thrown.

C

RETURNS The possibly null class loader of this ClassLoader. If null, the parent is the bootstrap class loader.

EXCEPTIONS

SecurityException

If the previously stated condition is not true.

SEE ALSO ClassLoader(), getSystemClassLoader(), RuntimePermission("getClassLoader"), SecurityManager.checkPermission().

EXAMPLE See Main.java in the class example.

Δ getResource()

PURPOSE Retrieves a resource using this ClassLoader or its ancestors.

SYNTAX

```
public URL getResource(String resName)
```

DESCRIPTION This method retrieves the resource with the name resName by using this ClassLoader or its ancestors. It does this by first using its parent, and, if it is not found, then looking for resource using its own policy (as defined by findResources()).

A *resource* is a piece of data such as an image or audio file or an HTML file that is used by the program. Resources are typically packaged with a JAR file or stored with the class files that use them.

1.2 CHANGES In Version 1.1, the default implementation did not do anything; it simply returned null. The subclass was expected to override this method to do something useful. In Version 1.2, the subclass is expected to override findResource() instead.

PARAMETERS

resName A non-null forward slash character ("/")-separated pathname that identifies the resource (for example, "app/index.html").

RETURNS A possibly null URL of the resource. It is null if no such resource is found or if the caller does not have permission to access the resource.

SEE ALSO `findResource()`, `getResourceAsStream()`.

EXAMPLE See `Main.java` in the class example.

Δ getResourceAsStream()

PURPOSE Retrieves a resource as a stream using this `ClassLoader` or its ancestors.

C

SYNTAX

```
public InputStream getResourceAsStream(String resName)
```

DESCRIPTION This method uses `getResource()` to find the resource with the name `resName` and returns an input stream for reading the resource.

A *resource* is a piece of data such as an image or audio file or an HTML file that is used by the program. Resources are typically packaged with a JAR file or stored with the class files that use them.

1.2 CHANGES In Version 1.1, the default implementation did not do anything; it simply returned `null`. The subclass was expected to override this method to do something useful. In Version 1.2, the subclass is expected to override `findResource()` instead.

PARAMETERS

`resName` A non-`null` forward slash character ("/")-separated pathname that identifies the resource (for example, `"app/index.html"`).

RETURNS A possibly `null` input stream for reading the resource; `null` if no such resource is found or if the caller does not have permission to access the resource.

SEE ALSO `findResource()`, `getResource()`.

EXAMPLE See `Main.java` in the class example.

1.2 getResources()

PURPOSE Retrieves all resources with a given name accessible by this `ClassLoader` or its ancestors.

SYNTAX

```
public final Enumeration getResources(String resName) throws
    IOException
```

DESCRIPTION This method retrieves all resources with the name `resName` using the same policy used by this `ClassLoader` to load classes. By default, this `ClassLoader` retrieves resources first by using its parent and then by looking for resources using its own policy (as defined by `findResources()`).

A *resource* is a piece of data such as an image or audio file or HTML file that is used by the program. Resources are typically packaged with a JAR file or stored with the class files that use them.

While `getResource()` finds the first resource with `resName`, this method finds *all* resources with the name `resName` accessible to this `ClassLoader` and returns their `URL`s in an enumeration.

PARAMETERS

`resName` A non-`null` forward slash character ("/")-separated pathname that identifies the resource (for example, `"app/index.html"`).

RETURNS A non-`null` enumeration of `URL` instances.

EXCEPTIONS

`IOException`

If an IO error occurred while getting the URLs associated with the requested resources.

SEE ALSO `findResources()`, `getResource()`.

EXAMPLE See the similar usage at `getSystemResources()`.

1.2 getSystemClassLoader()

PURPOSE Retrieves the system class loader.

SYNTAX `public static ClassLoader getSystemClassLoader()`

DESCRIPTION This method retrieves the system class loader. The *system class loader* is the class loader that started the application. It is the class loader responsible for loading classes specified in the classpath. The parent of the system class loader is the bootstrap class loader (`null`).

When you create a new class loader (using a concrete subclass of `ClassLoader`) without specifying an explicit parent, that new class loader's parent with be the system class loader.

When a security manager has been installed, this call can be executed only if the caller was loaded using the system class loader (or the bootstrap class loader) or if the caller has been granted `RuntimePermission("getClassLoader")`. Otherwise, a `SecurityException` is thrown.

RETURNS The system class loader, or `null` if none.

EXCEPTIONS

`SecurityException`

If the caller has not been granted `RuntimePermission("getClassLoader")`.

SEE ALSO `RuntimePermission("getClassLoader")`.

EXAMPLE

```
// Equivalent to ClassLoader.getSystemResource();
ClassLoader cl = ClassLoader.getSystemClassLoader();
System.out.println(cl.getResource("index.html"));
```

1.2 getSystemResources()

C

PURPOSE Retrieves all resources with a given name accessible by the system class loader or its ancestors.

SYNTAX

```
public static Enumeration getSystemResources(String resName)
    throws IOException
```

DESCRIPTION This method retrieves all resources that have the name `resName` and that are accessible by the system class loader or its ancestors. A *resource* is a piece of data such as an image or audio file or an HTML file that is used by the program. Resources are typically packaged with a JAR file or stored with the class files that use them.

System resources are those retrieved using the same policy used by the system class loader to load system classes. Specifically, the system class loader retrieves resources first by using its parent (the bootstrap class loader) and then from files in the directories, ZIP files, and JAR files specified by the `java.class.path` system property.

While `getSystemResource()` finds the first resource with `resName`, this method finds *all* resources with the name `resName` that are accessible to the bootstrap class loader and the system class loader and returns their URLs in an enumeration.

PARAMETERS

`resName` A non-`null` forward slash character ("/")-separated pathname that identifies the resource (for example, `"app/index.html"`).

RETURNS A non-`null` enumeration of `URL` instances.

EXCEPTIONS

`IOException`

If an IO error occurred while getting the resource.

SEE ALSO `getSystemClassLoader()`, `getSystemResource()`, `getSystemResourceAsStream()`.

EXAMPLE

```
try {
    Enumeration enum = ClassLoader.getSystemResources("index.html");
    while (enum.hasMoreElements()) {
        System.out.println(enum.nextElement());
    }
```

```
} catch (java.io.IOException e) {
    System.err.println(e);
}
```

Δ loadClass()

PURPOSE Loads a class using the policy defined by this `ClassLoader` and its ancestors.

SYNTAX
```
public Class loadClass(String cname) throws
    ClassNotFoundException
protected synchronized Class loadClass(String cname, boolean
    resolve) throws ClassNotFoundException
```

DESCRIPTION This method loads the class with the fully qualified class name `cname`. The following algorithm is used when loading in a class. If the class has already been loaded through this `ClassLoader`, it is returned. Otherwise, this `ClassLoader`'s parent is asked to load the class. The parent in turn asks its ancestor to load the class, and so on. If this `ClassLoader` does not have a parent, the bootstrap class loader is used. If the class cannot be loaded by the parent or its ancestors, then this `ClassLoader`'s `findClass()` method is invoked to find the class.

`resolve` should be set to `true` if an instance of the class being requested is being created or if the class's methods are to be invoked. `resolve` should be set to `false` if the class is being loaded simply to check its existence or to get its superclasses. If `resolve` is not supplied, it defaults to `false`. The `resolve` parameter is used by the Java virtual machine to optimize its class loading. It does not in any way affect how the loaded class can be used in the future. For example, if `resolve` was set to `false` when the class was loaded, the first time the program requests that an instance of the class be created, the Java virtual machine will automatically link it.

In the process of loading the class specified by `className`, the Java virtual machine may require additional classes to be loaded. Such classes are loaded using this same class loader (or its ancestors). Therefore this `ClassLoader` should ensure that it or its ancestor class loader can load all classes referenced directly or indirectly by classes that it loads.

Instead of loading a class using `loadClass()`, as in

```
Class c1 = classloader.loadClass(cname, resolve);
Class c2 = classloader.loadClass(cname);
```

you also use `Class.forName()`, as follows:

```
Class c1 = Class.forName(cname, resolve, classloader);
Class c2 = Class.forName(cname, false, classloader);
```

1.2 CHANGES In Version 1.1, you defined a new class loader by defining a subclass of `ClassLoader` and providing an implementation for the abstract method `load-`

`Class(String name, boolean resolve)`. In Version 1.2, `loadClass(String name, boolean resolve)` is no longer abstract. Instead, to define a new class loader, you leave the `loadClass` methods alone and provide an implementation for `findClass()`. Another difference is that, in Version 1.1 the first form of `loadClass()` called the second form with `resolve` set to `true`, while in Version 1.2 the first form calls the second form with `resolve` set to `false`.

PARAMETERS

`cname` A non-`null` fully qualified name of the class (for example, "`java.lang.String`").

`resolve` `true` if classes referenced by this class need to be loaded; `false` otherwise.

RETURNS The non-`null` `Class` representing the class `cname`.

EXCEPTIONS

`ClassNotFoundException`
If the class `cname` was not found by this class loader or any of its ancestors.

SEE ALSO `Class.forName()`, `findClass()`, `defineClass()`, `resolveClass()`.

EXAMPLE See `Main.java` in the class example.

java.lang

ClassNotFoundException

C

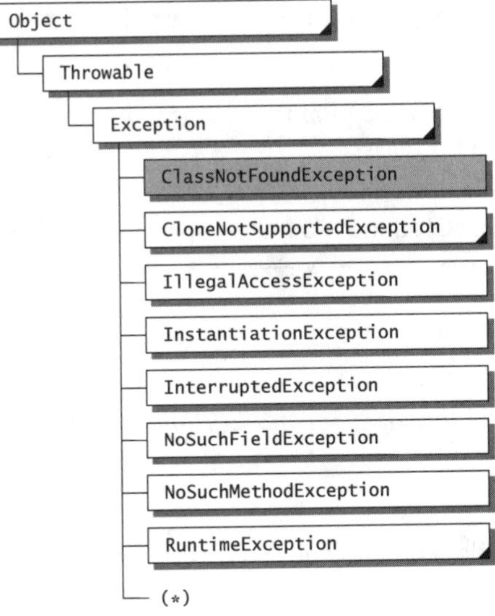

(*) 27 classes from other packages not shown.

Syntax

```
public class ClassNotFoundException extends Exception
```

Description

`ClassNotFoundException` is an exception that is thrown when a class loader cannot find the class to load.

See *The Java Class Libraries, Second Edition, Volume 1* for more information about this class.

Changes for Version 1.2

The `ClassNotFoundException` class allows a *root cause* exception to be specified when the exception is created. This allows the class loading mechanism to specify the root cause of the failure to load or find a class. A new method, `getException()`, can be used to retrieve this exception. The `printStackTrace()` methods have been overridden to display the stack trace of the root cause instead of the `ClassNotFoundException`, if it has been set.

MEMBER SUMMARY		
	Constructor	
Δ	`ClassNotFoundException()`	Constructs a `ClassNotFoundException` instance.
	Access Method	
1.2	`getException()`	Retrieves the exception that was thrown while attempting to load the class.
	Debugging Method	
Δ	`printStackTrace()`	Prints this `ClassNotFoundException`'s stack trace.

C

See Also

`Class.forName()`, `ClassLoader.loadClass()`.
`ClassNotFoundException` in *The Java Class Libraries, Second Edition, Volume 1.*

Example

You can make this program throw a `ClassNotFoundException` by giving it a bogus class name. A valid class name is qualified by its package name (for example, "`java.lang.String`").

```
class Main {
    public static void main(String[] args) {
        if (args.length != 1) {
            System.out.println("usage: java Main <classname>");
            System.exit(-1);
        }
        try {
            Class c = Class.forName(args[0]);
        } catch (ClassNotFoundException e) {
            System.out.println("cause: " + e.getException());
            e.printStackTrace(System.out);
        }
    }
}
```

Δ ClassNotFoundException()

PURPOSE Constructs a `ClassNotFoundException` instance.

SYNTAX
```
public ClassNotFoundException()
public ClassNotFoundException(String msg)
```
SINCE 1.2
```
public ClassNotFoundException(String msg, Throwable cause)
```

DESCRIPTION These forms of the constructor construct an instance of `ClassNotFoundException`. An optional string `msg` can be supplied that describes this particular instance of the exception. This is the string returned by `Throwable.getMessage()`. If `msg` is not supplied, it defaults to `null`.

A `ClassNotFoundException` can also be constructed with an exception `cause`, which may be thrown while loading the class. It could be, for example, a `java.io.IOException` if an IO error was encountered while trying to load the class.

1.2 CHANGES The form of the constructor that accepts a `Throwable` is new in Version 1.2.

PARAMETERS

`cause` The exception that was thrown while loading the class. If `null`, no such information was available.

`msg` A possibly `null` string that gives details about this `ClassNotFoundException`.

SEE ALSO `Throwable.getMessage()`.

C

1.2 getException()

PURPOSE Retrieves the exception that was thrown while attempting to load the class.

SYNTAX

```
public Throwable getException()
```

DESCRIPTION This method retrieves the exception that was thrown while attempting to load the class. If the constructor that accepts an `Throwable` argument was used when this instance of `ClassNotFoundException` was created, this method returns that `Throwable`. Otherwise, this method returns `null`.

RETURNS The exception that was thrown while loading the class. `null` if no such information was available.

SEE ALSO `ClassNotFoundException()`.

EXAMPLE See the class example.

Δ printStackTrace()

PURPOSE Prints this `ClassNotFoundException`'s stack trace.

SYNTAX

```
public void printStackTrace()
public void printStackTrace(PrintStream ps)
public void printStackTrace(PrintWriter pw)
```

DESCRIPTION You use this method to display the stack trace of this `ClassNotFoundException`. If you do not supply any arguments, the stack trace is sent to `System.err`. If you supply a `PrintStream` argument `ps`, the output will go to ps. If you supply a `PrintWriter` argument pw, the output will go to pw.

If `getException()` is non-`null`, the stack trace of that exception is displayed. Otherwise, the stack trace of this `ClassNotFoundException` is displayed.

1.2 CHANGES In Version 1.1, all forms of this method were inherited from `Throwable`. Also, since there was no constructor that accepted an exception, the stack trace printed was always that of the `ClassNotFoundException` (instead of the stack trace of `getException()`).

OVERRIDES `Throwable.printStackTrace()`.

SEE ALSO `getException()`, `System.err`.

EXAMPLE See the class example.

java.text
CollationElementIterator

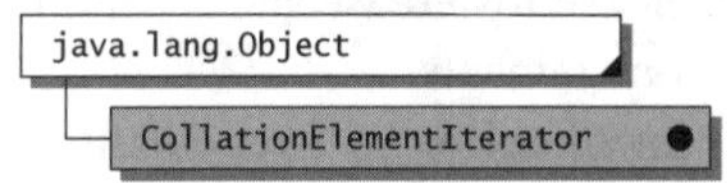

C

Syntax

```
public final class CollationElementIterator extends Object
```

Description

The `CollationElementIterator` class is an iterator used to walk through the decomposed characters of a locale-specific string according to the rules of a specific `Collator` object. (Decomposition converts precomposed characters, such as a-grave "`\u00E0`" into a sequence of Unicode combining characters, in this case "`a\u0300`".) This class is used primarily to search through strings. The iterator returns the collation element of the positioned character. This collation element contains properties that define how a character is collated by the given `Collator` object. These properties include the sorting order based on accents and uppercase/lowercase characters.

See *The Java Class Libraries, Second Edition, Volume 1* for more information about this class.

Changes for Version 1.2

This class defines five new methods: `getOffset()`, `previous()`, `setOffset()`, `setText()`, and `getMaxExpansion()`. We have added the following section to clarify collation elements.

Collation Elements

When a `Collator` instance is created, such as from `RuleBasedCollator`, it translates user characters in the source string into a series of *collation elements*, as shown next. (User characters are described in `BreakIterator`.)

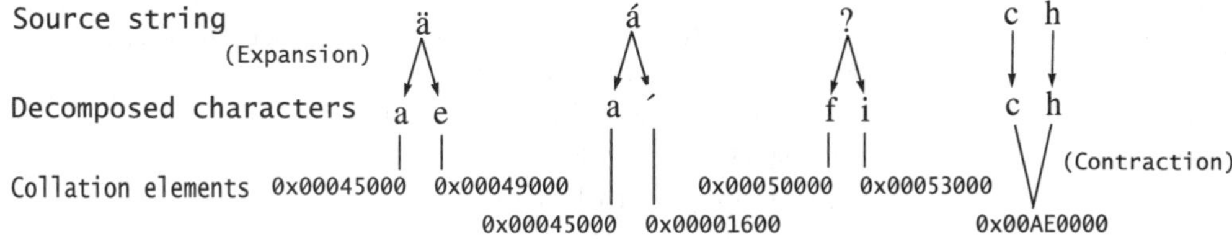

Each simple, unaccented character, such as all of the English alphabet A–Z, maps to a single collation element. More complex user characters require more than one element. This includes accented characters (for example, "á"), ligatures (for example, ?), and expansion characters (for example, "ä", which expands to "ae" for sorting in German). Contraction characters (for example, “ch” in traditional Spanish) map two characters to a single collation element. These collation elements hold the sort data for each decomposed character, with numeric values for ordering strength, such as for uppercase/lowercase and accent. A `CollationElementIterator` instance iterates over these collation elements.

The `next()` and `previous()` methods iterate over collation elements, while `setOffset()` sets the iterator to the position of specific user characters. Calling `next()` the first time moves the iterator position to the first collation element and returns that collation element. Because there is not a one-to-one mapping between user characters and collation elements, calling `next()` does not always increase the value returned by `getOffset()` (in the case of expansion characters). When it does increase the offset, it can increase it by more than 1 (in the case of contraction characters).

Calling `setOffset()` resets the iterator such that calling `next()` will return the first collation element at that offset. For example, if the current source character expands to three elements but `next()` has returned only two of them, calling `setOffset()` will reset the iterator so that it points to the specified offset in the source text and will reset any internal decomposition/expansion buffers.

The first 16 bits (that is, the first four hex digits) of a collation element is its primary order, usually the base character in Latin alphabets. The next 8 bits (two hex digits) is the secondary order, usually accents, and the last 8 bits (two hex digits) is the tertiary order, usually uppercase/lowercase differences.

	MEMBER SUMMARY	
	End-of-String Constant	
	`NULLORDER`	Returned by `next()` when end-of-string is reached.
	Iterator Methods	
1.2	`getMaxExpansion()`	Retrieves the maximum number of collation elements in an expansion sequence that ends with the collation element.
1.2	`getOffset()`	Retrieves the offset of the current character within the source text.
	`next()`	Moves the iterator to the next collation element in the string and retrieves that collation element.
1.2	`previous()`	Moves the iterator to the previous collation element in the string and retrieves that collation element.
	`reset()`	Resets the iterator to the beginning of the string.
1.2	`setOffset()`	Sets the position of the iterator within the source text.
1.2	`setText()`	Sets a new string over which to iterate.
	Order Methods	
	`primaryOrder()`	Retrieves the primary order value from a collation element.
	`secondaryOrder()`	Retrieves the secondary order value from a collation element.
	`tertiaryOrder()`	Retrieves the tertiary order value from a collation element.

See Also

`Collator`, `RuleBasedCollator`.
`CollationElementIterator` in *The Java Class Libraries, Second Edition, Volume 1.*

1.2 getMaxExpansion()

C

PURPOSE Retrieves the maximum number of collation elements in an expansion sequence that ends with the collation element.

SYNTAX `public int getMaxExpansion(int element)`

DESCRIPTION You use this method only when searching. It returns the maximum number of collation elements in an expansion sequence that ends with the collation `element`. An expansion sequence is one character that expands to more than one character.

For example, the German character “ä” expands to “ae”, which is the collation elements `0x00045000`, `0x00049000`. In this case, `getMaxExpansion(0x00049000)` returns `2`, since the user character expanded to two collation elements. The simple English character “a” translates to the collation element `0x00450000`. In this case, `getMaxExpansion(0x00450000)` returns `1`.

PARAMETERS

`element` The collation element returned from `previous()` or `next()`, an `int`.

RETURNS The maximum number of collation elements in an expansion sequence, an `int`.

EXAMPLE This example uses `next()` to iterate through a string of characters, printing out the value of `getMaxExpansion()` for each collation element. The `GERMAN` locale is modern German, so the accented character “ä” expands to “a”, followed by the umlaut accent, rather than the traditional “ae”.

```
import java.text.CollationElementIterator;
import java.text.Collator;
import java.text.RuleBasedCollator;
import java.util.Locale;

public class Main {
    public static void main(String[] args) {
        Locale loc = Locale.GERMAN;
        int element;

        // Set up string to iterate over.
        String str = "äabcABCàÀ";
        System.out.println("String: " + str + "\n");

        // Create an instance of a subclass of collator.
        Collator collator = Collator.getInstance(loc);

        if (collator instanceof RuleBasedCollator) {
            // Cast to the subclass.
            RuleBasedCollator rbc = (RuleBasedCollator)collator;
```

```
            // Try changing the decomposition mode.
            // rbc.setDecomposition(Collator.NO_DECOMPOSITION);

            // Get the first key of the string.
            CollationElementIterator cei =
                rbc.getCollationElementIterator(str);

            System.out.print("collation  primary  secondary  tertiary");
            System.out.println("   getMaxExpansion");
            System.out.println(" element    order     order      order");
            System.out.println("  (hex)");

            // Iterate to next character and get collation element.
            while ((element = cei.next()) !=
                    CollationElementIterator.NULLORDER) {

                System.out.print(" ");
                printInColumn(Integer.toHexString(element), 12);

                // Print the primary, secondary and tertiary orders.
                printInColumn(
                    CollationElementIterator.primaryOrder(element), 11
                );

                printInColumn(
                    CollationElementIterator.secondaryOrder(element), 11
                );

                printInColumn(
                    CollationElementIterator.tertiaryOrder(element), 11
                );

                printInColumn(
                    cei.getMaxExpansion(element), 0
                );

                System.out.println();
            }
        }
    }

    // Print string in a particular vertical column
    static void printInColumn(String str, int col) {
        System.out.print(str);
        for (int p = str.length(); p < col; ++p) {
            System.out.print(" ");
        }
    }

    // Print integer in a particular vertical column
    static void printInColumn(int integer, int col) {
        System.out.print(integer);
        for (int p = Integer.toString(integer).length(); p < col; ++p) {
            System.out.print(" ");
        }
    }
}
```

OUTPUT

```
> java Main
String: äabcABCàÀ

collation  primary  secondary  tertiary   getMaxExpansion
 element    order     order      order
  (hex)
 520000      82       0          0          1
 1c00        0        28         0          3
 520000      82       0          0          1
 530000      83       0          0          1
 540000      84       0          0          1
 520001      82       0          1          1
 530001      83       0          1          1
 540001      84       0          1          1
 520000      82       0          0          1
 1600        0        22         0          3
 520001      82       0          1          1
 1600        0        22         0          3
```


1.2 getOffset()

PURPOSE Retrieves the offset of the current character within the source text.

SYNTAX `public int getOffset()`

DESCRIPTION This method gets the offset of the current character in the source text. The offset is the zero-based position of the current user character (that is, not decomposed.) That is, the next call to `next()` will return the `Collation` element for this character (possibly including more than one character, if required by the language).

For example, if the current source character expands to three elements but `next()` has returned only two of them, calling `getOffset()` will retrieve the same value as it would prior to calling `next()`.

RETURNS The non-negative offset of the current character, an `int`.

EXAMPLE This method is demonstrated here and in `previous()`.

```
import java.text.CollationElementIterator;
import java.text.Collator;
import java.text.RuleBasedCollator;
import java.util.Locale;

public class Main {
    public static void main(String[] args) {
        Locale loc = Locale.GERMAN;
        int element;

        // Set up string to iterate over.
        String str = "äb";
        System.out.println("String: " + str + "\n");

        // Create an instance of a subclass of collator.
```

```
            Collator collator = Collator.getInstance(loc);

            if (collator instanceof RuleBasedCollator) {
                // Cast to the subclass.
                RuleBasedCollator rbc = (RuleBasedCollator)collator;

                // Get the first collation key of the string.
                CollationElementIterator cei =
                    rbc.getCollationElementIterator(str);

                element = cei.next();

                // Get the decomposed 'a'
                System.out.println( Integer.toHexString(element) );   // 52000
                System.out.println( cei.getOffset() );                // 1

                element = cei.next();

                // Get the decomposed accent for the 'a'
                System.out.println( Integer.toHexString(element) );   // 1c00
                System.out.println( cei.getOffset() );                // 1

                element = cei.next();

                // Get the character 'b'
                System.out.println( Integer.toHexString(element) );   // 53000
                System.out.println( cei.getOffset() );                // 2
            }
        }
    }
```

1.2 previous()

PURPOSE Moves the iterator to the previous collation element in the string and retrieves that collation element.

SYNTAX `public int previous()`

DESCRIPTION Each call to this method moves the iterator to the previous collation element and returns that collation element. Repeated use of this method iterates over the collation elements until it hits the beginning of the string where it returns `NULLORDER`.

RETURNS The previous collation element; returns `NULLORDER` if beginning-of-string is reached.

EXAMPLE This example iterates backward through a string. Notice how it iterates through the accents letters and then the base characters (iterating backwards) for the characters “à” and “À”, thereby causing the offset to be duplicated (7, 7 and 6, 6).

```
    import java.text.CollationElementIterator;
    import java.text.Collator;
    import java.text.RuleBasedCollator;
```

```
import java.util.Locale;

public class Main {
    public static void main(String[] args) {
        Locale loc = Locale.FRENCH;
        int element;

        // Set up string to iterate over.
        String str = "abcABCàÀ";

        // Create an instance of a subclass of collator.
        Collator collator = Collator.getInstance(loc);

        if (collator instanceof RuleBasedCollator) {
            // Cast to the subclass.
            RuleBasedCollator rbc = (RuleBasedCollator)collator;

            // Get the collation element of the string.
            CollationElementIterator cei =
                rbc.getCollationElementIterator(str);

            // Set the text. Set offset to the end of the string.
            cei.setText(str);
            cei.setOffset(str.length());
            System.out.println(str);               // abcABCàÀ

            while ((element = cei.previous()) !=
                    CollationElementIterator.NULLORDER) {
                System.out.print(cei.getOffset());
            }                                      // 7766543210
            System.out.println("");
        }
    }
}
```


1.2 setOffset()

PURPOSE Sets the position of the iterator within the source text.

SYNTAX `public void setOffset(int newOffset)`

DESCRIPTION This method sets the position of the iterator within the source text. Note that this method sets the position to composed characters, unlike `next()`, which iterates over decomposed characters. You can increment `newOffset` to iterate over the length of a string while doing character comparisons.

Calling `setOffset()` resets the iterator such that calling `next()` will return the first collation element at that offset. For example, if the current source character expands to three elements but `next()` has returned only two of them, calling `setOffset()` will reset the iterator so that it points to the specified offset in the source text and will reset any internal decomposition/expansion buffers.

PARAMETERS

`newOffset` The new offset to move the iterator to. This value must be between zero and the length of the source string (inclusive at both ends).

EXAMPLE This example creates a `CollationElementIterator` for a string and one for a pattern, and then iterates over the string to see if it can find the pattern within it. When it finds a match, it prints the match and the corresponding offset. To find matches, it iterates through and compares collation elements for each character until it hits the end of the pattern.

```
import java.text.CollationElementIterator;
import java.text.RuleBasedCollator;
import java.text.Collator;
import java.util.Locale;

public class Main {
    public static void main(String[] args) {
        Locale loc = Locale.FRENCH;

        String str = "abcàÀABCÀADE";
        String pat = "ÀA";

        System.out.println("String:  " + str);
        System.out.println("Pattern: " + pat + "\n");

        // Create an instance of a subclass of collator.
        Collator collator = Collator.getInstance(loc);

        boolean match;
        int patElement, strElement;

        if (collator instanceof RuleBasedCollator) {
            // Cast to the subclass.
            RuleBasedCollator rbc = (RuleBasedCollator)collator;

            CollationElementIterator strIter =
                    rbc.getCollationElementIterator(str);

            CollationElementIterator patIter =
                    rbc.getCollationElementIterator(pat);

            int END_OF_STRING = CollationElementIterator.NULLORDER;
            System.out.println("Searching... ");

            if (str.length() < pat.length()) {
               return;
        }

            // Step through the string.
            for (int i = 0; i <= (str.length() - pat.length()); i++) {
                // Print diagnostic.
                System.out.println(str.substring(i, i + pat.length()));

                // See if the pattern's collation elements match
                // the ones at this offset in the string.
                patIter.reset();
                strIter.setOffset(i);
```

```
                    match = true;
                    while (((patElement = patIter.next()) != END_OF_STRING)) {
                        strElement = strIter.next();
                        if (patElement != strElement) {
                            match = false;
                            break;
                        }
                    }
                    if (match) {
                        System.out.println(
                           "Found a match " + pat + " at offset: " + i);
                    }
                }
            }
        }
    }
```


OUTPUT

```
> java Main
String:  abcàÀABCÀADE
Pattern: ÀA

Searching...
ab
bc
cà
àÀ
ÀA
Found a match ÀA at offset: 4
AB
BC
CÀ
ÀA
Found a match ÀA at offset: 8
AD
DE
```

1.2 setText()

PURPOSE Sets a new string over which to iterate.

SYNTAX
```
public void setText(String newText)
public void setText(CharacterIterator newCharIter)
```

DESCRIPTION This method sets a new string over which to iterate. The argument passed in can be an instance of either `String` or `CharacterIterator`. The offset is set to `zero`.

PARAMETERS

`newCharIter` The new, non-`null` character iterator over which to iterate.

`newText` The new, non-`null` string over which to iterate.

EXAMPLE See `previous()`.

java.text
CollationKey

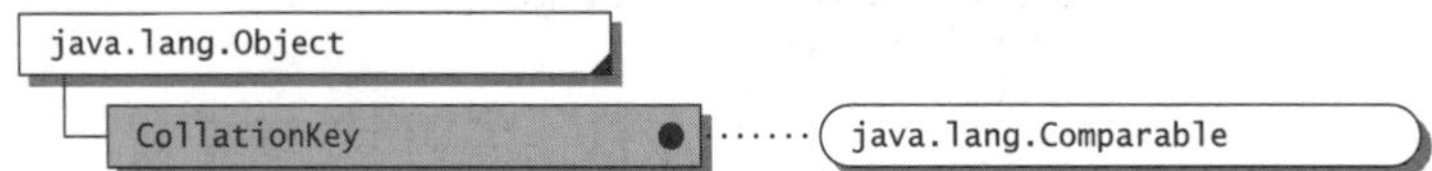

C

Syntax

```
public final class CollationKey extends Object implements Comparable
```

Description

The `CollationKey` class represents a sort key for a `String` object under the rules of a specific `Collator` object. Thus creating a `CollationKey` object produces a key from a string. These keys can then be compared; comparing two keys returns the relative order of the strings they represent. Once keys have been created, using `compareTo()` with `CollationKey` objects is always a much faster way of comparing than using the `compare()` method of `Collator`. Thus, when the strings must be compared multiple times, for example when sorting a list of strings or creating a database index, it is more efficient to use `CollationKey` objects.

See *The Java Class Libraries, Second Edition, Volume 1* for more information about this class.

Changes for Version 1.2

`CollationKey` has been modified so that it now implements interface `Comparable`, a new interface in Version 1.2 that has one method, `compareTo(Object)`.

MEMBER SUMMARY	
Comparison Method	
Δ `compareTo()`	Compares this `CollationKey` object to another `CollationKey` object for sort order.
String Getter Method	
`getSourceString()`	Retrieves the original string used to create this `CollationKey` object.
Byte Method	
`toByteArray()`	Converts this `CollationKey` object to an array of bytes.
Object Methods	
`equals()`	Compares this `CollationKey` object with another object for equality.
`hashCode()`	Creates the hash code of this `CollationKey` object.

See Also

`Collator`, `RuleBasedCollator`, `Comparator`.

`CollationKey` in *The Java Class Libraries, Second Edition, Volume 1.*

Δ compareTo()

PURPOSE

Compares this `CollationKey` object to another `CollationKey` object for sort order.

C

SYNTAX

```
public int compareTo(CollationKey target)
public int compareTo(Object obj)
```

DESCRIPTION

The first form of this method compares this `CollationKey` object to another `CollationKey` object, `target`, and returns an integer indicating which should appear first in the sorted order. The collation rules of the `Collator` object that created these keys apply.

The second form accepts an `Object` and is the implementation of the interface `Comparable`. It compares this `CollationKey` with `obj` for order. If `obj` cannot be cast to a `CollationKey`, this method throws a `ClassCastException`. Other than that, it operates the same as the first form.

If the strength of two `CollationKey` objects is `IDENTICAL`, then `compareTo()` returns zero if, and only if, the strings are canonically equivalent (see *The Unicode Standard, Version 2.0,* at `http://www.awl.com/cseng/titles/0-201-48345-9/`).

Note: `CollationKey` objects created by different collators cannot be compared. Nor can `CollationKey` objects be compared if they are from the same collator but have different strengths or decomposition settings. Currently, however, no exception is thrown.

1.2 CHANGES

In Version 1.1, only the first form of this method existed. The second form was added in Version 1.2.

PARAMETERS

`obj` A non-`null` object to be compared; must be a `CollationKey` object.

`target` A non-`null` `CollationKey` object to compare.

RETURNS

An `int` that is less than zero if this `CollationKey` object is less than that of the `target` or `obj`, zero if they are equal, and greater than zero if this `CollationKey` object is greater.

EXCEPTIONS

`ClassCastException`

If `obj` cannot be cast to a `CollationKey`.

SEE ALSO

`Collator.compare()`, `Comparable`.

EXAMPLE See the following code plus the class example in *The Java Class Libraries, Second Edition, Volume 1.*

```
import java.text.CollationKey;
import java.text.Collator;
import java.util.Locale;

public class Main {
    public static void main(String[] args) {
        Locale loc = Locale.FRENCH;

        // Create an instance of a subclass of collator.
        Collator myCollator = Collator.getInstance(loc);

        // Create collation keys for strings to be sorted.
        CollationKey key1 = myCollator.getCollationKey("Tom");
        CollationKey key2 = myCollator.getCollationKey("Dick");

        System.out.println( key1.compareTo(key2) );  //  1
        System.out.println( key2.compareTo(key1) );  // -1

        // System.out.println( key2.compareTo(new Integer(1)) );
                                                  // ClassCastException
    }
}
```

Collator

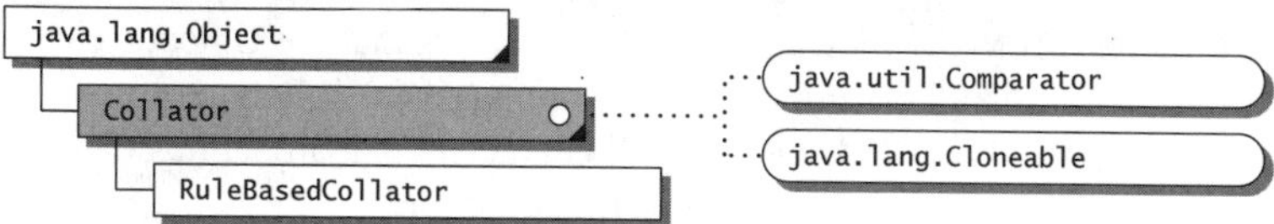

Syntax

```
public abstract class Collator extends Object implements Cloneable, Comparator
```

Description

The `Collator` class performs locale-sensitive string comparison. You use this class to build searching and alphabetical sorting routines for natural language text. The term *collate* means to determine the proper sort sequence for two or more strings.

`Collator` is an abstract base class. Subclasses implement specific collation strategies. One subclass, `RuleBasedCollator`, is currently provided and is applicable to a wide set of languages. Other subclasses may be created to handle more specialized needs.

See *The Java Class Libraries, Second Edition, Volume 1* for more information about this class.

Changes for Version 1.2

`Collator` now implements the interface `Comparator` and no longer implements `Serializable`—serialization never was implemented and always threw an exception. To implement this new interface, `Collator` implements the `compare(Object, Object)` method, which overloads the Version 1.1 method `compare(String, String)`. One tip is added to the usage section.

Usage

The example in `Collator`, "Usage," *The Java Class Libraries, Second Edition, Volume 1*, shows a collator being created. For efficiency, you would create one `Collator` instance using `Collator.getInstance()` and would reuse that collator using `compare()` on different strings.

MEMBER SUMMARY	
Constructor	
`Collator()`	Constructor called by subclasses.
Creation Method	
`getInstance()`	Creates and returns a `Collator` object for a locale.

Continued

C

MEMBER SUMMARY	
Decomposition Constants	
`CANONICAL_DECOMPOSITION`	Indicates that all characters that are Unicode canonical variants will be decomposed for collation.
`FULL_DECOMPOSITION`	Indicates that all characters that are Unicode variants will be decomposed for collation.
`NO_DECOMPOSITION`	Indicates that accented characters will not be decomposed for collation.
Comparison Constants	
`PRIMARY`	Indicates that comparisons should consider only primary differences.
`SECONDARY`	Indicates that comparisons should consider only secondary and greater differences.
`TERTIARY`	Indicates that comparisons should consider only tertiary and greater differences.
`IDENTICAL`	Indicates that comparisons should consider all differences.
Comparison Method	
Δ `compare()`	Compares two strings according to this `Collator` object's rules and returns an integer indicating which should be sorted first.
Collation Method	
`getCollationKey()`	Transforms a string into a collation key for bitwise comparison with other collation keys.
Decomposition Methods	
`getDecomposition()`	Retrieves the mode that determines how Unicode composed characters are separated prior to comparison.
`setDecomposition()`	Sets the mode that determines how Unicode composed characters are separated prior to comparison.
Strength Methods	
`getStrength()`	Sets the minimum level of difference considered significant during comparison.
`setStrength()`	Retrieves the minimum level of difference considered significant during comparison.
Locale Method	
`getAvailableLocales()`	Gets the set of locales for which `Collator` objects are installed.
Object Methods	
`clone()`	Creates a copy of this `Collator` object.
`equals()`	Compares this `Collator` object with another object for equality.
`hashCode()`	Computes the hash code of this `Collator` object.

See Also

`CollationKey`, `CollationElementIterator`, `Comparator`, `Locale`, `RuleBasedCollator`.

`Collator` in *The Java Class Libraries, Second Edition, Volume 1.*

Δ compare()

PURPOSE

Compares two strings according to this `Collator` object's rules and returns an integer indicating which should be sorted first.

SYNTAX

```
public abstract int compare(String source, String target)
public abstract int compare(Object source, Object target)
```

DESCRIPTION

This method compares source and target strings character by character according to the collation rules for this `Collator` object. It returns an integer less than, equal to, or greater than zero, depending on whether the source string compares less than, equal to, or greater than the target.

For a one-time comparison, this method has the best performance. However, if a given string will be involved in multiple comparisons, `compareTo()` in `CollationKey` has the best performance. See the `CollationKey` class description for an example.

The second form of this method accepts two `Object` types and is the implementation of the interface `Comparator`. It takes two non-`null` objects but throws a `ClassCastException` if either cannot be cast to `String`. Other than that, it operates the same as the first form.

1.2 CHANGES

In Version 1.1, only the first form of this method existed. The second form was added in Version 1.2.

PARAMETERS

`source` A non-`null` string to compare.

`target` A non-`null` string to compare.

RETURNS

An `int` that is less than zero if `source` is less than `target`, zero if `source` and `target` are equal, and greater than zero if `source` is greater than `target`.

EXCEPTIONS

`ClassCastException`

If `source` or `target` is not a `String`.

SEE ALSO

`CollationKey`, `getCollationKey()`, `Comparator`.

EXAMPLE

See the class example in *The Java Class Libraries, Second Edition, Volume 1.*

java.util
Collection

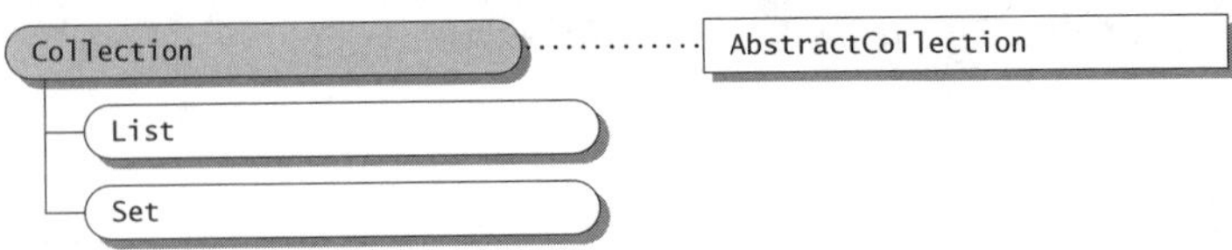

C

Syntax

```
public interface Collection
```

Description

A *collection* is a container of objects. Several kinds of containers are available for different situations. If the available set of containers does not meet your needs, you can define your own kind of container. The `Collection` interface represents a generic collection of objects.

Several interfaces and classes are related to collections. These collectively make up what is called *The Collections Framework*. The Collections Framework is based on *interfaces* that characterize common types of collections, such as sets and maps. The framework provides *implementations* of these interfaces, including hash tables, linked lists, and balanced trees, and *abstract classes* designed to help you implement your own collection. Finally, the framework provides various utilities that help with the use of collections, for example, for sorting or reversing lists.

The Interfaces

The Collections Framework has six collection interfaces. Each implementation in the Framework implements one of these interfaces, summarized in Table 5. To create a compatible collection, you will also implement one of these interfaces.

Interface	Description
`List`	An ordered list of elements. You have full control of where you place elements in the list. Elements in the list are accessed by an integer index. A list can hold duplicate elements.
`Set`	A possibly unordered set of elements. A set cannot hold duplicate elements.
`Collection`	A collection of elements. Root interface of `Set` and `List`. If you are creating a new collection that is not a `Set` or `List`, you should still have it implement this interface so that it can take advantage of the many services provided by The Collections Framework.

TABLE 5: The Collections Framework.

Interface	Description
`Map`	An unordered set of key/value pairs. A map cannot hold duplicate keys.
`SortedSet`	An ordered set of elements. Like a set, it cannot hold duplicate elements.
`SortedMap`	An ordered set of key/value pairs, ordered by key. Like a map, it cannot hold duplicate keys.

TABLE 5: The Collections Framework.

The Abstract Classes

For most interfaces in the Collections Framework, there is a corresponding abstract class to help with the implementation of that interface. For example, to implement `Set` you should consider having your collection subclass `AbstractSet`, since it provides implementations for most of the methods. You need to provide only a couple of methods—this greatly simplifies the effort of implementing `Set`.

There are five abstract classes, as shown in Table 6.

Class	Description
`AbstractList`	Implements the `List` interface. In particular, used by implementations backed by an array such as a data structure.
`AbstractSequentialList`	Implements the `List` interface. In particular, used by implementations backed by a linked list such as a data structure.
`AbstractSet`	Implements the `Set` and `SortedSet` interfaces.
`AbstractCollection`	Implements the `Collection` interface. `AbstractList` and `AbstractSet` both extend this class.
`AbstractMap`	Implements the `Map` and `SortedMap` interfaces.

TABLE 6: The Abstract Classes.

When you implement your own collection, you should provide a constructor with no arguments; this constructs an empty collection. You should also provide a constructor that accepts a `Collection` object. This latter constructor constructs a new collection that is initialized with the elements from the supplied collection, thereby making it easy to copy any collection.

The Implementations

Seven implementations of collections are available. They typically have names of the form *ImplementationInterface*. For example, the class `HashSet` is a set implemented by a hash table and `TreeSet` is a set implemented by a balanced tree.

Table 7 provides a quick summary of all collection implementations.

Class	Description
`ArrayList`	A list that is implemented using an array for quick random access.
`LinkedList`	A list that is implemented using a doubly linked list for quick insertions and deletions.
`HashSet`	A set that is implemented using a hash table.
`TreeSet`	A set that is implemented using a balanced red-black tree so that the elements are automatically ordered.
`HashMap`	A map whose keys are kept in a hash table.
`TreeMap`	A map whose keys are kept in a balanced red-black tree so that the elements are automatically ordered.
`WeakHashMap`	A map whose keys are kept in a hash table. When all references to a key outside the map are gone, the key/value pair is automatically removed from the map.

TABLE 7: The Implementation Classes.

In addition, there are two collection implementations that have always been a part of the Java programming language: `Vector` and `Hashtable`. These two classes have been retrofitted to fit into the collections framework. The `Vector` class implements the `List` interface; the `Hashtable` class implements the `Map` interface.

Ordered Collections

Some collections such as `TreeSet` and `TreeMap` order their elements and thus require a way to sort the elements. Two ways are available.

1. Provide a *comparator*, which is basically a method that compares two objects. The ordered collection uses the comparator when determining the order of any two elements. See `Comparator` for more details.
2. Have all of the elements implement the interface `Comparable`. This interface declares a single method that allows an element to be compared with any other element. See `Comparable` for more details.

Iterators

An iterator is used to access the elements in a collection in sequential manner. For example, to check every element in a set, you can create an iterator on the set and use it to access every element in the set. By continually calling the iterator's `next()` method, you are guaranteed to see each element in the collection exactly once.

The order of the elements presented by the iterator depends on the collection. Lists, for example, return the elements in exactly the same order that they appear in the list. For collections such as sets, the order can be arbitrary.

Utility Classes

The `Collections` class contains a number of useful methods that deal with collections. For example, a suite of methods, one for each collection type, creates an immutable view of any collection. Other methods sort and reorder lists. See `Collections` for more details.

The Collections Framework also provides a class—`Arrays`—for operating on arrays. `Arrays` has methods for sorting and searching through an array. See `Arrays` for more details.

Unsupported Methods

A collection does not have to support all operations. For example, a fixed-sized collection would not support any methods that add or remove elements. When an operation is not supported, the method will throw an `UnsupportedOperationException`.

Some implementations might restrict what elements (or in the case of `Maps`, keys and values) may be stored. Possible restrictions include requiring elements to

- be of a particular type,
- be comparable to other elements in the collection,
- be non-`null`, or
- obey some arbitrary predicate.

Attempting to add an element that violates an implementation's restrictions will result in a runtime exception, typically a `ClassCastException`, an `IllegalArgumentException`, or a `NullPointerException`. Attempting to remove or test for such an element might result in such an exception, although some "restricted collections" might permit this usage.

MEMBER SUMMARY	
Modification Methods	
`add()`	Adds an element to this collection.
`addAll()`	Adds all elements in a collection to this collection.
`clear()`	Removes all of the elements in this collection.
`remove()`	Removes an element from this collection.
`removeAll()`	Removes all elements from this collection that are in another collection.
`retainAll()`	Removes all elements in this collection that are not in another collection.
Iterator Method	
`iterator()`	Creates an iterator for the elements in this collection.
	Continued

MEMBER SUMMARY	
Query Methods	
`contains()`	Determines if this collection contains a particular element.
`containsAll()`	Determines if this collection contains all of the elements that are in another collection.
`isEmpty()`	Determines if this collection has no elements.
`size()`	Returns the number of elements in this collection.
Conversion Method	
`toArray()`	Returns all of the elements in this collection in an array.
Object Methods	
`equals()`	Determines if this collection is equal to another object.
`hashCode()`	Computes the hash code for this collection.

See Also

`ArrayList`, `Arrays`, `AbstractCollection`, `AbstractList`, `AbstractMap`, `AbstractSequentialList`, `AbstractSet`, `Collection`, `Collections`, `Comparator`, `Comparable`, `HashSet`, `HashMap`, `Iterator`, `LinkedList`, `List`, `ListIterator`, `Map`, `Set`, `SortedSet`, `SortedMap`, `TreeSet`, `TreeMap`, `WeakHashMap`.

add()

PURPOSE Adds an element to this collection.

SYNTAX `public boolean add(Object e)`

DESCRIPTION This method adds the element `e` to this collection. When this call returns, the collection contains `e`.

Some collections, such as sets (see `Set`), do not store duplicate elements. For such a collection, this call adds an element only if the collection does not already contain the element. See the `contains()` method.

Some collections do not accept `null`. If `null` is added to such a collection, an `IllegalArgumentException` should be thrown.

Some collections might accept only elements of a certain type. If an incompatible element is added to such a collection, a `ClassCastException` should be thrown.

This method might not be supported.

PARAMETERS

`e` The possibly `null` element to be added to this collection.

RETURNS `true` if this collection was modified; `false` if this collection does not permit duplicates and already contains the element.

EXCEPTIONS

`ClassCastException`
If the type of `e` is not compatible with this collection.

`IllegalArgumentException`
If some aspect of `e` prevents it from being added to this collection.

`NullPointerException`
If some element in `c` is `null` and this collection does not accept `null` elements.

`UnsupportedOperationException`
If this method is not supported by this collection.

SEE ALSO `addAll()`.

EXAMPLE See `Set.add()`.

addAll()

PURPOSE Adds all elements in a collection to this collection.

SYNTAX `public boolean addAll(Collection c)`

DESCRIPTION This method adds all elements in the collection `c` to this collection. It is equivalent to calling `add()` for each element in `c`.

Neither this collection nor collection `c` should be modified while this method is being called; otherwise, the results are undefined.

This method might not be supported.

PARAMETERS

`c` A non-`null` collection of elements to be added to this collection.

RETURNS `true` if this collection was modified.

EXCEPTIONS

`ClassCastException`
If the type of an element in `c` is not compatible with this collection.

`ConcurrentModificationException`
If `c`'s iterators are fail-fast and `c` is being modified during this method call.

`IllegalArgumentException`
If some aspect of an element in `c` prevents it from being added to this collection.

`NullPointerException`
If some element in `c` is `null` and this collection does not accept `null` elements.

`UnsupportedOperationException`
If this method is not supported by this collection.

SEE ALSO `add()`.

EXAMPLE See `Set.addAll()`.

clear()

PURPOSE Removes all of the elements in this collection.

SYNTAX `public void clear()`

DESCRIPTION This method removes all of the elements in this collection. After it is called, the collection will be empty. This method might not be supported.

EXCEPTIONS

`UnsupportedOperationException`
If this method is not supported by this collection.

EXAMPLE See `Set.clear()`.

C

contains()

PURPOSE Determines if this collection contains a particular element.

SYNTAX `public boolean contains(Object e)`

DESCRIPTION This method determines if this collection contains the element `e`. It returns `true` if some element in this collection is equal to `e`. An element is equal to `e` if both are `null` or if the `equals()` method determines that they are equal.

PARAMETERS

`e` A possibly `null` element.

RETURNS `true` if some element in this collection is equal to `e`.

EXCEPTIONS

`ClassCastException`
If the type of `e` is not compatible with this collection.

`NullPointerException`
If `e` is `null` and this collection does not accept `null` elements.

SEE ALSO `containsAll()`, `equals()`.

EXAMPLE See `Set.contains()`.

containsAll()

PURPOSE
Determines if this collection contains all of the elements that are in another collection.

SYNTAX

```
public boolean containsAll(Collection c)
```

DESCRIPTION
This method determines if this collection contains all of the elements that are in the collection `c`. If all elements in `c` appear in this collection, this method returns `true`. Two elements are equal if both are `null` or if the `equals()` method determines that they are equal.

PARAMETERS

`c` A non-`null` collection.

RETURNS
`true` if all elements in `c` appear in this collection.

EXCEPTIONS

`NullPointerException`
If some element in `c` is `null` and this collection does not accept `null` elements.

SEE ALSO
`contains()`, `equals()`.

EXAMPLE
See `Set.containsAll()`.

equals()

PURPOSE
Determines if this collection is equal to another object.

SYNTAX

```
public boolean equals(Object c)
```

DESCRIPTION
This method determines if this collection is equal to the object `c`. It returns `true` if this collection is equal to `c`. The way a collection determines equality is up to the collection. Some collections such as sets require that both collections be sets. Other collections have different requirements; for example, a list is equal only to itself.

If `equals(c)` is `true`, `c.equals(this)` must also be `true`. As always, if `equals(c)` is `true`, `hashCode()` must equal `c.hashCode()`.

PARAMETERS

`c` A possibly `null` object.

RETURNS
`true` if `c` is equal to this collection.

OVERRIDES
`java.lang.Object.equals()`.

SEE ALSO
`hashCode()`.

EXAMPLE
See `Set.equals()`.

hashCode()

PURPOSE Computes the hash code for this collection.

SYNTAX `public int hashCode()`

DESCRIPTION This method computes the hash code for this collection. This interface does not define how the hash code for this collection should be generated. The only restriction is that if two collections are equal (determined by using `equals()`), then their hash codes must also be equal.

In most cases, the hash code of the collection is derived using the hash code of all of its elements, but this is not required.

RETURNS An `int` that represents the hash code of this collection.

OVERRIDES `java.lang.Object.hashCode()`.

SEE ALSO `equals()`, `java.lang.Object.equals()`.

EXAMPLE See `Set.hashCode()`.

isEmpty()

PURPOSE Determines if this collection has no elements.

SYNTAX `public boolean isEmpty()`

RETURNS `true` if this collection contains no elements.

SEE ALSO `size()`.

EXAMPLE See `Set.isEmpty()`.

iterator()

PURPOSE Creates an iterator for the elements in this collection.

SYNTAX `public Iterator iterator()`

DESCRIPTION This method creates and returns an iterator (see `Iterator` for more details) for all elements in this collection. The order in which the elements are presented by the iterator depends on the class that created the iterator. Some classes might guarantee an ordering, while others might not.

In most cases, the collection should not be modified while the returned iterator is in use. Otherwise, a `ConcurrentModificationException` is thrown. However, some collections might allow this. Check with the collection's documentation.

RETURNS A non-`null` iterator.

SEE ALSO `ConcurrentModificationException, Iterator.`

EXAMPLE See `Set.iterator()`.

remove()

PURPOSE Removes an element from this collection.

SYNTAX `public boolean remove(Object e)`

DESCRIPTION This method removes the element `e` from this collection. If this collection contains one or more elements that are equal to `e` (determined using the `equals()` method), one of those elements is removed and `true` is returned. Otherwise, this method does not modify this collection and `false` is returned.

This method might not be supported.

PARAMETERS

`e` The possibly `null` element to be removed from this collection.

RETURNS `true` if this collection was modified.

EXCEPTIONS

`UnsupportedOperationException`
If this method is not supported by this collection.

SEE ALSO `removeAll(), retainAll().`

EXAMPLE See `Set.remove()`.

removeAll()

PURPOSE Removes all elements from this collection that are in another collection.

SYNTAX `public boolean removeAll(Collection c)`

DESCRIPTION This method removes all elements in this collection that are in `c`. The `equals()` method is used to determine whether two elements are equal. After this call returns, this collection will contain no elements in common with `c`. This operation can be thought of as a subtraction operation, where `c` is subtracted from this collection.

This method might not be supported.

PARAMETERS

`c` A non-`null` collection of elements to be removed from this collection.

RETURNS `true` if this collection was modified.

EXCEPTIONS

`ConcurrentModificationException`
If c's iterators are fail-fast and c is being modified during this method call.

`UnsupportedOperationException`
If this method is not supported by this collection.

SEE ALSO `remove()`, `retainAll()`.

EXAMPLE See `Set.removeAll()`.

retainAll()

PURPOSE Removes all elements in this collection that are not in another collection.

SYNTAX `public boolean retainAll(Collection c)`

DESCRIPTION This method removes all elements in this collection that are not in c. The `equals()` method is used to determine whether two elements are equal. This operation can be thought of as an intersection operation.

This method might not be supported.

PARAMETERS

`c` A non-`null` collection of elements to retain.

RETURNS `true` if this collection was modified.

EXCEPTIONS

`ConcurrentModificationException`
If c's iterators are fail-fast and c is being modified during this method call.

`UnsupportedOperationException`
If this method is not supported by this collection.

SEE ALSO `remove()`, `removeAll()`.

EXAMPLE See `Set.retainAll()`.

size()

PURPOSE Returns the number of elements in this collection.

SYNTAX `public int size()`

RETURNS The non-negative number of elements in this collection.

SEE ALSO `isEmpty()`.

EXAMPLE `Set.size()`.

toArray()

PURPOSE Returns all of the elements in this collection in an array.

SYNTAX
```
public Object[] toArray()
public Object[] toArray(Object arr[])
```

DESCRIPTION This method fills `arr` with all of the elements in this collection and returns `arr`. If `arr` is not large enough, a new array is created, filled, and then returned. The new array is just large enough to hold all of the elements in this collection, and its type is identical to the type of `arr`.

If `arr` is larger than all of the elements in this collection, `arr[size()]` is set to `null`. This `null` value can be used to determine the number of returned elements. However, it is not helpful if the collection may contain `null` elements.

The order of the elements in the returned array matches the order (if any) of the elements returned by an iterator on this collection.

If `arr` is not specified, it defaults to `new Object[0]`.

PARAMETERS

`arr` The non-`null` array into which the elements of this collection will be copied.

RETURNS The array `arr` or a new array whose length equals `size()`.

EXCEPTIONS

`ArrayStoreException`

If some element in this collection cannot be assigned to an element in `arr`. This exception is never thrown if `arr` is an `Object` array.

EXAMPLE See `Set.toArray()`.

java.util
Collections

```
java.lang.Object
  └ Collections
```

C

Syntax

```
public class Collections
```

Description

The `Collections` class contains various utility methods for collections. (See `Collection`). There are methods for searching, sorting, shuffling, and reversing a list. There are also methods for finding the highest and lowest elements of an arbitrary collection. And there are methods for creating a synchronized or immutable view of a collection.

Synchronization

The various implementations of collections such as `ArrayList` and `TreeMap` are all unsynchronized. That is, although you can have many threads simultaneously reading from the collection, you cannot, at the same time, have a thread modifying the collection. To enable this, you first must synchronize the methods of the collection. The `Collections` class offers several convenience methods for creating a wrapper around a collection, thereby effectively synchronizing each method.

However, be aware that although each method is synchronized, you might still need to synchronize more than one method call. For example, in the following statements:

```
if (!set.isEmpty()) {
    Object o = set.first();
}
```

the set might have been cleared just after `isEmpty()` was executed but before `first()` is executed. This would cause a `NoSuchElementException`. To synchronize both statements, you can do the following, which guarantees that the set will not be changed in between the two statements:

```
synchronized (set) {
    if (!set.isEmpty()) {
        Object o = set.first();
    }
}
```

Another typical situation in which method synchronization alone is not sufficient is during iteration. Iteration requires many calls to the collection, and you need to prevent any modifications between any of these calls. Here is some code that synchronizes a collection during iteration.

```
Collection c = Collections.synchronizedCollection(aCollection);
synchronized(c) {
    for (Iterator i=c.iterator(); i.hasNext();) {
        System.out.println( i.next() );
    }
}
```

MEMBER SUMMARY	
Constants	
EMPTY_LIST	A field holding an immutable empty list.
EMPTY_SET	A field holding an immutable empty set.
Collection Methods	
enumeration()	Returns an Enumeration over the specified Collection.
max()	Determines the highest element of a collection.
min()	Determines the lowest element of a collection.
List Methods	
binarySearch()	Searches a sorted list for an element.
copy()	Copies all of the elements from one list to another list.
fill()	Sets all of the elements in a list to a particular element.
nCopies()	Creates a list containing multiple copies of an element.
reverse()	Reverses the order of the elements in a list.
shuffle()	Randomly shuffles the elements of a list.
sort()	Sorts a list.
Set Method	
singleton()	Creates a set containing one element.
Comparator Method	
reverseOrder()	Returns a Comparator that reverses the order of elements in a collection.
Synchronized Wrapper Methods	
synchronizedCollection()	Creates a synchronized view of a collection.
synchronizedList()	Creates a synchronized view of a list.
synchronizedMap()	Creates a synchronized view of a map.
synchronizedSet()	Creates a synchronized view of a set.
synchronizedSortedMap()	Creates a synchronized view of a sorted map.
synchronizedSortedSet()	Creates a synchronized view of a sorted set.
Unmodifiable Wrapper Methods	
unmodifiableCollection()	Creates an unmodifiable view of a collection.
unmodifiableList()	Creates an unmodifiable view of a list.
unmodifiableMap()	Creates an unmodifiable view of a map.
unmodifiableSet()	Creates an unmodifiable view of a set.
unmodifiableSortedMap()	Creates an unmodifiable view of a sorted map.
unmodifiableSortedSet()	Creates an unmodifiable view of a sorted set.

binarySearch()

PURPOSE Searches a sorted list for an element.

SYNTAX

```
public static int binarySearch(List ls, Object e)
public static int binarySearch(List ls, Object e, Comparator
   comp)
```

DESCRIPTION This method searches the sorted list `ls` for the element `e`. `ls` must be sorted; otherwise, the results are undefined. If `e` appears more than once in `ls`, there is no guarantee as to which instance will be found.

If `ls` has the type `Object[]`, the comparator `comp` is used to sort the elements. However, if `comp` is not specified, the elements in `ls` must implement `Comparable`. In this case, the elements' `compareTo()` method is used to compare elements.

If `e` is found, this method returns its index. If `e` is not found, this method returns a negative value. If you negate the negative result and then subtract 1, the result specifies an *insertion index* in `ls`. The insertion index is the index at which `e` should be inserted into `ls` in order to maintain a sorted list.

This method uses a binary search that runs in *log*(`ls.size()`) time for random-access lists such as `ArrayList`. For sequential-access lists similar to `LinkedList`, this method runs in *n*log*(`ls.size()`) time. However, if the list is an instance of `AbstractSequentialList`, such as `LinkedList`, this method runs in linear time.

PARAMETERS

`comp`	A non-`null` comparator.
`e`	A possibly `null` element for which to search.
`ls`	A non-`null` list to be searched.

RETURNS The index of `e` in `ls` if `e` appears in `ls`. Otherwise, a negative value representing the insertion index is returned. See the description for more information. `-ls.size()-1` ≤ result ≤ `ls.size()`.

EXCEPTIONS

`ClassCastException`
If some element in `ls` cannot be compared to some other element in `ls`.

SEE ALSO `java.lang.Comparable`, `sort()`.

EXAMPLE

```
List l = Arrays.asList(new String[]{"cat", "dog", "gnu", "pig"});
System.out.println( Collections.binarySearch(l, "dog") ); // 1
System.out.println( Collections.binarySearch(l, "ape") ); // -1
System.out.println( Collections.binarySearch(l, "yak") ); // -5
```

copy()

PURPOSE Copies all of the elements from one list to another list.

SYNTAX `public static void copy (List dest, List src)`

DESCRIPTION This method copies all of the elements from `src` to `dest`. All elements in `dest` beyond `src.size()-1` are left alone. If `dest.size() < src.size()`, this method throws an `IndexOutOfBoundsException`.

PARAMETERS

`dest` The non-`null` destination list.

`src` The non-`null` source list.

EXCEPTIONS

`IndexOutOfBoundsException`

If `dest.size()` < `src.size()`.

EXAMPLE

```
List l1 = Arrays.asList(new String[]{"A", "B", "C"});
List l2 = Arrays.asList(new String[]{"1", "2"});

Collections.copy(l1, l2);
System.out.println( l1 );        // [1, 2, C]
Collections.copy(l2, l1);        // IndexOutOfBoundsException
```

EMPTY_LIST

PURPOSE A field holding an immutable empty list.

SYNTAX `public static final List EMPTY_LIST`

DESCRIPTION This field holds the empty `List` (immutable).

EXAMPLE See `Set.equals()`.

EMPTY_SET

PURPOSE A field holding an immutable empty set.

SYNTAX `public static final Set EMPTY_SET`

DESCRIPTION This field holds the empty `Set` (immutable).

EXAMPLE See `Set.equals()`.

C

enumeration()

PURPOSE Returns an `Enumeration` over the specified `Collection`.

SYNTAX `public static Enumeration enumeration(final Collection c)`

DESCRIPTION This method creates an enumeration over the collection `c`. It is used to provide interoperability with older classes that require an `Enumeration` object as input. The use of an `Iterator` is now recommended.

PARAMETERS

`c` A non-`null` collection.

SEE ALSO `Iterator`.

EXAMPLE

```
List l = new ArrayList(Arrays.asList(new String[]{"dog", "cat", "yak"}));
for (Enumeration e=Collections.enumeration(l); e.hasMoreElements(); ) {
    System.out.println( e.nextElement() );    // dog cat yak
}

Map m = new HashMap();
m.put("dog", null);
m.put("cat", null);
m.put("yak", null);
for (Enumeration e=Collections.enumeration(m.keySet());
        e.hasMoreElements(); ) {
    System.out.println( e.nextElement() );    // cat dog yak
}
```

fill()

PURPOSE Sets all of the elements in a list to a particular element.

SYNTAX `public static void fill(List ls, Object e)`

DESCRIPTION This method sets all of the elements in the list `ls` with the element `e`.

PARAMETERS

`e` A possibly `null` element.

`ls` A non-`null` list.

EXAMPLE

```
List l = Arrays.asList(new String[]{"cat", "dog", "pig"});
Collections.fill(l, "gnu");
System.out.println( l );        // [gnu, gnu, gnu]
```

C

max()

PURPOSE Determines the highest element of a collection.

SYNTAX
```
public static Object max(Collection c)
public static Object max(Collection c, Comparator comp)
```

DESCRIPTION This method iterates over all of the elements in `c` looking for the highest element of `c`. If `comp` is specified, it is used to compare the elements in `c`. If `comp` is not specified, then the `compareTo()` method of the elements is used to compare the elements. In this case, all elements must implement the `Comparable` interface.

PARAMETERS

`c` A non-`null` collection.

`comp` A non-`null` comparator.

RETURNS The possibly `null` last element of `c`.

EXCEPTIONS

`ClassCastException`
If some element in `c` is not comparable to some other element in `c`.

`NoSuchElementException`
If `c` is empty.

SEE ALSO `java.lang.Comparable`.

EXAMPLE
```
List l = new ArrayList(
    Arrays.asList(new String[]{"dog", "pig", "cat", "yak"}));

System.out.println( Collections.min(l) );      // cat
System.out.println( Collections.max(l) );      // yak

System.out.println( Collections.min(l, Collections.reverseOrder()) );      //
yak
System.out.println( Collections.max(l, Collections.reverseOrder()) );      //
cat
```

min()

PURPOSE Determines the lowest element of a collection.

SYNTAX
```
public static Object min(Collection c)
public static Object min(Collection c, Comparator comp)
```

DESCRIPTION This method iterates over all of the elements in `c` looking for the lowest element of `c`. If `comp` is specified, it is used to compare the elements in `c`. If `comp` is not specified, then the `compareTo()` method of the elements is used to compare the elements. In this case, all elements must implement the `Comparable` interface.

PARAMETERS

`c`	A non-`null` collection.
`comp`	A non-`null` comparator.

RETURNS The possibly `null` first element of `c`.

EXCEPTIONS

`ClassCastException`
If some element in `c` is not comparable to some other element in `c`.

`NoSuchElementException`
If `c` is empty.

SEE ALSO `java.lang.Comparable`.

EXAMPLE See `max()`.

nCopies()

PURPOSE Creates a list containing multiple copies of an element.

SYNTAX `public static List nCopies(int n, Object e)`

DESCRIPTION This method creates an immutable list containing `n` copies of element `e`.

PARAMETERS

`e`	A possibly `null` element to include in the returned list.
`n`	The number of copies of `e` in the returned list. $n \geq 0$.

EXCEPTIONS

`IllegalArgumentException`
If $n < 0$.

EXAMPLE

```
List l = Collections.nCopies(3, "dog");
System.out.println( l );        // [dog, dog, dog]

l.add("cat");                   // UnsupportedOperationException
```

reverse()

PURPOSE Reverses the order of the elements in a list.

SYNTAX `public static void reverse(List ls)`

DESCRIPTION This method reverses all of the elements in the list `ls`.

PARAMETERS

`ls`	A non-`null` list to reverse.

EXAMPLE

```
List l = Arrays.asList(new String[]{"dog", "pig", "cat"});

Collections.reverse(l);
System.out.println( l );        // [cat, pig, dog]
```


reverseOrder()

PURPOSE Returns a `Comparator` that reverses the order of elements in a collection.

SYNTAX `public static Comparator reverseOrder()`

DESCRIPTION This method returns a `Comparator` that reverses the order of elements in a collection. The returned comparator calls the elements' `compareTo()` method and reverses the result. (It describes an ordering that is the reverse of the elements' natural order.) If `compareTo()` returns a positive number, the comparator returned by this method returns a negative number, and if it returns a negative number, the comparator returns a positive number. For this comparator to be used, all elements in the collection must implement `Comparable`.

This comparator is serializable.

RETURNS A non-`null` comparator.

EXAMPLE

```
List l = Arrays.asList(new String[]{"dog", "pig", "cat"});
System.out.println( Collections.min(l, Collections.reverseOrder()) );
                                        // pig

Map m = new TreeMap(Collections.reverseOrder());
m.put("cat", null);
m.put("pig", null);
m.put("dog", null);
System.out.println( m );                // {pig=null, dog=null, cat=null}

Set s = new TreeSet(Collections.reverseOrder());
s.add("cat");
s.add("pig");
s.add("dog");
System.out.println( s );                // [pig, dog, cat]
```

shuffle()

PURPOSE Randomly shuffles the elements of a list.

SYNTAX

```
public static void shuffle(List ls)
public static void shuffle(List ls, Random r)
```

DESCRIPTION This method randomly shuffles all of the elements in list `ls`.

If r is specified, it is used to produce the new positions of the elements. If r is not specified, the seed of the random-number generator is initialized from the current time. This means that every call to shuffle, even between program invocations, has a high probability of yielding a different permutation.

If the permutations need to be consistent, you should create your own Random object using a particular seed.

PARAMETERS

ls The non-null list to be shuffled.

r A non-null Random object.

EXAMPLE

```
import java.util.*;

class Main {
    public static void main(String[] args) {
        System.out.println( sequence(1, 5, null));              // 3, 4, 2, 5, 1
        System.out.println( sequence(1, 5, null));              // 3, 5, 4, 2, 1

        // Now explicitly use a Random object.
        System.out.println( sequence(1, 5, new Random(257)) );  // 4, 1, 3, 2, 5
        System.out.println( sequence(1, 5, new Random(257)) );  // 4, 1, 3, 2, 5
    }

    public static List sequence(int s, int e, Random r) {
        List list = new ArrayList();
        for (int i=s; i<=e; i++) {
            list.add(new Integer(i));
        }
        if (r == null) {
            Collections.shuffle(list);
        } else {
            Collections.shuffle(list, r);
        }
        return list;
    }
}
```

singleton()

PURPOSE Creates a set containing one element.

SYNTAX `public static Set singleton(final Object e)`

DESCRIPTION This method creates an immutable set containing only one element, e.

PARAMETERS

e A possibly null element.

RETURNS A non-null, immutable set containing only e.

EXAMPLE

```
Set s = Collections.singleton("dog");

//s.add("cat");          // UnsupportedOperationException
//s.remove("dog");       // UnsupportedOperationException
```

sort()

PURPOSE Sorts a list.

SYNTAX

```
public static void sort(List ls)
public static void sort(List ls, Comparator comp)
```

DESCRIPTION This method sorts the elements in the list `ls`. `ls` must be modifiable but does not need to be resizable.

If `comp` is specified, it is used to compare the elements in `c`. If `comp` is not specified or is `null`, then the `compareTo()` method of the elements is used to compare the elements. In this case, all elements must implement the `Comparable` interface.

This method sorts `ls` using the merge-sort algorithm, providing `ls.size()`$*log_2$(`ls.size()`) performance. The sort is *stable*—that is, the order of equal elements in `ls` will be the same after the sort as it was before.

PARAMETERS

`ls` A non-`null` list.

EXCEPTIONS

`ClassCastException`
If some element in `ls` cannot be compared to some other element in `ls`.

`UnsupportedOperationException`
If `ls` does not support the set operation.

SEE ALSO `java.lang.Comparable`.

EXAMPLE

```
import java.util.*;

class Main {
    public static void main(String[] args) {
//
        List l = Arrays.asList(new String[]{"dog", "yak", "cat"});

        Collections.sort( l );
        System.out.println( l );                    // [cat, dog, yak]
        Collections.sort( l, Collections.reverseOrder() );
        System.out.println( l );                    // [yak, dog, cat]
//
    }
}
```

C

synchronizedCollection()

PURPOSE Creates a synchronized view of a collection.

SYNTAX `public static Collection synchronizedCollection(Collection c)`

DESCRIPTION This method creates a wrapper around the collection `c`. The wrapper implements the `Collection` interface, except that all methods are synchronized. With the synchronized wrapper, multiple threads can simultaneously read and modify the collection. However, be aware that although each method is synchronized, you might still need to synchronize a group of method calls. See the class description for more details about this.

Unlike the other versions of this method (`synchronizedSet()`, `synchronizedList()`, and so on), the `hashCode()` and `equals()` methods of the returned collection do not call the corresponding method on `c`. Instead, these two methods are simply the default `Object` methods. This essentially means that the returned collection will never be equal to any other collection. This is necessary in order to preserve the equals contracts of the `Set` and `List` interfaces.

Since the returned collection uses `c` and does not have its own storage, any changes to `c` will appear in the returned collection. Typically, `c` is not accessed directly.

The returned collection will be serializable if `c` is serializable.

PARAMETERS

`c` A non-`null` collection.

RETURNS A non-`null` synchronized collection.

EXAMPLE This example creates two threads: one to continually modify a collection and another that occasionally iterates over the collection. With the proper synchronization, the program runs fine. Without proper synchronization, the program throws a `ConcurrentModificationException`.

```
import java.util.*;

class Main {
    public static void main(String[] args) {
        // c is unsynchronized, so these 3 lines would result in a
        // ConcurrentModificationException.
        // Collection c = new ArrayList();
        // new Writer(c).start();
        // new Reader(c).start();

        // sc is synchronized
        Collection sc = Collections.synchronizedCollection(new ArrayList());
        new Writer(sc).start();
        new Reader(sc).start();
    }
}
```

```
class Reader extends Thread {
    Collection col;
    Reader(Collection c) {
        col = c;
    }
    public void run() {
        while (true) {
            synchronized(col) {
                for (Iterator i=col.iterator(); i.hasNext(); ) {
                    System.out.print(i.next()+" ");
                    Thread.yield();
                }
                System.out.println();
            }
        }
    }
}

class Writer extends Thread {
    static Random rnd = new Random();
    Collection col;
    Writer(Collection c) {
        col = c;
    }
    public void run() {
        while (true) {
            Integer ri = new Integer(rnd.nextInt(10));
            if (rnd.nextBoolean()) {
                col.add(ri);
            } else {
                col.remove(ri);
            }
            Thread.yield();
        }
    }
}
```

synchronizedList()

PURPOSE Creates a synchronized view of a list.

SYNTAX `public static List synchronizedList(List ls)`

DESCRIPTION This method creates a wrapper around the list `ls`. The wrapper implements the `List` interface, except that all methods are synchronized. With the synchronized wrapper, multiple threads can simultaneously read and modify the list. However, be aware that although each method is synchronized, you might still need to synchronize a group of method calls. See the class description for more details about this.

Since the returned list uses `ls` and does not have its own storage, any changes to `ls` will appear in the returned list.

The returned list will be serializable if `ls` is serializable.

PARAMETERS

`ls` A non-`null` list.

RETURNS A non-`null` synchronized list.

EXAMPLE See `synchronizedCollection()`.

synchronizedMap()

PURPOSE Creates a synchronized view of a map.

SYNTAX `public static Map synchronizedMap(Map m)`

DESCRIPTION This method creates a wrapper around the map `m`. The wrapper implements the `Map` interface, except that all methods are synchronized. With the synchronized wrapper, multiple threads can simultaneously read and modify the map. However, be aware that although each method is synchronized, you might still need to synchronize a group of method calls. Further, be aware that groups of method calls on a collection view of a synchronized map must synchronize on the synchronized map object, rather than the collection view object. See the class description for more details about this.

Since the returned map uses `m` and does not have its own storage, any changes to `m` will appear in the returned map.

The returned map will be serializable if `m` is serializable.

PARAMETERS

`m` A non-`null` map.

RETURNS A non-`null` synchronized map.

EXAMPLE See `synchronizedCollection()`.

synchronizedSet()

PURPOSE Creates a synchronized view of a set.

SYNTAX `public static Set synchronizedSet(Set s)`

DESCRIPTION This method creates a wrapper around the set `s`. The wrapper implements the `Set` interface, except that all methods are synchronized. With the synchronized wrapper, multiple threads can simultaneously read and modify the set. However, be aware that although each method is synchronized, you might still need to synchronize a group of method calls. See the class description for more details about this.

Since the returned set uses `s` and does not have its own storage, any changes to `s` will appear in the returned set.

The returned set will be serializable if `s` is serializable.

PARAMETERS

`s` A non-`null` set.

RETURNS A non-`null` synchronized set.

EXAMPLE See `synchronizedCollection()`.

synchronizedSortedMap()

PURPOSE Creates a synchronized view of a sorted map.

SYNTAX

```
public static SortedMap synchronizedSortedMap(SortedMap m)
```

DESCRIPTION This method creates a wrapper around the sorted map `m`. The wrapper implements the `SortedMap` interface, except that all methods are synchronized. With the synchronized wrapper, multiple threads can simultaneously read and modify the sorted map. However, be aware that although each method is synchronized, you might still need to synchronize a group of method calls. Further, be aware that groups of method calls on a collection view or submap view of a synchronized sorted map must synchronize on the synchronized sorted map object, rather than the view object. See the class description for more details about this.

Since the returned sorted map uses `m` and does not have its own storage, any changes to `m` will appear in the returned sorted map.

The returned sorted map will be serializable if `m` is serializable.

PARAMETERS

`m` A non-`null` sorted map.

RETURNS A non-`null` synchronized sorted map.

EXAMPLE See `synchronizedCollection()`, `synchronizedMap()`.

synchronizedSortedSet()

PURPOSE Creates a synchronized view of a sorted set.

SYNTAX

```
public static SortedSet synchronizedSortedSet(SortedSet s)
```

DESCRIPTION This method creates a wrapper around the sorted set `s`. The wrapper implements the `SortedSet` interface, except that all methods are synchronized. With the synchronized wrapper, multiple threads can simultaneously read and modify the sorted set. However, be aware that although each method is synchronized, you might still need to synchronize a group of method calls. Further, be aware that groups of method calls on a subset view of a synchronized sorted set must synchronize on the synchronized set object, rather than the subset view object. See the class description for more details about this.

Since the returned sorted set uses `s` and does not have its own storage, any changes to `s` will appear in the returned sorted set.

The returned sorted set will be serializable if `s` is serializable.

PARAMETERS

`s` A non-`null` sorted set.

RETURNS A non-`null` synchronized sorted set.

EXAMPLE See `synchronizedCollection()`.

unmodifiableCollection()

PURPOSE Creates an unmodifiable view of a collection.

SYNTAX `public static Collection unmodifiableCollection(Collection c)`

DESCRIPTION This method creates a wrapper around the collection `c`. The wrapper implements the `Collection` interface, except that all of the modification methods throw an `UnsupportedOperationException`. All of the query methods of the returned collection, except for `equals()` and `hashCode()`, simply call `c`'s query methods. Since the returned collection uses `c` and does not have its own storage, any changes to `c` will appear in the returned collection.

Unlike the other versions of this method (`unmodifiableSet()`, `unmodifiableList()`, and so on), the `hashCode()` and `equals()` methods of the returned collection do not call the corresponding method on `c`. Instead, these two methods are simply the default `Object` methods. This essentially means that the returned collection will never be equal to any other collection. This is necessary in order to preserve the equals contracts of the `Set` and `List` interfaces.

The returned collection will be serializable if `c` is serializable.

PARAMETERS

`c` A non-`null` collection.

RETURNS A non-`null` unmodifiable collection.

EXAMPLE

```
List l = new ArrayList(Arrays.asList(new String[]{"dog", "cat"}));
Collection roc = Collections.unmodifiableCollection(l);

//roc.add("pig");                           // UnsupportedOperationException
//roc.remove("cat");                        // UnsupportedOperationException

// Modify l and check for change in roc.
```

```
l.add("pig");
System.out.println( new ArrayList(roc) );  // [dog, cat, pig]

System.out.println( l.equals(roc) );                  // false
System.out.println( l.hashCode() == roc.hashCode() );  // false
```

unmodifiableList()

PURPOSE Creates an unmodifiable view of a list.

SYNTAX `public static List unmodifiableList(List ls)`

DESCRIPTION This method creates a wrapper around the list `ls`. The wrapper implements the `List` interface, except that all of the modification methods throw an `UnsupportedOperationException`. All of the query methods of the returned list simply call `ls`'s query methods. Since the returned list uses `ls` and does not have its own storage, any changes to `ls` will appear in the returned collection.

The returned list will be serializable if `ls` is serializable.

PARAMETERS

`ls` A non-`null` list.

RETURNS A non-`null` unmodifiable list.

EXAMPLE

```
List l = new ArrayList(Arrays.asList(new String[]{"dog", "cat"}));
List rol = Collections.unmodifiableList(l);

//rol.add("pig");                        // UnsupportedOperationException
//rol.remove("cat");                     // UnsupportedOperationException

// Modify l and check for change in rom.
l.add("pig");
System.out.println( new ArrayList(rol) );  // [dog, cat, pig]

System.out.println( l.equals(rol) );                  // true
System.out.println( l.hashCode() == rol.hashCode() );  // true
```

unmodifiableMap()

PURPOSE Creates an unmodifiable view of a map.

SYNTAX `public static Map unmodifiableMap(Map m)`

DESCRIPTION This method creates a wrapper around the map `m`. The wrapper implements the `Map` interface, except that all of the modification methods throw an `UnsupportedOperationException`. All of the query methods of the returned map simply call `m`'s query methods. Note that it is not possible to modify the returned map even through its collection views. Since the returned map uses `m` and does not have its own storage, any changes to m will appear in the returned map.

The returned map will be serializable if m is serializable.

PARAMETERS

m — A non-null map.

RETURNS — A non-null unmodifiable map.

EXAMPLE

```
Map m = new HashMap();
m.put("dog", null);
m.put("cat", null);
Map rom = Collections.unmodifiableMap(m);

//rom.put("pig", null);                      // UnsupportedOperationException
//rom.remove("cat");                         // UnsupportedOperationException

// Modify m and check for change in rom.
m.put("pig", null);
System.out.println( new HashMap(rom) );  // {dog=null, cat=null, pig=null}

System.out.println( m.equals(rom) );                     // true
System.out.println( m.hashCode() == rom.hashCode() );    // true
```

unmodifiableSet()

PURPOSE — Creates an unmodifiable view of a set.

SYNTAX — `public static Set unmodifiableSet(Set s)`

DESCRIPTION — This method creates a wrapper around the set s. The wrapper implements the Set interface, except that all of the modification methods throw an UnsupportedOperationException. All of the query methods of the returned set simply call s's query methods. Since the returned set uses s and does not have its own storage, any changes to s will appear in the returned collection.

The returned set will be serializable if s is serializable.

PARAMETERS

s — A non-null set.

RETURNS — A non-null unmodifiable set.

EXAMPLE

```
Set s = new HashSet(Arrays.asList(new String[]{"dog", "cat"}));
Set ros = Collections.unmodifiableSet(s);

//ros.add("pig");                            // UnsupportedOperationException
//ros.remove("cat");                         // UnsupportedOperationException

// Modify s and check for change in rom.
```

```
s.add("pig");
System.out.println( new HashSet(ros) );  // [dog, cat, pig]

System.out.println( s.equals(ros) );                   // true
System.out.println( s.hashCode() == ros.hashCode() );  // true
```

unmodifiableSortedMap()

PURPOSE Creates an unmodifiable view of a sorted map.

SYNTAX `public static SortedMap unmodifiableSortedMap(SortedMap m)`

DESCRIPTION This method creates a wrapper around the sorted map `m`. The wrapper implements the `SortedMap` interface, except that all of the modification methods throw an `UnsupportedOperationException`. All of the query methods of the returned sorted map simply call `m`'s query methods. Since the returned sorted map uses `m` and does not have its own storage, any changes to `m` will appear in the returned collection.

The returned sorted map will be serializable if `m` is serializable.

PARAMETERS

`m` A non-`null` sorted map.

RETURNS A non-`null` unmodifiable sorted map.

EXAMPLE See `unmodifiableMap()`.

unmodifiableSortedSet()

PURPOSE Creates an unmodifiable view of a sorted set.

SYNTAX `public static SortedSet unmodifiableSortedSet(SortedSet s)`

DESCRIPTION This method creates a wrapper around the sorted set `s`. The wrapper implements the `SortedSet` interface, except that all of the modification methods throw an `UnsupportedOperationException`. All of the query methods of the returned sorted set simply call `s`'s query methods. Since the returned sorted set uses `s` and does not have its own storage, any changes to `s` will appear in the returned collection.

The returned set will be serializable if `s` is serializable.

PARAMETERS

`s` A non-`null` sorted set.

RETURNS A non-`null` unmodifiable sorted set.

EXAMPLE See `unmodifiableSet()`.

java.lang

Comparable

Syntax

```
public interface Comparable
```

Description

The `Comparable` interface is used for determining the ordering of two objects.

Most sort routines (for example, `Collections.sort()`) have two forms, one that takes a comparator (see `Comparator`) and one that does not. If you use the form that takes the comparator, the sort method uses the comparator to order the elements. If you use the form that does not take a comparator, the sort method requires that all of the elements implement the `Comparable` interface. In particular, by implementing this interface the elements provide a `compareTo()` method that the sort method calls to determine the ordering.

Whichever sort routine you use, all elements of a collection must be *mutually comparable*, that is, `e1.compareTo(e2)` (or `comparator.compare(e1, e2)`) must not throw an exception for any elements `e1` and `e2` in the sorted collection.

So essentially, this interface is implemented by objects that have a default ordering and would like to allow themselves to be used by sort routines without a comparator. It is primarily a convenience for users of the object. The ordering that the objects implement with the `compareTo()` method should be the most typically used ordering.

`Comparable` objects also come in handy with the use of sorted collections such as `TreeMap` and `TreeSet`. To use these collections, either you must provide a comparator or all of the elements must implement the `Comparable` interface.

Note that if `null` is a valid element in a sorted collection, a comparator must be used (since `null` cannot implement `Comparable`).

Classes that implement this interface include `String`, `Byte`, `Character`, `Short`, `Integer`, `Long`, `Float`, `Double`, `BigInteger`, `BigDecimal`, `File`, and `Date`.

C

Usage

When `compareTo()` is implemented, the implementation must abide by several rules. See the method description for a list of these rules.

MEMBER SUMMARY	
Compare Method	
`compareTo()`	Determines the order of this object and another object.

See Also

`java.util.Comparator`.

Example

This example enhances the `java.awt.Point` class by making it comparable. `MyPoint` defines an ordering such that the point closest to `(0, 0)` comes first and the point farthest from `(0, 0)` comes last.

```
import java.util.*;
import java.awt.*;

class Main {
    public static void main(String[] args) {
        TreeSet set = new TreeSet();
        Random rnd = new Random();

        for (int i=0; i<10; i++) {
            set.add(new MyPoint((int)(
                rnd.nextInt(100)),(int)rnd.nextInt(100)));
        }

        for (Iterator it=set.iterator(); it.hasNext(); ) {
            MyPoint p = (MyPoint)it.next();
            System.out.println(p.x + " " + p.y);
        }
    }
}

class MyPoint extends Point implements Comparable {
    MyPoint(int x, int y) {
```

```
            super(x, y);
        }
        public int compareTo(Object o) {
            Point p = (Point)o;
            double d1 = Math.sqrt(x*x + y*y);
            double d2 = Math.sqrt(p.x*p.x + p.y*p.y);
            if (d1 < d2) {
                return -1;
            } else if (d2 < d1) {
                return 1;
            } else {
                return 0;
            }
        }
    }
```

C

compareTo()

PURPOSE Determines the order of this object and another object.

SYNTAX `public int compareTo(Object obj)`

DESCRIPTION This method compares this object with `obj` and determines which one comes first or whether they are equal.

- If this object comes before `obj`, a negative integer is returned.
- If this object is equal to `obj`, zero is returned.
- If this object comes after `obj`, a positive integer is returned.

Several properties apply to the results of this method. These properties are necessary for a well-defined ordering. Assume there are objects *x*, *y*, and *z*.

- If you swap the order of the comparison, the sign of the result will be opposite. In particular, this pseudocode holds:

  ```
  sign(x.compareTo(y)) == -(sign(y.compareTo(x))
  ```

  In addition, if *x*`.compareTo(`*y*`)` throws an exception, so will *y*`.compareTo(`*x*`)`.
- If $x > y$ and $y > z$, then x will be $> z$. In particular, if *x*`.compareTo(`*y*`) > 0` and *y*`.compareTo(`*z*`) > 0`, then

  ```
  x.compareTo(z) > 0.
  ```
- If *x* and *y* are equal, then if *x* is greater (or lesser) than *z*, *y* must also be greater (or lesser) than *z*. In particular, if *x*`.compareTo(`*y*`)==0` then this pseudocode holds:

  ```
  sign(x.compareTo(z)) == sign(y.compareTo(z))
  ```

  where `sign` returns `-1` if its argument is negative, `0` if its argument is `0`, and `1` if its argument is positive.

It is strongly recommend but not required that the following property holds:

- The `compareTo()` method should say that two objects are equal if, and only if, the `equals()` method says they're equal:

`(x.compareTo(y)==0) == x.equals(y).`

A natural ordering for which this property holds is said to be *consistent with equals*. A sorted set (such as `TreeSet`) will obey the contract for the `Set` interface if, and only if, its ordering is consistent with `equals`. Similarly, a sorted map (such as `TreeMap`) will obey the contract for the `Map` interface if, and only if, its ordering is consistent with `equals`.

PARAMETERS

`obj` A possibly `null` object.

RETURNS A negative integer if this object is less than `obj`, `0` if this object equals `obj`, and a positive integer if this object is greater than `obj`.

EXCEPTIONS

`ClassCastException`

If this object can't be compared with `obj`.

SEE ALSO `Object.equals()`. `java.util.Comparator`.

EXAMPLE See the class example.

Comparator

Comparator ······ java.text.Collator

Syntax

`public interface Comparator`

Description

A `Comparator` object is used in sort routines to sort elements. The sort routine calls the `compare()` method on pairs of elements from a collection and then uses the results to determine the elements' order. `Comparators` are also used by sorted collections, such as `TreeMap` and `TreeSet`.

An alternative to the use of comparators is for the elements to be comparable. In particular, elements can implement `Comparable`, thus supplying the sort routines a method (`compareTo()`) for ordering the elements. See `Comparable` for more details.

Note that if `null` is a valid element in a sorted collection, a comparator must be used (since `null` cannot implement `Comparable`).

Comparators should generally implement `java.io.Serializable`, since they can be used in serializable data structures such as `TreeMap` and `TreeSet`.

MEMBER SUMMARY	
Compare Methods	
`compare()`	Determines the order of two objects.
`equals()`	Determines whether this comparator is equal to another comparator.

See Also

`java.lang.Comparable.`

Example

This example implements an ordering for `java.awt.Point` objects such that the point closest to (`0`, `0`) comes first and the point farthest from (`0`, `0`) comes last.

```
import java.util.*;
import java.awt.*;

class Main {
    public static void main(String[] args) {
        TreeSet set = new TreeSet(new PointComparator());
        Random rnd = new Random();
```

```
        for (int i=0; i<10; i++) {
            set.add(new Point((int)(rnd.nextInt(100)), (int)rnd.nextInt(100)));
        }

        for (Iterator it=set.iterator(); it.hasNext(); ) {
            Point p = (Point)it.next();
            System.out.println(p.x + " " + p.y);
        }
    }
    static class PointComparator implements Comparator {
        public int compare(Object o1, Object o2) {
            Point p1 = (Point)o1;
            Point p2 = (Point)o2;
            double d1 = Math.sqrt(p1.x*p1.x + p1.y*p1.y);
            double d2 = Math.sqrt(p2.x*p2.x + p2.y*p2.y);
            if (d1 < d2) {
                return -1;
            } else if (d2 < d1) {
                return 1;
            } else {
                return 0;
            }
        }
    }
}
```

compare()

PURPOSE Determines the order of two objects.

SYNTAX `public int compare(Object o1, Object o2)`

DESCRIPTION This method compares `o1` and `o2` and determines which one comes first or whether they are equal.

- If `o1` comes before `o2`, a negative integer is returned.
- If `o1` is equal to `o2`, zero is returned.
- If `o1` comes after `o2`, a positive integer is returned.

Several properties apply to the results of this method. Assume there are objects *x*, *y*, and *z*.

- If you swap the order of the comparison, the sign of the result will be opposite. In particular, this pseudocode holds:

  `sign(compare(x, y)) == -sign(compare(y, x))`

  In addition, if `compare(x, y)` throws an exception, so will `compare(y, x)`.
- If $x > y$ and $y > z$, then x will be $> z$. In particular, if `compare(x, y) > 0` and `compare(y, z) > 0`, then

  `compare(x, z) > 0.`

- If *x* and *y* are equal, then if *x* is greater (or lesser) than *z*, *y* must also be greater (or lesser) than *z*. In particular, if *x*`.equals(`*y*`)` then this pseudocode holds:

```
sign(compare(x, z)) == sign(compare(y, z))
```

where sign returns `-1` if its argument is negative, `0` if its argument is `0`, and `1` if its argument is positive.

An optional property is as follows:

- The `compare()` method should say that two objects are equal if, and only if, the `equals()` method says they're equal:

```
(compare(x,y)==0) == x.equals(y).
```

A ordering for which this property holds is said to be *consistent with* `equals`. A sorted set (such as `TreeSet`) will obey the contract for the `Set` interface if, and only if, its ordering is consistent with `equals`. Similarly, a sorted map (such as `TreeMap`) will obey the contract for the `Map` interface if, and only if, its ordering is consistent with `equals`.

PARAMETERS

`o1` A possibly `null` object.

`o2` A possibly `null` object.

RETURNS A negative integer if `o1` < `o2`, `0` if `o1.equals(o2)`, and a positive integer if `o1` > `o2`.

EXCEPTIONS

`ClassCastException`

If `o1` can't be compared with `o2`.

SEE ALSO `java.lang.Object.equals()`.

EXAMPLE See the class example.

equals()

PURPOSE Determines whether this comparator is equal to another comparator.

SYNTAX `public boolean equals(Object obj)`

DESCRIPTION This method indicates whether `obj` is equal to this `Comparator`. This method must obey the general contract of `Object.equals()`. Additionally, this method can return `true` only if the `obj` is a `Comparator` instance and it imposes the same ordering as this `Comparator`. Thus `comp1.equals(comp2)` implies that for every object reference `o1` and `o2`,

```
sign(comp1.compare(o1, o2))==sign(comp2.compare(o1, o2)).
```

Note that it is *always* safe *not* to override `Object.equals()`. However, overriding this method might, in some cases, improve performance by allowing programs to determine that two distinct `Comparators` impose the same order.

PARAMETERS

`obj` The object with which to compare.

RETURNS `true` only if the specified object is also a `Comparator` and it imposes the same ordering as this `Comparator`; `false` otherwise.

SEE ALSO `java.lang.Object.equals()`, `java.lang.Object.hashcode()`.

java.util
ConcurrentModificationException

C

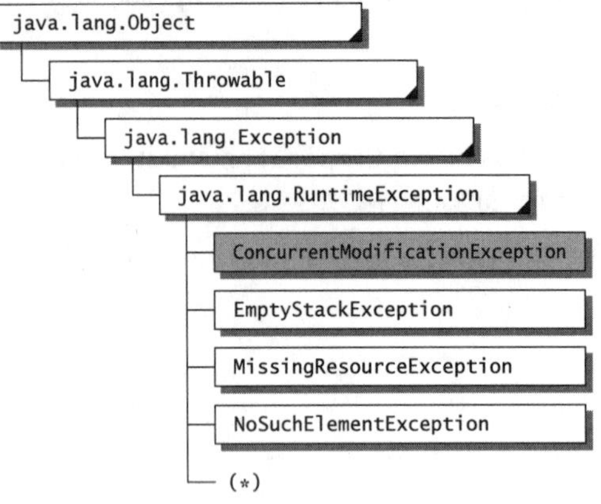

(*) 20 classes from other packages not shown.

Syntax

`public class ConcurrentModificationException extends RuntimeException`

Description

A `ConcurrentModificationException` is thrown when information is being read from an object that is unexpectedly being modified at the same time.

For example, if you are using an iterator (see `Iterator`) to read the contents of a collection (see `Collection`) and another thread modifies the collection at the same time, the reading thread will get a `ConcurrentModificationException`.

MEMBER SUMMARY	
Constructor	
`ConcurrentModificationException()`	Constructs a new `ConcurrentModificationException` instance.

See Also

`Iterator`.

Example

See `Set.iterator()`.

ConcurrentModificationException()

PURPOSE Constructs a new `ConcurrentModificationException` instance.

SYNTAX
```
public ConcurrentModificationException()
public ConcurrentModificationException(String msg)
```

DESCRIPTION This constructor constructs a `ConcurrentModificationException` containing `msg`, which gives details about what caused the exception. If `msg` is not specified, it defaults to `null`.

PARAMETERS

`msg` A possibly `null` string that gives details about the cause of this exception.

SEE ALSO `java.lang.Throwable.getMessage()`.

EXAMPLE See the `AbstractMap` class example.

java.net
DatagramPacket

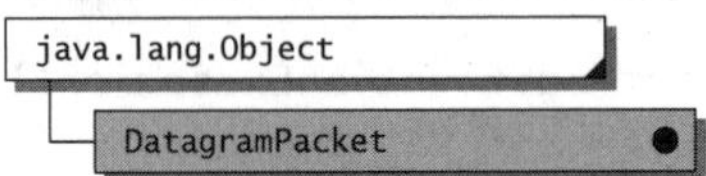

D

Syntax

```
public final class DatagramPacket
```

Description

The `DatagramPacket` class represents datagram packets in a connectionless protocol. A datagram packet that is sent contains the address of its destination and its contents. One that is received contains the address of its source and its contents. Datagram packets can be used for both single-client to single-server communication (*unicast*) and single-client to multiple-server communication (*multicast*). The only difference between the two modes of communication is that with unicast, the destination in the datagram packet is the address of a single machine, while with multicast, the destination in the datagram packet is a multicast group address.

See *The Java Class Libraries, Second Edition, Volume 1* for more information about this class.

Changes for Version 1.2

The `getOffset()` method and an overloaded `setData()` method allow for easier manipulation of the datagram packet's data. Two new constructors allow an offset to be specified regarding which part of the data buffer to use.

	MEMBER SUMMARY	
	Constructor	
Δ	`DatagramPacket()`	Constructs a `DatagramPacket` instance.
	Field Access Methods	
	`getAddress()`	Retrieves the destination address or source address of this `DatagramPacket`.
	`getData()`	Retrieves the contents of this `DatagramPacket`.
	`getLength()`	Retrieves the length of this `DatagramPacket`.
1.2	`getOffset()`	Retrieves the offset of the data to be sent or received.
	`getPort()`	Retrieves the destination port or source port of this `DatagramPacket`.

MEMBER SUMMARY	
Field Update Methods	
`setAddress()`	Sets the destination address or source address of this `DatagramPacket`.
Δ `setData()`	Sets the contents of this `DatagramPacket`.
`setLength()`	Sets the length of this `DatagramPacket`.
`setPort()`	Sets the destination port or source port of this `DatagramPacket`.

D

See Also

`DatagramPacket` in *The Java Class Libraries, Second Edition, Volume 1.*

Δ DatagramPacket()

PURPOSE Constructs an instance of `DatagramPacket`.

SYNTAX

```
public DatagramPacket(byte inBuffer[], int max)
SINCE 1.2  public DatagramPacket(byte inBuffer[], int offset, int max)
public DatagramPacket(byte outBuffer[], int count, InetAddress
    dst, int port)
SINCE 1.2  public DatagramPacket(byte outBuffer[], int offset, int count,
    InetAddress dst, int port)
```

DESCRIPTION The first two forms of this method construct a `DatagramPacket` instance for receiving a datagram packet. You specify an existing buffer `inBuffer` in which to put the incoming datagram packet. You also specify the maximum number of bytes, `max`, you expect to receive into `inBuffer`. `offset` specifies the start of `inBuffer` to store the bytes. If `offset` is not specified, it defaults to `0`. This is the value returned by `getOffset()`.

The last two forms construct a `DatagramPacket` instance for sending a datagram packet. You specify the buffer `outBuffer` that contains the bytes to be sent, the number of bytes to send (`count`), and the destination of the datagram packet (`dst` and `port`). `offset` specifies the start of `outBuffer` to get the bytes. If `offset` is not specified, it defaults to `0`. This is the value returned by `getOffset()`. Any direct updates to `outBuffer` after this `DatagramPacket` has been created affect the contents of this datagram packet as well.

By using the appropriate `set` methods, you can changes the fields of a datagram packet after the datagram packet has been created.

1.2 CHANGES The two constructors that accept the `offset` parameter are new in Version 1.2.

PARAMETERS

`count`	The number of bytes in `outBuffer` to send. `0` ≤ `count` ≤ `outBuffer.length-offset`.
`dst`	The non-`null` destination address to which to send the datagram packet.
`inBuffer`	The non-`null` buffer in which to receive the data.
`max`	The maximum number of bytes to receive into `inBuffer`. `max` ≤ `inBuffer.length-offset`.
`offset`	The starting index in `inBuffer` or `outBuffer` at which to start storing or reading data.
`outBuffer`	The non-`null` buffer containing the data to send.
`port`	The port to which to send the datagram packet. `0` ≤ `port` ≤ `65535`.

EXCEPTIONS

`IllegalArgumentException`
If `count`, `max`, or `port` is not within the specified bounds.

SEE ALSO `getOffset()`.

1.2 getOffset()

PURPOSE Retrieves the offset of the data to be sent or received.

SYNTAX

```
public synchronized int getOffset()
```

DESCRIPTION This method retrieves the offset of the data to be sent or received. The offset is the starting index in the data buffer of this `DatagramPacket` at which to start storing or reading data to be sent.

RETURNS The offset of the first byte of data to be sent or received.

SEE ALSO `DatagramPacket()`, `setData()`.

EXAMPLE See `setData()`.

Δ setData()

PURPOSE Sets the contents of this `DatagramPacket`.

SYNTAX

```
public synchronized void setData(byte[] newbuf)
```

SINCE 1.2

```
public synchronized void setData(byte[] newbuf, int offset, int
   count)
```

DESCRIPTION This method replaces the buffer being used by this `DatagramPacket` with the new buffer `newbuf`.

In the first form of the method, the `DatagramPacket`'s length is not changed unless the current length is greater than `newbuf.length`, in which case, the length is set to `newbuf.length`. Otherwise, the length must be changed explicitly using `setLength()`. Offset cannot be changed because there is no corresponding "set" method.

In the second form of this method, the `DatagramPacket`'s length and offset are updated using the `offset` and `count` parameters.

1.2 CHANGES The form that accept the `offset` and `count` parameters are new in Version 1.2.

PARAMETERS

`count` The number of bytes in `newbuf` to send, or the maximum number of bytes to read into `newbuf`. `count` ≤ `newbuf.length-offset`.

`newbuf` A non-`null` `byte` array containing the data to be sent, or the array to hold incoming data.

`offset` The starting index in `newbuf` at which to start storing or reading data.

EXCEPTIONS

`NullPointerException`
If `newbuf` is `null`.

`IllegalArgumentException`
If `offset` or `count` is outside of the specified bounds.

SEE ALSO `getData()`, `getLength()`, `getOffset()`.

EXAMPLE This sample `DatagramSocketImpl` uses `setData()` to place the data read into the `DatagramPacket`.

```
class SomeDatagramSocketImpl extends DatagramSocketImpl {
  int fd;
  int senderPort;
  InetAddress senderAddr;
  byte[] incoming;

  private native void receiveImpl() throws IOException;

  protected void receive(DatagramPacket dg) throws IOException {
    receiveImpl();      // sets sender information and incoming buffer

    dg.setPort(senderPort);
    dg.setAddress(senderAddr);
    dg.setData(incoming, 0, incoming.length);
    if (debug) {
        System.out.println("offset: " + dg.getOffset() + " length: " +
            dg.getLength());
    }
  }
```

java.net
DatagramSocket

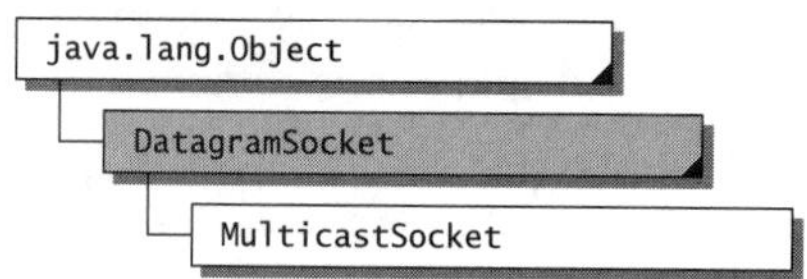

D

Syntax

```
public class DatagramSocket
```

Description

The `DatagramSocket` class is used to represent a datagram socket. A *socket* is a communications endpoint. A *datagram socket* is an endpoint for sending and receiving *datagram packets* between applications.

See *The Java Class Libraries, Second Edition, Volume 1* for more information about this class.

Changes for Version 1.2

Two new methods, `connect()` and `disconnect()`, are used to explicitly set the remote address of a `DatagramSocket`. The `send()` and `receive()` methods have been modified to use the remote address recorded for the `DatagramSocket`, if available, instead of inspecting the remote address in a `DatagramPacket`. Two additional new methods, `getInetAddress()` and `getPort()`, are used to retrieve the remote address of a `DatagramSocket`.

There also are new methods for setting and getting the send and receive buffer sizes.

	MEMBER SUMMARY	
	Constructor	
	`DatagramSocket()`	Constructs a `DatagramSocket` instance.
	Communication Methods	
	`close()`	Closes this `DatagramSocket`.
Δ	`receive()`	Receives a datagram packet from this `DatagramSocket`.
Δ	`send()`	Sends a datagram packet using this `DatagramSocket`.
	Remote Address Methods	
1.2	`connect()`	Sets this `DatagramSocket`'s remote address.
1.2	`disconnect()`	Clears this `DatagramSocket`'s remote address.
1.2	`getInetAddress()`	Retrieves the remote address recorded for this `DatagramSocket`.
1.2	`getPort()`	Retrieves the remote port recorded for this `DatagramSocket`.

MEMBER SUMMARY	
Socket Time-Out Methods	
`getSoTimeout()`	Retrieves the time-out period of this `DatagramSocket`.
`setSoTimeout()`	Sets the time-out period of this `DatagramSocket`.
Local Address Access Methods	
`getLocalPort()`	Retrieves the local port to which this `DatagramSocket` is bound.
`getLocalAddress()`	Retrieves the local address to which this `DatagramSocket` is bound.
Buffer Size Methods	
1.2 `getReceiveBufferSize()`	Retrieves the receive buffer size of this `DatagramSocket`.
1.2 `getSendBufferSize()`	Retrieves the send buffer size of this `DatagramSocket`.
1.2 `setReceiveBufferSize()`	Sets the receive buffer size of this `DatagramSocket`.
1.2 `setSendBufferSize()`	Sets the send buffer size of this `DatagramSocket`.

D

See Also

`DatagramSocket` in *The Java Class Libraries, Second Edition, Volume 1.*

1.2 connect()

PURPOSE Sets this `DatagramSocket`'s remote address.

SYNTAX `public void connect(InetAddress remoteAddr, int remotePort)`

DESCRIPTION This method records `remoteAddr` and `remotePort` as the remote address of this `DatagramSocket`. Subsequent datagram packets sent through this `DatagramSocket` (`send()`) will use `remoteAddr` and `remotePort` as the destination. An attempt to send a datagram packet that has another remote address will result in an `IllegalArgumentException`.

When datagram packets are read from this socket, only those from `remoteAddr` and `remotePort` are received. Packets received from other remote addresses are silently ignored. If `remoteAddr` is a multicast address, this `DatagramSocket` can be used only to send datagram packets.

Contrary to the method name, no actual "connection" is created because `DatagramSocket` is used for connectionless protocols. Only the remote address is recorded. When a `DatagramSocket` is initially created, it has no remote address. This `DatagramSocket`'s remote address can be cleared using `disconnect()`.

If a security manager has been installed, this method succeeds only if the caller has permission to accept connections from and create connections to remoteAddr and remotePort. After connect() has been called, no security checks are performed when packets are sent or received. Therefore you can use connect() to improve performance by avoiding multiple security checks for the same remote address.

PARAMETERS

remoteAddr A non-null address to which to connect.

remotePort The remote port to which to connect. 0 ≤ remotePort ≤ 65535.

EXCEPTIONS

IllegalArgumentException

If remoteAddr is null, or if remotePort is outside of the specified range.

SecurityException

If the caller is not allowed to send datagrams to or receive datagrams from the address and port.

SEE ALSO disconnect(), receive(), SecurityManager.checkAccept(), SecurityManager.checkConnect(), SecurityManager.checkMulticastAddress(), send(), SocketPermission("accept"), SocketPermission("connect").

EXAMPLE This is a variation on the DatagramSocket class example in *The Java Class Libraries, Second Edition, Volume 1.* It creates a DatagramSocket and then uses connect() to set the destination address instead of setting the destination address in the DatagramPackets.

```
class EchoServer extends Thread {
    private DatagramSocket sock = null;
    EchoServer(int port) {
        try {
            sock = new DatagramSocket(port);
        } catch (SocketException e) {
            e.printStackTrace();
        }
    }
    public void run() {
        if (sock == null)
            return;

        byte[] inbuf = new byte[1024];
        DatagramPacket request = new DatagramPacket(inbuf, inbuf.length);
        try {
            while (true) {
                sock.receive(request);
                sock.send(request); // just return what was sent
            }
        } catch (IOException e) {
            e.printStackTrace();
        }
    }
}

public static void echo(String msg, DatagramSocket client) {
    byte[] inbuf = new byte[1024];  // default size
```

```
    byte[] outbuf = msg.getBytes();

    try {
        // When constructing packet, don't need destination
        DatagramPacket request = new DatagramPacket(outbuf, outbuf.length);
        DatagramPacket reply = new DatagramPacket(inbuf, inbuf.length);
        client.send(request);
        client.receive(reply);
        client.close();
        System.out.println(new String(reply.getData()));
    } catch (SocketException e) {
        e.printStackTrace();
    } catch (IOException e) {
        e.printStackTrace();
    }
}

public static void main(String[] args) {
        if (args.length != 1) {
            System.err.println("Usage: java Main <message>");
            System.exit(1);
        }

        // start server
        EchoServer srv = new EchoServer(echo_port);
        srv.setDaemon(true);
        srv.start();

        try {
            InetAddress dst = InetAddress.getLocalHost();
            DatagramSocket dest = new DatagramSocket();
            dest.connect(dst, echo_port);

            System.out.println("remote addr: " + dest.getInetAddress());
            System.out.println("remote port: " + dest.getPort());

            echo(args[0], dest);

            dest.disconnect();

            System.out.println("disconnected addr: " + dest.getInetAddress());
            System.out.println("disconnected port: " + dest.getPort());

        } catch (UnknownHostException e) {
            System.err.println("Host not found: " + e);
        } catch (SocketException e) {
            e.printStackTrace();
        }
}
```

1.2 disconnect()

PURPOSE Clears this `DatagramSocket`'s remote address.

SYNTAX `public void disconnect()`

DESCRIPTION This method clears this `DatagramSocket`'s remote address by setting its remote address to `null` and remote port to `-1`. This method is idempotent.

SEE ALSO `connect()`, `getInetAddress()`, `getPort()`.

EXAMPLE See `connect()`.

1.2 getInetAddress()

D

PURPOSE Retrieves the remote address recorded for this `DatagramSocket`.

SYNTAX

```
public InetAddress getInetAddress()
```

DESCRIPTION This method retrieves the remote address recorded for this `DatagramSocket`. This is the value supplied to `connect()`.

RETURNS The remote address of this `DatagramSocket`, or `null` if no address has been recorded.

SEE ALSO `connect()`, `disconnect()`, `getPort()`.

EXAMPLE See `connect()`.

1.2 getPort()

PURPOSE Retrieves the remote port recorded for this `DatagramSocket`.

SYNTAX

```
public int getPort()
```

DESCRIPTION This method retrieves the remote port recorded for this `DatagramSocket`. This is the value supplied to `connect()`.

RETURNS The remote port of this `DatagramSocket`, or `-1` if `-1` or no port has been recorded.

SEE ALSO `connect()`, `disconnect()`, `getInetAddress()`.

EXAMPLE See `connect()`.

1.2 getReceiveBufferSize()

PURPOSE Retrieves the receive buffer size of this `DatagramSocket`.

SYNTAX

```
public synchronized int getReceiveBufferSize() throws
    SocketException
```

DESCRIPTION This method retrieves the buffer size (in bytes) being used by the underlying platform-specific network code for receiving packets sent to this `DatagramSocket`. It is the maximum amount of data that can be received in a single datagram packet from this socket. This value might not be the actual value used by the underlying platform-specific network code if it is outside of the allowable maximum or minimum of the platform.

The result might or might not be the same value that was previously set using `setReceiveBufferSize()`.

RETURNS The buffer size in bytes used for receiving packets.

EXCEPTIONS

`SocketException`

If an error occurred as the buffer size was being retrieved from this socket.

D

SEE ALSO `DatagramSocketImpl.getOption()`, `getSendBufferSize()`, `receive()`, `setReceiveBufferSize()`, `SocketOption.SO_RCVBUF`.

EXAMPLE This example sets the receive buffer size to `1024` and receives datagram packets. Such datagram packets contain at most `1024` bytes. Here is the fragment of the program that sets and gets the receive buffer size.

```
DatagramSocket client = new DatagramSocket();
DatagramPacket request = new DatagramPacket(outbuf, outbuf.length,
    dst, port);
DatagramPacket reply = new DatagramPacket(inbuf, inbuf.length);

System.out.println("original receive buffer size: " +
    client.getReceiveBufferSize());
client.setReceiveBufferSize(1024);
System.out.println("using receive buffer size: " +
    client.getReceiveBufferSize());
System.out.println("attempting to send: " + request.getLength() + " bytes");

client.send(request);
client.receive(reply);

System.out.println("read: " + reply.getLength() + " bytes");

client.close();
```

1.2 getSendBufferSize()

PURPOSE Retrieves the send buffer size of this `DatagramSocket`.

SYNTAX `public synchronized int getSendBufferSize() throws SocketException`

DESCRIPTION This method retrieves the buffer size in bytes being used by the underlying platform-specific network code for sending out packets from this `DatagramSocket`. It is the maximum amount of data that can be sent in a single datagram packet from this socket. This value might not be the actual value used by the underlying platform-specific network code if it is outside of the allowable maximum or minimum of the platform.

The result might or might not be the same value that was previously set using `setSendBufferSize()`.

RETURNS The buffer size in bytes used for sending packets.

EXCEPTIONS

`SocketException`

If an error occurred as the buffer size was being retrieved from this socket.

SEE ALSO `DatagramSocketImpl.getOption()`, `getReceiveBufferSize()`, `send()`, `setSendBufferSize()`, `SocketOption.SO_SNDBUF`.

EXAMPLE This example sets the send buffer size to `1024` and sends a datagram packet. Such a datagram packet contains at most `1024` bytes. Here is the fragment of the program that sets and gets the send buffer size.

```
DatagramSocket client = new DatagramSocket();
DatagramPacket request = new DatagramPacket(outbuf, outbuf.length,
    dst, port);
DatagramPacket reply = new DatagramPacket(inbuf, inbuf.length);

System.out.println("original send buffer size: " +
    client.getSendBufferSize());
client.setSendBufferSize(1024);
System.out.println("using send buffer size: " +
    client.getSendBufferSize());
System.out.println("attempting to send: " + request.getLength() + " bytes");

client.send(request);
client.receive(reply);
client.close();
```

Δ receive()

PURPOSE Receives a datagram packet from this `DatagramSocket`.

SYNTAX `public synchronized void receive(DatagramPacket dgram) throws IOException`

DESCRIPTION This method reads a datagram packet `dgram` from this `DatagramSocket`. It blocks until `dgram` is read. `dgram` must contain a preallocated buffer in which to receive the incoming data. Upon returning, `dgram` will contain the incoming data, as well as the address of the sender of the datagram packet.

If `connect()` has been called (with no intervening `disconnect()`), only packets received from the remote address specified by `connect()` are processed. Packets from other remote addresses are silently ignored. No security checks are performed on the incoming packets because `connect()` has already performed the appropriate checks on the sender.

If `connect()` has not been called, `receive()` returns the next packet read from this `DatagramSocket` without regard to the sender. If the caller is not allowed to receive packets from the sender, the packet is silently ignored.

The amount of data received is controlled by the platform-specific buffer size. If the data size exceeds this buffer size, a `SocketException` is thrown. (Some platform implementations truncate the data instead of throwing an exception, but that behavior is nonstandard and cannot be depended on.) If the data size exceeds `dgram.getLength()`, the data is truncated accordingly. See `getReceiveBufferSize()`.

Because the socket is a datagram socket, there is no guarantee that the same packet `dgram` will arrive just once. There also is no guarantee that successive calls to `receive()` will retrieve the datagram packets in the same order in which they were sent or even that a datagram packet will arrive at all.

1.2 CHANGES In Version 1.1, `DatagramSocket` did not have a `connect()` method. The security manager was used for each packet received to check whether the caller was allowed to receive packets from the sender.

PARAMETERS

`dgram` The non-`null` datagram packet into which to receive the data. Upon returning, `dgram` will contain the data of the packet and the address of the sender. The buffer in `dgram` for holding the data must have been preallocated. If the amount of data exceeds the buffer's size or `getReceiveBufferSize()`, the excess is ignored.

EXCEPTIONS

`InterruptedIOException`
If the time-out period for this `DatagramSocket` has expired before a datagram packet was received. This `DatagramSocket` may still receive future datagram packets.

`IOException`
If an IO error occurred while this socket was reading the datagram packet.

SEE ALSO `connect()`, `disconnect()`, `getReceiveBufferSize()`, `java.lang.SecurityManager.checkAccept()`, `setReceiveBufferSize()`.

EXAMPLE See `connect()`.

Δ send()

PURPOSE Sends a datagram packet using this `DatagramSocket`.

SYNTAX `public void send(DatagramPacket dgram) throws IOException`

DESCRIPTION This method uses this `DatagramSocket` to send the datagram packet `dgram`.

If `connect()` has been called (with no intervening `disconnect()`) and `dgram` contains a remote address, the address must be the same as that supplied to `connect()`. If it is not, an `IllegalArgumentException` is thrown. The packet is sent to the destination specified in `connect()`.

If `connect()` has not been called, `dgram` can be sent only if the caller is allowed by the security manager to connect to the destination specified in `dgram`. A `SecurityException` is thrown if the caller is not allowed to connect to the destination.

The amount of data sent is controlled by the platform-specific buffer size. If `dgram.getLength()` exceeds this size, a `SocketException` is thrown. (Some platform implementations truncate the data instead of throwing an exception, but that behavior is nonstandard and cannot be depended on.) See `getSendBufferSize()`.

Delivery of `dgram` to its destination is not guaranteed because datagram protocols have unreliable delivery.

If the destination address is a multicast address, `dgram` is sent to a multicast address and may be received by multiple receivers. This `DatagramSocket` sends `dgram` using the default time-to-live value,[1] which is determined by this `DatagramSocket`'s `DatagramSocketImpl`. Most implementations use a default of `1`, which means to multicast on the local network. If this datagram socket is a subclass of `MulticastSocket`, `MulticastSocket.getTimeToLive()` is used as the time-to-live value. Use `MulticastSocket.send()` for specifying the time-to-live value on a per-packet basis.

1.2 CHANGES In Version 1.1, `DatagramSocket` did not have a `connect()` method. `send()` would use the destination address specified by each packet and use the security manager to check whether it was allowed to connect to the destination.

PARAMETERS

`dgram` The non-`null` datagram packet being sent through this `DatagramSocket`. `dgram` contains the packet contents to send and, optionally, the address of the destination if a remote address has not been recorded for this `DatagramSocket`.

EXCEPTIONS

`IllegalArgumentException`

If the destination specified in `dgram` differs from the remote address recorded

1. If the time-to-live value of a multicast packet is `0`, the multicast packet is sent to the local host, not to the network. If the time-to-live value of a multicast packet is `1`, the packet is transmitted using the local network multicast, which reaches all immediately neighboring members of the sender. If the multicast packet's time-to-live value is greater than `1`, the packet is also forwarded by *multicast routers* to all other networks that have members of the multicast group. If the multicast packet's time-to-live value is greater than `2`, the packet is again forwarded from those networks, and so on.

for this `DatagramSocket`.

`IOException`
If an IO error occurred during the transmission of the datagram packet.

`SecurityException`
If not allowed to communicate with the destination specified in `dgram` due to security reasons.

SEE ALSO `connect()`, `disconnect()`, `java.lang.Security.checkConnect()`, `getSendBufferSize()`, `setSendBufferSize()`.

EXAMPLE See `connect()`.

D

1.2 setReceiveBufferSize()

PURPOSE Sets the receive buffer size of this `DatagramSocket`.

SYNTAX

```
public synchronized void setReceiveBufferSize(int size) throws
    SocketException
```

DESCRIPTION This method is used to provide a hint to the underlying platform-specific network code as to the buffer size to use when receiving packets sent to this `DatagramSocket`. Since datagram sockets have no notion of streams (that is, a large packet cannot be broken up into chunks), `size` is also the maximum size of a packet that may be received by this `DatagramSocket`.

This method provides only a hint to the underlying network code. To determine the actual receive buffer size, use `getReceiveBufferSize()`.

PARAMETERS

`size` The size of the buffer to use, in bytes, when receiving packets. `size` > `0`.

EXCEPTIONS

`IllegalArgumentException`
If `size` ≤ `0`.

`SocketException`
If an error occurred while setting the associated socket option.

SEE ALSO `getReceiveBufferSize()`, `receive()`, `setSendBufferSize()`.

EXAMPLE See `getReceiveBufferSize()`.

1.2 setSendBufferSize()

PURPOSE Sets the send buffer size of this `DatagramSocket`.

SYNTAX

```
public synchronized void setSendBufferSize(int size) throws
    SocketException
```

DESCRIPTION This method is used to provide a hint to the underlying platform-specific network code as to the buffer size to use when sending packets from this `DatagramSocket`. Since datagram sockets have no notion of streams (that is, a large packet cannot be broken up into chunks), `size` is also the maximum size of a packet that may be sent on this `DatagramSocket`.

This method provides only a hint to the underlying network code. To determine the actual send buffer size, use `getSendBufferSize()`.

PARAMETERS

`size` The size of the buffer to use when sending packets. `size` > `0`.

EXCEPTIONS

`IllegalArgumentException`

If `size`≤ `0`.

`SocketException`

If an error occurred while setting the associated socket option.

SEE ALSO `getSendBufferSize()`, `send()`, `setReceiveBufferSize()`.

EXAMPLE See `getSendBufferSize()`.

java.net
DatagramSocketImpl

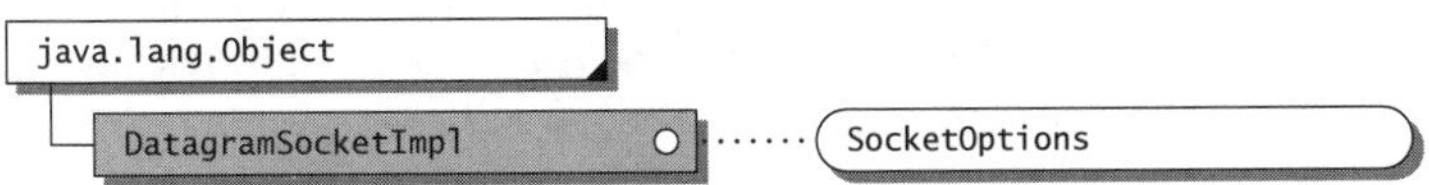

Syntax

```
public abstract class DatagramSocketImpl implements SocketOptions
```

D

Description

The `DatagramSocketImpl` class contains the methods necessary for implementing both unicast and multicast datagram sockets. The Java programmer uses the methods in the `DatagramSocket` and `MulticastSocket` classes for writing applications that communicate with each other using datagram packets. The actual implementations of the `DatagramSocket` and `MulticastSocket` classes are configurable at runtime and are supplied by a subclass of `DatagramSocketImpl`.

See *The Java Class Libraries, Second Edition, Volume 1* for more information about this class.

Changes for Version 1.2

The `getTTL()` and `setTTL()` methods are deprecated, replaced by the `getTimeToLive()` and `setTimeToLive()` methods. The latter two differ from the deprecated versions in that they accept and return `int` instead of `byte`. This allows time-to-live values to be specified more conveniently in the range `0` ≤ time-to-live ≤ `255`. See `MulticastSocket` for a description of time-to-live values.

MEMBER SUMMARY	
Methods for Changing Datagram Socket State	
`bind()`	Binds this datagram socket to the local port and address.
`close()`	Closes this datagram socket.
`create()`	Creates an unconnected datagram socket.
Methods for Communicating	
`peek()`	Looks in a datagram packet sent to this datagram socket for the sender's address.
`receive()`	Receives a datagram packet from this datagram socket.
`send()`	Sends a datagram packet using this datagram socket.

Continued

MEMBER SUMMARY

	Multicast Methods	
1.2	`getTimeToLive()`	Retrieves the time-to-live value for multicast packets sent from this datagram socket.
	`join()`	Makes this datagram socket join a multicast group.
	`leave()`	Makes this datagram socket leave a multicast group.
1.2	`setTimeToLive()`	Sets the time-to-live value for multicast packets sent from this datagram socket.
	Datagram Socket Information Fields	
	`fd`	This datagram socket's file descriptor.
	`localPort`	This datagram socket's local port number.
	Datagram Socket Information Methods	
	`getFileDescriptor()`	Retrieves this datagram socket's file descriptor.
	`getLocalPort()`	Retrieves this datagram socket's local port number.
	Deprecated Methods	
Δ	`getTTL()`	Replaced by `getTimeToLive()`.
Δ	`setTTL()`	Replaced by `setTimeToLive()`.

D

See Also

`MulticastSocket`.
`DatagramSocketImpl` in *The Java Class Libraries, Second Edition, Volume 1.*

1.2 getTimeToLive()

PURPOSE
Retrieves the time-to-live value for multicast packets sent from this datagram socket.

SYNTAX
```
protected abstract int getTimeToLive() throws IOException
```

DESCRIPTION
This method retrieves the time-to-live value for multicast packets sent from this datagram socket. A multicast packet sent from this datagram socket has a time-to-live value that specifies the transmission range of the packet.[1] The higher the time-to-live value, the higher the potential coverage of the multicast packet. The default time-to-live value is determined by `setTimeToLive()`. If

1. If the time-to-live value of a multicast packet is `0`, the multicast packet is sent to the local host, not to the network. If the time-to-live value of a multicast packet is `1`, the packet is transmitted using the local network multicast, which reaches all immediately neighboring members of the sender. If the multicast packet's time-to-live value is greater than `1`, the packet is also forwarded by *multicast routers* to all other networks that have members of the multicast group. If the multicast packet's time-to-live value is greater than `2`, the packet is again forwarded from those networks, and so on.

`setTimeToLive()` has never been invoked on this socket, `getTimeToLive()` returns an implementation-dependent default. Most implementations use a default of `1`, which means to multicast on the local network.

`getTimeToLive()` returns the default time-to-live value used for packets sent from this datagram socket.

RETURNS The time-to-live value for a multicast packet sent from this datagram socket. `0` ≤ time-to-live ≤ `255`.

D

EXCEPTIONS

`IOException`

If an error occurred while attempting to retrieve this datagram socket's time-to-live value.

SEE ALSO `MulticastSocket.getTimeToLive()`, `setTimeToLive()`.

Δ getTTL() *DEPRECATED*

PURPOSE Replaced by `getTimeToLive()`.

SYNTAX

```
protected abstract byte getTTL() throws IOException
```

1.2 CHANGES This method is deprecated in Version 1.2.

DEPRECATION The `getTimeToLive()` method allows the time-to-live value to be specified more conveniently.

RETURNS An unsigned 8-bit number specifying the time-to-live value for a multicast packet sent from this datagram socket. `0` ≤ time-to-live ≤ `255`.

EXCEPTIONS

`IOException`

If an error occurred while attempting to retrieve this datagram socket's time-to-live value.

1.2 setTimeToLive()

PURPOSE Sets the time-to-live value for multicast packets sent from this datagram socket.

SYNTAX

```
protected abstract void setTimeToLive(int ttl) throws IOException
```

DESCRIPTION This method sets the time-to-live value used for multicast packets sent from this datagram socket to be `ttl`. A multicast packet sent from this datagram socket has a time-to-live value that specifies the transmission range of the packet.[1] The higher the time-to-live value, the higher the potential coverage of the multicast packet.

Subsequent calls to `send()` will use this time-to-live value. Subsequent calls to `getTimeToLive()` will return this time-to-live value.

PARAMETERS

`ttl` The time-to-live for a multicast packet sent from this datagram socket. `0` ≤ `ttl` ≤ `255`.

EXCEPTIONS

`IOException`

If an IO error occurred while attempting to set the time-to-live of this datagram socket.

SEE ALSO `getTimeToLive()`, `MulticastSocket.setTimeToLive()`.

Δ setTTL() *DEPRECATED*

PURPOSE Replaced by `setTimeToLive()`.

SYNTAX `protected abstract void setTTL(byte ttl) throws IOException`

1.2 CHANGES This method is deprecated in Version 1.2.

DEPRECATION The `setTimeToLive()` method allows the time-to-live value to be specified more conveniently.

PARAMETERS

`ttl` An unsigned 8-bit number specifying the time-to-live value for a multicast packet sent from this datagram socket. `0` ≤ time-to-live ≤ `255`.

EXCEPTIONS

`IOException`

If an IO error occurred while attempting to set the time-to-live of this datagram socket.

1. If the time-to-live value of a multicast packet is `0`, the multicast packet is sent to the local host, not to the network. If the time-to-live value of a multicast packet is `1`, the packet is transmitted using the local network multicast, which reaches all immediately neighboring members of the sender. If the multicast packet's time-to-live value is greater than `1`, the packet is also forwarded by *multicast routers* to all other networks that have members of the multicast group. If the multicast packet's time-to-live value is greater than `2`, the packet is again forwarded from those networks, and so on.

Date

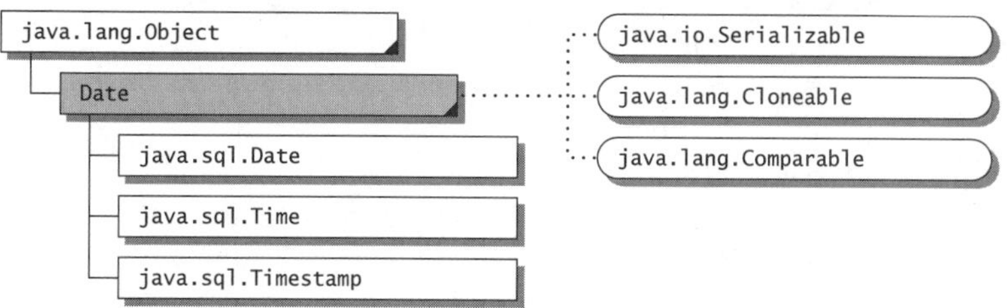

Syntax

```
public class Date implements java.io.Serializable, Cloneable, Comparable
```

Description

The `Date` class is used to represent a particular date and time with the resolution of milliseconds.

See *The Java Class Libraries, Second Edition, Volume 1* for more information about this class.

Changes for Version 1.2

A new `clone()` method allows `Date` objects to be cloned. Also, this class now implements `Comparable`, thereby allowing `Date` objects to be compared to one another and thus be sorted.

MEMBER SUMMARY	
Constructor	
`Date()`	Constructs a `Date` instance.
Getting and Setting Date and Time Values	
`getTime()`	Retrieves the value of this `Date` in milliseconds since epoch.
`setTime()`	Sets the value of this `Date` in milliseconds since epoch.
Comparison Methods	
`after()`	Determines whether this `Date` comes after another `Date`.
`before()`	Determines whether this `Date` comes before another `Date`.
1.2 `compareTo()`	Compares this `Date` with another `Date`.
`equals()`	Determines if this `Date` is equal to another object.
Object Methods	
Δ `clone()`	Creates a copy of this `Date`.

Continued

MEMBER SUMMARY	
Object Methods (*Continued*)	
`hashCode()`	Computes the hash code of this `Date`.
`toString()`	Generates the string representation of this `Date` using the UNIX `ctime` convention.
Deprecated Date Field Access Methods	
`getDate()`	Replaced by `Calendar.get(Calendar.DAY_OF_MONTH)`.
`getDay()`	Replaced by `Calendar.get(Calendar.DAY_OF_WEEK)-1`.
`getHours()`	Replaced by `Calendar.get(Calendar.HOUR_OF_DAY)`.
`getMinutes()`	Replaced by `Calendar.get(Calendar.MINUTE)`.
`getMonth()`	Replaced by `Calendar.get(Calendar.MONTH)`.
`getSeconds()`	Replaced by `Calendar.get(Calendar.SECOND)`.
`getTimezoneOffset()`	Replaced by `Calendar.get(Calendar.ZONE_OFFSET)` and `Calendar.get(Calendar.DST_OFFSET)`.
`getYear()`	Replaced by `Calendar.get(Calendar.YEAR)-1900`.
Deprecated Update Methods	
`setDate()`	Replaced by `Calendar.set(Calendar.DAY_OF_MONTH, int)`.
`setHours()`	Replaced by `Calendar.set(Calendar.HOUR_OF_DAY, int)`.
`setMinutes()`	Replaced by `Calendar.set(Calendar.MINUTE, int)`.
`setMonth()`	Replaced by `Calendar.set(Calendar.MONTH, int)`.
`setSeconds()`	Replaced by `Calendar.set(Calendar.SECOND, int)`.
`setYear()`	Replaced by `Calendar.set(Calendar.YEAR, int)`.
Deprecated Date Format Methods	
`parse()`	Replaced by `SimpleDateFormat.parse()`.
`toGMTString()`	Replaced by `SimpleDateFormat.format(this)`.
`toLocaleString()`	Replaced by `DateFormat.getDateTimeInstance().format(this)`.
`UTC()`	Replaced by `GregorianCalendar().getTime().getTime()`.

See Also

`Calendar`, `GregorianCalendar`.
`Date` in *The Java Class Libraries, Second Edition, Volume 1.*

Δ clone()

PURPOSE Creates a copy of this `Date`.

SYNTAX `public Object clone()`

DESCRIPTION This method creates a copy of this Date. The new returned Date instance has the same date as this Date. Changing the time of this Date does not affect the time of the new Date.

1.2 CHANGES In Version 1.1, this method was protected and inherited from java.lang.Object.

RETURNS A non-null copy of this Date.

OVERRIDES java.lang.Object.clone().

EXAMPLE

```
Date d = new Date();
System.out.println( d );        // Sun Jan 10 15:25:03 PST 1999

Date copy = (Date)d.clone();
System.out.println( copy );     // Sun Jan 10 15:25:03 PST 1999

// Changing the d does not affect copy.
d.setTime(123);
System.out.println( d );        // Wed Dec 31 16:00:00 PST 1969
System.out.println( copy );     // Sun Jan 10 15:25:03 PST 1999
```

1.2 compareTo()

PURPOSE Compares this Date with another Date.

SYNTAX

```
public int compareTo(Date d)
public int compareTo(Object d)
```

DESCRIPTION This method compares this Date with another Date d. If this Date is earlier than d, a value less than 0 is returned. If this Date is identical to d, 0 is returned. If this Date is later than d, a value greater than 0 is returned.

PARAMETERS

d The non-null Date against which to compare.

RETURNS A positive or negative number or 0, depending on how this Date compares with d.

EXAMPLE

```
Date newYears = new GregorianCalendar(1999, 1, 1).getTime();
Date valentinesDay = new GregorianCalendar(1999, 2, 14).getTime();
System.out.println( newYears.compareTo(valentinesDay) );    // -1
System.out.println( valentinesDay.compareTo(newYears) );    // 1

// Sorting an array of dates.
Random r = new Random();
Date[] dates = new Date[3];
for (int i=0; i<dates.length; i++) {
    dates[i] = new Date(r.nextLong());
}
Arrays.sort(dates);
```

```
for (int i=0; i<dates.length; i++) {
    System.out.println(dates[i]);
}
        // Thu Feb 19 02:02:36 PST 142989232
        // Thu Feb 22 05:59:35 PST 158577545
        // Tue Jan 24 16:22:15 PST 277980502
```

DateFormat

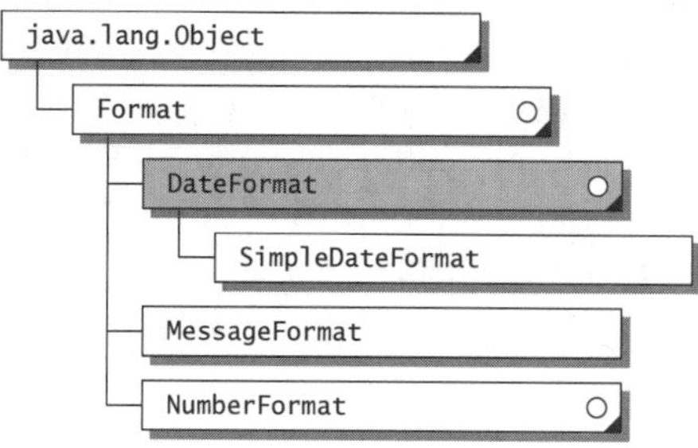

Syntax

```
public class DateFormat extends Format
```

Description

Dates are represented internally in a locale-independent way without inherent formatting. You can think of the internal representation as the number of milliseconds since *epoch* (January 1, 1970, 00:00:00 UTC), which is a `long` value. When a date is printed or displayed, it must be converted to a string, which can be localized and formatted.

`DateFormat` is an abstract base class that defines the programming interface for formatting and parsing a date and time in a locale-sensitive manner. A `DateFormat` object ultimately operates on a `Date` object, which holds information about both date and time. Dates can be formatted or parsed with or without times. Times by themselves can be formatted, but they don't parse properly in all cases.

Subclasses of `DateFormat`, such as `SimpleDateFormat`, allow for formatting (milliseconds to text) and parsing (text to milliseconds).

`DateFormat` enables you to format and parse dates for any locale. Your code can be completely independent of the local conventions for months, days of the week, or even the calendar format (lunar versus solar). The formatting styles include `FULL`, `LONG`, `MEDIUM`, `SHORT`, and `DEFAULT`. More details about and examples of using these styles are provided in the method descriptions.

See *The Java Class Libraries, Second Edition, Volume 1* for more information about this class.

Changes for Version 1.2

`DateFormat` no longer implements `Cloneable`, as it did in Version 1.1, but `Format` does, so you can still clone `DateFormat` objects. Other than that, this class has no API changes. However, we have added a clarification for the Year 2000 (Y2K) issue.

Year 2000

The pattern `yy` is a pattern for the two least-significant digits of the year. In some locales, such as U. S. English, the `SHORT`, `MEDIUM`, and `DEFAULT` styles all use two-digit abbreviated years, such as 99 for 1999. When using `yy` to get a date instance or date-time instance from the `DateFormat` class, the class must resolve the abbreviated year to some century. It does this by default by choosing the full year to be within the window 80 years before (inclusive) and 20 years after (exclusive) the exact moment of creation of the `DateFormat` instance, down to the millisecond. For an example and more details, see the `SimpleDateFormat` class. `DateFormat` uses `calendar.add(Calendar.YEAR, -80)` to determine the start of the window.

See Also

`DateFormat` in *The Java Class Libraries, Second Edition, Volume 1.*

DecimalFormat

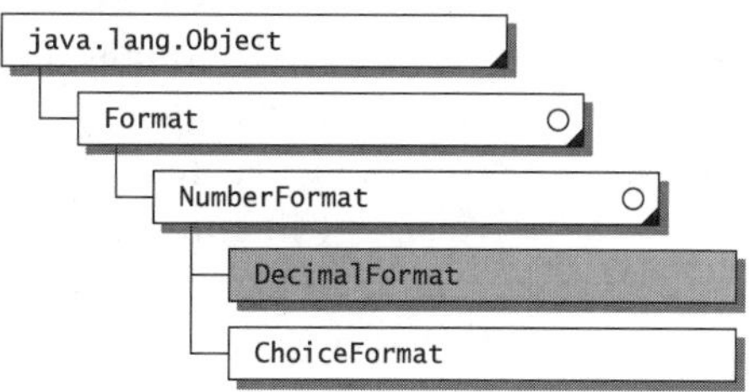

Syntax

```
public class DecimalFormat extends NumberFormat
```

Description

Numbers are represented internally in a locale-independent way without inherent formatting. When a number is printed or displayed, it must be converted to a string, which can be localized and formatted. The `DecimalFormat` class enables decimal numbers to be formatted to locale-specific strings. It also enables locale-specific strings to be parsed into number objects. For example, the number –1234 can be formatted as –1,234.00 in the U. S. locale.

See *The Java Class Libraries, Second Edition, Volume 1* for more information about this class.

Changes for Version 1.2

Four new methods are added: `setMaximumFractionDigits()`, `setMaximumIntegerDigits()`, `setMinimumFractionDigits()`, and `setMinimumIntegerDigits()`. There is a change in usage about which localized digits are handled. The "E" exponent character has been added as a pattern symbol. Pattern symbols are described in the following sections. Also, a new separator has been introduced: the monetary decimal separator. This is used when the currency sign (`\u00a4`) is seen in the pattern; otherwise, the normal decimal separator is used.

Usage

In Version 1.1, this class handled only localized digits, where the ten digits were contiguous in Unicode, from 0 to 9. If you had a different digits set (such as superscripts), you had to implement your own subclass. In Version 1.2, this class parses all Unicode characters that represent decimal digits. For formatting, the `DecimalFormatSymbols` zero digit is still used. The Unicode set of characters is defined in the Unicode standard.

Exponent Symbol

Any decimal number can be represented in exponential notation. For example, the number 12345 can be represented as 123.45E2, where 123.45 is the *mantissa* and 2 is the *exponent*.

Thus these numbers have the form *mantissa*E*exponent*. In the pattern, the exponent pattern symbol "E" must be immediately followed by one or more digit characters, for example, 0.###E0. Exponential notation does not use grouping separators (such as the comma, as in 1,234.5E1); if they are in the pattern, they are ignored during formatting. The number of digit characters after the exponent character gives the minimum exponent digit count; there is no maximum number of digits. Negative exponents are denoted using the same form specified for positive exponents, except with a negative sign. (This may change in a future release.) The minimum number of digits in the integer portion of the mantissa is achieved by having `DecimalFormat` adjust the exponent value to the exponent grouping (described next).

The exponent has *exponent grouping*, which determines what multiple the exponent value can be. An exponent grouping of 3 means the exponent can be a multiple of 3, such as –6, –3, 0, or 3. (These correspond to common units, such as micrograms, milligrams, grams, and kilograms.) The maximum number of integer places (marked with a leftmost #) in the mantissa pattern, if any, specifies the exponent grouping. For example, ##0.####E0 has an exponent grouping of 3; formatting the number 12345 results in 12.345E3. The mantissa integer pattern ##0 means that the maximum number of digits in the integer portion of this mantissa is 3; therefore the exponent grouping is 3. A pattern of ##.###E0 would have an exponent grouping of 2 and so would format 12345 to 1.2345E4.

However, you can instead force an exact number of mantissa integer digits, overriding the exponent grouping, by supplying a mantissa pattern that is all zeros. Thus the pattern 00.###E0 formats 12345 to 12.345E3. The same pattern formats 1234 to 12.34E2.

For example, the following pattern and original strings will result in the formatted strings shown. Notice that the exponent grouping is 4 because the pattern has four integer mantissa digits (###0). (The example code for this is in the `DecimalFormat()` constructor in *The Java Class Libraries, Second Edition, Volume 1.*)

```
PATTERN
###0.0#E0

ORIGINAL STRINGFORMATTED STRING
.1234567890123 .123457E0
1.234567890123 1.23457E0
12.34567890123 12.3457E0
123.4567890123 123.457E0
1234.567890123 1234.57E0
12345.67890123 1.23457E4
123456.7890123 12.3457E4
1234567.890123 123.457E4
12345678.90123 1234.57E4
123456789.0123 1.23457E8
1234567890.123 12.3457E8
12345678901.23 123.457E8
123456789012.3 1234.57E8
1234567890123. 1.23457E12
```

MEMBER SUMMARY	
Constructor	
`DecimalFormat()`	Constructs a `DecimalFormat` instance that has a pattern and symbols.
Format and Parse Methods	
`format()`	Formats a decimal number to produce a string.
`parse()`	Converts a string to a `Number` object.
Full Pattern Methods	
`applyLocalizedPattern()`	Assigns a localized pattern to this `DecimalFormat` instance.
`applyPattern()`	Assigns a nonlocalized pattern to this `DecimalFormat` instance.
`toLocalizedPattern()`	Produces a string of the current localized pattern.
`toPattern()`	Produces a string of the current nonlocalized pattern.
Getter Methods	
`getDecimalFormatSymbols()`	Retrieves the decimal format symbols for this `DecimalFormat` instance.
`getGroupingSize()`	Retrieves the number of digits between grouping separators.
`getMultiplier()`	Retrieves the multiplier used for percent or per mill.
`getNegativePrefix()`	Retrieves the prefix for negative numbers.
`getNegativeSuffix()`	Retrieves the suffix for negative numbers.
`getPositivePrefix()`	Retrieves the prefix for positive numbers.
`getPositiveSuffix()`	Retrieves the suffix for positive numbers.
`isDecimalSeparatorAlwaysShown()`	Determines if the decimal separator is displayed with integers.
Setter Methods	
`setDecimalFormatSymbols()`	Sets the decimal format symbols for this `DecimalFormat` instance.
`setDecimalSeparatorAlwaysShown()`	Sets the decimal separator display property for integers.
`setGroupingSize()`	Sets the number of digits between grouping separators.
1.2 `setMaximumFractionDigits()`	Sets the maximum number of digits allowed in the fraction portion of a number.
1.2 `setMinimumFractionDigits()`	Sets the minimum number of digits required in the fraction portion of a number.
1.2 `setMaximumIntegerDigits()`	Sets the maximum number of digits allowed in the integer portion of a number.

Continued

MEMBER SUMMARY	
Setter Methods (*Continued*)	
1.2 `setMinimumIntegerDigits()`	Sets the minimum number of digits required in the integer portion of a number.
`setMultiplier()`	Sets the multiplier for use in percent and per mill.
`setNegativePrefix()`	Sets the prefix for negative numbers.
`setNegativeSuffix()`	Sets the suffix for negative numbers.
`setPositivePrefix()`	Sets the prefix for positive numbers.
`setPositiveSuffix()`	Sets the suffix for positive numbers.
Object Methods	
`clone()`	Creates a copy of this `DecimalFormat` instance.
`equals()`	Compares this `DecimalFormat` instance with another object for equality.
`hashCode()`	Computes the hash code of this `DecimalFormat` instance.

D

See Also

`Format`, `NumberFormat`, `ChoiceFormat`, `DecimalFormatSymbols`.
`DecimalFormat` in *The Java Class Libraries, Second Edition, Volume 1.*

1.2 setMaximumFractionDigits()

PURPOSE Sets the maximum number of digits allowed in the fraction portion of a number.

SYNTAX `public void setMaximumFractionDigits(int maxFractionDigits)`

DESCRIPTION This method sets the maximum number of digits allowed in the fraction portion of a number for both formatting and parsing. If the number has more digits than `maxFractionDigits`, then the least-significant digits are truncated.

This method is equivalent to calling `applyPattern()`, with `maxFractionDigits` number of digit pattern symbols (#) filling out the fraction field.

PARAMETERS

`maxFractionDigits`

The maximum number of digits in the fraction portion of a number. This value should be less than or equal to 340; if it is larger, the number of digits will be pinned to 340. It must be `true` that `maxFractionDigits` ≥ `minFractionDigits`. If the new value for `maxFractionDigits` is less than the current value of `minFractionDigits`, then `minFractionDigits` will also be set to `maxFractionDigits`.

SEE ALSO `getMaximumFractionDigits()` in the `NumberFormat` class.

EXAMPLE See `getMaximumIntegerDigits()` in the `NumberFormat` class.

1.2 setMaximumIntegerDigits()

PURPOSE Sets the maximum number of digits allowed in the integer portion of a number.

SYNTAX `public void setMaximumIntegerDigits(int maxIntegerDigits)`

DESCRIPTION This method sets the maximum number of digits allowed in the integer portion of a number for both formatting and parsing. If the number has more digits than `maxIntegerDigits`, then the *most*-significant digits are truncated! Be certain that this is the effect you want.

Because this method truncates most-significant digits, it has no equivalent to using `applyPattern()`.

PARAMETERS

`maxIntegerDigits`

The maximum number of digits in the integer portion of a number. This value should be less than or equal to 309; if it is larger, the number of digits will be pinned to 309. It must be `true` that `maxIntegerDigits` ≥ `minIntegerDigits`. If the new value for `maxIntegerDigits` is less than the current value of `minIntegerDigits`, then `minIntegerDigits` will also be set to `maxIntegerDigits`.

SEE ALSO `getMaximumIntegerDigits()` in the `NumberFormat` class.

EXAMPLE See `getMaximumIntegerDigits()` in the `NumberFormat` class.

1.2 setMinimumFractionDigits()

PURPOSE Sets the minimum number of digits required in the fraction portion of a number.

SYNTAX `public void setMinimumFractionDigits(int minFractionDigits)`

DESCRIPTION This method sets the minimum number of digits required in the fraction portion of a number for both formatting and parsing. If the number has fewer digits than `minFractionDigits`, then the remaining places are filled with zero digits (`0`) for that locale.

This method is equivalent to calling `applyPattern()`, with `minFractionDigits` number of zero digit pattern symbols (`0`) filling out the fraction field.

PARAMETERS

`minFractionDigits`

The minimum number of digits in the fraction portion of a number. This value should be less than or equal to 340; if it is larger, the number of digits will be pinned to 340. It must be `true` that `minFractionDigits` ≤ `maxFractionDigits`. If the new value for `minFractionDigits` exceeds the current value of `maxFractionDigits`, then `maxFractionDigits` will also be set to `minFractionDigits`.

D

SEE ALSO `getMinimumFractionDigits()` in the `NumberFormat` class.

EXAMPLE See `getMaximumIntegerDigits()` in the `NumberFormat` class.

1.2 setMinimumIntegerDigits()

PURPOSE Sets the minimum number of digits required in the integer portion of a number.

SYNTAX

```
public void setMinimumIntegerDigits(int minIntegerDigits)
```

DESCRIPTION This method sets the minimum number of digits required in the integer portion of a number for both formatting and parsing. If the number has fewer digits than `minIntegerDigits`, then the remaining places are filled with zero digits (`0`) for that locale.

This method is equivalent to calling `applyPattern()`, with `minIntegerDigits` number of zero digit pattern symbols (`0`) filling out the integer field.

PARAMETERS

`minIntegerDigits`

The minimum number of digits in the integer portion of a number. This value should be less than or equal to 309; if it is larger, the number of digits will be pinned to 309. It must be `true` that `minIntegerDigits` ≤ `maxIntegerDigits`. If the new value for `minIntegerDigits` exceeds the current value of `maxIntegerDigits`, then `maxIntegerDigits` will also be set to `minIntegerDigits`.

SEE ALSO `getMinimumIntegerDigits()` in the `NumberFormat` class.

EXAMPLE See `getMaximumIntegerDigits()` in the `NumberFormat` class.

DecimalFormatSymbols

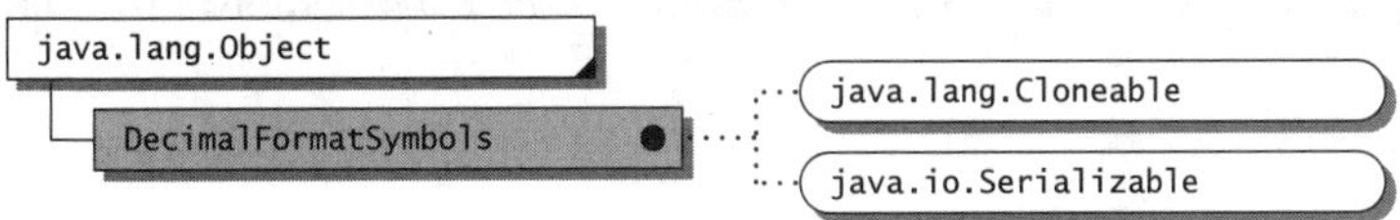

Syntax

```
public final class DecimalFormatSymbols extends Object implements Cloneable,
    Serializable
```

Description

The `DecimalFormatSymbols` class represents a set of symbols recognized by `DecimalFormat` when formatting and parsing localized numbers. There is a different `DecimalFormatSymbols` object for each locale. The symbols are shown in Table 8 with their U. S. English values.

U. S. English	Unicode	Symbol Name	Where Used
`0`	`\u0030`	Zero digit	In localized patterns and formatted strings.
`,`	`\u002C`	Grouping separator	In localized patterns and formatted strings.
`$`	`\u002E`	Currency symbol	In localized patterns and formatted strings.
`USD`	`USD`	International currency symbol	In localized patterns and formatted strings.
`.`	`\u002E`	Decimal separator	In localized patterns and formatted strings.
`.`	`\u002E`	Monetary decimal separator	In localized patterns and formatted strings.
`%`	`\u0025`	Percent sign	In localized patterns and formatted strings.
`‰`	`\u2030`	Per mill sign	In localized patterns and formatted strings.
`-`	`\u002D`	Minus sign	In localized patterns and formatted strings.
`#`	`\u0023`	Pattern digit	Only in localized patterns.
`;`	`\u003B`	Pattern separator	Only in localized patterns.
∞	`\u221E`	Infinity	Only in localized formatted strings.
�	`\uFFFD`	`NaN`	Only in localized formatted strings.

TABLE 8: Symbols in the U. S. English `DecimalFormatSymbols` Object.

These symbols appear in patterns generated by using `applyLocalizedPattern()` in the `DecimalFormat` class; here, they are called *pattern symbols*. They also appear in formatted numbers produced from the `format()` method, where they are called *format symbols*. This class contains setters for changing these symbols. The purpose of changing these symbols is to satisfy the requirements of a particular locale.

See *The Java Class Libraries, Second Edition, Volume 1* for more information about this class.

Changes for Version 1.2

In Version 1.1, currency symbols and monetary decimal separators were defined in the resource files for each locale and appeared when formatting numbers using `NumberFormat.getCurrencyInstance()` but were otherwise not individually settable or gettable. These setters and getters have been added to Version 1.2.

D

MEMBER SUMMARY

	Constructor	
	`DecimalFormatSymbols()`	Constructs a `DecimalFormatSymbols` instance.
	Symbol Getter Methods	
1.2	`getCurrencySymbol()`	Retrieves the string that represents the local currency.
	`getDecimalSeparator()`	Retrieves the character used for the local decimal separator.
	`getDigit()`	Retrieves the character used for a digit in a pattern.
	`getGroupingSeparator()`	Retrieves the character used for the local grouping separator.
	`getInfinity()`	Retrieves the string that represents infinity for a locale.
1.2	`getInternational-CurrencySymbol()`	Retrieves the international string that represents the local currency.
	`getMinusSign()`	Retrieves the character used for the local default minus sign.
1.2	`getMonetaryDecimal-Separator()`	Retrieves the character used for the local monetary decimal separator.
	`getNaN()`	Retrieves the string used to represent `NaN` for a locale.
	`getPatternSeparator()`	Retrieves the character that separates positive and negative subpatterns.
	`getPercent()`	Retrieves the character used for the local percent sign.
	`getPerMill()`	Retrieves the character used for the local per mill sign.
	`getZeroDigit()`	Retrieves the character used for the local zero digit.
	Symbol Setter Methods	
1.2	`setCurrencySymbol()`	Sets the string that represents the local currency.
	`setDecimalSeparator()`	Sets the character used for the local decimal separator.
	`setDigit()`	Sets the character used for a digit in a pattern.
	`setGroupingSeparator()`	Sets the character used for the local grouping separator.
	`setInfinity()`	Sets the string that represents infinity for a locale.
1.2	`setInternationalCurrency-Symbol()`	Sets the international string that represents the local currency.
	`setMinusSign()`	Sets the character used for the local default minus sign.

MEMBER SUMMARY	
1.2 setMonetaryDecimal-Separator()	Sets the character used for the local monetary decimal separator.
setNaN()	Sets the string that represents NaN for a locale.
setPatternSeparator()	Sets the character that separates positive and negative subpatterns.
setPercent()	Sets the character used for the local percent sign.
setPerMill()	Sets the character used for the local per mill sign.
setZeroDigit()	Sets the character used for the local zero digit.
Object Methods	
clone()	Creates a copy of this DecimalFormatSymbols instance.
equals()	Compares this DecimalFormatSymbols instance with another object for equality.
hashCode()	Computes the hash code of this DecimalFormatSymbols instance.

D

See Also

DecimalFormat, Locale.
DecimalFormatSymbols in *The Java Class Libraries, Second Edition, Volume 1*.

1.2 getCurrencySymbol()

PURPOSE Retrieves the string that represents the local currency.

SYNTAX `public String getCurrencySymbol()`

DESCRIPTION Each currency symbol can be represented two ways: as a national currency symbol, such as $, and as an international currency symbol, such as USD. This method gets the string used for the former—the national currency symbol in localized patterns and localized formatted numbers.

RETURNS The string used for the national currency symbol.

SEE ALSO setCurrencySymbol().

EXAMPLE

```
// Create a new decimal format symbols for US
DecimalFormatSymbols dfs;

dfs = new DecimalFormatSymbols(Locale.US);

// Print the currency symbols.
System.out.println( dfs.getCurrencySymbol() );                 // $
System.out.println( dfs.getInternationalCurrencySymbol() );  // USD
System.out.println( dfs.getMonetaryDecimalSeparator() );      // .
```

```
// Create a new decimal format symbols for UK
dfs = new DecimalFormatSymbols(Locale.UK);

// Print the currency symbols.
System.out.println( dfs.getCurrencySymbol() );                  // £
System.out.println( dfs.getInternationalCurrencySymbol() );  // GPB
System.out.println( dfs.getMonetaryDecimalSeparator() );     // .
```

D

1.2 getInternationalCurrencySymbol()

PURPOSE Retrieves the international string that represents the local currency.

SYNTAX `public String getCurrencySymbol()`

DESCRIPTION Each currency symbol can be represented two ways: as a national symbol, such as $, and as an international symbol, such as USD. This method gets the string used for the latter—the international currency symbol in localized patterns and localized formatted numbers.

RETURNS The string used for the international currency symbol.

SEE ALSO `setInternationalCurrencySymbol()`.

EXAMPLE See `getCurrencySymbol()`.

1.2 getMonetaryDecimalSeparator()

PURPOSE Retrieves the character used for the local monetary decimal separator.

SYNTAX `public char getMonetaryDecimalSeparator()`

RETURNS The character used for the monetary decimal sign in localized patterns and localized formatted numbers. The monetary decimal separator is used when the currency sign (`\u00A4`) is seen in the pattern; otherwise, the normal decimal separator is used. For example, this character is different in English and in Arabic.

SEE ALSO `setMonetaryDecimalSeparator()`.

EXAMPLE See `getCurrencySymbol()`.

1.2 setCurrencySymbol()

PURPOSE Sets the string that represents the local currency.

SYNTAX `public void setCurrencySymbol(String currencySymbol)`

DESCRIPTION Each currency symbol can be represented two ways: as a national currency symbol, such as $, and as an international currency symbol, such as USD. This method sets the former—the string used for the national currency symbol in localized patterns and localized formatted numbers.

PARAMETERS

`currencySymbol`
The string specifying the new currency symbol.

SEE ALSO `getCurrencySymbol()`.

EXAMPLE See `getCurrencySymbol()`.

D

1.2 setInternationalCurrencySymbol()

PURPOSE Sets the international string that represents the local currency.

SYNTAX
```
public void setInternationalCurrencySymbol(
   String currencySymbol)
```

DESCRIPTION Each currency symbol can be represented two ways: as a national currency symbol, such as $, and as an international currency symbol, such as USD. This method sets the string, `currencySymbol`, used for the international currency symbol in localized patterns and localized formatted numbers.

PARAMETERS

`currencySymbol`
The string specifying the new currency symbol.

SEE ALSO `getInternationalCurrencySymbol()`.

EXAMPLE See `getCurrencySymbol()`.

1.2 setMonetaryDecimalSeparator()

PURPOSE Sets the character used for the local monetary decimal separator.

SYNTAX
```
public void setMonetaryDecimalSeparator(char decimalSep)
```

DESCRIPTION This method sets the character, `decimalSep`, used for the monetary decimal separator in localized patterns and localized formatted numbers. The monetary decimal separator is used when the currency sign (`\u00A4`) is seen in the pattern; otherwise, the normal decimal separator is used. For example, this character is different in English and in Arabic.

PARAMETERS

`decimalSep` The character specifying the new monetary decimal separator symbol.

EXAMPLE See `getCurrencySymbol()`.

Double

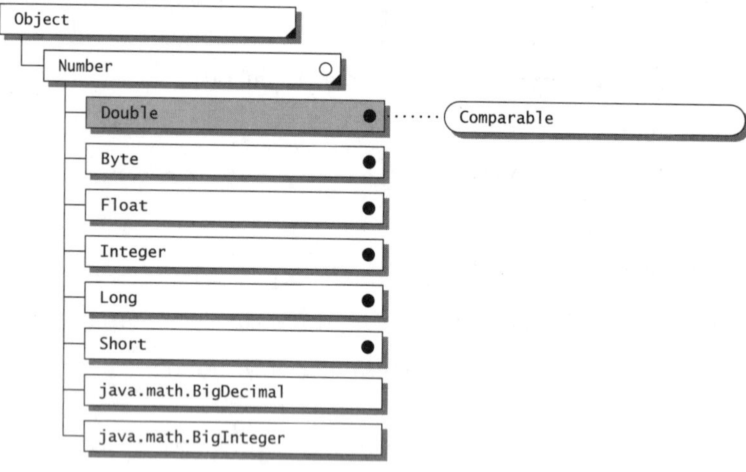

Syntax

```
public final class Double extends Number implements Comparable
```

Description

The `Double` class provides an object wrapper for a `double` data value. A *`double` data value* in Java is a 64-bit floating-point number. This wrapper allows `double`s to be passed to methods in Java class libraries that accept Java objects as parameters. In addition, the `Double` class provides methods that convert values to and from `double`s and perform other operations on `double`s.

See *The Java Class Libraries, Second Edition, Volume 1* for more information about this class.

Changes for Version 1.2

A new method, `parseDouble()`, parses the string representation of a `double` into a `double`. It is a complement to the existing `valueOf()` method that parses a string into a `Double` instance.

The `Double` class implements the `Comparable` interface and has two overloaded forms of the `compareTo()` method used for comparing `Double` objects. This allows arrays of `Double` objects to be sorted, as shown in this example.

```
Double[] da = new Double[]{new Double(1.58e5),
    new Double(-4.23e4), new Double(48)};
Arrays.sort(da);
for (int i = 0; i < da.length; i++) {
    System.out.println(da[i]);
} // -4.23e4, 48, 1.58e5
```

MEMBER SUMMARY	
Constructor	
`Double()`	Constructs a `Double` instance using a `double` or a string.
Constant Fields	
`MAX_VALUE`	The maximum value a `double` can have.
`MIN_VALUE`	The smallest positive value a `double` can have.
`NaN`	The special Not-a-Number (`NaN`) value.
`NEGATIVE_INFINITY`	Negative infinity for a `double`.
`POSITIVE_INFINITY`	Positive infinity for a `double`.
`TYPE`	The `Class` object representing the primitive type `double`.
Number Methods	
`byteValue()`	Retrieves the value of this `Double` as a `byte`.
`doubleValue()`	Retrieves the value of this `Double` as a `double`.
`floatValue()`	Retrieves the value of this `Double` as a `float`.
`intValue()`	Retrieves the value of this `Double` as an `int`.
`longValue()`	Retrieves the value of this `Double` as a `long`.
`shortValue()`	Retrieves the value of this `Double` as a `short`.
Conversion Methods	
`doubleToLongBits()`	Retrieves the bit representation of a `double`.
`longBitsToDouble()`	Retrieves the `double` corresponding to a given bit representation.
1.2 `parseDouble()`	Parses the string representation of a `double` into a `double`.
`toString()`	Generates the string representation of a `double` or a `Double`.
`valueOf()`	Creates a `Double` instance using its string representation.
Comparison Methods	
1.2 `compareTo()`	Compares the signed numeric value of this `Double` with that of another `Double`.
`equals()`	Determines if this `Double` is equal to another object.
`isInfinite()`	Determines if a `double` is infinitely large in magnitude.
`isNaN()`	Determines if a `double` is the special Not-a-Number (`NaN`) value.
Hash Code Method	
`hashCode()`	Computes the hash code of this `Double`.

See Also

`Comparable`, `java.util.Arrays`.
`Double` in *The Java Class Libraries, Second Edition, Volume 1.*

D

1.2 compareTo()

PURPOSE Compares the signed numeric value of this Double with that of another Double.

SYNTAX
```
public int compareTo(Double adouble)
public int compareTo(Object adouble)
```

DESCRIPTION This method compares this Double's numeric value with that of adouble. It returns an int indicating whether the two numeric values are equal and, if they are not, the ordering of the two values. It returns 0 if the two numeric values are the same. It returns a negative number if the numeric value of this Double object is less than that of adouble. It returns a positive number if the numeric value of this Double object is greater than that of adouble.

There are two ways in which comparisons performed by this method differ from those performed by the Java language numerical comparison operators <, <=, ==, >=, and > when applied to primitive doubles.

- Double.NaN is considered by this method to be equal to itself and greater than all other double values (including Double.POSITIVE_INFINITY).
- 0.0d is considered by this method to be greater than -0.0d.

If adouble is not an instance of Double, a ClassCastException is thrown.

PARAMETERS

adouble A non-null Double with which to compare.

RETURNS 0 if the numeric values of this Double and adouble are the same; a negative number if this Double's value is less than that of adouble; a positive number if this Double's value is greater than that of adouble.

EXCEPTIONS

ClassCastException

If adouble is not an instance of Double.

SEE ALSO Comparable.

EXAMPLE
```
Double d = new Double(1.23e3);
System.out.println(d.compareTo(new Double(1.23e3)));                  // 0
System.out.println(d.compareTo(new Double(0.0)));                     // 1

System.out.println(new Double(0.0).compareTo(new Double(-0.0))); // 1
System.out.println(new Double(0.0).compareTo(new Double(0.0)));  // 0

System.out.println(new Double(Double.POSITIVE_INFINITY).compareTo(
    new Double(Double.POSITIVE_INFINITY)));                           // 0

System.out.println(new Double(Double.POSITIVE_INFINITY).compareTo(
    new Double(Double.NEGATIVE_INFINITY)));                           // 1

System.out.println(new Double(Double.POSITIVE_INFINITY).compareTo(
```

```
    new Double(Double.NaN)));                                // -1

System.out.println(new Double(Double.POSITIVE_INFINITY).compareTo(
    new Double(Double.MAX_VALUE)));                          // 1

System.out.println(new Double(Double.NEGATIVE_INFINITY).compareTo(
    new Double(Double.MIN_VALUE)));                          // -1
System.out.println(new Double(Double.NaN).compareTo(
    new Double(Double.NaN)));                                // 0

System.out.println(new Double(Double.NaN).compareTo(new Double(0.0))); // 1

System.out.println(d.compareTo("abc")); // ClassCastException
```


1.2 parseDouble()

PURPOSE Parses the string representation of a `double` into a `double`.

SYNTAX

```
public static double parseDouble(String str) throws
    NumberFormatException
```

DESCRIPTION This method parses the string `str` into a `double` and returns it as a `double`. It expects `str` to be in the same format as that acceptable to `valueOf()`. The only difference between `parseDouble()` and `valueOf()` is that the former returns the result as a `double`, while the latter returns the result as a `Double`.

The format of the string is

[*Sign*] *Digits* **.** [*Digits*] [*ExponentPart*]

[*Sign*] **.** *Digits* [*ExponentPart*]

Sign is a negative sign, *Digits* is a sequence of digits from 0 through 9, and *ExponentPart* is one of “e” or “E” followed by a signed integer. Details of this format are in *The Java Language Specification, First Edition*, Section 20.10.16. Leading and trailing whitespace characters in `str` are ignored.

PARAMETERS

`str` A non-`null` string to be parsed.

RETURNS The `double` value represented by `str`.

EXCEPTIONS

`NumberFormatException`

If the string does not contain a valid format for a `double`.

SEE ALSO `valueOf()`.

EXAMPLE

```
String s1 = "1.0981e3";
String s2 = "-5.12";
```

```
try {
    double d1 = Double.parseDouble(s1);
    double d2 = Double.parseDouble(s2);

    System.out.println(d1);      // 1098.1
    System.out.println(d2);      // -5.12
} catch (NumberFormatException e) {
    System.err.println(e);
}
```

ExceptionInInitializerError

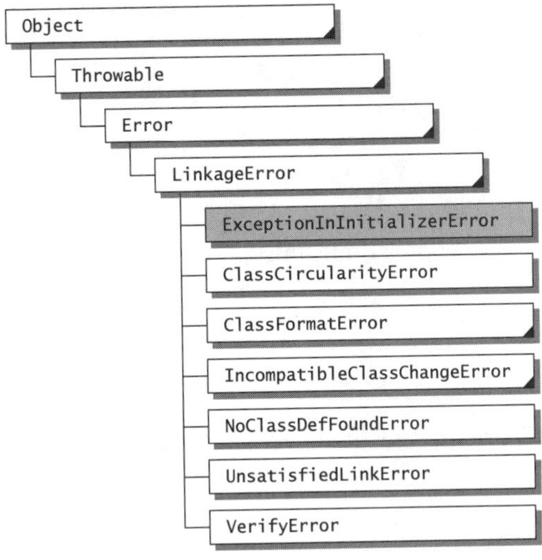

Syntax

```
public class ExceptionInInitializerError extends LinkageError
```

Description

`ExceptionInInitializerError` is a runtime linkage error that is thrown when an exception occurs while the Java runtime is initializing a static variable or a class's static initializer. If an `Error` or any of its subclasses is thrown during static initialization, the error itself is rethrown. If an exception (not a subclass of `Error`) is thrown, that exception is wrapped inside an `ExceptionInInitializerError` and then thrown by the initializer.

See *The Java Class Libraries, Second Edition, Volume 1* for more information about this class.

Changes for Version 1.2

The `printStackTrace()` methods have been overridden to display the stack trace of the root cause instead of the `ExceptionInInitializerError`, if it has been set.

MEMBER SUMMARY	
Constructor	
`ExceptionInInitializerError()`	Constructs an `ExceptionInInitializerError` instance.
Access Method	
`getException()`	Retrieves the exception that caused the initializer to fail.
Debugging Method	
Δ `printStackTrace()`	Prints this `ExceptionInInitializerError` and its stack trace.

E

See Also

`ExceptionInInitializerError` in *The Java Class Libraries, Second Edition, Volume 1.*

Δ printStackTrace()

PURPOSE Prints this `ExceptionInInitializerError`'s stack trace.

SYNTAX
```
public void printStackTrace()
public void printStackTrace(PrintStream ps)
public void printStackTrace(PrintWriter pw)
```

DESCRIPTION This method prints this `ExceptionInInitializerError`'s stack trace. If you do not supply any arguments, the stack trace is sent to `System.err`. If you supply a `PrintStream` argument `ps`, the output will go to `ps`. If you supply a `PrintWriter` argument `pw`, the output will go to `pw`.

If `getException()` is non-`null`, the stack trace of that exception is displayed. Otherwise, the stack trace of this `ExceptionInInitializerError` is displayed.

1.2 CHANGES In Version 1.1, all forms of this method were inherited from `Throwable`. The stack trace printed was always that of the `ExceptionInInitializerError` (instead of the stack trace of `getException()`).

OVERRIDES `Throwable.printStackTrace()`.

SEE ALSO `getException()`, `System.err`.

FieldPosition

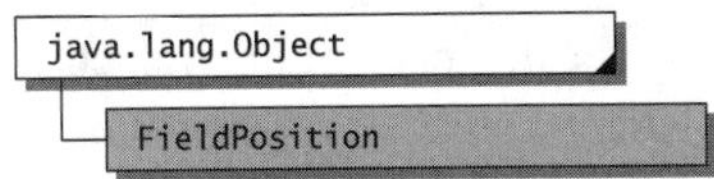

Syntax

```
public class FieldPosition extends Object
```

Description

Numbers and dates are made up of fields. A number can have an integer field and a fraction field. A date can have a year, month, week, day, hour, minute, and second field, among others.

The `FieldPosition` class holds the field constant that identifies a particular field (such as `NumberFormat.INTEGER_FIELD` for a number) and the begin index and end index of that field within a formatted number or date. This is useful for aligning a column of formatted numbers or dates on that field. For example, you can align numbers on a decimal point or dates on the year. This class identifies the position of a field in a formatted string by the characters from the begin index (inclusive) to the end index (exclusive).

If all you want is the contents of one or more date fields, use the `SimpleDateFormat` class instead. This gives you a simple way, using patterns, to get any combination of the day, month, year, hour, minute, second, and so on without having to handle `FieldPosition` objects.

`FieldPosition` is not used when parsing a string to a number or date—`ParsePosition` is used instead.

See *The Java Class Libraries, Second Edition, Volume 1* for more information about this class.

Changes for Version 1.2

There are two new setter methods: `setBeginIndex()` and `setEndIndex()`. This class now also overrides `Object` methods: `equals()`, `hashCode()`, and `toString()`.

MEMBER SUMMARY		
	Constructor	
	`FieldPosition()`	Constructs a `FieldPosition` instance for a specific field.
	Setter Methods	
1.2	`setBeginIndex()`	Sets the index of the first character in this `FieldPosition`'s field.
1.2	`setEndIndex()`	Sets the index of the character following the last character in this `FieldPosition`'s field.

Continued

MEMBER SUMMARY	
Access Methods	
`getBeginIndex()`	Retrieves the index of the first character in this `FieldPosition`'s field.
`getEndIndex()`	Retrieves the index of the character following the last character in this `FieldPosition`'s field.
`getField()`	Retrieves the field identifier of this `FieldPosition`'s field.
Object Methods	
Δ `toString()`	Generates the string representation of this `FieldPosition` instance.
Δ `equals()`	Compares this `FieldPosition` instance with another object for equality.
Δ `hashCode()`	Computes the hash code of this `FieldPosition` instance.

See Also

`Format`, `DecimalFormat`, `NumberFormat`.
`FieldPosition` in *The Java Class Libraries, Second Edition, Volume 1.*

Δ equals()

PURPOSE Compares this `FieldPosition` instance with another object for equality.

SYNTAX `public boolean equals(Object obj)`

DESCRIPTION This method compares this `FieldPosition` instance with `obj` for equality. If `obj` is a `FieldPosition` instance and has the same values of field identifier, begin index, and end index, then the instances are equal and this method returns `true`. If the `FieldPosition` values are not equal or if `obj` is `null` or not a `FieldPosition` instance, this method returns `false`.

1.2 CHANGES In Version 1.1, this method was not implemented in `FieldPosition`; instead, the same method in `Object` was called.

PARAMETERS

`obj` The possibly `null` object with which to compare.

RETURNS `true` if `obj` is not `null` and is type `FieldPosition` and is equal to this `FieldPosition` object; `false` otherwise.

OVERRIDES `java.lang.Object.equals()`.

SEE ALSO `hashCode()`.

EXAMPLE This example creates two `FieldPosition` instances, compares them for equality, and computes the hash code of the first one.

```
import java.text.FieldPosition;
import java.text.NumberFormat;
```

```
class Main {
    public static void main(String args[]) {
        // Create two field positions.
        FieldPosition fp1 = new FieldPosition(NumberFormat.INTEGER_FIELD);
        System.out.println(fp1.toString());

        FieldPosition fp2 = new FieldPosition(NumberFormat.INTEGER_FIELD);
        System.out.println(fp2.toString());

        // Tests for equality.
        System.out.println( fp1.equals(fp2) );                    // true
        System.out.println( fp1.equals(null) );                   // false

        // Compute hashcode.
        System.out.println( fp1.hashCode() == fp2.hashCode() );  // true

        fp1.setBeginIndex(1);

        // Tests for equality.
        System.out.println( fp1.equals(fp2) );                    // false
        System.out.println( fp1.equals(null) );                   // false

        // Compute hashcode.
        System.out.println( fp1.hashCode() == fp2.hashCode() );  // false
    }
}
```

Δ hashCode()

PURPOSE Computes the hash code of this `FieldPosition` instance.

SYNTAX `public int hashCode()`

DESCRIPTION This method computes the hash code, an `int`, of this `FieldPosition` instance based on its field identifier, begin index, and end index. Two `FieldPosition` instances with the same properties will have the same hash code. However, two `FieldPosition` instances that do not have the same properties might also have the same hash code, although the hash code algorithm reduces this possibility. The hash code is typically used as the key in a hash table.

1.2 CHANGES In Version 1.1, this method was not implemented in `FieldPosition`; instead, the same method in `Object` was called.

RETURNS The hash code of this `FieldPosition` instance, an `int`.

OVERRIDES `java.lang.Object.hashCode()`.

SEE ALSO `equals()`.

EXAMPLE See `equals()`.

1.2 setBeginIndex()

PURPOSE Sets the index of the first character in this `FieldPosition`'s field.

SYNTAX `public void setBeginIndex(int idx)`

DESCRIPTION This method sets the index of the first character in this field to `idx`. It is used by subclasses of `Format` in operations involving field positions. You use this method when creating a new subclass of `Format` to specify where each of the subclass's formatted fields begins.

PARAMETERS

`idx` A non-negative `int` specifying the position of the first character in this field.

1.2 setEndIndex()

PURPOSE Sets the index of the character following the last character in this `FieldPosition`'s field.

SYNTAX `public void setEndIndex(int idx)`

DESCRIPTION This method sets the index of the character following the last character in this field to `idx`. It is used by subclasses of `Format`. You use this method when creating a new subclass of `Format` to specify where each of the subclass's formatted fields ends.

PARAMETERS

`idx` An `int` specifying the position of the last character in this field.

Δ toString()

PURPOSE Generates the string representation of this `FieldPosition` instance.

SYNTAX `public String toString()`

DESCRIPTION This method generates the string representation of this `FieldPosition` instance, which includes the class name, the field identifier, and the values for the begin index and end index. Here is an example of such a string:

```
java.text.FieldPosition[field=2,beginIndex=0,endIndex=0]
```

1.2 CHANGES In Version 1.1, this method was not implemented in `FieldPosition`; instead, the same method in `Object` was called.

RETURNS The string representation of this `FieldPosition` instance.

OVERRIDES `java.lang.Object.toString()`.

EXAMPLE See `equals()`.

File

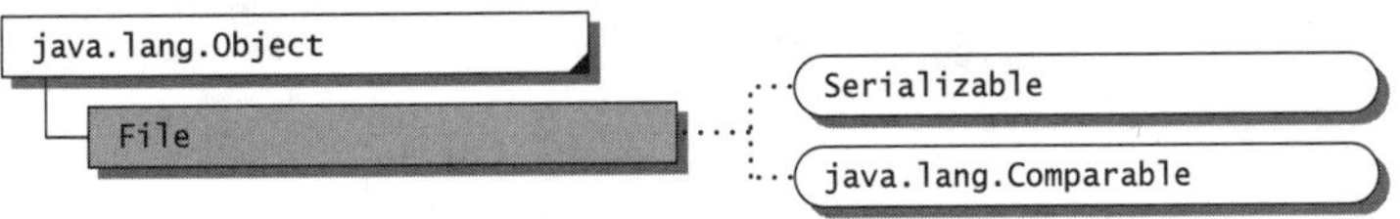

Syntax

```
public class File implements java.io.Serializable, Comparable
```

Description

The `File` class represents a filename. The filename can be absolute, in which case it is resolved relative to the root directory of the file system. Or it can be relative, in which case it is resolved relative to the current directory in which the Java program is running. The filename is specified in the filename convention of the file system on which the Java program is running.

This class not only manipulates the filename itself. It also provides methods for performing file-related operations that actually interact with the underlying file system. Such operations include creating directories, obtaining the status of the file/directory, renaming the file, and checking permissions on the file.

See *The Java Class Libraries, Second Edition, Volume 1* for more information about this class.

Changes for Version 1.2

The `File` class has been modified to implement the `Comparable` interface, which requires the implementation of the `compareTo()` method. This allows `File` instances to be lexicographically sorted, for example by using `Arrays.sort()`.

Methods have been added that returned `File` instances for getting the absolute, canonical, and parent pathnames of a `File`. Similarly, methods have been added for listing a directory (`listFiles()`) that return a list of `File` instances instead of `String` instances.

The `File` class also provides new capabilities. Using it, you now can create new files or temporary files, as well as use `deleteOnExit()` to ensure that temporary files are deleted automatically upon the Java virtual machine's termination. You can determine whether a file is *hidden* (determined in a platform-specific way), get a "file" URL corresponding to the file, and set the file's last modification time and read-only status.

MEMBER SUMMARY

	Constructor	
	`File()`	Constructs a `File` instance.
	Filename Methods	
1.2	`compareTo()`	Compares this `File` to another `File`.
1.2	`getAbsoluteFile()`	Creates a new `File` using this `File`'s absolute pathname.
	`getAbsolutePath()`	Generates the absolute (complete) pathname of this `File`.
1.2	`getCanonicalFile()`	Creates a new `File` using this `File`'s canonical pathname.
	`getCanonicalPath()`	Generates the absolute pathname of this `File` with all references resolved.
	`getName()`	Retrieves the filename (no directory) of this `File`.
	`getParent()`	Retrieves the pathname of the parent directory of this `File`.
1.2	`getParentFile()`	Creates a new `File` instance using the pathname of this `File`'s parent.
	`getPath()`	Retrieves the pathname of this `File`.
	`isAbsolute()`	Determines whether the pathname of this `File` is absolute.
1.2	`isHidden()`	Determines whether the file represented by this `File` is a hidden file.
1.2	`toURL()`	Retrieves the "file" URL corresponding to this `File`.
	File Status Methods	
	`canRead()`	Determines whether the current execution context is allowed to read this `File`.
	`canWrite()`	Determines whether the current execution context is allowed to write to this `File`.
	`exists()`	Determines whether this `File` exists.
	`isDirectory()`	Determines whether this `File` names a directory.
	`isFile()`	Determines whether this `File` names a regular file (nondirectory).
	`lastModified()`	Retrieves the last modification time of this `File`.
	`length()`	Retrieves the size of this `File` in bytes.
1.2	`setLastModified()`	Sets the last modification time of the file represented by this `File`.
1.2	`setReadOnly()`	Requests that the file represented by this `File` be set to allow only read operations.
	File Namespace Modification Methods	
1.2	`createNewFile()`	Creates a new file using the name of this `File`.
1.2	`createTempFile()`	Creates a new, empty, temporary file.
	`delete()`	Deletes this `File` or directory.
1.2	`deleteOnExit()`	Requests that the file represented by this `File` be deleted when the Java virtual machine exits normally.
	`mkdir()`	Creates a directory with the pathname of this `File`.
	`mkdirs()`	Creates all directories in the pathname of this `File`.
	`renameTo()`	Renames this `File`.

MEMBER SUMMARY

File Namespace Browsing Methods

	`list()`	Lists the files in the directory named by this `File`.
1.2	`listFiles()`	Lists the files in the directory named by this `File`.
1.2	`listRoots()`	Lists the available file system roots.

File System Property Fields (Static)

`pathSeparator`	The path variable separator string of the operating system.
`pathSeparatorChar`	The path variable separator character of the operating system.
`separator`	The file directory separator string of the file system.
`separatorChar`	The file directory separator character of the file system.

Object Methods

Δ	`equals()`	Compares this `File` with another object for equality.
	`hashCode()`	Computes the hash code of this `File`.
	`toString()`	Generates the string representation for this `File`.

F

See Also

`File` in *The Java Class Libraries, Second Edition, Volume 1.*

1.2 compareTo()

PURPOSE Compares this `File` to another `File`.

SYNTAX
```
public int compareTo(File target)
public int compareTo(Object target) {
```

DESCRIPTION This method compares this `File` to `target`. If this `File` is lexicographically equal to `target`, zero is returned. If this `File` is lexicographically less than `target`, a negative number is returned. If this `File` is lexicographically greater than `target`, a positive number is returned. If `target` is not an instance of `File`, a `ClassCastException` is thrown. The lexicographical ordering is platform-specific and depends on the underlying file system.

PARAMETERS

`target` The non-`null` `File` object to be compared.

RETURNS `0` if `target` is equal to this `File`, or a number < `0` if this `File` is lexicographically less than `target`, or a number > `0` if this `File` is lexicographically greater than `target`.

EXCEPTIONS

`ClassCastException`

If `target` is not an instance of `File`.

SEE ALSO `java.lang.Comparable`, `equals()`.

EXAMPLE

```
File f1 = new File("abc.txt");
File f2 = new File("abc.TXT");
File f3 = new File("xyz.txt");
File f4 = new File("aaa.txt");

System.out.println(f1.compareTo(f2)); // 0 on Windows; > 0 on Unix
System.out.println(f1.compareTo(f3)); // < 0
System.out.println(f1.compareTo(f4)); // > 0
```

F

1.2 createNewFile()

PURPOSE Creates a new file using the name of this `File`.

SYNTAX `public boolean createNewFile() throws IOException`

DESCRIPTION This method creates a new empty file for this `File`. If the file already exists, `false` is returned and the existing file is left unchanged. The check for whether the file already exists and the file creation are done in one step (that is, *atomically*) so that no intervening file system operation can create the file between the time that the existence check is performed and the time of file creation.

This method can be used with `deleteOnExit()` to implement a simple file-locking protocol.

The file can be created only if allowed by the security manager.

RETURNS `true` if the file was created successfully; `false` if the file already exists.

SEE ALSO `deleteOnExit()`, `java.lang.SecurityManager.checkWrite()`.

EXAMPLE

```
File lock = new File("testfile.lock");

try {
    // Create lock file
    if (lock.createNewFile()) {
        // Make sure it gets deleted when we're done
        lock.deleteOnExit();

        // Do something useful
        System.out.println("Obtained lock");
    } else {
        System.out.println("Cannot grab lock");
    }
} catch (IOException e) {
    e.printStackTrace();
}
```

1.2 createTempFile()

PURPOSE Creates a new, empty, temporary file.

SYNTAX

```
public static File createTempFile(String prefix, String suffix)
    throws IOException
public static File createTempFile(String prefix, String suffix,
    File directory) throws IOException
```

DESCRIPTION This method creates a new, empty, temporary file in `directory`. The file's name is generated using `prefix`, `suffix`, and a random sequence of characters. If `directory` is not supplied or `null`, the file is created in the default, platform-dependent, temporary-file directory. On UNIX systems, the default is either `/tmp` or `/var/tmp/`. On Windows systems, the default is `c:\temp`. This default can be changed using the `"java.io.tmpdir"` system property.

When this method returns, the following two conditions are guaranteed:

- The file did not exist before this method was invoked.
- This method will not return the same `File` again when invoked against the current invocation of the Java virtual machine.

The caller should use `deleteOnExit()` to ensure that the temporary file is removed when the program terminates.

`prefix` and `suffix` may be truncated in order to produce a valid name in the underlying file system. Only the first three characters of `prefix` are guaranteed to be used; the rest might be truncated. If `suffix` starts with the period character, the period and the next three characters are guaranteed to be used as the suffix of the name; the rest might be truncated. The possibly truncated prefix, a sequence of five or more characters generated by the Java runtime system, and the possibly truncated suffix are concatenated to produce the temporary file's name.

The file can be created only if permitted by the security manager.

PARAMETERS

`directory` The possibly `null` directory in which to create the temporary file.

`prefix` A non-`null` sequence of characters to be used as the beginning of the filename. It must contain at least three characters and must be valid for the underlying file system.

`suffix` A possibly `null` sequence of characters to be used as the end of the filename. It must contain characters valid for the underlying file system. If it is `null`, the suffix `.tmp` is used.

RETURNS A non-`null` `File` for the newly created empty file.

EXCEPTIONS

`IllegalArgumentException`
: If `prefix` contains fewer than three characters.

`IOException`
: If the temporary file could not be created due to IO problems.

`SecurityException`
: If the caller does not have permission to create the file.

SEE ALSO `deleteOnExit()`.

EXAMPLE

```
try {
    File temp = File.createTempFile("jcl", ".out");

    // Make sure it gets deleted when we're done
    temp.deleteOnExit();

    // Print out file name to see what we got
    System.out.println(temp);

    FileWriter fout = new FileWriter(temp);
    for (int i = 0; i < 100; i++) {
        fout.write("hello" + i);
    }
    fout.close();
    System.out.println("Temp file size: " + temp.length());
} catch (IOException e) {
    e.printStackTrace();
}
```

F

1.2 deleteOnExit()

PURPOSE Requests that the file represented by this `File` be deleted when the Java virtual machine exits normally.

SYNTAX `public void deleteOnExit()`

DESCRIPTION This method requests that the file or directory represented by this `File` be deleted when the Java virtual machine exits normally. The Java virtual machine exits normally when either all of the nondaemon threads terminate or a thread successfully invokes `System.exit()`.

This method is useful when used with temporary files that were created using `createTempFile()` and with file locks that were created using `createNewFile()`. Once `deleteOnExit()` has been invoked on a `File`, it is not possible to cancel the request. This method should therefore be used with care.

This method can be invoked only if the caller has permission from the security manager to delete the file.

EXCEPTIONS

`SecurityException`
If the security manager does not permit this file to be deleted by the caller.

SEE ALSO `createNewFile(), createTempFile(), delete(), java.lang.SecurityManager.checkDelete().`

EXAMPLE See `createNewFile()`, `createTempFile()`.

Δ equals()

PURPOSE Compares this `File` with another object for equality.

SYNTAX `public boolean equals(Object obj)`

DESCRIPTION This method determines whether this `File` has the same path as that of `obj`. It returns `true` if the two paths are equal. It returns `false` if the two are not equal or if `obj` is `null` or not a `File`. `compareTo()` is used to determine whether this `File` is equal to `obj`.

1.2 CHANGES In Version 1.1, the path comparison used string comparison instead of `compareTo()` (which is file system-dependent) for determining whether two file pathnames are equal. Therefore, for file systems such as Windows that support case-insensitive file pathnames, two paths that have characters that are the same but of different cases were not equal in Version 1.1 but are equal in Version 1.2.

PARAMETERS

`obj` The possibly `null` object against which this `File` is compared.

RETURNS `true` if `obj` has the same path as this object; `false` otherwise.

SEE ALSO `compareTo(), hashCode().`

EXAMPLE See `renameTo()` in *The Java Class Libraries, Second Edition, Volume 1.*

1.2 getAbsoluteFile()

PURPOSE Creates a new `File` using this `File`'s absolute pathname.

SYNTAX `public File getAbsoluteFile()`

DESCRIPTION This method is equivalent to

```
new File(this.getAbsolutePath())
```

RETURNS An instance of `File` whose pathname is `this.getAbsolutePath()`.

SEE ALSO `getAbsolutePath(), getCanonicalFile().`

EXAMPLE

```
System.out.println(new File("Main.java").getAbsoluteFile());
                                        // e:\book\egs\io\File\Main.java
System.out.println(
    new File("c:\\frontpage_webs\\", "Content").getAbsoluteFile());
                                        // c:\frontpage_webs\Content
System.out.println(
    new File("c:\\frontpage_webs", "Content").getAbsoluteFile());
                                        // c:\frontpage_webs\Content
System.out.println(new File("\\tmp\\graphics").getAbsoluteFile());
                                        // \tmp\graphics
```

F

1.2 getCanonicalFile()

PURPOSE Creates a new `File` using this `File`'s canonical pathname.

SYNTAX `public File getCanonicalFile() throws IOException`

DESCRIPTION This method is equivalent to

`new File(this.getCanonicalPath())`

RETURNS An instance of `File` whose pathname is `this.getCanonicalPath()`.

EXCEPTIONS

`IOException`

If an IO error occurs while determining the file's canonical path.

SEE ALSO `getAbsoluteFile()`, `getCanonicalPath()`.

EXAMPLE

```
System.out.println(
    new File("Main.java").getCanonicalFile());
                                        // /home/rosanna/tmp/Main.java
System.out.println(
    new File(".").getCanonicalFile());
                                        // /home/rosanna/tmp
System.out.println(
    new File("/export/home/tmp/../java", ".").getCanonicalFile());
                                        // /export/home/java
System.out.println(
    new File("/notthere/home/tmp/../java", ".").getCanonicalFile());
                                        // /notthere/home/tmp/../java/.
```

1.2 getParentFile()

PURPOSE Creates a new `File` instance using the pathname of this `File`'s parent.

SYNTAX `public File getParentFile()`

DESCRIPTION This method creates a new `File` instance using the pathname of `File's` parent. If this `File`'s pathname names a parent directory (that is, `this.getParent()`

returns non-`null`), the pathname of the parent directory is used to create a new instance of `File`. If this `File` does not have a parent (that is, `this.getParent()` returns `null`), this method returns `null`.

RETURNS A possibly `null` `File` representing this `File`'s parent directory.

SEE ALSO `getParent()`.

EXAMPLE

```
System.out.println(
    new File("Main.java").getParentFile());
                                        // null
System.out.println(
    new File("/export/home/tmp/../java", ".").getParentFile());
                                        // /export/home/tmp/../java
System.out.println(
    new File("/notthere/home/tmp/../java", ".").getParentFile());
                                        // /notthere/home/tmp/../java/
```

F

1.2 isHidden()

PURPOSE Determines whether the file represented by this `File` is a hidden file.

SYNTAX `public boolean isHidden()`

DESCRIPTION This method determines whether the file represented by this `File` is hidden. Whether a file is *hidden* is file system-dependent. On UNIX, a file is hidden if its filename begins with the period character ("."). On Windows systems, a file is hidden if it has been marked hidden in the file system.

RETURNS `true` if the file represented by this `File` is a hidden file; `false` otherwise.

EXCEPTIONS

`SecurityException`

If this file cannot be examined for security reasons.

SEE ALSO `java.lang.SecurityManager.checkRead()`.

EXAMPLE

```
System.out.println(new File("Main.java").isHidden()); // false
System.out.println(new File(".").isHidden());         // T on Unix; F on Win
System.out.println(new File("..").isHidden());        // T on Unix; F on Win
System.out.println(new File(".out").isHidden());      // T on Unix; F on Win
System.out.println(new File("/tmp", ".").isHidden()); // T on Unix; F on Win
```

1.2 listFiles()

PURPOSE

Lists the files in the directory named by this `File`.

SYNTAX

```
public File[] listFiles()
public File[] listFiles(FilenameFilter filter)
public File[] listFiles(FileFilter filter)
```

DESCRIPTION

This method is like `list()`, except that `list()` returns an array of string names, while this method returns an array of `File` instances. If a filename filter `filter` is supplied, the `File` instances returned are the files in the directory named by this `File` that satisfy `filter`. If `filter` is `null` or if not supplied, this method returns the names of all files found in the directory named by this `File`.

The `File` instances in the array are constructed using

```
new File(this.getPath(), childName);
```

Consequently, if this `File` contains an absolute path, then the returned `File` instances will also be absolute. If this `File` contains a relative path, then the returned instances of `File` will be relative to the same directory.

If this `File` does not represent a directory, this method returns `null`. Any hidden files are included in this list. But the names "`.`" and "`..`"—which are used to indicate the current directory and parent directory, respectively—are not included in this list.

This method can be invoked only if the caller is allowed by the security manager and the underlying file system to read this file.

PARAMETERS

`filter` A possibly `null` filter used to select the filenames or `File`s. If `null`, the same as not supplying any filter.

RETURNS

A possibly `null` array containing filter-selected instances of `File` in the directory named by this file. `null` if this `File` does not name a directory or if an IO error occurred while the files in the directory were being obtained.

EXCEPTIONS

`SecurityException`
If this file cannot be examined due to security reasons.

SEE ALSO

`FilenameFilter`, `FileFilter`.

EXAMPLE

```
import java.io.*;

class Main {
    public static void main(String[] args) {
        if (args.length != 2) {
            System.err.println("usage: java Main <directory> <suffix>");
            System.exit(-1);
```

```
        }

        File dir = new File(args[0]);
        File[] fs = dir.listFiles(new SuffixFileFilter(args[1]));
        if (dir == null) {
            System.out.println(args[0] + " is not a directory");
        } else {
            for (int i = 0; i < fs.length; i++) {
                System.out.println(fs[i]);
            }
        }
    }

    static class SuffixFileFilter implements FileFilter {
        String suffix;
        SuffixFileFilter(String suffix) {
            this.suffix = suffix;
        }

        public boolean accept(File target) {
            return target.getName().endsWith(suffix);
        }
    }
}
```

F

1.2 listRoots()

PURPOSE Lists the available file system roots.

SYNTAX `public static File[] listRoots()`

DESCRIPTION This method lists the roots of file systems visible to the caller. This list is platform-dependent. On UNIX, there is a single file system root, whose name is " /". On Windows, there is a file system root for each drive mounted on the underlying system. These drives might appear or disappear as drives and disks are physically connected or disconnected from the system. Therefore the result returned by this method depends the state of the underlying system.

Note that there are some file systems that do not have roots and hence will not show up in the list returned by this method. The Win32 Universal Naming Convention (UNC) filenames begin with "\" but there is no root for the UNC namespace, per se.

If the caller is not permitted to read a particular drive or part of the underlying file systems, the corresponding root is omitted from the result.

RETURNS A possibly `null` array of `File` instances representing roots of file systems; `null` if the roots cannot be determined.

SEE ALSO `list()`, `listFiles()`.

EXAMPLE

```
File[] roots = File.listRoots();
if (roots == null) {
```

```
        System.out.println("Cannot get roots");
    } else {
        for (int i = 0; i < roots.length; i++) {
            System.out.println(roots[i]);
        }
    }
```

1.2 setLastModified()

PURPOSE Sets the last modification time of the file represented by this `File`.

SYNTAX `public boolean setLastModified(long time)`

DESCRIPTION This method sets the last modification time, `time`, of this `File`. All platforms support file modification times to the nearest second, but some provide more precision. `time` will be truncated to fit the supported precision.

This method can be invoked only if the caller is allowed by the security manager and the underlying file system to update this file.

PARAMETERS

`time` A `long` representing the time in milliseconds since epoch (January 1, 1970, 00:00:00 UTC).

RETURNS `true` if the file's last modification time was set successfully; `false` otherwise.

EXCEPTIONS

`IllegalArgumentException`
If `time` < `0`.

`SecurityException`
If the caller does not have permission to update this file.

SEE ALSO `lastModified()`, `java.lang.SecurityManager.checkWrite()`.

EXAMPLE

```
File temp = File.createTempFile("jcl", ".out");

// Make sure it gets deleted when we're done
temp.deleteOnExit();

// Print out file name and its last modified time
long mod = temp.lastModified();
System.out.println(temp + ":" + mod);

// Introduced some delay
try {
    Thread.sleep(3000);
} catch (InterruptedException ie) {
};

// Write something out to file
FileWriter fout = new FileWriter(temp);
fout.write("hello");
```

```
fout.close();

System.out.println(temp + ":" + temp.lastModified());

// Change modified date back to original
if (temp.setLastModified(mod)) {
    System.out.println(temp + ":" + temp.lastModified());
} else {
    System.out.println("modification time unchanged");
}
```

1.2 setReadOnly()

F

PURPOSE Requests that the file represented by this `File` be set to allow only read operations.

SYNTAX `public boolean setReadOnly()`

DESCRIPTION This method marks the file represented by this `File` to be in read-only mode. A file or directory is in read-only mode if only read operations can be performed on it. For a file, this means you cannot update its contents. For a directory, this means you cannot add or delete files from the directory. Whether a read-only file or directory may be deleted depends on the underlying file system.

The `File` class does not provide a method to undo the read-only setting or query whether a file is in read-only mode or any other mode. To undo this setting, you need to use a platform-dependent utility.

RETURNS `true` if the file represented by this `File` has been set to read-only mode; `false` otherwise.

EXCEPTIONS

`SecurityException`

If the caller does not have permission to update this file.

SEE ALSO `java.lang.SecurityManager.checkWrite()`.

EXAMPLE This program sets a file to read-only mode.

```
import java.io.*;

class Main {
    public static void main(String[] args) {
        if (args.length != 1) {
            System.err.println("usage: java Main <filename>");
            System.exit(-1);
        }

        if ((new File(args[0])).setReadOnly()) {
            System.out.println("Set file to read-only mode");
        } else {
            System.out.println("Cannot set to read-only mode");
```

```
            }
        }
    }
```

1.2 toURL()

PURPOSE Retrieves the "file" URL corresponding to this `File`.

SYNTAX `public URL toURL() throws MalformedURLException`

DESCRIPTION This method creates a "file" URL representing this `File`. It uses this `File`'s absolute pathname and converts the file separators into slash characters ("/"). If the absolute pathname does not have a leading slash character, one is added to the file part of the URL. If this `File` represents a directory and does not have a trailing slash character, one is added to the file part of the URL.

RETURNS A non-`null` "file" `URL` instance representing this `File`.

SEE ALSO `getAbsolutePath()`, `java.net.URL`, `separatorChar`.

EXAMPLE

```
    try {
        System.out.println(new File("Main.java").toURL());
                                        // file:/c:/export/home/java/Main.java

        System.out.println(new File("\\tmp", "Main.java").toURL());
                                        // file:/c:/tmp/Main.java

        System.out.println(new File("c:\\book\\sup1", "Main.java").toURL());
                                        // file:/c:/book/sup1/Main.java
    } catch (MalformedURLException e) {
        e.printStackTrace();
    }
```

FileFilter

FileFilter

Syntax

```
public interface FileFilter
```

Description

The `FileFilter` interface provides a method for selecting files from a list of files. For example, if you are interested in files whose names end in `.java`, you can write a filter whose `accept()` method returns only `true` only for files ending in `.java`.

This interface is very similar to `FilenameFilter`. The only difference between the two interfaces is that `FilenameFilter.accept()` takes a directory `File` object and a string file name as arguments, while `FileFilter` takes only a `File` object.

Usage

You pass a class that implements this interface to `File.listFiles()`. Typically, you would use an inner class for this. See the class example for an example of this.

MEMBER SUMMARY	
Filter Method	
`accept()`	Determines whether a file passes this file filter.

See Also

`File.listFiles()`, `FilenameFilter`.

Example

This example implements a program that walks the file system and prints all files whose name matches a supplied set of suffixes. The `accept()` method returns `true` if the file is a directory (otherwise, the walker wouldn't traverse subdirectories) or if the filename suffix matches one of the strings in `patterns`.

```
import java.io.*;
import java.util.*;

class Main implements Observer {
    String[] patterns;
    File dir;

    Main(String dirname, String[] patterns) {
        dir = new File(dirname);
```

```
        this.patterns = patterns;

        // Start walking the file system.
        FileWalker fw = new FileWalker();
        fw.addObserver(this);
        fw.walk(new File(dirname), false, new FileFilter());
    }

    class FileFilter implements java.io.FileFilter {
        // Returns true if filename matches one of the patterns.
        public boolean accept(File file) {
            if (file.isDirectory()) {
                return true;
            }

            String s = file.getName();
            if (patterns.length == 0) {
                return true;
            } else {
                for (int i=0; i<patterns.length; i++) {
                    if (s.endsWith(patterns[i])) {
                        return true;
                    }
                }
            }
            return false;
        }
    }

    // This method is called for each file that the file walker discovers.
    public void update(Observable o, Object arg) {
        System.out.println(arg);
    }

    public static void main(String[] args) {
        if (args.length < 1) {
            System.err.println(
                "Usage: java Main <directory> [<pattern>...]");
        } else {
            // Retrieve patterns, if any.
            String[] patterns = new String[args.length-1];
            System.arraycopy(args, 1, patterns, 0, patterns.length);
            new Main(args[0], patterns);
        }
    }
}
```

Output

```
> java Main \jdk1.2 .jar
\jdk1.2\jre\lib\ext\iiimp.jar
\jdk1.2\jre\lib\i18n.jar
\jdk1.2\jre\lib\jaws.jar
\jdk1.2\jre\lib\rt.jar
\jdk1.2\lib\dt.jar
\jdk1.2\lib\tools.jar
\jdk1.2\src.jar
```

accept()

PURPOSE Determines whether a file passes this file filter.

SYNTAX `boolean accept(File file)`

DESCRIPTION This method implements a test to determine if `file` should pass this file filter. If `true` is returned, the caller should accept `file`; otherwise, the caller should reject `file`.

PARAMETERS

`file` The non-`null` file to be tested.

RETURNS `true` if file should be accepted; `false` otherwise.

SEE ALSO `File.listFiles()`.

EXAMPLE See the class example.

java.io

FileOutputStream

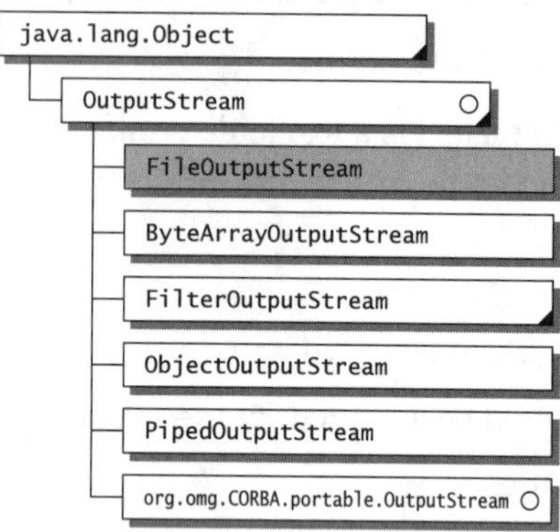

F

Syntax

```
public class FileOutputStream extends OutputStream
```

Description

The `FileOutputStream` class provides methods for writing data to a file.

See *The Java Class Libraries, Second Edition, Volume 1* for more information about this class.

Changes for Version 1.2

The `FileOutputStream` constructors that accept a string name now throw `FileNotFoundException` instead of the more generic `IOException`.

MEMBER SUMMARY	
Constructor	
Δ `FileOutputStream()`	Constructs a `FileOutputStream` instance.
Output Method	
`write()`	Writes bytes to this `FileOutputStream`.
Methods for Closing the Stream	
`close()`	Closes this `FileOutputStream`.
`finalize()`	Called to close this `FileOutputStream` when it is ready to be discarded.
File Descriptor Method	
`getFD()`	Retrieves the file descriptor used by this `FileOutputStream`.

See Also

`FileOutputStream` in *The Java Class Libraries, Second Edition, Volume 1.*

Δ FileOutputStream()

PURPOSE Constructs a `FileOutputStream` instance.

SYNTAX

```
public FileOutputStream(String filename) throws
    FileNotFoundException
public FileOutputStream(File file) throws IOException
public FileOutputStream(FileDescriptor fdObj)
public FileOutputStream(String filename, boolean append) throws
    FileNotFoundException
```

F

DESCRIPTION There are four forms of this constructor for `FileOutputStream`. The first form constructs a file output stream for writing to the file that has the name `filename`. `filename` is a platform-dependent name of the file. It can be an absolute or a relative pathname of the file. If absolute, it is resolved relative to the root of the file system. If relative, it is resolved relative to the current directory in which the Java program was started.

The second form constructs a file output stream for the file identified by the `File` object `file`. The third form constructs a file output stream using the opened file descriptor `fd`.

For these first three forms, if the file specified already exists any data contained therein is erased when the file output stream is created. If the file did not exist, it is created.

The fourth form of this method allows write operations to the newly created stream to append data to the file rather than overwrite any existing data in the file. If `append` is `true`, data written to this stream is appended to any existing data in the file that has the name `filename`. If `append` is `false`, existing data in the file is cleared when the file output stream is created.

The file output stream can be created only if the caller is allowed, by the security manager and the underlying file system, to write to the specified file.

1.2 CHANGES In Version 1.1, the forms that accept a string name threw `IOException` instead of `FileNotFoundException`.

PARAMETERS

`append`	If `true`, write operations to the stream will append to the file; if `false`, the file is cleared first.
`fd`	The non-`null` opened file descriptor of the file.
`file`	The non-`null` `File` object of the file.
`filename`	The non-`null` string name of the file.

EXCEPTIONS

`IOException`
: If the file is not found or some other IO error occurred while opening the file for writing.

`SecurityException`
: The file cannot be opened for writing due to security reasons.

SEE ALSO `File`, `FileDescriptor`, `java.lang.SecurityManager.checkWrite()`.

EXAMPLE See the `FileOutputStream` class example in *The Java Class Libraries, Second Edition, Volume 1.*

F

FilePermission

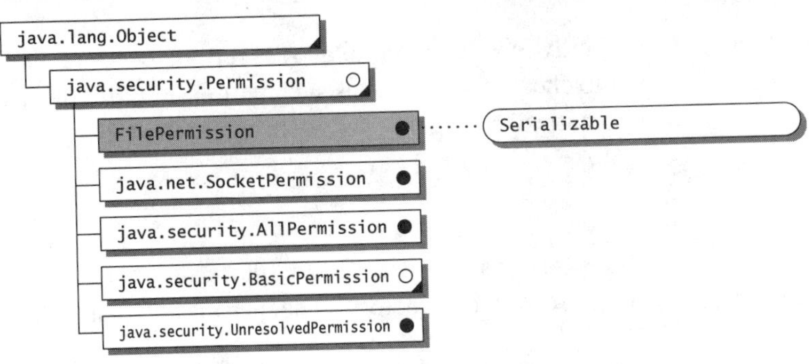

Syntax

```
public final class FilePermission extends Permission
```

Description

The `FilePermission` class represents a request to access a file or directory. A `FilePermission` object consists of a *permission name*, which names the file or directory, and a set of *actions*, which lists the types of access requested. For example, a `FilePermission` object with the permission name `"/users/duke/mail"` and an action `"read"` represents a request to read the file `/users/duke/mail`.

`FilePermission` objects are used internally by the security manager whenever an attempt to access the file system is made. The security manager checks whether the caller is allowed to perform the action(s) specified in the `FilePermission`. If the caller is not allowed, a `SecurityException` is thrown.

In Version 1.2, most of the "check" methods relating to the file systems in the `SecurityManager` class have been rewritten to use the `FilePermission` class. The only exceptions are those relating to file descriptors, which use the `RuntimePermissions` named `"readFileDescriptor"` and `"writeFileDescriptor"` instead. This rewrite is useful to systems that formerly wrote and installed their own security manager but is otherwise transparent to users of the `SecurityManager` class.

A brief discussion of the Version 1.2 security model is given in the `SecurityManager` class description. More information about Version 1.2's security model and framework is available at `http://java.sun.com/products/jdk/1.2/docs/guide/security/index.html`.

See the `java.util.jar.JarFile` class example for an example of how to sign an applet and how to set up the security policy that allows that applet to access the local file system.

Usage

Applets and applications usually do not directly use the `FilePermission` class. It is used internally by the Java runtime system to enforce its security policy. For example, when a program tries to create a FileOutputStream for the file /users/duke/mail, the system uses a FilePermission("/users/duke/mail","write") object to check whether the caller has permission to do so.

An application may explicitly create a FilePermission object and use SecurityManager.checkPermission() to check whether it has such permission. But the act of trying to perform the file operation automatically triggers such a check, so there is seldom a reason to duplicate the check.

The FilePermission Name

The permission name of a FilePermission identifies a file, a directory, the contents of a directory, or the (recursive) subtree of a directory. The permission name has the syntax described in Table 9.

F

Syntax	Description
	(The empty string) The current directory.
*	All files and directories in the current directory, excluding the current directory.
-	All files in the current directory and recursively in all of its subdirectories.
path	The file/directory named by *path*.
*path/**[a]	All files and directories in the directory named by *path*, excluding *path*.
path/-[a]	All files and directories in the directory named by *path* and recursively in path's subdirectories, excluding *path*.
<<ALL_FILES>>	A special token that identifies all files in the file system.

TABLE 9: FilePermission Name Syntax.

a. The slash character depicted here means the value of the system property file.separator.

path is the platform-dependent name of a file or directory. That is, characteristics such as the path's file separator and case-sensitivity of filenames are significant. *path* can be an absolute name, which means it names a file starting from the root of the file system on which the applet/application is running (see File.isAbsolute()). It also can be a relative name, which means that it names a file relative to the current directory in which the applet/application is running. The current directory is the value of the user.dir system property (see java.util.System). In the last two rows of Table 9, the forward slash character (/) means the value of the system property file.separator. On UNIX platforms, the value is the forward slash character (/); on Windows platforms, it is the backslash character (\). If you specify a pathname that contains a backslash character, you need to use two consecutive backslash characters (for example, "c:\\temp*") for each intended backslash character. This is because the backslash character is the escape character in the Java language.

FilePermission Actions

The actions of a `FilePermission` identify the file operations. See Table 10.

Action	Request
`read`	Read from specified files/directories.
`write`	Write to specified files/directories.
`delete`	Delete specified files/directories.
`execute`	Execute specified files/directories.

TABLE 10: `FilePermission` Actions.

F

The **Action** column contains keywords to use when specifying the actions of the `FilePermission`. The actions are specified in a string containing a comma-separated sequence of one or more of these keywords. Whitespace characters (blank, `\f`, `\t`, `\r`, and `\n`) may appear before and after a keyword. Character case is not significant. For example, the string `"read,write"` means the code can read and write to the object named in the permission.

The permissions granted by the security policy do not override the access control model of the underlying file system and operating system. For example, if a program has been granted `"read"` permission to file *X*, the user running the program must also have been granted read access to file *X* by the underlying file system. Otherwise, even when the permission checking passes, the program would not be able to perform the read.

Implies

The permission name and actions of a `FilePermission` object are used to determine whether one `FilePermission` *implies* another `FilePermission`. Permission *A* implies permission *B* means if permission *A* is granted, so will permission *B*. Following are the rules for how "implies" works for `FilePermission` objects.

- Two `FilePermissions` with the same permission name and actions imply each other.
- A `FilePermission` *A* implies the `FilePermission` *B* if *B*'s actions are a subset of *A*'s and the files and directories identified by *B*'s permission name are a subset *A*'s.

read

A `FilePermission` with the `"read"` action represents a request to read from the specified files or directories. This includes getting information about the file, such as its length and whether it exists, and retrieving the file's contents. A `FilePermission` with this action is checked by the following methods: `canRead()`, `exists()`, `isDirectory()`, `isFile()`, `isHidden()`, `lastModified()`, `length()`, `list()`, `listFiles()`, and `listRoots()` from the `File` class; `FileInputStream` constructor; and `RandomAccessFile` constructor.

write

A `FilePermission` with the `"write"` action represents a request to write to or change the specified files or directories. This includes operations on the file, such as renaming it, creating the file, or updating the contents of the file. A `FilePermission` with this action is checked by the following methods: `canWrite()`, `createNewFile()`, `createTempFile()`, `mkdir()`, `renameTo()`, `setLastModified()`, and `setReadOnly()` from the `File` class; `FileOutputStream` constructor; and `RandomAccessFile` constructor.

delete

A `FilePermission` with the `"delete"` action represents a request to delete the specified files or directories. A `FilePermission` with this action is used by `File.delete()` and `File.deleteOnExit()`.

execute

A `FilePermission` with the `"execute"` action represents a request to execute a program that has the specified filename(s). It is used by `Runtime.exec()`.

MEMBER SUMMARY	
Constructor	
`FilePermission()`	Constructs a new `FilePermission` instance.
Action Retrieval Method	
`getActions()`	Generates the canonical string representation of this `FilePermission`'s actions.
Permission Checking Methods	
`implies()`	Checks if this `FilePermission` *implies* another permission.
`newPermissionCollection()`	Creates a new `PermissionCollection` for storing `FilePermission` objects.
Object Methods	
`equals()`	Determines whether an object is equal to this `FilePermission`.
`hashCode()`	Computes the hash code for this `FilePermission`.

See Also

`java.lang.SecurityManager`, `java.security.Permission`, `java.security.PermissionCollection`.

Example

See the class example of `java.util.jar.JarFile` to see how to specify the security policy to allow a signed applet to read the current directory in which it is executing.

This example shows how to use `FilePermission` to check whether the program has permission to list the `/tmp` directory before doing so. As mentioned in the class description, there is usually no need for the program to do this check explicitly because the new `File.list()` will perform the check automatically. This example is just for illustrative purposes.

You run the program by using the `.policy` file. If you omit this file, you will get an `AccessControlException` (a subclass of `SecurityException`).

```
>java -Djava.security.policy=.policy Main
```

Main.java

```
FilePermission fp = new FilePermission("/tmp", "read");
try {
    AccessController.checkPermission(fp); // would throw SecurityException
                                          // if permission denied
    String[] list = (new File("/tmp")).list();
} catch (SecurityException e) {
    e.printStackTrace();
}
```

.policy

```
keystore ".keystore";
grant {
          permission java.io.FilePermission "/tmp", "read";
          permission java.io.FilePermission "/tmp/-", "read";
     };
```

equals()

PURPOSE
Determines whether an object is equal to this `FilePermission`.

SYNTAX
`public boolean equals(Object obj)`

DESCRIPTION
This method determines whether the object `obj` is equal to this `FilePermission`. Two `FilePermissions` are equal if they have the same actions and refer to the same files/directories. Two `FilePermissions` that have the same name and actions will be equal, but two with the same actions but different names might also be equal, as shown in the following example.

PARAMETERS

`obj` The possibly `null` object to check.

RETURNS
`true` if `obj` is a `FilePermission` instance that has the same actions and that refers to the same files/directories.

OVERRIDES
`java.lang.Object.equals()`.

SEE ALSO
`hashCode()`.

EXAMPLE When you run this program from the `/tmp` directory, the second `System.out.println()` call will print `true` because the current directory (that named by `p2`) will be the same as `/tmp`.

```
FilePermission p1 = new FilePermission("<<ALL FILES>>", "read, write");
FilePermission p2 = new FilePermission("", "read");
FilePermission p3 = new FilePermission("/tmp", "read");

System.out.println(p1.equals(p2)); // false
System.out.println(p2.equals(p3)); // true if run from /tmp directory

System.out.println(p1.hashCode()); // 0
System.out.println(p2.hashCode()); // 1515144 if run from /tmp directory
System.out.println(p3.hashCode()); // 1515144
```


FilePermission()

PURPOSE Constructs a new `FilePermission` instance.

SYNTAX `public FilePermission(String pname, String actions)`

DESCRIPTION This constructor constructs a new `FilePermission` instance. The name of this permission is `pname` and has the syntax described in the class description. `actions` contains a list of one or more comma-separated keywords listed in Table 10. It specifies the actions that can be performed on the objects named by `pname`, as described in the class description.

PARAMETERS

`actions` A non-`null` string specifying the actions of the new `FilePermission`.

`pname` A non-`null` string identifying the files and directories for the new `FilePermission`.

EXAMPLE See `equals()`.

getActions()

PURPOSE Generates the canonical string representation of this `FilePermission`'s actions.

SYNTAX `public String getActions()`

PURPOSE This method generates the canonical string representation of this `FilePermission`'s actions. The result might not be the same string passed into the constructor, but it will denote the same actions that were specified to the constructor. The keywords for the actions of the `FilePermission` are listed in the following order (in lowercase): `read`, `write`, `execute`, `delete`. An action that is not part of this `FilePermission` is not listed. Each keyword is separated by a comma, and there is no whitespace in the string.

RETURNS The non-`null` canonical string representation of the actions of this `FilePermission`.

OVERRIDES `java.security.Permission.getActions()`.

EXAMPLE

```
System.out.println(new FilePermission("", "  write , read").getActions());
                                                    // read,write
System.out.println(new FilePermission("", "delete, write").getActions());
                                                    // write,delete
System.out.println(new FilePermission("", "read,write,execute").getActions());
                                                    // read,write,execute
```


hashCode()

PURPOSE Computes the hash code for this `FilePermission`.

SYNTAX `public int hashCode()`

DESCRIPTION This method computes the hash code for this `FilePermission`. The hash code for a `FilePermission` object is computed using information obtained from the permission name of the object such that if two `FilePermissions` are equal, they will have the same hash code. Note, however, that two different `FilePermissions` might also have the same hash code. The hash code is typically used as the key in a hash table.

When the permission name is the empty string (`""`), the value of the `user.dir` system property is used to compute the hash code.

RETURNS An `int` representing the hash code of this object.

OVERRIDES `java.lang.Object.hashCode()`.

SEE ALSO `equals()`, `java.util.HashMap()`, `java.util.Hashtable()`.

EXAMPLE See `equals()`.

implies()

PURPOSE Checks if this `FilePermission` "implies" another permission.

SYNTAX `public boolean implies(Permission perm)`

DESCRIPTION This method checks if this `FilePermission` "implies" the permission `perm`. This `FilePermission` *implies* `perm` if, and only if, any actions on the files and directories identified by `perm` are also allowed by this `FilePermission`. That is, `perm`'s actions must be a subset of this `FilePermission`'s, and the files and directories identified by `perm` must be a subset of those identified by this

FilePermission. If perm is null or not an instance of FilePermission, this method returns false. See the class description for details.

PARAMETERS

perm — The possibly null permission to check.

RETURNS — true if perm is implied by this object; false otherwise.

OVERRIDES — java.lang.Permission.implies().

EXAMPLE

```
char s = File.separatorChar;
FilePermission p1 = new FilePermission("<<ALL FILES>>", "read, write");
FilePermission p2 = new FilePermission("", "read");
FilePermission p3 = new FilePermission(s+"tmp", "read");
FilePermission p4 = new FilePermission(s+"tmp"+s+"*", "read");
FilePermission p5 = new FilePermission(s+"tmp"+s+"foo", "read");
FilePermission p6 = new FilePermission(s+"tmp"+s+"foo", "execute");

System.out.println(p1.implies(p2));          // true
System.out.println(p1.implies(p3));          // true
System.out.println(p4.implies(p3));          // false; tmp excluded from *
System.out.println(p4.implies(p4));          // true
System.out.println(p4.implies(p5));          // true
System.out.println(p4.implies(p6));          // false; diff action

System.out.println(
    p1.implies(new SocketPermission("java.sun.com:80", "connect")));
                                             // false; diff Permission class
System.out.println(p1.implies(null));        // false; null Permission
```

newPermissionCollection()

PURPOSE — Creates a new PermissionCollection for storing FilePermission objects.

SYNTAX — `public PermissionCollection newPermissionCollection()`

DESCRIPTION — This method creates a new PermissionCollection for storing FilePermission objects. With a single FilePermission, you can ask (via the implies() method) whether it implies another permission. With a PermissionCollection, you can ask whether a collection of permissions implies another permission. The Java runtime system, for example, would make such a test when it tries to determine whether the caller is allowed to perform an action based on the FilePermissions granted to the caller by the security policy.

RETURNS — A new non-null PermissionCollection object suitable for storing FilePermissions. If you attempt to add an object that is not an instance of FilePermission to the collection, an IllegalArgumentException is thrown.

OVERRIDES — java.security.Permission.newPermissionCollection().

SEE ALSO — implies(), java.security.PermissionCollection.

EXAMPLE

```
char s = File.separatorChar;
FilePermission[] p = new FilePermission[5];

// Allow entire /tmp subtree to be read, including its root
p[0] = new FilePermission(s+"tmp"+s+"-", "read");
p[1] = new FilePermission(s+"tmp", "read");

// Allow writes to /tmp/myapp directory
p[2] = new FilePermission(s+"tmp"+s+"myapp", "write");
p[3] = new FilePermission(s+"tmp"+s+"myapp"+s+"*", "write");

// Allow execution in /tmp/myapp/bin/*
p[4] = new FilePermission(s+"tmp"+s+"myapp"+s+"bin"+s+"*", "execute");

PermissionCollection col = p[0].newPermissionCollection();
for (int i = 0; i < p.length; i++) {
    col.add(p[i]);
}

// OK to write to /tmp/myapp/bin?
System.out.println(col.implies(
    new FilePermission(s+"tmp"+s+"myapp"+s+"bin", "write")));
                                                          // true

// OK to read/execute /tmp/myapp/bin/install?
System.out.println(col.implies(
    new FilePermission(s+"tmp"+s+"myapp"+s+"bin"+s+"install",
        "read, execute")));
                                                          // true

// OK to read/write to /tmp/myapp/bin/install?
System.out.println(col.implies(
    new FilePermission(s+"tmp"+s+"myapp"+s+"bin"+s+"install",
        "read, write")));
                                                          // false
```

java.lang

Float

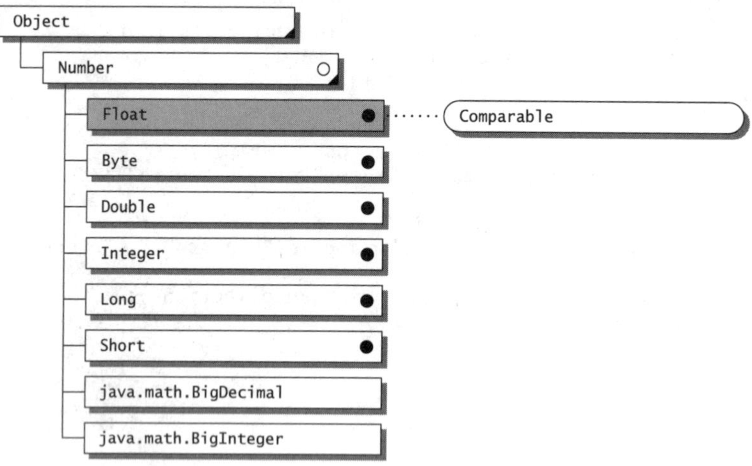

F

Syntax

`public final class Float extends Number implements Comparable`

Description

The `Float` class provides an object wrapper for a `float` data value. A *`float` data value* in Java is a 32-bit floating-point number. This wrapper allows floating-point numbers to be passed to methods in Java class libraries that accept Java objects as parameters. In addition, this class provides methods that convert values to and from `float`s. It also performs other operations on `float`s.

See *The Java Class Libraries, Second Edition, Volume 1* for more information about this class.

Changes for Version 1.2

A new `parseFloat()` method parses the string representation of a `float` into a `float`. It is a complement to the existing `valueOf()` method that parses a string into a `Float` instance.

The `Float` class implements the `Comparable` interface and has two overloaded forms of the `compareTo()` method used for comparing `Float` objects. This allows arrays of `Float` objects to be sorted, as shown in this example

```
Float[] fa = new Float[]{new Float(1.58e5),
    new Float(-4.23e4), new Float(48)};
Arrays.sort(fa);
for (int i = 0; i < fa.length; i++) {
    System.out.println(fa[i]);
} // -4.23e4, 48, 1.58e5
```

MEMBER SUMMARY

Constructor	
`Float()`	Constructs a `Float` instance using a number or a string.
Constant Fields	
`MAX_VALUE`	The maximum value a `float` can have.
`MIN_VALUE`	The smallest positive value a `float` can have.
`NaN`	The special Not-a-Number (`NaN`) value.
`NEGATIVE_INFINITY`	Negative infinity for a `float`.
`POSITIVE_INFINITY`	Positive infinity for a `float`.
`TYPE`	The `Class` object representing the primitive type `float`.
Number Methods	
`byteValue()`	Retrieves the value of this `Float` as a `byte`.
`doubleValue()`	Retrieves the value of this `Float` as a `double`.
`floatValue()`	Retrieves the value of this `Float` as a `float`.
`intValue()`	Retrieves the value of this `Float` as an `int`.
`longValue()`	Retrieves the value of this `Float` as a `long`.
`shortValue()`	Retrieves the value of this `Float` as a `short`.
Conversion Methods	
`floatToIntBits()`	Retrieves the bit representation of a `float`.
`intBitsToFloat()`	Retrieves the `float` corresponding to a given bit representation.
1.2 `parseFloat()`	Parses the string representation of a `float` into a `float`.
`toString()`	Generates the string representation of a `float` or a `Float`.
`valueOf()`	Creates a new `Float` instance using its string representation.
Comparison Methods	
1.2 `compareTo()`	Compares the signed numeric value of this `Float` with that of another `Float`.
`equals()`	Determines if this `Float` is equal to another `Float`.
`isInfinite()`	Determines if a `float` is infinitely large in magnitude.
`isNaN()`	Determines if a `float` is the special Not-a-Number (`NaN`) value.
Hash Code Method	
`hashCode()`	Computes the hash code of this `Float`.

See Also

`Comparable`, `java.util.Arrays`.
`Float` in *The Java Class Libraries, Second Edition, Volume 1.*

1.2 compareTo()

PURPOSE Compares the signed numeric value of this `Float` with that of another `Float`.

SYNTAX
```
public int compareTo(Float afloat)
public int compareTo(Object afloat)
```

DESCRIPTION This method compares this `Float`'s numeric value with that of `afloat`. It returns an `int` indicating whether the two numeric values are equal and, if they are not, the ordering of the two values. It returns `0` if the two numeric values are the same. It returns a negative number if the numeric value of this `Float` is less than that of `afloat`. It returns a positive number if the numeric value of this `Float` is greater than that of `afloat`.

There are two ways in which comparisons performed by this method differ from those performed by the Java language numerical comparison operators <, <=, ==, >=, and > when applied to primitive `float`s.

- `Float.NaN` is considered by this method to be equal to itself and greater than all other `float` values (including `Float.POSITIVE_INFINITY`).
- `0.0d` is considered by this method to be greater than `-0.0d`.

If `afloat` is not an instance of `Float`, a `ClassCastException` is thrown.

PARAMETERS

`afloat` A non-`null` `Float` with which to compare.

RETURNS `0` if the numeric values of this `Float` and `afloat` are the same; a negative number if this `Float`'s value is less than that of `afloat`; a positive number if this `Float`'s value is greater than that of `afloat`.

EXCEPTIONS

`ClassCastException`
If `afloat` is not an instance of `Float`.

SEE ALSO `Comparable`.

EXAMPLE
```
Float d = new Float(1.23e3);
System.out.println(d.compareTo(new Float(1.23e3)));                   // 0
System.out.println(d.compareTo(new Float(0.0)));                      // 1

System.out.println(new Float(0.0).compareTo(new Float(-0.0)));        // 1
System.out.println(new Float(0.0).compareTo(new Float(0.0)));         // 0

System.out.println(new Float(Float.POSITIVE_INFINITY).compareTo(
    new Float(Float.POSITIVE_INFINITY)));                             // 0

System.out.println(new Float(Float.POSITIVE_INFINITY).compareTo(
    new Float(Float.NEGATIVE_INFINITY)));                             // 1

System.out.println(new Float(Float.POSITIVE_INFINITY).compareTo(
    new Float(Float.NaN)));                                           // -1
```

```
System.out.println(new Float(Float.POSITIVE_INFINITY).compareTo(
    new Float(Float.MAX_VALUE)));                               // 1

System.out.println(new Float(Float.NEGATIVE_INFINITY).compareTo(
    new Float(Float.MIN_VALUE)));                               // -1
System.out.println(new Float(Float.NaN).compareTo(
    new Float(Float.NaN)));                                     // 0

System.out.println(new Float(Float.NaN).compareTo(new Float(0.0))); // 1

System.out.println(d.compareTo("abc")); // ClassCastException
```

1.2 parseFloat()

PURPOSE Parses the string representation of a `float` into a `float`.

SYNTAX
```
public static float parseFloat(String str) throws
    NumberFormatException
```

DESCRIPTION This method parses the string `str` into a `float` and returns it as a `float`. It expects `str` to be in the same format as that acceptable to `valueOf()`. The only difference between `parseFloat()` and `valueOf()` is that the former returns the result as a `float`, while the latter returns the result as a `Float`.

The format of the string is

[*Sign*] *Digits* **.** [*Digits*] [*ExponentPart*]

[*Sign*] **.** *Digits* [*ExponentPart*]

Sign is a negative sign, *Digits* is a sequence of digits from 0 through 9, and *ExponentPart* is one of "e" or "E" followed by a signed integer. Details of this format are in *The Java Language Specification, First Edition*, Section 20.9.17. Leading and trailing whitespace characters in `str` are ignored.

PARAMETERS

`str` A non-`null` string to be parsed.

RETURNS The `float` value represented by `str`.

EXCEPTIONS

`NumberFormatException`

If `str` does not contain a valid format for a `float`.

SEE ALSO `valueOf()`.

EXAMPLE

```
String s1 = "1.0981e3";
String s2 = "-5.12";

try {
    float d1 = Float.parseFloat(s1);
```

```
            float d2 = Float.parseFloat(s2);

            System.out.println(d1);     // 1098.1
            System.out.println(d2);     // -5.12
        } catch (NumberFormatException e) {
            System.err.println(e);
        }
```

F

java.util
GregorianCalendar

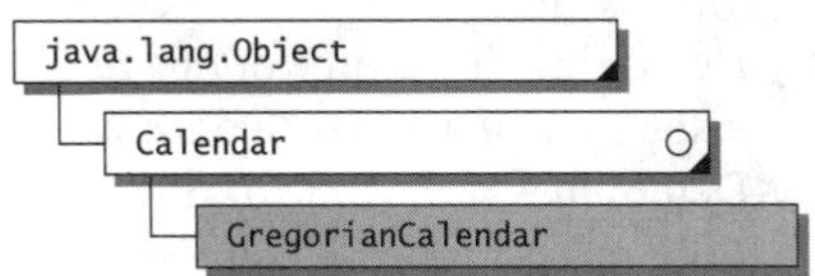

Syntax

```
public class GregorianCalendar extends Calendar
```

Description

The `GregorianCalendar` class is used to perform operations on dates under the *Gregorian calendar* system. The Gregorian calendar is the world's most widely used calendar system. See the `Calendar` class for a complete discussion of calendar classes in general and most of the documentation for this class. Refer to `Calendar` when using this class.

See *The Java Class Libraries, Second Edition, Volume 1* for more information about this class.

G

Changes for Version 1.2

The implementations for the methods `after()` and `before()` are now in `Calendar`. In Version 1.1, these two methods were abstract in `Calendar`. Although the overrides are gone, the methods are still available (since they are inherited), and they maintain their previous behavior. These two methods are not documented here; see `Calendar` for details.

Two new methods are `getActualMaximum()` and `getActualMinimum()`. An overloaded form of `roll()` also is new.

MEMBER SUMMARY	
Constructor	
`GregorianCalendar()`	Constructs a `GregorianCalendar` instance.
Era Constants	
`AD`	Represents A.D. (Anno Domini).
`BC`	Represents B.C. (before Christ).
Date Modification Methods	
`add()`	Increments/decrements a calendar field.
Δ `roll()`	Rolls a calendar field.
	Continued

G

MEMBER SUMMARY	
Comparison Methods	
`after()`	Determines if the time of this `GregorianCalendar` is later than the time of another `GregorianCalendar`.
`before()`	Determines if the time of this `GregorianCalendar` is before the time of another `GregorianCalendar`.
`isLeapYear()`	Determines if a year is a leap year.
Gregorian Change Methods	
`getGregorianChange()`	Retrieves the Gregorian calendar change date.
`setGregorianChange()`	Sets the Gregorian calendar change date.
Range Methods	
1.2 `getActualMaximum()`	Calculates the maximum value of a field using the current date.
1.2 `getActualMinimum()`	Calculates the minimum value of a field using the current date.
`getGreatestMinimum()`	Retrieves the greatest minimum value for a calendar field.
`getLeastMaximum()`	Retrieves the least maximum value for a calendar field.
`getMaximum()`	Retrieves the maximum value for a calendar field.
`getMinimum()`	Retrieves the minimum value for a calendar field.
Internal Calendar Computation Methods	
`computeFields()`	Computes the values for the calendar fields from this `GregorianCalendar`'s `Date` value.
`computeTime()`	Converts the calendar fields into a `Date` value.
Object Methods	
`equals()`	Determines if this `GregorianCalendar` is equal to another object.
`hashCode()`	Computes the hash code of this `GregorianCalendar`.

See Also

`Calendar`.
`GregorianCalendar` in *The Java Class Libraries, Second Edition, Volume 1.*

1.2 getActualMaximum()

PURPOSE Calculates the maximum value of a field using the current date.

SYNTAX `public int getActualMaximum(int fld)`

DESCRIPTION This method calculates the maximum value of the field `fld` using the values of the current date. It differs from `getMaximum()`, which returns the maximum value of `fld` regardless of the current date. For example, if the current month is

February, this method will return 28, while if the current month is January, this method will return 31.

PARAMETERS

`fld` One of the valid calendar field constants.

RETURNS The maximum value of the field `fld` using the current date.

OVERRIDES `Calendar.getActualMaximum()`.

SEE ALSO `getActualMinimum()`, `getLeastMaximum()`, `getGreatestMinimum()`, `getMaximum()`, `getMinimum()`.

EXAMPLE

```
Calendar cal = new GregorianCalendar();
System.out.println( cal.getTime().toString() );
    // Sun Jan 10 23:05:23 PST 1999

System.out.println( cal.getActualMinimum(Calendar.DAY_OF_MONTH) );    // 1
System.out.println( cal.getActualMaximum(Calendar.DAY_OF_MONTH) );    // 31

cal.set(Calendar.MONTH, Calendar.FEBRUARY);
System.out.println( cal.getActualMinimum(Calendar.DAY_OF_MONTH) );    // 1
System.out.println( cal.getActualMaximum(Calendar.DAY_OF_MONTH) );    // 28
```

G

1.2 getActualMinimum()

PURPOSE Calculates the minimum value of a calendar field using the current date.

SYNTAX `public int getActualMinimum(int fld)`

DESCRIPTION This method calculates the minimum value of the field `fld` using the values of the current date. It differs from `getMinimum()`, which returns the minimum value of `fld` regardless of the current date. For the Gregorian calendar, this method always returns the same value as `getMinimum()` and `getGreatestMinimum()`.

PARAMETERS

`fld` One of the valid calendar field constants.

RETURNS The minimum value of the field `fld` using the current date.

OVERRIDES `Calendar.getActualMinimum()`.

SEE ALSO `getActualMaximum()`, `getLeastMaximum()`, `getGreatestMinimum()`, `getMaximum()`, `getMinimum()`.

EXAMPLE See `getActualMaximum()`.

Δ roll()

PURPOSE Rolls a calendar field.

SYNTAX
```
public void roll(int fld, boolean up)
```
SINCE 1.2
```
public void roll(int fld, int amt)
```

DESCRIPTION This method increments or decrements the calendar field `fld`. If `up` is `true`, the field is incremented by `1`. If `up` is `false`, the field is decremented by `1`. If `amt` is positive, the field is incremented by `amt`. If `amt` is negative, the field is decremented by `-amt`.

If `up` is `true` and `get(fld) == getMaximum(fld)`, the calendar field is set to `getMinimum(fld)`. If `up` is `false` and `get(fld) == getMinimum(fld)`, the calendar field is set to `getMaximum(fld)`. This process is called *rolling*.

Rolling the calendar field can also affect other calendar fields. For example, if the current date is January 31 and the `WEEK_OF_MONTH` field is `5`, rolling up the `DATE` field causes the `WEEK_OF_MONTH` field to be `1`.

The leniency of a `Calendar` object has no effect on this method. `fld` cannot be either `DST_OFFSET` or `ZONE_OFFSET`.

1.2 CHANGES The overload with the `amt` parameter is new in Version 1.2.

PARAMETERS

`amt`	A positive or negative increment to apply to `fld`.
`fld`	One of the valid calendar field constants.
`up`	If `true`, rolls the calendar field up by `1`; if `false`, rolls the calendar field down by `1`.

EXCEPTIONS

`IllegalArgumentException`
If `fld` is either `DST_OFFSET` or `ZONE_OFFSET`.

OVERRIDES `Calendar.roll()`.

SEE ALSO `add()`.

EXAMPLE
```
Calendar cal = new GregorianCalendar();
DateFormat df = DateFormat.getInstance();

cal.set(1997, Calendar.JANUARY, 31);

System.out.println(df.format(cal.getTime()));      // 1/31/97 9:54 AM
cal.roll(Calendar.MONTH, false);
System.out.println(df.format(cal.getTime()));      // 12/31/97 9:54 AM
cal.roll(Calendar.DATE, true);
System.out.println(df.format(cal.getTime()));      // 12/1/97 9:54 AM

cal.set(1997, Calendar.JANUARY, 31);

System.out.println(df.format(cal.getTime()));      // 1/31/97 9:54 AM
```

```
cal.roll(Calendar.MONTH, -2);
System.out.println(df.format(cal.getTime()));      // 11/30/97 9:54 AM
cal.roll(Calendar.DATE, 2);
System.out.println(df.format(cal.getTime()));      // 11/2/97 9:54 AM

//cal.roll(Calendar.DST_OFFSET, true);             // IllegalArgumentEx
//cal.roll(Calendar.ZONE_OFFSET, true);            // IllegalArgumentEx
```

G

HashMap

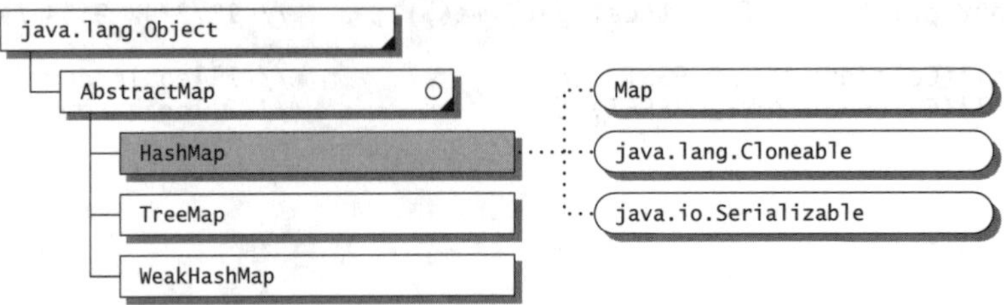

Syntax

`public class HashMap extends AbstractMap implements Map, Cloneable, Serializable`

Description

A `HashMap` is an implementation of the `Map` interface. It is a collection for storing key/value pairs called *entries*. It supports all optional operations and allows `null` elements, keys, and values. The keys in the map must be unique, but the values don't have to be. If you try to add an entry that has a duplicate key, the map replaces the old entry with the new entry. This is unlike a set, in which if you try to add a duplicate element, the operation is completely ignored.

Unlike with lists (see `List`), the keys in the map must not be modified while they are in the map. For example, if a `StringBuffer` is used as a key in the map, you must not modify the `StringBuffer` while it is in the map.

`HashMap` internally uses a hash table to store the entries. This means that accessing and adding an entry is almost as fast as accessing an array. However, the entries are not internally ordered in any way. `HashMap` is useful if you need to keep track of a set of entries and to determine if an entry is already in the set, but you don't care about the order of the entries.

`HashMap` is one of four implementations of the `Map` interface. The other three are `Hashtable`, `TreeMap` and `WeakHashMap`. `Hashtable`, `HashMap`, and `TreeMap` are general purpose implementations, while `WeakHashMap` is more esoteric.

`Hashtable` has been retrofitted to implement the `Map` interface. You should generally use `HashMap` instead of `Hashtable`.

`TreeMap` internally uses a balanced tree (a *red-black tree*) to store the entries in order (based on the key). This means that adding and removing an entry involves walking the tree to determine where to insert the entry (guaranteed log_2(`size()`) time). Since the entries in a `TreeMap` are kept sorted, obtaining a sorted list of entries is merely a matter of creating an iterator on the map.

`WeakHashMap` is like a `HashMap`, except that if a key is no longer referenced outside the `WeakHashMap`, the key's entry is automatically removed from the table.

Usage

You can create either an empty `HashMap` or one that is initialized from a map, as follows.

```
HashMap map;
map = new HashMap();
map = new HashMap(map);
```

Once the map is created, you can use various methods to modify it, such as `put()` to add entries to the map or `remove()` to remove entries from the map.

Capacity and Load Factor

The *capacity* of the `HashMap` affects the performance of all of the methods. The larger the capacity, typically, the better the performance. However, a larger capacity takes up more memory. Also, a larger capacity will slow down the time it takes to use an iterator to iterate over the map. In general, a capacity of twice the number of entries in the map is a good balance.

The `HashMap` automatically increases the capacity as the number of entries in the map increases. The *load factor* controls when the capacity should be increased. In particular, the `HashMap` doubles the capacity when

`size()` > *capacity***load_factor*.

A larger load factor makes more efficient use of memory at the expense of performance. A smaller load factor improves performance by using more memory.

See the `HashMap()` constructor for how to map the initial capacity and load factor of the map.

Iterators

This map implements fail-fast iterators (see `Iterator`). The map should not be modified while the returned iterator is in use; otherwise, the map will throw a `ConcurrentModificationException`. See `Iterator` for more details.

Serialization

When the map is serialized, all of the entries are serialized. The capacity and load factor of the map is restored when it is deserialized.

Synchronization

This map allows more than one thread to read from it. However, if a thread wants to modify the map, there should not be any other thread reading from it at the time of the modification. If reads and modifications need to be able to occur concurrently, you can create a synchronized version of the map by calling `Collections.synchronizedMap()` on the `Map`. This creates a version of the map in which all of the methods are synchronized. Note that although each method is synchronized, you might still need to synchronize a sequence of method calls. See the `Collections` class description for more details.

MEMBER SUMMARY	
Constructor	
`HashMap()`	Constructs a new `HashMap` instance.
Value Retrieval Method	
`get()`	Retrieves the value associated with a key.
Query Methods	
`containsKey()`	Determines if this map contains a particular key.
`containsValue()`	Determines if this map contains a particular value.
`isEmpty()`	Determines if this map has no entries.
`size()`	Returns the number of entries in this map.
Modification Methods	
`clear()`	Removes all of the entries in this map.
`put()`	Adds a key/value pair to this map.
`putAll()`	Adds key/value pairs from another map to this map.
`remove()`	Removes an entry from this map.
Collection View Methods	
`entrySet()`	Returns a set containing all of the key/value pairs in this map.
`keySet()`	Returns a map containing all of the keys in this map.
`values()`	Returns a collection containing all of the values in this map.
Object Method	
`clone()`	Creates a copy of this map.

H

See Also

`Collections`, `Iterator`, `Map`, `TreeMap`, `WeakHashMap`.

clear()

PURPOSE Removes all of the entries in this map.

SYNTAX `public void clear()`

DESCRIPTION This method removes all of the entries in this map. After this method is called, this map will be empty.

EXAMPLE See `Map.clear()`.

clone()

PURPOSE Creates a copy of this map.

SYNTAX `public Object clone()`

DESCRIPTION This method makes a shallow copy of this map. Only the map and all of the entries are cloned, not the elements. Both this map and the new map share references to the same keys and values.

Since the entries are cloned, changing the value associated with a key in one copy does not affect the value associated with the same key in the other. However, since the copies share references to the same keys and values, modifications to a value in one map affect the values of the other map. (Modifications to a key also have the same effect, but you should not be modifying keys.)

RETURNS A new non-`null` map.

OVERRIDES `java1.lang.Object.clone()`.

EXAMPLE

```
StringBuffer buf = new StringBuffer("spot");
HashMap map = new HashMap();
map.put("dog", buf);
map.put("cat", null);
System.out.println( map );        // {cat=null, dog=spot}

HashMap map2 = (HashMap)map.clone();
System.out.println( map2 );       // {cat=null, dog=spot}

// Changing a value in map does not affect map2.
map.put("cat", "luck");
System.out.println( map2 );       // {cat=null, dog=spot}

// Changing the value itself does affect map2.
buf.append("ty");
System.out.println( map2 );       // {cat=null, dog=spotty}
```

containsKey()

PURPOSE Determines if this map contains a particular key.

SYNTAX `public boolean containsKey(Object k)`

DESCRIPTION This method determines if this map contains the key `k`. It returns `true` if some key in this map is equal to `k`. Two keys are equal if both are `null` or the `equals()` method determines that they are equal.

PARAMETERS

`k` A possibly `null` key.

RETURNS `true` if some key in this map is equal to `k`.

SEE ALSO `equals()`.

EXAMPLE See `Map.containsKey()`.

containsValue()

PURPOSE Determines if this map contains a particular value.

SYNTAX `public boolean containsValue(Object v)`

DESCRIPTION This method determines if this map contains the value `v`. It returns `true` if some value in this map is equal to `v`. Two values are equal if both are `null` or if the `equals()` method determines that they are equal.

PARAMETERS

`v` A possibly `null` value.

RETURNS `true` if some value in this map is equal to `v`.

EXAMPLE See `Map.containsKey()`.

entrySet()

PURPOSE Returns a set containing all of the key/value pairs in this map.

SYNTAX `public Set entrySet()`

DESCRIPTION This method creates and returns a set containing all of the key/value pairs in this map. The key/value pairs are represented by `Map.Entry` objects. See `Map.Entry` for information on retrieving a key or value from an entry.

The returned set and this map share the same storage. This means that changes to the map are immediately reflected in the set and changes in the set are immediately reflected in this map.

The returned set supports all operations, including all entry removal methods, except for `add()` and `addAll()`. The iterators of the returned set are fail-fast. The `remove()` method of the iterators is supported.

RETURNS A non-`null` set containing all of the entries in this map.

SEE ALSO `Collection`, `keySet()`, `Map.Entry`, `values()`.

EXAMPLE See `Map.entrySet()`.

get()

PURPOSE Retrieves the value associated with a key.

SYNTAX `public Object get(Object k)`

DESCRIPTION This method searches this map for an entry with the key `k` and returns the associated value. It returns `null` if `k` is not in this map. A return value of `null` is ambiguous if the map accepts `null` values. You can use `containsKey()` to unambiguously determine if `k` is in this map.

PARAMETERS

`k` A possibly `null` key.

RETURNS The possibly `null` value associated with `k` or `null` if `k` is not in this map.

SEE ALSO `containsKey()`.

EXAMPLE See `Map.get()`.

HashMap()

PURPOSE Constructs a new `HashMap` instance.

SYNTAX

```
public HashMap()
public HashMap(Map m)
public HashMap(int initCap)
public HashMap(int initCap, float loadFactor)
```

DESCRIPTION This constructor constructs a new `HashMap` object initialized with the entries from `m`.

If `m` is not specified, the new `HashMap` object is empty. If `m` is specified, `initCap` defaults to `2*m.size()`; otherwise, `initCap` defaults to `101`. If `loadFactor` is not specified, it defaults to `0.75f`.

See the class description for documentation on the capacity and the load factor.

PARAMETERS

`initCap` The non-negative initial capacity of the set.

`loadFactor` The load factor. `0.0` ≤ `loadFactor`.

`m` A non-`null` map.

EXCEPTIONS

`ConcurrentModificationException`
If `m`'s iterators are fail-fast and `m` is being modified during this method call.

`IllegalArgumentException`
If `initCap` < `0` or `loadFactor` < `0.0`.

EXAMPLE

```
HashMap map = new HashMap();
map.put("dog", "spot");

// Create a second map based on the first.
HashMap map2 = new HashMap(map);
System.out.println( map2 );        // {dog=spot}
```

```
// Put an element to the first map.
map.put("cat", "luck");
System.out.println( map );          // {cat="luck, dog=spot}

// The change to the first map does not affect the second.
System.out.println( map2 );         // {dog=spot}
```

isEmpty()

PURPOSE Determines if this map has no entries.

SYNTAX `public boolean isEmpty()`

RETURNS `true` if this map contains no entries.

SEE ALSO `size()`.

EXAMPLE See `Map.isEmpty()`.

keySet()

PURPOSE Returns a map containing all of the keys in this map.

SYNTAX `public Set keySet()`

DESCRIPTION This method creates and returns a set containing all of the keys in this map. The set and this map share the same storage. This means that changes to this map are immediately reflected in the set and changes in the set are immediately reflected in this map.

The returned set supports all operations, including all entry removal methods, except for `add()` and `addAll()`. The iterators of the returned set are fail-fast. The `remove()` method of the iterators is supported.

RETURNS A non-`null` set containing all of the keys in this map.

SEE ALSO `Collection`, `entrySet()`, `values()`.

EXAMPLE See `Map.keySet()`.

put()

PURPOSE Adds a key/value pair to this map.

SYNTAX `public Object put(Object k, Object v)`

DESCRIPTION This method adds the given key `k` and value `v` to this map. If an entry with the key `k` already exists in this map, it is replaced with the new entry. In this case, the previous value is returned.

PARAMETERS

k	A possibly `null` key.

v	A possibly `null` value.

RETURNS	If `k` already exists in this map, then the possibly `null` old value is returned; otherwise, `null` is returned.

EXAMPLE	See `Map.put()`.

putAll()

PURPOSE	Adds key/value pairs from another map to this map.

SYNTAX	`public void putAll(Map m)`

DESCRIPTION	This method adds the key/value pairs from the map `m` to this map. Every entry from `m` is placed in this map. If the key for some entry from `m` already exists in this map, the entry in this map is replaced by the one from `m`.

PARAMETERS

m	A non-`null` map.

EXCEPTIONS

`ConcurrentModificationException`
If `m`'s iterators are fail-fast and `m` is being modified during this method call.

SEE ALSO	`put()`.

EXAMPLE	See `Map.putAll()`.

remove()

PURPOSE	Removes an entry from this map.

SYNTAX	`public Object remove(Object k)`

DESCRIPTION	This method searches for the first occurrence of an entry with key `k` in this map and removes the entry from this map. It uses `k.equals()` to determine equality.

PARAMETERS

k	The possibly `null` key of the entry to remove.

RETURNS	The possibly `null` value associated `k`. `null` if `k` does not match any keys in this map.

EXAMPLE	See `Map.remove()`.

size()

PURPOSE Returns the number of entries in this map.

SYNTAX `public int size()`

RETURNS The non-negative number of entries in this map.

SEE ALSO `isEmpty()`.

EXAMPLE See `Map.size()`.

values()

PURPOSE Returns a collection containing all of the values in this map.

SYNTAX `public Collection values()`

DESCRIPTION This method returns a collection that contains all of the values in this map. Unlike `keySet()`, the returned collection is not a set because there could be duplicates of values (sets don't allow duplicate elements).

The returned collection and this map share the same storage. This means that changes to this map are immediately reflected in the collection and changes in the collection are immediately reflected in this map.

The returned collection does not support `add()` and `addAll()`. The iterators of the returned collection are fail-fast. The `remove()` method of the iterators is supported.

RETURNS A non-`null` collection containing all of the values in this map.

SEE ALSO `Collection`, `entrySet()`, `keySet()`.

EXAMPLE See `Map.values()`.

HashSet

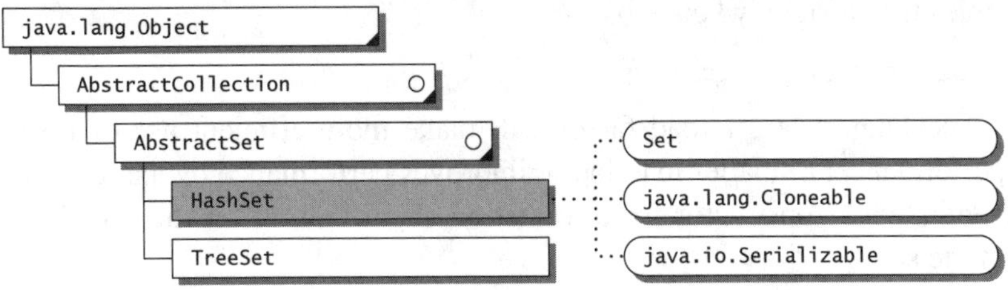

Syntax

```
public class HashSet extends AbstractSet implements Set, Cloneable, Serializable
```


Description

A `HashSet` is a hash table implementation of the `Set` interface. It is a collection for storing unique objects (*elements*). It supports all optional operations and allows `null` elements, keys, and values.

Accessing a set and adding and removing an element is almost as efficient as performing the same operation on an array. The elements are not ordered in any way, however, so if you need a sorted list, you have to explicitly sort the elements. `HashSet` is useful if all you need to do is to keep track of a set of objects and determine if an object is already in the set.

`HashSet` is one of two implementations of the `Set` interface. The other is `TreeSet`, which behaves like a `HashSet`, except that it stores its elements in order. Accessing, adding, and removing an element involves walking the tree to determine where to insert the element. However, since the elements are always kept in order, obtaining a sorted list of elements is very efficient.

Usage

You can create either an empty `HashSet` or one that is initialized from a collection, as follows.

```
HashSet set;
set = new HashSet();
set = new HashSet(collection);
```

Once the set is created, you can use various methods to modify it, such as `add()` to add elements to the set or `remove()` to remove elements from the set.

Capacity and Load Factor

The *capacity* of the `HashSet` affects the performance of all of the methods. The larger the capacity, typically, the better the performance. However, a larger capacity takes up more memory. Also, a larger capacity will slow the time it takes to use an iterator to iterate over the set. In general, a capacity of twice the number of elements in the set is a good balance.

The `HashSet` automatically increases the capacity as the number of elements in the set increases. The *load factor* controls when the capacity should be increased. In particular, the `HashSet` doubles the capacity when

```
size()*load_factor > capacity.
```

Roughly speaking, a larger load factor will make more efficient use of memory at the expense of performance; a smaller load factor improves performance by using more memory.

See the `HashSet()` constructor for information about how to set the initial capacity and load factor of the set.

Iterators

This set implements fail-fast iterators. It should not be modified while the returned iterator is in use. Otherwise, the set will throw a `ConcurrentModificationException`. See `Iterator` for more details.

H

Serialization

When the set is serialized, all elements are serialized. The capacity and load factor of the set is restored when it is deserialized.

Synchronization

This set allows more than one thread to read from it. However, if a thread wants to modify the set, there should not be any other thread reading from it at the time of the modification. If reads and modifications need to be able to occur concurrently, you can create a synchronized version of the set by calling `Collections.synchronizedSet()` on the set. This creates a version of the set in which all of the methods are synchronized. Note that although each method is synchronized, you might still need to synchronize a sequence of method calls. See the `Collections` class description for more details.

MEMBER SUMMARY	
Constructor	
`HashSet()`	Constructs a new `HashSet` instance.
Query Methods	
`contains()`	Determines if this set contains a particular element.
`isEmpty()`	Determines if this set has no elements.
`size()`	Returns the number of elements in this set.
Modification Methods	
`add()`	Adds an element to this set.
`clear()`	Removes all of the elements in this set.
`remove()`	Removes an element from this set.

MEMBER SUMMARY	
Iterator Method	
`iterator()`	Creates an iterator for all of the elements in this set.
Object Method	
`clone()`	Creates a copy of this set.

See Also

`Collections`, `Iterator`, `Set`, `TreeSet`.

add()

PURPOSE Adds an element to this set.

SYNTAX `public boolean add(Object e)`

DESCRIPTION This method adds an element, `e`, to this set, if `e` is not equal to any elements already contained in this set. If `e` is not `null`, `e`'s `equals()` method is used to determine if it is equal to any elements in this set.

PARAMETERS

`e` The possibly `null` element to be added to this set.

RETURNS `true` if `e` was added to the set.

SEE ALSO `addAll()`.

EXAMPLE See `Set.add()`.

clear()

PURPOSE Removes all of the elements in this set.

SYNTAX `public void clear()`

DESCRIPTION This method removes all of the elements in this set. After it is called, this set will be empty.

EXAMPLE See `Set.clear()`.

clone()

PURPOSE Creates a copy of this set.

SYNTAX `public Object clone()`

DESCRIPTION This method makes a shallow copy of this set. Only the set itself is cloned, not the elements. This set and the new set share references to the same elements.

RETURNS A new non-`null` `HashSet` instance that contains the same elements.

OVERRIDES `java.lang.Object.clone()`.

EXAMPLE

```
HashSet set = new HashSet(Arrays.asList(new Object[]{"dog", null, "cat"}));
System.out.println( set );        // [cat, dog, null]

HashSet set2 = (HashSet)set.clone();
System.out.println( set2 );       // [cat, dog, null]
```

contains()

H

PURPOSE Determines if this set contains a particular element.

SYNTAX `public boolean contains(Object e)`

DESCRIPTION This method determines if this set contains the element `e`. It returns `true` if some element in this set is equal to `e`. An element is equal to `e` if both are `null` or if the `equals()` method determines that they are equal.

PARAMETERS

`e` A possibly `null` element.

RETURNS `true` if some element in this set is equal to `e`.

SEE ALSO `containsAll()`, `equals()`.

EXAMPLE See `Set.contains()`.

HashSet()

PURPOSE Constructs a new `HashSet` instance.

SYNTAX

```
public HashSet()
public HashSet(Collection c)
public HashSet(int initCap)
public HashSet(int initCap, float loadFactor)
```

DESCRIPTION This constructor constructs a new `HashSet` object initialized with the entries from `c`.

If `c` is not specified, the new `HashSet` object is empty. If `c` is specified, `initCap` defaults to `2*c.size()`; otherwise, `initCap` defaults to `101`. If `loadFactor` is not specified, it defaults to `0.75f`.

See the class description for documentation on the capacity and the load factor.

PARAMETERS

`c`	A non-`null` collection.
`initCap`	The non-negative initial capacity of the set.
`loadFactor`	The load factor. `0.0` ≤ `loadFactor`.

EXCEPTIONS

`ConcurrentModificationException`
If `c`'s iterators are fail-fast and `c` is being modified during this method call.

`IllegalArgumentException`
If `initCap` < `0` or `loadFactor` < `0.0`.

EXAMPLE

```
HashSet set = new HashSet();
set.add("dog");

// Create a second set based on the first.
HashSet set2 = new HashSet(set);
System.out.println( set2 );        // [dog]

// Add an element to the first set.
set.add("cat");
System.out.println( set );         // [cat, dog]

// The change to the first set does not affect the second.
System.out.println( set2 );        // [dog]
```

H

isEmpty()

PURPOSE Determines if this set has no elements.

SYNTAX `public boolean isEmpty()`

RETURNS `true` if this set contains no elements.

SEE ALSO `size()`.

EXAMPLE See `Set.clear()`.

iterator()

PURPOSE Creates an iterator for all of the elements in this set.

SYNTAX `public Iterator iterator()`

DESCRIPTION This method creates and returns a fail-fast iterator (see `Iterator` for more details) for all of the elements in this set. The iterator presents the elements in no particular order.

RETURNS A non-`null` iterator.

SEE ALSO `Iterator`.

EXAMPLE See `Set.iterator()`.

remove()

PURPOSE Removes an element from this set.

SYNTAX `public boolean remove(Object e)`

DESCRIPTION This method searches for the first occurrence of `e` in this set and removes it from this set. It returns `true` if it found a matching element. Two elements match if both are `null` or if the `equals()` method determines that they are equal.

This method might not be supported.

H

PARAMETERS

`e` The possibly `null` element to remove.

RETURNS `true` if `e` was removed.

SEE ALSO `removeAll()`, `retainAll()`.

EXAMPLE See `Set.remove()`.

size()

PURPOSE Returns the number of elements in this set.

SYNTAX `public int size()`

RETURNS The non-negative number of elements in this set.

SEE ALSO `isEmpty()`.

EXAMPLE See `Set.size()`.

Hashtable

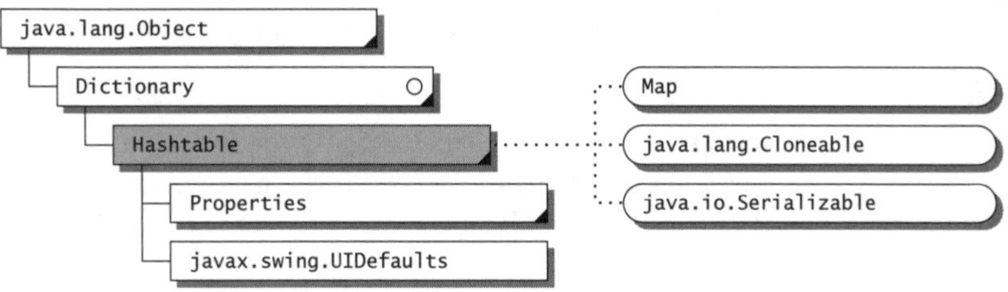

Syntax

`public class Hashtable extends Dictionary implements Cloneable, Map, Serializable`

Description

The `Hashtable` class represents a *hash table*. The keys in the hash table must be unique, but the values don't have to be unique. If you try to add an entry with a duplicate key, the hash table replaces the old entry with the new entry. The keys and values must not be `null`.

See *The Java Class Libraries, Second Edition, Volume 1* for more information about this class.

Changes for Version 1.2

For the most part, this class has been replaced with `Map` (see `Map`, `HashMap`, and `TreeMap`), which is a class in the new Collections Framework (see `Collection`). There are two key differences between `Map` and `Hashtable`. The first is that for a `Hashtable`, both the key and value must be non-`null`, whereas most maps will accept `null` keys and `null` values. The second difference is that the methods in this class are synchronized, whereas the methods in `Map` are not. However, by calling `Collections.synchronizedMap()` you can transform any `Map` object into a "synchronized map," whereby all methods become synchronized.

This class now implements the `Map` interface so that it can be used along with the other collection classes (see `Collection`). All of the new methods added for Version 1.2 are for implementing and supporting the `Map` interface.

The `equals()` and `hashCode()` methods have been overridden so that they take a `Hashtable`'s contents into account. In Version 1.1, these methods inherited their implementations from `java.lang.Object`.

MEMBER SUMMARY	
Constructor	
Δ `Hashtable()`	Constructs an empty `Hashtable` instance.
Retrieval Methods	
`elements()`	Retrieves a list of all elements in this `Hashtable`.
`get()`	Retrieves the element associated with a key from this `Hashtable`.
`keys()`	Retrieves a list of all keys in this `Hashtable`.
Query Methods	
`contains()`	Determines whether an element is in this `Hashtable`.
`containsKey()`	Determines if a key is in this `Hashtable`.
1.2 `containsValue()`	Determines if this `Hashtable` contains a particular value.
`isEmpty()`	Determines if this `Hashtable` has any elements.
`size()`	Retrieves the number of elements in this `Hashtable`.
Modification Methods	
`clear()`	Removes all keys and elements from this `Hashtable`.
`put()`	Adds a key/element pair to this `Hashtable`.
1.2 `putAll()`	Adds key/value pairs from map to this `Hashtable`.
`remove()`	Removes a key/element pair from this `Hashtable`.
Set Methods	
1.2 `entrySet()`	Returns a set containing all key/value pairs in this `Hashtable`.
1.2 `keySet()`	Returns a set containing all keys in this `Hashtable`.
1.2 `values()`	Returns a collection containing all values in this `Hashtable`.
Object Override Methods	
`clone()`	Creates a clone of this `Hashtable`.
Δ `equals()`	Determines if this `Hashtable` is equal to another object.
Δ `hashCode()`	Computes the hash code of this `Hashtable`.
`toString()`	Generates the string representation of this `Hashtable`.
Protected Method	
`rehash()`	Rehashes the content of this `Hashtable` into a larger `Hashtable`.

See Also

`Collection`, `HashMap`, `Map`.

`Hashtable` in *The Java Class Libraries, Second Edition, Volume 1*.

1.2 containsValue()

PURPOSE Determines if this `Hashtable` contains a particular value.

SYNTAX `public boolean containsValue(Object v)`

DESCRIPTION This method determines if this `Hashtable` contains a particular value `v`. It returns `true` if some value in this `Hashtable` is equal to `v`. For all non-`null` values, the `equals()` method is used to determine if two values are equal. This method calls `contains()`.

PARAMETERS

`v` A non-`null` value.

RETURNS `true` if some value in this `Hashtable` is equal to `v`.

EXCEPTIONS

`NullPointerException`
If `v` is `null`.

SEE ALSO `equals()`.

EXAMPLE

```
Hashtable h = new Hashtable();
h.put("dog", "spot");

System.out.println( h.containsValue("spot") );     // true
System.out.println( h.containsValue("dog") );      // false
//System.out.println( h.containsValue(null) );     // NullPointerException
```

1.2 entrySet()

PURPOSE Returns a set containing all key/value pairs in this `Hashtable`.

SYNTAX `public Set entrySet()`

DESCRIPTION This method creates a `Set` containing all key/value pairs in this hash table. The key/value pairs are represented by `Map.Entry` objects. See `Map.Entry` for information on retrieving a key or value from an entry.

The returned `Set` and this `Hashtable` both share the same storage. This means that changes to the `Hashtable` are immediately reflected in the `Set` and vice versa.

The returned `Set` does not support `add()` and `addAll()`. Iterators created from the returned `Set` are fail-fast (see `Iterator`).

RETURNS A non-`null` synchronized `Set` containing all entries in this `Hashtable`.

SEE ALSO `Collection`, `keySet()`, `Map.Entry`, `values()`.

H

EXAMPLE

```
Hashtable h = new Hashtable();
h.put("?", "spot");
h.put("cat", "?");
h.put("pig", "babe");

// Remove '?' key and replace '?' values with the key.
Set set = h.entrySet();
for (Iterator it=set.iterator(); it.hasNext(); ) {
    Map.Entry e = (Map.Entry)it.next();

    if (e.getValue().equals("?")) {
        e.setValue(e.getKey());
    } else if (e.getKey().equals("?")) {
        it.remove();
    }
}
System.out.println( h );                          // {pig=babe, cat=cat}

// Add to the map and check the set
h.put("yak", "yolk");
for (Iterator it=set.iterator(); it.hasNext(); ) {
    Map.Entry e = (Map.Entry)it.next();
    System.out.print(e.getKey()+"="+e.getValue()+" ");
}
System.out.println();                             // pig=babe cat=cat yak=yolk

// You can't add to the set.
//set.add("cow");                                 // UnsupportedOperationException
```


Δ equals()

PURPOSE Determines if this `Hashtable` is equal to another object.

SYNTAX `public synchronized boolean equals(Object c)`

DESCRIPTION This method determines if this `Hashtable` is equal to another object `c`. It returns `true` if, and only if, `c` is a `Map` object and both this `Hashtable` and `c` have exactly the same entries (see `Map.Entry`). `Map.Entry.equals()` is used to determine if two entries match. Basically, two entries match if their keys and values are equal to each other.

1.2 CHANGES In Version 1.1, this method was inherited from `java.lang.Object`. The equality of two `Hashtables` was based on the equality of their references, not their entries.

PARAMETERS

`c` The possibly `null` `Map` to be compared with this `Hashtable`.

RETURNS `true` if `c` is equal to this `Hashtable`.

OVERRIDES `java.lang.Object.equals()`.

SEE ALSO `hashCode()`.

EXAMPLE

```
Hashtable h1 = new Hashtable();
h1.put("dog", "spot");
h1.put("cat", "luck");

Map h2 = new HashMap();
h2.put("dog", "spot");

// Hashtable objects can be compared with any Map object.
System.out.println( h1.equals(null) );         // false
System.out.println( h1.equals(h2) );           // false

// Two maps are not equal even if all the keys match.
h2.put("cat", "john");
System.out.println( h1.equals(h2) );           // false

h2.put("cat", "luck");
System.out.println( h1.equals(h2) );           // true
```


Δ hashCode()

PURPOSE Computes the hash code of this `Hashtable`.

SYNTAX `public synchronized int hashCode()`

DESCRIPTION This method computes the hash code of this `Hashtable`. The hash code of a hash table is the sum of the hash codes of all entries in the hash table. The hash code for an entry is the exclusive-OR of the key and the value. The hash code for a `null` key or value is `0` (see `Map.Entry.hashCode()` for more information).

Two equal `Hashtables` will have the same hash code. Note that unequal `Hashtables` might also have the same hash code, although the hash code algorithm minimizes this possibility. The hash code is typically used as the key in a `Hashtable`.

1.2 CHANGES This method was inherited from `java.lang.Object` in Version 1.1. It did not use the contents of the entries in its calculation.

RETURNS This `Hashtable`'s hash code.

OVERRIDES `java.lang.Object.hashCode()`.

SEE ALSO `equals()`, `java.lang.Object.equals()`, `MapEntry.hashCode()`.

EXAMPLE See `java.lang.Object.hashCode()`.

Δ Hashtable()

PURPOSE Constructs an empty `Hashtable` instance.

SYNTAX
```
public Hashtable()
public Hashtable(Map m)                                  SINCE 1.2
public Hashtable(int initialSize)
public Hashtable(int initialSize, float loadFactor)
```

DESCRIPTION This constructor creates a new `Hashtable` with the initial size of `initialSize` and a load factor of `loadFactor`. If `m` is specified, the new hash table is initialized with the key/value pairs from `m`. If `initialSize` is not specified, it defaults to `101`. If `loadFactor` is not specified, it defaults to `0.75`. When `Hashtable` reaches the load specified by its load factor, it will automatically grow.

1.2 CHANGES The form that accepts a `Map` object is new in Version 1.2.

H

PARAMETERS

`initialCapacity`
The initial size of `Hashtable`. It must be a positive value. The default capacity is `101`. It is a good idea to use a prime number as the size. This is because prime numbers help make the keys more evenly distributed in the table.

`loadFactor` A number in the range `0.0` (exclusive) and `1.0` (inclusive) that states how full `Hashtable` should be before it is increased in size and rehashed. `1.0` means 100 percent full; `0.5` means 50 percent full. The smaller the load factor, the sooner the table will be increased. A small load factor also means that because the table is likely to be sparse, collisions (hashing a key to the same bucket) are less likely. Smaller buckets means that fewer comparisons are required before a key is found. Increasing the hash table's size is a costly operation because it involves rehashing all existing entries in the table for the new table size. A larger load factor means that the table should be fuller before it is increased and rehashed. `1.0` means that the table should be completely full before it is increased.

`m` A non-`null` `Map` object.

SEE ALSO `rehash()`.

EXAMPLE
```
Map m = new HashMap();
m.put("dog", "spot");
m.put("cat", null);

// Can't add null values to hash tables.
//Hashtable h = new Hashtable(m);   // NullPointerException

m.remove("cat");
Hashtable h = new Hashtable(m);
System.out.println( m );    // {dog=spot}
```

1.2 keySet()

PURPOSE Returns a set containing all keys in this `Hashtable`.

SYNTAX `public Set keySet()`

DESCRIPTION This method creates a `Set` from all keys in this `Hashtable`. The `Set` and this `Hashtable` both share the same storage. This means that changes to `Hashtable` are immediately reflected in the `Set` and vice versa.

The returned `Set` does not support `add()` and `addAll()`. Iterators created from the returned `Set` are fail-fast (see `Iterator`).

RETURNS A non-`null` synchronized `Set` containing all keys in this `Hashtable`.

SEE ALSO `Collection`, `entrySet()`, `values()`.

EXAMPLE

```
Hashtable h = new Hashtable();
h.put("dog", "spot");
h.put("gnu", "rick");

Set set = h.keySet();
System.out.println( new HashSet(set) );    // [dog, gnu]
System.out.println( set.contains("dog") ); // true

// Remove an entry from the set and check the h.
set.remove("dog");
System.out.println( h );                   // {gnu=rick}

// Add to the h and check the set
h.put("yak", "yolk");
System.out.println( new HashSet(set) );    // [gnu, yak]

// You can't add to the set.
//set.add("bess");                         // UnsupportedOperationException
```

1.2 putAll()

PURPOSE Adds key/value pairs from a map to this `Hashtable`.

SYNTAX `public synchronized void putAll(Map m)`

DESCRIPTION This method adds key/value pairs from the map `m` to this `Hashtable`. Every entry from `m` is added to this `Hashtable`. If the key for some entry from `m` already exists in this `Hashtable`, the entry in this `Hashtable` is replaced by the one from `m`.

PARAMETERS

`m` A non-`null` map.

EXCEPTIONS

`ConcurrentModificationException`
If `m`'s iterators are fail-fast and `m` is being modified during this method call.

`NullPointerException`
If the key or value of some entry from `m` is `null`.

SEE ALSO `put()`.

EXAMPLE

```
Map m = new TreeMap();
m.put("dog", "spot");
m.put("cat", null);
System.out.println( m );     // {cat=null, dog=spot}

Hashtable h = new Hashtable();
h.put("gnu", "rick");
h.put("dog", "?");

// Can't add null values to hash tables.
//h.putAll(m);               // NullPointerException

m.remove("cat");
h.putAll(m);
System.out.println( h );     // {dog=spot, gnu=rick}
```

H

1.2 values()

PURPOSE Returns a collection containing all values in this `Hashtable`.

SYNTAX `public Collection values()`

DESCRIPTION This method creates a `Collection` from all values in this `Hashtable`. Unlike `keySet()`, the returned `Collection` is not a `Set` because there could be duplicate values (sets don't allow duplicate elements).

The returned `Collection` and this `Hashtable` both share the same storage. This means that changes to the `Hashtable` are immediately reflected in the `Collection` and vice versa.

The returned `Collection` does not support `add()` and `addAll()`. Iterators created from the returned `Collection` are fail-fast (see `Iterator`).

RETURNS A non-`null` synchronized `Collection` containing all values in this `Hashtable`.

SEE ALSO `Collection`, `entrySet()`, `keySet()`.

EXAMPLE

```
import java.util.*;

class Main {
    public static void main(String[] args) {
        Hashtable h = new Hashtable();
        h.put("dog", "spot");
```

```
        h.put("cat", "luck");
        h.put("cow", "spot");
        h.put("yak", "spot");

        Collection col = h.values();
        printCol( col );                      // [luck, spot, spot, spot, ]
        System.out.println( col.contains("spot") );  // true

        // remove() removes one entry from the h.
        col.remove("spot");
        System.out.println( h );              // {cat=luck, cow=spot, yak=spot}

        // removeAll() removes all entries with the value "spot".
        col.removeAll(Collections.singleton("spot"));
        System.out.println( h );              // {cat=luck}

        // Add to the h and check the collection
        h.put("dog", "spot");
        printCol( col );                      // [luck, spot, ]

        // You can't add to the collection.
        //col.add("bess");                    // UnsupportedOperationException
    }

    static void printCol(Collection c) {
        System.out.print("[");
        for (Iterator it=c.iterator(); it.hasNext(); ) {
            System.out.print(it.next()+", ");
        }
        System.out.println("]");
    }
}
```

java.net

HttpURLConnection

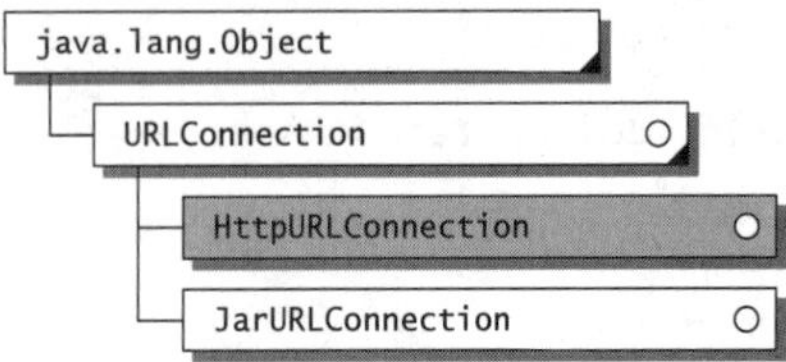

Syntax

```
abstract public class HttpURLConnection extends URLConnection
```

Description

H

The `HttpURLConnection` class is an abstract subclass of `URLConnection` that contains methods and constants specific for *HTTP*. HTTP is the Hypertext Transfer Protocol, a protocol for transmitting HTML documents and related resources. This protocol is described in detail in documents found at `http://www.w3.org/pub/WWW/Protocols/` and in *RFC 2068*.

See *The Java Class Libraries, Second Edition, Volume 1* for more information about this class.

Changes for Version 1.2

The `getErrorStream()` method is new for retrieving the optional document that accompanies an HTTP error header. This is useful when the server returns both an error header and a document explaining the error.

The `getPermission()` method has been added to retrieve the permission necessary to make the connection represented by an `HttpURLConnection`. The permission may be used to check who is allowed to use the connection (if the connection is shared, such as in a cache).

	MEMBER SUMMARY	
	Constructor	
	`HttpURLConnection()`	Constructs an `HttpURLConnection` instance.
	Request/Response-Related Methods[a]	
1.2	`getErrorStream()`	Creates an input stream for reading an error message from this `HttpURLConnection`.
	`getRequestMethod()`	Retrieves the method token from the request.
	`getResponseCode()`	Retrieves the response code from the response.
	`getResponseMessage()`	Retrieves the response message from the HTTP response read from this connection.
	`setRequestMethod()`	Sets the method token of the request.

MEMBER SUMMARY

Connection Methods	
`disconnect()`	Tears down the connection to the HTTP server.
`usingProxy()`	Determines whether this connection is going through a proxy.
Redirects (For All HTTP Connections)	
`getFollowRedirects()`	Determines whether HTTP connections automatically follow redirects.
`setFollowRedirects()`	Sets the connection to follow or not follow redirects automatically.
Security Method	
1.2 `getPermission()`	Retrieves the permission necessary to use this `HttpURLConnection`.
Protected Fields	
`method`	The method token of the request.
`responseCode`	The response code from the HTTP response.
`responseMessage`	The message associated with the response code from the HTTP response.

a. To conserve space, these HTTP request and response codes are not included here. Please see *The Java Class Libraries, Second Edition, Volume 1* for a listing of them.

H

See Also

`java.lang.SecurityManager`, `URLConnection.getPermission()`.
`HttpURLConnection` in *The Java Class Libraries, Second Edition, Volume 1.*

1.2 getErrorStream()

PURPOSE Creates an input stream for reading an error message from this `HttpURLConnection`.

SYNTAX `public InputStream getErrorStream()`

DESCRIPTION This method retrieves an input stream for reading the optional error message that accompanies an error response from the server. For example, an HTTP server might respond with a `HTTP_NOT_FOUND` error (`404`) and include an HTML page that explains who to contact. In that case, you may use this method to get an input stream for reading the HTML page.

Unlike `getInputStream()` and `getOutputStream()` (inherited from `URLConnection`), this method does not initiate a connection. It should be called only after the connection has been established and an error has been detected.

The default implementation returns `null`. A subclass should override this method to return an error stream when appropriate.

RETURNS The error stream, or `null`. If `null`, the connection received no errors, or the connection was not connected, or the server did not send a document to accompany the error header.

SEE ALSO `getResponseCode()`, `getResponseMessage()`.

1.2 getPermission()

PURPOSE Retrieves the permission necessary to use this `HttpURLConnection`.

SYNTAX `public Permission getPermission() throws IOException`

DESCRIPTION This method retrieves the permission necessary to use this `HttpURLConnection`. It returns a `SocketPermission` with the action "connect" and a name consisting of the host and port of the URL associated with this connection. A `HttpURLConnection`'s permission may be used, for example, if the contents obtained from this connection are to be shared in a cache and the cache manager wants to determine whether a client has permission to access the contents.

OVERRIDES `URLConnection.getPermission()`.

EXCEPTIONS

`IOException`

If an error occurred while this connection was creating the `SocketPermission` to be returned.

SEE ALSO `SocketPermission`.

EXAMPLE See `URLConnection.getPermission()`.

InflaterInputStream

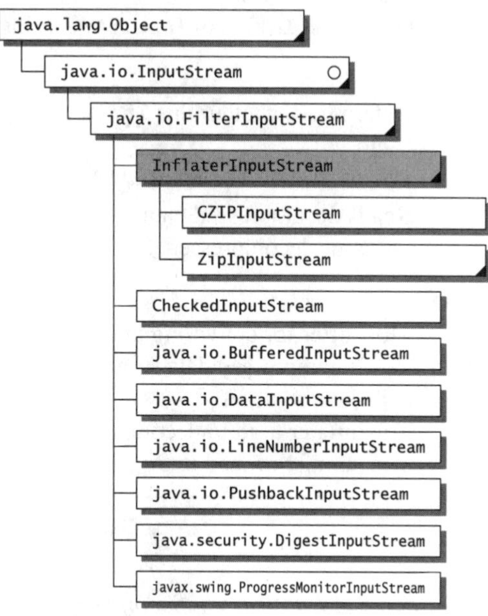

Syntax

```
public class InflaterInputStream extends FilterInputStream
```

Description

The `InflaterInputStream` class implements an input stream filter for decompressing data using the `Inflater` class. It makes it convenient to use an `Inflater` instance in a data streaming fashion. See the `Inflater` class in *The Java Class Libraries, Second Edition, Volume 1* for more information.

See *The Java Class Libraries, Second Edition, Volume 1* for more information about this class.

Changes for Version 1.2

The `available()` and `close()` methods have been overridden to track better when the stream has been closed and when end-of-stream has been reached. All of the methods in this class now throw an `IOException` if you try to use them after the stream has already been closed.

MEMBER SUMMARY	
Constructor	
`InflaterInputStream()`	Creates an `InflaterInputStream` instance.
Stream Methods	
Δ `available()`	Determines whether this `InflaterInputStream` has been closed.
Δ `close()`	Closes this `InflaterInputStream`.
`read()`	Reads decompressed data from this `InflaterInputStream`.
`skip()`	Discards decompressed data from this `InflaterInputStream`.
Protected Fields and Method	
`buf`	The buffer for delivering uncompressed data to the inflater.
`fill()`	Reads compressed data from the underlying input stream and decompresses it.
`inf`	The inflater used to decompress data.
`len`	The number of read bytes in `buf`.

I

See Also

`InflaterInputStream` in *The Java Class Libraries, Second Edition, Volume 1.*

Δ available()

PURPOSE Determines whether this `InflaterInputStream` has been closed.

SYNTAX `public int available() throws IOException`

DESCRIPTION This method determines whether this `InflaterInputStream` has been closed. It returns `0` if this `InflaterInputStream` has been closed; otherwise, it returns `1`. Unlike the conventional definition of `available()` (see `InputStream` in *The Java Class Libraries, Second Edition, Volume 1*), this method does not return the actual number of bytes that could be read without blocking.

1.2 CHANGES In Version 1.1, this method was inherited from `FilterInputStream`, which would call `available()` on the underlying input stream. In Version 1.2, this method uses only the fact of whether this stream has been closed.

RETURNS `0` if this `InflaterInputStream` has been closed; `1` otherwise.

EXCEPTIONS

`IOException`

If an IO error occurred.

Δ close()

PURPOSE Closes this `InflaterInputStream`.

SYNTAX `public void close() throws IOException`

DESCRIPTION This method closes the underlying input stream and records the fact that it has been closed so that subsequent methods invoked on this `InflaterInputStream` will result in an `IOException`.

1.2 CHANGES In Version 1.1, this method was inherited from `FilterInputStream`, which called `close()` on the underlying input stream.

EXCEPTIONS

`IOException`

If an IO error occurred while the underlying input stream was being closed.

EXAMPLE See the `InputStream` class example in *The Java Class Libraries, Second Edition, Volume 1*.

java.lang

InheritableThreadLocal

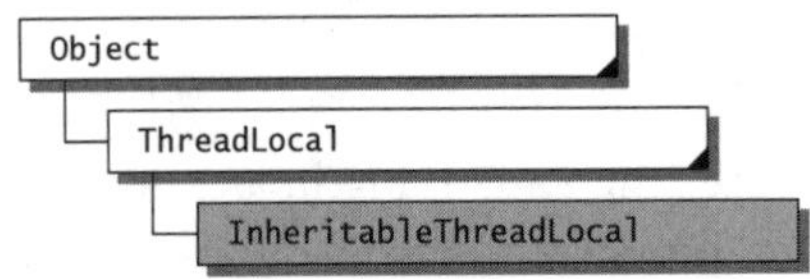

Syntax

```
public class InheritableThreadLocal extends ThreadLocal
```

Description

The `InheritableThreadLocal` class is used to implement inheritable thread-local variables. See the `ThreadLocal` class description for an explanation of thread-local variables.

I

An *inheritable* thread-local variable differs from a noninheritable thread-local variable (see `ThreadLocal`) in that the former's initial value in a child thread is copied from the parent thread. For example, if a thread *A* sets an inheritable thread-local variable to the value `"abc"` and then creates a child thread *B*, thread *B* will see the value `"abc"` if it examines the inheritable thread-local variable.

The value of an inheritable thread-local variable is copied at the time the child thread is constructed. Changing the value of the inheritable thread-local variable after the child thread is constructed does *not* affect the value of the child's copy of the inheritable thread-local variable. Conversely, any changes by the child thread to its copy of the inheritable thread-local variable has no effect on the parent's copy.

Inheritable thread-local variables should be used whenever some thread-state must be automatically copied into child threads. For example, a security-based application could use inheritable thread-local variables to store the principal (owner) of a thread and uses this information whenever the thread tries to access protected resources. In fact, there is no way that a thread can prevent the inheritance of a inheritable thread-local variable. In the security example, there is no way you can write some rogue code that creates a thread without a copy of the inheritable thread local variable that contains the principal. Moreover, without the appropriate `InheritableThreadLocal` object to an inheritable thread-local variable, there is no way an unauthorized thread could change the contents of the inheritable thread-local variable.

Usage

An inheritable thread-local variable is represented by an `InheritableThreadLocal` object. If you need a new inheritable thread-local variable, you simply create an `InheritableThreadLocal` object. You can then get and set the contents of the new inheritable thread-local variable by calling `get()` and `set()`, respectively, on the `InheritableThreadLocal` object.

See `ThreadLocal` for more usage information.

MEMBER SUMMARY	
Constructor	
`InheritableThreadLocal()`	Constructs a new `InheritableThreadLocal` instance.
Initial Value Override	
`childValue()`	Returns the initial value of this inheritable thread-local variable in the calling thread.

See Also

`ThreadLocal`.

Example

This example declares an inheritable thread-local variable and examines its behavior in a new child thread. Note that the value of the inheritable thread-local variable in the child thread is set at the time the child `Thread` object is constructed.

```
class Main {
    static InheritableThreadLocal thdloc = new InheritableThreadLocal();

    Main() {
        print();                                    // 1: "null"
        thdloc.set("MainThread");
        print();                                    // 3: "MainThread"

        Thread t = new MyThread(this);

        // Change the variable to see if the child thread
        // inherits the value before or after it is constructed.
        thdloc.set("MainThread-2");

        t.start();
        try {
            t.join();
        } catch (InterruptedException e) {
            e.printStackTrace();
        }
        print();                                    // 6: "MainThread-2"
    }

    public void print() {
        System.out.println(thdloc.get());
    }

    public static void main(String[] args) {
        new Main();
    }
}

class MyThread extends Thread {
    Main main;

    MyThread(Main main) {
```

```
            this.main = main;
            main.print();                          // 2: "MainThread"

            // Executing in the wrong thread for setting the thread local variable.
            // Main.thdloc.set("MyThread");
        }
        public void run() {
            main.print();                          // 4: "MainThread"
            Main.thdloc.set("MyThread");
            main.print();                          // 5: "MyThread"
        }
    }
```

childValue()

PURPOSE Returns the initial value of this inheritable thread-local variable in the calling thread.

SYNTAX `protected Object childValue(Object parentVal)`

DESCRIPTION This method returns the initial value of this inheritable thread-local variable in the calling thread. It is called automatically by the parent thread from within the child thread's constructor (more specifically, from within `Thread()`). `parentVal` is a reference to the object in the parent thread's copy of the inherited thread local variable. If you want the initial value of the child's copy of the inherited thread local variable to be different from `parentVal`, you must override this method to return the desired value.

The default implementation of this method returns `parentVal`.

PARAMETERS

`parentVal` A possibly `null` object in this inheritable thread-local variable of the parent thread at the time the calling thread was constructed.

RETURNS A possibly `null` object.

EXAMPLE This example demonstrates that `childValue()` is called when the child thread is constructed.

```
    class Main {
        static InheritableThreadLocal thrloc = new InheritableThreadLocal() {
            public Object childValue(Object parentVal) {
                System.out.println("cv " + thrloc.get());     // 3: "cv MainThread"
                return parentVal + "-2";
            }
        };

        Main() {
            System.out.println(thrloc.get());                   // 1: "null"
            thrloc.set("MainThread");
            System.out.println(thrloc.get());                   // 2: "MainThread"

            Thread t = new MyThread();
```

```
        t.start();
        try {
            t.join();
        } catch (InterruptedException e) {
            e.printStackTrace();
        }

        System.out.println(thrloc.get());                // 7: "MainThread"
    }

    public static void main(String[] args) {
        new Main();
    }
}

class MyThread extends Thread {
    public MyThread() {
        System.out.println("c " + Main.thrloc.get());    // 4: "c MainThread"
    }
    public void run() {
        System.out.println(Main.thrloc.get());           // 5: "MainThread-2"
        Main.thrloc.set("MyThread");
        System.out.println(Main.thrloc.get());           // 6: "MyThread"
    }
}
```

I

InheritableThreadLocal()

PURPOSE Constructs a new `InheritableThreadLocal` instance.

SYNTAX `public InheritableThreadLocal()`

DESCRIPTION This constructor constructs a new `InheritableThreadLocal` instance. Its initial value is the result of calling `childValue()`. See the class description and `childValue()` for details.

SEE ALSO `childValue()`.

EXAMPLE This example declares demonstrates both the uses of `initialValue()` and `childValue()`. Notice that `initialValue()` is called only once; `childValue()` is called when the variable is inherited from thread to thread.

```
class Main {
    static InheritableThreadLocal thrloc = new InheritableThreadLocal() {
        public Object initialValue() {
            System.out.println("iv");                    // 1: "iv"
            return "MainThread";
        }
        public Object childValue(Object parentVal) {
            System.out.println("cv " + thrloc.get());    // 3: "cv MainThread"
            return parentVal + "-2";
        }
    };

    Main() {
        System.out.println(thrloc.get());                // 2: "MainThread"
```

```
            Thread t = new MyThread(1);
            t.start();
            try {
                t.join();
            } catch (InterruptedException e) {
                e.printStackTrace();
            }

            System.out.println(thrloc.get());                  // 9: "MainThread"
        }

        public static void main(String[] args) {
            new Main();
        }
    }

    class MyThread extends Thread {
        private int val;
        public MyThread(int val) {
            System.out.println("c " + Main.thrloc.get());     // 4: "c MainThread"
            this.val = val;
        }
        public void run() {
            System.out.println(Main.thrloc.get());             // 5: "MainThread-2"
            Main.thrloc.set("Thread" + val);
            System.out.println(Main.thrloc.get());             // 6: "Thread1"

            if (val == 1) {
                new MyThread(2).start();
                                                       // Output from 2nd thread:
                                                               // 7:  "cv Thread1"
                                                               // 8:  "c Thread1"
                                                               // 10: "Thread1-2"
                                                               // 11: "Thread2"
            }
        }
    }
```

OUTPUT

```
    iv
    MainThread
    cv MainThread
    c MainThread
    MainThread-2
    Thread1
    cv Thread1
    c Thread1
    MainThread
    Thread1-2
    Thread2
```

Integer

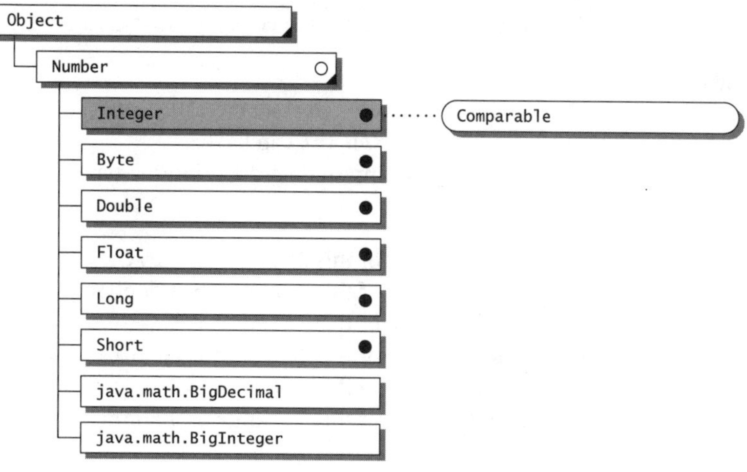

Syntax

```
public final class Integer extends Number implements Comparable
```

Description

The `Integer` class provides an object wrapper for an `int` data value. An *`int` data value* in Java is a 32-bit signed integer. This wrapper allows integers to be passed to methods in Java class libraries that accept Java objects as parameters. In addition, this class provides methods that convert values to and from `int` values and perform other operations on `int` values.

See *The Java Class Libraries, Second Edition, Volume 1* for more information about this class.

Changes for Version 1.2

The `Integer` class implements the `Comparable` interface and has two overloaded forms of the `compareTo()` method used for comparing and ordering `Integer` objects. This allows arrays of `Integer` objects to be sorted, as shown in this example.

```
Integer[] ia = new Integer[]{new Integer(10),
    new Integer(-4), new Integer(48)};
Arrays.sort(ia);
for (int i = 0; i < ia.length; i++) {
    System.out.println(ia[i]);
}
// -4, 10, 48
```

MEMBER SUMMARY	
Constructor	
`Integer()`	Constructs an `Integer` instance using an `int` value or a string.
Constant Fields	
`MAX_VALUE`	The maximum value an `int` can have.
`MIN_VALUE`	The minimum value an `int` can have.
`TYPE`	The `Class` object representing the primitive type `int`.
Number Methods	
`byteValue()`	Retrieves the value of this `Integer` as a `byte`.
`doubleValue()`	Retrieves the value of this `Integer` as a `double`.
`floatValue()`	Retrieves the value of this `Integer` as a `float`.
`intValue()`	Retrieves the value of this `Integer` as an `int`.
`longValue()`	Retrieves the value of this `Integer` as a `long`.
`shortValue()`	Retrieves the value of this `Integer` as a `short`.
Comparison Methods	
1.2 `compareTo()`	Compares the signed numeric value of this `Integer` with that of another `Integer`.
`equals()`	Determines if this `Integer` is equal to another object.
Conversion Methods	
`decode()`	Parses the string representation of a 16-bit signed integer into an `Integer`.
`getInteger()`	Creates an `Integer` instance using the value of a system property.
`parseInt()`	Parses a string representation of an integer into an `int`.
`toBinaryString()`	Generates the string representation of an `int` as an unsigned binary number.
`toHexString()`	Generates the string representation of an `int` as an unsigned hexadecimal number.
`toOctalString()`	Generates the string representation of an `int` as an unsigned octal number.
`toString()`	Generates the string representation of an `int` or `Integer`.
`valueOf()`	Creates a new `Integer` instance using its string representation.
Object Method	
`hashCode()`	Computes the hash code of this `Integer`.

See Also

`Comparable`, `java.util.Arrays`.

`Integer` in *The Java Class Libraries, Second Edition, Volume 1.*

1.2 compareTo()

PURPOSE
Compares the signed numeric value of this `Integer` with that of another `Integer`.

SYNTAX
```
public int compareTo(Integer anInt)
public int compareTo(Object anInt)
```

DESCRIPTION
This method compares this `Integer`'s (signed) numeric value with that of `anInt`. It returns an integer indicating whether the two numeric values are equal and, if they are not, the ordering of the two values. It returns `0` if the two numeric values are the same. It returns a negative number if the numeric value of this `Integer` object is less than that of `anInt`. It returns a positive number if the numeric value of this `Integer` is greater than that of `anInt`.

If `anInt` is not an instance of `Integer`, a `ClassCastException` is thrown.

PARAMETERS

`anInt` The non-`null` `Integer` with which to compare.

RETURNS
`0` if the numeric values of this `Integer` and `anInt` are the same; a negative number if this `Integer`'s value is less than that of `anInt`; a positive number if this `Integer`'s value is greater than that of `anInt`.

EXCEPTIONS

`ClassCastException`
If `anInt` is not an instance of `Integer`.

SEE ALSO
`Comparable`.

EXAMPLE
```
Integer b = new Integer((int)71000);
System.out.println(b.compareTo(new Integer((int)-1)));      // positive
System.out.println(b.compareTo(new Integer((int)71000)));   // 0
System.out.println(b.compareTo(new Integer((int)-71000)));  // positive
System.out.println(b.compareTo(new Integer((int)71001)));   // negative
System.out.println(b.compareTo("abc")); // ClassCastException
```

java.lang.reflect InvocationTargetException

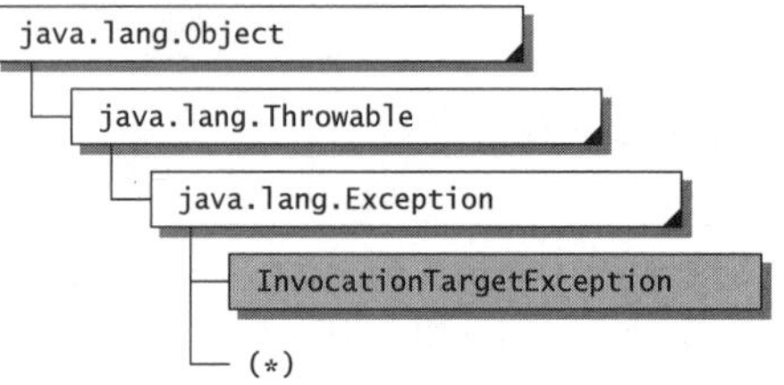

(*) 34 classes from other packages not shown.

Syntax

`public class InvocationTargetException extends Exception`

I

Description

The `InvocationTargetException` class is a wrapper for an exception that is produced by a *target* object in response to the invocation of a method or constructor. An `InvocationTarget-Exception` is thrown by `Method.invoke()` and `Constructor.newInstance()` when the invoked method or constructor throws an exception. This original exception can be retrieved from the `InvocationTargetException` by calling `getTargetException()`.

See *The Java Class Libraries, Second Edition, Volume 1* for more information about this class.

Changes for Version 1.2

The `printStackTrace()` methods have been overridden so that if the target exception is non-`null`, the target exception's stack trace is printed instead of the `InvocationTargetException`'s stack trace.

MEMBER SUMMARY	
Constructor	
`InvocationTargetException()`	Constructs an `InvocationTargetException` instance.
Wrapped Exception Method	
`getTargetException()`	Retrieves the exception wrapped by this `InvocationTargetException`.
Debugging Method	
Δ `printStackTrace()`	Prints the stack trace of the exception wrapped by this `InvocationTargetException`.

See Also

`InvocationTargetException` in *The Java Class Libraries, Second Edition, Volume 1.*

Δ printStackTrace()

PURPOSE Prints the stack trace of the exception wrapped by this `InvocationTarget-Exception`.

SYNTAX
```
public void printStackTrace()
public void printStackTrace(PrintStream ps)
public void printStackTrace(PrintWriter pw)
```

DESCRIPTION f this `InvocationTargetException`'s target exception (`getTargetException()`) is non-`null`, this method prints the target exception's stack trace. If the target exception is `null`, this `InvocationTargetException`'s stack trace is printed. The output goes to `ps` or `pw`. If no print stream or print writer has been specified, the output is sent to `System.err`.

1.2 CHANGES In Version 1.1, all forms of this method were inherited from `Throwable`. Thus, regardless of whether the target exception was `null` or non-`null`, this `InvocationTargetException`'s stack trace was printed.

PARAMETERS

`ps` The non-`null` print stream to which to send the stack trace.

`pw` The non-`null` print writer to which to send the stack trace.

SEE ALSO `System.err`.

java.util

Iterator

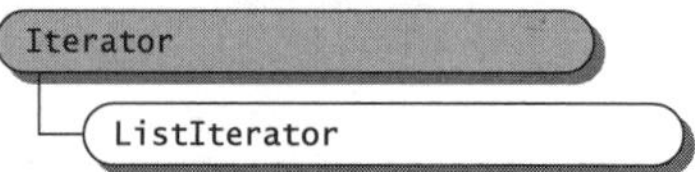

Syntax

```
public interface Iterator
```

Description

An `Iterator` is used to access the elements in a collection in a sequential manner. For example, to check every element in a set, you can create an iterator on the set and use it to access every element in the set. By repeatedly calling the iterator's `next()` method until `hasNext()` returns `false`, you are guaranteed to see each element in the collection exactly once.

I

The order of the elements presented by the iterator depends on the collection. Lists, for example, return the elements in exactly the same order that they appear in the list. For collections such as sets, the order can be arbitrary.

Usage

To create an iterator, you must first have a collection. You then call the collection's `iterator()` method to obtain an iterator for that collection. You can then access every element of the collection with a loop such as the following.

```
for (Iterator it=collection.iterator(); it.hasNext(); ) {
    Object e = it.next();
}
```

Concurrent Modification Error

Some collections do not allow modifications while an iterator on the collection is in use. These collections typically return iterators that are fail-fast. That is, the iterator watches for modifications on the collection and throws an exception if it detects a modification. This feature is used mainly to avoid programming errors.

The implementation of fail-fast behavior does not need to be properly synchronized and perfectly reliable. This feature is designed primarily as an extra precaution against a common programming error, the improper synchronization of common data structures. In other words, fail-fast iterators are not *guaranteed* to catch every instance of co-modification, but they typically do.

MEMBER SUMMARY	
Element Retrieval Method	
`next()`	Retrieves an element from this iterator's collection.
Query Method	
`hasNext()`	Determines if there are more elements in the iteration.
Modification Method	
`remove()`	Removes the most recently returned element from this iterator's collection.

See Also

`ListIterator`.

Example

For an example of how to implement an iterator, see the `AbstractCollection` class example. For examples of how to use an iterator, see the following member descriptions.

hasNext()

PURPOSE Determines if there are more elements in the iteration.

SYNTAX `boolean hasNext()`

DESCRIPTION This method determines if there are more elements in the iteration. If it returns `true`, there are more elements in the iteration and calling `next()` will not result in an exception.

RETURNS `true` if there are more elements.

EXCEPTIONS

`ConcurrentModificationException`
If this iterator's collection was modified by something other than this iterator.

SEE ALSO `next()`.

EXAMPLE

```
List list = Arrays.asList(new String[]{"dog"});
Iterator it = list.iterator();

System.out.println( it.hasNext() );        // true
System.out.println( it.next() );           // dog
System.out.println( it.hasNext() );        // false
//System.out.println( it.next() );         // NoSuchElementException

// Common way to loop forward through a list.
for (Iterator i=list.iterator(); i.hasNext(); ) {
```

```
        System.out.println( i.next() );
    }
```

next()

PURPOSE Retrieves an element from this iterator's collection.

SYNTAX `Object next()`

RETURNS A possibly `null` element.

EXCEPTIONS

`ConcurrentModificationException`
If this iterator's collection was modified by something other than this iterator while the iteration was in progress.

`NoSuchElementException`
If there are no more elements in the iteration.

I

SEE ALSO `hasNext()`.

EXAMPLE

```
    List list = Arrays.asList(new String[]{"dog", null, "cat"});

    // Common way to loop forward through a list.
    for (Iterator it=list.iterator(); it.hasNext(); ) {
        System.out.println( it.next() );
    }
```

remove()

PURPOSE Removes the most recently returned element from this iterator's collection.

SYNTAX `void remove()`

DESCRIPTION This method removes the element most recently retrieved from `next()`. The element is actually removed from the collection used to create this iterator. This method can be called at most once after a call to `next()`. If it is called before `next()` is ever called, it throws an `IllegalStateException`.

The collection or the iterator might not support this method, in which case an `UnsupportedOperationException` is thrown.

EXCEPTIONS

`ConcurrentModificationException`
If this iterator's collection was modified by something other than this iterator.

`IllegalStateException`
If `remove()` is not called right after `next()`.

`UnsupportedOperationException`
If this method is not supported by this iterator.

SEE ALSO `next()`.

EXAMPLE

```
List list = new ArrayList(Arrays.asList(new String[]{"dog", "cat"}));
Iterator it = list.iterator();

//it.remove();                            // IllegalStateException
System.out.println( it.next() );          // dog
it.remove();
System.out.println( list );               // [cat]

// You can't call remove() after another remove().
//it.remove();                            // IllegalStateException

// Remove all null elements.
list = new ArrayList(Arrays.asList(new String[]{"dog", null, "cat"}));
for (Iterator i=list.iterator(); i.hasNext(); ) {
    if (i.next() == null) {
        i.remove();
    }
}
System.out.println( list );               // [dog, cat]
```

java.util.jar

JarEntry

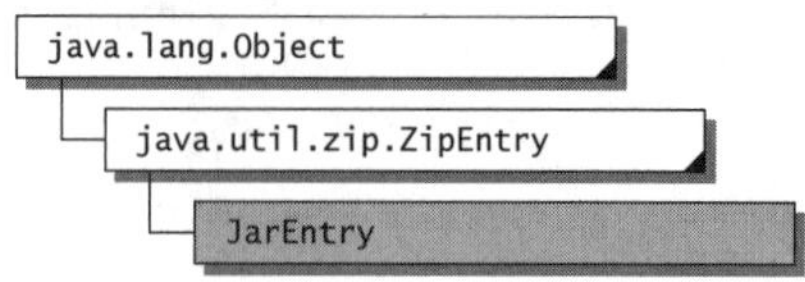

Syntax

`public class JarEntry extends ZipEntry`

Description

The `JarEntry` class is used to represent an entry in a Java Archive (JAR) file. It contains information about the JAR entry (name, size, CRC, and so on) and also is used to retrieve the actual JAR entry data. Most of these properties are inherited from `ZipEntry`, so you should see the `ZipEntry` descriptions for complete details. However, a `JarEntry` has two properties that a `ZipEntry` does not: manifest attributes and certificates.

Manifest Attributes

A *manifest* is a set of attributes (name/value pairs) associated with a JAR file. The attributes provide additional information about the JAR file and about entries in the JAR file. For example, if a class is signed, its digest is kept in the manifest.

Some of the attributes in a manifest pertain to entries in the JAR file. The attributes for a JAR entry can be retrieved by calling `getAttributes()`.

Certificates

Signing a JAR file results in some of the JAR entries also being signed. You can retrieve the certificates used to sign the JAR entry by calling `getCertificates()`.

MEMBER SUMMARY	
Constructor	
`JarEntry()`	Constructs a new `JarEntry` instance.
Retrieval Methods	
`getAttributes()`	Retrieves the manifest attributes for this JAR entry.
`getCertificates()`	Retrieves the certificates for this JAR entry.

See Also

`Attributes`, `JarFile`, `JarInputStream`, `JarOutputStream`, `Manifest`.

Example

This example implements a program that looks for JAR entries with certificates. When it finds one, it prints out various pieces of information about the certificate(s).

```
import java.io.*;
import java.util.*;
import java.util.jar.*;
import java.security.*;
import java.security.interfaces.*;
import java.security.cert.X509Certificate;
import java.security.cert.Certificate;

class Main {
    public static void main(String[] args) {
        if (args.length < 1) {
            System.err.println("Usage: java Main <jar-file>");
            System.exit(1);
        }

        try {
            JarFile jf = new JarFile(args[0], true);
            // List the names of all entries in the jar file.
            for (Enumeration e=jf.entries(); e.hasMoreElements(); ) {
                JarEntry je = (JarEntry)e.nextElement();

                // This step is necessary, otherwise getCertificates()
                // always returns null.
                InputStream is = jf.getInputStream(je);
                is.skip(je.getSize());

                Certificate[] cert = je.getCertificates();
                if (cert != null) {
                    System.out.println(je);
                    printCertificate(cert);
                }
            }
        } catch (Exception e) {
            e.printStackTrace();
        }
    }

    // Print some details about the certificate.
    static void printCertificate(java.security.cert.Certificate[] certs) {
        for (int i=0; i<certs.length; i++) {
            System.out.println("  Type: "+certs[i].getType());
            if (certs[i] instanceof X509Certificate) {
                X509Certificate c = (X509Certificate)certs[i];

                System.out.println("  Issuer: " + c.getIssuerDN().getName());
                System.out.println("  Subject: " + c.getSubjectDN().getName());
                System.out.println("  Serial#: " + c.getSerialNumber());
                System.out.println("  Expires: " + c.getNotAfter());
            }

            PublicKey pk = certs[i].getPublicKey();
            if (pk instanceof DSAPublicKey) {
                DSAPublicKey dpk = (DSAPublicKey)pk;
                System.out.println("  Algorithm: " + dpk.getAlgorithm());
                System.out.println("  Format: " + dpk.getFormat());
```

```
                }
            }
        }
    }
```

Output

Here is the output when run on the signed JAR file created in the `JarFile` class example.

```
ShowFiles.class
  Type: X.509
  Issuer: CN=Duke, OU=JavaSoft, O=Sun, L=Cupertino, ST=CA, C=US
  Subject: CN=Duke, OU=JavaSoft, O=Sun, L=Cupertino, ST=CA, C=US
  Serial#: 904936213
  Expires: Tue Jan 20 11:10:13 PST 2026
  Algorithm: DSA
  Format: X.509
```

getAttributes()

J

PURPOSE Retrieves the manifest attributes for this JAR entry.

SYNTAX `public Attributes getAttributes() throws IOException`

DESCRIPTION This method retrieves all of the manifest attributes associated with this JAR entry. If there are none, `null` is returned.

RETURNS A possibly `null` `Attributes` object.

EXAMPLE See the `JarInputStream` class example.

getCertificates()

PURPOSE Retrieves the certificates for this JAR entry.

SYNTAX `public java.security.cert.Certificate[] getCertificates()`

DESCRIPTION If the JAR entry is signed, this method retrieves the certificates used to sign this JAR entry. If the JAR entry is not signed, `null` is returned.

It is necessary to read all of the data associated with this JAR entry before calling this method. Otherwise, this method always returns `null`. See `JarFile.getInputStream()` or `JarInputStream.read()` for information on how to retrieve the JAR entry data. If you don't actually need the JAR entry data, you can call `skip()` on the data. For example, to skip the JAR entry data using `JarFile`, use

```
jarFile.getInputStream(jarEntry).skip(jarEntry.getSize())
```

To skip JAR entry data using `JarInputStream`, use

```
jarInputStream.skip(jarEntry.getSize())
```

RETURNS A possibly `null` array of certificates for this JAR entry.

EXAMPLE See the class example.

JarEntry()

PURPOSE Constructs a new `JarEntry` instance.

SYNTAX
```
public JarEntry(String jname)
public JarEntry(JarEntry je)
public JarEntry(ZipEntry ze)
```

DESCRIPTION This constructor creates a JAR entry with the name `jname`. Only the lower byte of each character is used in the name. The comment string and extra data properties of the new entry are set to `null`. All other properties have the value `-1`. See `ZipEntry` for a description of all available properties.

If `je` or `ze` is specified, the new JAR entry has the name `je.getName()` or `ze.getName()`. Also, the properties of a new JAR entry are initialized from `je` or `ze`.

PARAMETERS

`je` A non-`null` `JarEntry` to copy.

`jname` A non-`null` string containing the JAR entry name. Only the lower byte of each character is used. `jname.length` ≤ `65535`.

`ze` A non-`null` `ZipEntry` to copy.

EXCEPTIONS

`IllegalArgumentException`
If `jname.length` > `65535`.

EXAMPLE See the `JarOutputStream` class example.

JarException

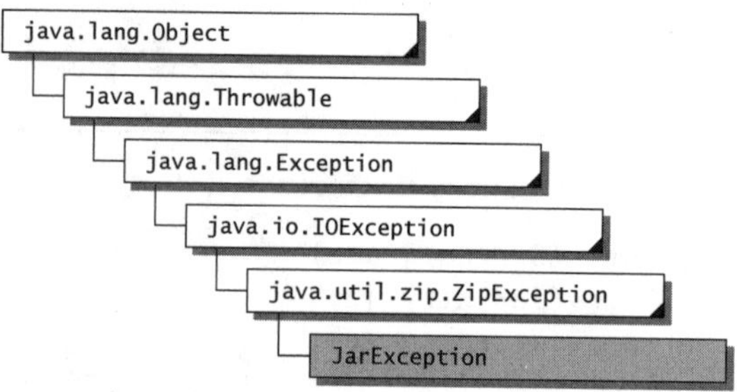

Syntax

```
public class JarException extends java.util.zip.ZipException
```

Description

A `JarException` is thrown by methods that process Java Archive (JAR) files. For example, it is thrown if there is an error in a manifest file (see `Manifest`).

MEMBER SUMMARY	
Constructor	
`JarException()`	Constructs a new instance of `JarException`.

See Also

`Manifest`.

JarException()

PURPOSE Constructs a new instance of `JarException`.

SYNTAX

```
public JarException()
public JarException(String msg)
```

DESCRIPTION This constructor constructs an instance of `JarException`. An optional detail string `msg` can be supplied that describes this particular instance of the exception. If `msg` is not supplied, the detail message defaults to `null`.

PARAMETERS

`msg` A possibly `null` string that gives details about this exception.

SEE ALSO `Throwable.getMessage()`.

JarFile

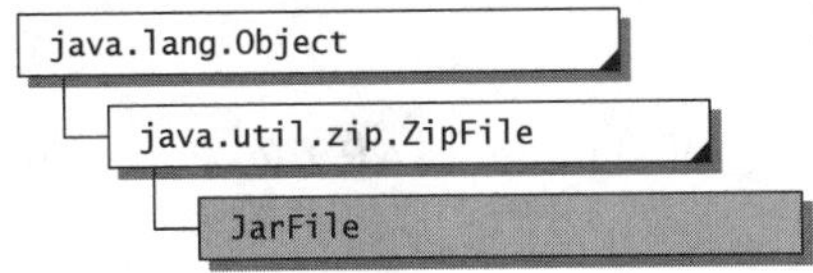

Syntax

```
public class JarFile extends ZipFile
```

Description

The `JarFile` class is used to read the contents of a Java Archive (JAR) file. A JAR file is essentially a ZIP file (see `ZipFile`) with additional information kept in a *manifest*. This class is similar to `ZipFile` except for two main differences.

1. The entries are `JarEntry` objects rather than `ZipEntry` objects.
2. There is a method for retrieving the manifest of the JAR file.

Because of the similarities with `ZipFile`, the descriptions in this class assume you are familiar with `ZipFile`. Please read the `ZipFile` descriptions before using this class.

Usage

This class can only read the contents of a JAR file. To create a JAR file, see `JarOutputStream`.

MEMBER SUMMARY	
Constructor	
`JarFile()`	Opens a JAR file.
Entry Methods	
`getEntry()`	Retrieves a JAR entry.
`getJarEntry()`	Retrieves a JAR entry.
`getInputStream()`	Creates an input stream on the contents represented by a JAR entry.
Manifest Members	
`getManifest()`	Retrieves the manifest for this JAR file.
`MANIFEST_NAME`	The entry name of the manifest in a JAR file.
Enumeration Method	
`entries()`	Creates an enumeration of all of the JAR entries.

See Also

`JarEntry`, `JarInputStream`, `JarOutputStream`, `java.util.zip.ZipEntry`, `Manifest`.

Example

This example shows the process of signing a JAR file. For an example that reads the contents of a JAR file, see `JarFile()`.

In this example, we create a simple applet that lists the contents of the applet's current directory to the Web browser's Java console window. Normally, this would result in a security exception. However, if the applet is signed, the user can allow the applet access to the file system, if desired.

ShowFiles.java

```
import java.applet.*;
import java.io.*;

public class ShowFiles extends Applet {
    public void init() {
        File dir = new File(".");
        String[] files = dir.list();
        for (int i=0; i<files.length; i++) {
            System.out.println(files[i]);
        }
    }
}
```

index.html

```
<applet code=ShowFiles archive=showfiles.jar width=100 height=100>
</applet>
```

The following is a brief description of the basic steps of using the JDK tools to sign an applet. For a more complete description of the process, see the tutorial for signing JAR files, located at `http://java.sun.com/docs/books/tutorial/jar/sign/index.html`.

1. The first step is to place the applet in a JAR file that we will sign.

   ```
   > jar cf showfiles.jar ShowFiles.class
   ```

2. You then need a certificate to sign the applet. If you don't have one, you can create one using the `keytool` command. The following command generates a key pair and a certificate for the individual named "Duke". The generated key pair and certificate is stored in a key store whose password is "almanac".

   ```
   > keytool -genkey -alias duke -keystore .keystore
   Enter keystore password: almanac
   What is your first and last name?
     [Unknown]: Duke
   What is the name of your organizational unit?
     [Unknown]: JavaSoft
   What is the name of your organization?
     [Unknown]: Sun
   What is the name of your City or Locality?
     [Unknown]: Cupertino
   ```

```
What is the name of your State or Province?
  [Unknown]: CA
What is the two-letter country code for this unit?
  [Unknown]: US
Is <CN=Duke, OU=JavaSoft, O=Sun, L=Cupertino, ST=CA, C=US> correct?
  [no]: yes
Enter key password for <duke>
        (RETURN if same as keystore password):
```

The previous command creates a self-signed certificate that shouldn't be used when you actually deploy your applet. Instead, you should use a certificate issued by a certification authority (CA) to sign your applet. A list of CAs is available at `https://certs.netscape.com/client.html`

3. The applet can now be signed by "Duke".

```
> jarsigner -keystore .keystore -storepass almanac showfiles.jar duke
```

When the signed JAR `showfiles.jar` is deployed, the administrator or user needs to grant Duke access to read the file system by setting up the appropriate permissions. The following policy file was generated using `policytool`.

.policy

```
/* AUTOMATICALLY GENERATED ON Fri Sep 11 17:23:50 PDT 1998*/
/* DO NOT EDIT */

keystore ".keystore";

grant signedBy "Duke" {
  permission java.io.FilePermission "${user.dir}", "read";
};
```

This permission allows the reading of the applet's current directory. See `FilePermission` for the syntax of these permission names.

You can then run the applet, for example, by using `appletviewer`:

```
appletviewer -J-Djava.security.policy=.policy index.html
```

For more information on permissions and policy files, see the individual permission's class descriptions (such as `FilePermission` and `NetPermission`) and the document

```
http://java.sun.com/products/jdk/1.2/docs/guide/security/permissions.html
```

entries()

PURPOSE	Creates an enumeration of all of the JAR entries.
SYNTAX	`public Enumeration entries()`
DESCRIPTION	This method creates an enumeration of all of the JAR entries in this `JarFile`. The enumeration consists of `JarEntry` objects that can be used to access the JAR entries in the JAR file. The manifest file also appears in the enumeration.

See `ZipFile.entries()` for more information about the JAR entries returned by the enumeration.

RETURNS A non-`null` enumeration of `JarEntry` objects.

OVERRIDES `java.util.zip.ZipFile.entries()`.

SEE ALSO `java.util.Enumeration`.

EXAMPLE See `JarFile()`.

getEntry()

PURPOSE Retrieves a JAR entry.

SYNTAX `public ZipEntry getEntry(String ename)`

DESCRIPTION This method returns the JAR entry with the name `ename`. If no entry is found, `null` is returned. Note, unlike the result of `getJarEntry()`, you must cast the result of `getEntry()` to a `JarEntry` to access the `JarEntry` specific methods.

See `ZipFile.getEntry()` for more details about this method.

J

PARAMETERS

`ename` The non-`null` case-sensitive name of a JAR entry.

RETURNS A possibly `null` `JarEntry` object with the name `ename`.

OVERRIDES `java.util.zip.ZipFile.getEntry()`.

SEE ALSO `getJarEntry()`.

EXAMPLE See `getJarEntry()`. In the example, you could replace the call

```
getJarEntry
```

with

```
(JarEntry)getEntry
```

getInputStream()

PURPOSE Creates an input stream on the contents represented by a JAR entry.

SYNTAX

```
public synchronized InputStream getInputStream(ZipEntry je)
    throws IOException
```

DESCRIPTION Each JAR entry represents a sequence of compressed or uncompressed data. This method creates an input stream that will deliver that data. The bytes flowing from the input stream are uncompressed and verified. When end-of-stream is reached in the input stream, if the digest of the bytes does not match the digest in the manifest, a `SecurityException` is thrown. The entry `je` should be one that was returned by `getJarEntry()`.

PARAMETERS

`je` A non-`null` `JarEntry` object.

EXCEPTIONS

`ZipException`
If a ZIP format error occurs while creating the input stream.

`IOException`
If an IO error occurs while creating the input stream.

OVERRIDES `java.util.zip.ZipFile.getInputStream()`.

SEE ALSO `getJarEntry()`.

EXAMPLE See `JarFile()`.

getJarEntry()

PURPOSE Retrieves a JAR entry.

SYNTAX `public JarEntry getJarEntry(String ename)`

DESCRIPTION This method returns a JAR entry with the name `ename`. If no entry is found, `null` is returned.

See `ZipFile.getEntry()` for more details about this method.

This method is implemented as

```
return (JarEntry)getEntry(ename);
```

PARAMETERS

`ename` A non-`null` case-sensitive JAR entry name.

RETURNS A possibly `null` `JarEntry` object with the name `ename`.

SEE ALSO `getEntry()`, `JarEntry`.

EXAMPLE See `JarFile()`.

getManifest()

PURPOSE Retrieves the manifest for this JAR file.

SYNTAX `public Manifest getManifest() throws IOException`

DESCRIPTION This method retrieves the manifest for this JAR file. See `Manifest` for more information about manifests.

RETURNS A possibly `null` `Manifest` object representing the manifest in this JAR input stream.

SEE ALSO `Manifest`.

EXAMPLE This simple example retrieves the JAR file's manifest and prints it out.

```
import java.util.*;
import java.util.jar.*;
import java.util.zip.*;

class Main {
    public static void main(String[] args) {
        try {
            JarFile jf = new JarFile(args[0]);
            Manifest man = jf.getManifest();

            if (man == null) {
                System.err.println("No manifest");
            } else {
                man.write(System.out);
            }
        } catch (Exception e) {
            e.printStackTrace();
        }
    }
}
```


OUTPUT Here is the output when the program is run on the signed JAR file created in the class example.

```
> java Main showfiles.jar
Manifest-Version: 1.0
Name: ShowFiles.class
SHA1-Digest: 7ZDT3kupdak9+5ETIEKrkUDTe4c=
```

JarFile()

PURPOSE Opens a JAR file.

SYNTAX

```
public JarFile(String fname) throws IOException
public JarFile(String fname, boolean verify) throws IOException
public JarFile(File file) throws IOException
public JarFile(File file, boolean verify) throws IOException
```

DESCRIPTION This constructor opens a JAR file and reads in all of its JAR entries. If `fname` is specified, this constructor opens the JAR file named `fname`. If `file` is specified, this constructor opens the file represented by `file`.

If `fname` is specified, `fname` becomes the JAR file's name; otherwise, `file.getPath()` becomes the JAR file's name. Use `ZipFile.getName()` to retrieve the JAR file's name.

If `verify` is `true` and the JAR is signed, the signature and the contents of the JAR file are checked for any tampering. If the JAR file has been modified, a `SecurityException` is thrown. The verification check is done when the bytes for an entry are completely read. At that time, if the digest of the bytes does not match the digest in the manifest, a `SecurityException` is thrown. Therefore, if it is necessary to verify the whole JAR file, you need to read all of the bytes of each entry in the JAR file (for example, by calling `closeEntry()` for each entry). If the JAR is not signed, `verify` is ignored.

PARAMETERS

`file` The non-`null` `File` object representing the JAR file.

`fname` The non-`null` name of the JAR file.

`verify` If `true`, verifies the contents of the signed JAR file. If JAR file not signed, `verify` is ignored.

EXCEPTIONS

`FileNotFoundException`
If the JAR file does not exist.

`IOException`
If an IO error occurs while opening the JAR file.

`SecurityException`
If the caller does not have permission to access the JAR file.

EXAMPLE This example implements a command that extracts the data for some entry in a JAR file. The command dumps the data to standard output. If an entry name is not specified, the command dumps the contents of the manifest. If an entry name is not found, the command lists the names of the entries in the JAR file.

```
import java.io.*;
import java.util.*;
import java.util.jar.*;

class Main {
    public static void main(String[] args) {
        if (args.length < 1) {
            System.err.println("Usage: java Main <jar-file> [entry-name]");
            System.exit(1);
        }

        try {
            JarFile jf = new JarFile(args[0], true);
            String entryName =
                (args.length >= 2) ? args[1] : JarFile.MANIFEST_NAME;
            JarEntry je = jf.getJarEntry(entryName);

            if (je == null) {
                System.err.println("No such entry " + entryName);

                // List the names of all entries in the jar file.
                for (Enumeration e=jf.entries(); e.hasMoreElements(); ) {
                    System.out.println("  " + e.nextElement());
                }
                System.exit(1);
            }

            // Dump the jar entry data to standard output.
            InputStream is = jf.getInputStream(je);
            byte[] buf = new byte[1024];
            int len;
```

```
                while ((len = is.read(buf)) >= 0) {
                    System.out.write(buf, 0, len);
                }
                is.close();
            } catch (Exception e) {
                e.printStackTrace();
            }
        }
    }
```

OUTPUT Here is the output when run on the signed JAR file created in the class example. Since an entry is not given, the command dumps the contents of the manifest.

```
> java Main showfiles.jar
Manifest-Version: 1.0
Name: ShowFiles.class
SHA1-Digest: 7ZDT3kupdak9+5ETIEKrkUDTe4c=
```

MANIFEST_NAME

PURPOSE The entry name of the manifest in a JAR file.

SYNTAX `public static final String MANIFEST_NAME`

DESCRIPTION This constant (`"META-INF/MANIFEST.MF"`) is the name of the entry given to the manifest in a JAR file. `JarOutputStream` uses this name when it creates the manifest entry in a new JAR file.

SEE ALSO `JarOutputStream`, `Manifest`.

EXAMPLE See `JarFile()`.

JarInputStream

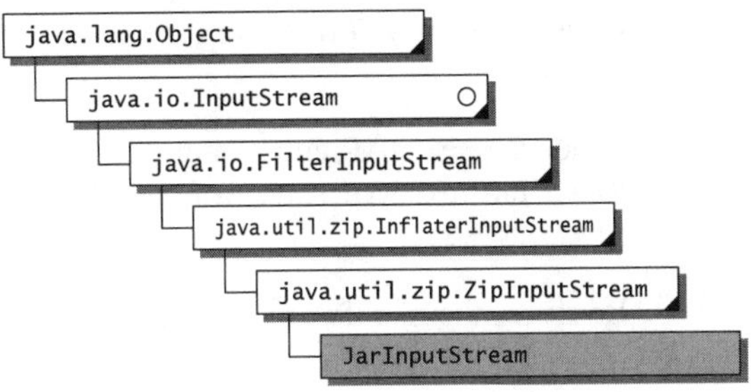

Syntax

```
public class JarInputStream extends ZipInputStream
```

Description

The `JarInputStream` class implements an input stream filter for reading the contents of a Java Archive (JAR) file. A JAR file is essentially a ZIP file (see `ZipFile`) with additional information kept in a *manifest*. This class is similar to `ZipInputStream` except for two main differences.

1. The input stream returns `JarEntry` objects rather than `ZipEntry` objects.
2. There is a method for retrieving the manifest of the JAR file.

Because of the similarities with `ZipInputStream`, the descriptions in this class assume you are familiar with `ZipInputStream`. Please read the `ZipInputStream` descriptions before using this class.

Manifest

A manifest is a set of attributes (name/value pairs) associated with a JAR file (see `JarFile`). The attributes provide additional information about the JAR file and about entries in the JAR file. For example, if a class is signed, its digest is kept in the manifest. See `Manifest` for more information.

Signed JAR Files

If a JAR file is signed, this class can be used to verify the signature. See the constructor for an example. For an example of how JAR files are signed, see `JarFile`.

MEMBER SUMMARY	
Constructor	
`JarInputStream()`	Constructs a new `JarInputStream` instance.
Entry Methods	
`getNextEntry()`	Reads the next JAR entry from this JAR input stream.
`getNextJarEntry()`	Reads the next JAR entry from this JAR input stream.
Manifest Method	
`getManifest()`	Retrieves the manifest for this JAR input stream.
Protected Method	
`createZipEntry()`	Called to create a new JAR entry.
Read Method	
`read()`	Reads decompressed data from this JAR input stream.

See Also

`JarEntry`, `JarFile`, `JarOutputStream`, `Manifest`, `ZipInputStream`.

Example

This example creates a JAR input stream on a JAR file. It then prints all of the attributes in the manifest and the attributes for every entry in the JAR file.

```
import java.io.*;
import java.util.*;
import java.util.jar.*;

class Main {
    public static void main(String[] args) {
        if (args.length < 1) {
            System.out.println("Usage: java Main <jar-file>");
            System.exit(1);
        }

        try {
            JarInputStream jis = new JarInputStream(
                new FileInputStream(args[0]));

            // Print the manifest.
            Manifest man = jis.getManifest();
            if (man != null) {
                printManifest(man);
            }
            System.out.println("\n");

            // Print the attributes for each jar entry.
            JarEntry je;
            while ((je = jis.getNextJarEntry()) != null) {
                System.out.println("++++++++++ " + je);
                if (je.getAttributes() != null) {
```

```
                printAttributes(je.getAttributes());
            }
        }
        jis.close();
    } catch (Exception e) {
        e.printStackTrace();
    }
}

static void printManifest(Manifest man) {
    System.out.println("---------- Main Attributes");
    printAttributes(man.getMainAttributes());
    for (Iterator it=man.getEntries().keySet().iterator(); it.hasNext(); )
    {
        String ename = (String)it.next();
        System.out.println("---------- " + ename);
        printAttributes(man.getAttributes(ename));
    }
}

static void printAttributes(Attributes attr) {
    for (Iterator it=attr.keySet().iterator(); it.hasNext(); ) {
        Object key = it.next();
        System.out.println(key+": "+attr.get(key));
    }
}
}
```

OUTPUT This is the output of the program when run on the JAR file created in the `JarFile` class example. Notice that the manifest file does not appear as an entry from the input stream. Also note that the attributes for an entry are not removed from the manifest. Therefore you can retrieve the attributes for an entry from either a JAR entry or from the manifest.

```
> java Main showfiles.jar
---------- Main Attributes
Manifest-Version: 1.0
---------- ShowFiles.class
SHA1-Digest: 7ZDT3kupdak9+5ETIEKrkUDTe4c=
++++++++++ META-INF/DUKE.SF
++++++++++ META-INF/DUKE.DSA
++++++++++ META-INF/
++++++++++ ShowFiles.class
SHA1-Digest: 7ZDT3kupdak9+5ETIEKrkUDTe4c=
```

createZipEntry()

PURPOSE Called to create a new JAR entry.

SYNTAX `protected ZipEntry createZipEntry(String ename)`

DESCRIPTION This method is called by `ZipInputStream.getNextEntry()` when it needs to create a `ZipEntry` object. This override creates and returns a `JarEntry` object that will eventually be returned by `getNextEntry()`. This method should not be called directly.

An override to this method must return a subclass of `ZipEntry`. The name of the returned object should be `ename`. See `ZipEntry()` for more information about ZIP entry names.

PARAMETERS

`ename` The non-`null` name of the new JAR entry.

RETURNS A non-`null` `JarEntry` object with the name `ename`.

OVERRIDES `java.util.zip.ZipInputStream.createZipEntry()`.

getManifest()

PURPOSE Retrieves the manifest for this JAR input stream.

SYNTAX `public Manifest getManifest()`

DESCRIPTION This method retrieves the manifest for this JAR input stream. The manifest holds additional information about the JAR and about the entries in the JAR. See `Manifest` for more information about manifests.

RETURNS A possibly `null` `Manifest` object representing the manifest in this JAR.

SEE ALSO `Manifest`.

EXAMPLE See the class example.

getNextEntry()

PURPOSE Reads the next JAR entry from this JAR input stream.

SYNTAX `public ZipEntry getNextEntry() throws IOException`

DESCRIPTION This method overrides the default implementation in order to handle the differences between JAR and ZIP files. Also, this method actually returns `JarEntry` objects rather than `ZipEntry` objects so that the returned objects can be safely cast to `JarEntry` objects. To avoid the cast, use the convenience method `getNextJarEntry()`.

The manifest file bundled with the JAR is not returned as an entry. To retrieve the manifest, use `getManifest()`.

This method results in a call to `createZipEntry()` which, in this class, returns `JarEntry` objects.

For more information on this method, see `ZipInputStream.getNextEntry()`.

RETURNS A `JarEntry` or `null` if there are no more JAR entries in this input stream.

EXCEPTIONS

`ZipException`
If a ZIP file error occurs while the next JAR entry is being retrieved.

`IOException`
If an IO error occurs while the next JAR entry is being retrieved.

`SecurityException`
If the next JAR entry has been modified since the JAR was signed.

OVERRIDES `java.util.zip.ZipInputStream.getNextEntry()`.

SEE ALSO `getManifest()`, `getNextJarEntry()`.

EXAMPLE See the class example.

getNextJarEntry()

PURPOSE Reads the next JAR entry from this JAR input stream.

SYNTAX `public JarEntry getNextJarEntry() throws IOException`

DESCRIPTION This method reads the next JAR entry from this JAR input stream. Its implementation calls `getNextEntry()`:

```
return (JarEntry)getNextEntry();
```

See `getNextEntry()` for more information.

RETURNS A `JarEntry` or `null` if there are no more JAR entries in this input stream.

EXCEPTIONS

`ZipException`
If a ZIP file error occurs while the next JAR entry is being retrieved.

`IOException`
If an IO error occurs while the next JAR entry is being retrieved.

`SecurityException`
If the next JAR entry has been modified since the JAR was signed.

SEE ALSO `getNextEntry()`.

EXAMPLE See the class example.

JarInputStream()

PURPOSE Constructs a new `JarInputStream` instance.

SYNTAX
```
public JarInputStream(InputStream in) throws IOException
public JarInputStream(InputStream in, boolean verify) throws
    IOException
```

J

DESCRIPTION This constructor reads the header of the JAR from `in` and also processes the manifest file (if present).

If `verify` is `true` and the JAR is signed, the signature and the contents of the JAR file is checked for any tampering. If the JAR file has been modified, a `SecurityException` is thrown. The verification check is done when the bytes for an entry are completely read. At that time, if the digest of the bytes does not match the digest in the manifest, a `SecurityException` is thrown. Therefore, if it is necessary to verify the whole JAR file, you need to read all of the bytes of each entry in the JAR file (for example, by calling `closeEntry()` for each entry). If the JAR is not signed, `verify` is ignored.

PARAMETERS

`in` A non-`null` input stream.

`verify` If `true`, verifies the contents of the JAR file.

EXCEPTIONS

`IOException`

If an IO error occurs while the JAR input stream is being processed.

`SecurityException`

If the JAR file has been modified since it was signed.

EXAMPLE This example demonstrates what happens when verification of the JAR file fails. See the class example for a more typical use of this constructor.

```
import java.io.*;
import java.util.jar.*;

class Main {
    public static void main(String[] args) {
        if (args.length < 1) {
            System.out.println("Usage: java Main <jar-file>");
            System.exit(1);
        }

        try {
            JarInputStream jis = new JarInputStream(
                new FileInputStream(args[0]), true);
            JarEntry je;
            while ((je = jis.getNextJarEntry()) != null) {
                System.out.println(je);
                jis.closeEntry(); // complete reading bytes of entry
            }
            jis.close();
        } catch (Exception e) {
            e.printStackTrace();
        }
    }
}
```

OUTPUT To demonstrate a security exception, we modified the `ShowFiles.class` data in the JAR file created in the `JarFile` class example. The security exception is not thrown until the entry for `ShowFiles.class` is completely read from the input stream (`closeEntry()`).

```
META-INF/DUKE.SF
META-INF/DUKE.DSA
META-INF/
ShowFiles.class
java.lang.SecurityException: SHA1 digest error for ShowFiles.class
        at sun.security.util.ManifestEntryVerifier.verify(
                ManifestEntryVerifier.java:198)
        at java.util.jar.JarVerifier.processEntry(JarVerifier.java:214)
        at java.util.jar.JarVerifier.update(JarVerifier.java:201)
        at java.util.jar.JarInputStream.read(JarInputStream.java:166)
        at java.util.zip.ZipInputStream.closeEntry(ZipInputStream.java:93)
        at Main.main(Main.java:17)
```

read()

PURPOSE Reads decompressed data from this JAR input stream.

SYNTAX `public int read(byte[] buf, int off, int len) throws IOException`

DESCRIPTION This method reads at most `len` bytes from this JAR input stream and places them in `buf` starting at `buf[off]`. The bytes are uncompressed.

The blocking behavior of this method depends on the input stream(s) that this JAR input stream filters. In general, this method blocks until some bytes (possibly fewer than `len`) are read.

This method returns `-1` if the JAR input stream has no more data to return.

PARAMETERS

`buf` The non-`null` buffer in which to store the data.

`len` The maximum number of bytes to read into `buf` starting at `buf[off]`. `0` ≤ `len` ≤ `buf.length-off`.

`off` The `0`-based starting offset to store the data in `buf`. `0` ≤ `off` < `buf.length`.

RETURNS The number of bytes read, or `-1` if the end-of-stream has been reached.

EXCEPTIONS

`ZipException`
If a ZIP file error occurs while reading.

`IOException`
If an IO error occurs while reading.

EXAMPLE See the `ZipFile.getEntry()`.

J

java.util.jar
JarOutputStream

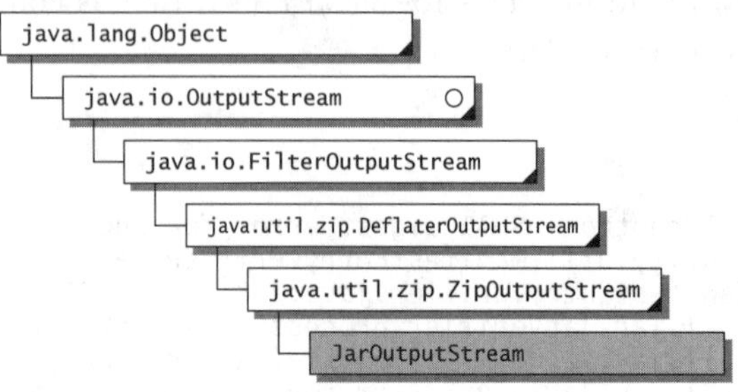

Syntax

```
public class JarOutputStream extends ZipOutputStream
```

Description

J

This class implements an output stream filter for creating a Java Archive (JAR) file. A JAR file is essentially a ZIP file (see `ZipFile`) with additional information kept in a *manifest*. This class is similar to `ZipOutputStream` except that you can supply an optional manifest to include in the JAR file.

Because of this class's similarities with `ZipOutputStream`, the descriptions in this class assume you are familiar with `ZipOutputStream`. Please read the `ZipOutputStream` descriptions before using this class.

Manifest

A *manifest* is a set of attributes (name/value pairs) associated with a JAR file (see `JarFile`). The attributes provide additional information about the JAR file and about entries in the JAR file. For example, if a class is signed, its digest is kept in the manifest. See `Manifest` for more information.

MEMBER SUMMARY	
Constructor	
`JarOutputStream()`	Constructs a new `JarOutputStream` instance.
Entry Method	
`putNextEntry()`	Writes a ZIP entry into this JAR output stream.

See Also

`java.util.zip.ZipOutputStream`, `Manifest`.

Example

This example creates a JAR file that has the files listed on the command line. The program creates a manifest containing a manifest entry for each file. Each manifest entry contains a "Date" attribute, which holds the last modified time of the associated file. The program also dumps the generated manifest to `System.out`.

```
import java.io.*;
import java.util.*;
import java.util.jar.*;

class Main {
    public static void main(String[] args) {
        if (args.length < 2) {
            System.out.println("Usage: java Main <jar-file> <file1>...");
            System.exit(1);
        }

        try {
            // Create the manifest.
            Manifest man = new Manifest();
            man.getMainAttributes().put(Attributes.Name.MANIFEST_VERSION,
                "1.0");

            for (int i=1; i<args.length; i++) {
                File f = new File(args[i]);
                Attributes attr = new Attributes();

                attr.put(new Attributes.Name("Date"),
                    new Date(f.lastModified()).toString());
                man.getEntries().put(entryName(f), attr);
            }

            // Dump manifest.
            man.write(System.out);

            JarOutputStream jos = new JarOutputStream(
                new FileOutputStream(args[0]), man);

            // Now save all the list files in the JAR.
            byte[] buf = new byte[1024];
            int len;
            for (int i=1; i<args.length; i++) {
                File f = new File(args[i]);
                FileInputStream fis = new FileInputStream(f);
                jos.putNextEntry(new JarEntry(entryName(f)));

                // Now read and write the jar entry data.
                while ((len = fis.read(buf)) >= 0) {
                    jos.write(buf, 0, len);
                }
                fis.close();
            }
            jos.close();
        } catch (Exception e) {
            e.printStackTrace();
        }
    }

    // Converts f's pathname to a form acceptable to ZIP files.
```

```
        // In particular, file separators are converted to forward slashes.
        static String entryName(File f) throws IOException {
            return f.getName().replace(File.separatorChar, '/');
        }
    }
```

OUTPUT

```
Manifest-Version: 1.0

Name: Main.class
Date: Fri Sep 04 23:17:30 PDT 1998

Name: Main.java
Date: Fri Sep 04 23:18:00 PDT 1998
```

JarOutputStream()

PURPOSE Constructs a new `JarOutputStream` instance.

SYNTAX

```
public JarOutputStream(OutputStream out) throws IOException
public JarOutputStream(OutputStream out, Manifest man) throws
    IOException
```

DESCRIPTION This constructor creates a new JAR output stream on `out`. When all data has been written to the JAR output stream, it is necessary to call either `finish()` to complete the JAR or `close()` to complete the JAR and close `out`. See `ZipOutputStream.ZipOutputStream()` for more details about this constructor.

If the manifest `man` is not `null`, it is included in the JAR. The manifest will have the JAR entry name `JarFile.MANIFEST_NAME`.

If `man` is not specified, it defaults to `null`.

PARAMETERS

`man` A non-`null` manifest.
`out` A non-`null` output stream.

EXCEPTIONS

`IOException`
If an IO error occurs while creating the JAR.

EXAMPLE See the class example.

putNextEntry()

PURPOSE Writes a ZIP entry into this JAR output stream.

SYNTAX

```
public void putNextEntry(ZipEntry ze) throws IOException
```

DESCRIPTION This method writes a ZIP entry into this JAR output stream. It behaves exactly like `ZipOutputStream.putNextEntry()`. See the description for `ZipOutputStream.putNextEntry()` for information about this method.

PARAMETERS

`ze` A non-`null` ZIP entry.

EXCEPTIONS

`ZipException`

If `ze` is not properly initialized.

`IOException`

If an IO error occurs while writing the ZIP entry.

OVERRIDES `java.util.zip.ZipOutputStream.putNextEntry()`.

EXAMPLE See the class example.

java.net
JarURLConnection

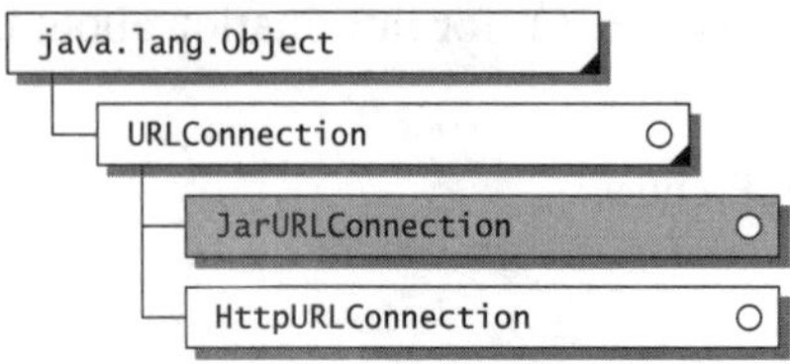

Syntax

```
public abstract class JarURLConnection extends URLConnection
```

Description

The Java Archive (JAR) specifies a platform-independent file format for packaging class files and resources into an *archive*. Such an archive is called a *JAR file*, and the entries within the archive are called *JAR entries*. See `http://java.sun.com/products/jdk/1.2/docs/guide/jar/` for details on JAR.

J

The `URLConnection` class represents an active connection to the resource identified by a URL. The `JarURLConnection` class is an abstract subclass of `URLConnection` that represents an active connection to the JAR file or entry identified by a JAR URL. It contains methods and fields specific for processing JAR files and entries over a URL connection.

The JAR URL

The JAR URL has the following syntax:

`jar:`*jarFileURL*`!/[`*entryName*`]`

where *jarFileURL* is a URL that identifies the location of the JAR file and *entryName* names an entry within that JAR file. *jarFileURL* is referred to as the JAR file URL. The protocol of the *jarFileURL* is usually `"file"` or `"http"`, but it could in fact be any protocol.

Here are some examples of JAR URLs.

`jar:http://java.sun.com/jndi/jndi.jar!/`

This URL names a JAR file. Its *jarFileURL* is `http://java.sun.com/jndi/jndi.jar`. It has no entry name.

`jar:http://java.sun.com/jndi/jndi.jar!/javax/naming/`

This URL names a JAR entry. Its *jarFileURL* is `http://java.sun.com/jndi/jndi.jar`. It entry name is `javax/naming/`.

`jar:http://java.sun.com/jndi/jndi.jar!/javax/naming/Context.class`

This URL names a JAR entry. Its *jarFileURL* is `http://java.sun.com/jndi/jndi.jar`. Its entry name is `javax/naming/Context.class`.

Usage

When the program calls `URL.getContent()` or `URL.openStream()`, these methods create a `URLConnection` for the URL and invoke methods on the `URLConnection`. When the URL is a JAR URL, the underlying `URLConnection` that is created is a subclass of `JarURLConnection`. So the most common usage of this class is probably indirectly when JAR URLs are used.

The program can also call `URL.openConnection()` to get a direct handle on the URL connection. If you do this, you can then cast the result to a `JarURLConnection`. This will allow you to get specific information about the `JarURLConnection`, such as a JAR entry's attributes and certificates, as follows.

```
URL url = new URL(
    "jar:http://java.sun.com/jndi/jndi.jar!/javax/naming/Context.class");
JarURLConnection conn = (JarURLConnection)url.openConnection();
Attributes attrs = conn.getAttributes();    // get entry's attributes
Certificates certs = conn.getCertificates(); // get entry's certificates
```

The `JarFile` class is useful for examining and retrieving the contents of a JAR file located on the file system. `JarURLConnection` is useful for examining and retrieving the contents of a JAR file that is on the network but perhaps not available directly through the network file system. Suppose a JAR file is located on an HTTP server. You can use a `JARURLConnection` to examine that JAR file and/or retrieve entries within that JAR file. This feature is used, for example, by `URLClassLoader` to load JAR files whose locations are identified URLs.

J

Subclass Implementations

When implementing the URL stream handler for the JAR protocol, you would define `URLStreamHandler.openConnection()` to return a subclass of `JarURLConnection`. To provide an implementation for `JarURLConnection`, you must, at a minimum, provide implementations for the abstract methods `connect()` and `getJarFile()`. Most likely, in order to implement the connection properly, you will also need to override the methods `getInputStream()` and `getContent()`.

`getJarFile()` should call `connect()` so that the program doesn't have to explicitly invoke `connect()` before calling any other methods in this class. This is a pattern that similar methods in `URLConnection` already follow.

Methods such as `connect()`, `getHeaderField()`, and `getPermission()` should be overridden to get that information from the underlying `URLConnection` (that is, the connection of the JAR file URL). The field `jarFileURLConnection` should be set to this underlying `URLConnection`. Some methods need to behave differently depending on whether the JAR URL refers to a JAR file or to a JAR entry.

If the URL names a JAR entry, `getInputStream()` should return an input stream for reading the entry (see `JarFile.getInputStream()`). A JAR entry's content type (`getContentType()`) is the entry's content type, which could be obtained either from the entry's `"Content-Type"` attribute or by examining the entry's contents. `getContent()` should return the object represented by the JAR entry (see `URLConnection.getContent()`). `getContentLength()` should return the size of JAR entry.

A JAR file's content type is "x-java/jar". `getContent()` should return a `JarFile` instance representing the JAR file, and `getContentLength()` should return the size of the JAR file.

MEMBER SUMMARY

Constructor	
`JarURLConnection()`	Constructs a new `JarURLConnection` instance.
JAR File Methods	
`getJarFile()`	Retrieves the JAR file associated with this `JarURLConnection`.
`getJarFileURL()`	Retrieves the URL of the JAR file associated with this `JarURLConnection`.
`getMainAttributes()`	Retrieves the main attributes of the manifest for this `JarURLConnection`'s JAR file.
`getManifest()`	Retrieves the manifest for this `JarURLConnection`.
JAR Entry Methods	
`getAttributes()`	Retrieves the attributes of the JAR entry associated with this `JarURLConnection`.
`getCertificates()`	Retrieves the certificates that were used to sign the JAR entry associated with this `JarURLConnection`.
`getEntryName()`	Retrieves the name of the JAR entry associated with this `JarURLConnection`.
`getJarEntry()`	Retrieves the JAR entry associated with this `JarURLConnection`.
Protected Field	
`jarFileURLConnection`	The field containing the `URLConnection` for retrieving this `JarURLConnection`'s JAR file.

See Also

`java.util.jar.Attributes`, `java.util.jar.JarEntry`, `java.util.jar.JarFile`, `java.util.jar.Manifest`, `URLConnection`, `URLStreamHandler`.

Example

This example opens a `JarURLConnection` and prints out some data read from it, including its manifest and main attributes.

```
import java.net.*;
import java.util.jar.*;
import java.util.Map;
import java.util.Iterator;
import java.util.Set;
```

```
public class Main {
    public static void main(String[] args) {
        try {
            URL url = new URL("jar:file:showfiles.jar!/");
            JarURLConnection jconn = (JarURLConnection)url.openConnection();

            System.out.println("JAR File URL: " + jconn.getJarFileURL());
                                                    // file:showfiles.jar
            System.out.println("JAR File: " + jconn.getJarFile());

            System.out.println("JAR Entry: " + jconn.getEntryName());
                                                    // null (not an entry)

            // Get manifest and print names of entries it contains
            Manifest man = jconn.getManifest();
            if (man != null) {
                System.out.println("Entries: " );
                for (Iterator it = man.getEntries().keySet().iterator();
                     it.hasNext();) {
                    System.out.println(it.next());
                }
            }

            // Print main attributes of JAR file
            Attributes attrs = jconn.getMainAttributes();
            System.out.println("Main Attributes: " );
            if (attrs != null) {
                Set set = attrs.entrySet();
                for (Iterator it = set.iterator(); it.hasNext();) {
                    System.out.println(it.next());
                }
            }
        } catch (java.io.IOException e) {
            e.printStackTrace();
        }
    }
}
```

getAttributes()

PURPOSE Retrieves the attributes of the JAR entry associated with this `JarURLConnection`.

SYNTAX `public Attributes getAttributes() throws IOException`

DESCRIPTION This method retrieves the attributes of the JAR entry associated with this `JarURLConnection`. The JAR URL that was used to create this `JarURLConnection` can name either an entire JAR file or an entry (either a file or a directory) within a JAR file. If it names a JAR entry, this method return that entry's attributes. Otherwise, it returns `null`.

RETURNS A possibly `null` set of attributes.

EXCEPTIONS

`IOException`

If an IO error occurred while accessing the JAR file associated with the JAR entry.

SEE ALSO `getEntryName()`, `getJarEntry()`, `getMainAttributes()`, `java.util.jar.JarEntry.getAttributes()`.

EXAMPLE See `getCertificates()`.

getCertificates()

PURPOSE Retrieves the certificates that were used to sign the JAR entry associated with this `JarURLConnection`.

SYNTAX `public java.security.cert.Certificate[] getCertificates() throws IOException`

DESCRIPTION This method retrieves the certificates that were used to sign the JAR entry associated with this `JarURLConnection`, if this `JarURLConnection` is associated with a signed JAR entry. Otherwise, `null` is returned. It is necessary to read all of the data associated with the JAR entry before calling this method. See `java.util.jar.JarEntry` for details.

J

RETURNS A possibly `null` array of `Certificate` objects.

EXCEPTIONS

`IOException`

If an IO error occurred while trying to access the JAR entry.

SEE ALSO `getJarEntry()`, `java.util.jar.JarEntry.getCertificates()`.

EXAMPLE This example creates a `JarURLConnection` for a JAR entry (`ShowFiles.class`) in a JAR file (`showfiles.jar`). This JAR file comes from the `JarFile` class example. The example first prints information about the `JarURLConnection`, including its JAR file URL, its JAR entry name, and its attributes. It then skips over the JAR entry's data and retrieves its certificates. Failure to skip over the JAR entry's data results in `getCertificates()` returning `null`. Instead of invoking `getAttributes()` and `getCertificates()` on the `JarURLConnection`, we could have invoked these methods on the JAR entry itself—this would have produced identical results.

```
try {
    URL url = new URL("jar:file:showfiles.jar!/ShowFiles.class");
    JarURLConnection jconn = (JarURLConnection)url.openConnection();

    System.out.println("JAR File URL: " + jconn.getJarFileURL());
                                                    // file:showfiles.jar

    System.out.println(jconn.getEntryName()); // ShowFiles.class
```

```
        // Print entry's attributes
        Attributes attrs = jconn.getAttributes();
        System.out.println("Attributes: " );
        if (attrs != null) {
            Set set = attrs.entrySet();
            for (Iterator it = set.iterator(); it.hasNext();) {
                System.out.println(it.next());
            }
        }

        // This step is necessary; otherwise getCertificates() return null
        JarEntry entry = jconn.getJarEntry();
        JarFile jfile = jconn.getJarFile();
        java.io.InputStream is = jfile.getInputStream(entry);
        is.skip(entry.getSize());

        // Get and Print entry's certificates
        Certificate[] certs = jconn.getCertificates();
        System.out.println("Certificates: " );
        if (certs != null) {
            printCertificates(certs);
        }
    } catch (java.io.IOException e) {
        e.printStackTrace();
    }
```

OUTPUT

```
JAR File URL: file:showfiles.jar
ShowFiles.class
Attributes:
SHA1-Digest=7ZDT3kupdak9+5ETIEKrkUDTe4c=
Certificates:
  Type: X.509
  Issuer: CN=Duke, OU=JavaSoft, O=Sun, L=Cupertino, ST=CA, C=US
  Subject: CN=Duke, OU=JavaSoft, O=Sun, L=Cupertino, ST=CA, C=US
  Serial#: 904936213
  Expires: Tue Jan 20 11:10:13 GMT-08:00 2026
  Algorithm: DSA
  Format: X.509
```

getEntryName()

PURPOSE Retrieves the name of the JAR entry associated with this `JarURLConnection`.

SYNTAX `public String getEntryName()`

RETURNS The possibly `null` name of the JAR entry associated with this `JarURLConnection`. `null` if the URL associated with this `JarURLConnection` names a JAR file instead of a JAR entry.

SEE ALSO `getJarEntry()`, `getJarFile()`, `getJarFileURL()`.

EXAMPLE See `getCertificates()`.

J

getJarEntry()

PURPOSE Retrieves the JAR entry associated with this `JarURLConnection`.

SYNTAX `public JarEntry getJarEntry() throws IOException`

RETURNS The possibly `null` `JAREntry` object for this connection. `null` if the URL associated with this `JarURLConnection` names a JAR file instead of a JAR entry.

EXCEPTIONS

`IOException`

If an IO error occurred while trying to access the JAR file.

SEE ALSO `getEntryName()`, `getJarFile()`, `getJarFileURL()`.

EXAMPLE See `getCertificates()`.

getJarFile()

PURPOSE Retrieves the JAR file associated with this `JarURLConnection`.

SYNTAX `public abstract JarFile getJarFile() throws IOException`

DESCRIPTION This method retrieves the JAR file associated with this `JarURLConnection`. The JAR URL that was used to create this `JarURLConnection` can name either an entire JAR file or an entry (either a file or a directory) within a JAR file. This method returns that JAR file. Methods that need the JAR file (such as `getMainAttributes()`) automatically call this method.

RETURNS The non-`null` `JarFile` instance for this `JarURLConnection`.

EXCEPTIONS

`IOException`

If an IO error occurred while trying to access the JAR file.

SEE ALSO `connect()`, `getAttributes()`, `getJarEntry()`, `getJarFileURL()`, `getMainAttributes()`, `getManifest()`.

EXAMPLE See `getCertificates()` and the class example.

getJarFileURL()

PURPOSE Retrieves the URL of the JAR file associated with this `JarURLConnection`.

SYNTAX `public URL getJarFileURL()`

DESCRIPTION This method retrieves the URL of the JAR file that is associated with this `JarURLConnection`. The URL is determined by parsing the JAR URL that was passed to the `JarURLConnection`'s constructor. See the class description for a description of the JAR URL syntax.

RETURNS A non-`null` `URL` instance representing the JAR URL of this `JarURLConnection`.

SEE ALSO `getJarFile()`.

EXAMPLE See `getCertificates()`.

getMainAttributes()

PURPOSE Retrieves the main attributes of the manifest for this `JarURLConnection`'s JAR file.

SYNTAX `public Attributes getMainAttributes() throws IOException`

DESCRIPTION This method retrieves the main attributes of the manifest for this `JarURLConnection`'s JAR file. A manifest is a set of attributes (name/value pairs) associated with a JAR file (see `java.util.jar.Manifest`). The attributes provide information about the JAR file and its entries, such as signatures and a digest of the contents for integrity protection. The *main* attributes of a manifest are those that are associated with the whole JAR file, as opposed to *entry* attributes, which are associated with JAR entries. The JAR URL that was used to create this `JarURLConnection` can name either an entire JAR file or an entry (either a file or a directory) within a JAR file.

RETURNS The possibly `null` main attributes of this `JarURLConnection`'s corresponding JAR file.

EXCEPTIONS

`IOException`
If an IO error was encountered while getting the JAR file (or its manifest) for this connection.

SEE ALSO `getAttributes()`, `getJarFile()`, `getManifest()`.

EXAMPLE See the class example.

getManifest()

PURPOSE Retrieves the manifest for this `JarURLConnection`.

SYNTAX `public Manifest getManifest() throws IOException`

DESCRIPTION This method retrieves the manifest for this `JarURLConnection`. A manifest is a set of attributes (name/value pairs) associated with a JAR file (see `java.util.jar.Manifest`). The attributes provide information about the JAR file and its entries, such as signatures and a digest of the contents for integrity protection. This method returns the manifest of the JAR file corresponding to this `JarURLConnection`. If the file has no manifest, `null` is returned.

RETURNS The possibly `null` `Manifest` instance of this `JarURLConnection`'s corresponding JAR file.

EXCEPTIONS

`IOException`

If an IO error was encountered while getting the JAR file for this connection.

SEE ALSO `getAttributes()`, `getJarFile()`, `getMainAttributes()`.

EXAMPLE See the class example.

jarFileURLConnection

PURPOSE The field containing the `URLConnection` for retrieving this `JarURLConnection`'s JAR file.

SYNTAX `protected URLConnection jarFileURLConnection`

DESCRIPTION This field contains the `URLConnection` for retrieving this `JarURLConnection`'s JAR file. The JAR URL of this `JarURLConnection` contains a JAR file URL. This is the URL returned by `getJarFileURL()`. `jarFileURLConnection` holds the `URLConnection` of the JAR file URL.

This field is typically set by the `connect()` method.

SEE ALSO `getJarFile()`, `getJarFileURL()`, `URLConnection.connect()`.

JarURLConnection()

PURPOSE Constructs a new `JarURLConnection` instance.

SYNTAX `protected JarURLConnection(URL url) throws MalformedURLException`

DESCRIPTION This constructor is used by subclasses to construct a new `JarURLConnection` instance. The syntax of `url` is that of a JAR URL (see the class description). If `url` does not conform to this syntax, a `MalformedURLException` is thrown.

PARAMETERS

`url` The non-`null` URL for which to open this `JarURLConnection`.

EXCEPTIONS

`MalformedURLException`

If `url` does not have conform to the JAR URL syntax.

LinkedList

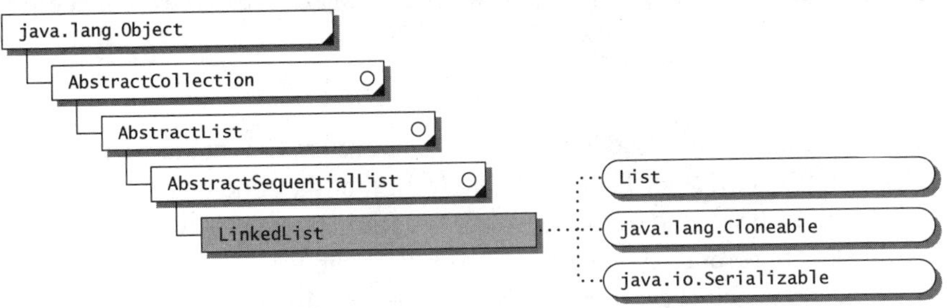

Syntax

```
public class LinkedList extends AbstractSequentialList implements List,
    Cloneable, Serializable
```

Description

`LinkedList` is a collection for storing objects in a particular order. Each element in the list has an index that is used to access the element. This list will store any arbitrary number of elements and supports all of the modification operations, so you can add, remove, and replace elements in the list.

`LinkedList` internally uses a doubly linked list to store its elements. This means that adding and removing an element involves updating two links, while accessing an element with an index involves traversing the linked list.

It maintains a reference to both the first and last elements in the list, so retrieving the last element of the list is efficient. For example, creating an iterator at the end of the list is the same as creating an iterator at the start of the list.

`LinkedList` is one of three implementations of the `List` interface. The others are `Vector` and `ArrayList`, which internally uses an array to store the elements. This means that accessing an element using an index involves a quick array access, while adding and removing an element from the list requires shifting elements around in the array. However, adding and removing elements at the end of the list is efficient.

Usage

You can create either a `LinkedList` or a list that is initialized from a collection, as follows.

```
LinkedList list;
list = new LinkedList();
list = new LinkedList(collection);
```

Once the list is created, you can use various modification methods, such as `add()` to add elements to the list or `remove()` to remove elements from the list.

Iterators

This list implements fail-fast iterators. The list should not be modified while the returned iterator is in use; otherwise, the iterator will throw a `ConcurrentModificationException`. See `Iterator` for more details.

Synchronization

This list allows more than one thread to read from it. However, if a thread wants to modify the list, there should not be any other thread reading from it at the time of modification. If reads and modifications must be able to occur concurrently, you can create a synchronized version of the list by calling `Collections.synchronizedList()` on the list. This creates a version of the list in which all of the methods are synchronized. Note that although each method is synchronized, you might still need to synchronize a sequence of method calls. See the `Collections` class description for more details.

MEMBER SUMMARY	
Constructor	
`LinkedList()`	Constructs a new `LinkedList` instance.
Element Retrieval Methods	
`getFirst()`	Retrieves the first element of this list.
`getLast()`	Retrieves the last element of this list.
Query Methods	
`contains()`	Determines if this list contains a particular element.
`indexOf()`	Determines the index of the first occurrence of an element in this list.
`lastIndexOf()`	Determines the index of the last occurrence of an element in this list.
`size()`	Returns the number of elements in this list.
Modification Methods	
`add()`	Inserts an element into this list.
`addAll()`	Inserts all of the elements of a collection into this list.
`addFirst()`	Inserts an element at the beginning of this list.
`addLast()`	Appends an element to the end of this list.
`clear()`	Removes all of the elements in this list.
`remove()`	Removes an element from this list.
`removeFirst()`	Removes the first element from this list.
`removeLast()`	Removes the last element from this list.
`set()`	Replaces an element with another.
Iterator Method	
`listIterator()`	Creates a list iterator for all of the elements in this list.

L

MEMBER SUMMARY	
Conversion Method	
`toArray()`	Returns an array containing all of the elements in this collection.
Object Method	
`clone()`	Creates a copy of this list.

See Also

`ArrayList`, `Collections`, `Iterator`, `ListIterator`.

Example

This example implements a synchronized queue. A producer thread adds integers to the queue at random times, while two consumer threads remove the elements from the head of the queue.

```
import java.util.*;

class Main {
    public static void main(String[] args) {
        LinkedList list = new LinkedList();

        // Create and start up the producer and consumer threads.
        new Producer(list).start();
        new Consumer(list).start();
        new Consumer(list).start();
    }
}

class Consumer extends Thread {
    LinkedList list;
    Consumer(LinkedList l) {
        list = l;
    }

    public void run() {
        try {
            while (true) {
                synchronized (list) {
                    // Wait until not empty.
                    while (list.isEmpty()) {
                        list.wait();
                    }

                    // Remove and print the head of the queue.
                    System.out.println( this+": "+list.removeFirst() );
                }
            }
        } catch (Exception e) {
            e.printStackTrace();
        }
    }
}
```

```
class Producer extends Thread {
    Random rnd = new Random();

    LinkedList list;
    Producer(LinkedList l) {
        list = l;
    }

    public void run() {
        int count = 0;
        try {
            while (true) {
                Thread.sleep(rnd.nextInt(2000));

                // Add an element to the end of the queue.
                synchronized (list) {
                    list.addLast(new Integer(count++));
                    list.notify();
                }
            }
        } catch (Exception e) {
            e.printStackTrace();
        }
    }
}
```

L

add()

PURPOSE Inserts an element into this list.

SYNTAX

```
public boolean add(Object e)
public void add(int ix, Object e)
```

DESCRIPTION This method inserts an element `e` at index `ix`. If `ix` is not specified, it defaults to `size()`. Adding to the end of the list is as efficient as adding to the head of the list.

PARAMETERS

`ix` The index at which `e` is to be inserted. `0` ≤ `ix` ≤ `size()`.

`e` The possibly `null` element to add to this list.

RETURNS The overloaded method that returns a `boolean` always returns `true`.

EXCEPTIONS

`IndexOutOfBoundsException`
If `ix` < `0` or `ix` > `size()`.

EXAMPLE See `List.add()`.

addAll()

PURPOSE Inserts all of the elements of a collection into this list.

SYNTAX
```
public boolean addAll(Collection c)
public boolean addAll(int ix, Collection c)
```

DESCRIPTION This method inserts all of the elements from the collection `c` into this list at index `ix`. The elements are inserted in the same order as they would appear from an iterator on `c`. If `ix` is not specified, it defaults to `size()`. Adding to the end of the list is as efficient as adding to the head of the list.

PARAMETERS

`c` The non-`null` collection of elements to be inserted into this list.

`ix` The index at which the elements in `c` are to be inserted. `0` ≤ `ix` ≤ `size()`.

RETURNS `true` if this list was modified.

EXCEPTIONS

`ConcurrentModificationException`

If `c`'s iterators are fail-fast and `c` is being modified during this method call.

`IndexOutOfBoundsException`

If `ix` < `0` or `ix` > `size()`.

EXAMPLE See `List.addAll()`.

addFirst()

PURPOSE Inserts an element at the beginning of this list.

SYNTAX
```
public void addFirst(Object e)
```

DESCRIPTION This method inserts the element `e` at the beginning of this list.

PARAMETERS

`e` The possibly `null` element to insert into this list.

EXAMPLE
```
LinkedList list = new LinkedList(Arrays.asList(new Object[]{null}));

list.addFirst("dog");
System.out.println( list );       // [dog, null]
list.addLast("cat");
System.out.println( list );       // [dog, null, cat]
```

L

addLast()

PURPOSE Appends an element to the end of this list.

SYNTAX `public void addLast(Object e)`

DESCRIPTION This method appends the element `e` to the end of this list. It is identical to the `add(Object)` method; it is included here for consistency.

PARAMETERS

`e` The possibly `null` element to append to this list.

EXAMPLE See `addFirst()`.

clear()

PURPOSE Removes all of the elements in this list.

SYNTAX `void clear()`

DESCRIPTION This method removes all of the elements in this list. After it is called, the list will be empty.

EXAMPLE See `List.clear()`.

clone()

PURPOSE Creates a copy of this list.

SYNTAX `public Object clone()`

DESCRIPTION This method makes a shallow copy of this list. Only the list itself is cloned, not the elements. This list and the new list share references to the same elements.

RETURNS A new non-`null` list that contains the same elements.

OVERRIDES `java.lang.Object.clone();`

EXAMPLE

```
StringBuffer buf = new StringBuffer("dog");
LinkedList list = new LinkedList(Arrays.asList(new Object[]{buf, "cat"}));

System.out.println( list );        // [dog, cat]

LinkedList list2 = (LinkedList)list.clone();
System.out.println( list2 );       // [dog, cat]

// This shows that the cloned list shares the same elements
// as the original list.
buf.append("fish");
System.out.println( list2 );       // [dogfish, cat]
```

contains()

PURPOSE Determines if this list contains a particular element.

SYNTAX `public boolean contains(Object e)`

DESCRIPTION This method determines if this list contains the element `e`. It returns `true` if some element in this collection is equal to the element `e`. For all non-`null` elements, the `equals()` method is used to determine if two elements are equal.

PARAMETERS

`e` A possibly `null` element.

RETURNS `true` if some element in this list is equal to `e`.

SEE ALSO `containsAll()`, `java.lang.Object.equals()`.

EXAMPLE See `List.contains()`.

getFirst()

PURPOSE Retrieves the first element of this list.

SYNTAX `public Object getFirst()`

DESCRIPTION This method retrieves the first element of this list.

RETURNS The possibly `null` first element of this list.

EXCEPTIONS

`NoSuchElementException`
If the list is empty.

EXAMPLE

```
LinkedList list = new LinkedList(Arrays.asList(new Object[]{"dog", null,
"cat"}));

System.out.println( list.getFirst() );       // dog
System.out.println( list.getLast() );        // cat
```

getLast()

PURPOSE Retrieves the last element of this list.

SYNTAX `public Object getLast()`

DESCRIPTION This method retrieves the last element of this list.

RETURNS The possibly `null` last element of this list.

EXCEPTIONS

`NoSuchElementException`
If the list is empty.

EXAMPLE See `getFirst()`.

indexOf()

PURPOSE Determines the index of the first occurrence of an element in this list.

SYNTAX `public int indexOf(Object e)`

DESCRIPTION This method searches this list, from the beginning, for any element that equals the element `e` (determined by using `equals()`). If one is found, its index is returned; otherwise, `-1` is returned.

PARAMETERS

`e` The possibly `null` element for which to search.

RETURNS The index of the first occurrence of `e` in this list or `-1` if `e` is not in this list.

SEE ALSO `java.lang.Object.equals()`.

EXAMPLE See `List.indexOf()`.

L

lastIndexOf()

PURPOSE Determines the index of the last occurrence of an element in this list.

SYNTAX `public int lastIndexOf(Object e)`

DESCRIPTION This method searches this list backwards, starting from the end, for any element that equals the element `e` (determined by using `equals()`). If one is found, its index is returned; otherwise, `-1` is returned.

PARAMETERS

`e` The possibly `null` element for which to search.

RETURNS The index of the last occurrence of `e` in this list or `-1` if `e` is not in this list.

SEE ALSO `java.lang.Object.equals()`.

EXAMPLE See `List.lastIndexOf()`.

LinkedList()

PURPOSE
Constructs a new `LinkedList` instance.

SYNTAX
```
public LinkedList()
public LinkedList(Collection c)
```

DESCRIPTION
This constructor constructs a new instance of `LinkedList`. The new instance is initialized to contain all of the elements in the collection `c`. The order of the elements in the new list is the same as the order of elements presented by an iterator on `c`. The references to the elements from `c` are copied into the new list, so subsequent modifications to `c` will not affect this list.

If `c` is not specified, the new list is empty.

PARAMETERS

`c` The non-`null` collection of elements to be added to this list.

EXCEPTIONS

`ConcurrentModificationException`
If `c`'s iterators are fail-fast and `c` is being modified during this method call.

EXAMPLE
See the class example.

L

listIterator()

PURPOSE
Creates a list iterator for all of the elements in this list.

SYNTAX
```
ListIterator listIterator(int ix)
```

DESCRIPTION
This method creates and returns a list iterator (see `ListIterator` for more details) for all elements in this list. The cursor of the list iterator is initialized to `ix`. This means that the first element returned by the list iterator is the element at `ix`. The elements preceding `ix` are also available to the list iterator. If `ix` is not specified, it defaults to `0`.

Creating the iterator at the end of the list is as efficient as creating it at the beginning of the list.

The order of the elements returned by the list iterator is exactly the same order that the elements appear in the list.

The returned list iterator is fail-fast (see `ListIterator` for more details).

PARAMETERS

`ix` The initial value of the list iterator's cursor. `0` ≤ `ix` ≤ `size()`.

RETURNS
A non-`null` list iterator for this list.

EXCEPTIONS

`IndexOutOfBoundsException`
If `ix` < `0` or `ix` > `size()`.

SEE ALSO `Iterator()`.

EXAMPLE See `List.listIterator()`.

remove()

PURPOSE Removes an element from this list.

SYNTAX

```
public Object remove(int ix)
public boolean remove(Object e)
```

DESCRIPTION `remove(int)` removes the element at index `ix` from this list. Removing the element at the end of the list is as efficient as removing the element at the head of the list.

`remove(Object)` removes the first occurrence of element `e` from this list. If `e` is non-`null`, `e.equals()` is used to find a match. `remove(Object)` returns `true` if an occurrence of `e` was found and removed.

L

PARAMETERS

`e` The possibly `null` element to remove from this list.
`ix` The index of the element to remove. `0` ≤ `ix` < `size()`.

RETURNS `remove(int)` returns the possibly `null` element that was removed; `remove(Object)` returns `true` if `e` was removed from this list and `false` otherwise.

EXCEPTIONS

`IndexOutOfBoundsException`
If `ix` < `0` or `ix` ≥ `size()`.

SEE ALSO `removeAll()`, `retainAll()`.

EXAMPLE See `List.remove()`.

removeFirst()

PURPOSE Removes the first element from this list.

SYNTAX

```
public Object removeFirst()
```

DESCRIPTION This method removes and returns the first element of this list.

RETURNS The possibly `null` element removed from this list.

EXCEPTIONS

`NoSuchElementException`
If the list is empty.

EXAMPLE

```
LinkedList list =
    new LinkedList(Arrays.asList(new Object[]{"dog", null, "cat"}));

System.out.println( list.removeFirst() );    // dog
System.out.println( list );                  // [null, cat]
System.out.println( list.removeLast() );     // cat
System.out.println( list );                  // [null]
```

removeLast()

PURPOSE Removes the last element from this list.

SYNTAX `public Object removeLast()`

DESCRIPTION This method removes and returns the last element of this list.

RETURNS The possibly `null` element removed from this list.

EXCEPTIONS

`NoSuchElementException`
If the list is empty.

EXAMPLE See `removeFirst()`.

set()

PURPOSE Replaces an element with another element.

SYNTAX `public Object set(int ix, Object e)`

DESCRIPTION This method replaces the element at `ix` with the element `e` and returns the element previously at `ix`. Replacing the element at the end of the list is as efficient as replacing the element at the head of the list.

PARAMETERS

`e` The possibly `null` element to be stored at `ix`.
`ix` The index of the element to replace. `0` ≤ `ix` < `size()`.

RETURNS The possibly `null` element that was replaced.

EXCEPTIONS

`IndexOutOfBoundsException`
If `ix` < `0` or `ix` ≥ `size()`.

EXAMPLE See `List.set()`.

size()

PURPOSE Returns the number of elements in this list.

SYNTAX `public int size()`

RETURNS The non-negative number of elements in this list.

SEE ALSO `isEmpty()`.

EXAMPLE See `List.size()`.

toArray()

PURPOSE Returns an array containing all of the elements in this collection.

SYNTAX
```
Object[] toArray()
Object[] toArray(Object arr[])
```

DESCRIPTION This method fills `arr` with all of the elements in this list and returns `arr`. If `arr` is not large enough, a new array is created, filled, and then returned. The new array is just large enough to hold all of the elements in this list, and its type is identical to the type of `arr`.

If `arr` is larger than all of the elements in this list, `arr[size()]` is set to `null`. This `null` value can be used to determine the number of returned elements but only if it is known that the list does not contain any `null` elements.

The order of the elements in the returned array matches the order of the elements in the list.

If `arr` is not specified, it defaults to `new Object[0]`.

PARAMETERS

`arr` The non-`null` array into which the elements of this list will be copied.

RETURNS The non-`null` array `arr` or a new array whose length equals `size()`.

EXCEPTIONS

`ArrayStoreException`

If some element in this list cannot be assigned to an element in `arr`.

EXAMPLE See `List.toArray()`.

List

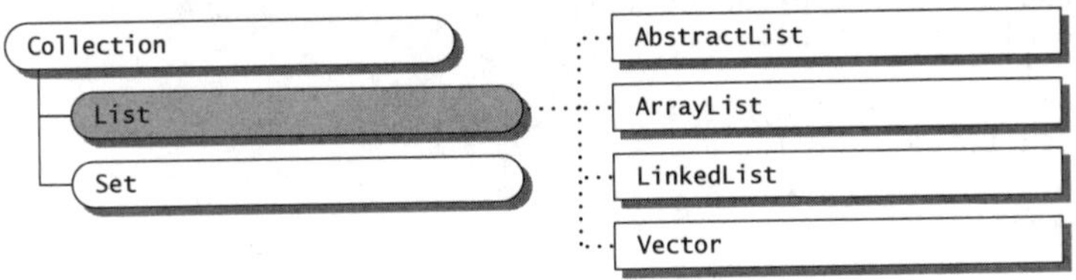

Syntax

```
public interface List extends Collection
```

Description

A `List` is a type of collection in which the elements can be accessed by means of an index. As with an array, the indices are `0`-based, that is, the first element in the list has the index `0`. A list also provides methods for inserting and removing elements at a particular index.

Unlike sets, lists generally accept duplicate elements.

Lists provide a special iterator, called a *list iterator*, that allows you to move both forward and backward through the list of elements. You can also use the list iterator to insert elements into a list and remove elements from a list.

Three types of collections are available: set, list, and map. See `Collection` for an overview of *The Collections Framework*, which includes set, list, and map.

Usage

The `java.util` package provides three implementation of lists: `ArrayList`, `LinkedList`, and `Vector`. They differ in how they store their elements, so one might be more efficient than another for your application. See the `ArrayList`, `LinkedList`, and `Vector` classes for more details.

There are several ways to create a list. Here are some of them.

```
List l;
l = new ArrayList();
l = new LinkedList();
l = Collections.EMPTY_LIST;
l = Collections.nCopies(10, "dog");
l = Arrays.asList(new String[]{"dog", "cat"});
```

Once a list is created, you can use the methods in this interface to query or modify the list. Be aware that some of these methods might result in a `UnsupportedOperationException` if the list does not support the method call. For example, `Arrays.asList()` returns a list whose elements can be replaced, but it does not allow you to add or remove elements.

The Collections Framework does not provide a nondestructive way to append lists. You might find it useful to define a method such as the following.

```
public static List append(List l1, List l2) {
    List result;
    if (l1 instanceof AbstractSequentialList) {
        result = new LinkedList(l1);
        result.addAll(l2);
    } else {
        result = new ArrayList(l1);
        result.addAll(l2);
    }
    return result;
}
```

The `Collections` class provides various utilities for manipulating lists, including sorting, reversing, and copying. It also provides various utility methods for changing the capabilities of a list by creating a wrapper around the list. For example, you can prevent any modifications to a list by using `Collections.unmodifiableList()`. Also, you can have all of the methods of the list be wrapped with synchronized methods by using `Collections.synchronizedList()`. See `Collections` for more details.

To implement a class that implements the `List` interface, you should consider subclassing either `AbstractList` or `AbstractSequentialList`. These two abstract classes minimize the effort needed to implement a `List` class.

L

Unsupported Methods

Not all lists can be modified. There are basically three ways by which you can modify a list: add an element to it, remove an element from it, and replace an element. A list can support any or none of these operations. If you attempt to use a method to modify a list that does not support the operation, the method will throw an `UnsupportedOperationException`.

MEMBER SUMMARY	
Element Retrieval Method	
`get()`	Retrieves the element at a particular index in this list.
Query Methods	
`contains()`	Determines if this list contains a particular element.
`containsAll()`	Determines if this list contains all of the elements in another collection.
`indexOf()`	Determines the index of the first occurrence of an element in this list.
`isEmpty()`	Determines if this list has no elements.
`size()`	Returns the number of elements in this list.
`lastIndexOf()`	Determines the index of the last occurrence of an element in this list.
Sublist Method	
`subList()`	Creates a list from a range of elements in this list.

MEMBER SUMMARY	
Conversion Method	
toArray()	Returns all of the elements in this list in an array.
Iterator Methods	
iterator()	Creates an iterator for the elements in this list.
listIterator()	Creates a list iterator for all of the elements in this list.
Modification Methods	
add()	Adds an element to this list.
addAll()	Inserts all of the elements of a collection into this list.
clear()	Removes all of the elements in this list.
remove()	Removes an element from this list.
removeAll()	Removes all elements from this list that are in another collection.
retainAll()	Removes all elements in this list that are not in another collection.
set()	Replaces the element at an index with another element.
Object Methods	
equals()	Determines if this list is equal to another object.
hashCode()	Computes the hash code for this list.

L

See Also

`AbstractList`, `AbstractSequentialList`, `ArrayList`, `Collection`, `LinkedList`, `Map`, `Set`, `Vector`.

Example

For an example that implements a `List`, see `AbstractList` and `AbstractSequentialList`. The examples in the following member descriptions demonstrate how a `List` is used.

add()

PURPOSE Adds an element to this list.

SYNTAX
```
public boolean add(Object e)
public void add(int ix, Object e)
```

DESCRIPTION This method adds the element `e` to this list. If the index at which `e` is to be inserted is not provided, this method adds `e` to the end of the list.

This method might not be supported.

PARAMETERS

`e`	The possibly `null` element to be added to this list.
`ix`	The index at which `e` is to be inserted. `0` ≤ `ix` ≤ `size()`.

RETURNS `true` if this list was modified.

EXCEPTIONS

`ClassCastException`
If the type of `e` is inappropriate for this list.

`IllegalArgumentException`
If some aspect of `e` prevents it from being added to this list.

`IndexOutOfBoundsException`
If `ix` < `0` or `ix` > `size()`.

`NullPointerException`
If `e` is `null` and this list does not accept `null` elements.

`UnsupportedOperationException`
If this method is not supported by this list.

SEE ALSO `addAll()`, `java.lang.Object.equals()`.

EXAMPLE

```
List list = Collections.EMPTY_LIST;

// This list is read-only.
//list.add("dog");                    // UnsupportedOperationException

// Create a modifiable list.
list = new ArrayList();
list.add(null);
list.add("dog");
list.add(0, "dog");
System.out.println( list );           // [dog, null, dog]

list.add(100, "cat");                 // IndexOutOfBoundsException
```

addAll()

PURPOSE Inserts all of the elements of a collection into this list.

SYNTAX

```
public boolean addAll(Collection c)
public boolean addAll(int ix, Collection c)
```

DESCRIPTION This method inserts all of the elements from the collection `c` into this list at index `ix`. The elements are inserted in the same order as they would appear from an iterator on `c`. If `ix` is not specified, it defaults to `size()`.

This method might not be supported.

PARAMETERS

`c`	The non-`null` collection of elements to be inserted into this list.
`ix`	The index at which the elements in `c` are to be inserted. `0` ≤ `ix` ≤ `size()`.

RETURNS `true` if this list was modified.

EXCEPTIONS

`ClassCastException`
If the type of c is inappropriate for this list.

`ConcurrentModificationException`
If c's iterators are fail-fast and c is being modified during this method call.

`IllegalArgumentException`
If some aspect of an element in c prevents it from being added to this list.

`IndexOutOfBoundsException`
If `ix` < `0` or `ix` > `size()`.

`NullPointerException`
If some element in c is `null` and this list does not accept `null` elements.

`UnsupportedOperationException`
If this method is not supported by this list.

SEE ALSO `add()`.

EXAMPLE

```
Collection c = Arrays.asList(new String[]{"dog", "cat"});

// The size of the collection cannot change.
//c.add("dog");                   // UnsupportedOperationException

List list = new ArrayList();
list.addAll(c);
list.addAll(1, c);
System.out.println( list );       // [dog, dog, cat, cat]

list.addAll(0, list);             // ConcurrentModificationException
```

clear()

PURPOSE Removes all of the elements in this list.

SYNTAX `public void clear()`

DESCRIPTION This method removes all of the elements in this list. After it is called, this list will be empty.

This method might not be supported.

EXCEPTIONS

`UnsupportedOperationException`
If this method is not supported by this list.

EXAMPLE

```
List list = new LinkedList();
list.add("dog");
System.out.println( list.size() );    // 1
```

L

```
list.clear();
System.out.println( list.isEmpty() ); // true
```

contains()

PURPOSE Determines if this list contains a particular element.

SYNTAX `public boolean contains(Object e)`

DESCRIPTION This method determines if this list contains the element `e`. It returns `true` if some element in this list is equal to `e`. An element is equal to `e` if both are `null` or if the `equals()` method determines that they are equal.

PARAMETERS

`e` A possibly `null` element.

RETURNS `true` if some element in this list is equal to `e`.

SEE ALSO `containsAll()`, `equals()`.

EXAMPLE

```
List list = Arrays.asList(
    new Object[]{"dog", null, new Integer(7)});

System.out.println( list.contains("dog") );        // true
System.out.println( list.contains(null) );         // true
System.out.println( list.contains("pig") );        // false

// This shows that although the two Integer objects are different,
// they are considered the same according to their equals() method.
System.out.println( list.contains(new Integer(7)) );// true
```

containsAll()

PURPOSE Determines if this list contains all of the elements in another collection.

SYNTAX `public boolean containsAll(Collection c)`

DESCRIPTION This method determines if this list contains all of the elements in the collection `c`. If all of the elements in the collection `c` appear in this list, this method returns `true`. Two elements are equal if both are `null` or if the `equals()` method determines that they are equal.

PARAMETERS

`c` A non-`null` collection.

RETURNS `true` if all elements in `c` appear in this list.

EXCEPTIONS

`ConcurrentModificationException`
If `c`'s iterators are fail-fast and `c` is being modified during this method call.

SEE ALSO contains(), equals().

EXAMPLE

```
List list = Arrays.asList(new String[]{"dog", "cat"});

System.out.println( list.containsAll(Collections.EMPTY_LIST) );
    // true
System.out.println( list.containsAll(Collections.singleton(null)) );
    // false
System.out.println( list.containsAll(Collections.singleton("dog")) );
    // true
System.out.println( list.containsAll(
            Arrays.asList(new String[]{"dog", "dog", "cat"})));
    //true
```

equals()

PURPOSE Determines if this list is equal to another object.

SYNTAX `public boolean equals(Object c)`

DESCRIPTION This method determines if this list is equal to the object `c`. It returns `true` if, and only if, `c` is a `List` object and the elements in `c` and this list match in number and in order. Two elements are equal if both are `null` or if the `equals()` method determines that they are equal.

PARAMETERS

`c` The possibly `null` object to be compared with this list.

RETURNS `true` if `c` is equal to this list.

OVERRIDES `java.lang.Object.equals()`.

SEE ALSO `hashCode()`.

EXAMPLE

```
List l1 = Arrays.asList(new String[]{"dog", null, "cat"});
List l2 = new ArrayList(Arrays.asList(new String[]{"dog", "cat"}));

System.out.println( l1.equals(null) );          // false
System.out.println( l1.equals(l2) );            // false

l2.add(1, null);
System.out.println( l1.equals(l2) );            // true

// lists and sets are not equal, even if they have the same contents.
System.out.println( Collections.EMPTY_LIST.equals(Collections.EMPTY_SET) );
                                                // false
```

get()

PURPOSE Retrieves the element at a particular index in this list.

SYNTAX `public Object get(int ix)`

DESCRIPTION This method retrieves the element located at index `ix`.

PARAMETERS

`ix` The index of the element to return. `0` ≤ `ix` < `size()`.

RETURNS The possibly `null` element at index `ix`. `null` if element is `null`.

EXCEPTIONS

`IndexOutOfBoundsException`
If `ix` < `0` or `ix` ≥ `size()`.

EXAMPLE

```
List list = new ArrayList();

for (int i=0; i<100; i++) {
    list.add("item " + i);
}
System.out.println( list.get(50) ); // item 50
list.get(101);                      // IndexOutOfBoundsException
```


hashCode()

PURPOSE Computes the hash code for this list.

SYNTAX `public int hashCode()`

DESCRIPTION This method computes the hash code for this list. This list's hash code is an integer value that is based on the hash codes of all of its elements. Two equal lists will have the same hash code. Unequal lists might also have the same hash code, although the hash code algorithm reduces this possibility. The hash code is typically used as the key in a hash table.

The following algorithm must be used to compute the hash code for a list.

```
int hashCode = 1;
for (Iterator it=list.iterator(); it.hasNext(); ) {
    Object e = it.next();
    hashCode = 31*hashCode + (e==null ? 0 : e.hashCode());
}
return hashCode;
```

RETURNS This list's hash code.

OVERRIDES `java.lang.Object.hashCode()`.

SEE ALSO `equals()`, `java.lang.Object.equals()`.

EXAMPLE See `java.lang.Object.hashCode()`.

indexOf()

PURPOSE Determines the index of the first occurrence of an element in this list.

SYNTAX `public int indexOf(Object e)`

DESCRIPTION This method searches this list, from the beginning, for any element that equals the element `e` (determined by using `equals()`). If one is found, its index is returned; otherwise, `-1` is returned.

PARAMETERS

`e` The possibly `null` element for which to search.

RETURNS The index of the first occurrence of `e` in this list or `-1` if `e` is not in this list.

SEE ALSO `java.lang.Object.equals()`.

EXAMPLE

```
List list = Arrays.asList(new String[]{"dog", "cat", "dog"});

System.out.println( list.indexOf("pig") );       // -1
System.out.println( list.indexOf("dog") );       // 0
System.out.println( list.indexOf(null) );        // -1
```


isEmpty()

PURPOSE Determines if this list has no elements.

SYNTAX `public boolean isEmpty()`

RETURNS `true` if this list contains no elements.

SEE ALSO `size()`.

EXAMPLE See `clear()`.

iterator()

PURPOSE Creates an iterator for the elements in this list.

SYNTAX `public Iterator iterator()`

DESCRIPTION This method creates and returns an iterator (see `Iterator` for more details) for all elements in this list in proper sequence.

In most cases, the list should not be modified while the returned iterator is in use. However, there might be some lists that allow this; check the list's documentation.

RETURNS A non-`null` iterator.

SEE ALSO `Iterator`.

EXAMPLE

```
List list = new LinkedList(Arrays.asList(new String[]{"dog", null, "cat"}));

for (Iterator it=list.iterator(); it.hasNext(); ) {
    Object e = it.next();
    System.out.print(e + " ");       // dog null cat

    // Remove null elements.
    if (e == null) {
        it.remove();
    }
}
System.out.println( list );          // [dog, cat]

// Attempt to modify the list while an iterator is being used.
Iterator  it = list.iterator();
list.add("pig");
//it.next();                         // ConcurrentModificationException

// Create a list whose size cannot be changed.
it = Arrays.asList(new String[]{"dog"}).iterator();
System.out.println( it.next() );     // dog
it.remove();                         // UnsupportedOperationException
```


lastIndexOf()

PURPOSE Determines the index of the last occurrence of an element in this list.

SYNTAX `public int lastIndexOf(Object e)`

DESCRIPTION This method searches this list backward, starting from the end, for any element that equals the element `e`. If one is found, its index is returned; otherwise, `-1` is returned. An element is equal to `e` if both are `null` or if the `equals()` method determines that they are equal.

PARAMETERS

`e` The possibly `null` element for which to search.

RETURNS The index of the last occurrence of `e` in this list or `-1` if `e` is not in this list.

SEE ALSO `java.lang.Object.equals()`.

EXAMPLE

```
List list = Arrays.asList(new String[]{"dog", "cat", "dog"});

System.out.println( list.indexOf("pig") );        // -1
System.out.println( list.lastIndexOf("dog") );    // 2
System.out.println( list.indexOf(null) );         // -1
```

listIterator()

PURPOSE
Creates a list iterator for all of the elements in this list.

SYNTAX
```
public ListIterator listIterator()
public ListIterator listIterator(int ix)
```

DESCRIPTION
This method creates and returns a list iterator (see `ListIterator` for more details) for all of the elements in this list. The cursor of the list iterator is initialized to `ix`. This means that the first element returned by the list iterator is the element at `ix`. The elements preceding `ix` are also available to the list iterator. If `ix` is not specified, it defaults to `0`.

The order of the elements returned by the list iterator is exactly the same order that the elements appear in the list.

PARAMETERS

`ix` The initial value of the list iterator's cursor. `0` ≤ `ix` ≤ `size()`.

RETURNS
A non-`null` list iterator for this list.

EXCEPTIONS

`IndexOutOfBoundsException`
If `ix` < `0` or `ix` > `size()`.

SEE ALSO
`iterator()`.

EXAMPLE
```
List list = new LinkedList(Arrays.asList(new String[]{"dog", null, "cat"}));

// Traverse the list forwards, removing all null elements
// and replacing "cat" with "cow".
for (ListIterator it=list.listIterator(); it.hasNext(); ) {
    Object e = it.next();
    System.out.print(e + " ");      // dog null cat

    if (e == null) {
        // Remove null elements.
        it.remove();
    } else if (e.equals("cat")) {
        // Replace cat with cow.
        it.set("cow");
    }
}
System.out.println( list );          // [dog, cow]

// Traverse the list backwards.
list = new LinkedList(Arrays.asList(new String[]{"dog", null, "cat"}));
for (ListIterator it=list.listIterator(list.size()); it.hasPrevious(); ) {
    Object e = it.previous();
    System.out.print(e + " ");      // cat null dog
}
```

remove()

PURPOSE Removes an element from this list.

SYNTAX
```
public Object remove(int ix)
public boolean remove(Object e)
```

DESCRIPTION `remove(int)` removes the element at index `ix` from this list and returns the element that was removed.

`remove(Object)` searches for the first occurrence of `e` in this list and removes it. It returns `true` if it found a matching element (it uses `equals()` to determine equality).

This method might not be supported.

PARAMETERS

- `e` The possibly `null` element to remove.
- `ix` The index of the element to remove. $0 \le ix < size()$.

RETURNS `remove(int)` returns the possibly `null` element that was removed; `remove(Object)` returns `true` if `e` was removed.

EXCEPTIONS

`IndexOutOfBoundsException`
If $ix < 0$ or $ix \ge size()$.

`UnsupportedOperationException`
If this method is not supported by this list.

SEE ALSO `removeAll()`, `retainAll()`.

EXAMPLE

```
List list = Arrays.asList(new String[]{"dog", null, "cat", "dog"});

// The size of the list cannot be changed.
//System.out.println( list.remove(0) );    // UnsupportedOperationException

// Make it modifiable list.
list = new ArrayList(list);
System.out.println( list.remove("pig") );    // false
System.out.println( list.remove("dog") );    // true
System.out.println( list );                 // [null, cat, dog]
System.out.println( list.remove(1) );       // cat
System.out.println( list );                 // [null, dog]
list.remove(100);                           // IndexOutOfBoundsException
```

removeAll()

PURPOSE Removes all elements from this list that are in another collection.

SYNTAX `public boolean removeAll(Collection c)`

DESCRIPTION This method removes all elements in this list that are in the collection `c`. Two elements are equal if both are `null` or if the `equals()` method determines that they are equal. After this call returns, this list will contain no elements in common with `c`. This operation can be thought of as a subtraction operation in which `c` is subtracted from this list.

This method might not be supported.

PARAMETERS

`c` A non-`null` collection of elements to be removed from this list.

RETURNS `true` if this list was modified.

EXCEPTIONS

`ConcurrentModificationException`
If `c`'s iterators are fail-fast and `c` is being modified during this method call.

`UnsupportedOperationException`
If this method is not supported by this list.

SEE ALSO `equals()`, `remove()`, `retainAll()`.

EXAMPLE

```
List list = new ArrayList(
    Arrays.asList(new String[]{"dog", "cat", "dog"}));

System.out.println( list.removeAll(Collections.EMPTY_LIST) );
                                        // false
System.out.println( list );             // [dog, cat, dog]

System.out.println( list.removeAll(Collections.singleton("dog")));
                                        // true
System.out.println( list );             // [cat]
```

retainAll()

PURPOSE Removes all elements in this list that are not in another collection.

SYNTAX `public boolean retainAll(Collection c)`

DESCRIPTION This method removes all elements in this list that are not present in the collection `c`. The `equals()` method is used to determine whether two elements are equal. This operation can be thought of, loosely, as an intersection operation.

This method might not be supported.

L

PARAMETERS

c A non-null collection of elements to retain.

RETURNS true if this list was modified.

EXCEPTIONS

ConcurrentModificationException
If c's iterators are fail-fast and c is being modified during this method call.

UnsupportedOperationException
If this method is not supported by this list.

SEE ALSO equals(), remove(), removeAll().

EXAMPLE

```
List list = Arrays.asList(new String[]{"dog", "cat", "dog"});

// The size of this list cannot be changed.
//list.retainAll(Collections.EMPTY_LIST); // UnsupportedOperationException

// Make the size of the list modifiable.
list = new LinkedList(list);
System.out.println( list.retainAll(Collections.singleton("dog")));
                                          // true
System.out.println( list );               // [dog, dog]
```


set()

PURPOSE Replaces the element at an index with another element.

SYNTAX `public Object set(int ix, Object e)`

DESCRIPTION This method replaces the element at ix with the element e and returns the element previously at ix.

This method might not be supported.

PARAMETERS

e The possibly null element to be stored at ix.

ix The index of the element to replace. $0 \le ix < size()$.

RETURNS The possibly null element that was replaced.

EXCEPTIONS

ClassCastException
If the type of e is inappropriate for this list.

IllegalArgumentException
If some aspect of e prevents it from being added to this list.

IndexOutOfBoundsException
If $ix < 0$ or $ix \ge size()$.

UnsupportedOperationException
If this method is not supported by this list.

EXAMPLE

```
List list = Arrays.asList(new String[]{"dog", null});

System.out.println( list.set(0, null) );     // dog
System.out.println( list.set(1, "dog") );    // null
System.out.println( list );                  // [null, dog]

//list.set(100, null);                       // IndexOutOfBoundsException

// Make it unmodifiable
list = Collections.unmodifiableList(list);
list.set(0, "dog");                          // UnsupportedOperationException.
```

size()

PURPOSE Returns the number of elements in this list.

SYNTAX `public int size()`

RETURNS The non-negative number of elements in this list.

SEE ALSO `isEmpty()`.

EXAMPLE

```
List list = Arrays.asList(new String[]{"dog", null, "cat", "dog"});
System.out.println( list.size() );    // 4
```

L

subList()

PURPOSE Creates a list from a range of elements in this list.

SYNTAX `public List subList(int fromIx, int toIx)`

DESCRIPTION This method creates and returns a sublist containing all elements between `fromIx` and `toIx`. The element at `fromIx` is included. The element at `toIx` is not included. The order of these elements in the sublist exactly matches the order of the elements as they appear in this list. The size of the new sublist is `toIx-fromIx`. The index of the first element in the sublist is `0`. The sublist cannot access any element in this list that is outside the range of `fromIx` and `toIx`.

A sublist does not have its own storage. Rather, it shares the storage with this list. If you modify the sublist, the modifications also appear in this list. If an element is added to or removed from this list directly, or indirectly through some other sublist, the sublist might no longer be valid and should be discarded.

Some implementations of `subList()` will watch for modifications of the underlying list. In this case, if a method of the sublist detects a modification, it throws a `ConcurrentModificationException`.

PARAMETERS

`fromIx` The index of the first element to be included in the sublist. `0` ≤ `fromIx` ≤ `size()`.

`toIx` The element at `toIx-1` is the last element to be included in the sublist. `fromIx` ≤ `toIx` ≤ `size()`.

RETURNS A non-`null` list containing the elements from this list in the range `fromIx` to `toIx-1`.

EXCEPTIONS

`IndexOutOfBoundsException`
If `fromIx` < `0`, or `toIx` < `fromIx`, or `toIx` > `size()`.

EXAMPLE

```
List list = new LinkedList(Arrays.asList(new String[]{"dog", "cat", "pig"}));
List slist = list.subList(1, 2);
System.out.println( slist );              // [cat]
System.out.println( slist.get(0) );       // cat
//System.out.println( slist.get(-1) );    // IndexOutOfBoundsException

// Append an element into the sublist.
slist.add("cow");

// The original list shows the new element.
System.out.println( list );               // [dog, cat, cow, pig]

// Clear the sublist.
slist.clear();
System.out.println( list );               // [dog, pig]

// Try removing an element from the original list and then reuse the sublist
list.remove(1);
System.out.println( slist.get(0) );       // ConcurrentModificationException
```

L

toArray()

PURPOSE Returns all of the elements in this list in an array.

SYNTAX

```
public Object[] toArray()
public Object[] toArray(Object arr[])
```

DESCRIPTION This method fills `arr` with all of the elements in this list and returns `arr`. If `arr` is not large enough, a new array is created, filled, and then returned. The new array is just large enough to hold all of the elements in this list, and its type is identical to the type of `arr`.

If `arr` is larger than all of the elements in this list, `arr[size()]` is set to `null`. This `null` value can be used to determine the number of returned elements. However, it is not helpful if the list may contain `null` elements.

The order of the elements in the returned array matches the order of the elements in this list.

If `arr` is not specified, it defaults to `new Object[0]`.

PARAMETERS

`arr` The non-`null` array into which the elements of this list will be copied.

RETURNS The non-`null` array `arr` or a new array whose length equals `size()`.

EXCEPTIONS

`ArrayStoreException`

If some element in this list cannot be assigned to an element in `arr` because the types do not match. This exception is never thrown if `arr` is an `Object` array.

EXAMPLE

```
import java.util.*;

class Main {
    public static void main(String[] args) {
        ArrayList list = new ArrayList(
            Arrays.asList(new String[]{"dog", null}));

        Object[] objs = list.toArray();
        print(objs);                          // [dog, null]

        // Since we passed in a string array, we can cast
        // the result to a string array.
        String[] strings = (String[])list.toArray(new String[0]);
        print(strings);                       // [dog, null]

        // Try adding something other than a string to the list.
        list.add(new Integer(0));

        print( list.toArray() );              // [dog, null, 0]

        // The Integer object can not be stored in the string array.
        print( list.toArray(new String[0]) );// ArrayStoreException
    }

    static void print(Object[] arr) {
        System.out.println(Arrays.asList(arr));
    }
}
```

L

java.util

ListIterator

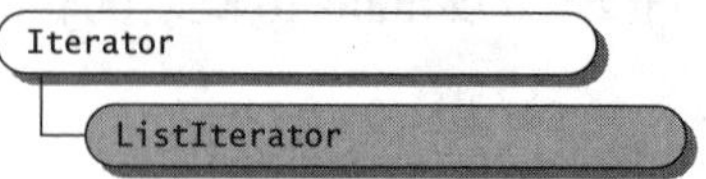

Syntax

```
public interface ListIterator extends Iterator
```

Description

A `ListIterator` is an iterator (see `Iterator`) with extra capabilities. Unlike a regular iterator, which allows you to retrieve elements only in a forward direction, a list iterator allows you to move both forward and backward. Also unlike a regular iterator, which allows you only to remove elements from the list, a list iterator lets you both add and replace elements in the list.

The order of the elements returned by the list iterator is exactly the same order in which the elements appear in the list.

The Cursor

L

The list iterator maintains a cursor that is positioned either before the first element, after the last element, or between two elements in the list. A list iterator typically has a constructor that allows you to specify the initial position of the cursor. The value of the cursor must be in the range `0` ≤ cursor ≤ size of the list.

Only two methods move the cursor: `next()` and `previous()`. All other methods leave the cursor in place, even the ones that modify the list.

The Last-Returned Element

A list iterator records the most recent element returned by `next()` or `previous()`. It is an internal value that can't be accessed. In the following documentation, this value is referred to as the *last-returned element*. This value is used by `remove()` and `set()` to determine which element to remove or replace. The last-returned element can be invalid, in which case `remove()` and `set()` will throw an `IllegalStateException`. The last-returned element is initially invalid.

Concurrent Modification Error

Some list iterators do not allow modifications on the list while the list iterator is in use. These lists typically return list iterators that are fail-fast, that is, the list iterator watches for modifications on the list and throws an exception if it detects one. This feature is used mainly to avoid programming errors.

If you are implementing a list iterator for a list that subclasses `AbstractList`, see `AbstractList.modCount` for information about how to implement fail-fast behavior.

The implementation of fail-fast behavior does not need to be properly synchronized and perfectly reliable. The fail-fast feature is designed primarily as an extra precaution against a common programming error, the improper synchronization of common data structures. In other words, it is fine if under certain race conditions, the list iterator happens to miss a modification of the list. It also is fine if some of the list iterator operations fail (because of concurrent activity) before the list iterator can throw a `ConcurrentModificationException`.

MEMBER SUMMARY	
Element Retrieval Methods	
`next()`	Retrieves the element following the cursor and advances the cursor.
`previous()`	Retrieves the element preceding the cursor and moves the cursor back over this element.
Query Methods	
`hasNext()`	Determines if there are more elements following the cursor.
`hasPrevious()`	Determines if there are more elements before the cursor.
`nextIndex()`	Returns the index of the element that would be returned by a call to `next()`.
`previousIndex()`	Returns the index of the element that would be returned by a call to `previous()`.
Modification Methods	
`add()`	Inserts an element into the list just before the cursor.
`remove()`	Removes the most recently returned element from the list.
`set()`	Replaces the most recently returned element in the list with another element.

See Also

`AbstractList`, `Iterator`.

Example

For an example of how to implement a list iterator, see the `AbstractSequentialList` class example. For examples of how to use a list iterator, see the following member descriptions.

add()

PURPOSE Inserts an element into the list just before the cursor.

SYNTAX `void add(Object e)`

DESCRIPTION This method inserts the element `e` into the list just before the cursor.

It invalidates the last-returned element (see the class description) so that `set()` and `remove()` will fail.

The list or the list iterator might not support this method, in which case an `UnsupportedOperationException` is thrown.

PARAMETERS

`e` A possibly `null` element to insert into the list.

EXCEPTIONS

`ClassCastException`
If the class of `e` is not compatible with the list.

`ConcurrentModificationException`
If the list was modified by something other than this list iterator.

`IllegalArgumentException`
If some aspect of `e` prevents it from being added to the list.

`UnsupportedOperationException`
If this method is not supported by this list iterator.

EXAMPLE

```
List list = new LinkedList(Arrays.asList(new String[]{"dog", "cat"}));
ListIterator it = list.listIterator();

System.out.println( it.next() );        // dog
it.add("pig");

// The element is added just after dog
System.out.println( list );             // [dog, pig, cat]

// Adding an element moves the cursor.
System.out.println( it.next() );        // cat

System.out.println( it.previous() );    // cat
System.out.println( it.previous() );    // pig
System.out.println( it.previous() );    // dog

// The cursor is now at the beginning of the list.
it.add("cow");
System.out.println( list );             // [cow, dog, cat, pig]
```

hasNext()

PURPOSE Determines if there are more elements following the cursor.

SYNTAX `boolean hasNext()`

DESCRIPTION This method determines if there are more elements following the cursor. It returns `true` if calling `next()` would return a value.

RETURNS `true` if there are more elements after the cursor.

EXCEPTIONS

`ConcurrentModificationException`
If the list was modified by something other than this list iterator.

SEE ALSO `hasPrevious()`, `next()`.

EXAMPLE

```
List list = Arrays.asList(new String[]{"dog"});
ListIterator it = list.listIterator();

System.out.println( it.hasNext() );         // true
System.out.println( it.next() );            // dog
System.out.println( it.hasNext() );         // false
//System.out.println( it.next() );          // NoSuchElementException
System.out.println( it.previous() );        // dog
System.out.println( it.hasNext() );         // true

// Common way to loop forward through a list.
for (ListIterator i=list.listIterator(); i.hasNext(); ) {
    System.out.println( i.next() );
}
```

hasPrevious()

PURPOSE Determines if there are more elements before the cursor.

SYNTAX `boolean hasPrevious()`

DESCRIPTION This method determines if there are more elements before the cursor. It returns `true` if calling `previous()` would return a value.

RETURNS `true` if there are more elements behind the cursor.

EXCEPTIONS

`ConcurrentModificationException`
If the list was modified by something other than this list iterator.

SEE ALSO `hasNext()`, `previous()`.

EXAMPLE

```
List list = Arrays.asList(new String[]{"dog", "cat"});
ListIterator it = list.listIterator();

System.out.println( it.hasPrevious() );     // false
//System.out.println( it.previous() );      // NoSuchElementException
System.out.println( it.next() );            // dog
System.out.println( it.hasPrevious() );     // true
System.out.println( it.previous() );        // dog
System.out.println( it.hasPrevious() );     // false

// Common way to loop backwards through a list.
for (ListIterator i=list.listIterator(list.size()); i.hasPrevious(); ) {
    System.out.println( i.previous() );     // cat dog
}
```

next()

PURPOSE Retrieves the element following the cursor and advances the cursor.

SYNTAX `Object next()`

DESCRIPTION This method retrieves the element following the cursor and advances the cursor by 1.

The last-returned element is set to the returned element. This value is used by `remove()` and `set()` (see the class description for more details).

RETURNS The possibly `null` element following the cursor.

EXCEPTIONS

`ConcurrentModificationException`

If the list was modified by something other than this list iterator.

`NoSuchElementException`

If there are no more elements following the cursor.

SEE ALSO `hasNext()`, `remove()`, `previous()`, `set()`.

EXAMPLE

```
List list = Arrays.asList(new String[]{"dog", null, "cat"});

// Common way to loop forward through a list.
for (ListIterator i=list.listIterator(); i.hasNext(); ) {
    System.out.println( i.next() );  // dog null cat
}
```

L

nextIndex()

PURPOSE Returns the index of the element that would be returned by a call to `next()`.

SYNTAX `int nextIndex()`

RETURNS The index of the element that would be returned by a call to `next()`.

EXCEPTIONS

`ConcurrentModificationException`

If the list was modified by something other than this list iterator.

SEE ALSO `previousIndex()`.

EXAMPLE

```
List list = Arrays.asList(new String[]{"dog"});
ListIterator it = list.listIterator();

System.out.println( it.nextIndex() );       // 0
System.out.println( it.next() );            // dog
System.out.println( it.nextIndex() );       // 1
System.out.println( it.previous() );        // dog
System.out.println( it.nextIndex() );       // 1
```

previous()

PURPOSE Retrieves the element preceding the cursor and moves the cursor back over this element.

SYNTAX `Object previous()`

DESCRIPTION This method retrieves the element preceding the cursor and moves the cursor back over this element.

The last-returned element is set to the returned element. This value is used by `remove()` and `set()` (see the class description for more details).

RETURNS The possibly `null` element preceding the cursor.

EXCEPTIONS

`ConcurrentModificationException`
If the list was modified by something other than this list iterator.

`NoSuchElementException`
If there are no more elements following the cursor.

SEE ALSO `hasPrevious()`, `next()`, `remove()`, `set()`.

EXAMPLE

```
List list = Arrays.asList(new String[]{"dog", null, "cat"});

// Common way to loop backwards through a list.
for (ListIterator i=list.listIterator(list.size()); i.hasPrevious(); ) {
    System.out.println( i.previous() );  // cat null dog
}
```

L

previousIndex()

PURPOSE Returns the index of the element that would be returned by a call to `previous()`.

SYNTAX `int previousIndex()`

RETURNS The index of the element that would be returned by a call to `previous()`.

EXCEPTIONS

`ConcurrentModificationException`
If the list was modified by something other than this list iterator.

SEE ALSO `nextIndex()`.

EXAMPLE

```
List list = Arrays.asList(new String[]{"dog", "cat"});
ListIterator it = list.listIterator();

System.out.println( it.previousIndex() );    // -1
System.out.println( it.next() );             // dog
```

```
System.out.println( it.previousIndex() );     // 0
System.out.println( it.previous() );          // dog
System.out.println( it.previousIndex() );     // -1
```

remove()

PURPOSE Removes the most recently returned element from the list.

SYNTAX `void remove()`

DESCRIPTION This method removes the last-returned element, which is the most recent element returned by either `next()` or `previous()` (see the class description for more details).

The last-returned element can be invalid, in which case this method throws an `IllegalStateException`. The last-returned value is invalidated by a call to `add()` or `remove()`. This means that you cannot, for example, call `remove()` twice in succession.

The list or the list iterator might not support this method, in which case an `UnsupportedOperationException` is thrown.

L

EXCEPTIONS

`ConcurrentModificationException`
If the list was modified by something other than this list iterator.

`IllegalStateException`
If the last-returned element is invalid (see the class description).

`UnsupportedOperationException`
If this method is not supported by this list iterator.

SEE ALSO `add()`, `next()`, `previous()`.

EXAMPLE

```
List list = new ArrayList(Arrays.asList(new String[]{"dog", "cat"}));
ListIterator it = list.listIterator();

//it.remove();                              // IllegalStateException
System.out.println( it.next() );            // dog
it.remove();
System.out.println( list );                 // [cat]

// You can't call remove() after another remove().
//it.remove();                              // IllegalStateException

// You also can't call remove() after add().
it.add("pig");
System.out.println( list );                 // [pig, cat]
//it.remove();                              // IllegalStateException

// But you can remove an element that's just been set.
System.out.println( it.next() );            // cat
it.set("dog");
```

```
it.remove();
System.out.println( list );                // [pig]

System.out.println( it.next() );           // IllegalStateException
System.out.println( it.previous() );       // pig

// Remove the previous element.
it.remove();
System.out.println( list );                // []

// Remove all null elements.
list = new ArrayList(Arrays.asList(new String[]{"dog", null, "cat"}));
for (ListIterator i=list.listIterator(); i.hasNext(); ) {
    if (i.next() == null) {
        i.remove();
    }
}
System.out.println( list );                // [dog, cat]
```

set()

PURPOSE Replaces the most recently returned element in the list with another element.

SYNTAX `void set(Object e)`

DESCRIPTION This method replaces the last-returned element with `e`. The last-returned element is the most recent element returned by either `next()` or `previous()` (see the class description for more details).

This method neither affects the cursor nor invalidates the last-returned element. Although not particularly useful, this does mean that you can call `set()` more than once or call `remove()` after calling `set()`.

The list or the list iterator might not support this method, in which case an `UnsupportedOperationException` is thrown.

PARAMETERS

`e` A possibly `null` element.

EXCEPTIONS

`ClassCastException`
If the class of `e` is not compatible with the list.

`ConcurrentModificationException`
If the list was modified by something other than this list iterator.

`IllegalArgumentException`
If some aspect of `e` prevents it from being added to this list.

`IllegalStateException`
If the last-returned element is invalid (see the class description).

L

EXAMPLE

```
List list = new ArrayList(Arrays.asList(new String[]{"dog", null, "cat"}));
ListIterator it = list.listIterator();

//it.set("pig");                                // IllegalStateException
System.out.println( it.next() );                // dog
it.set("pig");
it.set("pig");                                  // (this changes nothing)
System.out.println( list );                     // [pig, null, cat]

// You cannot call set() after remove() or add().
it.remove();
//it.set("cow");                                // IllegalStateException
it.add("dog");
//it.set("cow");                                // IllegalStateException
System.out.println( list );                     // [dog, null, cat]

// Replace null with pig
System.out.println( it.next() );                // null
System.out.println( it.previous() );            // null
it.set("pig");
System.out.println( list );                     // [dog, pig, cat]

// Replace "dog" with "cow".
for (ListIterator i=list.listIterator(); i.hasNext(); ) {
    if (i.next().equals("dog")) {
        i.set("cow");
    }
}
System.out.println( list );                     // [cow, pig, cat]
```

Locale

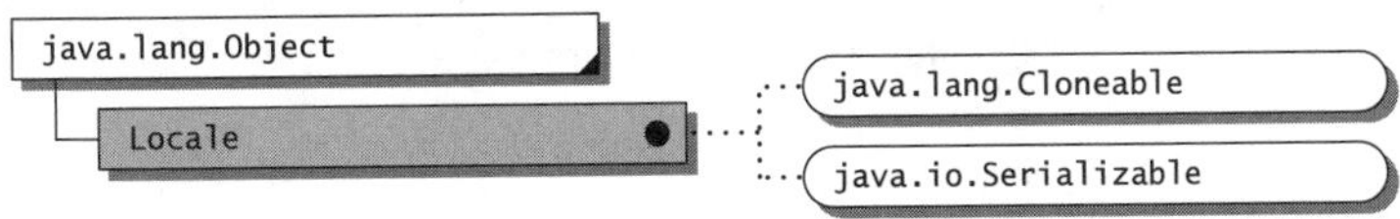

Syntax

```
public final class Locale implements Cloneable, Serializable
```

Description

The Locale class represents a locale. A *locale* is Java's standard means of identifying a language for the purposes of internationalization and localization. All classes that support localization use the `Locale` class to determine in which language to display its information. For example, when the `DateFormat` class is asked to format a date, it will use the word "Monday" for an English locale and the word "Lundi" for a French locale.

See *The Java Class Libraries, Second Edition, Volume 1* for more information about this class.

Changes for Version 1.2

Three methods are new: `getAvailableLocales()`, `getISOCountries()`, and `getISOLanguages()`. These allow you to retrieve the lists of available locales and codes.

The constructor now handles changes that have been made to the set of ISO-639 language codes. In particular, three codes have been changed. The constructor recognizes these new codes but does so by converting them to the old codes. Therefore, if you construct a locale with a new code and you retrieve it with `getLanguage()`, you will get the old code.

The `toString()` method behaves differently when both the language and variant codes are not empty but the country code is empty. In Version 1.1, the result would have been only the language code. In Version 1.2, the result includes both the language code and the variant, separated by two underscores.

MEMBER SUMMARY	
Constructor	
Δ `Locale()`	Constructs a `Locale` instance.
Set Locale Method	
`setDefault()`	Sets the default locale.
	Continued

MEMBER SUMMARY

Getter Methods

	Method	Description
1.2	`getAvailableLocales()`	Creates a list of all installed locales.
	`getCountry()`	Retrieves this `Locale`'s two-letter country code.
	`getDefault()`	Retrieves the default locale.
	`getDisplayCountry()`	Retrieves a human-readable localized version of this `Locale`'s country code.
	`getDisplayLanguage()`	Retrieves a human-readable localized version of this `Locale`'s language code.
	`getDisplayName()`	Retrieves a human-readable localized version of this `Locale`.
	`getDisplayVariant()`	Retrieves a human-readable localized version of this `Locale`'s variant code.
1.2	`getISOCountries()`	Creates a list of all two-letter country codes defined in ISO-3166.
	`getISO3Country()`	Retrieves this `Locale`'s three-letter country code.
1.2	`getISOLanguages()`	Creates a list of all two-letter language codes defined in ISO-639.
	`getISO3Language()`	Retrieves this `Locale`'s three-letter ISO language code.
	`getLanguage()`	Retrieves this `Locale`'s two-letter ISO language code.
	`getVariant()`	Retrieves this `Locale`'s variant code.

Predefined Locales for Countries

Field	Description
`CANADA`	Locale for Canada.
`CHINA`	Locale for China. Equivalent to `PRC`.
`FRANCE`	Locale for France.
`GERMANY`	Locale for Germany.
`ITALY`	Locale for Italy.
`JAPAN`	Locale for Japan.
`KOREA`	Locale for Korea.
`PRC`	Locale for People's Republic of China. Equivalent to `CHINA`.
`TAIWAN`	Locale for Taiwan.
`UK`	Locale for the United Kingdom.
`US`	Locale for the United States.

Predefined Locales for Languages

Field	Description
`CANADA_FRENCH`	Locale for French-speaking Canada.
`CHINESE`	Locale for the Chinese language.
`ENGLISH`	Locale for the English language.
`FRENCH`	Locale for the French language.
`GERMAN`	Locale for the German language.
`ITALIAN`	Locale for the Italian language.
`JAPANESE`	Locale for the Japanese language.
`KOREAN`	Locale for the Korean language.
`SIMPLIFIED_CHINESE`	Locale for the Chinese language in mainland China.
`TRADITIONAL_CHINESE`	Locale for the Chinese language in Taiwan.

MEMBER SUMMARY	
Object Methods	
`clone()`	Creates a clone of this `Locale`.
`equals()`	Determines if this `Locale` is equal to another object.
`hashCode()`	Computes the hash code of this `Locale`.
Δ `toString()`	Generates a string representing this `Locale`.

See Also

`Locale` in *The Java Class Libraries, Second Edition, Volume 1.*

1.2 getAvailableLocales()

PURPOSE Creates a list of all installed locales.

SYNTAX `public static Locale[] getAvailableLocales()`

DESCRIPTION This method creates and returns a list of all installed locales.

RETURNS A new non-`null` `string` array. The `string` array may be modified.

EXAMPLE

```
Locale[] locales = Locale.getAvailableLocales();
for (int i=0; i<locales.length; i++) {
    System.out.print(locales[i]+" ");
    if ((i+1) % 10 == 0) {
        System.out.println();
    }
}
System.out.println();
```

OUTPUT

```
en en_US ar ar_AE ar_BH ar_DZ ar_EG ar_IQ ar_JO ar_KW
ar_LB ar_LY ar_MA ar_OM ar_QA ar_SA ar_SD ar_SY ar_TN ar_YE
be be_BY bg bg_BG ca ca_ES cs cs_CZ da da_DK
de de_AT de_AT_EURO de_CH de_DE de_DE_EURO de_LU de_LU_EURO el el_GR
en_AU en_CA en_GB en_IE en_IE_EURO en_NZ en_ZA es es_AR es_BO
es_CL es_CO es_CR es_DO es_EC es_ES es_ES_EURO es_GT es_HN es_MX
es_NI es_PA es_PE es_PR es_PY es_SV es_UY es_VE et et_EE
fi fi_FI fi_FI_EURO fr fr_BE fr_BE_EURO fr_CA fr_CH fr_FR fr_FR_EURO
fr_LU fr_LU_EURO hr hr_HR hu hu_HU is is_IS it it_CH
it_IT it_IT_EURO iw iw_IL ja ja_JP ko ko_KR lt lt_LT
lv lv_LV mk mk_MK nl nl_BE nl_BE_EURO nl_NL nl_NL_EURO no
no_NO no_NO_NY pl pl_PL pt pt_BR pt_PT pt_PT_EURO ro ro_RO
ru ru_RU sh sh_YU sk sk_SK sl sl_SI sq sq_AL
sr sr_YU sv sv_SE th th_TH tr tr_TR uk uk_UA
zh zh_CN zh_HK zh_TW
```

1.2 getISOCountries()

PURPOSE Creates a list of all two-letter country codes defined in ISO-3166.

SYNTAX `public static String[] getISOCountries()`

DESCRIPTION This method creates and returns a list of all two-letter country codes defined in ISO-3166.

RETURNS A new non-`null` `string` array. The `string` array may be modified.

EXAMPLE This example simply lists all ISO country and language two-letter codes.

```
System.out.println("ISO Countries");
String[] countries = Locale.getISOCountries();
for (int i=0; i<countries.length; i++) {
    System.out.print(countries[i]+" ");
    if ((i+1) % 20 == 0) {
        System.out.println();
    }
}
System.out.println();

System.out.println("\nISO Languages");
String[] languages = Locale.getISOLanguages();
for (int i=0; i<languages.length; i++) {
    System.out.print(languages[i]+" ");
    if ((i+1) % 20 == 0) {
        System.out.println();
    }
}
System.out.println();
```

OUTPUT

```
ISO Countries
AD AE AF AG AI AL AM AN AO AQ AR AS AT AU AW AZ BA BB BD BE
BF BG BH BI BJ BM BN BO BR BS BT BV BW BY BZ CA CC CF CG CH
CI CK CL CM CN CO CR CU CV CX CY CZ DE DJ DK DM DO DZ EC EE
EG EH ER ES ET FI FJ FK FM FO FR FX GA GB GD GE GF GH GI GL
GM GN GP GQ GR GS GT GU GW GY HK HM HN HR HT HU ID IE IL IN
IO IQ IR IS IT JM JO JP KE KG KH KI KM KN KP KR KW KY KZ LA
LB LC LI LK LR LS LT LU LV LY MA MC MD MG MH MK ML MM MN MO
MP MQ MR MS MT MU MV MW MX MY MZ NA NC NE NF NG NI NL NO NP
NR NU NZ OM PA PE PF PG PH PK PL PM PN PR PT PW PY QA RE RO
RU RW SA SB SC SD SE SG SH SI SJ SK SL SM SN SO SR ST SV SY
SZ TC TD TF TG TH TJ TK TM TN TO TP TR TT TV TW TZ UA UG UM
US UY UZ VA VC VE VG VI VN VU WF WS YE YT YU ZA ZM ZR ZW

ISO Languages
aa ab af am ar as ay az ba be bg bh bi bn bo br ca co cs cy
da de dz el en eo es et eu fa fi fj fo fr fy ga gd gl gn gu
ha he hi hr hu hy ia id ie ik in is it iu iw ja ji jw ka kk
kl km kn ko ks ku ky la ln lo lt lv mg mi mk ml mn mo mr ms
mt my na ne nl no oc om or pa pl ps pt qu rm rn ro ru rw sa
sd sg sh si sk sl sm sn so sq sr ss st su sv sw ta te tg th
ti tk tl tn to tr ts tt tw ug uk ur uz vi vo wo xh yi yo za
zh zu
```

1.2 getISOLanguages()

PURPOSE Creates a list of all two-letter language codes defined in ISO-639.

SYNTAX
```
public static String[] getISO3Languages()
```

DESCRIPTION This method creates and returns a list of all two-letter language codes defined in ISO-639. Some languages codes in ISO-639 have changed; see Table 11.

Old	New
iw	he
ji	yi
in	id

TABLE 11: Changed ISO-639 Language Codes.

The returned list includes both the new and the old codes.

RETURNS A new non-`null` `string` array. The `string` array may be modified.

EXAMPLE See `getISOCountries()`.

Δ Locale()

PURPOSE Constructs a `Locale` instance.

SYNTAX
```
public Locale(String languageCode, String countryCode)
public Locale(String languageCode, String countryCode, String
   variantCode)
```

DESCRIPTION This constructor constructs a `Locale` instance that has the specified codes. `languageCode` should be one of the ISO-639 language codes; it is converted to lowercase. `countryCode` should be one of the two-letter ISO-3166 country codes; it is converted to uppercase. The `variantCode` may be any string and is converted to uppercase. This constructor simply stores the code strings; the strings are not checked for validity.

If the locale is not country-specific, it must be empty (""). If a `variantCode` is specified, `countryCode` must not be empty; otherwise, the variant code is ignored.

1.2 CHANGES ISO-639 changed three language codes; see Table 11. This constructor converts the new codes to the old codes. This class internally uses the old codes, so methods such as `getLanguage()` will return the old codes.

PARAMETERS

`countryCode` A non-`null` possibly empty string containing a two-letter ISO-3166 country code.

`languageCode` A non-`null` string containing a two-letter ISO-639 language code.

`variantCode` A non-`null` possibly empty string containing a variant code.

EXAMPLE This example demonstrates that the codes supplied to the constructor have their cases adjusted.

```
Locale l = new Locale("En", "Us", "Unix");
System.out.println(l.getLanguage());    // en
System.out.println(l.getCountry());     // US
System.out.println(l.getVariant());     // UNIX
System.out.println(l.toString());       // en_US_UNIX

l = new Locale("En", "", "Unix");
System.out.println(l.getLanguage());    // en
System.out.println(l.getCountry());     //
System.out.println(l.getVariant());     // UNIX
System.out.println(l.toString());       // en__UNIX

// Demonstrate that new codes are converted to old codes.
l = new Locale("he", "");
System.out.println(l.getLanguage());    // iw
```

L

Δ toString()

PURPOSE Generates a string representing this `Locale`.

SYNTAX `public final String toString()`

DESCRIPTION This method concatenates this locale's two-letter language code and two-letter country code, separated by an underscore ("_"). The codes are the same values passed to the constructor (after their cases have been adjusted). For example, if this locale was created with language code "en" and country code "US," this method would return "en_US".

If this `Locale` object has a variant code, an underscore and the variant code is appended to the result. The variant code is the same value passed to the constructor (after it has been converted to uppercase). To continue the previous example, if the variant code was "UNIX," this method would return "en_US_UNIX".

If both the language and country codes are empty, an empty string is returned, regardless of whether the variant is empty.

The format returned by this method is used by classes such as `ResourceBundle` to search for localized resource bundles. See `ResourceBundle` for more information.

1.2 CHANGES In Version 1.1, if the country code was empty, the variant would not be included. In Version 1.2, if the country code is empty, the variant is appended to the language code, separated by two underscores.

RETURNS A non-`null` string representing this `Locale`.

OVERRIDES `java.lang.Object.toString()`.

EXAMPLE This example demonstrates the results of every possible combination of empty language, country, and variant codes.

```
Locale l = new Locale("en", "US", "VARIANT");
System.out.println(l.toString());        // en_US_VARIANT

l = new Locale("", "US", "VARIANT");
System.out.println(l.toString());        // _US_VARIANT

l = new Locale("en", "", "VARIANT");
System.out.println(l.toString());        // en__VARIANT

l = new Locale("en", "US", "");
System.out.println(l.toString());        // en_US

l = new Locale("", "", "VARIANT");
System.out.println(l.toString());        //

l = new Locale("en", "", "");
System.out.println(l.toString());        // en

l = new Locale("", "US", "");
System.out.println(l.toString());        // _US

l = new Locale("", "", "");
System.out.println(l.toString());        //
```

L

java.lang
Long

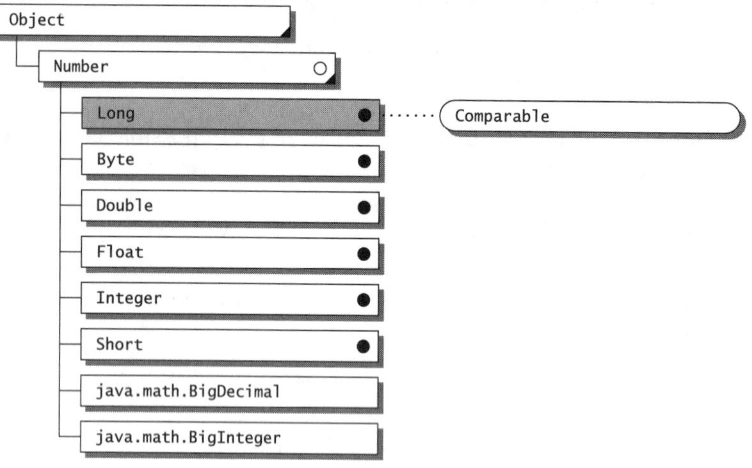

Syntax

L

```
public final class Long extends Number implements Comparable
```

Description

The `Long` class provides an object wrapper for a `long` data value. A *`long` data value* in Java is a 64-bit signed integer. This wrapper allows `long` integers to be passed to methods in Java class libraries that accept Java objects as parameters. In addition, this class provides methods that convert values to and from `long`s and perform other operations on `long`s.

See *The Java Class Libraries, Second Edition, Volume 1* for more information about this class.

Changes for Version 1.2

A new `decode()` method parses the string representation of a `long` into a `long`. It is a complement to the existing parsing methods.

The `Long` class implements the `Comparable` interface and has two overloaded forms of the `compareTo()` method used for comparing and ordering `Long` objects. This allows arrays of `Long` objects to be sorted, as shown in this example.

```
Long[] la = new Long[]{new Long(10), new Long(-4), new Long(48)};
Arrays.sort(la);
for (int i = 0; i < la.length; i++) {
    System.out.println(la[i]);
}
// -4, 10, 48
;
```

MEMBER SUMMARY	
Constructor	
`Long()`	Constructs a `Long` instance using a `long` or a string.
Number Methods	
`byteValue()`	Retrieves the value of this `Long` as a `byte`.
`doubleValue()`	Retrieves the value of this `Long` as a `double`.
`floatValue()`	Retrieves the value of this `Long` as a `float`.
`intValue()`	Retrieves the value of this `Long` as an `int`.
`longValue()`	Retrieves the value of this `Long` as a `long`.
`shortValue()`	Retrieves the value of this `Long` as a `short`.
Constants	
`MAX_VALUE`	The maximum value a `long` can have.
`MIN_VALUE`	The minimum value a `long` can have.
`TYPE`	The `Class` object representing the primitive type `long`.
String Conversion Methods	
1.2 `decode()`	Parses the string representation of a 64-bit signed integer into a `long`.
`getLong()`	Creates a `Long` using the value of a system property.
`parseLong()`	Parses the string representation of an integer into a `long`.
`toBinaryString()`	Generates the string representation of a `long` as an unsigned binary number.
`toHexString()`	Generates the string representation of a `long` as an unsigned hexadecimal number.
`toOctalString()`	Generates the string representation of a `long` as an unsigned octal number.
`toString()`	Generates the string representation of a `long` or a `Long`.
`valueOf()`	Creates a `Long` instance using its string representation.
Comparison Methods	
1.2 `compareTo()`	Compares the signed numeric value of this `Long` with that of another `Long`.
`equals()`	Determines if this `Long` is equal to another object.
Object Method	
`hashCode()`	Computes the hash code of this `Long`.

L

See Also

`Comparable`, `java.util.Arrays`.
`Long` in *The Java Class Libraries, Second Edition, Volume 1.*

1.2 compareTo()

PURPOSE Compares the signed numeric value of this `Long` with that of another `Long`.

SYNTAX
```
public int compareTo(Long aLong)
public int compareTo(Object aLong)
```

DESCRIPTION This method compares this `Long`'s (signed) numeric value with that of `aLong`. It returns an integer indicating whether the two numeric values are equal and, if they are not, the ordering of the two values. It returns `0` if the two numeric values are the same. It returns a negative number if the numeric value of this `Long` is less than that of `aLong`. It returns a positive number if the numeric value of this `Long` is greater than that of `aLong`.

If `aLong` is not an instance of `Long`, a `ClassCastException` is thrown.

PARAMETERS

`aLong` The non-`null` `Long` with which to compare.

RETURNS `0` if the numeric values of this `Long` and `aLong` are the same; a negative number if this `Long`'s value is less than that of `aLong`; a positive number if this `Long`'s value is greater than that of `aLong`.

EXCEPTIONS

`ClassCastException`

If `aLong` is not an instance of `Long`.

SEE ALSO `Comparable`.

EXAMPLE
```
Long b = new Long(1234567000);
System.out.println(b.compareTo(new Long(-1)));          // positive
System.out.println(b.compareTo(new Long(1234567000)));  // 0
System.out.println(b.compareTo(new Long(-1234567000))); // positive
System.out.println(b.compareTo(new Long(2147483647)));  // negative
System.out.println(b.compareTo("abc")); // ClassCastException
```

1.2 decode()

PURPOSE Parses the string representation of a 64-bit signed integer into a `long`.

SYNTAX
```
public static Long decode(String str) throws
    NumberFormatException
```

DESCRIPTION This method parses the string representation of a 64-bit signed integer into a `long`. The string may be in hexadecimal format (with an `0x` or `#` prefix), in octal format (with a zero character (`0`) prefix), or in decimal format (radix 10 digits). If the string contains a leading negative sign character ("–"), the number is negative. `str` must not contain any whitespace characters.

decode() is similar to valueOf(), except that valueOf() accepts a radix argument to determine the radix, while decode() examines the string's format in order to determine the radix. decode() is also similar to parseLong(), except that parseLong() returns a long, while decode() returns a Long and examines the string's format in order to determine the radix.

PARAMETERS

str — The non-null string to parse.

RETURNS — The non-null Long representing the value specified by str.

EXCEPTIONS

NumberFormatException

If str does not contain the valid format for a long.

SEE ALSO — Long(), parseLong(), valueOf().

EXAMPLE

```
try {
    Long l_dec = Long.decode("225");
    Long l_oct = Long.decode("065");            // octal
    Long l_hex1 = Long.decode("0x1f");          // hex
    Long l_hex2 = Long.decode("#1e");           // hex
    Long l_big = Long.decode("1234123455555");// decimal

    System.out.println("parsed: " +
        l_dec + "," + l_oct + "," + l_hex1 + ","  + l_hex2);
} catch (NumberFormatException e) {
    e.printStackTrace();
}
```

Manifest

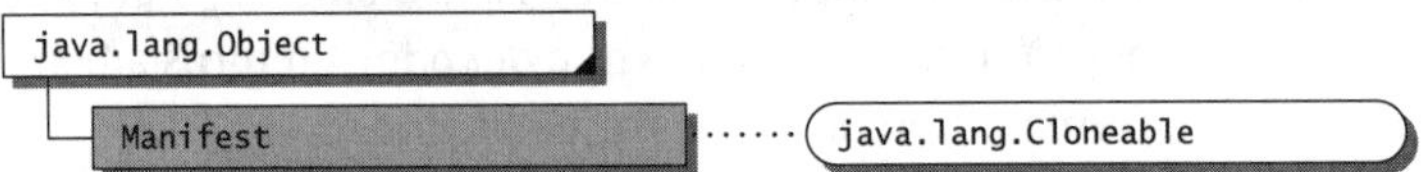

Syntax

```
public class Manifest implements Cloneable
```

Description

The `Manifest` class represents a *manifest*, which is a set of attributes (name/value pairs) associated with a JAR file (see `JarFile`). The attributes provide additional information about the JAR file and about entries in the JAR file. For example, if a class is signed, its digest is kept in the manifest.

Main Attributes

Some of the attributes in the manifest refer to the whole JAR file itself. These are called the *main attributes*. A main attribute also applies to all manifest entries; see later in this section for more details. Figure 11 contains an example of a manifest file.

Entry Attributes

All attributes other than the main attributes are separated into groups called *manifest entries*. A manifest entry has a name that is used to retrieve all of the attributes in that entry.

A manifest entry typically corresponds to an entry in the JAR file. In this case, the name of the manifest entry and JAR file entry are the same and all of the attributes in the manifest entry apply to the corresponding JAR entry.

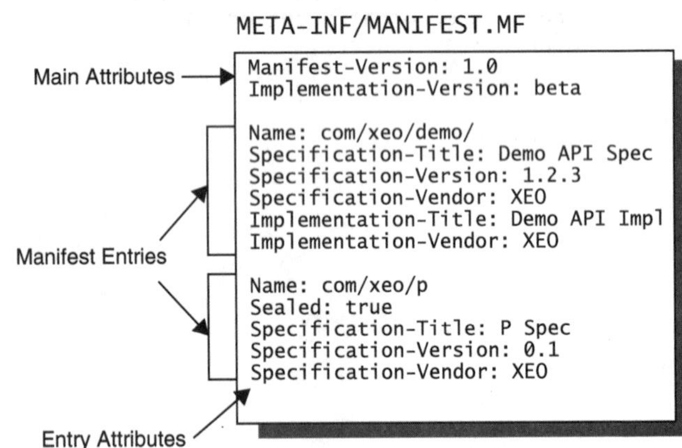

FIGURE 11: Manifest file.

Not all JAR entries have a corresponding manifest entry. Likewise, not all manifest entries have corresponding JAR entries.

Usage

To add a new main attribute, use

```
manifest.getMainAttributes().put(attrName, attrValue);
```

To add a new manifest entry, use

```
Attributes attr = new Attributes();
attr.put(new Attributes.Name("Sealed"), "true");
manifest.getEntries().put(entryName, attr);
```

Another way of adding attributes to a manifest is by reading the attributes from a file. See `read()` for more information.

Manifest String Representation

All of the contents of a manifest can be represented by a specially formatted string. This format is described in detail in the document

```
http://java.sun.com/products/jdk/1.2/docs/guide/jar/manifest.html
```

This class provides methods for generating the string representation of the manifest and for creating a manifest from the string representation.

Here are a few highlights about the format.

1. An attribute is represented by the attribute name followed by the attribute value. They are separated by a colon and space (": "). An attribute must also be terminated with a newline. For example, "Manifest-Version: 1.0" is an attribute as it appears in a manifest file. Note that attribute names are case-insensitive, so the names "manifest-version" and "Manifest-Version" are equal. See `Attributes.Name` for more information about attribute names.
2. Each line must be 72 bytes or less (including the newline character(s)). To continue a line, precede the continuation line with a space. All spaces following the first space in a continuation line are significant. Also, the newline character preceding a continuation line is discarded (not converted to a space).
3. The first attributes are the main attributes. The main attributes section is terminated by one or more blank lines.
4. After the main attributes come the manifest entries. Each manifest entry consists of lines of attributes; each entry is separated by one or more blank lines. The first attribute in each entry must have the attribute name "Name". The value of this attribute is the name of the manifest entry. When retrieving the attributes for an entry, the "Name" attribute will appear in the set. Here's an example of the string representation of a manifest. This manifest has two main attributes ("Manifest-Version" and "Author") and one manifest entry with two attributes ("Name" and "Desc").

```
Manifest-Version: 1.0
Author: Patrick Chan

Name: Main.java
Desc: Example for class example.
```

5. When creating a manifest from its string representation, only the lower byte of each Unicode character is used. When generating the string representation of a manifest, each byte is converted to a Unicode character by filling the upper byte with a zero.

Special Attributes

In general, a manifest could contain any arbitrary set of attributes as long as the previous formatting rules are followed. However, there is a set of attributes that have special meaning when used with standard Java development tools. For example, if you specify a main attribute with the name "Main-Class", the standard Java interpreter expects the value of this attribute to be a fully qualified class name and will proceed to invoke its `main()` method. These special attributes are described in `Attributes.Name`. They are also described in the tutorial at

```
http://java.sun.com/docs/books/tutorial/jar/basics/manifest.html
```

and the specification at

```
http://java.sun.com/products/jdk/1.2/docs/guide/jar/manifest.html
```

MEMBER SUMMARY	
Constructor	
`Manifest()`	Constructs a new `Manifest` instance.
Attribute Methods	
`getAttributes()`	Retrieves the attributes for an entry.
`getEntries()`	Retrieves a map containing the entries contained in this manifest.
`getMainAttributes()`	Retrieves the main attributes for this manifest.
Clear Method	
`clear()`	Removes all attributes from this manifest.
String Representation Methods	
`read()`	Reads a string representation of manifest information.
`write()`	Writes a string representation of this manifest.
Object Methods	
`clone()`	Creates a copy of this manifest.
`equals()`	Determines if this manifest is equal to another.
`hashCode()`	Computes the hash code of this manifest.

See Also

`Attributes`, `Attributes.Name`.

Example

This example creates a `Manifest` object from a manifest file (`manifest.txt`) and then prints the attributes from the new `Manifest` object.

```
import java.io.*;
import java.util.*;
import java.util.jar.*;

class Main {
    public static void main(String[] args) {
        if (args.length < 1) {
            System.out.println("Usage: java Main <manifest-file>");
            System.exit(1);
        }

        try {
            printManifest(new Manifest(new FileInputStream(args[0])));
        } catch (Exception e) {
            e.printStackTrace();
        }
    }

    static void printManifest(Manifest man) {
        System.out.println("---------- Main Attributes");
        printAttributes(man.getMainAttributes());
        for (Iterator it=man.getEntries().keySet().iterator(); it.hasNext();) {
            String ename = (String)it.next();
            System.out.println("---------- " + ename);
            printAttributes(man.getAttributes(ename));
        }
    }

    static void printAttributes(Attributes attr) {
        for (Iterator it=attr.keySet().iterator(); it.hasNext(); ) {
            Object key = it.next();
            System.out.println(key + ": " + attr.get(key));
        }
    }
}
```

manifest.txt

```
Manifest-Version: 1.0
Author: Patrick Chan

Name: Main.java
Desc: Example for class example.
```

Output

```
> java Main manifest.txt
---------- Main Attributes
Author: Patrick Chan
Manifest-Version: 1.0
---------- Main.java
Desc: Example for class example.
```

clear()

PURPOSE Removes all attributes from this manifest.

SYNTAX `public void clear()`

DESCRIPTION This method removes all attributes from this manifest. After this method is called, the main attributes of this manifest will be empty and this manifest will have no entries.

EXAMPLE See `clone()`.

clone()

PURPOSE Creates a copy of this manifest.

SYNTAX `public Object clone()`

DESCRIPTION This method creates a copy of this manifest that contains the same main attributes and manifest entries. Changing the main attributes and adding and removing manifest entries from this manifest do not affect the clone and changing the clone does not affect this manifest. However, the manifest entries themselves are not cloned. Therefore, if you modify a manifest entry in this manifest (for example, by giving the entry some new attributes), the change will be reflected in both this manifest and the clone.

The implementation of this method uses the constructor

```
return new Manifest(this);
```

RETURNS A non-`null` copy of this manifest.

EXAMPLE This example demonstrates that modifying the main attributes of the original and cloned manifest do not affect each other, while modifying a manifest entry in the original affects both the original and the clone.

```
import java.io.*;
import java.util.*;
import java.util.jar.*;

class Main {
    public static void main(String[] args) {
        Manifest man = new Manifest();
        man.getMainAttributes().put(Attributes.Name.MANIFEST_VERSION, "1.0");
        Attributes attr = new Attributes();
        attr.put(new Attributes.Name("Sealed"), "false");
        man.getEntries().put("Main.class", attr);
        Attributes attr2 = new Attributes();
        attr2.put(new Attributes.Name("Desc"), "Example Source");
        man.getEntries().put("Main.java", attr2);

        Manifest manCopy = (Manifest)man.clone();
        printAttributes(manCopy.getMainAttributes());// Manifest-Version: 1.0
```

M

```
        System.out.println(man.equals(manCopy));     // true

        // Changing a main attribute value in the original doesn't change clone
        man.getMainAttributes().put(Attributes.Name.MANIFEST_VERSION, "2.0");
        printAttributes(manCopy.getMainAttributes());// Manifest-Version: 1.0
        System.out.println(man.equals(manCopy));      // false


        // Deleting a manifest entry in the original doesn't change clone
        manCopy = (Manifest)man.clone();
        man.getEntries().remove("Main.class");
        System.out.println(man.equals(manCopy));      // false

        // Modifying a manifest entry in the original does change clone
        // Note that Main.java did not have a "Sealed" attribute before now
        manCopy = (Manifest)man.clone();
        Attributes mj = man.getAttributes("Main.java");
        mj.put(new Attributes.Name("Sealed"), "false");
        printAttributes(man.getAttributes("Main.java"));     // Desc, Sealed
        printAttributes(manCopy.getAttributes("Main.java")); // Desc, Sealed
        System.out.println(man.equals(manCopy));      // true

        // Clearing the original also does not affect the clone.
        man.clear();
        printAttributes(manCopy.getMainAttributes());// Manifest-Version: 2.0
    }

    static void printAttributes(Attributes attr) {
        for (Iterator it=attr.keySet().iterator(); it.hasNext(); ) {
            Object key = it.next();
            System.out.println(key + ": " + attr.get(key));
        }
    }
}
```

M

equals()

PURPOSE Determines if this manifest is equal to another.

SYNTAX `public boolean equals(Object obj)`

DESCRIPTION This method determines if this manifest is equal to `obj`. It returns `true` if, and only if, `obj` is a `Manifest` object and both this manifest and `obj` have identical main and manifest entry attributes. Attribute names and values are compared using their `equals()` methods.

PARAMETERS

`obj` A possibly `null` object to be compared with this manifest.

RETURNS `true` if `obj` is equal to this manifest.

SEE ALSO `hashCode()`.

EXAMPLE See `clone()`.

getAttributes()

PURPOSE Retrieves the attributes for an entry.

SYNTAX `public Attributes getAttributes(String ename)`

DESCRIPTION This method retrieves the attributes of the manifest entry `ename`. The implementation calls `getEntries()`:

```
return (Attributes)getEntries().get(ename);
```

PARAMETERS

`ename` A non-`null` case-sensitive entry name.

RETURNS The attributes for `ename` or `null` if `ename` does not exist.

EXAMPLE See the class example.

getEntries()

PURPOSE Retrieves a map containing the entries contained in this manifest.

SYNTAX `public Map getEntries()`

DESCRIPTION The keys in the returned map are the manifest entry names (`String` objects). The values in the returned map are `Attributes` objects that contain the attributes for an entry.

New entries and their attributes can be added to this manifest by calling the following.

```
Attributes attr = new Attributes();
attr.put(new Attributes.Name("Sealed"), "true");
String entryName = "Main.java";
manifest.getEntries().put(entryName, attr);
```

RETURNS A non-`null` `Map` object.

EXAMPLE See the class example.

getMainAttributes()

PURPOSE Retrieves the main attributes for this manifest.

SYNTAX `public Attributes getMainAttributes()`

DESCRIPTION This method returns the main attributes for this `Manifest`. Attributes can be added to the main attributes of this manifest by calling

```
Attributes.Name attrName = Attributes.Name.SEALED;
getMainAttributes().put(attrName, attrValue);
```

M

RETURNS A non-`null` `Attributes` object.

EXAMPLE See the class example.

hashCode()

PURPOSE Computes the hash code of this manifest.

SYNTAX `public int hashCode()`

DESCRIPTION This method computes the hash code of this manifest. The hash code is computed by adding the hash code of the manifest's attribute to the hash code of its entries.

RETURNS An `int` that is the hash code of this manifest.

SEE ALSO `equals()`.

Manifest()

PURPOSE Constructs a new `Manifest` instance.

SYNTAX
```
public Manifest()
public Manifest(Manifest man)
public Manifest(InputStream is) throws IOException
```

M

DESCRIPTION This constructor constructs a new `Manifest` instance. If `man` is specified, the new manifest will have `man`'s main attributes and list of manifest entries. The manifest entries themselves are shared and not duplicated. See `clone()` for more details.

If `is` is specified, the new manifest is initialized with attributes read from `is`. See `read()` for more details on this form of the constructor.

If neither `man` nor `is` is specified, the new manifest is empty.

PARAMETERS

`man` A non-`null` manifest.

`is` A non-`null` input stream containing the string representation of manifest information.

EXCEPTIONS

`IOException`

If an IO error occurred while reading from `is`.

EXAMPLE See the class example.

read()

PURPOSE Reads a string representation of manifest information.

SYNTAX `public void read(InputStream is) throws IOException`

DESCRIPTION This method reads from `is` a stream of bytes representing manifest information. Each byte is converted into a Unicode character by filling the top byte with zero. See the class description for information about the format of the input.

The new information from `is` does not replace all of this manifest's contents; rather the new information is *applied* to this manifest. In particular, new manifest entries and new main attributes from `is` are added to this manifest. If a main attribute from `is` also appears in this manifest, the current attribute value of this manifest is replaced with the attribute value from `is`. If a manifest entry exists in both `is` and this manifest, the manifest entry's attributes are the union of the attributes, with the values from `is` overriding existing attribute values that have the same attribute names.

This method can read output generated by `write()`.

PARAMETERS

`is` A non-`null` input stream that delivers the string representation of manifest information.

M

EXCEPTIONS

`IOException`

If an IO exception occurs while reading from `is`.

SEE ALSO `clear()`, `write()`.

EXAMPLE This example creates a manifest initialized with a few attributes and then calls `read()` on a manifest file (`manifest.txt`). Notice that new attributes from the manifest file are added to the manifest and values of existing attributes are updated.

```
import java.io.*;
import java.util.*;
import java.util.jar.*;

class Main {
    public static void main(String[] args) {
        Manifest man = new Manifest();
        man.getMainAttributes().put(Attributes.Name.MANIFEST_VERSION, "1.0");

        Attributes attr = new Attributes();
        attr.put(new Attributes.Name("Desc"), "Example for write() method");
        attr.put(new Attributes.Name("Date"), "10/11/98");
        man.getEntries().put("Main.java", attr);

        try {
            man.read(new FileInputStream("manifest.txt"));
```

```
        } catch (IOException e) {
            e.printStackTrace();
        }

        printManifest(man);
    }

    static void printManifest(Manifest man) {
        System.out.println("---------- Main Attributes");
        printAttributes(man.getMainAttributes());
        for (Iterator it=man.getEntries().keySet().iterator(); it.hasNext(); )
        {
            Object key = it.next();
            System.out.println("---------- " + key);
            printAttributes((Attributes)man.getEntries().get(key));
        }
    }

    static void printAttributes(Attributes attr) {
        for (Iterator it=attr.keySet().iterator(); it.hasNext(); ) {
            Object key = it.next();
            System.out.println(key + ": " + attr.get(key));
        }
    }
}
```

manifest.txt

```
Manifest-Version: 2.0
Sealed: true

Name: Main.java
Sealed: true

Name: Main.class
Desc: The class file for Main.java
```

OUTPUT

```
---------- Main Attributes
Sealed: true
Manifest-Version: 2.0
---------- Main.class
Desc: The class file for Main.java
---------- Main.java
Sealed: true
Date: 10/11/98
Desc: Example for write() method
```

write()

PURPOSE Writes a string representation of this manifest.

SYNTAX `public void write(OutputStream os) throws IOException`

DESCRIPTION This methods writes to `os` a stream of bytes that represents the entire contents of this manifest. Only the lower byte of each Unicode character is written. See the class description for information about the format of the output.

The result of this method is suitable for input by `read()`. In fact, a `Manifest` object created from the output of this method is equal (according to `equals()`) to this manifest.

PARAMETERS

`os` A non-`null` output stream.

EXCEPTIONS

`IOException`

If an IO error has occurred while writing to `os`.

SEE ALSO `read()`.

EXAMPLE

```
import java.io.*;
import java.util.*;
import java.util.jar.*;

class Main {
    public static void main(String[] args) {
        Manifest man = new Manifest();
        man.getMainAttributes().put(Attributes.Name.MANIFEST_VERSION, "1.0");

        Attributes attr = new Attributes();
        attr.put(new Attributes.Name("Desc"), "Example for write() method");
        man.getEntries().put("Main.java", attr);

        try {
            man.write(new FileOutputStream("manifest.txt"));

            // Read the manifest file back in and compare.
            Manifest man2 = new Manifest(new FileInputStream("manifest.txt"));

            System.out.println(man.equals(man2));    // true
        } catch (IOException e) {
            e.printStackTrace();
        }
    }
}
```

manifest.txt

```
Manifest-Version: 1.0

Name: Main.java
Desc: Example for write() method
```

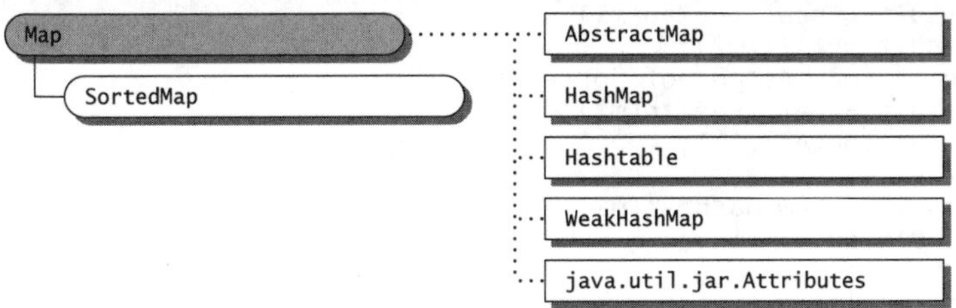

Syntax

`public interface Map`

Description

A `Map` is a type of collection that holds key/value pairs (*entries*). The keys in the map must be unique, but the values don't have to be. If you try to add an entry with a duplicate key, the map replaces the old entry with the new entry. This is unlike a set, in which if you try adding a duplicate element, the operation is completely ignored.

Unlike with lists (see `List`), the keys in the map must not be modified while they are in the map. For example, if a `StringBuffer` is used as a key in the map, you must not modify the `StringBuffer` while it is in the map.

Three types of collections are available: set, list, and map. See `Collection` for an overview of *The Collections Framework*, which includes set, list, and map.

Usage

The `java.util` package provides four implementations of maps: `HashMap`, `TreeMap`, `WeakHashMap`, and `Hashtable`. They differ in how they store their entries, so one might be more efficient than another for your application. See the `HashMap`, `TreeMap`, `WeakHashMap`, and `Hashtable` classes for more details.

There are several ways to create a map. Here are some of them.

```
Map map;
map = new HashMap();
map = new TreeMap();
map = new WeakHashMap();
```

Once a map is created, you can use the methods in this interface to query or modify the map. Be aware that some of these methods might result in an `UnsupportedOperationException` if the map does not support the method call. For example, `Collections.unmodifiableMap` returns a map that cannot be modified.

The Collections Framework does not provide a nondestructive way to create a union or intersection of two maps. You might find it useful to define methods such as the following.

```
public static Map union(Map m1, Map m2) {
    Map result;
    if (m1 instanceof SortedMap) {
        result = new TreeMap(m1);
        result.putAll(m2);
    } else if (m2 instanceof SortedMap) {
        result = new TreeMap(m2);
        result.putAll(m1);
    } else {
        result = new HashMap(m1);
        result.putAll(m2);
    }
    return result;
}

public static Map intersection(Map m1, Map m2) {
    Map result;
    if (m1 instanceof SortedMap) {
        result = new TreeMap(m1);
        result.keySet().retainAll(m2.keySet());
    } else if (m2 instanceof SortedMap) {
        result = new TreeMap(m2);
        result.keySet().retainAll(m1.keySet());
    } else {
        result = new HashMap(m1);
        result.keySet().retainAll(m2.keySet());
    }
    return result;
}
```


The `Collections` class provides various utility methods for changing the capabilities of a map by creating a wrapper around your map. For example, you can prevent any modifications to your map by using `Collections.unmodifiableMap()`. Also, you can have all of the methods of the map be wrapped with synchronized methods by using `Collections.synchronizedMap()`.

To implement a class that implements the `Map` interface, you should consider subclassing `AbstractMap`. This abstract class minimizes the effort needed to implement a `Map` class.

Collection View

A map allows you to view the contents of the map as a collection in several ways. For example, you can view as a collection all of the keys in the map or all of its values. These special collections actually share the same storage as the map, so making changes to the collection affects the map and making changes to the map affects the collection. This *collection view* of the map gives you more ways to view and modify the map. For example, `keySet()` creates a set of all keys in the map. Since it is a set, you can use all of the useful set operations such as `Set.removeAll()` and `Set.retainAll()` to operate on the map. See `keySet()`, `values()`, and `entrySet()` for more details.

MEMBER SUMMARY	
Value Retrieval Method	
`get()`	Retrieves the value associated with a key.
Query Methods	
`containsKey()`	Determines if this map contains a particular key.
`containsValue()`	Determines if this map contains a particular value.
`isEmpty()`	Determines if this map has no entries.
`size()`	Returns the number of entries in this map.
Modification Methods	
`clear()`	Removes all of the entries in this map.
`put()`	Adds a key/value pair to this map.
`putAll()`	Adds key/value pairs from another map to this map.
`remove()`	Removes an entry from this map.
Set Methods	
`entrySet()`	Returns a set containing all of the key/value pairs in this map.
`keySet()`	Returns a set containing all of the keys in this map.
`values()`	Returns a collection containing all of the values in this map.
Object Methods	
`equals()`	Determines if this map is equal to another object.
`hashCode()`	Computes the hash code for this map.

Unsupported Methods

Not all maps can be modified. There are only two ways in which you can modify a map: add an entry to it or remove an entry from it. A map can support one, both, or neither of these operations. If you attempt to use a method to modify a map that does not support the operation, the method will throw an `UnsupportedOperationException`.

See Also

`Collection`, `Collections`, `List`, `HashMap`, `Set`, `TreeMap`.

Example

For an example that implements a `Map`, see `AbstractMap`. For demonstrations of how a map is used, see the examples in the following member descriptions.

clear()

PURPOSE Removes all of the entries in this map.

SYNTAX `public void clear()`

DESCRIPTION This method removes all of the entries in this map. After it is called, this map will be empty.

This method might not be supported.

EXCEPTIONS

`UnsupportedOperationException`
If this method is not supported by this map.

EXAMPLE

```
Map map = new HashMap();
map.put("dog", "spot");
map.put("pig", "babe");
System.out.println( map.size() );    // 2
map.clear();
System.out.println( map.isEmpty() ); // true
```

containsKey()

M

PURPOSE Determines if this map contains a particular key.

SYNTAX `public boolean containsKey(Object k)`

DESCRIPTION This method determines whether this map contains the key `k`. It returns `true` if some key in this map is equal to `k`. A key is equal to `k` if both are `null` or if the `equals()` method determines that they are equal.

PARAMETERS

`k` A possibly `null` key.

RETURNS `true` if some key in this map is equal to `k`.

EXCEPTIONS

`ClassCastException`
If the type of `k` is not appropriate for this map.

`NullPointerException`
If `k` is `null` and this map does not accept `null` keys.

SEE ALSO `equals()`.

EXAMPLE

```
HashMap map = new HashMap();
map.put("dog", "spot");
map.put("cat", "luck");
```

```
System.out.println( map.containsKey("dog") );      // true
System.out.println( map.containsKey(null) );       // false

System.out.println( map.containsValue("luck") );   // true
System.out.println( map.containsValue(null) );     // false
```

containsValue()

PURPOSE Determines if this map contains a particular value.

SYNTAX `public boolean containsValue(Object v)`

DESCRIPTION This method determines if this map contains the value v. It returns `true` if some value in this map is equal to v. A value is equal to `v` if both are `null` or if the `equals()` method determines that they are equal. Unlike `containsKey()`, this method runs slowly for most map implementations. It typically iterates over every entry in the map.

PARAMETERS

v A possibly `null` value.

RETURNS `true` if some value in this map is equal to v.

EXCEPTIONS

`NullPointerException`

If `v` is `null` and this map does not accept `null` values.

SEE ALSO `equals()`.

EXAMPLE See `containsKey()`.

entrySet()

PURPOSE Returns a set containing all of the key/value pairs in this map.

SYNTAX `public Set entrySet()`

DESCRIPTION This method returns a set containing all of the key/value pairs in this map. The pairs are represented by `Map.Entry` objects. See `Map.Entry` for information about retrieving a key or value from an entry.

The returned set and this map share the same storage. This means that changes to the map are immediately reflected in the set and changes to the set are immediately reflected in the map.

The returned set does not support `add()` and `addAll()`.

RETURNS A non-`null` set containing all of the entries in this map.

SEE ALSO `Collection`, `keySet()`, `Map.Entry`, `values()`.

EXAMPLE

```
Map map = new HashMap();
map.put("dog", "spot");
map.put("cat", null);
map.put(null, "babe");

// Remove all null keys and replace all null values with the key.
Set set = map.entrySet();
for (Iterator it=set.iterator(); it.hasNext(); ) {
    Map.Entry e = (Map.Entry)it.next();

    if (e.getValue() == null) {
        e.setValue(e.getKey());
    } else if (e.getKey() == null) {
        it.remove();
    }
}
System.out.println( map );                          // {dog=spot, cat=cat}

// Add to the map and check the set
map.put("yak", "yolk");
System.out.println( set );                          // [dog=spot, cat=cat, yak=yolk]

// You can't add to the setlection.
set.add("bess");                                    // UnsupportedOperationException
```


equals()

PURPOSE Determines if this map is equal to another object.

SYNTAX `public boolean equals(Object c)`

DESCRIPTION This method determines if this map is equal the object `c`. It returns `true` if, and only if, `c` is a `Map` object and both this map and `c` have exactly the same entries (see `Map.Entry`). `Map.Entry.equals()` is used to determine if two entries match. Basically, two entries match if the keys and values of both are equal to each other.

PARAMETERS

`c` The possibly `null` object to be compared with this map.

RETURNS `true` if `c` is equal to this map.

OVERRIDES `java.lang.Object.equals()`.

SEE ALSO `hashCode()`.

EXAMPLE

```
Map m1 = new HashMap();
m1.put("dog", "spot");
m1.put("cat", "luck");

Map m2 = new HashMap();
m2.put("dog", "spot");
```

```
System.out.println( m1.equals(null) );          // false
System.out.println( m1.equals(m2) );            // false

// Two maps are not equal even if all the keys match.
m2.put("cat", "john");
System.out.println( m1.equals(m2) );            // false

m2.put("cat", "luck");
System.out.println( m1.equals(m2) );            // true

// Maps and sets are not equal, even if they have the same contents.
System.out.println( new HashMap().equals(Collections.EMPTY_SET) );
                                                // false
```

get()

PURPOSE Retrieves the value associated with a key.

SYNTAX `public Object get(Object k)`

DESCRIPTION This method searches this map for an entry with the key `k` and returns the associated value. `null` is returned if `k` is not in this map. A return value of `null` is ambiguous if the map accepts `null` values. You can use `containsKey()` to unambiguously determine if `k` is in this map.

PARAMETERS

`k` A possibly `null` key.

RETURNS The possibly `null` value associated with `k` or `null` if `k` is not in this map.

EXCEPTIONS

`ClassCastException`
If the type of `k` is not appropriate for this map.

`NullPointerException`
If `k` is `null` and this map does not accept `null` keys.

SEE ALSO `containsKey()`.

EXAMPLE

```
Map map = new HashMap();
map.put("dog", "spot");
map.put("cat", null);

System.out.println( map.get("dog") );           // spot
System.out.println( map.get("cat") );           // null
System.out.println( map.get("yak") );           // null

// If values can be null, use containsKey() to determine presense of keys.
System.out.println( map.containsKey("cat") );    // true
System.out.println( map.containsKey("yak") );    // false
```

M

hashCode()

PURPOSE	Computes the hash code for this map.
SYNTAX	`public int hashCode()`
DESCRIPTION	This method computes the hash code for this map. The hash code of a map is the sum of the hash codes of all entries in the map. The hash code for an entry is the exclusive-OR of the key and the value. The hash code for a `null` key or value is `0` (see `Map.Entry.hashCode()` for more information). Two equal maps will have the same hash code. Unequal maps might also have the same hash code, although the hash code algorithm reduces this possibility. The hash code is typically used as the key in a hash table.
RETURNS	This map's hash code.
OVERRIDES	`java.lang.Object.hashCode()`.
SEE ALSO	`equals()`, `java.lang.Object.equals()`, `MapEntry.hashCode()`.
EXAMPLE	See `java.lang.Object.hashCode()`.

isEmpty()

M

PURPOSE	Determines if this map has no entries.
SYNTAX	`public boolean isEmpty()`
RETURNS	`true` if this map contains no entries.
SEE ALSO	`size()`.
EXAMPLE	See `clear()`.

keySet()

PURPOSE	Returns a set containing all of the keys in this map.
SYNTAX	`public Set keySet()`
DESCRIPTION	This method returns a set containing all of the keys in this map. The set and this map share the same storage. This means that changes to the map are immediately reflected in the set and changes in the set are immediately reflected in the map. The returned set does not support `add()` and `addAll()`.
RETURNS	A non-`null` set containing all of the keys in this map.
SEE ALSO	`Collection`, `entrySet()`, `values()`.

EXAMPLE

```
Map map = new HashMap();
map.put("dog", "spot");
map.put("gnu", "rick");

Set set = map.keySet();
System.out.println( set );                     // [dog, gnu]
System.out.println( set.contains("dog") );    // true

// Remove an entry from the set and check the map.
set.remove("dog");
System.out.println( map );                     // {gnu=rick}

// Add to the map and check the set
map.put("yak", "yolk");
System.out.println( set );                     // [gnu, yak]

// You can't add to the setlection.
//set.add("bess");                             // UnsupportedOperationException
```

put()

PURPOSE Adds a key/value pair to this map.

SYNTAX `public Object put(Object k, Object v)`

DESCRIPTION This method adds a new entry with the key `k` and value `v` into this map. If an entry with the key `k` already exists in this map, it is replaced with the new entry. In this case, the previous value is returned.

This method might not be supported.

PARAMETERS

`k` A possibly `null` key.

`v` A possibly `null` value.

RETURNS If `k` already existed in this map, then the possibly `null` old value is returned; otherwise, `null` is returned.

EXCEPTIONS

`IllegalArgumentException`
If some aspect of `k` prevents it from being added to this map.

`ClassCastException`
If the type of `k` is not appropriate for this map.

`NullPointerException`
If `k` or `v` is `null` and this map does not accept `null` keys or values.

`UnsupportedOperationException`
If this method is not supported by this map.

EXAMPLE

```
Map map = new HashMap();
```

M

```
System.out.println( map.put("dog", "john") );     // null
System.out.println( map.put("cat", null ) );      // null

// Replace the keys.
System.out.println( map.put("dog", "spot") );     // john
System.out.println( map.put("cat", "luck") );     // null

// If values can be null, use containsKey() to determine presense of keys.
System.out.println( map.containsKey("cat") );     // true
System.out.println( map.containsKey("yak") );     // false
```

putAll()

PURPOSE Adds key/value pairs from another map to this map.

SYNTAX `public void putAll(Map m)`

DESCRIPTION This method adds every entry from map `m` to this map. If the key for some entry from `m` already exists in this map, the entry in this map is replaced by the one from `m`.

This method might not be supported.

PARAMETERS

`m` A non-`null` map.

M

EXCEPTIONS

`ConcurrentModificationException`
If `m`'s iterators are fail-fast and `m` is being modified during this method call.

`ClassCastException`
If the class of some key in `m` is not appropriate for this map.

`IllegalArgumentException`
If some aspect of some entry from `m` prevents it from being added to this map.

`NullPointerException`
If the key or value of some entry from `m` is `null` and this map does not accept `null` keys or values.

`UnsupportedOperationException`
If this method is not supported by this map.

SEE ALSO `put()`.

EXAMPLE

```
Map m1 = new TreeMap();
m1.put("dog", "spot");
m1.put("cat", null);
System.out.println( m1 );     // {cat=null, dog=spot}

Map m2 = new HashMap();
m2.put("gnu", "rick");
m2.put("cat", "luck");
```

```
m1.putAll(m2);
System.out.println( m1 );    // {cat=luck, dog=spot, gnu=rick}
```

remove()

PURPOSE Removes an entry from this map.

SYNTAX `public Object remove(Object k)`

DESCRIPTION This method searches for an entry with the key `k` in this map and removes the entry from this map. A key is equal to `k` if both are `null` or if the `equals()` method determines that they are equal.

This method might not be supported.

PARAMETERS

`k` The possibly `null` key of the entry to remove.

RETURNS The possibly `null` value previously associated with `k` or `null` if `k` did not match any keys in this map.

EXCEPTIONS

`UnsupportedOperationException`
If this method is not supported by this map.

EXAMPLE

```
HashMap map = new HashMap();
map.put("dog", "spot");
map.put("cat", null);

System.out.println( map.remove("dog") );     // spot
System.out.println( map.remove("cat") );     // null
System.out.println( map.remove("pig") );     // null
System.out.println( map.remove(null) );      // null
```

size()

PURPOSE Returns the number of entries in this map.

SYNTAX `public int size()`

RETURNS The non-negative number of entries in this map.

SEE ALSO `isEmpty()`.

EXAMPLE See `clear()`.

M

values()

PURPOSE Returns a collection containing all of the values in this map.

SYNTAX `public Collection values()`

DESCRIPTION This method returns a collection that contains all of the values in this map. Unlike with `keySet()`, the returned collection is not a set because there could be duplicates of values (sets don't allow duplicate elements).

The returned collection and this map share the same storage. This means that changes to the map are immediately reflected in the collection and changes in the collection are immediately reflected in the map.

The returned collection does not support `add()` and `addAll()`.

RETURNS A non-`null` collection containing all of the values in this map.

SEE ALSO `Collection`, `entrySet()`, `keySet()`.

EXAMPLE

```
Map map = new HashMap();
map.put("dog", "spot");
map.put("cat", "luck");
map.put("cow", "spot");
map.put("yak", "spot");

Collection col = map.values();
System.out.println( col );                       // [luck, spot, spot, spot]
System.out.println( col.contains("spot") );      // true

// remove() removes one entry from the map.
col.remove("spot");
System.out.println( map );                       // {cat=luck, cow=spot, yak=spot}

// removeAll() removes all entries with the value "spot".
col.removeAll(Collections.singleton("spot"));
System.out.println( map );                       // {cat=luck}

// Add to the map and check the collection
map.put("dog", "spot");
System.out.println( col );                       // [luck, spot]

// You can't add to the collection.
//col.add("bess");                               // UnsupportedOperationException
```

M

Map.Entry

Map.Entry

Syntax

```
public interface Map.Entry
```

Description

A `Map.Entry` represents a *map entry*: a key/value pair from a map (see `Map`). The only way to access a set of map entries is through the method `Map.entrySet()`. This method returns a set of map entry objects, one for each entry in the map.

You can change the value of a map entry but not of the key. Changing a map entry modifies the corresponding value in the map.

MEMBER SUMMARY	
Retrieval Methods	
`getKey()`	Retrieves the key of this map entry.
`getValue()`	Retrieves the value of this map entry.
Modification Method	
`setValue()`	Replaces the value of this map entry.
Object Methods	
`hashCode()`	Computes the hash code for this map entry.
`equals()`	Determines if this map entry is equal to another object.

See Also

`Map.entrySet()`.

Example

This example manipulates a map's entry set, modifying all `null` values to be the same as the key. The example creates an iterator from the entry set to iterate over all of the entries.

```
import java.util.*;

class Main {
    public static void main(String[] args) {
        TreeMap map = new TreeMap();
        map.put("dog", "spot");
        map.put("cat", null);
        map.put("pig", "babe");
```

```
            map.put("cow", null);

            Iterator it = map.entrySet().iterator();
            while (it.hasNext()) {
                Map.Entry e = (Map.Entry)it.next();
                Object o = e.getValue();

                if (e.getValue() == null) {
                    e.setValue(e.getKey());
                }
            }
            System.out.println( map );    // {cat=cat, cow=cow, dog=spot, pig=babe}

            // Obtain an entry set.
            Set set = map.entrySet();
            System.out.println( set );    // [cat=cat, cow=cow, dog=spot, pig=babe]

            // Remove an entry from the underlying set.
            map.remove("cat");
            System.out.println( set );    // [cow=cow, dog=spot, pig=babe]

            // Remove all map entries from the entry set.
            set.clear();
            System.out.println( map );    // {}
        }
    }
```

equals()

PURPOSE Determines if this map entry is equal to another object.

SYNTAX `public boolean equals(Object e)`

DESCRIPTION This method determines if this map entry is equal to the object `e`. It returns `true` if, and only if, `e` is a `Map.Entry` object and both this map entry and `e` have exactly the same key and value. More precisely, `e1.equals(e2)` returns `true` if the following is true.

```
(e2 instanceOf Map.Entry)
&&
(e1.getKey() == null ?
    e2.getKey() == null :
    e.getKey().equals(e2.getKey()))
&&
(e1.getValue() == null ?
        e2.getValue() == null :
        e.getValue().equals(e2.getValue()))
```

PARAMETERS

`e` The possibly `null` object to be compared with this map entry.

RETURNS `true` if `e` is equal to this map entry.

OVERRIDES `java.lang.Object.equals()`.

SEE ALSO `hashCode()`.

EXAMPLE See `java.lang.Object.equals()`.

getKey()

PURPOSE Retrieves the key of this map entry.

SYNTAX `public Object getKey()`

RETURNS The possibly `null` key of this map entry.

EXAMPLE See the class example.

getValue()

PURPOSE Retrieves the value of this map entry.

SYNTAX `public Object getValue()`

RETURNS The possibly `null` key of this map entry.

EXAMPLE See the class example.

M

hashCode()

PURPOSE Computes the hash code for this map entry.

SYNTAX `public int hashCode()`

DESCRIPTION This method computes the hash code for this map entry. The hash code of a map entry is the exclusive-Or of the key and the value. More precisely, the hash code value of an entry `e` is the following.

```
int kc = e.getKey()==null ? 0 : e.getKey().hashCode();
int vc = e.getValue()==null ? 0 : e.getValue().hashCode();
return kc ^ vc;
```

Two equal map entries will have the same hash code. Unequal map entries might also have the same hash code, although the hash code algorithm reduces this possibility. The hash code of an entry is typically used to compute the hash code of the map that contains the entry.

RETURNS This map entry's hash code.

OVERRIDES `java.lang.Object.hashCode()`.

SEE ALSO `equals()`, `java.lang.Object.equals()`.

EXAMPLE See `java.lang.Object.hashCode()`.

setValue()

PURPOSE Replaces the value of this map entry.

SYNTAX

```
public Object setValue(Object newVal)
```

DESCRIPTION This method replaces the value of this map entry with `newVal`. The key of the underlying map is also modified to refer to `newVal`.

This method might not be supported.

PARAMETERS

`newVal` A possibly `null` new value for this map entry.

RETURNS The possibly `null` old value of this map entry.

EXCEPTIONS

`ClassCastException`
If the class of `newVal` is not compatible with the underlying map.

`IllegalArgumentException`
If some aspect of `newVal` prevents it from replacing the old value.

`NullPointerException`
If `newVal` is `null` and the underlying map does not accept `null` elements.

`UnsupportedOperationException`
If this method is not supported by this underlying map.

M

EXAMPLE See the class example.

Math

Syntax

```
public final class Math
```

Description

The `Math` class defines methods in the standard Math library. This library includes methods for calculating trigonometric functions, for rounding floating-point numbers into whole numbers, and for performing calculations using numbers. All methods and variables that this class defines are static.

The definitions of many of the numeric functions in this package use algorithms available from the package *Freely Distributable Math Library* (`fdlibm`) in the network library `netlib`. These algorithms, which are written in the C programming language, are then to be understood as executed with all floating-point operations following the rules of Java floating-point arithmetic. The network library may be found at `http://sunsite.unc.edu/`.

The Java Math library is defined with respect to the version of `fdlibm` dated January 4, 1995. When `fdlibm` provides more than one definition for a function (such as `acos`), use the "IEEE 754 core function" version (that is, the version in the file whose name begins with the letter "e").

See *The Java Class Libraries, Second Edition, Volume 1* for more information about this class.

Changes for Version 1.2

Two new methods, `toDegrees()` and `toRadians()`, convert an angle to and from radians and degrees.

MEMBER SUMMARY	
Methods for Angle Conversion	
1.2 `toDegrees()`	Converts an angle measured in radians to the equivalent angle measured in degrees.
1.2 `toRadians()`	Converts an angle measured in degrees to the equivalent angle measured in radians.
	Continued

MEMBER SUMMARY	
Constants	
`E`	The value of *e*.
`PI`	The value of π.
Methods for Rounding	
`ceil()`	Rounds a number to the smallest whole number greater than or equal to it.
`floor()`	Rounds a number to the largest whole number less than or equal to it.
`rint()`	Rounds a floating-point number to its closest whole number.
`round()`	Rounds a floating-point number to a whole number and casts it to an `int` or a `long`.
Methods for Trigonometry	
`acos()`	Calculates the arc cosine of a number.
`asin()`	Calculates the arc sine of a number.
`atan()`	Calculates the arc tangent of a number.
`atan2()`	Converts rectangular coordinates to polar coordinates.
`cos()`	Calculates the trigonometric cosine of an angle.
`sin()`	Calculates the trigonometric sine of an angle.
`tan()`	Calculates the trigonometric tangent of an angle.
Other Methods	
`abs()`	Calculates the absolute value of a number.
`exp()`	Calculates the result of *e* raised to a specified power.
`IEEEremainder()`	Calculates the remainder of the division between two floating-point numbers.
`log()`	Calculates the natural logarithm of a number.
`max()`	Determines the greater of two numbers.
`min()`	Determines the smaller of two numbers.
`pow()`	Calculates the result of raising a number to a specified power.
`random()`	Generates a random number between 0.0 and 1.0.
`sqrt()`	Calculates the square root of a number.

M

See Also

`Math` in *The Java Class Libraries, Second Edition, Volume 1.*

1.2 toDegrees()

PURPOSE Converts an angle measured in radians to the equivalent angle measured in degrees.

SYNTAX `public static double toDegrees(double angrad)`

PARAMETERS

angrad — An angle specified in radians.

RETURNS — The measurement of the angle `angrad`, in degrees.

SEE ALSO — `toRadians()`.

EXAMPLE

```
System.out.println(Math.toDegrees(Math.PI));      // 180.0
System.out.println(Math.toDegrees(Math.PI/2));    // 90.0
System.out.println(Math.toDegrees(Math.PI/3));    // 59.99999999999999
System.out.println(Math.toDegrees(Math.PI/4));    // 45
```

1.2 toRadians()

PURPOSE — Converts an angle measured in degrees to the equivalent angle measured in radians.

SYNTAX — `public static double toRadians(double angdeg)`

PARAMETERS

angdeg — An angle specified in degrees.

RETURNS — The measurement of the angle `angdeg`, in radians.

SEE ALSO — `toDegrees()`.

EXAMPLE

```
System.out.println(Math.toRadians(30.0));     // 0.5235987755982988
System.out.println(Math.toRadians(60.0));     // 1.0471975511965976
System.out.println(Math.toRadians(90.0));     // 1.5707963267948966
System.out.println(Math.toRadians(180.0));    // 3.141592653589793
```

java.text

MessageFormat

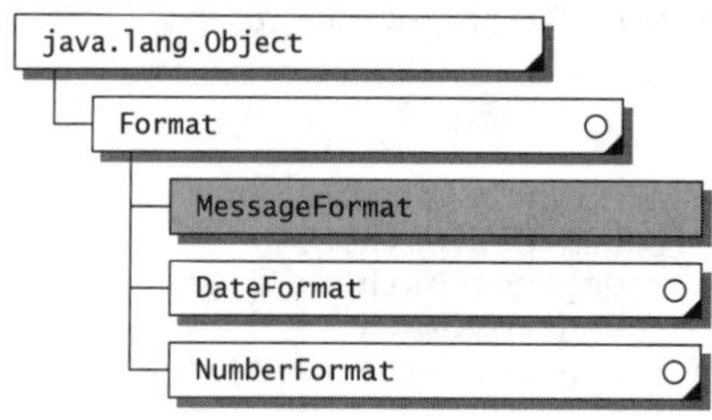

Syntax

`public class MessageFormat extends Format`

Description

The `MessageFormat` class provides a standard means of producing language-specific user messages that contain number, currency, percentage, date, time, and string variables. `MessageFormat` takes a set of objects, formats them to strings, and then inserts those strings into a pattern at the appropriate places to produce a string. This class uses the term *message* to mean text that is generally visible to an international set of users and hence is localized for each locale.

M

See *The Java Class Libraries, Second Edition, Volume 1* for more information about this class.

Changes for Version 1.2

This class has no API changes. However, we have added some clarifications for the Year 2000 (Y2K) issue, parsing in the class description, and the `parse()` method.

Year 2000

The pattern `yy` is a pattern for the two least-significant digits of the year. When using `yy` to parse a date string, apply a pattern, or construct a date in a `MessageFormat` instance, the `MessageFormat` instance must resolve the abbreviated year to some century. It does this by default by choosing the full year to be within the window 80 years before (inclusive) and 20 years after (exclusive) the time that the corresponding `SimpleDateFormat` instance is created. It uses `calendar.add(Calendar.YEAR, -80)` to determine the start of the window. For more details, see `SimpleDateFormat`.

Parsing

When a single argument is parsed more than once in the string, the last match will be the final result of the parsing. For example:

```
MessageFormat mf = new MessageFormat("{0,number,#.##}, {0,number,#.#}");
Object[] objs = {new Double(3.1415)};
String result = mf.format(objs);
// result now equals "3.14, 3.1"
objs = null;
objs = mf.parse(result, new ParsePosition(0));
// objs now equals {new Double(3.1)}
```

Likewise, parsing with a `MessageFormat` object using patterns that contain multiple occurrences of the same argument will return the last match. For example:

```
MessageFormat mf = new MessageFormat("{0}, {0}, {0}");
String forParsing = "x, y, z";
Object[] objs = mf.parse(forParsing, new ParsePosition(0));
// result now equals {new String("z")}
```

The parse() Method

When the parse fails, use `getErrorIndex()` in `ParsePosition` to find out where in the string it failed. The returned error index is the starting offset of the subpatterns with which the string is comparing. For example, if the parsing string "`AAA {0} BBB`" is comparing against the pattern "`AAD {0} BBB`", the error index is `0`. When an error occurs, the call to this method will return `null`. If `sourceStr` is `null`, an empty array is returned.

See Also

`MessageFormat` in *The Java Class Libraries, Second Edition, Volume 1.*

java.lang.reflect Modifier

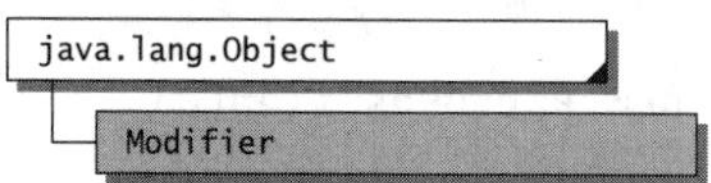

Syntax

```
public class Modifier
```

Description

The modifiers of a class, interface, field, method, or constructor (Java entities) are bit-encoded as `int`s. The `Modifier` class contains methods to process the encoding. Not all modifiers can appear on a Java entity.

See *The Java Class Libraries, Second Edition, Volume 1* for more information about this class.

Changes for Version 1.2

The `isStrict()` method and `STRICT` constant are new to support the modifier, `strictfp`, introduced in the Java program language in Version 1.2.

M

MEMBER SUMMARY	
Bit Mask Constants[a]	
`ABSTRACT`	Represents the `abstract` modifier (value `0x400`).
`FINAL`	Represents the `final` modifier (value `0x10`).
`INTERFACE`	Represents the `interface` modifier (value `0x200`).
`NATIVE`	Represents the `native` modifier (value `0x100`).
`PRIVATE`	Represents the `private` modifier (value `0x2`).
`PROTECTED`	Represents the `protected` modifier (value `0x4`).
`PUBLIC`	Represents the `public` modifier (value `0x1`).
`STATIC`	Represents the `static` modifier (value `0x8`).
1.2 `STRICT`	Represents the `strictfp` modifier (value `0x800`).
`SYNCHRONIZED`	Represents the `synchronized` modifier (value `0x20`).
`TRANSIENT`	Represents the `transient` modifier (value `0x80`).
`VOLATILE`	Represents the `volatile` modifier (value `0x40`).
Query Methods	
`isAbstract()`	Determines if the modifier set includes the `abstract` modifier.
`isFinal()`	Determines if the modifier set includes the `final` modifier.
`isInterface()`	Determines if the modifier set includes the `interface` modifier.

MEMBER SUMMARY	
`isNative()`	Determines if the modifier set includes the `native` modifier.
`isPrivate()`	Determines if the modifier set includes the `private` modifier.
`isProtected()`	Determines if the modifier set includes the `protected` modifier.
`isPublic()`	Determines if the modifier set includes the `public` modifier.
`isStatic()`	Determines if the modifier set includes the `static` modifier.
1.2 `isStrict()`	Determines if the modifier set includes the `strictfp` modifier.
`isSynchronized()`	Determines if the modifier set includes the `synchronized` modifier.
`isTransient()`	Determines if the modifier set includes the `transient` modifier.
`isVolatile()`	Determines if the modifier set includes the `volatile` modifier.
Debugging Method	
`toString()`	Generates a string containing the printable representation of the modifier set.

a. To conserve space, these constants do not have member descriptions. For the description of a modifier, see the corresponding query method.

See Also

`Modifier` in *The Java Class Libraries, Second Edition, Volume 1.*

M

1.2 isStrict()

PURPOSE Determines if the modifier set includes the `strictfp` modifier.

SYNTAX `public static boolean isStrict(int mod)`

DESCRIPTION This method determines if the modifier set includes the `strictfp` modifier. The `strictfp` modifier is used to specify that a method's `float` and `double` parameter values are to be rounded to standard float values before any floating-point arithmetic is performed and that if the method returns a `float` or `double`, that it return a standard float value. `float` and `double` variables used in the method also use strict floating-point. Strict floating-point guarantees write-once-run-anywhere and no multiple rounding.

If the `strictfp` modifier is not present, the default is wide floating-point, which means to optimize the calculations for speed.

The `strictfp` modifier may be applied to a method, a class, or an interface. When applied to a class, it is applied to all members (including nested classes and constructors) and initializer code. When applied to an interface, it is applied to the initializer code of the interface. Constructors cannot be marked as `strictfp` at a source level but rather inherit strictness from their enclosing class. The `strictfp` modifier can be applied only to methods that have implementations and hence cannot be applied to instance methods of interfaces or of abstract classes that have no implementation.

PARAMETERS

`mod` An `int` representing a set of modifiers.

RETURNS `true` if mod includes `STRICT`.

EXAMPLE In this example, the class `C` defines two methods, `f1` and `f2`. `f1` is declared with the `strictfp` modifier. The example retrieves the reflection objects for the class `C` and its declared methods (`f1` and `f2`) and prints whether the object has the `strictfp` modifier.

```
import java.lang.reflect.Method;
import java.lang.reflect.Modifier;

public class Main {
    public static void main(String argv[]) {

        int cmods = C.class.getModifiers();
        printMods(C.class.getName(), cmods);

        Method[] mds  = C.class.getDeclaredMethods();

        for (int i = 0; i < mds.length; i++) {
            printMods(mds[i].getName(), mds[i].getModifiers());
        }
    }

    static void printMods(String item, int mods) {
        System.out.println(item + ":" +
            ((Modifier.isStrict(mods)) ? "strict" : "not strict"));
    }

    class C {
        public strictfp double f1(double dx) {
            return dx/(1L<<54);
        }

        public  double f2(double dx) {
            return dx/(1L<<54);
        }
    }
}
```

OUTPUT

```
> java Main
Main$C:not strict
f1:strict
f2:not strict
```

MulticastSocket

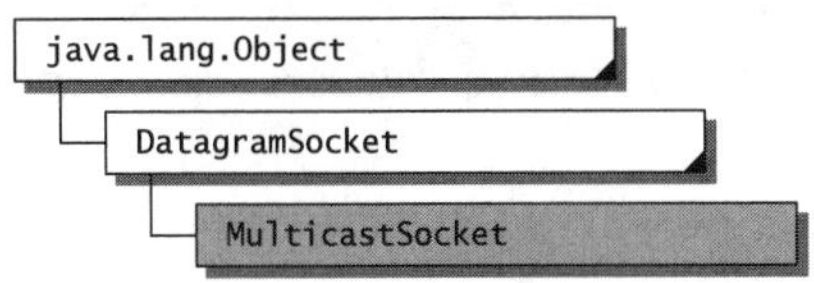

Syntax

```
public class MulticastSocket extends DatagramSocket
```

Description

The `MulticastSocket` class contains methods for sending and receiving multicast packets, although you can use it also to send and receive unicast datagrams. A program can communicate with other programs on the network by sending a *single* datagram packet to a *multicast group* consisting of zero or more members. The group is identified by a *multicast address*—an IP address to which group members subscribe. A *multicast packet* is a datagram packet that contains a multicast address. You can also send multicast packets using the `DatagramSocket` class (see `DatagramSocket.send()`).

See *The Java Class Libraries, Second Edition, Volume 1* for more information about this class.

Multicast Packet Transmission and Time-to-Live

Whether a datagram packet is sent to a single-host address or a multicast group is determined by the address contained in the packet. The socket from which the packet is sent can be either a `DatagramSocket` or a `MulticastSocket` (see the class example). Using `MulticastSocket` allows you control over the socket settings (time-to-live and network interface usage).

A multicast packet has a *time-to-live value*[1] that specifies the transmission range of this multicast packet, as received by members of the multicast group in other networks. The higher the time-to-live value, the higher the potential coverage of the multicast packet. The time-to-live value can be set per multicast socket (via `setTimeToLive()`) or can be specified on a per-packet basis using `MulticastSocket.send()`.

1. If the time-to-live value of a multicast packet is `0`, the multicast packet is sent to the local host, not to the network. If the time-to-live value of a multicast packet is `1`, the packet is transmitted using the local network multicast, which reaches all immediately neighboring members of the sender. If the multicast packet's time-to-live value is greater than `1`, the packet is also forwarded by *multicast routers* to all other networks that have members of the multicast group. If the multicast packet's time-to-live value is greater than `2`, the packet is again forwarded from those networks, and so on.

Changes for Version 1.2

The `getTTL()` and `setTTL()` methods are deprecated, replaced by `getTimeToLive()` and `setTimeToLive()`. The latter differ from the deprecated versions in that they accept and return `int` instead of `byte`. This allows time-to-live values to be specified more conveniently in the range `0` ≤ time-to-live ≤ `255`.

MEMBER SUMMARY	
Constructor	
`MulticastSocket()`	Constructs a `MulticastSocket` instance for sending/receiving multicast packets.
Method for Communicating	
`send()`	Sends a datagram packet using this `MulticastSocket`.
Multicast Group Membership Methods	
`joinGroup()`	Adds this `MulticastSocket` to a multicast group.
`leaveGroup()`	Removes this `MulticastSocket` from a multicast group.
Methods That Affect Multicast Packet Transmission	
`getInterface()`	Retrieves the address of the network interface used for this `MulticastSocket`.
1.2 `getTimeToLive()`	Retrieves the time-to-live value for multicast packets sent from this `MulticastSocket`.
`setInterface()`	Sets the address of the network interface to be used for this `MulticastSocket`.
1.2 `setTimeToLive()`	Sets the time-to-live value for multicast packets sent from this `MulticastSocket`.
Deprecated Methods	
Δ `getTTL()`	Replaced by `getTimeToLive()`.
Δ `setTTL()`	Replaced by `setTimeToLive()`.

M

See Also

`DatagramSocketImpl`.
`MulticastSocket` in *The Java Class Libraries, Second Edition, Volume 1.*

1.2 getTimeToLive()

PURPOSE Retrieves the time-to-live value for multicast packets sent from this `MulticastSocket`.

SYNTAX `public int getTimeToLive() throws IOException`

DESCRIPTION This method retrieves the time-to-live value for multicast packets sent from this `MulticastSocket`. A multicast packet sent from this `MulticastSocket` has a time-to-live value that specifies the transmission range of the packet. See the class description for details. The default time-to-live value is determined by `setTimeToLive()`. If `setTimeToLive()` has never been invoked on this `MulticastSocket`, the default is obtained from this `MulticastSocket`'s `DatagramSocketImpl`. Most implementations use a default of `1`, which means to multicast on the local network.

`getTimeToLive()` returns the default time-to-live value of packets sent from this `MulticastSocket`. You can override this default value on a per-packet basis by using the form of `send()` that accepts a time-to-live value.

RETURNS The time-to-live value for multicast packets sent from this `MulticastSocket`. `0` ≤ time-to-live ≤ `255`.

SEE ALSO `DatagramSocketImpl.getTimeToLive()`, `setTimeToLive()`.

EXAMPLE See `setTTL()`.

Δ getTTL() *DEPRECATED*

PURPOSE Replaced by `getTimeToLive()`.

SYNTAX `public byte getTTL() throws IOException`

1.2 CHANGES This method is deprecated in Version 1.2.

DEPRECATION The `getTimeToLive()` method allows the time-to-live value to be specified more conveniently. Replace the usage of `getTTL()`, as in

```
byte ttl = multisock.getTTL();
```

with

```
int ttl = multisock.getTimeToLive();
```

RETURNS An unsigned 8-bit number specifying the time-to-live value for multicast packets sent from this `MulticastSocket`. `0` ≤ time-to-live ≤ `255`.

EXCEPTIONS

`IOException`

If an IO error occurred while attempting to set the time-to-live value of this `MulticastSocket`.

1.2 setTimeToLive()

PURPOSE Sets the time-to-live value for multicast packets sent from this `MulticastSocket`.

SYNTAX `public void setTimeToLive(int ttl) throws IOException`

M

DESCRIPTION This method sets the time-to-live value for multicast packets sent from this `MulticastSocket`. A multicast packet sent from this `MulticastSocket` has a time-to-live value that specifies the transmission range of the packet. See the class description for details. The default time-to-live value is determined by this socket's `DatagramSocketImpl`. Most implementations use a default of `1`, which means to multicast on the local network.

This method sets to `ttl` the default time-to-live value of packets sent from this `MulticastSocket`. Subsequent calls to `getTimeToLive()` will return this time-to-live value. Subsequent calls to `send()` will use this time-to-live value. You can override this default value on a per-packet basis by using the form of `send()` that accepts a time-to-live value.

PARAMETERS

`ttl` The time-to-live value for packets sent from this `MulticastSocket`. `0` ≤ `ttl` ≤ `255`.

EXCEPTIONS

`IOException`

If an IO error occurred while attempting to set the time-to-live value of this `MulticastSocket`.

SEE ALSO `DatagramSocketImpl.setTimeToLive()`, `getTimeToLive()`.

M

Δ setTTL() *DEPRECATED*

PURPOSE Replaced by `setTimeToLive()`.

SYNTAX `public void setTTL(byte ttl) throws IOException`

1.2 CHANGES This method is deprecated in Version 1.2.

DEPRECATION The `setTimeToLive()` method allows the time-to-live value to be specified more conveniently. Replace the usage of `setTTL()`, as in

```
byte ttl = ...;
multisock.setTTL(ttl);
```

with

```
int ttl = ...;
multisock.setTimeToLive(ttl);
```

PARAMETERS

`ttl` An unsigned 8-bit number specifying the time-to-live value for multicast packets sent from this `MulticastSocket`. `0` ≤ time-to-live ≤ `255`.

EXCEPTIONS

`IOException`

If an IO error occurred while attempting to set the time-to-live value of this `MulticastSocket`.

NetPermission

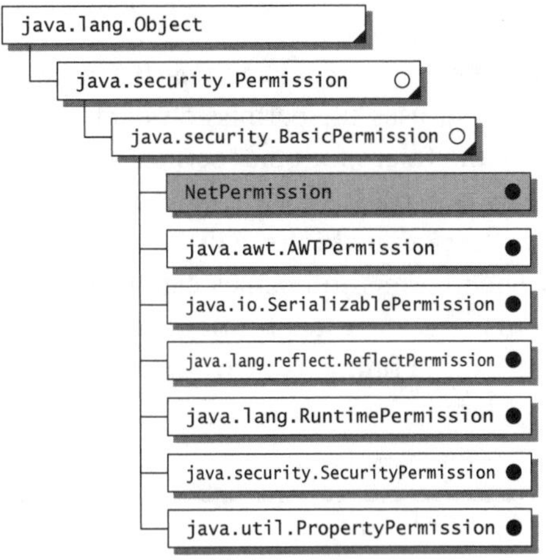

Syntax

```
public final class NetPermission extends BasicPermission
```

Description

The `NetPermission` class represents a request to perform a network operation. It is used internally by the Java runtime system to enforce its security policy. A `NetPermission` object has a *permission name* that identifies the network operation to check. For example, the `NetPermission` with the name `"setDefaultAuthenticator"` is used by the `Authenticator` class to check whether the caller is allowed to set the default authenticator for the application. This check is performed with the help of the *access controller* (see `java.security.AccessController`). If the access controller determines that the caller is not allowed, an `AccessControlException` (a subclass of `SecurityException`) is thrown.

A brief discussion of the Version 1.2 access control model is given in the `SecurityManager` class description. More information about Version 1.2's security model and framework is available at `http://java.sun.com/products/jdk/1.2/docs/guide/security/index.html`.

Usage

Applets and applications usually do not directly use the `NetPermission` class. This class is used internally by the Java runtime system to enforce its security policy when certain network operations are attempted. For example, when a program tries to install an `Authenticator` class, `Authenticator.setDefault()` will uses the `NetPermission("setDefaultAuthenticator")` object to check whether the caller has permission to do so.

An application may explicitly create a `NetPermission` object and use `SecurityManager.checkPermission()` or `AccessController.checkPermission()` to check whether

N

the security policy has granted it such permission. But the act of trying to perform the operation automatically triggers such a check, so there is seldom a reason to duplicate it.

The NetPermission Name

The permission name of a `NetPermission` identifies the network operation that is being checked. The Java runtime system uses the permission names listed in Table 12. It may use additional permission names in the future for other permissions relating to network operations. An application is also free to add and use new permission names to represent other types of network operations, but such `NetPermissions` will be known only to the application that defines them. Nevertheless, such permission names can appear in the security policy and be checked using the `AccessController`. An application that needs to define and use new permission names is usually better off defining its own `Permission` subclass to avoid future conflicts with the Java runtime system.

Permission Name	Request
`setDefaultAuthenticator`	Install an authenticator for requesting password information.
`specifyStreamHandler`	Use a user-specified `URLStreamHandler` when creating a `URL`.
`requestPasswordAuthentication`	Request password information from the user.

TABLE 12: `NetPermission` Names Used by the Java Runtime System.

Implies

The permission name of a `NetPermission` is a case-sensitive string. It is used to check whether one `NetPermission` is equal to another `NetPermission`. It is also used to check whether one `NetPermission` *implies* another `NetPermission`. Permission *A* implies permission *B* means if permission *A* is granted, so will permission *B*. Following are the rules for how "implies" works for `NetPermission` objects.

- Two `NetPermissions` with the same permission name imply each other.
- A `NetPermission` with a permission name of the form *pname*`.*` implies any `NetPermission` whose permission name has the prefix "*pname*.". For example, a `NetPermission` with a permission name `"some.op.*"` implies any `NetPermission` whose permission name has the prefix `"some.op."`.
- A `NetPermission` with the permission name `"*"` implies any `NetPermission`.

setDefaultAuthenticator

The `Authenticator` class is used by networking code to obtain authentication information from users. An application invokes `Authenticator.setDefault()` to install an authenticator that subsequent requests for authentication information will use. This method uses a `Net-`

Permission with the permission name "setDefaultAuthenticator" to check whether the caller has permission to call this method.

specifyStreamHandler
The URL class represents a Uniform Resource Locator (URL). Associated with each URL instance is a *URL stream handler* that is responsible for implementing the protocol associated with the URL. See URLStreamHandler. The Java runtime system has a default policy for creating URL stream handlers. You can override this default by using a form of the URL constructor that accepts a URLStreamHandler. That constructor uses a NetPermission with the permission name "specifyStreamHandler" to check whether the caller has permission to use the nondefault URL stream handler.

requestPasswordAuthentication
After an authenticator has been installed, any part of the program can then invoke Authenticator.requestPasswordAuthentication() that will use the installed authenticator to ask the user for password information. Authenticator.requestPasswordAuthentication() uses a NetPermission with the permission name "requestPasswordAuthentication" to check whether the caller has permission to call it.

MEMBER SUMMARY	
Constructor	
NetPermission()	Constructs a new NetPermission instance.

N

See Also
Authenticator, java.security.BasicPermission, PasswordAuthentication, java.lang.SecurityManager, URL, URLStreamHandler.

Example
The Authenticator class example was modified by adding a security manager. This means that it will check the security policy when Authenticator.setDefault() and Authenticator.requestPasswordAuthentication() are called. The policy file that the program uses grants (to everybody) permission to install the authenticator but no permission to request authentication information (which is typically not a logical setup). You can grant different permissions in the policy file to see how it affects the program.

Main.java
```
    // Install security manager
    System.setSecurityManager(new SecurityManager());

    // Install authenticator
    Authenticator.setDefault(new SomeAuthenticator(new Main()));
```

.policy

```
keystore ".keystore";
grant {
        permission java.net.NetPermission "setDefaultAuthenticator";
      };
```

OUTPUT

```
>java -Djava.security.policy=.policy Main
java.security.AccessControlException: access denied
        (java.net.NetPermission requestPasswordAuthentication )
        at java.security.AccessControlContext.checkPermission(Compiled Code)
        at java.security.AccessController.checkPermission(Compiled Code)
        at java.lang.SecurityManager.checkPermission(Compiled Code)
        at java.net.Authenticator.requestPasswordAuthentication(Compiled Code)
        at Main.actionPerformed(Compiled Code)
        at java.awt.Button.processActionEvent(Compiled Code)
        at java.awt.Button.processEvent(Compiled Code)
        at java.awt.Component.dispatchEventImpl(Compiled Code)
        at java.awt.Component.dispatchEvent(Compiled Code)
        at java.awt.EventQueue.dispatchEvent(Compiled Code)
        at java.awt.EventDispatchThread.run(Compiled Code)
```

NetPermission()

PURPOSE Constructs a new `NetPermission` instance.

SYNTAX

```
public NetPermission (String pname)
public NetPermission (String pname, String actions)
```


DESCRIPTION This constructor constructs a new `NetPermission` object using the name `pname`. The `actions` parameter is ignored.

PARAMETERS

`actions`	Ignored. Should be `null`.
`pname`	A non-`null` string, such as `"*"` or a permission name from Table 12.

ObjectInputStream

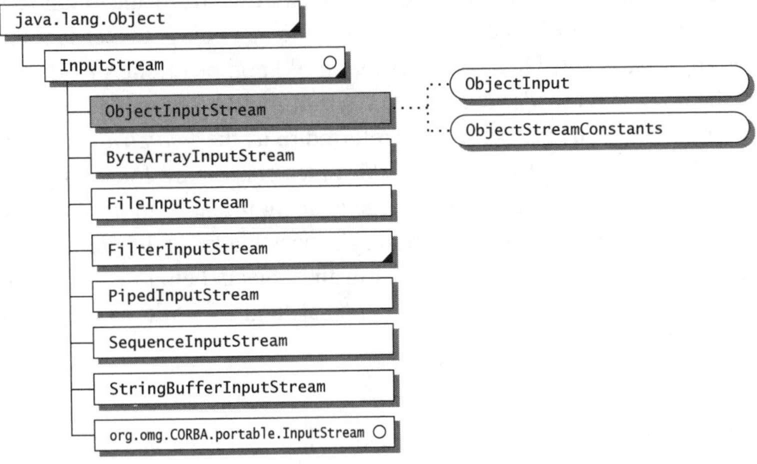

Syntax

```
public class ObjectInputStream extends InputStream implements ObjectInput,
    ObjectStreamConstants
```

Description

The `ObjectInputStream` class is used for deserializing primitive data and objects (including arrays and strings) read from an input stream. The data in the input stream was produced by using a corresponding `ObjectOutputStream`.

See *The Java Class Libraries, Second Edition, Volume 1* for more information about this class.

O

Changes for Version 1.2

Object Substitution

When deserializing data into an object, `ObjectInputStream` allows a trusted subclass of `ObjectInputStream`'s to replace the object just deserialized with a compatible object. This is called *object substitution.* In Version 1.1, this was done by the subclass's invoking `enableResolveObject()` and supplying an implementation of `resolveObject()` that `readObject()` invoked in order to do the replacement. In Version 1.2, object substitution is more flexible. The subclass can use `enableResolveObject()` and `resolveObject()`, or not use the `readObject()` implementation at all, by supplying an implementation for the new method, `readObjectOverride()`.

Class Loading

When data is deserialized into an object, the class for that object is loaded by using the top-most non-`null` class loader on the execution stack, starting from the method that invoked `readObject()`). If no non-`null` class loader is found, the `null` class loader is used. This policy has not changed in Version 1.2. However, the notion of "non-`null` class loader" has changed. In Version 1.1, the `null` class loader loads the Java runtime classes as well as the application's classes. In Version 1.2, the `null` class loader (referred to as the *bootstrap class loader* in Version 1.2) loads only the Java runtime classes. All other classes are loaded by non-`null` class loaders. See `ClassLoader` for details. This change is of significance to library code that deserializes objects on behalf of the caller. If the library's class loader is different from the caller's, the library might not be able to find the classes of the objects being deserialized. To find the classes, the library must subclass `ObjectInputStream` and override `resolveClass()` to use the caller's class loader.

Security

The `ObjectInputStream` class has been changed to use the Version 1.2 security model (see `SecurityManager` for an overview). In Version 1.1, object substitution could be performed only by a *trusted subclass*, a subclass that has been loaded by the system class loader. In Version 1.2, when a security manager has been installed, the caller that is using the `ObjectInputStream` subclass and the subclass itself must have been granted `SerializablePermission("enableSubstitution")` in order for `enableResolveObject()` to succeed. For the type of object substitution that involves `readObjectOverride()`, when a security manager has been installed, the caller and subclass must have been granted `SerializablePermission("enableSubclassImplementation")`.

O

Other Changes

A new protected constructor has been added to `ObjectInputStream`. This constructor is used by a subclass of `ObjectInputStream`'s if the subclass wants to have complete control over the implementation of the `ObjectInputStream` (by providing an implementation for the `readObjectOverride()` method).

The `readFields()` method has been added for reading all of the serializable fields from the serialized form of an object.

The `defaultReadObject()` and `enableResolveObject()` methods are no longer final. `defaultReadObject()` is described in *The Java Class Libraries, Second Edition, Volume 1.*

The `readLine()` method has been deprecated.

MEMBER SUMMARY	
Constructor	
Δ `ObjectInputStream()`	Constructs an `ObjectInputStream` instance.
Methods Used by a Class's `readObject()`	
Δ `defaultReadObject()`	Reads the object being deserialized.[a]
1.2 `readFields()`	Reads the serializable fields of the object being deserialized from this `ObjectInputStream`.
`registerValidation()`	Registers an object to be validated.
Stream Customization Methods	
Δ `enableResolveObject()`	Enables/disables this `ObjectInputStream` to replace objects read from this `ObjectInputStream`.
1.2 `readObjectOverride()`	Reads an object from this `ObjectInputStream`.
`readStreamHeader()`	Reads and verifies the stream header from the underlying input stream.
`resolveClass()`	Loads the local class represented by the class descriptor read from this `ObjectInputStream`.
`resolveObject()`	Replaces an object with another object during deserialization.
ObjectInput Methods	
`available()`	Determines the number of bytes that can be read for primitive data from this `ObjectInputStream`.
`close()`	Closes this `ObjectInputStream`.
`read()`	Reads one or more bytes from this `ObjectInputStream`.
Δ `readObject()`	Reads an object from this `ObjectInputStream`.
DataInput Methods	
`readBoolean()`	Reads a `boolean` from this `ObjectInputStream`.
`readByte()`	Reads a `byte` from this `ObjectInputStream`.
`readChar()`	Reads a 16-bit Unicode `char` from this `ObjectInputStream`.
`readDouble()`	Reads a 64-bit `double` from this `ObjectInputStream`.
`readFloat()`	Reads a 32-bit `float` from this `ObjectInputStream`.
`readFully()`	Reads the requested number of bytes from this `ObjectInputStream`.
`readInt()`	Reads a 32-bit `int` from this `ObjectInputStream`.
`readLong()`	Reads a 64-bit `long` from this `ObjectInputStream`.
`readShort()`	Reads a 16-bit `short` from this `ObjectInputStream`.
`readUnsignedByte()`	Reads an unsigned 8-bit `byte` from this `ObjectInputStream`.
`readUnsignedShort()`	Reads an unsigned 16-bit `short` from this `ObjectInputStream`.
`readUTF()`	Reads a Unicode string from this `ObjectInputStream`.

Continued

O

MEMBER SUMMARY

DataInput Methods *(Continued)*

`skipBytes()`	Skips the requested number of bytes of primitive data from this `ObjectInputStream`.
Deprecated Method	
Δ `readLine()`	Replaced by `BufferedReader.readLine()`.

a. This method is described in *The Java Class Libraries, Second Edition, Volume 1*. Its only change is that it is no longer final.

See Also

`ObjectInputStream.GetField`, `SerializablePermission`.
`ObjectInputStream` in *The Java Class Libraries, Second Edition, Volume 1*.

Δ enableResolveObject()

PURPOSE
Enables/disables this `ObjectInputStream` to replace objects read from this `ObjectInputStream`.

SYNTAX
```
protected boolean enableResolveObject(boolean enable) throws
    SecurityException
```

DESCRIPTION
This method enables or disables this `ObjectInputStream` to replace objects read from the `ObjectInputStream`. After an object has been read and before it is returned by `readObject()`, it can be replaced by another object by using `resolveObject()`. By default, `ObjectInputStream` does not allow this replacement. A subclass of `ObjectInputStream`'s must call `enableResolve-Object()` with `true` in order to allow it.

When a security manager has been installed, the caller must have been granted `SerializablePermission("enableSubstitution")`.

1.2 CHANGES
In Version 1.1, this method was final. Also, in Version 1.1 this method could be invoked only from an instance of an `ObjectInputStream` subclass that was loaded by the system class loader. In Version 1.2, the new security model is used (see the class description).

PARAMETERS

`enable`
If `true`, allows objects read from this stream to be replaced. If `false`, objects read from this stream cannot be replaced.

RETURNS
The previous setting before `enableResolveObject()` was invoked: `true` if replacement was previously enabled and `false` otherwise.

O

EXCEPTIONS

`SecurityException`
If `enable` is `true` and the security manager does not grant the caller permission to call this method.

SEE ALSO `java.lang.ClassLoader`, `ObjectOutputStream.enableReplaceObject()`, `resolveObject()`, `SerializablePermission`.

EXAMPLE See `resolveObject()` in *The Java Class Libraries, Second Edition, Volume 1.*

Δ ObjectInputStream()

PURPOSE Creates an `ObjectInputStream` instance.

SYNTAX

```
public ObjectInputStream(InputStream in) throws IOException,
   StreamCorruptedException
```

SINCE 1.2

```
protected ObjectInputStream() throws IOException,
   SecurityException
```

DESCRIPTION The public constructor creates an instance of `ObjectInputStream` for the input stream `in`. The constructor first reads a stream header that verifies whether `in` contains serialized data written by an `ObjectInputStream` and verifies that this version of the `ObjectInputStream` implementation is compatible with the version of the `ObjectOutputStream` used to write out the data. If this verification fails, a `StreamCorruptedException` is thrown. The constructor blocks until the header is completely read from `in`.

After the header has been verified, methods can be invoked on this newly created stream to read data from `in` for deserialization into primitive data and objects expected by those methods.

The protected constructor is used by a subclass's constructor if that subclass will be providing an implementation of `readObjectOverride()`. When `readObject()` is invoked on such a subclass, its `readObjectOverride()` method is called and the implementation provided by `ObjectInputStream` is not used. This constructor should be used (and `readObjectOverride()` overridden) only if the subclass is completely reimplementing `ObjectInputStream`. Notice that the protected constructor does not accept any arguments, so it is free to deal with streams and headers any way it chooses. Unlike the public constructor, this constructor does not perform any initialization. Therefore the subclass must also override `close()` because `ObjectInputStream.close()` uses private fields initialized by the public constructor.

To successfully use the protected constructor, the caller of the constructor must have been granted `SerializablePermission("enableSubclassImplementation")`. Otherwise, a `SecurityException` is thrown.

O

1.2 CHANGES The protected constructor is new in Version 1.2.

PARAMETERS

`in` The non-`null` input stream from which to read the serialized data.

EXCEPTIONS

`IOException`
If an IO error occurs while reading from `in`.

`SecurityException`
If the caller has not been granted `SerializablePermission("enableSubclassImmplementation")`.

`StreamCorruptedException`
If the serialized data in `in` is corrupted.

SEE ALSO `readObjectOverride()`, `SerializablePermission`.

EXAMPLE This example reads a serialized object from a file. See `readObjectOverride()` for an example of using the protected constructor.

```
try {
    ObjectInputStream in =
        new ObjectInputStream(new FileInputStream("test.ser"));
    System.out.println(in.readObject());
    in.close();
} catch (ClassNotFoundException e) {
    System.out.println(e);
} catch (IOException e) {
    System.out.println(e);
}
```

O

1.2 readFields()

PURPOSE Reads the serializable fields of the object being deserialized from this `ObjectInputStream`.

SYNTAX

```
public ObjectInputStream.GetField readFields() throws
   IOException, ClassNotFoundException, NotActiveException
```

DESCRIPTION This method is usually called by the `readObject()` method of a `Serializable` or `Externalizable` object. It is used to read all of the serializable fields of the object at once, as compared with methods such as `readBoolean()` and `readInt()`, which read the next field. If you use `readFields()`, you should not use the other `readXXX()` methods to read individual fields, and vice versa. (You can use the `readXXX()` methods to read optional data.) Once you've invoked `readFields()`, you can use the `ObjectInputStream.GetField.get()` methods to retrieve individual fields.

RETURNS A non-`null` instance of `ObjectInputStream.GetField` containing the serialized fields of the object being deserialized.

EXCEPTIONS

`ClassNotFoundException`
If the class definition of the object being deserialized cannot be found.

`NotActiveException`
If no object is currently being deserialized.

`IOException`
If an IO error was encountered while reading the fields from this stream.

SEE ALSO `ObjectInputStream.GetField`.

EXAMPLE See the `ObjectInputStream.GetField` class example.

Δ readLine() *DEPRECATED*

PURPOSE Replace by `BufferedReader.readLine()`.

SYNTAX `public String readLine() throws IOException`

1.2 CHANGES This method is deprecated in Version 1.2.

DEPRECATION This method reads a sequence of bytes terminated by `\n`, `\r`, `\r\n`, or end-of-stream. Each byte read is converted into a character by filling the high-order byte of each character with zero. The use of this method is deprecated because, in general, it does not properly convert the bytes read into strings. Characters should be serialized as `String` objects, as a sequence of 16-bit characters, or as a sequence of bytes using a specific character encoding. When the characters are deserialized, the `String` object is read using `readObject()`; the sequence of 16-bit characters is read using `readChar()`; and the sequence of encoded bytes are read into a `byte` array and converted into a `String` using the appropriate byte-to-character encoding.

RETURNS A string containing the bytes of the line read (not including the line terminating character). `null` if no bytes are read before the end-of-stream is reached.

EXCEPTIONS

`IOException`
If an IO error occurs.

SEE ALSO `BufferedReader.readLine()`, `java.lang.String()`, `java.lang.String.getBytes()`.

Δ readObject()

PURPOSE Reads an object from this `ObjectInputStream`.

SYNTAX
```
public final Object readObject() throws OptionalDataException,
    ClassNotFoundException, IOException
```

O

DESCRIPTION This method reads data from the underlying input stream, deserializes it into an object, and returns it to the caller. If the object's fields contain references to other objects, those objects and their references are also read and deserialized to form a complete graph of objects. Each object is deserialized by using one of the following methods of the class:

- `readExternal()` if the class implements `Externalizable`
- `defaultReadObject()` if the class implements `Serializable` but does not define a `readObject()` method
- `readObject()` if the class implements `Serializable` and defines a `readObject()` method

If this `ObjectInputStream` has enabled the replacement of objects read from its stream, `resolveObject()` is invoked for each object as the object is deserialized. If this `ObjectInputStream` has any registered validation instances, those are invoked to validate the object(s) before this method returns. (See `registerValidation()`.)

If `readObject()` is being called on a subclass of `ObjectInputStream`'s that was created using the protected `ObjectInputStream` constructor, `readObject()` simply returns the result of `readObjectOverride()`.

If a class defines a `writeObject()` method that writes out its required data followed by its optional data, then the corresponding `readObject()` method must first invoke `defaultReadObject()` to deserialize the required data. Then it reads and deserializes any optional data. See `Serializable` for an explanation of required data and optional data.

If an exception is encountered during `readObject()`, the validity of the rest of the data in this `ObjectInputStream` is suspect and that data should not be used any further.

O

1.2 CHANGES `readObjectOverride()` did not exist in Version 1.1 and hence `readObject()` did not use it.

RETURNS The object read from this `ObjectInputStream`; `null` if the next object in this stream is `null`.

EXCEPTIONS

`ClassNotFoundException`
If the class of the object (or an object reachable from the object) being read and deserialized cannot be found. The exception's message will contain the name of the class that is not found.

`EOFException`
If end-of-stream is reached before an object can be read.

`InvalidClassException`
If the deserialized class cannot be restored—for example, if the constructor required is not accessible or is nonexistent—or if the class cannot be instanti-

ated.

`IOException`
If an IO error occurs while reading from the underlying input stream.

`OptionalDataException`
If primitive data is found in the stream when an object was expected (that is, if this method is invoked when a call to `available()` would return a nonzero value).

`StreamCorruptedException`
If the handle to a previously serialized object cannot be deserialized because the serialized object was not found in the stream, or if the class descriptor for the class is not in the stream, or if the stream's control data is otherwise inconsistent with its actual content.

SEE ALSO `ObjectInputStream()`, `readObjectOverride()`, `registerValidation()`, `resolveObject()`.

EXAMPLE See `ObjectInputStream()`.

1.2 readObjectOverride()

PURPOSE Reads an object from this `ObjectInputStream`.

SYNTAX
```
protected Object readObjectOverride() throws
    OptionalDataException, ClassNotFoundException, IOException
```

DESCRIPTION This method reads an object from this `ObjectInputStream`. Its default implementation returns `null`. This method is called only in subclasses of `ObjectInputStream` that have used the protected `ObjectInputStream` constructor. Such subclasses must provide implementations for this method that read, deserialize, and return an object.

RETURNS A possibly `null` object deserialized from this `ObjectInputStream`.

EXCEPTIONS

`ClassNotFoundException`
If the class definition of the object being deserialized is not found.

`IOException`
If an IO error was encountered while reading the object from this `ObjectInputStream`.

`OptionalDataException`
If the method found primitive data instead of object data in the serialized stream.

SEE ALSO `ObjectInputStream()`, `readObject()`, `SerializablePermission`.

EXAMPLE This example demonstrates how to completely override the functionality of `readObject()` by using the protected `ObjectInputStream` constructor and

O

supplying an implementation for `readObjectOverride()`. Notice that the subclass overrides the `close()` method to avoid `ObjectInputStream.close()` being called. Calling `ObjectInputStream.close()` would have caused a `NullPointerException` because the protected constructor does not initialize the stream used by `close()`.

```
import java.io.*;

class Main {
    public static void main(String[] args) {
       try {
           ObjectInputStream in =
               new TestObjInputStream(new FileInputStream("test.ser"));
           System.out.println(in.readObject());
           in.close();
       } catch (ClassNotFoundException e) {
           System.out.println(e);
       } catch (IOException e) {
           System.out.println(e);
       }
    }

    static class TestObjInputStream extends ObjectInputStream {
        InputStream in;

        TestObjInputStream(InputStream in) throws IOException {
            super(); // use protected constructor
            this.in = in;
        }

        protected Object readObjectOverride() throws OptionalDataException,
            ClassNotFoundException, IOException {
            return ("testing"); // bogus implementation, just for demo
        }

        public void close() throws IOException {
            in.close();
        }
    }
}
```

ObjectInputStream.GetField

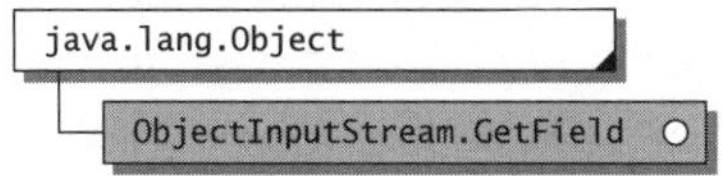

Syntax

```
abstract public static class ObjectInputStream.GetField
```

Description

The abstract class `ObjectInputStream.GetField` represents *serializable fields* of an object read from an `ObjectInputStream`. A serializable field is a field in a *serializable class* that has been specified by that class to be serializable. A serializable class is a class that implements the `Serializable` interface. It has two ways of specifying which of its fields are serializable: default serialization and explicit serialization. See `ObjectStreamField` for a description of the two ways. This class is used to represent fields that were serialized using either default or explicit serialization.

Usage

Once a serializable field exists for a class, it must exist in all future versions of the class so as to maintain compatibility. During deserialization, if a class evolves such that it no longer has a field with a name that maps to the serialized field, it uses `ObjectInputStream.GetField` to access the serializable field's value so that the value can be mapped to (or used within) the evolved class's implementation. Such a class would declare a `readObject()` method that uses `ObjectInputStream.readFields()` to read all of the serializable fields of the serialized object. `readObject()` then would use the `ObjectInputStream.GetField` instance returned by `ObjectInputStream.readFields()` to access individual serializable fields.

In the following example, supposed the fields `strField` and `intField` from the old implementation have been renamed to `newStrField` and `newIntField`. The new implementation's `readObject()` method would use the `ObjectInputStream.GetField`'s `get()` methods to retrieve the values of the old fields and assign them to the new fields.

```
private static final ObjectStreamField[] serialPersistentFields = {
    new ObjectStreamField("strField", String.class),
    new ObjectStreamField("intField", Integer.TYPE),
};
...
private void readObject(ObjectInputStream in)
    throws IOException, ClassNotFoundException {
    // Read in serial fields
    ObjectInputStream.GetField pfields = in.readFields();
    // Assign serialized values to fields
    String newStrField = (String)pfields.get("strField", "out-of-luck");
    int newIntField = (int)pfields.get("intField", 1000);
}
```

Defaults

When you use the `get()` method to get a serializable field's value from its corresponding serialized data, you must always supply a *default*. This default will be returned if the serialized data does not contain a value for the field even though the field is a valid serializable field. That is, the serializable class knows about this serializable field, but the serialized data does not contain a value for it. This can happen, for example, if the evolved class has added a new serializable field.

MEMBER SUMMARY	
Reading Serializable Field Methods	
`get()`	Retrieves the value of a serializable field.
`defaulted()`	Determines whether the default of a serializable field will be used.
ObjectStreamClass Method	
`getObjectStreamClass()`	Retrieves the `ObjectStreamClass` that describes the serializable fields.

See Also

`ObjectInputStream.readFields()`, `ObjectOutputStream.PutField`, `ObjectStreamClass`, `ObjectStreamField`.
`Serializable` in *The Java Class Libraries, Second Edition, Volume 1.*

Example

See the following `defaulted()` and the `ObjectStreamField.getName()` examples.

defaulted()

PURPOSE Determines whether the default of a serializable field will be used.

SYNTAX
```
abstract public boolean defaulted(String fname) throws
    IOException, IllegalArgumentException
```

DESCRIPTION This method determines whether the default supplied to the `get()` method will be used when the field with `fname` is read from the serialized data.

PARAMETERS

`fname` The non-`null` string name of the field.

RETURNS `true` if a default will be used for the field; `false` otherwise.

EXCEPTIONS

`IllegalArgumentException`

If `fname` does not identify a serializable field.

`IOException`

If an IO error occurred while accessing the serialized data.

SEE ALSO `get()`.

EXAMPLE This example is similar to the `ObjectStreamField` class example. `ClassA` declares an explicit serializable field, `strField`. The class then evolves to have two serializable fields, `strField` and `intField`. Previously serialized data of the old `ClassA` will contain only `strField`. When the evolved class tries to get a value for `intField` from old serialized data, it gets the default supplied (`1000`). `readObject()` also gets the `ObjectStreamClass` and uses it to list all of the serializable fields for illustrative purposes.

Note: `GetField` and `PutField` are not strictly necessary for the implementation evolution shown in this example, although `GetField` is useful in assigning a nonzero default to `intField`. Default serialization can deal with the `intField`'s not getting initialized by the old serialization data, but `intField` will be initialized to its Java default value, which is `0` for numeric primitive types.

To run this example, first compile `ClassA.java-old` and `Main.java` and run `Main` to write the serializable data into the file `ClassA1.ser`. Next, compile `ClassA.java-new` and `MainRead.java`. When you run `MainRead`, it will read the old serialized data in the file `ClassA1.ser` and use the default `1000` for `intField`. See the `ObjectStreamField` class example for a listing of `MainRead.java`.

ClassA.java-old

```
import java.io.*;

public class ClassA implements Serializable {
    String strField;
    int intField;

    /**
     * @serialField strField String null, empty string, or any String value
     */
    private static final ObjectStreamField[] serialPersistentFields = {
        new ObjectStreamField("strField", String.class),
    };

    public ClassA(String one, int two) {
        strField = one;
        intField = two;
    }

    private void readObject(ObjectInputStream in)
        throws IOException, ClassNotFoundException {

            // Read in serial fields
            ObjectInputStream.GetField pfields = in.readFields();

            // Assign serialized values to fields
```

```
                strField = (String)pfields.get("strField", "out-of-luck");
        }

        public String toString() {
            return "strField: " + strField + " intField: " + intField;
        }
    }
```

ClassA.java-new

```
import java.io.*;

public class ClassA implements Serializable {
    String strField;
    int intField;

    /**
     * @serialField strField String null, empty string or any String value
     * @serialField intField Integer Any integer value
     */
    private static final ObjectStreamField[] serialPersistentFields = {
        new ObjectStreamField("strField", String.class),
        new ObjectStreamField("intField", Integer.TYPE),
    };

    public ClassA(String one, int two) {
        strField = one;
        intField = two;
    }

    private void readObject(ObjectInputStream in)
        throws IOException, ClassNotFoundException {

            // Read in serial fields
            ObjectInputStream.GetField pfields = in.readFields();

            // Assign serialized values to fields
            strField = (String)pfields.get("strField", "out-of-luck");
            if (pfields.defaulted("intField")) {
                System.out.println("intField will use default");
            }
            intField = (int)pfields.get("intField", 1000);

            // Get ObjectStreamClass to get ObjectStreamFields for each field
            ObjectStreamClass objclass = pfields.getObjectStreamClass();
            ObjectStreamField[] fields = objclass.getFields();

            // See what we got
            for (int i = 0; i < fields.length; i++) {
                print(fields[i]);
            }
    }

    private void print(ObjectStreamField fd) {
        System.out.println("name: " + fd.getName());
        System.out.println("type: " + fd.getType());
        System.out.println("type code: " + fd.getTypeCode());
        System.out.println("type string: " + fd.getTypeString());
        System.out.println("primitive: " + fd.isPrimitive());
        System.out.println("offset: " + fd.getOffset());
```

```
    }

    public String toString() {
        return "strField: " + strField + " intField: " + intField;
    }
}
```

Main.java

```
import java.io.*;

class Main {
    public static void main(String[] args) {
        try {
            // Write them out
            FileOutputStream f = new FileOutputStream("ClassA1.ser");
            ObjectOutput out = new ObjectOutputStream(f);

            out.writeObject(new ClassA("hello", 500));
            out.flush();
            out.close();

            // Read it back
            FileInputStream f2 = new FileInputStream("ClassA1.ser");
            ObjectInputStream in = new ObjectInputStream(f2);
            ClassA obj = (ClassA) in.readObject();
            in.close();

            System.out.println(obj);
        } catch (IOException e) {
            e.printStackTrace();
        } catch (ClassNotFoundException e) {
            e.printStackTrace();
        }
    }
}
```


OUTPUT

```
>java MainRead
intField will use default
name: strField
type: class java.lang.Object
type code: L
type string: Ljava/lang/String;
primitive: false
offset: 0
strField: hello intField: 1000
```

get()

PURPOSE Retrieves the value of a serializable field.

SYNTAX
```
abstract public boolean get(String fname, boolean defvalue)
   throws IOException, IllegalArgumentException
abstract public byte get(String fname, byte defvalue) throws
   IOException, IllegalArgumentException
abstract public char get(String fname, char defvalue) throws
   IOException, IllegalArgumentException
abstract public short get(String fname, short defvalue) throws
   IOException, IllegalArgumentException
abstract public int get(String fname, int defvalue) throws
   IOException, IllegalArgumentException
abstract public float get(String fname, float defvalue) throws
   IOException, IllegalArgumentException
abstract public long get(String fname, long defvalue) throws
   IOException, IllegalArgumentException
abstract public double get(String fname, double defvalue) throws
   IOException, IllegalArgumentException
abstract public Object get(String fname, Object defvalue) throws
   IOException, IllegalArgumentException
```

DESCRIPTION This method returns the value of the serializable field, `fname`, from the serialized data. If the field is valid but does not have a value in the serialized data, then `defvalue` is returned. See the class description for a description of defaults and valid fields.

O

PARAMETERS

`defvalue` The value to use if `fname` does not have a value in the serialized data. If `defvalue` is nonprimitive, it can be `null`.

`fname` A non-`null` string that is the name of the serializable field.

RETURNS The value of the serializable field named `fname`, or `defvalue` if the field does not have a value in the serialized data.

EXCEPTIONS

`IllegalArgumentException`
If `fname` does not name a valid serializable field, or if the type of `defvalue` is not equal to the type of the actual serialized field.

SEE ALSO `ObjectOutputStream.PutField.put()`.

EXAMPLE See the `defaulted()` and the `ObjectStreamField` class examples.

getObjectStreamClass()

PURPOSE Retrieves the `ObjectStreamClass` that describes the serializable fields.

SYNTAX `abstract public ObjectStreamClass getObjectStreamClass()`

DESCRIPTION When an instance of a class is serialized to a stream, a description of the class is serialized and added to the serialized data as an `ObjectStreamClass` instance. Among the information that the `ObjectStreamClass` instance contains is a list of the class's serializable fields. When deserializing an object, you can obtain its `ObjectStreamClass` by invoking `getObjectStreamClass()` on the `ObjectInputStream.GetField` read from the serialized stream. You can then invoke `getFields()` on the `ObjectStreamClass` to list the serializable fields. Note that this information is read from the serialized stream. So, if a serializable class has evolved, its (new) `ObjectStreamClass` might differ from the one that is read from the serialized stream.

RETURNS The non-`null` `ObjectStreamClass` associated with these serializable fields.

SEE ALSO `ObjectStreamClass`.

EXAMPLE See `defaulted()`.

java.io

ObjectOutputStream

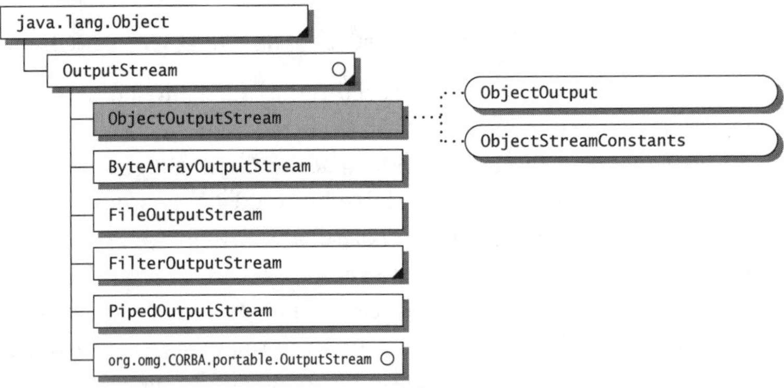

Syntax

```
public class ObjectOutputStream extends OutputStream implements ObjectOutput,
    ObjectStreamConstants
```

Description

The `ObjectOutputStream` class is used for serializing primitive data and objects (including arrays and strings) to an output stream. The serialized data can be read by a corresponding `ObjectInputStream`.

See *The Java Class Libraries, Second Edition, Volume 1* for more information about this class.

O

Changes for Version 1.2

Object Substitution

When converting an object into a serialized stream, `ObjectOutputStream` allows a trusted subclass of `ObjectOutputStream`'s to substitute the object being serialized with another object. This is called *object substitution*. In Version 1.1, this was done by the subclass's invoking `enableReplaceObject()` and supplying an implementation of `replaceObject()` that `writeObject()` invoked in order to do the replacement. In Version 1.2, object substitution is more flexible. The subclass can use `enableReplaceObject()` and `replaceObject()`, or not use the `writeObject()` implementation at all, by supplying an implementation for the new method `writeObjectOverride()`.

Security

The `ObjectOutputStream` class has been changed to use the Version 1.2 security model (see `SecurityManager` for an overview). In Version 1.1, object substitution could be performed only by a *trusted subclass*, a subclass that has been loaded by the system class loader. In Version 1.2, when a security manager has been installed, the caller that is using the `ObjectOutputStream` subclass and the subclass itself must have been granted `SerializablePermission("enableSubstitution")` in order for `enableReplaceObject()` to succeed. For the type of object substitution that involves `writeObjectOverride()`, when a security manager has been installed, the caller and subclass must have been granted `SerializablePermission("enableSubclassImplementation")`.

Other Changes

A new, protected constructor has been added to `ObjectOutputStream`. This constructor is used by a subclass of `ObjectOutputStream`'s if the subclass wants to have complete control over the implementation of the `ObjectOutputStream` (by providing an implementation for the `writeObjectOverride()` method).

Two methods have been added to this class for dealing with serializable fields: `putFields()` and `writeFields()`. `putFields()` gets a structure for assigning values to serializable fields of an object; `writeFields()` writes out those values to the output stream.

The format of `Externalizable` data changed with the release of the Java Developer Kit (JDK) Version 1.1.6. Data written using versions prior to 1.1.6 uses Version 1 of the Object Serialization protocol, while data written since 1.1.6 uses Version 2. The method `useProtocolVersion()` has been added to allow the caller to select the version of the protocol to use when serializing objects.

The `defaultWriteObject()` and `enableReplaceObject()` methods are no longer final. `defaultWriteObject()` is described in *The Java Class Libraries, Second Edition, Volume 1.*

O

	MEMBER SUMMARY	
	Constructor	
Δ	`ObjectOutputStream()`	Constructs an `ObjectOutputStream` instance.
	Methods Used by a Class's `writeObject()`	
Δ	`defaultWriteObject()`	Writes the object being serialized to this `ObjectOutputStream`.[a]
1.2	`putFields()`	Retrieves a structure for assigning values to the serializable fields of an object.
1.2	`writeFields()`	Writes the fields set using `putFields()` to this `ObjectOutputStream`.
	Stream Methods	
	`close()`	Closes this `ObjectOutputStream`.
	`drain()`	Writes any buffered data to the underlying output stream.
	`flush()`	Flushes this `ObjectOutputStream`.
	`reset()`	Resets the state of this `ObjectOutputStream`.
1.2	`useProtocolVersion()`	Specifies the protocol version to use when writing data to this `ObjectOutputStream`.

Continued

MEMBER SUMMARY	
Stream Customization Methods	
annotateClass()	Writes information related to a class to this ObjectOutput-Stream.
Δ[a] enableReplaceObject()	Enables/disables this ObjectOutputStream to replace objects written to this ObjectOutputStream.
replaceObject()	Replaces an object with another object during serialization.
1.2 writeObjectOverride()	Writes an object to this ObjectOutputStream.
writeStreamHeader()	Writes the stream header to the underlying output stream.
ObjectOutput Methods	
write()	Writes one or more bytes to this ObjectOutputStream.
Δ writeObject()	Writes an object to this ObjectOutputStream.
DataOutput Methods	
writeBoolean()	Writes a boolean to this ObjectOutputStream.
writeByte()	Writes an 8-bit byte to this ObjectOutputStream.
writeBytes()	Writes a string as a sequence of bytes to this ObjectOutput-Stream.
writeChar()	Writes a 16-bit char to this ObjectOutputStream.
writeChars()	Writes a string as a sequence of chars to this ObjectOutput-Stream.
writeDouble()	Writes a 64-bit double to this ObjectOutputStream.
writeFloat()	Writes a 32-bit float to this ObjectOutputStream.
writeInt()	Writes a 32-bit int to this ObjectOutputStream.
writeLong()	Writes a 64-bit long to this ObjectOutputStream.
writeShort()	Writes a 16-bit short to this ObjectOutputStream.
writeUTF()	Writes a string in UTF to this ObjectOutputStream.

a. This method is described in *The Java Class Libraries, Second Edition, Volume 1*. Its only change is that it is no longer final.

See Also

ObjectOutputStream.PutField, SerializablePermission.
ObjectOutputStream in *The Java Class Libraries, Second Edition, Volume 1.*

Δ enableReplaceObject()

PURPOSE Enables/disables this ObjectOutputStream to replace objects written to this ObjectOutputStream.

SYNTAX
```
protected boolean enableReplaceObject(boolean enable) throws
    SecurityException
```

DESCRIPTION This method enables or disables this `ObjectOutputStream` to replace objects written to this `ObjectOutputStream`. Before serializing an object to the underlying stream, `writeObject()` allows a subclass of `ObjectOutputStream`'s to replace the object with the value returned by `replaceObject()`. By default, `ObjectOutputStream` does not allow this replacement. A subclass of `ObjectOutputStream`'s must call `enableReplaceObject()` with `true` in order to allow this replacement.

When a security manager has been installed, the caller must have been granted `SerializablePermission("enableSubstitution")`.

1.2 CHANGES In Version 1.1, this method was final. Also, in Version 1.1 this method could be invoked only from an instance of an `ObjectOutputStream` subclass that was loaded by the system class loader. In Version 1.2, the new security model is used (see the class description).

PARAMETERS

`enable` If `true`, allows objects written to this `ObjectOutputStream` to be replaced. If `false`, objects written to this `ObjectOutputStream` cannot be replaced.

RETURNS The previous setting before `enableReplaceObject()` was invoked. `true` if replacement was enabled; `false` otherwise.

EXCEPTIONS

`SecurityException`

If `enable` is `true` and the security manager does not allow the caller to call this method.

SEE ALSO `java.lang.ClassLoader`, `ObjectInputStream.enableResolveObject()`, `replaceObject()`, `SerializablePermission("enableSubstitution")`.

EXAMPLE See `replaceObject()` in *The Java Class Libraries, Second Edition, Volume 1.*

Δ ObjectOutputStream()

PURPOSE Constructs an `ObjectOutputStream` instance.

SYNTAX

```
public ObjectOutputStream(OutputStream out) throws IOException
protected ObjectOutputStream() throws IOException,
    SecurityException
```

SINCE 1.2 (protected constructor)

DESCRIPTION The public constructor creates an instance of `ObjectOutputStream` that writes serialized data to the stream `out`. It writes the stream header (see `writeStreamHeader()`) to `out` and readies itself to accept objects and data to be serialized.

The protected constructor is used by a subclass's constructor if that subclass will be providing an implementation for the `writeObjectOverride()` method.

When `writeObject()` is invoked on such a subclass, its `writeObjectOverride()` method is called and the implementation provided by `ObjectOutputStream` is not used. The constructor should be used (and `writeObjectOverride()` overridden) only if the subclass is completely reimplementing `ObjectOutputStream`. Notice that the protected constructor does not accept any arguments, so it is free to deal with streams and headers any way it chooses. Unlike the public constructor, this constructor does not perform any initialization. Therefore the subclass must also override `close()` because `ObjectOutputStream.close()` uses private fields initialized by the public constructor.

To successfully use the protected constructor, the caller of the constructor must have been granted `SerializablePermission("enableSubclassImplementation")`. Otherwise, a `SecurityException` is thrown.

1.2 CHANGES The protected constructor is new to Version 1.2.

PARAMETERS

`out` The non-`null` output stream to which to write.

EXCEPTIONS

`IOException`

If an IO error occurs while writing to `out`.

`SecurityException`

If the caller has not been granted `SerializablePermission("enableSubclassImplementation")`.

O

SEE ALSO `SerializablePermission`, `writeObject()`, `writeObjectOverride()`.

EXAMPLE See `writeObjectOverride()` for an example of using the protected constructor.

```
try {
    ObjectOutputStream out =
        new ObjectOutputStream(new FileOutputStream("test.ser"));
    out.writeObject(new java.awt.Label("hello there"));
    out.close();
} catch (IOException e) {
    System.out.println(e);
}
```

1.2 putFields()

PURPOSE Retrieves a structure for assigning values to the serializable fields of an object.

SYNTAX
```
public ObjectOutputStream.PutField putFields() throws
    IOException
```

DESCRIPTION This method retrieves an `ObjectOutputStream.PutField` for assigning values to serializable fields to be written to an `ObjectOutputStream`. It is called inside a `Serializable` object's `writeObject()` method. The `writeObject()` method then invokes `put()` methods on the result to set the serializable fields' values. Fields set in such a way must be *flushed* to the output stream by using `writeFields()`.

RETURNS A non-`null` `PutField` for assigning values to an object's serializable fields.

SEE ALSO `writeFields()`.

EXAMPLE See the `ObjectOutputStream.PutField` class example.

1.2 useProtocolVersion()

PURPOSE Specifies the protocol version to use when writing data to this `ObjectOutputStream`.

SYNTAX `public void useProtocolVersion(int version) throws IOException`

DESCRIPTION The format of `Externalizable` data changed with the release of the Java Developer Kit (JDK) Version 1.1.6. Data written using versions prior to 1.1.6 use `ObjectStreamConstants.PROTOCOL_VERSION_1`, while data written since 1.1.6 use `ObjectStreamConstants.PROTOCOL_VERSION_2`. The method `useProtocolVersion()` is used by the caller to select the version of the protocol to use when serializing objects. The default is `ObjectStreamConstants.PROTOCOL_VERSION_2`.

This method must be called before any objects have been written to this `ObjectOutputStream`.

PARAMETERS

`version` One of `ObjectStreamConstants.PROTOCOL_VERSION_1` or `ObjectStreamConstants.PROTOCOL_VERSION_2`.

EXCEPTIONS

`IllegalArgumentException`
If `version` is not one of the two valid versions.

`IllegalStateException`
If this method is invoked after an object has been written to this stream.

`IOException`
If an IO error occurred while attempting to set the version.

EXAMPLE

```
ObjectOutputStream objout = new ObjectOutputStream(out);
objout.useProtocolVersion(ObjectStreamConstants.PROTOCOL_VERSION_1);
```

1.2 writeFields()

PURPOSE Writes the fields set using `putFields()` to this `ObjectOutputStream`.

SYNTAX `public void writeFields() throws IOException`

DESCRIPTION This method writes the fields set by `putFields()` to this `ObjectOutputStream`. A `Serializable` object's `writeObject()` method typically calls `putFields()` on the `ObjectOutputStream` to assign values to the fields to be serialized and then invokes `writeFields()` on the `ObjectOutputStream` to write out the fields' values.

EXCEPTIONS

`IOException`

If an IO error occurs while writing to this stream.

`NotActiveException`

If no object is currently being serialized, or if the object's fields have not been set by using `putFields()`.

SEE ALSO `putFields()`.

EXAMPLE See the `ObjectOutputStream.PutField` class example.

Δ writeObject()

PURPOSE Writes an object to this `ObjectOutputStream`.

O

SYNTAX `public final void writeObject(Object obj) throws IOException`

DESCRIPTION This method serializes `obj` and writes it to the underlying output stream. If `obj`'s fields contain references to other objects, those objects and their references are also serialized and written to the underlying output stream such that the entire graph of objects rooted at `obj` is serialized. The object is serialized by using one of the following methods of the class:

- `writeExternal()` if the class implements `Externalizable`
- `defaultWriteObject()` if the class implements `Serializable` but does not define a `writeObject()` method
- `writeObject()` if the class implements `Serializable` and does define a `writeObject()` method

If this `ObjectOutputStream` has enabled the replacement of objects written to it, `replaceObject()` is invoked with `obj` as an argument and the result is serialized.

If `writeObject()` is being called on a subclass of `ObjectOutputStream` that was created using the protected `ObjectOutputStream` constructor, `writeObject()` simply calls `writeObjectOverride()` and returns.

If an exception is encountered during `writeObject()`, the validity of the data of the entire `ObjectOutputStream` is suspect and that data should not be used further.

1.2 CHANGES `writeObjectOverride()` did not exist in Version 1.1 and hence `writeObject()` did not use it.

PARAMETERS

`obj` The possibly `null` object to write. If `null`, `null` is written to the stream.

EXCEPTIONS

`InvalidClassException`

If the class of `obj` (or the class of one of the objects in the graph of objects rooted at `obj`) is an array of an unknown primitive type, or if the class's fields do not match those of the object being serialized.

`IOException`

If an IO error occurs while writing to the underlying output stream.

`NotSerializableException`

If `obj` or one of the objects that it references does not implement the `Serializable` (or `Externalizable`) interface.

SEE ALSO `enableReplaceObject()`, `replaceObject()`, `writeObjectOverride()`.

EXAMPLE See `ObjectOutputStream()`.

1.2 writeObjectOverride()

PURPOSE Writes an object to this `ObjectOutputStream`.

SYNTAX

```
protected void writeObjectOverride(Object obj) throws
    IOException
```

DESCRIPTION The default implementation of this method does nothing. This method is called only in subclasses of `ObjectOutputStream` that have used the protected `ObjectOutputStream` constructor. Such subclasses must provide implementations for this method to write data for `obj` into the output stream.

PARAMETERS

`obj` The possibly `null` object to serialize.

EXCEPTIONS

`IOException`

If an IO error occurred while writing the serialized data.

EXAMPLE This example demonstrates how to completely override the functionality of `writeObject()` by using the protected `ObjectOutputStream` constructor and supplying an implementation for `writeObjectOverride()`. Notice that the subclass overrides the `close()` method to avoid `ObjectOutput-`

`Stream.close()` being called. Calling `ObjectOutputStream.close()` would have caused a `NullPointerException` because the protected constructor does not initialize the stream used by `close()`.

```
import java.io.*;

class Main {
    public static void main(String[] args) {
        try {
            SillyObjectOutputStream out =
                new SillyObjectOutputStream(new FileOutputStream("test.ser"));
            out.writeObject(new java.awt.Label("hello there"));
            out.close();
        } catch (IOException e) {
            System.out.println(e);
        }
    }

    static class SillyObjectOutputStream extends ObjectOutputStream {
        OutputStream out;
        byte[] sillyOutput = "silly".getBytes();

        SillyObjectOutputStream(OutputStream out) throws IOException {
            super(); // use protected constructor
            this.out = out;
        }

        protected void writeObjectOverride(Object obj) throws IOException {
            out.write(sillyOutput); // bogus implementation, just for demo
        }

        public void close() throws IOException {
            out.close();
        }
    }
}
```

java.io ObjectOutputStream.PutField

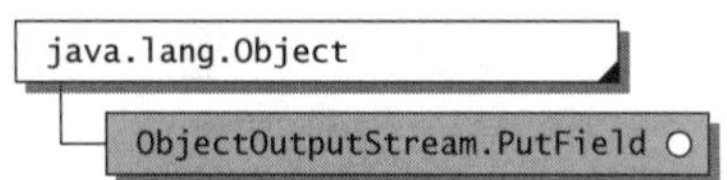

Syntax

```
static public abstract class ObjectOutputStream.PutField
```

Description

The abstract class `ObjectOutputStream.PutField` represents *serializable fields* of an object to be written to an `ObjectOutputStream`. A serializable field is a field in a *serializable class* that has been specified by that class to be serializable. A serializable class is a class that implements the `Serializable` interface. It has two ways of specifying which of its fields are serializable: default serialization and explicit serialization. See `ObjectStreamField` for a description of the two ways. This class is used to represent fields that are to be serialized using either default or explicit serialization.

Usage

Once a serializable field exists for a class, it must exist in all future versions of the class so as to maintain compatibility. During serialization, if a class evolves such that it no longer has a field with a name that maps to the serialized field, it uses `ObjectOutputStream.PutField` to assign a value to the serializable field using data from its current implementation. Such a class would declare a `writeObject()` method that uses `ObjectInputStream.putFields()` to get an instance of `ObjectOutputStream.PutField`. `writeObject()` would assign values to the serializable fields using the `ObjectOutputStream.PutField` instance, including those with no corresponding fields in the evolved class. When all of the serializable fields' values have been assigned, `writeObject()` would write them out to the stream by using `ObjectOutputStream.writeFields()`.

If a class defines a `writeObject()` method to write out more data than just the specified serializable fields, then it also needs to define a corresponding `readObject()` to read that data back during deserialization. See the `Serializable` class description for further discussion.

In the following example, `writeObject()` writes out two serializable fields, `strField` and `intField`, using the corresponding new fields in an evolved class. It then flushes the two fields to the output stream using `ObjectOutputStream.writeFields()`.

```
private static final ObjectStreamField[] serialPersistentFields = {
    new ObjectStreamField("strField", String.class),
    new ObjectStreamField("intField", Integer.TYPE),
};
...
private void writeObject(ObjectOutputStream out) throws IOException {
    // Get PutField instance for assigning values to serializable fields
    ObjectOutputStream.PutField pfields = out.putFields();
```

O

```
        pfields.put("strField", newStrField);
        pfields.put("intField", newIntField);
        // Write fields out
        out.writeFields();
    }
```

MEMBER SUMMARY	
Field Assignment Method	
`put()`	Assigns a value to a serializable field.
Flush Output Method	
`write()`	Called to write out the serializable fields.

See Also

`ObjectInputStream.GetField`, `ObjectOutputStream.writeFields()`, `ObjectStreamClass`, `ObjectStreamField`.
`Serializable` in *The Java Class Libraries, Second Edition, Volume 1.*

Example

See the `ObjectStreamField` class example. In that example, the class `ClassA` that originally declared the explicit serializable field `field1` evolved to replace `field1` with `field10`. In the evolved class, the value of `field10` is recorded for the serializable field `field1` so as to maintain compatibility for serialization purposes.

put()

PURPOSE Assigns a value to a serializable field.

SYNTAX

```
abstract public void put(String fname, boolean fvalue)
abstract public void put(String fname, byte fvalue)
abstract public void put(String fname, char fvalue)
abstract public void put(String fname, short fvalue)
abstract public void put(String fname, int fvalue)
abstract public void put(String fname, long fvalue)
abstract public void put(String fname, float fvalue)
abstract public void put(String fname, double fvalue)
abstract public void put(String fname, Object fvalue)
```

DESCRIPTION This method assigns the value `fvalue` to the serializable field named `fname`.

PARAMETERS

`fname` A non-`null` string that is the name of the serializable field.

`fvalue` The value to assign to the serializable field. If `fvalue` is nonprimitive, it can be `null`.

EXCEPTIONS

`IllegalArgumentException`

If `fname` does not name a serializable field, or if the type of `defvalue` is not compatible with the type of the actual serialized field.

SEE ALSO `ObjectInputStream.GetField.get()`.

EXAMPLE See the previous section, "Usage," and the `ObjectStreamField` class example.

write()

PURPOSE Called to write out the serializable fields.

SYNTAX

```
abstract public void write(ObjectOutput out) throws IOException
```

DESCRIPTION This method is used by `ObjectOutputStream.writeFields()` to write the serializable fields of this `ObjectOutputStream.PutField` instance to `out`. It should not be used directly.

PARAMETERS

`out` The non-`null` `ObjectOutput` object to write the serializable fields.

EXCEPTIONS

`IOException`

If an IO error occurred while writing to the fields.

java.io
ObjectStreamClass

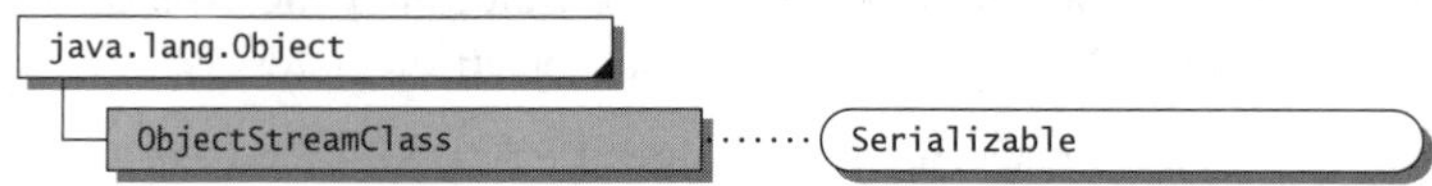

Syntax

```
public class ObjectStreamClass implements java.io.Serializable
```

Description

An `ObjectStreamClass` is a descriptor that describes a serializable class. It consists of the class's name and its Stream Unique Identifier (SUID). In addition, if the class implements `Serializable`, the class descriptor contains a list of the names and type names of the serializable fields of the class. See `Serializable` in *The Java Class Libraries, Second Edition, Volume 1* and `ObjectStreamField` for descriptions of serializable fields. If the class implements `Externalizable`, the class descriptor does not have this list. This descriptor is stored with a serialized object to identify the class of the serialized object.

See *The Java Class Libraries, Second Edition, Volume 1* for more information about this class.

Changes for Version 1.2

Two methods and one constant have been added to this class: `getField()`, `getFields()`, and `NO_FIELDS`. These changes allow a program to retrieve the serializable fields from a descriptor.

	MEMBER SUMMARY	
	Lookup Method	
	`lookup()`	Retrieves the descriptor for a class.
	Get Methods and Constant	
	`forClass()`	Retrieves the `Class` described by this descriptor.
1.2	`getField()`	Retrieves a serializable field for the class represented by this descriptor.
1.2	`getFields()`	Retrieves the serializable fields of the class represented by this descriptor.
	`getName()`	Retrieves the name of the class described by this descriptor.
	`getSerialVersionUID()`	Retrieves the SUID of the class described by this descriptor.
1.2	`NO_FIELDS`	Indicates that a class has no serializable fields.
	Object Method	
	`toString()`	Generates the string representation of this descriptor.

See Also

`ObjectStreamField`.
`ObjectStreamClass` in *The Java Class Libraries, Second Edition, Volume 1.*

1.2 getField()

PURPOSE Retrieves a serializable field for the class represented by this descriptor.

SYNTAX `public ObjectStreamField getField(String name)`

DESCRIPTION This method retrieves the serializable field with the name `name` for the class represented by this descriptor. It is used mainly for debugging.

PARAMETERS

`name` A non-`null` string representing the name of the serializable field.

RETURNS A possibly `null` `ObjectStreamField` representing the serializable field with the name `name`; `null` if the class has no such serializable field.

SEE ALSO `getFields()`.

EXAMPLE This example is a modification of the `ObjectStreamField.getName()` example. It uses `getField()` to explicitly retrieve the `ObjectStreamField` of each serializable field.

Main.java

```
import java.io.*;

class Main {
    public static void main(String[] args) {
        try {
            // Write them out
            FileOutputStream f = new FileOutputStream("ClassA1.ser");
            ObjectOutput out = new ObjectOutputStream(f);

            out.writeObject(new ClassA("hello", 500));
            out.flush();
            out.close();

            // Read it back
            FileInputStream f2 = new FileInputStream("ClassA1.ser");
            ObjectInputStream in = new ObjectInputStream(f2);
            ClassA obj = (ClassA) in.readObject();
            in.close();

            System.out.println(obj);
        } catch (IOException e) {
            e.printStackTrace();
        } catch (ClassNotFoundException e) {
            e.printStackTrace();
        }
    }
}
```

ClassA.java

```
import java.io.*;
import java.awt.Button;

public class ClassA implements Serializable {
    /**
     * A string field.
     * @serial
     */
    String strField;

    /**
     * An int field.
     * @serial
     */
    int intField;

    /**
     * A byte array field.
     * @serial
     */
    byte[] byteArrayField = new byte[] {(byte)3, (byte)2, (byte)1};

    /**
     * An object field.
     * @serial
     */
    Button[] buttons  = new Button[] {new Button("push me")};

    public ClassA(String one, int two) {
        strField = one;
        intField = two;
    }
    private void readObject(ObjectInputStream in)
        throws IOException, ClassNotFoundException {

            // Read in serial fields
            ObjectInputStream.GetField pfields = in.readFields();

            // Assign serialized values to fields
            strField = (String)pfields.get("strField", "out-of-luck");
            intField = (int)pfields.get("intField", 1000);
            byteArrayField = (byte[]) pfields.get("byteArrayField", null);
            buttons = (Button[]) pfields.get("buttons", null);

            // Get ObjectStreamClass to get ObjectStreamFields for each field
            ObjectStreamClass objclass = pfields.getObjectStreamClass();
            print("strField", objclass.getField("strField"));
            print("intField", objclass.getField("intField"));
            print("byteArrayField", objclass.getField("byteArrayField"));
            print("buttons", objclass.getField("buttons"));
            print("notThere", objclass.getField("notThere")); // null
    }
    private void print(String field, ObjectStreamField fd) {
        System.out.println("Field: " + field);
        if (fd != null) {
            System.out.println("name: " + fd.getName());
            System.out.println("type: " + fd.getType());
            System.out.println("type code: " + fd.getTypeCode());
            System.out.println("type string: " + fd.getTypeString());
```

```
                System.out.println("primitive: " + fd.isPrimitive());
                System.out.println("offset: " + fd.getOffset());
            }
        }
        public String toString() {
            return "strField: " + strField +
                " intField: " + intField +
                " byteArrayField: " + byteArrayField +
                " buttons: " + buttons;
        }
    }
```

1.2 getFields()

PURPOSE Retrieves the serializable fields of the class represented by this descriptor.

SYNTAX `public ObjectStreamField[] getFields()`

DESCRIPTION This method retrieves the serializable fields of the class represented by this descriptor, with each element of the result representing one of the serializable fields. If the class contains no serializable fields, the result is an empty array. To get an individual serializable field by its name, use `getField()`.

This method is used primarily for debugging purposes so that the caller can discover a class's serializable fields.

RETURNS A non-`null` array representing the serializable fields.

SEE ALSO `getField()`.

EXAMPLE See `ObjectStreamField.getName()` example.

O

1.2 NO_FIELDS

PURPOSE Indicates that a class has no serializable fields.

SYNTAX `public static final ObjectStreamField[] NO_FIELDS`

DESCRIPTION This constant indicates that a class has no serializable fields. Its value is an empty array. You can use this constant for equality checks on the result of `getFields()`.

SEE ALSO `getFields()`.

EXAMPLE

```
ObjectStreamField[] fields = objClass.getFields();
if (fields == ObjectStreamClass.NO_FIELDS) {
    // action for no fields case
} else {
    // action to process fields
}
```

java.io
ObjectStreamConstants

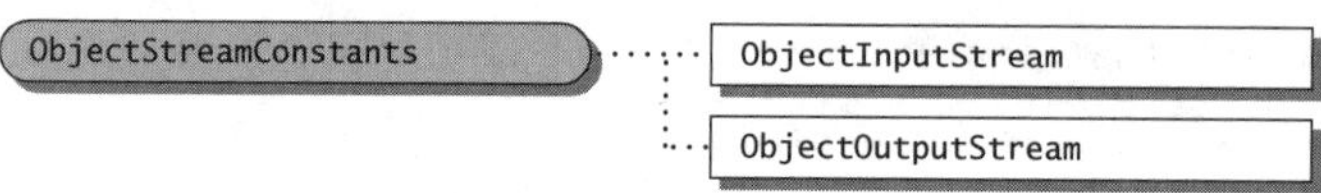

Syntax

```
public interface ObjectStreamConstants
```

Description

The ObjectStreamConstants interface contains definitions for constants used by Object Serialization. All constants are usually used only internally by Object Serialization, with the exceptions of PROTOCOL_VERSION_1 and PROTOCOL_VERSION_2, which are used as arguments to ObjectOutputStream.useProtocolVersion(). You would need to use the constants only if you subclass ObjectOutputStream/ObjectInputStream to override their default implementations.

See the Serializable, ObjectStreamClass, ObjectInputStream, and ObjectOutputStream classes for explanations of some of the terminology used here, such as *block data*. Complete details on the serialization/deserialization algorithms are described in the document http://java.sun.com/products/jdk/1.2/docs/guide/serialization/.

O

MEMBER SUMMARY		
Stream Headers		
STREAM_MAGIC	0xaced	
STREAM_VERSION	5	
Tags Used to Mark Items in a Serialized Stream		
baseWireHandle	0x7e0000	The first wire handle to be assigned.
TC_ARRAY	0x75	A new array.
TC_BASE	0x70	The first tag value.
TC_BLOCKDATA	0x77	The start of an optional data block. The next byte indicates the number of bytes in the block.
TC_BLOCKDATALONG	0x7a	The start of long optional block data. The next long indicates the number of bytes in this block data.
TC_CLASS	0x76	A reference to a Class.
TC_CLASSDESC	0x72	A new class descriptor (serialized ObjectStreamClass).
TC_ENDBLOCKDATA	0x78	The end of optional blocks for an object.

MEMBER SUMMARY		
TC_EXCEPTION	0x7b	An indication that the write was aborted.
TC_MAX	0x7b	The last tag value.
TC_NULL	0x70	A null object reference.
TC_OBJECT	0x73	A new object.
TC_REFERENCE	0x71	A reference to an object already written into the stream.
TC_RESET	0x79	An indication that the stream was reset.
TC_STRING	0x74	A new `String`.
Bit Masks for `ObjectStreamClass` Flags		
SC_BLOCK_DATA	0x08	Externalized data written in block data mode.
SC_EXTERNALIZABLE	0x04	Externalizable.
SC_SERIALIZABLE	0x02	Serializable class.
SC_WRITE_METHOD	0x01	Serializable class has defined a `writeObject()`.
Serialization Protocol Versions		
PROTOCOL_VERSION_1	1	Use pre-JDK 1.1.5 external data format.
PROTOCOL_VERSION_2	2	Use JDK 1.1.5 and post-JDK 1.1.5 external data format.
Security Permissions (see `SerializablePermission`)		
SUBCLASS_IMPLEMENTATION_PERMISSION		Enables subclass implementations of `ObjectInputStream`/`ObjectOutputStream` to override `readObject()`/`writeObject()`.
SUBSTITUTION_PERMISSION		Enables `replaceObject()`/`resolveObject()` to be used.

See Also

`ObjectStreamClass`, `ObjectStreamField`, `ObjectInputStream`, `ObjectOutputStream`, `SerializablePermission`.

`Externalizable`, `Serializable` in *The Java Class Libraries, Second Edition, Volume 1.*

ObjectStreamField

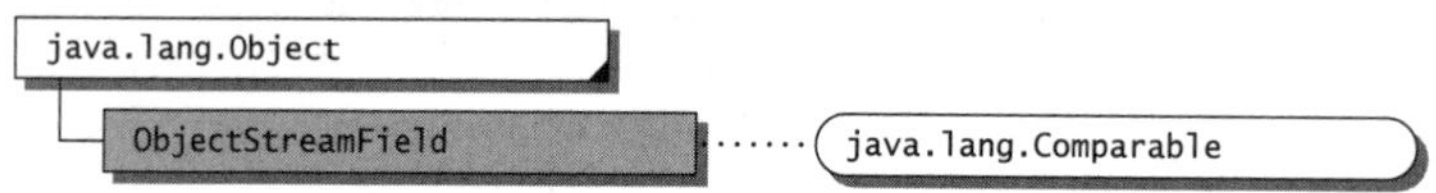

Syntax

`public class ObjectStreamField implements Comparable`

Description

The `ObjectStreamField` class represents a *serializable field*. A serializable field is a field in a *serializable class* that has been declared serializable. A serializable class is a class that implements the `Serializable` interface. It has two ways of specifying which of its fields are serializable:

- Default serialization
- Explicit serialization

Default Serialization

With default serialization, the serializable fields of a class are all of its nontransient and nonstatic fields. When an instance of the class is serialized, `ObjectOutputStream.defaultWriteObject()` is used to serialize these fields. For documentation purposes, a serializable field should have an `@serial` tag in its `javadoc` that describes the contents of that field. The `@serial` tag accepts an optional comment for additional information about the field's contents. This optional comment and the field's `javadoc` comments are used by `javadoc` to generate the field's serialized form documentation.

If the class defines a `writeObject()` method, it may serialize these fields and/or add other information into the serialization stream. Any data written by `writeObject()` that is not associated with a serializable field is called *optional data*. The `writeObject()` method should be documented by having an `@serialData` tag in its `javadoc` that describes the layout, sequence, and type of the optional data.

A similar but reversed process occurs when reading/deserializing the object (using the class `ObjectInputStream`). See the `Serializable` class in *The Java Class Libraries, Second Edition, Volume 1* for details.

The following is a serializable class with one serializable field, `field1`.

```
public class ClassA implements Serializable {
    /**
      * A string for testing.
      * @serial
      */
    String field1;
    transient String field2;
    public ClassA(String f1, String f2) {
```

```
            field1 = f1;
            field2 = f2;
        }
    }
```

Explicit Serialization

Explicit serialization is a way of overriding default serialization and explicitly specifying the serializable fields of a serializable class. It also allows you to declare serializable fields that do not exist as a member of the class definition, thereby enabling a separation between the implementation fields of a class and the serializable fields of its serialized form.

You use explicit serialization for a class by declaring a private static final field named `serialPersistentFields`. This field is an array of `ObjectStreamField` instances containing the string names of the fields and their corresponding `Class` objects. For documentation purposes, each such field should have a corresponding `@serialField` tag in its `javadoc` that describes the contents of that field. These fields are used by the methods `ObjectOutputStream.defaultWriteObject()` and `ObjectInputStream.defaultReadObject()`, unless the object defines `writeObject()/readObject()` methods. In this case, `writeObject()` and `readObject()` will take care of serializing these fields. As mentioned previously, the `writeObject()` method should be documented by having a `@serialData` tag in its `javadoc`.

In the following example, class `ClassA` has one serializable field: `field1`.

```
    Class ClassA implements Serializable {
        String field1;
        String field2;
        /**
         * @serialField field1 String
                      Can be null, empty string or any String value.
         */
        private static final ObjectStreamField[] serialPersistentFields = {
           new ObjectStreamField("field1", String.class);
        }
        public ClassA(String f1, String f2) {
           field1 = f1;
           field2 = f2;
        }
    }
```

When a class uses explicit serialization, nonstatic and nontransient fields are not serialized. Only those fields specified in `serialPersistentFields` are serialized. In the previous example, even though `field2` is neither transient nor static, it is not serialized.

Usage

You use this class to declare explicit serializable fields in `serialPersistentFields`, as shown previously. You ordinarily do not use any of the methods declared in this class; you just use its constructor. The methods are used by more advanced users to examine the fields of a serializable class (using `ObjectStreamClass.getFields()` or `ObjectStreamClass.getField()`).

This class is also used by `ObjectStreamClass`, `ObjectInputStream`, and `ObjectOutputStream` to process both default and explicit serializable fields (see the `getName()` example later in this discussion).

Information Recorded about a Serializable Field

The following information is recorded about a serializable field:

- The field's name as it is declared in the source code.
- The fully qualified name of the type of the field for the purpose of serialization (for example, `"[[Ljava/lang/Object;"`, `"Ljava/lang/String;"`). This is called the *type string*. Note that this string is *derived from*, but is different than, the type descriptor returned by `java.lang.Class.getName()` (see the *Type Descriptor* in the class description for `Class` in *The Java Class Libraries, Second Edition, Volume 1*). Primitive types do not have type strings. The type string of a class is an "L" followed by `Class.getName()`, with all of the period characters (".") replaced by slash characters ("/") and followed by a semicolon character (";"). The type string of an array is *d* number of open bracket characters ("[") followed by the type string of the array type, where *d* is the number of dimensions of the array. Table 13 contain examples of type strings.

Type	Type String
`Object[][]`	`[[Ljava/lang/Object`
`String`	`Ljava/lang/String`
`double[]`	`[D`
`int[][]`	`[[I`

TABLE 13: Type Strings.

- The *type code* of the field. This is the first character of the type string if the field is of a nonprimitive type. If the field is of a primitive type, the type code is the type descriptor for the primitive type (for example, "F" for `float`). See Table 13, page 366, in *The Java Class Libraries, Second Edition, Volume 1*. Table 14 lists the type codes.

Type	Type Code
`byte`	`B`
`char`	`C`
`double`	`D`
`float`	`F`
`int`	`I`
`long`	`J`
class or interface	`L`
`short`	`S`
`boolean`	`Z`
`array`	`[`

TABLE 14: Type Codes.

- The `Class` object representing the field's type.
- The reflection object (`java.lang.reflect.Field`) representing the field being serialized.
- The offset of the field within the instance data that is to be serialized.

MEMBER SUMMARY	
Constructor	
`ObjectStreamField()`	Constructs an `ObjectStreamField` instance.
Accessor Methods	
`getName()`	Retrieves the name of the serializable field represented by this `ObjectStreamField` as it has been declared in the source code.
`getOffset()`	Retrieves the offset of the serializable field represented by this `ObjectStreamField` within the instance data that is to be serialized.
`getType()`	Retrieves the `Class` object of the serializable field represented by this `ObjectStreamField`.
`getTypeCode()`	Retrieves the type code of the serializable field represented by this `ObjectStreamField`.
`getTypeString()`	Retrieves the type string of the serializable field represented by this `ObjectStreamField`.
`isPrimitive()`	Determines whether the serializable field represented by this `ObjectStreamField` is of a primitive type.
`setOffset()`	Sets the offset of the serializable field represented by this `ObjectStreamField` within the instance data that is to be serialized.
Comparable Method	
`compareTo()`	Compares the order of this `ObjectStreamField` with the order of another `ObjectStreamField`.
Object Method	
`toString()`	Returns a string that describes this `ObjectStreamField`.

O

See Also

`ObjectStreamClass.getFields()`, `ObjectStreamClass.getField()`,
`ObjectInputStream.GetField`, `ObjectOutputStream.PutField`.
`Serializable` in *The Java Class Libraries, Second Edition, Volume 1.*

Example

This example declares a serializable class `ClassA`. `ClassA` declares a single explicit serializable field, `field1`. `MainWrite` serializes an instance of `ClassA`.

ClassA then evolves to a newer implementation in which field1 has been replaced by field10. To accommodate this change, the evolved implementation declares a readObject() method that first explicitly reads in the explicit field and then assigns its value to the renamed field, field10.

To run this example, first compile ClassA.java-old and MainWrite.java and run MainWrite to store serializable data into the file ClassA1.ser. Then compile ClassA.java-new and MainRead.java. When you run MainRead, it reads the old serialized data from the file ClassA1.ser and assigns the serialized value of field1 to field10.

ClassA.java-old

```
import java.io.Serializable;
import java.io.ObjectStreamField;

public class ClassA implements Serializable {
    String field1;
    String field2;

    public ClassA(String one, String two) {
        field1 = one;
        field2 = two;
    }

    private static final long serialVersionUID = -5637912302326316l3L;

    /**
     * @serialField field1 String null, empty string, or any String value.
     */
    private static final ObjectStreamField[] serialPersistentFields = {
        new ObjectStreamField("field1", String.class)};

    public String toString() {
        return ("field1 " + field1 + "; field2 " + field2);
    }
}
```

MainWrite.java

```
import java.io.*;

class MainWrite {
    public static void main(String[] args) {
        try {
            // Write them out
            FileOutputStream f = new FileOutputStream("ClassA1.ser");
            ObjectOutput out = new ObjectOutputStream(f);

            out.writeObject(new ClassA("hello", "there"));
            out.flush();
            out.close();
        } catch (IOException e) {
            e.printStackTrace();
        }
    }
}
```

ClassA.java-new

```
import java.io.*;

public class ClassA implements Serializable {
    String field10;
    String field2;

    public ClassA(String one, String two) {
        field10 = one;
        field2 = two;
    }
    private static final long serialVersionUID = -563791230232631613L;

    /**
     * @serialField field1 String null, empty string, or any String value.
     */
    private static final ObjectStreamField[] serialPersistentFields = {
        new ObjectStreamField("field1", String.class)};

    /**
     * @serialData write out field10's value for field1
     */
    private void writeObject(ObjectOutputStream out) throws IOException {

        // Get PutField instance for assigning values to serializable fields
        ObjectOutputStream.PutField pfields = out.putFields();

        pfields.put("field1", field10);

        // Write fields out
        out.writeFields();
    }

    private void readObject(ObjectInputStream in)
        throws IOException, ClassNotFoundException {
            // Read in serialized fields
            ObjectInputStream.GetField pfields = in.readFields();

            // Get the one we want
            field10 = (String)pfields.get("field1", "out-of-luck");
    }

    public String toString() {
        return ("field10 " + field10 + "; field2 " + field2);
    }
}
```

MainRead.java

```
import java.io.*;

class MainRead {
    public static void main(String[] args) {
        try {
            // Read it back
            FileInputStream f2 = new FileInputStream("ClassA1.ser");
            ObjectInputStream in = new ObjectInputStream(f2);
            ClassA obj = (ClassA) in.readObject();
            in.close();
```

```
                System.out.println(obj);
            } catch (IOException e) {
                e.printStackTrace();
            } catch (ClassNotFoundException e) {
                e.printStackTrace();
            }
        }
    }
```

compareTo()

PURPOSE Determines the order of this `ObjectStreamField` with another `ObjectStreamField`.

SYNTAX `public int compareTo(Object obj)`

DESCRIPTION This method determines the order of this `ObjectStreamField` with the order of `obj`. Fields that are of primitive types come before fields that are of nonprimitive types. Within each group (primitive and nonprimitive), the fields are ordered according to their names, using `String.compareTo()`.

PARAMETERS

`obj` The non-`null` object with which to compare for ordering.

RETURNS `-1` if this `ObjectStreamField` comes before `obj`; `0` if this `ObjectStreamField` has the same name as `obj`; `1` if this `ObjectStreamField` comes after `obj`.

EXCEPTIONS

`ClassCastException`
If `obj` is not an instance of `ObjectStreamField`.

`NullPointerException`
If `obj` is `null`.

SEE ALSO `Comparable.compareTo()`.

EXAMPLE See `java.lang.Comparable`.

getName()

PURPOSE Retrieves the name of the serializable field represented by this `ObjectStreamField` as it has been declared in the source code.

SYNTAX `public String getName()`

RETURNS The non-`null` string used to name of the serializable field represented by this `ObjectStreamField` in the source code.

SEE ALSO `java.lang.reflect.Field.getName()`.

O

EXAMPLE This example declares a class `ClassA` with a bunch of (default) serializable fields. For demonstration purposes, it overrides `readObject()` to manually read in the serializable fields and then uses the methods in `ObjectStreamField` to display information about the fields. Note that the type descriptor of the nonprimitive types is `java.lang.Object`. This is because the serialization code always uses that class when creating `ObjectStreamField` instances for reading in fields of nonprimitive types. Notice that even though `ClassA` uses default serialization fields, its `readObject()` method can use `readField()` to get at the fields. This is not necessary nor recommended, and we use it here only for illustrative purposes.

```
import java.io.*;
import java.awt.Button;

public class ClassA implements Serializable {
    String strField;
    int intField;
    byte[] byteArrayField = new byte[] {(byte)3, (byte)2, (byte)1};
    Button[] buttons  = new Button[] {new Button("push me")};

    public ClassA(String one, int two) {
        strField = one;
        intField = two;
    }

    private void readObject(ObjectInputStream in)
        throws IOException, ClassNotFoundException {

            // Read in serial fields
            ObjectInputStream.GetField pfields = in.readFields();

            // Assign serialized values to fields
            strField = (String)pfields.get("strField", "out-of-luck");
            intField = (int)pfields.get("intField", 1000);
            byteArrayField = (byte[]) pfields.get("byteArrayField", null);
            buttons = (Button[]) pfields.get("buttons", null);

            // Get ObjectStreamClass to get ObjectStreamFields for each field
            ObjectStreamClass objclass = pfields.getObjectStreamClass();
            ObjectStreamField[] fields = objclass.getFields();

            // See what we got
            for (int i = 0; i < fields.length; i++) {
                print(fields[i]);
            }

    }

    private void print(ObjectStreamField fd) {
        System.out.println("name: " + fd.getName());
        System.out.println("type: " + fd.getType());
        System.out.println("type code: " + fd.getTypeCode());
        System.out.println("type string: " + fd.getTypeString());
        System.out.println("primitive: " + fd.isPrimitive());
        System.out.println("offset: " + fd.getOffset());
    }
```

```
        public String toString() {
            return "strField: " + strField +
                " intField: " + intField +
                " byteArrayField: " + byteArrayField +
                " buttons: " + buttons;
        }
    }
```

OUTPUT

```
java Main
name: intField
type: int
type code: I
type string: null
primitive: true
offset: 0
name: buttons
type: class java.lang.Object
type code: [
type string: [Ljava/awt/Button;
primitive: false
offset: 0
name: byteArrayField
type: class java.lang.Object
type code: [
type string: [B
primitive: false
offset: 1
name: strField
type: class java.lang.Object
type code: L
type string: Ljava/lang/String;
primitive: false
offset: 2
strField: hellointField: 500byteArrayField: [B@85d2bc05buttons:
[Ljava.awt.Button;@8616bc05
```


getOffset()

PURPOSE Retrieves the offset of the serializable field represented by this `ObjectStreamField` within the instance data that is to be serialized.

SYNTAX `public int getOffset()`

DESCRIPTION This method retrieves the offset of the serializable field represented by this `ObjectStreamField` within the instance data that is to be serialized. All of the instance data that needs to be serialized can be thought of as filling a `byte` array. For a field that has a primitive type, the offset is the position of the first byte of this field's primitive data, relative to the beginning of the `byte` array.

For a field that has a nonprimitive type, the offset is *n*, where this field's value is the *n*'th object reference being serialized. If this field is the fifth nonprimitive typed field, *n* would be `5`.

RETURNS An `int` representing the offset of this field.

SEE ALSO `setOffset()`.

EXAMPLE See `getName()`.

getType()

PURPOSE Retrieves the `Class` object of the serializable field represented by this `ObjectStreamField`.

SYNTAX `public Class getType()`

RETURNS The non-`null` `Class` object of the serializable field represented by this `ObjectStreamField`.

SEE ALSO `getTypeString()`, `java.lang.Object.getClass()`.

EXAMPLE See `getName()`.

getTypeCode()

PURPOSE Retrieves the type code of the serializable field represented by this `ObjectStreamField`.

SYNTAX `public char getTypeCode()`

DESCRIPTION See the class description and Table 14.

RETURNS The type code of the serializable field represented by this `ObjectStreamField`.

EXAMPLE See `getName()`.

getTypeString()

PURPOSE Retrieves the type string of the serializable field represented by this `ObjectStreamField`.

SYNTAX `public String getTypeString()`

DESCRIPTION This method retrieves the type string of the serializable field represented by this `ObjectStreamField`. The type string is derived from the field's class name. If the field is of a primitive type, `null` is returned. See the class description and Table 13.

RETURNS The type string of the serializable field represented by this `ObjectStreamField` or `null` if this field has a primitive type.

SEE ALSO `getType()`.

EXAMPLE See `getName()`.

isPrimitive()

PURPOSE Determines whether the serializable field represented by this `ObjectStreamField` is of a primitive type.

SYNTAX `public boolean isPrimitive()`

RETURNS `true` if the serializable field represented by this `ObjectStreamField` is of a primitive type; `false` otherwise.

SEE ALSO See `getName()`.

ObjectStreamField()

PURPOSE Constructs an `ObjectStreamField` instance.

SYNTAX `public ObjectStreamField(String fname, Class clazz)`

DESCRIPTION This constructor constructs an `ObjectStreamField` instance. It is typically used within a `serialPersistentFields` declaration. It creates a new instance of `ObjectStreamField` for the serializable field with name `fname` and whose type is the class `clazz`.

O

PARAMETERS

`clazz` The non-`null` `Class` object of the serializable field to be represented by the new `ObjectStreamField`.

`fname` The non-`null` name of the serializable field to be represented by the new `ObjectStreamField`.

EXAMPLE See the class example, `getName()`.

setOffset()

PURPOSE Sets the offset of the serializable field represented by this `ObjectStreamField` within the instance data that is to be serialized.

SYNTAX `protected void setOffset(int offset)`

DESCRIPTION This method sets the offset of the serializable field represented by this `ObjectStreamField` within the instance data that is to be serialized to be `offset`. See `getOffset()` for a description of `offset`. This method is used by subclasses to set the offset and should be used only by code that is performing serialization.

PARAMETERS

`offset` A nonnegative number specifying the offset of the serializable field represented by this `ObjectStreamField`.

SEE ALSO `getOffset()`.

toString()

PURPOSE Returns a string that describes this `ObjectStreamField`.

SYNTAX `public String toString()`

DESCRIPTION This method returns a string that describes this `ObjectStreamField`. The string consists of its type string or type code and its name.

RETURNS A non-`null` string that describes this `ObjectStreamField`.

OVERRIDES `java.lang.Object.toString()`.

EXAMPLE See `java.lang.Object.toString()`.

Package

Syntax

```
public class Package
```

Description

A `Package` object represents a Java package that has been loaded by a class loader. A class loader maintains a list of all packages from which it has ever loaded classes. For example, if a class loader loads `java.beans.Beans`, `java.beans` would appear in its package list.

A `Package` object contains not only the name of the package but also other information about the package. This information is typically included in the manifest in a Java Archive (JAR) file (see `Manifest`) that contains the package code.

The most typical use of a `Package` object is to examine the specification version of a package. For example, if your program expects version 4.2 of a particular package, your program can check to ensure that the version of the package is 4.2 or greater.

Usage

`Package` objects are not meant to be created by anyone other than class loaders. If you want a `Package` object, you need to retrieve it from a class or class loader. Also, if you want the `Package` object for a particular package, some class of that package must be loaded before the class loader will have a `Package` object for it.

This class support two ways to retrieve a `Package` object. The first returns the entire list of `Package` objects (see `getPackages()`). The second returns the `Package` object of a particular package (see `getPackage()`).

Specification and Implementation Information

Every package contains information about the specification that it implements and information about the implementation itself. Typically, this information is provided in the manifest of the JAR file that contains the package (see `Manifest` for more information). The specification and implementation information is divided into three pieces each: title, version, and vendor. The information should be complete enough to unambiguously identify the specification or implementation of the package and to contact the vendors.

Of all six pieces of information, only the specification version has a required syntax.

The Specification Version

The specification version of a package has a special syntax so that versions can be compared with each other. This feature allows your program to check the compatibility of a support package before using it. For example, if your program requires version 4.2 of a particular package and you provide it with version 4.1, the program will fail. See `isCompatibleWith()` for more details.

The specification version is a sequence of non-negative decimal numbers separated by dots. For example, `"1.2.3.0"` is a valid specification version. A specification version is compatible with *v* if the specification version is *later* than *v*. This check is done by comparing each of the numbers in the sequence from left to right. If a number in the specification version is less that the corresponding number in *v*, then the specification version is not compatible with *v*.

If one version string is shorter than the other, simply pretend that the shorter string is padded with dot-zero sequences (`".0"`). This means that a specification version of, for example, `"1.2.0"` is compatible with `"1.2"`.

Sealed Packages

By default, if you have a package of classes, you are allowed to put some of the package's class files in one JAR file and the rest in another. This can cause unexpected results if you inadvertently placed two incompatible packages with the same name in the class path.

You can prevent this problem by *sealing* a package. When you seal a package, all classes in that package must be located together in one JAR file. When a class loader loads a class from a sealed package in a JAR file, it will subsequently refuse to load classes in the same package from other JAR files. Conversely, if you load a class from an unsealed package, the class loader will refuse to load classes from a sealed package with the same name. When such failures occur, the class loader throws `SecurityException`.

It is important to note that sealed packages have no effect on the way class loaders look for a class. For example, you might think that once a class loader loads from a sealed package in a JAR file, it will simply look in that JAR file whenever it needs a class from that package. This assumption is false. The class loader looks for a class without regard to what it has loaded before. Only when the class loader finds the class does it check whether it is permissible to load the class. If the check fails, a `SecurityException` is thrown.

The default package (the package without a name) cannot be sealed.

See `Attribute.Name.SEALED` for information on how to seal a package.

MEMBER SUMMARY	
Package Retrieval Methods	
`getPackage()`	Retrieves the `Package` object for a particular package.
`getPackages()`	Retrieves the list of currently known packages.
Object Methods	
`hashCode()`	Computes the hash code for this `Package` object.
`toString()`	Generates a string representing this package.
	Continued

P

MEMBER SUMMARY	
Query Methods	
`getImplementationTitle()`	Retrieves the name of the implementation of this package.
`getImplementationVendor()`	Retrieves the vendor of the implementation of this package.
`getImplementationVersion()`	Retrieves the version of the implementation of this package.
`getName()`	Retrieves the name of this package.
`getSpecificationTitle()`	Retrieves the name of the specification that this package implements.
`getSpecificationVendor()`	Retrieves the vendor of the specification that this package implements.
`getSpecificationVersion()`	Retrieves the version of the specification that this package implements.
`isCompatibleWith()`	Compares this package's specification version with a desired version.
`isSealed()`	Determines if this package is sealed.

See Also

`Class.getPackage()`, `ClassLoader.getPackage()`, `java.util.jar.JarFile`, `java.util.jar.Manifest`.

Example

This example demonstrates how to set and retrieve the specification and implementation information for a package. The program declares a new package `p` that contains a single class `C`.

p/C.java

```
package p;

public class C {
}
```

This class is placed in a JAR file by using the following manifest, which contains all of the specification and implementation information for the package `p`.

p/manifest.mf

```
Manifest-Version: 1.0

Name: p/
Specification-Title: Demo API Specification
Specification-Version: 1.2.3
Specification-Vendor: Chan, Lee, Kramer
Implementation-Title: package.example
Implementation-Version: 5.3.b1
Implementation-Vendor: Xeo Enterprises
```

Main.java

```
class Main {
    public static void main(String[] args) {
        // Load p.C.
        new p.C();

        Package[] pkgs = Package.getPackages();

        for (int i=0; i<pkgs.length; i++) {
            System.out.println(pkgs[i].getName());
            System.out.println("  Specification Title:      "
                + pkgs[i].getSpecificationTitle());
            System.out.println("  Specification Version:    "
                + pkgs[i].getSpecificationVersion());
            System.out.println("  Specification Vendor:     "
                + pkgs[i].getSpecificationVendor());
            System.out.println("  Implementation Title:     "
                + pkgs[i].getImplementationTitle());
            System.out.println("  Implementation Version:   "
                + pkgs[i].getImplementationVersion());
            System.out.println("  Implementation Vendor:    "
                + pkgs[i].getImplementationVendor());

            if (pkgs[i].isSealed()) {
                System.out.println("  Sealed: true");
            }
        }
    }
}
```

Output

The first command creates the JAR file containing `p.C`. The second command runs `Main` and produces the following output.

```
> jar cfm c.jar p/manifest.mf p/C.class
> java -cp c.jar;. Main
p
  Specification Title:      Demo API Specification
  Specification Version:    1.2.3
  Specification Vendor:     Chan, Lee, Kramer
  Implementation Title:     package.example
  Implementation Version:   5.3.b1
  Implementation Vendor:    Xeo Enterprises
java.net
  Specification Title:      Java Platform API Specification
  Specification Version:    1.2
  Specification Vendor:     Sun Microsystems, Inc.
  Implementation Title:     Java Runtime Environment
  Implementation Version:   1.2beta4
  Implementation Vendor:    Sun Microsystems, Inc.
java.util.jar
  Specification Title:      Java Platform API Specification
  Specification Version:    1.2
  Specification Vendor:     Sun Microsystems, Inc.
  Implementation Title:     Java Runtime Environment
  Implementation Version:   1.2beta4
  Implementation Vendor:    Sun Microsystems, Inc.
...    <removed for brevity>
```

getImplementationTitle()

PURPOSE Retrieves the name of the implementation of this package.

SYNTAX `public String getImplementationTitle()`

DESCRIPTION The implementation title identifies the particular implementation of a package. For example, if a vendor has implementations for several platforms, the name of the platform could be included in the title.

RETURNS The possibly `null` title of this package's implementation.

EXAMPLE See the class example.

getImplementationVendor()

PURPOSE Retrieves the vendor of the implementation of this package.

SYNTAX `public String getImplementationVendor()`

DESCRIPTION This method returns the identity of the organization, company, or person responsible for the implementation of this package. There should be enough information in this string for a user of this package to contact the vendor.

RETURNS The possibly `null` vendor of this package's implementation.

EXAMPLE See the class example.

getImplementationVersion()

PURPOSE Retrieves the version of the implementation of this package.

SYNTAX `public String getImplementationVersion()`

DESCRIPTION This method returns a string that identifies the version of the implementation of this package. The format of the returned string is strictly up to the owner of the implementation. Examples of version strings are `"1.2beta4.1 7/9/1998"` and `"build 1003"`.

RETURNS The possibly `null` version of this package's implementation.

EXAMPLE See the class example.

getName()

PURPOSE Retrieves the name of this package.

SYNTAX `public String getName()`

RETURNS The non-`null` fully qualified name of this package (for example, `"java.net"`).

EXAMPLE See the class example.

getPackage()

PURPOSE Retrieves the `Package` object for a particular package.

SYNTAX `public static Package getPackage(String pname)`

DESCRIPTION This method searches the package list of the caller's class loader for a package called `pname` and returns a `Package` object that represents the package. If `pname` is not found in the class loader's list, the class loader's parent is searched, and so on, up the ancestor class loader hierarchy. If the caller's class loader is `null` (that is, `Class.getClassLoader()` returns `null`), the package list of the system class loader is searched.

PARAMETERS

`pname` A non-`null` fully qualified package name (for example, `"java.net"`).

RETURNS The `Package` object representing the package `pname`. If `pname` is not found, `null` is returned.

SEE ALSO `Class.getPackage()`, `ClassLoader.getPackage()`.

EXAMPLE See `getPackages()`.

getPackages()

PURPOSE Retrieves the list of currently known packages.

SYNTAX `public static Package[] getPackages()`

DESCRIPTION This method retrieves the package list for the caller's class loader. If the caller's class loader is `null` (that is, `Class.getClassLoader()` returns `null`), the package list of the system class loader is returned. No two `Package` objects in the returned list will have the same name. The list of packages are those loaded by the class loader and by the class loader's ancestors. (A class loader's parent is the class loader that loaded it).

RETURNS A new non-`null` array of `Package` objects representing each known package.

SEE ALSO `Class.getPackage()`, `ClassLoader.getPackage()`.

EXAMPLE This example demonstrates the effect of class loading on the package list of two different class loaders. One class loader is the default system class loader (see `ClassLoader`), while the other is a class loader that loads the `Main` class.

In our example, `Main` loads `p.C` from a JAR file. Also, `p.C` loads in `java.beans.Beans`.

The method to obtain the package list from the system class loader is private. To work around this restriction, the program uses reflection to call these methods (`invokeMethod()`). (Don't worry, this isn't a security hole; applications have the ability to enable or disable this type of access.)

```
import java.lang.reflect.*;
import java.util.*;

class Main {
    public static void main(String[] args) {
        // Load in the p.C class.
        new p.C();

        // Dump the package list for Main's class loader.
        System.out.println("Packages loaded by Main's class loader");
        Package[] pkgs = Package.getPackages();
        printPackages(pkgs);

        System.out.println(Package.getPackage("p")!=null);   // true

        // Now dump the package list of the system class loader.
        System.out.println("Packages loaded by the system class loader.");
        pkgs = (Package[])invokeMethod(
            Package.class, "getSystemPackages", new Object[0]);
        printPackages(pkgs);

        System.out.println(invokeMethod(ClassLoader.getSystemClassLoader(),
            "getPackage", new Object[]{"p"})!=null);         // false
    }

    public static void printPackages(Package[] pkgs) {
        // First sort the list.
        Arrays.sort(pkgs,
            new Comparator() {
                public int compare(Object a, Object b) {
                    return ((Package)a).getName().compareTo(
                        ((Package)b).getName());
                }
            }
        );
        for (int i=0; i<pkgs.length; i++) {
            System.out.print("  " + pkgs[i].getName());
            if (pkgs[i].isSealed()) {
                System.out.print(" *sealed*");
            }
            System.out.println();
        }
    }

    public static Object invokeMethod(
            Object o, String name, Object[] params) {
        // Create parameter type array.
        Class[] paramTypes = new Class[params.length];
        for (int i=0; i<params.length; i++) {
            paramTypes[i] = params[i].getClass();
        }
```

P

```
        // Retrieve the object o's class, unless the o
        // is itself a class.
        Class c = o instanceof Class ? (Class)o : o.getClass();

        // Find the declared method by checking all superclasses as well.
        while (c != null) {
            try {
                Method m = c.getDeclaredMethod(name, paramTypes);
                m.setAccessible(true);

                // Invoke the method an return the results.
                return m.invoke(o, params);
            } catch (NoSuchMethodException e) {
                c = c.getSuperclass();
            } catch (Exception e) {
                break;
            }
        }
        return null;
    }
}
```

OUTPUT The p.C class is placed in a JAR file called c.jar. Note that p shows up in Main's class loader but not in the system class loader.

```
> java -cp .;c.jar Main
Packages loaded by Main's class loader
  java.beans
  java.io
  java.lang
  java.lang.ref
  java.lang.reflect
  java.net
  java.security
  java.util
  java.util.jar
  java.util.zip
  p
  sun.io
  ...             <list truncated for brevity>
true

Packages loaded by the system class loader.
  java.beans
  java.io
  java.lang
  java.lang.ref
  java.lang.reflect
  java.net
  java.security
  java.security.cert
  java.util
  java.util.jar
  java.util.zip
  sun.io
  ...             <list truncated for brevity>
false
```

getSpecificationTitle()

PURPOSE Retrieves the name of the specification that this package implements.

SYNTAX `public String getSpecificationTitle()`

DESCRIPTION The specification title identifies the particular specification that this package implements. For example, there might be two specifications for a package—basic and advanced—where the advanced version contains more classes. This information would be included in the specification title. However, suppose that a vendor supplied different implementations of a specification for different platforms. If they all behave the same and implement the same specification, their specification titles should all be the same.

RETURNS The possibly `null` title of the specification that this package implements.

EXAMPLE See the class example.

getSpecificationVendor()

PURPOSE Retrieves the vendor of the specification that this package implements.

SYNTAX `public String getSpecificationVendor()`

DESCRIPTION This method returns the identity of the organization, company, or person responsible for the specification that this package implements. There should be enough information in this string for a user of this package to contact the vendor.

RETURNS The possibly `null` vendor of the specification that this package implements.

EXAMPLE See the class example.

getSpecificationVersion()

PURPOSE Retrieves the version of the specification that this package implements.

SYNTAX `public String getSpecificationVersion()`

DESCRIPTION The specification version is a sequence of non-negative decimal numbers separated by dots. For example, `"1.2.3.0"` is a valid specification version. See the class description for more information about the specification version.

RETURNS The possibly `null` specification version that this package implements.

SEE ALSO `isCompatibleWith()`.

EXAMPLE See the class example.

hashCode()

PURPOSE Computes the hash code for this `Package` object.

SYNTAX
```
public int hashCode()
```

DESCRIPTION The hash code of a `Package` object is strictly dependent on the name of the package.

Two `Package` objects with the same name will have the same hash code. Note that unequal `Package` objects might also have the same hash code, although the hash code algorithm reduces this possibility. The hash code is typically used as the key in a hash table.

RETURNS This `Package` object's hash code.

OVERRIDES `java.lang.Object.hashCode()`.

SEE ALSO `equals()`, `java.lang.Object.equals()`.

EXAMPLE See `java.lang.Object.hashCode()`.

isCompatibleWith()

PURPOSE Compares this package's specification version with a desired version.

SYNTAX
```
public boolean isCompatibleWith(String v) throws
    NumberFormatException
```

DESCRIPTION This method compares the specification version of this package with v. If the specification version of this package is less than that of v, this method returns `false`; otherwise, it returns `true`.

The specification version is a sequence of non-negative decimal numbers separated by dots. For example, `"1.2.3.0"` is a specification version. The specification version is check with `v` by comparing each of the corresponding numbers in the sequence, left to right. If some number in this specification version is less than the corresponding number in v, the specification version is less than v and `false` is immediately returned.

If one version string is shorter than the other, this method simply pads the shorter string with dot-zero sequences (`".0"`). This means that a specification version of, for example, `"1.2.0"` is compatible with `"1.2"`.

Note that for a class loader to have a `Package` object for a package, it must first have loaded a class from that package. If you know exactly how the package is packaged (for example, in a JAR file), you might be able to determine the specification version of a package before any class from it is loaded. However, it is more convenient and portable to force the class loader to load a class from the package and then examine its specification version.

RETURNS `true` if this package's specification version is greater than or equal to v.

EXCEPTIONS

`NumberFormatException`

If a component in either this specification version or v is not a non-negative decimal number.

SEE ALSO `getSpecificationVersion()`.

EXAMPLE

```
// Load p.C.
new p.C();

Package p = Package.getPackage("p");
if (p == null) {
    System.out.println("Package p is not found.");
    System.exit(1);
}
System.out.println("Specification Version of p: "
    + p.getSpecificationVersion());                     // 1.2.3

System.out.println( p.isCompatibleWith("1") );          // true
System.out.println( p.isCompatibleWith("1.0") );        // true
System.out.println( p.isCompatibleWith("1.2") );        // true
System.out.println( p.isCompatibleWith("1.2.3") );      // true
System.out.println( p.isCompatibleWith("1.2.3.0") );    // true
System.out.println( p.isCompatibleWith("1.2.3.0.0.0") ); // true
System.out.println( p.isCompatibleWith("1.2.3.1") );    // false

System.out.println( p.isCompatibleWith("0") );          // true
System.out.println( p.isCompatibleWith("2") );          // false
System.out.println( p.isCompatibleWith("1.beta") );   // NumberFormatException
```

P

isSealed()

PURPOSE Determines if this package is sealed.

SYNTAX

```
public boolean isSealed()
public boolean isSealed(URL url)
```

DESCRIPTION This methods returns `true` if this package is sealed with respect to `url`. This means that the class loader can load classes only from the JAR file at the URL `url`. See the class description for more information about sealed packages.

If `url` is not specified and if this package is sealed, this method returns `true`.

PARAMETERS

`url` A non-`null` `URL` object.

RETURNS `true` if the package is sealed with respect to `url` or if `url` is not specified.

EXAMPLE This example demonstrates how sealing works by constructing a scenario that tries to break it.

First, we declare a new package `p` with two classes, `Far` and `Near`. The `Far` class is put into a JAR file that specifies that the package `p` is to be sealed. The sealed JAR file is installed on a remote site. The `Near` class is included in the same JAR file as the `Main` class. The `Main` program first loads `Far`. This results in the class loader's creating a `Package` object for `p` and sealing it with respect to the JAR file's location.

Then `Main` loads `Near`. The class loader finds `p.Near.class` and determines its package to be `p`. The class loader then notices that `p` is sealed, determines that `p.Near.class` did not come from the sealed URL, and throws a `SecurityException`.

The same failure would occur if `Near` was loaded before `Far`.

Main.java

```
import java.net.*;

class Main {
    public static void main(String[] args) {
        new p.Far();

        try {
            Package pkg = Package.getPackage("p");

            System.out.println( pkg.isSealed() );
                                            // true
            System.out.println( pkg.isSealed(new URL("http://www.xeo.com")) );
                                            // false
            System.out.println(
                pkg.isSealed(new URL("http://www.xeo.com/bookegs/far.jar")) );
                                            // true
        } catch (MalformedURLException e) {
            e.printStackTrace();
        }

        // Now cause the failure.
        new p.Near();
    }
}
```

main.mf This is the manifest for the `main.jar` file.

```
Manifest-Version: 1.0
Main-Class: Main
Class-Path: http://www.xeo.com/bookegs/far.jar
```

p/Near.java

```
package p;

public class Near {
    public void print() {
        System.out.println(getClass());
    }
}
```

p/Far.java

```
package p;

public class Far {
    public void print() {
        System.out.println(getClass());
    }
}
```

p/far.mf This is the manifest for the `far.jar` file.

```
Manifest-Version: 1.0

Name: p/
Sealed: true
```

OUTPUT

```
> java -jar main.jar
true
false
true
Exception in thread "main" java.lang.SecurityException: sealing violation
        at java.net.URLClassLoader.defineClass(URLClassLoader.java:176)
        at java.net.URLClassLoader.access$1(URLClassLoader.java:156)
        at java.net.URLClassLoader$1.run(URLClassLoader.java:137)
        at java.security.AccessController.doPrivileged(Native Method)
        at java.net.URLClassLoader.findClass(URLClassLoader.java:131)
        at java.lang.ClassLoader.loadClass(ClassLoader.java:245)
        at java.lang.ClassLoader.loadClass(ClassLoader.java:195)
        at Main.main(Main.java:16)
```

toString()

P

PURPOSE Generates a string representing this package.

SYNTAX `public String toString()`

DESCRIPTION This method generates a string containing this package's name and all of its specification information.

RETURNS The non-`null` string representation of this package.

OVERRIDES `Object.toString()`.

EXAMPLE

```
Package p = Package.getPackage("java.lang");
if (p == null) {
    System.out.println("Package p is not found.");
    System.exit(1);
}
System.out.println(p);
    // package java.lang, Java Platform API Specification, version 1.2
```

ParsePosition

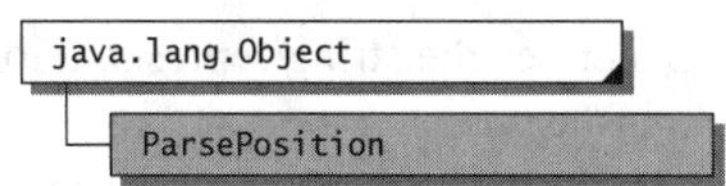

Syntax

```
public class ParsePosition extends Object
```

Description

Parsing is the operation of recognizing a pattern of digits in a string and returning it as a number, date, or message object. `ParsePosition` is a class used by `Format` and its subclasses to keep track of the current position in a string during parsing. The index property records the current position. See Figure 12. By design, as you parse a string with different `Format` objects, all `Format` objects can use the same `ParsePosition`. A `ParsePosition` object tracks Unicode characters and thus is not locale-sensitive.

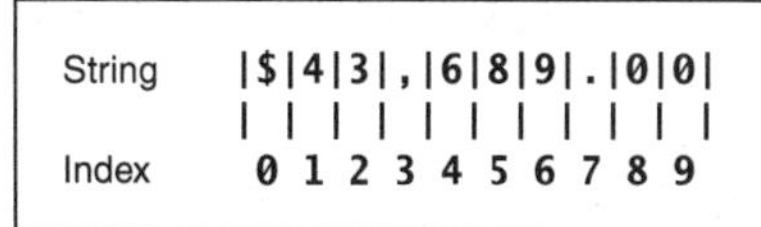

FIGURE 12: **`ParsePosition`.**

The classes that use a `ParsePosition` object include `Format` and its subclasses. For example, the `parseObject()` method takes a `ParsePosition` object, as does the `parse()` method in `NumberFormat` and all of its subclasses: `DecimalFormat`, `DateFormat`, `SimpleDateFormat`, and `MessageFormat`.

See *The Java Class Libraries, Second Edition, Volume 1* for more information about this class.

P

Changes for Version 1.2

There are two new getter/setter methods: `getErrorIndex()` and `setErrorIndex()`. This class now also overrides `Object` methods: `equals()`, `hashCode()`, and `toString()`.

MEMBER SUMMARY	
Constructor	
`ParsePosition()`	Constructs a `ParsePosition` instance that has an initial index.
Parse Methods	
`getIndex()`	Retrieves the current parse position.
`setIndex()`	Sets the current parse position.
1.2 `getErrorIndex()`	Retrieves the index at which a parse error occurred.
1.2 `setErrorIndex()`	Sets the index at which a parse error occurred.

Continued

MEMBER SUMMARY	
Object Methods	
Δ `toString()`	Generates the string representation of this `ParsePosition` instance.
Δ `equals()`	Compares this `ParsePosition` instance with another object for equality.
Δ `hashCode()`	Computes the hash code of this `ParsePosition` instance.

See Also

`Format`.
`ParsePosition` in *The Java Class Libraries, Second Edition, Volume 1*.

Δ equals()

PURPOSE Compares this `ParsePosition` instance with another object for equality.

SYNTAX `public boolean equals(Object obj)`

DESCRIPTION This method compares this `ParsePosition` instance with `obj` for equality. If `obj` is a `ParsePosition` instance and has the same values of the current index and the error index, then the objects are equal and this method returns `true`. If the `ParsePosition` values are not equal or if `obj` is `null` or not a `ParsePosition` instance, this method returns `false`.

1.2 CHANGES In Version 1.1, this method was not implemented in `ParsePosition`; instead, the same method in `Object` was called.

PARAMETERS

`obj` The possibly `null` object with which to compare.

RETURNS `true` if `obj` is not `null`, is of type `ParsePosition` and is equal to this `ParsePosition` instance; `false` otherwise.

OVERRIDES `java.lang.Object.equals()`.

SEE ALSO `hashCode()`.

EXAMPLE This example creates two `ParsePosition` instances, compares them for equality, and then computes the hash code of the first one.

```
import java.text.ParsePosition;

class Main {
    public static void main(String args[]) {
        // Create two parse positions.
        ParsePosition parsePos1 = new ParsePosition(0);
        System.out.println(parsePos1.toString());
            // java.text.ParsePosition[index=0,errorIndex=-1]
```

P

```
        ParsePosition parsePos2 = new ParsePosition(0);
        System.out.println(parsePos2.toString());
            // java.text.ParsePosition[index=0,errorIndex=-1]

        // Tests for equality.
        System.out.println( parsePos1.equals(parsePos2) ); // true

        // Compute hashcode.
        System.out.println( parsePos1.hashCode() );        // -65536
    }
}
```

1.2 getErrorIndex()

PURPOSE Retrieves the index at which an error occurred.

SYNTAX `public int getErrorIndex()`

RETURNS The index, an `int`, at which an error occurred, or `-1` if the error index has not been set.

SEE ALSO `setErrorIndex()`.

Δ hashCode()

PURPOSE Computes the hash code of this `ParsePosition` instance.

SYNTAX `public int hashCode()`

DESCRIPTION This method computes the hash code, `int`, of this `ParsePosition` instance based on the current index and the error index of this object. Two `ParsePosition` instances that are equal (according to `equals()`) will have the same hash code. However, two `ParsePosition` instances that do not have the same properties might also have the same hash code, although the hash code algorithm reduces this possibility. The hash code is typically used as the key in a hash table.

1.2 CHANGES In Version 1.1, this method was not implemented in `ParsePosition`; instead, the same method in `Object` was called.

RETURNS The hash code of this `ParsePosition` instance.

OVERRIDES `java.lang.Object.hashCode()`.

SEE ALSO `equals()`.

EXAMPLE See `equals()`.

P

1.2 setErrorIndex()

PURPOSE Sets the index at which a parse error occurred.

SYNTAX `public void setErrorIndex(int index)`

DESCRIPTION This method sets the index at which a parse error occurred. Formatters should set this before returning an error code from their `parseObject()` method. The default value is `-1` if this is not set.

PARAMETERS

`index` The character index at which a parse error occurred, an `int`.

SEE ALSO `getErrorIndex()`.

Δ toString()

PURPOSE Generates the string representation of this `ParsePosition` instance.

SYNTAX `public String toString()`

DESCRIPTION This method returns the string representation of this `ParsePosition` instance, including the class name, current index, and error index. Here is an example of such as string:

```
java.text.ParsePosition[index=0,errorIndex=-1]
```

1.2 CHANGES In Version 1.1, this method was not implemented in `ParsePosition`; instead, the same method in `Object` was called.

RETURNS The non-`null` string representation of a `ParsePosition` instance.

OVERRIDES `java.lang.Object.toString()`.

EXAMPLE See `equals()`.

java.net
PasswordAuthentication

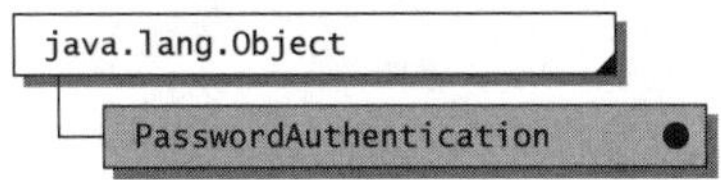

Syntax

```
public final class PasswordAuthentication
```

Description

The `PasswordAuthentication` class represents a name/password pair. It is used by the `Authenticator` class to return authentication information.

Usage

The `PasswordAuthentication` class is used by the `Authenticator` class to return authentication information. For example, an invocation of the static method `requestPasswordAuthentication()` returns a `PasswordAuthentication` instance from which you can extract the user name and password.

```
PasswordAuthentication pw = Authenticator.requestPasswordAuthentication(
    server, 80, "http", null, "basic");
// use password
...
// clear it out after we're done
char pwbuf = pw.getPassword();
for (int i = 0; i < pwbuf.length; i++) {
   pwbuf[i] = (char)0;
}
```


MEMBER SUMMARY	
Constructor	
`PasswordAuthentication()`	Constructs a new instance of `PasswordAuthentication` using a user name and a password.
Access Methods	
`getPassword()`	Retrieves the password of this `PasswordAuthentication` instance.
`getUserName()`	Retrieves the user name of this `PasswordAuthentication` instance.

See Also

`Authenticator`.

Example

See the `Authenticator` class example.

getPassword()

PURPOSE Retrieves the password of this `PasswordAuthentication` instance.

SYNTAX `public char[] getPassword()`

DESCRIPTION This method returns a direct pointer to the `char` array used to store the password. If the caller changes this array, it will be changed in this `PasswordAuthentication` instance as well. To eliminate the password from memory (thus maintaining its secrecy), the caller should zero out the contents of the array when it is no longer needed.

RETURNS The non-`null` array containing the password.

SEE ALSO `getUserName()`.

EXAMPLE See the `Authenticator` class example.

getUserName()

PURPOSE Retrieves the user name of this `PasswordAuthentication` instance.

SYNTAX `public String getUserName()`

RETURNS A non-`null` string containing the user name.

EXAMPLE See the `Authenticator` class example.

PasswordAuthentication()

PURPOSE Constructs a new instance of `PasswordAuthentication` using a user name and a password.

SYNTAX `public PasswordAuthentication(String userName, char[] password)`

DESCRIPTION This method constructs a new instance of `PasswordAuthentication` using a `userName` and `password`. A copy of the password array is made. The caller should try to maintain the password's secrecy by zeroing out the array's contents as soon as possible when the password is no longer needed. This won't affect the contents of the newly created `PasswordAuthentication` instance.

PARAMETERS

`password` A non-`null` array containing the password.

`userName` A non-`null` string that identifies the entity with the password.

EXAMPLE See the `Authenticator` class example.

java.lang.ref

PhantomReference

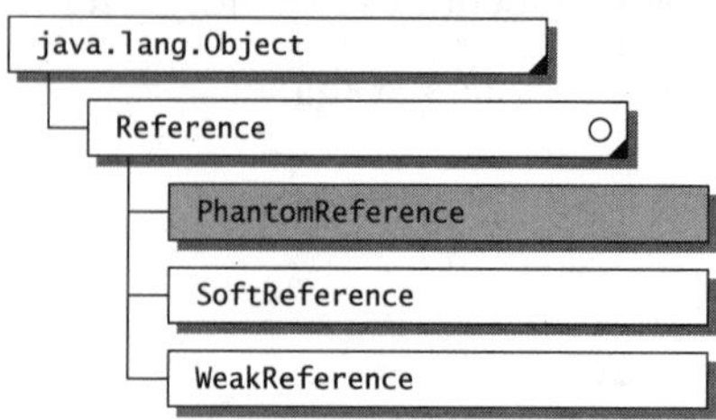

Syntax

```
public class PhantomReference extends Reference
```

Description

The `PhantomReference` class represents a *phantom reference*. A phantom reference is a type of reference object (see `Reference`) that you use to receive notification of an object after it has been finalized but before it is reclaimed (finalization is described in *The Java Language Specification, First Edition*, Section 12.6). See Figure 13.

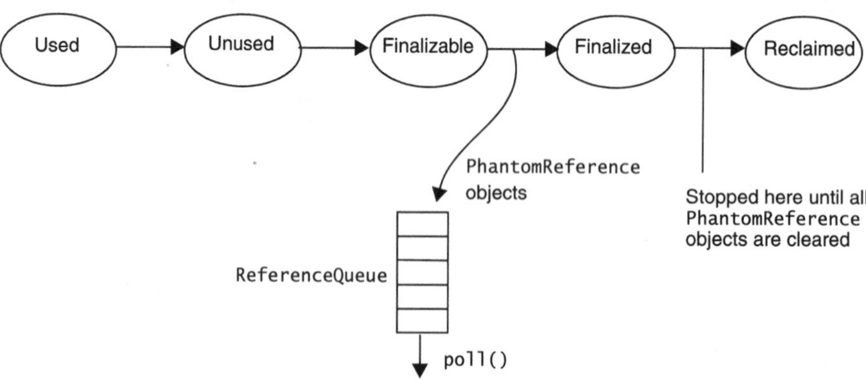

FIGURE 13: Phantom Reference Notification.

Phantom reference notification is very similar to weak reference notification. You could use either reference type to determine when an object is being collected. Only when an object can be *resurrected* does it matter which reference type you use. (Resurrection occurs when an object makes itself *used* during finalization; see *The Java Language Specification, First Edition*, Section 12.6, for more details.) In particular, if the object is resurrectable and you want to know when the object is really going to be reclaimed, you must use a phantom reference. If you are interested in when the garbage collector collects a resurrectable object, you must use a

P

weak reference. However, resurrection is rarely used (and highly discouraged), so this situation almost never arises.

A phantom reference differs from other reference types in that you must explicitly clear it in order for the object to be reclaimed (that is, its storage is returned to the heap). See Figure 13. However, the phantom reference is automatically cleared if the phantom reference itself is collected.

Usage

To receive notification of when an object `obj` is about to be reclaimed, you first must create a reference queue (see `ReferenceQueue`). You then construct a phantom reference object, supplying both `obj` and the reference queue. Finally, you poll the reference queue. Then when the phantom reference object appears in the queue, you know that `obj` is about to be reclaimed. Following is some sample code that demonstrates these steps.

```
ReferenceQueue q = new ReferenceQueue();
PhantomReference pr = new PhantomReference(obj, q);
try {
    Reference r = rq.remove();
    r.clear();         // Free the object for final reclamation
} catch (InterruptedException e) {
    e.printStackTrace();
}
```

MEMBER SUMMARY	
Constructor	
`PhantomReference()`	Constructs a `PhantomReference` instance.
Reference Retrieval Method	
`get()`	Returns `null`.

See Also

`Reference`, `ReferenceQueue`, `SoftReference`, `WeakReference`.

Example

This example creates a thread that watches for objects to become unused. Each object has a label, and object labels are kept in a set. When an object becomes unused, the thread removes its label from the set.

```
import java.lang.ref.*;
import java.io.*;
import java.util.*;

class Main {
    public static void main(String[] args) throws IOException {
```

```
        Set isUsed = new HashSet();
        Object o = new Object();
        WatcherThread thread = new WatcherThread(isUsed);
        thread.start();

        thread.watch("A", o);
        System.out.println( isUsed.contains("A") );   // true

        // Wait a few seconds before making o unused.
        try {
            Thread.sleep(5000);
        } catch (Exception e) {
            e.printStackTrace();
        }
        o = null;

        // Use all available memory to force a garbage-collection.
        eatMemory(new LinkedList());

        System.out.println( isUsed.contains("A") );   // false
    }
    static void eatMemory(LinkedList l) {
        try {
            l.add(new double[100000]);
            eatMemory(l);
        } catch (OutOfMemoryError e) {
            System.out.println("**** OUT OF MEMORY ****");
            l.clear();
            System.gc();
        }
    }
}

class WatcherThread extends Thread {
    ReferenceQueue refq = new ReferenceQueue();
    Map map = new HashMap();
    Set set;

    public WatcherThread(Set s) {
        set = s;
    }

    public void watch(String label, Object o) {
        Reference r = new PhantomReference(o, refq);
        set.add(label);
        map.put(r, label);
    }

    public void run() {
        try {
            while (true) {
                // Wait for phantom reference notification.
                Reference r = refq.remove();

                r.clear();
                set.remove(map.get(r));
                map.remove(r);
            }
        } catch (Exception e) {
            e.printStackTrace();
```

P

```
            }
        }
    }
```

get()

PURPOSE Returns `null`.

SYNTAX `public Object get()`

RETURNS This method always returns `null`.

OVERRIDES `Reference.get()`.

EXAMPLE See `Reference`.

PhantomReference()

PURPOSE Constructs a `PhantomReference` instance.

SYNTAX `public PhantomReference(Object referent, ReferenceQueue queue)`

DESCRIPTION This constructor creates a `PhantomReference` instance that refers to `referent`. The garbage collector will enqueue the new `PhantomReference` instance to `queue` sometime after `referent` is finalized.

PARAMETERS

`queue` A non-`null` reference queue.

`referent` A non-`null` object.

EXAMPLE See the class example.

java.io

PipedReader

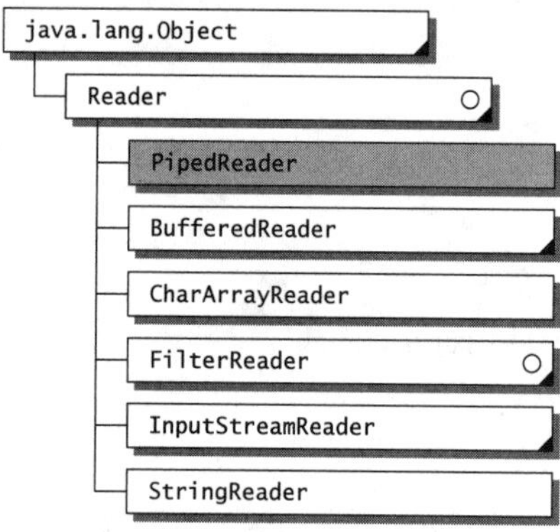

Syntax

`public class PipedReader extends Reader`

Description

The `PipedReader` class is used to provide a character input stream to a *pipe*. A pipe is a useful programming paradigm for communication between two threads. See `PipedInputStream` for more on the use of pipes. The `PipedReader` class is paired with the `PipedWriter` class, which writes characters to the pipe.

See *The Java Class Libraries, Second Edition, Volume 1* for more information about this class.

P

Changes for Version 1.2

The `ready()` method overrides `Reader.ready()` to return `true` or `false` depending on whether data is ready to be read from the pipe. In Version 1.1, `ready()` was inherited from `Reader` and always returned `false`.

The implementation of this class has been modified to do more error checking and to note the state of the thread writing to the pipe.

MEMBER SUMMARY	
Constructor	
`PipedReader()`	Constructs a `PipedReader` instance.
Input Methods	
Δ `read()`	Reads characters from this `PipedReader`.
Δ `ready()`	Determines whether this `PipedReader` is ready to be read.

MEMBER SUMMARY	
Pipe Methods	
`close()`	Closes this `PipedReader`.
`connect()`	Connects this `PipedReader` to a piped writer.

See Also

`PipedWriter`.
`PipedReader` in *The Java Class Libraries, Second Edition, Volume 1*.

Δ read()

PURPOSE Reads characters from this `PipedReader`.

SYNTAX

```
public synchronized int read() throws IOException
public synchronized int read(char buf[], int offset, int count)
   throws IOException
```

DESCRIPTION The first form of this method reads a character from this `PipedReader`. The second form reads `count` number of characters from this `PipedReader` into `buf` starting at offset `offset`. These methods block until input data is available, end-of-stream is reached, or an exception is thrown.

1.2 CHANGES In Version 1.1, the form that accepts no arguments was inherited from `Reader`. In Version 1.2, that form is overridden. Also, the implementation of this method now does more checks with respect to the state of the pipe, such as whether it has been connected and closed and the active state of the thread has been written to the pipe.

PARAMETERS

`buf` The non-`null` `char` array in which to store the characters read.

`count` The number of characters to read. `0` ≤ `count` ≤ `buf.length-offset`.

`offset` The index in `buf` at which to start storing characters. `0` ≤ `offset` ≤ `buf.length`.

RETURNS The first form of this method returns the character read; the second form returns the number of characters read. Both forms return `-1` if end-of-stream is reached before any characters are read.

EXCEPTIONS

`ArrayIndexOutOfBoundsException`
If `count` or `offset` is outside of the specified bounds.

`InterruptedIOException`
If the current thread is interrupted while reading from the pipe.

`IOException`

If the pipe was not connected, or if the pipe has been closed, or if the thread writing data to the pipe is not active.

OVERRIDES `Reader.read()`.

EXAMPLE See the `PipedReader` class example in *The Java Class Libraries, Second Edition, Volume 1*.

Δ ready()

PURPOSE Determines whether this `PipedReader` is ready to be read.

SYNTAX `public synchronized boolean ready() throws IOException`

DESCRIPTION This method determines if this `PipedReader` is ready to be read. A `PipedReader` is ready to be read if there is data in the pipe to be read.

1.2 CHANGES In Version 1.1, `PipedReader` inherited `ready()` from `Reader`. `Reader.ready()`, which always returns `false`.

RETURNS `true` if there is data in the pipe to be read; `false` otherwise.

EXCEPTIONS

`IOException`

If the pipe has not been connected, or if the pipe has been closed, or if the thread writing to the pipe is not alive.

OVERRIDES `Reader.ready()`.

java.io
PipedWriter

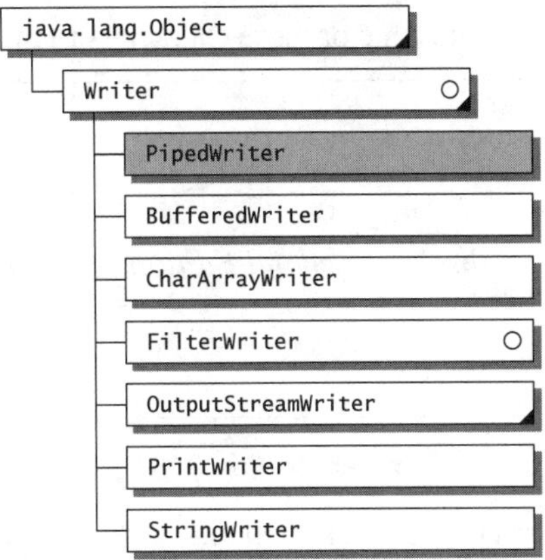

Syntax

`public class PipedWriter extends Writer`

Description

The `PipedWriter` class is used to provide a character output stream for a *pipe*. A pipe is a useful programming paradigm for communication between two threads. See `PipedInputStream` for more on the use of pipes. The `PipedWriter` class is paired with the `PipedReader` class, which reads characters from the pipe.

See *The Java Class Libraries, Second Edition, Volume 1* for more information about this class.

P

Changes for Version 1.2

The implementation of this class has been modified to do more error checking and to note the state of the thread writing to the pipe.

MEMBER SUMMARY	
Constructor	
`PipedWriter()`	Constructs a `PipedWriter` instance.
Pipe Methods	
`close()`	Closes this `PipedWriter`.
`connect()`	Connects this `PipedWriter` to a piped reader.
`flush()`	Flushes this `PipedWriter`.
	Continued

MEMBER SUMMARY	
Output Method	
Δ `write()`	Writes one or more characters to this `PipedWriter`.

See Also

`PipedReader`.
`PipedWriter` in *The Java Class Libraries, Second Edition, Volume 1.*

Δ write()

PURPOSE Writes one or more characters to this `PipedWriter`.

SYNTAX

```
public void write(int ch) throws IOException
public void write(char[] buf, int offset, int count) throws
   IOException
```

DESCRIPTION The first form of this method writes the lower 16 bits of `ch`. The second form writes to this `PipedWriter` `count` number of characters from the `char` array `buffer` starting at index `offset`.

The characters written to this `PipedWriter` can be read from the piped reader connected to this `PipedWriter`. Characters not yet read from the piped reader are buffered in the pipe. If the pipe becomes full, the `write()` method blocks until there is room in the pipe to write more characters.

1.2 CHANGES In Version 1.2, the implementation of this method does more checks regarding the state of the pipe, such as whether it has been connected and closed and the active state of the thread reading from the pipe. In Version 1.1, the first form of this method was inherited from the `Writer` class.

PARAMETERS

- `buffer` The non-`null` `char` array containing the characters to be written.
- `ch` The character to be written.
- `count` The number of characters to write. `0` ≤ `count` ≤ `buffer.length-offset`.
- `offset` The index in `buffer` at which to start getting the characters for writing. `0` ≤ `offset` < `buffer.length`.

EXCEPTIONS

`ArrayIndexOutOfBoundsException`
If `count` or `offset` is outside of the specified bounds.

`InterruptedIOException`
If the pipe is full and the current thread is interrupted while waiting for space to free up in the pipe.

`IOException`

If this `PipedWriter` has already been closed, or if the thread that was reading from the pipe is no longer alive (it died without closing the pipe).

`NullPointerException`

If you try to write to this `PipedWriter` before it has been connected.

OVERRIDES `Writer.write()`.

EXAMPLE See the `PipedReader` class example in *The Java Class Libraries, Second Edition, Volume 1.*

java.io PrintStream

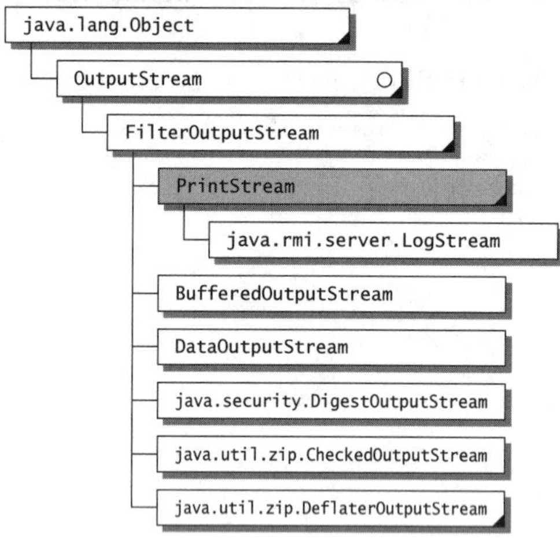

Syntax

```
public class PrintStream extends FilterOutputStream
```

Description

The `PrintStream` class represents a *print stream*, which is a filter stream that accepts Java data values and writes out their string representations as a byte stream. The characters in the string representation are converted into bytes using a platform-dependent default byte encoding.

P

See *The Java Class Libraries, Second Edition, Volume 1* for more information about this class.

Changes for Version 1.2

In Version 1.1, the `PrintStream` constructors were deprecated. In Version 1.2, the constructors have been undeprecated.

MEMBER SUMMARY	
Constructor	
Δ `PrintStream()`	Constructs a `PrintStream` instance.
Output Methods	
`print()`	Prints a data value to this `PrintStream`.
`println()`	Prints a data value followed by a line separator to this `PrintStream`.
`write()`	Writes bytes to this `PrintStream`.

MEMBER SUMMARY

Error-Checking Methods	
`checkError()`	Determines whether this `PrintStream` has had any exceptions.
`setError()`	Records that this `PrintStream` has encountered an IO exception.
Stream Methods	
`close()`	Closes this `PrintStream`.
`flush()`	Flushes any buffered output from this `PrintStream`.

See Also

`PrintWriter`.
`PrintStream` in *The Java Class Libraries, Second Edition, Volume 1.*

Δ PrintStream()

PURPOSE Constructs a `PrintStream` instance.

SYNTAX

```
public PrintStream(OutputStream out)
public PrintStream(OutputStream out, boolean autoFlush)
```

DESCRIPTION This constructor creates an instance of `PrintStream` that writes to the underlying output stream `out`.

If `autoflush` is `true`, output sent to this stream is automatically flushed when `println()` is used. If `autoflush` is `false` or unspecified, no automatic flushing is done.

1.2 CHANGES This method was deprecated in Version 1.1.

PARAMETERS

`autoflush` If `true`, this `PrintStream` will automatically flush output after each line separator is written. If `false`, no automatic flushing will be performed.

`out` The non-`null` output stream for which to create the print stream filter.

EXAMPLE

```
Socket sock = ...;
PrintStream out = new PrintStream(sock.getOutputStream());
out.println("hello");
```

P

java.io

PrintWriter

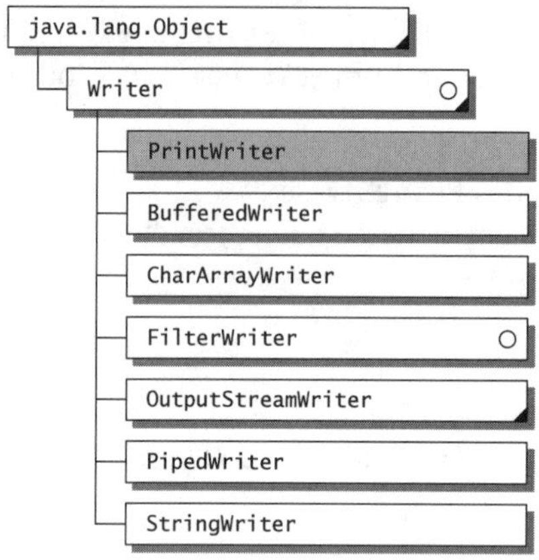

Syntax

```
public class PrintWriter extends Writer
```

Description

The `PrintWriter` class represents a *print writer*, which is a character output stream, or *writer*, that accepts Java data values and writes out their string representations as characters.

See *The Java Class Libraries, Second Edition, Volume 1* for more information about this class.

P

Changes for Version 1.2

The out field was made protected (instead of private) for use by subclasses of `PrintWriter`. The `println()` methods that accept a single argument have been rewritten to use the `println()` method that accepts no argument so that a subclass can just override the no-arg `println()` method to affect the behavior of all of the `println()` methods.

MEMBER SUMMARY	
Constructor	
`PrintWriter()`	Constructs a `PrintWriter` instance.
Output Methods	
`print()`	Prints a data value to this `PrintWriter`.
Δ `println()`	Prints a data value followed by a newline to this `PrintWriter`.
`write()`	Writes characters to this `PrintWriter`.

MEMBER SUMMARY	
Error-Checking Methods	
`checkError()`	Determines whether this `PrintWriter` has had any exceptions.
`setError()`	Records that this `PrintWriter` has encountered an IO exception.
Close Methods	
`close()`	Closes this `PrintWriter`.
`flush()`	Flushes any buffered output from this `PrintWriter`.
Protected Field	
1.2 `out`	Holds the underlying `Writer` to which this `PrintWriter` writes.

See Also

`PrintStream`.
`PrintWriter` in *The Java Class Libraries, Second Edition, Volume 1.*

1.2 out

PURPOSE Holds the underlying `Writer` to which this `PrintWriter` writes.

SYNTAX `protected Writer out`

DESCRIPTION This field is initialized by the `PrintWriter` constructor and used by all methods when writing data to the underlying stream.

P

Δ println()

PURPOSE Prints a data value followed by a line terminator to this `PrintWriter`.

SYNTAX

```
public void println()
public void println(boolean bool)
public void println(int inum)
public void println(long lnum)
public void println(float fnum)
public void println(double dnum)
public void println(Object obj)
public void println(String str)
public void println(char ch)
public void println(char[] charArray)
```

DESCRIPTION The first form of this method prints a line terminator to this `PrintWriter`. The last nine forms print a data value followed by a line terminator to this `PrintWriter`. The output generated is the string representation of the data value to be printed. `String.valueOf()` is used on the data value to obtain its string representation.

The data is written to the underlying `PrintWriter` by using `write()`. If this `PrintWriter` is an autoflush writer, the output is automatically flushed after it has been written.

If you want to subclass `PrintWriter` to affect how it prints line terminators (for example, to produce double spacing), you need only to override the form of `println()` that accepts no argument. This will affect all other `println()` forms.

1.2 CHANGES All of the `println()` methods that accept an argument have been rewritten to use the form that accepts no argument so as to make subclassing easier.

PARAMETERS

`bool`	The `boolean` value (`true` or `false`) to print.
`ch`	The `char` value to print.
`charArray`	The non-`null` `char` array to print.
`dnum`	The `double` value to print.
`fnum`	The `float` value to print.
`inum`	The `int` value to print.
`lnum`	The `long` value to print.
`obj`	The object to print (`null` is accepted).
`str`	The string to print (`null` is accepted).

SEE ALSO `flush()`, `java.lang.String.valueOf()`, `write()`.

EXAMPLE

```
import java.io.*;

class Main {
    public static void main(String[] args) {
        PrintWriter out = new DoublePrintWriter(System.out);
        out.println("hello");
        out.println("there");
        out.println("readers");
        out.flush();
    }

    static public class DoublePrintWriter extends PrintWriter {
        public DoublePrintWriter(PrintStream s) {
            super(s);
        }
        public void println() {
            super.println();
            super.println();
        }
    }
}
```

Properties

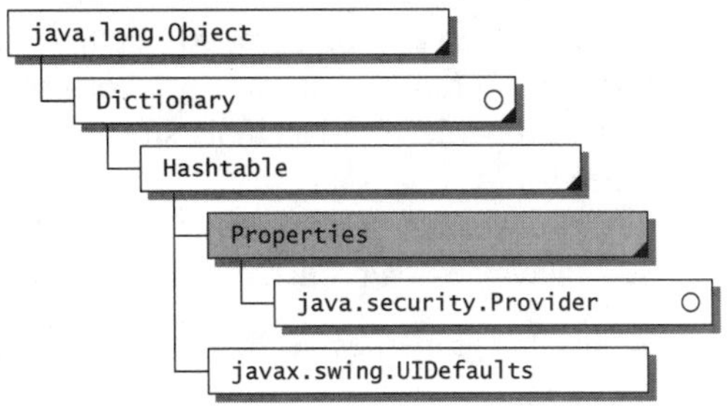

Syntax

```
public class Properties extends Hashtable
```

Description

The `Properties` class is used to represent a *properties list*. Each item on the list is called a *property* and consists of a *property name* and a *property value*. Each property name and property value is a Unicode string.

See *The Java Class Libraries, Second Edition, Volume 1* for more information about this class.

Changes for Version 1.2

Two methods are new. The first is `setProperty()`, which adds or modifies a property in a `Properties` object. In Version 1.1, a property was added or modified by calling `put()`. However, since `put()` accepts arbitrary objects, it was possible to mistakenly supply nonstring values. The `setProperty()` method, which should be used in place of `put()`, accepts only strings.

The second new method is `store()`. It works just like `save()` and replaces `save()`. The problem with `save()` was that it did not throw an `IOException` when an IO error occurred. As a result, `save()` has been deprecated.

`Hashtable` now implements `Map`. This adds a number of new methods, such as `putAll()` and `keySet()` (see `Map` for more details), to `Hashtable`. Since the `Properties` class inherits from `Hashtable`, these new methods are now available in this class.

MEMBER SUMMARY	
Constructor	
`Properties()`	Constructs a properties list.

Continued

P

MEMBER SUMMARY	
Property Methods	
`getProperty()`	Retrieves the value of a property in this properties list.
`list()`	Writes this properties list to a print output stream or writer.
`load()`	Reads properties from an input stream and adds them to this properties list.
`propertyNames()`	Retrieves the list of property names from this properties list.
1.2 `setProperty()`	Sets the value of a property in this properties list.
1.2 `store()`	Writes this properties list to an output stream.
Protected Field	
`defaults`	The default properties.
Deprecated Method	
Δ `save()`	Replaced by `store()`.

See Also

`Properties` in *The Java Class Libraries, Second Edition, Volume 1.*

Δ save() *DEPRECATED*

PURPOSE Replaced by `store()`.

SYNTAX `public synchronized void save(OutputStream out, String comment)`

P

1.2 CHANGES This method is deprecated in Version 1.2.

DEPRECATION This method has been replaced by `store()`. The behavior of `save()` and `store()` is the same, except that `store()` throws an `IOException` when an IO error occurs, while `save()` did nothing.

PARAMETERS

`comment` The possibly `null` comment to write to the stream.

`out` The non-`null` output stream to which to write.

SEE ALSO `store()`.

1.2 setProperty()

PURPOSE Sets the value of a property in this properties list.

SYNTAX `public Object setProperty(String key, String val)`

DESCRIPTION This method sets the value of the property key to val in this properties list. If key does not appear in this properties list, the property key/val is added to this list and null is returned. If key does appear in this properties list, the value of the property in this properties list is replaced with val and the old value is returned.

PARAMETERS

- key — A non-null string containing the property's key.
- val — A non-null string containing the property's value.

RETURNS The old value associated with key, or null if key was not present in this properties list.

SEE ALSO getProperty().

EXAMPLE

```
Properties props = new Properties();
props.setProperty("title", "The Java Class Libraries");
System.out.println( props );       // {title=The Java Class Libraries}
```

1.2 store()

PURPOSE Writes this properties list to an output stream.

SYNTAX

```
public synchronized void store(OutputStream out, String comment)
    throws java.io.IOException
```

DESCRIPTION This method writes this properties list to the output stream out. Only the main properties list is written. If the string comment is not null, it is written out as the first line in the stream as a comment preceded by a hash character ("#"). Before the properties are written, a comment with the current time of day is written out to the stream. The properties are then written out in the format described in the Properties class description.

P

PARAMETERS

- comment — The possibly null comment to write to the stream.
- out — The non-null output stream to which to write.

EXCEPTIONS

IOException
If an IO error occurred while writing the properties list to out.

SEE ALSO list(), load().

EXAMPLE

```
Properties props = new Properties();
props.setProperty("title", "The Java Class Libraries");

try {
```

```
        props.store(new FileOutputStream("out.properties"), "comment");
    } catch (IOException e) {
        e.printStackTrace();
    }
```

OUTPUT

```
#comment
#Sun Jan 10 17:47:19 PST 1999
title=The\ Java\ Class\ Libraries
```

java.util
PropertyPermission

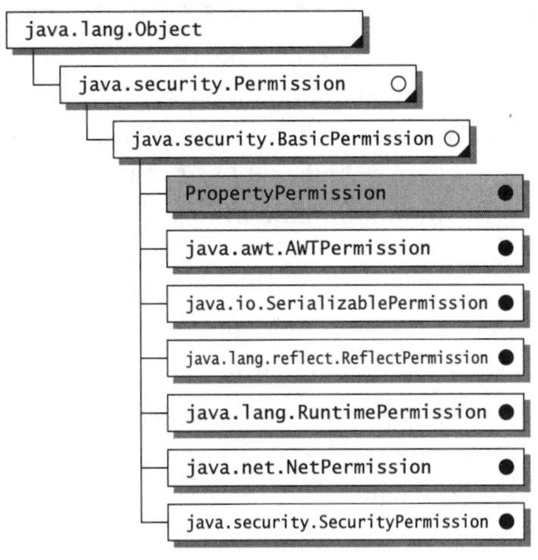

Syntax

`public final class PropertyPermission extends BasicPermission`

Description

The `PropertyPermission` class represents how a system property (see `System`) is to be accessed. It is used internally by the Java runtime system whenever you attempt to access a system property. A `PropertyPermission` object consists of a *permission name*, which is the name of a system property (such as `"user.dir"`), and a set of actions—`read` and `write`—which lists the types of access requested. For example, a `PropertyPermission` with the name `"user.dir"` and an action called `"read"` represents a request to read the system property `user.dir`. It is used by the security manager to check whether the caller is allowed to perform the requested operation. If the caller is not allowed, a `SecurityException` is thrown.

In Version 1.2, both of the "check" methods relating to system properties—`checkPropertiesAccess()` and `checkPropertyAccess()`—in the `SecurityManager` class have been rewritten to use the `PropertyPermission` class. This rewrite is useful to systems that formerly wrote and installed their own security manager but is otherwise transparent to users of the `SecurityManager` class. Also, the `System` class has a new method—`setProperty()`—that updates a single property (formerly, you had to update all system properties in one call). This new method uses `PropertyPermission` to check that the caller has `"write"` permission for the system property that it is attempting to update.

A brief discussion of the Version 1.2 security model is given in the `SecurityManager` class description. More information about Java 1.2's security model and framework is available at `http://java.sun.com/products/jdk/1.2/docs/guide/security/index.html`.

Usage

Applets and applications usually do not directly use the PropertyPermission class. It is used internally by the Java runtime system to enforce its security policy. For example, when a program does a System.getProperty("user.dir"), the runtime system uses a PropertyPermission("user.dir","read") object to check that the caller has permission to do so.

An application may explicitly create a PropertyPermission object and use SecurityManager.checkPermission() to check whether it has such permission. But the act of trying to access the system properties operation automatically triggers such a check, so there is seldom a reason to duplicate it.

The PropertyPermission Name

The permission name of a PropertyPermission is the name of the system property. See the System's class description for a list of predefined system properties. As explained in the System class, additional system properties can be added using the -D option to the java command. Note that because system property names are case-sensitive, so are PropertyPermission names.

There is a special convention for identifying more than one system property using a single permission name, as shown in Table 15.

Syntax	Description
*	All system properties.
spname	The system property named by *spname*.
component.*	All system properties with the prefix "*component*".

TABLE 15: PropertyPermission Name Syntax.

P

PropertyPermission Actions

The actions of a PropertyPermission object identify the operation to be performed on the system property. See Table 16. The **Action** column contains keywords to use when specifying the actions of the PropertyPermission object. The actions are specified in a string containing a comma-separated sequence of one or more of these keywords. Whitespace characters (blank, \n, \f, \t, and \r) may appear before and after a keyword. Character case is not significant. For example, the string "read, write" means the code can read and update the system property named in the permission.

Action	Request
read	Read the identified system properties.
write	Update the identified system properties.

TABLE 16: PropertyPermission Actions.

Implies

The permission name and actions of a `PropertyPermission` object are used to determine whether one `PropertyPermission` *implies* another `PropertyPermission`. Permission *A* implies permission *B* means if permission *A* is granted, so will permission *B*. `PropertyPermission` *A* implies `PropertyPermission` *B* if *B*'s actions are a subset of *A*'s and the system properties identified by *B*'s permission name are a subset *A*'s.

read

A `PropertyPermission` with the "read" action represents a request to read the specified system property or properties. A `PropertyPermission` with this action is used by the following methods: `System.getProperty()` and `System.getProperties()`.

write

A `PropertyPermission` with the "write" action represents a request to update the specified system property or properties. A `PropertyPermission` with this action is used by the following methods: `System.setProperty()` and `System.setProperties()`.

MEMBER SUMMARY	
Constructor	
`PropertyPermission()`	Constructs a new `PropertyPermission` instance.
Action Retrieval Method	
`getActions()`	Generates the canonical string representation of this `PropertyPermission`'s actions.
Permission Checking Methods	
`implies()`	Checks if this `PropertyPermission` *implies* another permission.
`newPermissionCollection()`	Creates a new `PermissionCollection` for storing `PropertyPermission` objects.
Object Methods	
`equals()`	Determines whether an object is equal to this `PropertyPermission`.
`hashCode()`	Computes the hash code of this `PropertyPermission`.

P

See Also

`java.lang.SecurityManager`, `java.lang.System.getProperties()`, `java.lang.System.getProperty()`, `java.lang.System.setProperties()`, `java.lang.System.setProperty()`, `java.security.Permission`, `Properties`.

Example

This example shows how to use a `PropertyPermission` instance to check whether the program has permission to read the system properties that have the prefix `"user."`. As mentioned in the class description, there is usually no need for the program to do this check explicitly because the `System.getProperty()` will perform the check automatically. This example is just for illustrative purposes.

You run the program with the `.policy` file. If you omit the policy file, you will get an `AccessControlException` (a subclass of `SecurityException`).

```
>java -Djava.security.policy=.policy Main
```

Main.java

```
PropertyPermission propperm = new PropertyPermission("user.*", "read");
try {
    AccessController.checkPermission(propperm);
    System.out.println(System.getProperty("user.home")); // also checks perm
} catch (SecurityException e) {
    e.printStackTrace();
}
```

.policy

```
keystore ".keystore";
grant {
        permission java.util.PropertyPermission "user.*", "read";
      };
```

equals()

PURPOSE Determines whether an object is equal to this `PropertyPermission`.

SYNTAX `public boolean equals(Object obj)`

DESCRIPTION This method determines whether an object `obj` is equal to this `PropertyPermission`. Two `PropertyPermissions` are equal if they have the same permission name and (case-insensitive) actions. Permission names are checked using `equals()`.

PARAMETERS

`obj` The possibly `null` object to check.

RETURNS `true` if `obj` is a `PropertyPermission` with the same permission name and actions as this `PropertyPermission`.

OVERRIDES `java.lang.Object.equals()`.

SEE ALSO `hashCode()`.

EXAMPLE

```
PropertyPermission p0 = new PropertyPermission("*", "write,read");
PropertyPermission p1 = new PropertyPermission("*", "read, write");
PropertyPermission p2 = new PropertyPermission("os.*", "read");
```

```
PropertyPermission p3 = new PropertyPermission("user.dir", "write");
PropertyPermission p4 = new PropertyPermission("user.dir", "read");

System.out.println(p1.equals(p0)); // true (action order irrelevant)
System.out.println(p1.equals(p2)); // false
System.out.println(p2.equals(p3)); // false
System.out.println(p3.equals(p4)); // false (actions different)
System.out.println(p4.equals(new FilePermission("user.dir", "read")));
                                        // classes different

System.out.println(p1.hashCode()); // 42
System.out.println(p2.hashCode()); // 3418784
System.out.println(p3.hashCode()); // -267617302
```

getActions()

PURPOSE Generates the canonical string representation of this `PropertyPermission`'s actions.

SYNTAX `public String getActions()`

DESCRIPTION This method generates the canonical string representation of this `PropertyPermission`'s actions. The result might not be the same string passed into the constructor, but it will denote the same actions that were specified to the constructor. The keywords for the actions of the `PropertyPermission` are listed in the following order (in lowercase): `read`, `write`. An action that is not part of this `PropertyPermission` is not listed. Each keyword is separated by a comma, and there is no whitespace in the string.

RETURNS The non-`null` canonical string representation of the actions of this `FilePermission`.

OVERRIDES `java.security.Permission.getActions()`.

EXAMPLE

```
System.out.println(
    new PropertyPermission("file.separator", "  write , read").getActions());
                                                       // read,write
System.out.println(new PropertyPermission("user.dir", " write").getActions());
                                                       // write
```

hashCode()

PURPOSE Computes the hash code of this `PropertyPermission`.

SYNTAX `public int hashCode()`

DESCRIPTION This method computes the hash code of this `PropertyPermission`. The hash code of a `PropertyPermission` object is computed using its permission name. Two `PropertyPermissions` that are equal (according to `equals()`) will have the same hash code. However, two different PropertyPermissions might also have the same hash code. The hash code is typically used as the key in a hash table.

RETURNS An `int` representing the hash code of this object.

OVERRIDES `java.lang.Object.hashCode()`.

SEE ALSO `equals()`, `java.util.HashMap()`, `java.util.Hashtable()`.

EXAMPLE See `equals()`.

implies()

PURPOSE Checks if this `PropertyPermission` *implies* another permission.

SYNTAX `public boolean implies(Permission perm)`

DESCRIPTION This method checks if this `PropertyPermission` *implies* another permission `perm`. This `PropertyPermission` *implies* `perm` if, and only if, any actions on the system properties identified by `perm` are also allowed by this `PropertyPermission`. That is, `perm`'s actions must be a subset of this `PropertyPermission`'s actions, and the system properties identified by `perm` must be a subset of those identified by this `PropertyPermission`. If `perm` is `null` or not an instance of `PropertyPermission`, this method returns `false`.

PARAMETERS

`perm` The possibly `null` permission to check.

RETURNS `true` if `perm` is implied by this object; `false` otherwise.

OVERRIDES `java.lang.Permission.implies()`.

EXAMPLE

```
PropertyPermission p1 = new PropertyPermission("*", "read, write");
PropertyPermission p2 = new PropertyPermission("*", "read");
PropertyPermission p3 = new PropertyPermission("java.*", "read");
PropertyPermission p4 = new PropertyPermission("java.home", "read");
PropertyPermission p5 = new PropertyPermission("foo.bar", "write");

System.out.println(p1.implies(p2));              // true
System.out.println(p1.implies(p3));              // true
System.out.println(p4.implies(p3));              // false; diff name
System.out.println(p3.implies(p4));              // true
System.out.println(p1.implies(p5));              // true
System.out.println(p2.implies(p5));              // false; diff action
System.out.println(p4.implies(p5));              // false; diff name, action

System.out.println(
    p1.implies(new SocketPermission("java.sun.com:80", "connect")));
                                                 // false; diff Permission
System.out.println(p1.implies(null));            // false; null Permission
```

PropertyPermission()

PURPOSE Constructs a new `PropertyPermission` instance.

SYNTAX `public PropertyPermission(String pname, String actions)`

DESCRIPTION This constructor constructs a new `PropertyPermission`. The name of this permission is `pname` and has the syntax described in the class description. `actions` contains a list of one or more comma-separated keywords: `read` or `write`. It specifies the actions that can be performed on the objects named by `pname`, as described in the class description.

PARAMETERS

`actions` A non-`null` string specifying the actions of the new `PropertyPermission`.

`pname` A non-`null` string identifying the system property or group of system properties for the new `PropertyPermission`.

EXAMPLE See `equals()`.

newPermissionCollection()

PURPOSE Creates a new `PermissionCollection` for storing `PropertyPermission` objects.

SYNTAX `public PermissionCollection newPermissionCollection()`

DESCRIPTION This method creates a new `PermissionCollection` for storing `PropertyPermission` objects. With a single `PropertyPermission`, you can ask (via the `implies()` method) whether it implies another permission. With a `PermissionCollection`, you can ask whether the collection of permissions implies another permission. The Java runtime system, for example, will perform such a test when it tries to determine whether the caller is allowed to perform an action based on the `PropertyPermissions` granted the caller in the security policy.

RETURNS A new non-`null` `PermissionCollection` object suitable for storing `PropertyPermissions`. If you attempt to add an object that is not an instance of `PropertyPermission` to the collection, an `IllegalArgumentException` is thrown.

OVERRIDES `java.security.Permission.newPermissionCollection()`.

SEE ALSO `implies()`, `java.security.PermissionCollection`.

EXAMPLE

```
PropertyPermission[] p = new PropertyPermission[3];

// Allow entire java. hierarchy to be read
p[0] = new PropertyPermission("java.*", "read");
```

P

```
// Allow update to java.vendor.* hierarchy
p[1] = new PropertyPermission("java.vendor.*", "write");

// Allow read/update to os.version
p[2] = new PropertyPermission("os.version", "read, write");

PermissionCollection col = p[0].newPermissionCollection();
for (int i = 0; i < p.length; i++) {
    col.add(p[i]);
}

// OK to read/write java.vendor.url?
System.out.println(col.implies(
    new PropertyPermission("java.vendor.url", "read, write")));
                                                         // true

// OK to read user.dir?
System.out.println(col.implies(
    new PropertyPermission("user.dir", "read")));    // false

// OK to write java.vendor ?
System.out.println(col.implies(
    new PropertyPermission("java.vendor", "write")));
                // false; java.vendor.* doesn't include java.vendor
```

PushbackInputStream

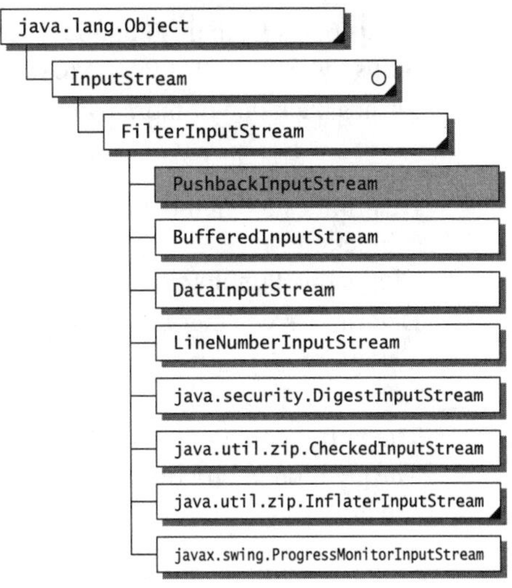

Syntax

```
public class PushbackInputStream extends FilterInputStream
```

Description

The `PushbackInputStream` class represents a filter stream that allows bytes to be "pushed back" to (or unread from) the stream. For example, you can read some bytes and then push them back onto the stream so that the next read operation will retrieve the bytes that were pushed back. This capability is useful when building parsers that need to read ahead in the stream in order to decide how to process the stream.

See *The Java Class Libraries, Second Edition, Volume 1* for more information about this class.

Changes for Version 1.2

The `close()` and `skip()` methods override their counterparts in `FilterInputStream`.

MEMBER SUMMARY	
Constructor	
`PushbackInputStream()`	Constructs a `PushbackInputStream` instance for an input stream.
	Continued

MEMBER SUMMARY	
Input Methods	
`read()`	Reads bytes from this `PushbackInputStream`.
Δ `skip()`	Skips bytes from this `PushbackInputStream`.
`unread()`	Pushes back one or more bytes.
Stream Methods	
`available()`	Determines the number of bytes that can be read without blocking.
Δ `close()`	Closes this `PushbackInputStream`.
`markSupported()`	Determines whether this `PushbackInputStream` supports mark/reset.
Protected Fields	
`buf`	The buffer containing the unread bytes.
`pos`	The position in `buf` from which to read the next pushed-back byte.

See Also

`PushbackInputStream` in *The Java Class Libraries, Second Edition, Volume 1.*

Δ close()

PURPOSE Closes this `PushbackInputStream`.

P

SYNTAX `public synchronized void close() throws IOException`

DESCRIPTION This method closes the underlying input stream and release the buffers used by this input stream.

1.2 CHANGES In Version 1.1, this method was inherited from `FilterInputStream`, which simply closes the underlying input stream.

EXCEPTIONS

`IOException`

If an IO error occurs while the underlying input stream is being closed.

OVERRIDES `FilterInputStream.close()`.

EXAMPLE See the `PushbackInputStream.available()` example in the *The Java Class Libraries, Second Edition, Volume 1.*

Δ skip()

PURPOSE
Skips bytes from this `PushbackInputStream`.

SYNTAX
`public long skip(long count) throws IOException`

DESCRIPTION
This method skips `count` number of bytes from this `PushbackInputStream`. Bytes that are skipped will not be returned by subsequent `read()` calls (unless mark/reset is used). This method first skips the bytes that have been pushed back and then calls `skip()` on the underlying input stream to skip the rest of the bytes.

If `count` ≤ `0`, no bytes are skipped.

1.2 CHANGES
In Version 1.1, this method was inherited from `FilterInputStream`, which simply skips the bytes by calling `skip()` on the underlying input stream. Although the effect is no different in Version 1.2, Version 1.2 is more efficient.

PARAMETERS

`count`
The number of bytes to skip.

RETURNS
The actual number of bytes skipped.

EXCEPTIONS

`IOException`
If an IO error occurred while skipping the bytes.

OVERRIDES
`FilterInputStream.skip()`.

EXAMPLE
See `InputStream.skip()` in *The Java Class Libraries, Second Edition, Volume 1.*

P

java.io

PushbackReader

Syntax

```
public class PushbackReader extends FilterReader
```

Description

The `PushbackReader` class represents a filter reader (filter character stream) that allows characters to be "pushed back" (or unread) from the stream. For example, you can read some characters and subsequently push them back onto the stream so that the next read operation will retrieve the characters that were pushed back. This capability is useful when building parsers that need to read ahead in order to decide how to process the input.

See *The Java Class Libraries, Second Edition, Volume 1* for more information about this class.

Changes for Version 1.2

The `mark()` and `reset()` methods override their counterparts in `FilterReader` to properly reflect that `PushbackReader` does not support mark/reset.

P

	MEMBER SUMMARY	
	Constructor	
	`PushbackReader()`	Creates a `PushbackReader` instance.
	Input Methods	
	`read()`	Reads one or more characters from this `PushbackReader`.
	`unread()`	Pushes back one or more characters.
	Stream Methods	
	`close()`	Closes this `PushbackReader`.
	`ready()`	Determines whether this `PushbackReader` is ready to be read without being blocked.
	Mark/Reset Methods	
Δ	`mark()`	This method should not be called.
	`markSupported()`	Returns `false`.
Δ	`reset()`	This method should not be called.

See Also

`PushbackReader` in *The Java Class Libraries, Second Edition, Volume 1.*

Δ mark()

PURPOSE This method should not be called.

SYNTAX `public void mark(int readAheadLimit) throws IOException`

DESCRIPTION `PushbackReader` does not support mark/reset.

1.2 CHANGES In Version 1.1, this method invoked `mark()` on the underlying stream. This behavior is incorrect because `PushbackReader` does not support mark/reset.

PARAMETERS

`readAheadLimit`
Ignored.

EXCEPTIONS

`IOException`
Always thrown because `PushbackReader` does not support mark/reset.

OVERRIDES `FilterReader.mark()`.

SEE ALSO `markSupported()`, `reset()`.

Δ reset()

PURPOSE This method should not be called.

SYNTAX `public void reset() throws IOException`

DESCRIPTION `PushbackReader` does not support mark/reset.

1.2 CHANGES In Version 1.1, this method invoked `reset()` on the underlying stream. This behavior is incorrect because `PushbackReader` does not support mark/reset.

EXCEPTIONS

`IOException`
Always thrown because `PushbackReader` does not support mark/reset.

OVERRIDES `FilterReader.reset()`.

SEE ALSO `mark()`, `markSupported()`.

P

java.util
Random

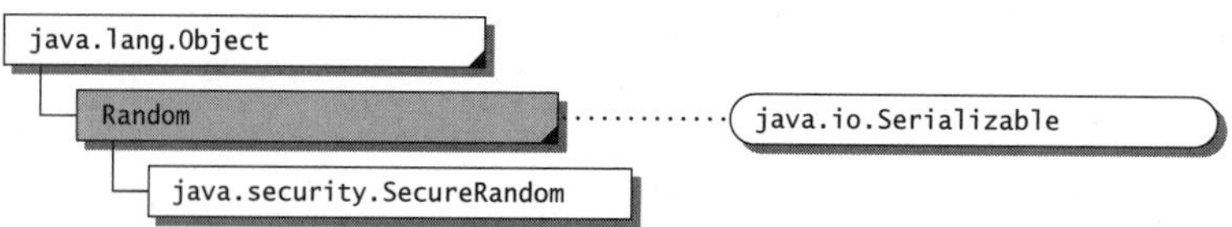

Syntax

```
public class Random implements Serializable
```

Description

The `Random` class is used to represent a pseudorandom-number generator for generating a sequence of pseudorandom numbers. You create a pseudorandom-number generator by giving it a *seed*. The generator uses the seed in the algorithm for generating the pseudorandom numbers.

See *The Java Class Libraries, Second Edition, Volume 1* for more information about this class.

Changes for Version 1.2

The `nextBoolean()` method and an overloaded version of `nextInt()` are new.

R

MEMBER SUMMARY	
Constructor	
`Random()`	Constructs a pseudorandom-number generator.
Seed Method	
`setSeed()`	Sets the seed of this pseudorandom-number generator.
Generation Methods	
`nextBytes()`	Generates the next pseudorandom, uniformly distributed sequence of bytes.
1.2 `nextBoolean()`	Generates the next pseudorandom, uniformly distributed `boolean` value.
`nextDouble()`	Generates the next pseudorandom, uniformly distributed `double` value.
`nextFloat()`	Generates the next pseudorandom, uniformly distributed `float` value.
`nextGaussian()`	Generates the next pseudorandom, Gaussian-distributed `double` value.
Δ `nextInt()`	Generates the next pseudorandom, uniformly distributed `int` value.
`nextLong()`	Generates the next pseudorandom, uniformly distributed `long` value.

MEMBER SUMMARY	
Protected Method	
`next()`	Generates the next pseudorandom number in the sequence.

See Also

`Random` in *The Java Class Libraries, Second Edition, Volume 1.*

1.2 nextBoolean()

PURPOSE Generates the next pseudorandom, uniformly distributed `boolean` value.

SYNTAX `public int nextBoolean()`

RETURNS Either `true` or `false`.

EXAMPLE

```
Random r = new Random();
System.out.println( r.nextBoolean() );      // true
System.out.println( r.nextBoolean() );      // true
System.out.println( r.nextBoolean() );      // false
```

Δ nextInt()

PURPOSE Generates the next pseudorandom, uniformly distributed `int` value.

SYNTAX `public int nextInt()`

SINCE 1.2 `public int nextInt(int n)`

DESCRIPTION This method returns a uniformly distributed `int` value (positive or negative). If `n` is specified, the return value is a uniformly distributed `int` value in the range `[0..n - 1]`.

1.2 CHANGES The form that accepts an `int` parameter is new in Version 1.2.

PARAMETERS

`n` An integer that restricts the range of return values to `[0..n - 1]`.

RETURNS A random `int` value.

SEE ALSO `java.lang.Integer.MAX_VALUE`, `java.lang.Integer.MIN_VALUE`, `next()`, `nextLong()`.

EXAMPLE

```
Random r = new Random();
System.out.println( r.nextInt() );      // -1434938125
System.out.println( r.nextInt() );      // 1792700005
System.out.println( r.nextInt(10) );    // 3
System.out.println( r.nextInt(10) );    // 8
// r.nextInt(-10);                      // IllegalArgumentException
```

R

java.io
RandomAccessFile

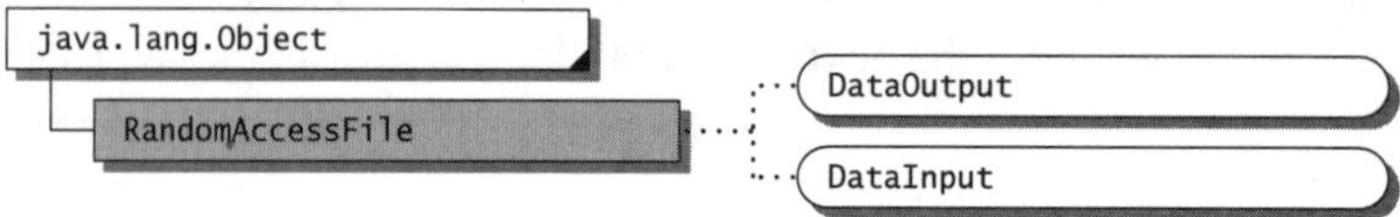

Syntax

```
public class RandomAccessFile implements DataOutput, DataInput
```

Description

The `RandomAccessFile` class represents a *random-access file*. A random-access file is a file in which you can point anywhere in the file and perform IO operations on the file at that point. It provides methods for setting the *current file pointer* (the position in the file where the IO will be effected). It also provides methods defined in the `DataInput` and `DataOutput` interfaces to allow primitive data values to be read from and written to the file.

See *The Java Class Libraries, Second Edition, Volume 1* for more information about this class.

Changes for Version 1.2

The `setLength()` method has been added to allow a file to be truncated or expanded.

The `RandomAccessFile` constructor that accepts a string name now throws a `FileNotFoundException` instead of the more generic `IOException`.

MEMBER SUMMARY	
Constructor	
Δ `RandomAccessFile()`	Constructs a `RandomAccessFile` instance.
Random Access Methods	
`getFilePointer()`	Retrieves the current file pointer of this `RandomAccessFile`.
`seek()`	Sets the file pointer of this `RandomAccessFile`.
1.2 `setLength()`	Sets the length of this `RandomAccessFile`.
Input Methods	
`read()`	Reads bytes from this `RandomAccessFile`.
`readBoolean()`	Reads a `boolean` from this `RandomAccessFile`.
`readByte()`	Reads an 8-bit `byte` from this `RandomAccessFile`.
`readChar`	Reads a 16-bit `char` from this `RandomAccessFile`.
`readDouble()`	Reads a 64-bit `double` from this `RandomAccessFile`.
`readFloat()`	Reads a 32-bit `float` from this `RandomAccessFile`.

MEMBER SUMMARY	
`readFully()`	Reads the requested number of bytes from this `RandomAccessFile`, blocking until all bytes are read.
`readInt()`	Reads a 32-bit `int` from this `RandomAccessFile`.
`readLine()`	Reads a line from this `RandomAccessFile`.
`readLong()`	Reads a 64-bit `long` from this `RandomAccessFile`.
`readShort()`	Reads a 16-bit `short` from this `RandomAccessFile`.
`readUnsignedByte()`	Reads an unsigned 8-bit `byte` from this `RandomAccessFile`.
`readUnsignedShort()`	Reads an unsigned 16-bit `short` from this `RandomAccessFile`.
`readUTF()`	Reads a Unicode string in UTF from this `RandomAccessFile`.
`skipBytes()`	Skips bytes from this `RandomAccessFile`.
Output Methods	
`write()`	Writes bytes to this `RandomAccessFile`.
`writeBoolean()`	Writes a `boolean` to this `RandomAccessFile`.
`writeByte()`	Writes an 8-bit `byte` to this `RandomAccessFile`.
`writeBytes()`	Writes a string to this `RandomAccessFile` as a sequence of bytes.
`writeChar()`	Writes a 16-bit `char` to this `RandomAccessFile`.
`writeChars()`	Writes a string to this `RandomAccessFile` as a sequence of 16-bit `char`s.
`writeDouble()`	Writes a 64-bit `double` to this `RandomAccessFile`.
`writeFloat()`	Writes a 32-bit `float` to this `RandomAccessFile`.
`writeInt()`	Writes a 32-bit `int` to this `RandomAccessFile`.
`writeLong()`	Writes a 64-bit `long` to this `RandomAccessFile`.
`writeShort()`	Writes a 16-bit `short` to this `RandomAccessFile`.
`writeUTF()`	Writes a string in UTF to this `RandomAccessFile`.
Information Methods	
`length()`	Determines the number of bytes in this `RandomAccessFile`.
`getFD()`	Retrieves the file descriptor of this `RandomAccessFile`.
Close Method	
`close()`	Closes this `RandomAccessFile`.

R

See Also

`RandomAccessFile` in *The Java Class Libraries, Second Edition, Volume 1.*

Δ RandomAccessFile()

PURPOSE Constructs a `RandomAccessFile` instance.

SYNTAX
```
public RandomAccessFile(File file, String mode) throws
    IOException
public RandomAccessFile(String fileName, String mode) throws
    FileNotFoundException
```

DESCRIPTION There are two forms of the constructor for `RandomAccessFile`. The first form constructs an instance of `RandomAccessFile` for the file with the file pathname `fileName`. The second form constructs an instance of `RandomAccessFile` for the file as described by the `File` instance `file`. When the `RandomAccessFile` instance is created, the file is opened in the mode specified in the string `mode`. `mode` can be "r", which means to open the file in read-only mode, or "rw", which means to open the file in read-write mode. Any other values of `mode` will raise an `IllegalArgumentException`.

The file can be opened only if allowed by the security manager.

1.2 CHANGES In Version 1.1, the form that accepts a string name threw an `IOException`.

PARAMETERS

`file` The non-`null` `File` of the file to open.

`fileName` The non-`null` string name of the file to open.

`mode` The non-`null` access mode ("r" or "rw").

EXCEPTIONS

`FileNotFoundException`
If `fileName` names a directory instead of a file or if the file cannot be found.

`IllegalArgumentException`
If `mode` is neither "r" nor "rw."

`IOException`
If an IO error occurred while attempting to open the specified file.

`SecurityException`
If the file could not be opened in the mode specified due to security reasons.

SEE ALSO `java.lang.SecurityManager`, `FilePermission`.

EXAMPLE See the `RandomAccessFile` class example in *The Java Class Libraries, Second Edition, Volume 1.*

R

1.2 setLength()

PURPOSE Sets the length of this `RandomAccessFile`.

SYNTAX
```
public native void setLength(long newLength) throws IOException
```

DESCRIPTION This method sets the length of this `RandomAccessFile` to `newLength`. If `this.length()` > `newLength`, this method truncates this file so that it contains `newLength` bytes. If `getFilePointer()` > `newLength`, the file pointer is set to `newLength`. (The file pointer is the position in the file at which the next read/write method will operate.)

If `this.length()` < `newLength`, this method expands this file so that it contains `newLength` bytes. The contents of the extended portion of the file is undefined.

PARAMETERS

`newLength` The desired length of the file in bytes.

EXCEPTIONS

`IOException`

If an IO error occurred while setting the length.

SEE ALSO `length()`.

EXAMPLE This example creates a file of a specified size.

```
import java.io.*;

class Main {
    public static void main(String[] args) {
        if (args.length != 2) {
            System.err.println(
                "usage: java Main <new filename> <size in bytes>");
            System.exit(-1);
        }
        long size = 0;
        try {
            size = Long.parseLong(args[1]);
        } catch (NumberFormatException e) {
            System.err.println(
                "usage: java Main <new filename> <size in bytes>");
            System.exit(-1);
        }

        try {
            RandomAccessFile raf = new RandomAccessFile(args[0], "rw");
            raf.setLength(size);     // extend file to be specified size
            raf.close();
        } catch (IOException e) {
            e.printStackTrace();
        }
    }
}
```

R

Reference

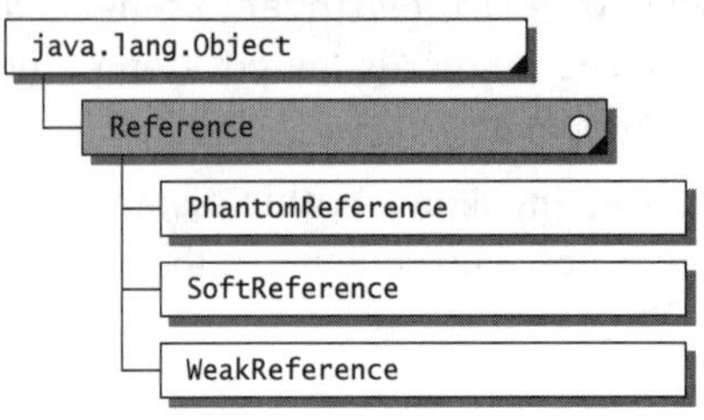

Syntax

```
public abstract class Reference
```

Description

The `Reference` abstract class represents a *reference object*, which is an object that you used to determine when another object is garbage collected. It is typically used to free resources associated with the object when the object is no longer being used.

Reference objects are used in the following way. To learn when some object `obj` is garbage collected, you create a reference object to refer to `obj` (the *referent*). When `obj` is no longer used, the garbage collector collects `obj` and enqueues all reference objects to it to a *reference queue*. You then can determine that `obj` has been garbage collected by polling the reference queue until the reference object appears. See Figure 14. Initially, the references `R1` and `R2` are created for a "used" object. When the object becomes unused and undergoes garbage collection, the two references are moved to the reference queue.

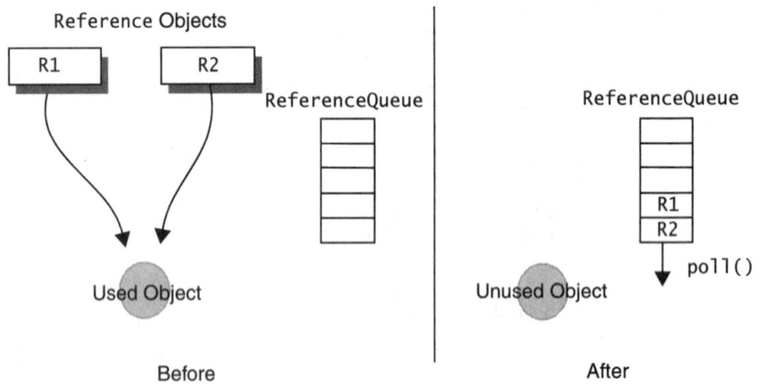

FIGURE 14: The Enqueuing of Reference Objects to an Unused Object.

Garbage Collection

An object is garbage collected when it is no longer being used. The garbage collector decides which objects are no longer being used by following all references from a *root set* and noting which objects are reachable and which are not. Those not reachable are marked for collection. The root set of references is essentially all static object variables and all active object variables in live threads.

For performance reasons, some garbage collectors use inexact heuristics to determine if an object is still in use. For example, some garbage collectors include in the root set any value that might look like an object reference; that value might actually be an integer value whose value happens to be a valid object reference. For such garbage collectors, some objects might not be collected even if they are in fact unused.

More information about garbage collection is given in *The Java Virtual Machine Specification*, Section 3.5.

The Phases of an Object That Is Being Garbage Collected

An object that is being referenced by some Java reference is considered *used* and will not be collected. When no Java references refer to an object, the object is considered *unused* and so is a candidate for collection. When the garbage collector finds an unused object, it schedules it for finalization (see *The Java Language Specification, First Edition*, Section 12.6 for details on finalization). After the object is finalized, the garbage collector schedules the object for reclamation (storage is returned to the heap). Figure 15 illustrates these transition states.

FIGURE 15: The States of an Object Undergoing Garbage Collection.

The Reference Queue

If a thread wants to be notified when an object `obj` is garbage collected, it must poll a reference queue and wait for a reference object referring to `obj` to appear. There is no single system-wide reference queue. Rather, you create your own reference queue, and you can create as many as you need. When you create a reference object, you must pass it the reference queue that you want the garbage collector to use when it enqueues the reference object.

See `ReferenceQueue` for more information about reference queues and enqueueing semantics.

Types of Reference Objects

There are three types of reference objects: *soft* references, *weak* references, and *phantom* references. Each of these reference objects affect and are affected by the garbage collector in different ways. As we discuss the effects of the different reference objects, keep in mind that the reference objects to the referent are completely ignored until the garbage collector determines that the referent is no longer being used.

Soft Reference

A *soft reference* is slightly weaker than a Java reference when it comes to preventing an object from being garbage collected. A Java reference to an object prevents the object from being collected in all situations. A soft reference to an object prevents the object from being collected only until memory is low. Until memory is low, you can continue to access the soft reference's referent (note that accessing the referent might change the referent's status from *unused* to *used*.)

When memory is low, the garbage collector looks for all unused objects referred to by a soft reference and then *clears* the soft references. When a soft reference is *cleared*, you can no longer get to the referent and the referent begins its way through the stages of being garbage collected. The goal is to free up enough memory with these objects to avoid an `OutOfMemoryException`. In fact, the garbage collector guarantees that all soft references will be cleared before it throws an `OutOfMemoryException`.

Soft references are most often used in caches when the objects are fairly expensive to create but are not always used. The soft reference allows an unused object to remain in the cache in case it might be called upon but does not prevent the object from being collected if memory is tight.

Weak Reference

To receive notification of an unused object just before it is finalized, you use a *weak* reference. Unlike a soft reference, a weak reference does not delay the process of garbage collection. When the referent of a weak reference becomes unused, the garbage collector treats the referent just like any other object that becomes unused.

Weak reference notification is used in the same way as finalization. However, finalization must be done by the object that is being garbage collected; by contrast, weak reference notification allows a separate object to do finalization.

Note that the weak reference object is enqueued at most once. Thus if the referent is resurrected and you still want weak reference notification on the referent, you must create a new weak reference on the referent.

Phantom Reference

To receive notification of an object after it has been finalized, you use a *phantom* reference. When a phantom reference is enqueued, you can be sure that the object is in the final stage of being collected and that there is no way that the object can be resurrected. This means that you can safely free any resources associated by the referent without fear that the resources will ever be used again.

Unlike with soft and weak references, the garbage collector does not automatically clear a phantom reference. The phantom reference actually holds onto the object (even though you can't get to it), thereby preventing its return to the heap. Before the object can be returned to the heap, you must explicitly clear the phantom reference (or let the phantom reference itself be garbage collected).

Effects of Multiple Reference Objects on an Object

This discussion about reference object types assumes that only one type of reference object is referring to an object. This section explains what happens when there are several different types of reference objects referring to an object.

First, if there's some chain of only Java references from the root set to an object, the object will not be collected and any reference objects on the object will be ignored. In this case, the object is said to be *strongly reachable*.

If an object is not strongly reachable but some chain of references consisting of only Java references and soft references from the root set to the object exists, the object is said to be *softly reachable*. This means that the object will be garbage collected only if memory is low. Also, any weak or phantom references on the object will be ignored.

If an object is no longer softly reachable (memory became low and the strong references to the object were cleared), the garbage collector starts the collection process on the object. First (but not necessarily immediately), any weak references to the object are cleared and enqueued. The object is then finalized.

If after finalization the object is not resurrected, all phantom references to the object are enqueued. At this point, the object is said to be *phantom-reachable*. The object is held by the phantom reference until it is cleared or the phantom reference becomes unused.

Usage

See `SoftReference`, `WeakReference`, and `PhantomReference` for usage information.

MEMBER SUMMARY	
Reference Methods	
`clear()`	Clears this reference object.
`get()`	Retrieves this reference object's referent.
Reference Queue Methods	
`enqueue()`	Enqueues this reference object to the registered queue.
`isEnqueued()`	Determines if this reference object is enqueued.

R

See Also

`PhantomReference`, `ReferenceQueue`, `SoftReference`, `WeakReference`.

Example

This example is designed simply to show some of the different aspects of reference objects. It creates three types of reference objects and immediately calls `get()` on each. Notice that the phantom reference returns `null`.

The example creates a thread that exhausts memory in order to force the soft reference to be cleared. Notice that although the weak reference is cleared before the phantom reference, the phantom reference is retrieved from the reference queue before the weak reference.

```
import java.lang.ref.*;
import java.util.*;

class Main {
    public static void main(String[] args) {
        C obj = new C();
        ReferenceQueue rq = new ReferenceQueue();

        SoftReference sr = new SoftReference(obj, rq);
        System.out.println(sr.get());                          // C

        WeakReference wr = new WeakReference(obj, rq);
        System.out.println(wr.get());                          // C

        PhantomReference pr = new PhantomReference(obj, rq);
        System.out.println(pr.get());                          // null

        try {
            // Explicitly enqueue the reference and then remove it.
            pr.enqueue();
            System.out.println(pr.isEnqueued());               // true
            Reference r = rq.remove();
            System.out.println(r+": "+r.get());                // Phanthom: null
            r.clear();
        } catch (InterruptedException e) {
            e.printStackTrace();
        }

        // Make C object no longer strongly-reachable.
        obj = null;

        // Use all available memory to force a garbage-collection.
        eatMemory(new LinkedList());

        try {
            while (true) {
                Reference r = rq.remove();
                if (r != null) {
                    System.out.println(r+": "+r.get());

                    if (r instanceof PhantomReference) {
                        r.clear();
                    }
                }
            }
        } catch (InterruptedException e) {
            e.printStackTrace();
        }
    }

    static void eatMemory(LinkedList l) {
        try {
            l.add(new double[100000]);
            eatMemory(l);
        } catch (OutOfMemoryError e) {
            System.out.println("**** OUT OF MEMORY ****");
```

R

```
                l.clear();
                System.gc();
            }
        }
    }

    class C {
        protected void finalize() {
            System.out.println("C.finalize() called.");
        }

        public String toString() {
            return "C";
        }
    }

    class MemoryPig extends Thread {
        public void run() {
            List l = new LinkedList();

            while (true) {
                try {
                    while (true) {
                        l.add(new double[100000]);
                    }
                } catch (OutOfMemoryError e) {
                    System.out.println("**** OUT OF MEMORY ****");
                    l.clear();
                    System.gc();
                }
            }
        }
    }
```

Output

```
> java -Xmx1m Main

C
C
null
true
java.lang.ref.PhantomReference@a583c65d: null
C.finalize() called.
**** OUT OF MEMORY ****
java.lang.ref.SoftReference@a5e3c65d: null
java.lang.ref.WeakReference@a5bfc65d: null
```

clear()

PURPOSE Clears this reference object.

SYNTAX `public void clear()`

DESCRIPTION This method removes the reference to this object's referent.

EXAMPLE See the class example.

enqueue()

PURPOSE Enqueues this reference object to the registered queue.

SYNTAX `public boolean enqueue()`

DESCRIPTION If this reference object was registered with a reference queue, this method enqueues the reference object to that queue and returns `true`. However, if this reference object is already enqueued or if this reference object is not registered with any reference queue, this method simply returns `false`.

Enqueuing this reference object means that it will not be enqueued by the garbage collector.

RETURNS `true` if this method was successful; `false` otherwise.

get()

PURPOSE Retrieves this reference object's referent.

SYNTAX `public Object get()`

DESCRIPTION This method returns the referent of this reference object. If this reference object has been cleared, `null` is returned. If this is a phantom reference object, this method always returns `null`.

RETURNS A possibly `null` object.

EXAMPLE See the class example.

isEnqueued()

R

PURPOSE Determines if this reference object is enqueued.

SYNTAX `public boolean isEnqueued()`

RETURNS `true` if this reference object is enqueued; `false` otherwise.

EXAMPLE See the class example.

ReferenceQueue

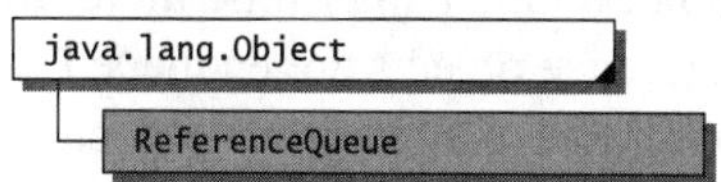

Syntax

```
public class ReferenceQueue
```

Description

The `ReferenceQueue` class represents a *reference queue,* which is a queue used to receive notification that an object is undergoing garbage collection. When the garbage collector detects an unused object and marks it for garbage collection, it enqueues to a reference queue all reference objects (see `Reference`) that refer to the unused object (see Figure 16). By polling a reference queue and looking for a reference object to the target object, an application can discover when the object is garbage collected.

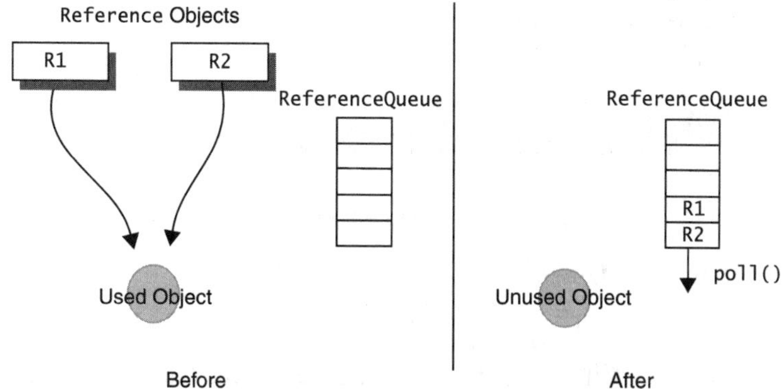

FIGURE 16: The Enqueuing of Reference Objects to an Unused Object.

See `Reference` for information about the different types of reference objects and about the stages an object undergoes during garbage collection.

There is no single system-wide reference queue. Rather, you create your own reference queue, and you can create as many as you need. When you create a reference object, you must pass it the reference queue that you want the garbage collector to use when it enqueues the reference object.

R

Enqueuing Order

If there are several soft references to an object, all of them will be enqueued at the same time. This is also true of weak references. Other than this, there are no guarantees regarding the order and timeliness in which reference objects are enqueued. The reference objects for a collected object *A* might be enqueued after the reference objects for an object *B* that is collected later.

Enqueued at Most Once

The garbage collector enqueues a reference object at most once. When a reference object to an object `obj` is enqueued by the garbage collector (because `obj` is being collected), the reference object will never again be enqueued, even if `obj` is resurrected. (Resurrection occurs when an object makes itself *used* during finalization; see *The Java Language Specification, First Edition*, Section 12.6, for more details.)

If a reference object itself becomes unused, it will never be enqueued.

A reference object can appear in a queue only once. For example, if the garbage collector is about to enqueue a reference object but notices that it is already enqueued (which can happen if you explicitly enqueue the reference object by calling its `enqueue()` method), the garbage collector will not enqueue the reference object. Since it will not later enqueue the reference object again, you must be careful when explicitly enqueuing reference objects because you might miss the notification.

MEMBER SUMMARY	
Constructor	
`ReferenceQueue()`	Constructs a `ReferenceQueue` instance.
Reference Object Retrieval Methods	
`poll()`	Checks if any reference objects are enqueued in this `ReferenceQueue`.
`remove()`	Removes the next reference object that appears in this `ReferenceQueue`.

R

See Also

`Reference`.

Example

See the `Reference` class example.

poll()

PURPOSE Checks if any reference objects are enqueued in this ReferenceQueue.

SYNTAX
```
public Reference poll()
```

DESCRIPTION This method checks this ReferenceQueue for any reference objects. If any are available, it removes the first one from this ReferenceQueue and returns it. If none are available, it returns null.

RETURNS A possibly null reference object.

EXAMPLE See the Reference class example.

ReferenceQueue()

PURPOSE Constructs a ReferenceQueue instance.

SYNTAX
```
public ReferenceQueue()
```

DESCRIPTION This method constructs an empty ReferenceQueue instance. The ReferenceQueue is ready to be used by newly created reference objects.

EXAMPLE See the Reference class example.

remove()

PURPOSE Removes the next reference object that appears in this ReferenceQueue.

SYNTAX
```
public Reference remove() throws IllegalArgumentException,
   InterruptedException
public Reference remove(long timeout) throws
   IllegalArgumentException, InterruptedException
```

DESCRIPTION This methods waits and removes the next reference object that appears in this ReferenceQueue. It waits at most timeout milliseconds. If timeout milliseconds is exceeded, this method returns null. If timeout is 0, it waits until a reference object appears. If timeout is not specified, it defaults to 0.

PARAMETERS

timeout The number of milliseconds to wait for a reference object.

RETURNS A reference object; returns null if this method returned because the timeout period expired.

EXCEPTIONS

IllegalArgumentException

If timeout < 0.

`InterruptedException`
If this method is interrupted.

EXAMPLE See the `Reference` class example.

java.lang.reflect
ReflectPermission

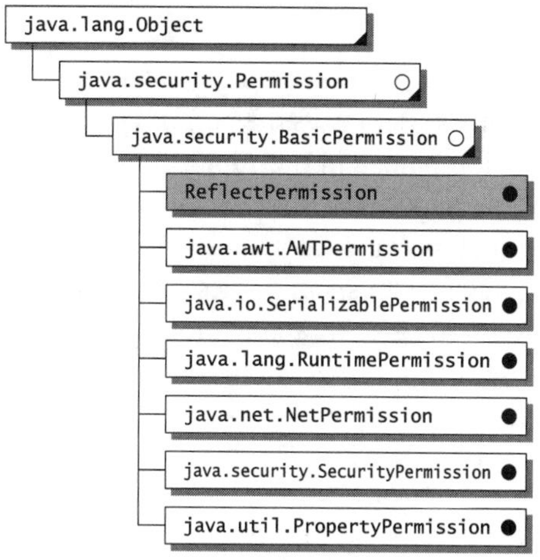

Syntax

```
public final class ReflectPermission extends BasicPermission
```

Description

The `ReflectPermission` class represents a request to access objects through the reflection APIs. It is used internally by the Java runtime system to enforce its security policy. A `ReflectPermission` object has a *permission name* that identifies the reflection operation to check. For example, the `ReflectPermission` with the name `"suppressAccessChecks"` is used by `AccessibleObject.setAccessible()` to determine whether the caller is allowed to turn off Java language access checks to allow even nonpublic members of the object being reflected to be accessed. This check is performed with the help of the *access controller* (see `java.security.AccessController`). If the access controller determines that the caller is not allowed, an `AccessControlException` (a subclass of `SecurityException`) is thrown.

A brief discussion of the Version 1.2 security and access control model is given in the `SecurityManager` class description. More information about Version 1.2's security model and framework is available at `http://java.sun.com/products/jdk/1.2/docs/guide/security/index.html`.

Usage

Applets and applications usually do not directly use the `ReflectPermission` class. It is used internally by the Java runtime system to enforce its security policy when the reflection APIs (such as `AcceessibleObject.setAccessible()`) are used.

An application may explicitly create a `ReflectPermission` object and use `SecurityManager.checkPermission()` or `AccessController.checkPermission()` to check whether

R

the security policy has granted it such permission. But the act of trying to perform the reflection operation automatically triggers such a check, so there is seldom a reason to duplicate it.

The ReflectPermission Name

The permission name of a `ReflectPermission` object identifies the reflection operation that is being checked. The Java runtime system uses the permission name `"suppressAccessChecks"`. It may use additional permission names in the future for other permissions relating to reflection. An application is also free to add and use new permission names to represent other types of reflection operations, but such permission names will be known only to the application that defines them. Nevertheless, such permission names can appear in the security policy and be checked using the `AccessController`. An application that needs to define and use new permission names is usually better off defining its own `Permission` subclass to avoid future conflicts with the Java runtime system.

Implies

The permission name of a `ReflectPermission` is a case-sensitive string. It is used to check whether one `ReflectPermission` is equal to another `ReflectPermission`. It is also used to check whether one `ReflectPermission` *implies* another `ReflectPermission`. Permission *A* implies permission *B* means if permission *A* is granted, so will permission *B*. Following are the rules for how "implies" works for `ReflectPermission` objects.

- Two `ReflectPermissions` with the same permission name imply each other.
- A `ReflectPermission` with a permission name of the form *pname*`.*` implies any `ReflectPermission` whose permission name has the prefix "*pname*`.`". For example, a `ReflectPermission` with a permission name `"some.op.*"` implies any `ReflectPermission` whose permission name has the prefix `"some.op."`.
- A `ReflectPermission` with the permission name `"*"` implies any `ReflectPermission`.

R

suppressAccessChecks

Each class, member, and constructor is declared with an access modifier: `private`, `protected`, or `public`. If such an explicit modifier is not used, the item implicitly has *package-protected* access, which means only classes in the same package can access the item. The Java runtime system enforces these access checks. For more details on accessibility, see *The Java Language Specification, First Edition*, Section 6.6.1.

The `ReflectPermission` with the permission name `"suppressAccessChecks"` represents the permission to turn off such access checks when accessing an object through reflection. If this permission has been granted, you must first invoke `AccessibleObject.setAccessible(true)` on the reflection object and then use methods in the reflection object (such as `Method.invoke()` or `Field.get()`) that would otherwise throw `IllegalAccessException`. Note that this permission has no effect on accessibility when the language is used without reflection.

See the `RuntimePermission` class with the permission name `"accessDeclaredMembers"` for another permission that's related to reflection. `"accessDeclaredMembers"` determines whether you can obtain the reflection object, for example by using `Class.getField()`. Once you obtain the reflection object, `"suppressAccessChecks"` determines whether you can use it to read/update/invoke methods on the object that it reflects.

MEMBER SUMMARY	
Constructor	
`ReflectPermissions()`	Constructs a new `ReflectPermission` instance.

See Also

`java.lang.SecurityManager`, `java.security.AccessController`, `java.security.Permission`, `java.security.Policy`, `java.lang.reflect.AccessibleObject`.

Example

Programs usually do not use this class directly.

ReflectPermission()

PURPOSE: Constructs a new `ReflectPermission` instance.

SYNTAX:

```
public ReflectPermission(String pname)
public ReflectPermission(String pname, String actions)
```

DESCRIPTION: Both forms of this method construct a new `ReflectPermission` object with the name `pname`. The `actions` parameter is ignored.

PARAMETERS

`actions`	Ignored. Should be `null`.
`pname`	A non-`null` string, such as `"suppressAccessChecks"` or `"*"`.

R

java.text
RuleBasedCollator

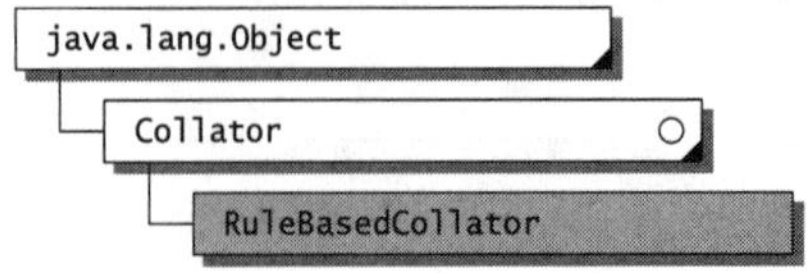

Syntax

```
public class RuleBasedCollator extends Collator
```

Description

The `RuleBasedCollator` class is a concrete subclass of `Collator` that performs locale-sensitive string comparison. You use this class to build searching and alphabetical sorting routines for natural language text. The term *collate* means to determine the proper sort sequence for two or more strings.

The comparison is determined by a rules table for each locale. Java comes with rules tables for many locales. You can customize any of these tables as you desire.

See *The Java Class Libraries, Second Edition, Volume 1* for more information about this class.

Changes for Version 1.2

The only API addition is `getCollationElementIterator(CharacterIterator)`. This is a new overloading of that method, which in Version 1.1 accepted only a `String` argument. There are also documentation changes to the following sections. In "Collation Rules," a new diagram demonstrates a more complex rule. "Customizing the Rules" and "Equivalency" contain more accurate descriptions. In "Expansion," the earlier documentation for expanding the German 'ä' (a-umlaut) contained an error that is corrected here. In "Normalization and Accents," the description has been completely rewritten to reflect a change in implementation.

R

Collation Rules

The characters '&', '<', and ';' perform various levels of reset:

- '&' essentially resets all of the levels (primary through tertiary) to be the same as whatever element follows it.
- '<' resets everything less significant than primary (that is, secondary and tertiary).
- ';' resets everything less significant than secondary (that is, tertiary).

Figure 17 illustrates that semicolons and commas are also rule delimiters.

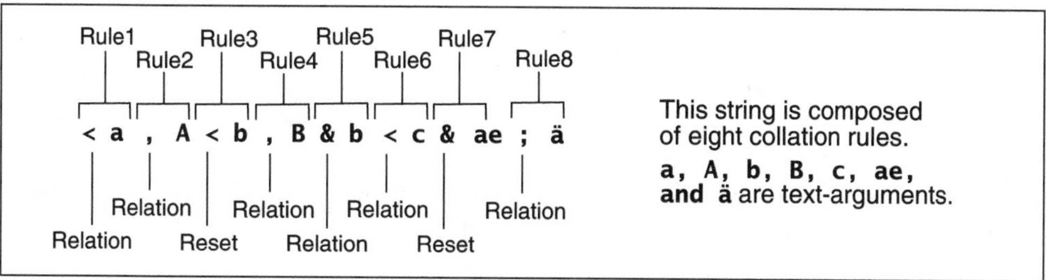

FIGURE 17: Each Rule Is a Relation Followed by Characters.

Basic Rules

You can concatenate rule strings together to customize them. Appending rules of the form "`< arg`" means that the text argument `arg` is "primary-strength-greater-than" the previous character. The form "`; arg`" means that `arg` is "secondary-strength-greater-than" the previous character. The form "`, arg`" means that `arg` is "tertiary-strength-greater-than" the previous character.

For example, the following shows the sort order of lowercase and uppercase letters in some Latin languages, such as English. To add this rule to the English sorting rules, write the following:

```
< a, A < b, B < c, C < d, D < e, E < f, F < g, G < h, H < i, I < j, J < k,
K < l, L < m, M < n, N < o, O < p, P < q, Q < r, R < s, S < t, T < u, U <
v, V < w, W < x, X < y, Y < z, Z
```

To interpret this, break it up into strength/argument pairs, as shown in Table 17.

`< a`	'a' is primary-greater-than nothing.
`, A`	'A' is tertiary-greater-than 'a' (other strength levels stay the same as 'a').
`< b`	'b' is primary-greater-than 'A' (other strength levels reset to zero).
`, B`	'B' is tertiary-greater-than 'b' (other strength levels stay the same as 'b').
`< c`	'c' is primary-greater-than 'B' (other strength levels reset to zero).
`, C`	'C' is tertiary-greater-than 'd' (other strength levels stay the same as 'c').
`< d`	'd' is primary-greater-than 'C' (other strength levels reset to zero).
`, D`	'D' is tertiary-greater-than 'd' (other strength levels stay the same as 'd').
	(and so on)

TABLE 17: Interpretation of `< a, A < b, B < c, C < d, D. . . .`

Customizing the Rules

Using the reset character, you can also add rules at the end of the rule string that override earlier rules, rather than simply add characters to the end of the sorting.

For example, in traditional Spanish, the 'ch' combination should sort between the characters 'c' and 'd'. (The default Spanish locale does not use this rule as of JDK 1.1.6.) Treating two characters as one is called *contraction*. To add this rule to the English sorting rules (we omitted the letters between D and Y), write the following rule string:

```
< a, A < b, B < c, C < d, D < ... < y, Y < z, Z & c < ch
```

To interpret this, break it up into strength/argument pairs, as in Table 18. The last rule means that when a collator sees 'ch', it outputs a single collation element that has primary strength greater than 'c'.

`& c`	Reset to 'c'. Make the next rule relative to 'c'.
`< ch`	'ch' is primary-greater-than 'c' (other strength levels are reset to zero).

TABLE 18: Strength/Argument Pairs.

This would sort words in this order:

```
car
cyanide
churo
day
```

The "Rule Modification" example given later in this discussion shows another example with 'ch'.

R

Equivalency

The following are equivalent ways of expressing the same thing. Notice that they all begin with a relation character.

```
< a < b < c
< a < b & b < c
< a < c & a < b
```

The order is important, as the subsequent item goes immediately after the text-argument. These examples can be expressed in words, as follows.

- `< a < b < c`
  'a' is primary-greater-than nothing, 'b' is primary-greater-than 'a', and 'c' is primary-greater-than 'b'.
- `< a < b & b < c`

'a' is primary-greater-than nothing, 'b' is primary-greater-than 'a', and the reset character '&' indicates that the next rule (`< c`) is relative to reset's text-argument (`b`). Hence, 'c' is primary-greater-than 'b'—this is equivalent to the first rule.

- `< a < c & a < b`
  'a' is primary-greater-than nothing, 'c' is primary-greater-than 'a', and the reset character '&' indicates that the next rule (`< b`) is relative to reset's text-argument (`a`). Hence, 'b' is primary-greater-than 'a', which makes this equivalent to the first rule.

The following are not equivalent to each other:

```
< a < b & a < c
< a < c & a < b
```

Expansion

Expansion is the process of sorting a character as if it were expanded to two characters. In traditional German, 'ä' (a-umlaut) is sorted as though it expands to two characters: 'a' followed by 'e'. This is expressed as the rules at the end of this rule string:

```
a,A < b,B < c,C < ... < x,X < y,Y < z,Z & ae;ä & AE;Ä
```

This can be expressed in words as in Table 19.

`& ae`	Reset. Makes the next rule relative to 'ae'.
`; ä`	'ä' is secondary-greater-than 'ae'. This means that when a collator sees 'ä', it outputs the collation element for 'a' and then the one for 'e' but with the secondary weights incremented by 1 so that it does not look exactly the same as 'ae'.
`& AE`	Reset. Makes the next rule relative to 'AE'.
`; Ä`	'Ä' is secondary-greater-than 'AE'.

TABLE 19: Interpretation of `& ae;ä & AE;Ä`.

R

Normalization and Accents

`RuleBasedCollator` automatically processes its rule table to include both pre-composed and combining-character versions of accented characters. Even if the provided rule string contains only base characters and separate combining accent characters, the pre-composed accented characters matching all canonical combinations of characters from the rule string will be entered in the table.

This allows you to use a `RuleBasedCollator` to compare accented strings even when the collator is set to `NO_DECOMPOSITION`. There are two caveats, however. First, if the strings to be collated contain combining sequences that might not be in canonical order, you should set the collator to `CANONICAL_DECOMPOSITION` or `FULL_DECOMPOSITION` to enable sorting of combining sequences. Second, if the strings contain characters with compatibility decompositions (such as full-width and half-width forms), you must use `FULL_DECOMPOSITION`, since the rule tables include only canonical mappings. (For more information, see the print version of *The Unicode Standard, Version 2.0,* at `http://www.awl.com/cseng/titles/0-201-48345-9/`.)

MEMBER SUMMARY	
Constructor	
`RuleBasedCollator()`	Constructs a `RuleBasedCollator` instance.
Comparison Method	
`compare()`	Compares two strings according to the rules of this `RuleBasedCollator` instance and returns an integer indicating which should be sorted first.
Iterator Method	
Δ `getCollationElementIterator()`	Retrieves the `CollationElementIterator` object for a string.
Collation Method	
`getCollationKey()`	Transforms a string into a `CollationKey` object for bitwise comparison with other `CollationKey` objects.
Rule Method	
`getRules()`	Retrieves the rules string for this `RuleBasedCollator` instance.
Object Methods	
`clone()`	Standard override; no change in semantics.
`equals()`	Compares this `RuleBasedCollator` instance with another object for equality.
`hashCode()`	Computes the hash code of this `RuleBasedCollator` instance.

R

See Also

`Collator`, `CollationElementIterator`.
`RuleBasedCollator` in *The Java Class Libraries, Second Edition, Volume 1.*

Δ getCollationElementIterator()

PURPOSE Retrieves the `CollationElementIterator` object for a string.

SYNTAX

```
public CollationElementIterator
   getCollationElementIterator(String source)
```

SINCE 1.2

```
public CollationElementIterator
   getCollationElementIterator(CharacterIterator source)
```

DESCRIPTION This method is used mostly for searching. You also call this method when you want to create your own collation rules that need access to the particular values of the primary, secondary, and tertiary orders (as described in `CollationElementIterator`). When you call `compare()` on a built-in `Collator` object, such as `RuleBasedCollator`, `CollationElementIterator` objects are created automatically for you for each string to be compared.

This method creates and returns an instance of `CollationElementIterator` for the locale-specific `source` string. This iterator is used to walk through each character of the string according to the rules of this `RuleBasedCollator` instance. Use the iterator to return the sort-order properties of the positioned character. The order properties of a character define how a character is collated by the given `Collation` object.

1.2 CHANGES In Version 1.1, only the first form of this method existed. The second form, which accepts a `CharacterIterator`, was added in Version 1.2.

PARAMETERS

`source` The string to be compared.

RETURNS The instance of `CollationElementIterator` for the `source` string.

SEE ALSO `CollationElementIterator`.

EXAMPLE See the class example in the `CollationElementIterator` class.

java.lang
Runtime

Syntax

```
public class Runtime
```

Description

The `Runtime` class defines methods in the `Runtime` library. It contains methods that perform environment- and system-related functions, such as loading libraries, executing system programs, turning on tracing, and performing garbage collection.

See *The Java Class Libraries, Second Edition, Volume 1* for more information about this class.

Changes for Version 1.2

In Version 1.1, the `loadLibrary()` method loaded a library using a system-wide search path. In Version 1.2, it looks for the file containing the library using `classloader.findLibrary()`, where `classloader` is the class loader of the caller.

The use of `runFinalizersOnExit()` has been deprecated.

R

MEMBER SUMMARY	
Getting the Runtime Instance	
`getRuntime()`	Retrieves the reference to the `Runtime` instance.
Memory Management Methods	
`freeMemory()`	Retrieves an approximation of the number of free bytes in the Java system memory.
`gc()`	Runs the garbage collector.
`runFinalization()`	Runs the `finalize()` method of objects that are pending finalization.
`totalMemory()`	Retrieves the total number of bytes in the Java system memory.
General Methods	
`exec()`	Executes a platform-dependent program.
`exit()`	Causes the virtual machine to exit.
`load()`	Loads a dynamic library when given its full pathname.
Δ `loadLibrary()`	Loads a dynamic library when given its library name.

MEMBER SUMMARY	
Debugging Methods	
`traceInstructions()`	Enables/disables the tracing of instructions.
`traceMethodCalls()`	Enables/disables the tracing of method calls.
Deprecated Methods	
`getLocalizedInputStream()`	Replaced by `InputStreamReader` and `BufferedReader`.
`getLocalizedOutputStream()`	Replaced by `OutputStreamWriter` and `BufferedWriter`.
Δ `runFinalizersOnExit()`	Enables/disables finalization when the program exits.

See Also

`ClassLoader.findLibrary()`, `System.mapLibraryName()`, `Thread.stop()`.
`Runtime` in *The Java Class Libraries, Second Edition, Volume 1.*

Δ loadLibrary()

PURPOSE Loads a dynamic library when given its library name.

SYNTAX `public void loadLibrary(String libname)`

DESCRIPTION This method loads the dynamic library, `libname`. A library can be loaded only once per Java virtual machine. If classes from different class loaders request that the same library be loaded, an `UnsatisfiedLinkError` is thrown.

Loading a library makes the symbols and functions exported by that library available to the program. This can be used to support native methods. For details on native methods, see `http://java.sun.com/docs/books/tutorial/native1.1/index.html`.

See `System.mapLibraryName()` to see how `libname` is mapped to the platform-specific library name for loading the library.

A library can be loaded only if permitted by the security manager. See `SecurityManager.checkLink()` and the `RuntimePermission`'s `loadLibrary` type.

`loadLibrary()` finds the file containing `libname` by first looking for the file containing the library by using `classloader.findLibrary()`, where `classloader` is the class loader of the caller. If `findLibrary()` returns an absolute filename, the Java virtual machine will load the library from that file. If `findLibrary()` returns `null`, the Java virtual machine will search for the library in the search path specified by the system properties `sun.boot.library.path` and `java.library.path`. Each of these properties contains a list of directories

R

to search; each item on the list is separated using `File.pathSeparator`. These two properties are initialized by the Java runtime system. `sun.boot.library.path` typically contains `$JAVA_HOME/jre/bin`, while `java.library.path` is initialized in a platform-dependent way. On Solaris, it is initialized using the environment variable `LD_LIBRARY_PATH`. On Windows, it is initialized using the following, in order:

- The `SYSTEM` directory (on NT, `SYSTEM32` first, then `SYSTEM`)
- The `Windows` directory
- The `PATH` environment variable

The Java virtual machine first maps `libname` to a platform-specific string representing a native library using `System.mapLibraryName()` and then tries to load a library with that name from the directories specified in the two system properties.

1.2 CHANGES In Version 1.1, instead of using the algorithm in the description, this method found the library in the directories specified by the platform-dependent library search path. On Solaris, the library search path is specified by the environment variable `LD_LIBRARY_PATH`. On Windows, the library search order is as follows:

- The directory from which the application is loaded
- The current directory
- The `SYSTEM` directory (on NT, `SYSTEM32` first, then `SYSTEM`)
- The `Windows` directory
- The `PATH` environment variable

EXCEPTIONS

`OutOfMemoryError`
If the library could not be loaded due to insufficient memory in the system.

`SecurityException`
If the currently executing thread is not permitted to load `libname`.

`UnsatisfiedLinkError`
If `ClassLoader.findLibrary()` returned a nonabsolute filename, or if the library could not be loaded and linked successfully.

SEE ALSO `ClassLoader.findLibrary()`, `load()`, `SecurityManager.checkLink()`, `RuntimePermission("loadLibrary")`.

R

Δ runFinalizersOnExit() *DEPRECATED*

PURPOSE Enables/disables finalization when the program exits.

SYNTAX `public static void runFinalizersOnExit(boolean run)`

1.2 CHANGES This method is deprecated in Version 1.2.

DEPRECATION This method specifies that the finalizers of *all* unfinalized objects are to be run. However, there might be threads, for example daemon threads, that continue to execute until the Java virtual machine actually exits. It is unsafe to finalize objects that other threads might still be using.

PARAMETERS

`run` `true` means finalize objects pending finalization before exiting; `false` means finalization need not be run upon exit.

SEE ALSO `Object.finalize(), runFinalization(), Thread.stop().`

java.lang

RuntimePermission

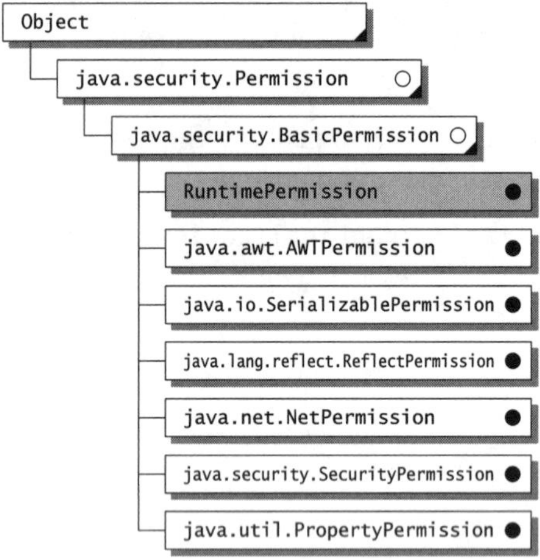

Syntax

```
public final class RuntimePermission extends BasicPermission
```

Description

The `RuntimePermission` class represents a request to perform an operation that affects, or obtains information about, the Java runtime system. It is used internally by the Java runtime system to enforce its security policy. A `RuntimePermission` object has a *permission name* that identifies the runtime operation to check. For example, the `RuntimePermission` with the name `"exitVM"` is used by `Runtime.exit()` to determine whether the caller is allowed to terminated the Java Virtual Machine. This check is performed with the help of the security manager/access controller. If the access controller determines that the caller is not allowed, an `AccessControlException` (a subclass of `SecurityException`) is thrown.

In Version 1.2, most of "check" methods in the `SecurityManager` class relating to the runtime systems have been rewritten to use the `RuntimePermission` class. This rewrite is useful to applications that formerly wrote and installed their own security manager but is otherwise transparent to users of the `SecurityManager` class.

A brief discussion of the Version 1.2 security model is given in the `SecurityManager` class description. More information about Version 1.2's security model and framework is available at `http://java.sun.com/products/jdk/1.2/docs/guide/security/index.html`.

Usage

Applets and applications usually do not directly use the `RuntimePermission` class. It is used internally by the Java runtime system to enforce its security policy. For example, when a program invokes `Runtime.exit()`, the system will use the `RuntimePermission("exitVM")` object to check that the caller has permission to do so.

An application may explicitly create a `RuntimePermission` object and use `SecurityManager.checkPermission()` or `AccessController.checkPermission()` to check whether the security policy has granted it such permission. But the act of trying to perform the operation will automatically trigger such a check, so there is seldom a reason to duplicate it.

The RuntimePermission Name

The permission name of a `RuntimePermission` object identifies the runtime operation to check. The Java runtime system uses the permission names listed in Table 20. It may use additional permission names in the future for other permissions relating to runtime operations.

Permission Name	Request
`accessClassInPackage.`*pkg*	Load classes from the package *pkg*.
`accessDeclaredMembers`	Access declared members of a class using reflection.
`createClassLoader`	Create a class loader.
`createSecurityManager`	Create a security manager.
`defineClassInPackage.`*pkg*	Add classes to the package *pkg*.
`exitVM`	Exit the Java Virtual Machine.
`getClassLoader`	Get a reference to the class loader(s) of a class.
`getProtectionDomain`	Get a reference to the protection domain of a class.
`loadLibrary.`*libname*	Load the native library *libname*.
`modifyThread`	Modify the state of a thread (such as changing its priority and suspending and resuming it).
`modifyThreadGroup`	Modify the state of the thread group (such as changing its priority and suspending and resuming its threads).
`queuePrintJob`	Submit a print job.
`readFileDescriptor`	Open a file for reading by using its file descriptor.
`setContextClassLoader`	Set the context of the class loader for access control checking.
`setFactory`	Install a factory, such as a socket factory, content handler factory, or `URL` stream handler factory.
`setIO`	Reassign one of the fields: `System.out`, `System.err`, or `System.in`.
`setSecurityManager`	Install a security manager.
`stopThread`	Invoke `Thread.stop()`.
`writeFileDescriptor`	Open a file for writing by using its file descriptor.

TABLE 20: `RuntimePermission` Names Used by the Java Runtime System.

R

An application is also free to add and use new permission names to represent other types of runtime operations, but such RuntimePermissions will be known only to the application that defines them. Nevertheless, such permission names can appear in the security policy and be checked using the AccessController. An application that needs to define and use new permission names is usually better off defining its own Permission subclass to avoid future conflicts with the Java runtime system.

Implies

The permission name of a RuntimePermission object is a case-sensitive string. It is used to check whether one RuntimePermission is equal to another RuntimePermission. It is also used to check whether one RuntimePermission *implies* another RuntimePermission. Permission *A* implies permission *B* means if permission *A* is granted, so will permission *B*. Following are the rules for how "implies" works for RuntimePermission objects.

- Two RuntimePermissions with the same permission name imply each other.
- A RuntimePermission with a permission name of the form *pname*.* implies any RuntimePermission whose permission name has the prefix "*pname*.". For example, a RuntimePermission with a permission name "accessClassInPackage.sun.*" implies any RuntimePermission whose permission name has the prefix "accessClassInPackage.sun.".
- A RuntimePermission with the permission name "*" implies any RuntimePermission.

accessClassInPackage

A RuntimePermission object with the permission name "accessClassInPackage.*pkg*" is used by class loaders to check whether the caller has permission to load classes from the specified package(s). *pkg* can be a "*", which means all packages, or a fully qualified package name (such as "sun.misc"), or a package prefix followed by a "*" (such as "sun.*"). Note that this form of *access* differs from the public/protected/private access declared as part of a package. This form of access is intended to guard against the use of internal packages that are shared by different packages among a subsystem but that are not intended to be generally available. This check is performed both by class loaders and when reflection is used to access classes and their members. See SecurityManager.checkPackageAccess() for more details.

R

accessDeclaredMembers

A RuntimePermission object with the permission name "accessDeclaredMembers" is used to check whether the caller has permission to obtain the reflection objects of members of a class. Members are granted access if they are declared public or they are members of classes that have the same class loader as the caller's. Access to all other members is allowed only if this permission has been granted. This permission is usually granted to tools such as debuggers and introspectors that need to dynamically examine and manipulate a program's objects.

This permission is used by the following methods in the Class class: getConstructor(), getConstructors(), getDeclaredConstructor(), getField(), getFields(), get-

DeclaredConstructors(), getDeclaredField(), getDeclaredFields(), getMethods(), getMethod(), getDeclaredMethods(), getDeclaredMethod(), and getDeclaredClasses(),

See Security.checkMemberAccess() for details about this permission. See ReflectPermission for another permission that is related to reflection. The ReflectPermission with permission name "suppressAccessChecks" controls whether the nonpublic fields of the objects being reflected can be read/updated and whether the nonpublic methods and constructors being reflected can be invoked. That is, "accessDeclaredMembers" determines whether you can obtain the reflection object, for example by using Class.getField(). Once you obtain the reflection object, "suppressAccessChecks" determines whether you can use it to access the object that it reflects, for example to examine the value stored in the field.

createClassLoader

A RuntimePermission with the permission name "createClassLoader" is used to check whether the caller has permission to create class loaders. The ability to create class loaders allows a program to load classes from possibly arbitrary sources; that ability is therefore considered dangerous from a security standpoint. This permission is checked by the constructor of ClassLoader and all of its subclasses. See SecurityManager.checkCreateClassLoader().

createSecurityManager

A RuntimePermission with the permission name "createSecurityManager" is used to check whether the caller has permission to create a new security manager if one has already been installed. The SecurityManager class has a number of protected methods that access information about its execution environment, such as its class loader and execution stack. A malicious program can create a subclass of SecurityManager that accesses and misuses this information. This permission is checked by the SecurityManager constructor.

defineClassInPackage

A RuntimePermission object with the permission name "defineClassInPackage.*pkg*" is used by class loaders to check whether the caller has permission to add class or interface definitions to the specified package(s). *pkg* can be a "*", which means all packages, or a fully qualified package name (such as "sun.misc"), or a package prefix followed by a "*" (such as "sun.*").

Class definitions in the same package can access package-private classes, interfaces, and members. Applications might want to restrict such access for security reasons. Such restrictions are best enforced by *sealing* a package. (See Package for details.) See SecurityManager.checkPackageDefinition() for more details.

exitVM

A RuntimePermission with the permission name "exitVM" is used to check whether the caller has permission to invoke the method System.exit() (Runtime.exit()). This permission should seldom be granted, except for completely stand-alone applications.

R

getClassLoader

A `RuntimePermission` with the permission name `"getClassLoader"` is used to check whether the caller has permission to get the class loader of a class (for example, `Class.getClassLoader()`). If the caller is loaded either by using the same class loader or by the "bootstrap" class loader (`null`), the class loader is returned without any checks. Otherwise, this permission must be granted to the caller before the class's class loader can be obtained. This permission is used by `ClassLoader.getParent()`, `ClassLoader.getSystemClassLoader()`, `Class.getClassLoader()`, and `Thread.getContextClassLoader()`.

getProtectionDomain

A `RuntimePermission` with the permission name `"getProtectionDomain"` is used to check whether the caller has permission to get a class's *protection domain*. The protection domain of a class consists of its code source (the URL that it was loaded from and the certificates used to sign it) and the permissions that the class has been granted (`java.security.Permission`). `Class.getProtectionDomain()` returns a class's protection domain if this permission has been granted.

loadLibrary

A `RuntimePermission` with the permission name `"loadLibrary.`*libname*`"` is used to protect the loading and linking of native libraries. *libname* can be a "*", which means all libraries, or a library name (such as `"libnet.so"`), or a platform-dependent library pathname (`"/usr/lib/libnet.so"`).

This permission is checked by `Runtime.load()` and `Runtime.loadLibrary()`. See `SecurityManager.checkLink()`.

modifyThread

A `RuntimePermission` with the permission name `"modifyThread"` is used to check whether the caller is allowed to modify a thread. This includes stopping it, suspending and resuming it, and changing its priority, name, and/or daemon status. It is used by `SecurityManager.checkAccess()` to check whether the caller is allowed to modify a system thread. `SecurityManager.checkAccess()` is used by the `Thread` class whenever a request to change the thread is made.

modifyThreadGroup

A `RuntimePermission` with the permission name `"modifyThreadGroup"` is used to check whether the caller is allowed to modify a thread group. This includes stopping its threads, suspending and resuming it, adding members to the group, and changing its priority, name, and/or daemon status. It is used by `SecurityManager.checkAccess()` to check whether the caller is allowed to modify a system thread group. `SecurityManager.checkAccess()` is used by the `ThreadGroup` class whenever a request to change the thread group is made.

queuePrintJob
A `RuntimePermission` with the permission name `"queuePrintJob"` is used to check whether the caller can submit a print job. See `SecurityManager.checkPrintJobAccess()`.

readFileDescriptor
A `RuntimePermission` with the permission name `"readFileDescriptor"` is used to check whether the caller is allowed to open a file for reading using its file descriptor. Granting this permission allows the following constructor, `FileInputStream(FileDescriptor desc)`, to be used; the `desc` argument is ignored for the purposes of the permission check. See `Security-Manager.checkRead(FileDescriptor desc)`.

setContextClassLoader
A `RuntimePermission` with the permission name `"setContextClassLoader"` is used to check whether the class loader for a thread can be changed or set. When a thread is first created, its context class loader is inherited from its parent thread (that is, the creating thread). This default can be changed by using `Thread.setContextClassLoader()` if the caller has been granted this permission.

setFactory
A `RuntimePermission` with the permission name `"setFactory"` is used to check whether the caller is allowed to set the various factories, such as factories for socket implementations, and content handlers. It is used by the following methods: `HttpURLConnection.setFollow-Redirects()`, `ServerSocket.setSocketFactory()`, `Socket.setSocketImplFactory()`, `URLConnection.setFileNameMap()`, and `URLConnection.setContentHandlerFactory()`. These factories determine how the program will behave or misbehave with respect to the network.

setIO
A `RuntimePermission` with the permission name `"setIO"` is used to check whether the caller can redirect standard input, output, and error streams using the methods `System.setIn()`, `System.setOut()`, and `System.setErr()`, respectively. Changing these fields affects the entire Java Virtual Machine and could be used by malicious programs to collect information or feed in bad data.

R

setSecurityManager
A `RuntimePermission` with the permission name `"setSecurityManager"` is used to check whether the caller can replace the existing security manager. It is used by `System.set-SecurityManager()`. This is a dangerous permission to grant because the security manager controls almost all permission checking on the Java Virtual Machine. A malicious security manager when installed could circumvent all security policies and, in fact, could even execute malicious code when asked to perform security checks.

stopThread

A `RuntimePermission` with the permission name `"stopThread"` is used to check whether the caller can stop a thread. In an environment in which threads are created from code originating from different code sources, you do not want one thread to be able to stop other threads. `stopThread` differs from `modifyThread` in that `stopThread` affects only the `Thread.stop()` method. Also, `SecurityManager.checkAccess()` uses `modifyThread` only to protect system threads, while `stopThread` applies to *all* threads, including both system and nonsystem threads. Of course, a program can override the default `SecurityManager.checkAccess()` to also protect nonsystem threads.

writeFileDescriptor

A `RuntimePermission` with the permission name `"writeFileDescriptor"` is used to check whether the caller is allowed to open a file for writing by using its file descriptor. Granting this permission allows the following constructor, `FileOutputStream(FileDescriptor desc)`, to be used; the `desc` argument is ignored for the purposes of the permission check. See `SecurityManager.checkWrite(FileDescriptor desc)`.

MEMBER SUMMARY	
Constructor	
`RuntimePermission()`	Constructs a new instance of `RuntimePermission`.

See Also

`java.security.AccessControlException`, `java.security.AccessController`, `java.security.BasicPermission`, `java.security.Permission`, `System`, `SecurityManager`.

R

Example

This example creates some `RuntimePermissions` and checks them against the security policy of the Java runtime system. When the program is run using the policy file shown, it throws an `AccessControlException` for the `RuntimePermission` with permission name `"setIO"` because that has not been granted by the policy.

Main.java

```
import java.security.AccessController;

public class Main {
    public static void main(String[] args) {
        // Permit access to sun.* packages
        RuntimePermission pkgcheck =
                new RuntimePermission("accessClassInPackage.sun.*");

        // Permit Class.getProtectionDomain()
        RuntimePermission domaincheck =
```

```
                new RuntimePermission("getProtectionDomain");
        // Permit standard IO to be changed
        RuntimePermission iocheck = new RuntimePermission("setIO");

        try {
            AccessController.checkPermission(pkgcheck);
            AccessController.checkPermission(domaincheck);
            AccessController.checkPermission(iocheck);
        } catch (SecurityException e) {
            e.printStackTrace();
        }
    }
}
```

.policy

```
keystore ".keystore";
grant {
        permission java.lang.RuntimePermission "accessClassInPackage.*";
        permission java.lang.RuntimePermission "getProtectionDomain";
      };
```

OUTPUT

```
> java -Djava.security.policy=.policy Main
java.security.AccessControlException: access denied
        (java.lang.RuntimePermission setIO)
    at java.security.AccessControlContext.checkPermission(Compiled Code)
    at java.security.AccessController.checkPermission(Compiled Code)
    at Main.main(Compiled Code)
```

RuntimePermission()

PURPOSE Constructs a new instance of `RuntimePermission`.

SYNTAX

```
public RuntimePermission(String pname)
public RuntimePermission(String pname, String actions)
```

DESCRIPTION Both forms of this method construct a new `RuntimePermission` object using the name `pname`. The `actions` parameter is ignored. `pname` has the syntax described in the class description.

PARAMETERS

`actions` Ignored. Should be `null`.

`pname` A non-`null` string, such as "*" or a permission name from Table 20.

EXAMPLE See the class example.

R

java.lang
SecurityManager

Syntax

`public class SecurityManager`

Description

A security manager enforces security policies related to what a program is allowed to do.

See *The Java Class Libraries, Second Edition, Volume 1* for more information about this class.

Changes for Version 1.2

Version 1.1 Security Model

In Version 1.1 and earlier versions, the security manager was the one and only entity in the Java runtime system that controlled the security policy. The `SecurityManager` class contained permission checking methods ("check" methods) that various parts of the Java runtime system would call whenever it needed to access a protected resource such as the file system or the network. The default implementations of the "check" methods threw a `SecurityException`. An application that wanted to allow access to a resource would subclass `SecurityManager` and override the corresponding "check" methods. For example, an application such as a Web browser would override the "check" methods relating to the network to allow applets to connect to the applet host.

S

There were several problems with this model. First, writing such a security manager is an arduous and error-prone task. The writer must define a security policy that is suitable for the application, for example determining which resources to protect and the granularity at which the protection should be applied (for example, permit a network connection to only the applet host, to all hosts, or to specific hosts). The writer then must override the appropriate "check" methods to implement that policy. If there is a new type of resource that needs to be protected, the writer must define corresponding new "check" methods.

Second, performing the security checks themselves—that is, deciding whether a particular caller has been granted permission to perform an operation—often involved examining the execution context and its stack and using heuristics to decide whether to grant the permission. A third problem was that different applications define and implement different security policies that need to be administered in different ways.

Version 1.2 Security Model

The Version 1.2 security model addresses the problems of the Version 1.1 security model. It makes formal the notions of *permission*, *access controller*, and *security policy*.

A permission represents a request to perform an operation on a protected resource or group of resources. It is represented by (the subclasses of) the `Permission` class. Permissions for different types of protected resources are represented by different subclasses of `Permission`. For example, the `FilePermission` class specifies the actions (such as "read" and "write") to be performed on a file (such as "/tmp"). The `SocketPermission` class specifies the actions (such as "connect") to be performed on a machine (such as "java.sun.com").

Permissions are granted to entities called *code sources*. A code source specifies where the code came from (its *codebase*) and who signed it. The entity that signed the code is called a *principal*. An applet or application may be composed of code signed by different principals. Each such piece of code is marked (that is, *signed*) using information unique to the principal—its credentials—in such a way that, when the code (class files) is subsequently loaded by the Java runtime system, the identity of the principal can be determined. A principal can be an individual (for example, "Duke"), a company (such as "Sun Microsystems, Inc"), or any other entity. See `java.security.Principal` for more descriptions of principals.

The access controller (`AccessController`) is responsible for deciding whether a permission has been granted by the underlying security policy to the principal that signed the code and the code's codebase. Permission are granted to the code source—that is, to both the principal and codebase. If no codebase is specified, then the permission is granted to any code signed by the principal. If no principal is specified, then the permission is granted to any code from the codebase. If neither principal nor codebase is specified, then the permission is granted to all.

Every Java runtime system has associated with it a security policy that consists of a list of code sources and their corresponding permissions to protected resources. For example, the policy might grant the principal "Duke" permission to read the contents of the "/tmp" directory subtree, and grant all code from "http://www.wombat.com/classes/" permission to read the "user.dir" system property. All permissions that are granted must be specified in the security policy; if a permission is not in the policy, then it has not been granted. The security policy is typically defined by a set of *policy files*. See `java.security.Policy` for details on security policies.

In Version 1.2, the security manager is still the focal point of the security model in that it contains all of the "check" methods that the Java runtime system invokes to do security checks. But the security manager now also creates and uses `Permission` objects and passes them to the access controller to perform the actual checks. The access controller in turn consults the security policy. Instead of writing new security managers by subclassing `SecurityManager` class, the application writer can have the application simply configure the security policy to grant the appropriate permissions. There is no need to override the "check" methods.

If a new resource needs to be protected, the application can define a new subclass of `Permission` and use `SecurityManager.checkPermission()` or `AccessController.checkPer-`

mission() to check it against the policy. Users of the application simply need to use the new permission class's name when granting the permission in the security policy at run time.

There is also no need for subclasses of SecurityManager to explicitly check the calling thread's execution stack or context when deciding whether to grant a permission. The AccessController by default performs the appropriate checks and provides a doPrivileged() method for situations that require a different execution context (than the calling thread's). See java.security.AccessController.doPrivileged(). Because of the addition of this new, safer, capability, the methods in SecurityManager formerly used for the same purpose have been deprecated (see "Deprecated Methods" a little later in this discussion).

More information about Version 1.2's security model and framework is available at http://java.sun.com/products/jdk/1.2/docs/guide/security/index.html.

Execution Context

Permission checking is done on the *execution context* of the caller—that is, the entire execution stack starting from the method performing the permission checking to the topmost AccessController.doPrivileged() call on the execution stack, or to the bottom of the execution stack if there is no AccessController.doPrivileged() call on the stack. The security policy must have granted the permission to each code source in that execution stack range; otherwise the permission check fails. For example, if method A calls method B, which invokes SecurityManager.checkRead(), the code sources of both A and B must have been granted the java.io.FilePermission to read the requested file. If method A calls method B, and method B wraps the SecurityManager.checkRead() inside of an AccessController.doPrivileged() call, then only the code source of B needs to have been granted the relevant java.io.FilePermission. See java.security.AccessController for details.

In our discussions, for brevity, we refer to the execution context of the caller as simply *the caller.*

SecurityManager No Longer Abstract

In Version 1.1, SecurityManager was abstract because it did not make sense to have a security manager with default "check" method implementations that just threw a SecurityException.

In Version 1.2, SecurityManager is no longer abstract because the default "check" methods, through the use of the access controller, will check the security policy to see whether the corresponding permission has been granted. Most applications want this behavior and would not need to subclass SecurityManager. You can ask the java interpreter to use the default security manager as follows:

```
java -Djava.security.manager SomeClass
```

General Permission Checking Method

A new method, checkPermission(), has been added to this class. This method allows a generic permission to be checked against the Java runtime system's security policy. This means that new security checks can be added (for example, by using new Permission subclasses) without the application's having to subclass SecurityManager.

Modified Permission Checking Methods

All of the "check" methods have been rewritten to use the new `Permission` classes and the access controller. This rewrite is useful to applications that formerly wrote and installed their own security manager. However, it is otherwise transparent to users of the `SecurityManager` class.

In Version 1.1, the default implementations of the "check" methods threw a `SecurityException`. To change the behavior of any one of the "check" methods, you needed to subclass `SecurityManager` and override the method. In Version 1.2, there is usually no need to override a "check" method. The default implementations submit to the `SecurityManager.checkPermission()` method a `Permission` object that corresponds to the operation that is being checked. This method will use the `AccessController` class, which will in turn consult the security policy to determine whether the caller has been granted the requested permission.

There are two reasons why a `SecurityManager` subclass overrides a `checkXXX()` method. One is to enforce a stricter policy than the default and the other is to enforce a less strict policy than the default. To enforce a stricter policy, the override should first call `super.checkXXX()` and then add its own security checks. To enforce a less strict policy, the override should first make its own security checks and at the point where it would normally throw a `SecurityException`, it should call `super.checkXXX()`.

Deprecated Methods

The use of the `AccessController` class means there is now a safer means to check whether the caller has been granted permissions. Thus the following methods and field in `SecurityManager` have been deprecated: `currentClassLoader()`, `currentLoadedClass()`, `classDepth()`, `classLoaderDepth()`, `getInCheck()`, `inCheck`, `inClass()`, and `inClassLoader()`. See `AccessController`, and specifically `AccessController.doPrivileged()`, for details.

MEMBER SUMMARY

	Constructor	
Δ	`SecurityManager()`	Constructs a new `SecurityManager` instance.
	Permission Checking Methods	
Δ	`checkAccept()`	Determines if allowed to accept a socket connection.
Δ	`checkAccess()`	Determines if allowed to modify a thread or thread group.
Δ	`checkAwtEventQueueAccess()`	Determines if allowed to access the AWT system event queue.
Δ	`checkConnect()`	Determines if allowed to establish a socket connection.
Δ	`checkCreateClassLoader()`	Determines if allowed to create a class loader.
Δ	`checkDelete()`	Determines if allowed to delete a file.

Continued

MEMBER SUMMARY

Permission Checking Methods *(Continued)*

Δ	`checkExec()`	Determines if allowed to execute a platform-dependent program.
Δ	`checkExit()`	Determines if allowed to exit the virtual machine.
Δ	`checkLink()`	Determines if allowed to load and link in a library.
Δ	`checkListen()`	Determines if allowed to bind to a local port.
Δ	`checkMemberAccess()`	Determines if allowed to access reflection objects of members of a class.
Δ	`checkMulticast()`	Determines if allowed to join, leave, or send data to a multicast address.
Δ	`checkPackageAccess()`	Determines if allowed to access a package.
Δ	`checkPackageDefinition()`	Determines if allowed to add class definitions to a package.
1.2	`checkPermission()`	Determines if a permission has been granted.
Δ	`checkPrintJobAccess()`	Determines if allowed to submit a print job.
Δ	`checkPropertiesAccess()`	Determines if allowed to read and update the system properties.
Δ	`checkPropertyAccess()`	Determines if allowed to read a system property.
Δ	`checkRead()`	Determines if allowed to read a file.
Δ	`checkSecurityAccess()`	Determines if allowed to perform a specified security-related action.
Δ	`checkSetFactory()`	Determines if allowed to set the networking-related object factories.
Δ	`checkSystemClipboardAccess()`	Determines if allowed to read or write to the system clipboard.
Δ	`checkTopLevelWindow()`	Determines if allowed to create a top-level window.
Δ	`checkWrite()`	Determines if allowed to write to a file.

S

Methods for Checking Security Manager's State

	`getClassContext()`	Retrieves the execution context of the caller as an array of classes.
	`getSecurityContext()`	Retrieves the execution context of the caller that can be used for subsequent permission checking.
	`getThreadGroup()`	Retrieves the default thread group to use when creating threads.

Deprecated Members

Δ	`classDepth()`	Finds the first occurrence of a class on the execution stack.
Δ	`classLoaderDepth()`	Finds the first occurrence of a class created by a non-`null` class loader on the execution stack.

MEMBER SUMMARY	
Δ currentClassLoader()	Finds the topmost non-null class loader on the execution stack.
Δ currentLoadedClass()	Finds the topmost class with a non-null class loader on the execution stack.
Δ getInCheck()	Determines whether there is a security check in progress.
Δ inCheck	Records whether there is a security check in progress.
Δ inClass()	Determines whether a class is on the execution stack.
Δ inClassLoader()	Determines whether a class loader is on the execution stack.

See Also

`ClassLoader`, `java.io.FilePermission`, `java.net.SocketPermission`, `java.security.AccessController`, `java.security.Permission`, `java.security.Policy`, `java.security.SecureClassLoader`, `java.util.PropertyPermission`, `RuntimePermission`, `System.getSecurityManager()`, `System.setSecurityManager()`.

Δ checkAccept()

PURPOSE Determines if allowed to accept a socket connection.

SYNTAX `public void checkAccept(String host, int port)`

DESCRIPTION This method determines whether the caller is allowed by the Java runtime's security policy to accept a socket connection from the machine `host` on the remote port `port`. The default implementation makes the check by using a `SocketPermission` with an action of `"accept"`, and a name of `host:port`.

1.2 CHANGES In Version 1.1, the default implementation always threw `SecurityException`.

PARAMETERS

`host` The non-null machine name to check. The syntax of the name is platform-dependent. For example, if the machine has an Internet host name, `host` could be a domain-qualified name like `foobar.widget.com` or a nonqualified name like `foobar`.

`port` The remote port number to check.

EXCEPTIONS

`SecurityException`
If the connection cannot be accepted due to security reasons.

SEE ALSO `checkListen()`, `checkRead()`, `checkWrite()`, `java.net.ServerSocket.accept()`, `java.net.SocketPermission`.

S

Δ checkAccess()

PURPOSE
Determines if allowed to modify a thread or thread group.

SYNTAX
```
public void checkAccess(Thread thrd)
public void checkAccess(ThreadGroup thrdGroup)
```

DESCRIPTION
This method determines whether the caller is allowed by the Java runtime's security policy to modify a thread or thread group. The first form determines whether the caller is allowed to modify the thread `thrd`. Modifications include stopping, suspending, and resuming the thread and changing its priority, name, and/or daemon status. The default implementation makes the check by using a `RuntimePermission` with a name of `"modifyThread"`.

The second form determines whether the caller is allowed by the Java runtime's security policy to modify the thread group `thrdGroup`. Modifications include stopping, suspending, resuming, and destroying threads in the thread group, joining the thread group, and changing the thread group's daemon status and maximum priority. The default implementation makes the check by using a `RuntimePermission` with a name of `"modifyThreadGroup"`.

The default implementation checks only for changes to system threads and thread groups. That is, it only performs the security check if `thrd` is a system thread or if `thrdGroup` is the system thread group. Changes to nonsystem threads and nonsystem thread groups are not checked (that is, no `SecurityException` is thrown). A security manager that wants to protect threads running code from different code sources from changing each other's state should override this method.

1.2 CHANGES
In Version 1.1, the default implementation always threw `SecurityException`.

PARAMETERS

`thrd` The non-`null` thread to be checked.

`thrdGroup` The non-`null` thread group to be checked.

S

EXCEPTIONS

`SecurityException`
If the caller is not allowed to modify `thrd` or `thrdGroup` for security reasons.

SEE ALSO
`RuntimePermission("modifyThread")`, `RuntimePermission("modifyThreadGroup")`, `Thread.checkAccess()`, `Thread.resume()`, `Thread.setDaemon()`, `Thread.setName()`, `Thread.setPriority()`, `Thread.stop()`, `Thread.suspend()`, `Thread.Thread()`, `ThreadGroup.checkAccess()`, `ThreadGroup.destroy()`, `ThreadGroup.setDaemon()`, `ThreadGroup.setMaxPriority()`, `ThreadGroup.setPriority()`, `ThreadGroup.resume()`, `ThreadGroup.stop()`, `ThreadGroup.suspend()`, `ThreadGroup.ThreadGroup()`.

Δ checkAwtEventQueueAccess()

PURPOSE Determines if allowed to access the AWT system event queue.

SYNTAX `public void checkAwtEventQueueAccess()`

DESCRIPTION This method checks whether the caller is allowed by the Java runtime's security policy to get a reference to the system event queue. The default implementation makes the check by using an `AWTPermission` with a name of `"accessEventQueue"`.

The AWT system uses a single *system event queue* for posting events (see `java.awt.Toolkit.getSystemEventQueue()`). The system event queue can include not only events generated by the AWT, but also system events that are added programmatically.

Depending on the AWT toolkit implementation, applets running on the same virtual machine may not necessarily share the same system event queue. Gaining a reference to the system event queue has security implications. This is because with the reference, you can read the queue's contents or post events to it.

1.2 CHANGES In Version 1.1, the default implementation always threw `SecurityException`.

EXCEPTIONS

`SecurityException`
If the system event queue cannot be accessed due to security reasons.

SEE ALSO `java.awt.AWTPermission`, `java.awt.EventQueue`, `java.awt.Toolkit.getSystemEventQueue()`.

Δ checkConnect()

PURPOSE Determines if allowed to establish a socket connection.

SYNTAX
```
public void checkConnect(String host, int prt)
public void checkConnect(String host, int prt, Object ctx)
```

DESCRIPTION The two forms of this method check whether the caller is allowed by the Java runtime's security policy to establish a connection to the port `prt` on the machine `host`. If `prt` is `-1`, this method checks whether the resolution of `host` to an IP address is allowed. If a context `ctx` is specified, the security manager determines whether `ctx` is allowed to establish the connection. The default implementation makes the check by using a `SocketPermission` with an action of `"connect"` or `"resolve"` (depending on the value of `prt`), and a name constructed from `host` and `prt`.

1.2 CHANGES In Version 1.1, the default implementation always threw `SecurityException`.

PARAMETERS

`ctx`	The non-`null` context to check.
`host`	The non-`null` machine name to check.
`prt`	The port to check. If `prt` is `-1`, checks whether the resolution of `host` to an IP address is allowed.

EXCEPTIONS

`SecurityException`
If the connection cannot be established for security reasons, or if `ctx` is not an instance of `java.security.AccessControlContext`.

SEE ALSO `java.net.DatagramSocket.getLocalAddress()`, `java.net.DatagramSocket.send()`, `java.net.DatagramSocket.receive()`, `getSecurityContext()`, `java.net.InetAddress.getByName()`, `java.net.InetAddress.getHostName()`, `java.net.InetAddress.getAllByName()`, `java.net.MulticastSocket.send()`, `java.net.Socket.Socket()`, `java.net.SocketPermission`.

Δ checkCreateClassLoader()

PURPOSE Determines if allowed to create a class loader.

SYNTAX `public void checkCreateClassLoader()`

DESCRIPTION This method determines whether the caller is allowed by the Java runtime's security policy to create a class loader. The default implementation makes the check by using a `RuntimePermission` with a name of `"createClassLoader"`.

1.2 CHANGES In Version 1.1, the default implementation always threw `SecurityException`.

EXCEPTIONS

`SecurityException`
If a class loader cannot be created due to security reasons.

SEE ALSO `ClassLoader.ClassLoader()`, `RuntimePermission("createClassLoader")`.

Δ checkDelete()

PURPOSE Determines if allowed to delete a file.

SYNTAX `public void checkDelete(String fileName)`

DESCRIPTION This method determines whether the caller is allowed by the Java runtime's security policy to delete the file `fileName`. Implementers should use the canonical form of `fileName` in order to unambiguously identify the file being

S

checked. The default implementation makes the check by using a `FilePermission` with an action of `"delete"` and a name of `file`.

1.2 CHANGES In Version 1.1, the default implementation always threw `SecurityException`.

PARAMETERS

`fileName` The non-`null` system-dependent filename to check.

EXCEPTIONS

`SecurityException`
If `fileName` cannot be deleted for security reasons.

SEE ALSO `java.io.File.delete()`, `java.io.File.getCanonicalPath()`, `java.io.FilePermission`.

Δ checkExec()

PURPOSE Determines if allowed to execute a platform-dependent program.

SYNTAX `public void checkExec(String prog)`

DESCRIPTION This method determines whether the caller is allowed by the Java runtime's security policy to execute the platform-dependent program `prog`. Executing platform-dependent programs has security implications because certain programs can make unexpected and sometimes undesirable updates to the system environment. The default implementation makes the check by using a `FilePermission` with an action of `"execute"` and a name of `file` if `file` is an absolute path name, otherwise a name of `"<<ALL FILES>>"` is used.

1.2 CHANGES In Version 1.1, the default implementation always threw `SecurityException`.

PARAMETERS

`prog` The non-`null` platform-dependent name of the program to check. `prog` may be an absolute filename naming the program or a program name to be searched in the invoker's program execution path.

EXCEPTIONS

`SecurityException`
If `prog` cannot be executed for security reasons.

SEE ALSO `java.io.FilePermission`, `Process`, `Runtime.exec()`.

Δ checkExit()

PURPOSE Determines if allowed to exit the virtual machine.

SYNTAX `public void checkExit(int stat)`

DESCRIPTION This method determines whether the caller is allowed by the Java runtime's security policy to exit the virtual machine with status `stat`. Exiting the virtual machine has security implications because it effectively stops the entire Java program. The exit status is significant because it is sometimes used by other programs to check whether a program executed correctly. The default implementation makes the check by using a `RuntimePermission` with a name of `"exitVM"`.

1.2 CHANGES In Version 1.1, the default implementation always threw `SecurityException`.

PARAMETERS

`stat` The exit status to check.

EXCEPTIONS

`SecurityException`
If the virtual machine cannot be exited with `stat` for security reasons.

SEE ALSO `Runtime.exit(), RuntimePermission("exitVM").`

Δ checkLink()

PURPOSE Determines if allowed to load and link a library.

SYNTAX `public void checkLink(String lib)`

DESCRIPTION This method determines whether the caller is allowed by the Java runtime's security policy to load and link the library `lib` into the system. Loading libraries has security implications because it makes the symbols being exported by the libraries visible to the program. This could possibly result in the overriding of the definition of symbols (to be loaded in the future) of functions that have security importance, such as functions for getting passwords, resolving host names, and getting machine licenses. The default implementation makes the check by using a `RuntimePermission` with a name of `"loadLibrary." + lib`.

1.2 CHANGES In Version 1.1, the default implementation always threw `SecurityException`.

PARAMETERS

`lib` A non-`null` string containing either the filename or library name of the library to load.

EXCEPTIONS

`SecurityException`
If `lib` cannot be loaded for security reasons.

SEE ALSO `Runtime.load(), Runtime.loadLibrary(), RuntimePermission("loadLibrary").`

S

Δ checkListen()

PURPOSE Determines if allowed to bind to a local port.

SYNTAX `public void checkListen(int lport)`

DESCRIPTION This method determines whether the caller is allowed by the Java runtime's security policy to bind to the local port `lport`. The default implementation makes the check by using a `SocketPermission` with an action of `"listen"` and a name of `"localhost:"+lport` if `lport` is nonzero, and a name of `"localhost:1024-"` if `lport` is zero.

1.2 CHANGES In Version 1.1, the default implementation always threw `SecurityException`.

PARAMETERS

`lport` The local port to check.

EXCEPTIONS

`SecurityException`

If `lport` cannot be bound due to security reasons.

SEE ALSO `java.net.DatagramSocket.DatagramSocket()`, `java.net.MulticastSocket.MulticastSocket()`, `java.net.ServerSocket.ServerSocket()`, `java.net.SocketPermission`.

Δ checkMemberAccess()

PURPOSE Determines if allowed to access reflection objects of members of a class.

SYNTAX `public void checkMemberAccess(Class cl, int atype)`

DESCRIPTION This method determines whether the caller is allowed by the Java runtime's security policy to access the reflection objects of members of access type `atype` from the class or interface `cl`. In the default implementation, if `atype` is `Member.PUBLIC` or if `cl` was loaded by the same class loader as the caller, this method returns. Otherwise, it uses `RuntimePermission("accessDeclared-Members")` to check whether the caller has been granted permission.

1.2 CHANGES In Version 1.1, no special preference was given to classes loaded by the same class loader or public methods. In all cases, the default implementation always threw `SecurityException`.

PARAMETERS

`atype` The access type of members being checked; one of `Member.DECLARED` or `Member.PUBLIC`.

`cl` The non-`null` class or interface being checked.

EXCEPTIONS

`SecurityException`

S

If reflection objects of members of type `mtype` from class or interface `cl` cannot be accessed due to security reasons.

SEE ALSO `Class.getConstructor()`, `Class.getConstructors()`, `Class.getDeclaredClasses()`, `Class.getDeclaredConstructors()`, `Class.getDeclaredConstructor()`, `Class.getDeclaredField()`, `Class.getDeclaredFields()`, `Class.getDeclaredMethod()`, `Class.getDeclaredMethods()`, `Class.getField()`, `Class.getFields()`, `Class.getMethod()`, `Class.getMethods()`, `java.lang.reflect.Member.DECLARED`, `java.lang.reflect.Member.PUBLIC`, `java.lang.reflect.ReflectPermission`, `RuntimePermission("accessDeclaredMembers")`.

Δ checkMulticast()

PURPOSE Determines if allowed to use join, leave, or send to a multicast address.

SYNTAX

```
public void checkMulticast(InetAddress maddr)
public void checkMulticast(InetAddress maddr, byte ttl)
```

DESCRIPTION A program can communicate with other programs on the network by sending a *single* multicast packet to a *multicast group* comprising zero or more members. The group is identified by a *multicast address*—an IP address to which group members subscribe. The `MulticastSocket` class contains methods for sending and receiving IP multicast packets.

This method determines whether the caller is allowed by the Java runtime's security policy to join, leave, or send data to the IP multicast address `maddr`. If `ttl` is specified, it means to check whether the caller is allowed to send datagram packets to members of the group `maddr` using a time-to-live value of `ttl`.[1] A higher value of `ttl` means more network resources will be used.

The default implementation makes the check by using a `SocketPermission` with an action of `"accept,connect"` and a name of `maddr`. `ttl` is ignored.

S

1.2 CHANGES In Version 1.1, the default implementation always threw `SecurityException`.

PARAMETERS

`maddr` The non-`null` multicast group address to check.

`ttl` The transmission range of datagram packets that will be used.

1. If the time-to-live value of a multicast packet is zero, the packet is sent to the local host, not to the network. If the time-to-live value of a multicast packet is one, the packet is transmitted using the local network multicast which reaches all immediately-neighboring members of the sender. If the packet's time-to-live value is greater than one, the packet is also forwarded by *multicast routers* to all other networks that have members of the multicast group. If the packet's time-to-live value is greater than two, the packet is again forwarded from those networks, and so on.

EXCEPTIONS

`SecurityException`

If a multicast address for `maddr` (and `ttl`) cannot be used due to security reasons.

SEE ALSO `java.net.DatagramSocket.send()`, `java.net.DatagramSocketImpl`, `java.net.MulticastSocket.getTimeToLive()`, `java.net.MulticastSocket.joinGroup()`, `java.net.MulticastSocket.leaveGroup()`, `java.net.MulticastSocket.send()`, `java.net.MulticastSocket.setTimeToLive()`, `java.net.SocketPermission`.

Δ checkPackageAccess()

PURPOSE Determines if allowed to access a package.

SYNTAX `public void checkPackageAccess(String pkg)`

DESCRIPTION This method determines whether the caller is allowed by the Java runtime's security policy to access the package `pkg`. Note that "access" is orthogonal to the access control specified in the program using the `public`, `protected`, and `private` modifiers. This check is meant to protect access to classes that are `public` but intended for internal use. Examples of such packages are those with the `"sun."` prefix. The list of restricted packages is obtained from the property name `"package.access"` in the security properties file `$JAVA_HOME/jre/lib/security/java.security`. If `pkg` is one of these restricted class, the default implementation uses a `RuntimePermission` with a name of `"accessClassInPackage."+pkg`.

1.2 CHANGES In Version 1.1, the default implementation always threw `SecurityException`.

PARAMETERS

`pkg` The non-`null` name of the package to check (e.g., "java.io").

EXCEPTIONS

`SecurityException`

If `pkg` cannot be accessed due to security reasons.

SEE ALSO `RuntimePermission("accessClassInPackage")`.

Δ checkPackageDefinition()

PURPOSE Determines if allowed to add class definitions to a package.

SYNTAX `public void checkPackageDefinition(String pkg)`

DESCRIPTION This method determines whether the caller is allowed by the Java runtime's security policy to add class or interface definitions to the package `pkg`. Class definitions in the same package can access package-private classes, interfaces, and members. Applications might want to restrict such access for security reasons. Such restrictions are best enforced by *sealing* a package. See `Package` for details.

The list of restricted packages is obtained from the property name `"package.definition"` in the security properties file `$JAVA_HOME/jre/lib/security/java.security`. If `pkg` is one of these restricted class, the default implementation uses a `RuntimePermission` with a name of `"defineClassInPackage."+pkg`.

1.2 CHANGES In Version 1.1, the default implementation always threw `SecurityException`.

PARAMETERS

`pkg` The non-`null` name of the package to check (e.g., "java.io").

EXCEPTIONS

`SecurityException`
If class definitions cannot be added to `pkg` due to security reasons.

SEE ALSO `Package, RuntimePermission("defineClassInPackage").`

1.2 checkPermission()

PURPOSE Determines if a permission has been granted by the security policy currently in effect.

SYNTAX

```
public void checkPermission(Permission perm)
public void checkPermission(Permission perm, Object ctx)
```

DESCRIPTION This method determines whether a permission has been granted. The first form determines whether the caller has been granted the permission `perm`.

The second form determines whether the execution context `ctx` has been granted permission `perm`. `ctx` should be a value returned by `getSecurityContext()`, which returns a snapshot of the execution context. This second form is useful when you don't know a priori which permissions to grant and need to enforce permission checking later. For example, you might want to associate permission checking with the creator of an object, rather than subsequent users of the object. This is useful, for instance, in a multithreaded program in which a main thread creates the object and passes the object to worker threads to process.

S

PARAMETERS

`ctx` A possibly `null` execution context. If `null` or not an instance of `AccessControlContext`, a `SecurityException` is thrown.

`perm` A possibly `null` permission to check.

EXCEPTIONS

`SecurityException`
If `perm` has not been granted or if `ctx` is `null` or not an instance of `AccessControlContext`.

SEE ALSO `getSecurityContext()`, `java.security.AccessController.getContext()`, `java.security.AccessController.checkPermission()`, `java.security.AccessControlContext.checkPermission()`.

EXAMPLE This example creates a security manager and uses `checkPermission()` to check whether it can read a property. Note that this explicit check is not necessary because `System.getProperty()` will automatically do the check. This explicit check is for illustrative purposes only.

To run the program with a policy file, enter

```
>java -Djava.security.policy=.policy Main
```

Main.java

```
PropertyPermission pp = new PropertyPermission("user.*", "read");
try {
    // Create and install security manager
    SecurityManager sm = new SecurityManager();
    System.setSecurityManager(sm);

    // Perform check--not really necessary since getProperty()'ll do it
    sm.checkPermission(pp);

    System.out.println(System.getProperty("user.home"));
} catch (SecurityException e) {
    e.printStackTrace();
}
```

.policy

```
keystore ".keystore";
grant {
        permission java.util.PropertyPermission "user.*", "read";
      };
```

Δ checkPrintJobAccess()

PURPOSE Determines if allowed to submit a print job.

SYNTAX `public void checkPrintJobAccess()`

DESCRIPTION This method determines whether the caller is allowed by the Java runtime's security policy to submit a print job. It is intended to be used by applications such as Web browsers to control whether an applet is allowed to use printer resources in the application's environment. The default implementation makes this check by using a `RuntimePermission` with a name of `"queuePrintJob"`.

1.2 CHANGES In Version 1.1, the default implementation always threw `SecurityException`.

EXCEPTIONS

`SecurityException`
If not allowed to submit a print job.

SEE ALSO `RuntimePermission("queuePrintJob")`.

Δ checkPropertiesAccess()

PURPOSE Determines if allowed to read and update the system properties.

SYNTAX
```
public void checkPropertiesAccess()
```

DESCRIPTION This method determines whether the caller is allowed by the Java runtime's security policy to access the system properties. This method controls both the reading and updating of system properties. The default implementation makes this check by using a `PropertyPermission` with an action of `"read,write"` and a name of `"*"`.

1.2 CHANGES In Version 1.1, the default implementation always threw `SecurityException`.

EXCEPTIONS

`SecurityException`
If the system properties cannot be accessed due to security reasons.

SEE ALSO `checkPropertyAccess()`, `java.util.Properties`, `java.util.PropertyPermission`, `System.getProperties()`, `System.setProperties()`.

S

Δ checkPropertyAccess()

PURPOSE Determines if allowed to read a system property.

SYNTAX
```
public void checkPropertyAccess(String prop)
```

DESCRIPTION The two forms of this method determine whether the caller is allowed by the Java runtime's security policy to read the system property `prop`. The default implementation makes this check by using a `PropertyPermission` with an action of `"read"` and a name of `prop`. To check whether the caller is allowed to update a system property, you must use create a `PropertyPermission` with an action of `"write"` and use `checkPermission()` directly.

1.2 CHANGES In Version 1.1, the default implementation always threw `SecurityException`.

PARAMETERS

`defval` The possibly `null` default value for `prop` to check.
`prop` The non-`null` system property to check.

EXCEPTIONS

`SecurityException`
If `prop` cannot be accessed due to security reasons.

SEE ALSO `checkPermission()`, `checkPropertiesAccess()`, `java.util.Properties`, `java.util.PropertyPermission`, `System.getProperty()`.

Δ checkRead()

PURPOSE Determines if allowed to read a file.

SYNTAX

```
public void checkRead(FileDescriptor fd)
public void checkRead(String fileName)
public void checkRead(String fileName, Object ctx)
```

DESCRIPTION The three forms of this method check whether the caller is allowed by the Java runtime's security policy to read the specified file. The first form determines whether the security manager allows reading from the open file descriptor, `fd`. This is useful for checking objects such as sockets that more commonly have file descriptors rather than filenames. The default implementation makes the check by using a `RuntimePermission` with a name of `"readFileDescriptor"`.

The other two forms check whether the caller is allowed to read the file named `fileName`. If `ctx` is supplied, `ctx` must be allowed to read `fileName`. The default implementation makes these checks using a `FilePermission` with an action of `"read"` and a name of `fileName`.

Implementers should use the canonical form of `fileName` in order to unambiguously identify the file being checked (for example by using `File.getCanonicalPath()`).

1.2 CHANGES In Version 1.1, the default implementation always threw `SecurityException`.

PARAMETERS

`ctx` The non-`null` execution context to be checked.
`fd` The non-`null` file descriptor of the file to check.
`fileName` The non-`null` system-dependent filename to check.

EXCEPTIONS

`SecurityException`
If `fileName` or `fd` cannot be read due to security reasons, or if `ctx` is not an

S

instance of `java.security.AccessControlContext`.

SEE ALSO `java.io.File.canRead()`, `java.io.File.exists()`, `java.io.File.getCanonicalPath()`, `java.io.File.isDirectory()`, `java.io.File.isFile()`, `java.io.File.lastModified()`, `java.io.File.length()`, `java.io.File.list()`, `java.io.FileInputStream.FileInputStream()`, `java.io.FilePermission`, `java.io.RandomAccessFile.RandomAccessFile()`, `RuntimePermission("readFileDescriptor")`.

Δ checkSecurityAccess()

PURPOSE Determines if allowed to perform a specified security-related action.

SYNTAX `public void checkSecurityAccess(String action)`

DESCRIPTION Classes in the `java.security` package use this method to check whether the caller is allowed by the Java runtime's security policy to invoke the methods defined in their classes. See `java.security.SecurityPermission` for details. The default implementation makes this check by using a `SecurityPermission` with a name of `action`.

1.2 CHANGES In Version 1.1, the default implementation always threw `SecurityException`.

PARAMETERS

`action` A non-`null` string specifying the security-related action to check. The format of the string is unspecified and meant for internal use only.

EXCEPTIONS

`SecurityException`
If not allowed to perform the security-related action `action`.

SEE ALSO `java.security.Identity`, `java.security.Policy`, `java.security.Provider`, `java.security.Security`, `java.security.Signer`, `java.security.SecurityPermission`.

S

Δ checkSetFactory()

PURPOSE Determines if allowed to set the networking-related object factories.

SYNTAX `public void checkSetFactory()`

DESCRIPTION The networking classes use the concept of a *factory* to allow different underlying implementations to be used at the discretion of the Java program. A `Foo` factory is an object that generates instances of class `Foo`. There are factories for sockets, URL protocol handlers, and URL content handlers. The program can set a particular factory *once* during the life of the program. This factory defines the implementation for that class for the rest of the program.

`checkSetFactory()` determines whether the caller is allowed by the Java runtime's security policy to set networking-related object factories. The default implementation makes the check by using a `RuntimePermission` with a name of `"setFactory"`.

1.2 CHANGES In Version 1.1, the default implementation always threw `SecurityException`.

EXCEPTIONS

`SecurityException`
If not allowed to set any networking-related object factory due to security reasons.

SEE ALSO
```
java.net.HttpURLConnection.setFollowRedirects(),
java.net.ServerSocket.setSocketFactory(),
java.net.Socket.setSocketImplFactory(),
java.net.URL.setURLStreamHandlerFactory(),
java.net.URLConnection.setContentHandlerFactory(),
java.rmi.server.RMISocketFactory.setSocketFactory(),
RuntimePermission("setFactory").
```

Δ checkSystemClipboardAccess()

PURPOSE Determines if allowed to read or write to the system clipboard.

SYNTAX
```
public void checkSystemClipboardAccess()
```

DESCRIPTION The system clipboard allows data to be transferred between Java programs and native programs. `Toolkit.getSystemClipboard()` is an abstract method that retrieves the system clipboard. Its implementation should call `checkSystemClipboardAccess()` to determine whether the caller can access the system clipboard.

`checkSystemClipboardAccess()` determines whether the caller is allowed by the Java runtime's security policy to access the system clipboard. The default implementation makes the check by using an `AWTPermission` with a name of `"accessClipboard"`.

1.2 CHANGES In Version 1.1, the default implementation always threw `SecurityException`.

EXCEPTIONS

`SecurityException`
If not allowed to access the system clipboard.

SEE ALSO
```
java.awt.AWTPermission("accessClipboard"),
java.awt.datatransfer.Clipboard,
java.awt.Toolkit.getSystemClipboard().
```

S

Δ checkTopLevelWindow()

PURPOSE Determines if allowed to create a top-level window.

SYNTAX
```
public boolean checkTopLevelWindow(Object window)
```

DESCRIPTION This method determines whether the caller is allowed by the Java runtime's security policy to create the top-level window `window`. Creating top-level windows has security implications because a program may impersonate security-related applications (e.g., login windows) and mislead the user to supply security-sensitive information (e.g., passwords).

`checkTopLevelWindow()` returns `false` if the window creation is allowed, but the window must have visual warnings that it is a window generated by the Java program. The method returns `true` if creation is allowed without restrictions. To disallow the creation entirely, `checkTopLevelWindow()` should throw a `SecurityException`. The default implementation makes the check by using an `AWTPermission` with a name of `"showWindowWithoutWarningBanner"`. If the check succeeds without a `SecurityException` being thrown, this method returns `true`; otherwise it returns `false`.

1.2 CHANGES In Version 1.1, the default implementation always returned `false`.

PARAMETERS

`window` The non-`null` new window being created.

RETURNS `true` if top-level windows can be created without restrictions; `false` if top-level windows should be created with an accompanying visual warning.

SEE ALSO `java.awt.AWTPermission("showWindowWithoutWarningBanner")`, `java.awt.Window.Window()`.

Δ checkWrite()

S

PURPOSE Determines if allowed to write to a file.

SYNTAX
```
public void checkWrite(FileDescriptor fd)
public void checkWrite(String fileName)
```

DESCRIPTION The two forms of this method determine whether the caller is allowed by the Java runtime's security policy to write to the file named `fileName` or to the open file descriptor `fd`. `fd` is useful for checking objects such as sockets that more commonly have file descriptors rather than filenames. The default implementation makes the check by using a `RuntimePermission` with a name of `"writeFileDescriptor"`.

The default implementation of the form that accepts a string name `fileName` make the check by using a `FilePermission` with an action of `"write"` and a name of `fileName`. Implementers should use the canonical form of `fileName` in order to unambiguously identify the file being checked.

1.2 CHANGES In Version 1.1, the default implementation always threw `SecurityException`.

PARAMETERS

`fd` The non-`null` file descriptor to check.

`fileName` The non-`null` system-dependent filename to check.

EXCEPTIONS

`SecurityException`

If `fd` or `fileName` cannot be written to for security reasons.

SEE ALSO `java.io.File.canWrite()`, `java.io.File.getCanonicalPath()`, `java.io.File.mkdir()`, `java.io.File.mkdirs()`, `java.io.File.renameTo()`, `java.io.FileOutputStream.FileOutputStream()`, `java.io.FilePermission`, `java.io.RandomAccessFile.RandomAccessFile()`.

Δ classDepth() *DEPRECATED*

PURPOSE Replaced by `checkPermission()`.

SYNTAX

```
protected native int classDepth(String className)
```

1.2 CHANGES This method has been deprecated in Version 1.2.

DEPRECATION This method was used by Version 1.1 security managers to do permission checks. In Version 1.2, permission checking should be left to the `AccessController` class (which is used by `checkPermission()`).

PARAMETERS

`className` The non-`null` fully qualified name of the class for which to look.

RETURNS The position of the stack frame found; `-1` if not found.

SEE ALSO `java.security.AccessController.checkPermission()`.

S

Δ classLoaderDepth() *DEPRECATED*

PURPOSE Replaced by `checkPermission()`.

SYNTAX

```
protected native int classLoaderDepth()
```

1.2 CHANGES This method has been deprecated in Version 1.2.

DEPRECATION This method was used by Version 1.1 security managers to do permission checks. In Version 1.2, permission checking should be left to the `AccessController` class (which is used by `checkPermission()`).

RETURNS The topmost stack frame that is executing a method whose class was created with a non-`null` class loader.

SEE ALSO `java.security.AccessController.checkPermission()`.

Δ currentClassLoader() *DEPRECATED*

PURPOSE Replaced by `checkPermission()`.

SYNTAX `protected native ClassLoader currentClassLoader()`

1.2 CHANGES This method has been deprecated in Version 1.2.

DEPRECATION This method was used by Version 1.1 security managers to do permission checks. In Version 1.2, permission checking should be left to the `AccessController` class (which is used by `checkPermission()`).

RETURNS The class loader for the topmost stack frame that is executing a method of a class created by a non-`null` class loader; `null` if such a stack frame does not exist.

SEE ALSO `java.security.AccessController.checkPermission()`.

Δ currentLoadedClass() *DEPRECATED*

PURPOSE Replaced by `checkPermission()`.

SYNTAX `protected native Class currentLoadedClass()`

1.2 CHANGES This method has been deprecated in Version 1.2.

DEPRECATION This method was used by Version 1.1 security managers to do permission checks. In Version 1.2, permission checking should be left to the `AccessController` class (which is used by `checkPermission()`).

S

RETURNS The class of the topmost stack frame that is executing a method of a class created by a non-`null` class loader; `null` if such a stack frame does not exist.

SEE ALSO `java.security.AccessController.checkPermission()`.

Δ getInCheck() *DEPRECATED*

PURPOSE Replaced by `checkPermission()`.

SYNTAX `public boolean getInCheck()`

1.2 CHANGES This method has been deprecated in Version 1.2.

DEPRECATION	This method was used by Version 1.1 security managers to do permission checks. In Version 1.2, permission checking should be left to the `AccessController` class (which is used by `checkPermission()`).
RETURNS	`true` if a security check is in progress; `false` otherwise.
SEE ALSO	`java.security.AccessController.checkPermission()`.

Δ inCheck *DEPRECATED*

PURPOSE	Replaced by `checkPermission()`.
SYNTAX	`protected boolean inCheck`
1.2 CHANGES	This method has been deprecated in Version 1.2.
DEPRECATION	This field was used by Version 1.1 security managers to do permission checks. In Version 1.2, permission checking should be left to the `AccessController` class (which is used by `checkPermission()`).
SEE ALSO	`java.security.AccessController.checkPermission()`.

Δ inClass() *DEPRECATED*

PURPOSE	Replaced by `checkPermission()`.
SYNTAX	`protected boolean inClass(String className)`
1.2 CHANGES	This method has been deprecated in Version 1.2.
DEPRECATION	This method was used by Version 1.1 security managers to do permission checks. In Version 1.2, permission checking should be left to the `AccessController` class (which is used by `checkPermission()`).
PARAMETERS	
`className`	The non-`null` name of the class for which to look.
RETURNS	`true` if `className` is on the execution stack; `false` otherwise.
SEE ALSO	`java.security.AccessController.checkPermission()`.

S

Δ inClassLoader() *DEPRECATED*

PURPOSE	Replaced by `checkPermission()`.
SYNTAX	`protected boolean inClassLoader()`
1.2 CHANGES	This method has been deprecated in Version 1.2.

DEPRECATION This method was used by Version 1.1 security managers to do permission checks. In Version 1.2, permission checking should be left to the `AccessController` class (which is used by `checkPermission()`).

RETURNS `true` if some class on the execution stack has been created by a non-`null` class loader; `false` otherwise.

SEE ALSO `java.security.AccessController.checkPermission()`.

Δ SecurityManager()

PURPOSE Constructs a new `SecurityManager` instance.

SYNTAX `public SecurityManager()`

DESCRIPTION This method constructs a new `SecurityManager` instance. If no security manager has been previously set, this newly created object can be installed as the security manager by calling `System.setSecurityManager()`. If a security manager has been installed, that manager is used to check whether the caller has been granted `RuntimePermission("createSecurityManager")` to create a new security manager.

1.2 CHANGES In Version 1.1, the constructor was `abstract protected`, not `public`. Also you were not allowed to call the constructor if a security manager had already been set (a `SecurityException` would be thrown).

EXCEPTIONS

`SecurityException`

If no `RuntimePermission("createSecurityManager")` has been granted to the caller by the currently installed security manager.

SEE ALSO `System.getSecurityManager()`, `System.setSecurityManager()`.

EXAMPLE See `checkPermission()`.

S

SerializablePermission

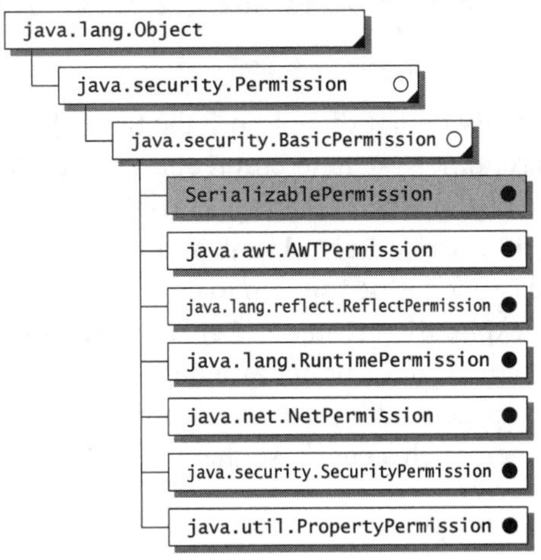

Syntax

```
public final class SerializablePermission extends BasicPermission
```

Description

The `SerializablePermission` class represents a request to perform special serialization/deserialization operations. It contains a *permission name* that identifies the serialization/deserialization operation to check. This class is used internally by the `ObjectInputStream`/`ObjectOutputStream` classes whenever you attempt to call their specially protected constructors/members. These constructors/members check, with the help of the *access controller*, whether the caller is allowed to perform the operation. If the access controller determines that the caller is not allowed, an `AccessControlException` (a subclass of `SecurityException`) is thrown. See `java.security.AccessController` for details.

Object Substitution

When deserializing data into an object, `ObjectInputStream` allows a trusted subclass of `ObjectInputStream` to replace the object just deserialized with a compatible object. Similarly, when converting an object into a serialized stream, `ObjectOutputStream` allows a trusted subclass of `ObjectOutputStream` to substitute the object being serialized with another object. This feature is called *object substitution*. Object substitution in Version 1.1 systems was allowed only by *trusted* classes, which were defined as classes loaded by the default system class loader. In Version 1.2, the definition of *trusted* has been expanded to be that determined by the security policy. In Version 1.2, `SerializablePermission` is used in enforcing the security policy.

A brief discussion of the Version 1.2 security model is given in the `SecurityManager` class description. More information about Version 1.2's security model and framework is available at `http://java.sun.com/products/jdk/1.2/docs/guide/security/index.html`.

Usage

Applets and applications usually do not directly use the `SerializablePermission` class. It is used internally by the Java runtime system to enforce its security policy. For example, when a program tries to replace an object when creating a serialization stream, `ObjectOutputStream.enableReplaceObject()` uses a `SerializablePermission("enableSubstitution")` object to check whether the caller has permission to do so.

An application may explicitly create a `SerializablePermission` object and use `SecurityManager.checkPermission()` or `AccessController.checkPermission()` to check whether the security policy has granted it such permission. But the act of trying to perform the operation automatically triggers such a check, so there is seldom a reason to duplicate it.

The SerializablePermission Name

Permission Name	Request
`enableSubclassImplementation`	Subclass `ObjectInputStream`/`ObjectOutputStream` to control how objects are deserialized/serialized.
`enableSubstitution`	Replace objects being serialized/deserialized.

TABLE 21: `SerializablePermission` Names Used by the Java Runtime System.

The permission name of a `SerializablePermission` object identifies the serialization operation that is being checked. The Java runtime system uses the permission names listed in Table 21. It may use additional permission names in the future for other permissions relating to serialization. An application is also free to add and use new permission names to represent other types of serialization operations, but such `SerializablePermissions` will be known only to the application that defines them. Nevertheless, such permission names can appear in the security policy and be checked using the `AccessController`. An application that needs to define and use new permission names is usually better off defining its own `Permission` subclass to avoid future conflicts with the Java runtime system.x

Implies

The permission name of a `SerializablePermission` object is a case-sensitive string. It is used to check whether one `SerializablePermission` is equal to another `SerializablePermission`. It is also used to check whether one `SerializablePermission` *implies* another `SerializablePermission`. Permission *A* implies permission *B* means if permission *A* is granted, so will permission *B*. Following are the rules for how "implies" works for `SerializablePermission` objects.

- Two SerializablePermissions with the same permission name imply each other.
- A SerializablePermission with a permission name of the form *pname*.* implies any SerializablePermission whose permission name has the prefix "*pname*.". For example, a SerializablePermission with a permission name "some.op.*" implies any SerializablePermission whose permission name has the prefix "some.op.".
- A SerializablePermission with the permission name "*" implies any SerializablePermission.

enableSubclassImplementation

ObjectOutputStream and ObjectInputStream can be customized via subclassing to perform special processing when serializing and deserializing objects, respectively. For example, you can subclass ObjectOutputStream to write out additional header information—such as checksums or code-signing information (ObjectOutputStream.writeStreamHeader() or ObjectInputStream.resolveClass())—or to replace objects being deserialized from the stream (ObjectInputStream.resolveObject()).

There are two ways to subclass ObjectOutputStream. The subclass's constructor can use one of the following two constructors:

```
public ObjectOutputStream(OutputStream out)
protected ObjectOutputStream()
```

A subclass that uses the public constructor will use the default serialization (see ObjectOutputStream.writeObject()). That is, an object written to the stream will be serialized using the object's writeObject() method; it will use defaultWriteObject() if the object does not have a writeObject() method. A subclass that uses the protected constructor must specify how objects are written by supplying an implementation for ObjectOutputStream.writeObjectOverride().

Similarly, there are two ways to subclass ObjectInputStream. If a subclass uses the protected constructor, it must provide its own method for reading objects (ObjectInputStream.readObjectOverride()).

ObjectOutputStream and ObjectInputStream can be subclassed to override the default serialization/deserialization only if the subclass is signed by a principal that has been granted, by the security policy, a SerializablePermission that has the permission name "enableSubclassImplementation". Otherwise, if a security manager has been installed, a SecurityException will be thrown when the protected constructors are called.

enableSubstitution

A subclass of ObjectOutputStream can replace objects written to the serialized stream by calling the enableReplaceObject() method with true and overriding the replaceObject() method. This feature can be used, for example, to replace obsolete objects with up-to-date ones. Similarly, a subclass of ObjectInputStream can replace objects read from a serialized stream by calling the enableResolveObject() method with true and overriding the resolveObject() method.

A subclass of ObjectOutputStream/ObjectInputStream can do this only if it has been signed by a principal that has been granted, by the security policy, a SerializablePermission that has the permission name "enableSubstitution". Otherwise, if a security manager has been installed, a SecurityException will be thrown when the enableReplaceObject() or enableResolveObject() method is called.

MEMBER SUMMARY	
Constructor	
SerializablePermission()	Constructs a new SerializablePermission instance.

See Also

java.lang.SecurityManager, java.security.AccessController, java.security.Permission, java.security.Policy, ObjectInputStream, ObjectInputStream.enableResolveObject(), ObjectInputStream.readObjectOverride(), ObjectOutputStream, ObjectOutputStream.enableReplaceObject(), ObjectOutputStream.writeObjectOverride().

Example

Programs shouldn't use this class directly.

SerializablePermission()

PURPOSE Constructs a new SerializablePermission instance.

SYNTAX

```
public SerializablePermission(String pname)
public SerializablePermission(String pname, String actions)
```

DESCRIPTION Both forms of this constructor create a new SerializablePermission instance using the name pname. The actions parameter is ignored.

PARAMETERS

actions Ignored. Should be null.

pname A non-null string, such as "*"or a permission name from Table 21.

S

Set

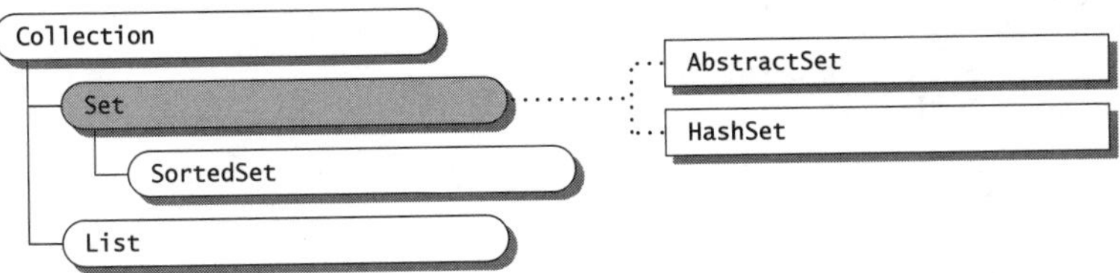

Syntax

```
public interface Set extends Collection
```

Description

A `Set` is a type of collection that holds objects (*elements*) but does not allow duplicates. The elements of the set might not be kept in any particular order.

Unlike with lists (see `List`), the elements of the set must not be modified while they are in the set. For example, if a `StringBuffer` is in the set, you must not modify the `StringBuffer` while it is in the set.

Three types of collections are available: set, list, and map. See `Collection` for an overview of *The Collections Framework*, which includes set, list, and map.

Usage

The `java.util` package provides two implementations of sets: `HashSet` and `TreeSet`. These differ in how they store their elements. `HashSet` is typically more efficient, while `TreeSet` provides stronger guarantees. See these classes for more details.

There are several ways to create a set. Here are some of them.

```
Set s;
s = new HashSet();
s = new HashSet(Arrays.asList(new String[]{"dog", "cat"}));
s = new TreeSet();
s = Collections.EMPTY_SET;
s = Collections.singleton("dog");
```

Once a set is created, you can use the methods in this interface to query or modify the set. Be aware that some of these methods might result in an `UnsupportedOperationException` if the set does not support the method call. For example, `Collections.singleton()` returns a set that cannot be modified, so if you try to add to it, you'll get an exception.

The Collections Framework does not provide a nondestructive way to create a union or intersection of two maps. You might find it useful to define methods such as the following.

```
public static Set union(Set s1, Set s2) {
    Set result;
    if (s1 instanceof SortedSet) {
        result = new TreeSet(s1);
```

```
            result.addAll(s2);
        } else if (s2 instanceof SortedSet) {
            result = new TreeSet(s2);
            result.addAll(s1);
        } else {
            result = new HashSet(s1);
            result.addAll(s2);
        }
        return result;
    }

    public static Set intersection(Set s1, Set s2) {
        Set result;
        if (s1 instanceof SortedSet) {
            result = new TreeSet(s1);
            result.retainAll(s2);
        } else if (s2 instanceof SortedSet) {
            result = new TreeSet(s2);
            result.retainAll(s1);
        } else {
            result = new HashSet(s1);
            result.retainAll(s2);
        }
        return result;
    }
```

The `Collections` class provides various utility methods for changing the capabilities of a set by creating a wrapper around your set. For example, you can prevent any modifications to your set by using `Collections.unmodifiableSet()`. Also, you can have all of the methods of the set wrapped with synchronized methods by using `Collections.synchronizedSet()`.

To implement a class that implements the `Set` interface, consider subclassing `AbstractSet`. This abstract class minimizes the effort needed to implement a `Set` class.

Unsupported Methods

Not all sets can be modified. There are only two ways in which you can modify a set: add an element to it or remove an element from it. A set can support one, both, or neither of these operations. If you attempt to use a method to modify a set that does not support the operation, the method will throw an `UnsupportedOperationException`.

S

MEMBER SUMMARY	
Query Methods	
`contains()`	Determines if this set contains a particular element.
`containsAll()`	Determines if this set contains all of the elements that are in another collection.
`isEmpty()`	Determines if this set has no elements.
`size()`	Returns the number of elements in this set.

MEMBER SUMMARY	
Modification Methods	
`add()`	Adds an element to this set.
`addAll()`	Inserts all of the elements of a collection into this set.
`clear()`	Removes all of the elements in this set.
`remove()`	Removes an element from this set.
`removeAll()`	Removes all elements from this set that are in another collection.
`retainAll()`	Removes all elements in this set that are not in another collection.
Iterator Method	
`iterator()`	Creates an iterator for all of the elements in this set.
Conversion Method	
`toArray()`	Returns all of the elements in this set in an array.
Object Methods	
`equals()`	Determines if this set is equal to another object.
`hashCode()`	Computes the hash code for this set.

See Also

`Collection`, `Collections`, `List`, `HashSet`, `Map`, `TreeSet`.

Example

For an example that implements a `Set`, see `AbstractSet`. For descriptions that demonstrate how a set is used, see the examples in the following members.

add()

PURPOSE Adds an element to this set.

SYNTAX `public boolean add(Object e)`

DESCRIPTION This method adds an element `e` to this set. If `e` is not equal to any elements in this set, `e` is added to this set. If `e` is not `null`, `e`'s `equals()` method is used to determine if it is equal to any elements in this set.

Some sets might accept elements of only a certain type. If an incompatible element is added to such a collection, a `ClassCastException` is thrown.

This method might not be supported.

PARAMETERS

`e` The possibly `null` element to be added to this set.

S

RETURNS `true` if `e` was added to the set.

EXCEPTIONS

`ClassCastException`
If the type of `e` is not appropriate for this set.

`IllegalArgumentException`
If some aspect of `e` prevents it from being added to this set.

`NullPointerException`
If `e` is `null` and this set does not accept `null` elements.

`UnsupportedOperationException`
If this method is not supported by this set.

SEE ALSO `addAll()`.

EXAMPLE

```
Set set = new HashSet();
set.add(new Integer(0));
System.out.println( set );                           // [0]

// Since this new Integer object is equal to the previous object,
// this object is not added to the list.
System.out.println( set.add(new Integer(0)) );  // false
System.out.println( set );                           // [0]

set = Collections.singleton("dog");
// This set is read-only.
set.add("cat");                                     // UnsupportedOperationException
```

addAll()

PURPOSE Inserts all of the elements of a collection into this set.

SYNTAX `public boolean addAll(Collection c)`

DESCRIPTION All elements from `c` that are not in this set are added to this set. This operation can be thought of as a union operation.

This method might not be supported.

PARAMETERS

`c` The non-`null` but possibly empty collection of elements to be added to this set.

RETURNS `true` if this set was modified.

EXCEPTIONS

`ClassCastException`
If the type of some element in `c` is not appropriate for this set.

`ConcurrentModificationException`
If `c`'s iterators are fail-fast and `c` is being modified during this method call.

`IllegalArgumentException`
: If some aspect of an element in `c` prevents it from being added to this set.

`NullPointerException`
: If some element in `c` is `null` and this set does not accept `null` elements.

`UnsupportedOperationException`
: If this method is not supported by this set.

SEE ALSO `add()`.

EXAMPLE

```
Set set = new TreeSet();
set.add("pig");
set.addAll(Arrays.asList(new String[]{"dog", "cat"}));
System.out.println( set );        // [dog, cat, pig]

set.addAll(set);                  // ConcurrentModificationException
```

clear()

PURPOSE Removes all of the elements in this set.

SYNTAX `public void clear()`

DESCRIPTION This method removes all of the elements in this set. After it is called, this set will be empty.

This method might not be supported.

EXCEPTIONS

`UnsupportedOperationException`
: If this method is not supported by this set.

EXAMPLE

```
Set set = new TreeSet();
set.add("dog");
System.out.println( set.size() );    // 1
set.clear();
System.out.println( set.isEmpty() ); // true
```

contains()

PURPOSE Determines if this set contains a particular element.

SYNTAX `public boolean contains(Object e)`

DESCRIPTION This method determines if this set contains the element `e`. It returns `true` if some element in this set is equal to `e`. An element is equal to `e` if both are `null` or if the `equals()` method determines that they are equal.

PARAMETERS

e A possibly `null` element.

RETURNS `true` if some element in this set is equal to e.

EXCEPTIONS

`ClassCastException`

If the type of e is not appropriate for this set.

SEE ALSO `containsAll()`, `equals()`.

EXAMPLE

```
HashSet set = new HashSet(Arrays.asList(
    new Object[]{"dog", null, new Integer(7)}));

System.out.println( set.contains("dog") );              // true
System.out.println( set.contains(null) );               // true
System.out.println( set.contains("pig") );              // false

// This shows that although the two Integer objects are different,
// they are considered the same according to their equals() method.
System.out.println( set.contains(new Integer(7)) );    // true
```

containsAll()

PURPOSE Determines if this set contains all of the elements in another collection.

SYNTAX `public boolean containsAll(Collection c)`

DESCRIPTION This method determines if this set contains all of the elements in the collection c. If all of the elements in collection c appear in this set, this method returns `true`. Two elements are equal if both are `null` or if the `equals()` method determines that they are equal. This operation can be thought of as a subset operation, in which c is a subset of this collection.

PARAMETERS

c A non-`null` but possibly empty collection.

RETURNS `true` if all of the elements in c appear in this set.

SEE ALSO `contains()`, `equals()`.

EXCEPTIONS

`ConcurrentModificationException`

If c's iterators are fail-fast and c is being modified during this method call.

EXAMPLE

```
HashSet set = new HashSet(Arrays.asList(new String[]{"dog", "cat"}));

System.out.println( set.containsAll(Collections.EMPTY_SET) );
    // true
System.out.println( set.containsAll(Collections.singleton(null)) );
    // false
```

```
System.out.println( set.containsAll(Collections.singleton("dog")) );
    // true
System.out.println( set.containsAll(
            Arrays.asList(new String[]{"dog", "dog", "cat"})));
    //true
```

equals()

PURPOSE Determines if this set is equal to another object.

SYNTAX `public boolean equals(Object c)`

DESCRIPTION This method determines if this set is equal to the object `c`. It returns `true` if, and only if, `c` is a `Set` object and both this set and `c` have exactly the same elements. Two elements are equal if both are `null` or if the `equals()` method determines that they are equal.

PARAMETERS

`c` The possibly `null` object to be compared with this set.

RETURNS `true` if `c` is equal to this set.

OVERRIDES `java.lang.Object.equals()`.

SEE ALSO `hashCode()`.

EXAMPLE

```
Set s1 = new HashSet(Arrays.asList(new String[]{"dog", null, "cat"}));
Set s2 = new HashSet(Arrays.asList(new String[]{"dog", "cat"}));

System.out.println( s1.equals(null) );          // false
System.out.println( s1.equals(s2) );            // false

s2.add(null);
System.out.println( s1.equals(s2) );            // true

// lists and sets are not equal, even if they have the same contents.
System.out.println( Collections.EMPTY_LIST.equals(Collections.EMPTY_SET) );
                                                // false
```

S

hashCode()

PURPOSE Computes the hash code for this set.

SYNTAX `public int hashCode()`

DESCRIPTION This method computes the hash code for this set. The hash code of a set is the sum of the hash codes of all elements in the set. The hash code of a `null` element has the value `0`. Two equal sets will have the same hash code. Unequal sets might also have the same hash code, although the hash code algorithm reduces this possibility. The hash code is typically used as the key in a hash table.

RETURNS This set's hash code.

OVERRIDES `java.lang.Object.hashCode().`

SEE ALSO `equals(), java.lang.Object.equals().`

EXAMPLE See `java.lang.Object.hashCode().`

isEmpty()

PURPOSE Determines if this set has no elements.

SYNTAX `public boolean isEmpty()`

RETURNS `true` if this set contains no elements.

SEE ALSO `size().`

EXAMPLE See `clear().`

iterator()

PURPOSE Creates an iterator for all of the elements in this set.

SYNTAX `public Iterator iterator()`

DESCRIPTION This method creates and returns an iterator (see `Iterator` for more details) for all of the elements in this set. In most cases, the iterator presents the elements in no particular order (for example, `HashSet`). However, some sets might have iterators that guarantee an ordering (for example, `TreeSet`).

In most cases, the set should not be modified while the returned iterator is in use. However, there might be some sets that allow this; check the set's documentation.

RETURNS A non-`null` iterator.

SEE ALSO `ConcurrentModificationException, Iterator.`

EXAMPLE

```
// This set's iterators return the elements in order.
Set set = new TreeSet(Arrays.asList(new String[]{"e", "a", "d", "c", "b"}));
for (Iterator it=set.iterator(); it.hasNext(); ) {
    System.out.print( it.next()+" " );
}
System.out.println();                // a b c d e

// This set's iterators return the elements in no particular order.
set = new HashSet(Arrays.asList(new String[]{"e", "a", "d", "c", "b"}));
for (Iterator it=set.iterator(); it.hasNext(); ) {
```

S

```
        System.out.print( it.next()+" " );
    }
    System.out.println();                   // e d b c a

    // Attempt to modify the set while an iterator is being used.
    Iterator  it = set.iterator();
    set.add("pig");
    //it.next();                            // ConcurrentModificationException

    // Create a set whose size cannot be changed.
    it = Collections.singleton("dog").iterator();
    it.remove();                            // UnsupportedOperationException
```

remove()

PURPOSE Removes an element from this set.

SYNTAX `public boolean remove(Object e)`

DESCRIPTION This method removes element `e` from this set if the set contains it (determined by using `contains()`). It returns `true` if it found a matching element. (Two elements are matched if both are `null` or if `equals()` determines that they are equal.)

This method might not be supported.

PARAMETERS

`e` The possibly `null` element to remove.

RETURNS `true` if `e` was removed from this set.

EXCEPTIONS

`UnsupportedOperationException`
If this method is not supported by this set.

SEE ALSO `removeAll()`, `retainAll()`.

EXAMPLE

```
    Set set = new TreeSet(Arrays.asList(new String[]{"dog", "cat", "dog"}));

    // Make it modifiable set.
    set = new TreeSet(set);
    System.out.println( set.remove("pig") );     // false
    System.out.println( set.remove("dog") );     // true
    System.out.println( set );                   // [cat]

    set = Collections.singleton("dog");
    // The size of this set cannot be changed.
    System.out.println( set.remove("dog") );     // UnsupportedOperationException
```

S

removeAll()

PURPOSE Removes all elements from this set that are in another collection.

SYNTAX `public boolean removeAll(Collection c)`

DESCRIPTION This method removes all elements in this set that are in collection `c`. The `equals()` method is used to determine whether two elements are equal. After this call returns, this set will contain no elements in common with `c`. This operation can be thought of as a set difference operation, in which `c` is subtracted from this set.

This method might not be supported.

PARAMETERS

`c` A non-`null` collection of elements to be removed from this set.

RETURNS `true` if this set was modified.

EXCEPTIONS

`ConcurrentModificationException`
If `c`'s iterators are fail-fast and `c` is being modified during this method call.

`UnsupportedOperationException`
If this method is not supported by this set.

SEE ALSO `equals()`, `remove()`, `retainAll()`.

EXAMPLE

```
Set set = new HashSet(
    Arrays.asList(new String[]{"dog", null, "cat"}));

System.out.println( set.removeAll(Collections.EMPTY_SET) );
                                        // false
System.out.println( set );              // [cat, dog, null]

System.out.println( set.removeAll(
    Arrays.asList(new String[]{"dog", null})) );
                                        // true
System.out.println( set );              // [cat]
```

S

retainAll()

PURPOSE Removes all elements in this set that are not in another collection.

SYNTAX `public boolean retainAll(Collection c)`

DESCRIPTION This method removes all elements in this set that are not in collection `c`. The `equals()` method is used to determine whether two elements are equal. This operation can be thought of as an intersection operation.

This method might not be supported.

PARAMETERS

`c` A non-`null` collection of elements to retain.

RETURNS `true` if this set was modified.

EXCEPTIONS

`ConcurrentModificationException`
If `c`'s iterators are fail-fast and `c` is being modified during this method call.

`UnsupportedOperationException`
If this method is not supported by this set.

SEE ALSO `equals()`, `remove()`, `removeAll()`.

EXAMPLE

```
Set set = new HashSet(Arrays.asList(new String[]{"dog", "cat"}));
Set set2 = new HashSet(Arrays.asList(new String[]{"cat", "pig"}));

// This creates a set that includes elements not common to either set.
Set common = new HashSet(set);
common.retainAll(set2);
Set notCommon = new HashSet(set);
notCommon.addAll(set2);
notCommon.removeAll(common);
System.out.println( notCommon );          // [dog, pig]

System.out.println( set.retainAll(Collections.singleton("dog")));
                                          // true
System.out.println( set );                // [dog]

// This is an expensive way to clear the set.
set.retainAll(Collections.EMPTY_SET);
System.out.println( set );                // []

set = Collections.singleton("dog");
// The size of this set cannot be changed.
set.retainAll(Collections.EMPTY_SET);    // UnsupportedOperationException
```

size()

PURPOSE Returns the number of elements in this set.

SYNTAX `public int size()`

RETURNS The non-negative number of elements in this set.

SEE ALSO `isEmpty()`.

EXAMPLE

```
TreeSet set = new TreeSet();
set.add("dog");
System.out.println( set.size() );    // 1
set.add("cat");
System.out.println( set.size() );    // 2
set.add("dog");
System.out.println( set.size() );    // 2
```

toArray()

PURPOSE Returns all of the elements in this set in an array.

SYNTAX
```
public Object[] toArray()
public Object[] toArray(Object arr[])
```

DESCRIPTION This method fills `arr` with all of the elements in this set and returns `arr`. If `arr` is not large enough, a new array is created, filled, and then returned. The new array is just large enough to hold all of the elements in this set, and its type is identical to the type of `arr`.

If `arr` is larger than all of the elements in this set, `arr[size()]` is set to `null`. This `null` value can be used to determine the number of returned elements. However, it is not helpful if the set may contain `null` elements.

The order of the elements in the returned array matches the order (if any) of the elements returned by an iterator on this set.

If `arr` is not specified, it defaults to `new Object[0]`.

PARAMETERS

`arr` The non-`null` array into which the elements of this set will be copied.

RETURNS The array `arr` or a new array whose length equals `size()`; cannot be `null`.

EXCEPTIONS

`ArrayStoreException`
If some element in this set cannot be assigned to an element in `arr` because of a type mismatch. This exception is never thrown if `arr` is an `Object` array.

EXAMPLE
```
import java.util.*;

class Main {
    public static void main(String[] args) {
        HashSet set = new HashSet(Arrays.asList(new String[]{"dog", null}));

        Object[] objs = set.toArray();
        print(objs);                          // [dog, null]

        // Since we passed in a string array, we can cast
        // the result to a string array.
        String[] strings = (String[])set.toArray(new String[0]);
        print(strings);                       // [dog, null]

        // Try adding something other than a string to the set.
        set.add(new Integer(0));

        print( set.toArray() );               // [dog, 0, null]

        // The Integer object can not be stored in the string array.
        print( set.toArray(new String[0]) ); // ArrayStoreException
    }
```

S

```
    static void print(Object[] arr) {
        System.out.println(Arrays.asList(arr));
    }
}
```

S

java.lang
Short

Object
Number
Short · · · · · · Comparable
Byte
Double
Float
Integer
Long
java.math.BigDecimal
java.math.BigInteger

Syntax

`public final class Short extends Number implements Comparable`

Description

The `Short` class provides an object wrapper for a `short` data value. A *`short` data value* in Java is a 16-bit signed integer. This wrapper allows `shorts` to be passed to methods in Java class libraries that accept Java objects as parameters. In addition, this class provides methods that convert values to and from `short` values.

See *The Java Class Libraries, Second Edition, Volume 1* for more information about this class.

S

Changes for Version 1.2

The `Short` class implements the `Comparable` interface and has two overloaded forms of the `compareTo()` method used for comparing and ordering `Short` objects. This allows arrays of `Short` objects to be sorted, as shown in this example.

```
Short[] sa = new Short[]{new Short((short)10),
    new Short((short)-4), new Short((short)48)};
Arrays.sort(sa);
for (int i = 0; i < sa.length; i++) {
    System.out.println(sa[i]);
}
// -4, 10, 48
```

MEMBER SUMMARY	
Constructor	
`Short()`	Constructs a `Short` instance using a `short` value or a string.
Number Methods	
`byteValue()`	Retrieves the value of this `Short` as a `byte`.
`doubleValue()`	Retrieves the value of this `Short` as a `double`.
`floatValue()`	Retrieves the value of this `Short` as a `float`.
`intValue()`	Retrieves the value of this `Short` as an `int`.
`longValue()`	Retrieves the value of this `Short` as a `long`.
`shortValue()`	Retrieves the value of this `Short` as a `short`.
`short`-Related Constants	
`MAX_VALUE`	The maximum value a `short` can have.
`MIN_VALUE`	The minimum value a `short` can have.
`TYPE`	The `Class` object representing the primitive type `short`.
Comparison Methods	
1.2 `compareTo()`	Compares the signed numeric value of this `Short` with that of another `Short`.
`equals()`	Determines if this `Short` is equal to another object.
String Conversion Constants	
`decode()`	Parses the string representation of a 16-bit signed integer into a `Short`.
`parseShort()`	Parses the string representation of an integer into a `short`.
`toString()`	Generates the string representation of a `short` or `Short`.
`valueOf()`	Creates a `Short` instance using its string representation.
Object Method	
`hashCode()`	Computes the hash code of this `Short`.

S

See Also

`Comparable`, `java.util.Arrays`.

`Short` in *The Java Class Libraries, Second Edition, Volume 1.*

1.2 compareTo()

PURPOSE Compares the signed numeric value of this `Short` with that of another `Short`.

SYNTAX
```
public int compareTo(Short aShort)
public int compareTo(Object aShort)
```

DESCRIPTION This method compares this `Short`'s (signed) numeric value with that of `aShort`. It returns an integer indicating whether the two numeric values are equal and, if they are not, the ordering of the two values. It returns `0` if the two numeric values are the same. It returns a negative number if the numeric value of this `Short` is less than that of `aShort`. It returns a positive number if the numeric value of this `Short` is greater than that of `aShort`.

If `aShort` is not an instance of `Short`, a `ClassCastException` is thrown.

PARAMETERS

`aShort` The non-`null` `Short` object with which to compare.

RETURNS `0` if the numeric values of this `Short` and `aShort` are the same; a negative number if this `Short`'s value is less than that of `aShort`; a positive number if this `Short`'s value is greater than that of `aShort`.

EXCEPTIONS

`ClassCastException`

If `aShort` is not an instance of `Short`.

SEE ALSO `Comparable`.

EXAMPLE

```
Short b = new Short((short)1000);
System.out.println(b.compareTo(new Short((short)-1)));     // positive
System.out.println(b.compareTo(new Short((short)1000)));   // 0
System.out.println(b.compareTo(new Short((short)-1000)));  // positive
System.out.println(b.compareTo(new Short((short)1001)));   // negative
System.out.println(b.compareTo("abc")); // ClassCastException
```

java.text
SimpleDateFormat

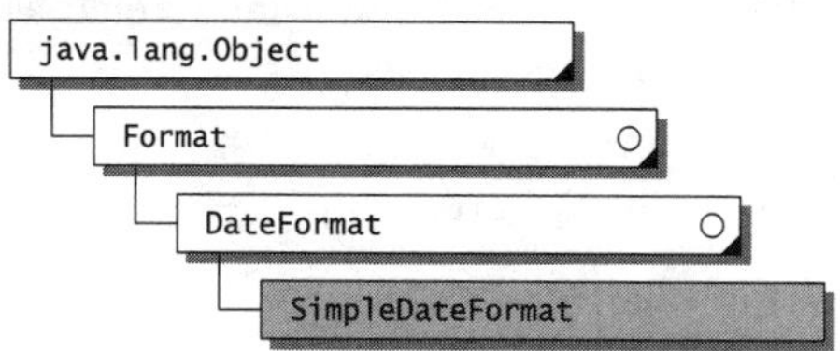

Syntax

```
public class SimpleDateFormat extends DateFormat
```

Description

`SimpleDateFormat` is a concrete class for formatting and parsing dates in a locale-sensitive manner. It allows for formatting (milliseconds to text), parsing (text to milliseconds), and normalization (described in the `DateFormat` class).

See *The Java Class Libraries, Second Edition, Volume 1* for more information about this class.

Changes for Version 1.2

This class has two new methods: `set2DigitYearStart()` and `get2DigitYearStart()`. The year 2000 (Y2K) issue is also described.

Year 2000

The date pattern `yy` is an abbreviation for the year and indicates the two least-significant digits. Because the first two digits are omitted, this can lead to ambiguity when trying to convert this abbreviated string (such as 12/25/61) to a full date. That is, when using `yy` to parse a date string, `SimpleDateFormat` must resolve the abbreviated year to some century. By default, it does this by choosing the full year to be within the window 80 years before (inclusive) and 20 years after (exclusive) the exact time (to the millisecond) that the `SimpleDateFormat` instance is created. It uses `calendar.add(Calendar.YEAR, -80)` to determine the start of the window.

This window has millisecond resolution and is fixed in time for any instance of `SimpleDateFormat`. For example, if the creation date is November 3, 1999, 22:51:45.050 PST (Pacific Standard Time), the default starting date would be 80 years earlier, or November 3, 1919, 22:51:45.050 PST (where the time is *hours*:*minutes*:*seconds*.*milliseconds*). See Figure 18. Notice that the starting date measures back 80 years to the millisecond from the creation date. It has a 100-year window of November 3, 1919, 22:51:45.050 PST to November 3, 2019, 22:51:45.049 PST (where the differences are underlined). When interpreting a two-digit year at the edge of the window, its starting date is based on the moment and day of creation, in milliseconds, not necessarily at midnight or on January 1.

According to this example, when parsing the string "Nov 3, 19 22:51:45 PST" (with a two-digit year), the year will be interpreted as 1919 if the SimpleDateFormat instance was created before November 3, 1999, 22:51:45 PST but interpreted as 2019 if the instance was created on or after November 3, 1999, 22:51:45 PST.

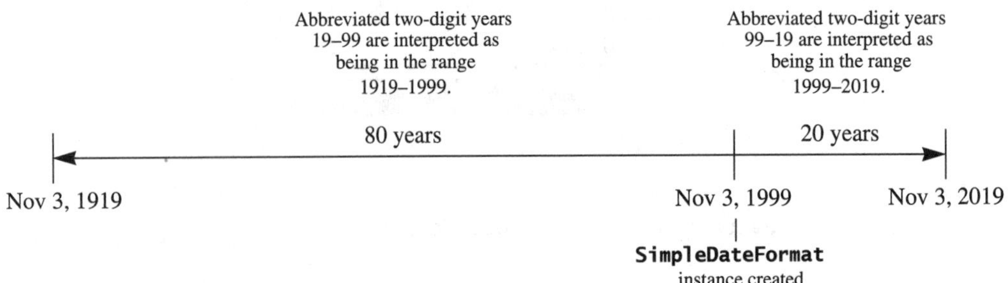

FIGURE 18: An abbreviated year is interpreted as being in the 80/20-year window.

Here is another example. Using the default 80/20-year window and a SimpleDateFormat instance created on January 1, 1997 with the pattern MM/dd/yy, the string "01/11/12" would be interpreted as January 11, 2012 (which is 15 years into the future), while the string "05/04/64" would be interpreted as May 4, 1964 (which is 33 years in the past).

SimpleDateFormat guarantees a "round-trip" from Date to string to Date only if the full date format is used. If you save a date string to disk as a two-digit year and then parse it using a new instance of SimpleDateFormat, the year can be misinterpreted as being in the wrong century. (There is no ambiguity when *formatting* a date to a two-digit string.)

In Version 1.2, you can get the value of the starting date with get2DigitYearStart(). In Version 1.1, the start date of 80 years before creation date was not changeable. In Version 1.2, you can choose to use either the default 80/20-year window or choose a fixed starting date by using set2DigitYearStart().

S

MEMBER SUMMARY	
Constructor	
SimpleDateFormat()	Constructs a SimpleDateFormat instance that has a pattern for a locale.
DateFormatSymbols Methods	
getDateFormatSymbols()	Retrieves the instance of DateFormatSymbols for this SimpleDateFormat instance.
setDateFormatSymbols()	Sets an instance of DateFormatSymbols to this SimpleDate-Format instance.
Two-Digit Year Methods	
1.2 get2DigitYearStart()	Gets the start date for the 100-year period for two-digit years.
1.2 set2DigitYearStart()	Sets the start date for the 100-year period for two-digit years.

MEMBER SUMMARY	
Pattern Methods	
`applyLocalizedPattern()`	Assigns a localized pattern to this `SimpleDateFormat` instance.
`applyPattern()`	Assigns a nonlocalized pattern to this `SimpleDateFormat` instance.
`toLocalizedPattern()`	Produces a string of the current localized pattern.
`toPattern()`	Produces a string of the current nonlocalized pattern.
Format and Parse Methods	
`format()`	Formats a `Date` object to produce a string.
`parse()`	Parses a date-time string to produce a `Date` object.
Object Methods	
`clone()`	Creates a copy of this `SimpleDateFormat` instance.
`equals()`	Compares this `SimpleDateFormat` instance with another object for equality.
`hashCode()`	Computes the hash code of this `SimpleDateFormat` instance.

See Also

`Calendar`, `GregorianCalendar`, `TimeZone`, `DateFormat`, `DateFormatSymbols`, `DecimalFormat`.

`SimpleDateFormat` in *The Java Class Libraries, Second Edition, Volume 1.*

1.2 get2DigitYearStart()

PURPOSE Gets the start date for the 100-year period for two-digit years.

SYNTAX `public Date get2DigitYearStart()`

DESCRIPTION This method gets the start date for the 100-year period that two-digit year patterns will be interpreted as being located in. A two-digit year is specified by the pattern yy. During parsing, two-digit years are placed in the range `started` to `startDate + 100` years.

SEE ALSO `set2DigitYearStart()`.

EXAMPLE This example loops through the two-digit years 00 to 90 for the default 80/20-year window. It then loops through those same two-digit years with the start date of 1950.

```
import java.text.SimpleDateFormat;
import java.text.ParsePosition;
import java.util.*;

class Main {
    public static void main(String[] args) {
```

```
        Locale locale = Locale.FRENCH;

        // Create a date formatter.
        SimpleDateFormat formatter =
            new SimpleDateFormat ("dd.MM.yy", locale);

        printList(formatter);

        // Set a new start date.
        ParsePosition pos = new ParsePosition(0);
        Date newTwoDigitYearStart = formatter.parse("01.01.1950", pos);
        formatter.set2DigitYearStart(newTwoDigitYearStart);

        printList(formatter);
    }

    static void printList(SimpleDateFormat formatter) {
        // Print the start of the 2-digit year
        System.out.println("Starting year: "
                           + formatter.get2DigitYearStart() + "\n");

        // Create a list of 2-digit years at 10-year intervals
        for (int i=00; i<=90; i+=10) {
            String dateString = "03.11." + i;

            // Parse this string into a Date.
            ParsePosition pos = new ParsePosition(0);
            Date parsedDate = formatter.parse(dateString, pos);
            System.out.println(dateString + "    " + parsedDate);
        }
        System.out.println();
    }
}
```

OUTPUT

```
> java Main
Starting year: Fri Nov 22 01:09:55 PST 1918

03.11.0    Fri Nov 03 00:00:00 PST 2000
03.11.10    Wed Nov 03 00:00:00 PST 2010
03.11.20    Wed Nov 03 00:00:00 PST 1920
03.11.30    Mon Nov 03 00:00:00 PST 1930
03.11.40    Sun Nov 03 00:00:00 PST 1940
03.11.50    Fri Nov 03 00:00:00 PST 1950
03.11.60    Thu Nov 03 00:00:00 PST 1960
03.11.70    Tue Nov 03 00:00:00 PST 1970
03.11.80    Mon Nov 03 00:00:00 PST 1980
03.11.90    Sat Nov 03 00:00:00 PST 1990

Starting year: Sun Jan 01 00:00:00 PST 1950

03.11.0    Fri Nov 03 00:00:00 PST 2000
03.11.10    Wed Nov 03 00:00:00 PST 2010
03.11.20    Tue Nov 03 00:00:00 PST 2020
03.11.30    Sun Nov 03 00:00:00 PST 2030
03.11.40    Sat Nov 03 00:00:00 PST 2040
03.11.50    Fri Nov 03 00:00:00 PST 1950
03.11.60    Thu Nov 03 00:00:00 PST 1960
03.11.70    Tue Nov 03 00:00:00 PST 1970
```

```
03.11.80    Mon Nov 03 00:00:00 PST 1980
03.11.90    Sat Nov 03 00:00:00 PST 1990
```

1.2 set2DigitYearStart()

PURPOSE Sets the start date for the 100-year period for two-digit years.

SYNTAX `public void set2DigitYearStart(Date startDate)`

DESCRIPTION This method sets the start date, `startDate`, for the 100-year window that two-digit year patterns will be interpreted as being located in. A two-digit year is specified by the pattern `yy`. During parsing, two-digit years will be placed in the range `startDate` (inclusive) to `startDate + 100` years (exclusive).

PARAMETERS

`startDate` The starting date of the 100-year period, a non-`null` `Date` object.

SEE ALSO `get2DigitYearStart()`.

EXAMPLE See `get2DigitYearStart()`.

java.util

SimpleTimeZone

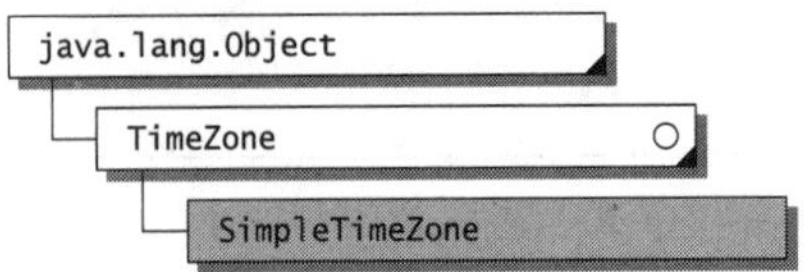

Syntax

```
public class SimpleTimeZone extends TimeZone
```

Description

`SimpleTimeZone` is a concrete subclass of `TimeZone` and represents a time zone for use with a Gregorian calendar. `SimpleTimeZone` implements daylight savings time rules of the form "start on the first Sunday in April" or "end on the Sunday on or before March 15."

See *The Java Class Libraries, Second Edition, Volume 1* for more information about this class.

Changes for Version 1.2

The biggest change to this class is the enhancements to the rules that specify the start and end of daylight light savings time. In Version 1.1, you could specify only rules of the form "The last Sunday of April." See `SimpleTimeZone()`, `setStartRule()`, and `setEndRule()` for a list of the new rule forms.

Two new methods, `getDSTSavings()` and `setDSTSavings()`, respectively retrieve and change the time difference between daylight savings time and standard time.

The new method `hasSameRule()` allows the comparison of the daylight savings period of `TimeZone` objects.

S

MEMBER SUMMARY	
Constructor	
Δ `SimpleTimeZone()`	Constructs a `SimpleTimeZone` instance.
Time Offset Methods	
`getOffset()`	Retrieves the time difference (in daylight savings time) of this time zone from GMT.
`getRawOffset()`	Retrieves the time difference (in standard time) of this time zone from GMT.
`setRawOffset()`	Sets the time difference from GMT.

MEMBER SUMMARY	
Daylight Savings Time Methods	
1.2 `hasSameRules()`	Determines if the daylight savings period of this time zone is equal to that of another time zone.
`inDaylightTime()`	Determines if a particular date falls in this time zone's daylight savings time period.
1.2 `getDSTSavings()`	Retrieves the time difference between daylight savings time and standard time.
1.2 `setDSTSavings()`	Sets the time difference between daylight savings time and standard time.
Δ `setEndRule()`	Sets the daylight savings time end rule.
Δ `setStartRule()`	Sets the daylight savings time start rule.
`setStartYear()`	Sets the year in which daylight savings time takes effect.
`useDaylightTime()`	Determines if this `SimpleTimeZone` has a daylight savings time period.
Object Methods	
`clone()`	Creates a clone of this `SimpleTimeZone`.
`equals()`	Determines if this `SimpleTimeZone` is equal to another object.
`hashCode()`	Computes the hash code of this `SimpleTimeZone`.
Δ `toString()`	Generates a string representation of this `SimpleTimeZone`.

See Also

`Calendar`, `TimeZone`.
`SimpleTimeZone` in *The Java Class Libraries, Second Edition, Volume 1.*

Example

This example demonstrates the creation of a new time zone, complete with its own daylight savings time period. The created time zone uses the raw offset of the default time zone. The daylight savings time period of the new time zone is calculated to start exactly 10 seconds in the future and end 20 seconds in the future.

S

In the calculation of the start of daylight savings time, an hour must be subtracted from the start time. This is because the start time must be specified relative to daylight savings time rather than to standard time.

A thread is created to monitor the time as it enters and leaves daylight savings time.

```
import java.util.*;
import java.text.*;

class Main extends Thread {
    static SimpleTimeZone tz;

    public static void main(String[] args) {
        // Create a new SimpleTimeZone object with the name JAV.
        // Use the local raw offset.
```

```
        tz = new SimpleTimeZone(TimeZone.getDefault().getRawOffset(), "JAV");

        Calendar calendar = Calendar.getInstance();

        // Determine the number of milliseconds so far today.
        int todayMillis = calendar.get(Calendar.HOUR)*60*60*1000
            + calendar.get(Calendar.MINUTE)*60*1000
            + calendar.get(Calendar.SECOND)*1000;

        // If PM, add another 12 hours.
        if (calendar.get(Calendar.AM_PM) == Calendar.PM) {
            todayMillis += 12*60*60*1000;
        }

        // Set the start of daylight savings time 10 seconds from now.
        tz.setStartRule(
            calendar.get(Calendar.MONTH),
            calendar.get(Calendar.DAY_OF_WEEK_IN_MONTH),
            calendar.get(Calendar.DAY_OF_WEEK),
            todayMillis + 10000);

        // Set the end of daylight savings time 20 seconds from now.
        tz.setEndRule(
            calendar.get(Calendar.MONTH),
            calendar.get(Calendar.DAY_OF_WEEK_IN_MONTH),
            calendar.get(Calendar.DAY_OF_WEEK),
            todayMillis + 20000 + tz.getDSTSavings());

        // Start a thread to monitor the time.
        new Main().start();
    }

    public void run() {
        DateFormat formatter =
            new SimpleDateFormat("MMM dd HH:mm:ss zzz", Locale.US);
        formatter.setTimeZone(tz);

        while (true) {
            try {
                // Get the current time and date.
                Date date = new Date();

                // Print current time.
                System.out.print( (tz.inDaylightTime(date) ?
                    "Daylight Savings Time - " : "Standard Time          - "));
                System.out.println(formatter.format(date));

                // Sleep for 3 seconds.
                Thread.sleep(3000);
            } catch (Exception e) {
                e.printStackTrace();
            }
        }
    }
}
```

Output

```
Standard Time          - Oct 06 16:42:04 GMT-08:00
Standard Time          - Oct 06 16:42:07 GMT-08:00
```

```
Standard Time          - Oct 06 16:42:10 GMT-08:00
Daylight Savings Time - Oct 06 17:42:13 GMT-07:00
Daylight Savings Time - Oct 06 17:42:16 GMT-07:00
Daylight Savings Time - Oct 06 17:42:19 GMT-07:00
Daylight Savings Time - Oct 06 17:42:22 GMT-07:00
Standard Time          - Oct 06 16:42:25 GMT-08:00
Standard Time          - Oct 06 16:42:28 GMT-08:00
```

1.2 getDSTSavings()

PURPOSE Retrieves the time difference between daylight savings time and standard time.

SYNTAX `public int getDSTSavings()`

DESCRIPTION This method retrieves the time difference between daylight savings time and standard time. The return value is valid only if `useDaylightTime()` returns `true`.

RETURNS The number of milliseconds by which daylight savings time differs from standard time. The return value is ≥ `0`.

SEE ALSO `setDSTSavings()`.

EXAMPLE

```
// Time difference of 1 hour.
        SimpleTimeZone tz = (SimpleTimeZone)TimeZone.getTimeZone("PST");
        System.out.println(tz.getDSTSavings() + " " + tz.useDaylightTime());
    // 3600000 true

// Time difference of 1/2 hour.
        tz = (SimpleTimeZone)TimeZone.getTimeZone("Pacific/Rarotonga");
        System.out.println(tz.getDSTSavings() + " " + tz.useDaylightTime());
    // 1800000 true

// No daylight savings time.
        tz = (SimpleTimeZone)TimeZone.getTimeZone("GMT");
        System.out.println(tz.getDSTSavings() + " " + tz.useDaylightTime());
    // 3600000 false
```

S

1.2 hasSameRules()

PURPOSE Determines if the daylight savings period of this time zone is equal to that of another time zone.

SYNTAX `public boolean hasSameRules(TimeZone other)`

DESCRIPTION This method determines if the daylight savings start and end rules for this time zone are equal to `other`. This method returns `true` if both time zones have the same raw offset (see `getRawOffset()`) and the same rules. If both time zones do not have daylight savings times (that is, `useDaylightTime()` returns `false`), this method returns `true` regardless of what rules are specified.

PARAMETERS

`other` A possibly `null` `TimeZone` object.

RETURNS `true` if both time zones have the same raw offset and implement the same start and end daylight savings time rules.

OVERRIDES `TimeZone.hahsSameRules()`.

EXAMPLE

```
SimpleTimeZone tz1 = (SimpleTimeZone)TimeZone.getTimeZone("PST");
SimpleTimeZone tz2 = (SimpleTimeZone)TimeZone.getTimeZone("PST");

System.out.println( tz1.hasSameRules(tz2) );    // true

tz1.setStartRule(Calendar.MARCH, 15, tz1.getDSTSavings());
System.out.println( tz1.hasSameRules(tz2) );    // false

tz1.setStartRule(Calendar.MARCH, 0, 0);
tz2.setStartRule(Calendar.MARCH, 0, 0);
System.out.println( tz1.hasSameRules(tz2) );    // true

tz1.setRawOffset(2*60*60*1000);
System.out.println( tz1.hasSameRules(tz2) );    // false
```

1.2 setDSTSavings()

PURPOSE Sets the time difference between daylight savings time and standard time.

SYNTAX `public void setDSTSavings(int millisSavedDuringDST)`

DESCRIPTION This method changes the time difference, in milliseconds, between daylight savings time and standard time for this `TimeZone` to be `millisSavedDuringDST`. It has no effect on `TimeZones` returned by `TimeZone.getTimeZone()`.

Changing the daylight savings time difference has no effect unless `useDaylightTime()` returns `true`.

S

PARAMETERS

`millisSavedDuringDST`

The number of milliseconds by which daylight savings time differs from standard time. `millisSavedDuringDST` > `0`.

SEE ALSO `getDSTSavings()`.

EXAMPLE

```
SimpleTimeZone tz = (SimpleTimeZone)TimeZone.getTimeZone("PST");

// Change the daylight savings difference to 30 minutes.
```

```
tz.setDSTSavings(30*60*1000);

// The above only affects tz; it does not change other
// TimeZone objects that were or will be created
// from calling TimeZone.getTimeZone().
System.out.println(
    ((SimpleTimeZone)TimeZone.getTimeZone("PST")).getDSTSavings() );
        // 3600000

// tz.setDSTSavings(0);      // IllegalArgumentException
// tz.setDSTSavings(-1);     // IllegalArgumentException
```

Δ setEndRule()

PURPOSE Sets the daylight savings time end rule.

SYNTAX

```
public void setEndRule(int month, int dayOfWeekInMonth, int
    dayOfWeek, int time)
```

SINCE 1.2

```
public void setEndRule(int month, int dayOfMonth, int time)
```

SINCE 1.2

```
public void setEndRule(int month, int dayOfWeekInMonth, int
    dayOfWeek, int time, boolean after)
```

DESCRIPTION This method sets the end of daylight savings time for this `SimpleTimeZone`. The four parameters together specify the time (in daylight savings time) on which daylight savings time ends.

The parameter `month` specifies the starting month; for example, `Calendar.APRIL`. The parameter `dayOfWeek` specifies one of the 7 days of the week; for example, `Calendar.SUNDAY`.

The parameter `dayOfWeekInMonth` specifies the *n*th week in the month; for example, `1` means the first week of the month. The parameter `dayOfWeekInMonth` may also be negative; for example, `-1` means the last week of the month. If `dayOfWeekInMonth` is `0`, this time zone no longer implements daylight savings time.

The parameter `time` is the number of milliseconds after midnight. It is important to note that the time is specified in daylight savings time rather than standard time. For example, suppose `time` is 2 A.M. (2*60*60*1000). Then when the clock is at 1:59:59 A.M. (in daylight savings time) and advances by a second, the time immediately becomes 1 A.M.

When a daylight savings time period is being set, both this method and `setStartRule()` must be used. Otherwise, the effects are undefined. After this method is called, `useDaylightTime()` returns `true`.

Following are the different types of daylight savings end rules possible with this class and how to specify them with this method.

- A Specific Day in a Month. For example, March 15, 2 A.M. (daylight savings time) is specified as

```
stz.setEndRule(Calendar.March, 15, 2*60*60*1000);
```

- The *n*th Day-of-week in a Month. For example, the third Sunday in March, 2 A.M. (daylight savings time) is specified as

```
stz.setEndRule(Calendar.March, 3, Calendar.SUNDAY,
   2*60*60*1000)
```

- The Last *n*th Day-of-week in a Month. For example, the second to last Sunday in March, 2 A.M. (daylight savings time) is specified as

```
stz.setEndRule(Calendar.March, -2, Calendar.SUNDAY,
   2*60*60*1000)
```

- A Day-of-week Before a Specific Day. For example, the Sunday on or before March 15, 2 A.M. (daylight savings time) is specified as

```
stz.setEndRule(Calendar.March, 15, Calendar.SUNDAY,
   2*60*60*1000, false)
```

- A Day-of-week After a Specific Day. For example, the Sunday on or after March 15, 2 A.M. (daylight savings time) is specified as

```
stz.setEndRule(Calendar.March, 15, Calendar.SUNDAY,
   2*60*60*1000, true)
```

1.2 CHANGES The second and third forms of the method are new. They enable the ability to specify a particular day or a day of the week before or after a particular day.

PARAMETERS

`after` If `true`, daylight savings time ends on or after the `dayOfWeek` in `month`; otherwise, daylight savings time ends on or before the `dayOfWeek` in `month`.

`dayOfWeek` The day of the week in which daylight savings time ends. `Calendar.SUNDAY` ≤ `dayOfWeek` ≤ `Calendar.SATURDAY`.

`dayOfWeekInMonth`
The *n*th week of the month in which daylight savings time ends. `-5` ≤ `dayOfWeekInMonth` ≤ `5`. If `0`, the time zone no longer implements daylight savings time.

`month` The month in which daylight savings time ends. `Calendar.JANUARY` ≤ `month` ≤ `Calendar.DECEMBER`.

`time` The time, in milliseconds after midnight, at which daylight savings time ends. `0` ≤ `time` ≤ `24*60*60*1000`. The time is in standard time.

SEE ALSO `setStartRule()`.

EXAMPLE

```
SimpleTimeZone tz = new SimpleTimeZone(0, "JAV");
int time = 2*60*60*100;    // 2am

    // March 15th 2am
```

```
tz.setEndRule(Calendar.MARCH, 15, time);
    // 3rd Sunday in March 2am
tz.setEndRule(Calendar.MARCH, 3, Calendar.SUNDAY, time);

    // 2nd last Sunday in March 2am
tz.setEndRule(Calendar.MARCH, -2, Calendar.SUNDAY, time);

    // The Sunday on before March 15th 2am
tz.setEndRule(Calendar.MARCH, 15, Calendar.SUNDAY, time, false);

    // The Sunday on after March 15th 2am
tz.setEndRule(Calendar.MARCH, 15, Calendar.SUNDAY, time, true);

tz = (SimpleTimeZone)TimeZone.getTimeZone("PST");
System.out.println(tz.useDaylightTime());        // true
tz.setEndRule(Calendar.JANUARY, 0, Calendar.FRIDAY, 0, true);
System.out.println(tz.useDaylightTime());        // false
```

Δ setStartRule()

PURPOSE Sets the daylight savings time start rule.

SYNTAX

```
public void setStartRule(int month, int dayOfWeekInMonth, int
    dayOfWeek, int time)
```

SINCE 1.2
```
public void setStartRule(int month, int dayOfMonth, int time)
```

SINCE 1.2
```
public void setStartRule(int month, int dayOfMonth, int dayOfWeek,
    int time, boolean after)
```

DESCRIPTION This method sets the start of daylight savings time for this `SimpleTimeZone`. The parameters together specify a particular day and time (in standard time) on which daylight savings time should start.

The parameter `month` specifies the starting month; for example, `Calendar.APRIL`. The parameter `dayOfWeek` specifies one of the 7 days of the week; for example, `Calendar.SUNDAY`.

The parameter `dayOfWeekInMonth` specifies the *n*th week in the month; for example, `1` means the first week of the month. The parameter `dayOfWeekInMonth` may also be negative; for example, `-1` means the last week of the month. If `dayOfWeekInMonth` is `0`, this time zone no longer implements daylight savings time.

The parameter `time` is the number of milliseconds after midnight. It is important to note that the time is specified in daylight savings time rather than standard time. For example, suppose `time` is 2 A.M. (2*60*60*1000). When the clock is at 1:59:59 A.M. (standard time) and advances by 1 second, the time immediately becomes 3 A.M. (assuming that `getDSTSavings()` returns an hour.)

When a daylight savings time period is being set, both this method and `setEndRule()` must be used. Otherwise, the effects are undefined. After this method is called, `useDaylightTime()` returns `true`.

Following are the different types of start rules possible with this class and how to specify them with this method.

- A Specific Day in a Month. For example, March 15, 2 A.M. (standard time) is specified as

```
stz.setStartRule(Calendar.March, 15, 2*60*60*1000)
```

- The *n*th Day-of-week in a Month. For example, the third Sunday in March, 2 A.M. (standard time) is specified as

```
stz.setStartRule(Calendar.March, 3, Calendar.SUNDAY,
    2*60*60*1000)
```

- The Last *n*th Day-of-week in a Month. For example, the second to last Sunday in March, 2 A.M. (standard time) is specified as

```
stz.setStartRule(Calendar.March, -2, Calendar.SUNDAY,
    2*60*60*1000)
```

- A Day-of-week Before a Specific Day. For example, the Sunday on or before March 15, 2 A.M. (standard time) is specified as

```
stz.setStartRule(Calendar.March, 15, Calendar.SUNDAY,
    2*60*60*1000, false)
```

- A Day-of-week After a Specific Day. For example, the Sunday on or after March 15, 2 A.M. (standard time) is specified as

```
stz.setStartRule(Calendar.March, 15, Calendar.SUNDAY,
    2*60*60*1000, true)
```

1.2 CHANGES The second and third forms of the method are new. They enable the ability to specify a particular day or a day of the week before or after a particular day.

PARAMETERS

`after` If `true`, daylight savings time starts on or after the `dayOfWeek` in `month`; otherwise, daylight savings time starts on or before the `dayOfWeek` in `month`.

`dayOfWeek` The day of the week in which daylight savings time starts. `Calendar.SUNDAY` ≤ `dayOfWeek` ≤ `Calendar.SATURDAY`.

`dayOfWeekInMonth`
The *n*th week of the month in which daylight savings time starts. `-5` ≤ `dayOfWeekInMonth` ≤ `5`. If `0`, the time zone no longer implements daylight savings time.

`month` The month in which daylight savings time starts. `Calendar.JANUARY` ≤ `month` ≤ `Calendar.DECEMBER`.

`time` The time, in milliseconds after midnight, at which daylight savings time starts. `0` ≤ `time` ≤ `24*60*60*1000`. The time is in standard time.

SEE ALSO setEndRule().

EXAMPLE

```
SimpleTimeZone tz = new SimpleTimeZone(0, "JAV");
int time = 2*60*60*100;    // 2am

    // March 15th 2am
tz.setStartRule(Calendar.MARCH, 15, time);

    // 3rd Sunday in March 2am
tz.setStartRule(Calendar.MARCH, 3, Calendar.SUNDAY, time);

    // 2nd last Sunday in March 2am
tz.setStartRule(Calendar.MARCH, -2, Calendar.SUNDAY, time);

    // The Sunday on before March 15th 2am
tz.setStartRule(Calendar.MARCH, 15, Calendar.SUNDAY, time, false);

    // The Sunday on after March 15th 2am
tz.setStartRule(Calendar.MARCH, 15, Calendar.SUNDAY, time, true);

tz = (SimpleTimeZone)TimeZone.getTimeZone("PST");
System.out.println(tz.useDaylightTime());        // true
tz.setStartRule(Calendar.JANUARY, 0, Calendar.FRIDAY, 0, true);
System.out.println(tz.useDaylightTime());        // false
```

Δ SimpleTimeZone()

PURPOSE Constructs a SimpleTimeZone instance.

SYNTAX

```
public SimpleTimeZone(int rawOffset, String ID)
public SimpleTimeZone(int rawOffset, String ID, int startMonth,
   int startDayOfWeekInMonth, int startDayOfWeek, int startTime,
   int endMonth, int endDayOfWeekInMonth, int endDayOfWeek, int
   endTime)
```

SINCE 1.2

```
public SimpleTimeZone(int rawOffset, String ID, int startMonth,
   int startDayOfWeekInMonth, int startDayOfWeek, int startTime,
   int endMonth, int endDayOfWeekInMonth, int endDayOfWeek, int
   endTime, int dstSavings)
```

DESCRIPTION This method constructs a SimpleTimeZone instance. The parameter rawOffset is the number of milliseconds by which this time zone differs from GMT. For example, PST differs by -8*1000*60*60 milliseconds from GMT. The raw offset is based on standard time (that is, the effects of daylight savings time is ignored). ID is the time-zone ID for this new SimpleTimeZone.

If only rawOffset and ID are specified, the new SimpleTimeZone does not have a daylight savings period. useDaylightTime() will return false.

By default, the daylight savings time start year is 0.

S

The parameters `startMonth`, `startDayOfWeekInMonth`, `startDayOfWeek`, and `startTime` together specify the start of daylight savings time. See `setStartRule()` for details on `startMonth` and `startTime`. The meanings of `startDayOfWeekInMonth` and `startDayOfWeek` vary depending on each other's values. Table 22 summarizes how they are interpreted based on their values.

startDayOfWeekInMonth	startDayOfWeek	Interpretation
1..31	0	Specifies a particular day of the month; for example, March 15.
1..5	Calendar.SUNDAY.. Calendar.SATURDAY	Specifies the *n*th day of the week in the month, where *n* is `startDayOfWeekInMonth`; for example, the second Sunday of the month.
-5..-1	Calendar.SUNDAY.. Calendar.SATURDAY	Specifies the *n*th last day of the week in the month, where *n* is `startDayOfWeekInMonth`; for example, the second to last Sunday of the month.
1..31	-Calendar.SUNDAY.. -Calendar.SATURDAY	Specifies the day of the week on or after the *n*th day, where *n* is `startDayOfWeekInMonth`; for example, the Sunday on or after the fifteenth.
-1..-31	-Calendar.SUNDAY.. -Calendar.SATURDAY	Specifies the day of the week on or before the *n*th day, where *n* is `startDayOfWeekInMonth`; for example, the Sunday on or before the fifteenth.

TABLE 22: Interpretation of `startDayOfWeekInMonth` and `startDayOfWeek`.

S

The parameters `endMonth`, `endDayOfWeekInMonth`, `endDayOfWeek`, and `endTime` together specify the end of daylight savings time. See `setEndRule()` for details on `endMonth` and `endTime`. The meanings of `endDayOfWeekInMonth` and `endDayOfWeek` vary depending on each other's values. Table 23 summarizes how they are interpreted based on their values.

endDayOfWeekIn-Month	endDayOfWeek	Interpretation
`1..31`	`0`	Specifies a particular day of the month; for example, March 15.
`1..5`	`Calendar.SUNDAY..` `Calendar.SATURDAY`	Specifies the *n*th day of the week in the month, where *n* is `endDayOfWeekInMonth`; for example, the second Sunday of the month.
`-5..-1`	`Calendar.SUNDAY..` `Calendar.SATURDAY`	Specifies the *n*th last day of the week in the month, where *n* is `endDayOfWeekInMonth`; for example, the second to last Sunday of the month.
`1..31`	`-Calendar.SUNDAY..` `-Calendar.SATURDAY`	Specifies the day of the week on or after the *n*th day, where *n* is `endDayOfWeekIn-Month`; for example, the Sunday on or after the fifteenth.
`-1..-31`	`-Calendar.SUNDAY..` `-Calendar.SATURDAY`	Specifies the day of the week on or before the *n*th day, where *n* is `endDayOfWeekIn-Month`; for example, the Sunday on or before the fifteenth.

TABLE 23: Interpretation of `endDayOfWeekInMonth` and `endDayOfWeek`.

The parameter `dstSavings` is the number of milliseconds by which daylight savings time differs from standard time. This number must be greater than zero. If not specified, `dstSavings` defaults to `60*60*1000` (1 hour.)

Following are the different types of start/end rules possible with this class and how to specify them using this constructor. To conserve space, the end rule is always assumed to be the same as the start rule, except that it is a month later. Note that the starting time is relative to standard time and the ending time is relative to daylight savings time.

S

- No daylight savings period. This is specified as

```
new SimpleTimeZone(rawOffset, "ID")
```

- A Specific Day in a Month. For example, March 15, 2 A.M. is specified as

```
new SimpleTimeZone(rawOffset, "ID", Calendar.March, 15,
   0, 2*60*60*1000,Calendar.April, 15, 0, 2*60*60*1000)
```

- The *n*th Day-of-week in a Month. For example, the third Sunday in March, 2 A.M. is specified as

```
new SimpleTimeZone(rawOffset, "ID",Calendar.March, 3,
    Calendar.SUNDAY,2*60*60*1000, Calendar.April, 3,
    Calendar.SUNDAY, 2*60*60*1000)
```

- The Last *n*th Day-of-week in a Month. For example, the second to last Sunday in March, 2 A.M. is specified as

```
new SimpleTimeZone(rawOffset, "ID",Calendar.March, -2,
    Calendar.SUNDAY, 2*60*60*1000, Calendar.April, -2,
    Calendar.SUNDAY, 2*60*60*1000)
```

- A Day-of-week Before a Specific Day. For example, the Sunday on or before March 15, 2 A.M. is specified as

```
new SimpleTimeZone(rawOffset, "ID", Calendar.March, -15,
    -Calendar.SUNDAY, 2*60*60*1000, Calendar.April, -15,
    -Calendar.SUNDAY, 2*60*60*1000)
```

- A Day-of-week After a Specific Day. For example, the Sunday on or after March 15, 2 A.M. is specified as

```
new SimpleTimeZone(rawOffset, "ID", Calendar.March, 15,
    -Calendar.SUNDAY, 2*60*60*1000, Calendar.April, 15,
    Calendar.SUNDAY, 2*60*60*1000)
```

1.2 CHANGES The last form of this constructor is new. It enables the ability to specify a daylight savings time difference. Also, new ways to express the start and end of daylight savings are now possible. The new rule types are made available by interpreting negative values for `startDayOfWeekInMonth` and `startDayOfWeek`.

PARAMETERS

`dstSavings` The number of milliseconds by which daylight savings time differs from standard time. `dstSavings` > `0`.

`endDayOfWeek`
The daylight savings time starting day of the week. `Calendar.SUNDAY` ≤ `endDayOfWeek` ≤ `Calendar.SATURDAY`.

`endDayOfWeekInMonth`
The *n*th week of the month. `endDayOfWeekInMonth` ≥ `1` or `endDayOfWeekInMonth` ≤ `-1`.

`endMonth` The daylight savings time starting month. `Calendar.JANUARY` ≤ `month` ≤ `Calendar.DECEMBER`.

`endTime` The time, in milliseconds after midnight, at which daylight savings time ends. `0` ≤ `endTime` ≤ `24*60*60*1000`. The time is in daylight savings time.

`ID` A non-`null` string containing the ID of the time zone.

`rawOffset` The number of milliseconds by which this time zone differs from GMT. May be negative.

`startDayOfWeek`
: The day of the week in which daylight savings time starts. `Calendar.SUNDAY` ≤ `startDayOfWeek` ≤ `Calendar.SATURDAY`.

`startDayOfWeekInMonth`
: The *n*th week of the month. `-5` ≤ `dayOfWeekInMonth` ≤ `5`.

`startMonth`
: The daylight savings time starting month. `Calendar.JANUARY` ≤ `startMonth` ≤ `Calendar.DECEMBER`.

`startTime`
: The time, in milliseconds after midnight, at which daylight savings time starts. `0` ≤ `startTime` ≤ `24*60*60*1000`. The time is in standard time.

SEE ALSO `getDSTSavings()`, `setStartRule()`, `setEndRule()`.

EXAMPLE

```
// -8 hours GMT. No daylight savings time.
SimpleTimeZone tz = new SimpleTimeZone(-28800000, "JAV");

// March 15th 2am - April 15th 2am
tz = new SimpleTimeZone(-28800000, "JAV",
    Calendar.MARCH, 15, 0, 2*60*60*1000,
    Calendar.APRIL, 15, 0, 2*60*60*1000);

// 3rd Sunday in March 2am - 3rd Sunday in April 2am
tz = new SimpleTimeZone(-28800000, "JAV",
    Calendar.MARCH, 3, Calendar.SUNDAY, 2*60*60*1000,
    Calendar.APRIL, 3, Calendar.SUNDAY, 2*60*60*1000);

// 2nd last Sunday in March 2am - 2nd last Sunday in April 2am
tz = new SimpleTimeZone(-28800000, "JAV",
    Calendar.MARCH, -2, Calendar.SUNDAY, 2*60*60*1000,
    Calendar.APRIL, -2, Calendar.SUNDAY, 2*60*60*1000);

// Sun on or before Mar 15 2am - Sun on or before Apr 15 2am
tz = new SimpleTimeZone(-28800000, "JAV",
    Calendar.MARCH, -15, -Calendar.SUNDAY, 2*60*60*1000,
    Calendar.APRIL, -15, -Calendar.SUNDAY, 2*60*60*1000);

// Sun on or after Mar 15 2am - Sun on or after Apr 15 2am
tz = new SimpleTimeZone(-28800000, "JAV",
    Calendar.MARCH, 15, -Calendar.SUNDAY, 2*60*60*1000,
    Calendar.APRIL, 15, -Calendar.SUNDAY, 2*60*60*1000);
```


Δ toString()

PURPOSE Generates a string representation of this `SimpleTimeZone`.

SYNTAX `public String toString()`

DESCRIPTION This method creates a string showing the current state of this `SimpleTimeZone`. This method is typically used for debugging purposes. Here is a sample of the resulting string for the PST time zone.

```
java.util.SimpleTimeZone[id=PST,offset=-28800000,dstSavings=3600000,useDay-
light=true,startYear=0,startMode=3,startMonth=3,startDay=1,startDayOf-
Week=1,startTime=7200000,endMode=2,endMonth=9,endDay=-
1,endDayOfWeek=1,endTime=7200000]
```

Table 24 shows the meanings of the `SimpleTimeZone.toString()` fields.

Field	Meaning
`id`	The time-zone ID.
`offset`	The raw offset—the time difference between this time zone (regardless of daylight savings time) and GMT, in milliseconds.
`dstSavings`	The time difference between daylight savings time and standard time, in milliseconds. Must be ≥ `0`.
`useDaylight`	`true` if this time zone has a daylight savings period. Possibly values are `true` and `false`.
`startYear`	The year in which daylight savings time was/will be instated.
`startMode`	1=exact day of the week; for example, March 15. 2=day of the week in the month; for example, the last Sunday in March. 3=day of week after the day of month; for example, Sunday on or after March 15. 4=day of week before the day of month; for example, Sunday on or before March 15.
`startMonth`	The month in which daylight savings time takes effect. Range: `Calendar.JANUARY..Calendar.DECEMBER`.
`startDay`	The day of month or week in the month that daylight savings time takes effect. If `startDayOfWeek` is `0`, this field specifies a particular day of the month. Range: `1..31`. Otherwise, this field specifies a week in the month; for example, 1=first week in the month, 2=second week in the month, `-1`=last week in the month, and so on. Range: `-5..-1`, `1..5`.
`startDayOfWeek`	The day of the week in which daylight savings time takes effect. Range: `Calendar.SUNDAY..Calendar.SATURDAY`.
`startTime`	The time (in milliseconds) at which daylight savings time takes effect. Range: `0..86400000`.

TABLE 24: `SimpleTimeZone.toString()` Fields.

S

Field	Meaning
endMode	1=exact day of the week; for example, March 15. 2=day of the week in the month; for example, the last Sunday in March. 3=day of week after the day of month; for example, Sunday on or after March 15. 4=day of week before the day of month; for example, Sunday on or before March 15.
endDay	The day of the month or week in the month on which daylight savings time ends. If startDayOfWeek is 0, this field specifies a particular day of the month. Range: 1..31. Otherwise, this field specifies a week in the month; for example, 1=first week in the month, 2=second week in the month, -1=last week in the month, and so on. Range: -5..-1, 1..5.
endDayOfWeek	The day in the week on which daylight savings time ends. Range: Calendar.SUNDAY..Calendar.SATURDAY.
endMonth	The month in which daylight savings time ends. Range: Calendar.JANUARY..Calendar.DECEMBER.
endTime	The time (in milliseconds) at which daylight savings time ends. Range: 0..86400000.

TABLE 24: SimpleTimeZone.toString() Fields.

1.2 CHANGES This method was inherited from java.lang.Object in Version 1.1. It printed the object reference.

RETURNS A non-null string representation of this SimpleTimeZone's state.

OVERRIDES java.Object.toString().

EXAMPLE This example demonstrates the effect of different time zone start rules on the internal time zone fields.

```
SimpleTimeZone tz = (SimpleTimeZone)TimeZone.getTimeZone("PST");
System.out.println( tz );
    // java.util.SimpleTimeZone[id=PST,offset=-28800000,
    // dstSavings=3600000,useDaylight=true,startYear=0,
    // startMode=3,startMonth=3,startDay=1,startDayOfWeek=1,
    // startTime=7200000,endMode=2,endMonth=9,endDay=-1,
    // endDayOfWeek=1,endTime=7200000]

int time = 2*60*60*1000;

tz.setStartRule(Calendar.MARCH, 15, time);
System.out.println( tz );
    // ...startMode=1,startMonth=2,startDay=15,
    // startDayOfWeek=0,startTime=7200000...
```

```
tz.setStartRule(Calendar.MARCH, 15, 0, time);
System.out.println( tz );
    // ...startMode=1,startMonth=2,startDay=15,
    // startDayOfWeek=0, startTime=7200000...

tz.setStartRule(Calendar.MARCH, 2, Calendar.WEDNESDAY, time);
System.out.println( tz );
    // ...startMode=2,startMonth=2,startDay=2,
    // startDayOfWeek=4,startTime=7200000...

tz.setStartRule(Calendar.MARCH, -2, Calendar.WEDNESDAY, time);
System.out.println( tz );
    // ...startMode=2,startMonth=2,startDay=-2,
    // startDayOfWeek=4,startTime=7200000...

tz.setStartRule(Calendar.MARCH, 2, Calendar.WEDNESDAY, time, true);
System.out.println( tz );
    // ...startMode=3,startMonth=2,startDay=2,
    // startDayOfWeek=4,startTime=7200000...

tz.setStartRule(Calendar.MARCH, 2, Calendar.WEDNESDAY, time, false);
System.out.println( tz );
    // ...startMode=4,startMonth=2,startDay=2,
    // startDayOfWeek=4,startTime=7200000...
```

Socket

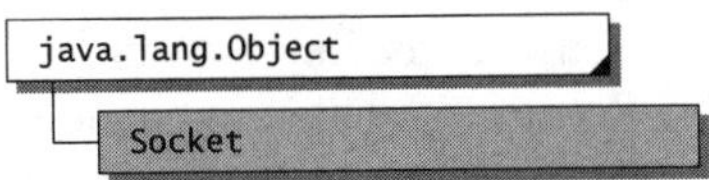

Syntax

`public class Socket`

Description

The `Socket` class is used to represent a socket to be used for connection-oriented (streaming) protocols. A *socket* is a communications endpoint. The `DatagramSocket` class is used for connection-less protocols.

See *The Java Class Libraries, Second Edition, Volume 1* for more information about this class.

Changes for Version 1.2

New methods set and get the send and receive buffer sizes.

MEMBER SUMMARY	
Constructor	
`Socket()`	Constructs a stream `Socket` to the specified destination.
Communications Methods	
`close()`	Closes this `Socket`.
`getInputStream()`	Creates an input stream for this `Socket`.
`getOutputStream()`	Creates an output stream to this `Socket`.
Socket Information Methods	
`getInetAddress()`	Retrieves the remote IP address to which this `Socket` is connected.
`getLocalAddress()`	Retrieves the local IP address used by this `Socket`.
`getLocalPort()`	Retrieves this `Socket`'s local port.
`getPort()`	Retrieves this `Socket`'s remote port.
`toString()`	Generates the string representation of this `Socket`.
Socket Option Methods	
1.2 `getReceiveBufferSize()`	Retrieves the receive buffer size of this `Socket`.
1.2 `getSendBufferSize()`	Retrieves the send buffer size of this `Socket`.

Continued

S

MEMBER SUMMARY	
Socket Option Methods (*Continued*)	
getSoLinger()	Retrieves the linger-on-close time-out period of this Socket.
getSoTimeout()	Retrieves the time-out period of this Socket.
getTcpNoDelay()	Determines whether this Socket is using Nagle's algorithm.
1.2 setReceiveBufferSize()	Sets the receive buffer size of this Socket.
1.2 setSendBufferSize()	Sets the send buffer size of this Socket.
setSoLinger()	Sets the linger-on-close time-out period of this Socket.
setSoTimeout()	Sets the time-out period of this Socket.
setTcpNoDelay()	Enables or disables Nagle's algorithm on this Socket.
Socket Implementation Method	
setSocketImplFactory()	Sets the system's client socket implementation factory.

See Also

SocketOptions.
Socket in *The Java Class Libraries, Second Edition, Volume 1.*

1.2 getReceiveBufferSize()

PURPOSE Retrieves the receive buffer size of this Socket.

SYNTAX
```
public synchronized int getReceiveBufferSize() throws
    SocketException
```

DESCRIPTION This method retrieves the buffer size being used by the underlying platform-specific network code for receiving data sent to this Socket. This size may or may not be the same value that was previously set using setReceiveBufferSize(). Also, it might not be the actual value used by the underlying platform-specific network code if it is outside of the allowable maximum or minimum of the platform.

RETURNS The buffer size, in bytes, used for receiving data.

EXCEPTIONS

SocketException
If an error occurred while using the associated socket option to get the buffer size.

SEE ALSO SocketImpl.getOption(), getSendBufferSize(), setReceiveBufferSize(), SocketOption.SO_RCVBUF.

EXAMPLE
```
Socket sock = srvSocket.accept();
```

S

```
System.out.println("Socket's original receive buffer size: " +
    sock.getReceiveBufferSize());

// set to the size we want
sock.setReceiveBufferSize(newBufSize);
```

1.2 getSendBufferSize()

PURPOSE Retrieves the send buffer size of this `Socket`.

SYNTAX `public synchronized int getSendBufferSize() throws SocketException`

DESCRIPTION This method retrieves the buffer size being used by the underlying platform-specific network code for sending out data from this `Socket`. This size may or may not be the same value that was previously set using `setSendBufferSize()`. Also, it might not be the actual value used by the underlying platform-specific network code if it is outside of the allowable maximum or minimum of the platform.

RETURNS The buffer size, in bytes, used for sending data.

EXCEPTIONS

`SocketException`
If an error occurred while using the associated socket option to get the buffer size.

SEE ALSO `SocketImpl.getOption()`, `getReceiveBufferSize()`, `setSendBufferSize()`, `SocketOption.SO_SNDBUF`.

EXAMPLE

```
Socket sock = srvSocket.accept();

System.out.println("Socket's original send buffer size: " +
    sock.getSendBufferSize());

// set to the size we want
sock.setSendBufferSize(newBufSize);
```

S

1.2 setReceiveBufferSize()

PURPOSE Sets the receive buffer size of this `Socket`.

SYNTAX `public synchronized void setReceiveBufferSize(int size) throws SocketException`

DESCRIPTION This method is used to provide a hint to the underlying platform-specific network code as to the buffer size to use when receiving data sent to this `Socket`. A larger size can increase throughput, but it also will increase memory usage.

This method provides only a hint to the underlying network code. To determine the actual receive buffer size, use `getReceiveBufferSize()`.

PARAMETERS

`size` The size of the buffer, in bytes, to use when receiving data. `size` > `0`.

EXCEPTIONS

`IllegalArgumentException`
If `size` ≤ `0`.

`SocketException`
If an error occurred while setting the associated socket option.

SEE ALSO `SocketImpl.setOption()`, `getReceiveBufferSize()`, `setSendBufferSize()`, `SocketOption.SO_RCVBUF`.

EXAMPLE See `getReceiveBufferSize()`.

1.2 setSendBufferSize()

PURPOSE Sets the send buffer size of this `Socket`.

SYNTAX

```
public synchronized void setSendBufferSize(int size) throws
    SocketException
```

DESCRIPTION This method is used to provide a hint to the underlying platform-specific network code as to the buffer size to use when sending data from this `Socket`. A larger size can increase throughput, but it also will increase memory usage.

This method provides only a hint to the underlying network code. To determine the actual send buffer size, use `getSendBufferSize()`.

PARAMETERS

`size` The size of the buffer, in bytes, to use when sending data. `size` > `0`.

EXCEPTIONS

`IllegalArgumentException`
If `size` ≤ `0`.

`SocketException`
If an error occurred while setting the associated socket option.

SEE ALSO `SocketImpl.setOption()`, `getSendBufferSize()`, `setReceiveBufferSize()`, `SocketOption.SO_SNDBUF`.

EXAMPLE See `getSendBufferSize()`.

S

SocketOptions

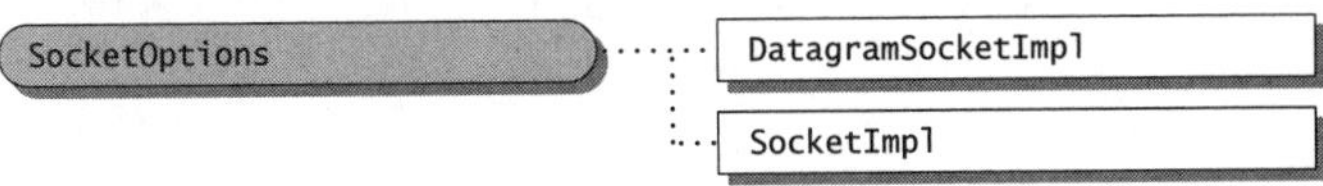

Syntax

```
public interface SocketOptions
```

Description

The `SocketOptions` interface contains methods and constants for setting and getting socket options. It must be implemented by concrete subclasses of `SocketImpl` and `DatagramSocketImpl` to allow options to be set in and retrieved from the implementation.

Usage

The methods and constants in this interface are used by the socket classes (`Socket`, `ServerSocket`, `DatagramSocket`, and `MulticastSocket`) for their socket implementations. You use these methods and constants only if you are defining a subclass of one of these socket classes.

If you are implementing a concrete subclass of `SocketImpl` or `DatagramSocketImpl`, you need to provide implementations for `getOption()` and `setOption()`.

MEMBER SUMMARY	
Socket Option Methods	
`getOption()`	Retrieves the value of a socket option.
`setOption()`	Sets a socket option.
Socket Option Constants	
`IP_MULTICAST_IF`	Socket option for getting and setting the outgoing network interface in multicast packets.
`SO_BINDADDR`	Socket option for retrieving the local address bound to a socket.
`SO_LINGER`	Socket option for setting and getting the linger-on-close timeout value.
`SO_RCVBUF`	Socket option for setting and getting the buffer size for reading incoming packets.
`SO_REUSEADDR`	Socket option for enabling and disabling local address reuse.
`SO_SNDBUF`	Socket option for setting and getting the buffer size for sending packets.
`SO_TIMEOUT`	Socket option for setting and getting the socket timeout value.
`TCP_NODELAY`	Socket option for enabling and disabling Nagle's algorithm.

See Also

`DatagramSocket, DatagramSocketImpl, MulticastSocket, ServerSocket, Socket, SocketImpl.`

getOption()

PURPOSE Retrieves the value of a socket option.

SYNTAX `public Object getOption(int optID) throws SocketException`

DESCRIPTION This method retrieves the value of the socket option `optID`. If `optID` specifies an option that has a primitive type, it is returned using its corresponding wrapper class. For example, an `Integer` instance is used to represent a numeric socket option value, while a `Boolean` is used to represent a `boolean` socket option.

PARAMETERS

`optID` An `int` specifying the socket option whose value to return.

RETURNS A non-`null` object representing the option's value.

SEE ALSO `setOption()`.

EXCEPTIONS

`SocketException`

If the socket option cannot be gotten because the socket is closed or the socket implementation does not support getting the option identified by `optID`.

EXAMPLE See any of the `SocketOptions` constants examples.

IP_MULTICAST_IF

PURPOSE Constant representing a socket option for getting and setting the outgoing network interface in multicast packets.

SYNTAX `public final static int IP_MULTICAST_IF`

DESCRIPTION This is a constant that represents a socket option for getting and setting the outgoing network interface in multicast packets. It is useful on a multihomed host—a machine with more than one network interface, each having its own `IP` address. This socket option is used by `MulticastSocket.setInterface()` to control which one of those multiple network interfaces should be used to send multicast packets. It is also used by `MulticastSocket.getInterface()` to determine which interface is being used.

The result of getOption() and the argument to setOption() are of class InetAddress when getting and setting the IP_MULTICAST_IF option. The value of this constant is 0x10.

SEE ALSO MulticastSocket.getInterface(), MulticastSocket.setInterface().

EXAMPLE

```
// Specify InetAddress for multicast to use
impl.setOption(SocketOptions.IP_MULTICAST_IF,
    InetAddress.getByName("129.11.11.11"));
// Read it back
InetAddress addr = (InetAddress)impl.getOption(SocketOptions.IP_MULTICAST_IF);
```

setOption()

PURPOSE Sets a socket option.

SYNTAX
```
public void setOption(int optID, Object val) throws
    SocketException
```

DESCRIPTION This method sets the socket option optID to the value val. The type of val depends on optID. For example, a boolean socket option takes a Boolean instance, while a socket option such as IP_MULTICAST_IF takes an InetAddress instance.

PARAMETERS

optID An int that identifies the socket option.

value The new value of the socket option.

EXCEPTIONS

SocketException

If the socket option cannot be set because the socket has been closed or optID is not an option recognized by the implementation or the option cannot be set to val.

EXAMPLE See any of the SocketOptions constants examples.

SO_BINDADDR

PURPOSE Constant representing a socket option for retrieving the local address bound to a socket.

SYNTAX
```
public final static int SO_BINDADDR
```

DESCRIPTION This is a constant that represents a socket option for retrieving the local address bound to a socket. When you create a socket for Socket, DatagramSocket, or ServerSocket, you can specify a local IP address to which to bind the socket. This is useful when creating a socket on a multihomed host—a machine with more than one network interface, each having its own IP address. If you don't explicitly specify a local IP address to use, it defaults to the platform-dependent system default.

The socket implementation classes use this socket option to determine which local address is being used. The result of `getOption()` is of class `InetAddress` when getting the `SO_BINDADDR` option. The value of this constant is `0x000F`.

SEE ALSO `DatagramSocket.getLocalAddress()`, `Socket.getLocalAddress()`, `ServerSocket.getLocalAddress()`.

EXAMPLE

```
// Read bound addr
InetAddress addr = (InetAddress)impl.getOption(SocketOptions.SO_BINDADDR);
```

SO_LINGER

PURPOSE Constant representing a socket option for setting and getting the linger-on-close timeout value.

SYNTAX `public final static int SO_LINGER`

DESCRIPTION This is a constant representing a socket option for setting and getting the linger-on-close timeout value. The linger-on-close timeout value affects how a socket behaves when it closes. See the `Socket` class description in *The Java Class Libraries, Second Edition, Volume 1* for a detailed description of this option.

The socket implementation classes use this socket option to set and get the linger-on-close timeout value. When the `SO_LINGER` option is being get or set, a `Boolean` value of `false` indicates that the option has been disabled, while an `Integer` value indicates that the option has been enabled with the timeout (in seconds) contained in the `Integer`. The value of this constant is `0x0080`.

S

SEE ALSO `Socket.getSoLinger()`, `Socket.setSoLinger()`.

EXAMPLE

```
// Disable SO_LINGER
impl.setOption(SocketOptions.SO_LINGER, new Boolean(false));

// Enable it with time-out of 1 sec
impl.setOption(SocketOptions.SO_LINGER, new Integer(1000));

// Read it back
int timeout;
Object obj = impl.getOption(SocketOptions.SO_LINGER);
if (obj instanceof Integer) {
    timeout = ((Integer)obj).intValue();
}
```

SO_RCVBUF

PURPOSE Constant representing a socket option for setting and getting the buffer size for reading incoming packets.

SYNTAX `public final static int SO_RCVBUF`

DESCRIPTION This is a constant that represents a socket option for setting and getting the buffer size for reading incoming packets. When this socket option is used with `setOption()`, it suggests a buffer size (in number of bytes) for the platform's networking code to use when reading incoming packets. When this socket option is used with `getOption()`, it returns an `Integer` of the actual buffer size being used.

The result of `getOption()` and the argument to `setOption()` are of class `Integer` when getting and setting the `SO_RCVBUF` option. The value of this constant is `0x1002`.

SEE ALSO `DatagramSocket.getReceiveBufferSize()`, `DatagramSocket.setReceiveSize()`, `Socket.getReceiveBufferSize()`, `Socket.setReceiveSize()`.

EXAMPLE

```
// Set receive buffer size of 1k
impl.setOption(SocketOptions.SO_RCVBUF, new Integer(1024));

// Read back actual size used
int size = ((Integer)(impl.getOption(SocketOptions.SO_RCVBUF))).intValue();
```

SO_REUSEADDR

PURPOSE Constant representing a socket option for enabling and disabling local address reuse.

SYNTAX `public final static int SO_REUSEADDR`

DESCRIPTION This is a constant that represents a socket option for enabling and disabling local address reuse. When you create a unicast socket for `Socket`, `DatagramSocket`, or `ServerSocket`, it is bound to a port on the local machine. Once bound, that port cannot be reused until the socket is closed. By contrast, more than one multicast sockets can share one port. This happens, for example, when these sockets are all part of the same multicast group.

This socket option is used by multicast socket implementations to enable local address reuse. The result of `getOption()` and the argument to `setOption()` are of class `Integer` when getting and setting the `SO_REUSEADDR` option. If the `Integer` contains a nonzero value, the option is enabled; if the `Integer` contains a `0`, the option is disabled. The value of this constant is `0x04`.

S

SEE ALSO `MulticastSocket.MulticastSocket()`.

EXAMPLE

```
// Enable SO_REUSEADDR
impl.setOption(SocketOptions.SO_REUSEADDR, new Integer(-1));
```

SO_SNDBUF

PURPOSE Constant representing a socket option for setting and getting the buffer size for sending packets.

SYNTAX `public final static int SO_SNDBUF`

DESCRIPTION This is a constant that represents a socket option for setting and getting the buffer size for sending packets. When this socket option is used with `setOption()`, it suggests a buffer size (in number of bytes) for the platform's networking code to use when sending packets. When this socket option is used with `getOption()`, it returns an `Integer` of the actual buffer size being used.

The result of `getOption()` and the argument to `setOption()` are of class `Integer` when getting and setting the `SO_SNDBUF` option. The value of this constant is `0x1001`.

SEE ALSO `DatagramSocket.getSendBufferSize()`, `DatagramSocket.setSendSize()`, `Socket.getSendBufferSize()`, `Socket.setSendSize()`.

EXAMPLE

```
// Set send buffer size of 1k
impl.setOption(SocketOptions.SO_SNDBUF, new Integer(1024));

// Read back actual size used
int size = ((Integer)(impl.getOption(SocketOptions.SO_SNDBUF))).intValue();
```


SO_TIMEOUT

PURPOSE Constant representing a socket option for setting and getting the socket timeout value.

SYNTAX `public final static int SO_TIMEOUT`

DESCRIPTION This is a constant that represents a socket option for setting and getting the socket timeout value. The socket timeout value affects how a socket behaves when it performs an operation on the socket that blocks. See the `Socket` class description in *The Java Class Libraries, Second Edition, Volume 1* for a detailed description of this option.

The socket implementation classes use this socket option to set and get the socket timeout value. The result of `getOption()` and the argument to `setOption()` are of class `Integer` when getting and setting the `SO_TIMEOUT` option. The value of this constant is `0x1006`.

SEE ALSO `DatagramSocket.setSoTimeout()`, `Socket.setSoTimeout()`, `ServerSocket.setSoTimeout()`.

EXAMPLE

```
// Set time-out of 1 sec
impl.setOption(SocketOptions.SO_TIMEOUT, new Integer(1000));

// Read it back
int timeout = ((Integer)impl.getOption(SocketOptions.SO_TIMEOUT)).intValue();
```

TCP_NODELAY

PURPOSE Constant representing a socket option for enabling and disabling Nagle's algorithm.

SYNTAX `public final static int TCP_NODELAY`

DESCRIPTION This is a constant that represents a socket option for enabling and disabling Nagle's algorithm. The socket option for Nagle's algorithm for TCP data coalescing is described in the `Socket` class description in *The Java Class Libraries, Second Edition, Volume 1.*

The socket implementation classes use this socket option to enable and disable Nagle's algorithm and to determine whether the algorithm has been enabled for the socket. The result of `getOption()` and the argument to `setOption()` are of class `Boolean` when getting and setting the `TCP_NODELAY` option. If the `Boolean` is `true`, the algorithm is disabled; if the `Boolean` is `false`, the algorithm is enabled. The value of this constant is `0x0001`.

SEE ALSO `Socket.getTcpNoDelay()`, `Socket.setTcpNoDelay()`.

EXAMPLE

```
// Enable TCP_NODELAY (i.e., disable Nagle's algorithm)
impl.setOption(SocketOptions.TCP_NODELAY, new Boolean(true));
// Read it back
boolean tcpNoDelay =
    ((Boolean)impl.getOption(SocketOptions.TCP_NODELAY)).booleanValue();
```

java.net

SocketPermission

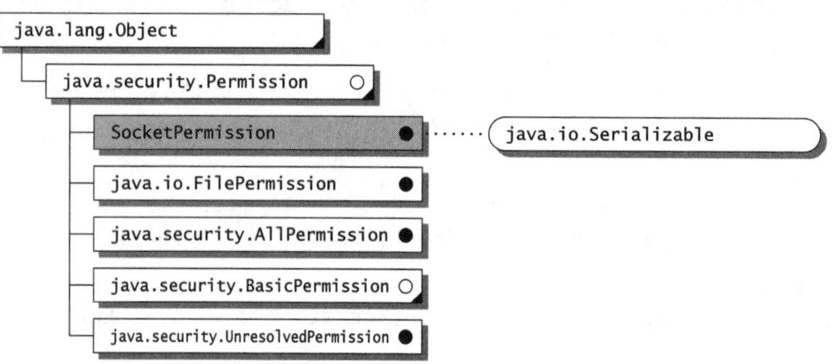

Syntax

```
public final class SocketPermission extends Permission
```

Description

The `SocketPermission` class represents a request to access the network by using sockets. It is used internally by the Java runtime system to enforce its security policy whenever an attempt is made to use sockets. A `SocketPermission` object consists of a *permission name*, which names the machine and optionally the port number, and a set of *actions*, which lists the type of access requested. For example, a `SocketPermission` with the permission name `"java.sun.com:80"` and action `"connect"` represents a request to connect a socket to the machine `java.sun.com` at port 80. It is used by the security manager to check whether the calling thread is allowed to perform the requested operation. If the thread is not allowed, a `SecurityException` is thrown.

In Version 1.2, all of the "check" methods relating to sockets in the `SecurityManager` class have been rewritten to use the `SocketPermission` class. This rewrite is useful to systems that formerly wrote and installed their own security manager but is otherwise transparent to users of the `SecurityManager` class.

S

A brief discussion of the Version 1.2 security model is given in the `SecurityManager` class description. More information about Version 1.2's security model and framework is available at `http://java.sun.com/products/jdk/1.2/docs/guide/security/index.html`.

Usage

Applets and applications usually do not directly use the `SocketPermission` class. It is used internally by the Java runtime system to enforce its security policy. For example, when a program tries to connect a socket to the machine `java.sun.com`, the system uses the `SocketPermission("java.sun.com","connect")` object to check that the caller has permission to do so.

An application may explicitly create a `SocketPermission` object and use `SecurityManager.checkPermission()` to check whether it has such permission. But the act of trying to perform the socket operation automatically triggers such a check, so there is seldom a reason to duplicate it.

The SocketPermission Name

The permission name of a `SocketPermission` identifies a machine and optionally the port number. The name can be the machine's name, its IP address (see `InetAddress`), or a DNS domain name prefixed by `"*."`. In the latter case, the name specifies all machines in the DNS domain (including subdomains). For example, `"*.sun.com"` means all machines in the domain `sun.com`, including machine names such as `java.sun.com` and `foo.test.sun.com`. You can also specify a port number or a range of port numbers for the associated machine(s). The port number is separated from the machine name by a colon character (`:`). If the port number has not been specified, it means all port numbers are permitted. Tables 25 and 26 summarize the machine name and port number syntaxes.

Syntax	Description
	(The empty string) The local machine.
`localhost`	The local machine.
hostname	The machine with name *hostname* (for example, "java.sun.com").
ipaddress	The machine at the address *ipaddress* (for example, "123.33.21.23").
*	All machines.
`*.`*domainname*	All machine names in the DNS domain *domainname* and subdomains, excluding *domainname* (for example, "*.sun.com").

TABLE 25: `SocketPermission` Machine Name Syntax.

Syntax	Description
	All port numbers.
`:`*num*	The port number *num*.
`:-`*num*	All port numbers ≤ *num*.
`:`*num*`-`	All port numbers ≥ *num*.
`:`*num1*`-`*num2*	All port numbers ≥ *num1* and ≤ *num2*.

TABLE 26: `SocketPermission` Port Number Syntax.

S

SocketPermission Actions

The actions of a `SocketPermission` identify the socket operations. See Table 27. In that table, the **Action** column contains keywords to use when specifying the actions. The actions are specified in a string containing a comma-separated sequence of one or more of these keywords. Whitespace characters (blank, `\n`, `\r`, `\f`, and `\t`) may appear before and after a keyword. Character case is not significant. For example, the actions `"connect,accept"` mean the code can accept connections from, and create connections to, the machine/port named in the permission. The `"resolve"` action is special in that any of the other actions also *implies* `"resolve"`. That is, if you specify `"accept"`, `"resolve"` is also implicitly specified.

Action	Request
`accept`	Accept a socket connection from the specified machine.
`connect`	Connect a socket to the specified machine/port.
`listen`	Bind a socket to the local machine/port for listening for new socket connection requests.
`resolve`	Resolve a machine name to its IP address.

TABLE 27: `SocketPermission` Actions.

Implies

The permission name and actions of a `SocketPermission` object are used to determine whether one `SocketPermission` *implies* another `SocketPermission`. Permission *A* implies permission *B* means if permission *A* is granted, so will permission *B*. Following are the rules for how "implies" works for `SocketPermission` objects.

- Two `SocketPermissions` with the same permission name and actions imply each other.
- A `SocketPermission` *A* implies the `SocketPermission` *B* if *B*'s actions are a subset of *A*'s and the machines and ports identified by *B*'s permission name are a subset *A*'s.

Any one of `"accept"`, `"connect"`, and `"listen"` implies `"resolve"`.

In addition to these two simple rules, `SocketPermission` also performs additional checks at the time its `implies()` method is invoked so as to minimize the chances of security attacks. See the `implies()` method for details.

accept

A `SocketPermission` with the `"accept"` action represents a request to accept a socket connection from the specified host and port number. A `SocketPermission` with this action is used by `DatagramSocket.receive()` and `ServcerSocket.accept()` to check whether this permission has been granted by the security policy. See `SecurityManager.checkAccept()`.

connect

A SocketPermission with the "connect" action represents a request to create a socket connection to the specified host and port number. A SocketPermission with this action is used by DatagramSocket.send(), Multicast.send(), and Socket.Socket() to check whether this permission has been granted by the security policy. See SecurityManager.checkConnect().

listen

A SocketPermission with the "listen" action represents a request to bind to a port on the local machine so that it can listen for connections to that port. The host name of the permission name is ignored. This permission is used by DatagramSocket.DatagramSocket(), MulticastSocket.MulticastSocket(), and ServerSocket.ServerSocket() to check whether this permission has been granted by the security policy. See SecurityManager.checkListen().

resolve

A SocketPermission with the "listen" action represents a request to resolve the machine named in the permission name to an IP address. Any port number specified in the permission name is ignored. This permission is used by the following methods: DatagramSocket.getLocalAddress(); getByName(), getAllByName(), getHostName(), and getLocalHost() in the InetAddress class. This action is implied by the other actions such that it need not be explicitly specified if any of the other actions is specified. See SecurityManager.checkConnect().

MEMBER SUMMARY	
Constructor	
SocketPermission()	Constructs a new SocketPermission instance.
Action Retrieval Method	
getActions()	Generates the canonical string representation of this SocketPermission's actions.
Permission Checking Methods	
implies()	Checks if this SocketPermission *implies* another permission.
newPermissionCollection()	Creates a new PermissionCollection for storing SocketPermission objects.
Object Methods	
equals()	Determines whether an object is equal to this SocketPermission.
hashCode()	Computes the hash code for this SocketPermission.

S

See Also

`DatagramSocket, MulticastSocket, ServerSocket, Socket, java.lang.SecurityManager, java.security.Permission.`

Example

This example shows how to use `SocketPermission` to check whether the program has permission to connect to the `java.sun.com` machine before doing so. As mentioned in the class description, there is usually no need for the program to do this check explicitly because the `DatagramSocket` constructor will perform the check automatically. This example is just for illustrative purposes.

You run the program with the `.policy` file. If you omit this file, you will get an `AccessControlException` (a subclass of `SecurityException`).

Main.java

```
SocketPermission fp = new SocketPermission("java.sun.com", "connect");
try {
    AccessController.checkPermission(fp);
    System.out.println(InetAddress.getByName("java.sun.com"));
    Socket socket = new Socket("java.sun.com", 80);
    socket.close();
} catch (IOException e) {
    e.printStackTrace();
} catch (SecurityException e) {
    e.printStackTrace();
}
```

.policy

```
keystore ".keystore";
 grant {
          permission java.net.SocketPermission "java.sun.com", "connect";
       };
```

Output

```
>java -Djava.security.policy=.policy Main
```

S

equals()

PURPOSE	Determines whether an object is equal to this `SocketPermission`.
SYNTAX	`public boolean equals(Object obj)`
DESCRIPTION	This method determines whether an object `obj` is equal to this `SocketPermission`. Two `SocketPermissions` are equal if they have the same actions and same machine name/port number designations. The case of the letters in the machine name is ignored.
PARAMETERS	
`obj`	The possibly `null` object to check.

RETURNS `true` if `obj` is a `SocketPermission` instance with the same actions and same machine name/port number designations as this `SocketPermission`.

OVERRIDES `java.lang.Object.equals()`.

SEE ALSO `hashCode()`.

EXAMPLE

```
SocketPermission p1 = new SocketPermission("*", "listen, accept");
SocketPermission p2 = new SocketPermission("java.sun.com:80", "connect");
SocketPermission p3 = new SocketPermission("java.sun.com", "connect");
SocketPermission p4 = new SocketPermission("JAVA.SUN.COM", "resolve, connect");

System.out.println(p1.equals(p2)); // false
System.out.println(p2.equals(p3)); // false because port is different
System.out.println(p3.equals(p4)); // true because connect implies resolve
                                   // and case in host name is ignored

System.out.println(p1.hashCode()); // 42
System.out.println(p2.hashCode()); // 1352280493
System.out.println(p3.hashCode()); // 1352280493
System.out.println(p4.hashCode()); // 1352280493
```

getActions()

PURPOSE Generates the canonical string representation of this `SocketPermission`'s actions.

SYNTAX `public String getActions()`

DESCRIPTION This method generates the canonical string representation of this `SocketPermission`'s actions. The result might not be the same string passed into the constructor, but it will denote the same actions that were specified to the constructor. The keywords for the actions of the `SocketPermission` are listed in the following order (in lowercase): `connect`, `listen`, `accept`, `resolve`. An action that is not part of this `SocketPermission` is not listed. Each keyword is separated by a comma and there is no whitespace in the string. The `"connect"`, `"listen"`, and `"accept"` actions implicitly include `"resolve"` as well. So even if `"resolve"` was not explicitly specified in the constructor, it will show up in the list.

RETURNS The non-`null` canonical string representation of the actions of this `SocketPermission`.

OVERRIDES `java.security.Permission.getActions()`.

EXAMPLE

```
System.out.println(
    new SocketPermission("java.sun.com", "  connect").getActions());
                                        // connect, resolve
System.out.println(
```

S

```
        new SocketPermission("java.sun.com", "accept, connect").getActions());
                                             // connect, accept, resolve
    System.out.println(
        new SocketPermission("java.sun.com", "resolve").getActions());
                                             // resolve
    System.out.println(new SocketPermission("java.sun.com", "").getActions());
                                             // IllegalArgumentException
                                             // bad args constructor
```

hashCode()

PURPOSE Computes the hash code for this `SocketPermission` object.

SYNTAX `public int hashCode()`

DESCRIPTION This method computes the hash code for this `SocketPermission` object. The hash code for a `SocketPermission` object is computed using information obtained from the machine name of the object only (not the port nor the actions) such that if two `SocketPermission` objects are equal, they will have the same hash code. Note, however, that two different `SocketPermissions` might also have the same hash code. The hash code is typically used as the key in a hash table.

RETURNS An `int` representing the hash code of this object.

OVERRIDES `java.lang.Object.hashCode()`.

SEE ALSO `equals()`, `java.util.HashMap()`, `java.util.Hashtable()`.

EXAMPLE See `equals()`.

implies()

PURPOSE Checks if this `SocketPermission` object *implies* another permission.

SYNTAX `public boolean implies(Permission perm)`

DESCRIPTION This method checks if this `SocketPermission` object *implies* the permission `perm`. This `SocketPermission` *implies* `perm` if, and only if, any actions on the machine/port identified by `perm` are also requested by this `SocketPermission`. That is, `perm`'s actions must be a subset of this `SocketPermission` and the machines and ports identified by `perm` must be a subset of those identified by this `SocketPermission`. If `perm` is `null` or not an instance of `SocketPermission`, this method returns `false`.

When wildcard names are involved (such as `"*.sun.com"`), this method performs checks to minimize chances for attacks. It checks that `perm`'s machine name maps to an IP address and does a reverse lookup on that IP address to verify that `perm`'s machine name is what it claims to be. For example, if this permission has as its name "*.sun.com" and perm's name is "foo.test.-sun.com" (the name of a nonexistent machine), then this method will return false because it cannot obtain foo.test.sun.com's IP address. Alternatively, if foo.test.sun.com does exist but the reverse lookup reveals that its name is "bar.chaos.com", this method will also return false.

There are some limitations to these verification checks. First, since the specification of machine names is in DNS notation, these verification checks are highly dependent on the naming service—the entity that does the machine name-to-IP address and IP address-to-machine name resolutions—that returns fully qualified machine names. This might be a problem for some intranets that deploy enterprise-level naming services that do not return fully qualified machine names. NIS and NIS+ are examples of these naming services. The workaround is to configure the client machine to use DNS as the first naming service and NIS/NIS+ as the secondary naming services. Second, a *multi-homed* machine is one that has multiple network interfaces. Such a machine has multiple IP addresses—one per network interface—and corresponding machine names. For such machines, a reverse lookup on one IP address might return a different machine name (depending on the IP address used to perform the reverse lookup), hence causing the verification to fail. The workaround is to name such machines explicitly in the permission instead of depending on wildcards.

A similar problem exists with mirrored hosts, whereby one popular machine/host name (such java.sun.com) is actually mapped to multiple physical machines. This has similar problems as the multihomed machine case, and the workaround is the same. A machine that is behind a fire-wall also faces similar problems. A client outside the fire-wall will not be able to resolve the machine's name, and consequently the implies check will fail. The workaround is to use the machine's IP address in the permission.

PARAMETERS

perm The possibly null permission to check.

RETURNS true if perm is implied by this object; false otherwise.

OVERRIDES java.lang.Permission.implies().

EXAMPLE

```
SocketPermission p0 = new SocketPermission("localhost:0", "connect");
SocketPermission p1 = new SocketPermission("*", "connect");
SocketPermission p2 = new SocketPermission("*:1024-2048", "connect");
SocketPermission p3 = new SocketPermission("*.sun.com", "accept");
SocketPermission p4 = new SocketPermission("java.sun.com", "accept");
SocketPermission p5 = new SocketPermission("foo.test.sun.com", "accept");
SocketPermission p6 = new SocketPermission("java.sun.com", "resolve");
SocketPermission p7 = new SocketPermission("java.sun.com:-555", "accept");
SocketPermission p8 = new SocketPermission("*.test.sun.com:-555", "accept");
SocketPermission p9 = new SocketPermission("sun.com:-555", "accept");
```

```
System.out.println(p1.implies(p2));              // true
System.out.println(p1.implies(p3));              // false (accept != connect)
System.out.println(p3.implies(p4));              // false (mirrored host)
System.out.println(p3.implies(p5));              // false (nonexistent machine)
System.out.println(p3.implies(p6));              // false (mirrored host)
System.out.println(p4.implies(p6));              // true
System.out.println(p4.implies(p7));              // true
System.out.println(p3.implies(p8));              // true
System.out.println(p3.implies(p9));              // false

System.out.println(p1.implies(p0));              // true

System.out.println(p1.implies(new FilePermission("java.sun.com:80", "read")));
                                                 // false
System.out.println(p1.implies(null));            // false
```

newPermissionCollection()

PURPOSE Creates a new `PermissionCollection` for storing `SocketPermission` objects.

SYNTAX `public PermissionCollection newPermissionCollection()`

DESCRIPTION This method creates a new `PermissionCollection` for storing `SocketPermission` objects. With a single `SocketPermission`, you can ask (via the `implies()` method) whether it implies another permission. With a `PermissionCollection`, you can ask whether the collection of permissions implies another permission. The Java runtime system, for example, will make such a test when it tries to determine whether the caller is allowed to perform an action based on the `SocketPermissions` granted to the caller by the security policy.

RETURNS A new non-`null` `PermissionCollection` suitable for storing `SocketPermissions`. If you attempt to add an object that is not an instance of `SocketPermission` to the collection, an `IllegalArgumentException` is thrown.

S

OVERRIDES `java.security.Permission.newPermissionCollection()`.

SEE ALSO `implies()`, `java.security.PermissionCollection`.

EXAMPLE

```
SocketPermission[] p = new SocketPermission[3];

// Allow connections to "*.xeo.com" subtree, including its root
p[0] = new SocketPermission("xeo.com", "connect");
p[1] = new SocketPermission("*.xeo.com", "connect");

// Allow resolution of all names under .com
p[2] = new SocketPermission("*.com", "resolve");

PermissionCollection col = p[0].newPermissionCollection();
for (int i = 0; i < p.length; i++) {
    col.add(p[i]);
}
```

```
// OK to connect to www.xeo.com?
System.out.println(col.implies(
    new SocketPermission("www.xeo.com", "connect")));
                                                       // true
// OK to connect/resolve www.xeo.com?
System.out.println(col.implies(
    new SocketPermission("www.xeo.com:90", "connect, resolve")));
                                                       // true
// OK to resolve www.altavista.com
System.out.println(col.implies(
    new SocketPermission("www.altavista.com", "resolve")));
                                                       // true
// Not OK to resolve com
System.out.println(col.implies(
    new SocketPermission("com", "resolve")));          // false
```

SocketPermission()

PURPOSE Constructs a new `SocketPermission` instance.

SYNTAX `public SocketPermission(String pname, String action)`

DESCRIPTION This constructor creates a new `SocketPermission` instance. The name of this permission is `pname` and has the syntax described in the class description. `actions` contains a list of one or more of the comma-separated keywords listed in Table 27. It specifies the actions that can be performed on the objects named by `pname`, as described in the class description.

PARAMETERS

`actions` A non-`null` string specifying the actions of the new `SocketPermission`.

`pname` A non-`null` string identifying the host and port for the new `SocketPermission`.

EXCEPTIONS

`IllegalArgumentException`

If `actions` is the empty string or has an invalid action, or if `pname` specifies the host or port number syntaxes incorrectly.

EXAMPLE See `equals()`.

S

java.lang.ref SoftReference

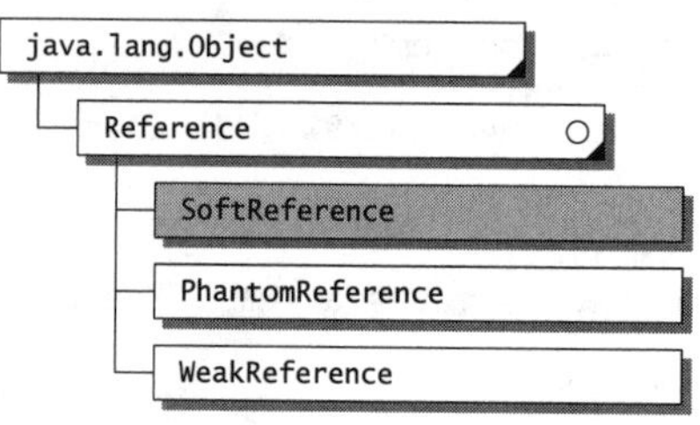

Syntax

```
public class SoftReference extends Reference
```

Description

The `SoftReference` class represents a *soft reference*, which is a type of reference object (see `Reference`) that is slightly weaker than a Java reference when it comes to preventing an object from being garbage collected. A Java reference to an object prevents the object from being collected in all situations, whereas a soft reference to an object (the *referent*) prevents the object from being collected only until memory is low. See Figure 19.

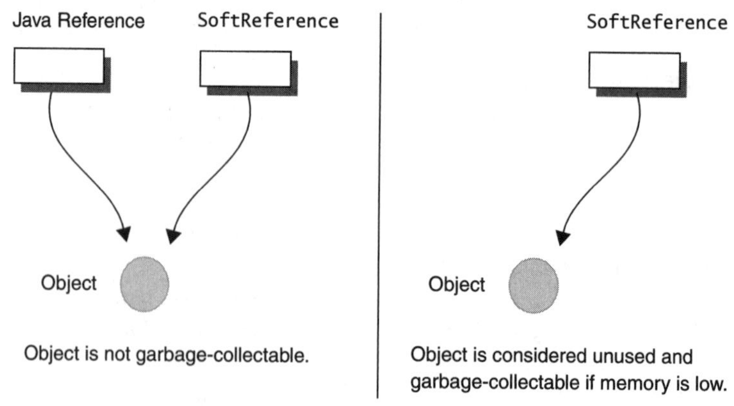

FIGURE 19: An Object's Garbage-Collectable State.

As long as a Java reference refers to an object, that object will never be garbage collected. However, an object no longer being referenced by any Java reference is considered to be *unused*. At this point, if the object is being referenced by a soft reference, the object will not be garbage collected. In fact, the object can be continually retrieved and used through the soft reference. However, note that accessing the object changes the object's status from *unused* to *used*.

When memory is low, the garbage collector looks for all unused objects referred to by soft references and then *clears* the soft references. When a soft reference is *cleared*, you can no longer get to the referent and the referent begins its way through the stages of being garbage collected. The goal is to free up enough memory with these objects to avoid an `OutOfMemory-`

S

Exception. In fact, the garbage collector guarantees that all soft references will be cleared and collected before it throws an OutOfMemoryException.

Soft references are most often used in caches when the objects are fairly expensive to create but are not always used. The soft reference allows an unused object to remain in the cache in case it might be called upon but does not prevent the object from being garbage collected if memory is tight.

A soft reference object is enqueued at most once even if the referent is *resurrected* while being collected. (This situation can arise with the use of finalizers; see *The Java Language Specification, First Edition*, Section 12.6, for more details.) Thus if the referent is resurrected and you still want soft reference notification on the referent, you must create a new soft reference on the referent.

Usage

To have an object retained until memory is low, you need only to create a soft reference to the object. If you need to retrieve the object, use the soft reference's get() method. If get() returns null, the object is being garbage collected.

To receive notification of when an object obj is being garbage collected, you first must create a reference queue (see ReferenceQueue). You then construct a soft reference object, supplying both obj and the reference queue. Finally, you poll the reference queue. When the soft reference object appears in the queue, you know that obj is being garbage collected. Following is some sample code that demonstrates the steps.

```
ReferenceQueue q = new ReferenceQueue();
SoftReference sr = new SoftReference(obj, q);
try {
    Reference r = rq.remove();
} catch (InterruptedException e) {
    e.printStackTrace();
}
```

MEMBER SUMMARY	
Constructor	
SoftReference()	Constructs a SoftReference instance.
Referent Retrieval Method	
get()	Retrieves this SoftReference's referent.

See Also

PhantomReference, Reference, ReferenceQueue, WeakReference.

Example

This example declares a class that parses and counts the frequency of words in a text file. The words and their frequency are kept in a HashMap. The HashMap is referenced by a soft reference, which means it will be cleared when memory is low. If the soft reference is cleared and subsequently used, the HashMap is automatically reconstructed.

This example creates a HashMap, causes all memory to be consumed, and then retrieves the HashMap again. Since the soft reference was cleared, the HashMap must be reconstructed.

```
import java.lang.ref.*;
import java.io.*;
import java.util.*;

class Main {
    public static void main(String[] args) throws IOException {
        WordCount wc = new WordCount(args[0]);
        System.out.println(wc.getMap());

        // Cause an OutOfMemoryException
        eatMemory(new LinkedList());

        // Print out the words again.
        System.out.println(wc.getMap());
    }

    static void eatMemory(LinkedList l) {
        try {
            l.add(new double[100000]);
            eatMemory(l);
        } catch (OutOfMemoryError e) {
            System.out.println("**** OUT OF MEMORY ****");
            l.clear();
            System.gc();
        }
    }
}

class WordCount {
    String filename;
    SoftReference sr;

    WordCount(String n) throws IOException {
        filename = n;
        sr = new SoftReference(parse(filename));
    }

    Map getMap() throws FileNotFoundException, IOException {
        Map map = (Map)sr.get();

        if (map == null) {
            // Reconstruct the map.
            System.out.println("**** Reconstructing Map ****");
            map = parse(filename);
            sr = new SoftReference(map);
        }
        return map;
    }

    // Returns a map of all the words and their frequency in the file n.
```

```
    Map parse(String n) throws FileNotFoundException, IOException {
        Map map = new HashMap();
        BufferedReader rd = new BufferedReader(new FileReader(n));
        String line;

        while ((line = rd.readLine()) != null) {
            StringTokenizer st = new StringTokenizer(line);
            while (st.hasMoreTokens()) {
                String word = st.nextToken();
                Integer ri = (Integer)map.get(word);
                if (ri == null) {
                    map.put(word, new Integer(1));
                } else {
                    map.put(word, new Integer(ri.intValue()+1));
                }
            }
        }
        return map;
    }
}
```

Input

```
Jack be nimble Jack be quick
```

Output

```
> java -Xmx1m Main input.txt

{nimble=1, Jack=2, quick=1, be=2}
**** OUT OF MEMORY ****
**** Reconstructing Map ****
{nimble=1, Jack=2, quick=1, be=2}
```

get()

PURPOSE	Retrieves this `SoftReference`'s referent.
SYNTAX	`public Object get()`
DESCRIPTION	This method returns the referent of this `SoftReference`. If this `SoftReference` has been cleared (that is, the referent is being garbage collected), this method returns `null`.
RETURNS	A possibly `null` object.
OVERRIDES	`Reference.get()`.
EXAMPLE	See the class example.

SoftReference()

PURPOSE Constructs a `SoftReference` instance.

SYNTAX
```
public SoftReference(Object referent)
public SoftReference(Object referent, ReferenceQueue queue)
```

DESCRIPTION This constructor creates a `SoftReference` instance that refers to `referent`. If `queue` is specified, the garbage collector will enqueue this new `SoftReference` to `queue` sometime after it marks `referent` for collection.

PARAMETERS

`queue`	A non-`null` reference queue.
`referent`	A non-`null` object.

EXAMPLE See the class example.

SortedMap

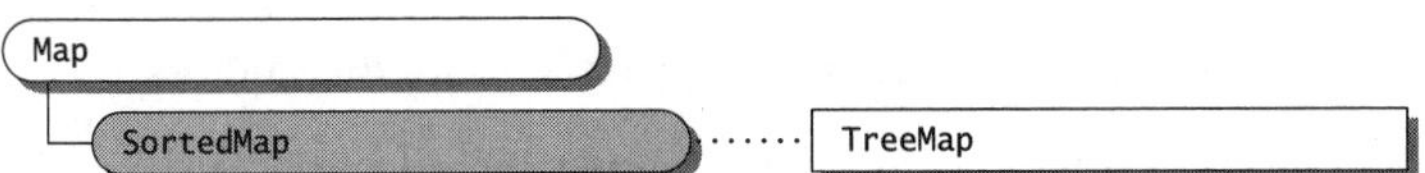

Syntax

```
public interface SortedMap extends Map
```

Description

A `SortedMap` is a collection for holding unique key/value pairs, or *entries*. Sorted maps are similar to maps (see `Map`), except that sorted maps keep their entries in sorted order.

Ordering the Entries—The Comparator

There are two possible ways by which a sorted map determines the order of the entries: use a `Comparator` class or use the `Comparable` interface.

1. If a *comparator* (a class that compares two keys; see `Comparator` for more details) is available, the sorted map orders the keys using the comparator.
2. If there is no comparator, the sorted map requires that all keys implement `Comparable`; any entry whose key does not implement `Comparable` is immediately rejected when it is added (by using the `put()` method) to the map. The sorted map then uses the key's `compareTo()` method to order the entries.

All keys in a map must be *mutually comparable*; that is, `e1.compareTo(e2)` (or `comparator.compare(e1, e2)`) must not throw an exception for any keys `e1` and `e2` in the sorted map. Note that this implies that if `null` is a valid key in a map, that map's keys must use a comparator. Since a call `null.compareTo()` throws an exception, the key must use a comparator.

Element Equality

It is important to note that sorted maps use either the comparator or the key's `compareTo()` method to compare keys. They do not use the keys' `equals()` method to test for equality.

This means that if you want a sorted map to accept exactly the same elements as a nonsorted map, the comparator or `compareTo()` method (whichever is being used) should say that two elements are equal if, and only if, `equals()` claim they are equal. If this condition is not met, then you'll have the case in which if you add an element to a nonsorted map, it might be ignored but if you add the same element to a sorted map, it might be accepted.

If it is not necessary that the sorted map behave exactly like a nonsorted map, the previous condition does not need to hold.

Usage

There is one implementation of this interface available: `TreeMap`. See `TreeMap` for more details.

All implementations of this interface should provide four constructors:

1. A constructor that takes no arguments. This creates an empty sorted map with no comparator.
2. A constructor that takes a comparator. The new sorted map is empty.
3. A constructor that takes a map. The new sorted map is initialized with the entries from the map and has no comparator.
4. A constructor that takes a sorted map. The new sorted map is initialized with the given sorted map's comparator and entries.

MEMBER SUMMARY	
Retrieval Methods	
`firstKey()`	Retrieves the key of the first entry (in sorted order) in this map.
`lastKey()`	Retrieves the key of the last entry (in sorted order) in this map.
SubMap Methods	
`headMap()`	Returns a sorted submap of all entries in this map that precede a particular value.
`subMap()`	Returns a sorted submap of a range of values in this map.
`tailMap()`	Returns a sorted submap of all entries in this map that follow a particular value.
Comparator Retrieval Method	
`comparator()`	Retrieves this map's comparator.

See Also

`TreeMap`.

S

comparator()

PURPOSE Retrieves this map's comparator.

SYNTAX `public Comparator comparator()`

DESCRIPTION This method retrieves this map's comparator. The comparator imposes an ordering on the entries in this map. In particular, the comparator is used on the keys of the entries. If there is no comparator, the `compareTo()` methods of the keys implement the ordering.

RETURNS The comparator used to order this map or `null` if this map does not use a comparator.

SEE ALSO Comparable.

EXAMPLE

```
TreeMap map = new TreeMap();
map.put("dog", null);
map.put("cat", null);
System.out.println( map );                 // {cat=null, dog=null}
System.out.println( map.comparator() );    // null

map = new TreeMap(Collections.reverseOrder());
map.put("cat", null);
map.put("dog", null);
System.out.println( map );                 // {dog=null, cat=null}
System.out.println( map.comparator() );
                     // java.util.Collections$ReverseComparator@335d7cf0
```

firstKey()

PURPOSE Retrieves the key of the first entry (in sorted order) in this map.

SYNTAX `public Object firstKey()`

DESCRIPTION This method returns the key of the first entry in this map. See the class description for information about how the entries are sorted.

RETURNS The first key in this map; the element could be `null`.

EXCEPTIONS

`NoSuchElementException`

If this map is empty.

EXAMPLE

```
TreeMap map = new TreeMap();
map.put("dog", null);
map.put("cat", null);
map.put("pig", null);
System.out.println( map.firstKey() );      // cat
System.out.println( map.lastKey() );       // pig

map = new TreeMap();
System.out.println( map.firstKey() );      // NoSuchElementException
```


headMap()

PURPOSE Returns a sorted submap of all entries in this map that precede a particular value.

SYNTAX `public SortedMap headMap(Object toV)`

DESCRIPTION This method returns a submap containing all of the entries with a key that is < `toV`. This map does not have to contain `toV`.

The returned submap and this map share the same storage. This means that changes to the submap are immediately reflected in this map and changes to this map are immediately reflected in the submap.

If you add an entry to the returned submap whose key is ≥ `toV`, an `IllegalArgumentException` is thrown.

PARAMETERS

`toV` All entries whose keys are < `toV` are included in the submap.

RETURNS A non-`null` map containing all entries from this map whose keys are < `toV`.

EXCEPTIONS

`ClassCastException`
If `toV` cannot be compared with the other keys in this map.

`NullPointerException`
If `toV` is `null` and `null` cannot be compared with the other keys in this map.

EXAMPLE

```
TreeMap map = new TreeMap();
map.put("c", null);
map.put("p", null);
Map headmap = map.headMap("g");
System.out.println( headmap );                          // {c=null}

// You can't add anything to the headmap beyond g.
System.out.println( headmap.put("a", null) );           // null
//System.out.println( headmap.put("g", null) );         // IllegalArgumentException
//System.out.println( headmap.put("h", null) );         // IllegalArgumentException
System.out.println( map );                              // {a=null, c=null, p=nul}

// Add to map and check headmap.
map.put("f", null);
System.out.println( headmap );                          // {a=null, c=null, f=null}
```

lastKey()

PURPOSE Retrieves the key of the last entry (in sorted order) in this map.

SYNTAX `public Object lastKey()`

DESCRIPTION This method returns the key of the last entry in this map. See the class description for information about how the entries are sorted.

RETURNS The last key in this map; the key could be `null`.

EXCEPTIONS

`NoSuchElementException`
If this map is empty.

EXAMPLE See `firstKey()`.

subMap()

PURPOSE Returns a sorted submap of a range of values in this map.

SYNTAX `public SortedMap subMap(Object fromV, Object toV)`

DESCRIPTION This method returns a submap containing all of the entries whose keys are ≥ `fromV` and < `toV`. Neither `fromV` nor `toV` needs to be in this map.

The returned submap and this map share the same storage. This means that changes to the submap are immediately reflected in this map and changes to this map are immediately reflected in the submap.

If you add an entry to the returned submap whose key is < `fromV` or ≥ `toV`, an `IllegalArgumentException` is thrown.

PARAMETERS

`fromV` The lower bound (inclusive) of the submap.

`toV` The upper bound (exclusive) of the submap.

RETURNS A non-`null` submap containing the entries from this map whose keys are ≥ `fromV` and < `toV`.

EXCEPTIONS

`ClassCastException`

If `fromV` or `toV` cannot be compared with the other keys in this map.

`IllegalArgumentException`

If `fromV` > `toV`.

`NullPointerException`

If `fromV` or `toV` is `null` and `null` cannot be compared with the other keys in this map.

`IndexOutOfBoundsException`

If `fromV` > `toV`.

EXAMPLE

```
TreeMap map = new TreeMap();
map.put("c", null);
map.put("p", null);
Map headmap = map.headMap("g");
System.out.println( headmap );                     // {c=null}

// You can't add anything to the headmap beyond g.
System.out.println( headmap.put("a", null) );         // null
//System.out.println( headmap.put("g", null) );      // IllegalArgumentException
//System.out.println( headmap.put("h", null) );      // IllegalArgumentException
System.out.println( map );                         // {a=null, c=null, p=nul}

// Add to map and check headmap.
map.put("f", null);
System.out.println( headmap );                     // {a=null, c=null, f=null}
```

tailMap()

PURPOSE
Returns a sorted submap from all entries in this map that follow a particular value.

SYNTAX
`public SortedMap tailMap(Object fromV)`

DESCRIPTION
This method returns a submap containing all of the entries whose keys are ≥ `fromV`. This map does not have to contain `fromV`.

The returned submap and this map share the same storage. This means that changes to the submap are immediately reflected in this map and changes to this map are immediately reflected in the submap.

If you add an entry to the returned submap whose key is < `fromV`, an `IllegalArgumentException` is thrown.

PARAMETERS

`fromV` All entries whose keys are ≥ `fromV` are included in the submap.

RETURNS
A non-`null` submap containing the entries from this map whose keys are ≥ `fromV`.

EXCEPTIONS

`ClassCastException`
If `fromV` cannot be compared with the other keys in this map.

`NullPointerException`
If `fromV` is `null` and `null` cannot be compared with the other keys in this map.

EXAMPLE

```
TreeMap map = new TreeMap();
map.put("c", null);
map.put("p", null);
Map tailmap = map.tailMap("g");
System.out.println( tailmap );                    // {p=null}

// You can't put anything to the tailmap before g.
//System.out.println( tailmap.put("a", null) );   // IllegalArgumentException
System.out.println( tailmap.put("g", null) );     // null
System.out.println( tailmap.put("z", null) );     // null
System.out.println( map );                       // {c=null, g=null, p=null, z=null}

// Put to map and check tailmap.
map.put("h", null);
System.out.println( tailmap );                   // {g=null, h=null, p=null, z=null}
```

S

SortedSet

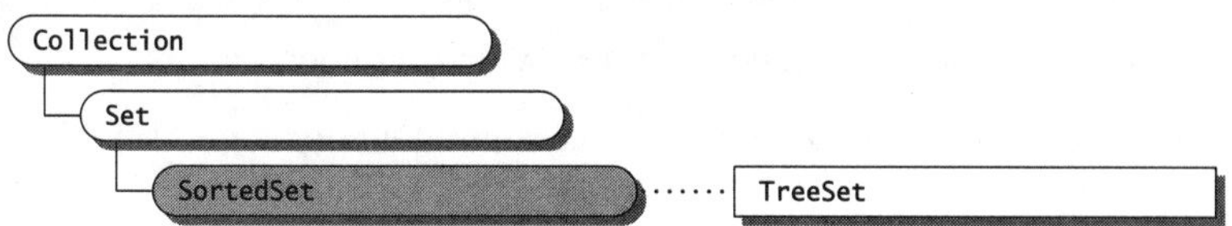

Syntax

```
public interface SortedSet extends Set
```

Description

A `SortedSet` is a collection for holding unique objects (*elements*). Sorted sets are similar to sets (see `Set`), except that they keep their elements in sorted order.

Ordering the Elements—The Comparator

There are two possible ways by which a sorted set determines the order of the elements:

1. If a *comparator* (a class that compares two elements; see `Comparator` for more details) is available, the sorted set orders the elements using the comparator.
2. If there is no comparator, the sorted set then requires that the elements all implement `Comparable`; any element that does not is immediately rejected when it is added (by using the `add()` method) to the set. The sorted set then uses the element's `compareTo()` method to order the elements.

All elements in a set must be *mutually comparable*; that is, `e1.compareTo(e2)` (or `comparator.compare(e1, e2)`) must not throw an exception for any elements `e1` and `e2` in the sorted set. Note that this implies that if `null` is a valid element in a set, that set must use a comparator. Since a call `null.compareTo()` throws an exception, the set must use a comparator.

Element Equality

S

It is important to note that sorted sets use either the comparator or the element's `compareTo()` method to compare elements. Unlike nonsorted sets, they do not use the element's `equals()` method to test for equality.

This means that if you want a sorted set to accept exactly the same elements as a nonsorted set, then the comparator or `compareTo()` method (whichever is being used) should say that two elements are equal if, and only if, `equals()` claims they are equal. If this condition is not met, then you'll have the case in which if you add an element to a nonsorted set, it might be ignored (because `equals()` returned `true`) but if you add the same element to a sorted set, it might be accepted (because `compareTo()` or the comparator returned a nonzero number).

If it is not necessary that a sorted set behave exactly like a nonsorted set, the previous condition does not need to hold.

Usage

There is one implementation of this interface available: `TreeSet`. See `TreeSet` for more details.

All implementations of this interface should provide four constructors:

1. A constructor that takes no arguments. This creates an empty sorted set with no comparator.
2. A constructor that takes a comparator. The new sorted set is empty.
3. A constructor that takes a collection. The new sorted set is initialized with the elements from the collection and has no comparator.
4. A constructor that takes a sorted set. The new sorted set is initialized with the given sorted set's comparator and elements.

MEMBER SUMMARY	
Element Retrieval Methods	
`first()`	Retrieves the first (in sorted order) element in this set.
`last()`	Retrieves the last (in sorted order) element in this set.
SubSet Methods	
`headSet()`	Creates a subset of all of the elements in this set that precede a particular value.
`subSet()`	Creates a subset of a range of values in this set.
`tailSet()`	Creates a subset of all of the elements in this set that follow a particular value.
Comparator Method	
`comparator()`	Retrieves this sorted set's comparator.

See Also

`TreeSet.`

S

comparator()

PURPOSE	Retrieves this sorted set's comparator.
SYNTAX	`public Comparator comparator()`
DESCRIPTION	This method returns this sorted set's comparator. The comparator is used to implement an ordering on the elements in this set. If the comparator is `null`, the element's `compareTo()` method is used to implement the ordering.
RETURNS	The possibly `null` comparator used to order this set.
SEE ALSO	`Comparable.`

EXAMPLE

```
TreeSet set = new TreeSet(Arrays.asList(new Object[]{"dog", "pig", "cat"}));
System.out.println( set );                  // [cat, dog, pig]
System.out.println( set.comparator() );    // null

set = new TreeSet(Collections.reverseOrder());
set.addAll(Arrays.asList(new Object[]{"dog", "pig", "cat"}));
System.out.println( set );                  // [pig, dog, cat]
System.out.println( set.comparator() );
                         // java.util.Collections$ReverseComparator@335d7cf0
```

first()

PURPOSE Retrieves the first (in sorted order) element in this set.

SYNTAX `public Object first()`

DESCRIPTION This method returns the first element in this set. See the class description for information about how the elements are sorted.

RETURNS The first element in this set; the element could be `null`.

EXCEPTIONS

`NoSuchElementException`
If this set is empty.

EXAMPLE

```
TreeSet set = new TreeSet(Arrays.asList(new Object[]{"dog", "pig", "cat"}));
System.out.println( set.first() );      // cat
System.out.println( set.last() );       // pig

set = new TreeSet();
System.out.println( set.first() );      // NoSuchElementException
```

headSet()

PURPOSE Creates a subset of all of the elements in this set that precede a particular value.

SYNTAX `public SortedSet headSet(Object toV)`

DESCRIPTION This method returns a subset containing all of the elements that are < `toV`. This set does not have to contain `toV`.

The returned subset and this set share the same storage. This means that changes to the subset are immediately reflected in this set and changes to this set are immediately reflected in the subset.

If you add an element to the returned subset that is ≥ `toV`, an `IllegalArgumentException` is thrown.

S

PARAMETERS

`toV` All elements that are < `toV` are included in the subset.

RETURNS A non-`null` set containing the elements from this set that are < `toV`.

EXCEPTIONS

`ClassCastException`
If `toV` cannot be compared with the other elements in this set.

`NullPointerException`
If `toV` is `null` and `null` cannot be compared with the other elements in this set.

EXAMPLE

```
TreeSet set = new TreeSet(Arrays.asList(new Object[]{"c", "p"}));
Set headset = set.headSet("g");
System.out.println( headset );                    // [c]

// You can't add anything to the headset beyond g.
System.out.println( headset.add("a") );          // true
//System.out.println( headset.add("g") );        // IllegalArgumentException
//System.out.println( headset.add("h") );        // IllegalArgumentException
System.out.println( set );                        // [a, c, p]

// Add to set and check headset.
set.add("f");
System.out.println( headset );                    // [a, c, f]
```

last()

PURPOSE Retrieves the last (in sorted order) element in this set.

SYNTAX `public Object last()`

DESCRIPTION This method returns the last element in this set. See the class description for information about how the elements are sorted.

RETURNS The last element in this set; the element could be `null`.

EXCEPTIONS

`NoSuchElementException`
If this set is empty.

EXAMPLE See `first()`.

S

subSet()

PURPOSE

Creates a subset of a range of values in this set.

SYNTAX

`public SortedSet subSet(Object fromV, Object toV)`

DESCRIPTION

This method returns a subset containing all of the elements that are ≥ `fromV` and < `toV`. Neither `fromV` nor `toV` needs to be in this set.

The returned subset and this set share the same storage. This means that changes to the subset are immediately reflected in this set and changes to this set are immediately reflected in the subset.

If you add an element to the returned subset that is < `fromV` or ≥ `toV`, an `IllegalArgumentException` is thrown.

PARAMETERS

`fromV` The lower bound (inclusive) of the subset.

`toV` The upper bound (exclusive) of the subset.

RETURNS

A set containing the elements from this set that are ≥ `fromV` and < `toV`.

EXCEPTIONS

`ClassCastException`

If `fromV` or `toV` cannot be compared with the other elements in this set.

`IllegalArgumentException`

If `fromV` > `toV`.

`NullPointerException`

If `fromV` or `toV` is `null` and `null` cannot be compared with the other elements in this set.

EXAMPLE

```
TreeSet set = new TreeSet(Arrays.asList(new Object[]{"c", "u", "p"}));
Set subset = set.subSet("b", "g");
System.out.println( subset );                  // [c]

// You can't add anything to the subset outside of [b e)
//System.out.println( subset.add("a") );  // IllegalArgumentException
System.out.println( subset.add("b") );    // true
System.out.println( subset.add("d") );    // true
//System.out.println( subset.add("g") );  // IllegalArgumentException
//System.out.println( subset.add("h") );  // IllegalArgumentException
System.out.println( set );                 // [b, c, d, p, u]

// Add to set and check subset.
set.add("f");
System.out.println( subset );              // [b, c, d, f]
```

S

tailSet()

PURPOSE Creates a subset of all of the elements in this set that follow a particular value.

SYNTAX `public SortedSet tailSet(Object fromV)`

DESCRIPTION This method returns a subset containing all of the elements that are ≥ `fromV`. This set does not have to contain `fromV`.

The returned subset and this set share the same storage. This means that changes to the subset are immediately reflected in this set and changes to this set are immediately reflected in the subset.

If you add an element to the returned subset that is < `fromV`, an `IllegalArgumentException` is thrown.

PARAMETERS

`fromV` All elements that are ≥ `fromV` are included in the subset.

RETURNS A non-`null` set containing the elements from this set that are ≥ `fromV`.

EXCEPTIONS

`ClassCastException`
If `fromV` cannot be compared with the other elements in this set.

`NullPointerException`
If `fromV` is `null` and `null` cannot be compared with the other elements in this set.

EXAMPLE

```
TreeSet set = new TreeSet(Arrays.asList(new Object[]{"c", "p"}));
Set tailset = set.tailSet("g");
System.out.println( tailset );                  // [p]

// You can't add anything to the tailset before g.
//System.out.println( tailset.add("a") );   // IllegalArgumentException
System.out.println( tailset.add("g") );     // true
System.out.println( tailset.add("z") );     // true
System.out.println( set );                  // [c, g, p, z]

// Add to set and check tailset.
set.add("h");
System.out.println( tailset );              // [g, h, p, z]
```

S

String

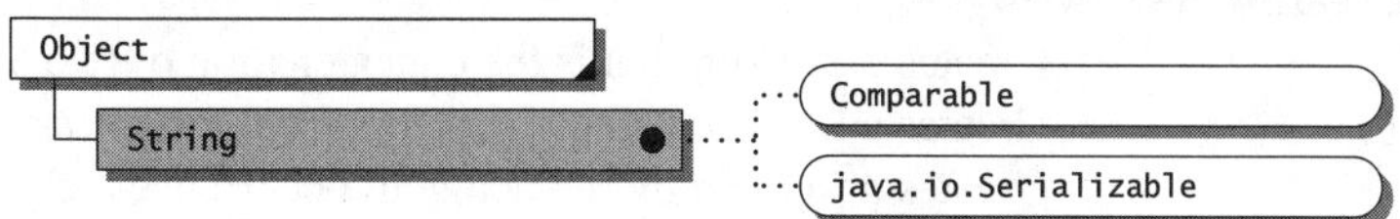

Syntax

```
public final class String implements java.io.Serializable, Comparable
```

Description

The `String` class is used to represent a sequence of characters. Once a `String` instance is created, its contents cannot be modified. This class contains methods for examining and searching the contents of a `String` and methods for creating new `String` instances using existing `String`s and other data types.

See *The Java Class Libraries, Second Edition, Volume 1* for more information about this class.

Changes for Version 1.2

The `String` class implements the `Comparable` interface and has a new overload of the `compareTo()` method that accepts an `Object` as a parameter. It also has a new `compareToIgnoreCase()` method and a built-in `Comparable` implementation, `CASE_INSENSITIVE_ORDER`, for performing comparisons that ignore case.

	MEMBER SUMMARY	
	Constructor	
	`String()`	Constructs a new `String` instance using characters from a `char` array, `byte` array, or `String`.
	Comparison Methods and Constant	
1.2	`CASE_INSENSITIVE_ORDER`	An implementation of `Comparator` whose `compare()` method ignores case.
Δ	`compareTo()`	Compares this `String` to another `String` for equality and Unicode ordering.
1.2	`compareToIgnoreCase()`	Compares this `String` to another `String` for equality and Unicode ordering, ignoring case considerations.
	`equals()`	Determines if this `String` is equal to another `String`.
	`equalsIgnoreCase()`	Performs a case-insensitive comparison of this `String` with another `String`.

Continued

S

MEMBER SUMMARY

Methods for Creating New Strings	
`concat()`	Creates a `String` that is the concatenation of two `Strings`.
`copyValueOf()`	Creates a `String` using characters from a `char` array.
`replace()`	Creates a `String` by replacing all occurrences of a character with another character.
`substring()`	Creates a `String` that is a substring of this `String`.
`toLowerCase()`	Creates a `String` by turning all characters of this `String` into lowercase.
`toUpperCase()`	Creates a `String` by turning all characters of this `String` into uppercase.
`trim()`	Creates a `String` by trimming leading and trailing whitespace characters from this `String`.
`valueOf()`	Creates the string representation of a data value.
Search Methods	
`endsWith()`	Determines if this `String` ends with a specified suffix.
`indexOf()`	Finds the first occurrence of a character or substring within this `String`.
`lastIndexOf()`	Finds the last occurrence of a character or substring within this `String`.
`regionMatches()`	Determines if a region of this `String` matches a region of another `String`.
`startsWith()`	Determines if this `String` starts with a specified prefix.
Conversion Methods	
`charAt()`	Retrieves the character at an index.
`getBytes()`	Retrieves the byte encoding of the characters in this `String`.
`getChars()`	Copies characters from this `String` into the specified `char` array.
`toCharArray()`	Creates a `char` array containing the characters from this `String`.
`toString()`	Generates the string representation of this `String`.
Object Methods	
`hashCode()`	Computes the hash code of this `String`.
`intern()`	Retrieves this `String` from the "string pool."
`length()`	Retrieves the number of characters in this `String`.

S

See Also

`Comparable`, `java.util.Arrays`, `java.util.Comparator`.
`String` in *The Java Class Libraries, Second Edition, Volume 1.*

1.2 CASE_INSENSITIVE_ORDER

PURPOSE An implementation of Comparator whose compare() method ignores case.

SYNTAX `public static final Comparator CASE_INSENSITIVE_ORDER`

DESCRIPTION This implementation uses compareToIgnoreCase() when determining the ordering of strings.

It does not take locale into account. You should use the java.text.Collator class to do locale-sensitive ordering.

SEE ALSO java.text.Collator.

EXAMPLE

```
String[] array = new String[]{"This is a test", "Theo Washer",
                "the case is closed", "tHe aLtErNaTiNg StRiNg"};
java.util.Arrays.sort(array, String.CASE_INSENSITIVE_ORDER);

for (int i = 0; i < array.length; i++) {
    System.out.println(array[i]);
}
```

Δ compareTo()

PURPOSE Compares this String to another String for equality and Unicode ordering.

SYNTAX `public int compareTo(String str)`

SINCE 1.2 `public int compareTo(Object str)`

DESCRIPTION This method compares this String with the string str, character-by-character, according to Unicode ordering. It returns an integer indicating whether the two strings are equal and, if they are not, the ordering of the two strings. If the two strings are identical (they have the same length and the same characters in the same order), this method returns 0. Otherwise, it returns a negative value if the difference—that is, the first different character—of this String precedes that of str in the Unicode code set. A negative value is also returned if this String is a prefix of str. The compareTo() method returns a positive value if the difference of str precedes that of this String in the Unicode code set. A positive value also is returned if str is a prefix of this String. For roman character sets, the positive and negative return values could be used to order strings alphabetically.

Both forms of this method behave the same. If a non-String is passed to the second form of this method, a ClassCastException is thrown.

1.2 CHANGES The form that accepts Object is new in Version 1.2 to satisfy the Comparable interface.

PARAMETERS

`str` The non-`null` `String` with which to compare.

RETURNS `0` if the strings are identical; a negative value if the difference of this `String` is lower in the Unicode code set than that of `str`; a positive value if the difference of this `String` is higher in the Unicode code set.

EXCEPTIONS

`ClassCastException`
If `str` is not an instance of this `String`.

SEE ALSO `Comparable, compareToIgnoreCase().`

EXAMPLE

```
String str = "this is a test";
int r1 = str.compareTo("this is a test and more"); // negative (str shorter)
int r2 = str.compareTo("this is not a test");      // negative ('a' < 'n')
int r3 = str.compareTo("this is a test");          // 0
int r4 = str.compareTo("no, this is not a test");  // positive ('t' > 'n')
int r5 = str.compareTo("this");                    // positive (str longer)
int r6 = str.compareTo(new Integer(10));           // ClassCastException
```

1.2 compareToIgnoreCase()

PURPOSE Compares this `String` to another `String` for equality and Unicode ordering, ignoring case considerations.

SYNTAX `public int compareToIgnoreCase(String str)`

DESCRIPTION This method is just like `compareTo()`, except that it ignores case when comparing the characters. This method returns an integer whose sign is that of

```
this.toUpperCase().toLowerCase().compareTo(
    str.toUpperCase().toLowerCase())
```

This method does not take locale into account. You should use the `java.text.Collator` class to do locale-sensitive ordering.

S

PARAMETERS

`str` The non-`null` string with which to compare.

RETURNS `0` if the strings are identical when ignoring case considerations; a negative number if this `String` appears before `str` when case is ignored; a positive number if this `String` appears after `str` when case is ignored.

SEE ALSO `java.text.Collator.compare(String, String).`

EXAMPLE

```
System.out.println("abc".compareToIgnoreCase("Abc"));       // 0
System.out.println("This".compareToIgnoreCase("tHe"));      // 4
System.out.println("JAVE".compareToIgnoreCase("javeline")); // -4
System.out.println("Java".compareToIgnoreCase("Javits"));   // -8
```

java.lang

StringBuffer

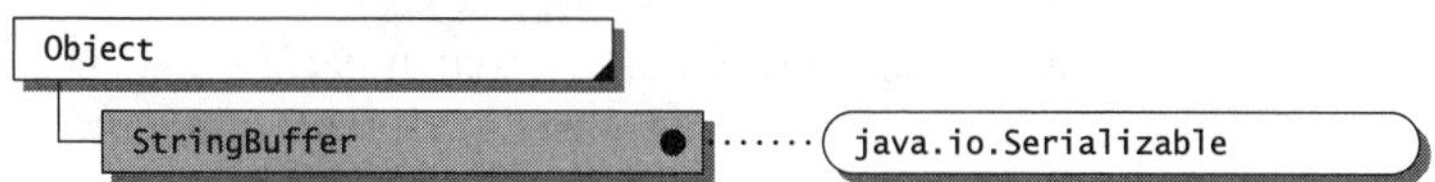

Syntax

```
public final class StringBuffer implements java.io.Serializable
```

Description

The `String` class creates immutable `String` objects. Each time you update a string, a new `String` object is created. A more efficient way to deal with these updates is to store a string in a `StringBuffer`, make updates to it until a `String` form is needed, and then use the `StringBuffer` to create a `String` object.

See *The Java Class Libraries, Second Edition, Volume 1* for more information about this class.

Changes for Version 1.2

In Version 1.1, you could append and insert to an existing `StringBuffer`. In Version 1.2, you can delete characters or replace characters anywhere in the buffer. You can also retrieve a portion of the `StringBuffer` using the `substring()` method, instead of getting the entire buffer.

An overload of the `insert()` method that accepts a range of characters from a `char` array also is new.

MEMBER SUMMARY		
	Constructor	
	`StringBuffer()`	Constructs a `StringBuffer` instance.
	Update Methods	
	`append()`	Appends the string representation of an object or data value to this `StringBuffer`.
1.2	`delete()`	Deletes the characters from a region of this `StringBuffer`.
1.2	`deleteCharAt()`	Deletes a character from this `StringBuffer`.
Δ	`insert()`	Inserts the string representation of an object or data value into this `StringBuffer`.
1.2	`replace()`	Replaces the characters in a region of this `StringBuffer`.
	`reverse()`	Reverses the order of characters in this `StringBuffer`.
	`setCharAt()`	Replaces a character in this `StringBuffer`.
	`setLength()`	Truncates or expands this `StringBuffer`.

Continued

S

MEMBER SUMMARY	
Access Methods	
`charAt()`	Retrieves a character from this `StringBuffer`.
`getChars()`	Copies a region of this `StringBuffer` to a `char` array.
1.2 `substring()`	Retrieves a region of characters in this `StringBuffer` as a `String`.
`toString()`	Retrieves the contents of this `StringBuffer` as a `String`.
Capacity and Length Methods	
`capacity()`	Retrieves the current capacity of this `StringBuffer`.
`ensureCapacity()`	Ensures that the capacity of this `StringBuffer` is at least a specified amount.
`length()`	Retrieves the number of characters in this `StringBuffer`.

See Also

`StringBuffer` in *The Java Class Libraries, Second Edition, Volume 1.*

1.2 delete()

PURPOSE Deletes the characters from a region of this `StringBuffer`.

SYNTAX `public synchronized StringBuffer delete(int start, int end)`

DESCRIPTION This method deletes the characters in the region of this `StringBuffer`, starting at the index `start` (inclusive) and ending at the index `end` (exclusive). If `end` > `length()`, `length()` is used as the ending index. If `end` is the same as `start`, no deletion is done and this `StringBuffer` is returned unchanged.

All characters with index greater than `end` are shifted down (toward the head of this `StringBuffer`) to fill the void left by the deleted characters. The size of this `StringBuffer` is decremented by the number of characters deleted.

If you just want to remove a single character, use `deleteCharAt()`.

S

PARAMETERS

`end` The ending (exclusive) index at which to end the deletion. `start` ≤ `end` ≤ `length()`.

`start` The beginning (inclusive) index at which to start the deletion. `0` ≤ `start` ≤ `length()-1`.

RETURNS This `StringBuffer` after the deletion.

EXCEPTIONS

`StringIndexOutOfBoundsException`
If `start` < `0`, or `start` > `length()-1`, or `start` > `end`.

SEE ALSO `deleteCharAt()`.

EXAMPLE

```
StringBuffer buf = new StringBuffer("On a clear day");
buf.delete(5, 11);
System.out.println(buf.toString()); // "On a day"
```

1.2 deleteCharAt()

PURPOSE Deletes a character from this `StringBuffer`.

SYNTAX `public synchronized StringBuffer deleteCharAt(int ix)`

DESCRIPTION This method deletes the character at index `ix` from this `StringBuffer`. All characters with index greater than `ix` are shifted down (toward the head of this `StringBuffer`). The size of this `StringBuffer` is decremented by `1`.

PARAMETERS

`ix` The zero-based index of the character to delete. `0` ≤ `ix` ≤ `length()-1`.

RETURNS This `StringBuffer` after the deletion.

EXCEPTIONS

`StringIndexOutOfBoundsException`

If `ix` is outside of the specified range.

SEE ALSO `delete()`.

EXAMPLE

```
StringBuffer buf = new StringBuffer("The Java Class Libraries");
buf.deleteCharAt(3);
buf.deleteCharAt(7);
buf.deleteCharAt(12);
System.out.println(buf.toString()); // "TheJavaClassLibraries"
```

Δ insert()

PURPOSE Inserts the string representation of an object or data value into this `StringBuffer`.

SYNTAX

```
public StringBuffer insert(int ix, boolean bool)
public synchronized StringBuffer insert(int ix, char ch)
public StringBuffer insert(int ix, int inum)
public StringBuffer insert(int ix, long lnum)
public StringBuffer insert(int ix, float fnum)
public StringBuffer insert(int ix, double dnum)
public synchronized StringBuffer insert(int ix, Object obj)
public synchronized StringBuffer insert(int ix, String str)
public synchronized StringBuffer insert(int ix, char[] data)
public synchronized StringBuffer insert(int ix, char[] data, int
   offset, int count)
```

DESCRIPTION Each of the ten forms of this method inserts the string representation of its argument into this `StringBuffer`, starting at index `ix`. Any characters occurring at or greater than `ix` are placed after the newly added characters. A call to `insert()` with an `ix` of `length()` is equivalent to a call to `append()`. This method returns the reference to the (updated) `StringBuffer`. This `StringBuffer` is automatically expanded as needed to accommodate additional characters. The data is copied into this `StringBuffer`, so any subsequent modifications to the arguments do not affect this `StringBuffer`. For example, subsequent changes to `data` will not affect this `StringBuffer`.

`String.valueOf()` is used to convert the argument into its string representation, except for the forms that accept `char` arrays.

Although some forms of the method do not have the `synchronized` modifier, they eventually call a version of `insert()` that does have the `synchronized` modifier, thus ensuring that all updates to this `StringBuffer` are done one at a time.

1.2 CHANGES The form that accepts `offset` and `count` parameters with a `char[]` is new in Version 1.2.

PARAMETERS

`bool`	The `boolean` whose string representation to insert.
`ch`	The character to insert.
`count`	The number of characters from `data` to use.
`data`	The non-`null` `char` array for getting characters to insert.
`dnum`	The `double` whose string representation to insert.
`fnum`	The `float` whose string representation to insert.
`inum`	The `int` whose string representation to insert.
`ix`	The zero-based index at which to start the insertion in this `StringBuffer`. `0` ≤ `ix` ≤ `length()-1`.
`lnum`	The `long` whose string representation to insert.
`obj`	The possibly `null` object whose string representation to insert. If `null`, insert the string `"null"`.
`offset`	The index (inclusive) in `data` from which to start getting characters. `0` ≤ `offset` < `data.length`.
`str`	The possibly `null` string to insert. If `null`, insert the string `"null"`.

RETURNS This `StringBuffer` after the insertion.

EXCEPTIONS

`StringIndexOutOfBoundsException`
If `ix`, `offset`, or `count` is outside of the specified range.

S

EXAMPLE

```
int inum = 512;
long lnum = Long.MAX_VALUE;
double dnum = 123.123e54;
float fnum = 3.1243f;
char sep = ' ';
Object obj1 = null;
Object obj2 = new Vector();
char[] charArray = {'a', 'b', 'c'};
StringBuffer buf = new StringBuffer(100);

// Keep inserting at head of buffer all the data types above
buf.insert(0, inum).insert(0, sep).insert(0, lnum).insert(0, sep);
buf.insert(0, dnum).insert(0, sep).insert(0, dnum).insert(0, sep);
buf.insert(0, obj1).insert(0, sep).insert(0, obj2);
buf.insert(0, sep).insert(0, charArray);
buf.insert(0, charArray, 1, 1);
```

1.2 replace()

PURPOSE Replaces the characters in a region of this `StringBuffer`.

SYNTAX

```
public synchronized StringBuffer replace(int start, int end,
    String str)
```

DESCRIPTION This method replaces the characters between the indices `start` (inclusive) and `end` (exclusive) with the characters from `str`. If `str` contains more characters than the region specified by `start` and `end`, this `StringBuffer` is automatically expanded to accommodate the additional characters and characters at index `end` or higher are shifted up (toward the end of this `StringBuffer`). If `str` contains fewer characters than the region specified by `start` and `end`, this `StringBuffer` is automatically reduced and characters at index `end` or higher are shifted down (toward the head of this `StringBuffer`).

PARAMETERS

`end` The ending (exclusive) index in this `StringBuffer` of the old contents to replace. `start` ≤ `end` < `length()`.

`start` The beginning (inclusive) index in this `StringBuffer` of the old contents to replace. `0` ≤ `start` ≤ `length()-1`.

`str` The non-`null` string that will replace the previous contents.

RETURNS This `StringBuffer` after the update.

EXCEPTIONS

`StringIndexOutOfBoundsException`

If `start` < `0`, or `start` > `end`, or `start` > `length()-1`.

SEE ALSO `delete()`, `insert()`.

S

EXAMPLE

```
StringBuffer buf = new StringBuffer("The C++ Class Libraries");
buf.replace(4, 7, "Java");
System.out.println(buf.toString()); // "The Java Class Libraries"
```

1.2 substring()

PURPOSE Retrieves a region of characters in this `StringBuffer` as a `String`.

SYNTAX

```
public String substring(int start)
public synchronized String substring(int start, int end)
```

DESCRIPTION This method returns the characters between the index `start` (inclusive) and the index `end` (exclusive) as a `String`. If `end` has not been specified, `length()` is used as the ending index.

To get the entire string, use `toString()`.

PARAMETERS

`end` The ending (exclusive) index. `start` ≤ `end` ≤ `length()`.

`start` The beginning (inclusive) index in this `StringBuffer`. `0` ≤ `start` < `length()`.

RETURNS The non-`null` new string.

EXCEPTIONS

`StringIndexOutOfBoundsException`
If `start` or `end` is outside of the specified range.

SEE ALSO `toString()`.

EXAMPLE

```
StringBuffer buf = new StringBuffer("The Java Class Libraries");
System.out.println(buf.substring(4, 8)); // "Java"
System.out.println(buf.substring(9));    // "Class Libraries"
```

StringCharacterIterator

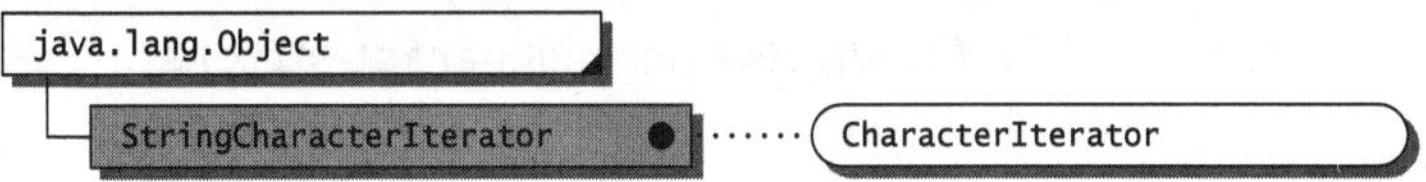

Syntax

```
public final class StringCharacterIterator extends Object implements
    CharacterIterator
```

Description

`StringCharacterIterator` is a class for iterating forward and backward over a string of Unicode characters. This class enables moving about within a range of text and returning individual characters or their index values.

See *The Java Class Libraries, Second Edition, Volume 1* for more information about this class.

Changes for Version 1.2

In Version 1.2, the semantics for `current()`, `first()`, `last()`, `next()`, `previous()`, and `setIndex()` change in order to fix one bug in Version 1.1. They now accept the position returned by `getEndIndex()`. All of the changes in this class and `CharacterIterator` derive from this change.

For example, in the following diagram, the method `getEndIndex()` returns 8, whereas `last()` returns the last character, "!", which is at position 7. In Version 1.1, the iterator was allowed to point only to actual character positions. Thus there was nowhere for it to point if the iteration range was empty or if you tried to move the iterator to position 8; you would just get an exception. This meant that client code would have to special-case these conditions so that they never tried to create an iterator over an empty string or tried to move to the end of the substring. In Version 1.2, this is fixed by making the end index a legal position for the iterator and having `current()` return `DONE` when sitting there. Because these changes affect semantics, these bugs will never be fixed in the Version 1.1 series.

```
|T|h|e| |e|n|d|!|
0 1 2 3 4 5 6 7 8
|               |
            getEndIndex()
```

MEMBER SUMMARY		
	Constructor	
	StringCharacterIterator()	Constructs a StringCharacterIterator instance.
	Text Setter Method	
Δ	setText()	Resets this iterator to use a new string.
	Movement Methods	
Δ	first()	Moves the index to the beginning of the text subrange, and retrieves the character at that position.
Δ	last()	Moves the index to and retrieves the last character within the text subrange.
Δ	next()	Increments the index by one, and retrieves the character at the new index.
Δ	previous()	Decrements the index by one, and retrieves the character at the new index.
Δ	setIndex()	Moves the index to a position, and retrieves the character at that new index.
	Character and Index Getter Methods	
Δ	current()	Retrieves the character at the current index.
	getIndex()	Retrieves the current index.
	getBeginIndex()	Retrieves the index at the beginning of the text subrange.
	getEndIndex()	Retrieves the index at the end of the text subrange.
	Comparison Method	
	equals()	Compares this StringCharacterIterator instance with another instance for equality.
	Object Methods	
	clone()	Creates a copy of this StringCharacterIterator instance.
	hashCode()	Computes the hash code of this StringCharacterIterator instance.

See Also

CharacterIterator.
StringCharacterIterator in *The Java Class Libraries, Second Edition, Volume 1.*

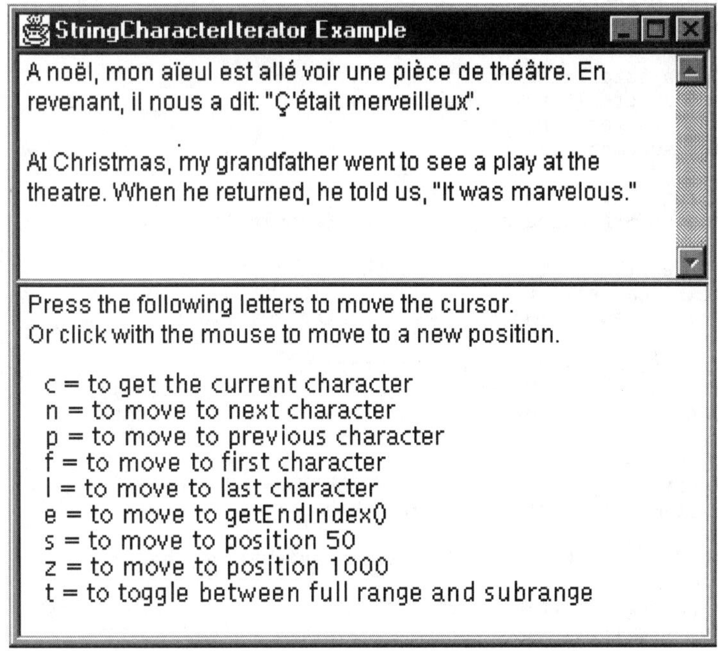

FIGURE 20: Using `StringCharacterIterator`.

Example

This example demonstrates the different ways a `StringCharacterIterator` can move through text. Run this program by supplying the filename of a text file you want to display and iterate over, such as `input.txt`. The full text is initially highlighted, with the cursor at position 0. Press the letters n (next), p (previous), f (first), l (last), e (`getEndIndex()`), and s (`setEndIndex(50)`) to move the cursor. Pressing z causes an exception to be thrown, as it tries to move the index outside the text range. See Figure 20.

To toggle between iterating over the full range and subrange, press "t" (toggle). (The subrange is highlighted in Solaris but not in Windows.) This subrange is calculated to range from 30 to 70 percent of the way through the text. Notice that if you click in the text but *outside* of the subrange, then pressing a movement key properly causes an `IllegalArgumentException`. This is because the iterator is trying to set the current index to a value outside of its subrange. Click inside of the subrange for a valid value. Values are printed in the console window. This example enables you to go to the end of the subrange or range so that you can see the diagnostic `DONE` appear.

```
import java.awt.*;
import java.awt.event.*;
import java.io.*;
import java.util.*;
import java.text.StringCharacterIterator;

class Main extends Frame {
    TextArea textArea =
        new TextArea("", 20, 50, TextArea.SCROLLBARS_VERTICAL_ONLY);
```

S

```
TextArea message =
    new TextArea("", 15, 50, TextArea.SCROLLBARS_NONE);

StringCharacterIterator sci = null;
StringCharacterIterator sci1 = null;
StringCharacterIterator sci2 = null;
boolean subrangeflag = false;

Main(String s, String sNative) {
    super("StringCharacterIterator Example");

    // Set the text and create the iterator.
    textArea.setText(s);
    sci1 = new StringCharacterIterator(sNative);

    // Create the subrange iterator.
    int end = (int)Math.round (0.7 * sNative.length());
    int begin  = (int)Math.round (0.3 * sNative.length());

    // Diagnostics:
    System.out.println("start of subrange: " + begin);
    System.out.println("end of subrange:   " + end);

    sci2 = new StringCharacterIterator(sNative, begin, end, begin);

    // Set the initial iterator.
    sci = sci1;

    // Display the instructions
    message.setText(
      "Press the following letters to move the cursor.\n" +
      "Or click with the mouse to move to a new position.\n" +
      "\n" +
      "  c = to get the current character\n" +
      "  n = to move to next character\n" +
      "  p = to move to previous character\n" +
      "  f = to move to first character\n" +
      "  l = to move to last character\n" +
      "  e = to move to getEndIndex()\n" +
      "  s = to move to position 50\n" +
      "  z = to move to position 1000\n" +
      "  t = to toggle between full range and subrange\n"
    );

    message.setEditable(false);

    // Create text area and listen for key events.
    add(textArea, BorderLayout.CENTER);
    add(message, BorderLayout.SOUTH);
    textArea.addKeyListener(new KeyEventHandler());

    setSize(400, 400);
    show();
    textArea.select(sci.getBeginIndex(), sci.getEndIndex());
    textArea.setCaretPosition(sci.getIndex());
}

class KeyEventHandler extends KeyAdapter {
    public void keyPressed(KeyEvent evt) {
```

S

```
// In case the user clicks, get the caret position.
int caret = textArea.getCaretPosition();

// Set the iterator to match the caret.
if (subrangeflag) {
    if (caret < (sci.getEndIndex())) {
        sci.setIndex(caret);
    }
} else {
    if (caret < textArea.getText().length()) {
        sci.setIndex(caret);
    }
}
char rtn = '_';

// Branch according to key pressed.
switch (Character.toLowerCase(evt.getKeyChar())) {
  case 'c':
      rtn = sci.current();
      break;
  case 'n':
      rtn = sci.next();
      break;
  case 'p':
      rtn = sci.previous();
      break;
  case 'f':
      rtn = sci.first();
      break;
  case 'l':
      rtn = sci.last();
      break;
  case 'e':
      try {
          rtn = sci.setIndex(sci.getEndIndex());
      } catch (IllegalArgumentException e) {
          System.out.println("Caught IllegalArgumentException "
                             + e.getMessage());
      }
      break;
  case 's':
      try {
          rtn = sci.setIndex(50);
      } catch (IllegalArgumentException e) {
          System.out.println("Caught IllegalArgumentException "
                             + e.getMessage());
      }
      break;
  case 'z':
      try {
          rtn = sci.setIndex(1000);
      } catch (IllegalArgumentException e) {
          System.out.println("Caught IllegalArgumentException "
                             + e.getMessage());
      }
      break;
  case 't':
      // Toggle between range and subrange.

      if (subrangeflag) {
```

S

```
                sci = sci1;
                subrangeflag = false;
            } else {
                sci = sci2;
                subrangeflag = true;
            }

            // Diagnostics:
            System.out.println("");
            System.out.println("getBeginIndex:    "
                                + sci.getBeginIndex());
            System.out.println("getEndIndex:      "
                                + sci.getEndIndex());

            // Highlight the range.
            textArea.select(sci.getBeginIndex(), sci.getEndIndex());
            break;
        }

        // Set the caret position.
        textArea.setCaretPosition(sci.getIndex());

        // Diagnostics:
        System.out.println("");
        System.out.println("getIndex:      " + sci.getIndex());
        switch (rtn) {
          case StringCharacterIterator.DONE:
            System.out.println("character:     " + "DONE");
            break;
          case '\n':
            System.out.println("character:     " + "newline");
            break;
          default:
            System.out.println("character:     " + rtn);
        }
        evt.consume();
    }
}

public static void main(String[] args) {
    if (args.length != 1) {
        System.err.println("Usage: java Main <filename>");
        System.exit(1);
    }
    try {
        // To workaround a TextArea bug, create two versions
        // of the text:
        // - one with '\n' for newlines (to display in text area)
        // - the other with native newlines (to iterate over)
        // Read in the entire contents of the file.
        BufferedReader rd = new BufferedReader(new FileReader(args[0]));
        String sep = System.getProperty("line.separator");
        String line;
        StringBuffer sbuf = new StringBuffer();
        StringBuffer sbufNative = new StringBuffer();

        while ((line = rd.readLine()) != null) {
            sbuf.append(line);
            sbuf.append('\n');
            sbufNative.append(line);
            sbufNative.append(sep);
```

S

```
            }
            rd.close();
            new Main(new String(sbuf), new String(sbufNative));
        } catch (Exception e) {
            e.printStackTrace();
        }
    }
}
```

Δ current()

PURPOSE Retrieves the character at the current index.

SYNTAX `public char current()`

DESCRIPTION This method gets the character at the current index, or returns `StringCharacterIterator.DONE` (documented in `CharacterIterator`) if the text subrange is empty. (The subrange is empty if `getBeginIndex()` and `getEndIndex()` return the same value.) The current index is the same as that returned by `getIndex()`. This method does not move the current index.

1.2 CHANGES In Version 1.1, if the text subrange was empty this method threw a `StringIndexOutOfBoundsException`. In Version 1.2, it returns `StringCharacterIterator.DONE` if the text subrange is empty.

RETURNS The character at the current index, or `StringCharacterIterator.DONE` if the text range is empty.

SEE ALSO `CharacterIterator.DONE`, `getIndex()`.

EXAMPLE See `next()`, as well as the following code.

```
String str = "abcdefghij";
StringCharacterIterator it = new StringCharacterIterator(str);
System.out.println( it.current() );    // a
it.last();
System.out.println( it.current() );    // j
it.next();
System.out.println( it.current() );    // DONE

// The current character of an empty subrange is DONE.
it = new StringCharacterIterator(str, 5, 5, 5);
System.out.println( it.current() );    // DONE
```

Δ first()

PURPOSE Moves the index to the beginning of the text subrange, and retrieves the character at that position.

SYNTAX `public char first()`

DESCRIPTION This method moves the current index to the beginning of the text subrange and returns the first character. This new index is the same as that returned by `getBeginIndex()`. If the text subrange is empty, this method does not move the iterator but just returns `StringCharacterIterator.DONE` (documented in `CharacterIterator`). (The subrange is empty if `getBeginIndex()` and `getEndIndex()` return the same value.)

1.2 CHANGES In Version 1.1, if the text subrange was empty this method threw a `StringIndexOutOfBoundsException`. In Version 1.2, it returns `StringCharacterIterator.DONE` if the text subrange is empty.

RETURNS The first character in the text subrange, or `StringCharacterIterator.DONE` if the text subrange is empty.

SEE ALSO `CharacterIterator.DONE`, `getBeginIndex()`.

EXAMPLE See `next()`, as well as the following code.

```
String str = "abcdefghij";
StringCharacterIterator it = new StringCharacterIterator(str, 5);
System.out.println( it.getIndex() );    // 5
System.out.println( it.first() );       // a
System.out.println( it.getIndex() );    // 0

// first() moves to beginning of subrange.
it = new StringCharacterIterator(str, 5, 6, 6);
System.out.println( it.getIndex() );    // 6
System.out.println( it.first() );       // f
System.out.println( it.getIndex() );    // 5

// The current character of an empty subrange is DONE.
it = new StringCharacterIterator(str, 5, 5, 5);
System.out.println( it.first() );       // DONE
```

Δ last()

S

PURPOSE Moves the index to and retrieves the last character within the text subrange.

SYNTAX `public char last()`

DESCRIPTION This method moves the index to the last character in the text subrange and retrieves that character. Compare this to `setIndex(getEndIndex())`, which returns the first character beyond the end of the text subrange, if one exists. The index that `last()` moves to is the same as that returned by `getEndIndex() - 1`, or `getEndIndex()` if the text subrange is empty. This is special-cased for the empty subrange so that `last()` does not move the current index *ahead of* the subrange. (The subrange is empty if `getBeginIndex()` and `getEndIndex()` return the same value.) If the text subrange is empty, this method returns `StringCharacterIterator.DONE` (documented in `CharacterIterator`).

1.2 CHANGES In Version 1.1, if the text subrange was empty this method set the index to `getEndIndex() - 1` and threw a `StringIndexOutOfBoundsException`. In Version 1.2, it returns `StringCharacterIterator.DONE`.

RETURNS The last character within the text subrange, or `StringCharacterIterator.DONE` if the text subrange is empty.

SEE ALSO `CharacterIterator.DONE`.

EXAMPLE See `next()`, as well as the following code.

```
String str = "abcdefghij";
StringCharacterIterator it = new StringCharacterIterator(str, 5);
System.out.println( it.getIndex() );     // 5
System.out.println( it.last() );         // j
System.out.println( it.getIndex() );     // 9

// first() moves to beginning of subrange.
it = new StringCharacterIterator(str, 5, 6, 6);
System.out.println( it.getIndex() );     // 6
System.out.println( it.last() );         // f
System.out.println( it.getIndex() );     // 5

// The current character of an empty subrange is DONE.
it = new StringCharacterIterator(str, 5, 5, 5);
System.out.println( it.last() );         // DONE
```

Δ next()

PURPOSE Increments the index by one, and retrieves the character at the new index.

SYNTAX `public char next()`

DESCRIPTION This method increments the current index by one and returns the character at the new index. The current index is always pinned to the range from `getBeginIndex()` to `getEndIndex()`, inclusive. If the iterator attempts to increment past the end of the text subrange, the current index is not incremented and a value of `StringCharacterIterator.DONE` is returned (documented in `CharacterIterator`). If the text subrange is empty, this method does not move the iterator but just returns `StringCharacterIterator.DONE`. (The subrange is empty if `getBeginIndex()` and `getEndIndex()` return the same value.)

1.2 CHANGES In Version 1.1, if the text subrange was empty, this method threw a `StringIndexOutOfBoundsException`. In Version 1.2, it returns `StringCharacterIterator.DONE` if the text subrange is empty.

A bug in JDK 1.1.5 and earlier versions was a peculiar behavior in the method `next()`. That is, after `next()` reached the end of the subrange and returned `DONE`, continuing to call it caused it to mistakenly continue incrementing the

S

current position well beyond the index of the last character. This was fixed in JDK 1.1.6.

RETURNS The character at the new index, or `StringCharacterIterator.DONE`.

SEE ALSO `CharacterIterator.DONE`.

EXAMPLE This example demonstrates all of the movement methods. It also shows the value of the index at the last character (20) and the end of the range (21) and tests for the value `DONE`.

```
import java.text.StringCharacterIterator;

class Main {
    public static void main(String args[]) {
        String str =  "We want to thank you.";
        String str2 = "   |<-SUBRANGE-->|   ";

        // create string character iterator
        StringCharacterIterator sci =
                               new StringCharacterIterator(str, 3, 17, 11);

        System.out.println("'sci' is the string character iterator ");
        System.out.println("'|' is positioned ahead of the current index");
        System.out.println("                          " + str2);

        char rtn = sci.current();
        System.out.print("sci.current():       ");     // t
        printOutChar(sci, str, rtn);

        rtn = sci.next();
        System.out.print("sci.next():          ");     // h
        printOutChar(sci, str, rtn);

        rtn = sci.previous();
        System.out.print("sci.previous():      ");     // t
        printOutChar(sci, str, rtn);

        rtn = sci.setIndex(sci.getEndIndex() - 2);
        System.out.print("sci.setIndex(" + (sci.getEndIndex() - 2) + "):    ");
        printOutChar(sci, str, rtn);                   // k

        rtn = sci.next();
        System.out.print("sci.next():          ");     // ' '
        printOutChar(sci, str, rtn);

        rtn = sci.next();
        System.out.print("sci.next():          ");     // DONE
        printOutChar(sci, str, rtn);

        rtn = sci.first();
        System.out.print("sci.first():         ");     // w
        printOutChar(sci, str, rtn);

        rtn = sci.last();
        System.out.print("sci.last():          ");     // ' '
        printOutChar(sci, str, rtn);

        int i = sci.getIndex();
```

S

```
        System.out.print("sci.getIndex():      ");     // 16
        printOutInt(sci, str, i);

        i = sci.getBeginIndex();
        System.out.print("sci.getBeginIndex(): ");     // 3
        printOutInt(sci, str, i);

        i = sci.getEndIndex();
        System.out.print("sci.getEndIndex():   ");     // 17
        printOutInt(sci, str, i);
    }

    // Print the text with a separator '|' at the current position
    public static void printOutChar(StringCharacterIterator iter,
                                    String str, char rtn) {
        printFirstPart(iter, str);
        if (rtn == StringCharacterIterator.DONE)
            System.out.println("   returns " + "DONE");
        else
            System.out.println("   returns \"" + rtn + "\"");
    }

    // Print the text with a separator '|' at the current position
    public static void printOutInt(StringCharacterIterator iter,
                                   String str, int rtn) {
        printFirstPart(iter, str);
        if (rtn == StringCharacterIterator.DONE)
            System.out.println("   returns " + "DONE");
        else
            System.out.println("   returns \"" + rtn + "\"");
    }

  public static void printFirstPart(StringCharacterIterator iter, String str) {
        int pos = iter.getIndex();
        System.out.print("\"" + str.substring(0,pos));
        System.out.print("|");
        System.out.print(str.substring(pos,str.length()) + "\"");
  }
}
```

OUTPUT

```
> java Main
'sci' is the string character iterator
'|' is positioned ahead of the current index
                         |<-SUBRANGE-->|
sci.current():       "We want to |thank you."   returns "t"
sci.next():          "We want to t|hank you."   returns "h"
sci.previous():      "We want to |thank you."   returns "t"
sci.setIndex(15):    "We want to than|k you."   returns "k"
sci.next():          "We want to thank| you."   returns " "
sci.next():          "We want to thank |you."   returns DONE
sci.first():         "We |want to thank you."   returns "w"
sci.last():          "We want to thank| you."   returns " "
sci.getIndex():      "We want to thank| you."   returns "16"
sci.getBeginIndex(): "We want to thank| you."   returns "3"
sci.getEndIndex():   "We want to thank| you."   returns "17"
```

S

Δ previous()

PURPOSE Decrements the index by one, and retrieves the character at the new index.

SYNTAX `public char previous()`

DESCRIPTION This method decrements the current index by one and returns the character at the new index. The current index is always pinned to the range from `getBeginIndex()` to `getEndIndex()`, inclusive. If the iterator attempts to decrement past the beginning of its range, `getBeginIndex()`, the current index remains at that position and a value of `StringCharacterIterator.DONE` is returned (documented in `CharacterIterator`). If the text subrange is empty, this method does not move the iterator but just returns `StringCharacterIterator.DONE`. (The subrange is empty if `getBeginIndex()` and `getEndIndex()` return the same value.)

1.2 CHANGES In Version 1.1, if the text subrange was empty this method threw a `StringIndexOutOfBoundsException`. In Version 1.2, it returns `StringCharacterIterator.DONE` if the text subrange is empty.

RETURNS The character at the new index, or `StringCharacterIterator.DONE`.

SEE ALSO `CharacterIterator.DONE`.

EXAMPLE See `next()`, as well as the following code.

```
String str = "abcdefghij";
StringCharacterIterator it = new StringCharacterIterator(str, 5);
System.out.println( it.getIndex() );     // 5
System.out.println( it.previous() );     // e
System.out.println( it.getIndex() );     // 4
System.out.println( it.first() );        // a
System.out.println( it.previous() );     // DONE
System.out.println( it.getIndex() );     // 0

// A subrange.
it = new StringCharacterIterator(str, 5, 6, 6);
System.out.println( it.getIndex() );     // 6
System.out.println( it.previous() );     // f
System.out.println( it.getIndex() );     // 5
System.out.println( it.previous() );     // DONE
System.out.println( it.getIndex() );     // 5

// The current character of an empty subrange is DONE.
it = new StringCharacterIterator(str, 5, 5, 5);
System.out.println( it.previous() );         // DONE
```

S

Δ setIndex()

PURPOSE Moves the index to a position, and retrieves the character at that new index.

SYNTAX `public char setIndex(int idx)`

DESCRIPTION This method sets the current index to `idx` and returns the character at that new index. If a value outside of the subrange is passed in, it throws an error (rather than returning `StringCharacterIterator.DONE`). If the text subrange is empty, this method does not move the iterator but just returns `StringCharacterIterator.DONE`. (The subrange is empty if `getBeginIndex()` and `getEndIndex()` return the same value.)

1.2 CHANGES In Version 1.1, the call `iterator.setIndex(iterator.getEndIndex())` threw an exception, which is considered a bug. If the text subrange was empty, `setIndex(iterator.getBeginIndex())` also threw an exception. In Version 1.2, both of these return `StringCharacterIterator.DONE`.

PARAMETERS

`idx` The index to which to move the current index. `begin` ≤ `idx` ≤ `end`, where `begin` and `end` are arguments passed into the constructor `StringCharacterIterator()`.

RETURNS The character at the new index, or `StringCharacterIterator.DONE`.

EXCEPTIONS

`IllegalArgumentException`

If `idx` is outside of its valid range.

SEE ALSO `CharacterIterator.DONE`.

EXAMPLE See `next()`, as well as the following code.

```
String str = "0123456789";
StringCharacterIterator it = new StringCharacterIterator(str);
System.out.println( it.current() );    // 0
it.setIndex(10);
System.out.println( it.current() );    // DONE

// The index is relative to the underlying string, not the subrange.
it = new StringCharacterIterator(str, 5, 6, 5);
System.out.println( it.current() );    // 5

// The current index of an empty subrange is DONE.
it = new StringCharacterIterator(str, 5, 5, 5);
System.out.println( it.current() );    // DONE
```

S

Δ setText()

PURPOSE Resets this iterator to use a new string.

SYNTAX `public void setText(String text)`

DESCRIPTION This method resets this iterator to use the string `text`. This method is used by other `java.text` classes such as `BreakIterator` and `CollationElement-`

Iterator that want to avoid allocating a new StringCharacterIterator object every time their setText() method is called.

PARAMETERS

text The new, non-null string over which to iterate.

EXAMPLE The following example creates an iterator with the string str1, prints the string, resets the iterator to the string str2, and prints that string.

```
import java.text.StringCharacterIterator;

class Main {
    public static void main(String args[]) {

        String str =  "We want to thank you";

        // create string character iterator
        StringCharacterIterator sci = new StringCharacterIterator(str);

        System.out.println("'sci' is the string character iterator ");
        System.out.println("'[' is positioned ahead of the current index");

        char rtn = sci.last();
        System.out.print("sci.last():          ");
        printOutChar(sci, str, rtn);
    }

    // Print the text with a separator '[' at the current position
    public static void printOutChar(StringCharacterIterator iter,
                                    String str, char rtn) {
        printFirstPart(iter, str);
        if (rtn == StringCharacterIterator.DONE)
            System.out.println("   returns " + "DONE");
        else
            System.out.println("   returns \"" + rtn + "\"");
    }

  public static void printFirstPart(StringCharacterIterator iter, String str) {
        int pos = iter.getIndex();
        System.out.print("\"" + str.substring(0,pos));
        System.out.print("[");
        System.out.print(str.substring(pos,str.length()) + "\"");
  }
}
```

OUTPUT

```
> java Main
'sci' is the string character iterator
'[' is positioned ahead of the current index
sci.last():          "We want to thank yo[u"   returns "u"
```

java.io
StringReader

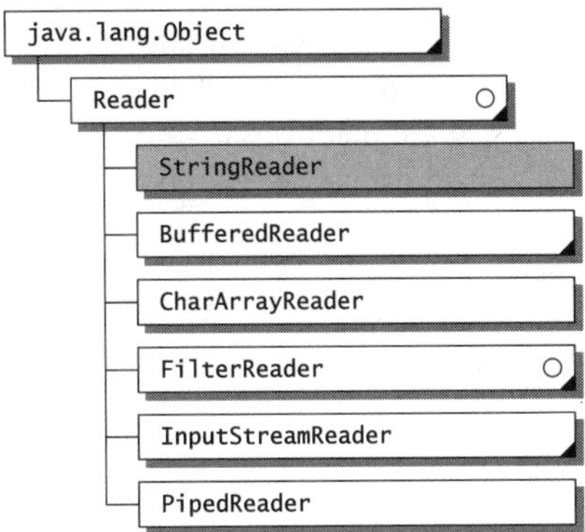

Syntax

```
public class StringReader extends Reader
```

Description

The `StringReader` class allows a string to be used as an character input stream. For example, you can turn a string into an character input stream (reader) so that you can read characters from that reader.

See *The Java Class Libraries, Second Edition, Volume 1* for more information about this class.

Changes for Version 1.2

The `ready()` method now throws an exception if the `StringReader` has been closed.

MEMBER SUMMARY	
Constructor	
`StringReader()`	Constructs a `StringReader` instance using a string.
Input Methods	
`read()`	Reads characters from this `StringReader`.
`skip()`	Skips characters from this `StringReader`.
Stream Methods	
`close()`	Closes this `StringReader`.
Δ `ready()`	Determines whether this `StringReader` is ready to be read.

Continued

MEMBER SUMMARY	
Mark/Reset Methods	
`mark()`	Marks the current read position in this `StringReader`.
`markSupported()`	Determines whether this `StringReader` supports mark/reset.
`reset()`	Resets the read position to the previously marked position.

See Also

`StringReader` in *The Java Class Libraries, Second Edition, Volume 1.*

Δ ready()

PURPOSE Determines whether this `StringReader` is ready to be read.

SYNTAX `public boolean ready() throws IOException`

DESCRIPTION This method determines whether this `StringReader` is ready to be read. A `StringReader` is ready to be read if it has not been closed.

1.2 CHANGES In Version 1.1, this method always returned `true`, even when the reader had been closed.

RETURNS `true` if this `StringReader` is ready to be read.

EXCEPTIONS

`IOException`

If this `StringReader` has been closed.

EXAMPLE

```
StringReader in = new StringReader("Java Class Libraries");
System.out.println(in.ready()); // true
```

S

StringWriter

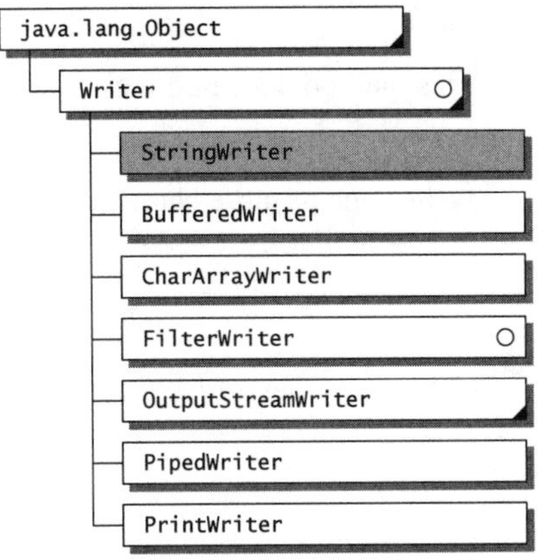

Syntax

```
public class StringWriter extends Writer
```

Description

The `StringWriter` class implements a character output stream that uses a `StringBuffer` to store the characters written to it. You can subsequently request that the characters written to it be returned as a string. This is helpful when you want to capture output from methods that operate on writers in the form of a string.

See *The Java Class Libraries, Second Edition, Volume 1* for more information about this class.

Changes for Version 1.2

The constructor that accepts an initial size has been changed from `protected` to `public`.

A `throws IOException` clause has been added to the `close()` method.

S

MEMBER SUMMARY	
Constructor	
Δ `StringWriter()`	Constructs a `StringWriter` instance.
Externalizing Methods	
`getBuffer()`	Retrieves the contents of this `StringWriter` as a `StringBuffer`.
`toString()`	Retrieves the contents of this `StringWriter` as a `String`.

Continued

MEMBER SUMMARY	
Stream Methods	
Δ `close()`	This method does nothing.
`flush()`	This method does nothing.
Output Method	
`write()`	Writes one or more characters to this `StringWriter`.

See Also

`StringWriter` in *The Java Class Libraries, Second Edition, Volume 1.*

Δ close()

PURPOSE This method does nothing.

SYNTAX `public void close() throws IOException`

DESCRIPTION This empty implementation satisfies the abstract method declared in `Writer`.

1.2 CHANGES A `throws IOException` was added in Version 1.2.

SEE ALSO `Writer.close()`.

Δ StringWriter()

PURPOSE Constructs a `StringWriter` instance.

SYNTAX
```
public StringWriter()
public StringWriter(int initialSize)
```

DESCRIPTION The first form of this constructor constructs an instance of `StringWriter`. It creates a `StringBuffer` with a default size of 16 to hold characters written to this `StringWriter`. The second form constructs an instance of `StringWriter` that has a string buffer size of `initialSize`. The `StringBuffer` of the newly created writer will grow automatically as the number of characters written to it exceeds the initial buffer size.

The lock of this `StringWriter` is assigned to the `StringBuffer` being used for this `StringWriter`. (See `Writer.lock`.)

1.2 CHANGES In Version 1.1, the form of the constructor that accepts an initial size argument was `protected`.

PARAMETERS

`initialSize` The initial size to use when creating the internal `StringBuffer`.

S

EXAMPLE

```
String str = "Java Class Libraries";

// Allocate the size we expect to use
StringWriter out = new StringWriter(str.length()*3);

out.write(str);
out.write(str);
out.write(str);
System.out.println(out.toString());
    // Java Class LibrariesJava Class LibrariesJava Class Libraries
```

System

Syntax

```
public final class System
```

Description

The `System` class provides a collection of methods for examining and manipulating system-related information in a platform-independent manner. These methods include support for standard IO, memory management, and system properties.

See *The Java Class Libraries, Second Edition, Volume 1* for more information about this class.

System Properties

A *system property* is a key-value pair that the Java runtime defines to describe the user, the system environment, and the Java system. Table 28 lists the default system properties. Note that some items on this list are implementation-specific and subject to change without notice. Other properties also can be made available to a Java program via the `-D` option to the Java interpreter. For example, running the interpreter as follows adds the property `myenviron` with the value `abc` to the list of properties visible to the program `Main`:

```
java -Dmyenviron=abc Main
```

The `System` class provides methods that allow you to get all or selected properties, as well as methods to update them. The ability to read or update any system property is controlled by the security manager.

Property Name	Description
`appletviewer.security.allowUnsigned`	`true` means unsigned applets can be run.
`appletviewer.security.mode`	Specifies that network access is available to the applet ("none", "unrestricted", or "host").
`appletviewer.version`	The version of the applet viewer.
`awt.appletWarning`	If set, indicates that the applet window contains a "Warning: Applet Window" message.
`awt.font.`*`font_name`*	Maps *font_name* to the actual font name.

TABLE 28: Java System Properties.

Property Name	Description
`awt.image.incrementaldraw`	`true` means `Component.imageUpdate()` should use `awt.image.redrawrate.`
`awt.image.redrawrate`	An integer specifying the redraw rate for images.
`awt.toolkit`	The class name of the toolkit to use `Toolkit.getDefaultToolkit()`.
`browser`	Used by the JDBC/ODBC driver to determine the prefix to use when loading the native library.
`com.sun.CORBA.ORBServerHost`	Host name of the ORB server.
`com.sun.CORBA.ORBServerPort`	Port number of the ORB server.
`content.types.temp.file.template`	Pathname of the temporary file template for building the MIME table.
`content.types.user.table`	Pathname of the user-specified default MIME table.
`doc.url`	Base URL for documentation used by the HotJava browser.
`env.class.path`	Value of the `CLASSPATH` environment variable.
`exec.path`	List of paths to use when launching an application using MIME entries.
`file.dir.title`	String specifying the title for pages returned by the "file" URL stream handler.
`file.encoding`	Encoding identifier to use for `char-to-byte` and `byte-to-char` conversions.
`file.encoding.pkg`	Package prefix for the converter class (prefix + `.CharToByte` + encoding identifier).
`file.separator`	String used in file pathnames to separate directories.
`ftp.protocol.user`	Default password to use when making anonymous FTP connections via the "ftp" URL stream handler.
`ftp.proxyHost`	Host name of the FTP proxy to use.
`ftp.proxyPort`	Port of the FTP proxy to use.
`ftpProxyHost`	Host name of the FTP proxy to use
`ftpProxyPort`	Port of the FTP proxy to use.
`gopherProxyHost`	Host name of the gopher proxy to use.
`hotjava.home`	Directory name of where the HotJava browser software has been installed.
`hotjava.title`	Name to use for the HotJava browser program when posting news articles using the news URL stream handler.

Continued

TABLE 28: Java System Properties.

Property Name	Description
`http.agent`	Prefix to use for the client's "user agent" in the HTTP.
`http.keepAlive`	Used to turn off the client's use of the keep-alive feature of the HTTP.
`http.nonProxyHosts`	If set, indicates not to use a proxy when accessing this list of hosts by using the HTTP.
`http.proxyHost`	Host name of the HTTP proxy to use for the HotJava browser.
`http.proxyPort`	Port number of the HTTP proxy to use for the HotJava browser.
`impl.prefix`	Prefix of the implementation class names used in `InetAddress` and `DatagramSocket` (for example, "java.net." + prefix + "DatagramSocketImpl").
`java.awt.fonts`	Name of the directory in which fonts used by AWT are located (the value of the `JAVA_FONTS` environment variable).
`java.awt.graphicsenv`	Class name of the local graphics environment.
`java.awt.printerjob`	Class name of the `java.awt.print.PrinterJob` implementation.
`java.class.path`	List of the JAR files and directories of the application class files.
`java.class.version`	Java class library version number.
`java.compiler`	Library name of the JIT compiler to use instead of the default interpreter.
`java.content.handler.pkgs`	List of the package prefixes for class names to use for content handlers (`URL.getContent()`).
`java.ext.dirs`	Directory in which to find the installed Java Standard Extensions.
`java.home`	Directory name in which the Java software is installed.
`java.iccprofile.path`	List of directories to search for files containing the ICC profiles.
`java.io.tmpdir`	Name of the directory in which to create temporary files.
`java.library.path`	List of paths to search when loading libraries.
`java.net.ftp.imagepath.*`	Used when setting the image filename in a MIME entry.
`java.net.ftp.imagepath.directory`	Used by the gopher client to translate the gopher document to HTML.
`java.net.ftp.imagepath.file`	Used by the gopher client to translate the gopher document to HTML.

TABLE 28: Java System Properties.

S

Property Name	Description
`java.net.ftp.imagepath.gif`	Used by the gopher client to translate the gopher document to HTML.
`java.net.ftp.imagepath.text`	Used by the gopher client to translate the gopher document to HTML
`java.protocol.handler.pkgs`	List of package prefixes for the class names to use for URL stream handlers.
`java.rmi.activation.activator.class`	Class name of the RMI activator to use.
`java.rmi.activation.port`	Port number of the activation system (`rmid`).
`java.rmi.activation.security.class`	Class name of the RMI security manager to use (defaults to `java.rmi.RMISecurityManager`).
`java.rmi.activation.security.codebase`	URL of the code base used by the RMI class loader.
`java.rmi.dgc.leaseValue`	The maximum lease duration granted for distributed garbage collection (default is 10 minutes).
`java.rmi.loader.packagePrefix`	Package name of the class that implements the `LoaderHandler` interface (defaults to `sun.rmi.server`).
`java.rmi.registry.packagePrefix`	Package name of the class that implements the `Registry` interface (defaults to `sun.rmi.registry`).
`java.rmi.server.codebase`	URL of the code base used by the RMI class loader and when marshalling data.
`java.rmi.server.disableHttp`	Boolean property for enabling HTTP tunneling (default is `false`).
`java.rmi.server.hostname`	Local host name to use in the case of multihomed host or when the fully qualified host name is not available.
`java.rmi.server.logCalls`	Specifies whether to log RMI calls on the server and print to `stderr`.
`java.rmi.server.packagePrefix`	Package name of the classes that implement the server reference classes.
`java.security.debug`	Used by the Java Security for debugging.
`java.security.manager`	Class name of the `java.lang.SecurityManager` implementation to use.
`java.security.policy`	URL of the additional or overriding security policy.
`java.soundpath`	Pathname of the soundbank.
`java.vendor`	Java vendor-specific information.
`java.vendor.url`	Java vendor's URL.
`java.vendor.url.bug`	URL for filing Java bugs.

Continued

TABLE 28: Java System Properties.

S

Property Name	Description
`java.version`	Java version number.
`java.vm.info`	Used by the compiler to record the JIT compiler being used.
`javac.debug`	Turns on the debug mode in `javac`.
`javac.dump.modifiers`	Enables the diagnostic dump of class modifier bits.
`javac.dump.stack`	Used by `javac` for debugging to indicate whether to dump the stack trace.
`javac.trace.depend`	Traces dependencies when running `javac`.
`jdbc.drivers`	Class names of the initial JDBC drivers to load.
`line.separator`	String used to separate lines.
`mail.host`	Name of the host to use for the mailhost in the SMTP client.
`nntp.server`	Name of the host to use in the news URL stream handler.
`org.omg.CORBA.ORBClass`	Class name of an ORB implementation.
`org.omg.CORBA.ORBInitialHost`	Host name of ORB's initial services.
`org.omg.CORBA.ORBInitialPort`	Port number of ORB's initial services.
`org.omg.CORBA.ORBInitialServices`	URL of ORB's initial services.
`org.omg.CORBA.ORBPort`	ORB's server port number.
`org.omg.CORBA.ORBSingletonClass`	Class name of the ORB returned by `ORB.init()`.
`os.arch`	Machine architecture (for example, "x86", "sparc").
`os.name`	Name of the operating system.
`os.version`	Version of the operating system.
`package.restrict.access.`*`pkg`*	Specifies whether the applet or application is restricted from accessing classes in the package with the package prefix *pkg*.
`packages.restrict.definition.`*`pkg`*	Specifies whether the applet or application is restricted from defining classes in the package with the package prefix *pkg*.
`path.separator`	String used to separate components in a path variable.
`policy.provider`	Class name of the security policy provider (the default is `java.security.PolicyFile`).
`programname`	Name of the program to use when posting news articles using the news URL stream handler.
`proxyHost`	Host name of the proxy to use in the RMI socket factory, FTP, or HTTP client.

TABLE 28: Java System Properties.

S

Property Name	Description
`proxyPort`	Port number of the proxy to use in the RMI socket factory, FTP, or HTTP client.
`QUERY_STRING`	Query string for the RMI/HTTP tunneling.
`REQUEST_METHOD`	Request method for the RMI/HTTP tunneling.
`rmi.home`	Pathname of the directory in which to find the `serialver.properties` file.
`SERVER_NAME`	Server name for the RMI/HTTP tunneling.
`SERVER_PORT`	Port number for the RMI/HTTP tunneling.
`socksProxyHost`	Host name of the proxy to use for the SOCKS protocol.
`socksProxyPort`	Port number of the proxy to use for the SOCKS protocol.
`sun.boot.class.path`	List of JAR files and directories for the bootstrap class loader.
`sun.io.unicode.encoding`	Name of the encoding for the Unicode character-to-byte encoding (the default is "UnicodeBig").
`sun.rmi.dgc.logLevel`	An integer indicating the log level for the distributed garbage collection used by the RMI.
`sun.rmi.loader.logLevel`	Integer indicating the log level to use for the RMI loader.
`sun.rmi.server.logLevel`	Integer indicating the log level to use for the RMI server.
`sun.rmi.transport.logLevel`	Integer indicating the log level to use for the RMI transport.
`sun.rmi.transport.proxy.logLevel`	Integer indicating the log level to use for the RMI transport proxy.
`sun.rmi.transport.tcp.logLevel`	Integer indicating the log level to use for the RMI over TCP.
`sun.rmi.transport.tcp.multiplex.logLevel`	Integer indicating the log level to use for the RMI when multiplexed over a single TCP connection.
`user.dir`	Pathname of the user's current working directory.
`user.emailname`	String to use as the user's e-mail address when posting articles via the news URL stream handler.
`user.fromaddr`	String to use as the "from address" when posting articles via the news URL stream handler.
`user.home`	Pathname of the user's home directory.
`user.language`	ISO language code for the user's preferred language (for example, "fr").

Continued

TABLE 28: Java System Properties.

S

Property Name	Description
`user.mailcap`	Pathname of a mailcap format file to include when building a MIME table.
`user.name`	User's logon/account name.
`user.region`	ISO country code for the user's region (for example, "FR").
`user.timezone`	Time zone of the user (the default is "GMT").

TABLE 28: Java System Properties.

Changes for Version 1.2

A new method, `mapLibraryName()`, allows you to obtain the platform-specific name of a library.

In Version 1.1, you could update only the values of all of the system properties (using `setProperties()`). In Version 1.2, you can use `setProperty()` to update an individual system property's value.

The use of `runFinalizersOnExit()` is deprecated.

S

MEMBER SUMMARY	
Standard IO	
`err`	Standard error output stream.
`in`	Standard input stream.
`out`	Standard output stream.
`setErr()`	Sets the standard error output stream.
`setIn()`	Sets the standard input stream.
`setOut()`	Sets the standard output stream.
Runtime Methods	
`exit()`	Exits the virtual machine.
`gc()`	Runs the garbage collector.
`load()`	Loads a dynamic library when given its full pathname.
`loadLibrary()`	Loads a dynamic library when given its library name.
1.2 `mapLibraryName()`	Maps a library name to a platform-specific library name.
`runFinalization()`	Runs the finalization method of objects that are pending finalization.
System Properties	
`getProperties()`	Retrieves the list of system properties.
`getProperty()`	Retrieves the named system property.
1.2 `setProperty()`	Sets/updates a system property's value.
`setProperties()`	Updates the list of system properties.

MEMBER SUMMARY	
Security Methods	
`getSecurityManager()`	Retrieves the reference to the security manager.
`setSecurityManager()`	Sets the system's security manager.
Array Method	
`arraycopy()`	Copies a region of one array to another array.
Time Method	
`currentTimeMillis()`	Retrieves the current time in milliseconds.
Object Method	
`identityHashCode()`	Returns `Object.hashCode()` for an object.
Deprecated Methods	
`getenv()`	Replaced by `getProperty()`.
Δ `runFinalizersOnExit()`	Enables/disables finalization when the program exits.

See Also

`ClassLoader.findLibrary()`, `Runtime`, `Thread.stop()`.
`System` in *The Java Class Libraries, Second Edition, Volume 1.*

1.2 mapLibraryName()

PURPOSE Maps a library name to a platform-specific library name.

SYNTAX `public static native String mapLibraryName(String libname);`

DESCRIPTION This method is used by `Runtime.loadLibrary()` to map the library name supplied by the caller to a platform-specific name.

For the Solaris platform, the platform-specific name is "lib" + `libname` + ".so". For the Windows platform, the platform-specific name is `libname` + ".dll". If the debug version of the Java interpreter is used (`java_g`), "_g" is placed after `libname`. For example, on the Solaris platform, when `java_g` is used, the platform-specific name is "lib" + `libname` + "_g.so".

PARAMETERS

`libname` A non-`null` string containing the library name.

RETURNS A non-`null` string representing the platform-specific library name.

SEE ALSO `ClassLoader.findLibrary()`, `loadLibrary()`, `Runtime.loadLibrary()`.

S

EXAMPLE

```
System.out.println(System.mapLibraryName("net"));
                                     // libnet.so on Solaris
                                     // libnet_g.so on Solaris for debug
                                     // net.dll on Windows
                                     // net_g.dll on Windows for debug
```

Δ runFinalizersOnExit() *DEPRECATED*

PURPOSE Enables/disables finalization when the program exits.

SYNTAX `public static void runFinalizersOnExit(boolean run)`

1.2 CHANGES This method is deprecated in Version 1.2.

DEPRECATION This method specifies that the finalizers of *all* unfinalized objects are to be run. However, there might be threads, for example daemon threads, that continue to execute until the Java virtual machine actually exits. It is unsafe to finalize objects that other threads might still be using.

PARAMETERS

`run` `true` means to finalize objects that are pending finalization before exiting; `false` means finalization need not be run upon exit.

SEE ALSO `runFinalization()`, `Runtime.runFinalizersOnExit()`.

1.2 setProperty()

PURPOSE Sets/updates a system property's value.

SYNTAX `public static String setProperty(String prop, String val)`

DESCRIPTION This method sets the system property `prop` to have the value `val`. If the property did not previously exist, it is added. If the property did previously exist, it is updated. The change is visible to all code on the same Java virtual machine. The property can be changed only if permitted by the security manager. See `PropertyPermission`.

S

PARAMETERS

`prop` A non-`null` string representing the property's name.
`val` A non-`null` string representing the value.

RETURNS The previous value that `prop` used to have before this method was invoked. `null` if the property did not have a value before or if it was `null`.

EXCEPTIONS

`SecurityException`

If the security manager does not permit the setting of `prop` by the caller.

SEE ALSO `PropertyPermission`.

EXAMPLE This example changes the value of the `user.dir` property to `/tmp`.

```
String oldVal = System.setProperty("user.dir", "/tmp");
System.out.println("Old value: " + oldVal);
System.out.println("New value: " + System.getProperty("user.dir"));
```

java.lang
Thread

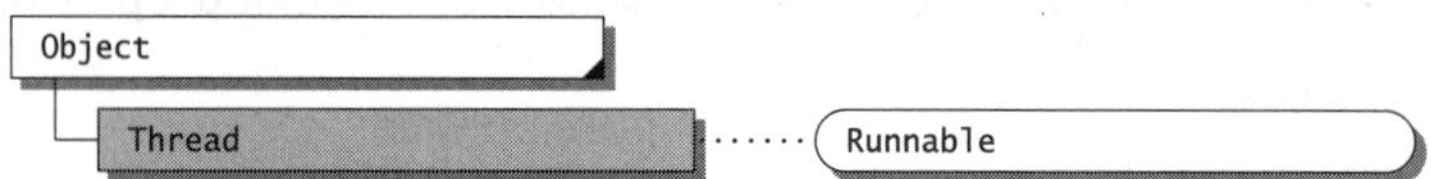

Syntax

```
public class Thread implements Runnable
```

Description

The `Thread` class is used to represent a thread and includes methods to control the execution state of a thread. A *thread* is a single sequential flow of control within a process. A single process can have multiple, concurrently executing threads. For example, a process may have a thread reading input from the user, while at the same time another thread is updating a database containing the user's account balance, while at the same time a third thread is updating the display with the latest stock quotes. Such a process is called a *multithreaded process*; the program from which this process executes is called a *multithreaded program*.

See *The Java Class Libraries, Second Edition, Volume 1* for more information about this class.

Changes for Version 1.2

The `getContextClassLoader()` and `setContextClassLoader())` methods for getting and setting the class loader of a thread are new in Version 1.2.

The following methods have been deprecated: `countStackFrames()`, `resume()`, `stop()`, and `suspend()`. `stop()` is unsafe because it might leave objects in an inconsistent state. The other methods relate to the use of `suspend()`, which is unsafe because it makes programs susceptible to deadlocks.

The `checkAccess()` method is now final. Although the method's implementation has not changed, it uses `SecurityManager.checkAccess()`, which has changed to use the Version 1.2 security permissions model. See `SecurityManager` for details.

MEMBER SUMMARY	
Constructor	
`Thread()`	Constructs a `Thread` instance.
Interrupt Methods	
`interrupt()`	Sends an interrupt to this `Thread`.
`interrupted()`	Determines if the currently executing thread has been interrupted.
`isInterrupted()`	Determines if this `Thread` has been interrupted.

MEMBER SUMMARY

	Thread Property Fields and Methods	
	`getName()`	Retrieves this `Thread`'s name.
	`getPriority()`	Retrieves this `Thread`'s priority.
	`getThreadGroup()`	Retrieves this `Thread`'s thread group.
	`isDaemon()`	Determines if this `Thread` is a daemon thread.
	`MAX_PRIORITY`	The maximum priority that a thread can have.
	`MIN_PRIORITY`	The minimum priority that a thread can have.
	`NORM_PRIORITY`	The default priority that is assigned to the first user thread.
	`setDaemon()`	Changes this `Thread`'s daemon status.
	`setName()`	Changes this `Thread`'s name.
	`setPriority()`	Changes this `Thread`'s priority.
	Thread State Methods	
	`destroy()`	Destroys this `Thread` without any cleanup.
	`isAlive()`	Determines if this `Thread` is active.
	`join()`	Waits for this `Thread` to terminate.
	`run()`	The actual body of this `Thread`.
	`sleep()`	Causes the currently executing thread to sleep for a period of time.
	`start()`	Starts the execution of this `Thread`.
	`yield()`	Causes the currently executing thread to yield to other threads.
	Stack Frame Method	
	`dumpStack()`	Prints a snapshot of the current execution stack trace.
	Class Loader Methods	
1.2	`getContextClassLoader()`	Retrieves the context class loader for this `Thread`.
1.2	`setContextClassLoader()`	Sets the context class loader for this `Thread`.
	Security Method	
Δ	`checkAccess()`	Checks whether the caller is allowed to modify this `Thread`.
	Current Thread Methods	
	`activeCount()`	Estimates the number of active threads in the current thread's thread group and its subgroup.
	`currentThread()`	Retrieves the currently executing thread.
	`enumerate()`	Enumerates the active threads in the currently executing thread's thread group.
	Description Method	
	`toString()`	Generates a string representation of this `Thread`.
	Deprecated Methods	
Δ	`countStackFrames()`	Counts the number of stack frames in this `Thread`.

Continued

T

MEMBER SUMMARY	
Deprecated Methods (*Continued*)	
Δ `resume()`	Resumes the execution of this `Thread`.
Δ `stop()`	Stops the execution of this `Thread`.
Δ `suspend()`	Suspends the execution of this `Thread`.

See Also

`ClassLoader`, `SecurityManager`.
`Thread` in *The Java Class Libraries, Second Edition, Volume 1.*

Δ checkAccess()

PURPOSE Checks whether the caller is allowed to modify this `Thread`.

SYNTAX `public final void checkAccess()`

DESCRIPTION This method checks whether the security manager allows the caller to modify this `Thread`. Modifications that require access checking include changing the state of the thread (for example, suspend/resume) and changing the properties associated with a thread (its daemon status and priority).

The default security manager (`SecurityManager`) uses the following heuristics. If this `Thread` is a system thread (that is, it belongs to the system thread group) and a security manager has been installed, a `SecurityException` is thrown unless the caller has been granted `RuntimePermission("modifyThread")` by the Java runtime's security policy. If this `Thread` is not a system thread, this method just returns. A security manager should override `SecurityManager.checkAccess()` to control whether nonsystem threads can be modified.

1.2 CHANGES In Version 1.1, this method was not final. Also in Version 1.1, `SecurityManager.checkAccess()` always threw a `SecurityException` and had to be overridden to perform the appropriate checks, even for system threads.

EXCEPTIONS

`SecurityException`
If the caller is not allowed to modify this `Thread` due to security reasons.

SEE ALSO `currentThread()`, `resume()`, `RuntimePermission("modifyThread")`, `SecurityManager.checkAccess()`, `setDaemon()`, `setName()`, `setPriority()`, `stop()`, `suspend()`, `Thread()`, `ThreadGroup.checkAccess()`.

Δ countStackFrames() *DEPRECATED*

PURPOSE Counts the number of stack frames in this `Thread`.

SYNTAX `public native int countStackFrames()`

DESCRIPTION Counts the number of stack frames in this `Thread`. This `Thread` must be suspended.

1.2 CHANGES This method is deprecated in Version 1.2.

DEPRECATION This method is deprecated because its depends on the use of `suspend()`, which is a deprecated method.

RETURNS The number of stack frames in this `Thread`.

EXCEPTIONS

`IllegalThreadStateException`
If this `Thread` is not suspended.

1.2 getContextClassLoader()

PURPOSE Retrieves the context class loader for this `Thread`.

SYNTAX `public ClassLoader getContextClassLoader()`

DESCRIPTION This method retrieves the context class loader for this `Thread`. The *context class loader* of a thread is, by default, set to the context class loader of the thread's parent thread when the thread is created. The context class loader of the primordial thread (the one that runs `main()`) is set to the class loader that loaded the application (see `ClassLoader.getSystemClassLoader()`). So unless the code that created the thread explicitly changes the context class loader by using `setContextClassLoader()`, the class loader will be that of the application.

The Java runtime system typically uses the class loader that loaded the class of the caller when loading classes and resources referenced by the class. Consequently, the thread's context class loader is usually ignored. `getContextClassLoader()` is useful for library code (such as the Java Development Kit (JDK) itself or standard extensions) that call `Class.forName()` or otherwise use class loaders to load classes and resources *on behalf of* the caller. In such cases, to avoid using its own class loader (which is usually the bootstrap class loader), the library code uses `getContextClassLoader()` to load the classes and resources. In this way, the library code has a better chance of successfully loading the classes and resources intended by the user of the library code.

If the context class loader is not the same as or is not an ancestor of the calling class's class loader, the caller must have been granted `RuntimePermis-`

sion("getClassLoader") by the Java runtime system's security policy. Otherwise, a SecurityException is thrown.

RETURNS The possibly null context class loader for this Thread. It is null if it was previously set to null using setContextClassLoader().

EXCEPTIONS

SecurityException

If the caller does not have permission to access the class loader of this Thread.

SEE ALSO ClassLoader.getSystemClassLoader(), RuntimePermission("getClassLoader"), setContextClassLoader().

EXAMPLE Here is an example of how library code typically uses getContextClassLoader().

```
try {
    ClassLoader cl = Thread.currentThread().getContextClassLoader();
    Class c = Class.forName(className, true, cl);
} catch (ClassNotFoundException e) {
    e.printStackTrace();
}
```

Δ resume() *DEPRECATED*

PURPOSE Resumes the execution of this Thread.

SYNTAX `public final void resume()`

1.2 CHANGES This method is deprecated in Version 1.2.

DEPRECATION This method is deprecated because its use is related to that of suspend(), which is a deprecated method.

EXCEPTIONS

SecurityException

If the caller is not allowed to modify this Thread due to security reasons.

SEE ALSO checkAccess(), suspend(), stop(), ThreadGroup.resume().

EXAMPLE See suspend() for how to replace the use of this deprecated method.

1.2 setContextClassLoader()

PURPOSE Sets the context class loader for this Thread.

SYNTAX `public void setContextClassLoader(ClassLoader cl)`

DESCRIPTION This method sets cl to be this Thread's context class loader. The context class loader for a thread is, by default, set to the context class loader of the thread's parent, as explained in getContextClassLoader(). One use of setContext-

`ClassLoader()` is to affect the class loader used by library code that loads classes and resources, if the caller has prior knowledge that the library code will use the thread's context class loader for loading classes and resources. A caller that calls this method should use a `try/finally` block to undo the change so that the change will not affect other code executed by the thread.

To use this method, the caller must have been granted `RuntimePermission("setContextClassLoader")` by the Java runtime's security policy. If it has not, a `SecurityException` is thrown.

PARAMETERS

`cl` The possibly `null` context `ClassLoader` for this `Thread`. If `null`, subsequent calls to `getContextClassLoader()` will return `null` and subsequent children of this `Thread` will inherit `null` as their context class loader.

EXCEPTIONS

`SecurityException`
If the caller does not have permission to modify this `Thread`.

SEE ALSO `getContextClassLoader()`, `RuntimePermission("setContextClassLoader")`.

Δ stop() *DEPRECATED*

PURPOSE Stops the execution of this `Thread`.

SYNTAX

```
public final void stop()
public final synchronized void stop(Throwable e)
```

DESCRIPTION The two forms of this method stop the execution of this `Thread`. A thread that has been stopped is no longer active and is removed from its thread group.

Normally, to stop a thread you call `stop()` with no arguments. Doing this causes the error `ThreadDeath` to be thrown. The Java runtime then catches this error and completes the termination. You can also call `stop()` with a `Throwable` object `e`, but this is not done unless you want to terminate the thread abnormally. If `e` is not an instance of `ThreadDeath` or its subclasses, it is not caught by the Java runtime. The uncaught exception is thrown to the top-level error handler, which prints out a stack trace of `e`.

When a thread is stopped, it terminates immediately and any locks it is holding are released. Releasing locks in such an abnormal manner typically leads to unintended program behavior. The `stop()` method is deprecated and should be used only with great caution.

This method can be executed only if permitted by the security manager.

1.2 CHANGES This method is deprecated in Version 1.2.

DEPRECATION As mentioned in the description, stopping a thread releases any locks that it is holding, an action that can lead to unintended program behavior. Applications should generally avoid using `stop()` and should instead be programmed in such a way as to allow threads to terminate deterministically. For example, the thread's run loop could use a `boolean` to indicate whether the thread should continue. The code wishing to stop the thread would set the `boolean` to `false` when it wants the thread to terminate.

PARAMETERS

`e` The object to be thrown when stopping this `Thread`. This is thrown by this `Thread`, not the caller of `stop()`.

EXCEPTIONS

`SecurityException`
If the caller is not allowed to stop this thread due to security reasons.

SEE ALSO `checkAccess()`, `activeCount()`, `isActive()`, `start()`, `ThreadDeath`, `ThreadGroup.stop()`, `ThreadGroup.uncaughtException()`, `Throwable`.

EXAMPLE This example defines a thread called `Worker`. `Worker`'s `run()` method has a `while` loop that does work and periodically checks whether it has been stopped. `Worker` can be stopped using the `safeStop()` method, which sets a `boolean` to indicate whether the thread should continue.

```
class Main {
    public static void main(String args[]) {
        for (int i=0; i<5; i++) {
            Worker worker = new Worker();
            worker.setPriority(Thread.currentThread().getPriority()-1);

            try {
                worker.start();
                Thread.sleep(5000);     // Wait 5 seconds.

                System.out.println("Stopping thread: " + worker);

                worker.safeStop();      // Stop the thread.
            } catch (InterruptedException e) {
                e.printStackTrace();
            }
        }
    }
}

class Worker extends Thread {
    private int count;
    private boolean done = false;

    synchronized void safeStop() {
        done = true;
    }

    synchronized boolean ok() {
        return (!done);
    }
```

```
    void doWork() {
        // do something useful here
        ++count;
    }

    public void run() {
        while (ok()) {
            doWork();
        }
    }
}
```

Δ suspend() *DEPRECATED*

PURPOSE Suspends the execution of this `Thread`.

SYNTAX `public final void suspend()`

DESCRIPTION This method suspends the execution of this `Thread`. When a thread has been suspended, it cannot run until it is resumed via a call to `resume()`. A thread that is suspended is still marked *active*. If you suspend a thread that has already been suspended, no action is taken.

Note that a suspended thread still holds all of the locks it acquired. Hence, thread suspension can be a source of deadlocks in multithreaded programs and should be used only with great caution.

This method may be executed only if permitted by the security manager.

1.2 CHANGES This method is deprecated in Version 1.2.

DEPRECATION As mentioned in the description, suspending a thread leaves the thread holding all of its locks, thereby possibly leading to deadlocks. Instead of using `suspend()`, the program should maintain its own state about the thread, for example by maintaining a `boolean` that tracks whether the thread is "suspended."

EXCEPTIONS

`SecurityException`

If the caller is not allowed to suspend this `Thread` due to security reasons.

SEE ALSO `checkAccess()`, `countStackFrames()`, `resume()`, `stop()`, `ThreadGroup.suspend()`.

EXAMPLE This example defines a thread called `Worker` that provides `safeSuspend()` and `safeResume()`, which use a `boolean` to record the state of the thread instead of using the `suspend()` and `resume()` methods.

```
class Main {
    public static void main(String args[]) {
        Worker worker = new Worker();
        worker.setPriority(Thread.currentThread().getPriority()-1);

        try {
```

T

```
                worker.start();

                for (int i = 0; i < 5; i++) {
                    Thread.sleep(5000);    // Wait 5 seconds.
                    worker.safeSuspend();  // Suspend the thread.
                    Thread.sleep(1000);    // Wait a second for it to resume
                    worker.safeResume();   // Resume the thread
                }

                worker.safeStop();
            } catch (InterruptedException e) {
                e.printStackTrace();
            }
        }
    }
    class Worker extends Thread {
        private int count;
        private boolean done = false;
        private boolean suspended = false;

        synchronized void safeStop() {
            System.out.println("stopped");
            done = true;
        }
        synchronized void safeSuspend() {
            System.out.println("suspended");
            suspended = true;
        }
        synchronized void safeResume() {
            System.out.println("resumed");
            suspended = false;
            notify();
        }
        synchronized boolean ok() {
            return (!done);
        }
        synchronized void doWork() {
            if (!suspended) {
                // do something useful
                ++count;
            } else {
                while (suspended) {
                    try {
                        wait();
                    } catch (InterruptedException e) {
                    }
                }
            }
        }
        public void run() {
            while (ok()) {
                doWork();
            }
        }
    }
```

ThreadGroup

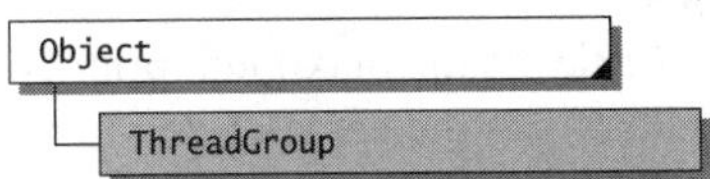

Syntax

```
public class ThreadGroup
```

Description

The `ThreadGroup` class represents a group of threads. A thread group can contain a set of threads and other thread groups. A thread or thread group may be in at most one thread group. Thread groups allow you to organize groups so that you can manipulate the group of threads as a whole. For example, you can set the maximum priority of a thread group and suspend and resume all threads in a group.

See *The Java Class Libraries, Second Edition, Volume 1* for more information about this class.

Changes for Version 1.2

The `interrupt()` method is new to Version 1.2.

The following methods are deprecated: `allowThreadSuspension()`, `resume()`, `stop()`, and `suspend()`. `stop()` is unsafe because it might leave objects in an inconsistent state. The other methods relate to the use of `suspend()`, which is unsafe because it makes programs susceptible to deadlocks.

The `checkAccess()` method's implementation is unchanged, but the method uses `SecurityManager.checkAccess()`, which has been changed to use the Version 1.2 security permissions model.

MEMBER SUMMARY	
Constructor	
`ThreadGroup()`	Constructs a `ThreadGroup` instance.
Thread Group State Methods	
`activeCount()`	Estimates the number of active threads in this `ThreadGroup`.
`activeGroupCount()`	Estimates the number of active thread groups in this `ThreadGroup`.
`enumerate()`	Enumerates the threads or thread groups in this `ThreadGroup`.
`isDestroyed()`	Determines whether this `ThreadGroup` has been destroyed.
`list()`	Prints the threads and thread groups in this `ThreadGroup`.

Continued

MEMBER SUMMARY

Thread Group Property Methods	
`getMaxPriority()`	Retrieves the maximum priority of this `ThreadGroup`.
`getName()`	Retrieves the name of this `ThreadGroup`.
`getParent()`	Retrieves the parent thread group of this `ThreadGroup`.
`isDaemon()`	Determines if this thread group is a daemon `ThreadGroup`.
`parentOf()`	Determines if this `ThreadGroup` is an ancestor of another `ThreadGroup`.
`setDaemon()`	Changes the daemon status of this `ThreadGroup`.
`setMaxPriority()`	Sets the maximum priority of this `ThreadGroup` and its subgroup.
Thread State Methods	
`destroy()`	Destroys this `ThreadGroup` and its subgroups.
1.2 `interrupt()`	Interrupts all threads in this `ThreadGroup` and its subgroups.
Security Method	
Δ `checkAccess()`	Determines if the caller is allowed to modify this `ThreadGroup`.
Thread Exit Handling Method	
`uncaughtException()`	Handles a thread exit from this `ThreadGroup` due to an uncaught exception.
Description Method	
`toString()`	Generates the string representation of this `ThreadGroup`.
Deprecated Methods	
Δ `allowThreadSuspension()`	Enables/disables whether this `ThreadGroup`'s threads can be suspended due to low memory in the virtual machine.
Δ `resume()`	Resumes all of the threads in this `ThreadGroup` and its subgroups.
Δ `stop()`	Stops the execution of all of the threads in this `ThreadGroup` and its subgroups.
Δ `suspend()`	Suspends all of the threads in this `ThreadGroup` and its subgroups.

T

See Also

`RuntimePermission("modifyThreadGroup")`, `SecurityManager`, `Thread`.
`ThreadGroup` in *The Java Class Libraries, Second Edition, Volume 1.*

Δ allowThreadSuspension() *DEPRECATED*

PURPOSE
Enables/disables whether this `ThreadGroup`'s threads can be suspended due to low memory in the virtual machine.

SYNTAX
`public boolean allowThreadSuspension(boolean allow)`

DESCRIPTION
This method enables or disables the ability of the virtual machine to suspend this `ThreadGroup`'s threads when the virtual machine is low on memory. If `allow` is `true`, this `ThreadGroup`'s threads can be suspended. If `allow` is `false`, this `ThreadGroup`'s threads cannot be suspended and any threads that are currently suspended due to low memory are unsuspended.

A thread group inherits this property (whether the virtual machine can suspend its threads if the virtual machine is low on memory) from its parent at the time the thread group is created. This property has no effect on the suspension of this `ThreadGroup`'s threads via the `suspend()` call.

1.2 CHANGES
This method is deprecated in Version 1.2.

DEPRECATION
This method is deprecated because its use is related to that thread suspension, which is deadlock-prone.

PARAMETERS

`allow` `true` means suspension can occur; `false` means suspension cannot occur.

RETURNS
`true`.

Δ checkAccess()

PURPOSE
Determines if the caller is allowed to modify this `ThreadGroup`.

SYNTAX
`public final void checkAccess()`

DESCRIPTION
This method checks whether the security manager allows the caller to modify this `ThreadGroup`. Modifications that require access checking include changing the state of the thread (for example, suspend/resume) and changing the properties associated with a thread (its daemon status and priority).

The default security manager (`SecurityManager`) uses the following heuristics. If this `ThreadGroup` is the system thread group and a security manager has been installed, a `SecurityException` is thrown unless the caller has been granted `RuntimePermission("modifyThreadGroup")` by the Java runtime's security policy. Otherwise, this method just returns. A security manager should override `SecurityManager.checkAccess()` to control whether nonsystem thread groups may be modified.

1.2 CHANGES In Version 1.1, `SecurityManager.checkAccess()` method always threw a `SecurityException` and had to be overridden to perform the appropriate checks, even for the system thread group.

EXCEPTIONS

`SecurityException`

If the caller is not allowed to modify this `ThreadGroup` due to security reasons.

SEE ALSO `interrupt()`, `RuntimePermission("modifyThreadGroup")`, `Security.checkAccess()`.

1.2 interrupt()

PURPOSE Interrupts all threads in this `ThreadGroup` and it subgroups.

SYNTAX `public final void interrupt()`

DESCRIPTION This method interrupts the threads in this `ThreadGroup` and its subgroups. A thread group may be interrupted only if allowed by the `SecurityManager`.

EXCEPTIONS

`SecurityException`

If the caller is not allowed to access this `ThreadGroup` or any of the threads in it.

SEE ALSO `checkAccess()`, `RuntimePermission("modifyThreadGroup")`. `Thread.interrupt()` in *The Java Class Libraries, Second Edition, Volume 1*.

Δ resume() *DEPRECATED*

PURPOSE Resumes all of threads in this `ThreadGroup` and its subgroups.

SYNTAX `public final void resume()`

1.2 CHANGES This method is deprecated in Version 1.2.

DEPRECATION This method is deprecated because its use is related to that of `suspend()`, which is a deprecated method.

EXCEPTIONS

`SecurityException`

If the caller is not allowed to modify this `ThreadGroup` due to security reasons.

SEE ALSO `checkAccess()`, `Thread.resume()`.

T

Δ stop()

DEPRECATED

PURPOSE Stops the execution of all of the threads in this `ThreadGroup` and its subgroups.

SYNTAX `public final void stop()`

1.2 CHANGES This method is deprecated in Version 1.2.

DEPRECATION Stopping a thread releases any locks it is holding, an action that can lead to unintended program behavior. See `Thread.stop()` for examples of how to avoid the use of `stop()`.

EXCEPTIONS

`SecurityException`

If the caller is not allowed to stop this `ThreadGroup` due to security reasons.

SEE ALSO `checkAccess()`, `Thread.stop()`.

Δ suspend()

DEPRECATED

PURPOSE Suspends all of the threads in this `ThreadGroup` and its subgroups.

SYNTAX `public final void suspend()`

1.2 CHANGES This method is deprecated in Version 1.2.

DEPRECATION Suspending a thread leaves the thread holding all of its locks, thereby possibly leading to deadlocks. See `Thread.suspend()` for a workaround.

EXCEPTIONS

`SecurityException`

If the caller is not allowed to suspend this `ThreadGroup` due to security reasons.

SEE ALSO `checkAccess()`, `Thread.suspend()`.

java.lang

ThreadLocal

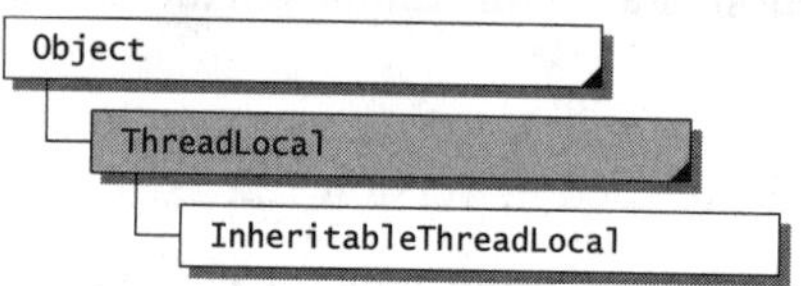

Syntax

```
public class ThreadLocal
```

Description

The `ThreadLocal` class is used to implement *thread-local variables*. A thread-local variable is like an instance variable in that both hold one object reference. They differ in that the storage of an instance variable is part of an object, while the storage of a thread-local variable is (conceptually) part of a thread. In other words, if a thread *A* stores the value `"abc"` in a thread-local variable and a thread *B* reads the thread-local variable, thread *B* will see `null`. If thread *B* stores the value `"xyz"` in the same thread-local variable and thread *A* reads it, thread *A* will still see the value `"abc"`. See Figure 21.

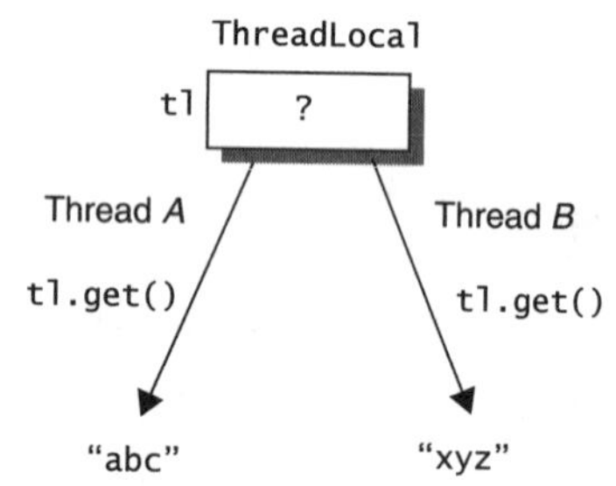

FIGURE 21: The `ThreadLocal` Object is Thread-Dependent.

Thread-local variables are useful for storing state that is associated with a thread. For example, the Java security system uses thread-local variables to store the principal (owner) of a thread and uses this information whenever the thread tries to access protected resources.

Thread-local variables in a thread do not appear in any child threads that the thread creates. If you want a thread-local variable to automatically appear in a child thread, see `InheritableThreadLocal`.

T

Usage

A thread-local variable is represented by a `ThreadLocal` object. If you need a new thread-local variable, you simply create a `ThreadLocal` object. You can then get and set the contents of the new thread-local variable by calling `get()` and `set()`, respectively, on the corresponding `ThreadLocal`.

A thread's thread-local storage can be accessed only by the owning thread. In a sense, a thread-local variable is like a private instance variable: One object cannot access another object's private instance variables. Therefore, if you want a particular thread-local variable in a thread to be set to a certain value, you have to arrange for the thread to do it itself.

A `ThreadLocal` object is typically made static so that you don't need an instance of the encapsulating class in order to use it. However, the `ThreadLocal` could be kept in a more private variable if protecting access to the thread-local value is important. See the next section for additional information.

Security

It is impossible for one thread to access another thread's thread-local variable storage. However, it is possible for any method that the thread happens to call to access the thread's thread-local storage. Therefore, if you want to restrict access to a particular thread-local variable to a certain set of objects, then you need to make sure that only those objects have a reference to the associated `ThreadLocal` object. So even if a thread executes some rogue code, there is no way the rogue code can access that thread's thread-local variables without a reference to the appropriate `ThreadLocal` objects.

MEMBER SUMMARY	
Constructor	
`ThreadLocal()`	Constructs a new `ThreadLocal` instance.
Get/Set Value Methods	
`get()`	Retrieves the value of this thread-local variable in the calling thread.
`set()`	Sets the value of this thread-local variable in the calling thread.
Initial Value Override	
`initialValue()`	Returns the initial value for this thread-local variable in the calling thread.

See Also

`InheritableThreadLocal`.

Example

This example declares a thread-local variable that is used by two threads: the main thread and a thread that it creates. Note that it is incorrect for a thread to set a thread-local variable in the thread's constructor because the constructor is executed using the thread that is creating the new thread object. A thread-local variable should be set in the `run()` method or by a method called directly or indirectly from `run()`. Note also that the new thread (`MyThread`) does not inherit the value of the thread-local variable from its parent.

```
class Main {
    static ThreadLocal thdloc = new ThreadLocal();

    Main() {
        print();                                    // 1: "null"
```

T

```
            thdloc.set("MainThread");
            print();                                 // 2: "MainThread"

            Thread t = new MyThread(this);
            t.start();
            try {
                t.join();
            } catch (InterruptedException e) {
                e.printStackTrace();
            }
            print();                                 // 6: "MainThread"
        }

        public void print() {
            System.out.println(thdloc.get());
        }

        public static void main(String[] args) {
            new Main();
        }
    }

    class MyThread extends Thread {
        Main main;

        MyThread(Main main) {
            this.main = main;
            main.print();                            // 3: "MainThread"

            // Executes in the wrong thread for setting the thread local variable.
            // Main.thdloc.set("MyThread");
        }
        public void run() {
            main.print();                            // 4: "null"
            Main.thdloc.set("MyThread");
            main.print();                            // 5: "MyThread"
        }
    }
```

get()

PURPOSE Retrieves the value of this thread-local variable in the calling thread.

SYNTAX `public Object get()`

DESCRIPTION This method returns the value in the calling thread's copy of this thread-local variable. If `set()` is never called on this thread-local variable, this method returns whatever `initialValue()` returns (which is `null` by default).

RETURNS The possibly `null` value in this thread-local's variable.

EXAMPLE See the class example.

initialValue()

PURPOSE

Returns the initial value for this thread-local variable in the calling thread.

SYNTAX

`protected Object initialValue()`

DESCRIPTION

This method returns the initial value for this thread-local variable in the calling thread. It must be overridden if a thread-local variable is to have a default value other than `null`. It is called exactly once by a thread when it calls `get()` on this `ThreadLocal` object for the first time.

If this method returns a reference to a particular object, then the object will be shared by all threads using the thread-local variable; that is, the object is not automatically cloned so that all threads will have its own copy. If each thread should have a copy of the default value, then this method should create a new instance of the object and return it.

The default implementation of this method returns `null`.

RETURNS

A possibly `null` object representing the initial value of this thread-local variable.

EXAMPLE

This example declares a thread-local variable that creates a new `StringBuffer` object for each copy of the thread-local variable. The example shows that changes to the `StringBuffer` object in one thread do not affect the copy in another thread.

```
class Main {
    static ThreadLocal thrloc = new ThreadLocal() {
        public Object initialValue() {
            return new StringBuffer("Buffer ");
        }
    };

    Main() {
        System.out.println(thrloc.get());                    // 1: "Buffer"
        ((StringBuffer)thrloc.get()).append("1");
        System.out.println(thrloc.get());                    // 2: "Buffer 1"

        Thread t = new MyThread();
        t.start();
        try {
            t.join();
        } catch (InterruptedException e) {
            e.printStackTrace();
        }

        System.out.println(thrloc.get());                    // 5: "Buffer 1"
    }

    public static void main(String[] args) {
        new Main();
    }
}
```

T

```
class MyThread extends Thread {
    public void run() {
        System.out.println(Main.thrloc.get());            // 3: "Buffer"
        ((StringBuffer)Main.thrloc.get()).append("2");
        System.out.println(Main.thrloc.get());            // 4: "Buffer 2"
    }
}
```

set()

PURPOSE Sets the value of this thread-local variable in the calling thread.

SYNTAX `public void set(Object val)`

DESCRIPTION This method sets the value in the calling thread's copy of this thread-local variable to `val`.

PARAMETERS

`val` A possibly `null` object to be stored in the calling thread's copy of this thread-local variable.

EXAMPLE See the class example.

ThreadLocal()

PURPOSE Constructs a new `ThreadLocal` instance.

SYNTAX `public ThreadLocal()`

DESCRIPTION This constructor creates a new `ThreadLocal` object representing a new thread-local variable. Unless `initialValue()` is overridden, the initial value of the new thread-local variable is `null`.

EXAMPLE See the class example.

TimeZone

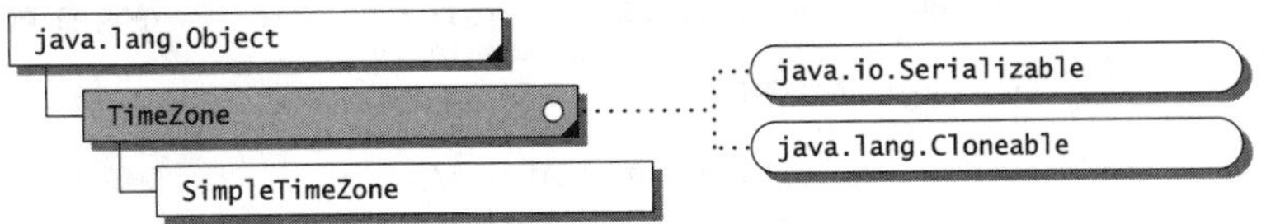

Syntax

```
abstract public class TimeZone implements Serializable, Cloneable
```

Description

The `TimeZone` class is an abstract class designed to be the superclass of different kinds of `TimeZone` objects. A `TimeZone` object represents a time zone. It is used to compute the local time based on a time relative to Greenwich Mean Time (GMT). It also contains daylight savings time information.

`TimeZone` objects can differ in the type of calendar used to interpret dates and in the rules that determine the daylight savings time period. For example, the `java.util` package provides one `TimeZone` subclass called `SimpleTimeZone`. `SimpleTimeZone` uses a Gregorian calendar (see `GregorianCalendar`) and its daylight savings time rules can be only of the form "start on the first Sunday in April." `SimpleTimeZone` cannot handle rules of the form "start on March 4"; a different `TimeZone` subclass is needed for this.

See *The Java Class Libraries, Second Edition, Volume 1* for more information about this class.

Changes for Version 1.2

Two methods are new: `getDisplayName()` and `hasSameRules()`. Also, two constants, `LONG` and `SHORT`, which are used by `getDisplayName()`, have been added. See the member descriptions for more details.

The `getTimeZone()` method now returns a `TimeZone` object for GMT when it does not recognize the supplied time-zone ID (in Version 1.1, it returned `null`). Also, this method now returns a new copy of the `TimeZone` object, which you can safely modify if you wish.

Many more time zones are new to Version 1.2. Table 29 lists the new set of time zones. Note also that the time-zone IDs are no longer exactly three uppercase characters long, as they all were in Version 1.1. (This is not a semantic change, since the form of the time-zone IDs was never restricted.)

ID	Raw Off-set	Short Display Name	Long Display Name
ACT	9.5	GMT+09:30	GMT+09:30
AET	10	GMT+10:00	GMT+10:00
AGT	-3	GMT-03:00	GMT-03:00
ART	2	GMT+02:00	GMT+02:00
AST	-9	AKST	Alaska Standard Time
Africa/Abidjan	0	GMT+00:00	GMT+00:00
Africa/Accra	0	GMT+00:00	GMT+00:00
Africa/Addis_Ababa	3	GMT+03:00	GMT+03:00
Africa/Algiers	1	GMT+01:00	GMT+01:00
Africa/Asmera	3	GMT+03:00	GMT+03:00
Africa/Bangui	1	GMT+01:00	GMT+01:00
Africa/Banjul	0	GMT+00:00	GMT+00:00
Africa/Bissau	0	GMT+00:00	GMT+00:00
Africa/Blantyre	2	GMT+02:00	GMT+02:00
Africa/Bujumbura	2	GMT+02:00	GMT+02:00
Africa/Cairo	2	GMT+02:00	GMT+02:00
Africa/Casablanca	0	GMT	Greenwich Mean Time
Africa/Conakry	0	GMT+00:00	GMT+00:00
Africa/Dakar	0	GMT+00:00	GMT+00:00
Africa/Dar_es_-Salaam	3	GMT+03:00	GMT+03:00
Africa/Djibouti	3	GMT+03:00	GMT+03:00
Africa/Douala	1	GMT+01:00	GMT+01:00
Africa/Freetown	0	GMT+00:00	GMT+00:00
Africa/Gaborone	2	GMT+02:00	GMT+02:00
Africa/Harare	2	GMT+02:00	GMT+02:00
Africa/Johannesburg	2	GMT+02:00	GMT+02:00
Africa/Kampala	3	GMT+03:00	GMT+03:00
Africa/Khartoum	2	GMT+02:00	GMT+02:00
Africa/Kigali	2	GMT+02:00	GMT+02:00
Africa/Kinshasa	1	GMT+01:00	GMT+01:00
Africa/Lagos	1	GMT+01:00	GMT+01:00
Africa/Libreville	1	GMT+01:00	GMT+01:00
Africa/Lome	0	GMT+00:00	GMT+00:00
Africa/Luanda	1	GMT+01:00	GMT+01:00
Africa/Lubumbashi	2	GMT+02:00	GMT+02:00
Africa/Lusaka	2	GMT+02:00	GMT+02:00
Africa/Malabo	1	GMT+01:00	GMT+01:00
Africa/Maputo	2	GMT+02:00	GMT+02:00
Africa/Maseru	2	GMT+02:00	GMT+02:00
Africa/Mbabane	2	GMT+02:00	GMT+02:00
Africa/Mogadishu	3	GMT+03:00	GMT+03:00
Africa/Monrovia	0	GMT+00:00	GMT+00:00
Africa/Nairobi	3	GMT+03:00	GMT+03:00
Africa/Ndjamena	1	GMT+01:00	GMT+01:00
Africa/Niamey	1	GMT+01:00	GMT+01:00
Africa/Nouakchott	0	GMT+00:00	GMT+00:00
Africa/Ouagadougou	0	GMT+00:00	GMT+00:00
Africa/Porto-Novo	1	GMT+01:00	GMT+01:00
Africa/Sao_Tome	0	GMT+00:00	GMT+00:00
Africa/Timbuktu	0	GMT+00:00	GMT+00:00
Africa/Tripoli	1	GMT+01:00	GMT+01:00
Africa/Tunis	1	GMT+01:00	GMT+01:00

TABLE 29: Available Time Zones.

ID	Raw Off-set	Short Display Name	Long Display Name	ID	Raw Off-set	Short Display Name	Long Display Name
Africa/Windhoek	1	GMT+01:00	GMT+01:00	America/Godthab	-3	GMT-03:00	GMT-03:00
America/Adak	-10	GMT-10:00	GMT-10:00	America/Grand_Turk	-5	GMT-05:00	GMT-05:00
America/Anchorage	-9	AKST	Alaska Standard Time	America/Grenada	-4	GMT-04:00	GMT-04:00
America/Anguilla	-4	GMT-04:00	GMT-04:00	America/Guadeloupe	-4	GMT-04:00	GMT-04:00
America/Antigua	-4	GMT-04:00	GMT-04:00	America/Guatemala	-6	GMT-06:00	GMT-06:00
America/Aruba	-4	GMT-04:00	GMT-04:00	America/Guayaquil	-5	GMT-05:00	GMT-05:00
America/Asuncion	-4	GMT-04:00	GMT-04:00	America/Guyana	-4	GMT-04:00	GMT-04:00
America/Barbados	-4	GMT-04:00	GMT-04:00	America/Halifax	-4	AST	Atlantic Standard Time
America/Belize	-6	GMT-06:00	GMT-06:00	America/Havana	-5	GMT-05:00	GMT-05:00
America/Bogota	-5	GMT-05:00	GMT-05:00	America/Indianapolis	-5	EST	Eastern Standard Time
America/Buenos_Aires	-3	GMT-03:00	GMT-03:00	America/Jamaica	-5	GMT-05:00	GMT-05:00
America/Caracas	-4	GMT-04:00	GMT-04:00	America/La_Paz	-4	GMT-04:00	GMT-04:00
America/Cayenne	-3	GMT-03:00	GMT-03:00	America/Lima	-5	GMT-05:00	GMT-05:00
America/Cayman	-5	GMT-05:00	GMT-05:00	America/Los_Angeles	-8	PST	Pacific Standard Time
America/Chicago	-6	CST	Central Standard Time	America/Managua	-5	GMT-05:00	GMT-05:00
America/Costa_Rica	-6	GMT-06:00	GMT-06:00	America/Manaus	-4	GMT-04:00	GMT-04:00
America/Cuiaba	-4	GMT-04:00	GMT-04:00	America/Martinique	-4	GMT-04:00	GMT-04:00
America/Curacao	-4	GMT-04:00	GMT-04:00	America/Mazatlan	-7	GMT-07:00	GMT-07:00
America/Dawson_Creek	-7	GMT-07:00	GMT-07:00	America/Mexico_City	-6	GMT-06:00	GMT-06:00
America/Denver	-7	MST	Mountain Standard Time	America/Miquelon	-3	GMT-03:00	GMT-03:00
America/Dominica	-4	GMT-04:00	GMT-04:00	America/Montevideo	-3	GMT-03:00	GMT-03:00
America/Edmonton	-7	GMT-07:00	GMT-07:00	America/Montreal	-5	GMT-05:00	GMT-05:00
America/El_Salvador	-6	GMT-06:00	GMT-06:00	America/Montserrat	-4	GMT-04:00	GMT-04:00
America/Fortaleza	-3	GMT-03:00	GMT-03:00	America/Nassau	-5	GMT-05:00	GMT-05:00

Continued

TABLE 29: Available Time Zones.

T

ID	Raw Offset	Short Display Name	Long Display Name
America/New_York	-5	EST	Eastern Standard Time
America/Noronha	-2	GMT-02:00	GMT-02:00
America/Panama	-5	GMT-05:00	GMT-05:00
America/Paramaribo	-3	GMT-03:00	GMT-03:00
America/Phoenix	-7	MST	Mountain Standard Time
America/Port-au-Prince	-5	GMT-05:00	GMT-05:00
America/Port_of_Spain	-4	GMT-04:00	GMT-04:00
America/Porto_Acre	-5	GMT-05:00	GMT-05:00
America/Puerto_Rico	-4	GMT-04:00	GMT-04:00
America/Regina	-6	GMT-06:00	GMT-06:00
America/Santiago	-4	GMT-04:00	GMT-04:00
America/Santo_Domingo	-4	GMT-04:00	GMT-04:00
America/Sao_Paulo	-3	GMT-03:00	GMT-03:00
America/Scoresbysund	-1	GMT-01:00	GMT-01:00
America/St_Johns	-3.5	NST	Newfoundland Standard Time
America/St_Kitts	-4	GMT-04:00	GMT-04:00
America/St_Lucia	-4	GMT-04:00	GMT-04:00
America/St_Thomas	-4	GMT-04:00	GMT-04:00
America/St_Vincent	-4	GMT-04:00	GMT-04:00
America/Tegucigalpa	-6	GMT-06:00	GMT-06:00
America/Thule	-4	GMT-04:00	GMT-04:00
America/Tijuana	-8	GMT-08:00	GMT-08:00
America/Tortola	-4	GMT-04:00	GMT-04:00
America/Vancouver	-8	GMT-08:00	GMT-08:00
America/Winnipeg	-6	GMT-06:00	GMT-06:00
Antarctica/Casey	8	GMT+08:00	GMT+08:00
Antarctica/DumontDurville	10	GMT+10:00	GMT+10:00
Antarctica/Mawson	6	GMT+06:00	GMT+06:00
Antarctica/McMurdo	12	GMT+12:00	GMT+12:00
Antarctica/Palmer	-4	GMT-04:00	GMT-04:00
Asia/Aden	3	GMT+03:00	GMT+03:00
Asia/Alma-Ata	6	GMT+06:00	GMT+06:00
Asia/Amman	2	GMT+02:00	GMT+02:00
Asia/Anadyr	13	GMT+13:00	GMT+13:00
Asia/Aqtau	4	GMT+04:00	GMT+04:00
Asia/Aqtobe	5	GMT+05:00	GMT+05:00
Asia/Ashkhabad	5	GMT+05:00	GMT+05:00
Asia/Baghdad	3	GMT+03:00	GMT+03:00
Asia/Bahrain	3	GMT+03:00	GMT+03:00
Asia/Baku	4	GMT+04:00	GMT+04:00
Asia/Bangkok	7	GMT+07:00	GMT+07:00
Asia/Beirut	2	GMT+02:00	GMT+02:00
Asia/Bishkek	5	GMT+05:00	GMT+05:00
Asia/Brunei	8	GMT+08:00	GMT+08:00
Asia/Calcutta	5.5	GMT+05:30	GMT+05:30
Asia/Colombo	6	GMT+06:00	GMT+06:00

TABLE 29: Available Time Zones.

ID	Raw Off-set	Short Display Name	Long Display Name	ID	Raw Off-set	Short Display Name	Long Display Name
Asia/Dacca	6	GMT+06:00	GMT+06:00	Asia/Rangoon	6.5	GMT+06:30	GMT+06:30
Asia/Damascus	2	GMT+02:00	GMT+02:00	Asia/Riyadh	3	GMT+03:00	GMT+03:00
Asia/Dubai	4	GMT+04:00	GMT+04:00	Asia/Saigon	7	GMT+07:00	GMT+07:00
Asia/Dushanbe	5	GMT+05:00	GMT+05:00	Asia/Seoul	9	GMT+09:00	GMT+09:00
Asia/Hong_Kong	8	GMT+08:00	GMT+08:00	Asia/Shanghai	8	CST	China Standard Time
Asia/Irkutsk	8	GMT+08:00	GMT+08:00	Asia/Singapore	8	GMT+08:00	GMT+08:00
Asia/Ishigaki	8	GMT+08:00	GMT+08:00	Asia/Taipei	8	GMT+08:00	GMT+08:00
Asia/Jakarta	7	GMT+07:00	GMT+07:00	Asia/Tashkent	5	GMT+05:00	GMT+05:00
Asia/Jayapura	9	GMT+09:00	GMT+09:00	Asia/Tbilisi	5	GMT+05:00	GMT+05:00
Asia/Jerusalem	2	IST	Israel Standard Time	Asia/Tehran	3.5	GMT+03:30	GMT+03:30
Asia/Kabul	4.5	GMT+04:30	GMT+04:30	Asia/Thimbu	6	GMT+06:00	GMT+06:00
Asia/Kamchatka	12	GMT+12:00	GMT+12:00	Asia/Tokyo	9	JST	Japan Standard Time
Asia/Karachi	5	GMT+05:00	GMT+05:00	Asia/Ujung_Pandang	8	GMT+08:00	GMT+08:00
Asia/Katmandu	5.75	GMT+05:45	GMT+05:45	Asia/Ulan_Bator	8	GMT+08:00	GMT+08:00
Asia/Krasnoyarsk	7	GMT+07:00	GMT+07:00	Asia/Vientiane	7	GMT+07:00	GMT+07:00
Asia/Kuala_Lumpur	8	GMT+08:00	GMT+08:00	Asia/Vladivostok	10	GMT+10:00	GMT+10:00
Asia/Kuwait	3	GMT+03:00	GMT+03:00	Asia/Yakutsk	9	GMT+09:00	GMT+09:00
Asia/Macao	8	GMT+08:00	GMT+08:00	Asia/Yekaterinburg	5	GMT+05:00	GMT+05:00
Asia/Magadan	11	GMT+11:00	GMT+11:00	Asia/Yerevan	4	GMT+04:00	GMT+04:00
Asia/Manila	8	GMT+08:00	GMT+08:00	Atlantic/Azores	-1	GMT-01:00	GMT-01:00
Asia/Muscat	4	GMT+04:00	GMT+04:00	Atlantic/Bermuda	-4	GMT-04:00	GMT-04:00
Asia/Nicosia	2	GMT+02:00	GMT+02:00	Atlantic/Canary	0	GMT+00:00	GMT+00:00
Asia/Novosibirsk	6	GMT+06:00	GMT+06:00	Atlantic/Cape_Verde	-1	GMT-01:00	GMT-01:00
Asia/Phnom_Penh	7	GMT+07:00	GMT+07:00	Atlantic/Faeroe	0	GMT+00:00	GMT+00:00
Asia/Pyongyang	9	GMT+09:00	GMT+09:00	Atlantic/Jan_Mayen	-1	GMT-01:00	GMT-01:00
Asia/Qatar	3	GMT+03:00	GMT+03:00	Atlantic/Reykjavik	0	GMT+00:00	GMT+00:00

Continued

TABLE 29: Available Time Zones.

T

ID	Raw Offset	Short Display Name	Long Display Name	ID	Raw Offset	Short Display Name	Long Display Name
Atlantic/South_-Georgia	-2	GMT-02:00	GMT-02:00	Europe/Belgrade	1	GMT+01:00	GMT+01:00
Atlantic/St_Helena	0	GMT+00:00	GMT+00:00	Europe/Berlin	1	GMT+01:00	GMT+01:00
Atlantic/Stanley	-4	GMT-04:00	GMT-04:00	Europe/Brussels	1	GMT+01:00	GMT+01:00
Australia/Adelaide	9.5	GMT+09:30	GMT+09:30	Europe/Bucharest	2	EET	Eastern European Standard Time
Australia/Brisbane	10	GMT+10:00	GMT+10:00	Europe/Budapest	1	GMT+01:00	GMT+01:00
Australia/Darwin	9.5	GMT+09:30	GMT+09:30	Europe/Chisinau	2	GMT+02:00	GMT+02:00
Australia/Lord_Howe	10.5	GMT+10:30	GMT+10:30	Europe/Copenhagen	1	GMT+01:00	GMT+01:00
Australia/Perth	8	GMT+08:00	GMT+08:00	Europe/Dublin	0	GMT+00:00	GMT+00:00
Australia/Sydney	10	GMT+10:00	GMT+10:00	Europe/Gibraltar	1	GMT+01:00	GMT+01:00
BET	-3	GMT-03:00	GMT-03:00	Europe/Helsinki	2	GMT+02:00	GMT+02:00
BST	6	GMT+06:00	GMT+06:00	Europe/Istanbul	2	GMT+02:00	GMT+02:00
CAT	2	GMT+02:00	GMT+02:00	Europe/Kaliningrad	2	GMT+02:00	GMT+02:00
CNT	-3.5	NST	Newfoundland Standard Time	Europe/Kiev	2	GMT+02:00	GMT+02:00
CST	-6	CST	Central Standard Time	Europe/Lisbon	0	GMT+00:00	GMT+00:00
CTT	8	CST	China Standard Time	Europe/London	0	GMT+00:00	GMT+00:00
EAT	3	GMT+03:00	GMT+03:00	Europe/Luxembourg	1	GMT+01:00	GMT+01:00
ECT	1	CET	Central European Standard Time	Europe/Madrid	1	GMT+01:00	GMT+01:00
EET	2	GMT+02:00	GMT+02:00	Europe/Malta	1	GMT+01:00	GMT+01:00
EST	-5	EST	Eastern Standard Time	Europe/Minsk	2	GMT+02:00	GMT+02:00
Europe/Amsterdam	1	GMT+01:00	GMT+01:00	Europe/Monaco	1	GMT+01:00	GMT+01:00
Europe/Andorra	1	GMT+01:00	GMT+01:00	Europe/Moscow	3	GMT+03:00	GMT+03:00
Europe/Athens	2	GMT+02:00	GMT+02:00	Europe/Oslo	1	GMT+01:00	GMT+01:00

TABLE 29: Available Time Zones.

ID	Raw Off-set	Short Display Name	Long Display Name	ID	Raw Off-set	Short Display Name	Long Display Name
Europe/Paris	1	CET	Central European Standard Time	Indian/Comoro	3	GMT+03:00	GMT+03:00
Europe/Prague	1	GMT+01:00	GMT+01:00	Indian/Kerguelen	5	GMT+05:00	GMT+05:00
Europe/Riga	2	GMT+02:00	GMT+02:00	Indian/Mahe	4	GMT+04:00	GMT+04:00
Europe/Rome	1	GMT+01:00	GMT+01:00	Indian/Maldives	5	GMT+05:00	GMT+05:00
Europe/Samara	4	GMT+04:00	GMT+04:00	Indian/Mauritius	4	GMT+04:00	GMT+04:00
Europe/Simferopol	3	GMT+03:00	GMT+03:00	Indian/Mayotte	3	GMT+03:00	GMT+03:00
Europe/Sofia	2	GMT+02:00	GMT+02:00	Indian/Reunion	4	GMT+04:00	GMT+04:00
Europe/Stockholm	1	GMT+01:00	GMT+01:00	JST	9	JST	Japan Standard Time
Europe/Tallinn	2	GMT+02:00	GMT+02:00	MET	3.5	GMT+03:30	GMT+03:30
Europe/Tirane	1	GMT+01:00	GMT+01:00	MIT	-11	GMT-11:00	GMT-11:00
Europe/Vaduz	1	GMT+01:00	GMT+01:00	MST	-7	MST	Mountain Standard Time
Europe/Vienna	1	GMT+01:00	GMT+01:00	NET	4	GMT+04:00	GMT+04:00
Europe/Vilnius	2	GMT+02:00	GMT+02:00	NST	12	GMT+12:00	GMT+12:00
Europe/Warsaw	1	GMT+01:00	GMT+01:00	PLT	5	GMT+05:00	GMT+05:00
Europe/Zurich	1	GMT+01:00	GMT+01:00	PNT	-7	MST	Mountain Standard Time
GMT	0	GMT	Greenwich Mean Time	PRT	-4	GMT-04:00	GMT-04:00
HST	-10	HST	Hawaii Standard Time	PST	-8	PST	Pacific Standard Time
IET	-5	EST	Eastern Standard Time	Pacific/Apia	-11	GMT-11:00	GMT-11:00
IST	5.5	GMT+05:30	GMT+05:30	Pacific/Auckland	12	GMT+12:00	GMT+12:00
Indian/Antananarivo	3	GMT+03:00	GMT+03:00	Pacific/Chatham	12.75	GMT+12:45	GMT+12:45
Indian/Chagos	5	GMT+05:00	GMT+05:00	Pacific/Easter	-6	GMT-06:00	GMT-06:00
Indian/Christmas	7	GMT+07:00	GMT+07:00	Pacific/Efate	11	GMT+11:00	GMT+11:00
Indian/Cocos	6.5	GMT+06:30	GMT+06:30	Pacific/Enderbury	13	GMT+13:00	GMT+13:00

Continued

TABLE 29: Available Time Zones.

ID	Raw Offset	Short Display Name	Long Display Name	ID	Raw Offset	Short Display Name	Long Display Name
`Pacific/Fakaofo`	-10	`GMT-10:00`	`GMT-10:00`	`Pacific/Pago_Pago`	-11	`GMT-11:00`	`GMT-11:00`
`Pacific/Fiji`	12	`GMT+12:00`	`GMT+12:00`	`Pacific/Palau`	9	`GMT+09:00`	`GMT+09:00`
`Pacific/Funafuti`	12	`GMT+12:00`	`GMT+12:00`	`Pacific/Pitcairn`	-8.5	`GMT-08:30`	`GMT-08:30`
`Pacific/Galapagos`	-6	`GMT-06:00`	`GMT-06:00`	`Pacific/Ponape`	11	`GMT+11:00`	`GMT+11:00`
`Pacific/Gambier`	-9	`GMT-09:00`	`GMT-09:00`	`Pacific/Port_Moresby`	10	`GMT+10:00`	`GMT+10:00`
`Pacific/Guadalcanal`	11	`GMT+11:00`	`GMT+11:00`	`Pacific/Rarotonga`	-10	`GMT-10:00`	`GMT-10:00`
`Pacific/Guam`	10	`GMT+10:00`	`GMT+10:00`	`Pacific/Saipan`	10	`GMT+10:00`	`GMT+10:00`
`Pacific/Honolulu`	-10	`HST`	`Hawaii Standard Time`	`Pacific/Tahiti`	-10	`GMT-10:00`	`GMT-10:00`
`Pacific/Kiritimati`	14	`GMT+14:00`	`GMT+14:00`	`Pacific/Tarawa`	12	`GMT+12:00`	`GMT+12:00`
`Pacific/Kosrae`	12	`GMT+12:00`	`GMT+12:00`	`Pacific/Tongatapu`	13	`GMT+13:00`	`GMT+13:00`
`Pacific/Majuro`	12	`GMT+12:00`	`GMT+12:00`	`Pacific/Truk`	10	`GMT+10:00`	`GMT+10:00`
`Pacific/Marquesas`	-9.5	`GMT-09:30`	`GMT-09:30`	`Pacific/Wake`	12	`GMT+12:00`	`GMT+12:00`
`Pacific/Nauru`	12	`GMT+12:00`	`GMT+12:00`	`Pacific/Wallis`	12	`GMT+12:00`	`GMT+12:00`
`Pacific/Niue`	-11	`GMT-11:00`	`GMT-11:00`	`SST`	11	`GMT+11:00`	`GMT+11:00`
`Pacific/Norfolk`	11.5	`GMT+11:30`	`GMT+11:30`	`UTC`	0	`GMT+00:00`	`GMT+00:00`
`Pacific/Noumea`	11	`GMT+11:00`	`GMT+11:00`	`VST`	7	`GMT+07:00`	`GMT+07:00`

TABLE 29: Available Time Zones.

MEMBER SUMMARY

Display Name Styles

1.2	`LONG`	A style constant specifying a long display name.
1.2	`SHORT`	A style constant specifying a short display name.

Time Zone Methods

	`getDefault()`	Retrieves the default `TimeZone`.
1.2	`getDisplayName()`	Retrieves a printable name representing this `TimeZone`.
Δ	`getTimeZone()`	Retrieves the `TimeZone` for a time zone.
1.2	`hasSameRules()`	Determines if the raw offset and daylight savings time of this `TimeZone` match those of another `TimeZone`.
	`setDefault()`	Sets the default time zone.

MEMBER SUMMARY	
ID Methods	
`getAvailableIDs()`	Retrieves all available time-zone IDs.
`getID()`	Retrieves this `TimeZone`'s ID.
`setID()`	Sets the ID for this `TimeZone`.
Daylight Savings Time Methods	
`inDaylightTime()`	Determines if a particular date falls in this `TimeZone`'s daylight savings time period.
`useDaylightTime()`	Determines if this `TimeZone` has a daylight savings time period.
Offset Methods	
`getOffset()`	Retrieves the time difference (observing daylight savings time) of this `TimeZone` from GMT.
`getRawOffset()`	Retrieves the time difference (in standard time) of this `TimeZone` from GMT.
`setRawOffset()`	Sets the time difference from GMT.
Object Method	
`clone()`	Creates a clone of this `TimeZone`.

See Also

`SimpleTimeZone`.
`TimeZone` in *The Java Class Libraries, Second Edition, Volume 1.*

1.2 getDisplayName()

PURPOSE Retrieves a printable name representing this `TimeZone`.

SYNTAX

```
public final String getDisplayName()
public final String getDisplayName(Locale loc)
public final String getDisplayName(boolean daylight, int style)
public String getDisplayName(boolean daylight, int style, Locale
   loc)
```

DESCRIPTION This method returns a localized name that represents this `TimeZone` and that is suitable for displaying to the user. `loc` specifies the desired locale of the returned name. If `daylight` is `true`, the returned name represents the `TimeZone` during daylight savings time. If `style` is `SHORT`, the returned name is a short name such as "PST." If `style` is `LONG`, the returned name is a long name such as "Pacific Standard Time."

If a printable name is not available for the specified combination of `loc`, `daylight`, and `style`, a default name is returned. The default name has the form

T

GMT+-*HH*:*MM*, where +-*HH*:*MM* is the time difference between this TimeZone and GMT. For example, the default name for PST is GMT-08:00.

If loc is not specified, it defaults to Locale.getDefault(). If daylight is not specified, it defaults to false. If style is not specified, it defaults to LONG.

PARAMETERS

daylight — If true, the returned name represents this TimeZone during daylight savings time.

loc — The non-null desired locale of the returned name.

style — The style of the returned name, which may be either LONG or SHORT.

RETURNS — A non-null string representing this TimeZone.

SEE ALSO — LONG, SHORT.

EXAMPLE

```
TimeZone tz = TimeZone.getTimeZone("PST");
System.out.println( tz.getDisplayName() );
    // Pacific Standard Time

// If the display name is not available in the desired locale,
// the default display name is returned.
System.out.println( tz.getDisplayName(Locale.CHINESE) ); // GMT-08:00

// Print the display name variants for PST.
System.out.println( tz.getDisplayName(false, TimeZone.SHORT) );
    // PST
System.out.println( tz.getDisplayName(false, TimeZone.LONG) );
    // Pacific Standard Time
System.out.println( tz.getDisplayName(true, TimeZone.SHORT) );
    // PDT
System.out.println( tz.getDisplayName(true, TimeZone.LONG) );
    // Pacific Daylight Time

// Print the display name variants for PST using an unsupported locale.
System.out.println( tz.getDisplayName(false, TimeZone.SHORT, Locale.CHINESE));
    // GMT-08:00
System.out.println( tz.getDisplayName(false, TimeZone.LONG, Locale.CHINESE) );
    // GMT-08:00
System.out.println( tz.getDisplayName(true, TimeZone.SHORT, Locale.CHINESE) );
    // GMT-07:00
System.out.println( tz.getDisplayName(true, TimeZone.LONG, Locale.CHINESE) );
    // GMT-07:00
```


Δ getTimeZone()

PURPOSE — Retrieves the TimeZone for a time zone.

SYNTAX — `public static synchronized TimeZone getTimeZone(String ID)`

DESCRIPTION This method retrieves the TimeZone for a time zone. ID should be one of the ID's returned by getAvailableIDs(). If it is not, a TimeZone representing GMT is returned.

By default, the daylight savings time rules are assumed to apply in all years. However, if necessary, it possible to set the actual year in which daylight savings time took effect by calling setStartYear().

Note: In Version 1.2, this method returns only SimpleTimeZones.

1.2 CHANGES In Version 1.1, the returned object could not be modified because it was globally shared by all clients of the TimeZone class. In Version 1.2, the returned object is a copy of TimeZone that may be modified by the caller if desired.

In Version 1.1, this method returned null if ID was not recognized. In Version 1.2, this method returns a TimeZone representing GMT.

PARAMETERS

ID A possibly null string containing a time-zone ID.

RETURNS A non-null TimeZone.

SEE ALSO getAvailableIDs().

EXAMPLE

```
TimeZone tz = TimeZone.getTimeZone("PST");
System.out.println( tz.getDisplayName() );
    // Pacific Standard Time

// Using an invalid time zone id yields the GMT time zone.
tz = TimeZone.getTimeZone("NoSuch");
System.out.println( tz );
    // java.util.SimpleTimeZone[id=GMT,offset=0,dstSavings=3600000,
    // useDaylight=false,startYear=0,startMode=0,startMonth=0,
    // startDay=0,startDayOfWeek=0,startTime=0,endMode=0,
    // endMonth=0,endDay=0,endDayOfWeek=0,endTime=0]
```

1.2 hasSameRules()

PURPOSE Determines if the raw offset and daylight savings time of this TimeZone match those of another TimeZone.

SYNTAX `public boolean hasSameRules(TimeZone tz)`

DESCRIPTION This method determines if the raw offset and daylight savings time of this TimeZone match those of tz. It returns true if the raw offset (getRawOffset()) and daylight savings time (useDaylightTime()) of this TimeZone match those of tz.

PARAMETERS

tz A non-null TimeZone.

RETURNS `true` if the raw offset and daylight savings time of this `TimeZone` match those of `tz`.

SEE ALSO `getRawOffset()`, `useDaylightTime()`.

EXAMPLE

```
// Two time zones with same raw offset but different daylight time.
TimeZone tz1 = TimeZone.getTimeZone("MST");
TimeZone tz2 = TimeZone.getTimeZone("America/Phoenix");
System.out.println( tz1.getRawOffset()==tz2.getRawOffset() ); // true
System.out.println( tz1.hasSameRules(tz2) );                  // false

// Two time zones with same raw offset and daylight time but different ID.
tz1 = TimeZone.getTimeZone("America/Vancouver");
tz2 = TimeZone.getTimeZone("PST");
System.out.println( tz1.hasSameRules(tz2) );                  // true

// Two time zones with same and daylight time but different raw offset.
tz2 = TimeZone.getTimeZone("MST");
System.out.println( tz1.hasSameRules(tz2) );                  // false
```

1.2 LONG

PURPOSE A style constant specifying a long display name.

SYNTAX `public static final int LONG`

DESCRIPTION This constant is used in `getDisplayName()` when requesting a long display name. An example of a long display name is “Pacific Standard Time.”

SEE ALSO `SHORT`.

EXAMPLE See `getDisplayName()`.

1.2 SHORT

PURPOSE A style constant specifying a short display name.

SYNTAX `public static final int SHORT`

DESCRIPTION This constant is used in `getDisplayName()` when requesting a short display name. An example of a short display name is “PST.”

SEE ALSO `LONG`.

EXAMPLE See `getDisplayName()`.

T

TreeMap

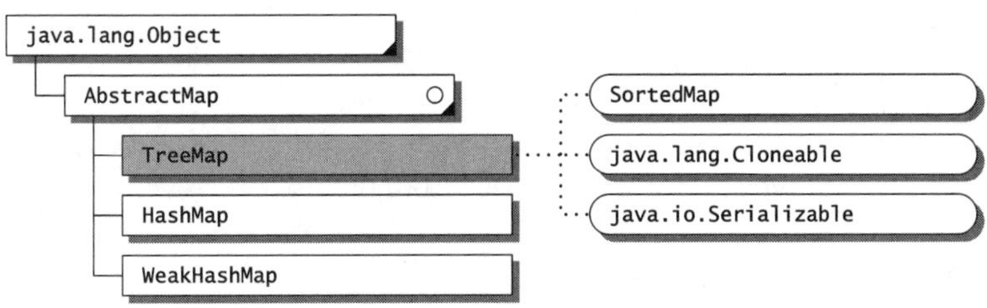

Syntax

```
public class TreeMap extends AbstractMap implements SortedMap, Cloneable,
    java.io.Serializable
```

Description

A `TreeMap` is an implementation of the `SortedMap` interface. It is a collection for storing a set of key/value pairs (*entries*) in order. It supports all optional operations and allows `null` elements, keys, and values. The keys in the map must be unique, but the values don't have to be. If you try to add an entry with a duplicate key, the map replaces the old entry with the new entry. This is unlike a set, in which if you try to add a duplicate element, the operation is completely ignored.

Unlike with lists (see `List`), the keys in the map must not be modified while they are in the map. For example, if a `StringBuffer` is used as a key in the map, you must not modify the `StringBuffer` while it is in the map.

`TreeMap` internally uses a balanced tree (a *red-black tree*) to store the entries in order. This means that adding and removing an entry involves walking the tree to determine where to insert the entry (guaranteed log_2(`size()`) time). Since the entries in a `TreeMap` are kept sorted, obtaining a sorted list of entries is merely a matter of creating an iterator on the map.

`TreeMap` is one of four implementations of the `Map` interface. The other three are `HashMap`, `Hashtable`, and `WeakHashMap`. `HashMap`, `Hashtable`, and `TreeMap` are general purpose implementations, while `WeakHashMap` is more esoteric.

`HashMap` internally uses a hash table to store the entries. This means that accessing and adding an entry is almost as efficient as accessing an array. However, the entries are not internally ordered in any way.

`Hashtable` has been retrofitted to implement the `Map` interface. You should generally use `HashMap` instead of `Hashtable`.

`WeakHashMap` is like a `HashMap`, except that if a key is no longer referenced outside the `WeakHashMap`, the key's entry is automatically removed from the table.

Usage

You can create either an empty `TreeMap` or one that is initialized from another map, as follows.

```
TreeMap map;
map = new TreeMap();
map = new TreeMap(map);
```

Once the map is created, you can use various methods to modify it, such as `put()` to add entries to the map and `remove()` to remove entries from the map.

Ordering the Entries—The Comparator

A `TreeMap` determines the order of the entries by using either a `Comparator` class or the `Comparable` interface.

1. If a *comparator* (a class that compares two keys; see `Comparator` for more details) is available, the `TreeMap` orders the keys using the comparator.
2. If there is no comparator, the `TreeMap` requires that all of the keys implement `Comparable`; any key that does not is immediately rejected by the `put()` method. The `TreeMap` then uses the key's `compareTo()` method to order the entries.

All keys in a map must be *mutually comparable*; that is, `e1.compareTo(e2)` (or `comparator.compare(e1, e2)`) must not throw an exception for any keys `e1` and `e2` in the `TreeMap`. Note that this implies that if `null` is a valid key in a map, that map's keys must use a comparator. Since a call `null.compareTo()` throws an exception, the key must use a comparator.

Key Equality

It is important to note that this class uses either the map's comparator or the key's `compareTo()` method to compare keys. It does not use the key's `equals()` method to test for equality.

This means that, for example, if you want a tree map to accept exactly the same keys as a hash map, then the comparator or `compareTo()` method (whichever is being used) should say that two keys are equal if, and only if, `equals()` claims they are. If this condition is not met, then you'll have the case in which if you add a key to a hash map, it might be ignored but if you add the same key to a tree map, it might be accepted.

If it is not necessary that the tree map behave exactly like hash map, the previous condition does not need to hold.

Iterators

The map implements fail-fast iterators. The map should not be modified while the returned iterator is in use; otherwise, the iterator will throw a `ConcurrentModificationException`. See `Iterator` for more details.

Synchronization

The map allows more than one thread to read from it. However, if a thread wants to modify the map, there should not be any other thread reading from it at the time of the modification. If reads and modifications need to be able to occur concurrently, you can create a synchronized version of the map by calling `Collections.synchronizedMap()` on the map. This creates a version of the map in which all of the methods are synchronized. Note that although each method is synchronized, you might still need to synchronize a sequence of method calls. See the `Collections` class description for more details.

MEMBER SUMMARY	
Constructor	
`TreeMap()`	Constructs a new `TreeMap` instance.
Retrieval Methods	
`get()`	Retrieves the value associated with a key.
`firstKey()`	Retrieves the key of the first entry (in sorted order) in this map.
`lastKey()`	Retrieves the key of the last entry (in sorted order) in this map.
Query Methods	
`containsKey()`	Determines if this map contains a particular key.
`size()`	Returns the number of entries in this map.
Modification Methods	
`clear()`	Removes all of the entries in this map.
`put()`	Adds a key/value pair to this map.
`putAll()`	Adds key/value pairs from another map to this map.
`remove()`	Removes an entry from this map.
Collection View Methods	
`entrySet()`	Returns a set containing all of the key/value pairs in this map.
`keySet()`	Returns a set containing all of the keys in this map.
`values()`	Returns a collection containing all of the values in this map.
SubMap Methods	
`headMap()`	Returns a sorted submap of all entries in this map that precede a particular value.
`subMap()`	Returns a sorted submap of a range of values in this map.
`tailMap()`	Returns a sorted submap of all entries from this map that follow a particular value.
Comparator Retrieval Method	
`comparator()`	Retrieves this map's comparator.
Object Method	
`clone()`	Creates a copy of this map.

See Also

`Collections`, `HashMap`, `Map`, `WeakHashMap`.

clear()

PURPOSE Removes all of the entries in this map.

SYNTAX `public void clear()`

DESCRIPTION This method retrieves this map's comparator. After it is called, this map will be empty.

EXAMPLE See `Map.clear()`.

clone()

PURPOSE Creates a copy of this map.

SYNTAX `public Object clone()`

DESCRIPTION This method makes a shallow copy of this map. Only this map and all of the entries are cloned, not the elements. Both this map and the new map share references to the same keys and values. The new map uses this map's comparator.

Since the entries are cloned, changing the value associated with a key in one copy (by using `Map.Entry.setValue()`) does not affect the other. However, since the copies share references to the same keys and values, modifications to a value in one map affect the same value in the other map. (Modifications to a key have the same effect, but you should not be modifying keys.)

RETURNS A new non-`null` map.

OVERRIDES `java.lang.Object.clone()`.

EXAMPLE See `HashMap.clone()`.

comparator()

PURPOSE Retrieves this map's comparator.

SYNTAX `public Comparator comparator()`

DESCRIPTION This method returns this map's comparator. The comparator is used to implement an ordering on the entries in this map. In particular, the comparator is used on the keys of the entries. If the comparator is `null`, the key's `compareTo()` methods are used to implement the ordering.

RETURNS The possibly `null` comparator used to order this map.

SEE ALSO `Comparable.`

EXAMPLE See `SortedMap.comparator()`.

containsKey()

PURPOSE Determines if this map contains a particular key.

SYNTAX `public boolean containsKey(Object k)`

DESCRIPTION This method determines if this map contains the key `k`. It returns `true` if some key in this map is equal to `k`. For all non-`null` keys, the `equals()` method is used to determine if two keys are equal.

PARAMETERS

`k` A possibly `null` key.

RETURNS `true` if some key in this map is equal to `k`; `false` otherwise.

EXCEPTIONS

`ClassCastException`
If `k` is not comparable to some keys in this map.

`NullPointerException`
If `k` is `null` and `null` is not comparable with the other keys in this map.

EXAMPLE See `Map.containsKey()`.

entrySet()

PURPOSE Returns a set containing all of the key/value pairs in this map.

SYNTAX `public Set entrySet()`

DESCRIPTION This method returns a set containing all of the key/value pairs in this map. The key/value pairs are represented by `Map.Entry` objects. See `Map.Entry` for information about retrieving a key or value from an entry.

The returned set and this map share the same storage. This means that changes to this map are immediately reflected in the set and changes in the set are immediately reflected in this map.

The returned set supports all operations, including all entry removal methods, except for `add()` and `addAll()`. The iterators of the returned set are fail-fast and return the entries in sorted order. The `remove()` method of the iterators is supported.

RETURNS A non-`null` set containing all of the entries in this map.

SEE ALSO `Collection, keySet(), Map.Entry, values().`

EXAMPLE `Map.entrySet()`.

firstKey()

PURPOSE Retrieves the key of the first entry (in sorted order) in this map.

SYNTAX `public Object firstKey()`

DESCRIPTION This method returns the key of the first entry in this map. See the class description for information about how the entries are sorted.

RETURNS A possibly `null` key from this map.

EXCEPTIONS

`NoSuchElementException`
If this map is empty.

EXAMPLE See `SortedMap.firstKey()`.

get()

PURPOSE Retrieves the value associated with a key.

SYNTAX `public Object get(Object k)`

DESCRIPTION This method searches this map for an entry with the key `k` and returns the associated value. `null` is returned if `k` is not in this map. A return value of `null` is ambiguous if this map accepts `null` values. You can use `containsKey()` to unambiguously determine if `k` is in this map.

PARAMETERS

`k` A possibly `null` key.

RETURNS The value associated with `k` (the value can be `null`) or `null` if `k` is not in this map.

EXCEPTIONS

`ClassCastException`
If `k` is not comparable to the other keys in this map.

`NullPointerException`
If `k` is `null` and `null` is not comparable to the other keys in this map.

SEE ALSO `containsKey()`.

EXAMPLE `Map.get()`.

headMap()

PURPOSE — Returns a sorted submap from all entries in this map that precede a particular entry.

SYNTAX

```
public SortedMap headMap(Object toV)
```

DESCRIPTION — This method returns a submap containing all of the entries whose keys are < `toV` (exclusive). This map does not have to contain `toV`.

The returned submap and this map share the same storage. This means that changes to the submap are immediately reflected in this map and changes to this map are immediately reflected in the submap.

If you add an entry to the returned submap whose key is ≥ `toV`, an `IllegalArgumentException` is thrown.

PARAMETERS

`toV` — All entries whose keys are < `toV` are included in the submap.

RETURNS — A non-`null` map containing the entries from this map whose keys are < `toV`.

EXCEPTIONS

`ClassCastException` — If `toV` cannot be compared with the other keys in this map.

`NullPointerException` — If `toV` is `null` and `null` cannot be compared with the other keys in this map.

EXAMPLE — See `SortedMap.headMap()`.

keySet()

PURPOSE — Returns a set containing all of the keys in this map.

SYNTAX

```
public Set keySet()
```

DESCRIPTION — This method returns a set containing all of the keys in this map. The set and this map share the same storage. This means that changes to this map are immediately reflected in the set and changes in the set are immediately reflected in this map.

The returned set supports all operations, including all entry removal methods, except for `add()` and `addAll()`. The iterators of the returned set are fail-fast. The `remove()` method of the iterators is supported.

RETURNS — A non-`null` set containing all of the keys in this map.

SEE ALSO — `Collection`, `entrySet()`, `values()`.

EXAMPLE — `Map.keySet()`.

lastKey()

PURPOSE Retrieves the key of the last entry (in sorted order) in this map.

SYNTAX `public Object lastKey()`

DESCRIPTION This method returns the key of the last entry in this map. See the class description for information about how the entries are sorted.

RETURNS A possibly `null` key from this map.

EXCEPTIONS

`NoSuchElementException`
If this map is empty.

EXAMPLE See `SortedMap.firstKey()`.

put()

PURPOSE Adds a key/value pair to this map.

SYNTAX `public Object put(Object k, Object v)`

DESCRIPTION This method adds a new entry with the key `k` and value `v` to this map. If an entry with the key `k` already exists in this map, it is replaced with the new entry. In this case, the previous value is returned.

PARAMETERS

`k` A possibly `null` key.
`v` A possibly `null` value.

RETURNS If `k` already exists in this map, then the possibly `null` old value is returned; otherwise, `null` is returned.

EXCEPTIONS

`ClassCastException`
If `k` cannot be compared with the other keys in this map.

`NullPointerException`
If `k` is `null` and `null` cannot be compared with the other keys in this map.

EXAMPLE See `Map.put()`.

putAll()

PURPOSE Adds key/value pairs from another map to this map.

SYNTAX `public void putAll(Map m)`

DESCRIPTION Every entry from map `m` is added to this map. If the key for some entry from `m` already exists in this map, the entry in this map is replaced by the one from `m`.

PARAMETERS

`m` A non-`null` map.

EXCEPTIONS

`ConcurrentModificationException`
If `m`'s iterators are fail-fast and `m` is being modified during this method call.

`ClassCastException`
If the class of some key in `m` is not comparable to the other keys in this map.

`NullPointerException`
If some key from `m` is `null` and `null` is not comparable to the other keys in this map.

SEE ALSO `put()`.

EXAMPLE See `Map.putAll()`.

remove()

PURPOSE Removes an entry from this map.

SYNTAX `public Object remove(Object k)`

DESCRIPTION This method searches for the first occurrence of an entry with the key `k` in this map and removes the entry from this map. It uses `equals()` to determine equality.

PARAMETERS

`k` The possibly `null` key of the entry to remove.

RETURNS The possibly `null` value associated with `k` or `null` if `k` does not match any keys in this map.

EXCEPTIONS

`ClassCastException`
If `k` is not comparable to the other keys in this map.

`NullPointerException`
If `k` is `null` and `null` is not comparable with the other keys in this map.

EXAMPLE See `Map.remove()`.

size()

PURPOSE Returns the number of entries in this map.

SYNTAX `public int size()`

T

RETURNS The non-negative number of entries in this map.

SEE ALSO `isEmpty()`.

EXAMPLE See `Map.size()`.

subMap()

PURPOSE Returns a sorted submap of a range of values in this map.

SYNTAX `public SortedMap subMap(Object fromV, Object toV)`

DESCRIPTION This method returns a submap containing all of the entries whose keys are ≥ `fromV` and < `toV`. Neither `fromV` nor `toV` needs to be in this map.

The returned submap and this map share the same storage. This means that changes to the submap are immediately reflected in this map and changes to this map are immediately reflected in the submap.

If you add an entry to the returned submap whose key is < `fromV` or ≥ `toV`, an `IllegalArgumentException` is thrown.

PARAMETERS

`fromV` The lower bound (inclusive) of the submap.
`toV` The upper bound (exclusive) of the submap.

RETURNS A non-`null` submap containing the entries from this map whose keys are ≥ `fromV` and < `toV`.

EXCEPTIONS

`ClassCastException`
If `fromV` or `toV` cannot be compared to the other keys in this map.

`IllegalArgumentException`
If `fromV` > `toV`.

`NullPointerException`
If `fromV` or `toV` is `null` and `null` cannot be compared with the other keys in this map.

`IndexOutOfBoundsException`
If `fromV` > `toV`.

EXAMPLE See `SortedMap.submap()`.

tailMap()

PURPOSE Returns a submap of all entries from this map that follow a particular entry.

SYNTAX `public SortedMap tailMap(Object fromV)`

DESCRIPTION

This method returns a submap containing all of the entries whose keys are ≥ `fromV`. This map does not have to contain `fromV`.

The returned submap and this map share the same storage. This means that changes to the submap are immediately reflected in this map and changes to this map are immediately reflected in the submap.

If you add an entry to the returned submap whose key is < `fromV`, an `IllegalArgumentException` is thrown.

PARAMETERS

`fromV` All entries whose keys are ≥ `fromV` are included in the submap.

RETURNS

A non-`null` submap containing the entries from this map whose keys are ≥ `fromV`.

EXCEPTIONS

`ClassCastException`

If `fromV` cannot be compared to the other keys in this map.

`NullPointerException`

If `fromV` is `null` and `null` cannot be compared with the other keys in this map.

EXAMPLE

See `SortedMap.tailmap()`.

TreeMap()

PURPOSE

Constructs a new `TreeMap` instance.

SYNTAX

```
public TreeMap()
public TreeMap(Map m)
public TreeMap(SortedMap m)
public TreeMap(Comparator comp)
```

DESCRIPTION

This constructor creates a new `TreeMap` object initialized with the entries from the map `m`. If `m` is a sorted map, the new `TreeSet` uses `m`'s comparator. If `m` is not specified, the new `TreeMap` object is empty.

If `comp` is specified, the new map is empty. The comparator must be able to compare any two keys that will be added to the map. Otherwise, various methods in this class will throw a `ClassCastException`. If `comp` is not specified, it defaults to `null`.

If `comp` is `null`, all of the keys added to this set must implement `Comparable`. Moreover, every key must be able to compare itself with any other key in the map. Otherwise, various methods in this class will throw a `ClassCastException`.

T

PARAMETERS

`c` A non-`null` collection.

`m` A non-`null` map.

`comp` A possibly `null` comparator.

SEE ALSO `java.lang.Comparable.`

EXAMPLE This example creates a `TreeMap` that sorts keys in reverse lexicographical order.

```
TreeMap map = new TreeMap(Collections.reverseOrder());
map.put("pig", null);
map.put("cow", null);
map.put("dog", null);
map.put("cat", null);

System.out.println( map );
// {pig=null, dog=null, cow=null cat=null}
```

values()

PURPOSE Returns a collection containing all of the values in this map.

SYNTAX `public Collection values()`

DESCRIPTION This method creates and returns a collection from all of the values in this map. Unlike with `keySet()`, the returned collection is not a set because there could be duplicates of values (sets don't allow duplicate elements).

The returned collection and this map share the same storage. This means that changes to this map are immediately reflected in the collection and changes in the collection are immediately reflected in this map.

The returned collection supports all operations, including all entry removal methods, except for `add()` and `addAll()`. The iterators of the returned collection are fail-fast. The `remove()` method of the iterators is supported.

RETURNS A non-`null` collection containing all of the values in this map.

SEE ALSO `Collection, entrySet(), keySet().`

EXAMPLE See `Map.values()`.

java.util

TreeSet

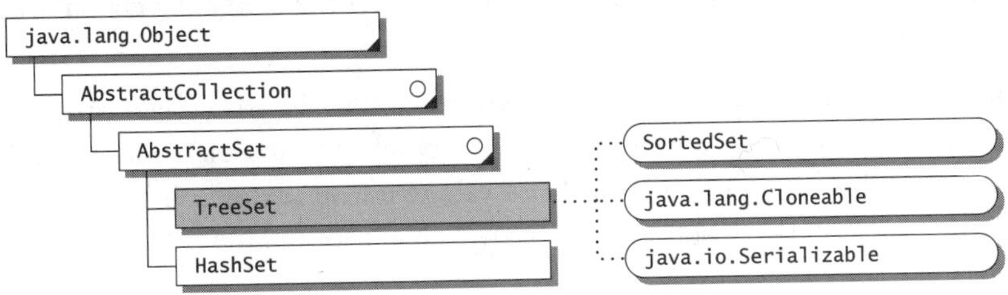

Syntax

```
public class TreeSet extends AbstractSet implements SortedSet, Cloneable,
    java.io.Serializable
```

Description

A `TreeSet` is an implementation of the `Set` interface; it also implements the `SortedSet` interface. It is a collection for storing a set of unique objects (*elements*). It supports all optional operations and allows `null` elements, provided the ordering permits it.

`TreeSet` internally uses a balanced tree (a *red-black tree*) to store the elements in order. This means that adding and removing an element involves walking the tree to determine where to insert the element (guaranteed log_2(`size()`) time). Since the elements in a `TreeSet` are kept in order, obtaining a sorted list of elements is merely a matter of creating an iterator on the set.

`TreeSet` is one of two implementations of the `Set` interface. The other, `HashSet`, internally uses a hash table (see `HashMap`) to store the elements. This means that accessing and adding an element is almost as fast as perform the same operation on an array. However, the elements are not internally ordered in any way. `HashSet` is useful if all you need to do is to keep track of a set of objects and determine if an object is already in the set.

Usage

You can create either an empty `TreeSet` or one that is initialized from another set, as follows.

```
TreeSet set;
set = new TreeSet();
set = new TreeSet(set);
```

Once the set is created, you can use various methods to modify it, such as `add()` to add elements to the set or `remove()` to remove elements from the set.

Ordering the Elements—The Comparator

A `TreeSet` determines the order of the elements in either of two ways:

1. If a *comparator* (a class that compares two elements; see `Comparator` for more details) is available, the `TreeSet` orders the elements using the comparator.

2. If there is no comparator, the `TreeSet` requires that all of the elements implement `Comparable`; any element that does not is immediately rejected when it is added (by using the `add()` method) to the `TreeSet`. The `TreeSet` then uses the element's `compareTo()` method to order the elements.

All elements in a set must be *mutually comparable*; that is, `e1.compareTo(e2)` (or `comparator.compare(e1, e2)`) must not throw an exception for any elements `e1` and `e2` in the sorted set. Note that this implies that if `null` is a valid element in a set, then that set must use a comparator. Since a call `null.compareTo()` throws an exception, the set must use a comparator.

Element Equality

It is important to note that this class uses either this set's comparator or the element's `compareTo()` method to compare elements. Unlike a nonsorted set, it does not use the element's `equals()` method to test for equality.

This means that if, for example, you want a tree set to accept exactly the same elements as a nonsorted set such as `HashSet`, then the comparator or `compareTo()` method (whichever is being used) should say two elements are equal if, and only if, they are both `null` or `equals()` claims that they are equal. If this condition is not met, then you'll have the case in which if you add an element to a nonsorted set, it might be ignored (because `equals()` returned `true`) but if you add the same element to a tree set, it might be accepted (because `compareTo()` or the comparator returned a nonzero number).

If it is not necessary that a tree set behave exactly like a nonsorted set (such as a `HashSet`), the previous condition does not need to hold. (Note that if this condition does not hold, the tree set does not obey the specification of the `Set` interface.)

Iterators

This set implements fail-fast iterators. The set should not be modified while the returned iterator is in use; otherwise, the iterator will throw a `ConcurrentModificationException`. See `Iterator` for more details.

Synchronization

A set allows more than one thread to read from it. However, if a thread wants to modify the set, there should not be any other thread reading from it at the time of the modification. If reads and modifications need to be able to occur concurrently, you can create a synchronized version of the set by calling `Collections.synchronizedSet()` on the set. This creates a version of the set in which all of the methods are synchronized. Note that although each method is synchronized, you might still need to synchronize a sequence of method calls. See the `Collections` class description for more details.

MEMBER SUMMARY	
Constructor	
`TreeSet()`	Constructs a new `TreeSet` instance.
Element Retrieval Methods	
`first()`	Retrieves the first (in sorted order) element in this set.
`last()`	Retrieves the last (in sorted order) element in this set.
Subset Methods	
`headSet()`	Creates a subset of all of the elements in this set that precede a particular value.
`subSet()`	Creates a subset of a range of elements in this set.
`tailSet()`	Creates a subset of all of the elements in this set that are greater than or equal to a particular element.
Query Methods	
`contains()`	Determines if this set contains a particular element.
`isEmpty()`	Determines if this set has no elements.
`size()`	Returns the number of elements in this set.
Modification Methods	
`add()`	Adds an element to this set.
`clear()`	Removes all of the elements in this set.
`remove()`	Removes an element from this set.
Iterator Method	
`iterator()`	Creates an iterator for all of the elements in this set.
Comparator Method	
`comparator()`	Retrieves this set's comparator.
Object Method	
`clone()`	Creates a copy of this set.

See Also

`Collections`, `Comparable`, `Comparator`, `HashSet`, `Set`, `SortedSet`.

add()

PURPOSE Adds an element to this set.

SYNTAX `public boolean add(Object e)`

DESCRIPTION This method adds an element `e` to this set, if `e` is not equal to any element in this set. If this set uses a comparator, that comparator is used to determine if `e` is equal to any elements in this set. If there is no comparator, `e` determines whether it is equal to any elements by using its `compareTo()` method. If `e` cannot be compared to every element in this set, this method throws a `ClassCastException`.

PARAMETERS

`e` The possibly `null` element to be added to this set.

RETURNS `true` if `e` was added to the set.

EXCEPTIONS

`ClassCastException`
If `e` cannot be ordered with respect to the other elements in the set.

SEE ALSO `java.lang.Comparable.compareTo()`, `Comparator`.

EXAMPLE See `Set.add()`.

clear()

PURPOSE Removes all of the elements in this set.

SYNTAX `public void clear()`

DESCRIPTION This method removes all of the elements in this set. After it is called, this set will be empty.

EXAMPLE See `Set.clear()`.

clone()

PURPOSE Creates a copy of this set.

SYNTAX `public Object clone()`

DESCRIPTION This method makes a shallow copy of this set. Only the set itself is cloned, not the elements. Both this set and the new set share references to the same elements. The new set uses this set's comparator.

RETURNS A new non-`null` set that contains the same elements.

EXAMPLE

```
TreeSet set = new TreeSet(Arrays.asList(new Object[]{"dog", "pig", "cat"}));
System.out.println( set );          // [cat, dog, pig]

TreeSet set2 = (TreeSet)set.clone();
System.out.println( set2 );         // [cat, dog, pig]
```

comparator()

PURPOSE Retrieves this set's comparator.

SYNTAX `public Comparator comparator()`

DESCRIPTION This method returns this set's comparator. The comparator is used to implement an ordering on the elements in this set. If the comparator is `null`, the elements' `compareTo()` methods are used to implement the ordering.

RETURNS The possibly `null` comparator used to order this set.

SEE ALSO `java.lang.Comparable`.

EXAMPLE See `SortedSet.comparator()`.

contains()

PURPOSE Determines if this set contains a particular element.

SYNTAX `public boolean contains(Object e)`

DESCRIPTION This method determines if this set contains the element `e`. It returns `true` if some element in this set is equal to `e`.

If this set has a comparator, it is used to determine if `e` is equal to any elements in this set. If there is no comparator, `e`'s `compareTo()` method (if not `null`) is used to determine if it is equal to any elements in this set. If `e` cannot be compared to every element in this set, this method throws a `ClassCastException`.

Note that this method can throw a `ClassCastException` even if `e` does not appear in the set.

PARAMETERS

`e` A possibly `null` element.

RETURNS `true` if some element in this set is equal to `e`.

EXCEPTIONS

`ClassCastException`

If `e` cannot be ordered with respect to the other elements in the set.

SEE ALSO `java.lang.Comparable.compareTo()`, `Comparator`, `containsAll()`, `equals()`.

EXAMPLE See `Set.contains()`.

T

first()

PURPOSE Retrieves the first (in sorted order) element in this set.

SYNTAX `public Object first()`

DESCRIPTION This method returns the first element in this set. See the class description for information about how the elements are sorted.

RETURNS A possibly `null` element from this set.

EXCEPTIONS

`NoSuchElementException`
If this set is empty.

EXAMPLE See `SortedSet.first()`.

headSet()

PURPOSE Creates a subset of all of the elements in this set that precede a particular value.

SYNTAX `public SortedSet headSet(Object toV)`

DESCRIPTION This method creates and returns a subset containing all of the elements that are < `toV`. This set does not have to contain `toV`.

The returned subset and this set share the same storage. This means that changes to the subset are immediately reflected in this set and changes to this set are immediately reflected in the subset.

If you add an element to the returned subset that is ≥ `toV`, an `IllegalArgumentException` is thrown.

PARAMETERS

`toV` All elements that are < `toV` are included in the subset.

RETURNS A non-`null` set containing the elements from this set that are < `toV`.

EXCEPTIONS

`ClassCastException`
If `toV` cannot be compared with the other elements in the set.

`NullPointerException`
If `toV` is `null` and `null` cannot be compared with the other elements in the set.

EXAMPLE See `SortedSet.headset()`.

isEmpty()

PURPOSE Determines if this set has no elements.

SYNTAX `public boolean isEmpty()`

RETURNS `true` if this set contains no elements.

SEE ALSO `size()`.

EXAMPLE See `Set.clear()`.

iterator()

PURPOSE Creates an iterator for the elements in this set.

SYNTAX `Iterator iterator()`

DESCRIPTION This method creates and returns a fail-fast iterator (see `Iterator` for more details) for all of the elements in this set. The iterator will present the elements in sorted order according to this set's comparator. If the comparator is `null`, the elements are sorted according to their `compareTo()` methods.

RETURNS A non-`null` iterator.

SEE ALSO `Iterator`, `java.lang.Comparable.compareTo()`.

EXAMPLE See `TreeSet()`.

last()

PURPOSE Retrieves the last (in sorted order) element in this set.

SYNTAX `public Object last()`

DESCRIPTION This method returns the last element in this set. See the class description for information about how the elements are sorted.

RETURNS A possibly `null` element from this set.

EXCEPTIONS

`NoSuchElementException`
If this set is empty.

EXAMPLE See `SortedSet.first()`.

remove()

PURPOSE
Removes an element from this set.

SYNTAX
`public boolean remove(Object e)`

DESCRIPTION
This method searches for the first occurrence of element `e` in this set and removes it from this set. It returns `true` if a matching element is found.

If this set has a comparator, it is used to determine if `e` is equal to any elements in this set. If there is no comparator, `e`'s `compareTo()` method is used to determine if it is equal to any elements in this set. If `e` cannot be compared to every element in this set, this method throws a `ClassCastException`. Note that this method can throw a `ClassCastException` even if `e` does not appear in the set.

PARAMETERS

`e`
The possibly `null` element to remove.

RETURNS
`true` if `e` was removed.

EXCEPTIONS

`ClassCastException`
If `e` cannot be ordered with respect to the other elements in the set.

SEE ALSO
`java.lang.Comparable.compareTo()`, `Comparator`, `SortedSet`.

size()

PURPOSE
Returns the number of elements in this set.

SYNTAX
`public int size()`

RETURNS
The non-negative number of elements in this set.

SEE ALSO
`isEmpty()`.

EXAMPLE
See `Set.size()`.

subSet()

PURPOSE
Creates a subset of a range of elements in this set.

SYNTAX
`public SortedSet subSet(Object fromV, Object toV)`

DESCRIPTION
This method returns a subset containing all of the elements that are ≥ `fromV` and < `toV`. Neither `fromV` nor `toV` needs to be in this set.

The returned subset and this set share the same storage. This means that changes to the subset are immediately reflected in this set and changes to this set are immediately reflected in the subset.

If you add an element to the returned subset that is < `fromV` or ≥ `toV`, an `IllegalArgumentException` is thrown.

PARAMETERS

`fromV` All elements *e* such that `fromV` ≤ *e* < `toV` are included in the subset.

`toV` All elements *e* such that `fromV` ≤ *e* < `toV` are included in the subset.

RETURNS A non-`null` set containing all of the elements from this set that are ≥ `fromV` and < `toV`.

EXCEPTIONS

`ClassCastException`
If `fromV` or `toV` cannot be compared with the other elements in the set.

`IllegalArgumentException`
If `fromV` > `toV`.

`NullPointerException`
If `fromV` or `toV` is `null` and `null` cannot be compared with the other elements in the set.

`IndexOutOfBoundsException`
If `fromV` > `toV`.

EXAMPLE See `SortedSet.subset()`.

tailSet()

PURPOSE Creates a subset of all of the elements in this set that are greater than or equal to a particular element.

SYNTAX
```
public SortedSet tailSet(Object fromV)
```

DESCRIPTION This method returns a subset containing all of the elements that are ≥ `fromV`. This set does not have to contain `fromV`.

The returned subset and this set share the same storage. This means that changes to the subset are immediately reflected in this set and changes to this set are immediately reflected in the subset.

If you add an element to the returned subset that is < `fromV`, an `IllegalArgumentException` is thrown.

PARAMETERS

`fromV` All elements that are ≥ `fromV` are included in the subset.

RETURNS A non-`null` set containing the elements from this set that are ≥ `fromV`.

EXCEPTIONS

`ClassCastException`
If `fromV` cannot be compared to the other elements in the set.

`NullPointerException`
: If `fromV` is `null` and `null` cannot be compared to the other elements in the set.

EXAMPLE See `SortedSet.tailset()`.

TreeSet()

PURPOSE Constructs a new `TreeSet` instance.

SYNTAX
```
public TreeSet()
public TreeSet(Collection c)
public TreeSet(SortedSet s)
public TreeSet(Comparator comp)
```

DESCRIPTION This constructor creates a new `TreeSet` instance containing all of the elements from either collection `c` or sorted set `s`. If `s` is provided, this set uses `s`'s comparator.

If `comp` is specified, the new set is empty. The comparator must be able to compare any two elements that will be added to the set. Otherwise, various methods in this class will throw a `ClassCastException`. If `comp` is not specified, it defaults to `null`.

If no comparator is provided, all of the elements added to this set must implement `Comparable`. Moreover, every element must be able to compare itself to any other element in the set. Otherwise, various methods in this class will throw a `ClassCastException`.

PARAMETERS

`c` A non-`null` collection.
`comp` A comparator.
`s` A non-`null` sorted set.

EXCEPTIONS

`ClassCastException`
: If every element in `c` or `s` cannot be ordered with respect to the other elements in the collection or set.

SEE ALSO `java.lang.Comparable`.

EXAMPLE This example declares a comparator that compares the string version of any two elements. `null` is treated as the string "null".

```
TreeSet set = new TreeSet(
    new Comparator() {
        public int compare(Object o1, Object o2) {
            String s1 = o1 == null ? "null" : o1.toString();
            String s2 = o2 == null ? "null" : o2.toString();
            return s1.compareTo(s2);
        }
    }
);
```

```
set.addAll(Arrays.asList(
    new Object[]{"dog", null, new Integer(3), "cat", new Float(2.0)}));
for (Iterator it=set.iterator(); it.hasNext(); ) {
    System.out.print( it.next()+" " );
}
System.out.println();      // 2.0 3 cat dog null
```

T

java.net

URL

java.lang.Object

URL ······ java.io.Serializable

Syntax

`public final class URL implements java.io.Serializable`

Description

The `URL` class represents a URL and provides methods to construct and obtain components of the URL (its protocol identifier, host name, port number, and so on). In addition, it provides methods that, after a URL has been created, can be used to retrieve the resource identified by the URL. It also supports lower-level methods such as opening a connection or IO streams to the server that is managing the resource identified by the URL.

See *The Java Class Libraries, Second Edition, Volume 1* for more information about this class.

URL Stream (Protocol) Handlers and Factories

Associated with each URL is a *URL stream* (or *protocol*) *handler* (see `URLStreamHandler` in *The Java Class Libraries, Second Edition, Volume 1*). A URL stream handler is responsible for implementing the protocol associated with the URL. For example, there is a HTTP stream handler for URLs that have the `http` protocol identifier. The Java runtime itself provides a handful of stream handlers (for example, HTTP and FTP) and allows new stream handlers to be added dynamically.

A *URL stream handler factory* is responsible for creating an instance of `URLStreamHandler` when it is supplied with a protocol identifier. See `URLStreamHandlerFactory` in *The Java Class Libraries, Second Edition, Volume 1*. The factory controls which implementations are selected for the protocol identifiers, as well as which protocols are supported. The program uses `URL.setURLStreamHandlerFactory()` to select the stream handler factory to use.

U

Default Policy for Creating Stream Handlers

If no stream handler factory has been installed or if the installed factory cannot produce a handler for a protocol, the system searches for a class that has the class name

packagePrefix "." *protocol* "." `Handler`

packagePrefix is obtained from the system property `java.protocol.handler.pkgs`, which is a "|"-separated list of package prefixes. *protocol* is the protocol identifier (for example, `http` or `ftp`). If the class is not found by using these package prefixes, the package prefix `sun.net.www.protocol` is tried. For example, if the `java.protocol.handler.pkgs` system property contains "com.widget|com.wiz" and the protocol identifier is `http`, the system will attempt to load each of the following classes in turn until one is successfully instantiated:

```
com.widget.http.Handler
com.wiz.http.Handler
sun.net.www.protocol.http.Handler
```

If no class can be instantiated in this way, a `MalformedURLException` is thrown.

Changes for Version 1.2

Two new public constructors allow a `URLStreamHandler` to be explicitly specified for creating the appropriate URL connection.

MEMBER SUMMARY	
Constructor	
Δ `URL()`	Constructs a `URL` instance.
Field Access Methods	
`getFile()`	Retrieves this `URL`'s filename.
`getHost()`	Retrieves this `URL`'s host name.
`getPort()`	Retrieves this `URL`'s port number.
`getProtocol()`	Retrieves this `URL`'s protocol identifier.
`getRef()`	Retrieves this `URL`'s reference.
`set()`	Sets the fields of this `URL`.
Communication Methods	
`getContent()`	Retrieves the content pointed to by this `URL`.
`openConnection()`	Opens this `URL`'s connection.
`openStream()`	Opens an input stream to this `URL`'s connection.
Comparison Methods	
`equals()`	Determines if this `URL` is equal to another object.
`sameFile()`	Determines whether two URLs point to the same file.
Hash Code Method	
`hashCode()`	Computes the hash code of this `URL`.
Description Methods	
`toExternalForm()`	Generates the string representation of this `URL`.
`toString()`	Generates the string representation of this `URL`.
Factory Method	
`setURLStreamHandlerFactory()`	Sets the URL stream handler factory for an application.

U

See Also

URL, URLStreamHandler, URLStreamHandlerFactory in *The Java Class Libraries, Second Edition, Volume 1.*

Δ URL()

PURPOSE

Constructs a URL instance.

SYNTAX

```
public URL(String protocol, String host, int port, String file)
   throws MalformedURLException
public URL(String protocol, String host, String file) throws
   MalformedURLException
```

SINCE 1.2

```
public URL(String protocol, String host, int port, String file,
   URLStreamHandler handler) throws MalformedURLException
public URL(String spec) throws MalformedURLException
public URL(URL context, String spec) throws MalformedURLException
```

SINCE 1.2

```
public URL(URL context, String spec, URLStreamHandler handler)
   throws MalformedURLException
```

DESCRIPTION

The six forms of the constructor of the URL class construct a URL instance from the information supplied. The first three forms create a URL for the protocol with identifier protocol to host host at the port number port. If port is not supplied or if it is -1, the default port number for protocol is used. For example, for the HTTP protocol the default port is 80. file specifies the pathname and any arguments to use after reaching the host. file is parsed into a file pathname and any arguments that occur after the hash character ("#") (these are recorded as the *reference* of the URL).

The last three forms construct a URL by parsing the URL string spec. An example of spec is http://www.widget.com/cgi-bin/123.cgi#urllist. This string gets parsed into a URL with host www.widget.com, default port -1, file cgi-bin/123.cgi, and reference urllist. If spec is a relative URL and if context is specified and non-null, context identifies the context in which to parse spec and constructs the new URL. If spec is an absolute URL (as in the previous example), context is ignored. If context is not specified or is null, spec must be an absolute URL. For example, if context is the URL http://www.widget.com/cgi-bin/ and spec is formX, the new URL will be http://www.widget.com/cgi-bin/formX.

Each URL instance has associated with it a URL stream handler. If a non-null handler is supplied, it is used to implement the protocol identified by this URL. If handler is null or unspecified, a handler is created using the installed URL-StreamHandlerFactory (if any) and the default policy for creating stream handlers described in the class description. handler can be non-null only if the caller has been granted NetPermission("specifyStreamHandler"). Otherwise, a `SecurityException` is thrown. If a handler cannot be created for the protocol identified by the URL, a `MalformedURLException` is thrown.

Once a `URL` has been constructed, you can then open a connection to the location pointed to by the URL and read the data from that location.

1.2 CHANGES The two forms of the constructor that accept a `handler` parameter are new in Version 1.2.

PARAMETERS

- `context` The possibly `null` context in which to interpret `spec` if `spec` is a relative URL. If `null`, `spec` must be an absolute URL.
- `file` The non-`null` file pathname (and any arguments) to use after reaching the host.
- `handler` The possibly `null` protocol handler to use for the new URL. If `null`, use the installed handler factory and default policy described in the class description.
- `host` The non-`null` string containing the name of the host to which to connect.
- `port` The port number to use.
- `protocol` The non-`null` string containing the protocol identifier.
- `spec` The non-`null` URL string to parse.

EXCEPTIONS

`MalformedURLException`
: If the protocol identifier (either `protocol` or that identifier determined from `spec`) is unspecified (`null`) or a stream handler could not be found for it.

`SecurityException`
: If `handler` is non-`null`, and the caller has not been granted `NetPermission("specifyStreamHandler")` by the installed security manager.

SEE ALSO `openConnection()`, `getContent()`, `URLStreamHandler.parseURL()`.

EXAMPLE

```
try {
    URL url = new URL("http://java.sun.com/index.html");

    Object content = url.getContent();
    if (content != null) {
        System.out.println("class: " + content.getClass());
        System.out.println("obj: " + content);
    }
    InputStream in = url.openStream();
    if (in != null) {
        for(int c = in.read(); c > 0; c = in.read()) {
            System.out.print((char)c);
        }
    }
} catch (MalformedURLException e) {
    e.printStackTrace();
} catch (IOException e) {
    e.printStackTrace();
}
```

URLClassLoader

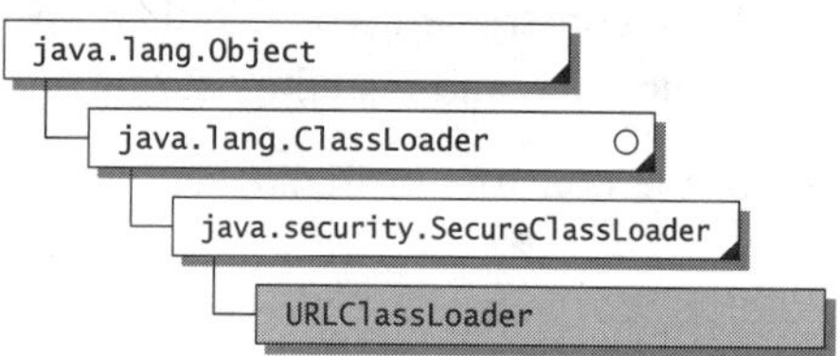

Syntax

```
public class URLClassLoader extends SecureClassLoader
```

Description

The `URLClassLoader` class represents a class loader for loading classes and resources from locations specified by a list of URLs. It provides an easy way for programs to load classes and resources from locations in addition to those available to the system class loader without your having to write a new class loader. The locations are specified by URLs, each of which can identify a Java Archive (JAR) file or a codebase directory containing Java class files.

The classes loaded using a `URLClassLoader` are in the protection domain(s) corresponding to the URL(s) from which they were loaded. They share the same namespace with other classes loaded using the same `URLClassLoader`.

Usage

To use this class, you first create a `URLClassLoader` for the URLs from which you want to load classes and then load the class.

```
try {
    ClassLoader cl = URLClassLoader.newInstance(urls);
    Class c = cl.loadClass("p.Test");
    Object obj = c.newInstance();
    ...
} catch (ClassNotFoundException e) {
    e.printStackTrace();
} catch (InstantiationException e) {
    e.printStackTrace();
} catch (IllegalAccessException e) {
    e.printStackTrace();
}
```

Security Considerations

To use a `URLClassLoader`, you must first create one. There are two ways to create a `URLClassLoader`:

- Use the `URLClassLoader` constructor.
- Use the static `newInstance()` method.

These differ in the `RuntimePermissions` that are required. The `URLClassLoader` constructor requires that the caller has been granted the permission named `"createClassLoader"`. The `newInstance()` method does not require any permissions except when the caller is loading classes to restricted packages (see `SecurityManager.checkPackageAccess()`). Typically, you should use `newInstance()` to create a `URLClassLoader`. The constructors are useful when you are creating new subclasses of `URLClassLoader`, in which case your code would require `"createClassLoader"` permission anyway.

If you subclass `URLClassLoader`, you should add to the subclass's constructor the following code.

```
SecurityManager security = System.getSecurityManager();
if (security != null) {
    security.checkCreateClassLoader();
}
```

This is done so that programs using security managers that were developed prior to Version 1.2 will still work correctly. The old way of doing security checks involves counting the caller's stack frames. For such checks to work correctly, the `SecurityManager.checkCreateClassLoader()` call must be made in the subclass's constructor.

MEMBER SUMMARY	
Constructors and Creation Methods	
`URLClassLoader()`	Constructs a new `URLClassLoader` instance for a list of URLs.
`newInstance()`	Constructs a new `URLClassLoader` instance that checks the loading of classes into restricted packages for a list of URLs.
URL Methods	
`addURL()`	Appends a URL to this `URLClassLoader`'s list of URLs.
`getURLs()`	Retrieves the ordered list of URLs searched by this `URLClassLoader`.
ClassLoader Methods	
`findClass()`	Loads a class.
`findResource()`	Returns the URL of a resource.
`findResources()`	Returns an enumeration of URLs of resources for a resource name.
`getPermissions()`	Retrieves the permissions for a `CodeSource` object.
Package Method	
`definePackage()`	Adds a new package to this `URLClassLoader`'s list of defined packages.

U

See Also

`java.lang.ClassLoader`.

Example

This example creates a `URLClassLoader` using `newInstance()`, loads a class using it, and creates a new instance of the class.

```
try {
    URL[] urls = new URL[] {new URL("file:p/")};

    // Create URLClassLoader
    ClassLoader cl = URLClassLoader.newInstance(urls);

    // Load p.Test using URLClassLoader
    Class c = cl.loadClass("p.Test");

    // Create new instance of p.Test
    c.newInstance();
} catch (MalformedURLException e) {
    e.printStackTrace();
} catch (ClassNotFoundException e) {
    e.printStackTrace();
} catch (IllegalAccessException e) {
    e.printStackTrace();
} catch (InstantiationException e) {
    e.printStackTrace();
}
```

addURL()

PURPOSE Appends a URL to this `URLClassLoader`'s list of URLs.

SYNTAX `protected void addURL(URL url)`

DESCRIPTION This method appends a URL to the end of this `URLClassLoader`'s list of URLs to search when loading classes and resources. If `url` ends with a trailing slash, it identifies a codebase directory where the class files and resources are stored. If `url` does not end with a trailing slash, it is assumed to name a JAR file.

This method can be used by a subclass of `URLClassLoader` to add additional URLs.

PARAMETERS

`url` The non-`null` URL to be added.

SEE ALSO `URLClassLoader()`.

definePackage()

PURPOSE Adds a new package to this `URLClassLoader`'s list of defined packages.

SYNTAX `protected Package definePackage(String pname, Manifest man, URL url) throws IllegalArgumentException`

DESCRIPTION

This method adds a new package with the name `pname` to this `URLClassLoader`'s list of defined packages. Each class loader maintains a list of packages of classes that it has loaded. A package's specification and implementation attributes and information about whether the package is sealed is obtained from the manifest `man`. If the package is sealed, `url` specifies the URL of the code source from which the package was loaded. Subsequent classes from this package must be loaded from the same code source.

This method is used by `findClass()` when it is loading a class.

PARAMETERS

`pname` A non-`null` string representing the package name.

`man` The non-`null` `Manifest` of the JAR file containing the package.

`url` The URL of the package's code source or `null` if the package has no code source. Ignored if the package is not sealed.

RETURNS

A non-`null` `Package` object representing the package with the name `pname`.

EXCEPTIONS

`IllegalArgumentException`

If `pname` already names a package loaded by this `URLClassLoader` or one of its ancestor class loaders.

SEE ALSO

`java.lang.ClassLoader.definePackage()`, `java.lang.ClassLoader.getPackages()`, `java.lang.Package`.

findClass()

PURPOSE

Loads a class.

SYNTAX

```
protected Class findClass(final String cname) throws
    ClassNotFoundException
```

DESCRIPTION

This method searches for and loads a class with the fully qualified class name `cname` in the JAR files and codebase directories specified by this `URLClassLoader`'s list of URLs. Any URLs referring to JAR files in this list are loaded and opened as needed until the class is found. If the class is found, it is loaded and its corresponding `Class` object is returned. The package of the class that has been loaded is added to this `URLClassLoader`'s list of defined packages. If the class is not found, a `ClassNotFoundException` is thrown.

If this `URLClassLoader` does not have permission to read, or otherwise cannot successfully access, the contents of a JAR file or codebase directory named by one of its URLs, it skips to the next URL (any exception encountered is ignored).

This method is used by `ClassLoader.loadClass()` to load a class using this class loader.

PARAMETERS

`cname` A non-`null` string representing the fully qualified name of the class (such as `"java.lang.String"`).

RETURNS The non-`null` class representing `cname`.

EXCEPTIONS

`ClassNotFoundException`
If the class could not be found

OVERRIDES `ClassLoader.findClass().`

SEE ALSO `definePackage(), ClassLoader.definePackage().`

findResource()

PURPOSE Returns the URL of a resource.

SYNTAX
```
Finds the resource with the specified name on the URL search
   path.
public URL findResource(String rname)
```

DESCRIPTION This method returns the URL of a resource. It searches for the first resource with the name `rname` in the JAR files and codebase directories specified by this `URLClassLoader`'s list of URLs. Any URLs referring to JAR files in this list are loaded and opened as needed until the resource is found. If no resource is found, `null` is returned.

This method is used by `ClassLoader.getResource()` to find a resource in this class loader.

PARAMETERS

`rname` A non-`null` string representing the resource's name.

RETURNS A possibly `null` `URL` instance identifying the location of the resource.

OVERRIDES `ClassLoader.findResource();`

SEE ALSO `java.lang.ClassLoader.getResource().`

U

EXAMPLE This example illustrates the difference between `findResource()` and `ClassLoader.getResource()`. The former searches only this `URLClassLoader`'s list of URLs, while the latter searches using its parent class loader first and then the list of URLs. The former finds the `index.html` in the `p.jar` file, while the latter finds it using the parent class loader.

```
try {
    URL[] urls = new URL[2];
    urls[0] = new URL("file:p.jar");
    urls[1] = new URL("http://wombat.eng.sun.com/");

    // Create URLClassLoader
    URLClassLoader cl = URLClassLoader.newInstance(urls);
```

```
        // Find the first "index.html" from these URLs
        System.out.println(cl.findResource("index.html"));

        System.out.println("-----------------");

        // Find first "index.html" from parent class loader + URLs
        System.out.println(cl.getResource("index.html"));
    } catch (MalformedURLException e) {
        e.printStackTrace();
    } catch (java.io.IOException e) {
        e.printStackTrace();
    }
```

OUTPUT

```
    jar:file:p.jar!/index.html
    -----------------
    file:/tmp/net/URLClassLoader/findResource/index.html
```

findResources()

PURPOSE Returns an enumeration of URLs of resources for a resource name.

SYNTAX

```
public Enumeration findResources(String rname) throws
   IOException
```

DESCRIPTION This method searches for all resources with the name `rname` in the JAR files and codebase directories specified by this `URLClassLoader`'s list of URLs and returns a list of URLs for the resources found.

It is used by `ClassLoader.getResources()` to find the resources in this class loader.

PARAMETERS

`rname` A non-`null` string representing the resource's name.

RETURNS A non-`null` enumeration of URLs (of type `URL`).

OVERRIDES `ClassLoader.findResources()`.

SEE ALSO `java.lang.ClassLoader.getResources()`.

EXAMPLE This example illustrates the difference between `findResources()` and `ClassLoader.getResources()`. The former retrieves only resources found in this `URLClassLoader`'s list of URLs, while the latter uses both the list of URLs and its parent class loader. The latter finds also the `index.html` that is the application's class path.

```
    try {
        URL[] urls = new URL[2];
        urls[0] = new URL("file:p.jar");
        urls[1] = new URL("http://wombat.eng.sun.com/");

        // Create URLClassLoader
```

U

```
        URLClassLoader cl = URLClassLoader.newInstance(urls);

        // Find "index.html" from these URLs
        Enumeration enum = cl.findResources("index.html");
        while (enum.hasMoreElements()) {
            System.out.println(enum.nextElement());
        }

        System.out.println("-----------------");

        // Find "index.html" from parent class loader + URLs
        enum = cl.getResources("index.html");
        while (enum.hasMoreElements()) {
            System.out.println(enum.nextElement());
        }
    } catch (MalformedURLException e) {
        e.printStackTrace();
    } catch (java.io.IOException e) {
        e.printStackTrace();
    }
```

OUTPUT

```
jar:file:p.jar!/index.html
http://wombat.eng.sun.com/index.html
-----------------
file:/tmp/net/URLClassLoader/findResources/index.html
jar:file:p.jar!/index.html
http://wombat.eng.sun.com/index.html
```

getPermissions()

PURPOSE Retrieves the permissions for a `CodeSource` object.

SYNTAX

```
protected PermissionCollection getPermissions(CodeSource
    codesource)
```

DESCRIPTION This method retrieves the permissions for a `CodeSource` object. A `CodeSource` object consists of a URL specifying the location of the classes and the list of certificates used to sign those classes. This method returns the permissions that have been granted to `codesource` by the security policy.

U

These permissions contain the permissions granted to `codesource` by the security policy. They also contain the permission that is necessary in order for this `URLClassLoader` to retrieve the class file(s) at `codesource`'s URL (*url*). The latter depends on *url*'s protocol. If *url* is a file URL that names a directory, the permission is a `FilePermission` containing a permission name that is the recursive subtree of the file (for example, `"path/-"`, where `path` is the file part *url*) and a `"read"` action. If *url* is a file URL that names a file, the permission is a `FilePermission` with the filename as the permission name and a `"read"` action. Otherwise, the permission is a `SocketPermission` with a permission name of *url*'s host name and an action list of "connect, accept". If *url* does not have a host name, "localhost" is used. The security policy must have granted this permission (or permissions that imply this permission) to the principal that created this URLClassLoader instance; otherwise, a SecurityException is thrown.

This method is used by ClassLoader.defineClass() to set the protection domain of the classes that the class loader loads (see Class.getProtectionDomain(), java.security.ProtectionDomain). A protection domain consists of a CodeSource and the permissions granted to the code source by the security policy. The protection domain of a class is used when a thread executing code in that class requests permission to access a protected resource. At that point, a check is made to see whether the permissions in the class's protection domain *implies* the requested permission. If so, permission is granted; otherwise, a SecurityException is thrown.

For more information about Version 1.2's security model and framework, see http://java.sun.com/products/jdk/1.2/docs/guide/security/index.html.

PARAMETERS

codesource A non-null CodeSource object.

RETURNS The non-null permissions granted to the codesource.

SEE ALSO java.io.FilePermission, java.lang.ClassLoader.getProtectionDomain(). java.net.SocketPermission, java.security.Policy, java.security.ProtectionDomain.

getURLs()

PURPOSE Retrieves the ordered list of URLs searched by this URLClassLoader.

SYNTAX

```
public URL[] getURLs()
```

DESCRIPTION This method retrieves the ordered list of URLs searched by this URLClassLoader. The list of URLs consists of a list of URLs supplied to the URLClassLoader constructor, followed by the URLs added using addURL(), in the order in which the URLs were added using addURL(). This list identifies the JAR files and/or codebase directories that will be searched when this URLClassLoader is asked to load a class or resource.

The returned value is a new array containing these URLs.

RETURNS A non-null ordered list of URLs.

SEE ALSO addURL(), URLClassLoader().

EXAMPLE

```
try {
    URL[] urls = new URL[3];
    urls[0] = new URL("file:p/");
    urls[1] = new URL("http://java.sun.com/");
    urls[2] = new URL("file:/tmp/c.jar");

    // Create URLClassLoader
    URLClassLoader cl = URLClassLoader.newInstance(urls);

    URL[] retUrls = cl.getURLs();
    for (int i = 0; i < retUrls.length; i++) {
        System.out.println(retUrls[i]);
    }
} catch (MalformedURLException e) {
    e.printStackTrace();
}
```

OUTPUT

```
file:p/
http://java.sun.com/
file:/tmp/c.jar
```

newInstance()

PURPOSE Creates a new `URLClassLoader` instance that checks the loading of classes into restricted packages for a list of URLs.

SYNTAX

```
public static URLClassLoader newInstance(final URL[] urls)
public static URLClassLoader newInstance(final URL[] urls, final
    ClassLoader parent)
```

DESCRIPTION This method creates a new instance of a `URLClassLoader` that searches for classes and resources from the JAR files and codebase directories specified in the list of URLs `urls`. See the `URLClassLoader` for a description of the `urls` and `parent` parameters.

Using `newInstance()` is different from calling the `URLClassLoader` constructor, in two (related) ways. First, the class loader created by `newInstance()` invokes `SecurityManager.checkPackageAccess()` to ensure that the class being requested is not from a *restricted* package and, if it is, that the caller has permission to load it. The Java runtime system has a list of restricted packages (such as those with the "sun" prefix) that applications are not allowed to access.

Second, `newInstance()` creates the class loader while in *privileged* mode. That means that the caller does not need the `"createClassLoader"` `RuntimePermission` in order to use this method. Contrast this with the `URLClassLoader` constructor, in which the caller does need such a permission in order to

U

avoid a `SecurityException`. Most libraries and applications should use `newInstance()` instead of the constructor. This is because `newInstance()` does not require the user to grant the permission for creating class loaders, `RuntimePermission("createClassLoader")`, an action that has severe security implications.

The `AccessControlContext` of the caller that created the new instance of `URLClassLoader` will be used when classes and resources are subsequently loaded. For example, if the class loader is created by *A* and then *B* subsequently uses that class loader to load a class, it will be *A*'s credentials that will be used when checks are made to determine whether permission has been granted. Effectively, any method invoked on this new class loader will look like it is being executed by its creator (*A*).

PARAMETERS

`parent` The possibly `null` parent class loader. `null` means the *bootstrap* class loader (that is, the Java Virtual Machine's built-in class loader).

`urls` The non-`null` array of URLs from which to load classes and resources.

RETURNS A new `URLClassLoader` instance that checks package access before loading classes. Cannot be `null`.

EXCEPTIONS

`SecurityException`
If the caller is not allowed to create a new class loader or if the caller is not allowed to get the system class loader.

SEE ALSO
```
java.lang.ClassLoader,
java.lang.RuntimePermission{"getClassLoader",
"createClassLoader", "accessClassInPackage"},
java.net.NetPermission{"specifyStreamHandler"},
java.lang.SecurityManager.checkCreateClassLoader().
```

EXAMPLE See the class example.

URLClassLoader()

PURPOSE Constructs a new `URLClassLoader` instance for a list of URLs.

SYNTAX
```
public URLClassLoader(URL[] urls)
public URLClassLoader(URL[] urls, ClassLoader parent)
public URLClassLoader(URL[] urls, ClassLoader parent,
   URLStreamHandlerFactory factory)
```

DESCRIPTION All of these forms of this constructor create a new instance of a `URLClassLoader` that searches for classes and resources from the JAR files and codebase directories specified in the list of URLs `urls`. If a URL ends with a trailing slash, it identifies a *codebase* directory where the class files and resources are stored. If a URL does not end with a trailing slash, it is assumed to name a JAR file. The order in which the URLs appear in the list is the order in which the locations they specified will be searched whenever this new class loader is asked to load a class or resource. The contents of the `urls` array is copied such that subsequent changes to that array will not affect the list of URLs known to the new class loader.

`parent` specifies the parent class loader of the new class loader. When this new class loader is asked to load a class or resource, the parent class loader is asked first to load the class or resource (which in turn asks its parent, and so on). If the class or resource is not found, the new class loader will attempt to load it using its list of URLs. If parent is `null`, it means the *bootstrap* class loader (that is, the Java Virtual Machine's built-in class loader). If `parent` is not specified, the system class loader (the class loader used to start the application) is used as the parent class loader. See `Classloader.getSystemClassLoader()`. Supplying the parent class loader is useful to code that wants to restrict or delegate the loading of classes (that is, it wants to use a different class loading policy than the system class loader).

Each nonfile URL (that is, a URL that does not begin with `"file://"`) that names a JAR file is loaded using a JAR URL stream handler (see `JarURLConnection`). If `factory` is specified, it names a `URLStreamHandlerFactory` that will be used to create the stream handler. If it is unspecified, a stream handler determined by the default URL stream handler loading policy is used. See `URL.setURLStreamHandlerFactory()`. If the URL names either a JAR file using the `"file"` protocol or a directory, `factory` is ignored. Note that specifying a factory might cause a subsequent class loading call to fail with a `SecurityException` if that caller does not have permission to specify a URL stream handler (see `NetPermission`).

The `AccessControlContext` of the caller that created the new instance of `URLClassLoader` will be used when classes and resources are subsequently loaded. For example, if the class loader is created by *A* and then *B* subsequently uses that class loader to load a class, it will be *A*'s credentials that will be used when checks are made to learn whether permission has be granted. Effectively, any method invoked on this new class loader will look like it is being executed by its creator (*A*).

PARAMETERS

`factory` The possibly `null` `URLStreamHandlerFactory` to use for creating a stream handler for the JAR URL protocol. If `null`, the default stream handler for the JAR URL protocol is used.

`parent` The possibly `null` parent class loader. `null` means the bootstrap class loader.

`urls` The non-`null` array of URLs from which to load classes and resources.

EXCEPTIONS

`SecurityException`
If the caller is not allowed to create a new class loader or if the caller is not allowed to get the system class loader.

SEE ALSO `java.lang.ClassLoader`, `java.lang.RuntimePermission {"getClassLoader", "createClassLoader"}`, `java.net.NetPermission{"specifyStreamHandler"}`, `java.lang.SecurityManager.checkCreateClassLoader()`, `java.security.AccessControlContext`.

EXAMPLE This example is a variation on the class example. Instead of using `newInstance()` to create a `URLClassLoader`, it uses the `URLClassLoader` constructor. If you run the program with only a security manager, it will fail with an `AccessControlException`. For the program to work, the program must be granted `"createClassLoader"` permission. You can grant that by including a `.policy` file, with the appropriate permissions in the command line.

```
try {
    URL[] urls = new URL[] {new URL("file:p/")};

    // Create URLClassLoader
    ClassLoader cl = new URLClassLoader(urls);

    // Load p.Test using URLClassLoader
    Class c = cl.loadClass("p.Test");

    // Create new instance of p.Test
    c.newInstance();
} catch (MalformedURLException e) {
    e.printStackTrace();
} catch (ClassNotFoundException e) {
    e.printStackTrace();
} catch (IllegalAccessException e) {
    e.printStackTrace();
} catch (InstantiationException e) {
    e.printStackTrace();
}
```

OUTPUT

```
>java -Djava.security.manager Main
Exception in thread "main" java.security.AccessControlException: access denied
(java.lang.RuntimePermission createClassLoader )
        at java.security.AccessControlContext.checkPermission(Compiled Code)
        at java.security.AccessController.checkPermission(Compiled Code)
        at java.lang.SecurityManager.checkPermission(Compiled Code)
        at java.lang.SecurityManager.checkCreateClassLoader(Compiled Code)
        at java.lang.ClassLoader.<init>(Compiled Code)
        at java.security.SecureClassLoader.<init>(Compiled Code)
        at java.net.URLClassLoader.<init>(Compiled Code)
        at Main.main(Compiled Code)
```

```
> java -Djava.security.manager -Djava.security.policy=.policy Main
Test Constructor
```

.policy

```
keystore ".keystore";
 grant {
          permission java.lang.RuntimePermission "createClassLoader";
       };
```

URLConnection

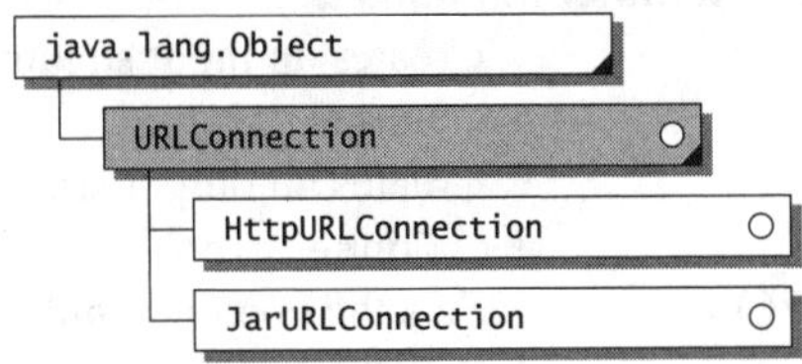

Syntax

```
public abstract class URLConnection
```

Description

The `URLConnection` class represents an active connection to the resource identified by a URL. It is an abstract class that must be subclassed to provide an implementation of `connect()`.

See *The Java Class Libraries, Second Edition, Volume 1* for more information about this class.

Changes for Version 1.2

Since Version 1.1.6, the public field `fileNameMap` has been replaced by the set/get methods, `getFileNameMap()` and `setFileNameMap()`.

The new `getPermission()` method retrieves the permission necessary to make the connection represented by a `URLConnection`. The permission may be used to check who is allowed to use the connection (if the connection is shared, such as in a cache).

MEMBER SUMMARY

	Constructor	
	`URLConnection()`	Constructs a `URLConnection` instance.
	Connection Establishment Field and Method	
	`connect()`	Establishes this `URLConnection`.
	`connected`	Indicates whether a connection has been established to this `URLConnection`.
	Content Processing Field and Methods	
Δ	`fileNameMap`	Map for translating filenames to content types.
	`getContent()`	Retrieves the content of this `URLConnection` as an object.
1.2	`getFileNameMap()`	Retrieves a `FileNameMap` instance for translating filenames to content types.

Continued

U

MEMBER SUMMARY

Content Processing Field and Methods *(Continued)*

`getInputStream()`	Creates an input stream for reading from this `URLConnection`.
`getOutputStream()`	Creates an output stream for writing to this `URLConnection`.
`setContentHandlerFactory()`	Sets the content handler factory for an application.
1.2 `setFileNameMap()`	Sets the `FileNameMap` instance for translating filenames to content types.
`guessContentTypeFromName()`	Guesses the content type by looking at the filename extension.
`guessContentTypeFromStream()`	Guesses the content type by inspecting the content of the document.

Security Method

1.2 `getPermission()`	Retrieves the permission necessary to use this `URLConnection`.

Response Header Methods

`getContentEncoding()`	Retrieves the content encoding type of the response data.
`getContentLength()`	Retrieves the content length of the response data.
`getContentType()`	Retrieves the content type of the response data.
`getDate()`	Retrieves the creation date of the response data.
`getExpiration()`	Retrieves the expiration date of the response data.
`getHeaderField()`	Retrieves a header field from the response.
`getHeaderFieldDate()`	Retrieves a response header field and parses its value as a GMT date.
`getHeaderFieldInt()`	Retrieves a response header field and parses its value as an integer.
`getHeaderFieldKey()`	Retrieves the *n*th header field name at the specified position in the response header.
`getLastModified()`	Retrieves the last modification date of the response data.

Request Header Methods

`getDefaultRequestProperty()`	Retrieves the default value of a request header field for future connections.
`getRequestProperty()`	Retrieves the value of a request header field for this `URLConnection`.
`setDefaultRequestProperty()`	Sets the default value of a request header field for new connections.
`setRequestProperty()`	Sets the value of a request header field for this `URLConnection`.

MEMBER SUMMARY	
Cache Field and Methods	
`getDefaultUseCaches()`	Determines whether new URL connections, by default, may use caches.
`getUseCaches()`	Determines whether this `URLConnection` allows caches to be used.
`setDefaultUseCaches()`	Sets the default cache usage flag for new connections.
`setUseCaches()`	Sets the cache usage flag of this `URLConnection`.
`useCaches`	Indicates whether this `URLConnection` allows the use of caches.
If-Modified-Since Field and Methods	
`getIfModifiedSince()`	Retrieves the modification time that forces refetching of the document.
`ifModifiedSince`	Indicates that documents modified after this time must be refetched.
`setIfModifiedSince()`	Sets the modification time that forces refetching of the document.
User Interaction Field and Methods	
`allowUserInteraction`	Indicates whether user interaction is allowed for this `URLConnection`.
`getAllowUserInteraction()`	Determines whether this `URLConnection` allows user interaction.
`getDefaultAllowUserInteraction()`	Determines whether new URL connections, by default, allow user interaction.
`setAllowUserInteraction()`	Sets the user interaction flag for this `URLConnection`.
`setDefaultAllowUserInteraction()`	Sets the default user interaction flag for new URL connections.
User IO Fields and Methods	
`doInput`	Indicates whether this `URLConnection` will be used for input.
`doOutput`	Indicates whether this `URLConnection` will be used for output.
`getDoInput()`	Determines whether this `URLConnection` intends to do any input.
`getDoOutput()`	Determines whether output is planned to this `URLConnection`.
`setDoInput()`	Sets the indication of whether input from this `URLConnection` is planned.
`setDoOutput()`	Sets the indication of whether output to this `URLConnection` is planned.

Continued

U

MEMBER SUMMARY	
URL Field and Method	
`url`	The URL of this `URLConnection`.
`getURL()`	Retrieves the URL of this `URLConnection`.
Description Method	
`toString()`	Generates the string representation of this `URLConnection`.

See Also

`java.lang.SecurityManager`.
`ContentHandler`, `URLConnection` in *The Java Class Libraries, Second Edition, Volume 1.*

Δ fileNameMap

PURPOSE Replaced by `getFileNameMap()` and `setFileNameMap()`.

SYNTAX `public static FileNameMap fileNameMap`

1.2 CHANGES This field has been removed.

SEE ALSO `getFileNameMap()`, `setFileNameMap()`.

1.2 getFileNameMap()

PURPOSE Retrieves a `FileNameMap` instance for translating filenames to content types.

SYNTAX `public static FileNameMap getFileNameMap()`

DESCRIPTION This method returns a new instance of `FileNameMap` using the map previously set by using `setFileNameMap()`. This map is used by `guessContentTypeFromName()` to determine the MIME content type of an object from its filename extension. Its value is set using `setFileNameMap()`.

RETURNS A non-`null` `FileNameMap` instance for translating filenames to content types.

SEE ALSO `FileNameMap`, `guessContentTypeFromName()`, `setFileNameMap()`.

1.2 getPermission()

PURPOSE Retrieves the permission necessary to use this `URLConnection`.

SYNTAX `public Permission getPermission() throws IOException`

DESCRIPTION

This method returns the permission required to use this `URLConnection`. A `URLConnection` for a file, for example, would have a `FilePermission` containing the file portion of the URL. A `URLConnection` for HTTP, for example, might have a `SocketPermission` for connecting to the target host.

This method returns `AllPermission` by default. The `URLConnection` subclass should override this with the appropriate `Permission` subclass.

The permission returned might depend on the state of the connection. For example, the permission before connecting might be different from that after connecting, for example when an HTTP server redirects the connection to another server. The permission before the connection would refer to the original HTTP server, while the permission after the connection would refer to the redirected HTTP server.

A `URLConnection`'s permission might be used, for example, if the contents of this connection are shared, such as in a cache of Web pages and the cache manager wants to determine whether a client can access the contents. In this case, the permission should be obtained after the URL's contents (`getContents()`) have been retrieved. A `URLConnection`'s permission also might be used to check whether the caller has permission to fetch the data referred to by the URL. This can be used to check, for example, whether a `SecurityException` will be thrown if `URLConnection.getContent()` is called. In this case, the permission should be obtained and used before the connection is made (before `connect()` or `getContent()` is called).

RETURNS

A possibly `null Permission` object. If `null`, no permission is required to use this `URLConnection`.

EXCEPTIONS

`IOException`

If an IO error occurred while getting the `Permission`.

SEE ALSO

`java.security.Permission`.

EXAMPLE

```
try {
    URL url = new URL("http://java.sun.com/index.html");
    URLConnection jc = url.openConnection();
    Permission perm = jc.getPermission();
    System.out.println("before permission: " + perm);
    // use AccessController.checkPermission() to check access
    System.out.println(url.getContent());
    perm = jc.getPermission();
    System.out.println("after permission: " + perm);
} catch (MalformedURLException e) {
    e.printStackTrace();
} catch (IOException e) {
    e.printStackTrace();
}
```

U

1.2 setFileNameMap()

PURPOSE Sets the `FileNameMap` instance for translating filenames to content types.

SYNTAX
```
public static void setFileNameMap(FileNameMap map)
```

DESCRIPTION This method sets the map `map` for translating filenames to content types used by all `URLConnections`. This map is used by `guessContentTypeFromName()` to determine the MIME content type of an object from its filename extension.

In Version 1.2.2, the Java runtime sets the map to be the contents of `$JAVA_HOME/jre/lib/content-types.properties`. You can override this default by calling this method with the map to use.

This method can be invoked only if permitted by the security manager.

PARAMETERS

`map` The possibly `null` `FileNameMap` instance to use for all `URLConnections`. If `null`, the filename map for `URLConnections` is not set.

EXCEPTIONS

`SecurityException`
If the caller does not have permission to set factories.

SEE ALSO `FileNameMap`, `getContent()`, `guessContentTypeFromName()`, `RuntimePermission("setFactory")`, `SecurityManager.checkSetFactory()`.

U

URLDecoder

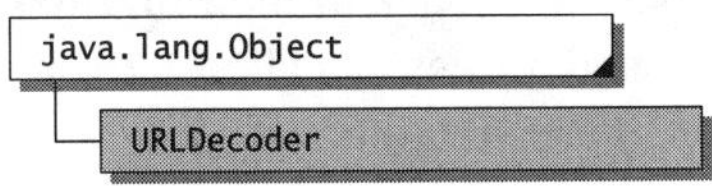

Syntax

`public class URLDecoder`

Description

The `URLDecoder` class provides a utility method for helping to decode the `application/x-www-form-urlencoded` MIME content type. This MIME type used by Web browsers when delivering HTML form data to an HTTP server. For brevity, we shall refer to `application/x-www-form-urlencoded` as `x-www-form-urlencoded`.

The x-www-form-urlencoded Format

The details of the `x-www-form-urlencoded` format are in *RFC 1738*. Briefly, an `x-www-form-urlencoded` string consists of a number of name/value pairs. The name and value are separated by an equals sign (=), and name/value pairs are separated by an ampersand (&). For example, two name/value pairs (n1, v1) and (n2, v2), are encoded as

```
n1=v1&n2=v2
```

If either the name or value contains *unsafe* characters, the name or value must be transformed to eliminate these unsafe characters. The set of *safe* characters is:

letters: `a-z`, `A-Z`
digits: `0-9`
underscore: `_`
minus: `-`
asterisk: `*`

The set of unsafe characters is everything except the safe characters. Each unsafe character in the name or value is transformed to a two-digit hexadecimal number preceded by a percent sign (%). The hexadecimal number is the ASCII value of the character. For example, the bar character (`|`) is converted to `%7C`. However, the space is treated differently; instead of being converted to `%hh` form, it is converted to a plus sign (+).

Usage

The name of this class is a little misleading. It is not used to decode an encoded URL. Nor is it used to decode an `x-www-form-urlencoded` string. Rather, it is used to decode part of an `x-www-form-urlencoded` string, in particular, its names and values. For example, the string `"a%7Cb+c"` would be converted to the string `"a|b c"`.

To decode an `x-www-form-urlencoded` string, you first need to break up the string into name/value pairs and then break up the name/value pairs. After this, you can call `decode()` on all of the names and values to decode them back to their original form.

The class that encodes names and values is called `URLEncoder`. Any string encoded by `URLEncoder.encode()` can be converted into its original form by calling `URLDecoder.decode()`.

This class it typically used on the server side of an HTML form-based application. For example, it could be used by a Common Gateway Interface (CGI) program or Servlet to decode the data from an HTML form.

MEMBER SUMMARY	
Decode Method	
`decode()`	Decodes the name or value of an `x-www-form-urlencoded` string.

See Also

`URLEncoder.encode()`.

Example

This example implements two useful methods for encoding and decoding strings in `x-www-form-urlencoded` format. The `encode()` method takes a map of strings and returns an x-www-form-urlencoded string of all of the entries. The `decode()` method takes an x-www-form-urlencoded string and parses it and returns a map containing all of the decoded name/value pairs in the string.

```
import java.net.*;
import java.util.*;

class Main {
    public static void main(String[] args) {
        // Create a map with a few entries.
        Map m = new HashMap();
        m.put("c|net", "www.cnet.com");
        m.put("dst(p, q)", "sqrt((q.x-p.x)^2+(q.y-p.y)^2)");

        // Encode the entries in the map.
        String data = encode(m);
        System.out.println(data);
            // c%7Cnet=www.cnet.com&dst%28p%2C+q%29=sqrt%28%28
            // q.x-p.x%29%5E2%2B%28q.y-p.y%29%5E2%29

        // Decode the x-www-form-urlencoded string into a map.
        try {
            m = decode(data);
            System.out.println(m);
                // {c|net=www.cnet.com,
                // dst(p, q)=sqrt((q.x-p.x)^2+(q.y-p.y)^2)}
```

U

```
        } catch (Exception e) {
            e.printStackTrace();
        }
    }

    // Returns x-www-form-urlencoded string of all the entries
    // in the map m.
    public static String encode(Map m) {
        int count = 0;
        StringBuffer buf = new StringBuffer();
        for (Iterator it=m.keySet().iterator(); it.hasNext(); count++) {
            String key = (String)it.next();

            if (count > 0) {
                buf.append('&');
            }
            buf.append(URLEncoder.encode(key)+"="+
                URLEncoder.encode((String)m.get(key)));
        }
        return new String(buf);
    }

    // Decodes the x-www-form-urlencoded string s and
    // returns a map containing all the encoded entries.
    public static Map decode(String s) throws IllegalArgumentException {
        Map m = new HashMap();
        try {
            StringTokenizer st = new StringTokenizer(s, "&");

            while (st.hasMoreElements()) {
                s = (String)st.nextElement();
               String key = URLDecoder.decode(s.substring(0, s.indexOf('=')));
              String value = URLDecoder.decode(s.substring(s.indexOf('=')+1));
                m.put(key, value);
            }
        } catch (Exception e) {
            throw new IllegalArgumentException();
        }
        return m;
    }
}
```

decode()

PURPOSE Decodes the name or value of an `x-www-form-urlencoded` string.

SYNTAX `public static String decode(String str) throws Exception`

DESCRIPTION This method converts all `%`*hh* substrings to a character whose ASCII hexadecimal value is *hh* and all plus characters (+) to spaces. For example, the string "`%7C`" is converted to a string containing the bar character (`|`). The string `str` is assumed to be either the name or value of `x-www-form-urlencoded` data. See the class example for more details about the translation rules.

PARAMETERS

`str`	A non-`null` string.

RETURNS A non-`null` decoded string.

EXCEPTIONS

`IllegalArgumentException`
If `str` has an invalid syntax.

`Exception`
If some other error occurred while decoding `str`.

SEE ALSO `URLEncoder.encode()`.

EXAMPLE See the class example.

U

java.lang
UnsupportedClassVersionError

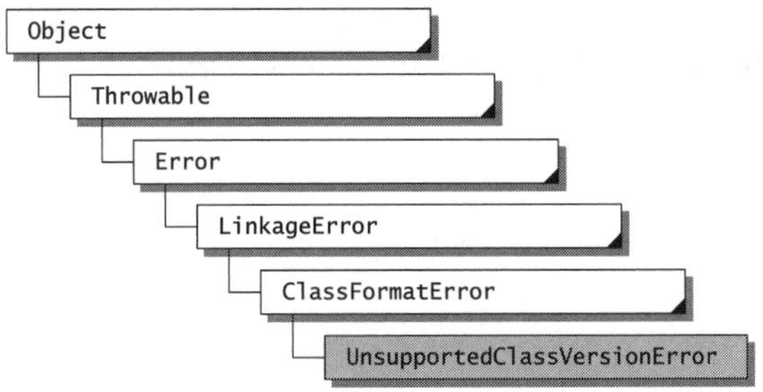

Syntax

`public class UnsupportedClassVersionError extends ClassFormatError`

Description

`UnsupportedClassVersionError` is a runtime linkage error that is thrown when the class loader attempts to load a class that has major or minor version numbers that are not supported. This can happen, for example, if the class was compiled using a compiler that generates class files with major/minor version numbers different from that expected by the Java virtual machine that is loading the class.

MEMBER SUMMARY	
Constructor	
`UnsupportedClassVersionError()`	Constructs a new instance of `UnsupportedClassVersionError`.

See Also

`ClassFormatError`.

U

UnsupportedClassVersionError()

PURPOSE: Constructs a new instance of `UnsupportedClassVersionError`.

SYNTAX:
```
public UnsupportedClassVersionError()
public UnsupportedClassVersionError(String msg)
```

DESCRIPTION: Both forms of the constructor construct an instance of `UnsupportedClassVersionError`. An optional string `msg` can be supplied that describes this particular instance of the error. If `msg` is not supplied, it defaults to `null`. This is the string returned by `Throwable.getMessage()`.

PARAMETERS

`msg` A possibly `null` string that gives details about this error.

SEE ALSO `Throwable.getMessage()`.

java.lang
UnsupportedOperationException

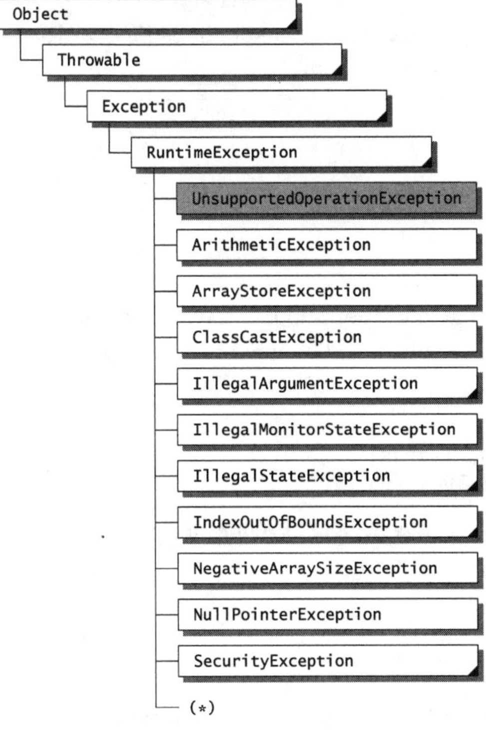

(*) 13 classes from other packages not shown.

Syntax

```
public class UnsupportedOperationException extends RuntimeException
```

Description

An `UnsupportedOperationException` exception is thrown when a method is called that is optionally supported. For example, `Collections.singleton()` returns an immutable set. If you try to modify the returned set, you will get an `UnsupportedOperationException`.

This exception is a runtime exception that typically isn't caught or declared in the throws clause of a method.

U

MEMBER SUMMARY	
Constructor	
`UnsupportedOperationException()`	Constructs a new `UnsupportedOperationException` instance.

See Also

`RuntimeException.`

Example

This example creates an immutable set that does not support any modification operations. Calling any of the modification operations results in an `UnsupportedUnsupportedException`.

```
import java.util.*;

class Main {
    public static void main(String[] args) {
        Set s = Collections.singleton("dog");

        s.add("cat");         // UnsupportedOperationException
    }
}
```

UnsupportedOperationException()

PURPOSE Constructs a new `UnsupportedOperationException` instance.

SYNTAX
```
public UnsupportedOperationException()
public UnsupportedOperationException(String msg)
```

DESCRIPTION This constructor constructs an `UnsupportedOperationException` that contains `msg`, which gives details about what caused the exception. If `msg` is not specified, it defaults to `null`.

PARAMETERS

`msg` A possibly `null` string that gives details about the cause of this exception.

SEE ALSO `Throwable.getMessage().`

EXAMPLE This example defines an interface called `Cell` that simply holds an object. The example implements one version that is modifiable and one that isn't. If you try to modify the read-only version, you get an `UnsupportedOperationException`.

```
import java.util.*;

class Main {
    public static void main(String[] args) {
        Cell c = new ReadWriteCell("dog");
        c.set("cat");
```

U

```
        c = new ReadOnlyCell("dog");
        c.set("cat");          // UnsupportedOperationException
    }
}

interface Cell {
    Object get();
    void set(Object o);
}

class ReadOnlyCell implements Cell {
    Object cell;
    ReadOnlyCell(Object o) {
        cell = o;
    }
    public Object get() {
        return cell;
    }
    public void set(Object o) {
        throw new UnsupportedOperationException();
    }
}
class ReadWriteCell implements Cell {
    Object cell;
    ReadWriteCell(Object o) {
        cell = o;
    }
    public Object get() {
        return cell;
    }
    public void set(Object o) {
        cell = o;
    }
}
```

Vector

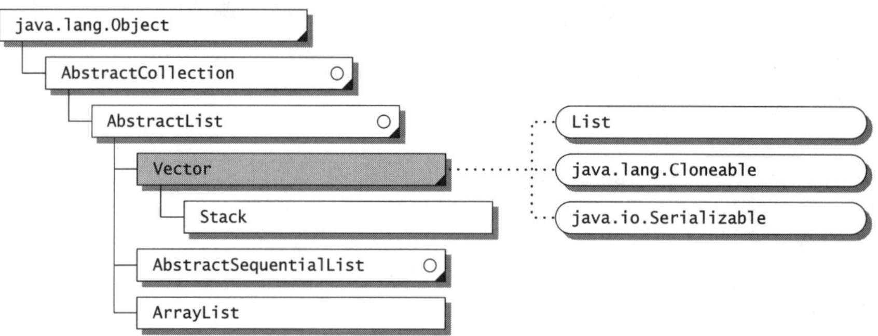

Syntax

`public class Vector extends AbstractList implements Cloneable, List, Serializable`

Description

The `Vector` class represents an expansible array consisting of objects called *elements*. You manipulate a vector much like an array. A vector and an array differ only in that you can add objects to a vector and the vector will grow automatically to accommodate the new objects, where as an array. You also can shrink a vector, whereas you cannot shrink an array. Elements may be `null`.

See *The Java Class Libraries, Second Edition, Volume 1* for more information about this class.

Changes for Version 1.2

For the most part, this class has been replaced with `List` (see `List`, `ArrayList`, and `LinkedList`), which is a class in the new Collections Framework (see `Collection`). The key difference between `Vector` and `List` is that the methods in `Vector` are still synchronized, whereas the methods in `List` are not. However, by calling `Collections.synchronizedList()` you can transform any `List` object into a "synchronized list," whereby all methods become synchronized.

`Vector` now implements the `List` interface so that it can be used along with the other collection classes (see `Collection`). Most of the new methods in Version 1.2 are there to implement and support the `List` interface. `Vector` has also been changed to inherit from `AbstractList`.

The methods `contains()`, `indexOf()`, and `lastIndexOf()` now handle `null` elements. In Version 1.1, you would get a `NullPointerException` if you searched for `null`.

Most of the methods in this class in Version 1.1 were final. In Version 1.2, none are, so you can now subclass this class and override any method you wish.

MEMBER SUMMARY		
	Constructor	
Δ	`Vector()`	Constructs an empty `Vector` instance.
	Query Methods	
Δ	`contains()`	Determines if this `Vector` contains a particular element.
1.2	`containsAll()`	Determines if this `Vector` contains all of the elements in another collection.
Δ	`indexOf()`	Searches for an object in this `Vector`.
	`isEmpty()`	Determines whether this `Vector` is empty.
Δ	`lastIndexOf()`	Searches for an object starting at the end of this `Vector`.
	`size()`	Determines the number of elements in this `Vector`.
	Element Retrieval Methods	
1.2	`get()`	Retrieves the element at a particular index in this `Vector`.
	`copyInto()`	Copies the references of the elements of this `Vector` into an array.
	`elementAt()`	Retrieves the element at the specified index in this `Vector`.
	`elements()`	Generates a list of the elements in this `Vector`.
	`firstElement()`	Retrieves the first element in this `Vector`.
	`lastElement()`	Retrieves the last element in this `Vector`.
	Modification Methods	
1.2	`add()`	Adds an element to this `Vector`.
1.2	`addAll()`	Inserts all of the elements of a collection into this `Vector`.
	`addElement()`	Adds an element to the end of this `Vector`.
1.2	`clear()`	Removes all of the elements in this `Vector`.
	`insertElementAt()`	Inserts an element in this `Vector`.
1.2	`remove()`	Removes an element from this `Vector`.
1.2	`removeAll()`	Removes all elements from this `Vector` that are in another collection.
	`removeAllElements()`	Removes all elements from this `Vector`.
	`removeElement()`	Removes an element from this `Vector`.
	`removeElementAt()`	Removes the element at the specified index from this `Vector`.
1.2	`removeRange()`	Removes a contiguous sequence of elements from this `Vector`.
1.2	`retainAll()`	Removes all elements in this `Vector` not in another collection.
1.2	`set()`	Replaces the element at an index with another element.
	`setElementAt()`	Replaces the element at the specified index in this `Vector`.
	`setSize()`	Truncates or expands this `Vector`.

Continued

V

MEMBER SUMMARY

Vector Capacity Methods	
`capacity()`	Determines the current capacity of this `Vector`.
`ensureCapacity()`	Ensures that this `Vector` has at least the specified capacity.
`trimToSize()`	Trims this `Vector`'s capacity to be the same as the its size.
Sublist Method	
1.2 `subList()`	Creates a list from a range of elements in this `Vector`.
Conversion Method	
1.2 `toArray()`	Returns all of the elements in this `Vector` in an array.
Object Methods	
`clone()`	Creates a clone of this `Vector`.
Δ `equals()`	Determines if this `Vector` is equal to another object.
Δ `hashCode()`	Computes the hash code of this `Vector`.
`toString()`	Generates the string representation of this `Vector`.
Protected Fields	
`capacityIncrement`	The size of the increment to use when growing the capacity of this `Vector`.
`elementCount`	The number of elements in `elementData`.
`elementData`	The buffer in which elements of this `Vector` are stored.

See Also

`ArrayList`, `Collection`, `List`, `LinkedList`.
`Vector` in *The Java Class Libraries, Second Edition, Volume 1.*

1.2 add()

PURPOSE Adds an element to this `Vector`.

SYNTAX
```
public synchronized boolean add(Object e)
public void add(int ix, Object e)
```

V

DESCRIPTION This method adds an element `e` to this `Vector`. The `equals()` method of `e` is used to determine whether two elements are the same.

PARAMETERS
- `e` The possibly `null` element to be added to this `Vector`.
- `ix` The index at which `e` is to be inserted. $0 \le ix \le size()$.

RETURNS This method always returns `true`.

EXCEPTIONS

`IndexOutOfBoundsException`
If `ix < 0` or `ix > size()`.

SEE ALSO `addAll()`, `java.lang.Object.equals()`.

EXAMPLE

```
Vector v = new Vector();
v.add("dog");
v.add(null);
v.add("dog");
System.out.println( v );          // [dog, null, dog]

v.add(1, "cat");
System.out.println( v );          // [dog, cat, null, dog]
```

1.2 addAll()

PURPOSE Inserts all of the elements of a collection into this `Vector`.

SYNTAX
```
public synchronized boolean addAll(Collection c)
public synchronized boolean addAll(int ix, Collection c)
```

DESCRIPTION This method inserts all elements from `c` into this `Vector` at index `ix`. The elements are inserted in the same order as they would appear from an iterator on `c`. If `ix` is not specified, it defaults to `size()`.

PARAMETERS

`c` The non-`null` collection of elements to be added to this `Vector`.

`ix` The index at which the elements in `c` are to be added. `0` ≤ `ix` ≤ `size()`.

RETURNS `true` if `c` is not empty.

EXCEPTIONS

`ConcurrentModificationException`
If `c`'s iterators are fail-fast and `c` is being modified during this method call.

`IndexOutOfBoundsException`
If `ix < 0` or `ix > size()`.

SEE ALSO `add()`.

V

EXAMPLE

```
Collection c = Arrays.asList(new String[]{"dog", "cat"});

Vector v = new Vector();
v.addAll(c);
v.addAll(1, c);
System.out.println( v );       // [dog, dog, cat, cat]
```

1.2 clear()

PURPOSE Removes all of the elements in this `Vector`.

SYNTAX `public void clear()`

DESCRIPTION This method removes all of the elements in this `Vector`. After it is called, this `Vector` will be empty. This method calls `removeAllElements()`.

SEE ALSO `removeAllElements()`.

EXAMPLE

```
Vector v = new Vector();
v.add("dog");
System.out.println( v.size() );    // 1
v.clear();
System.out.println( v.isEmpty() ); // true
```

Δ contains()

PURPOSE Determines if this `Vector` contains a particular element.

SYNTAX `public boolean contains(Object e)`

DESCRIPTION This method determines if this `Vector` contains a particular element, `e`. It returns `true` if some element in this `Vector` is equal to `e`. For all non-`null` elements, the `equals()` method is used to determine if two elements are equal.

1.2 CHANGES This method now allows `e` to be `null`.

PARAMETERS

`e` A possibly `null` element.

RETURNS `true` if some element in this vector is equal to `e`.

SEE ALSO `containsAll()`, `equals()`.

EXAMPLE

```
Vector v = new Vector(Arrays.asList(new Object[]{"dog", null, new Inte-
ger(7)}));

System.out.println( v.contains("dog") );         // true
System.out.println( v.contains(null) );          // true
System.out.println( v.contains("pig") );         // false

// This shows that although the two Integer objects are different,
// they are considered the same according to their equals() method.
System.out.println( v.contains(new Integer(7)) );// true
```

V

1.2 containsAll()

PURPOSE Determines if this `Vector` contains all of the elements in another collection.

SYNTAX `public synchronized boolean containsAll(Collection c)`

DESCRIPTION This method determines if this `Vector` contains all of the elements in `c`. If all of the elements in `c` appear in this `Vector`, this method returns `true`. For all non-`null` elements, the `equals()` method is used to determine if two elements are equal.

PARAMETERS

`c` A non-`null` collection.

RETURNS `true` if all of the elements in `c` appear in this `Vector`.

SEE ALSO `contains()`, `equals()`.

EXCEPTIONS

`ConcurrentModificationException`

If `c`'s iterators are fail-fast and `c` is being modified during this method call.

EXAMPLE

```
Vector v = new Vector(Arrays.asList(new String[]{"dog", "cat"}));

System.out.println( v.containsAll(Collections.EMPTY_LIST) );
    // true
System.out.println( v.containsAll(Collections.singleton(null)) );
    // false
System.out.println( v.containsAll(Collections.singleton("dog")) );
    // true
System.out.println( v.containsAll(
            Arrays.asList(new String[]{"dog", "dog", "cat"})));
    // true
```

Δ equals()

PURPOSE Determines if this `Vector` is equal to another object.

SYNTAX `public synchronized boolean equals(Object c)`

DESCRIPTION This method determines if this `Vector` is equal to `c`. It returns `true` if, and only if, `c` is a `List` object and the elements in `c` and this `Vector` match in number and in order. For all non-`null` elements, the `equals()` method of an element in this `Vector` is applied to the corresponding element in `c`.

1.2 CHANGES In Version 1.1, this method was inherited from `java.lang.Object`, whose implementation of `equals()` checks equality based on the object's reference.

PARAMETERS

`c` The possibly `null List` object to be compared with this `Vector`.

RETURNS true if c is equal to this Vector.

OVERRIDES java.lang.Object.equals().

SEE ALSO hashCode().

EXAMPLE

```
Vector v1 = new Vector(Arrays.asList(new String[]{"dog", null, "cat"}));
Vector v2 = new Vector(Arrays.asList(new String[]{"dog", "cat"}));

System.out.println( v1.equals(null) );                          // false
System.out.println( v1.equals(v2) );                            // false

v2.add(1, null);
System.out.println( v1.equals(v2) );                            // true

// Shows that vectors are never equal to non-list objects.
System.out.println( new Vector().equals(new HashSet()) );   // false
```

1.2 get()

PURPOSE Retrieves the element at a particular index in this Vector.

SYNTAX `public synchronized Object get(int ix)`

DESCRIPTION This method returns the element located at index ix.

PARAMETERS

ix The index of the element to return. $0 \le ix < size()$.

EXCEPTIONS

IndexOutOfBoundsException

If ix < 0 or ix ≥ size().

EXAMPLE

```
Vector v = new Vector();

for (int i=0; i<100; i++) {
    v.add("item " + i);
}
System.out.println( v.get(50) ); // item 50
v.get(101);                      // IndexOutOfBoundsException
```

V

Δ hashCode()

PURPOSE Computes the hash code of this Vector.

SYNTAX `public synchronized int hashCode()`

DESCRIPTION This method computes the hash code of this Vector. This Vector's hash code is an integer value that is based on the hash codes of all of its elements. Two equal Vector's will have the same hash code. Note that unequal Vector's might have the same hash code, although the hash code algorithm minimizes this possibility. The hash code is typically used as the key in a hash table.

The following algorithm is used to compute the hash code for a Vector:

```
int hashCode = 1;
for (Iterator it=list.iterator(); it.hasNext(); ) {
    Object e = it.next();
    hashCode = 31*hashCode + (e==null ? 0 : e.hashCode());
}
return hashCode;
```

1.2 CHANGES In Version 1.1, this method was inherited from `java.lang.Object`, whose implementation of `hashCode()` is based on the object's reference.

RETURNS This Vector's hash code.

OVERRIDES `java.lang.Object.hashCode()`.

SEE ALSO `equals()`, `java.lang.Object.equals()`.

EXAMPLE See `java.lang.Object.hashCode()`.

Δ indexOf()

PURPOSE Searches for an object in this Vector.

SYNTAX

```
public int indexOf(Object obj)
public synchronized int indexOf(Object obj, int idx)
```

DESCRIPTION This method searches for the object `obj` in this Vector. If `idx` is specified, the search begins at the index `idx` toward the end of this Vector. If `idx` is not specified, the search begins at index `0`. A comparison of `obj` with the elements in this Vector uses `Object.equals()` to test for equality.

1.2 CHANGES This method now allows searches for `null`.

PARAMETERS

- `idx` The index in this Vector at which to start the search. `idx` ≥ `0`.
- `obj` The possibly `null` object for which to search.

RETURNS The index of `obj` in this Vector; -1 if `obj` is not in this Vector in the range specified.

SEE ALSO `contains()`, `lastIndexOf()`, `java.lang.Object.equals()`.

EXAMPLE

```
Vector v = new Vector(Arrays.asList(new String[]{"dog", "cat", "dog"}));

System.out.println( v.indexOf("pig") );        // -1
System.out.println( v.indexOf("dog") );        // 0
System.out.println( v.indexOf(null) );         // -1
```

V

Δ lastIndexOf()

PURPOSE Searches for an object starting at the end of this `Vector`.

SYNTAX
```
public int lastIndexOf(Object obj)
public synchronized int lastIndexOf(Object obj, int idx)
```

DESCRIPTION This method searches for the object `obj` in this `Vector` starting at the end of this `Vector`. If `idx` is specified, the search begins at the index `idx` toward the start of this `Vector`. If `idx` is not specified, the search begins at index `size() - 1`. A comparison of `obj` with the elements in this `Vector` uses `Object.equals()` to test for equality.

1.2 CHANGES This method now allows searches for `null`.

PARAMETERS

`idx` The zero-based index in this `Vector` at which to start the backward search. `idx` < `size()`.

`obj` The possibly `null` object for which to search.

RETURNS The index of `obj` in this `Vector`; `-1` if `obj` is not in this `Vector` in the search range specified.

SEE ALSO `contains()`, `indexOf()`, `java.lang.Object.equals()`.

EXAMPLE
```
Vector v = new Vector(Arrays.asList(new String[]{"dog", "cat", "dog"}));

System.out.println( v.indexOf("pig") );        // -1
System.out.println( v.lastIndexOf("dog") );    // 2
System.out.println( v.indexOf(null) );         // -1
```

1.2 remove()

PURPOSE Removes an element from this `Vector`.

SYNTAX
```
public Object remove(int ix)
public boolean remove(Object e)
```

DESCRIPTION `remove(int)` removes the element at index `ix` from this `Vector` and returns the element that was removed.

`remove(Object)` searches for the first occurrence of `e` in this `Vector` and removes it. It returns `true` if it found a matching element (it uses `equals()` to determine equality).

PARAMETERS

`e` The possibly `null` element to remove.

`ix` The index of the element to remove. `0` ≤ `ix` < `size()`.

RETURNS `remove(int)` returns the possibly `null` element that was removed; `remove(Object)` returns `true` if `e` was removed.

EXCEPTIONS

`IndexOutOfBoundsException`
If `ix < 0` or `ix ≥ size()`.

`UnsupportedOperationException`
If this method is not supported by this `Vector`.

SEE ALSO `removeAll()`, `retainAll()`.

1.2 removeAll()

PURPOSE Removes all elements from this `Vector` that are in another collection.

SYNTAX `public synchronized boolean removeAll(Collection c)`

DESCRIPTION This method removes all elements in this `Vector` that are in `c`. The `equals()` method is used to determine whether two elements are equal. After this call returns, this `Vector` will contain no elements in common with `c`. This operation can be thought of as a *subtraction operation*, in which `c` is subtracted from this `Vector`.

PARAMETERS

`c` A non-`null` collection of elements to be removed from this `Vector`.

RETURNS `true` if this `Vector` was modified.

EXCEPTIONS

`ConcurrentModificationException`
If `c`'s iterators are fail-fast and `c` is being modified during this method call.

SEE ALSO `equals()`, `remove()`, `retainAll()`.

EXAMPLE

```
Vector v = new Vector(Arrays.asList(new String[]{"dog", "cat", "dog"}));

System.out.println( v.removeAll(Collections.EMPTY_LIST) );
                                        // false
System.out.println( v );                // [dog, cat, dog]

System.out.println( v.removeAll(Collections.singleton("dog")) );
                                        // true
System.out.println( v );                // [cat]
```

V

1.2 removeRange()

PURPOSE Removes a contiguous sequence of elements from this `Vector`.

SYNTAX `protected void removeRange(int fromIx, int toIx)`

DESCRIPTION This method removes all of the elements between `fromIx` (inclusive) and `toIx` (exclusive) from this `Vector`.

PARAMETERS

`fromIx` The index of the first element to be removed. `0` ≤ `fromIx` ≤ `size()`.

`toIx` The element at `toIx`–1 is the last element to be removed. `fromIx` ≤ `toIx` ≤ `size()`.

EXAMPLE See the `AbstractList` class example.

1.2 retainAll()

PURPOSE Removes all elements in this `Vector` not in another collection.

SYNTAX `public synchronized boolean retainAll(Collection c)`

DESCRIPTION This method removes all elements in this `Vector` that are not present in `c`. The `equals()` method is used to determine whether two elements are equal. This operation can be thought of as an *intersection operation.*

PARAMETERS

`c` A non-`null` collection of elements to retain.

RETURNS `true` if this `Vector` was modified.

EXCEPTIONS

`ConcurrentModificationException`
If `c`'s iterators are fail-fast and `c` is being modified during this method call.

SEE ALSO `equals()`, `remove()`, `removeAll()`.

EXAMPLE

```
Vector v = new Vector(Arrays.asList(new String[]{"dog", "cat", "dog"}));

System.out.println( v.retainAll(Collections.singleton("dog")));
                                          // true
System.out.println( v );                  // [dog, dog]
```

V

1.2 set()

PURPOSE Replaces the element at an index with another element.

SYNTAX `public synchronized Object set(int ix, Object e)`

DESCRIPTION This method replaces the element at index `ix` with `e` and returns the element previously at `ix`.

PARAMETERS

`e` The possibly `null` element to be stored at `ix`.

`ix` The index of the element to replace. `0` ≤ `ix` < `size()`.

RETURNS The possibly `null` element that was replaced.

EXCEPTIONS

`IndexOutOfBoundsException`

If `ix` < `0` or `ix` ≥ `size()`.

EXAMPLE

```
Vector v = new Vector(Arrays.asList(new String[]{"dog", null}));

System.out.println( v.set(0, null) );     // dog
System.out.println( v.set(1, "dog") );    // null
System.out.println( v );                  // [null, dog]

//v.set(100, null);                       // IndexOutOfBoundsException

// Make it unmodifiable
List list = Collections.unmodifiableList(v);
list.set(0, "dog");                       // UnsupportedOperationException.
```

1.2 subList()

PURPOSE Creates a list from a range of elements in this `Vector`.

SYNTAX `public List subList(int fromIx, int toIx)`

DESCRIPTION This method creates and returns a sublist containing all elements between `fromIx` (inclusive) and `toIx` (exclusive). The order of these elements in the sublist exactly matches the order of the elements as they appear in this `Vector`. The size of the new sublist is `toIx-fromIx`. The index of the first element in the sublist is `0`. The sublist cannot access any element in this `Vector` that is outside of the range of `fromIx` and `toIx`.

A sublist does not have its own storage; rather, it shares the storage with this `Vector`. If you modify the sublist, the modifications also appear in this `Vector`. If this `Vector` is modified, the sublist is no longer valid and should be discarded. If the sublist detects such a modification, it throws a `ConcurrentModificationException`.

V

PARAMETERS

`fromIx` The index of the first element to be included in the sublist. `0` ≤ `fromIx` ≤ `size()`.

toIx — The element at toIx-1 is the last element to be included in the sublist. fromIx ≤ toIx ≤ size().

RETURNS — A non-null synchronized list containing the elements from this Vector in the range fromIx to toIx-1.

EXCEPTIONS

IndexOutOfBoundsException
If fromIx < 0, or toIx < fromIx, or toIx > size().

EXAMPLE

```
Vector v = new Vector(Arrays.asList(new String[]{"dog", "cat", "pig"}));
List slist = v.subList(1, 2);
System.out.println( new ArrayList(slist) ); // [cat]
System.out.println( slist.get(0) );         // cat
//System.out.println( slist.get(-1) );      // IndexOutOfBoundsException

// Append an element into the sublist.
slist.add("cow");

// The original list shows the new element.
System.out.println( v );                    // [dog, cat, cow, pig]

// Clear the sublist.
slist.clear();
System.out.println( v );                    // [dog, pig]

// Create a sublist and then remove element from vector.
slist = v.subList(0, v.size());
v.remove(1);
//System.out.println( slist.get(0) );       // ConcurrentModificationException
```

1.2 toArray()

PURPOSE — Returns all of the elements in this Vector in an array.

SYNTAX

```
public synchronized Object[] toArray()
public synchronized Object[] toArray(Object arr[])
```

DESCRIPTION — This method fills arr with all of the elements in this Vector and returns arr. If arr is not large enough, a new array is created, filled, and then returned. The new array is just large enough to hold all of the elements in this Vector, and its type is identical to the type of arr.

If arr is larger than all of the elements in this Vector, arr[size()] is set to null. This null value can be used to determine the number of returned elements. However, it is not helpful if the list may contain null elements.

The order of the elements in the returned array matches the order (if any) of the elements returned by an iterator on this Vector.

If arr is not specified, it defaults to new Object[0].

V

PARAMETERS

arr — The non-null array into which the elements of this Vector are copied.

RETURNS — The array arr or a new array whose length equals size().

EXCEPTIONS

ArrayStoreException
If some element in this Vector cannot be assigned to an element in arr. This exception is never thrown if arr is an Object array.

EXAMPLE

```
import java.util.*;

class Main {
    public static void main(String[] args) {
        Vector v = new Vector(Arrays.asList(new String[]{"dog", null}));

        Object[] objs = v.toArray();
        print(objs);                        // [dog, null]

        // If we passed in a string array, we can cast
        // the result to a string array.
        String[] strings = (String[])v.toArray(new String[0]);
        print(strings);                     // [dog, null]

        // Try adding something other than a string to the vector.
        v.add(new Integer(0));

        print( v.toArray() );               // [dog, null, 0]

        // The Integer object can not be stored in the string array.
        //print( v.toArray(new String[0]) ); // ArrayStoreException
    }

    static void print(Object[] arr) {
        System.out.println(Arrays.asList(arr));
    }
}
```

Δ Vector()

PURPOSE — Constructs an empty Vector instance.

SYNTAX
```
public Vector()
public Vector(Collection c)          SINCE 1.2
public Vector(int initCap)
public Vector(int initCap, int capIncrement)
```

DESCRIPTION — This constructor creates a Vector instance with a initial capacity of initCap and capacity increment of capIncrement. When additional capacity is needed, the existing capacity is increased by capIncrement. However, if capIncre-

V

ment is 0, the capacity is doubled when additional capacity is needed. If initCap is not specified, it defaults to 10. If capIncrement is not specified, it defaults to 0.

If c is specified, the new vector is initialized with the elements from c.

1.2 CHANGES The form that accepts a Collection parameter is new in Version 1.2.

PARAMETERS

c — A non-null collection.

capIncrement — The amount by which this Vector is to grow when additional capacity is needed. If 0, the capacity is doubled.

initCap — The initial capacity of this Vector. initCap $\geq$ 0.

SEE ALSO capacity(), capacityIncrement, ensureCapacity().

EXAMPLE

```
Vector v = new Vector(Arrays.asList(new String[]{"dog", null}));
v.add("cat");
System.out.println( v );    // [dog, null, cat]
```

V

WeakHashMap

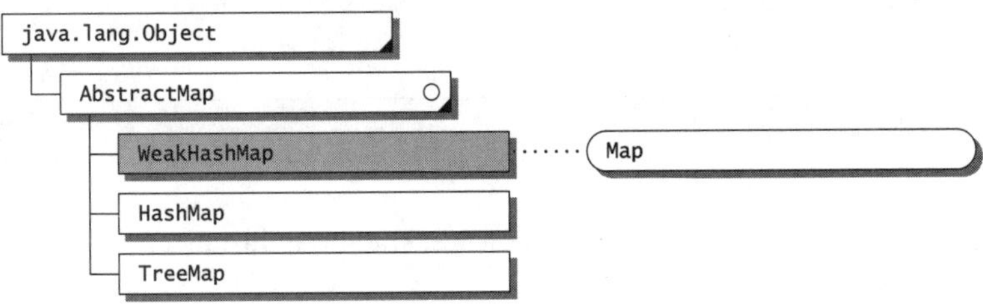

Syntax

```
public class WeakHashMap extends AbstractMap implements Map
```

Description

`WeakHashMap` is identical in every way to `HashMap`, except that entries are automatically removed when all strong references to a key are gone. See `HashMap` for more information about this class.

A common use for this map is to associate information with an object whose existence and form you do not control. For example, suppose your application allows users to annotate other users's documents. You could do this by maintaining a `WeakHashMap` that maps a document to its annotations. If the document becomes eligible for garbage collection (because it is no longer accessible to any thread), its entry in the `WeakHashMap` is automatically removed.

Usage

You can create an empty `WeakHashMap` as follows.

```
WeakHashMap map;
map = new WeakHashMap();
```

Once the map is created, you can use various methods to modify it, such as `put()` to add entries to the map and `remove()` to remove entries from the map.

Iterators

The iterators on this map are fail-fast (see `Iterator`) but only if a modification was explicitly made. If an entry is automatically removed while you are using an iterator, the iterator will not fail.

Implementation Notes

You cannot predict when an entry will be automatically removed from the map. In particular, the entry is not necessarily immediately removed as soon as all references to the key are gone. When it is depends on when the garbage collector runs. You can use `System.gc()` to suggest that the garbage collector run, but certain implementations might ignore the call.

Although the keys in the map are held by weak references, the values are held by ordinary strong references. To prevent entries from being unintentionally retained in the map, values should not refer to keys in the map.

MEMBER SUMMARY	
Constructor	
`WeakHashMap()`	Constructs a new `WeakHashMap` instance.
Value Retrieval Method	
`get()`	Retrieves the value associated with a key.
Query Methods	
`containsKey()`	Determines if this map contains a particular key.
`isEmpty()`	Determines if this map has no entries.
`size()`	Returns the number of entries in this map.
Modification Methods	
`clear()`	Removes all of the entries in this map.
`put()`	Adds a key/value pair to this map.
`remove()`	Removes an entry from this map.
Collection View Method	
`entrySet()`	Returns a set containing all of the key/value pairs in this map.

See Also

`java.lang.ref.WeakReference.`

Example

This example adds a key to a `WeakHashMap`. It then creates a thread that repeatedly checks whether the key is still in the map. The thread uses a copy of the key rather than the original key to check for the presence of the key in the map. (The thread cannot hold the original key; otherwise, the key would never be removed from the map.)

The `main()` method then waits for you to type `RETURN`. Doing this sets the `key` field to `null`, thereby releasing all references to the key. At some point in the future, the garbage collector will reclaim the key and cause the entry to be removed from the map. The thread then exits.

W

The call to `System.gc()` is not necessary; the garbage collector will eventually reclaim the key. Calling it is simply a suggestion that garbage collection take place. The system may ignore the call, depending on the implementation of the Java Virtual Machine.

```
import java.util.*;

class Main implements Runnable {
```

```
    static WeakHashMap map = new WeakHashMap();
    static Integer key = new Integer(123);

    public static void main(String[] args) {
        map.put(key, null);
        new Thread(new Main()).start();
        try {
            System.in.read();
        } catch (Exception e) {
            e.printStackTrace();
        }
        key = null;
    }

    public void run() {
        Integer keyCopy = new Integer(123);

        while (map.containsKey(keyCopy)) {
            try {
                Thread.sleep(1000);
                System.out.println( "still here" );
            } catch (Exception e) {
                e.printStackTrace();
            }
            System.gc();
        }
    }
}
```

clear()

PURPOSE Removes all of the entries in this map.

SYNTAX `public void clear()`

DESCRIPTION This method removes all of the entries in this map. After it is called, this map will be empty.

EXAMPLE See `Map.clear()`.

containsKey()

PURPOSE Determines if this map contains a particular key.

SYNTAX `public boolean containsKey(Object k)`

DESCRIPTION This method determines if this map contains the key `k`. It returns `true` if some key in this map is equal to `k`. For all non-`null` keys, the `equals()` method is used to determine if two keys are equal.

PARAMETERS

`k` A possibly `null` key.

RETURNS `true` if some key in this map is equal to `k`.

SEE ALSO `equals()`.

EXAMPLE See `Map.containsKey()`.

entrySet()

PURPOSE Returns a set containing all of the key/value pairs in this map.

SYNTAX `public Set entrySet()`

DESCRIPTION This method creates and returns a set containing all of the key/value pairs in this map. The key/value pairs are represented by `Map.Entry` objects. See `Map.Entry` for information about retrieving a key or value from an entry.

The set and this map share the same storage. This means that changes to this map are immediately reflected in the set and changes in the set are immediately reflected in this map.

The returned set supports all operations, including all entry removal methods, except for `add()` and `addAll()`. The iterators of the returned set are fail-fast. The `remove()` method of the iterators is supported.

RETURNS A non-`null` set containing all of the entries in this map.

SEE ALSO `Collection, keySet(), Map.Entry, values()`.

EXAMPLE `See.entrySet()`.

get()

PURPOSE Retrieves the value associated with a key.

SYNTAX `public Object get(Object k)`

DESCRIPTION This method searches this map for an entry with the key `k` and returns the associated value. `null` is returned if `k` is not in this map. A return value of `null` is ambiguous if the map accepts `null` values. You can use `containsKey()` to unambiguously determine if `k` is in this map.

PARAMETERS

`k` A possibly `null` key.

RETURNS The possibly `null` value associated with `k` or `null` if `k` is not in this map.

SEE ALSO `containsKey()`.

EXAMPLE `Map.get()`.

isEmpty()

PURPOSE Determines if this map has no entries.

SYNTAX `public boolean isEmpty()`

RETURNS `true` if this map contains no entries.

SEE ALSO `size()`.

EXAMPLE See `Map.isEmpty()`.

put()

PURPOSE Adds a key/value pair to this map.

SYNTAX `public Object put(Object k, Object v)`

DESCRIPTION This method adds a new entry with the key `k` and the value `v` to this map. If an entry with the key `k` already exists in this map, it is replaced with the new entry. In this case, the previous value is returned.

PARAMETERS

`k` A possibly `null` key.

`v` A possibly `null` value.

RETURNS If `k` already exists in this map, then the possibly `null` old value is returned; otherwise, `null` is returned.

EXAMPLE See `Map.put()`.

remove()

PURPOSE Removes an entry from this map.

SYNTAX `public Object remove(Object k)`

DESCRIPTION This method searches for the first occurrence of an entry with key `k` in this map and removes the entry from this map. It uses `equals()` to determine equality.

PARAMETERS

`k` The possibly `null` key of the entry to remove.

RETURNS The possibly `null` value associated with `k` or `null` if `k` does not match any keys in this map.

EXAMPLE See `Map.remove()`.

size()

PURPOSE Returns the number of entries in this map.

SYNTAX `public int size()`

DESCRIPTION This method returns the number of entries in this map. Note that this map can change at any time, including just after this method returns. Thus the returned value might no longer be valid by the time you look at the map.

RETURNS The non-negative number of entries in this map.

SEE ALSO `isEmpty()`.

EXAMPLE See `Map.size()`.

WeakHashMap()

PURPOSE Constructs a new `WeakHashMap` instance.

SYNTAX

```
public WeakHashMap()
public WeakHashMap(int initCap)
public WeakHashMap(int initCap, float loadFactor)
```

DESCRIPTION This constructor creates a new `WeakHashMap` instance with the capacity `initCap` and load factor `loadFactor`. If `initCap` is not specified, it defaults to `101`. If `loadFactor` is not specified, it defaults to `0.75f`.

See the `HashMap` class description for information about the capacity and the load factor.

PARAMETERS

`initCap` The non-negative initial capacity of the set.

`loadFactor` The load factor. `0.0` ≤ `loadFactor`.

EXCEPTIONS

`IllegalArgumentException`

If `initCap` < `0` or `loadFactor` ≤ `0.0`.

EXAMPLE See the class example.

WeakReference

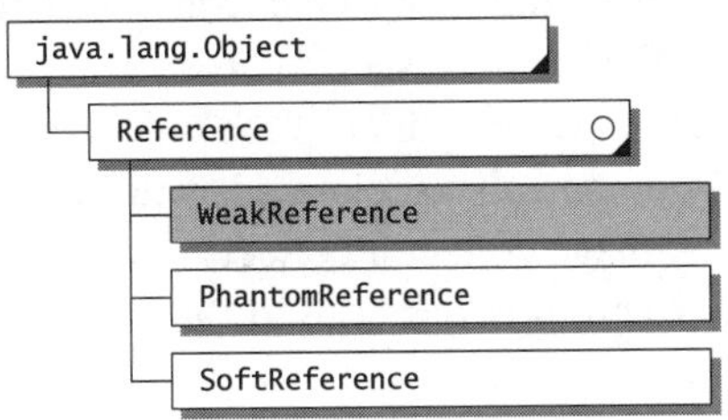

Syntax

```
public class WeakReference extends Reference
```

Description

The `WeakReference` class represents a *weak reference*, which is a type of reference object (see `Reference`) you use to receive notification of an unused object before it is finalized (finalization is described in *The Java Language Specification, First Edition*, Section 12.6). Unlike a soft reference (see `SoftReference`), a weak reference does not delay garbage collection. When the referent of a weak reference becomes unused, the garbage collector treats the referent just like any other object that becomes unused.

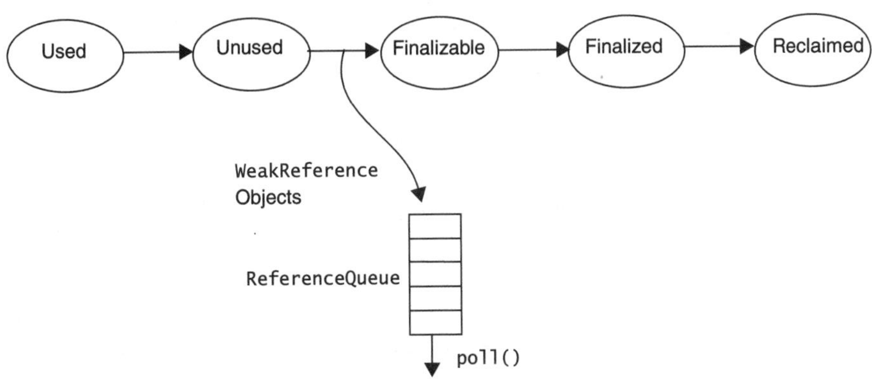

FIGURE 22: Weak Reference Notification.

Weak reference notification is used in the same way that finalization is used. See Figure 22. However, finalization is done by the object that is being garbage collected; by contrast, weak reference notification allows a separate object to do finalization. Also, in finalization, a reference to the object is available; a weak reference cannot retrieve a reference to the object.

Weak reference notification is very similar to phantom reference notification. You can use either reference type to determine when an object is being collected. Only when an object can be *resurrected* does it matter which reference type you use. (Resurrection occurs when an object makes itself *used* during finalization; see *The Java Language Specification, First Edition*, Section 12.6, for more details.) In particular, if the object is resurrectable and you want to know when the object is really going to be reclaimed, you must use a phantom reference. If you are interested in when the garbage collector collects a resurrectable object, you must use a weak reference. However, resurrection is rarely used (and highly discouraged), so this situation almost never arises.

A weak reference object is enqueued at most once even if the referent is *resurrected*. Thus if the referent is resurrected and you still want weak reference notification on the referent, you must create a new weak reference on the referent.

Usage

To receive notification of when an object `obj` is being garbage collected, you first must create a reference queue (see `ReferenceQueue`). You then construct a weak reference object, supplying both `obj` and the reference queue. Finally, you poll the reference queue. Then when the weak reference object appears in the queue, you know that `obj` is on its way to being finalized. Following is some sample code that demonstrates the steps.

```
ReferenceQueue q = new ReferenceQueue();
WeakReference wr = new WeakReference(obj, q);
try {
    Reference r = rq.remove();
} catch (InterruptedException e) {
    e.printStackTrace();
}
```

MEMBER SUMMARY	
Constructor	
`WeakReference()`	Constructs a `WeakReference` instance.

See Also

`PhantomReference`, `Reference`, `ReferenceQueue`, `SoftReference`, `WeakHashMap`.

W

Example

This example creates a thread whose existence is tied to a particular object. When that object is no longer used, the thread should kill itself. A weak reference is created to refer to the object. The thread occasionally checks the weak reference to see if the object is still being used. When the weak reference yields `null`, the thread exits.

```
import java.lang.ref.*;
import java.io.*;
import java.util.*;

class Main {
    public static void main(String[] args) throws IOException {
        Object o = new Object();
        (new WatcherThread(o)).start();

        // Wait a few seconds before making o unused.
        try {
            Thread.sleep(5000);
        } catch (Exception e) {
            e.printStackTrace();
        }
        o = null;

        // Use all available memory to force a garbage-collection.
        eatMemory(new LinkedList());
    }
    static void eatMemory(LinkedList l) {
        try {
            l.add(new double[100000]);
            eatMemory(l);
        } catch (OutOfMemoryError e) {
            System.out.println("**** OUT OF MEMORY ****");
            l.clear();
            System.gc();
        }
    }
}

class WatcherThread extends Thread {
    WeakReference wr;

    public WatcherThread(Object o) {
        wr = new WeakReference(o);
    }

    public void run() {
        try {
            while (wr.get() != null) {
                // Do some work here.
                System.out.println("working...");

                Thread.sleep(2000);
            }
            System.out.println("done.");
        } catch (Exception e) {
            e.printStackTrace();
        }
    }
}
```

Output

```
> java -Xmx1m Main

working...
working...
```

```
working...
done.
**** OUT OF MEMORY ****
```

WeakReference()

PURPOSE Constructs a `WeakReference` instance.

SYNTAX
```
public WeakReference(Object referent)
public WeakReference(Object referent, ReferenceQueue queue)
```

DESCRIPTION This constructor creates a `WeakReference` instance that refers to `referent`. If `queue` is specified, the garbage collector will enqueue this new `WeakReference` to `queue` sometime after `referent` becomes unused.

If `queue` is not specified, the new `WeakReference` is not registered with any queue.

PARAMETERS

`queue` A non-`null` reference queue.

`referent` A non-`null` object.

ZipEntry

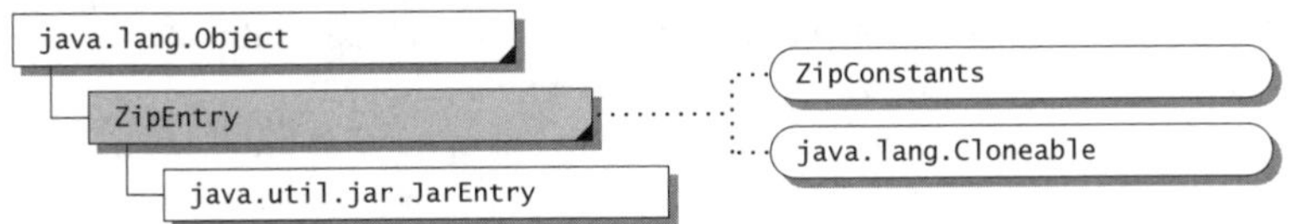

Syntax

```
public class ZipEntry implements ZipConstants, Cloneable
```

Description

The `ZipEntry` class is used to represent a ZIP entry in a ZIP file. A ZIP entry is used to describe a piece of compressed (or uncompressed) data stored in the ZIP file. There is one ZIP entry for every independent piece of data in the ZIP file. A ZIP entry contains such information as the time the data was last modified and the data's compressed and uncompressed sizes. The format of a ZIP file is described in detail in the document at `ftp://ftp.uu.net/pub/archiving/zip/doc/appnote-970531-pk.zip`.

See *The Java Class Libraries, Second Edition, Volume 1* for more information about this class.

Changes for Version 1.2

The `ZipEntry` class implements `Cloneable` and exports a public `clone()` method. It overrides `hashCode()` to return the hash code of its entry's name.

A new public constructor accepts a `ZipEntry` and creates an instance of it by copying fields from the original `ZipEntry`.

A new method, `setCompressedSize()`, allows you to set the compressed size of the ZIP entry data.

MEMBER SUMMARY	
Constructor	
Δ `ZipEntry()`	Constructs a `ZipEntry` instance.
Get Property Methods	
`getComment()`	Retrieves the comment string for this `ZipEntry`.
`getCompressedSize()`	Retrieves the compressed size of this `ZipEntry`'s data.
`getCrc()`	Retrieves the checksum value for the uncompressed form of this `ZipEntry`'s data.
`getExtra()`	Retrieves any extra information associated with this `ZipEntry`.

Continued

Z

MEMBER SUMMARY	
Get Property Methods (*Continued*)	
getMethod()	Retrieves the compression method of this ZipEntry.
getName()	Retrieves this ZipEntry's name.
getSize()	Retrieves the uncompressed size of this ZipEntry's data.
getTime()	Retrieves the last modification time of this ZipEntry.
isDirectory()	Determines if this ZipEntry is a directory.
Set Property Methods	
setComment()	Sets the optional comment string for this ZipEntry.
1.2 setCompressedSize()	Sets the compressed size of this ZipEntry's data.
setCrc()	Sets the checksum value for this ZipEntry.
setExtra()	Sets optional extra information for this ZipEntry.
setMethod()	Sets the compression method for this ZipEntry.
setSize()	Sets the uncompressed size of this ZipEntry's data.
setTime()	Sets the last modification time of this ZipEntry.
Compression Method Constants	
DEFLATED	Compression-method constant for compressed entries.
STORED	Compression-method constant for uncompressed entries.
Object Methods	
Δ clone()	Creates a copy of this ZipEntry.
Δ hashCode()	Computes the hash code of this ZipEntry.
toString()	Generates a string representation of this ZipEntry.

See Also

java.util.jar.JarEntry.
ZipEntry in *The Java Class Libraries, Second Edition, Volume 1.*

Δ clone()

PURPOSE Creates a copy of this ZipEntry.

SYNTAX `public Object clone()`

DESCRIPTION This method creates a copy of this ZipEntry using the fields from this ZipEntry. All of the fields are copied. The contents of the byte array in the extra field (getExtra()) are also copied.

1.2 CHANGES In Version 1.1, this method was inherited from java.lang.Object.

RETURNS A non-null instance of ZipEntry that has the same fields as this ZipEntry.

OVERRIDES java.lang.Object.clone().

EXAMPLE See the `Cloneable` class example in the *The Java Class Libraries, Second Edition, Volume 1.*

Δ hashCode()

PURPOSE Computes the hash code of this `ZipEntry`.

SYNTAX `public int hashCode()`

DESCRIPTION This method computes the hash code of this `ZipEntry`. The hash code of a `ZipEntry` is computed using the hash code of its name. Note that `ZipEntry`'s `equals()` method has not been overridden, which means two `ZipEntrys` are equal if they are the same object. Therefore two `ZipEntrys` that are equal must have the same hash code, but two `ZipEntrys` with the same hash code might not necessarily be equal.

1.2 CHANGES In Version 1.1, this method was inherited from `java.lang.Object`, in which the hash code computation uses the reference of the object.

RETURNS An `int` representing the hash code of this `ZipEntry`.

OVERRIDES `java.lang.Object.hashCode()`.

SEE ALSO `java.lang.Object.equals()`.

EXAMPLE See `java.lang.Object.equals()` in the *The Java Class Libraries, Second Edition, Volume 1.*

1.2 setCompressedSize()

PURPOSE Sets the compressed size of this `ZipEntry`'s data.

SYNTAX `public void setCompressedSize(long csize)`

PARAMETERS

`csize` The size of the compressed entry data, in bytes.

SEE ALSO `getCompressedSize()`.

Δ ZipEntry()

PURPOSE Constructs a `ZipEntry` instance.

SYNTAX `public ZipEntry(String zname)`

SINCE 1.2 `public ZipEntry(ZipEntry orig)`

DESCRIPTION The first form of this method creates a `ZipEntry` instance with the name `zname`. Only the lower byte of each character in `zname` is used in the name. The second form creates a `ZipEntry` instance using the fields from `orig`. `orig`'s name, time, crc, size, compressed size, compression method, comment, and extra information are copied to the new entry. The value of the extra field (`getExtra()`) is assigned to the new object, but the contents of its `byte` array are not copied. (Contrast this behavior with that of `clone()`'s, which also clones the `byte` array.)

1.2 CHANGES In Version 1.1, only the form that accepts a string name existed.

PARAMETERS

`orig` A non-`null` `ZipEntry` whose fields are to be copied.

`zname` A non-`null` string containing the ZIP entry name. Only the lower byte of each character is used. `zname.length()` ≤ `65535`.

EXCEPTIONS

`NullPointerException`
If `zname` or `orig` is `null`.

`IllegalArgumentException`
If `zname.length()` > `65535` characters.

EXAMPLE See the `ZipEntry` class example in *The Java Class Libraries, Second Edition, Volume 1.*

Z

ZipFile

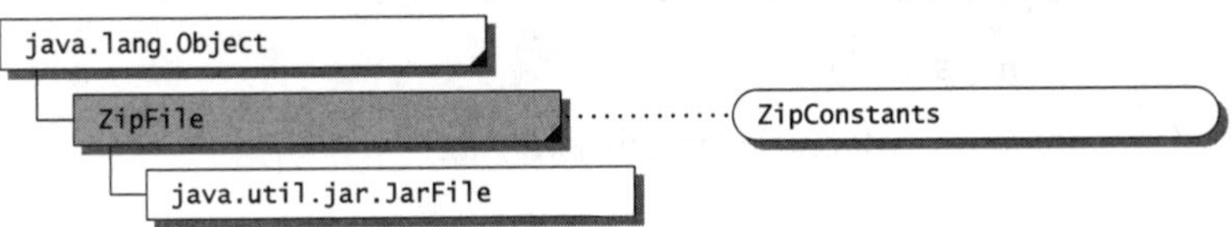

Syntax

```
public class ZipFile implements ZipConstants
```

Description

The `ZipFile` class is used to read the contents of a ZIP file. It does not support the ability to create a ZIP file. Instead, use `ZipOutputStream` to create a ZIP file. The format of a ZIP file is described in detail in the documents at `ftp://ftp.uu.net/pub/archiving/zip/doc/`. `ZipFile` uses the DEFLATE compression algorithm described in *RFC 1951* at `http://ds.internic.net/rfc/rfc1951.txt`.

See *The Java Class Libraries, Second Edition, Volume 1* for more information about this class.

Changes for Version 1.2

A new `size()` method returns the number of ZIP entries in a ZIP file.

MEMBER SUMMARY	
Constructor	
`ZipFile()`	Opens a ZIP file.
ZIP File Methods	
`close()`	Closes this `ZipFile`.
`getName()`	Retrieves this `ZipFile`'s name.
1.2 `size()`	Retrieves the number of entries in this `ZipFile`.
ZIP Entry Methods	
`entries()`	Creates an enumeration of all of the ZIP entries.
`getEntry()`	Retrieves a ZIP entry.
`getInputStream()`	Creates an input stream on the contents represented by a ZIP entry.

Z

See Also

`ZipFile` in *The Java Class Libraries, Second Edition, Volume 1.*

1.2 size()

PURPOSE Retrieves the number of entries in this `ZipFile`.

SYNTAX `public int size()`

RETURNS The number of ZIP entries in this ZIP file.

EXCEPTIONS

`IllegalStateException`
If this `ZipFile` instance has been closed.

EXAMPLE

```
import java.util.zip.*;
import java.io.IOException;

class Main {
    public static void main(String[] args) {
        if (args.length != 1) {
            System.err.println("usage: java Main <zipfilename>");
            System.exit(-1);
        }
        try {
            ZipFile zf = new ZipFile(args[0]);
            System.out.println(args[0] + " has " + zf.size() + " entries.");
        } catch (IOException e) {
            e.printStackTrace();
        }
    }
}
```

ZipInputStream

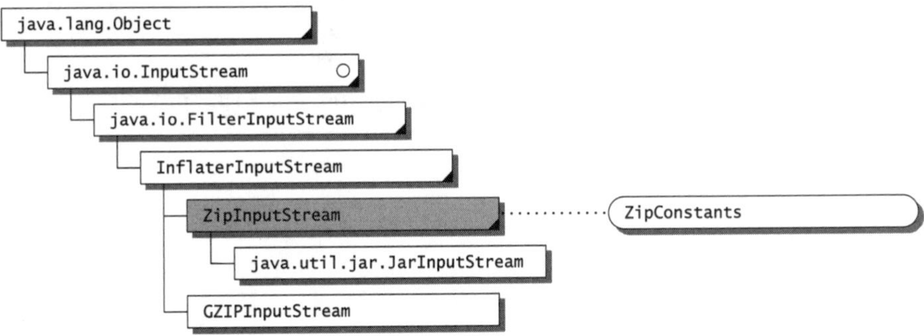

Syntax

`public class ZipInputStream extends InflaterInputStream implements ZipConstants`

Description

The `ZipInputStream` class implements an input stream filter for reading a ZIP file. See `ZipFile` for more information on the format of a ZIP file.

See *The Java Class Libraries, Second Edition, Volume 1* for more information about this class.

Changes for Version 1.2

The `available()` method has been overridden.

A new, protected `createZipEntry()` method creates new `ZipEntrys` for use by subclasses (such as `JarInputStream`). The portion of this class that creates `ZipEntry` instances has been rewritten to use `createZipEntry()` instead of the `ZipEntry` constructor so that subclasses that produce subclasses of `ZipEntry` (such as `JarEntry`) are possible.

MEMBER SUMMARY	
Constructor	
`ZipInputStream()`	Constructs a `ZipInputStream` instance.
Stream Methods	
Δ `available()`	Determines whether this `ZipInputStream` has been closed.
`close()`	Closes this `ZipInputStream`.
`read()`	Reads decompressed data from this `ZipInputStream`.
`skip()`	Discards decompressed data from this `ZipInputStream`.
	Continued

Z

MEMBER SUMMARY		
	Entry Methods	
	`closeEntry()`	Closes the current `ZipEntry`.
1.2	`createZipEntry()`	Creates a `ZipEntry` instance.
	`getNextEntry()`	Reads the next ZIP entry from this `ZipInputStream`.

See Also

`java.util.jar.JarInputStream`.
`ZipInputStream` in *The Java Class Libraries, Second Edition, Volume 1*.

Δ available()

PURPOSE Determines whether this `ZipInputStream` has been closed.

SYNTAX `public int available() throws IOException`

DESCRIPTION This method determines whether this `ZipInputStream` has been closed. It returns `0` if this `ZipInputStream` has been closed; otherwise, it returns `1`. Unlike the conventional definition of `available()` (see `InputStream`), this method does not return the actual number of bytes that could be read without blocking.

1.2 CHANGES In Version 1.1, this method was inherited from `InflaterInputStream`, which would call `available()` on the underlying input stream. In Version 1.2, this method uses only the fact of whether this stream has been closed.

RETURNS `0` if this `ZipInputStream` has been closed; `1` otherwise.

EXCEPTIONS

`IOException`
If an IO error occurred.

1.2 createZipEntry()

PURPOSE Creates a `ZipEntry` instance.

SYNTAX `protected ZipEntry createZipEntry(String zname)`

DESCRIPTION This method is used internally by this class when it needs to create an instance of `ZipEntry`. It should be overridden by a subclass to return the appropriate subclass of `ZipEntry`. For example, `JarInputStream` overrides this method to return a new instance of `JarEntry`.

PARAMETERS

`zname`	A non-`null` string representing the name of the ZIP entry.
RETURNS	A non-`null` instance of `ZipEntry` for `zname`.
SEE ALSO	`JarEntry`, `JarInputStream`.

Addendum

The following method descriptions were inadvertently omitted from the `Class` chapter.

Δ getClasses()

PURPOSE Retrieves an array of `Class` objects for all public class and interface members.

SYNTAX `public Class[] getClasses()`

DESCRIPTION This method retrieves an array containing `Class` objects for all of the public classes and interfaces that are members of the class represented by this `Class` object. This includes public class and interface members inherited from superclasses and public class and interface members declared by the class.

1.2 CHANGES In Version 1.1, this method was not implemented; it always returned an empty array.

RETURNS A non-`null` array of `Class` objects.

EXCEPTIONS

`SecurityException`

If caller does not have permission to access member information.

SEE ALSO `getDeclaredClasses()`, `SecurityManager.checkMemberAccess()`.

EXAMPLE

A.java

```
public interface A {
  public class B {
  }

  interface C {
  }
}
```

D.java

```
public class D implements A {
  public class E {
  }
}
```

F.java

```
public class F extends D {
  public class G {
  }

  class H {
  }
}
```

Main.java

```
public class Main {
  public static void main(String[] args) {

    printClasses("D.getClasses", D.class.getClasses()); // D$E
    printClasses("D.getDeclaredClasses", D.class.getDeclaredClasses());
                                                           // D$E

    printClasses("A.getClasses", A.class.getClasses()); // A$B A$C
    printClasses("A.getDeclaredClasses", A.class.getDeclaredClasses());
                                                           // A$B A$C

    printClasses("F.getClasses", F.class.getClasses()); // F$G D$E
    printClasses("F.getDeclaredClasses", F.class.getDeclaredClasses());
                                                           // F$G F$H

    System.out.println(A.class.getDeclaringClass());   // null
    System.out.println(A.B.class.getDeclaringClass()); // interface A
    System.out.println(D.E.class.getDeclaringClass()); // class D
    System.out.println(F.E.class.getDeclaringClass()); // class D
  }

  public static void printClasses(String msg, Class[] cls) {
    System.out.print(msg + ": ");
    for (int i = 0; cls != null && i < cls.length; i++) {
      System.out.print(cls[i].getName() + " ");
    }
    System.out.println();
  }
}
```

OUTPUT

```
D.getClasses: D$E
D.getDeclaredClasses: D$E
A.getClasses: A$B A$C
A.getDeclaredClasses: A$B A$C
F.getClasses: F$G D$E
F.getDeclaredClasses: F$G F$H
null
interface A
class D
class D
```

Δ getDeclaredClasses()

PURPOSE Retrieves an array of `Class` objects for all class and interface members.

SYNTAX `public Class[] getDeclaredClasses() throws SecurityException`

DESCRIPTION This method retrieves an array containing `Class` objects for all of the classes and interfaces that are declared as members of the class represented by this `Class` object.

1.2 CHANGES In Version 1.1, this method was not implemented; it always returned an empty array.

RETURNS A non-`null` array of `Class` objects.

SEE ALSO `getClasses()`, `getDeclaringClass`, `SecurityManager.checkMemberAccess()`.

EXCEPTIONS

`SecurityException`
If access to the information is denied.

EXAMPLE See `getClasses()`.

Δ getDeclaringClass()

PURPOSE Retrieves the declaring class of this `Class` object.

SYNTAX `public Class getDeclaringClass()`

DESCRIPTION If the class or interface represented by this `Class` object is a member of another class, this method retrieves the `Class` object representing the class of which it is a member (its declaring class). This method returns `null` if this class or interface is not a member of any other class.

1.2 CHANGES In Version 1.1, this method was not implemented; it always returned `null`.

RETURNS A possibly `null` `Class` object.

SEE ALSO `getClass()`.

EXAMPLE See `getClasses()`.

Index

B

C

E

† indicates a page in *The Java Class Libraries, Second Edition, Volume 1*

F

G

H

I

J

K

L

N

O

T

V

 † indicates a page in *The Java Class Libraries, Second Edition, Volume 1*

W

X

Y

Z

The XP Series

Kent Beck, Series Advisor

Extreme Programming Explained
By Kent Beck
0201616416
Paperback
© 2000

The XP Manifesto

Extreme Programming Installed
By Ron Jeffries, Ann Anderson, and Chet Hendrickson
0201708426
Paperback
© 2001

Get XP Up and Running in Your Organization

Extreme Programming in Practice
By James Newkirk and Robert C. Martin
0201709376
Paperback
© 2001

Learn from the Chronicle of an XP Project

Extreme Programming Applied
By Ken Auer and Roy Miller
0201616408
Paperback
© 2002

Delves Deeper into XP Theory

Planning Extreme Programming
By Kent Beck and Martin Fowler
0201710919
Paperback
© 2001

Planning Projects with XP

Extreme Programming Examined
By Giancarlo Succi and Michele Marchesi
0201710404
Paperback
© 2001

Best XP Practices as Presented and Analyzed at the recent Extreme Programming Conference

Extreme Programming Explored
By William C. Wake
0201733978
Paperback
© 2002

Best XP Practices for Developers